World History, Volume 1: to 1500

SENIOR CONTRIBUTING AUTHORS

ANN KORDAS, JOHNSON & WALES UNIVERSITY

RYAN J. LYNCH, COLUMBUS STATE UNIVERSITY

BROOKE NELSON, FORMERLY CALIFORNIA STATE UNIVERSITY

JULIE TATLOCK, MOUNT MARY UNIVERSITY

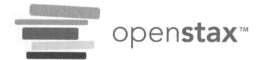

ISBN: 978-1-711471-42-6

OpenStax
Rice University
6100 Main Street MS-375
Houston, Texas 77005

To learn more about OpenStax, visit https://openstax.org.
Individual print copies and bulk orders can be purchased through our website.

HARDCOVER BOOK ISBN-13	978-1-711471-41-9
B&W PAPERBACK BOOK ISBN-13	978-1-711471-42-6
DIGITAL VERSION ISBN-13	978-1-951693-67-1
ORIGINAL PUBLICATION YEAR	**2023**

1 2 3 4 5 6 7 8 9 10 RS 23

Printed by

XanEdu

17177 Laurel Park Dr., Suite 233
Livonia, MI 48152
800-562-2147
www.xanedu.com

OpenStax

OpenStax provides free, peer-reviewed, openly licensed textbooks for introductory college and Advanced Placement® courses and low-cost, personalized courseware that helps students learn. A nonprofit ed tech initiative based at Rice University, we're committed to helping students access the tools they need to complete their courses and meet their educational goals.

Rice University

OpenStax is an initiative of Rice University. As a leading research university with a distinctive commitment to undergraduate education, Rice University aspires to path-breaking research, unsurpassed teaching, and contributions to the betterment of our world. It seeks to fulfill this mission by cultivating a diverse community of learning and discovery that produces leaders across the spectrum of human endeavor.

Philanthropic Support

OpenStax is grateful for the generous philanthropic partners who advance our mission to improve educational access and learning for everyone. To see the impact of our supporter community and our most updated list of partners, please visit openstax.org/impact.

Arnold Ventures

Chan Zuckerberg Initiative

Chegg, Inc.

Arthur and Carlyse Ciocca Charitable Foundation

Digital Promise

Ann and John Doerr

Bill & Melinda Gates Foundation

Girard Foundation

Google Inc.

The William and Flora Hewlett Foundation

The Hewlett-Packard Company

Intel Inc.

Rusty and John Jaggers

The Calvin K. Kazanjian Economics Foundation

Charles Koch Foundation

Leon Lowenstein Foundation, Inc.

The Maxfield Foundation

Burt and Deedee McMurtry

Michelson 20MM Foundation

National Science Foundation

The Open Society Foundations

Jumee Yhu and David E. Park III

Brian D. Patterson USA-International Foundation

The Bill and Stephanie Sick Fund

Steven L. Smith & Diana T. Go

Stand Together

Robin and Sandy Stuart Foundation

The Stuart Family Foundation

Tammy and Guillermo Treviño

Valhalla Charitable Foundation

White Star Education Foundation

Schmidt Futures

William Marsh Rice University

CONTENTS

Unit 2 States And Empires, 1000 BCE–500 CE

Unit 3 An Age Of Religion, 500–1200 CE

Unit 4 A Global Middle Ages, 1200–1500 CE

Preface

About OpenStax

OpenStax is part of Rice University, which is a 501(c)(3) nonprofit charitable corporation. As an educational initiative, it's our mission to improve educational access and learning for everyone. Through our partnerships with philanthropic organizations and our alliance with other educational resource companies, we're breaking down the most common barriers to learning. Because we believe that everyone should and can have access to knowledge.

About OpenStax Resources

Customization

World History is licensed under a Creative Commons Attribution 4.0 International (CC BY) license, which means that you can distribute, remix, and build upon the content, as long as you provide attribution to OpenStax and its content contributors.

Because our books are openly licensed, you are free to use the entire book or select only the sections that are most relevant to the needs of your course. Feel free to remix the content by assigning your students certain chapters and sections in your syllabus, in the order that you prefer. You can even provide a direct link in your syllabus to the sections in the web view of your book.

Instructors also have the option of creating a customized version of their OpenStax book. The custom version can be made available to students in low-cost print or digital form through their campus bookstore. Visit the Instructor Resources section of your book page on OpenStax.org for more information.

Art attribution

In *World History,* art contains attribution to its title, creator or rights holder, host platform, and license within the caption. Because the art is openly licensed, anyone may reuse the art as long as they provide the same attribution to its original source.

If art appears without licensing information, you may assume that there are no known restrictions. If you claim copyright, please contact OpenStax at info@openstax.org.

Errata

All OpenStax textbooks undergo a rigorous review process. However, like any professional-grade textbook, errors sometimes occur. Since our books are web-based, we can make updates periodically when deemed pedagogically necessary. If you have a correction to suggest, submit it through the link on your book page on OpenStax.org. Subject matter experts review all errata suggestions. OpenStax is committed to remaining transparent about all updates, so you will also find a list of past and pending errata changes on your book page on OpenStax.org.

Format

You can access this textbook for free in web view or PDF through OpenStax.org, and for a low cost in print.

About *World History*

World History is designed to support both semesters of the world history course offered at both two-year and four-year institutions. Serving a student base of both majors and non-majors in the field, as well as an institutional variation in requirements of one or two semesters depending on the plan of study, the course introduces students to a global perspective of history conveyed within an engaging narrative. Concepts and assessments are presented in ways to help students think critically about the issues they encounter so they can broaden their perspective of global history and how the topics studied apply to their current life as citizens of the world.

The text shows how historical content and the ways in which history is studied are relevant to modern-day needs and situations. The narrative shows readers the *why* of historical events and people, providing context and import to engage students. A primary goal of the book is to include content, scholarship, and activities that explore a variety of perspectives, including those traditionally underrepresented in this canon.

Being able to thoughtfully achieve a global approach requires explicit discussions about the challenge historians face in their work. Each instructor and student enters the classroom with a construct that informs their existing understanding as well as their ability to understand and to appreciate novel perspectives. *World History* works to present an honest and authentic view of history for students to explore. The authors and reviewers achieve balance by introducing and juxtaposing people's experiences of history for a rich and nuanced discussion. New resources and new voices are integrated into the text in a deep and meaningful manner. Primary source material represents the cultures being discussed from a firsthand perspective whenever possible, showing a variety of experiences and voices that stress the interconnected nature of people and societies throughout history. Moreover, the work of diverse and underrepresented scholars and scholarship bolsters the text's ability to embrace diversity of thought and interpretation while spotlighting parts of history and places that often receive less coverage in history textbooks. Students will be challenged to use empathy to understand others' ways of thinking in order to better understand, analyze, and evaluate today's changes in the world.

Pedagogical Foundation

Learning Objectives

Every module begins with a set of clear and concise learning objectives that have been designed to be both measurable and meaningful. These objectives closely align with current teaching practice and aim to help the instructor decide what content to include or assign, and to guide student expectations of learning. After completing the module and end-of-module exercises, students should be able to demonstrate mastery of the learning objectives.

Key Features

Various features throughout each chapter engage students with the content while having them practice some of the most essential skills in the study of history, such as the examination of primary sources, the analysis of multiple accounts of an event or period, the study of non-textual artifacts, and the exploration of how specific historical topics connect to today's world.

- **In Their Own Words:** Students are presented with a textual primary source for review and/or analysis, with discussion/reflection questions included. This feature bolsters the foundational importance of using primary sources in historical studies.
- **Dueling Voices:** Learners are given either a historiographical debate, or a side-by-side primary source reading that offers two different interpretations of the same event. Sometimes these are directly contrasting, and sometimes they help elucidate different perspectives. Discussion questions are included. This feature highlights that history is an interpretive discipline and that historians must regularly grapple with conflicting and at times contradictory information and approaches.
- **Beyond the Book:** Non-textual sources— such as art, physical objects, or architecture—are presented for study with the goal of helping students understand the value of these kinds of sources in historical work. Discussion questions open up conversations about how to understand these important artifacts.
- **The Past Meets the Present:** Students explore how an aspect of chapter content speaks to an issue in the present day, and have the opportunity to engage further in the topic with reflection/discussion questions.
- **Link to Learning:** This feature provides a very brief introduction to online resources—videos, interactives, collections, maps, and other engaging resources—that are pertinent to students' exploration of the topic at hand.

Section Summaries

Section summaries distill the information in each section for both students and instructors down to key, concise points addressed in the section.

Key Terms

Key terms are bold and are followed by a definition in context. Definitions of key terms are also listed in each end-of-chapter Glossary, as well as a book-level Glossary appendix.

Assessments

A variety of assessments allow instructors to confirm core conceptual understanding, elicit brief explanations that demonstrate student understanding, and offer more in-depth assignments that enable learners to dive more deeply into a topic or history-study skill.

- **Review Questions** test for conceptual apprehension of key concepts.
- **Check Your Understanding Questions** require students to explain concepts in words.
- **Application and Reflection Questions** dive deeply into the material to support longer reflection, group discussion, or written assignments.

Answers to Questions in the Book

The end-of-chapter Review, Check Your Understanding, and Reflection Questions are intended for homework assignments or classroom discussion; thus, student-facing answers are not provided in the book. Answers and sample answers are provided in the Instructor Answer Guide, for instructors to share with students at their discretion, as is standard for such resources.

About the Authors

Senior Contributing Authors

Senior Contributing Authors (left to right): Ann Kordas, Ryan J. Lynch, Brooke Nelson, Julie Tatlock.

Ann Kordas, Johnson & Wales University
Ann Kordas holds a PhD in History from Temple University, and a JD from Boston University School of Law. She is a professor in the Humanities Department at Johnson & Wales University, where she teaches courses in U.S. history, world history, the history of the Atlantic World, and the history of the Pacific World. Her research interests lie primarily in the fields of cultural history and gender history.

Ryan J. Lynch, Columbus State University
Dr. Ryan J. Lynch is Associate Professor of the History of the Islamic World and Associate Dean of the Honors College at Columbus State University in Columbus, Georgia. A specialist of pre-modern Islamic history, he completed his DPhil and MPhil in Islamic Studies and History at the University of Oxford, an MLitt in Middle Eastern History and Language at the University of St Andrews, and a BA in History and Religious Studies at Stetson University. Dr. Lynch's research focuses primarily on the period of the early Islamic conquests, the Islamization of the Middle East, Islamic state formation, and Arabic historiography, while he also has a growing

interest in how modern terror groups use an imagined Islamic past to justify their extremist views in the modern period. He is the author of the award-winning book *Arab Conquests and Early Islamic Historiography* (I.B. Tauris, 2020).

Brooke Nelson, formerly California State University

Brooke Nelson is the Director of Curriculum at Marco Learning, an edtech company focused on making great educational resources available to all students. Previous to this role, she taught at California State University, Dominguez Hills, and Marymount California University. Her favorite courses to teach were World History, Death and Dying, and Introduction to Western Civilization because they allowed her to share her love of history with both non-major and major students. Her research focus is the late Roman world, with a special emphasis on religious conflicts and gender studies. She has a doctorate from Claremont Graduate University and master's degrees from the University of California, Irvine, and the University of Edinburgh.

Julie Tatlock, Mount Mary University

Dr. Julie C. Tatlock chairs the Department of Justice, Sociology and History at Mount Mary University in Milwaukee, Wisconsin. Her research interests include World History, Gender History, British History, and Face-to-Face and Online Pedagogy. She has several recent publications including, *Shaping Online Spaces Through Online Humanities Curricula* (IGI Global, 2023), "The Original Order of Things," (*Lutheran Journal of Ethics*, 2020), and "Enhancing Student Engagement Online: Creative Pedagogy in the Digital World," IGI Global, 2019). She is passionate about innovative teaching and learning as well as making higher education accessible to all students.

Contributing Authors

Chris Bingley, UCLA
Celeste Chamberland, Roosevelt University
Scott Corbett, Ventura College
Rick Gianni, Grand Canyon University
Jennifer Lawrence, Tarrant County College
Jamie McCandless, Kennesaw State University
Cristina Mehrtens, University of Massachusetts Dartmouth
Anthony Miller, Hanover College
Abigail Owen, Carnegie Mellon University
David Price, Santa Fe College
Kim Richardson, University of South Carolina Lancaster
Chris Rose, The University of Texas at Austin
Joseph Snyder, Southeast Missouri State University
Christopher Thrasher, National Park College
David Toye, Northeast State Community College
Alexander Wathen, University of Houston-Downtown
Grace Hunt Watkinson, Kennesaw State University
Joel Webb, Auburn University

Reviewers

Wayne Ackerson, Georgia Gwinnett College
Jonathan Allen, University of Maryland, College Park
Milan Andrejevich, Ivy Tech Community College
Maria Arbelaez, University of Nebraska Omaha
John Bertalan, University of South Florida
Robert Bond, MiraCosta College
Wesley Borucki, Palm Beach Atlantic University
Ken Bridges, South Arkansas Community College

Michael Burchett, Ohio Christian University
William Burns, The George Washington University
Matthew Byron, Young Harris College
Robert Caldwell, University at Buffalo
Elaine Carey, Purdue University Northwest
Katherine Clark Walter, The College at Brockport
Melanie Cochran, Volunteer State Community College
Melissa Daggett, San Jacinto College
Sharon Deubreau, Rhodes State College
Charles deWitt, Belhaven University
Sherrie Dux-Ideus, Central Community College
Mark Ellingson, Interdenominational Theological Center
Ronald Eydenberg, Middlesex Community College
Bryan Gibbs, Dallas College
Lela Gibson, Santiago Canyon College
Travis Grasser, Collin College
Chris Gratien, University of Virginia
Matthew Hacholski, Seward County Community College
Brian Harding, Mott Community College
Paul Harvey, Steilacoom Historical School District No. 1
David Head, University of Central Florida
Catherine Holden, Stevenson University
Christopher Jackson, De Anza College
Lesley Kauffman, San Jacinto College
Mark Klobas, Scottsdale Community College
Jennifer Lang, Delgado Community College
Ira Lovitch, Mount St. Mary's University
Paul Lubienecki, Chautauqua Institution
Senya Lubisich, Citrus College
John Lund, Keene State College
Jodie Mader, Thomas More University
Michael Mangus, The Ohio State University at Newark
Nicky Kay Michael, Bacone College
Charlotte Miller, Middle Georgia State University
Brandon Morgan, Central New Mexico Community College
Phil Nash, The Pennsylvania State University
Caryn Neumann, Miami University
Kenneth Orosz, SUNY Buffalo State College
Lisa Ossian, Des Moines Area Community College
Tao Peng, Minnesota State University, Mankato
Janet Rankin, Oregon State University
Jason Ripper, Everett Community College
Maria Ritzema, College of DuPage
Lomarsh Roopnarine, Jackson State University
James Ross-Nazzal, Houston Community College
Kimlisa Salazar Duchicela, Pima Community College
Greg Sanford, MCC Penn Valley
Leah Seabook-Rocha, Central Texas College
Julia Sloan, Curry College
Steven Smith, Fullerton College

Mary Sommar, Millersville University
Ralph Sonenshine, American University
David Stefancic, Saint Mary's College, Notre Dame, IN
Bianka Stumpf, Central Carolina Community College
Deborah Vess, East Georgia State College
Paul Vickery, Oral Roberts University
Christopher Ward, Clayton State University
Laura Wood, Tarrant County College
Clinton Young, University of Arkansas at Monticello

Additional Resources

Student and Instructor Resources

We've compiled additional resources for both students and instructors, including Getting Started Guides, an instructor's answer guide, test bank, and image slides. Instructor resources require a verified instructor account, which you can apply for when you log in or create your account on OpenStax.org. Take advantage of these resources to supplement your OpenStax book.

Instructor's answer guide. Each component of the instructor's guide is designed to provide maximum guidance for delivering the content in an interesting and dynamic manner.

Test bank. With nearly 1,300 assessments across both *World History* volumes, instructors can customize tests to support a variety of course objectives. The test bank includes review questions (multiple-choice, identification, fill-in-the-blank, true/false), short answer questions, and long answer questions to assess students on a variety of levels. The test bank is available in Word format.

PowerPoint lecture slides. The PowerPoint slides provide learning objectives, images and descriptions, feature focuses, and discussion questions as a starting place for instructors to build their lectures.

Academic Integrity

Academic integrity builds trust, understanding, equity, and genuine learning. While students may encounter significant challenges in their courses and their lives, doing their own work and maintaining a high degree of authenticity will result in meaningful outcomes that will extend far beyond their college career. Faculty, administrators, resource providers, and students should work together to maintain a fair and positive experience.

We realize that students benefit when academic integrity ground rules are established early in the course. To that end, OpenStax has created an interactive to aid with academic integrity discussions in your course.

Visit our academic integrity slider (https://www.openstax.org/r/academic-integrity-slider). Click and drag icons along the continuum to align these practices with your institution and course policies. You may then include the graphic on your syllabus, present it in your first course meeting, or create a handout for students. (attribution: Copyright Rice

University, OpenStax, under CC BY 4.0 license)

At OpenStax we are also developing resources supporting authentic learning experiences and assessment. Please visit this book's page for updates. For an in-depth review of academic integrity strategies, we highly recommend visiting the International Center of Academic Integrity (ICAI) website at https://academicintegrity.org/ (https://academicintegrity.org).

Community Hubs

OpenStax partners with the Institute for the Study of Knowledge Management in Education (ISKME) to offer Community Hubs on OER Commons—a platform for instructors to share community-created resources that support OpenStax books, free of charge. Through our Community Hubs, instructors can upload their own materials or download resources to use in their own courses, including additional ancillaries, teaching material, multimedia, and relevant course content. We encourage instructors to join the hubs for the subjects most relevant to your teaching and research as an opportunity both to enrich your courses and to engage with other faculty. To reach the Community Hubs, visit www.oercommons.org/hubs/openstax.

Technology partners

As allies in making high-quality learning materials accessible, our technology partners offer optional low-cost tools that are integrated with OpenStax books. To access the technology options for your text, visit your book page on OpenStax.org.

FIGURE 1.1 The Whole World. This seventeenth-century projection map of the world, prepared by cartographer Philip Eckebrecht for the noted German astronomer Johannes Kepler, gives a sense of the breadth of territory this text will cover. As we see later in this chapter, maps often reflect the maker's perception of geographical realities. (credit: modification of work "A Modern Depiction of the World" by Library of Congress/Wikimedia Commons, Public Domain)

CHAPTER OUTLINE

INTRODUCTION What is history? Is it simply a record of things people have done? Is it what writer Maya Angelou suggested—a way to meet the pain of the past and overcome it? Or is it, as Winston Churchill said, a chronicle by the victors, an interpretation by those who write it? History is all this and more. Above all else, it is a path to knowing why we are the way we are—all our greatness, all our faults—and therefore a means for us to understand ourselves and change for the better.

But history serves this function only if it is a true reflection of the past. It cannot be a way to mask the darker parts of human nature, nor a way to justify acts of previous generations. It is the historian's task to paint as clear a picture as sources will allow.

Will history ever be a perfect telling of the human tale? No. There are voices we may never hear. Yet each new history book written and each new source uncovered reveal an ever more precise record of events around the world (Figure 1.1). You are about to take a journey into human history.

1.1 Developing a Global Perspective

LEARNING OBJECTIVES

By the end of this section, you will be able to:
- Identify the role history plays in higher education
- Discuss the ways in which the study of history can build skills for lifelong learning and success
- Explain how the features of this text will optimize your learning experience

From the legends of Troy heralded by Homer to the contents of digital archives accessed by modern students, the human story has fascinated and instructed those who have tried to understand its complexities. Knowing the past has long been considered a mark of civilization, and its study has never been more important. We have all heard the philosopher George Santayana's observation, "Those who do not learn from history are doomed to repeat it." Yet because history is an ever-changing collection of events influenced and shaped by a variety of causes and outcomes, it never truly repeats at all.

Santayana's comment rings true, however, in that we can discern patterns of human behavior by careful study of the past. To know history is to know ourselves, and understanding history's nuances opens our imaginations to the possibilities each new situation creates. It is this knowledge of possibilities that allows the student of history to see the present with more clarity and prescience.

World History as Preparation for Life after College

History is more than a series of names and dates; those are simply its building blocks, the pieces necessary for completing the whole picture. History is a story, the human story, that connects us both to each other and to the generations that lived before us. And today we study history in a way that grounds students in this shared past while also preparing them for their futures. The liberal arts are intended to help students find fulfillment, to better themselves and their communities through meaningful self-reflection and development. But they have also always prepared students to enter the workplace by honing career skills. To say that a world history class prepares students for the workplace is simply to acknowledge what has always been true.

This world history text has several key features that will help you understand the past in ways that are relevant to the present. Perhaps most important is its recognition that the study of world history prepares us to meet modern challenges. To cover the history of the whole world is daunting, perhaps, but a student must be prepared to engage with the globalization processes that have dominated history for the past few centuries. People around the globe are more integrated than ever by social and economic forces that transcend national boundaries. Both your private and public lives will require knowledge of the world and its people. Understanding the diversity of peoples and ideas and possessing cultural empathy and awareness will allow you to meet global complexities with competence.

The study of history will also enhance your critical-thinking and analytical ability, both of which consistently appear among the top ten skills desired by employers (Figure 1.2). Other skills that have become increasingly important include adaptive thinking, social intelligence, cross-cultural competency, and media literacy. This final skill is critical to modern workplaces. History teaches students how to assess and analyze the material they are reading, as well as how to develop and present content in a meaningful and persuasive way. It also hones a creative mindset that is flexible and open to interpretations and ideas outside our own worldview.

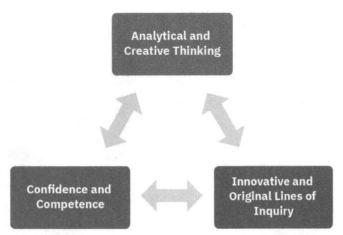

FIGURE 1.2 **Do You Have These Skills?** The top skills employers will value in 2025, according to the World Economic Forum, include innovative inquiry and creative thinking. You will develop and practice many of these skills in this course. (attribution: Copyright Rice University, OpenStax, under CC BY 4.0 license)

Without question, skills such as critical thinking, analysis, and creativity are developed best through the study of history. Historians must be truly multidisciplinary in the sense that they observe and gather as much information as they can and then interpret that data with the aim of drawing conclusions. The historian also must be a creative thinker because the source material—the data—is human, making it the most complex data imaginable. Historical data is as diverse as the people who make it, and it might be everything from the edicts of kings to the tunes played by street musicians. Historians must also be effective communicators. Who cares about a story nobody reads or a product nobody buys? What company in the world could not use and value someone who can think critically and creatively and then explain and communicate effectively? Historical thinking also provides students with a stronger sense of self, with avenues to explore human existence, and with the skills necessary to navigate the complexity of their world and future workplaces.

This text and its assessment questions will encourage you to analyze large amounts of information, to understand a myriad of concepts, and to make connections across topics. Developing cultural awareness and empathy is also critically important, and studying world history is a way to ensure you have this necessary skill. The influential job site Indeed.com says, "In our workplaces, in our world, we are a diverse people. Cultural competence is increasingly important as our means of communication and collaboration in working environments evolve. Learning how to respect, communicate and collaborate with an increasingly diverse work culture is crucial to optimizing a company's efficiency and productivity."

World History and Global Citizenship

The study of world history recognizes the integrated nature of modern life and prepares students for diverse, global workplaces. Knowing about the world will prepare you to be a **global citizen**, someone who may reside in only one nation but who self-identifies as part of the larger world community. Issues in need of solutions, like climate change, social justice, and human rights, are global in scale. You must know the world to be the change it needs. How do you fit in the global environment? What is your story, and how is it linked to that of others?

In many ways, the idea of global citizenship emerged from the human wreckage of the two world wars. Beginning in 1948, the United Nations (UN) established a series of universal declarations that conceived of all people as deserving of human rights and dignity (Figure 1.3). Three such declarations further affirmed the rights of women (Convention on the Elimination of All Forms of Discrimination Against Women, also known as CEDAW, 1979), of children (The Declaration of the Rights of the Child, 1959), and of people with disabilities (The Declaration on the Rights of Disabled Persons, 1975). The UN regularly requires that member nations report on progress in these areas. Words and declarations help to create an ethos, a set of guiding principles. So, in addition to participating in global economies that transcend lines on a map, many in our world recognize that we have also agreed to a series of rights and obligations that do the same.

FIGURE 1.3 Human Rights, Codified. Eleanor Roosevelt is shown holding a poster of the UN Universal Declaration of Human Rights in November 1949. Roosevelt, the former First Lady of the United States, chaired the committee that drafted the declaration. (credit: "Eleanor Roosevelt UDHR" by FDR Presidential Library & Museum/Flickr, CC BY 2.0)

A BBC poll in 2015–2016 surveyed eighteen countries and found that more than half the respondents believed themselves to be "global citizens." It also found that in times of prosperity, sentiments favoring a world community grow, while in times of strife, people tend to revert to more local, national identities. Though no one can see the future, it is difficult to imagine turning the clock back on the processes of globalization. Whether you would like to be a global citizen of the world or not, understanding the world is essential.

🔗 LINK TO LEARNING

What does it mean to be a citizen of the world? Watch this TED Talk by Hugh Evans (https://openstax.org/l/77HughEvansA) and think about the ways this concept resonates with you. Do you see yourself as connected to the world? Is that a positive attribute? Why or why not?

Features of This Textbook

This text is a great place to begin your journey into the world's past. It has several features that will help you understand the history of world civilizations from the earliest time to the modern era. For clarity, it adopts a traditional **chronological approach**, proceeding from ancient to modern times. Each chapter features maps prominently and will help you frame world cultures in their geographic and historical context. You will engage with firsthand accounts of key people and events—including instances in which people's recollections of the same events might differ. And the text will highlight links between the past and the present to emphasize how earlier knowledge applies to our world.

Of particular note are the feature boxes within each chapter. These present documents and images from the eras you are studying. Sometimes you will be guided outside the text—such as in the Link to Learning boxes—to explore other digital resources that clarify content, expand on ideas, and highlight interesting new work happening in the field. Finally, where appropriate, the text will offer material relevant to your current experiences, to help you understand the links between the past and the present. Following is a quick reference to these features.

In Their Own Words

In Their Own Words feature boxes present a source composed in the period the chapter covers and allow you to examine it in context, learning how to critically analyze source material. A short series of questions will help to guide your analysis.

Dueling Voices

Dueling Voices feature boxes present either an ongoing historical debate or conflicting reports of the same event or idea that were written around the time it occurred or emerged.

Beyond the Book

In Beyond the Book feature boxes, you can explore the value of art, architecture, music, film, and other physical objects as sources in interpreting history. The goal is to demonstrate that the human story resides in a great deal more than just the written word itself. You may also have the opportunity to do some experiential learning.

The Past Meets the Present

The Past Meets the Present feature boxes ask you to understand the connections between the material in the chapter and the present. They will prompt you to think about the relevance of a particular historical issue in today's world.

Because this is a global history, we tried to be true to the essence of world cultures by presenting people's names in forms as close as possible to their language of origin. These spelling choices have been made by experts in their field based on current research. For example, the text uses the pinyin system of transliteration for writing Chinese names, as opposed to the older Wade-Giles system, because pinyin is the system adopted by the People's Republic of China and more closely approximates the sounds of Mandarin Chinese. In languages using the Latin alphabet, accents have been retained on all personal names (Hernán Cortés, Napoléon Bonaparte); however, in transliterated languages such as Chinese and Arabic, we have avoided accents and apostrophes whenever possible, unless they are necessary to aid pronunciation and enhance readability. In naming events, places, and other items of historical interest, we have generally chosen the most commonly encountered English variants. Finally, dates are given using the Gregorian calendar, the international standard for civil calendars, with "BCE" to indicate developments occurring before the Common Era and "CE" to mark events in our own era.

The study of world history also requires a strong understanding of geography. You might assume that maps are fairly cut and dried. After all, we can clearly demonstrate where things are, can't we? For most of history, however, this was not actually the case. Maps are some of the most contested pieces of historical evidence we have because they were almost always made from the perspective of the one making the map, not as an objective practice. Most civilizations put themselves at the center of their known world, for instance. Maps have also been used to aid in the conquest and suppression of peoples. During the Age of Exploration, the Pope arbitrarily divided inhabited territory that was new to Europeans and granted it to Spain and Portugal. Centuries later in Berlin, Germany, European diplomats drew lines on a map of Africa to apportion territory among colonial powers. Think of how written history might change if our surviving maps were indigenous in origin. Even when humanity acquired knowledge of the size and space of things, maps remained inaccurate, often showing Europe as larger than it is and regions of the Global South—Latin America, Africa, and parts of Asia and Oceania—as smaller than their actual size.

Maps also present challenges because some territories are claimed by more than one political entity. There are many examples in the distant past, and even today, of contested regions, such as Crimea and Taiwan, that can make presenting regional geographies difficult. Crimea is claimed by both Russia and Ukraine, and Taiwan claims independence while China considers Taiwan part of its territory. The text will highlight these regions as they arise in the human story so you can explore geography's complexities.

⊘ LINK TO LEARNING

For a perspective on how Google Earth reflects the globalization of society, read "World Maps and the Dawn of Globalisation" (https://openstax.org/l/77GoogleEarthA) by Jerry Brotton, a cultural historian and author of *The History of the World in Twelve Maps*. This brief blog post comments on the precision of GPS map technology as used by Google Earth. As you read it, consider the possibilities and dangers of such technology.

1.2 Primary Sources

LEARNING OBJECTIVES

By the end of this section, you will be able to:
- Identify different types of primary sources
- Analyze primary sources in a historical context
- Interpret primary sources effectively

Historians develop interpretations of the past based on source material, and we do the same in this book. From ancient hieroglyphs to works of art to blog posts, from histories and biographies written by later scholars to Google Maps, sources help us build our interpretations of the human story.

Learning to Evaluate Documents and Images

There are two main kinds of historical sources, primary and secondary. A **primary source** is a gateway to the past because it is an object or document that comes directly from the time period to which it refers. Primary sources might be government documents, menus from restaurants, diaries, letters, musical instruments, photographs, portraits drawn from life, songs, and so on. If a historian is looking at Ancient Egypt, a statue of a pharaoh is a primary source for that time period, as are hieroglyphs that tell of the pharaoh's reign. Primary sources, when we have them, are considered more valuable than other sources because they are as close in time as we can get to the events being studied. Think, for example, of a court trial: The ideal is to have the trial quickly so that witness testimony is fresher and therefore more reliable. With the passage of time, people can forget, they might subconsciously add or take away parts of a memory, and they may be influenced to interpret events differently.

A **secondary source** is one written or created after the fact. A twentieth-century biography of an Egyptian pharaoh is a secondary source, as are a map drawn in the 1960s to identify the battle sites of World War II (1939–1945) and a museum curator's blog post about the artistic achievements of the Ming (1368–1644). These types of scholarly sources are critical for the evolution of historical knowledge and are often the place students begin to form an understanding of past events. Secondary sources are useful for setting context and placing a topic in relationship to others of the same era. They also provide access to scholarly research based on primary sources for students whose access might be limited by language or geography. Good research requires both types of sources and some attention to **historiography**, which is the study of how other historians have already interpreted and written about the past.

All primary sources are not equal. History technically begins with the advent of writing, when humans began to deliberately make records and, after that, to develop the idea that preserving the past was a worthwhile endeavor. This is not to say that there isn't anything valuable to be found in the oral histories of preliterate societies, or in prehistoric cave paintings and archaeological artifacts. For historians, however, the written word is more accurate evidence for building narratives of the past. For example, imagine a modern magazine with a rock or pop star on the front, dressed for performance in a vibrant or provocative style. If that were the only piece of evidence that existed five hundred years from now, how would historians interpret our era? Without context, interpretation of the past is quite difficult. Studying artifacts is certainly worthwhile, but text offers us greater clarity. Even if the cover of the magazine bore only a caption, like "Pop star rising to the top of the charts," future historians would have significantly more information than from the photo alone. However, even textual sources must be met with a critical eye. "Fake news" is not new, but the speed at which it travels today is unprecedented. We must investigate the full context of any source and look for corroboration.

It takes time to develop the skills necessary to interpret primary sources. As an example, consider the act of reading a poem. You can read the surface of a poem, the literal meaning of the words presented. But that seldom reflects the true meaning the poet meant to convey. You must also look for nuances, hidden meanings, or repeated metaphors. We approach a primary source in a similar way.

There are four key areas to consider when interpreting sources: the author, the audience, the intent, and the context. Here are some key questions to ask yourself when exploring a new source:

1. What kind of source is it? Government documents have a different purpose than personal diaries. A former president commenting on a political issue has a different view from a comedian doing the same.
2. Who authored the source and why? Is the author responsible for simply recording the information, or was the author involved in the event? Is the author reliable, or does the author have an agenda?
3. What is the historical context? How does the source relate to the events covered in the chapter?

None of the answers disqualify a source from adding value, but precisely what that source brings to the overall picture depends heavily on those answers.

⊘ LINK TO LEARNING

This is a presentation on working with primary sources (https://openstax.org/l/77PrimarySA) produced by the Smithsonian. Pay particular attention to section 2, "Documents." Read through it and take note of the kinds of questions to ask as you critically assess primary sources. You may want to write them down or have them on hand for reference as you work your way through this text.

In a world where many sources are available in digital format, searching online, as many students do, is a convenient way of doing research. But the internet has just as much misinformation as it has legitimate sources. Historians evaluate the strength of both primary and secondary sources, especially online. How do we decide what a good source is? Some clues are more obvious than others. For example, it is unlikely any truly scholarly material will be found on the first page of a Google search, unless the search terms include key phrases or use targeted search engines such as Google Scholar. Online encyclopedias may be a good place to start your research, but they should be only a springboard to more refined study.

Your work is only as strong as the sources you use. Whether you are writing a paper, a discussion post online, or even a creative writing piece, the better your sources, the more persuasive will be your writing. Sites like Wikipedia and Encyclopedia.com offer a quick view of content, but they will not give enough depth to allow for the critical thinking necessary to produce quality work. However, they are useful for introducing a topic with which you might not be familiar. And if you start with encyclopedic sources, you can often find pathways to better sources. They might spark new lines of inquiry, for instance, or have bibliographic information that can lead you to higher-quality material.

Always make sure you can tell who is producing the website. Is it a scholar, a museum, or a research organization? If so, there is a good chance the material is sound. Is the information cited? In other words, does the source tell you where it got the information? Are those sources in turn objective and reliable? Can you corroborate the site's information? This means doing some fact checking. You should see whether other sources present similar data and whether your source fits into the narrative developed by other scholars. Does your school library list the site as a resource? Finally, if you are not sure, ask. Librarians work in online spaces too, and you can generally reach out to these experts with any questions.

As you explore world history via this text, you will be asked many times to read and interpret primary sources. These will normally be set off as feature boxes, as noted earlier. Let's work through a few examples. The goal is to become more familiar with the types of questions you should ask of sources, as well as the variety of sources you will work with throughout the text.

First, an image exercise. The following images are exterior and interior views of the Hagia Sophia in Istanbul, a wonder of the late antique world whose name means "Holy Wisdom" in Greek. Buildings and other material objects change as they are affected by historical events. Images of them can tell us much about those events and the people who enter or interact with them.

The first set of images (Figure 1.4 and Figure 1.5) provide a likeness of the famous church at the time it was built, during the reign of the Byzantine emperor Justinian I (483–565 CE). The domed structure was unique for its engineering and stunning in its effect. Decorated with Greek **iconography**, the visual images and symbols used in a work of art, the basilica stood as an emblem of Justinian's power, the awesome nature of the Christian God, and the surviving wealth and stability of the East. Churches at the time were meant to inspire awe; because most people could not read, stories of religious figures and events were told through highly decorative and symbolic images, and obedience and a desire to join a religious community could be motivated by the buildings' grandeur. As you study the renderings, reflect on the following questions: What are the key features of the building? What does it make you think about? What does it tell you about the period in which it was built? What would you think about it if you were a poor sixth-century farmer, an urban merchant of some wealth, or a foreign leader?

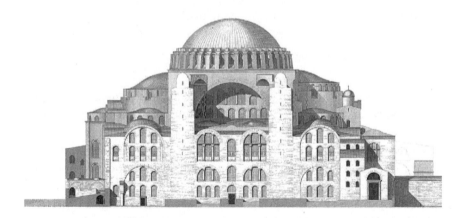

FIGURE 1.4 Exterior of Hagia Sophia. Note the domes and archways in this drawing of the exterior of the Hagia Sophia. Such architectural features were particularly hard to build during the sixth century and often collapsed because the engineering was flawed. Thanks to their durability, those of Hagia Sophia were a marvel at the time it was built. (credit: "Saint Sophia, Constantinopolis" by ETH Library/Wikimedia Commons, Public Domain)

FIGURE 1.5 Interior of Hagia Sophia. The Greek Christian iconography found in the interior of the Hagia Sophia includes halos on the figures, signifying holiness. Also note the lavish use of precious gold in this tenth-century mosaic of Mary, the child Jesus, and the emperors (left) Justinian and (right) Constantine. (credit: "Hagia Sophia Southwestern entrance mosaics 2" by "Myrabella"/Wikimedia Commons, CC0 1.0)

In 1453, nearly a thousand years after the reign of Justinian, the city of Constantinople (now called Istanbul in present-day Turkey) was conquered by Muslim Turks. According to contemporary accounts of the conquest, when the Ottoman leader Sultan Mehmed II came to the Hagia Sophia, he recognized its beauty and saved it from destruction. To Muslims, the Christian God and the Muslim God are the same, so Mehmed made the church a mosque—following a long tradition in the Middle East of continuing the use of sacred spaces. Minarets, towers from which the Muslim call to prayer is issued, were added at the four corners of the building, and Arabic writing was placed beside the ancient Greek iconography.

The second set of images (Figure 1.6 and Figure 1.7) show the Hagia Sophia as it stands today, having also been a museum and now serving as a mosque once again. The building tells a tale spanning hundreds of years and highlights many fascinating aspects of the region's history. But without the context, its meaning would be far less clear.

FIGURE 1.6 **Hagia Sophia's Minarets.** Hagia Sophia has four tall minarets, which were added a thousand years after its initial construction. Minarets are towers from which the Muslim call to prayer goes out multiple times a day. (credit: "Hagia Sophia (Istanbul)" by Frank Mago/Flickr, CC BY 2.0)

FIGURE 1.7 **Hagia Sophia's Many Influences.** Muslims consider themselves the heirs of Judaism and Christianity, and until recently, you could still see the early Greek iconography in the interior of Hagia Sophia. Now it is covered during prayer times by large medallions bearing Arabic writing. (credit: "Hagia Sophia Istanbul 2013 13" by Karelj/ Wikimedia Commons, Public Domain)

Documentary Sources: Competing Narratives

Textual, or written, primary sources are considered the best possible resource for historians. They tend to offer both far more context and far more information than other types of sources, and sometimes clues about the writer's intent. But even they must be approached with method and scrutiny. We must evaluate the author, audience, intent, and context in order to accurately interpret a primary source document. Some questions you might ask about the author include the following: Who wrote the piece and what is their background? What was important to the author? Why might the author have written what they did? In some cases, the answers will be fairly obvious. In others, a deeper inspection might reveal hidden motives.

You must also take into account the planned audience for a document: For whom was it written? Was it meant to be public or private? Is it a letter to a friend or an essay submitted for publication? For a modern example, is it a text to a friend or to a mother? Texts will one day be a source for historians to use, but knowing who sent them, and to whom, will be essential to interpreting them correctly. (For fun, search online using the term "misinterpreted texts.")

In addition to considering the audience, you should think about the intent: Why was the document written? Was it intended to be a factual account of an event? Was it meant to persuade? Is it a complete falsification? Often people write things that present them in the best light rather than reveal weaknesses.

Finally, you should reflect on the circumstances of the document's creation. Some questions you may want to ask include the following: What is the general time period of the document, and what was that time like? What was happening when the individual wrote the document? Was there any sort of intimidation or distress? Is it a time of war or peace? Is there religious conflict? Is there an economic crisis? A health crisis? A natural disaster? Could the writer have been fending off an attack or lobbying for one? Are we missing other perspectives or voices we would like to hear?

The answers to these questions will shape your interpretation of the primary source and bring you closer to its true meaning. Most text-based sources have meanings beyond the obvious, and it is the historian's job to uncover these. Be sure to keep these questions in mind throughout this course and whenever you undertake historical research or are considering the accuracy of information you encounter (Figure 1.8).

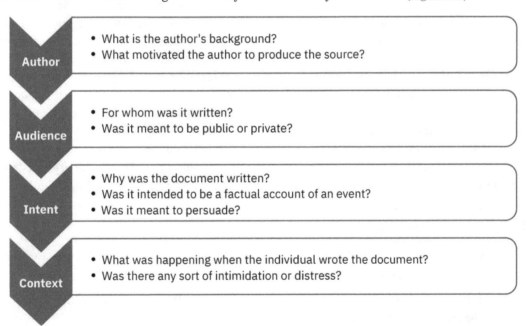

FIGURE 1.8 Evaluating Primary Sources. These key questions to ask about primary sources help us evaluate the author, audience, intent, and context. (attribution: Copyright Rice University, OpenStax, under CC BY 4.0 license)

To gain experience using these questions, consider the two accounts in The Spanish Arrival in the Aztec Capital, written relatively close to each other in time and dealing with similar subjects from different perspectives. According to the first account, written in 1519 by Hernán Cortés, Indigenous people in the Americas were thrilled to become subjects of Spain when European colonizers arrived. The Aztec, telling of their encounter with the Spanish, relate that the Spaniards killed even the unarmed, which seemed barbaric to the author. What should historians do with such widely competing texts? How do they decide what each one adds to the true story of the conquest of Mexico? As you read, keep these questions in mind.

The Spanish Arrival in the Aztec Capital

Hernán Cortés was a Spanish conquistador who conquered the Aztec Empire in what is now central Mexico in 1521. An ambitious but brutal young man seeking fame and fortune, Cortés wrote a series of letters to Charles V describing his exploits in the hope of raising himself in the king's esteem. In the following letter, written in 1519, Cortés recounts his conquest of Tenochtitlán, the Aztec capital, and describes the Indigenous people he encountered. The letter is followed by an Aztec account of the conquest that describes an event known as the Massacre in the Great Temple, an attack on nobles and warriors who had gathered in Tenochtitlán to celebrate a religious festival. The attack was conducted by Pedro de Alvarado, who had been left in charge while Cortés was absent from the city. At the time of the massacre, Moctezuma, the Aztec ruler, was under house arrest, having previously greeted Cortés on his arrival and invited him into the sacred city.

In my former despatch [sic], Most Excellent Prince, I gave a list of the cities and towns that had to that time voluntarily submitted to your authority, together with those I had reduced by conquest. I also mentioned having received information from the natives of a certain great Lord, called MUTECZUMA, who, according to their computation of distances, dwelt ninety or a hundred leagues from the coast and the port where I had disembarked; and that, trusting in the greatness of God, and the confidence inspired by the royal name of your Highness, I proposed to go and see him wherever he might be. I also recollect having [. . .] assured your Highness that he should be taken either dead or alive, or become a subject to the royal throne of your Majesty. With this determination I departed from the city of Cempoal, to which I gave the name of Sevilla, on the 16th of August, with fifteen horse and three hundred infantry, all in the best condition for war in which I was able, or the time permitted me to render them. [. . .] I also left the whole province of Cempoal, and all the mountainous region adjacent to the town, containing fifty thousand warriors, and fifty towns and fortresses, in peace and security, and firm in their allegiance to your Majesty, as they have remained to the present time. Although they were subjects of Muteczuma, yet according to the information I received, they had been reduced to that condition by force, within a short period; and when they had obtained through me some knowledge of your Highness, and of your great regal power, they declared their desire to become vassals of your Majesty, and to form an alliance with me. They also begged me to protect them against that mighty Lord, who used violent and tyrannical measures to keep them in subjection, and took from them their sons to be slain and offered as sacrifices to his idols; with many other complaints against him, in order to avoid whose tyranny they embraced the service of your Majesty.

—Hernán Cortés, *Second Letter to Charles V*

During this time, the people asked Motecuhzoma how they should celebrate their god's fiesta. He said: "Dress him in all his finery, in all his sacred ornaments."

During this same time, The Sun commanded that Motecuhzoma and Itzcohuatzin, the military chief of Tlatelolco, be made prisoners. The Spaniards hanged a chief from Acolhuacan named Nezahualquentzin. They also murdered the king of Nauhtla, Cohualpopocatzin, by wounding him with arrows and then burning him alive.

For this reason, our warriors were on guard at the Eagle Gate. [. . .] But messengers came to tell them to dress the figure of Huitzilopochtli [the god of sun and war]. They left their posts and went to dress him in his sacred finery: his ornaments and his paper clothing.

When this had been done, the celebrants began to sing their songs. That is how they celebrated the first day of the fiesta. On the second day they began to sing again, but without warning they were all put to death. The dancers and singers were completely unarmed. [. . .]

The Spaniards attacked the musicians first, slashing at their hands and faces until they had killed all of them. The singers—and even the spectators—were also killed. This slaughter in the Sacred Patio went on for three hours. Then the Spaniards burst into the rooms of the temple to kill the others: those who were carrying water, or bringing fodder for the horses, or grinding meal, or sweeping, or standing watch over this work.

The king Motecuhzoma [. . .] protested: "Our lords, that is enough! What are you doing? These people are not carrying shields or macanas. Our lords, they are completely unarmed!"

The Sun had treacherously murdered our people on the twentieth day after the captain left for the coast. We allowed the Captain to return to the city in peace. But on the following day we attacked him with all our might, and that was the beginning of the war.

—Miguel León-Portilla, *The Broken Spears: The Aztec Account of the Conquest of Mexico*

- To whom is each author writing?
- How do the authors' different intentions affect what they wrote?
- One author was on the side of the victorious and one among the vanquished. How does this context affect the tone of the writing?

Textual Sources: The Importance of Language

The different types of language used in a source are clues to its interpretation. Linguists call the use of language **rhetoric**. Rhetorical choices, decisions about the way words are used and put together, are often deliberate and intended to achieve a certain outcome. For example, think about the way you talk to a professor versus the way you talk to a friend. We must closely examine the rhetorical choices in any primary document to correctly interpret it. To practice this skill, consider President Roosevelt's famous speech in Roosevelt's "Day of Infamy" Speech and the guiding questions that follow.

IN THEIR OWN WORDS

Roosevelt's "Day of Infamy" Speech

The United States entered World War II in 1941 after the Japanese attacked Pearl Harbor (Figure 1.9), the naval base where the U.S. Pacific fleet moored most of its vessels. It was a surprise attack that killed hundreds, devastated the base, and shocked the country. President Franklin D. Roosevelt went to Congress and asked for a declaration of war against Japan. The speech he gave, however, was about more than this request. Roosevelt used certain words to highlight that the attack was secret and calculated. He also suggested that God was on the side of the United States. As you read, pay special attention to the words Roosevelt uses. Can you pick out a few key rhetorical choices?

FIGURE 1.9 Pearl Harbor under Attack. This photograph of Pearl Harbor, Hawaii, was taken from a Japanese plane on December 7, 1941, shortly after the beginning of the torpedo attack on the U.S. fleet anchored there. (credit: "Attack on Pearl Harbor Japanese planes view" by Naval History and Heritage Command/Wikimedia Commons, Public Domain)

Mr. Vice President, Mr. Speaker, Members of the Senate and of the House of Representatives: Yesterday, December 7th, 1941—a date which will live in infamy—the United States of America was suddenly and deliberately attacked by naval and air forces of the Empire of Japan.

The United States was at peace with that nation and, at the solicitation of Japan, was still in conversation with its government and its emperor looking toward the maintenance of peace in the Pacific. Indeed, one hour after Japanese air squadrons had commenced bombing in the American Island of Oahu, the Japanese Ambassador to the United States and his colleague delivered to our secretary of state a formal reply to a recent American message. And while this reply stated that it seemed useless to continue the existing diplomatic negotiations, it contained no threat or hint of war or of armed attack.

It will be recorded that the distance of Hawaii from Japan makes it obvious that the attack was deliberately planned many days or even weeks ago. During the intervening time, the Japanese government has deliberately sought to deceive the United States by false statements and expressions of hope for continued peace.

The attack yesterday on the Hawaiian Islands has caused severe damage to American naval and military forces. I regret to tell you that very many American lives have been lost. In addition, American ships have been reported torpedoed on the high seas between San Francisco and Honolulu.

Yesterday the Japanese government also launched an attack against Malaya.

Last night Japanese forces attacked Hong Kong.

Last night Japanese forces attacked Guam.

Last night Japanese forces attacked the Philippine Islands.

Last night the Japanese attacked Wake Island.

And this morning the Japanese attacked Midway Island.

Japan has, therefore, undertaken a surprise offensive extending throughout the Pacific area. The facts of yesterday and today speak for themselves. The people of the United States have already formed their opinions and well understand the implications to the very life and safety of our nation.

As commander in chief of the army and navy I have directed that all measures be taken for our defense. But always will our whole nation remember the character of the onslaught against us.

No matter how long it may take us to overcome this premeditated invasion, the American people in their righteous might will win through to absolute victory.

I believe that I interpret the will of the Congress and of the people when I assert that we will not only defend ourselves to the uttermost but will make it very certain that this form of treachery shall never again endanger us.

Hostilities exist. There is no blinking at the fact that our people, our territory, and our interests are in grave danger. With confidence in our armed forces—with the unbounding determination of our people—we will gain the inevitable triumph—so help us God.

I ask that the Congress declare that since the unprovoked and dastardly attack by Japan on Sunday, December 7th, 1941, a state of war has existed between the United States and the Japanese Empire.

—Franklin D. Roosevelt, "Day of Infamy"

- What message was Roosevelt conveying to the nation's people and to the world?
- What word choices did he make to convey this message?

🔗 LINK TO LEARNING

In his "Day of Infamy" speech, Roosevelt uses a rhythmic cadence to give the impression of imminent danger as Japan attacks other targets. Listen to an audio recording of the speech (https://openstax.org/l/77Infamy) from the Franklin D. Roosevelt Presidential Library and Museum.

Hidden in History

Historians begin their work with a research question and seek to find the sources necessary to build an authentic narrative that answers it. One challenge is that written sources are undeniably valuable but often leave out important details. For example, many speak only of the lives of elites. It is not terribly difficult to find information about kings, queens, and other rulers of the past, but what of their families? Their servants? What of the ordinary people who lived under their rule?

Some groups of people remain hidden in our account of history because few records talk about their lives and experiences. Historians of the 1960s began to revolutionize the discipline by studying history "from the bottom up." In other words, they began to focus on just those groups that had long been ignored. They used sources like church records, newspapers, and court hearings to illuminate the lives of the poor and illiterate. Court hearings were one venue in which the words of people from all backgrounds were recorded as they served as witnesses and as accused. Mothers and fathers also sought out those who could write letters for them to get pardons for loved ones convicted of crimes. These kinds of sources shed light on those whose voices were rarely heard, either while they lived or after they died. Great strides have been made in the field of social history, which looks beyond politics to the everyday aspects of life in the past. But it remains difficult, lacking records, to represent women, the poor, and minority communities on an equal footing with those who have traditionally held power.

These kinds of limitations can also apply to regions of the world. Civilizations with long-standing and abundant historical documents often have more complete histories than others. Much is known, for example, about European history and Chinese history, both of which have deep roots in the written word. Europe, after all, had Herodotus, and China had Sima Qian. Herodotus, who lived in the fifth century BCE, is called the father of history in the West; he wrote the history of the Greco-Persian wars. Sima Qian, born in the middle of the second century BCE, is referred to in China as the father of history for his work *Records of the Grand Historian*, a sweeping history of the Han dynasty. The Middle East and India also have rich textual histories. In Africa and Latin America, the historical record is less full.

In the case of Latin America, the historical record was significantly altered when the Europeans arrived. Believing that much of the writing of Indigenous people that they found spoke of a religion and culture they meant to replace, the conquerors deliberately destroyed it. Writing Africa's history is complicated by both its size and its diversity, as well as its colonial past. Due to the extremes of climate, surviving written documents and even archaeological evidence are not easily found, and what exists of written history is often tainted by the bias of the colonial observers who wrote it. New scholarship is emerging in both regions, generated by historians who look with fresh eyes and seek to understand history as it was. To gain some insight into the way history is relevant to the present, read Chinua Achebe on the Value of Indigenous History and consider the questions posed.

THE PAST MEETS THE PRESENT

Chinua Achebe on the Value of Indigenous History

The following is an interview with the noted Nigerian novelist Chinua Achebe (1930–2013) in *The Atlantic*. Achebe, author of several important books including *Things Fall Apart*, which explores the impact of British missionary work in Nigeria, speaks to both the historic legacy of colonialism—the practice of controlling another people or area, usually for economic gain—and the need to first see ourselves independently and then in relation to others (Figure 1.10).

FIGURE 1.10 Chinua Achebe. This is a photo of the young Chinua Achebe in Lagos, Nigeria, in 1966. (credit: "Chinua Achebe, 1966" by *The New York Times*/Wikimedia Commons, Public Domain)

But, of course, something doesn't continue to surprise you every day. After a while I began to understand why the book [*Things Fall Apart*] had resonance. I began to understand my history even better. It wasn't as if when I wrote it I was an expert in the history of the world. I was a very young man. I knew I had a story, but how it fit into the story of the world—I really had no sense of that. Its meaning for my Igbo people was clear to me, but I didn't know how other people elsewhere would respond to it. Did it have any meaning or resonance for them? I realized that it did when, to give you just one example, the whole class of a girls' college in South Korea wrote to me, and each one expressed an opinion about the book. And then I learned something, which was that they had a history that was similar to the story of *Things Fall Apart*—the history of colonization. This I didn't know before. Their colonizer was Japan. So these people across the waters were able to relate to the story of dispossession in Africa. People from different parts of the world can respond to the same story, if it says something to them about their own history and their own experience.

—Chinua Achebe in Katie Bacon, "An African Voice," *The Atlantic*

- Try to sum up Chinua Achebe's words in one sentence.
- In what ways do you think colonialism has influenced the writing of history?

1.3 Causation and Interpretation in History

LEARNING OBJECTIVES

By the end of this section, you will be able to:
- Describe causation as it is used in the study of history
- Identify the levels of causation
- Analyze the role of interpretation in producing an accurate historical record

The study of history has always been about more than giving a recounting of past events. It is about remembering our shared past, making human connections that traverse centuries, and helping us know more about ourselves. Once we know how to muster as many facts as we can, we must consider the next step—understanding causation. Causation is the *why* behind events; understanding it is the way historians get at the heart of the matter. The powerful and public forces that change society and government are also present when individuals make choices about their lives. What, then, are the forces that shape history, that shift it one way or another, that move people to change on both an individual and a societal level?

All of us see these historical causes through the lens of our own experiences, circumstances, and value systems. Historians, particularly those trained in recent times, work to eliminate as much bias as they can, but we cannot wholly disconnect ourselves from our environment and beliefs. Bias can even sometimes act as a positive force, allowing us to look at the past in new ways. For example, historians in the 1960s and 1970s began to question their discipline's traditional focus on elites and sought out new sources that highlight the lives of more ordinary people. Driven by a bias in favor of the counterculture and politics of the era, they wanted to know more about what *all* people experienced.

Levels of Causation

In their quest for the why of an event, historians look at both the immediate and the long-term circumstances of that event. Not all causes are equally significant; we need to rank them in importance. Let us begin with a thought exercise. At this moment in your history, you are reading this textbook. Why? Perhaps you would say, "Because the instructor told me to, and it will be on the test." Certainly that is a valid reason. But if you think a bit more deeply, you might also say, "I want to do well in my education so I can be successful." And at an even deeper level, "Society tells me that education is necessary to realize my full potential, find fulfillment, and participate in the community."

Think of all the other things that caused you to be here in this moment. There are no wrong answers; just explore the levels of causation behind your reading right now. Now rank them in order of importance. Which causes had the most influence on you, and which were more remote? Your response might look something like a pyramid (Figure 1.11). The **primary cause** is the most immediate. It is the spark. The secondary cause is once removed. The tertiary cause offers the broader context.

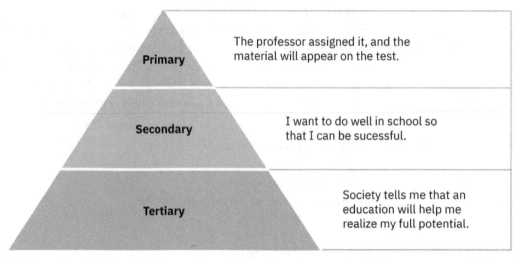

FIGURE 1.11 Causation Explained. This causation chart answers the question, "Why are you reading?" on three levels. The primary level is the most immediate. (attribution: Copyright Rice University, OpenStax, under CC BY 4.0 license)

To reach a true understanding of why you are reading your text, you needed to know yourself well, understand the connection between education and career, and assess how social factors, such as the value employers place on education, influence your decision-making. The more aspects of causation historians can find, the closer they can get to the true nature of the event.

Let's try another example, this one from history. Why did the United States enter World War II in 1941? In this case, the immediate cause was Japan's attack on the U.S. naval base at Pearl Harbor in Hawaii, but hostilities had been brewing for some time. The president of the United States, Franklin Roosevelt, had been looking for ways to help the British fend off a potential German invasion, and Japan and the United States had long-standing issues over the use of power in the Pacific (Figure 1.12).

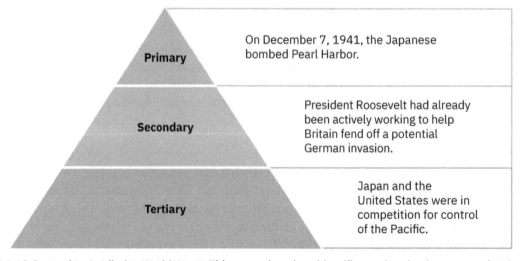

FIGURE 1.12 Causation Applied to World War II. This causation chart identifies and ranks the reasons for the entry of the United States into World War II. (attribution: Copyright Rice University, OpenStax, under CC BY 4.0 license)

Here is one more example. In 1453, Mehmed II laid siege to the city of Constantinople. Why? Mehmed II was the leader of the Ottoman Empire, the sultan. He had been badly treated by his father, and when he ascended the throne, he felt he had something to prove. The Ottomans had tried several times to take Constantinople because it lay at the crossroads of many civilizations. Conquest had long been a reliable mechanism for bringing new people and wealth into the Ottoman Empire and for keeping its economy prosperous. All these factors played a role in the siege undertaken by Mehmed II. Can you order them by importance? This is the point where historians usually disagree, even about events for which most of the facts are clear. A historian who believes powerful leaders are the most influential factor driving events would rank Mehmed's personal goals first (Figure 1.13). Base your ranking on the strongest arguments you can make.

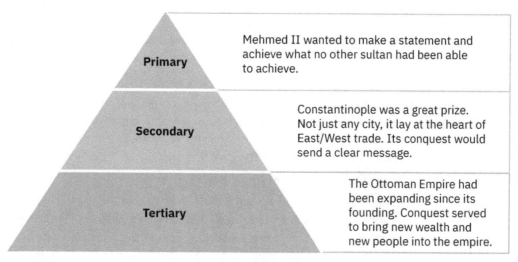

FIGURE 1.13 Causation Applied to the Conquest of Constantinople. This causation chart ranks the reasons for Mehmed II's 1453 Ottoman conquest of Constantinople. (attribution: Copyright Rice University, OpenStax, under CC BY 4.0 license)

There can be more than three causes to any event, of course, and because human choice always plays a role, we sometimes cannot separate events on the big stage from the smallest of personal moments in history. The context of the Ottoman Empire's continuous expansion set the scene in this example, and Mehmed II's desire to prove his ability was the spark.

Before moving on, try one more example on your own. Pick a moment in history with which you are familiar and follow the same process.

Interpretation in History

Hand in hand with bringing causation to light is discovering what informed the choices people made in the past. What makes people act as they do? For much of history, we found the answer in the actions of elites—tsars, sultans, kings, and queens. The first historians largely concerned themselves with the study of wars and rulers, in accordance with the **great man theory** of history that credits leaders and heroes with triggering history's pivotal events. Although these historians gave some attention to historical detail, there was also an equal measure of bravado, exaggeration, and political spin in their work. This seemed reasonable in a world where the king's choice became everyone's choice and where sources rarely spoke about anyone other than noble lords and ladies. That this type of history remained the norm for so long was also a function of who was writing it.

In the West, Thomas Carlyle, a nineteenth-century Scottish historian, considered the study of the lives of "big men" enough to understand all of history. Higher education was the privilege of only the rich; it must have seemed quite natural to believe that only the elites could move history. These ideas began to change, however, if slowly. In the early nineteenth century, a new school of thought called Romanticism emerged. The Romantics believed there was greatness in everyday life. Even a small flower was worthy of a poem, and the plight of a lowly squire was as important as the worries of the great lord of the manor, for both were essential actors in the human experience. The advent of Romantic art, poetry, music, and novels paved the way for a broad reexamination of what was worth knowing and studying. Writing a little later, in 1860, the Russian novelist Leo Tolstoy argued that there is more to history than the actions of one person. In his novel *War and Peace*, he contended that the "general mass of men" who participate in history are the ones who truly cause events.

DUELING VOICES

Great Men, or Everyone?

In an 1840 lecture on heroes, Thomas Carlyle coined the term "Great Men" to describe the kind of history he considered worthy, the study of elite men in positions of power. In his novel *War and Peace*, the Russian novelist Leo Tolstoy argued that there is far more to history than the actions of one person. In the following excerpts, consider the viewpoint of each writer.

As I take it, Universal History, the history of what man has accomplished in this world, is at bottom the History of the Great Men who have worked here. They were the leaders of men, these great ones; the modellers, patterns, and in a wide sense creators, of whatsoever the general mass of men contrived to do or to attain; all things that we see standing accomplished in the world are properly the outer material result, the practical realization and embodiment, of Thoughts that dwelt in the Great Men sent into the world: the soul of the whole world's history, it may justly be considered, were the history of these. [. . .]

We cannot look, however imperfectly, upon a great man, without gaining something by him. He is the living light-fountain, which it is good and pleasant to be near. The light which enlightens, which has enlightened the darkness of the world; and this not as a kindled lamp only, but rather as a natural luminary shining by the gift of Heaven; a flowing light-fountain, as I say, of native original insight, of manhood and heroic nobleness;—in whose radiance all souls feel that it is well with them.

—Thomas Carlyle, "Lecture on Heroes"

In historical events (where the actions of men are the subject of observation) the first and most primitive approximation to present itself was the will of the gods and, after that, the will of those who stood in the most prominent position—the heroes of history. But we need only penetrate to the essence of any historic event—which lies in the activity of the general mass of men who take part in it—to be convinced that the will of the historic hero does not control the actions of the mass but is itself continually controlled. It may seem to be a matter of indifference whether we understand the meaning of historical events this way or that; yet there is the same difference between a man who says that the people of the West moved on the East because Napoleon wished it and a man who says that this happened because it had to happen, as there is between those who declared that the earth was stationary and that the planets moved round it and those who admitted that they did not know what upheld the earth, but knew there were laws directing its movement and that of the other planets. There is, and can be, no cause of an historical event except the one cause of all causes. But there are laws directing events, and some of these laws are known to us while we are conscious of others we cannot comprehend. The discovery of these laws is only possible when we have quite abandoned the attempt to find the cause in the will of some one man, just as the discovery of the laws of the motion of the planets was possible only when men abandoned the conception of the fixity of the earth.

—Leo Tolstoy, *War and Peace*

- Which kind of history do you prefer, the "great man" kind or what we might call the "everyone" kind? Why?
- Whose argument is more convincing, Carlyle's or Tolstoy's? Why?

While on one hand historians began to look at people of the lower classes as more integral to the human story, history as a discipline became dominated by the same set of colonial powers that were conquering much of the globe in the nineteenth century. Therefore, two divergent streams of thought were operating simultaneously, and the picture of history both expanded in terms of class and contracted in terms of diversity. One of the early European schools of thought was **progressive history**, which viewed history as a straight line to a specific destination. Historians with this "progressive" view believed societies were becoming more democratic over time and that the advance of republican governments was inevitable. Their perspective might also be considered a form of *teleological* history, which proposes that history is moving to a particular end, a culmination of the human experience. Progressive historians believed in the betterment of people and of society, so long as it occurred on a European model. Progress looked only one way: the Western way. Consider what Chinua Achebe (quoted in Chinua Achebe on the Value of Indigenous History) would have said about European democracy and republicanism.

In the twentieth century, particularly after World War I, the idea of inevitable human progress seemed laughable. People grew more willing to question the authority of elites because these leaders were of little help once war began. Historians became more interested in the irrational aspects of the human condition, the psychology behind people's choices. This is one reason for the rise of contemporary **intellectual history**, which looks at the ideas that drive people to make certain choices and focuses on philosophical questions and the history of human thought.

The counterculture of the 1960s in the West deepened people's desire to challenge existing norms, such as the lack of rights for women and for racial minorities. The field of **social history**, guided by the concept that history is made by all people and not just elites, became much more important during this period (Figure 1.14). In this context, young historians and sociologists began to develop new ideas. In their 1966 book *The Social Construction of Reality*, for example, sociologists Peter Berger and Thomas Luckmann argued that our belief systems are informed by **social constructs**, ideas that have been created and accepted by the people in a society, such as the concepts of class distinction and gender. Social constructs influence the ways people think and behave.

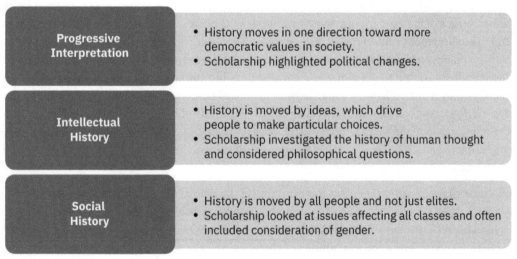

Progressive Interpretation	• History moves in one direction toward more democratic values in society. • Scholarship highlighted political changes.
Intellectual History	• History is moved by ideas, which drive people to make particular choices. • Scholarship investigated the history of human thought and considered philosophical questions.
Social History	• History is moved by all people and not just elites. • Scholarship looked at issues affecting all classes and often included consideration of gender.

FIGURE 1.14 Trends in Historical Thought. Historians' thinking has led from the progressive school of interpretation to the more contemporary fields of intellectual and social history. (attribution: Copyright Rice University, OpenStax, under CC BY 4.0 license)

To understand history, you must understand the social construction of reality, which is the way people define roles and perceive themselves within a social context. Consider our earlier thought exercise. You believe education is important. Why? Who has said that to you in the past? How did you come to believe it? In other words, what is your social construction of education, and where did it come from?

Social constructs exist everywhere and inform many decisions we make, often on a subconscious level. For example, consider the following questions:

1. What do you buy a five-year-old girl for her birthday? What do you buy for a boy the same age? What influenced your decision?
2. What would you wear to a job interview? What would you wear to a party? Why?
3. To which person standing at the front of a classroom would you give more respect: a woman dressed in a tailored suit, or a man wearing jeans and a t-shirt? Why?

In addition to examining reality as socially constructed, twentieth-century historians made interpretations through the lenses of Marxism, which considers history to be driven by class struggle, women's history (now usually referred to in the context of gender history), which sees history as driven by power differences between men and women, and postcolonialism, which focuses on the history of places formerly occupied by colonial powers. In the process we call **revisionism**, each additional lens revised the great man story of history, adding new key players and viewpoints.

Let us look at one more example. How would each school of historical thought approach the story of colonial Latin America between the Spanish conquest that began in 1493 and the independence movements of the 1820s? The progressive historian might explore the growth of democratic legal systems or people's increased interest in republican forms of government. The intellectual historian might consider the Indigenous literature and philosophy of the period. The social historian would look at what conquered people ate, how they worked, and what they looked for in marriage partners. A Marxist historian would examine unfair labor practices and moments of class conflict like rebellion or riot. The gender historian would focus on the role that social constructs of gender played in the lives of people in the past. And the postcolonialist would highlight why aspects of colonialism, such as racism and poverty, remain influential after independence. All these interpretative elements help us weave a more complete picture of the past.

The variety of interpretations open to historians also helps us put in the final piece, which is the practice of **historical empathy**, the ability to meet the past on its own terms and without judgment or the imposition of our own modern-day attitudes. To fully embrace the study of the past, the student of history must be able to set aside the assumptions of the modern era. Everyone has a set of biases, generated by the people who influence our lives and the experiences that shape who we become. Historians must spend the time necessary to investigate these biases and understand how they affect their interpretations. It is not the historian's job to pass judgment on the past, but to present it as clearly as possible and to preserve that clarity for future generations. This may mean reflecting impartially on historical positions, attitudes, or decisions we might find abhorrent as viewed from today's world. However, the more strands of history we can investigate and bring together, the more accurate the picture will be. And there is still much work to be done. For example, recent and ongoing research into LGBTQ+ studies, Indigenous studies, and the history of the Global South will continue to sharpen our image of the past.

The bottom line is that interpretation plays a central role in the field of history. And changes in our interpretation increase the number of ways we can get a clearer picture of those who lived before us. The danger lies in using only one lens. Yes, historians choose some causes as more important than others, but only after considering all the information available.

Key Terms

chronological approach an approach to history that follows a timeline from ancient to modern

global citizen a person who sees themselves as responsible to a world community rather than only a national one

great man theory the view that it is enough to study the deeds and impact of important leaders to paint an accurate picture of the past

historical empathy the ability to see the past on its own terms, without judgment or the imposition of our own modern-day attitudes

historiography the study of how historians have already interpreted the past

iconography the use of images and symbols in art

intellectual history the history of ideas, which looks at the philosophies that drive people to make certain choices

primary cause the most immediate reason an event occurred

primary source a document, object, or other source material from the time period under study

progressive history a school of thought that views history as a straight line to a specific and more democratic destination

revisionism the process of altering our interpretation of historical events by adding new elements and perspectives

rhetoric the way words are used and put together in speaking or writing

secondary source a document, object, or other source material written or created after the time period under study

social constructs ideas such as class and gender created and accepted by the people in a society that influence the way they think and behave

social history a field of history that looks at all classes and categories of people, not just elites

Section Summary

1.1 Developing a Global Perspective

Knowing the past, the human story, has long been considered a mark of civilization, and its study has never been more important. The study of world history provides the skills necessary to meet global workforce needs while at the same time developing a sense of self and place in our global community. You will gain critical-thinking and analysis skills that will help you fulfill the role of a global citizen in our interconnected world. This text will help you approach history with an open mind, and it will engage you in meaningful ways, often highlighting content that remains relevant in today's society.

1.2 Primary Sources

Primary sources are the first-hand evidence with which historians form a foundation of knowledge of the past. Interpreting them requires attention to four key areas: the author, the audience, the intent, and the context. Secondary sources offer valuable starting points for inquiry and context, but students must be aware of any bias they contain. Despite the efforts of generations of historians, there are still people and regions we do not know much about. We must hope that new generations of historians will continue to hone our interpretation of the past.

1.3 Causation and Interpretation in History

The historian's main job is to discover why history happened as it did. What caused the events that have shaped our shared human past? To answer this question, historians apply rigorous interpretative methodology rooted in the search for causation. They study events for both immediate causation and contributing factors, while avoiding judgment and remaining open to revision. You now have the tools you need to fully engage with the material in this text and begin your journey into the human past.

Assessments

Review Questions

1. What is an example of a primary source?
   a. a diary entry by a person who lived in the period under discussion
   b. a modern biography of a person in the period under discussion
   c. an account of a nineteenth-century battle in a twenty-first century textbook
   d. an article in an academic journal

2. Whom do the Chinese view as the Father of History?
   a. Homer
   b. Santayana
   c. Herodotus
   d. Sima Qian

3. What interpretation of history assumes that history can be viewed primarily through the lives and choices of leaders?
   a. great man theory
   b. progressive interpretation
   c. gender interpretation
   d. Marxist interpretation

4. The belief that history is moved primarily by class struggle is the _____ of history.
   a. social interpretation theory
   b. revisionist view
   c. progressive interpretation
   d. Marxist interpretation

5. What is the most immediate motivator of a historical event?
   a. the tertiary cause
   b. the primary cause
   c. the action of a great man
   d. the social construct

6. Our perspectives are deeply rooted in _____, which we learn from our upbringing and environment.
   a. education
   b. social constructs
   c. historical empathy
   d. causation

Check Your Understanding Questions

1. What does it mean to be a global citizen?

2. What are the features of this textbook, and how will they enhance your learning experience?

3. What is a primary source, and what are some examples of primary sources?

4. What are the four types of questions we should ask about textual sources and why?

5. Define causation as it is used in the study of history.

6. Describe the process you would go through to establish the primary, secondary, and tertiary causes of a

historical event.

Application and Reflection Questions

1. How do you see your knowledge of world history helping you achieve life goals? What do you hope to learn from this text?

2. Why is it important to consider competing sources about the same topic?

3. What primary source materials do you think you will leave behind for later generations? How would you want them to be interpreted?

4. If you could suggest a revisionist addition to the history you have been taught so far, what would it be? Why?

5. Provide three examples of social constructs that affect the way you view the world and explain why.

6. Which historical interpretation interests you most? Why?

7. Choose a recent event you have followed in the news or on social media and establish a history of that event. In a few short paragraphs, tell the story and rank the causes in order of importance. Then write the history again, using one of the major interpretive theories in the chapter (progressive, intellectual, gender, etc.). Your goal is to produce a different viewpoint on the same story.

FIGURE 2.1 The Landscape of Evolution. Millions of years ago, our early evolutionary ancestors roamed around today's Ethiopia, living off the land. (credit: modification of work "Blue Nile Falls at Tis Issat near Bahir Dar, Ethiopia" by A.Savin/Wikimedia Commons, Licence Art Libre/Copyleft)

CHAPTER OUTLINE

INTRODUCTION In 1974, while on a mapping expedition in Ethiopia (Figure 2.2), an American paleoanthropologist named Donald Johanson and a colleague stumbled upon a skeletal forearm and skull in a gully. Upon closer inspection, they not only found more bones but also realized that all of them had belonged to some type of early human. After careful work, Johanson's team was able to recover about 40 percent of the skeleton, which they named Lucy after the popular Beatles song, "Lucy in the Sky with Diamonds."

We now know that, though small, Lucy was an adult when she died about 3.2 million years ago. Scholars have learned a great deal since her discovery, about her but also about many of our other evolutionary ancestors. In the millions of years since Lucy walked the Earth, a number of early human species have come and gone. Some migrated out of Africa and populated portions of Asia, Europe, Australia, and the Americas. These different species developed new tools, learned to control fire, mastered language, and produced stunning works of art. Then, about twelve thousand years ago, some of our own species adopted agriculture. With this innovation, many early human groups began to end their hunting and gathering ways and establish settled communities.

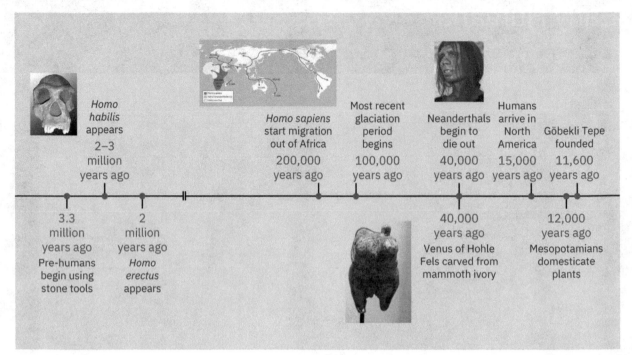

FIGURE 2.2 Timeline: Early Humans. (credit "2–3 million years ago": modification of work "Skull of Homo Habilis (Replica)" by "Luna04"/Wikimedia Commons, CC BY 2.5; credit "200,000 years ago": modification of work "Spreading of Homo sapiens" by "NordNordWest"/Wikimedia Commons, Public Domain; credit "40,000 years ago" top: modification of work "Reconstruction of Neanderthal woman (makeup by Morten Jacobsen)" by Public Library of Science/Wikimedia Commons, CC BY 2.5; credit "40,000 years ago" bottom: modification of work "Venus"-pendant, mammoth ivory, Alb-Donau Region, on loan from the National Archaeological Museum in Baden-Württemberg, shown at the Landesmuseum Württemberg, Stuttgart, Germany" by "Anagoria"/Wikimedia Commons, CC BY 3.0)

2.1 Early Human Evolution and Migration

LEARNING OBJECTIVES

By the end of this section, you will be able to:
- Discuss the process of human evolution in a biological and anthropological context
- Explain how and why Paleolithic humans migrated
- Describe the tools and technologies used in the Paleolithic Age

Millions of years ago, our distant ancestors descended from the trees, took to walking upright on the land, and gradually evolved into the species we are today. Their evolution was influenced by many variables, including changes in climate, diet, and survival strategies. Over time, humans developed new skills and tools to meet the challenges of endurance and sought better prospects for themselves through cooperation and migration.

Understanding these changes and the long-ago origins of our species has required careful research by archaeologists, anthropologists, genetic scientists, historians, sociologists, and many others. Through painstaking reconstructions and study, these specialists have used a relatively small number of archaeological finds and material remnants of our distant ancestors to paint a striking picture of our prehistoric past, going back millions of years. The nature of this work, however, requires using some extrapolation, educated speculation, and outright guesswork to piece together the bits of unearthed evidence into an intelligible story. This means that even as we have had to discard old theories when new information has emerged, there remain plenty of things we'll simply never know for sure.

Human Evolution

The concept of evolution over time is one we are all likely familiar with. Consider, for example, how technology has evolved. The first true smartphones appeared on the market at the beginning of this century, but these complicated devices didn't spring all at once from the minds of ambitious engineers. Rather, these engineers built on technology that had evolved and improved over many decades. In the mid-1800s, telegraph technology first demonstrated that electricity could be used for long-distance communication. That technology paved the way for the first telephones, which were basic and expensive but over many decades became more sophisticated, more common, and cheaper. By the early 1980s, electronics companies had begun selling telephones that used radio technology to communicate wirelessly. Over time these devices were made faster and smaller, and companies added features like cameras, microprocessors, and eventually internet access. With these evolutionary transformations, the smartphone was born.

⊘ LINK TO LEARNING

Use this guided activity from the Evolution Lab to explore how we study biological relationships between species using phylogenetics (https://openstax.org/l/77Phylogenetics) to learn more. Try to create your own "Tree of Life."

Modern humans are not smartphones, and in human history, chance biological adaptations to a changing environment drove the evolutionary process rather than the minds of inventors conceiving of technical innovations. But the evolutionary process that eventually gave birth to our species resembles the technological evolution of smartphones and other devices in some important ways. Just like we can trace the evolution of the smartphone back to the telegraph, so can we trace our own evolution back to a very distant ancestor called **Australopithecus**, who lived in eastern and southern Africa between 2.5 and 4 million years ago. Lucy, previously mentioned, was of the genus *Australopithecus* (Figure 2.3). A **genus** is a taxonomic rank that includes several similar and related species within it. Like us, members of Lucy's species *afarensis* (named for the Afar region of East Africa where she was found) were capable of walking upright and likely used tools. Beyond that, however, they were very different from us. They had plenty of hair like chimpanzees, fingers and arms well suited for climbing trees, and brains about one-third the size of ours. Despite these differences, scholars have concluded that the genus *Homo* ("human") evolved from *Australopithecus* somewhere around two to three million years ago.

FIGURE 2.3 Lucy. Despite the incomplete state of the remains of Lucy, a member of the ancient genus *Australopithecus*, the similarities between her and modern humans of the genus *Homo* are striking. This image is a photoshopped reproduction of her skeleton. (credit: modification of work "Reconstruction of the fossil skeleton of "Lucy" the Australopithecus afarensis" by "120"/Wikimedia Commons, CC BY 2.5)

Possibly the earliest member of the genus *Homo* was **Homo habilis** (Figure 2.4). This species appears in the archaeological record about two to three million years ago. *Habilis* means "handy"; it was thought at one time that this was the first species to have created stone tools. We now know that stone tools predate *Homo habilis*, but the name has stuck. *Homo habilis* resembles us in many ways, with a large brain similar to ours as well as small teeth and a face we might recognize as human. But members of the species also had many ape-like characteristics, such as long arms, hairy bodies, and adult heights of only three or four feet.

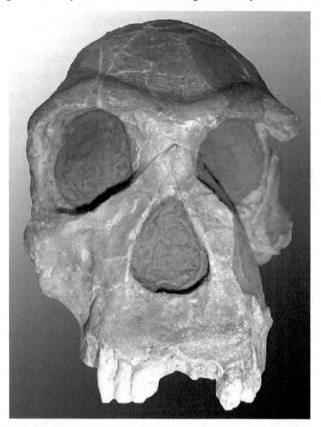

FIGURE 2.4 *Homo Habilis.* Partially restored remains, like the skull represented by this replica, are some of the most important evidence we have of the human ancestor *Homo habilis.* (credit: "Skull of Homo Habilis (Replica)" by "Luna04"/Wikimedia Commons, CC BY 2.5)

Around two million years ago, a species even more similar to us, **Homo erectus,** emerged in East Africa. It likely evolved from *Homo habilis.* As the name *erectus* for "upright" suggests, this species lived entirely on the ground and walked—even ran—exclusively in an upright position. The consequences of this evolutionary shift were huge. Being upright meant that the body's digestive organs were pulled down lower and into a smaller space. That in turn necessitated a change in diet, away from tough plants and toward easier-to-digest items like nuts, fruits, tubers, honey, and even meat. Living on the ground was also more dangerous because it made eluding predators more difficult. However, the upright position left *Homo erectus*'s hands free to use tools. This advantage likely led to further evolutions that made human hands more dexterous over time, prompting the wider adoption of ever more sophisticated tools.

Members of *Homo erectus* shared other close similarities with modern humans. They were about the same height as we are, sometimes reaching just over six feet. They made and used relatively sophisticated stone tools and relied on fire for both warmth and cooking food. They likely constructed huts of wood and fur in which to live and worked cooperatively with each other to hunt and forage. The position of the larynx in the throat also suggests that *Homo erectus* may have had some capacity to communicate vocally, which would have aided in cooperative endeavors. Finally, archaeologists have uncovered strong evidence that *Homo erectus* cared for the sick and elderly. This evidence includes the discovery of the remains of individuals who suffered from debilitating diseases yet lived a long time, indicating that assistance was both necessary and provided by others. Together these characteristics made the species highly adaptable to changing climates and environments, helping explain why its members survived for so long. *Homo erectus* populations lived until as recently as about 100,000 years ago.

Sometime between 1.8 and 1.5 million years ago, *Homo erectus* started migrating into other parts of Africa and beyond, reaching North Africa, the Near East, Europe, and East and South Asia over hundreds of thousands of years. The reasons for this extensive migration are still debated, but they likely included climate change and the desire to follow certain types of prey. *Homo erectus* appears to have stayed close to rivers and lakes during migration, hunting and eating animals like rhinoceroses, bears, pigs, and crocodiles, as discoveries in the Near East have confirmed. Populations evolved to adapt to the different environmental conditions into which they moved. Over time this led to a diversity of human species, including *Homo heidelbergensis*; *Homo neanderthalensis,* or **Neanderthals**; Denisovans; and modern humans, or **Homo sapiens** (*sapiens* means "wise"). Some of these species, like Denisovans and Neanderthals, emerged outside Africa. Others, like *Homo heidelbergensis* and *Homo sapiens*, emerged in Africa first and later migrated to other areas.

The extent to which these different human species interacted with each other remains unclear. DNA evidence from a bone found in Siberia has shown that a girl (who died at age thirteen) was born there of a Denisovan father and a Neanderthal mother. Another recent study demonstrated that modern European and Middle Eastern populations have between 1 and 4 percent Neanderthal DNA. This appears to suggest that mating between *Homo sapiens* and Neanderthals was quite common. The careful work of archaeologists and other scholars has also made clear that some species evolved from others. For example, both Neanderthals and Denisovans appear to have evolved from populations of *Homo heidelbergensis*.

At some point between forty thousand and fifteen thousand years ago, the diversity of human species declined and only *Homo sapiens* remained. Two models attempt to explain why. The first and most commonly accepted is the "out of Africa" model. This theory suggests that modern humans emerged first in Africa approximately 200,000 years ago and then, approximately 100,000 years ago, expanded out of Africa and replaced all other human species. The second model is often called the "multiregional evolution model" and proposes that *Homo sapiens* evolved from *Homo erectus* in several places around the same time. This model emerged as an explanation for the great diversity of modern human traits in different populations around the world. But it relies primarily on the study of fossils and archaeological records rather than on genetic data.

These theories about human evolution are not necessarily mutually exclusive, and the real answer to the puzzle may be a combination of the two. For example, it's entirely possible that modern humans or a common ancestor did emerge first in Africa. Then, as this species expanded around the world, it mixed its genetic information with that of other human species. The DNA evidence collected in recent years certainly suggests a more complicated picture, and the debate has not yet been settled. The tools of both archaeology and molecular genetics continue to reveal new insights into the puzzle of human evolution and the rise of *Homo sapiens*. And the conclusions we can draw about our distant past will continue to change as we learn more.

DUELING VOICES

What Happened to Neanderthals in Europe?

For tens of thousands of years before *Homo sapiens* arrived in Europe, the continent was home to Neanderthals (Figure 2.5). Then, about forty thousand years ago, right around the time modern humans entered Europe, the species *neanderthalensis* began to rapidly die out. For more than a century and a half, scholars have been trying to understand why.

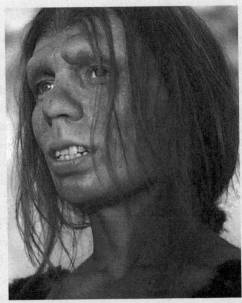

FIGURE 2.5 An Imagined Neanderthal Woman. This modern reconstruction of what a Neanderthal woman may have looked like demonstrates a striking resemblance to modern humans. (credit: "Reconstruction of Neanderthal woman (makeup by Morten Jacobsen)" by Public Library of Science/Wikimedia Commons, CC BY 2.5)

One theory is that modern humans replaced the Neanderthals in Europe through violent competition, including a type of warfare between the two groups. Another model argues that the competition was less about violence and more about resources. This theory posits that modern humans were simply better tool makers, had better survival strategies, and possibly experienced lower mortality rates and higher birth rates. Neanderthals simply couldn't keep up, and their small population dwindled and then disappeared entirely.

Modern DNA analysis has opened the door for a new theory, that mating occurred between the two species and that the population of Neanderthals was simply absorbed by modern humans. The presence of small amounts of Neanderthal DNA in modern human populations lends some credibility to this idea, but it seems unlikely to explain the total disappearance of Neanderthals.

Finally, analysis of climate change in Europe has revealed some variations that could have weakened Neanderthal populations and led to their disappearance in some areas. As of now, no one theory can account for everything. It seems possible that several factors were at play rather than a single primary cause, so the debate goes on.

- How might more than one of these reasons, or all of them, have contributed to the decline of Neanderthals in Europe?
- Can you think of any other explanations for the extinction of Neanderthals?

Why Did Humans Move and Where Did They Go?

Archeological evidence indicates that *Homo sapiens* began migrating out of eastern and southern Africa as early as 200,000 years ago. This expansion took early humans deeper south, west, and north as far as the Mediterranean Sea. Approximately 100,000 years ago, groups of *Homo sapiens* left the African continent and began a global migration that lasted for tens of thousands of years (Figure 2.6). After crossing the Sinai into southwest Asia, early migrants out of Africa likely followed the coasts of Asia, and by about seventy thousand years ago, they had made their way into India and China.

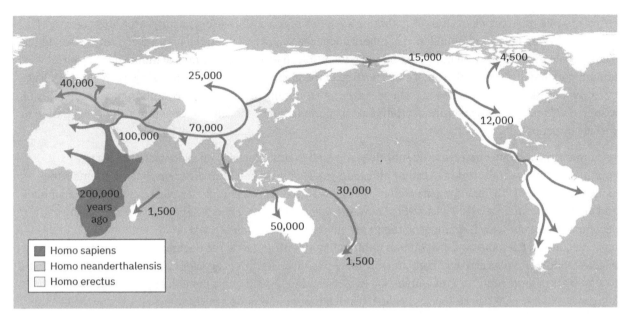

FIGURE 2.6 **Migration of the Earliest Humans.** *Homo sapiens* first expanded around south and eastern Africa before embarking on migrations that eventually took them around the world. (credit: modification of work "Spreading of Homo sapiens" by "NordNordWest"/Wikimedia Commons, Public Domain)

Some groups continued moving south through Malaysia, into Indonesia and beyond. In places like Papua New Guinea and Australia, there is evidence of settlements at least forty-five thousand years old. Others groups making their way into southwest Asia from northern Africa entered Europe around forty thousand years ago, moving either along the Mediterranean coast or by way of Turkey into the Danube valley. By twenty-five thousand years ago, *Homo sapiens* had reached Siberia and other parts of northern Asia. And approximately fifteen thousand years ago, some groups in Asia crossed into North America, eventually reaching the tip of South America and settling at various locations in between.

This timeline has been pieced together based on the analysis of several archaeological finds. But our knowledge is still limited, and new discoveries frequently require adjustments to the proposed dates and patterns of global human migration. For example, we now know that because the Earth was in its most recent ice age during this period, areas currently covered by water were then dry land. This is true for large portions of maritime Southeast Asia as well as the Bering Strait between Asia and North America. Humans were able to walk as far south as Java and from Asia into Alaska.

Yet they also roamed as far as Australia, which was not connected by land to Asia in this period. This means they must have used rafts of some type, probably by crossing short distances between islands. Likewise, discoveries of human habitation dating from fourteen thousand years ago in South America suggest that rafts or boats of some kind may also have been used to skirt the North and South American coasts. No crafts have been or may ever be found, but we must assume they existed.

More interesting still, analysis of the remains of the eight-thousand-year-old Kennewick Man discovered in 1996 in Washington State reveals anatomical features more consistent with Southeast Asian populations than with those traditionally assumed to have populated the Americas. This discovery complicates the version of human migration we think we know, and if anything, it suggests there is much about the process that we may never fully understand.

But what triggered this migration in the first place? Despite the uncertainties, we can draw some speculative conclusions. We know that around the same time *Homo sapiens* began leaving Africa, the climate there was becoming increasingly dry. Drier conditions meant fewer of the plants and animals humans needed to survive were available. Modern humans were **hunter-gatherers** like their evolutionary ancestors, meaning they survived by employing the strategies of hunting animals and gathering wild plants rather than by planting crops and raising livestock. As hunter-gathering societies regularly forage over a large area, any scarcity of resources in some places or abundance in others encourages movement. In the lifetime of a single individual, a large-scale migration would have been barely perceptible, if at all. But over tens of thousands of years, human populations traversed an enormous portion of the globe. Nor did they go in a single direction or all at once. Groups likely moved back and forth over areas, responding to the climatic conditions and availability of resources. There were long periods of relative stasis punctuated by movement, creating waves of migration in various directions.

As humans moved into new environments, they adjusted their strategies to be successful under new conditions. This meant learning to gather different types of plants and hunt different types of animals they came into contact with, including mastodons, woolly mammoths and rhinos, various types of grazing animals, and giant sloths and beavers. The arrival of humans who were highly effective at survival occasionally accompanied major transformations in their new environments. Scientists who study now-extinct animals have recognized for some time that human hunting likely contributed to the decline of a number of these species. Before humans arrived approximately forty-five thousand years ago, for example, Australia was home to a number of large reptiles, a marsupial lion (which carried its young in a pouch), and huge wombats and kangaroos (Figure 2.7). These species began to vanish around the same time humans reached Australia and well before the climatic warming that led to the extinction of large animals in other places.

FIGURE 2.7 A Marsupial Lion. Tens of thousands of years ago, Australia was home to many large marsupials, such as this marsupial lion. Its fossilized skeleton is shown here in the Victoria Fossil Cave where it was found. (credit: "A skeleton of a Marsupial Lion (Thylacoleo carnifex) in the Victoria Fossil Cave, Naracoorte Caves National Park" by "Karora"/Wikimedia Commons, Public Domain)

Early Human Technologies

To understand how early humans lived hundreds of thousands and even millions of years ago, scholars use the tools of archaeology to analyze the objects left behind. Many were made of materials like wood, animal skin, and earth, which rarely endure in the archaeological record. Bone items are somewhat more durable and have occasionally survived. But our window into the distant past is quite small. Stone items are the most likely to have lasted long enough for us to study them today. Beginning possibly as early as 3.3 million years ago, our distant pre-human ancestors began using stone tools for a variety of purposes. This event marks the start of the **Paleolithic Age** (*lithos* means "stone"), which lasted until nearly twelve thousand years ago.

The earliest known human-made stone tools date from about 2.6 million years ago. They were likely first created by *Homo habilis*, by smashing smooth rocks together to create crudely sharpened edges. The resulting implements are often described as **Oldowan tools**, and their use continued until about 1.7 million years ago. While a seemingly simple adaptation from our perspective, the development of Oldowan tools in fact represents a huge leap in human engineering ability. These sharpened stones served a variety of cutting, scraping, and chopping purposes. They were highly efficient tools for killing animals, butchering meat, smashing bones to access marrow, and a host of similar tasks.

Beginning around 1.7 million years ago, some ancient humans began to develop a new and more sophisticated style of stone tool by carefully chipping away smaller flakes of the stone core to create a teardrop-shaped implement often described as a hand-axe. Far thinner and sharper than the Oldowan tools, hand-axes were even better at the cutting, scraping, and chopping tasks for which they were designed. They were such an improvement over earlier tools that archaeologists have given them their own name. They are called **Acheulean tools** (pronounced *ah-SHOOL-ee-an*), after Saint-Acheul, the site in France where they were first found in the nineteenth century CE. Since then, more Acheulean tools have been uncovered in Africa, the Middle East, and India and scattered in parts of East Asia (Figure 2.8).

(a)   (b)

FIGURE 2.8 Early Paleolithic Stone Tools. Acheulean hand-axes (a) were far more sophisticated and required more skill to create than the earlier Oldowan variety (b). (credit a: modification of work "Handaxe in quartzite, from the bed TG-10 of Galería in Atapuerca (Burgos, Spain)" by "Locutus Borg"/Wikimedia Commons, Public Domain; credit b: modification of work "Canto tallado de tradición Olduvayense procedente de la región del Sáhara atlántico Guelmim-Es Semara (Museo Arqueológico Nacional de Madrid)" by "Locutus Borg/Wikimedia Commons, Public Domain)

Far superior to the Oldowan variety, Acheulean tools remained the dominant style of stone tool until as recently as about 250,000 years ago. At that time a new type of utensil emerged in Europe, North Africa, and southwestern Asia. Called **Mousterian tools**, these implements were smaller hand-axes and tools made from stone flakes rather than cores. In older traditions, the flakes had been removed in order to shape the core as desired, such as into a hand-axe. But in the Mousterian tradition, sometimes the flakes were chipped off in such a way that they themselves could be used as small knives for cutting meat, scraping leather, and serving as spearheads attached to shafts (Figure 2.9). Advances to the Mousterian techniques later led to other tool traditions. By around forty-five thousand years ago, humans were making a great diversity of specialized tools from stone flakes. These included a variety of scrapers as well as engraving tools for carving and carefully reshaping softer materials like bone and antler into either tools or works of art.

FIGURE 2.9 The Next Generation of Paleolithic Tools. Mousterian stone tools, like these found in Israel, were used as scrapers for more careful butchering of animals between 250,000 and 50,000 years ago. (credit: modification of work "Stone Scrapers for Cleaning & Working Leather, Mousterian Culture" by Gary Todd/Flickr, Public Domain)

Another important tool of our human ancestors was fire. When exactly humans began controlling fire remains a topic of debate. There is evidence that earlier ancestors like *Homo erectus* used it, but we don't know whether they were able to start fires or merely used and perpetuated those that naturally occurred. It's clear, however, that by at least about 125,000 years ago, if not much earlier, modern humans had learned to start and control fires.

Controlled fires were useful for staying warm in cold climates, scaring off predators, and cooking meat to make it easier to consume and digest. Archaeological finds also suggest that controlled fires aided in the manufacture of certain tools. Wooden spears could be hardened in the flame, making them more effective hunting implements. Some types of stone could be treated with heat to make them easier to chip and mold. Fire also played an important social function. Gathering around the heat and light likely aided in bonding and helped build the social connections vital for cooperative activities and group survival.

Sitting around a fire may also have been an occasion for early humans to display one of their most powerful tools, the unique ability to use sounds as language. There is some speculation that earlier human ancestors like *Homo erectus* were able to make sound and possibly had a type of language. We'll never know for sure. But we do know that modern humans are capable of making a great variety of different sounds. Biologists calculate that we can produce fifty different phonemes, or distinctive sounds. When strung together in a sophisticated manner, these phonemes can produce many tens of thousands of words to describe what we see, feel, do, and imagine. Beginning at least 100,000 years ago, modern humans began using language in this fashion, gaining a major advantage over competing animals. With language, they could coordinate daily tasks, work much more efficiently in groups, communicate abstract ideas, and pass important information to successive generations. Few tools aided modern humans more than their ability to communicate with complex languages.

While they left no record of their discussions, early humans did leave a number of impressive artistic depictions. The work that has survived includes small animal and human sculptures, usually made of carved bone or stone. The human-shaped items are often of large, possibly pregnant, women and might have served as symbols of fertility. There are also preserved hand prints, created by placing a hand on stone and blowing pigment around it to preserve the image of its shape.

Some of the most stunning prehistoric art still in existence today consists of cave paintings dating as far back as forty thousand years. Many painted caves have been discovered in Spain and France, but there are also examples in England, Italy, Germany, Russia, and Indonesia. The paintings in the Cave of Altamira in northern

Spain are prime examples of this type of art. Within the cave, and dating to about thirty-six thousand years ago, are more than two dozen large images of animals including bison, bulls, horses, deer, and boars. Each is painted in impressive detail using combinations of charcoal and ochre (a pigment made from clay) to produce bold reds, yellows, browns, and blacks. In many instances, the artists incorporated features of the cave walls as part of their designs, giving three-dimensional shape and definition to the animals they drew (Figure 2.10).

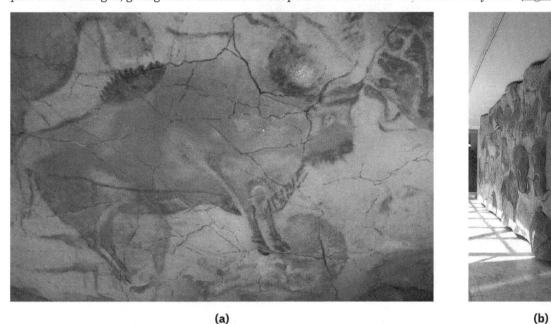

(a)   **(b)**

FIGURE 2.10 **Paleolithic Art**. The Paleolithic artist who painted this (a) bison in Altamira Cave (in what is now Spain) used protruding features of the cave's surface to create a three-dimensional effect, such as at the bison's shoulders. (b) Other examples of three-dimensionality in the art of Altamira are apparent in a Czech museum's model of the cave's ceiling. (credit a: modification of work "Cave Paintings" by Graeme Churchard/Flickr, CC BY 2.0; credit b: modification of work "A model of the ceiling of Altamira from right, in the Brno museum Anthropos" by "HTO"/Wikimedia Commons, Public Domain)

BEYOND THE BOOK

Interpreting Artistic Expression in the Paleolithic Age

We often think of visual art as a relatively modern gesture consisting of works like oil paintings, sculptures, and even computer-designed images. But artistic expression among our species is quite ancient. We may never know how much art was produced tens of thousands of years ago; many examples have probably been lost. But what we do have is fascinating to behold, though interpreting it is much like trying to reconstruct an entire puzzle from just a few pieces.

Some of the most interesting and perplexing artistic works include a number of female images sometimes called Venus figurines. These are relatively small statuettes (one to sixteen inches in height) that were carved from stone, ivory, bone, or clay to resemble women. The tiny Venus of Hohle Fels, discovered in Germany, is the oldest such object found to date (Figure 2.11). Carved from mammoth ivory, it dates to about forty thousand years ago, and what remains of it depicts a woman with large exaggerated breasts. This feature has led some anthropologists to conclude that it was intended to represent sex, reproduction, or fertility.

FIGURE 2.11 Venus of Hohle Fels. The Venus of Hohle Fels, found in Germany, was created from mammoth ivory approximately forty thousand years ago and is just under two and a half inches in height. (credit: "Venus"-pendant, mammoth ivory, Alb-Donau Region, on loan from the National Archaeological Museum in Baden-Württemberg, shown at the Landesmuseum Württemberg, Stuttgart, Germany" by "Anagoria"/Wikimedia Commons, CC BY 3.0)

Similar to the Venus of Hohle Fels and also discovered in Germany is the Venus of Willendorf (Figure 2.12). This female figurine, less than five inches tall, may be as much as thirty-three thousand years old. Like other such images, it shows a woman with exaggerated breasts and a stylized head with no facial features. Analysis of it has produced a number of interpretations, from the traditional representation of fertility to a type of self-portrait.

FIGURE 2.12 Venus of Willendorf. Those who suggest the Venus of Willendorf may be a self-portrait note that it could be showing how a woman would have seen herself if she were looking down instead of at her reflection.

(credit: "Venus von Willendorf; Kopie" by "Thirunavukkarasye-Raveendran"/Wikimedia Commons, CC0 1.0)

Unlike the preceding examples, the Venus of Dolní Věstonice, discovered in the modern Czech Republic, is made of ceramic (Figure 2.13). It stands just under four and a half inches tall and may be as much as twenty-nine thousand years old.

FIGURE 2.13 Venus of Dolní Věstonice. The small Venus of Dolní Věstonice is an early example of a fired-clay sculpture. (credit: modification of work "Dolní Věstonice Venus - Fossils in the Arppeanum" by "Daderot"/Wikimedia Commons, CC0 1.0)

Various other female figurines have been found as far from Europe as central Russia, and while individually unique, all have the same characteristics. They are small and were likely intended to be portable. They have exaggerated breasts and often show reproductive organs. They have large bellies that may reflect pregnancy. But without some record from the people who created them, their true symbolism and use will likely remain a mystery.

- Why do you think these figurines are often interpreted as being related to fertility? Do you think that interpretation is plausible? Why or why not?
- What interpretation of these figurines would you suggest, based on the information you've read and seen here?

The significance that cave paintings held for the people who created them may never be fully understood. It was once believed the images were designed to be popularly admired as interesting decorations, not unlike the ornaments we put in our homes today. But given that they are often deep in the dark interiors of the caves, where sunlight could not reach, this interpretation has mostly been abandoned.

With limited insight into the minds of the artists, scholars have concluded that the art likely served some unknown religious purpose. Many speculate that the caves could have been used by shamans—men and women thought to have a special knowledge of the spiritual world—who might have crawled deep into the interior to commune in ceremonies with a type of spiritual force. Such interpretations remain little more than educated guesses. What is indisputable is that the art demonstrates that even tens of thousands of years ago humans had the unique ability to reproduce the world around them in complex, symbolic fashion, through images we can immediately recognize today.

2.2 People in the Paleolithic Age

LEARNING OBJECTIVES

By the end of this section, you will be able to:
- Explain how the environment shaped the way people lived in the Paleolithic Age
- Describe the day-to-day life of people in the Paleolithic Age
- Discuss Paleolithic Age peoples and their likely attitudes toward the environment, gender, religion, and social hierarchy

Living in an age when global temperatures are gradually rising, we are well equipped to recognize the impact of climate on daily life. For much of their existence, however, Earth's early peoples lived in an ice age, when temperatures were colder and ice covered areas that are now forested or farmed. Hostile climates tend to create a scarcity of key resources and require that people spend more time securing those necessities. Early humans thus relied on one another and their communities for basic survival, forming small tight-knit groups that migrated to ensure their access to edible plants, water, and game. In regions where food was more secure, such as in lush environments with ample water supply, settlements were more permanent and people had more time for artistic and social endeavors.

But survival was generally difficult and cooperation vital. This is one reason egalitarianism was common among prehistoric hunter-gatherers, as it still is among the few remaining groups that pursue this survival strategy today. However, men and women in early human groups often had different responsibilities. For example, women tended to gather while men hunted. Across the planet, groups relied heavily on existing resources harvested from their natural surroundings, and any change or challenge could spell disaster. Yet people proved to be resilient and innovative.

🔗 LINK TO LEARNING

We know that our Paleolithic ancestors communicated with each other through language and that this exchange was vital for cooperation. But did they also have a type of written communication? Some researchers think it's possible that seemingly abstract signs preserved in caves represent just that. Watch this short video about fascinating scholarship around these intriguing cave signs (https://openstax.org/l/77CaveSigns) to learn more.

Ice, Ice, and More Ice

Scientists who study the changes that have occurred on Earth over billions of years have identified at least five significant periods of cooling on the planet. These are often called ice ages, and each has included multiple *glaciation* periods during which glaciers grew on the land.

A few factors can trigger an ice age, but generally such climate changes occur when insufficient sunlight is able to reach the planet's surface. Then temperatures drop in northern latitudes, resulting in the accumulation of ice. As the glacial ice sheets grow and spread across the land, water is pulled from the oceans, causing sea levels to decline. Even areas closer to the equator, where ice is unlikely to develop, can experience dramatic climate change during these cooling periods. Otherwise-tropical areas can experience drying, causing rivers to disappear, lakes to turn into swamps, jungles into savannahs, and grasslands into deserts. These changes have a huge effect on plants and animals, leading to evolutionary adaptations in some and extinction in others. These are all natural processes, and each recorded ice age in our planet's history has eventually come to an end when more sunlight reaches the Earth and causes the temperature to rise and ice to melt.

The most recent glaciation period began a little over 100,000 years ago and reached its peak about eighteen thousand years ago (Figure 2.14). The ice age of which this glaciation period was a part ended approximately twelve thousand years ago. At peak glaciation, ice sheets sometimes two miles thick covered the land around the North Pole and extended outward over much of present-day Russia, Scandinavia, the British Isles, Greenland, Canada, and the northern reaches of the United States.

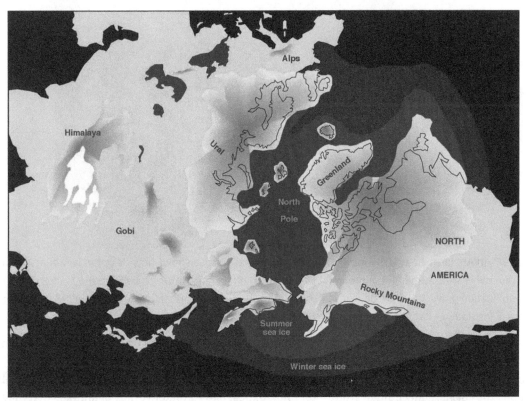

FIGURE 2.14 The Most Recent Glaciation Period. During the most recent glaciation period, eighteen thousand to one million years ago, ice sheets covered large portions of the northern hemisphere, and Earth's sea levels were far lower than they are today. (credit: modification of work "Northern Hemisphere glaciation during the last ice ages" by "Hannes Grobe/AWI"/Wikimedia Commons, CC BY 2.5)

The consequences of these climatic transformations for modern humans have been huge. It is probably not a coincidence that at approximately the same time Earth entered its last glaciation period, humans began their global expansion. Climate changes in Africa were likely a decisive factor in encouraging and enabling them to move into other parts of the world. Low sea levels allowed modern humans to expand into maritime Southeast Asia and Japan and reach Australia. And not long after Earth reached peak glaciation, the first human migrants entered North America from Siberia, by way of a strip of land exposed by low sea levels.

Modern humans who moved into colder conditions had to adjust to their harsh environments. For example, they created new forms of clothing, unnecessary in warmer climates but vital now, by removing the hides from hunted animals with various types of rock tools and scraping them clean. The earliest clothing must have been simple and likely functioned as blankets draped over the body to keep warm. However, by around thirty thousand years ago, modern humans had developed the earliest known sewing needles, making them of bone, wood, and ivory. Like their modern counterparts, these needles had sharp points at one end and a hole in the other. With thread made from animal remains or wild flax, humans could now piece together bits of soft animal hide from foxes, rabbits, and deer to produce far more sophisticated and tight-fitting clothing.

The five-thousand-year-old remains of a man discovered in the alpine region between Austria and Italy in 1991 and dubbed Ötzi provide us with some indication of the type of clothing that could be created (Figure 2.15). Ötzi was dressed in a heavy coat made of goat and sheep hides stitched together. He also wore tight-fitting leggings of similar materials, a bearskin cap with a chin strap, and shoes constructed from woven grass, tree fibers, and deer hide. This type of clothing was far more functional than earlier designs and would have allowed populations to survive in frigid areas.

FIGURE 2.15 An Ancient Shoe. This reproduction of one of Ötzi's shoes shows how deerskin and bearskin lined with bark and twine were fashioned to protect his feet in the cold climate in which he lived thousands of years ago. (credit: modification of work "Ötzi shoe (replica), bearskin with deerskin upper, internal cage of twined linden bark, padded grass insulation - Bata Shoe Museum" by "Daderot"/Wikimedia Commons, CC0 1.0)

The warming of Earth and retreat of the glaciers that began around seventeen thousand years ago submerged continental shelves around the world and created new lakes and rivers. These changes in turn created opportunities for exploiting fresh- and saltwater marine life in the new waterways and the warmer shallow waters along the coasts. Many human groups were now exposed to a greater variety of animals that they could use to supplement their diets. As other animals like reindeer adapted to life in cold environments and moved north, the human populations that hunted them moved north as well. The higher water levels also helped to isolate some groups, however. Those that had migrated into maritime Southeast Asia and Australia found themselves more secluded on islands in the south Pacific. Those that had crossed into the Americas from Asia were cut off from populations in the eastern hemisphere as sea waters rose in the Bering Strait. The civilizations they created in North and South America remained largely separated from the rest of the world until the fifteenth century CE.

Life in the Paleolithic Age

Until as recently as twelve thousand years ago, human populations around the world remained very small and relied on subsistence hunting and gathering for survival. A typical group of early humans could be as small as fifteen people and perhaps as large as only forty (Figure 2.16). These groups were further subdivided into family units. Their small size should not be surprising, since they had only the naturally occurring resources around them to depend upon. But it also contributed to the development of close relationships between members of the group, an advantage in a world where cooperation could mean the difference between life and death. Groups much larger than forty or so would have struggled to live on the scarce resources of an area and found cooperation difficult to achieve. Any groups that became too large would by necessity have split up and found other areas and other resources.

FIGURE 2.16 Early Hunter-Gatherers. This 1804 sketch of a hunter-gatherer people known as the San was made by Samuel Daniell of England, during his appointment as artist for a British expedition traveling throughout southern Africa. For hunter-gatherers such as the San and our early ancestors, living in small groups of no more than about forty was necessary to survive, given scarce resources. (credit: "Bushmen Hottentots armed for an expedition" by Samuel Daniell in *African Scenery and Animals*/Wikimedia Commons, Public Domain)

Diets for humans in this period consisted of nuts, fruits, berries, wild grains and honey, fish, birds, shellfish, insects, and other animals. What people ate depended heavily on the environments in which they lived. Those in lush, warm environments had access to a variety of edible plants and animals. In more frigid and icier environments, they depended more on animals and fish. Fishing strategies likely included the use of spears but also nets and even hooks made of bone. Land animals eaten for food were either scavenged from remains left behind by other predators or hunted by humans themselves. Most hunting likely focused on smaller animals.

But large-game hunts did occur. Archaeological remains and cave paintings indicate that humans hunted deer, horses, gazelle, bison, and even very large animals like woolly mammoths. We know from archaeological work done in the Americas that as early as twelve thousand years ago, modern humans occasionally drove bison herds over cliffs to their deaths in order to process their meat and hides. Similar methods were likely used in other places to hunt various species of herding animals around this time or even earlier. Hunting woolly mammoths tens of thousands of years ago would have required a lot of group cooperation and the use of sophisticated tools like spears. It would also have been very dangerous, and scholars debate how common it really was. But killing a mammoth would have been highly desirable; a typical animal weighed around six tons, and harvesting it would provide a good supply of meat, hide, and bone for a small group.

For shelter, early humans commonly used both built structures and naturally occurring refuges like caves. Archaeologists around the world have unearthed evidence suggesting that some populations occupied a single cave for tens of thousands of years. The Panga ya Saidi cave in Kenya, for example, may have been home to humans for as long as seventy-eight thousand years. When caves weren't available or when populations needed to be more mobile, humans designed their own shelters using wood, bone, animal skins, and other items gathered from the surrounding area. Evidence of shelters constructed of mammoth bones and covered with animal hides has been uncovered in several locations in Eastern Europe, including Ukraine, Poland, and the Czech Republic. These encampments may have been used as long as twenty-five thousand years ago.

There are strong indications that modern humans living even tens of thousands of years ago had developed some form of spirituality, perhaps even a kind of religion. As they are today, spirituality and belief in the supernatural were a way of making sense of the world. Natural occurrences like sunsets, earthquakes, comets, lighting, volcanoes, and many events for which we have ready scientific answers may have held supernatural significance for our Paleolithic ancestors. If modern practices are any guide, Paleolithic humans likely had religious traditions similar to **animism**—the idea that a degree of spirituality exists not only in people but also in plants, inanimate objects, and even natural phenomena like fires. The detailed cave paintings of bison, deer, and other animals left behind by these distant ancestors may be some of the few surviving traces of their ideas about the supernatural. It is even possible they recognized some members as religious figures. Such shaman men and women would have provided some connection between this world and another less understood world beyond.

We do know that modern humans and even Neanderthals buried their dead, and they frequently placed common household items in the grave when they did. A few rare burial sites found in eastern and southern Europe and dating back thirty thousand years were particularly ornate. Some included ivory spears and discs, along with bodies carefully covered in red ochre and beads made of both mammoth ivory and fox teeth. But most burials discovered so far were fairly simple. While it's tempting to draw conclusions about a belief in the afterlife from such finds, it's impossible to know for sure what significance these burials had for the people who performed them.

By studying archaeology and observing modern hunter-gatherers, many have concluded that ancient hunter-gatherer societies were very egalitarian. The small size of the groups, the lack of wealth, and the nomadic lifestyle were likely the reasons. But it is difficult to know exactly how egalitarian early human societies were. There was clearly some degree of differentiation within them. Just like today, within even a small group there would have been varying degrees of physical ability, intelligence, charisma, and other traits. Group members would surely have recognized these differences and used them to their advantage.

Older interpretations of social organization suggested that men did most of the hunting while women did the cooking or stayed home to nurse children. More recently, some have suggested that Paleolithic men and women both made a number of contributions to society. Meat, likely hunted mostly by men, would have been highly prized, but plants and other foods gathered mostly by women may have contributed as many if not more valued calories to the group. It is also likely that if men were away hunting, then by necessity women would have taken care of everything else. This meant protecting homes from attack, repairing shelters, and making tools.

Diverse Paleolithic Peoples

Our window into Paleolithic life is small and opaque. Scholars have thus had to rely mostly on observing hunter-gatherer societies that exist today and extrapolating from their experiences. Relatively few such populations still survive, and they are found in only a few places around the world where producing food simply isn't practicable or desirable. These include the Kalahari Desert of southern Africa, the forests of equatorial Africa, the far Arctic, Tanzania, parts of western Australia, and a few other places.

The San people of the Kalahari Desert in southern Africa have often been studied (Figure 2.17). They live today in parts of Botswana, Namibia, and Angola, and those who still practice a traditional lifestyle do so in groups of up to sixty people that include members of several related families. The San survive by foraging on wild vegetables, nuts, fruit, and insects. They also rely on hunting wild game like antelope with throwing sticks, spears, and small bows that shoot poison-dipped arrows. Their groups are largely leaderless, though in certain instances respected hunters or older men might wield some authority.

FIGURE 2.17 **The San People of Africa.** Some of the San people who live in the Kalahari Desert of southern Africa still follow a hunter-gatherer lifestyle today, living in relatively small and generally egalitarian family groups. (credit: "Tribu d'indigènes" by "hbieser"/Wikimedia Commons, CC0 1.0)

Despite this egalitarianism, the San do maintain some important divisions of labor based on sex. For example, men are expected to create fires for cooking and warmth, which they do by rubbing sticks together to create heat and adding a bit of dry grass so that it ignites. Men are also the primary hunters for the group, though women sometimes participate. Women's responsibilities include gathering, as well as building traditional shelters from tree branches covered in long grass. These shelters are light and can be built quickly to allow the group to move regularly when necessary. Water is a constant concern in the very arid Kalahari environment, and the San can live on relatively little of it. They collect it from certain plants and special watering holes, frequently using hollowed-out ostrich eggs to collect and store it for later use.

In the Arctic region of northern Alaska, Canada, and Greenland, where conditions are very different from those in the Kalahari, the Inuit people practice a form of hunter-gatherer lifestyle suitable to that environment. Like other hunter-gatherer groups, they live in relatively small bands made of multiple families and are generally much more egalitarian than settled societies that depend on agriculture. There are few plants to gather but an abundance of birds and animals to hunt and fish, including caribou, walrus, bowhead whale, seal, polar bear, muskox, and fox. In addition to providing meat and fuel, these animals have hides the Inuit use to make ocean-going vessels and thick clothing to protect them from the harsh cold (Figure 2.18). The plants that can be gathered in some warmer regions include grasses, roots, and seaweed.

FIGURE 2.18 The Inuit People of Alaska. Making carefully constructed fur clothing allows modern Inuit people to survive the cold conditions of their environment. This photograph of an Inuit family was made in 1929 and has been digitally restored. (credit: "Inupiat Family from Noatak, Alaska, 1929" by Edward S. Curtis in *The North American Indian*/Wikimedia Commons, Public Domain)

As is common among hunter-gatherer groups, men tend to do the hunting and fishing while women care for the children, maintain the home, and process the food that is hunted or gathered. The relatively limited supply of plants in relation to animals has exerted a strong influence on Inuit society. Since by far the largest part of the diet is produced by hunting and fishing, the emphasis on these male-dominated activities is strong. Hunting and fishing are also very dangerous occupations in which death and serious injury are common. The result is that women have traditionally outnumbered men in Inuit bands. In the past this ratio has led to higher rates of polygamy and even infanticide. The accumulation of numerous wives by some men has also sparked jealousy and violent rivalries among kin.

Both the San and the Inuit have had considerable exposure to the settled agricultural societies around them, and modern technology has influenced the way they live. For example, the Inuit today often use firearms to hunt in ways they could not have done several centuries ago. But one hunter-gatherer society that has still had only limited exposure to agricultural societies is the Awá people of the Brazilian rainforest. The known behaviors of the Awá thus provide scholars a picture of hunter-gatherer societies that may be closer to that of our distant ancestors.

Unlike the San and the Inuit, who live in environments where many resources are scarce, the Awá inhabit a very plentiful and lush environment. There are relatively few of them, only about three hundred and fifty, and their semi-nomadic hunter-gatherer lifestyle is not a vestige of ancient practices. Rather, it is believed that as recently as the nineteenth century CE they abandoned previously settled communities and moved deep into the Amazon River basin to live as they currently do. Despite their relatively late adoption of this lifestyle, the Awá display many of the societal characteristics common among other hunter-gatherer groups. They are highly egalitarian. They own relatively few material objects. They live in small groups of up to thirty. And they survive by hunting animals and gathering edible plants from the surrounding environment. A traditional and highly valued gathered plant is the fruit of the babassu palm. In addition to relying on this oily and protein-rich fruit, Awá groups also survive on the abundant fish in the wet rainforest and hunt numerous other animals using bows and arrows.

The different environments in which the world's remaining hunter-gatherers live have inspired very different understandings of the supernatural. The Inuit have a rich mythology that includes stories of fantastic hunts and incredible creatures that inhabit the world. The northern lights, a natural celestial display common in very high latitudes, is seen as a feature of the supernatural that can be both comforting and terrifying.

Many San religious beliefs revolve around a sometimes helpful and sometimes foolish being called Kaggen. Kaggen can take the form of numerous animals, including certain insects. The San also practice numerous types of rituals for important life events, such as a young boy's first kill and marriage. They recognize certain members of their group as shamans with a special connection to the supernatural world.

The Awá perform unique religious ceremonies during special times, such as evenings with a full moon. They also practice rituals that take them to a spirit world where they can request special intervention on Earth.

2.3 The Neolithic Revolution

LEARNING OBJECTIVES

By the end of this section, you will be able to:
- Discuss the Neolithic Age
- Explain the consequences of the Neolithic Revolution
- Describe Neolithic settlements around the world and their significance

From the time *Homo sapiens* emerged and for tens of thousands of years afterward, members of the species lived a life of hunting and gathering, much as their distant ancestors had. Then, about twelve thousand years ago and for reasons that remain imperfectly understood, some modern human populations adopted agriculture. This means they transitioned away from existing on merely the sustenance nature provided. Instead, they began actively promoting the growth and eventual transformation of crops, and later the domestication of animals, to provide themselves with the resources they needed. This shift in strategy inaugurated the **Neolithic Age**.

The birth of agriculture triggered a host of additional changes in the way humans understood land, the way they organized socially, the amount and forms of wealth they could acquire, and even the religious traditions they practiced. Not everyone made the leap to farming, however. Plenty of hunter-gatherer societies avoided transitioning into a settled agricultural life, either because the new strategy wasn't practicable in their environment or because for them the costs outweighed the benefits. Yet those groups that did become agriculturalists experienced a degree of population growth and labor specialization that ultimately allowed for the establishment of a number of sophisticated Neolithic settlements.

The Development of Agriculture

Possibly the most important transformation in the history of modern humans was the shift from hunting and gathering to a life based primarily on agriculture. We call this shift the **Neolithic Revolution**. But the revolution didn't happen in just one place or at one time. Instead, it occurred independently at different times and in several different areas, including the Near East, China, sub-Saharan Africa, Mesoamerica, and South America.

Each region domesticated different types of plants. In the Near East it was grains like wheat and barley. In Mesoamerica it was squash and later maize, or corn, and in China millet and rice. These plants grew naturally in those areas and were gathered in their wild form for many thousands of years before they were cultivated deliberately. The shift to agriculture brought enormous transformations to human populations around the world. It made it possible to feed much larger groups, necessitated the abandonment of hunter-gatherer-style egalitarianism, prompted the domestication of animals, and ultimately made way for human civilization as we understand it.

The reason some human populations undertook this important evolution remains imperfectly understood. However, it's likely not a coincidence that the earliest known adoptions of agriculture occurred not long after the end of the last ice age, about twelve thousand years ago. This climatic shift altered animal migration patterns and probably brought much drier conditions to places like the Near East, where we find the earliest evidence of plant domestication. Climate conditions may have put a strain on food resources and prompted a shift in survival strategy. For example, humans might have attempted to help edible plants grow by moving them to places where they didn't grow before or had stopped growing. Populations already settled in one area might have begun to notice that seeds from the plants they were gathering would grow where they were left. Further observations likely prompted additional human interventions in order to produce more.

BEYOND THE BOOK

Göbekli Tepe

The archaeological site of Göbekli Tepe is located in what is now southeast Turkey near the Syrian border. It includes a number of large circular and rectangular structures, large T-shaped stone pillars, and numerous pieces of stone art depicting boars, snakes, birds, foxes, and other animals, made with both skill and care (Figure 2.19). It has been known for several decades, but it was only in the 1990s that German archaeologist Klaus Schmidt began conducting extensive excavations and studies.

FIGURE 2.19 Göbekli Tepe. This aerial photograph of Göbekli Tepe shows four of the large circular features of the site, the largest of which is almost one hundred feet in diameter, as well as several rectangular structures nearby. (credit: modification of work "The archaeological site of Göbekli Tepe - main excavation area" by German Archaeological Institute, E. Kücük/PLoS ONE/Wikimedia Commons, CC BY 2.5)

One of the most fascinating characteristics of Göbekli Tepe is that some of its earliest structures, built about 11,600 years ago, predate the domestication of agriculture. Indeed, the earliest evidence we have for agriculture at the site dates to about one thousand years later. Until this discovery was made, scholars assumed that agricultural production was a necessary prerequisite for megalithic architecture like that at Göbekli Tepe. The evidence here, however, led to an important reevaluation of our understanding of the Neolithic Revolution: What if settled communities and megalithic architecture led to agriculture, rather than the other way around?

Schmidt concluded that the site was a temple of sorts, where hunter-gatherer peoples from surrounding areas assembled at times to practice their religion and cooperate in building a stone site suitable for their religious purposes. Rather than religion and temple building emerging from agriculture, as had been commonly believed, Schmidt concluded that religion emerged first, and agriculture and the domestication of animals came later.

Since Schmidt published his findings, others working at the site have developed new and even more interesting conclusions. Discovering that Göbekli Tepe was actually a year-round settlement, archaeologist Lee Clare suggested that rather than bringing about agriculture, the people who built it may have been resisting it. The many carvings of animals at the site, he argued, might represent narrative connections to the hunter-gatherer lifestyle to which they were trying to cling as the world around them was embracing farming.

Both these conclusions challenge our earlier understanding of the Neolithic Revolution. And neither is likely to be the last word on what was happening at Göbekli Tepe.

- Which theory about Göbekli Tepe sounds more plausible to you? Why?
- Why might hunter-gatherer people take time to build a religious site? What does this suggest about the importance of religion for them?

Not all regions of the world had the right conditions in place to encourage a shift from hunting and gathering to settled agriculture. Among those regions that did, and where agriculture first flourished, were Mesopotamia, southern Turkey, and Israel. On a map, these places take the shape of a large crescent bending through the Near East. For this reason, the area is often referred to as the **Fertile Crescent**.

It was here that about twelve thousand years ago people began domesticating edible wild grasses to create what we know today as wheat and barley. Later, other species of plants were domesticated: peas, lentils, carrots, olives, and dates. Around ten thousand years ago, Asian peoples living on the Yangtze and Yellow Rivers began farming crops like rice, millet, and soybeans. In sub-Saharan Africa, likely around modern Sudan, people began actively cultivating sorghum, possibly as early as six thousand years ago. Over time they added crops like peanuts and sesame. Around the same time, groups living in central Mexico began cultivating maize (corn). Later they added crops like beans, squash, and peppers. Farther south, in the Andean region, around five thousand years ago people began to grow potatoes.

Each instance of the independent emergence of agriculture was followed by the expansion of these techniques to other areas. Wheat cultivation spread from the Fertile Crescent across the Mediterranean region and into northern Europe. Rice farming was adopted across large parts of eastern Asia where the crop would grow. Maize eventually expanded across Mesoamerica; in time, it reached as far north as the modern United States and as far south as the Andean region.

The key change brought by the rise of agriculture was not only that humans began to grow their own plants rather than just finding them where they grew naturally. It was also that humans, rather than their environment, became the deciding factor in determining which plants would grow. Since humans were selecting plants for their edible properties, their intervention led to gradual but important transformations in the plants themselves. For example, ancient wild varieties of wheat and barley had heavy husks around their edible seeds. These husks protected the seeds so that they could survive over the winter and sprout in the summer. But humans were primarily interested in the seeds, not the inedible husks. By selecting wheat and barley plants with thinner husks and more seeds year over year, humans transformed the plants over time into varieties of wheat and barley more suitable for their purposes. This domestication process occurred with numerous types of plants in different areas around the world.

The rise of agriculture also led to the domestication of numerous types of animals, often selected for characteristics that were beneficial to humans, such as docility, strength, ability to feed on readily available foods, and rapid growth and reproduction so the animals could be slaughtered for food. Some of the many animals domesticated in the Neolithic Age were sheep and goats in the Near East around ten thousand years ago, chickens in south Asia around eight thousand years ago, horses in central Asia around six thousand years ago, and llamas in Peru about the same time (Figure 2.20).

FIGURE 2.20 Peruvian Llamas. Domesticated llamas in Peru provided early peoples there with meat, animal power, dung for fertilizer, and fiber for clothing. (credit: "Llamas in Peru" by "NIAID"/Flickr, CC BY 2.0)

While the advantages of plant and animal domestication seem obvious to us today, some groups either could not or simply did not adopt these practices. The Indigenous peoples of Australia, for example, lived in environments that would have supported agriculture, and some of them were in contact with groups from New Guinea that did farm crops like taro and yams. Yet the early Australians continued to practice a mostly hunter-gatherer lifestyle until Europeans arrived about two hundred and fifty years ago. They apparently consciously determined that hunting and gathering were more suitable and practical given their own needs and the environment in which they lived. This is just one example of a people choosing a means of survival apart from the Neolithic Revolution.

How Farming Changed the Human Experience

As the example of the Indigenous people of Australia proves, agriculture was not readily adopted by everyone exposed to it. This may seem strange to us, living in a world made possible by agriculture. But we're largely removed from the sometimes-painful transition many of our distant ancestors made. Consider, for example, the loss in leisure time. Scholars who study modern hunter-gatherers have found that the time required to acquire enough food to live amounts to about twenty hours per week. However, comparable agricultural societies spend thirty or more hours engaged in farming. That means less time for resting, sharing knowledge, and undertaking activities that bring more joy than hard work does. These same studies have also noted that the greatest loss in leisure hours was borne by women, who spent far more time engaged in laborious tasks outside the home than hunter-gatherer women in similar environments.

Large groups living in agricultural communities were also more vulnerable to epidemic diseases, which became common in areas that collected large amounts of human and animal waste. They were far more dependent on the weather as well; their crops needed to receive the water they required but no more. Unlike hunter-gatherers, agriculturalists couldn't easily migrate to areas with more suitable weather conditions.

Farmers also had a less-diverse diet than hunter-gatherers, made up mostly of one or two staple crops, usually starchy carbohydrates. While domesticated animals were available to farmers, meat consumption among Neolithic communities was significantly lower than among hunter-gatherers. Relying on a limited variety of food sources could result in mineral and vitamin deficiencies. But the advantages are also plain to see. Agriculture allowed for much larger populations. That meant more workers producing more food and more people to defend the settlement. When functioning well, agriculture created a constant supply of food and even a surplus that could be stored.

As early humans left their hunter-gatherer existence behind beginning around twelve thousand years ago, they also drifted away from the egalitarianism it fostered because agriculture required labor specialization in a way that hunting and gathering did not. Farming a field of wheat, for example, required a family to devote their energy to that process and associated chores, leaving little time for the diversity of tasks common among hunter-gatherers. And as agriculture became more sophisticated, such as by incorporating plows and domesticated animals to pull them, some successful farmers were able to produce surpluses that allowed them to accumulate wealth in the form of material property and land. This wealth, and the higher social status that went with it, were left for their descendants to inherit, strengthening social divisions between the well-off and others. For example, if food was plentiful, not everyone needed to farm, allowing some to become artisans or traders, who generated more wealth.

Some people were able to specialize in ways that freed them entirely from the need to focus on food production. They became traders, stoneworkers, religious leaders, and other types of elites. Those who acquired considerable wealth became leaders with the authority to command armies and create rules for society. Those without wealth could expect a life of difficult toil if they were lucky, and a life of bondage if they were not. Within the social tiers made possible by the spread of agriculture, new divisions defined by sex emerged. Among hunter-gatherer societies, women commonly gathered while men commonly hunted. But in agricultural societies, it was the men who typically worked among the crops in the fields. The need for strength to control the plow was likely one of the factors that contributed to this development. Women were relegated to the domestic sphere and spent their time preparing food, making pottery, and weaving cloth. Being less tied to the home, men had opportunities for leadership in society that women did not. They also thus had responsibilities women did not, including dangerous duties like fighting and dying to defend the settlement.

At home, women undertook the difficult and time-consuming work of milling grains. Originally done simply with mortars and pestles, this task evolved along with the rise in agricultural production to include the use of larger stone tools. Operating these mills required many long hours kneeling on the ground and bending over the millstones. It was also in the home that wool sheared from domesticated sheep was spun into thread and woven into cloth. Such chores were in addition to the labor of giving birth, rearing children, and preparing food.

Agriculture also had a huge effect on religious practices. The division of labor and the increased specialization it brought allowed for the emergence of highly defined priestly classes in many places. These religious elites derived their authority from their ability to interpret the intentions of the supernatural world, a quality that was highly prized. As a result, they could control material and human resources, which were put to work constructing sometimes elaborate monuments and performing highly choreographed rituals. Religions themselves became more intricate as well as qualitatively different. Pre-agricultural societies had tended to practice varieties of animism, seeing elements of spirituality in a great many ordinary things and animals. They had a keen interest in communing with the supernatural, often through shamanic and other rituals. Communities that experienced the Neolithic Revolution, however, developed a focus on agricultural fertility and on deities who could intervene for humanity's benefit by encouraging this fertility and perpetuating the important cycle of birth, death, and rebirth.

Domesticating Humans?

The process of plant and animal domestication is often seen as a one-way street, with humans orchestrating the process while staying relatively unchanged. But it may also be the case that humans transformed, or domesticated, themselves in order to develop populations most suitable for the agricultural lifestyle. Some have argued that the adoption of agriculture encouraged humans to select and reproduce traits that would produce the most advantages, such as docility and cooperativeness. The fact that modern humans are far less aggressive and more cooperative than we were tens of thousands of years ago appears to support the conclusion that we adapted ourselves.

And as some such as historian Yuval Noah Harari have suggested, edible plants themselves exerted pressures on us we didn't quite recognize. Just over twelve thousand years ago, for example, wheat was merely one wild edible plant among many found in the Near East. Today it is grown around the world (Figure 2.21). This incredible success was made possible by humans, who labored to remove rocks from the fields, bring water, remove insects, and work from dawn to dusk to ensure wheat's survival and success. These costs borne by humans have redounded to the great benefit of wheat. Did we domesticate wheat, or did it domesticate us?

FIGURE 2.21 Did Wheat Domesticate Humans? Human labor helped make wheat one of the most successful plants in the world. Did agriculture in turn encourage humans to select for advantageous traits like cooperativeness? (credit: Sunset over the wheat field featured" by "Dreamy Pixel"/Wikimedia Commons, CC BY 4.0)

- How does the theory of human domestication affect your understanding of our relationship with agriculture?
- In what other ways do you think agriculture may have brought about human domestication?

Neolithic Peoples

By around nine thousand years ago, groups in a few different areas around the world were not only practicing agriculture but also beginning to establish large and complex permanent settlements. A number of these Neolithic settlements emerged in Europe, the Near East, China, Pakistan, and beyond. One of the largest to be excavated today is in southeastern Turkey, at a site known as Çatalhöyük (pronounced *cha-tal-HOY-ook*). Evidence indicates this site was occupied for about twelve hundred years, roughly between 7200 and 6000 BCE. It covers more than thirty acres, and at its height it may have been home to as many as six thousand people.

Houses at Çatalhöyük were made with mud brick and were clustered together without roads or passages between them. This design required that residents enter their homes from the roof, but it provided them with protection from the outside world. Thanks to extensive excavation at the site, we can tell that the people who built and lived in Çatalhöyük included farmers, hunters, and skilled craftspeople with complex religious ideas. Their rooms include many examples of art, such as depictions of hunts and various kinds of animals, and even what may be representations of their myths, such as a woman giving birth to a bull. Cattle imagery abounds in Çatalhöyük, including bull heads with large horns and bull horns protruding from furniture, suggesting that the people who lived there venerated the animal (Figure 2.22).

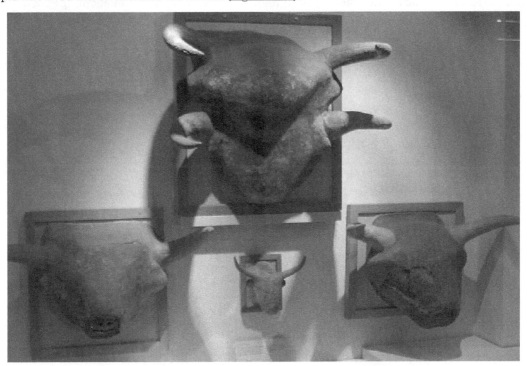

FIGURE 2.22 Neolithic Interior at Çatalhöyük. In this reconstruction of a Neolithic Age Çatalhöyük interior, several bull heads adorn the walls. (credit: "Bull heads from Catal Hüyük in Angora Museum" by Stipich Béla/Wikimedia Commons, CC BY 2.5)

The people of Çatalhöyük lived a life that was neither fully agricultural nor hunter-gatherer. Instead, they combined the two strategies. They had domesticated animals like cattle; grew a variety of domesticated plants like wheat, lentils, and barley; and may even have used some form of irrigation system to increase agricultural production. Yet they also relied on hunting wild animals for meat and gathering wild edible plants like walnuts, various types of berries, pears, and crab apples. It seems clear that their wealth was derived from trade in agricultural products, woven items, clay vessels, and especially obsidian, a naturally occurring volcanic glass. Because it can be chipped to create a razor-sharp edge, obsidian would have been a highly valued trade item for people in need of effective tools for butchering and other chores. The obsidian of Çatalhöyük was obtained from a nearby volcano and traded to people as far away as Syria and Cyprus.

⊘ LINK TO LEARNING

The Çatalhöyük Research Project (https://openstax.org/l/77Catalhoyuk) provides up-to-date information about excavations at the site, as well as detailed descriptions of its architecture and artifacts and the way its people may once have lived.

Far to the south of Çatalhöyük, in the Jordan River valley east of Jerusalem, was an even older Neolithic city, Jericho. Archaeologists estimate that Jericho was occupied as early as 8300 BCE. Its construction was very different from that of Çatalhöyük. Rather than being composed of homes with adjoining walls for protection,

Jericho was protected by a large ditch and a thick stone wall that encircled the settlement. Within the settlement there was also a large stone tower, the purpose of which remains unclear. Nearby were similar Neolithic settlements at Ain Ghazal and Nahal Hemar. And far to the north on the Euphrates River was Abu Hureyra.

Archaeologists have determined that all these sites and others were part of a culture often described as Natufian (Figure 2.23). The founding of most of them predates agriculture, and while their environments are very dry today, many thousands of years ago they were rich in wild edible plants and animals. It was likely the wealth of these resources that allowed the Natufian groups to settle there, only later adopting agriculture and building Neolithic settlements.

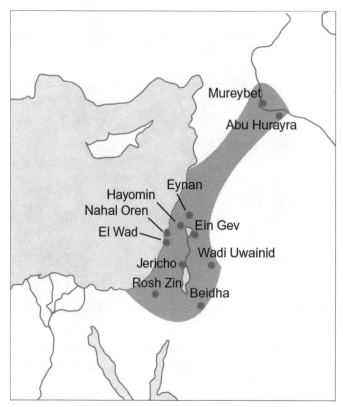

FIGURE 2.23 Sites of Natufian Settlements. Approximately twelve thousand years ago, the area where Natufian culture spread was far wetter and filled with much more abundant wildlife than today. (credit: modification of work "Extensión de la cultura Natufiense" by "Crates"/Wikimedia Commons, CC BY 3.0)

The earliest evidence of agriculture in South Asia has been found at the Neolithic settlement of Mehrgarh, situated in modern Pakistan to the north and west of the Indus River. As early as 7000 BCE, the people of this community were farming barley and raising goats and sheep. A few thousand years later they began domesticating cotton. Barley cultivation techniques may have been brought to the area from the Near East, though they also may have been developed independently. The structures of the settlement itself were made of dried mud bricks, with homes designed in a rectangular shape and divided into four parts. The people of Mehrgarh included skilled artisans capable of using sea shells, sandstone, and the rich blue lapis lazuli. Many of these materials came from great distances away, indicating that the settlement engaged in some type of long-distance trade, as did other Neolithic settlements.

The earliest Neolithic settlements in China, from around 8000 BCE, were located along two of its major rivers, the Yellow and the Yangtze. Along the Yellow River, people mainly cultivated millet, while on the Yangtze it was rice. These were areas with an abundance of water, access to fertile grasslands, and a variety of edible plants and animals for gathering and hunting, and Neolithic settlements proliferated. The people domesticated pigs and dogs and supplemented their diets of rice and millet by hunting, fishing, and gathering wild plants. They also made cord from hemp and pottery from clay.

Two of the early sites discovered there are Pengtoushan and Bashidang, both located in the Yangtze River valley in modern Hunan province. They may have been settled as early as 7500 BCE and preserve evidence of some of the earliest cultivation of wild rice. Homes were made by either digging partially into the ground or building on earth platforms with a central post to hold up the roof. A large ditch surrounds Bashidang, which may have served to channel water from the settlement and into the river. This surrounding-ditch design has been found at other locations and gradually developed into a type of moat around the settlements.

In other areas around the world, the shift to agriculture happened in similar fashion. Sites with permanent settlement, the practice of agriculture, the use of pottery, and other characteristics associated with particular Neolithic cultures have been discovered in a great number of places. The earliest known agricultural settlements in the Americas have been found in northeastern Mexico, where as early as 6500 BCE people were cultivating plants like pepper and squash. In the Andes Mountains region of South America, Neolithic settlements growing potatoes and manioc began to emerge as early as 3000 BCE. The cultivation of taro in New Guinea may have begun as early as 7000 BCE. Along the Danube River valley in Europe, Neolithic settlements began to emerge around 6000 BCE, likely having adopted cereal farming from the Near East. And in central Africa, farming of white Guinea yams began around 5000 BCE, later including crops like millet and sorghum.

Key Terms

Acheulean tools stone tools made by carefully chipping away flakes of the stone core to make them into
teardrop-shaped implements that replaced the cruder Oldowan hand-axes

animism the belief that a degree of spirituality exists not only in people but also in plants, inanimate objects,
and natural phenomena

Australopithecus a very distant ancestor of modern humans who lived in eastern and southern Africa
between 2.5 and 4 million years ago

Fertile Crescent a crescent-shaped geographical area in the Middle East where agriculture first flourished

genus a taxonomic rank that includes several similar and related species

Homo erectus a member of the genus *Homo* who emerged in East Africa around two million years ago, living
entirely on the ground and walking exclusively in an upright position

Homo habilis the earliest member of the genus *Homo*, appearing in the archaeological record about two to
three million years ago

Homo sapiens modern humans, members of the genus *Homo* who emerged in Africa first and later migrated
to other areas

hunter-gatherers people who survive by employing the strategies of hunting animals and gathering wild
plants rather than by planting crops and raising livestock

Mousterian tools stone tools and hand-axes made beginning around 250,000 years ago and consisting of
flakes rather than cores

Neanderthals members of the genus *Homo* who evolved from *Homo erectus* and lived in Europe and western
Asia between 30,000 and 200,000 years ago

Neolithic Age the final phase of the Paleolithic Age, beginning around twelve thousand years ago when human
populations began growing crops and domesticating animals

Neolithic Revolution the shift from hunting and gathering to a life based primarily on agriculture

Oldowan tools sharpened stones used until about 1.7 million years ago for a variety of cutting, scraping, and
chopping purposes

Paleolithic Age the period of time beginning as early as 3.3 million years ago until nearly twelve thousand
years ago, when our distant pre-human ancestors began using stone tools for a variety of purposes

Section Summary

2.1 Early Human Evolution and Migration

For about the last thirty thousand years, modern humans, or *Homo sapiens*, have been the only human species
walking the Earth. But not only did several different human species once share the planet; they also evolved
from much older and very different ancestors who began forging the path of global migration that modern
humans later followed. Many tens of thousands of years or more later, *Homo sapiens* began creating
sophisticated stone hand-axes from rock cores and mastered the use of fire for cooking, staying warm,
guarding against predators, and creating places for social interaction. They used their keen ability to produce a
variety of sounds to construct languages that allowed them to communicate complex ideas and pass important
information to later generations. They created art that still speaks to us today. With all these tools, modern
humans were able to migrate around the globe and create a diversity of cultures, traditions, and lifestyles.

2.2 People in the Paleolithic Age

Beginning perhaps as early as 100,000 years ago, modern humans began leaving Africa and migrating far and
wide. That this movement occurred during the start of the most recent glaciation period suggests that climatic
changes may have been a motivating factor. Over time, these migrating humans found themselves in a great
variety of environments that required them to develop appropriate tools and strategies. In very frigid parts of
the world, for example, they fashioned tools like sewing needles to create sophisticated clothing for keeping
out the cold.

For many tens of thousands of years, these groups lived a hunter-gatherer lifestyle, relying on edible plants as well as meat that could be either scavenged or hunted. Their diets varied from place to place but often included foods like wild grains, berries, honey, small and large mammals, fish, and shellfish. What we know or guess about these populations comes from both archaeological work and observations of the few modern hunter-gatherer societies that remain.

2.3 The Neolithic Revolution

The changes that came with the Neolithic Revolution beginning about twelve thousand years ago dramatically transformed human life. The adoption of agriculture and the domestication of animals allowed for larger populations, surpluses of food, and labor specialization, even as they reduced leisure time and restructured formerly egalitarian societies into hierarchical tiers. From the remains of Neolithic settlements we can get a sense of life at this important moment in our species' history. The remains of Çatalhöyük feature rooms decorated with art and a settlement designed for protection. The art and architecture from there and from other places like Göbekli Tepe demonstrate both skill and high degrees of cooperation. They also show modern humans in a transitional period between the hunter-gatherer world and the fully agricultural one. Over time, hunter-gatherer lifestyles were abandoned in most places as agricultural settlements grew.

Assessments

Review Questions

1. Which human species is likely the earliest member of the genus *Homo*?
   a. *Homo sapiens*
   b. *Homo erectus*
   c. *Homo habilis*
   d. *Homo neanderthalensis*

2. What was one of the consequences of the digestive organs moving lower and into a smaller space when members of the *Homo* genus began walking upright?
   a. It led them to build shelters.
   b. It led them to adopt foods that were easier to digest.
   c. It led them to seek protection in trees.
   d. It led them to migrate to warmer environments.

3. Which statement best describes the multiregional evolution model?
   a. Fully evolved modern humans left Africa about 100,000 years ago.
   b. All modern humans evolved from a population of *Homo erectus* in Asia.
   c. Modern humans evolved in many places in a piecemeal fashion.
   d. Fully evolved modern humans descended directly from *Australopithecus*.

4. How did migrating modern humans reach Australia?
   a. They walked on exposed land.
   b. They walked over frozen ice sheets.
   c. They took rafts over open water.
   d. They built crude bridges between islands.

5. Which phrase best describes Acheulean tools?
   a. hand-axes made by careful chipping of stones
   b. stone blades attached to handles
   c. stone spearheads attached to wooden shafts
   d. stone cores with a sharp edge for cutting

6. Human migration to which area was made possible by lower sea levels during the last ice age?
    a. India
    b. China
    c. North America
    d. The Near East

7. Why were small groups of humans better suited to survival in the Paleolithic Age?
    a. It was hard to feed larger groups of people.
    b. Large groups were more likely to settle.
    c. Small groups created more sophisticated tools.
    d. Small groups tended to get along better than larger ones.

8. Where have archaeologists uncovered evidence of Paleolithic shelters made of mammoth bones?
    a. eastern Europe
    b. Australia
    c. South America
    d. eastern Africa

9. Which hunter-gatherer group still living today tends to experience problems from having larger populations of women than men?
    a. Awá
    b. San
    c. Inuit
    d. Kalahari

10. What was an advantage of adopting agriculture?
    a. greater mobility
    b. a more reliable food supply
    c. greater food variety
    d. more leisure time

11. In which location did the Neolithic Revolution take place first?
    a. China
    b. North America
    c. the Fertile Crescent
    d. sub-Saharan Africa

12. What Neolithic settlements were the first to develop rice agriculture?
    a. those in the Yangtze River valley
    b. those in the Danube River valley
    c. those in the Fertile Crescent
    d. those in northeastern Mexico

13. Which region independently began cultivating maize about six thousand years ago?
    a. the Yangtze River region
    b. the Andean region
    c. sub-Saharan Africa
    d. central Mexico

14. What tasks were commonly done by men in agricultural communities?

a. preparing food
b. plowing fields
c. making pottery
d. weaving cloth

Check Your Understanding Questions

1. To which genus and species do modern humans belong? What were some of the other human species and what happened to them?

2. In what ways was language a useful tool for modern humans?

3. What evidence supports the claim that Neanderthals and *Homo sapiens* may have mated?

4. Why do most scholars now dismiss the idea that Paleolithic cave paintings were designed to be popularly admired by those groups that created them?

5. How would scholars describe the religious traditions of hunter-gatherer peoples, and what evidence might they use?

6. What types of tools might have helped ancient humans migrating into cold environments and why?

7. What do you imagine would have happened if a Paleolithic hunter-gatherer community grew too large for the surrounding resources to support? Why?

8. Why might some groups have decided not to adopt agriculture?

9. How did the relationship between men and women change with the advent of agriculture?

10. How did agriculture lead to the development of social hierarchies?

Application and Reflection Questions

1. What are some of the reasons our distant ancestors evolved in a way that took them out of the trees?

2. What types of tools do you imagine Paleolithic humans may have developed that have not survived in the archaeological record?

3. What type of environment would you look for if you were a Paleolithic hunter-gatherer? Why?

4. Why might egalitarianism among hunter-gatherer groups be a successful social strategy?

5. Was the Neolithic Revolution an example of modern humans making progress? Why or why not?

6. How might groups living in Neolithic settlements like Jericho or Çatalhöyük have thought of hunter-gatherer communities living around them? Why?

Early Civilizations and Urban Societies

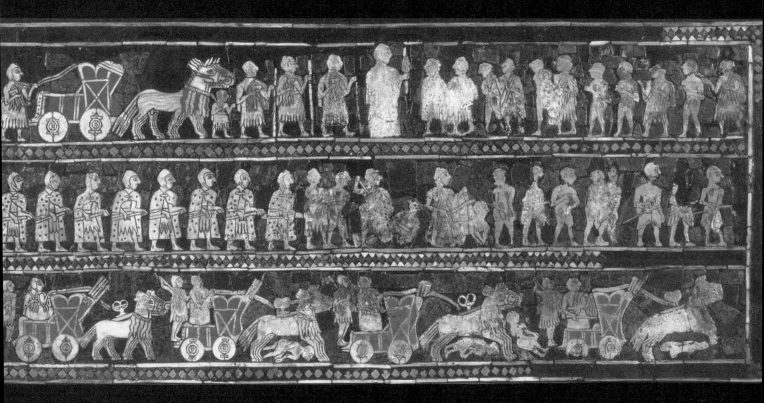

FIGURE 3.1 **The Art of Ur.** This intricately ornamented box of mosaic-covered wood was found in a royal tomb in the ancient city of Ur. It dates from about 2550 BCE and exhibits several markers of this era's civilizations, such as a hierarchical society (as the scenes illustrate) and the presence of wealth, leisure, and specialized skills needed to make such an elaborate decorative object. (credit: modification of work "Standard of Ur" by Unknown/Wikimedia Commons, Public Domain)

CHAPTER OUTLINE

3.1 Early Civilizations
3.2 Ancient Mesopotamia
3.3 Ancient Egypt
3.4 The Indus Valley Civilization

INTRODUCTION The land of Sumer, in today's southern Iraq, was home to some of the largest early cities in human history. In one of these ancient settlements, Ur, a beautiful wooden box was laid in a royal tomb in about 2550 BCE (Figure 3.1). It measures roughly nine by twenty inches (a little bigger than a laptop) and is inlaid with elaborate mosaic figures and borders composed of bits of red limestone, lapis lazuli, and marine shell. This kind of specialized craftsmanship was a hallmark of societies that no longer depended on hunting and gathering for food but rather produced crops capable of sustaining large populations. In turn, they gained enough time and prosperity for some members to focus on artisanal crafts.

The box indicates at least three important things about the civilization that produced it. First, a highly skilled artisan constructed the box and created the mosaics, indicating the presence of specialization of labor. Second, the mosaics show someone who is presumably the king at the center of the top row, directing the soldiers below. These power dynamics suggest new social hierarchies. Finally, the soldiers all appear smaller in the scene than the king, symbolically reflecting their subordinate position and telling us that social stratification had come into existence. All these developments took place gradually over time, bringing slow but enduring change to the lives of the people in Ur and those who lived nearby. Similar changes occurred in the world's other ancient cities.

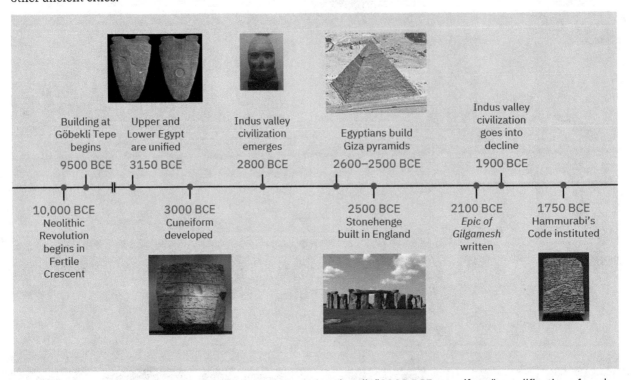

FIGURE 3.2 Timeline: Early Civilizations and Urban Societies. (credit "3000 BCE, cuneiform": modification of work "Sumerian Cuneiform Clay Tablet" by Gary Todd/Flickr, CC0 1.0; credit "3000 BCE, Dynastic Rule": "La palette de Narmer" by "Jean88"/Wikimedia Commons, CC0 1.0; credit "3000 BCE, Indus Valley": modification of work "Harappan (Indus Valley) Pottery" by Gary Todd/Flickr, CC0 1.0; credit "2500 BCE, Giza": "All Gizah Pyramids" by Ricardo Liberato/Wikimedia Commons, CC BY 2.5; credit "2500 BCE, Stonehenge": "Stonehenge" by "thegarethwiscombe"/Flickr, CC BY 2.0; credit "1750 BCE": "Prologue of the code of Hammurabi" by Marie-Lan Nguyen/Wikimedia Commons, Public Domain)

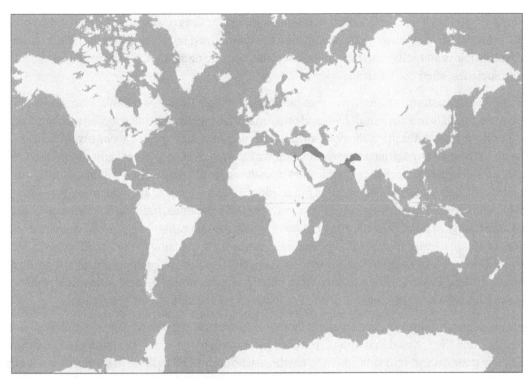

FIGURE 3.3 Locator Map: Early Civilizations and Urban Societies. (credit: modification of work "World map blank shorelines" by Maciej Jaros/Wikimedia Commons, Public Domain)

3.1 Early Civilizations

LEARNING OBJECTIVES

By the end of this section, you will be able to:
- Discuss the attributes of early civilizations
- Analyze the way human relationships changed with the development of urban areas

Early civilizations, most of which arose along large rivers, were marked by an agriculturally sustained population that remained settled in one area and could number in the tens of thousands. The stability of the population allowed for the development of a discernible **culture**, which consists of all the different ways a distinct group of people interact with one another and their environment and pass these ways down from generation to generation over time. This is not to say that earlier groups of people lacked social identities. But there were important differences between them and the early civilizations that followed.

The development of early civilizations occurred between 10,000 and 8,000 BCE in just a few specific areas of the world that historians have labeled the "cradles of civilization." In these locations—today's Mexico, Peru, China, India/Pakistan, Iraq, and Egypt—the introduction of farming allowed larger populations to settle in one place, and the ability to produce and distribute surpluses of food enabled some people to specialize in such tasks as manufacturing handicrafts, tending to the spiritual world, and governing. The peoples of these cultures experienced radical changes in their lifestyles as well as in the ways their communities interacted with each other and their environments.

Attributes of Early Civilizations

Even after the Neolithic Revolution, many people continued to lead a nomadic or seminomadic existence, hunting and gathering or herding domesticated animals. People produced or gathered only enough materials to meet the immediate food, shelter, and clothing needs of their family unit. Even in societies that adopted farming as a way of life, people grew only enough for their own survival. Moreover, the family unit was self-sufficient and relied on its own resources and abilities to meet its needs. No great differences in wealth existed between families, and each person provided necessary support for the group. Group leaders relied primarily on consensus for decision-making. Order and peace were maintained by negotiations between community elders such as warriors and religious leaders. Stability also became dependent on peaceful relationships with neighboring societies, often built on trade.

Early civilizations, by contrast, arose where large numbers of people lived in a relatively small, concentrated area and worked to produce a surplus of food and other materials, which they distributed through a system of exchange. For farming communities, this food surplus meant family size grew to six or seven children and caused the global human population to skyrocket. Population growth rooted in agricultural production led to larger cities, in which the food produced by farmers in outlying rural areas was distributed among the population of the urban center, where food was not produced. This system of **specialization** was a key feature of early civilizations and what distinguished them from previous societies. Individuals performed specific tasks such as farming, writing, or performing religious rituals. People came to rely on the exchange of goods and services to obtain necessary supplies. For example, artisans specializing in craft production relied on farmers to cultivate the food they needed to thrive. In turn, farmers depended upon artisans to produce tools and clothing for them. A weaver acquired wool from a shepherd and produced cloth that might then be given to a physician in exchange for medicine or a priest as payment for conducting a religious ritual.

The system of exchange, however, created hierarchies within society. Those who could accumulate more goods became wealthy, and they passed that wealth from one generation to the next. This wealth led, in turn, to the accumulation of political and religious power, while those who continued to labor in production remained lower on the social scale. This **social stratification**, another characteristic of early civilizations, means that families and individuals could vary greatly in their wealth and status. Those who share the same level of wealth and status make up a distinct class or strata, and these strata or classes are ordered from highest to lowest based on their social standing.

The nature of government also changed as populations grew. In smaller groups, decisions about war and migration were made in concert because no individual or family was likely to survive without the others. Also, in small communities, order and peace were often enforced at the family level. If someone acted badly, the customs of the society were brought to bear on them to correct the offending behavior. For example, the San of South Africa held a ritual dance to contact their elders for advice on how to correct a difficult situation. The act of coming together was often enough for the community to heal. In larger civilizations, officials such as priests and kings possessed the authority to command the obedience of subjects, who relied on the powerful to protect them. In return for physical protection and the promise of prosperity, farmers and artisans provided food and goods and, eventually, paid taxes. This exchange served to reinforce both the developing social hierarchy and the specialization of labor.

As civilizations developed around the world in this way, they shared the features noted. Their existence did not mean the end of older ways of living, however. Nomadic and seminomadic peoples not only remained an integral part of the ancient world, they also provided crucial resources and a vehicle for the exchange of knowledge and culture. They were particularly important as a means of connecting one large city to another.

The First Urban Societies

Around 10,000 BCE, wheat was first domesticated in what is today northern Iraq, southeastern Turkey, and western Iran, and also in Syria and Israel. This region is commonly called the Fertile Crescent (because of its shape). It includes Mesopotamia (modern Iraq), southern Anatolia (modern Turkey), and the Levant (modern Syria, Lebanon, Israel, and Palestine) and has yielded the earliest evidence of agriculture (Figure 3.4). This same region saw the rise of the first urban areas in the Neolithic Age, often called Neolithic cities. Examples include Jericho (8300–6500 BCE) along the Jordan River in what is today the Palestinian Territories, and Çatalhöyük (7200–6000 BCE) in southeastern Turkey. Archaeologists have established that these early urban areas had populations as high as six thousand.

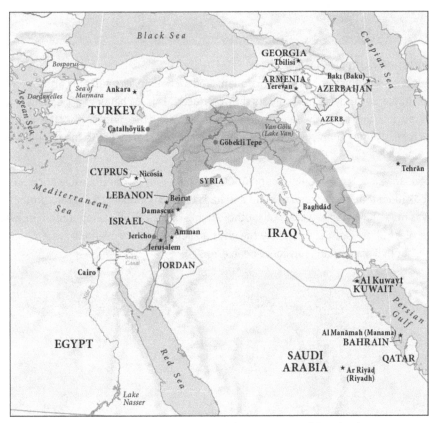

FIGURE 3.4 The Fertile Crescent. This broad swath of land (shown in green) in what is now Iraq, Syria, Israel, Palestine, and Turkey was home to the world's first cities, including Çatalhöyük and Jericho. (attribution: Copyright Rice University, OpenStax, under CC BY 4.0 license)

⊘ LINK TO LEARNING

Hunter-gatherer cultures also built large structures, such as the monumental architecture at Göbekli Tepe in southeast Turkey and at Poverty Point in Louisiana in the United States. Listen to this TEDx Talk lecture by the archaeologist who excavated at Göbekli Tepe (https://openstax.org/l/77gobeklitepe) to find out more about the site. You can learn more about the Poverty Point culture by exploring the Poverty Point website (https://openstax.org/l/77PovertyPoint). Look especially at "History and Artifacts."

Neolithic settlements depended upon the transition to agricultural production to sustain their populations. Such developments were also accompanied by increasing complexity in other areas of life, such as religion. An agricultural surplus enabled religious specialists to devote time to performing bull sacrifices at Çatalhöyük, for example, and freed artisans to hone their skills to create the frescoes that decorated the interior space where these sacrifices occurred. Some form of government must have organized the labor and materials necessary to construct the walls and tower at Jericho, which may have served as an observatory to mark the passage of the solar year. In both Jericho and Çatalhöyük, a shared belief system, or unity behind a leader, must have inspired the inhabitants to labor in the fields and distribute their agricultural surplus. At Jericho, the community may have been united by its veneration of ancestors, whose skulls were decorated and revered as idols. The people of Çatalhöyük may have offered their bull sacrifices to a mother-deity, possibly represented by small figurines of a woman that archaeologists have discovered there.

Interpreting Evidence from Neolithic Cities

Prehistoric peoples left no writings behind, and historians and archaeologists can only attempt to understand their beliefs and attitudes by studying the artifacts they produced. This is challenging because ancient societies had very different religious and social systems from our own. But even the most convincing interpretations may not persuade everyone. We may simply never know what certain artifacts meant to the people who created them.

Consider the famous tower of Jericho, built around 8000 BCE (Figure 3.5). Careful excavation has revealed that the tower likely took more than thirty years to build and had stairs for climbing to the top through the center. Some believe it was made for defensive purposes; others think it was a religious monument or even an observatory. Regardless of its use, it seems likely the city had some type of governing system that served to organize the labor. But that assumption too could be in error.

FIGURE 3.5 The Tower of Jericho. Built around 8000 BCE, this twenty-eight-foot-tall tower at the Neolithic city of Jericho is one of the earliest stone monuments in the world, but its precise purpose remains unclear. (credit: "Tower of Jericho" by Reinhard Dietrich/Wikimedia Commons, Public Domain)

As another example, consider a decorated skull found in Neolithic Jericho (Figure 3.6). An ancient artisan made it by plastering over a human skull and placing pieces of shell in the eye sockets. Historians and archaeologists have speculated that the people of Jericho venerated such skulls, which may have been seen as relics of ancestors and objects of worship. But perhaps the skull meant something else entirely.

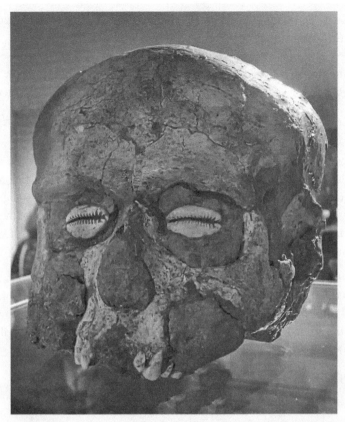

FIGURE 3.6 Skull from Jericho. More than nine thousand years ago, an artisan at Jericho covered this human skull with plaster and placed shells in the eye sockets, possibly to celebrate a distant ancestor. (credit: "A plastered skull from the ancient city of Jericho in Palestine 7000 BCE" by Mary Harrsch/Flickr, CC BY 2.0)

Evidence from the Neolithic city of Çatalhöyük demonstrates that its people venerated bulls. Archaeologists have discovered numerous bucranium (bull heads and horns) at the site (Figure 3.7). But what did these bull symbols mean? Popular interpretation suggests they symbolize the son and lover of an important mother-deity. Other explanations call them female symbols of life and rebirth. Still others propose different interpretations.

FIGURE 3.7 Bull Decorations at Çatalhöyük. This reconstruction of a room at Çatalhöyük depicts several

bucranium decorating the walls. Interpretations of their meaning vary. (credit: "A reconstructed sanctuary of Catal Hüyük" by Stipich Béla/Wikimedia Commons, CC BY 2.5)

- What do scholars' interpretations suggest about the way these artifacts are studied?
- Do their interpretations sound convincing to you? What others can you think of, given what you have read and seen?

The Neolithic cities of Jericho and Çatalhöyük were some of the earliest to emerge. But they are not the only such sites. As early as 7000 BCE, a Neolithic settlement appeared in modern Pakistan, at a site today known as Mehrgarh, whose inhabitants engaged in long-distance trade, grew barley, and raised goats and sheep. Comparable Neolithic settlements in China emerged around 8000 BCE along the Yellow and Yangtze Rivers, where people cultivated millet and rice. A few thousand years later in the Americas, Neolithic settlements sprang up in both Mesoamerica and the Andes Mountains region.

Not all the Neolithic settlements endured. Çatalhöyük, for example, was ultimately abandoned around 6000 BCE and never reoccupied. Jericho, on the other hand, was abandoned and resettled a few times and is still a functioning city today. What is important about these Neolithic settlements is what they can tell us about the long transition between the emergence of agriculture and the eventual rise of early civilizations thousands of years later in places like Mesopotamia, Egypt, and the Indus River valley.

3.2 Ancient Mesopotamia

LEARNING OBJECTIVES

By the end of this section, you will be able to:
- Identify characteristics of civilization in Ancient Mesopotamia
- Discuss the political history of Mesopotamia from the early Sumerian city-states to the rise of Old Babylon
- Describe the economy, society, and religion of Ancient Mesopotamia

In the fourth millennium BCE, the world's first great cities arose in southern Mesopotamia, or the land between the Tigris and Euphrates Rivers, then called Sumer. The ancient Sumerians were an inventive people responsible for a host of technological advances, most notably a sophisticated writing system. Even after the Sumerian language ceased to be spoken early in the second millennium BCE, Sumerian literary works survived throughout the whole of Mesopotamia and were often collected by later cities and stored in the first libraries.

The Rise and Eclipse of Sumer

The term *Mesopotamia*, or "the land between the rivers" in Greek, likely originated with the Greek historian Herodotus in the fifth century BCE and has become the common name for the place between the Tigris and Euphrates Rivers in what is now Iraq. The rivers flow north to south, from the Taurus Mountains of eastern Turkey to the Persian Gulf, depositing fertile soil along their banks. Melting snow and rain from the mountains carry this topsoil to the river valleys below. In antiquity, the river flow was erratic, and flooding was frequent but unpredictable. The need to control it and manage the life-giving water led to the building of cooperative irrigation projects.

Agricultural practices reached Mesopotamia by around 8000 BCE, if not earlier. However, for about two millennia afterward, populations remained quite small, typically living in small villages of between one hundred and two hundred people. Beginning around 5500 BCE, some had begun to establish settlements in southern Mesopotamia, a wetter and more forbidding environment. It was here that the Sumerian civilization emerged (Figure 3.8). By around 4500 BCE, some of the once-small farming villages had become growing urban centers, some with thousands of residents. During the course of the fourth millennium BCE (3000s

BCE), urbanization exploded in the region. By the end of the millennium, there were at least 124 villages with about one hundred residents each, twenty towns with as many as two thousand residents, another twenty small urban centers of about five thousand residents, and one large city, Uruk, with a population that may have been as high as fifty thousand. This growth helped make Sumer the earliest civilization to develop in Mesopotamia.

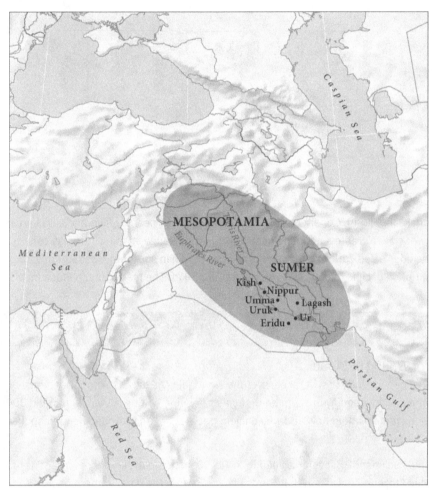

FIGURE 3.8 Early Sumer. By the end of the fourth millennium BCE, urban areas of varying sizes dotted the landscape in Sumer. Uruk was the largest. (attribution: Copyright Rice University, OpenStax, under CC BY 4.0 license)

The fourth millennium BCE in Sumer was also a period of technological innovation. One important invention made after 4000 BCE was the process for manufacturing bronze, an alloy of tin and copper, which marked the beginning of the **Bronze Age** in Mesopotamia. In this period, bronze replaced stone as the premier material for tools and weapons and remained so for nearly three thousand years. The ancient Sumerians also developed the plow, the wheel, and irrigation techniques that used small channels and canals with dikes for diverting river water into fields. All these developments allowed for population growth and the continued rise of cities by expanding agricultural production and the distribution of agricultural goods. In the area of science, the Sumerians developed a sophisticated mathematical system based on the numbers sixty, ten, and one.

One of the greatest inventions of this period was writing. The Sumerians developed **cuneiform,** a script characterized by wedge-shaped symbols that evolved into a phonetic script, that is, one based on sounds, in which each symbol stood for a syllable (Figure 3.9). They wrote their laws, religious tracts, and property transactions on clay tablets, which became very durable once baked, just like the clay bricks the Sumerians used to construct their buildings. The clay tablets held records of commercial exchanges, including contracts and receipts as well as taxes and payrolls. Cuneiform also allowed rulers to record their laws and priests to preserve their rituals and sacred stories. In these ways, it helped facilitate both economic growth and the formation of states.

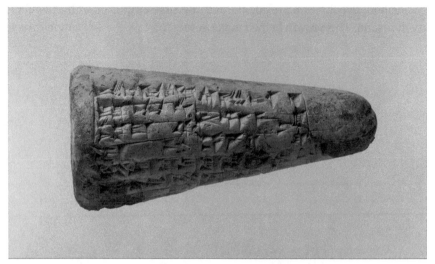

FIGURE 3.9 Sumerian Cuneiform. Cuneiform, from the Latin *cuneus* (meaning "wedge"), was created by pressing a stylus of reed into wet clay to create a meaningful arrangement of wedge shapes. This clay cone from circa 1934–1924 BCE includes a dedication to the ruler of the city of Isin in southern Mesopotamia. (credit: "Votive cone with cuneiform inscription of Lipit-Eshtar" by Anonymous Gift, 1971/The Metropolitan Museum of Art, Public Domain)

DUELING VOICES

The Invention of Writing in Sumer

Writing developed independently in several parts of the world, but the earliest known evidence of its birth has been found in Sumer, where cuneiform script emerged as a genuine writing system by around 3000 BCE, if not earlier. But questions remain about how and why ancient peoples began reproducing their spoken language in symbolic form.

Archaeologist Denise Schmandt-Besserat argued in the 1990s that small clay representations of numbers and objects, often called "tokens," date from thousands of years before the development of cuneiform writing and were its precursor. These tokens, she believed, were part of an accounting system, and each type represented a different good: livestock, grains, and oils. Some were found within hollow baseball-sized clay balls now called "bullae," which were marked with pictures of the tokens inside. Schmandt-Besserat believed the pictures portray the type of transaction in which the goods represented by the tokens were exchanged, and thus they were a crucial step toward writing. Over time, she suggested, the marked bullae gave way to flat clay tablets recording the transactions, and the first truly written records emerged (Figure 3.10).

(a)   **(b)**

FIGURE 3.10 Sumerian Clay Tablet. One theory holds that the antecedents of Sumerian clay tablets inscribed with writing like this one (a) were small clay tokens (b) and the pictures of them on the clay "bullae" vessels that held them. (credit a: modification of work "Sumerian Cuneiform Clay Tablet" by Gary Todd/Flickr, CC0 1.0; credit b: modification of work "Clay accounting tokens Susa Louvre" by Marie-Lan Nguyen/Wikimedia Commons, CC BY 2.5)

Schmandt-Besserat's linear interpretation is still one of the best-known explanations for the emergence of writing. But it is hardly the only one. One scholar who offers a different idea is the French Assyriologist Jean-Jacques Glassner. Glassner believes that rather than being an extension of accounting techniques, early writing was a purposeful attempt to render the Sumerian language in script. He equates the development of writing, which gives meaning to a symbol, to the process by which Mesopotamian priests interpreted omens for divining the future. Writing allowed people to place language, a creation of the gods, under human control. Glassner's argument is complex and relies on ancient works of literature and various theoretical approaches, including that of postmodernist philosopher Jacques Derrida.

Many disagree with Glassner's conclusions, and modern scholars concede that tokens likely played an important role, but probably not in the linear way Schmandt-Besserat proposed. Uncertainty about the origin of writing in Sumer still abounds, and the scholarly debate continues.

- Why do you think Schmandt-Besserat's argument was once so appealing?
- If you lived in a society with no writing, what might prompt you to develop a way to represent your language in symbolic form?

Cuneiform was a very complex writing system, and literacy remained the monopoly of an elite group of highly trained writing specialists, the scribes. But the script was also highly flexible and could be used to symbolize a great number of sounds, allowing subsequent Mesopotamian cultures such as the Akkadians, Babylonians, and many more to adapt it to their own languages. Since historians deciphered cuneiform in the nineteenth century, they have read the thousands of clay tablets that survived over the centuries and learned much about the history, society, economy, and beliefs of the ancient Sumerians and other peoples of Mesopotamia.

The Sumerians were **polytheists**, people who revered many gods. Each Sumerian city had its own patron god, however, one with whom the city felt a special connection and whom it honored above the others. For example, the patron god of Uruk was Inanna, the goddess of fertility; the city of Nippur revered the weather god Enlil; and Ur claimed the moon god Sin. Each city possessed an immense temple complex for its special deity, which included a site where the deity was worshipped and religious rituals were performed. This site, the **ziggurat**, was a stepped tower built of mud-brick with a flat top (Figure 3.11). At its summit stood a roofed structure that housed the sacred idol or image of the temple's deity. The temple complex also included the homes of the priests, workshops for artisans who made goods for the temple, and storage facilities to meet the needs of the temple workers.

FIGURE 3.11 **The Ziggurat of Ur.** The partially reconstructed remains of the once-great ziggurat of Ur (near the modern city of Nasiriyah in Iraq) demonstrate the size of these huge temples and the enormous human resources spent on their construction. When it was completed in the twenty-first century BCE, this structure had additional tiers upon the large base shown and was about one hundred feet high. (credit: "Ziggarat of Ur" by "Tla2006"/Wikimedia Commons, Public Domain)

Sumerians were clearly eager to please their gods by placing them at the center of their society. These gods could be fickle, faithless, and easily stirred to anger. If displeased with the people, they might bring famine or conquest. Making sure the gods were praised and honored was thus a way of ensuring prosperity. Praising them, however, implied different things for different social tiers in Sumer. For common people, it meant living a virtuous life and giving to the poor. For priests and priestesses, it consisted of performing the various rituals at the temple complexes. And for rulers honoring the gods, it meant ensuring that the temples were properly funded, maintained, and regularly beautified and enlarged if possible.

By the Early Dynastic Period (c. 2650 BCE–2400 BCE), powerful dynasties of kings called *lugals* had established themselves as rulers of the cities. In each city, the *lugals* rose to power primarily as warlords, since the Sumerian cities often waged war against each other for control of farmland and access to water as well as other natural resources. *Lugals* legitimized their authority through the control of the religious institutions of the city. For example, at Ur, the daughter of the reigning **lugal** always served as the high priestess of the moon god Sin, the chief deity at Ur.

The *lugals* at Ur during this period, the so-called First Dynasty of Ur, were especially wealthy, as reflected in the magnificent beehive-shaped tombs in which they were buried. In these tombs, precious goods such as jewelry and musical instruments were stored, along with the bodies of servants who were killed and placed in the tomb to accompany the rulers to the Land of the Dead. One of the more spectacular tombs belonged to a woman of Ur called Pu-Abi, who was buried wearing an elaborate headdress and might have been a queen (Figure 3.12). The most famous *lugal* in all Sumer in this early period was Gilgamesh of Uruk, whose legendary exploits were recounted later in fantastical form in the *Epic of Gilgamesh*.

FIGURE 3.12 Sumerian Gold Headdress. The striking beauty and quality of this gold and lapis lazuli headdress from circa 2600 BCE have convinced some that the woman wearing it in the Ur tomb where it was found might have been a queen. Others believe she was simply an attendant, though an elaborately dressed one. (credit: modification of work "Headdress" by Dodge Fund, 1933/The Metropolitan Museum of Art, Public Domain)

🔗 LINK TO LEARNING

The *Epic of Gilgamesh* is one of the world's earliest examples of epic literature. To understand this ancient tale, first written down in the form we know today around 2100 BCE, read the overview of the *Epic of Gilgamesh* (https://openstax.org/l/77gilgamesh) provided by the Metropolitan Museum of Art, which has a notable collection of ancient Mesopotamian artifacts.

The Rise of the World's First Empire

Around 2300 BCE, the era of the independent Sumerian **city-state**, a political entity consisting of a city and surrounding territory that it controls, came to an end. Sumer and indeed all of Mesopotamia was conquered by Sargon of Akkad, who created the first-known empire, in this case, a number of regional powers under the control of one person. The word "Akkad" in his name was a reference to the Akkadians, a group that settled in central Mesopotamia, north of Sumer, around the ancient city of Kish. Over time, the Akkadians adopted Sumerian culture and adapted cuneiform to their own language, a language of the Semitic family that includes the Arabic and Hebrew spoken today. They also identified their own gods with the gods of the Sumerians and adopted Sumerian myths. For example, the Akkadians identified the fertility goddess Inanna with their own goddess Ishtar.

Sargon conquered not only Sumer but also what is today northern Iraq, Syria, and southwestern Iran. While the precise details of his origin and rise to power are not known, scholars believe the story Sargon told about himself, at least, has likely been accurately preserved in the *Legend of Sargon*, written two centuries after his death as a purported autobiography. It is a familiar story of a scrappy young hero born in humble circumstances and rising on his own merits to become a great leader. The *Legend* relates how, when Sargon was a baby, his unwed mother put him in a basket and cast it on the Euphrates River. A farmer found and raised him, and Ishtar loved Sargon and elevated him from a commoner to a great king and conqueror.

This interesting tale would have certainly been a powerful piece of propaganda justifying Sargon's rule and endearing him to the common people, and some of it may even be true. But from what historians can tell, Sargon's rise to power likely occurred during a period of turmoil as his kingdom of Kish, of which he had likely seized control, came under attack by another king named Lugalzagesi. Sargon's eventual defeat of Lugalzagesi and conquest of all of Sumer proved to be the beginning of a larger conquest of Mesopotamia. The Akkadian Empire that Sargon created lasted for about a century and a half, officially coming to an end in the year 2193 BCE (Figure 3.13).

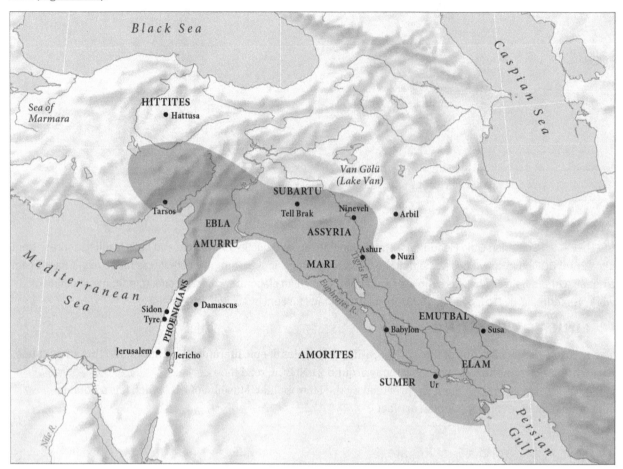

FIGURE 3.13 The World's First Empire. The Akkadian Empire reached its greatest geographic extent under its first emperor, Sargon of Akkad. At Sargon's death in 2279 BCE, it included all of Mesopotamia, and his armies were marching into Syria and Anatolia. (attribution: Copyright Rice University, OpenStax, under CC BY 4.0 license)

One of the rivals of the Akkadian Empire was the city-state of Ebla, located in northwestern Syria. At some point, its people had adapted Sumerian cuneiform to their own language, which, like Akkadian, belonged to the Semitic family of languages, and archaeologists have discovered thousands of cuneiform tablets at the site. These tablets reveal that Ebla especially worshipped the storm god Adad, who was honored with the title "Ba'al" or lord. More than one thousand years later in the Iron Age, people in this region still worshipped Baal, who was the main rival of Yahweh for the affections of the ancient Israelites.

Other rivals of the Akkadians were the Elamites, who inhabited the region to the immediate southeast of Mesopotamia in southwest Iran and whose city of Susa arose around 4000 BCE. The art and architecture of the Elamites suggest a strong Sumerian influence. They developed their own writing system around 3000 BCE, even though they adapted Sumerian cuneiform to their language later in the third millennium BCE. The Elamites also worshipped their own distinct deities, such as Insushinak, the Lord of the Dead. Both Elam and Ebla eventually suffered defeat at the hands of the Akkadians.

In the year 2193 BCE, however, the Akkadian Empire collapsed. The precise reason is not entirely clear. However, some ancient accounts point to the incursions of the nomadic Guti tribes, whose original homes were located in the Zagros Mountains of northwestern Iran, northwest of Mesopotamia. These Guti were originally **pastoralists**, who lived off their herds of livestock and moved from place to place to find pasture for their animals. While the Guti tribes certainly did move into the Akkadian Empire toward its end, modern scholarship suggests that the empire was likely experiencing internal decline and famine before this. The Guti appear to have exploited this weakness rather than triggering it. Regardless, for around a century, the Guti ruled over Sumer and adopted its culture as their own. Around 2120 BCE, however, the Sumerians came together under the leadership of the cities of Uruk and Ur and expelled the Guti from their homeland.

Later Empires in Mesopotamia

While Sargon's empire lasted only a few generations, his conquests dramatically transformed politics in Mesopotamia. The era of independent city-states waned, and over the next few centuries, a string of powerful Mesopotamian rulers were able to build their own empires, often using the administrative techniques developed by Sargon as a model. For example, beginning about 2112 BCE, all Sumer was again united under the Third Dynasty of Ur as the Guti were driven out. The rulers of this dynasty held the title of *lugal* of all Sumer and Akkad, and they were also honored as gods. They built temples in the Sumerian city of Nippur, which was sacred to the storm god Enlil, the ruler of the gods in the Sumerian pantheon. The most famous *lugal* of this dynasty was Ur-Nammu (c. 2150 BCE), renowned for his works of poetry as well as for the law code he published.

At its height, the Third Dynasty extended its control over both southern and northern Mesopotamia. But by the end of the third millennium, change was on the horizon. Foreign invaders from the north, east, and west put tremendous pressure on the empire, and its rulers increased their military preparedness and even constructed a 170-mile fortification wall to keep them out. While these strategies were somewhat effective, they appear to have only postponed the inevitable as Amorites, Elamites, and other groups eventually poured in and raided cities across the land. By about 2004 BCE, Sumer had crumbled, and even Ur was violently sacked by the invaders.

LINK TO LEARNING

The sack of Ur by the Elamites and others was the inspiration for a lament or song of mourning that became a classic of Sumerian literature. Read *The Lament for Urim* (https://openstax.org/l/77lamentur) and pay attention to the way the writer attributes the destruction to the caprice of the gods; the actual invaders are merely tools. For descriptions of the destruction itself, focus on lines 161–229.

In the centuries after 2004 BCE, the migration of Amorites into Mesopotamia resulted in the gradual disappearance of Sumerian as a spoken language. People in the region came to speak Amorite, which belonged to the family of Semitic languages. Nonetheless, scribes continued to preserve and write works in Sumerian and Akkadian cuneiform. Sumerian and Akkadian became the languages of religious rituals, hymns, and prayers, as well as classic literary works such as the *Epic of Gilgamesh*. Consequently, the literary output of these earlier cultures was preserved and transmitted to the new settlers. When nomadic Amorite tribes settled in Mesopotamia, they eventually established new cities such as Mari, Asshur, and Babylon, and they adopted much of the culture they encountered. The ancient Sumerian cities of Larsa and Isin of this era also preserved these cultural traditions, even as they came under the rule of Amorite kings.

Hammurabi, the energetic ruler of Babylon during the first half of the eighteenth century BCE, defeated the kings of the rival cities of Mari and Larsa and created an empire that encompassed nearly all of Mesopotamia. To unify this new empire, Hammurabi initiated the construction of irrigation projects, built new temples at Nippur, and published his legal edicts throughout his realm. Hammurabi had these edicts inscribed on stone pillars erected in different places in the empire to inform his subjects about proper behavior and the laws of the land. Being especially clear, the **Code of Hammurabi** far outlived the king who created it. It also provides us with a fascinating window into how Mesopotamian society functioned at this time.

The Law in Old Babylon

Remarkable for its clarity, the Code of Hammurabi may have introduced concepts like the presumption of innocence and the use of evidence. It informed legal systems in Mesopotamia for many centuries after Hammurabi's death (Figure 3.14).

FIGURE 3.14 The Code of Hammurabi. This stele found in Susa (modern Iran) is the most complete example of Hammurabi's code. An engraving of Hammurabi standing before the sun-god Shamash tops the column, with a statement that the code is to "bring about the rule of righteousness in the land, to destroy the wicked and the evil-doers; so that the strong should not harm the weak; [and] to further the well-being of mankind." (credit: "Stele of Hammurabi" by "Rlunaro"/Wikimedia Commons, Public Domain)

The Code of Hammurabi promoted the principle that punishment should fit the crime, but penalties often depended on social class:

> 199. If [a man] put out the eye of a man's slave, or break the bone of a man's slave, he shall pay one-half of its value.

> 202. If any one strike the body of a man higher in rank than he, he shall receive sixty blows with an ox-whip in public.

Many edicts concern marriage, adultery, children, and marriage property.

129. If a man's wife be surprised with another man, both shall be tied and thrown into the water, but the husband may pardon his wife and the king his slaves.

150. If a man give his wife a field, garden, and house and a deed therefor, if then after the death of her husband the sons raise no claim, then the mother may bequeath all to one of her sons whom she prefers, and need leave nothing to his brothers.

A good number of the code's edicts concern the settling of commercial disputes:

9. If anyone lose an article, and find it in the possession of another [who says] "A merchant sold it to me, I paid for it before witnesses," . . . The judge shall examine their testimony—both of the witnesses before whom the price was paid, and of the witnesses who identify the lost article on oath. The merchant is then proved to be a thief and shall be put to death. The owner of the lost article receives his property, and he who bought it receives the money he paid from the estate of the merchant.

48. If anyone owe a debt for a loan, and a storm prostrates the grain, or the harvest fail, or the grain does not grow for lack of water; in that year he need not give his creditor any grain, he washes his debt-tablet in water and pays no rent for this year.

—"Hammurabi's Code of Laws," c. 1780 BCE, translated by L.W. King

---

- What do these edicts suggest about the different social tiers in Babylonian society? How were they organized?
- Was marriage similar to or different from marriage today?
- Do the edicts for resolving economic disputes seem fair to you? Why or why not?

While Hammurabi's empire lasted a century and a half, much of the territory he conquered began falling away from Babylon's control shortly after he died. The empire continued to dwindle in size until 1595 BCE, when an army of Hittites from central Anatolia in the north (modern Turkey) sacked the city of Babylon. Shortly thereafter, Kassites from the Zagros Mountains of northwestern Iran conquered Babylon and southern Mesopotamia and settled there, unlike the Hittites who had returned to their Anatolian home. The Kassites established a dynasty that ruled over Babylon for nearly five hundred years, to the very end of the Bronze Age. Like the Guti and the Amorites before them, over time, the Kassite rulers adopted the culture of their Mesopotamian subjects.

Society and Religion in Ancient Mesopotamia

Thanks to the preservation of cuneiform clay tablets and the discovery and translation of law codes and works of literature, historians have at their disposal a wealth of information about Mesopotamian society. The study of these documents and the archaeological excavations carried out in Mesopotamia have allowed them to reconstruct the empire's economy.

We know now that temples and royal palaces were not merely princely residences and places for religious rituals; they also functioned as economic redistribution centers. For example, agricultural goods were collected from farmers as taxes by civic and religious officials, who then stored them to provide payments to the artisans and merchants they employed. Palaces and temples thus needed to possess massive storage facilities. Scribes kept records in cuneiform of all the goods collected and distributed by these institutions. City gates served as areas where farmers, artisans, and merchants could congregate and exchange goods. Precious metals such as gold often served as a medium of exchange, but these goods had to be weighed and measured during commercial exchanges, since coinage and money as we understand it today did not emerge until the Iron Age, a millennium later.

Society in southern Mesopotamia was highly urban. About 70 to 80 percent of the population lived in cities, but not all were employed as artisans, merchants, or other traditional urban roles. Rather, agriculture and animal husbandry accounted for a majority of a city's economic production. Much of the land was controlled by the temples, kings, or other powerful landowners and was worked by semi-free peasants who were tied to the land. The rest of the land included numerous small plots worked by the free peasants who made up about half the population. A much smaller portion was made up of enslaved people, typically prisoners of war or persons who had committed crimes or gone into debt. A man could sell his own children into slavery to cover a debt.

Much of the hard labor performed in the fields was done by men and boys, while the wives, mothers, and daughters of merchants and artisans were sometimes fully engaged in running family businesses. Cuneiform tablets tell us that women oversaw the business affairs of their families, especially when husbands were merchants who often traveled far from home. For example, cuneiform tablets from circa 1900 BCE show that merchants from Ashur in northern Mesopotamia conducted trade with central Anatolia and wrote letters to their female family members back home. Women were also engaged in the production of textiles like wool and linen. They not only produced these textiles in workshops with their own hands, but some appear to have held managerial positions within the textile industry.

Free peasant farmers, artisans, and merchants were all commoners. This put them in a higher social position than the semi-free peasants and slaves but lower than the elite nobility, who made up a very small percentage of the population and whose ranks included priests, official scribes, and military leaders. This aristocratic elite often received land in payment for their services to the kings and collected rents in kind from their peasant tenants. Social distinctions were also reflected in the law. For example, aspects of Hammurabi's law code called for punishments for causing physical harm to another to be equal to the harm inflicted. This principle is best summarized in the line "an eye for an eye and a tooth for a tooth." However, the principle applied only to victims and perpetrators of the same social class. An aristocrat convicted of the murder of a fellow noble paid with their life, while an aristocrat who harmed or murdered a commoner might be required only to pay a fine.

Men and women were not equal under the Code of Hammurabi. A man was free to have multiple wives and divorce a wife at will, whereas a woman could divorce her husband only if she could prove he had been unkind to her without reason. However, a woman from a family of means could protect her position in a marriage if her family put up a dowry, which could be land or goods. Upon marriage, the husband obtained the dowry, but if he divorced or was unkind to his wife, he had to return it to her and her family.

Cuneiform tablets have also allowed historians to read stories about the gods and heroes of Mesopotamian cultures. Mesopotamians revered many different gods associated with forces of nature. These were anthropomorphic deities who not only had divine powers but also frequently acted on very human impulses like anger, fear, annoyance, and lust. Examples include Utu, the god of the sun (Figure 3.15); Inanna (known to the Akkadians as Ishtar), the goddess of fertility; and Enlil (whose equivalent in other Mesopotamian cultures was Marduk), the god of wind and rain. The ancient Mesopotamians held that the gods were visible in the sky as heavenly bodies like stars, the moon, the sun, and the planets. This belief led them to pay close attention to these bodies, and over time, they developed a sophisticated understanding of their movement. This knowledge allowed them to predict astronomical events like eclipses and informed their development of a twelve-month calendar.

FIGURE 3.15 **The God Utu.** This limestone relief of the Mesopotamian god Utu (known as Shamash among the Akkadians) is part of the larger Tablet of Shamash created in the early ninth century BCE. Here Utu is shown seated, holding the rod-and-ring, an ancient symbol reflecting the balance of power between the palace and the temple. (credit: "Tablet of Shamash" by "Katolophyromai"/Wikimedia Commons, CC0 1.0)

People in Mesopotamia believed human beings were created to serve the gods (Figure 3.16). They were expected to supply the gods with food through the sacrifice of sheep and cattle in religious rituals, and to honor them with temples, religious songs or hymns, and expensive gifts. People sought divine support from their gods. But they also feared that their worship might be insufficient and anger the deity. When that happened, the gods could bring death and devastation through floods and pestilence. Stories of gods wreaking great destruction, sometimes for petty reasons, are common in Mesopotamian myths. For example, in one Sumerian myth, the storm god Enlil nearly destroyed the entire human race with a flood when the noise made by humans annoyed him and kept him from sleep.

FIGURE 3.16 A Sumerian Worshiper. This one-foot-tall Sumerian statue of a worshiper with clasped hands from circa 2900–2600 BCE was placed in a temple to perpetually worship the god to whom it was dedicated. (credit: "Standing male worshiper" by Fletcher Fund, 1940/The Metropolitan Museum of Art, Public Domain)

The ancient Mesopotamians' belief that the gods were fickle, destructive, and easily stirred to anger is one reason many historians believe they had a generally pessimistic worldview. From the literature they left behind, we can see that while they hoped for the best, they were often resigned to accept the worst. Given the environment in which Mesopotamian civilization emerged, this pessimism is somewhat understandable. River flooding was common and could often be unpredictable and destructive. Wars between city-states and the destruction that comes with conflict were also common. Life was difficult in this unforgiving world, and the profiles of the various gods of the Mesopotamians reflect this harsh reality.

Evidence of Mesopotamians' pessimism is also present in their view of the afterlife. In their religion, after death all people spent eternity in a shadowy underworld sometimes called "the land of no return." Descriptions of this place differ somewhat in the details, but the common understanding was that it was a gloomy and frightening place where the dead were consumed by sorrow, eating dust and clay and longing pitifully and futilely to return to the land of the living.

3.3 Ancient Egypt

LEARNING OBJECTIVES

By the end of this section, you will be able to:
- Discuss the unification of Ancient Egypt and the development of a distinct culture there
- Analyze the accomplishments of the pharaohs under the Old Kingdom
- Describe the changes in government and society in Egypt during the Middle Kingdom

The rich agricultural valleys historians refer to as the "Fertile Crescent," due to the shape of this region on the map, witnessed the development of an early civilization as long ago as the fourth millennium BCE. Adjacent to this region was another fertile river valley formed by the Nile in northeast Africa. Here arose another civilization that was quite unique. Unlike the city-states of Sumer, which were not organized into an empire until the time of Sargon of Akkad, the peoples of the Nile River valley were brought together under a single ruler around 3150 BCE. Although brief intervals of disunity occurred, Egypt remained a united and powerful kingdom, the great superpower of the ancient Near East, until the end of the Bronze Age in about 1100 BCE.

The Origins of Ancient Egypt

Aside from the Nile, Egypt and the areas around it are today part of the expansive and very arid Sahara. But around 10,000 BCE, as the Neolithic Revolution was getting underway in parts of southwestern Asia, much of North Africa including Egypt was lush, wet, and dotted with lakes. The region was highly hospitable to the many Paleolithic peoples living there and surviving on its abundant resources.

However, beginning around 6000 BCE the grasslands and lakes began to give way to sand as the once green environment was transformed into the Sahara we recognize today. As the environment became more difficult for humans to survive in, they retreated to oases and rivers on the fringes. One of these areas was the Nile River valley, a long thin area of fertility running through the deserts of eastern North Africa and made possible by the regular flooding of the Nile. The Nile is the longest river in Africa, and the second-longest in the world after the Amazon. It originates deep in central Africa and flows thousands of miles north through Egypt before it spills into the Mediterranean Sea.

It was around this same time, about 7000 to 6000 BCE, that agricultural technology and knowledge about the domestication of wheat, barley, sheep, goats, and cattle were introduced into the Nile River valley, likely through contact with the Levant. The earliest evidence for the emergence of Egyptian culture dates from this era as well. Two related but different Neolithic cultures arose: one in the Nile delta, where the river runs into the Mediterranean, and the other upriver and to the south of this location. The people of these cultures lived in crude huts, survived on fishing and agriculture, developed distinctive pottery styles, and even practiced burial rituals. Over thousands of years, they developed into two separate kingdoms, Lower Egypt or the delta region, and Upper Egypt or the area upriver (Figure 3.17).

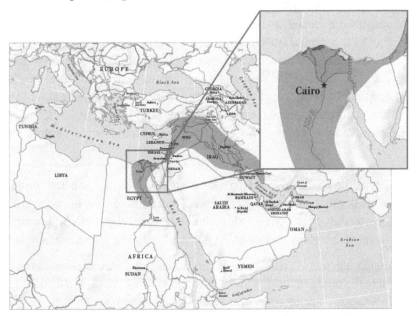

FIGURE 3.17 The Upper and Lower Kingdoms of Egypt. The fertile Nile River valley became home to two different but related early Egyptian cultures, the Lower Kingdom in the north and the Upper Kingdom in the south. (attribution: Copyright Rice University, OpenStax, under CC BY 4.0 license)

A major political and cultural shift occurred in about 3150 BCE when Upper and Lower Egypt were unified into a single powerful kingdom. Some evidence suggests this achievement belongs to a king named Narmer. More recent records attribute it to a king called Menes, but many scholars now believe Menes and Narmer are one and the same (Figure 3.18).

FIGURE 3.18 The Narmer Palette. Often called the Narmer palette, this two-foot-high siltstone Egyptian artifact appears to depict Egypt's unification, which would place it from around 3150–3000 BCE. The large figure on one side (left image) is believed to be King Narmer wearing the white crown of Upper Egypt and striking a prisoner, and the tall, left-most figure in the upper row on the other side (right image) is likely Narmer wearing the red crown of Lower Egypt in a procession. Two mythical creatures stand below, their necks artfully entwined. (credit: "La palette de Narmer" by "Jean88"/Wikimedia Commons, CC0 1.0)

Unification gave rise to what scholars refer to as the Early Dynasty Period (about 3150 to 2613 BCE), or the era of the earliest dynasties to rule a unified Egypt. The powerful kings of these dynasties established a bureaucratic system, possibly influenced by the palace/temple redistributive economic system in place in ancient Sumer. But unlike Mesopotamia, ancient Egypt in the Bronze Age was now a single state instead of a number of warring rivals. Also unlike Mesopotamia, which was subject to periodic invasion, Egypt was protected by its geography. On both east and west, the Nile River valley was surrounded by large deserts that were difficult to cross and that made the kingdom into a kind of island in a hot, dry sea. During this time, many of the best-known cultural characteristics of ancient Egypt emerged in their earliest forms. They include the institution of the pharaoh, distinctive religious practices, and the Egyptian writing system.

The Pharaoh

The king of the united Egypt, the pharaoh, governed a kingdom much larger than any contemporary realm. Historians estimate that the population of the Egyptian state, when first united in about 3150 BCE, numbered as many as two million people, whereas a typical Sumerian *lugal* ruled about thirty thousand subjects. The temple/palace system in Egypt therefore operated on a much vaster scale than anywhere in Mesopotamia.

The term **pharaoh** in ancient Egyptian is translated as "big house," likely a reference to the size of the palaces along the Nile valley where the pharaoh resided and administered the lands. As in ancient Mesopotamia, the palace included large facilities for storing taxes in kind, as well as workshops for artisans who produced goods for the palace. Also, as in Mesopotamia, a large portion of the population were peasant farmers. They paid taxes in kind to support the artisans and others working in the pharaoh's palaces and temples and living nearby, inside the city. The ruling elite included scribes, priests, and the pharaoh's officials.

The pharaoh was not merely a political figure but also served as the high priest and was revered as a god. In the role of high priest, the pharaoh united the lands by performing religious rituals to honor the different gods worshipped up and down the Nile River valley. As a deity, the pharaoh was the human form or incarnation of Horus, the god of justice and truth. Egyptians believed the divine presence of the pharaoh as Horus maintained justice throughout the land, which, in turn, maintained peace and prosperity, as evidenced by the welcome annual flooding of the Nile.

Egyptian Religion

Like the people of Mesopotamia, Ancient Egyptians were polytheists and worshipped many deities who controlled the forces of nature. For example, Re was the god of the sun, and Isis was the earth goddess of fertility. Osiris was associated with the Nile. The annual flooding of the river, the central event of the Egyptian year, was explained through the myth of Osiris, who was murdered by his brother Seth, the god of the desert wind, but then resurrected by his devoted wife Isis. The Nile (Osiris) was at its lowest in the summer when the hot desert wind was blowing (Seth), but then it was "resurrected" when it flooded its banks and brought life-giving water to the earth (Isis). Horus (the pharaoh) was the child of Isis and Osiris. Since Osiris was a god who had died, he was also the lord of the underworld and the judge of the dead. Ancient Egyptians believed Osiris would reward people who had lived a righteous life with a blessed afterlife in the underworld, whereas he would punish wicked evildoers.

As these gods and myths indicate, the Nile played an important role in the development of Egyptian religion. Whereas the unpredictable flooding of the Tigris and Euphrates Rivers in southern Mesopotamia commonly brought destruction along with fresh alluvial deposits, the Nile's summer flooding, predictable as clockwork, brought only welcome deposits of rich sediment. It provided Egyptians with a sense that the world was harmonious and organized around cycles. In later centuries, this notion developed into the concept of Ma'at (also personified as a goddess), which combined the ideas of order, truth, justice, and balance. In contrast to the apparently pessimistic people in Mesopotamia, Egyptians drew from their environment a feeling that their world was orderly, balanced, and geared toward a sense of cosmic justice. It was an Egyptian's responsibility to live in harmony with this order.

IN THEIR OWN WORDS

Flooding, Stories, and Cosmology in Ancient Egypt and Sumer

Ancient Egypt (the first excerpt that follows) and Ancient Sumer (the second) both depended on life-giving rivers, but their reactions to periodic flooding were quite different. Note the way each discusses the flooding, those responsible, and the reasons for it.

> Hymn to the flood. Hail flood!
> emerging from the earth, arriving to bring Egypt to life,
> hidden of form, the darkness in the day,
> the one whose followers sing to him, as he waters the plants,
> created by Re to make every herd live,
> who satisfies the desert hills removed from the water,
> for it is his due that descends from the sky
> —he, the beloved of Geb, controller of Nepri,
> the one who makes the crafts of Ptah verdant.
> Lord of fish, who allows south marsh fowl,
> without a bird falling from heat.
> Maker of barley, grower of emmer grain,
> creator of festivals of the temples.
> When he delays, then noses are blocked,
> everyone is orphaned,
> and if the offerings of the gods are distributed,
> then a million men perish among mankind. . . .
> Verdant the spirit at your coming, O Flood.

Verdant the spirit at your coming.
Come to Egypt,
make its happiness.
Make the Two Riverbanks verdant, . . .
Men and herds are brought to life by your deliveries of the fields, . . .
Verdant the spirit at your coming, O Flood.

—Author unknown, *Hymn to the Nile*, 2000–1700 BCE

I will reveal to you, O Gilgamesh, the mysterious story,
And one of the mysteries of the gods I will tell you.
The city of Shurippak, a city which, as you know,
Is situated on the bank of the river Euphrates. The gods within it
Decided to bring about a flood, even the great gods,
As many as there were. . . .
I saw the approach of the storm,
And I was afraid to witness the storm;
I entered the ship and shut the door.
I entrusted the guidance of the ship to the boat-man,
Entrusted the great house, and the contents therein.
As soon as early dawn appeared,
There rose up from the horizon a black cloud,
Within which the weather god thundered,
And the king of the gods went before it. . . .
The storm brought on by the gods swept even up to the heavens,
And all light was turned into darkness. It flooded the land; it blew with violence;
And in one day it rose above the mountains.
Like an onslaught in battle it rushed in on the people.
Brother could not save brother.
The gods even were afraid of the storm;
They retreated and took refuge in the heaven of Anu.
There the gods crouched down like dogs, in heaven they sat cowering.

—Author unknown, *Epic of Gilgamesh*, translated by R. Campbell Thompson and William Muse Arnold
and compiled by Laura Getty

- What do these excerpts reveal about each people's view of their world and the supernatural?
- What do they suggest about each culture's relationship to its river(s)?

Egyptian Writing

Egyptians developed their own unique writing system, known today by the Greek word **hieroglyphics** (meaning "sacred writings"), though the Egyptians called it *medu-netjer* ("the god's words"). The roots of hieroglyphic writing can be traced to the time before the Early Dynastic Period when the first written symbols emerged. But by at least 3000 BCE, the use of these symbols had developed into a sophisticated script. It used a combination of alphabetic signs, syllabic signs, word signs, and pictures of objects. In this complicated system, then known only to highly trained professional scribes, written symbols represented both sounds and ideas (Figure 3.19). The Egyptians also developed a simplified version of this hieroglyphic script known as **hieratic**, which they often employed for more mundane purposes such as recordkeeping and issuing receipts in commercial transactions.

FIGURE 3.19 Egyptian Hieroglyphics. The hieroglyphics in this Egyptian stele from circa 1944 BCE are far more stylized than the Egyptian writing produced a thousand years earlier. It took many centuries for the Egyptian script to evolve into the style of writing seen here. (credit: modification of work "Stela of the Steward Mentuwoser" by Gift of Edward S. Harkness, 1912/The Metropolitan Museum of Art, Public Domain)

Egyptian scribes recorded their ideas in stone inscriptions on the walls of temples and painted them on the walls of tombs, but they also used the fibers from a reed plant growing along the banks of the Nile to produce **papyrus**, a writing material like paper that could be rolled into scrolls and stored as records. Some of these papyrus rolls have survived for thousands of years because of the way the dry heat preserved them, and they proved very useful for modern historians and archaeologists after hieroglyphics were deciphered in the nineteenth century. They preserved Egyptian myths and poetry, popular stories, and lists of pharaohs, along with records of the daily life of ancient Egyptians.

The Age of Pyramid Building

By the 2600s BCE, the power of the pharaohs and the sophistication of the state in Egypt were such that the building of large-scale stone architecture became possible. Historians in the nineteenth century believed the significance of these developments was so great that it required a different name for the period. Today we call it the Old Kingdom (2613–2181 BCE), and it is best known for the massive stone pyramids that continue to awe visitors to Egypt today, many thousands of years after they were built (Table 3.1).

6000–3150 BCE	Pre-Dynastic Egypt
3150–2613 BCE	Early Dynastic Egypt
2613–2181 BCE	Old Kingdom Period
2181–2040 BCE	First Intermediate Period
2040–1782 BCE	Middle Kingdom Period
1782–1570 BCE	Second Intermediate Period
1570–1069 BCE	New Kingdom Period
1069–525 BCE	Third Intermediate Period

TABLE 3.1 **The Ages of Egypt.** These names for the different eras of ancient Egypt's history were developed by scholars in the nineteenth century. "Kingdom" describes a period of high centralized state organization. "Intermediate" describes a time of weak centralized state organization. While flawed in some ways, the labels continue to influence the way we understand the expansive chronology of ancient Egyptian history. (source: https://www.worldhistory.org/egypt/)

The pyramids were tombs for the pharaohs of Egypt, places where their bodies were stored and preserved after death. The preservation of the body was important and was directly related to Egyptian religious beliefs that a person was composed of a number of different elements. These included the *Ka, Ba, Ahk,* and others. A person's Ka was their spiritual double. After the physical body died, the Ka remained but had to stay in the tomb with the body and be nourished with offerings. The Ba was also a type of spiritual essence, but it separated from the body after death, going out in the world during the day and returning to the body each night. The duty of the Ahk, yet another type of spirit, was to travel to the underworld and the afterlife. The belief in concepts like the Ka and Ba was what made the practice of mummification and the creation of tombs important in Egyptian religion. Both elements needed the physical body to survive.

Before the pyramids, tombs and other architectural features were built of mud-brick and called *mastabas.* But during the Early Dynastic reign of the pharaoh Djoser, just before the start of the Old Kingdom, a brilliant architect named Imhotep decided to build a marvelous stone tomb for his king. Originally, it was intended to be merely a stone mastaba. However, Imhotep went beyond this plan and constructed additional smaller stone mastabas, one on top of the other. The result was a multitiered step pyramid (Figure 3.20). Surrounding it, Imhotep built a large complex that included temples.

FIGURE 3.20 The Pyramid of Djoser. The Pyramid of Djoser, sometimes called the step pyramid, is composed of six stone *mastabas* set atop each other, each slightly smaller than the one below. Built by the architect Imhotep during the reign of Pharaoh Djoser, it is the earliest large stone building in Egypt. (credit: " Pyramid of Djoser (Step Pyramid)" by Jorge Láscar/Flickr, CC BY 2.0)

The step pyramid of Djoser was revolutionary, but the more familiar smooth-sided style appeared a few decades later in the reign of Snefru, when three pyramids were constructed. The most impressive has become known as the Red Pyramid, because of the reddish limestone revealed after the original white limestone surface fell away over the centuries. It had smooth sides and rose to a height of 344 feet over the surrounding landscape. Still an impressive sight, it pales in comparison to the famed Great Pyramid built by Snefru's son Khufu at Giza near Cairo (Figure 3.21). The Great Pyramid at Giza was 756 feet long on each side and originally 481 feet high. Its base covers four city blocks and contains 2.3 million stone blocks, each weighing about 2.5 tons. Even more than the Pyramid of Djoser, the Great Pyramid is a testament to the organization and power of the Egyptian state.

FIGURE 3.21 The Great Pyramid at Giza. The Giza pyramid complex, located just outside modern Cairo, includes three large pyramids and many other monuments and minor pyramids. From left to right, the large pyramids shown

here are the Great Pyramid, the Pyramid of Khafre, and the Pyramid of Menkaure, all built between 2600 and 2500 BCE. (credit: "The Giza-pyramids and Giza Necropolis, Egypt" by "Robster1983"/Wikimedia Commons, CC0 1.0)

Later pharaohs of the Old Kingdom built two additional but slightly smaller pyramids at the same location. All align with the position of the Dog Star Sirius in the summer months, when the Nile floods each year. Each was also linked to a temple along the Nile dedicated to the relevant pharaoh.

Egyptian rulers invested heavily in time and resources to construct these tombs. In the mid-fifth century BCE, the ancient Greek historian Herodotus recorded that the pyramid of Khufu took 100,000 workers twenty years to construct. Herodotus lived two thousand years after this pyramid was built, however, so we might easily dismiss his report as exaggeration. Modern archaeologists suspect that a much smaller but still substantial workforce of around twenty thousand was likely employed. Excavations at the site reveal that these workers lived in cities built nearby that housed them as well as many others dedicated to feeding and caring for them. The workers were not enslaved, as is commonly assumed. Indeed, they likely enjoyed a higher standard of living than many other Egyptians at the time.

As the pyramid and temple complexes became larger and more numerous during the Old Kingdom, so too did the number of priests and administrators in charge of managing them. This required that ever-increasing amounts of wealth be redirected toward these individuals from the central state. Over time, the management of the large Egyptian state also required more support from the regional governors or **nomarchs** and administrators of other types, which meant the pharaohs had to delegate more authority to them. By around 2200 BCE, priests and regional governors possessed a degree of wealth and power that rivaled and sometimes surpassed that of the nobility. For all these reasons and more, centralized power in Old Kingdom Egypt weakened greatly during this time, and scholars since the nineteenth century have referred to it as the First Intermediate Period.

Scholars once claimed that this was a time of chaos and darkness. As evidence, they noted the decline in the building of large-scale monuments like the giant pyramids as well as a drop in the quality of artwork and historical records during these decades. Modern research, however, has demonstrated that this is a gross simplification. Power wasn't necessarily lost so much as redistributed from central to regional control. From the perspective of the reigning noble families, this may have seemed like chaos and disorder. But it was not necessarily the dark age older generations of historians believed it to be.

A Second Age of Egyptian Greatness

The First Intermediate Period came to an end around 2040 BCE as a series of powerful rulers, beginning with Mentuhotep II, was able to reestablish centralized control in Egypt. This led to the rise of what we now call the Middle Kingdom Period, which lasted nearly 260 years.

In the year 1991 BCE, Amenemhat, a former vizier (adviser) to the line of kings who established the Middle Kingdom, assumed control and founded a line of pharaohs who ruled Egypt for two centuries. Under the leadership of these pharaohs, Egypt acquired its first standing army, restarted the large-scale building projects known in earlier times, made contacts with surrounding peoples and kingdoms in the Levant and in Kush (modern Sudan), and generally held itself together with a strong centralized power structure.

⊚ LINK TO LEARNING

New Kingdom pharaohs circulated a work of literature that foretold the rise of Amenemhat, who would bring an end to disorder and restore Egypt to prosperity. This ancient work was called the Prophecy of Neferty (https://openstax.org/l/77prophecy) and is presented as an English translation by University College London.

During the Middle Kingdom Period, pharaohs introduced the cult of the deity Amon-Re at Thebes. Amon-Re was a combination of the sun-god Re, the creator god worshipped in the north of Egypt, and Amon, a sky god revered in the south. He was portrayed as the king of the gods and the father of each reigning pharaoh. The pharaohs of the Middle Kingdom no longer constructed massive pyramids for their tombs. Instead, they focused on erecting massive temples to Amon-Re and his wife, the mother-goddess Mut, at Thebes (Figure 3.22). The ruins of these temples are located at Karnak in southern Egypt. Amon-Re's temples featured immense halls in which multiple columns or colonnades supported the roof, courtyards, and ceremonial gates. They housed the sacred images of the deities, which on festival days were brought out in ritual processions.

FIGURE 3.22 **Temple of Amon-Re**. The temple of Amon-Re, built around 2055 BCE, was plundered in ancient times for its stone. What remains are these ruins. The large ceremonial gates still stand, towering above the visitors who walk beneath them. (credit: modification of work "Karnak Temple Complex at Luxor, Egypt" by Daniel Csörföly/ Wikimedia Commons, Public Domain)

Middle Kingdom Egypt reached its height in the 1870s and 1860s BCE during the reign of Senusret III, a powerful warrior pharaoh and capable administrator of the centralized state. He greatly expanded Egypt's territorial control, leading armies up the Nile into Kush and into the Levant. These efforts not only strengthened Egypt's ability to protect itself from invasion but also greatly increased the flow of trade from these regions. Kush was known for its rich gold deposits and capable warriors, and Senusret III's several campaigns there brought Egypt access not only to the gold but also to mercenaries from Kush.

Senusret also dramatically increased the degree of centralized power held by the pharaoh, reducing the authority and even the number of the nomarchs. Overall, Egypt now grew wealthier, safer, more centralized, and more powerful than it had ever been. As a result, his reign was also a time of cultural flourishing when Egyptian art, architecture, and literature grew in refinement and sophistication (Figure 3.23).

FIGURE 3.23 The Art of the Middle Kingdom. This pectoral, a form of jewelry worn over the chest, is an excellent example of the fine artwork of the Egyptian Middle Kingdom Period. It once belonged to an Egyptian princess called Sithathoryunet and is made of gold and semiprecious stones. (credit: modification of work "Pectoral and Necklace of Sithathoryunet with the Name of Senwosret II" by Purchase, Rogers Fund and Henry Walters Gift, 1916/The Metropolitan Museum of Art, Public Domain)

The deaths of Senusret III and his son Amenemhat III led indirectly to a rare but not unprecedented transfer of royal power to an Egyptian woman. Possibly Amenemhat IV's wife, sister, or both, Sobekneferu, the daughter of Amenemhat III, was the first woman to rule Egypt since before the Old Kingdom. She reigned for only a few years, and little is known of her accomplishments. But scholars have determined that she was the first pharaoh to associate herself with the Egyptian crocodile god Sobek. She may even have commissioned the construction of the city of Crocodilopolis to honor this important god. Because she died without having had children, she was the last in the long series of pharaohs in the line of Amenemhat I.

Even before the reign of Sobekneferu, Egypt was already experiencing some degree of decline. Over the next century, the pharaohs and their centralized control became steadily weaker. Increasing numbers of Semitic-speaking peoples from the Levant flowed into Egypt, possibly the result of increased trade between Egypt and the Levant at first. But by the late 1700s BCE, these Semitic-speaking groups had grown so numerous in the Nile delta region and centralized control of Egypt had grown so weak that some of their chieftains began to assert control in a few areas. The Egyptians called these Semitic-speaking chieftains *Heqau-khasut* (rulers of foreign lands). Today they are more commonly called Hyksos, a Greek corruption of this Egyptian name.

By the time the Hyksos were asserting their control over parts of the Nile delta, Egypt was already well into what historians of the nineteenth century dubbed the Second Intermediate Period. Like the First Intermediate Period, the second was a time of reduced centralized control. Not only did the Egyptian nobles, ruling from their capital in Thebes, lose control of the delta, they also lost territory upriver to an increasingly powerful kingdom of Kush in the south. This meant that the territory once controlled by the powerful centralized state bureaucracy was effectively split into three regions: one ruled by Hyksos in the north, one by Kushite in the south, and one by the remnants of the Egyptian nobility in the center.

Despite the fragmentation, for most of this period, the three regions of Egypt appear to have maintained peaceful relationships. That changed, however, beginning in the 1550s BCE when a string of Theban Egyptian rulers was able to go on the offensive against the Hyksos. After the Hyksos were defeated and the Nile delta recaptured, the emboldened Egyptians turned their attention south to Kush, eventually extending their control over these regions as well. These efforts ushered in a new period of Egyptian greatness called the New Kingdom, the highest high-water mark of Egyptian power and cultural influence in the ancient world.

3.4 The Indus Valley Civilization

LEARNING OBJECTIVES

By the end of this section, you will be able to:
- Analyze the growth, development, and decline of the Indus valley culture
- Describe the cities of Mohenjo-Daro and Harappa
- Identify key themes in Indus valley religion and culture

More than fifteen hundred miles east of Mesopotamia, in the fertile valley of the Indus River, another early civilization developed in the early third millennium BCE as a peer of ancient Sumer. Early in the second millennium BCE, however, the cities of this Indus valley culture experienced decline. Lacking written records, historians have only cultural artifacts on which to base any speculation about the rise and fall of this spectacular culture, which undoubtedly influenced subsequent civilizations that arose in South Asia.

The Origins of the Indus Valley Civilization

The Indus River flows from the Himalayan Mountains south into the Indian Ocean, depositing rich alluvial soil from the mountains along its banks. Its valley (in modern Pakistan and India) thus provided a hospitable environment for population growth for the emerging Indus valley civilization (c. 2800 BCE–1800 BCE).

Evidence for the domestication of plants and animals in this region dates to about 7000 BCE, but the process may have begun earlier. It is likely that agriculturalists in the region adopted barley and wheat cultivation techniques from the Near East, where people had been practicing agriculture for thousands of years by this point. However, it is also possible that the people of the Indus valley developed some of these techniques independently. Regardless, by about 5000 BCE, they were clearly in contact with the civilizations in Egypt and Sumer.

The farmers of the Indus valley cultivated wheat and barley as well as raised cattle and sheep, as did the farmers of Mesopotamia and western Asia. They also domesticated and cultivated bananas and cotton for cloth production, which were both unknown in ancient Mesopotamia. Thanks to the Neolithic Revolution, which secured a stable food source and stimulated population growth, people began living in settled communities along the Indus River valley as a new early civilization developed.

Beginning around 2800 BCE, the Indus valley entered a new phase in its development with the growth of a great number of urban centers. The two largest cities emerged at what are now the archaeological sites of Harappa in the northeast and Mohenjo-Daro to the southeast and downriver. Other large urban centers existed at Dholavira, Ganeriwala, and Rakhigarhi, along with many smaller but similarly organized cities scattered across the valley. By the time this civilization reached its height around 2000 BCE, more than one thousand urban centers of varying sizes were spread across the expansive region (Figure 3.24).

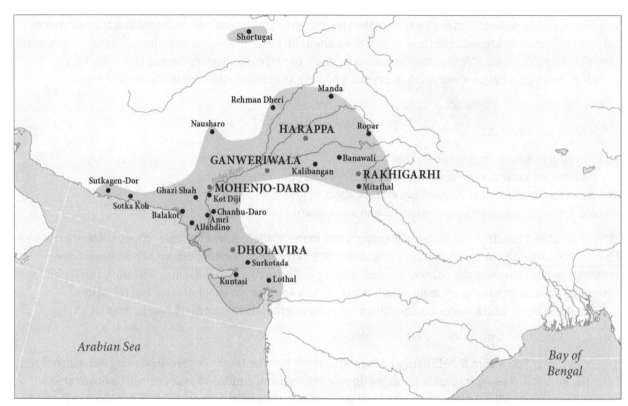

FIGURE 3.24 The Indus Valley Culture. The Indus valley civilization was spread over a very large area that today includes parts of Pakistan and India. By 2000 BCE it was highly urbanized, with several large cities and as many as a thousand smaller urban areas. (attribution: Copyright Rice University, OpenStax, under CC BY 4.0 license)

Despite the large size of this civilization, its existence was unknown to modern scholars until the early nineteenth century when British excavations revealed the ancient city of Harappa. Because Harappa was the first major site discovered by archaeologists, the term **Harappan** often appears as a synonym for Indus valley civilization.

The archaeological sites of Harappa in the north and Mohenjo-Daro in the south have received the most study of all the Indus valley cities and remain the best known. At their height, they likely had populations of about thirty thousand people each. The political organization across the Indus valley remains imperfectly understood, but it may have consisted of a collection of independent city-states, such as existed in ancient Sumer. It is equally plausible, however, that the few large cities functioned as regional capitals ruling over the surrounding smaller ones. The fact that the sites all possessed a similar structural organization, with a sophisticated grid of well-laid-out city streets, lends credibility to theories that some form of central authority was operating.

⊘ LINK TO LEARNING

There is much to explore at the sites of Harappa and Mohenjo-Daro. Take a look at these walkthrough slideshows on Harappa (https://openstax.org/l/77harappa) and Mohenjo-Daro (https://openstax.org/l/77mohenjo-daro) to better understand how these cities were organized and what they look like today.

All the cities are divided into two sections: a lower city that was largely a residential area, and an upper city or citadel that was walled off from the rest of the settlement (Figure 3.25). This citadel may have served as a monumental ceremonial center for ritual activities and the residence of the ruling elite, like the palaces and temples of Egypt and Mesopotamia. At Harappa, the wall of mud-brick enclosing the citadel was forty-two feet thick at its base and nearly fifty feet high (about as tall as a five-story building today), with rectangular towers at regular intervals. Within the citadels stood platforms built of mud-brick where ritual activities such as animal sacrifices may have been performed; at Harappa, the platform was twenty-three feet high. At the site of Kalibangan, in northwestern India, archaeologists uncovered a pit on top of the platform containing burned cattle bones.

FIGURE 3.25 The Citadel Mound at Mohenjo-Daro. The stupa at Mohenjo-Daro, located in present-day Pakistan, was built circa 2500 BCE. The identification and dating of the stupa in 1923 by Indian archaeologist Rakhal Das Banerji led to the first major excavations at the site in the 1920s and 1930s. (credit: "Stupa at Mohenjo-Daro" by Omair Anwer/Flickr, CC BY 2.0)]

The citadels also included public baths. At Mohenjo-Daro, the tank of the bath was forty feet long and twenty-three feet wide and entered by staircases on either side. A nearby well provided the water. Archaeologists have uncovered a large hall supported by pilasters composed of mud-brick at Mohenjo-Daro, as well as a multistory residence built around an open courtyard. This evidence suggests that ritual specialists, perhaps priests, lived and performed religious functions in the citadels that may have required them to bathe in the large public bath and congregate in the hall. An extensive granary for grain storage was found at Mohenjo-Daro. Farmers from outlying rural areas undoubtedly produced the surplus crops that were stored here to provide sustenance for the elite, religious specialists, and other city residents such as merchants and artisans, just as in Mesopotamia and Egypt.

The lower sections of the Indus valley cities consisted of residential quarters and workshops. At Mohenjo-Daro and Kalibangan, the houses typically consisted of four to six rooms built around a central courtyard and were equipped with wells to provide running water to a bathroom. Larger homes in the cities were multistory with as many as thirty rooms. There is also evidence of devices attached to some of the roofs that pumped wind into homes and other large buildings to cool them.

⊘ LINK TO LEARNING

Some of the most intriguing evidence at the large Indus valley civilization sites indicates the residents had sophisticated knowledge of water engineering and built citywide drainage systems (https://openstax.org/l/77IndusDrainage) with covers for servicing. Evidence was found of indoor toilets that connected to this drainage network (https://openstax.org/l/77DrainageNet) that ran throughout the city.

The Indus valley cities also included an industrial area where workshops were located. At Harappa, this district included quarters for the laborers who worked there. The ancient city at the site of Lothal near the Indian Ocean included a dockyard and a warehouse for incoming trade goods. The inhabitants of these cities may have included the artisans and merchants who provided goods for the ruling elite. As in ancient Mesopotamia and Egypt, the majority of the population were probably farmers who lived in the outlying rural areas surrounding each city.

Trade, Writing, and Religion

Archaeological work has revealed that a considerable amount of trade flowed between Mesopotamia and the Indus valley. Cuneiform tablets from Mesopotamia refer to the Indus valley as *Meluhha* and document that precious stones such as lapis lazuli and carnelian, as well as marine shells from the Indian Ocean, were imported from there. Merchants traveled by sea across the Indian Ocean and by land over the Iranian plateau (Figure 3.26).

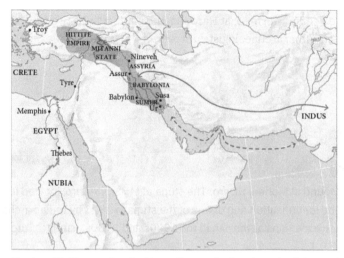

FIGURE 3.26 Indus Valley Trade with Mesopotamia. From the work of archaeologists, we know that significant trade took place between the inhabitants of the Indus River valley and their contemporaries in Mesopotamia. (attribution: Copyright Rice University, OpenStax, under CC BY 4.0 license)

The influence of Mesopotamia on the Indus valley culture is evident in the use of seals. The Indus valley seals were inscribed with depictions of human figures and animals such as bulls and goats, likely totems for families or lineages, and brief inscriptions that likely indicate names, titles, or occupations. Merchants marked ownership of goods by making an impression of the seal on the soft clay that covered the mouth of the jar or other vessel that held the objects, or on clay tags attached to sacks of grain (Figure 3.27). A similar practice occurred in contemporary Mesopotamia, where the seal was in the shape of a cylinder that could be rolled to leave an impression. Archaeologists have found seals from the Indus valley in ancient Sumerian cities such as Ur.

FIGURE 3.27 An Indus Valley Seal. On the left is a seal from the Indus valley civilization, and on the right is a modern clay impression made from it. Such seals typically showed animals and a script that remains to be deciphered. (credit: modification of work "Stamp seal and modern impression: unicorn and incense burner (?)" by Dodge Fund, 1949/The Metropolitan Museum of Art, Public Domain)

The script that appears on many of the seals is unique to the people of the Indus valley civilization, and scholars have yet to decipher it. It seems to consist of phonograms, signs for the sounds of syllables, and there appear to be about four hundred such signs. Many speculate that the language written in this script may be related to the Dravidian languages still spoken across southern India today. It may also be similar to the script invented by the Elamites of southwestern Iran. Unlike the case in Mesopotamia and Egypt, archaeologists have not uncovered clay tablets or papyrus rolls in the Indus valley.

THE PAST MEETS THE PRESENT

Deciphering Indus Valley Script

One of the great mysteries surrounding Indus valley script is what exactly it represents. Was it a means of capturing spoken language, or did the marks simply indicate whether taxes had been paid on an item or signify the quality of a particular good (in the same way we use stars to rate products and services online today)?

Rajesh Rao, a professor of computer science at the University of Washington who became fascinated with the Indus valley civilization as a child in India, created a computer program to help him answer this question by measuring conditional entropy in Indus valley writing. Conditional entropy measures the degree of randomness in a sequence. In a system of writing that encodes language, there is a fairly low level of randomness. Letters appear frequently in some combinations and rarely or never in others. For example, in the English language, the letter *q* is usually followed by the letter *u* and never by the letter *k*. At the beginning of a word, the letter *h* is never followed by a consonant.

Rao tested the conditional entropy of the Indus valley script along with that of several natural languages including English, artificial languages such as those written for computers, and other sequences not related to language such as human DNA sequences. He discovered that the Indus valley script has a degree of randomness similar to that of natural languages, leading him to the conclusion that the symbols do represent a language and are not simply marks of quality or signs that something has been taxed. He also concluded that the rate of conditional entropy in Indus valley writing resembled that of Old Tamil, an earlier form of the Tamil language currently spoken in southern India that belongs to the Dravidian language family. This idea angered many Indians, especially those who speak Hindi, a language derived from Sanskrit that is the first language of many people in northern India. This issue is both historical and modern. If the language of the ancient Indus valley was Dravidian in origin, it calls into question the ancestry of the people who lived there, and given the evolution of the caste system, it raises questions about social identities that have existed for centuries. The issue remains in question, and the controversy about ancestral origins is far more complex than the single issue of language.

- Why do you think the origin of language matters so much to the people of India?
- If Indus valley writing were deciphered, what could historians learn about the culture that we cannot currently know?
- In what other ways could computers help historians learn about the past?

Bronze technology probably also entered the Indus River valley by the third millennium BCE through trade with Mesopotamia. Merchants from the Indus valley may even have exported tin from Afghanistan to Mesopotamia, since this metal was in demand for the manufacture of bronze.

Notwithstanding the many obvious Mesopotamian influences and trading connections, the people of the Indus valley civilization developed their own unique culture. Their distinctive religion may have shaped later cultures in India. For example, clay figurines from the Indus valley that are believed to depict deities are often interpreted as portraying a goddess whose female attributes are similar to those of the Hindu goddess Durga, consort of the god Shiva. Some seals depict a horned three-faced figure surrounded by animals, which closely resembles the Hindu deity Shiva when represented as the Lord of the Animals (Figure 3.28). Archaeologists have also found stones molded into shapes that resemble *lingams* and *yonis*, which are representations of male and female sexual organs associated with the worship of Shiva. The people of the Indus valley buried their dead with modest grave goods such as clay pots, which suggests a belief in an afterlife. However, there is no evidence of temples or monumental tombs such as the Egyptian pyramids or the royal tombs of Ur in Mesopotamia.

(a)   **(b)**

FIGURE 3.28 Possible Influence of Indus Valley Religious Imagery. Historians speculate that the religion of the Indus valley might have influenced later Indian cultures. For example, a seal from 2600–1900 BCE discovered at Mohenjo-Daro (a) shows a seated figure with three faces surrounded by animals. A much later sixth-century CE portrayal of Shiva from the Elephanta Caves in western India (b) shows the Hindu god seated, also with three faces and surrounded by animals. (credit a: modification of work "Shiva Pashupati" by Unknown/Wikimedia Commons, Public Domain; credit b: modification of work "Elephanta Caves" by Christian Haugen/Flickr, CC BY 2.0)

The artisans of the Indus valley created unique sculptures in clay, stone, and bronze. One of the more spectacular stone works from Mohenjo-Daro depicts a serene bearded man who may be a priest or leader in the community. A tiny bronze figure appears to represent a young woman dancing (Figure 3.29). Her bracelets and necklaces indicate that the people of this culture employed artisans to manufacture such adornment, which may have indicated high social status. Artisans of the Indus valley were also very busy manufacturing pottery and seals. Their artistic designs influenced artisans in neighboring cultures over a wide area, from the upper Ganges River valley in what is today northwestern India to Baluchistan in western Pakistan and southeastern Iran.

FIGURE 3.29 The Mohenjo-Daro Dancer. This four-inch-tall bronze statue of a young woman discovered at Mohenjo-Daro and dated to circa 2300–1750 BCE could depict a goddess or a woman of the elite class who is dancing. If she is dancing, we can also conclude that music and dance may have been incorporated into social and religious rituals. (credit: modification of work "Bronze 'Dancing Girl,' Mohenjo-daro, c. 2500 BC" by Gary Todd/Flickr, Public Domain)

Merchants from the Indus valley were undoubtedly active in exchanging such wares in these regions. In the absence of coinage, they used a common system of stone cubical weights to assess goods in commercial exchanges that required barter. The cities of the Indus valley could have also used these weights to assess taxes in kind that they collected for their granaries.

The Era of Decline

Beginning around 1800 BCE, the centuries of trade between the Indus valley and Mesopotamia came to an end. Over the next four centuries, the cities of the Indus River valley were slowly depopulated, and the civilization declined, likely in stages. Why and how this decline occurred remains unknown. One common view is that it was related to regional climate change. Around 2000 BCE, the floodplain of the Indus River shifted dramatically, creating dry river beds where cities had been and water once flowed. Changes in the pattern of seasonal wind and rainfall, known as the **monsoon** in South Asia, may have caused these environmental effects. Without a secure source of water for drinking and irrigation, the cities would have suffered declines in population. Another theory suggests that centuries of environmental degradation caused by urbanization and large population growth made the land unsuitable to human populations. Still other views point to the possibility of tectonic activity that changed the course of the rivers, or even epidemic disease that decimated the population.

Before these environmental factors began to be considered, the view for many years was that the Indus valley civilization was violently destroyed in a conquest by nomadic Indo-European speakers calling themselves Aryans, a Sanskrit-speaking group of nomadic pastoralists who raised cattle and horses. Some Aryans began migrating from the Eurasian Steppe north of the Black and Caspian Seas around 3500 BCE. Over time, different groups spread into Europe, Anatolia, Iran, and eventually Pakistan and India.

The Aryan invasion theory of decline depends heavily on Indo-European works of religious literature like the *Rigveda*, produced sometime between 1500 and 1000 BCE in northwestern India. This work includes a great number of hymns, rituals, descriptions of deities, and other largely religious topics geared toward understanding the origin of the universe and the nature of the divine. But in parts it also discusses the arrival of the Aryans and describes them attacking the walled cities and forts of the indigenous population. While some of these descriptions were likely developed centuries after the fall of the Indus valley civilization and may be unrelated to it, some scholars continue to hold that these passages describe the conquest of Mohenjo-Daro. Archaeological evidence attesting to the fact that Mohenjo-Daro was attacked around 1500 BCE and mostly destroyed lends some credibility to these claims.

We may never know what best explains the collapse of the Indus valley civilization. A few or all these causes may have played a role. For example, environmental degradation caused by years of resource exploitation and high population density certainly had an effect. These issues could have been compounded by climate change and disease. And in a weakened state, the people of the region would have been far more vulnerable to attack by raiding groups like the Aryans.

However it happened, by around 1500 BCE, the social and political systems had broken down, and the sophisticated culture of the Indus valley civilization had collapsed. The architectural styles that characterized the cities at their height were abandoned, as was the writing system, the sophisticated metalworking, and other artisanal crafts. The Indus valley civilization had come to an end.

Key Terms

Bronze Age the period from 3500 to 1110 BCE when bronze, an alloy of copper and tin, was the preferred material for manufacturing tools and weapons

city-state an independent political entity consisting of a city and surrounding territory that it controls

Code of Hammurabi a list of judicial decisions that the Babylonian king Hammurabi had inscribed on stone pillars throughout his kingdom

culture all the ways in which members of a human society interact with one another and with their environment and pass these ways from generation to generation

cuneiform a phonetic writing system based on the sounds of words and invented by the Sumerians in about 3000 BCE

Harappan a term describing the ancient Indus valley civilization, named for one of its largest cities and the first to be discovered by archaeologists

hieratic a simplified form of hieroglyphics employed by Egyptian scribes for recording everyday documents such as receipts and contracts

hieroglyphics a complex writing system developed around 3000 BCE in which written symbols represented both sounds and ideas

lugal the Sumerians' term for their ruler

monsoon the seasonal pattern of wind and rainfall across South Asia

nomarchs regional governors in ancient Egypt

papyrus a type of paper Egyptians made from a common reed plant growing along the Nile

pastoralists nomadic people who rely on herds of domesticated animals for subsistence

pharaoh the title of the Egyptian ruler, translated as "big house"

polytheists people who worship multiple gods, usually associated with different aspects of the natural world

social stratification the hierarchical order of society in which people sharing the same level of wealth and status make up a distinct class or strata

specialization a societal characteristic in which people perform specific tasks, such as farming (farmer) or producing tools and clothing (artisan), that contribute to the well-being of the community

ziggurat an immense stepped tower with a flat top built of mud-brick that served as a temple in Sumerian cities

Section Summary

3.1 Early Civilizations

For tens of thousands of years, humans lived largely as mobile, subsistence hunter-gatherers. But with the innovation of agricultural production in a few areas around the world, some groups began to settle, and a new agricultural and sedentary lifestyle gave rise to early civilizations characterized by urban settings, the specialization of labor, and increasing social stratification. The earliest examples appeared in Neolithic settlements like Jericho, Çatalhöyük, Mehrgarh, and others in China, Mesoamerica, and the Andean region of South America.

3.2 Ancient Mesopotamia

The city of Uruk in the land of Sumer was one of the first true cities in world history. Advances in technology such as the invention of bronze-making techniques, a writing system called cuneiform, and a sophisticated religion with a pantheon of deities spread and facilitated the development of a complex Mesopotamian culture and the rise of other city-states there. The Sumerian city-states under the rule of their *lugals* or kings commonly waged war against one another and against a stream of foreign invaders.

The period of independent city-states came to an end with the rise of the world's first empire, the Akkadian Empire of Sargon of Akkad. While it lasted only about a century and a half, this empire inaugurated a new era in the region, which later saw the emergence of other powerful realms. These included the Third Dynasty of Ur and the famous Babylonian Empire of Hammurabi, who created an influential law code. These later empires preserved many elements of the earlier Sumerian civilization, including cuneiform and works of literature like the *Epic of Gilgamesh*.

3.3 Ancient Egypt

Ancient Egypt arose as an early civilization along the Nile River valley in the fourth millennium BCE. A polytheistic society with a great assortment of deities and its own writing system, Egypt was united under the pharaohs for much of its ancient history. Its people held that order, truth, and justice (Ma'at) ruled the day and ordered the universe.

The Old Kingdom was the era of pyramid building. The Middle Kingdom was a time of renewed strength and territorial expansion. "Intermediate" periods of weakened centralized control followed and preceded these kingdoms. The First Intermediate Period was a time when regional governors gained power at the expense of the pharaohs. During the Second Intermediate Period, traditional Egyptian nobles lost control of the Nile delta to the Hyksos people and control of far upper Egypt to the kingdom of Kush. These areas were later reconquered with the inauguration of the New Kingdom.

3.4 The Indus Valley Civilization

The Indus valley culture emerged as an early civilization in the early third millennium BCE. It drew inspiration from contacts with Mesopotamia, but its people also developed large well-planned cities such as Harappa and Mohenjo-Daro that were quite different from contemporary cities in ancient Sumer. Since the written script of the Indus peoples remains undeciphered, historians can only speculate about how these great cities arose and why they fell in the early second millennium, perhaps as a result of trade disruptions, changes in the course of rivers, the arrival of Indo-European–speaking nomads, climate change, environmental degradation, disease, or some combination of these factors.

Assessments

Review Questions

1. What is a characteristic of early civilizations?
   a. nomadic lifestyle
   b. egalitarian society
   c. specialization
   d. subsistence economy

2. What does the construction of the tower at Jericho suggest about that Neolithic settlement?
   a. It likely revered ancestors.
   b. It likely had some type of government.
   c. It likely performed animal sacrifices.
   d. It likely had a small population.

3. The population of what Neolithic town in today's Turkey may have shared a belief in a mother-deity?
   a. Çatalhöyük
   b. Jericho
   c. Caral
   d. Anyang

4. The earliest known script, cuneiform, was written by pressing a stylus made of reed into what type of material?
   a. wet clay
   b. hot bronze

    c. dry papyrus

    d. gold plates

5. How large do scholars estimate the population of the city of Uruk may have been by the end of the fourth millennium BCE?

    a. twenty thousand

    b. thirty thousand

    c. forty thousand

    d. fifty thousand

6. Who is credited with establishing the first-known empire in world history?

    a. Hammurabi

    b. Ur-Nammu

    c. Naram-Sin

    d. Sargon of Akkad

7. What two adjectives best describe the gods of Mesopotamia?

    a. pleasant and helpful

    b. fickle and easily angered

    c. distant and unconcerned

    d. weak and cautious

8. What adjective best describes the afterlife, according to the Sumerian belief system?

    a. gloomy

    b. happy

    c. exciting

    d. scary

9. Who do scholars believe was the first pharaoh to unite all Egypt?

    a. Narmer

    b. Amenemhat I

    c. Djoser

    d. Khufu

10. What was another role of the pharaoh, in addition to being the political head of the state?

    a. merchant

    b. scribe

    c. high priest

    d. farmer

11. Imhotep built a large stone step pyramid for what pharaoh?

    a. Djoser

    b. Khufu

    c. Menkaure

    d. Snefru

12. What role did the nomarchs play in the decline of the Old Kingdom and beginning of the First Intermediate Period?

    a. They instituted important religious practices.

    b. They assumed more control over their regions.

    c.   They allowed for greater Hyksos immigration.

    d.   They rejected the authority of the priests.

13. What was significant about the reign of Sobekneferu?

    a.   She was both pharaoh and priest.

    b.   She was the last pharaoh of the Middle Kingdom.

    c.   She gave unprecedented power to the nomarchs.

    d.   She was the first woman to rule since before the Old Kingdom.

14. The Mesopotamians called the Indus valley civilization by what name?

    a.   Meluhha

    b.   Harappa

    c.   Mohenjo-Daro

    d.   Dholavira

15. What may have served as the monumental ceremonial center in Indus valley cities?

    a.   a ziggurat

    b.   a pyramid

    c.   a citadel

    d.   a sunken court

16. What was the likely purpose of the large baths at Mohenjo-Daro?

    a.   watering of livestock

    b.   ritual cleansing

    c.   storage of drinking water

    d.   the king's use only

17. What was a common trade item exported from the Indus valley to Mesopotamia?

    a.   lapis lazuli

    b.   diamonds

    c.   rubies

    d.   sapphires

Check Your Understanding Questions

1. In what ways did the nomadic and seminomadic peoples beyond the borders of early civilizations contribute to these civilizations?

2. What do the artifacts and other archaeological finds from Jericho and Çatalhöyük suggest about life in these early urban environments?

3. What was the *Legend of Sargon*, and how does it explain Sargon of Akkad's rise to power?

4. In what way did the palace and temple complex in ancient Mesopotamian cities function as an economic redistribution center?

5. How were gods honored and served in the Sumerian religion?

6. In what respects were the Sumerian *lugals* and Egyptian pharaohs different?

7. What do ancient sources and modern analyses suggest about the labor required to build the large pyramids of the Old Kingdom?

8. Why is the reign of Pharaoh Senusret III considered the high point of Middle Kingdom Egypt?

9. What evidence suggests that the walled citadel areas in Indus valley cities may have been used for religious purposes?

10. What suggests that the religion of the Indus valley civilization may have survived for many centuries in a different form?

11. What are some of the theories about the decline of the Indus valley civilization?

Application and Reflection Questions

1. Imagine that you lived through a transition from a nomadic to a settled way of life. What in your life would have changed the most? Do you think your standard of living would be better or worse? Why?

2. What may have motivated the people of the Neolithic towns of Jericho and Çatalhöyük to produce an agricultural surplus? How was this surplus likely used?

3. The Code of Hammurabi identifies different punishments and expectations for people based on their social position. Why do you think this was the case? Why wouldn't everyone have faced the same types of punishments and expectations?

4. Why did the rise of the Akkadian Empire bring an end to the era of independent city-states in Mesopotamia? Why didn't the city-states simply reassert their independence after the empire collapsed?

5. Many scholars have explained the capricious actions of the Mesopotamian gods and the generally pessimistic worldview of the people as consequences of a difficult environment. Does this sound convincing? Why or why not? Can you think of an alternate explanation?

6. Terms like Old Kingdom, Middle Kingdom, and Intermediate Period were developed in the nineteenth century by scholars seeking to organize Egyptian chronology into distinct ages. Despite some flaws, this naming convention is still used. Do you think it should be? Why or why not? What other type of chronological organization might you suggest? Why?

7. While Egypt was unified early (about 3150 BCE), Mesopotamia was not unified until the rise of Sargon almost a thousand years later. What do you think accounts for this difference? Why didn't Egypt emerge as a number of independent city-states and Sumer as an empire early on?

8. We know there was trade between the Indus valley civilization and that of Mesopotamia. But it remains unclear to what extent the rise of the Indus valley culture can be attributed to connections with Mesopotamia. What elements of Indus valley culture may have been influenced by Mesopotamia? What elements are unique to the cities of the Indus valley?

9. In what ways do the Indus valley cities resemble those of Mesopotamia? In what ways do they resemble modern cities?

10. Historians' inability to read the writing of the Indus valley civilization means that we know less about this culture than we do about Mesopotamia and ancient Egypt. What elements of a culture are difficult to understand without the help of written documents? Why is this the case? What kinds of things are impossible to know until the script is deciphered?

FIGURE 4.1 An Army at War. This seventh-century BCE stone relief from an Assyrian palace shows the army of King Ashurbanipal fighting against nomadic Arabian desert groups. (credit: modification of work "Assyrian Arabian Battle" by "LaLouvre"/Wikimedia Commons, CC0 1.0)

CHAPTER OUTLINE

INTRODUCTION At the dawn of the Iron Age, which began around 1200 BCE in the Near East, highly trained Assyrian armies with bronze and iron weapons expanded out of northern Mesopotamia. Within a few centuries, their conquests had provided the Assyrians with an empire larger than the Near East had ever seen. Relying on archaeological finds like this detailed relief as well as textual documentation from the Bible and other sources, historians have pieced together the history of this once-mighty state (Figure 4.1). The Assyrians conquered the kingdom of Israel in the eighth century BCE, added Egypt to their lands in the seventh century BCE, and held it all together with a combination of ruthless military tactics, efficient state organization, and a wide network of royal roads. They left a powerful regional legacy, yet theirs is just one of many empires that rose and fell in the complicated and dangerous world of the ancient Near East. Though these local power brokers were linked by the shared heritage of a Sumerian past, including influences such as cuneiform and Hammurabi's law code, their rapid succession speaks to the level of rivalry and conflict experienced by the people of the area. Yet the same chaos led to important innovations in all aspects of society, particularly military technology.

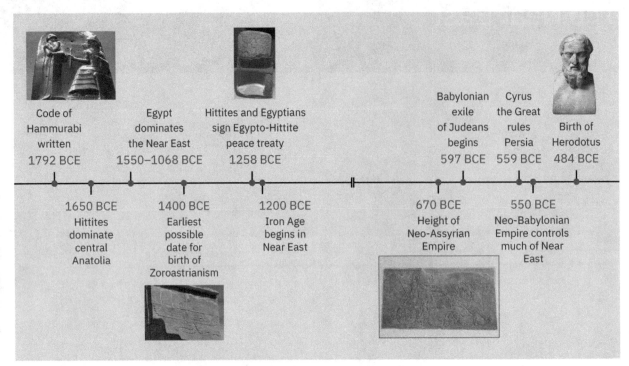

FIGURE 4.2 Timeline: The Near East. (credit "1792 BCE": modification of work "Louvre - Hammurabi's Code" by "Erin"/Flickr, CC BY 2.0; credit "1400 BCE": modification of work "Persepolis, Tripylon, eastern gate (2)" by Marco Prins/Wikimedia Commons, CC0 1.0; credit "1258 BCE": modification of work "Treaty of Kadesh" by Iocanus/ Museum of the Ancient Orient/Wikimedia Commons, CC BY 3.0; credit "670 BCE": modification of work "Ancient Assyria Bas-Relief of Lion Hunt, Nimrud, 883-859 BC" by Gary Todd/Flickr, Public Domain; credit "484 BCE": modification of work "Marble bust of Herodotos" by The Metropolitan Museum of Art, Gift of George F. Baker, 1891/ Wikimedia Commons, Public Domain)

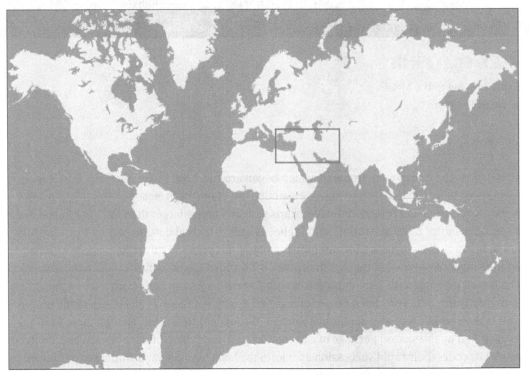

FIGURE 4.3 Locator Map: The Near East. (credit: modification of work "World map blank shorelines" by Maciej Jaros/Wikimedia Commons, Public Domain)

4.1 From Old Babylon to the Medes

LEARNING OBJECTIVES

By the end of this section, you will be able to:
- Describe the geography of the Ancient Near East
- Discuss the political norms, technological innovations, and unique social attributes of the major city-states of the Ancient Near East
- Explain how city-states of the Ancient Near East interacted with their neighbors

When Sargon of Akkad built Mesopotamia's first empire in approximately 2300 BCE, he inaugurated a new era in the Near East. Though it lasted only about a century and a half, his model of imperial expansion and administration was followed by a number of successive regional powers in the region. The Third Dynasty of Ur and Hammurabi's Babylonian kingdom were in many ways imitators of Sargon's earlier example. Later powers like the Hittites, Neo-Assyrians, and Neo-Babylonians continued to borrow from earlier empires and added unique traits as well. Within these different empires existed a diverse assortment of peoples, social classes, religions, and daily practices. From the archaeological record and surviving documents, historians have cataloged these groups and learned a little about how they lived.

Power Politics in the Near East

The end of the third millennium BCE was a transformative, if sometimes chaotic, period in Mesopotamia. Foreign invaders from the north, east, and west put tremendous pressure on the rulers of the Third Dynasty of Ur, the last Sumerian dynasty. One of the greatest threats came from nomadic peoples then living in the desert regions of Syria. Raiding by these Amorites was considered such a problem that in approximately 2034 BCE, Shu-Sin, ruler of Ur, constructed a 170-mile wall from the banks of the Euphrates to the Tigris to keep them out. The strategy ultimately failed, and in the reign of Shu-Sin's son Ibbi-Sin, the Amorites breached the wall and began attacking cities. They were soon joined by the Elamites from the east. As raids by these groups increased in volume and intensity, city after city fell, and the Third Dynasty of Ur disintegrated. By around 2004 BCE, all that remained of Ibbi-Sin's empire was the city of Ur itself. In that year, it too was sacked by the Elamites and others.

Amorites then spread out across Mesopotamia, establishing powerful cities of their own. They adopted the region's existing religious traditions, its local customs, and the Akkadian language. They also embraced the political culture of rivalry, and their two most prominent cities, Isin and Larsa, fought for supremacy. The drive for dominance stoked the same kinds of innovation and expansion that had characterized the first city, Ur.

The Rise of Babylon

During the later stages of the competition between Isin and Larsa, a new power emerged in southern Mesopotamia. This was the city of Babylon. Unlike Ur, Babylon had not previously been an important city-state. Its name is of unknown origin and was likely pronounced *Babil*. Akkadian speakers of the area called it *Bab-ili*, which meant "gateway of the gods." In 1894 BCE, an Amorite chieftain named Sumu-adum took the city and installed himself as ruler. His successors expanded their control over the surrounding area, building public works projects and digging canals. But this expansion was modest, and by about 1800 BCE, Babylon controlled only a relatively small territory around the city itself. Indeed, at this time, it was just one of a handful of small states making up a loose coalition in Mesopotamia.

It was during the reign of Hammurabi in eighteenth century BCE that Babylon rose as a center of power and the administrative capital of a new Mesopotamian empire (Figure 4.4). Early in his reign, Hammurabi made an alliance with the powerful Assyrians to the north. This pact gave him the protection he needed to expand his kingdom, taking control of Isin, Uruk, and other key cities of southern Mesopotamia. Soon Babylon had become a major center of power in the south and the target of rival kingdoms. In approximately 1764 BCE, a coalition led by the city-states of Elam and Eshunna invaded Babylonian territory, hoping to capture

Hammurabi's powerful realm, but it failed, and Hammurabi turned his attention to the south. Eventually, he sent his armies even against his former ally, Assyria. By 1755 BCE, he had transformed the small kingdom he inherited into the center of a Mesopotamian empire to rival any that had come before it.

FIGURE 4.4 Hammurabi. This relief at the top of a seven-foot stone stele from the time of King Hammurabi shows him (at left) receiving his royal insignia from a seated god, likely Marduk. This grant makes it clear that Hammurabi's right to rule comes directly from the heavens. The lower portion of the stele includes his famous law code. (credit: "Louvre - Hammurabi's Code" by "Erin"/Flickr, CC BY 2.0)

At its height during Hammurabi's reign, the Babylonian Empire stretched from the upper reaches of the Euphrates River, not far from modern Aleppo in the north, to the Zagros Mountains in the east and the Persian Gulf in the south (Figure 4.5). But these extensive borders did not long survive the death of Hammurabi himself. Under the rule of his son Samsu-iluna, Babylon faced resistance from the Kassites of the Zagros Mountains and from a newly formed kingdom called Sealand in the marshy region near the Persian Gulf. The empire's territorial control continued to decline until, by the reign of Samsu-ditana in the late sixteenth century BCE, all that remained was the small region around the city of Babylon itself. In this weakened state, Babylon was sacked by a new emerging power, the Hittites, and the dynasty of Hammurabi came to a definitive end.

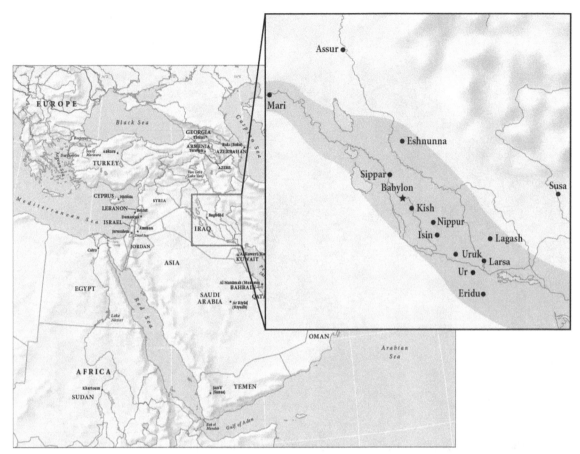

FIGURE 4.5 **Hammurabi's Realm**. Under Hammurabi, the Babylonians expanded out of Babylon to conquer much of Mesopotamia and construct the region's first empire, shown here in green. (attribution: Copyright Rice University, OpenStax, under CC BY 4.0 license)

The Hittites

Unlike the Babylonians, the Hittites were not from Mesopotamia, nor were they members of the Semitic language group. Rather, they were an Indo-European-speaking group that emerged as a powerful force in Anatolia starting in the 1600s BCE. Their precise origins are not known, but they were likely immigrants to Anatolia who blended into the local population and adopted much of its culture and religion. By 1650 BCE, the Hittites dominated central Anatolia from their capital at Hattusas. Their expansion across Anatolia and into Syria continued into the early sixteenth century BCE under the reign of Mursilis, during which time the growing kingdom also set its sights on Babylon.

Possibly as a demonstration of military might or simply to seize an opportunity, the Hittite army descended into Mesopotamia and took the city of Babylon. Despite the success of the campaign, Mursilis's power in Anatolia began to weaken during his absence. He was assassinated soon after he returned, and the Hittite Empire began to crumble as its subject kingdoms rebelled and it was consumed by war. By 1500 BCE, order had been restored, but the new rulers struggled to return the Hittites to their former glory.

Beginning with the rise of the Hittite king Tudhaliyas I in 1420 BCE, the Hittite Empire experienced a revival and new imperial growth (Figure 4.6). By the reign of Suppiluliumas I in the mid-fourteenth century BCE, it had become arguably the most powerful empire in the Near East and a major rival of New Kingdom Egypt. The two realms vied for control of the eastern Mediterranean in the 1300s and 1200s BCE, eventually facing off in the epic Battle of Qadesh in 1274 BCE.

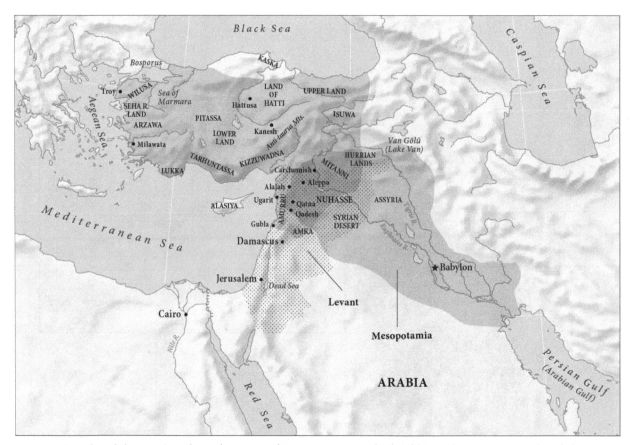

FIGURE 4.6 The Hittite Empire. Shown in green at its greatest extent in the thirteenth century BCE, the Hittite Empire included all of Asia Minor to the borders of Assyria and parts of Syria. (attribution: Copyright Rice University, OpenStax, under CC BY 4.0 license)

Generally accepted as a draw or possibly a narrow Hittite victory, the fighting at Qadesh is most memorable for ultimately leading the two forces to recognize that they had more to gain from peace than war. In 1258 BCE, the Hittite king Hattusilis II and the Egyptian Pharaoh Ramesses II signed one of early history's greatest peace treaties (Figure 4.7). The agreement confirmed Hittite control of Syria and Egyptian dominance over the Phoenician ports of the eastern Mediterranean. However, little more than fifty years later, the once-powerful Hittite Empire collapsed, never to reappear.

FIGURE 4.7 The Egypto-Hittite Peace Treaty. These carved fragments are from one of many copies of the Egypto-Hittite Peace Treaty of 1258 BCE. (credit: "Treaty of Kadesh" by Iocanus/Museum of the Ancient Orient/Wikimedia Commons, CC BY 3.0)

The Hittite Empire was not the only important Near Eastern power to disintegrate during this period. Across the eastern Mediterranean and Mesopotamia beginning around 1200 BCE, kingdoms and empires from Greece to Mesopotamia went into a decline so extensive it is now called the Late Bronze Age Collapse. Although its trigger remains unknown, the collapse coincided with widespread regional famine, epidemic disease, war, and waves of destructive migrations across the eastern Mediterranean. By the time calm returned around 1100 BCE, the region had entered a new era, the **Iron Age**. This was a period in which iron replaced bronze as the metal of choice for tools and weapons, and new and more sophisticated empires expanded across the Near East.

The Neo-Assyrian Empire

For a few centuries after the Late Bronze Age Collapse, Mesopotamia experienced transformations that dramatically reshaped the region and set the stage for a new imperial era. During the eleventh and tenth centuries BCE, decline came to both Assyria and especially to Babylonia, where dynasties competed for control. Complicating the situation for the Babylonians, a Semitic group of unknown origin called the Chaldeans took control of far southern Mesopotamia during this period. Assyria in the north fared a little better but also struggled to reestablish control over northern Mesopotamia. One of the major factors limiting Assyria's ability to grow was the presence of a group of West-Semitic seminomads called Aramaeans. The Aramaeans likely emerged first in southern Syria; they exploited Assyrian and Babylonian weakness to expand into Mesopotamia, disrupting Assyrian trading routes as they went. By the tenth century BCE, they had become the dominant population in western Mesopotamia and controlled a number of powerful kingdoms there.

It was only around 900 BCE that Assyria was able to reestablish control over northern Mesopotamia. This marks the birth of what historians often refer to as the Neo-Assyrian Empire (to distinguish it from the Old

Assyrian Empire of 2000–1600 BCE and the Middle Assyrian Empire of 1400–1100 BCE). Beginning in the reign of Ashurnasirpal II in the early ninth century BCE, the Neo-Assyrian Empire began a steady march toward imperial dominance across the Near East, asserting control over many Aramaean kingdoms in Syria and eventually over Babylonia itself. By the end of Tiglath-Pileser III's reign in 727 BCE, the Neo-Assyrian Empire had become the dominant power in the Near East. Over the next several decades, successive Assyrian kings were able to build an expansive empire across Mesopotamia and the eastern Mediterranean through wars of conquest. In 671 BCE, King Esarhaddon invaded Egypt and added that center of wealth and power to his kingdom.

With this conquest, the Neo-Assyrian Empire achieved a degree of territorial control far surpassing that of any earlier empire of the region (Figure 4.8). But its supremacy was not to last. Beginning in the last decades of the seventh century BCE, two growing powers threatened and eventually overthrew Assyria. These kingdoms were Babylonia and Media.

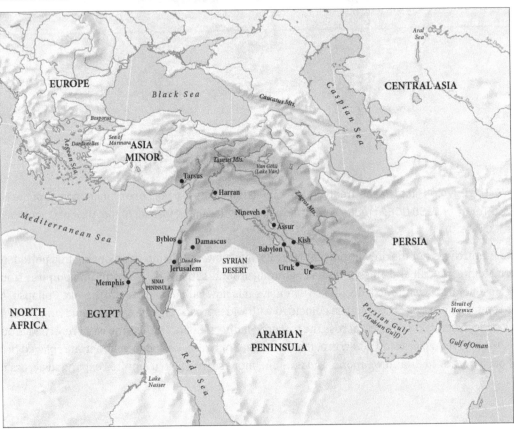

FIGURE 4.8 The Neo-Assyrian Empire. This map shows the Neo-Assyrian Empire (in orange) at its height, around 670 BCE. Note the major cities and peoples consumed by its conquests. (attribution: Copyright Rice University, OpenStax, under CC BY 4.0 license)

During the period of Assyrian expansion, Babylonia had been reduced to a **vassal state** of the empire, meaning it was nominally independent in the running of its internal affairs but had to bow to imperial demands and provide goods and soldiers when commanded. But in 616 BCE, the Chaldean Babylonian ruler Nabopolassar attempted to take advantage of a period of Assyrian weakness by launching a bold attack against the Old Assyrian capital of Asshur. Although the attack failed, it encouraged the Median dynasty to risk its own attack into Assyria. The Median Empire, a kingdom in northwestern Iran, had only recently unified and strengthened, largely because Assyria had devastated the rival kingdoms around it, such as Elam. The attack on Assyria proved successful, and Asshur was destroyed in 614 BCE. Shortly afterward, the Babylonians and the Medes entered into an alliance to overthrow Assyria. Assyria received support from Egypt, but it was unable to prevent the Babylonian-Median alliance from overwhelming its forces and capturing its cities. In 612 BCE, the

Babylonians and the Medes reduced the once-great Assyrian city of Nineveh to rubble, killing the Assyrian king in the process. The remaining Assyrian forces fled west and held out for a few more years. By 605 BCE, however, the Assyrian Empire had been defeated and its people carried off into slavery.

The victors divided the spoils. The Median Empire took the areas to the east, north, and northeast and expanded its control to central Anatolia, much of western Iran, and the southern area between the Black and Caspian Seas.

The Babylonians, often called the Neo-Babylonians to distinguish them from Hammurabi's subjects in the Old Babylonian period, took control of the western portion of the former Neo-Assyrian Empire. This included much of Mesopotamia, Syria, and the important Phoenician ports along the Mediterranean (Figure 4.9). Under king Nebuchadnezzar II, they waged war in Syria and the eastern Mediterranean to weaken Egypt's power. Then, in 601 BCE, Nebuchadnezzar attempted a bold invasion of Egypt itself, only to be repulsed by strong resistance.

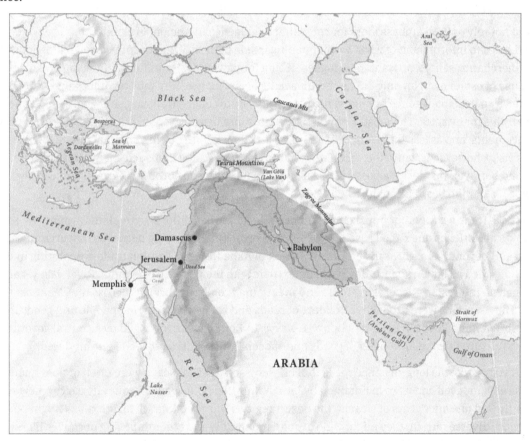

FIGURE 4.9 The Neo-Babylonian Empire. By 550 BCE, the Neo-Babylonian Empire (shown in green) had extended its control over Mesopotamia, Syria, and Judah, and even into the Arabian Peninsula. (attribution: Copyright Rice University, OpenStax, under CC BY 4.0 license)

Foreign Affairs and Trade

The many city-states, kingdoms, and empires of Mesopotamia operated in a complex world in which both risks and rewards for rulers were extremely high. War was especially common, and diplomatic mistakes could have costly consequences. Kings preferred to avoid war if possible and maintain healthy diplomatic relationships with others instead. A smaller kingdom, for example, might find it advantageous to seek an alliance with a large regional power like Assyria, Babylonia, or the Hittite Empire. Sending sons and daughters to rival kingdoms in marriage also helped forestall war and build cultural and familial bridges between competitors. The Hittite king Suppiluliumas attempted to marry one of his sons into the Egyptian royal family, which would have united these two regional powers and competitors. That marriage never took place, but many others did.

Ambassadors were a key part of Mesopotamia's complex diplomatic world. Kings frequently sent their representatives to friendly and even rival kingdoms to mend or strengthen relationships, a vital task frequently performed under extreme pressure. A wrong move could start a war. As they are today, however, such emissaries were guaranteed certain protections. In ordinary situations, they could expect to be free to leave unharmed when the situation demanded it, to be exempt from certain taxes, and to have their property respected. But if war broke out between the two kingdoms, an ambassador could get caught in the middle.

Gift giving was an important part of the ambassadors' role. When sent to another kingdom, emissaries frequently carried with them an offering of high value for the king who received them, and on their return home, their king expected a present of equal or greater worth. This exchange of gifts demonstrated respect and goodwill between the rulers. Returning empty-handed suggested the foreign king was breaking off diplomatic relations or had even become hostile. Occasionally an ambassador might be unable to return home, either because the relationship between the two kingdoms had gone sour or because the foreign king refused to supply an appropriate gift.

Rulers did not rely only on ambassadors for collecting intelligence in Ancient Mesopotamia. They often employed spies to inform them of what was happening inside both rival and friendly foreign kingdoms. These could be merchants, sailors, artisans, or refugees fleeing foreign lands. Hammurabi, for example, made frequent use of espionage. Not only did he recruit agents of all types to keep tabs on other kings, but he even established a special intelligence bureau in the palace at Mari to collect, translate, and analyze documents provided by his many spies. The most common uses of this intelligence were to anticipate war, learn about troop movements, and assess the strength of a foreign kingdom before putting an army into the field. Using spies was risky, however, because the very nature of the work suggested that such agents were never to be trusted, and betrayal was always a possibility. An even greater risk was borne by the spies themselves, who could expect a painful death if caught.

Long-distance trade was another important point of contact between different kingdoms around the region. Archaeological work has unearthed a wealth of information about the trading networks that crisscrossed the Near East and beyond. As early as the empire of Sargon of Akkad, Mesopotamian traders operating in the Persian Gulf sailed as far as modern-day Pakistan to trade with the people of the Indus River valley. Large empires had an interest in encouraging trade and maintained roads and bridges across the Near East for that purpose. The Assyrians were productive builders of roads and bridges that carried people and goods into and across their territory. Roads in the enormous Neo-Assyrian Empire were managed by a central government authority to ensure that the movement of goods and especially of soldiers proceeded unhindered.

By today's standards, the long-distance roads that crisscrossed this landscape were often of poor quality. They were generally unpaved and were maintained by local authorities, who would frequently carve a new road alongside the old one after years of wear. In the desert regions where soil was firm, the roads might be straight, while in more diverse terrain, they might wind around mountains and other imposing obstacles like swamps. Traveling between cities on such roads could take several weeks, even over relatively short distances. Traders could expect some form of protection from local rulers, however, in exchange for paying custom fees and duties.

Access to foreign goods and raw materials was a major concern of empires in the Near East. In Mesopotamia in particular, vital resources like stone, timber, and metal ores were scarce, and they had to be procured in large quantities from distant locations. The flow of these goods into imperial centers often took the form of tribute payments, much like a tax, from vassal or subjugated kingdoms (Figure 4.10). However, tribute was not the only mechanism for international trade. During the Old Assyrian period (c. 2000–1600 BCE), for example, Assyrian traders traveled between Mesopotamia, Anatolia, and even Afghanistan trading in valuable goods like copper, tin, and textiles. Copper and tin were especially important because they are the ingredients needed to make bronze, the primary material for manufacturing metal tools and weapons in this period. The Assyrians even established merchant colonies in Anatolia where they exchanged tin and textiles for silver and gold.

FIGURE 4.10 Receiving Tribute. In this relief from the Black Obelisk of Shalmaneser III, Assyrian king Shalmaneser III is shown receiving tribute from Jehu, the king of Israel, bowing before him. The limestone obelisk was erected in 825 BCE as a public monument and is one of only two complete Assyrian obelisks that have been discovered to date. (credit: "First depiction of Hoshea on the Black Obelisk" by The British Museum/Wikimedia Commons, Public Domain)

⊘ LINK TO LEARNING

Explore this website, created by the British Museum, about trade and contraband (https://openstax.org/l/77MesoTrade) in Ancient Assyria.

Daily Life and the Family in the Near East

The ability to purchase luxury trade items was the privilege of the elites, who were also treated differently under the law. Hammurabi's Code, the list of judicial decisions issued by Hammurabi and inscribed on stone pillars erected throughout his kingdom, identified three social classes during the Old Babylonian period: nobles (*awelum*), commoners (*mushkenum*), and the enslaved (*wardum*). These classes were not fixed but were important for understanding how individuals were treated under the law. For example, if a commoner put out the eye or broke the bone of a noble, the noble was empowered to do the same to the offending commoner. However, a noble who injured a commoner could expect to merely pay a fine.

Social distinctions also applied in the treatment of women under the law. For example, if a husband divorced his wife because she had not given birth to sons, he was required to return her dowry and pay her a sum equal to the bride price paid upon marriage. If no bride price had been paid and the husband was a noble, he was required to pay his wife one mina of silver, the equivalent of about a year's wage for an average worker. However, if he were a commoner, he was expected to pay only one-third of a mina of silver.

The homes of Babylonians in this period reflected these social distinctions. Commoners' dwellings were typically windowless and made of mud with thick walls that protected the occupants from the oppressive summer heat. Some were of baked brick with a type of plaster along the walls to keep out moisture and preserve the brick. They were very simply furnished and usually contained a set of interior stairs leading to the roof, where occupants could dry vegetables or perform religious rituals. The homes of the wealthy, by contrast, were larger structures built around a central courtyard and included several rooms for different purposes, such as kitchens, bathrooms, reception rooms, and storage rooms. They contained various types of wooden furniture, and walls were decorated with paintings of animals or even insects. Enslaved people commonly lived within the home, especially women and girls who worked as servants.

All Babylonians were expected to serve the gods, who were regarded as an aristocracy of powerful lords ruling over all. These deities tended to take human forms and express human emotions and desires such as love, hate, and envy. By the time of Hammurabi, the large pantheon included gods of Sumerian origin as well as gods introduced by other groups that had influenced Mesopotamian religious practices, such as the Akkadians and the Amorites. During Hammurabi's dynasty, the storm god Marduk was elevated to the highest tier of the pantheon and accepted as the patron god of Babylonia. Other powerful deities included Ea (Enki) (Figure 4.11), the god of fresh waters; Sin (Nanna), the god of the moon; and Shamash (Utu), the god of the sun and justice. Each city had its own patron god and corresponding temple. Individuals worshipped their city's patron god but also believed they had their own personal deity who offered protection in exchange for daily worship and service.

FIGURE 4.11 The Babylonian God Ea. In this detail from the Adda Seal, an ancient cylinder seal dating to approximately 2300 BCE and housed at the British Museum, the Babylonian god Ea, also known as Enki, is depicted wearing a horned helmet and surrounded by a river of flowing water. (credit: "Enki (detail of the Adda seal)" by British Museum/Wikimedia Commons, Public Domain)

The temples dedicated to the gods supported complex administrations consisting of singers, scribes, diviners, snake charmers, stone carvers, guards, exorcists, and male and female priests. Temple rituals included the carefully choreographed serving of meals for the gods accompanied by music, during which the gods were believed to consume the essence of the food provided. (Afterward, the actual food was consumed by the temple staff and the king.) The temple staff also participated in elaborate religious festivals performed in the cities, such as the New Year Festival. During these events, the divine images of the gods were carried from the temples and throughout the town in a grand procession where everyone might catch a glimpse of the deity.

Since Assyria was also part of the larger Mesopotamian world, there were many social and cultural similarities between the Babylonians and the Assyrians. The Assyrian population was made up of four hierarchically organized classes: the nobility, the professional class, the peasantry, and the enslaved. The nobility occupied the highest position and controlled large estates. Members of this class could expect to receive a thorough education in preparation for serving in elite positions within the empire, such as military officers, governors, and high-ranking priests. Priests were important not only as interpreters of divine will but also as points of connection between the center of political power and the rest of the empire.

The large professional class included a host of skilled groups, from bankers and physicians to scribes and merchants. Each group maintained its own guild, which enforced high professional standards and saw to it that proper taxes were paid. The largest class, and the least well documented, was the peasantry. Most in this group were almost certainly poor farmers who worked the lands of the higher classes. At the very bottom of the social order were the enslaved, the majority of whom had been captured during war. They often worked the most dangerous jobs and had almost no rights. Those enslaved not by war but by unpaid debt had a somewhat higher status and could own property, conduct business, and even buy their way out of slavery in rare instances.

Above all these classes was the household of the Assyrian king. The kings of Assyria were considered viceroys of the gods, especially the chief deity Asshur. They were expected to emulate the gods through their own virtuous behavior and to act in accordance with divine omens interpreted by religious advisers. In acting on the omens, the ruler was fulfilling the dual role of defender of order against chaos and representative of humanity's interests. When times were difficult and the gods displeased, the king might be expected to subject himself to penalties in order to calm the heavenly ire. For example, during the annual New Year Festival, the king underwent a form of ritual humiliation intended to satisfy the gods and protect his people from harm. In extreme situations, he might even need to symbolically die in order to appease the gods. In these instances, the king would step back and allow a substitute king to rule in his place for a period of weeks or months. Once that time was over, the substitute king was killed and the actual king returned to power.

The constant wars of conquest undertaken during the Neo-Assyrian Empire necessitated a highly skilled and well-organized standing army. This army included charioteers, cavalry, archers, and wielders of slings and spears (Figure 4.12). All Assyrian men were expected to serve some period of military service. The king was the official head of the army, and his chief officials were high-ranking military officers. The Neo-Assyrian Empire was effectively a military state, and it was demonstrably efficient at expanding its territory and keeping its vassals in line.

FIGURE 4.12 The Victorious Assyrian Army. These large stone reliefs from the late eighth century BCE were carved to decorate an Assyrian palace or public building. They depict victorious Assyrian soldiers returning from battle carrying the heads of their enemies and standing on their headless bodies. (credit: "Orthostats showing Assyrian soldiers, Tell Tayinat, Amuq Valley, Iron Age, 738 BC, limestone" by "Daderot"/Oriental Institute Museum, University of Chicago/Wikimedia Commons, CC0 1.0)

Those who defied the Assyrian war machine could expect swift and devastating consequences, including public torture and mutilation to demonstrate the price of rebellion (a response scholars have called "calculated frightfulness"). Another tactic to shut down regular or particularly difficult rebellions was the forced deportation of entire populations to other parts of the empire. The elite and skilled in a city were compelled to move to a previously depopulated region, there to be steadily assimilated into the surrounding culture until they became culturally indistinguishable from other Assyrians.

The Neo-Assyrian War Machine

Inscriptions, art, and even the Bible attest that the Neo-Assyrian military at its height was the most modern and efficient in the ancient world. Unlike other armies whose farmer-soldiers could fight only in summer, the Neo-Assyrians were a highly trained professional standing army of both male citizens and subject peoples. Training and the ability to fight year-round gave a considerable advantage and transformed the waging of war in the Near East.

Specialized groups worked together in battle. A standard Neo-Assyrian infantry team included spear fighters as well as archers and slingers who provided cover in battle (Figure 4.13).

FIGURE 4.13 Assyrian Spear Fighters. This large seventh-century BCE stone relief from the wall of a palace in Nineveh shows a line of Assyrian soldiers with large shields and spears. (credit: modification of work "Gypsum Wall Panel Relief, North Palace, Nineveh, Iraq, 645-635 BC" by Gary Todd/Flickr, Public Domain)

The archers used composite bows, a design capable of firing accurately at a range of four hundred feet (Figure 4.14).

FIGURE 4.14 **Neo-Assyrian Archers**. Helmeted Neo-Assyrian archers carry large bows in this relief from about the eighth century BCE, which once decorated the Palace of Sennacherib. (credit: modification of work "Ancient Assyria Bas-Relief of Armed Soldiers, Palace of King Sennacherib (704-689 BC)" by Gary Todd/Flickr, Public Domain)

Four-wheeled chariots had featured in Mesopotamian warfare since at least 3000 BCE, but the two-wheeled, horse-drawn chariot that appeared around 2000 BCE proved far superior (Figure 4.15). Neo-Assyrian fighters often assembled in squadrons of fifty chariots, each with a driver and an archer carrying swords and clubs for close combat.

FIGURE 4.15 **Assyrian Charioteers.** This Assyrian stone relief from the ninth century shows charioteers on a lion hunt; a similar vehicle served in battle. (credit: modification of work "Ancient Assyria Bas-Relief of Lion Hunt, Nimrud, 883-859 BC" by Gary Todd/Flickr, Public Domain)

Though mighty, the Neo-Assyrians tried to avoid warfare, usually by demanding a besieged city surrender without a fight. But if forced, they used "calculated frightfulness" to demonstrate the price of resistance, inflicting various forms of torture on the conquered peoples (Figure 4.16).

FIGURE 4.16 **Resistance to Neo-Assyrian Rule.** This stone relief made after a battle against the Elamites in 653 BCE shows two rebellious chiefs staked to the ground and being flayed alive. Such displays would remind other chiefs of what awaited resistance to Neo-Assyrian rule. (credit: modification of work "Image from page 248 of 'History of Egypt, Chaldea, Syria, Babylonia and Assyria' (1903)" by Internet Archive Book Images/Flickr, Public Domain)

- Why might some rulers have resisted Neo-Assyrian control despite knowing the cost?
- What set the military of the Neo-Assyrians apart from their rivals? How did their use of technology increase the severity and frequency of warfare in the Near East?

Hittite society differed dramatically from that of the Assyrians and Babylonians. The entire empire included only a few large cities, like Hattusas, and most people lived in small rural villages or towns. With the exception of some leased acreage, village land was mostly held in common and worked by the people. Early in Hittite history, enslaved people had been relatively rare, but they became more numerous later on as the number of war captives rose. The Hittites practiced **chattel slavery**, meaning enslaved people were considered property and could be sold at will. They were frequently put to work in agricultural settings to free Hittite citizens for military service.

The religion of the Hittites incorporated elements from a number of different religious traditions, including that of Mesopotamia. Divination rituals, for example, were essentially Mesopotamian in origin and included studying the organs of sacrificed animals, consulting female soothsayers, and observing the movement of birds. Among the most important gods were the sun goddess Arinna and her consort the weather god Tarhunna (Figure 4.17). The former oversaw the government of the king and queen, the latter the rains and war. The king was the high priest and was responsible for performing specific rites at major religious festivals, such as the New Year Festival when gods laid out the course of events for the coming year. The people were expected to do their part by performing religious rites at cult centers, such as giving sacrificed animals and food and drink to the gods.

FIGURE 4.17 The Hittite Weather God Tarhunna. This stone relief made between the tenth and eighth centuries BCE depicts the Hittite weather god Tarhunna. He is holding his traditional symbols, an axe in one hand and a three-pronged thunderbolt in the other. (credit: "God of Thunder. Hittite relief from Samal (now Zincirli)" by "Maur"/Pergamonmuseum/Wikimedia Commons, Public Domain)

4.2 Egypt's New Kingdom

LEARNING OBJECTIVES

By the end of this section, you will be able to:
- Explain the causes and consequences of the Hyksos invasion
- Analyze the successes and failures of key New Kingdom pharaohs
- Discuss Egypt's interaction with its neighbors via immigration and trade
- Identify the political and religious innovations of Egypt's New Kingdom

During the New Kingdom period, Egyptian pharaohs reunited Upper and Lower Egypt following two centuries of foreign rule. They also ended the isolation that had been typical of the Old and Middle Kingdoms and embarked on expansionist conquests. The New Kingdom pharaohs were among the greatest warriors and builders in Egyptian history. As a result of their conquests, trade flourished with the Near East and other areas, and significant advances took place in the arts.

The Hyksos in Egypt

As centralized power in Egypt declined during the late Middle Kingdom, Egyptians were less able to enforce their borders and preserve their state's integrity. The result was that Semitic-speaking immigrants from Canaan flowed into the Nile delta. It is not entirely clear to historians what prompted these Hyksos to leave Canaan, but some suspect they were driven into Egypt by foreign invasion of their land. Others suggest the early Hyksos may have been traders who settled in Egypt and later brought their extended families and others. However it happened, by about 1720 BCE, they were so numerous in Lower Egypt that some of their chieftains began to assert control over many local areas. This transformation coincided with the onset of the Second Intermediate Period (c. 1720–1540 BCE) and the general collapse of centralized Egyptian rule.

Over the next several decades, many more Canaanite migrants made their way across the Sinai and into Lower Egypt. During this period, several Egyptian princes held onto power despite the changes occurring around them. Then, around 1650 BCE, one group of recently arrived Canaanites challenged the remaining princes, overthrew them, and assumed control of the entire delta, inaugurating an important new period in Egyptian history.

These Canaanites are often referred to as the Hyksos. While that name is a much later Greek corruption of the Egyptian *hekau khasut*, meaning "chieftains of foreign lands," it has stuck. The Hyksos ruled the delta for more than a century, from approximately 1650 to 1540 BCE. After they had been defeated, Egyptian tradition described their rule as one of wanton destruction, including the enslavement of Egyptians, the burning of cities, and the desecration of shrines. However, these descriptions are almost certainly rooted more in later New Kingdom propaganda than in reality. Like many others who came to Egypt, the Hyksos readily adopted Egyptian culture, art, language, writing, and religion. They established their own dynasty but relied on Egyptian patterns of rule and even included Egyptians in their bureaucracies.

Hyksos rule appears to have benefited Egypt in a number of ways. It was likely the Hyksos who brought sophisticated bronze-making technology into Egypt from Canaan, for example. The advantages of bronze over softer materials like copper were obvious to Egyptians, and the metal soon became the material of choice for weapons, armor, and other tools where hardness was desired. The Hyksos also introduced composite-bow technology (which made archery faster and more accurate), new types of protective armor, and most importantly, the horse-drawn, lighter-weight chariot with spoked wheels. They may have brought the horse itself to Egypt in this period, but we do not know for sure. The chariot, however, was an especially important arrival. By the 1500s BCE, horse-drawn chariots with riders armed with powerful and highly accurate composite bows had become a staple of Egyptian militaries, just as they were across all the powerful empires and kingdoms of the Near East.

During this Second Intermediate Period, the once-vast domains of Middle Kingdom Egypt were effectively divided into three parts: the Hyksos kingdom in Lower Egypt (nearest the Mediterranean), the kingdom of Kush far upriver beyond the first cataract (an area of shallow rapids), and the Theban kingdom of Upper Egypt (Figure 4.18). Occupying all of Lower Egypt, the Hyksos kingdom had access to Canaan and by extension to the rest of the Near East. Inscriptions and archaeological evidence attest to a considerable flow of trade between Lower Egypt and the Canaanites in Palestine and Syria, though the extent of the Hyksos' political power beyond Egypt was likely limited to a few city-states in Palestine, if that.

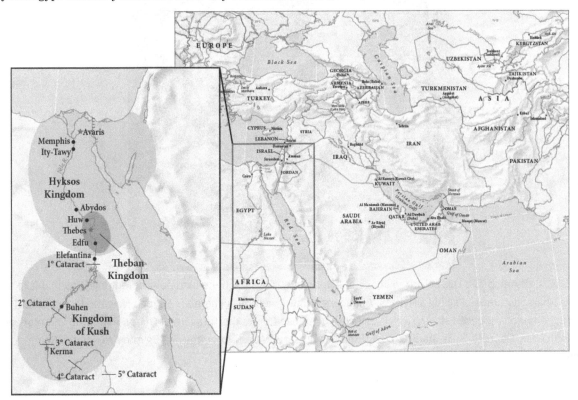

FIGURE 4.18 Three Kingdoms in Egypt. During the Second Intermediate Period, Egypt was effectively divided into three kingdoms, those of the Hyksos, the Kush, and the Thebans. (attribution: Copyright Rice University, OpenStax, under CC BY 4.0 license)

In the Theban kingdom, centered on the city of Thebes, indigenous Egyptian rulers still held sway. It is possible that in the early years of their rule in Lower Egypt, the Hyksos were able to exert some indirect control over Thebes, but distance made direct rule nearly impossible. Still, the connections between the two kingdoms continued, perhaps with some intermarrying.

The Theban kings resisted Hyksos control of Lower Egypt. However, an alliance between the Hyksos and the kingdom of Kush in the far south made any effort to oust the Hyksos extremely risky. It was only beginning in the 1550s BCE that a string of Theban Egyptian rulers were able to go on the offensive against the Hyksos. After multiple failed attempts, these rulers eventually succeeded in capturing large portions of Hyksos territory and bringing the fight to the edges of Avaris, the capital of Hyksos Egypt. By approximately 1540 BCE, Pharaoh Ahmose I had broken the defenses around Avaris, destroyed the Hyksos kingdom, and reasserted Egyptian power in Lower Egypt (Figure 4.19). He then turned his attention south to Kush and east to Palestine, extending Egyptian control over these regions as well. His reign ushered in a new period of Egyptian greatness called the New Kingdom.

FIGURE 4.19 Ahmose I. This colorized image of a decorative feature on the blade of a ceremonial Egyptian axe shows Pharaoh Ahmose I killing a Hyksos. Ahmose's military victories ushered in Egypt's New Kingdom period. (credit: "Pharaoh Ahmose I slaying a Hyksos (axe of Ahmose I, from the Treasure of Queen Aahhotep II) Colorized per source" by Georges Émile Jules Daressy/Annales du Service des Antiquités de l'Égypte /Wikimedia Commons, Public Domain)

The Pharaohs of the New Kingdom

The New Kingdom period (c. 1550–1069 BCE) represents the pinnacle of Egyptian power and influence in the Near East. During this time, Egypt not only reconquered the territory it had lost following the collapse of the Middle Kingdom, but it also extended its reach deep into the Libyan Desert, far south into Nubia, and eventually east as far as northern Syria. This expansion made Egypt the Mediterranean superpower of its day. So it is not surprising that the pharaohs of this period are some of the best known. They include the conqueror Amenhotep I, the indomitable Queen Hatshepsut, "the magnificent" Amenhotep III, the transformative Akhenaten, and the highly celebrated Ramesses II, also known as Ramesses the Great. Many came to power at a young age and ruled for an extended period of time that allowed for many accomplishments. They also commanded massive and highly trained armies and had at their disposal a seemingly endless supply of wealth, with which they constructed some of the most impressive architectural treasures of the entire Near East.

The New Kingdom began with the reign of Ahmose, the pharaoh who recovered not only Lower Egypt but also Nubia and Palestine. When he died in 1525 BCE, his oldest surviving son, Amenhotep I, assumed control. Amenhotep then married one of his sisters, Meritamun, as was common in this period and as the gods of Egyptian myth were believed to have done.

The rise of the early New Kingdom pharaohs coincided with the elevation of a previously minor deity, the Thebans' patron god Amun. Respect for him merged with regard for Re, the patron of the monarchy, and he became known as Amun-Re. Amenhotep I and his successors built temples and other major public works in his honor, particularly the great Temple of Amun at Karnak. Thebes also had special importance for the New Kingdom pharaohs as the state's religious capital and the favored royal burial place, commonly called the Valley of the Kings.

Dying without an heir, Amenhotep I was succeeded by Thutmose I, a general who may have been a distant relative. Thutmose I and his son Thutmose II both campaigned in Nubia and Syria. The father marched his armies all the way to the Euphrates River in Syria, likely as a show of force against emerging powers in the region. The son married his sister Hatshepsut, who gave birth to a daughter but not a son. So when Thutmose II died in 1479 BCE, his two-year-old son conceived by a concubine assumed the throne as Thutmose III.

Acting as regent for the infant pharaoh, Hatshepsut inaugurated a very unusual period in Egyptian history. Rather than merely rule in the background as a typical regent would, she proclaimed herself co-regent with her stepson and soon assumed the title of pharaoh. Statues of her from this period depict her wearing the pharaonic headdress and ceremonial beard and give her the broad torso more typical of a male (Figure 4.20). Such masculine features were not an attempt to obscure her femininity but rather a recognition that all the symbolic representations of Egyptian pharaohs were male. Inscriptions clearly indicated that she was a woman. She was called the "Daughter of Re," and feminine word endings appear in some inscriptions, such as "His Majesty, Herself."

FIGURE 4.20 Pharaoh Hatshepsut. This granite statue of a kneeling Pharaoh Hatshepsut, carved in the fifteenth century BCE and originally painted, measures just over twenty-seven inches high. As this detail shows, the work depicts her with male features including a flat chest and a beard. (credit: "Kneeling statue of Hatshepsut" by The Metropolitan Museum of Art, Rogers Fund, 1923/Wikimedia Commons, Public Domain)

As Egyptian pharaohs had done for many centuries, Hatshepsut also claimed divinity. While the reasons for this long-standing belief remain unclear and may never be fully understood, this is one of the features of Egyptian culture that made it very different from that of Mesopotamian contemporaries, who usually held kings to be only viceroys of the gods, not gods themselves. Unlike earlier pharaonic claims of divinity, however, Hatshepsut's included a detailed account of her heavenly origins in the form of a poem she had inscribed on the walls of her mortuary temple for all to see. In the poem, Amun-Re himself assumes the form of Thutmose I and, after conceiving Hatshepsut with her mother, predicts that his child will rule all Egypt and elevate it to unsurpassed glory. The poem then describes how a council of Egyptian gods proclaimed Hatshepsut's earthly authority, and how Thutmose I recognized her divinity and named her his rightful successor.

As both a woman and a regent, Hatshepsut was prudent to thus legitimate her rule. And by all accounts, the heavenly prophecies about her reign proved accurate. For twenty-one years she ruled over a prosperous and dominant Egypt, even conducting military campaigns into Nubia and possibly southern Palestine. At one point, she sent a large fleet south into a mysterious land the Egyptians called Punt, likely coastal East Africa near modern Somalia, where her ships collected and brought back a cargo of exotic plants, animals, precious metals, and spices.

Construction of Hatshepsut's three-tiered mortuary temple began shortly after she took the throne and likely lasted many years. The temple was built into the side of a cliff and included a series of ramps that took visitors through garden courtyards, past large obelisks and statues, and toward a shrine to Amun at the top (Figure 4.21). In the years after her death, elaborate rituals including libations, food offerings to the gods, purification rituals, recitations, and singing were performed by the priests who managed the enormous complex.

FIGURE 4.21 The Temple of Hatshepsut. Hatshepsut's mortuary temple is located at Deir el-Bahri, beneath cliffs near the Valley of the Kings. Its large ramps and tiers were designed to blend neatly into the cliff behind it. (credit: modification of work "Temple of Hatshepsut" by Hesham Ebaid/Wikimedia Commons, CC0 1.0)

When Hatshepsut died in 1458 BCE, her stepson Thutmose III took control as sole ruler in Egypt for the first time. He was about thirty years old by then and had extensive military training. This preparation served him well, for soon he faced a Hittite and northern Mesopotamian threat to Egypt's control in Syria and Palestine. Leading his armies himself, he was able to neutralize the threats, launch a major raid across the Euphrates River, and take numerous Canaanite princes hostage so as to deter any uprisings from his vassals.

It was only late in his reign that Thutmose III began to eliminate his predecessor from history. He had Hatshepsut's statues toppled and smashed, her name removed from monuments, and references to her scrubbed from the official king lists. The evidence suggests that he harbored no ill will toward his stepmother. Instead, her erasure from the record was probably part of Thutmose's process of paving the way for his son to rule in his own right in the future, without a dominant female like his stepmother to assert control.

Amenhotep II, son of Thutmose III, continued the successful military campaigns against both Hittite and Mesopotamian threats to Egyptian influence in Palestine and Syria. His rule was followed by the short reign of

Thutmose IV, likely a younger son, and the long and especially prosperous rule of Amenhotep III, known as "the Magnificent."

Amenhotep III's nearly forty-year reign in the fourteenth century BCE was a time of extended peace during which numerous monuments to Egyptian greatness were constructed. These included the sumptuous palace at Thebes, the Serapeum—a temple of the god Serapis—at Saqqara, many temples for other gods, Amenhotep's own large mortuary temple, and a great many statues of himself. His reign was also marked by an increased emphasis on the Egyptian sun god Aton, one of many manifestations of Re. Amenhotep's palace at Thebes and the large royal barge upon which he and his queen glided along the Nile for important religious events were named for Aton. Toward the end of Amenhotep III's reign, he officially proclaimed himself the personification of Aton, and his servants greeted him as such.

Under Amenhotep III's heir Amenhotep IV, the emphasis on Aton reached its fullest extent. Amenhotep IV built a new city downriver from Thebes that he called Amarna, "the place where the solar orb is transformed." It was also known as Akhetaton. The following year, he changed his own name to Akhenaten, meaning "the transfigured spirit of the solar orb," and moved himself and his entire family to the new city. Akhenaten later closed the temples of the other major Egyptian gods and ordered representations of them destroyed and their names chiseled off monuments. The pharaoh and his wife Queen Nefertiti now became the chief priests of a new cult built around Aton (Figure 4.22).

FIGURE 4.22 Nefertiti. One of the most recognizable New Kingdom artifacts is a nineteen-inch limestone bust of Queen Nefertiti that was made in about 1345 BCE and discovered at Amarna, Egypt, in 1912. (credit: "Nefertiti Statue photo from Rosicrucian Museum, replica from the original at the Egyptian Museum in Berlin" by E. Michael Smith "Chiefio"/Wikimedia Commons, Public Domain)

In the emerging new religion, people were instructed to worship the pharaoh. This made Akhenaten and Nefertiti intermediaries between the people and their god, eliminating the need for powerful priests like those of Amun (Figure 4.23). Many theories have been proposed to explain Akhenaten's motive for founding a new monotheistic religion, including sincere belief, but most have been discarded. It is possible he was merely attempting to revert to an older model of religious practice in which the king was the primary state deity.

FIGURE 4.23 Akhenaten and Nefertiti. This small stone engraving made during his lifetime shows Pharaoh Akhenaten at left, sitting beneath the Aton (the solar orb) with his queen, Nefertiti. Akhenaten cradles one of their three daughters, while Nefertiti holds the other two on her lap and her shoulder. (credit: "Akhenaten, Nefertiti, and three daughters beneath the Aten" by Richard Mortel/Flickr, CC BY 2.0)

DUELING VOICES

The Many Strange Faces of Akhenaten

Mystery and debate have surrounded the pharaoh Akhenaten ever since archaeologists first uncovered the lost city of Akhetaton in the 1880s. He has been called a heretic, a revolutionary, a lunatic, and more. Some of the fascination comes from the theory that he gave birth to modern monotheism. Others have seen in him a way to reject monotheism entirely.

In 1910, the British Egyptologist Arthur Weigall published a biography called *The Life and Times of Akhnaton* in which he argued that the Egyptian pharaoh had experienced a "pre-Christian revelation." The book was a bestseller in Europe, drawing Christian readers eager to learn about a possible connection between their religion and Ancient Egypt.

In 1939, Sigmund Freud, the founder of psychoanalysis, developed his own interpretation of Akhenaten's significance in his biography of Moses, *Moses and Monotheism*, arguing that Moses was in fact a priest of Akhenaten's new religion. When Akhenaten died and his religion was washed away, Moses was forced to flee Egypt. His religious ideas, according to Freud, passed to the people of Canaan and led to the monotheistic religion of Judaism.

In the 1930s and 1940s, some followers of the Nazi movement in Germany became fascinated with the life of Akhenaten. Eager to reject Christianity because of its connections of Judaism, they supported a revival of pre-Christian paganism rooted in nature worship, which they felt was more authentically German. Reading about Akhenaten and seeing his artifacts on display in the Berlin Museum, they could not help but see similarities between his religion and the pagan sun-worshipping religion they were trying to advance in Germany. Their ideas led to a number of books, like Savitri Devi's 1939 *A Perfect Man: Akhnaton, King of Egypt* and Josef Magnus Wehner's 1944 novel *Akhenaten and Nefertiti: A Tale from Ancient Egypt.*

Devi actually wrote several books about Akhenaten and his religion. Few today find her analysis worth considering, but they are a reminder of the way Akhenaten's religious movement has fascinated and influenced people thousands of years after his death.

- Try developing your own interpretation of Akhenaten's religious motivation. Consider what you learned about the actual Akhenaten as well as any other elements you want to imagine.
- Why do you think early twentieth-century writers saw what they wanted to see in the life and religion of Akhenaten? Can you think of any examples of this phenomenon today?

One reason many questions about him remain is that after Akhenaten died in about 1336 BCE, Egyptians reverted to their older religious traditions and attempted to erase this period from their history. The process was begun by his successor Smenkhkare and accelerated under the pharaoh who followed, Tutankhamun. These two young and short-lived pharaohs ushered Egypt back to the old faith, abandoning the city of Akhetaton, returning to Memphis, and beginning repairs on the temples desecrated under the previous regime. Tutankhamun also sent his armies into Nubia and Canaan to put down revolts and challenge the threat posed by the Hittites. He may have been leading one of these armies when he was killed, at the age of only eighteen or nineteen. The next pharaohs continued restoring the old religions, even scratching out references to the Aton and destroying what remained of Akhetaton.

⊘ LINK TO LEARNING

In November 1922, British archaeologist Howard Carter became the first person to enter the interior chambers of King Tutankhamun's tomb (https://openstax.org/l/77KingTut) in thousands of years. The discovery of the tomb caused excitement and fascination around the world and began a years-long excavation and cataloging of its many treasures. Take a look at these colorized images of photos taken during the excavation process to see why. (Note that the excavation techniques you see in the photos were often destructive and would never be used today.)

When Horemheb, the final pharaoh of this first dynasty of the New Kingdom, died childless, a military commander named Ramesses I took control and began a new dynasty. His heirs, sometimes called the **Ramesside kings**, worked hard to restore Egypt to greatness through impressive military and building campaigns. The greatest pharaoh of this period, and the last great pharaoh of the New Kingdom, was Ramesses II, who ruled Egypt for more than sixty-five years from 1279 to 1213 BCE.

During his long reign, Ramesses II fought several wars with the Hittites in Syria and launched additional wars against the Libyans to the west of Egypt. The threat from the Hittites was especially pronounced in this period. In an attempt to push them back and restore Egyptian influence in Syria, Ramesses II led an army of twenty thousand into Syria to retake the important city of Qadesh. During the fighting, Ramesses himself led several chariots straight into the Hittite lines. It was only by a combination of luck and Hittite negligence that he and his forces survived and were able to ultimately beat back the enemy (Figure 4.24). While the attempt to recapture Qadesh failed, once he was safely home, Ramesses II claimed the campaign was a success.

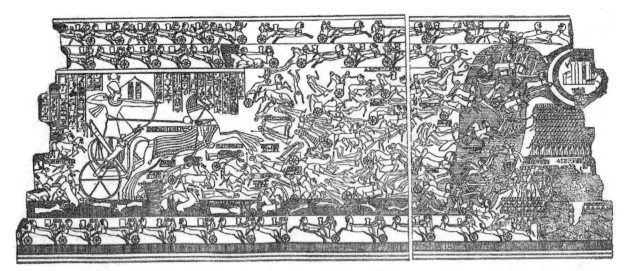

FIGURE 4.24 Ramses II. This sketch of an engraving on a wall of the mortuary temple of Pharaoh Ramesses II depicts him (on the left) as a larger-than-life charioteer firing arrows into the Hittite army at the Battle of Qadesh. The Egyptian records of the battle note that the pharaoh demonstrated great bravery as he led a small group of chariots into the fray. (credit: modification of work "Battle scene from the Great Kadesh reliefs of Ramses II on the Walls of the Ramesseum" by A History Of Egypt From The Earliest Times To The Persian Conquest by James Henry Breasted/Wikimedia Commons, Public Domain)

The failed attempt to retake Qadesh helped convince Ramesses to agree to a peace treaty with the Hittites in approximately 1258 BCE. The threat they continued to pose also motivated him to build a new capital in the Nile delta, much closer to Canaan. Called Pi-Ramesse ("House of Ramesses"), it included a great number of impressive monuments, some with reliefs showing the pharaoh defeating the Hittites. Beyond the building campaigns in Pi-Ramesse, Ramesses II also enlarged and beautified several additional temples in Thebes and other locations. However, the greatest monuments to his rule were the two temples he built at Abu Simbel, far to the south in Nubia. The more impressive of the two is called the Great Temple at Abu Simbel. It was carved into the side of a mountain and includes four massive seated statues of Ramesses II himself. A passageway between the two center statues leads to chambers that stretch hundreds of feet into the sandstone (Figure 4.25). The engineers who designed the temple constructed it such that twice a year, the rays of the sun would enter the building at dawn and bathe the gods placed there in light.

FIGURE 4.25 The Temple at Abu Simbel. In 1968, Ramesses II's thirteenth-century BCE temple at Abu Simbel was relocated because the creation of a large dam on the Nile was going to flood the original site. This photograph shows the structure as it looks today. (credit: "Abu Simbel Temple of Ramesses II" by "Than217"/Wikimedia Commons, Public Domain)

Egypt's Foreign Policy

Powerful pharaohs used war beyond their borders to keep their rivals and other major powers in check. Thutmose III had led armies into both Nubia and Canaan for this purpose. In Canaan, his efforts were directed at blunting the growing influence of Mitanni, a kingdom in northern Mesopotamia. The rise of Mitanni led a number of Canaanite leaders who had previously pledged their allegiance to Egypt to instead seek Mitanni protection. By campaigning in Canaan several times, Thutmose III was able to bring the Canaanite regions back into Egypt's orbit. He also directly attacked Mitanni itself in order to weaken its control in the region. His numerous successors continued these efforts, thus ensuring Egypt's influence in Canaan. Amenhotep II brought back thousands of prisoners and a wealth of treasure from his campaigns in the region, for example. Well over a century later, Seti I and Ramesses II were still pursuing these efforts to preserve Egyptian dominance.

Pharaohs also frequently took hostages, usually members of the royal families of subject kingdoms. Thutmose III brought back a number of the sons of Canaanite kings after his campaigns, who were raised and educated in Egypt and learned Egyptian customs. Apart from serving as cultural bridges, hostages also helped strengthen Egypt's relationships with its subject realms by reducing the likelihood their fathers would rebel in the future. Another means of improving relations with other kingdoms was marriage. Thutmose IV married one of the daughters of the Mitanni king as part of an agreement intended to check the power of the Hittites.

While wars in foreign lands could pacify enemies and preserve Egypt's international influence, military campaigns also had a strong economic component. Conquering new territory meant conquering new wealth that could be used to benefit the state. Records of just one of Thutmose III's campaigns in Canaan note that the booty included more than two thousand horses and twenty thousand sheep, almost two thousand goats, wheat, weapons, equipment, captives, and items made of precious metals, such as copper from mines in the Sinai. Descriptions of campaigns in Nubia recount similar acquisitions. Conquered peoples were also expected to provide annual tribute to the Egyptian state.

And there were benefits from maintaining control over vital trade routes and centers of commerce. The eastern Mediterranean regions of Canaan and Syria included routes connecting Mesopotamia with the sea and Cyprus. Major trading centers included Hazor and Qadesh. Megiddo was located at a mountain pass on the trade routes connecting Mesopotamia with important Canaanite cities on the way to Egypt (Figure 4.26). The value of these trade routes and commercial centers prompted Egypt to launch several campaigns into the area. Battles were fought at Qadesh and Megiddo in an effort to keep the Hittite and Mitanni kingdoms out and maintain Egyptian control over the area. These famous battles came at enormous cost in troops and wealth, and the results were mixed. The Battle of Qadesh was at best a draw. The Battle of Megiddo, fought in the fifteenth century BCE by the forces of Thutmose III, was largely an Egyptian success and led to the kingdom establishing firm control over the larger region.

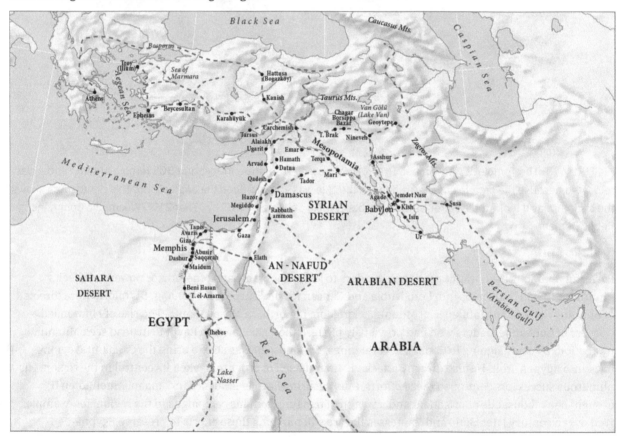

FIGURE 4.26 Trade Routes in the Eastern Mediterranean. The regions of Canaan and Syria connected vital trade routes (shown in red) that ran from Mesopotamia to Egypt and the Arabian Peninsula as well as Anatolia. (attribution: Copyright Rice University, OpenStax, under CC BY 4.0 license)

By maintaining their influence in Canaan, Syria, and Nubia, Egyptian pharaohs preserved the state's access to vital trading resources. Tin and copper were transported from Anatolia via trading routes through Canaan. Phoenicia in northwestern Canaan was a major source of the cedar used to construct Egyptian ships. It was also through the Phoenician port city of Byblos that Egyptian papyrus frequently flowed to other parts of the Eastern Mediterranean. The Greek name for book, *biblos*, reflects this connection with Byblos and is the ancient origin of the English word "bible." Ivory, ebony, leopard skins, incense, and gold were procured in Nubia. There were also mines in the Sinai for turquoise, alabaster, and quartzite. Trade goods coming from Egypt to other parts of the world included pottery, grains, papyrus, linen, and many other items. To protect the flow of trade, Egypt provided border protection, supervised toll roads, and generally ensured the safety of merchants. Records from New Kingdom Egypt note frequent deliveries of trade goods from foreign allies such as Mitanni, Babylon, and others. They are described as gifts, but scholars believe they were almost certainly trade.

Toward the end of the New Kingdom era, Egypt's ability to maintain control over the trade routes in Canaan and Syria declined steadily. Instability in the commercial centers and banditry on the roads became more common. One travel report from the tail end of the New Kingdom (c. 1100 BCE) describes some of the problems experienced by an Egyptian envoy sent to Phoenicia to buy a supply of cedar. First he was robbed by his own crew, then he was refused the cedar he was promised in Phoenicia, and finally he was attacked by roving migrants. He appealed to officials in Egypt, but little could be done. In earlier centuries, such difficulties would have been unthinkable, but by 1100 BCE, Egypt's influence in the region was no longer strong.

Many of the problems the envoy described were symptoms of the Late Bronze Age Collapse and were out of Egypt's control. One of the consequences of this larger civilizational decline was that large numbers of migrants, such as those who attacked the envoy, were sweeping across the eastern Mediterranean bringing chaos and destruction. An Egyptian inscription from 1208 BCE described them as "coming from the sea," which has led modern scholars to refer to them as the Sea Peoples (Figure 4.27). It appears that many came from the Aegean area.

FIGURE 4.27 An Attack by the Sea Peoples. This redrawing of a wall relief from the Temple of Ramesses III records the arrival of a group of Sea People (on the left) and the Egyptians led by Ramesses (the larger-than-life archer on the right) preparing to defend themselves. (credit: modification of work "A depiction of the army of Ramesses III fighting the Sea Peoples" by "Seebeer"/Wikimedia Commons, Public Domain)

As inscriptions from the period demonstrate, Egypt resisted the invading forces. Many of the Sea Peoples were likely killed. But many others settled in Egypt and assimilated there, just as they did across the entire eastern Mediterranean. All this disruption took a toll on the region, however. The Mycenaean kingdoms in Greece and the Hittite kingdom in Anatolia suffered greatly and collapsed. City-states across Canaan were especially hard hit. Even kingdoms far from the Mediterranean, like Assyria and Babylon, weakened during this time of troubles.

Though Egypt proved more able to withstand the dangers of the period, it did experience problems. Grain prices, for example, soared during this time. Tomb robbing became common as workers who had not been paid found other ways to support their families. At the same time the Libyans and Sea Peoples were leading their attacks in northern Egypt, Nubian subjects rose up in rebellion to Egypt's south. And the migrating Sea Peoples in Canaan greatly weakened Egypt's control of the region. By 1070 BCE, the challenges had been mounting for years, and the New Kingdom came to an end.

4.3 The Persian Empire

LEARNING OBJECTIVES

By the end of this section, you will be able to:
- Discuss the history of Persia through the reign of Darius I
- Describe the origin and tenets of Zoroastrianism
- Identify the achievements and innovations of the Persian Empire

In conquering Mesopotamia, Syria, Canaan, and Egypt, the Neo-Assyrians created the largest empire the Near East had ever seen. Their dominance did not last, however, because Babylonia and Media destroyed the empire and carved up the spoils. But this proved to be a transitional period that set the stage for an empire that dwarfed even that of the Neo-Assyrians. Emerging from the area to the east of Mesopotamia, the founders of the Persian Empire proved to be both excellent warriors and efficient imperial organizers. Their kings commanded power, wealth, and authority over an area stretching from the Indus River to the Nile. Governors stationed in the many conquered regions served as extensions of the king's authority, and trade flowed along a large network of roads under Persian military protection. For two centuries, Persia was the undisputed superpower of the ancient world.

The Rise of Persia

The origins of the Persians are murky and stretch back to the arrival of nomadic Indo-European speakers in the Near East, possibly as early as 2000 BCE. Those who reached Persia (modern Iran) are often described as Indo-Iranians or Indo-Aryans. They were generally pastoralists, relying on animal husbandry, living a mostly migratory life, and using the horse-drawn chariot. The extent to which they displaced or blended with existing groups in the region is not clear. From written records of the rise of the Neo-Assyrian Empire during the ninth century BCE, we know the Assyrians conducted military campaigns against and exacted tribute from an Indo-Iranian group called the Persians. The Persians lived in the southern reaches of the Zagros Mountains and along the Persian Gulf, in general proximity to the Medes with whom they shared many cultural traits.

Much of what we know about the early Persians comes from the work of the ancient Greek historian Herodotus, who was born about 484 BCE (Figure 4.28). According to Herodotus, Persia was made a vassal of Media in the seventh century BCE but freed itself in the sixth century BCE under the leadership of Cyrus II, also called Cyrus the Great. Inscriptions from the period suggest that Cyrus was likely a member of the Persian royal family, the Achaemenid dynasty. Once in power, he reorganized the Persian state and its military to mirror those of the Median Empire. This step included creating divisions for cavalry, archers, and infantry and setting up special training for the cavalry. Then, in 550 BCE, just a few years into his reign, Cyrus sent his military to challenge the Medes, whereupon the Median troops revolted, handed over their king, and accepted Cyrus's rule. He then proceeded to integrate the Median elite and officials into his own government. The Median domains had become the Persian Empire.

FIGURE 4.28 Herodotus. The ancient Greek historian Herodotus is one of our major sources for information about the Persian Empire. This roughly life-sized stone bust of him is a second-century Roman copy of a fourth-century BCE bronze statue. (credit: "Marble bust of Herodotos" by The Metropolitan Museum of Art, Gift of George F. Baker, 1891/Wikimedia Commons, Public Domain)

Between 550 and 539 BCE, Cyrus sent his armies east and west to expand his recently acquired realm. In 539 BCE, he turned his attention to the Neo-Babylonian Empire, defeating its armies and marching into Babylon. His Persian Empire now incorporated the territories controlled by Babylonia, including Mesopotamia, Syria, Phoenicia, and Judah, and had become the largest empire to have existed in the Near East to that point. Organizing and administering this massive domain required the use of governors, whom Cyrus generally selected from local areas, a prudent move in a world where rebellions were common.

🔗 LINK TO LEARNING

Cyrus the Great left a record of his conquest of Babylon inscribed on a clay spool about eight inches long. This artifact, now called the Cyrus Cylinder, was created in 539 BCE and promptly buried in the foundation of the city wall, to remain there until its discovery in 1879. Explore this link to the British Museum website to see a high-resolution image of the Cyrus Cylinder (https://openstax.org/l/77CyrusCyl) and a translation of its inscriptions.

Cyrus died in in battle in 530 BCE, leaving the throne and empire to his son Cambyses II. The first task for Cambyses was to continue preparing for the invasion of Egypt his father had planned. A large fleet was built in the Mediterranean and a massive land force assembled for crossing the Sinai. The invasion began in 525 BCE. The defending Egyptians were soon overwhelmed, and the pharaoh retreated up the Nile but was captured. Having now added Egypt to his already large empire, Cambyses took on the role of pharaoh, adopting the proper titles and caring for the Egyptian religious institutions. This practice of respecting local traditions was a common feature of Persian expansion and helped to win support in newly acquired areas.

Under Cambyses II, the Persian Empire stretched from the edges of India to the shores of the Aral Sea, the Aegean coast of Anatolia, and the Nile River and included everything in between. Then, just as Cambyses was reaching the height of his power, a Persian revolt broke out in 522 BCE in support of his brother Bardiya. On his way to put down the rebellion, Cambyses II died, leaving the future of the empire uncertain but allowing for the rise of possibly Persia's most famous and powerful leader, Darius I.

Darius I and the Reorganization of the Empire

The events surrounding the rebellion of Cambyses II's brother Bardiya are unclear because a handful of different accounts survive. According to Herodotus, Cambyses ordered one of his trusted advisers to secretly murder Bardiya. Since no one knew Bardiya was dead, an impostor pretending to be him launched a rebellion against Cambyses, though after several months the false Bardiya was killed in a palace coup at the hands of Darius, an army officer who claimed descent from the royal house. Afterward, since neither Cambyses nor Bardiya had sons, Darius made himself king. Other accounts differ in some ways, and some scholars have speculated that Darius invented the story about a false Bardiya in order to legitimize his own coup against the real Bardiya and take the throne.

We may never know exactly what happened, but Darius was indeed able to grasp control of the Persian Empire in 522 BCE. However, it took more than a year for him to put down the ensuing rebellions, some possibly instigated by those who refused to recognize the legitimacy of his claim to the throne. Once these had been quelled, Darius commissioned an enormous relief inscription to be made on the cliff face of Mount Behistun. It shows a dominating figure of himself facing a number of bound former rebels, accompanied by lengthy descriptions of the rebellion and, in three different languages, Darius's version of the events that led to his rise to power (Figure 4.29). To further strengthen his claim on the throne, Darius integrated himself deeply into the royal line through a number of marriages, to the daughters of Cyrus II, the widow of Cambyses II, and two of Cambyses's sisters.

FIGURE 4.29 The Behistun Relief. The massive Behistun Relief, more than eighty feet long and almost fifty feet high, shows a crowned Darius (on the left) with his foot on the impostor he claimed to have overthrown. Captive rebels and a narrative in three languages of Darius's version of events complete the carving. (credit: "Behistun Inscription" by "Hara1603"/Wikimedia Commons, Public Domain)

Darius now set about reorganizing the empire, carving it into twenty different governing districts called satrapies (Figure 4.30). Each **satrapy** was administered by a royal governor called a satrap, usually a trusted Persian or Median noble. Satraps answered directly to the king, had their own courts, wielded great power, and possessed vast lands within the satrapy. They often ruled from the large cities of the regions and were responsible for ensuring that their satrapy remained pacified and submitted its allotted taxes, though there were also local rulers within the region who managed affairs related to specific ethnic or religious groups. The only area not made into a satrapy was the Persian heartland, which was governed directly by the king.

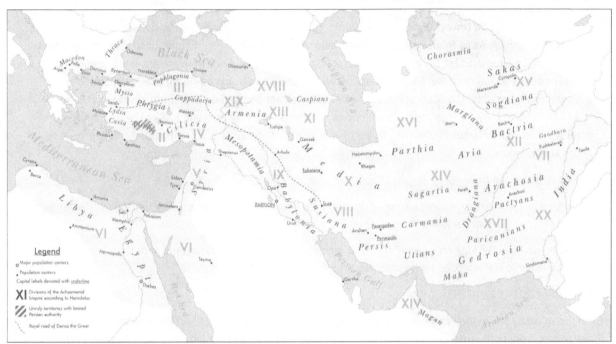

FIGURE 4.30 **The Persian Empire.** The Persian Empire under Darius I reached from the edge of India in the east to Libya in the west. To manage this large empire, Darius divided it into twenty different satrapies. (credit: modification of work "Achaemenid Empire 500 BCE" by "Cattette"/Wikimedia Commons, CC BY 4.0)

Darius I and later kings had a number of tools at their disposal to keep the powerful satraps in line. For example, they frequently sent royal officials, known as the "eyes and ears of the great king," to arrive unannounced and conduct audits, compiling detailed reports about how the satrapies were being governed that were sent directly to the king for review. If the reports were negative, the satraps could expect either removal or even execution at the hands of the region's military garrison. These garrisons were used by the satraps to enforce the laws and maintain order, but they ultimately answered to the king and could discipline the satraps when necessary.

Communication between the satraps and the king was carried out through letters dictated to scribes and transmitted along royal roads. These roads constituted an impressive communication system that linked the many key cities of the empire with the Persian heartland and its cities, like Susa, Persepolis, and Pasargadae. While it was not new—the Neo-Assyrian Empire had its own network of roads that the Persians adopted and improved—it was a valuable tool for administering the large and complicated empire. Along the many royal roads of the empire were inns, resting places, and waystations with stables for horses. Safety was ensured by the troops stationed along the way, especially at key and vulnerable points. To move letters along the roads, a member of the army of mounted royal messengers would travel the roughly twenty miles to the first station, change horses, and continue to the next station. In this way, communication could move roughly two hundred miles in a single day.

THE PAST MEETS THE PRESENT

Persia and the U.S. Postal Service

The Persian Empire required a sophisticated communications network to move messages across its vast territory, so it relied on speedy couriers who traveled roads first developed by the Assyrians and then improved. The ancient Greek historian Herodotus commented on Persian communications in his famous *Histories*:

> There is nothing that travels faster, and yet is mortal, than these couriers; the Persians invented this system, which works as follows. It is said that there are as many horses and men posted at intervals as there are days required for the entire journey, so that one horse and one man are assigned to each day. And neither snow nor rain nor heat nor dark of night keeps them from completing their appointed course as swiftly as possible. The first courier passes on the instructions to the second, the second to the third, and from there they are transmitted from one to another all the way through, just as the torchbearing relay is celebrated by the Hellenes in honor of Hephaistos. The Persians call this horse-posting system the *angareion*.

> —Herodotus, *Histories*

Herodotus was not the only ancient author to describe the Persian courier system. The biblical Old Testament Book of Esther notes that not just horses were used:

> And he wrote in the king Ahasuerus' name, and sealed it with the king's ring, and sent letters by posts on horseback, and riders on mules, camels, and young dromedaries.

> —Esther 8:10 (KJV)

Even today, many still marvel at the efficiency of the Persian courier system. When the chief architect for the Eighth Avenue post office in New York City came across Herodotus's description, he thought it perfect for a large inscription on the new building (Figure 4.31). His paraphrase of Herodotus is still visible there. Popularly thought of as the U.S. Postal Service's unofficial motto, it reads as follows: "Neither snow nor rain nor heat nor gloom of night stays these couriers from the swift completion of their appointed rounds."

FIGURE 4.31 "**Neither Snow nor Rain nor Heat nor Gloom of Night.**" The unofficial motto of the U.S. Postal Service, which once also described the Persian Empire's courier system, is inscribed on the face of this New York City building, over the colonnade. (credit: modification of work "Post Office, New York City (https://www.loc.gov/pictures/resource/det.4a24669/)" by Library of Congress Prints and Photographs Division/Library of Congress)

- What purposes might the Persian courier system have served? How might the empire have functioned in the absence or breakdown of such a system?
- Why might the chief architect for the Eighth Avenue post office in New York City have selected Herodotus' description?

Building projects were another important expression of Darius's power and authority. During his reign, he undertook the construction of elaborate palaces at Susa, Persepolis, and Pasargadae (Figure 4.32). These were constructed and decorated by skilled workers from many different locations and reflected artistic influences from around the empire, among them fluted columns designed by Greek stonemasons, Assyrian reliefs carved by Mesopotamians, and a variety of other features of Egyptian, Lydian, Babylonian, Elamite, and Median origin. The many workers—men, women, and children—who built these palaces migrated to the construction sites and often lived in nearby villages or encampments.

FIGURE 4.32 **Persepolis**. The ruins of the city of Persepolis, situated thirty-seven miles southwest of modern-day Shiraz (in modern Iran), reveal that the site was an impressive imperial center in Darius's time. (credit: modification of work "HDR image of Persepolis, Iran" by "Roodiparse"/Wikimedia Commons, Public Domain)

🔗 LINK TO LEARNING

Explore a reconstruction of the palace complex of Persepolis (https://openstax.org/l/77Persepolis) as it may have appeared to a visitor in ancient Persia via the Getty Museum's Persepolis Reimagined interactive exhibit.

Major infrastructure projects were also a feature of Darius's reign. For example, he ordered the construction of a long canal that would have allowed ships to pass from the Red Sea into Egypt's Nile River and thus to the Mediterranean. It is unclear whether he actually completed it. It seems unlikely, though Herodotus insists he did. Whatever the case, that Darius attempted this massive undertaking is a testament to the power and resources the kings of Persia had at their fingertips. Other infrastructure projects included the expansion and rebuilding of the many roads that crisscrossed the empire, as well as the construction of a number of *qanats* (Figure 4.33). These were long, underground tunnels used for carrying fresh water over many kilometers, usually for irrigation, and represented a major improvement over earlier technologies. They likely had been used before the Achaemenids, but their construction expanded with the rise of Persian power.

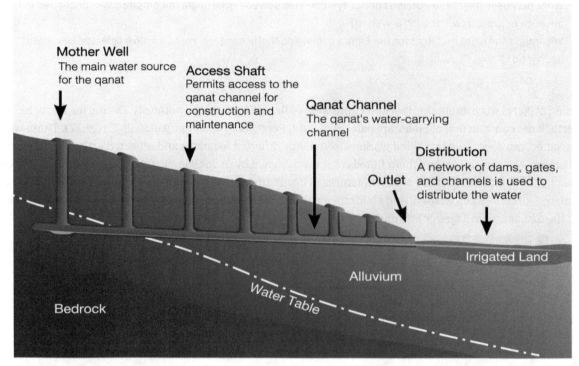

FIGURE 4.33 Qanats for Irrigation. The *qanats* built by Darius were designed to carry fresh water over long distances into populated areas or to irrigate land for farming. (credit: modification of work "Qanat cross section" by Samuel Bailey/Wikimedia Commons, CC BY 3.0)

Persian Culture and Daily Life

The social order of the Persian Empire included a number of hierarchically organized groups. At the bottom were the enslaved. While the Persians did not have a long history of using slavery before becoming a major power, it was common in the regions they conquered. Over time, the Persian nobility adapted to the practice and used enslaved people to work their land.

Next in the hierarchy were the free peasants, who generally worked the land and lived in the villages of the empire. On the next level were the various kinds of artisans, and higher still were the educated classes of scribes, imperial recordkeepers, and important merchants. And higher than all of these was the ruling order, including priests, nobles, and warriors (Figure 4.34).

FIGURE 4.34 Persian Recordkeeping. Thousands of clay tablets like this one from the administrative archives at Persepolis have been key to helping historians understand the way the empire functioned and was socially

organized. Like the rulers of earlier Near Eastern empires, the Persians also used cuneiform. (credit: "Persepolis tablet" by "Pentocelo"/Wikimedia Commons, Public Domain)

The Persian king occupied a place far above and removed from these groups. As the earthly representative of the god Ahura Mazda, he expected complete submission from everyone in the empire. Those in his presence had to position themselves on the ground to show his superiority over them. Servants who came near had to cover their mouths so as not to breathe on him. His power was absolute, though he was restrained by custom and the advice of leading nobles. One of the most important of these nobles was the "Commander of a Thousand," who managed the large court, served as a gatekeeper to any audience with the king, and oversaw the king's personal protection service. As was the case in the Assyrian Empire, kings were not necessarily eldest sons. Rather, the current king could select his heir and frequently chose a younger son for any number of reasons.

The Persian king and his court seem not to have remained in one centralized capital. Rather, they moved periodically between the cities and regions of Babylon, Susa, Rhagae, Parthia, Ecbatana, Persepolis, and possibly others. One motive was a desire to avoid extreme weather during certain seasons, but there were also political considerations. For example, by moving across the countryside, the king made himself visible not only to important individuals in the cities but also to the many peasants in the villages that dotted the landscape. Thus, he allowed them opportunities to present him with petitions or seek his guidance.

Moving the court in this way was no easy feat, however. It required the efforts of thousands of people including officials, soldiers, religious leaders, wives, other women, and servants of all types, and the transport of horses, chariots, religious objects, treasure, and military equipment. In many ways, it was as though the state itself migrated with the seasons. The arrival of this migrating state in any major location was met with elaborate public ceremonies of greeting and welcome. Some contemporary descriptions detail how flowers and incense were laid along the city roads where the king moved. His dramatic entry was followed by the proper sacrifices to the local gods and an opportunity for the people to bring gifts to the king, such as exotic animals, jewels, precious metals, food, and wine. It was considered a great honor to present the king with a gift, and the gift-giving ceremonies served to strengthen the king's relationship with his subjects.

The vast army of Persia had its own ceremonies and customs. Herodotus records that it was made up of a great number of subject peoples from around the empire, all with their own colorful uniforms. Military training began at a very young age and included lessons in archery, horseback combat, and hand-to-hand combat. The most talented of the infantrymen in the Persian army might hope to rise to the ranks of the Immortals, an elite, heavy-infantry combat force that served both in war and in the king's personal guard. The larger army was made up of various units of infantry, archers, and cavalry. The largest unit was the corps, made up of ten thousand men. Each corps had a commanding officer who answered to the supreme commander. In battle, the archers would rapidly fire their arrows into the enemy as the cavalry and infantry advanced in their respective formations. Occasionally, when rebellions were put down or new territories added, the Persians deported the conquered populations elsewhere within the empire.

Because most records from the Persian Empire focus on kings, wars, the military, and high-level officials and bureaucrats, we know little about commoners. But we know that most ordinary Persians had diets of bread or mash made of barley, supplemented by figs, dates, plums, apples, almonds, and other fruits and nuts. Much more rarely, meals might also include goat, mutton, or poultry. Besides the military, the empire supported a host of other necessary occupations, such as sentinels, messengers, various types of attendants, architects, merchants, and numerous types of lower professions. The many agricultural workers grew traditional crops of the Near East, like wheat and barley, in addition to rice (brought from India) and alfalfa (for horse feed). Merchants in the Persian Empire benefited greatly from the stability created by the government and the extensive network of crisscrossing roads that connected the far-flung regions. Although long-distance trade was prohibitively expensive for most things except luxury goods, trade across short distances was apparently common.

The religion of the Persians was a tradition we describe today as **Zoroastrianism**. Its name comes from *Zoroaster*, the Greek pronunciation of the name of its founder, Zarathustra. Scholars today believe that Zoroaster likely lived at some point between 1400 and 900 BCE and was almost certainly a Persian priest, prophet, or both. His followers likely practiced a polytheistic religion similar in many ways to the Vedic traditions held by Indo-European speakers who migrated into India. Among Zoroastrians' many gods were both powerful heavenly deities and more terrestrial nature gods. Ceremonies included various rituals similar to those of other polytheistic religions, such as the sacrifice of animals on outdoor altars.

Zoroaster appears to have emphasized the perpetual conflict between the forces of justice and those of wickedness. Over time, he developed supernatural personifications of these forces: Ahura Mazda was the lord of wisdom and the force of good (Figure 4.35), and Angra Mainu was the destructive spirit and the force of evil. Each was supported by lesser supernatural beings. On the side of Ahura Mazda were the *ahuras* who worked to bring good to the world, and on the side of Angra Mainu were the *daevas* who served the interests of evil.

FIGURE 4.35 Ahura Mazda. The Persian god Ahura Mazda was the principal source of good as understood by followers of Zoroastrianism, a Persian religion. This large stone carving of him adorns a gate at the ruins of Persepolis (in modern Iran). (credit: "Persepolis, Tripylon, eastern gate (2)" by Marco Prins/Wikimedia Commons, CC0 1.0)

The Persian followers of Zoroastrianism believed Ahura Mazda had created the world as an entirely good place. However, Angra Mainu was dedicated to destroying this perfection with evil, so the two forces fought for the supremacy of good or evil on Earth. The world the Persians saw around them was the product of their pitched battle. However, the fight would not last forever. At some appointed time in the future, Ahura Mazda would overcome the forces of Angra Mainu, and the followers of evil would face judgment and punishment for their crimes. It was up to humans to decide for themselves what path to follow. At the final judgment, the dead would be resurrected and made to walk through a river of fire. Those consumed by the fire were unworthy and would be condemned to torment in hell, while those who survived would live forever in a paradise with no evil.

While Zoroaster's beliefs were not readily accepted by his own people, he found protection and a following among others, and in the centuries after his death, his ideas spread and changed. For example, the Medes incorporated their own priestly class into the Zoroastrian traditions. The Achaemenids borrowed artistic traditions from the Mesopotamians to depict Ahura Mazda in the same way they styled their important gods.

Later, Judeans within the Persian Empire, who were from the Canaanite kingdom of Judah and followers of Judaism, incorporated many Zoroastrian ideas into their own religious traditions. These ideas went on to influence the religions of Christianity and Islam.

THE PAST MEETS THE PRESENT

Zoroastrianism, Judaism, and Christianity

Zoroastrianism, Judaism, and Christianity may have emerged in the ancient world, but they are all still practiced today. And while in modern times these religions appear quite different, they share important similarities.

Consider these modern similarities between Zoroastrianism and Christianity. Both accept the idea of a powerful god as the source of all good, the existence of evil and deceptive forces that plague the world, a final judgment that occurs when the forces of evil have been vanquished forever, and a pleasant afterlife for those who follow the path of righteousness. These similarities are not the product of random accident. Rather, the connections between Zoroastrianism and Christianity date to developments within Judaism in the centuries before the birth of Christ.

It was likely that when the Judeans were members of the Persian Empire, they became acquainted with some of the ideas of Zoroastrianism, and these ideas influenced the way they understood their own monotheistic religion. The notion that a force of evil was responsible for the many problems in the world may have been a comforting thought for those who wanted to believe that God was both all-powerful and thoroughly benevolent. The concept of a final judgment was also appealing to Judeans, who held that they were not only God's chosen people but also persecuted by the forces of evil. While these ideas begin to appear in Judean writings only in the centuries after the fall of Persia, the seeds had likely been planted much earlier through a growing familiarity with the tenets of Zoroastrianism. In the second century BCE, many followers of Judaism had come to accept the idea of a final judgment. It was this form of Judaism that ultimately influenced the fundamental tenets of Christianity.

- What do the connections between Zoroastrianism, Judaism, and Christianity suggest about the way religions borrow from each other? Can you think of other examples?
- How might modern Christianity be different had Judaism not been influenced by Zoroastrianism?

While the religion of the Persians was Zoroastrianism, the empire included people of different religions, including Armenians, Nubians, Libyans, Phoenicians, Egyptians, Babylonians, Ionian Greeks, Bactrians, Judeans, and many others. Indeed, it was the Persian king Cyrus II who permitted the Judeans exiled in Babylon to return to Judah and rebuild their temple. The empire expected loyalty and the payment of tribute, but its kings were not interested in transforming their diverse peoples into Persians. Instead, they developed an imperial system that supported the maintenance of a multiethnic, multilingual, and multireligious empire.

4.4 The Hebrews

LEARNING OBJECTIVES

By the end of this section, you will be able to:
- Discuss the history of the Hebrews in the context of the development of the Near East
- Explain how the Hebrew faith differed from others in the same region and time period

The Hebrews, a Semitic-speaking Canaanite people known for their monotheistic religion of Judaism or the Jewish religion, have preserved a history of their people that claims very ancient origins and includes descriptions of early leaders, kings, religious traditions, prophets, and numerous divine interventions. That history, often called the Tanakh or **Hebrew Bible** in the Jewish tradition and the Old Testament in the Christian tradition, has survived for many centuries and influenced the emergence of the two other major monotheistic faiths, Christianity and Islam. While fundamentalist Christians and Orthodox Jews hold that the

Bible is both divinely inspired and inerrant, historians must scrutinize the text and the rich history it records. This study and the careful work of archaeologists in the Near East have revealed a number of problems with accepting as infallible the story as recorded in the Hebrew Bible, but research has also opened our eyes to a history that is perhaps even more interesting than the account traditionally preserved.

The History of the Hebrews

The history of the Hebrews recorded in the Bible starts with the beginning of time and the creation of the first man, Adam. However, it is with the life of the patriarch Abraham that we begin to see the emergence of the Hebrews as a distinct group. Abraham, we are told, descended from Noah a thousand years before, and Noah himself descended from Adam a thousand years before that. Relying on the ages and generations referenced in the Hebrew Bible, we can deduce that Abraham was born around 2150 BCE in the Mesopotamian city of Ur. At the age of seventy-five, he left this city and traveled to the land of Canaan in the eastern Mediterranean. There Abraham and his wife Sarah had their first son together, Isaac. Isaac then had a son, Jacob, and Jacob gave birth to twelve sons. From these twelve sons, the traditional Twelve Tribes of Israel descend (Figure 4.36).

FIGURE 4.36 Biblical Abraham. The Bible explains that Abraham migrated from Mesopotamia to Canaan, as represented in this nineteenth-century painting by a Hungarian artist, and there he eventually had children and grandchildren. (credit: "The Departure of Abraham" by Hungarian National Gallery/Wikimedia Commons, Public Domain)

While this chronology explains how the Hebrews found themselves in Canaan, there is little to support it. There are no archaeological sites we can reference, and the only evidence we have for Abraham, his trip from Mesopotamia, and his children, grandchildren, and great-grandchildren comes from the Hebrew Bible. This has led some to suspect that the stories of Abraham and his family may have been developed much later than the Bible suggests. And in fact, historians have traced the story of Abraham to sources written down between the tenth and sixth centuries BCE. It is possible that Abraham was a historical person and part of an ancient migration recounted for centuries in oral form, but without additional records or archaeological discoveries that attest to his existence, we cannot know for sure.

The Hebrew Bible notes that Joseph, one of Abraham's twelve great-grandsons, ended up in Egypt. Later, around 1800 BCE based on the biblical chronology, Joseph's family joined him, and his descendants lived there for several generations. During this long time in Egypt, the Bible explains that the descendants of Joseph experienced increasingly poor treatment, including being enslaved by the (unnamed) Egyptian pharaoh and put to work on building projects in the Nile delta (Figure 4.37). Later, the pharaoh decided to kill all the male Hebrew children, but one was saved from the slaughter by being hidden in a basket to float down the Nile. He was discovered by the pharaoh's daughter, who named him Moses and raised him among the Egyptian royalty as her own.

FIGURE 4.37 The Hebrews in Egypt. The Bible explains that, as represented in this monumental nineteenth-century painting by the English artist Edward Poynter, the Hebrews were enslaved and oppressed in Egypt. (credit: "Israel in Egypt" by Guildhall Art Gallery/Wikimedia Commons, Public Domain)

The Bible continues the story by explaining that the adult Moses discovered who he actually was and demanded that the pharaoh release the Hebrews and allow them to return to Canaan. After experiencing a number of divine punishments issued by the Hebrew god, the pharaoh reluctantly agreed. The Hebrews' flight from Egypt included a protracted trek across the Sinai desert and into Canaan, during which they agreed to worship only the single god Yahweh and obey his laws. This period of their history is often called the **Exodus**, because it records their mass migration out of Egypt and eventually to Canaan. Once in Canaan, Moses's general Joshua led several military campaigns against the inhabitants, which allowed the Hebrews to settle the land.

The details in the biblical account of the Hebrews' life in Egypt and their exodus from that kingdom have led some scholars to associate these stories with the period of Hyksos rule. It was then, during the Second Intermediate Period, that the Canaanites flooded into the Nile delta and took control, and it may be that the story of Joseph and his family entering Egypt preserves a memory of that process. The exact time of the exodus from Egypt has been difficult for historians to determine for a number of reasons, not least of which is the fact that the Bible does not name the Egyptian pharaohs of the Exodus period.

Yet some features of the biblical account indicate there was in fact some type of exodus. For example, Moses's name is Egyptian and not Hebrew, suggesting he came from Egypt. The Bible also names the two midwives who traveled with the group, leading some scholars to conclude there was some oral tradition about a very small group that may have crossed the Sinai into Canaan, though not the very large group described in the Bible. As for the story of the conquests of Joshua, the archaeological record simply does not support this. Even at the site of Jericho, extensive archaeological work has been unable to prove that the city was destroyed when and in the way the Bible describes. This absence of strong evidence has led most to conclude that there likely was no conquest, and that there was already a population of Hebrews in Canaan who were later joined by a smaller group from Egypt.

What Is in a Name?

Without archaeological or other evidence, historians have had to rely on the Hebrew Bible for clues about the Exodus. One possible hint comes from the Bible's book of Exodus, which describes the birth of Moses, his mother's effort to save him from slaughter, and his discovery and adoption by the pharaoh's daughter (Figure 4.38).

FIGURE 4.38 The Infant Moses. This 1904 Anglo-Dutch painting called *The Finding of Moses* represents the biblical account of the pharaoh's daughter discovering the infant Moses floating in a basket on the Nile. (credit: "The Finding of Moses" by Lawrence Alma-Tadema/Wikimedia Commons, Public Domain)

> And there went a man of the house of Levi, and took to wife a daughter of Levi. And the woman conceived, and bare a son: and when she saw him that he was a goodly child, she hid him three months. And when she could no longer hide him, she took for him an ark of bulrushes, and daubed it with slime and with pitch, and put the child therein; and she laid it in the flags by the river's brink. And his sister stood afar off, to witness what would be done to him. And the daughter of Pharaoh came down to wash herself at the river; and her maidens walked along by the river's side; and when she saw the ark among the flags, she sent her maid to fetch it. And when she had opened it, she saw the child: and, behold, the babe wept. And she had compassion on him, and said, This is one of the Hebrews' children. Then said his [Moses's] sister to Pharaoh's daughter, Shall I go and call to thee a nurse of the Hebrew women, that she may nurse the child for thee? And Pharaoh's daughter said to her, Go. And the maid went and called the child's mother. And Pharaoh's daughter said unto her, Take this child away, and nurse it for me, and I will give thee thy wages. And the woman took the child, and nursed it. And the child grew, and she brought him unto Pharaoh's daughter, and he became her son. And she called his name Moses: and she said, Because I drew him out of the water.
>
> —Exodus 2:1-10 (KJV)

As this story explains, the pharaoh's daughter named Moses to reflect the fact that she "drew him out of the water." Some scholars believe this phrase is a reference to the Hebrew word *mashah*, meaning to "draw out," which sounds similar to the Hebrew pronunciation of Moses, *Mosheh*. That explanation would have made sense to Hebrew readers of the Bible, but it does not make sense that an Egyptian princess would speak Hebrew. While this problem makes it difficult to take the story seriously as evidence, it does raise an interesting question.

Is the biblical account actually an attempt to explain a Hebrew man's name that was not Hebrew but Egyptian? In Egyptian, Moses means "child of." It would have been part of a larger name such as Thutmose, which means "child of [the god] Thoth." The fact that Hebrew tradition tried to explain his Egyptian name suggests to some that Moses may have been a real person with Egyptian heritage. That, in turn, suggests there is some validity to the Exodus story itself.

- Does the scholarly interpretation of the name Moses as Egyptian in origin seem credible to you? Why or why not?
- What does this story reveal about family relationships in the period?

The biblical book of Judges describes how the Hebrews moved into the hills of Canaan and lived as members of twelve tribes. In the book of Samuel, we hear how they faced oppression from the Philistines, one of the many Sea Peoples groups. To better defend themselves against the Philistines, the Hebrews organized themselves into a kingdom they called Israel. Their first leader, Saul, became king around 1030 BCE but failed to rule properly. The second king, David, not only ruled effectively but also was able to drive back the Philistines.

The Hebrews, properly referred to as Israelites in this period because of their formation of the Kingdom of Israel, now entered a golden age in their history. David suppressed the surrounding kingdoms, made Jerusalem his capital, and established a shrine there to the Israelite god Yahweh. This more organized kingdom was then left to David's son Solomon, who furthered the organization of Israel, made alliances with surrounding kingdoms, and embarked on numerous construction projects, the most important of which was a large temple to Yahweh in Jerusalem.

Historians call the period of these three kings—Saul, David, and Solomon—the united monarchy period. Archaeological work and extrabiblical sources support many biblical claims about the era. For example, there was a threat to the Hebrews from the Philistines, who were likely one of the many groups of migrants moving, often violently, around the eastern Mediterranean during the period of the Late Bronze Age Collapse. We have Egyptian and other records of these migrants, some specifically mentioning the Philistines by name. It seems likely that the founding of Israel was a response to this threat.

As for the existence of Saul and David, things are less clear. The Bible provides several conflicting accounts of how these two men became king. For example, Saul is made king when he is found hiding among some baggage, but also after leading troops in a dramatic rescue. Similar confusion surrounds David, though it seems clear he became an enemy of Saul at some point and was able to make himself king. Despite these contradictions, there is one piece of archaeological evidence for the existence of King David. The Tel Dan stele discovered in the Golan Heights in the 1990s makes reference to the "house of David," meaning the kingdom of David (Figure 4.39). However, no similar archaeological evidence has been unearthed for David's son Solomon. Indeed, evidence of Solomon's most famous achievement, the building of the first temple in Jerusalem, has yet to be discovered. However, we have strong archaeological evidence for some of his other public works projects, such as the three-thousand-year-old gates discovered at Gezer, Hazor, and Megiddo.

FIGURE 4.39 Evidence for the Existence of David? This stone fragment from the Tel Dan stele dates from the ninth century BCE and was discovered in the 1990s. It includes an inscription that reads "house of David," making it the only non-biblical source attesting to the existence of King David. (credit: modification of work "Aramaic Inscription on Basalt Monument, Dan, 9th Century BC" by Gary Todd/Flickr, CC0 1.0)

After the death of Solomon, the period of the united monarchy came to an end, and Israel split into two kingdoms, Israel in the north and Judah in the south. This inaugurated the period of the divided monarchy (Figure 4.40). Jerusalem remained the capital of Judah, while Samaria was the capital of Israel. The northern kingdom was the larger and wealthier of the two and exerted influence over and sometimes warred with Judah. The biblical account often puts the kings of the northern kingdom in a negative light, noting that they abused their subjects and incorporated elements of foreign religious traditions in their worship of Yahweh.

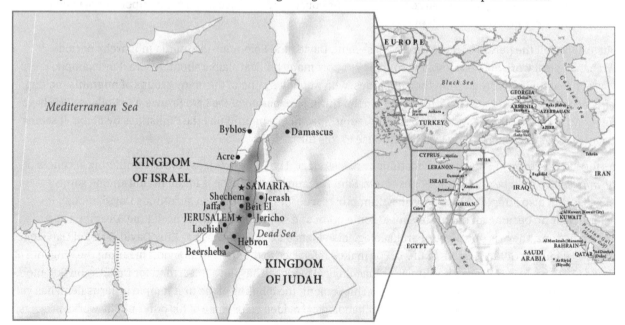

FIGURE 4.40 The Divided Monarchy. After the reign of Solomon, the united monarchy of the Israelites split into the kingdoms of Judah and Israel.(attribution: Copyright Rice University, OpenStax, under CC BY 4.0 license)

With the rise of the Neo-Assyrian Empire and its expansion into Canaan, Israel and Judah entered a new era under foreign domination within the Assyrian-controlled Near East. Anti-Assyrian sentiment in both kingdoms and the Neo-Assyrians' desire to control the eastern Mediterranean eventually led to multiple Assyrian attacks on Israel. The most devastating occurred in 722 BCE, when thousands of Israelites were deported to other parts of the empire, as was the Assyrians' custom.

Prophets in Judah interpreted the destruction of Israel as punishment for its having veered from the covenant with Yahweh. They called for religious reforms in Judah in order to avoid a similar fate. While Judah was incorporated into the Neo-Assyrian Empire, it avoided the destruction experienced by Israel. However, the defeat of Assyria by the Neo-Babylonians brought new challenges to Judah. Resistance to Babylon led to punishments and forced deportations in 597 BCE, and finally to the destruction of Jerusalem and its temple in 586 BCE.

The many Judeans deported to Babylon after the fall of Jerusalem were settled in Mesopotamia and expected to help repopulate areas that had been devastated by wars. Many assimilated into Babylonian culture and became largely indistinguishable from other Mesopotamians. Some, however, retained their Judean culture and religious beliefs. For these Judeans, the **Babylonian exile**, as it was called, was a time of cultural and religious revival. They edited various earlier Hebrew writings and combined them into a larger work, thus giving shape to the core of the Hebrew Bible. Finally, with the rise of the Persian Empire and its conquest of Babylonia, the Persian king Cyrus the Great permitted the unassimilated Judeans to return to Judah. They went in two major waves over the next few decades and began a process of reconstruction that eventually included the rebuilding of Yahweh's temple at Jerusalem.

The Culture of the Hebrews

The most salient feature of Hebrew culture during this period was its then-unusual monotheism. The Bible suggests this tradition began with Abraham, who was said to have entered into a covenant with Yahweh as far back as 2100 BCE. With the emergence of Moses in the Bible, Hebrew monotheism really began to take shape. As the Bible explains, during the exodus from Egypt, Moses was given the laws directly from Yahweh, including the command that only Yahweh be worshipped. This account suggests that pure monotheism was commonly practiced by the Hebrews from that time forward. Yet closer inspection of the biblical stories reveals a much more complicated and gradual process toward monotheism.

For example, the first of the commandments given to Moses by Yahweh demands that the Hebrews "have no other gods before me." This language implies that there are in fact other gods, but those gods are not to be worshipped. In other places in the Bible, God is referred to as plural or occasionally as part of an assembly of gods. This textual evidence likely preserves small elements of the earlier Canaanite polytheistic religious traditions. These include the veneration of El, the head of the pantheon and often associated with Yahweh, and of Yahweh's consort Asherah, the storm god Baal, the fertility goddess Astarte, and many others. Archaeologists' discoveries of temples and figurines representing these gods attest to the fact that they were worshipped in some form well into the eighth century BCE.

Many portions of the Bible describe how the Hebrews frequently fell away from Yahweh and back into their polytheistic traditions. This backsliding is usually condemned in the Bible and occasionally results in efforts by biblical heroes to restore Moses's covenant with God. King Hezekiah of Judah (727–697 BCE), for example, conducted a cleansing campaign against unauthorized worship around his kingdom. He removed local shrines, destroyed sacred monuments, and smashed cult objects. His son, King Manasseh, however, restored some of these cultic practices and shrines. Setting aside the bias of the Bible's writers, Manasseh may have been attempting to rescue long-standing religious traditions that had been under assault by his reform-minded father. However, as early as the mid-seventh century BCE, the religious reformers who promoted the centralized worship of Yahweh and obedience to the laws of Moses had clearly gained the upper hand. Their interpretation of Hebrew history and religion was then on the rise.

The backsliding theme of the Hebrew Bible was partly a way for its writers to account for the vestiges of Canaanite religious practices that did not fit neatly with their view of the Hebrews as having been monotheistic from the time of Moses. The abandonment of Yahweh accounted for the disasters that befell the Hebrews in Israel and Judah, especially the destruction of the temple and forced deportation to Babylon. Neo-Assyria and Neo-Babylonia were merely tools, the biblical writers and the prophets they record attest, used by Yahweh to compel the Hebrews to follow the correct path or face punishment. This version of Israelite history was kindled and strengthened during the Babylonian exile, when the core portion of the Hebrew Bible was being edited and assembled.

By the time the Judeans were allowed to return to Jerusalem and rebuild their temple, the basic framework of what we understand today as Judaism had emerged and been largely accepted. The Jews (or people from Judah) were expected to worship only Yahweh, live moral lives consistent with his dictates, and closely follow the laws of Moses. For example, they were prohibited from murdering, stealing, and committing adultery. They were barred from consuming specific foods such as pork, shellfish, insects, and meat that had been mixed with dairy. Food had to be properly prepared, which included ritual slaughter for animals. Jewish people were also prohibited from working on the seventh day of the week and were compelled to treat wives with respect and give to charity, among many other acts. And of course there were important rules about the worship of Yahweh, including loving him, fearing him, emulating him, and not profaning his name.

Since the Hebrews could trace their origins back to agricultural clans, a number of the laws of Moses dealt with agricultural issues, like prohibitions against eating ripe grains from the harvest before they are made into an offering. The festival of Sukkot, meaning "huts," was a harvest festival when Jewish people were expected to erect huts, possibly as a way to remember the time when they were primarily agriculturalists. However, as the Hebrews grew in number and began living in cities and adopting urban occupations, these agricultural traditions were relegated primarily to symbolic religious practice. In cities, Jewish people found economic opportunities as craftspeople, traders, and merchants. As Jerusalem grew in the centuries after the Babylonian exile, their religion became ever more adapted to urban life.

At the center of urban life in Jerusalem was the temple, completed around 515 BCE (Figure 4.41). It included courtyards as well as an enclosed sanctuary with altars and a special location kept in total darkness, referred to as the Holy of Holies, where Yahweh was present. In the temple, the priests organized various religious festivals and performed elaborate rituals, including special sacrifices of animals supplied by worshippers seeking the favor of Yahweh.

FIGURE 4.41 The Second Temple. This contemporary model of the Second Temple complex in Jerusalem shows the way it would have looked after extensive expansions were completed in the first century BCE. (credit: "Second Temple" by "Ariely"/Wikimedia Commons, CC BY 3.0)

Key Terms

Babylonian exile the deportation of Judeans to Babylon after the fall of Jerusalem
chattel slavery a form of slavery in which one person is owned by another as a piece of property
Exodus the mass migration of Hebrews out of Egypt under the leadership of Moses
Hebrew Bible the holy book that, according to Jewish tradition, tells the history of the Hebrew people
Iron Age the period beginning around 1200 BCE when iron became the preferred material for manufacturing
    tools and weapons
Ramesside kings the line of kings that ruled New Kingdom Egypt following the reign of Ramses I
satrapy one of twenty governing districts in Persia administered by royal governors called *satraps*, who
    answered directly to the king
vassal state a state or kingdom that is nominally independent in the running of its internal affairs but must
    submit to the demands of a dominating empire and usually provide tribute to it
Zoroastrianism the religion of the ancient Persians, named for its founder Zarathustra, pronounced *Zoroaster*
    in Greek

Section Summary

4.1 From Old Babylon to the Medes

After the challenges to Mesopotamian civilization created by the invasions of the Amorites and Elamites, a succession of new empires emerged. In the 1700s BCE, King Hammurabi transformed Babylon from a minor city-state to the center of a vast empire. At the start of the 1500s BCE, the Hittites exploded out of Anatolia, sacking Babylon and later competing with Egypt for supremacy in the eastern Mediterranean. During the Iron Age that followed, the Near East underwent an even deeper transformation as the Neo-Assyrians created the first empire to control both Mesopotamia and Egypt. Then, at the end of the seventh century BCE, a resurgent Babylonia allied with the Median Empire to destroy the Neo-Assyrian Empire and carve up the spoils.

Each empire controlled large territories that were home to diverse peoples, religions, and daily practices, often adopted from older civilizations and shaped to suit their own needs and interests.

4.2 Egypt's New Kingdom

During the Second Intermediate Period, Egyptian influence dwindled to only the region around Thebes. Semitic-speaking immigrants from Canaan called the Hyksos flowed into the Nile delta and eventually established control there, bringing improved bronze-making technology, the composite bow, and the horse-drawn, lighter-weight chariot.

The first kings of the Egyptian New Kingdom drove out the Hyksos and extended their own influence into Nubia. Pharaohs like Thutmose III led their armies into Canaan and Syria to halt rivals like the Hittite kingdom and Mitanni. The New Kingdom also saw the rise of the cult of Amun-Re in Thebes and Akhenaten's revolutionary transformations. Akhenaten and Ramesses II built new cities as testaments to their greatness, and many others like Hatshepsut commissioned elaborate tombs, temples, and monuments. These powerful pharaohs extended their influence into Nubia, Canaan, and Syria through a number of military campaigns that also allowed Egypt to control vital trade routes to Mesopotamia. After centuries of greatness, however, the New Kingdom's power declined, hastened by invasions, the loss of territory, and deteriorating foreign influence, until finally the kingdom fell.

4.3 The Persian Empire

According to Herodotus, Cyrus the Great led the Persians to overthrow the Median dynasty and then by 539 BCE to defeat the Neo-Babylonians. Cyrus's successor Cambyses II extended Persia's control over Egypt and assembled a vast empire that stretched from the edges of India to the Nile River. When Darius I rose to power, he reorganized the empire into twenty districts called satrapies, each with its own governor or satrap, and oversaw a number of public works projects such as elaborate palaces and *qanats* for carrying fresh water over many kilometers.

The kings of Persia were honored as the earthly representatives of the Persian god Ahura Mazda and commanded a large army of subject peoples from around the empire. The religion of the Persians was Zoroastrianism, which saw the world as the field of competition between the forces of good and evil and predicted a final judgment after evil had been conquered. But the empire included numerous ethnicities and followers of many religions, including the Judeans with their own unique monotheistic religious tradition.

4.4 The Hebrews

The history of the Hebrew people as recorded in the Hebrew Bible tracks their emergence in Canaan, their oppression in and exodus from Egypt, their construction of a united monarchy, and their many conflicts among themselves and with empires like Neo-Assyria and Neo-Babylonia. But the archaeological record and various portions of the Bible cast some doubt on a number of aspects of this general story. For example, archaeology does not support the occurrence of Joshua's conquest of Canaan after the Exodus, though at least some of King Solomon's building projects have been discovered in sites like Gezer, Hazor, and Megiddo. And the stories of Hebrews migrating to Egypt may preserve much older traditions related to the arrival of the Hyksos there.

The Bible also describes the monotheistic worship of Yahweh, the definitive characteristic of the Hebrews. But contrary to what the Bible suggests, this religious practice did not arise fully formed. Rather, it developed over centuries and under unique circumstances and geopolitical pressures. By the time the Persian Empire extended its domination across the Near East, the religion of Judaism as we know it today was starting to take shape. It demanded absolute obedience to Yahweh and his many laws, including specific dietary restrictions. And the worship of Yahweh was centralized in the temple at Jerusalem.

Assessments

Review Questions

1. What Near Eastern empire was centered in Anatolia?
   a. Old Babylonian Empire
   b. Neo-Babylonian Empire
   c. Hittite Empire
   d. Neo-Assyrian Empire

2. What was the purpose of the Neo-Assyrian practice now called "calculated frightfulness"?
   a. to settle depopulated lands
   b. to demonstrate the cost of rebellion
   c. to appease the gods
   d. to acquire tin

3. What were the four primary social classes in Neo-Assyrian society?
   a. nobles, professionals, peasants, the enslaved
   b. nobles, farmers, bankers, peasants
   c. kings, scribes, landowners, the enslaved
   d. kings, farmers, priests, the enslaved

4. What did the gift-giving ceremonies carried out between empires by their ambassadors demonstrate?
   a. good will
   b. hostile intentions
   c. military might
   d. divine support

5. What method did ancient city-states and empires use to acquire territory through peaceful means?
   a. tribute
   b. intermarriage
   c. espionage
   d. war

6. Where did the Hyksos people come from?
   a. Canaan
   b. Nubia
   c. Assyria
   d. Babylonia

7. What Egyptian pharaoh completed the task of driving the Hyksos from the Nile delta?
   a. Seqenenre Tao II
   b. Kamose
   c. Hatshepsut
   d. Ahmose

8. To what now-mysterious place did Queen Hatshepsut send an expedition to gather exotic plants, animals, precious metals, and spices?
   a. Punt
   b. Anatolia
   c. Libya
   d. Canaan

9. Whom did Akhenaten want the people of Egypt to worship exclusively?
   a. Aton
   b. Re
   c. Amun
   d. the pharaoh

10. What Persian king conquered the Neo-Babylonians?
    a. Cyrus II
    b. Cambyses II
    c. Darius I
    d. Bardiya

11. According to Zoroastrianism, what happens to people when they die?
    a. They go to heaven.
    b. They sleep until final judgment.
    c. They become gods.
    d. They are reborn as animals.

12. After Darius I's reorganization, who controlled the individual governing regions of the empire?
    a. priests
    b. Judeans
    c. generals
    d. satraps

13. What happened to the Judeans when they were attacked by the Neo-Babylonians in the early sixth century

BCE?

    a. They were deported to Babylon.

    b. They fled to Egypt.

    c. They became Phoenicians.

    d. They became allies of Persia.

14. According to the Hebrew Bible, where did Abraham originally come from?

    a. Canaan

    b. Egypt

    c. Mesopotamia

    d. Anatolia

15. Which of the following is consistent with the laws God gave to Moses?

    a. eating pork

    b. eating shrimp

    c. worshipping only Yahweh

    d. worshipping only Ahura Mazda

Check Your Understanding Questions

1. Use the map provided to identify the following empires at their height: Hammurabi's Empire, the Hittite Empire, the Neo-Assyrian Empire. Match A, B, and C to the respective empire.

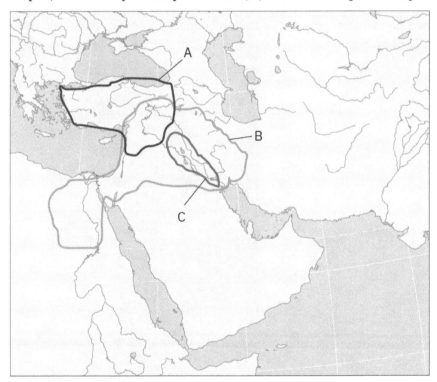

2. What led to the fall of the Neo-Assyrian Empire in the late seventh century BCE?

3. What methods did Near Eastern kingdoms, city-states, and empires use to gather intelligence about their neighbors, rivals, and vassals?

4. What were the consequences of the Hyksos migrations?

5. How did Egypt maintain its influence in Canaan during the New Kingdom?

6. Describe the scale of the Persian Empire during the reign of Darius I.

7. What are some similarities between Christianity and Zoroastrianism?

8. What evidence supports the existence of the united monarchy of Israel?

9. How did the Babylonian exile affect the faith of the Judeans?

Application and Reflection Questions

1. What role did war play in the expansion and maintenance of the major Near Eastern empires? How is this strategy similar to or different from the way countries create and maintain power today?

2. How was the relationship between the people of the ancient Near East and their gods similar to or different from religious practices today?

3. Why might someone want to become an ambassador or a spy in the ancient Near East?

4. What made the New Kingdom pharaohs successful?

5. Why were some New Kingdom pharaohs removed from the historical record, and by whom?

6. If you were the king of a vassal state in the Persian Empire, would you have considered rebellion? Why or why not?

7. What do you think best explains why the Persian Empire was successful?

8. What role do you think religious texts should play in the study of history, and why?

9. The narrative of the Hebrew Bible includes many stories about migration. Why do you think migration was an important theme for the Hebrews?

FIGURE 5.1 Harappa: A Doorway to Trade. This intricately painted cooking vessel is from the ancient city of Harappa, in today's Pakistan near the Ravi River. Harappan ways left an indelible mark on Indian culture. Featuring standardized weights and measures, uniform bricks, and even indoor plumbing, Harappa and the city of Mohenjo-Daro were doorways to trade, to waves of human migration, and to agriculture flowing from Egypt and Mesopotamia to the rest of Asia. (credit: modification of work "Harappa Vessel - 1-8harappanjar" by Prof Grossetti/Flickr, Public Domain)

CHAPTER OUTLINE

5.1 Ancient China
5.2 The Steppes
5.3 Korea, Japan, and Southeast Asia
5.4 Vedic India to the Fall of the Maurya Empire

INTRODUCTION Ancient Asia was dominated by two civilizational poles, one centered in today's India and the other to the east, across the Asian landmass in China. Within both these zones developed impressive cities, kingdoms, and even empires whose commercial might, religion, and technology shaped the lives of Asians for thousands of years (Figure 5.1). Other Asians—traveling peoples of the steppes—acted as conduits of trade and exchange as they brought goods and ideas from one end of the continent to the other.

The same was true far to the east and the south. There, groups that became the Koreans and Japanese, as well as others who arrived in Southeast Asia via migration and trade, also carved out civilizations, smaller societies that influenced their larger neighbors in China and India. At this time, Asia was a region woven together by networks of traveling monks, nomadic peoples, oceanic and overland trade, and shared writing systems.

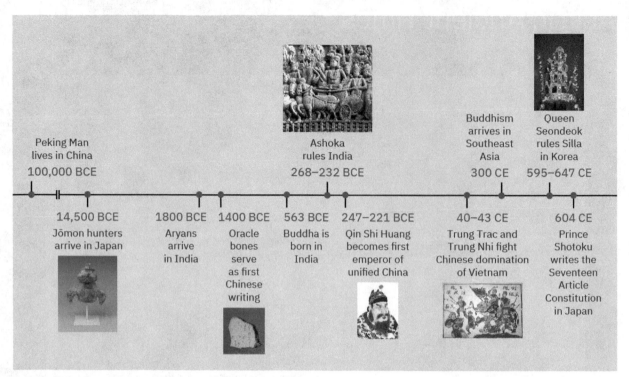

FIGURE 5.2 Timeline: Asia in Ancient Times. (credit "14,500 BCE": modification of work "Dogū (Clay Figurine)" by The Harry G. C. Packard Collection of Asian Art, Gift of Harry G. C. Packard, and Purchase, Fletcher, Rogers, Harris Brisbane Dick, and Louis V. Bell Funds, Joseph Pulitzer Bequest, and The Annenberg Fund Inc. Gift, 1975/ Metropolitan Museum of Art, Public Domain; credit "1400 BCE": modification of work "Shang Ox Bone Oracle Bone" by Gary Todd/Flickr, Public Domain; credit "268–232 BCE": modification of work "King Asoka visits Ramagrama" by Anandajoti Bhikkhu/Flickr, CC BY 2.0; credit "247–221 BCE": modification of work "A portrait painting of Qin Shi Huangdi, first emperor of the Qin dynasty" by Richard R. Wertz/18th century album of portraits of 86 emperors of China, with Chinese historical notes, British Library/Wikimedia Commons, Public Domain; credit "40-43 CE": modification of work "Hai ba trung Dong Ho painting" by "LuckyBirdie"/Wikimedia Commons, Public Domain; credit "595–647 CE": modification of work "Gold Crown of Silla Kingsom" by Gary Todd/Flickr, Public Domain)

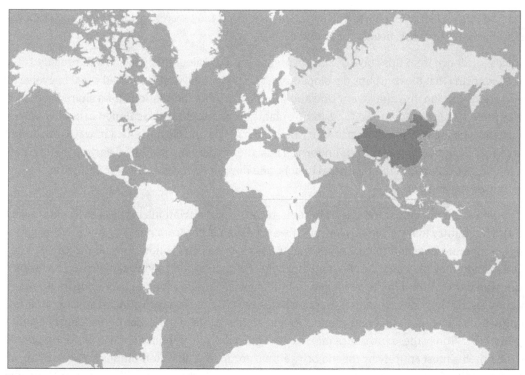

FIGURE 5.3 Locator Map: Asia in Ancient Times. (credit: modification of work "World map blank shorelines" by Maciej Jaros/Wikimedia Commons, Public Domain)

5.1 Ancient China

LEARNING OBJECTIVES

By the end of this section, you will be able to:
- Discuss the early dynasties of ancient China
- Analyze the impact of the Warring States Period on ancient Chinese politics and culture
- Explain the connections between ancient Chinese philosophy and its political and social context

Ancient China was not the first area in Asia to practice agriculture and develop cities. But it was home to some of the world's earliest political dynasties, and it produced written scripts, influential schools of thought and religion, and innovations in architecture and metallurgy, such as the manufacture of bronze and iron agricultural implements, weapons, chariots, and jewelry. A climate of constant regional warfare between small Chinese states imparted to kings and philosophers alike a sense of urgency to build institutions and systems that would bring stability to their realms. Against this background, China's first empire, the Qin, presided over the creation of some of the ancient world's greatest historical treasures, including the Terracotta Army and an early form of the Great Wall.

Prehistoric China

Recent studies of Paleolithic and Neolithic China suggest it was home to several distinct cultural complexes that developed independently of one another and exhibited notable regional variations in agriculture, social organization, language, and religion.

Human beings set foot on the Chinese subcontinent more than a million years ago. Evidence indicates the presence there of an archaic member of the human lineage known as *Homo erectus*, a term meaning "upright man." One example is the well-known **Peking Man**, a subspecies of *Homo erectus* identified by fossil remains found in northern China in 1929. The species *Homo sapiens* (meaning "wise man" and including all modern humans) appeared later, around 100,000 years ago. These communities of hunter-gatherers followed the mammoth, elk, and moose on which they subsisted into northern China. Later they learned to fish along

China's many rivers and long coastlines and supplemented their food stores by foraging from a rich variety of plants, including many grasses, beans, yams, and roots.

Archaeological evidence from this stage of China's prehistory, the Paleolithic period from roughly 100,000 to 10,000 BCE, confirms that these groups developed symbolic language, which enabled them to evolve ideas about abstractions like kinship and an afterlife and thus produce the foundations for a shared culture and society. Their tools, such as those used for grinding plants, were simple and fashioned primarily of stone, but also of bone and wood. Early humans arrived in China from Africa and western Asia in waves separated by hundreds of years, but they were far from uniform. Thus, they eventually produced early societies that spoke a variety of languages, differed in their spiritual beliefs, and developed the capacity for agriculture independently of one another.

China's diverse geography, climate, and terrain reinforced regional variations in these early cultures as well (Figure 5.4). The country today stretches for roughly a thousand miles from north to south and east to west, occupying a temperate zone dominated by two major river systems, the Yellow and the Yangtze. Mountains, deserts, grasslands, high plateaus, jungles, and a variety of climates exist, such as the frozen environs surrounding the city of Harbin in the north and the subtropical climate around Hong Kong in the south. Most of the early cultures and later dynasties that produced Chinese civilization lay in a much smaller area, within a series of provinces along the Yellow and Yangtze Rivers, ringed by the outer areas of Manchuria, Mongolia, Xinjiang, and Tibet. Today these provinces make up the most densely populated areas of the People's Republic of China, inhabited almost entirely by the majority ethnic group in China, Han Chinese. The outlying areas have been the traditional homelands of a great many religious and ethnic minorities, such as Mongolians, Tibetans, Uyghurs, and Manchu, who did not become incorporated into the first dynasties of ancient China. Early inhabitants of China found that each region offered advantages and challenges to meeting the necessities of daily life: food, shelter, and security.

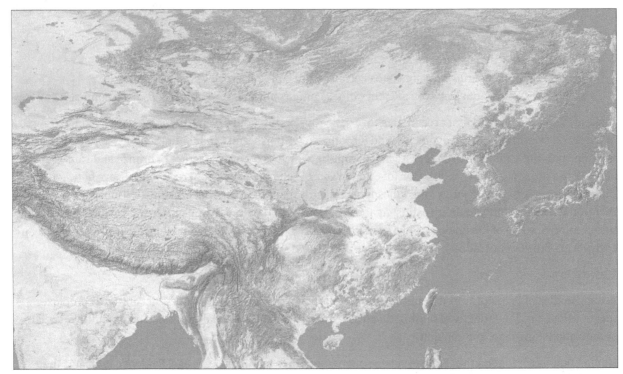

FIGURE 5.4 Topography of Ancient China. This map shows the varied topography of ancient China, which included fertile plains, river valleys, numerous mountain ranges, deserts, and a long running coastline on the eastern edge. (credit: "China topography" by Tom Patterson, US National Park Service Natural Earth/Wikimedia Commons, Public Domain)

More than twenty sites that produced unique Neolithic cultures have been found in China. The earliest such culture was the Nanzhuangtou (8500 to 7700 BCE) in Hebei, a province in the northeast, and the last known was the Yueshi culture (1900 to 1500 BCE) found in Shandong, an eastern coastal province. All were capable of farming, domesticating animals, and manufacturing textiles and ceramics.

China's Neolithic cultures are notable for their independent growth and regional diversity, and for the differences between those in the north and those in the south. For example, in the southeastern part of the country, near Shanghai, a site dated to around 8000 BCE was home to people who cultivated rice, used boats, constructed standing homes, and made pottery with geometric designs. Evidence suggests their language was more closely related to those of the peoples living in Southeast Asia today, so calling them "Chinese" is open to debate. To the north, the colder climate forced early communities in today's Hebei province to rely on another grain, millet, for their primary foodstuff. These farmers used stone tools such as sickles and made simple jars to store their grain. Wooden spears and hoes were more common in the south than stone tools, and while both north and south domesticated dogs and pigs, in the north grazing animals such as sheep were tamed, while in the south farmers harnessed the power of water buffalo.

There were distinctive Neolithic cultures in the east and west of China. From about 4100 to 2600 BCE, the Dawenkou culture arose near Shandong in the east, characterized by the manufacture of exquisite works of pottery and the use of turquoise, ivory, and jade. The burial practices of the Dawenkou became more elaborate over time, eventually leading to the use of wooden coffins and the creation of ledges of earth to surround the graves. Later eastern cultures lavished treasures on the deceased, burying them with necklaces and beads, showing an increasing sophistication in the decorative arts.

To the west lay the Yangshao culture, dating to 5000 BCE, whose people farmed millet and dug homes in the earth to protect themselves from a cool climate. In Yangshao, burying the dead was a simpler process, but artists decorated pottery with painted designs and intricate geometric patterns. To the east there are few examples of painted bowls, jars, or cups. Instead, eastern cultures devoted their creative efforts to the slow, painstaking process of shaping jade. The Hongshan culture in Liaoning province and the Liangzhu complex in Jiangsu fashioned beautiful jade talismans, ornaments, and treasures for spiritual ceremonies. The great distance between these two cultures—with Hongshan far in the northeast near today's border with North Korea and the Liangzhu located around the Yangtze River delta in the southeast—shows the breadth of jade's influence along China's eastern seaboard. In the west, jade remained a much rarer object.

Later networks of exchange connected these regional cultures, which increasingly borrowed from each other, accelerating change, innovation, and collision. From roughly 3000 to 2000 BCE, China's Neolithic cultures created and shared new implements for cooking and artistic styles such as geometric patterns on ceramics. With contact, however, came growing conflict as well, suggested in the archaeological record by the emergence of metalworking and cities defended by walls of rammed earth. The need to coordinate defense and construct such ramparts likely required a political evolution within these cultures, giving rise to an elite military class led by chiefs. Thereafter, military elites were shrouded in spiritual rituals revolving around human sacrifice, possibly of captives of war, who were entombed beneath buildings in sites found in northern China. Increasing exchange between Neolithic cultures and the prominence of war may also have led to greater social differentiation. Burial sites for elites show evidence of increasingly elaborate ceremonies to please the gods or ancestors and to honor the deceased and denote their status.

Women were often buried with the same quantity of items and laid in the same position as their male counterparts. Archaeological remains such as graves, figurines, tools, and other materials suggest that many Neolithic Chinese communities were matrilineal societies, in which lines of kinship were traced through the mother's family. While weaving textiles became an important occupation for many women, the division of labor was far less rigid in this period. Carvings depicting goddesses, symbols of fertility, and women's genitalia are prevalent in many of the cultures and seem to suggest women were on a par with men in the Neolithic era, especially when compared with later periods in Chinese history.

Early Dynastic China

The Yellow River had an enormous impact on the development of Chinese civilization. It stretches for more than 3,395 miles, beginning in the mountains of western China and emptying into the Bohai Sea from Shandong province. (Only the Yangtze River to the south is longer.) Critical to the development of farming and human settlement along the Yellow River was the soil, which is loess—a sediment that is highly fertile, but easily moved by winds roaming the plain and driven along as silt by the power of the river. This portability of the soil and the human-built dikes along the river have caused it to constantly evolve and change over the centuries, leaving the surrounding areas prone to regular flooding and subjecting farmers to recurring cycles of bountiful harvests and natural disasters. Rainfall around the Yellow River is limited to around twenty inches annually, meaning that the river's floods have usually been paired with periodic droughts.

Near the Yellow River, the site of Erlitou in Henan province reveals a culture defined by the building of palaces, the creation of bronze vessels for rituals, and the practice of forms of ancestor worship. Sites such as these have led to debate about whether they prove the existence of the Xia dynasty, a fabled kingdom said to have been founded by one of China's mythological heroes, the Great Yu. No site has yet been found with documents written by the Xia. Instead, all references to it come from records written many centuries after the possible mythical kingdom ceased to exist.

The first Chinese dynasty for which we have solid evidence is the Shang. It created a complex, socially stratified Bronze Age civilization whose signature achievement was the creation of a written script. The Shang were long thought to be a mythological dynasty like the Xia until scholars in the late nineteenth century discovered old turtle shells inscribed with Chinese characters in a medicine shop. Eventually, these shells and other "oracle bones," once used in the art of divination, were found to be written records from China's first dynasty (Figure 5.5).

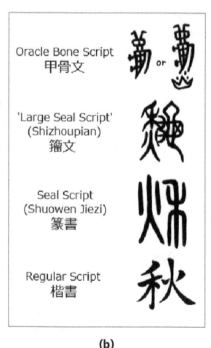

(a)   (b)

FIGURE 5.5 Bronze Age Script. (a) This ancient oracle bone is carved with early variations of Chinese characters. (b) Oracle bone script went through a number of stages to evolve into the contemporary form of script we see today, as evidenced by the early iterations of the characters for the word "autumn," shown here. (credit a: modification of work "Shang Ox Bone Oracle Bone" by Gary Todd/Flickr, Public Domain; credit b: modification of work "Comparison of Chinese characters for autumn" by "Pat457"/Wikimedia Commons, CC0 1.0)

Shang kings exerted their authority through rituals of ancestor worship drawn from the Erlitou culture and adapted to the art of bone divination. First carving written characters onto shells and animal bones and then applying heat to crack and shatter them, they posed questions to spirits and divined from the bones the spirits' predictions regarding impending harvests, military campaigns, or the arrival of an heir. From there, the Shang developed a logographic script whose characters visually represented words and ideas, combining symbols to make new concepts and sounds as needed. These characters served in a number of tasks such as keeping records, making calendars and organizing time, and preserving knowledge and communicating it from generation to generation.

The earliest forms of Chinese writing were likely forged on fragile materials such as bamboo or even silk and have not survived. But the Shang's passing on to future dynasties a logographic script, rather than a phonographic alphabet, meant that for centuries literacy was the preserve of elites. Reading required memorizing hundreds and eventually thousands of symbols and their meanings, rather than learning the sounds of a far fewer number of letters as is the case with an alphabet. Chinese ideas, values, and spiritual beliefs stored in this logographic script long outlived the Shang, becoming a key element of continuity from one dynasty to the next.

Through their invention of writing, the Shang were also able to command enormous resources for two centuries. They developed the organizational capacity to mine metal ores and transport them to foundries to make bronze cups, goblets, and cauldrons that grew to weigh hundreds of pounds. Shang artisans began weaving silk into cloth, and the city walls around an early capital in Zhengzhou were erected by ten thousand workers moving earth into bulwarks that stood thirty feet high and sixty feet wide.

But the Shang became China's first dynasty largely because of their military prowess, expanding their power through conquest, unlike the earlier and more trade-oriented cultures. Through warfare and the construction of a network of walled towns, the Shang built one of the world's first large territorial states controlled by a noble warrior class. This area included territory in Henan, Anhui, Shandong, Hebei, and Shanxi provinces. The Shang used bronze spears, bows, and later horse-drawn chariots to make raids against neighboring cultures, distributing the prizes to vassals and making enemies into allies for a share of the plunder. The prizes included captives of war, enslaved by the Shang warrior elite or sacrificed. An aristocratic and militaristic culture, the Shang also organized royal hunts for game such as deer, bear, and even tigers and elephants to hone their skills.

🔗 LINK TO LEARNING

Visit this website and read a detailed summary of the importance to ancient Chinese cultures of ritual killing (https://openstax.org/l/77RitualKill) to learn more about and see visual examples of the Shang's ritualistic vessels, art of divination, and burial customs.

The oracle bones suggest that religion and ritual were the backbone of Shang society. The kings were not just military leaders but high priests who worshipped their ancestors and the supreme deity known as Di. Shang queens and princesses were also active in politics and warfare, with a few notable women such as the general Fu Hao leading large armies onto the battlefield. Aristocratic women also regularly served as priests in the royal ancestral cult. Like many other ancient societies, the Shang dynasty exhibited a theocratic dimension, with the kings claiming the exclusive right to act as intermediaries between their subjects and the spirit world.

To stage this royal role, the Shang built palaces, temples, and altars for worship in their capital cities, served by artisans making a host of goods. They developed enormous tombs tunneled beneath the earth for royals and nobility, signifying their capacity to organize labor and resources on a vast scale. Fu Hao's tomb, for example, was small by comparison to many others for Shang royals, but it was dug twenty-five feet deep into the earth and was large enough to hold sixteen human sacrifices and hundreds of bronze weapons, mirrors, bells, and other items fashioned from bone, jade, ivory, and stone. A comparison of early Shang tombs in Zhengzhou with those of a later period discovered in Anyang suggests that human sacrifices became ever more spiritually significant, and also more extreme. Later kings were found buried not with a few victims but with hundreds of servants and prisoners of war, as well as animals such as dogs and horses. By spilling human blood, Shang royalty hoped to appease Di and their ancestors to ward off problems such as famine. But the scale of these rituals ballooned, with one record indicating that King Wu Ding went so far as to sacrifice more than nine thousand victims in one ritual bloodletting.

Under the sway of the Shang, the disparate Neolithic cultures of northern China grew more uniform, while even groups beyond the Shang's control in the Yangtze River valley and the west were influenced by their artistic styles and motifs. Yet over the course of their reign, the Shang's reliance on constant warfare and a religion centered on human sacrifices bred discontent and may have fueled the perception of their kings as corrupt and sadistic. It might even have precipitated revolt against the Shang rulers and the culture's eventual demise.

The Zhou Dynasty

The Zhou dynasty, which supplanted the Shang dynasty in 1045 BCE, borrowed extensively from its predecessors. But the Zhou people were originally independent of the Shang, with their homeland lying in today's Shaanxi province in north-central China, in a large fertile basin surrounded by mountains just beyond the core Shang territory that lay to the east. Once settled there, Zhou nobility became vassals of the Shang kings, equipped to defend them and campaign against their hated rivals the Qiang, a proto-Tibetan tribe.

The Zhou combined the practices of farming learned from the Shang with livestock raising learned from nomadic groups living outside the Chinese core. From the Shang, the Zhou also acquired the arts of bronze-making and divination before later developing their own ritual vessels and spiritual practices. Armed by the Shang with chariots, bows, and bronze armor, the Zhou eventually overthrew the Shang kings and founded a new dynastic ruling house. Inheriting the Shang logographic script, the Zhou dynasty became the first to transmit texts such as the *Book of Documents*, records of dozens of speeches and announcements attributed to historical leaders, from the ancient world directly to future generations.

But for all that the Zhou inherited from the Shang, their dynasty also introduced influential changes to ancient China. Likely in order to distance themselves from the Shang, the Zhou allowed the scale of human sacrifices in burials to decline and phased out the use of divination with oracle bones. Above the deity Di, they introduced the concept of a higher power referred to as heaven, and they situated themselves as mediators by performing rituals designed to show that the cosmos legitimated their right to rule (Table 5.1).

Chinese Dynasty	Approximate Duration
Shang dynasty	1600–1050 BCE
Zhou (*pronounced "Jeo"*) dynasty • Western Zhou dynasty (c. 1046–771 BCE) • Eastern Zhou dynasty (c. 771–256 BCE)	1046–256 BCE
Qin (*pronounced "chin"*) dynasty	221–206 BCE

TABLE 5.1 China's Dynasties This table marks the duration of China's dynasties, from the start of the Shang dynasty to the fall of the last, the Qing, in 1912. The physical borders of Chinese civilization fluctuated from one dynasty to the next. (http://afe.easia.columbia.edu/timelines/china_timeline.htm#timeline-keyevents)

Chinese Dynasty	Approximate Duration
Han dynasty • Western/Former Han dynasty (206–9 CE) • Eastern/Later Han dynasty (25–220 CE)	206 BCE–220 CE
Six Dynasties Period • Three Kingdoms dynasty (220–265 CE) • Jin dynasty (265–420 CE) • Period of the Northern and Southern dynasties (386–589 CE)	220–589 CE
Sui (*pronounced "sway"*) dynasty	581–618 CE
Tang dynasty	618–906 CE
Five Dynasties Period	907–960 CE
Song dynasty • Northern Song dynasty (960–1127) • Southern Song dynasty (1127–1279)	960–1279
Yuan dynasty	1279–1368
Ming dynasty	1368–1644
Qing dynasty	1644–1912

TABLE 5.1 China's Dynasties This table marks the duration of China's dynasties, from the start of the Shang dynasty to the fall of the last, the Qing, in 1912. The physical borders of Chinese civilization fluctuated from one dynasty to the next. (http://afe.easia.columbia.edu/timelines/china_timeline.htm#timeline-keyevents)

More than just spiritual changes, these policy shifts helped the Zhou spread a political ideology that fostered a shared cultural identity that was formative to Chinese civilization. According to the Zhou, the Shang rulers over time had grown despotic, ruining the lives of their subjects and squandering the bountiful resources of China. Around 1046 BCE, the Zhou, having grown tired of their abuses, rose up against the Shang and, led by King Wu, defeated them in battle.

The Zhou victory and Shang defeat were recorded in various Chinese classical texts as proof that the heavens had revoked the Shang's right to rule and conferred it upon the new Zhou dynasty. This "**Mandate of Heaven**" shaped Chinese ideology and understanding of dynastic cycles for centuries to come (Figure 5.6). It justified the overthrow of bad governments and corrupt or inept rulers and reinforced a common conviction that in order to govern, a ruling house must demonstrate morality and order to retain heaven's favor. The concept also pressured dynastic rulers to deserve the mandate by exhibiting moral leadership and proving their legitimacy through support for agriculture, the arts, and the welfare of the common people. Thereafter, natural disasters such as flood or famine and social upheaval in the form of rebellions or poverty were read as signs that a dynasty was in peril of having its mandate to rule rescinded.

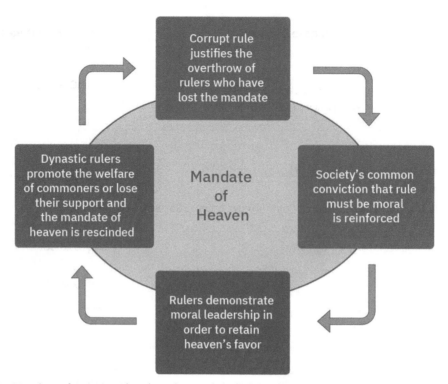

FIGURE 5.6 The Mandate of Heaven. The Zhou dynasty's belief that imperial rule must be sanctioned by a mandate from the gods shaped China's history and culture for centuries to follow. (attribution: Copyright Rice University, OpenStax, under CC BY 4.0 license)

The Mandate of Heaven also ensured continuity between dynasties because it became an element of a core ideology passed from one ruling house to the next, even as non-Chinese groups such as Mongols and Jurchen later invoked it as conquerors. Thus, the mandate created a basis for increasing political unity of the Chinese under a supreme sovereign, while also promoting dissent and latent revolution against unpopular rulers. From this ideology sprang new terms for subjects, identified as denizens of Zhongguo (China), a name formed from the terms for *central* and *state*, or as Huaxia (Chinese) in the Zhou dynasty, to express their membership in a shared culture defined by farming, writing, and metalworking and inherited from mythical figures and common ancestors.

To consolidate their political control, the early Zhou rulers led military campaigns to extend their territory east over the Yellow River and relied on a complex system of decentralized rule. Leniency was shown to the Shang, with a son of the dynasty left to rule his own city and preside over rituals to honor his ancestors. Other Shang nobles were uprooted and moved to new cities to keep them under the watch of the Zhou, whose relatives and trusted advisors governed walled garrisons and cities on the frontier to guard against rising threats. In other areas, the Zhou cooperated with largely autonomous leaders, granting aristocratic titles in return for tribute and military service from local chiefs and nobility. To cement these ties, the Zhou brokered marriages between the royal line and the families of local lords, who within their own domains performed the same spiritual and administrative functions as the ruling family. Like the Zhou, local lords were served by ministers, scribes, court attendants, and warriors, and they enjoyed the fruits of the efforts of ordinary laborers and farmers who lived on their estates.

The Zhou proved more durable than the Shang but, especially in later centuries, their power was diffused among many smaller, competing kingdoms only nominally under their control. The Zhou's decentralized feudal system, in which land and power was granted by the king to local leaders in return for special privileges, gradually weakened as those regional lords ignored the commands of kings, instead amassing armies and searching for alliances and technological advantages over their neighbors.

As a result, scholars typically divide the Zhou dynasty into several periods. The Western Zhou (c. 1046–771

BCE) refers to the first half of the dynasty's rule, from its founding to the sack of its capital in Haojing by nomadic armies in 771 BCE. Afterwards the Zhou reestablished their capital in the east, in Luoyang, inaugurating the period called the Eastern Zhou (771–256 BCE). The Eastern Zhou dynasty itself is often divided into two halves—the Spring and Autumn (771–476 BCE) and the Warring States (475–256 BCE) periods. The first half of the Eastern Zhou dynasty derives its name from the *Spring and Autumn Annals*. That chronicle, from about the fifth century BCE, documents the gradual erosion of the Zhou kings' power as outlying territories such as Chu, Qin, and Yan became increasingly autonomous. Not surprisingly, then, the Warring States era was characterized by open warfare between these regional powers to enlarge their territories, absorb neighboring kingdoms, and replace the Zhou as the new sovereigns of ancient China.

Bridging the two eras of the Spring and Autumn and the Warring States was a period defined by a flourishing of literature and philosophy known as the Hundred Schools of Thought (770–221 BCE). Inspired by political turmoil and rivalries between various Chinese states, those who wished to retain power were drawn to the study of the military arts, diplomacy, and political intrigue. Those who lamented the lack of order and waning loyalty to authority and tradition turned to the study of morality and ethics. In a political climate of competition and reform, new schools of thought informed a swelling class of capable administrators and military strategists contesting for the patronage of rulers. Philosophers such as Mozi and Sunzi, author of *The Art of War*, created their own rival traditions and contributed to courtly debates on morality, war, government, technology, and law.

In this marketplace of ideas, Chinese civilization as a whole rapidly grew more sophisticated. At the same time, rulers sought to expand their revenues, increase the size of their populations, implement new techniques for farming such as draining marshes, and create new forms of currency such as bolts of silk. This era also fostered dynamic new forms of art as the Zhou court became home to musicians skilled with chimes, drums, lutes, flutes, and bells. States such as Chu and Zheng became famous for their artists and styles of dance, while popular hymns were later translated into poems and recorded in the *Book of Songs*. These intellectual traditions and cultural forms, though varied, served as the foundational core for Chinese politics, education, and art in the ancient world.

Foremost among the new schools of thought was **Confucianism**, a philosophical system that shaped morality, governance, and social relations in China before spreading to Korea, Vietnam, and Japan in later centuries. Its founding philosopher, known as Kong Fuzi, or Confucius, was probably born about 551 BCE and lived in relative obscurity as a teacher in the small state of Lu. Later his descendants and disciples made his teachings on the family, society, and politics known in ancient China via *The Analects*, a collection of brief statements attributed to him and recorded long after his death. Later scholars influenced by Confucius, such as Mengzi, went on to win renown for their teachings, attracting throngs of new students while gaining influential positions as advisers in the service of rulers.

A central tenet of Confucianism is the importance of exemplifying virtuous leadership by living a moral life, studiously observing rituals, and being tirelessly devoted to the duties owed to the leader's subjects. Confucian texts such as the *Book of Documents* promoted habits like literacy, critical thinking, the search for universal truth, humility, respect for ancestors and elders, and the valuing of merit over aristocratic privilege. Confucius also considered family relationships to be central to an orderly society. Specifically, he delineated five cordial relationships—between king and subjects, father and son, husband and wife, elder brother and younger siblings, and friends. Each relationship consisted of an authority figure who required obedience and honor from the other person or persons, except for friends who were to honor one another. In return, the person in authority was supposed to embody *ren*, an attitude of generosity and empathy for those beneath him. So long as everyone behaved as they should, good order would flourish.

Later Confucian teachers such as Xun Kuang (also known as Xunzi), witnessing the violence of the Warring States period, argued that humanity's base impulses necessitated rigorous self-cultivation and discipline. Among devout Confucians, such ideas spawned a constant search for internal self-improvement and concern for the well-being of others and society as a whole. During this period, Zhou kings presided over rites to honor royal ancestors, but they also made greater use of written works to magnify their prestige and power. *Yijing*, or *The Book of Changes*, presented a new system of divination later included as a seminal text in the Confucian canon.

IN THEIR OWN WORDS

The Analects of Confucius

Over many decades following Confucius's death, his students and followers collected his words of wisdom in *The Analects*. *The Analects* consists of twenty short books, each of which includes a series of short quotations on a particular theme. Confucius's main concern was to teach people how to become *junzi*, compassionate and moral beings more concerned with doing what was right than with satisfying their own desires. The *junzi* understood their duties to others and fulfilled all the ancient ritual obligations. Confucius believed *junzi* could be created through education, and that society would be harmonious and peaceful if the government was guided by *junzi*. The following are some excerpts from Book 2.

> CHAP. I. The Master [Confucius] said, "He who exercises government by means of his virtue may be compared to the north polar star, which keeps its place and all the stars turn towards it."

> CHAP. II. The Master said, "In the Book of Poetry are three hundred pieces, but the design of them all may be embraced in one sentence—Having no depraved thoughts."

> CHAP. III. 1. The Master said, "If the people be led by laws, and uniformity sought to be given them by punishments, they will try to avoid the punishment, but have no sense of shame. 2. "If they be led by virtue, and uniformity sought to be given them by the rules of propriety, they will have the sense of shame, and moreover will become good."

> CHAP. IV. 1. The Master said, "At fifteen, I had my mind bent on learning. 2. "At thirty, I stood firm. 3. "At forty, I had no doubts. 4. "At fifty, I knew the decrees of Heaven. 5. "At sixty, my ear was an obedient organ for the reception of truth. 6. "At seventy, I could follow what my heart desired, without transgressing what was right."

> —Confucius, *The Analects*, translated by James Legge

- Why would Confucius think it important to be able to feel shame?
- How would the values expressed here help make a person a better leader?
- What connection, if any, can you see between the teachings of Confucius and the Zhou concept of the Mandate of Heaven?

🔗 LINK TO LEARNING

You can read the full text of *The Analects* (https://openstax.org/l/77Analects) at the Project Gutenberg website.

A mystical indigenous religion that venerated nature, **Daoism** borrowed from various ideological systems, such as the dualism of *yin-yang* with its emphasis on the complementary poles of light and dark cosmological forces. Daoism's thousands of texts, temples, and priests did not flower until the later Han dynasty, but during the Zhou era, this school emerged as a major influence thanks to teachers like Laozi and Zhuang Zhou (commonly known as Zhuangzi) and the circulation of the books attributed to them, the *Tao Te Ching* and the *Zhuangzi*. From them, Daoists learned a litany of poems, sayings, parables, and folktales teaching that *dao* (or "the way") was an underlying influence that shaped and infused all humans, the natural world, and the cosmos. Daoists encouraged dwelling on the beauty of the natural world, exploring mystic rituals, and contemplating the comparative insignificance of the individual against the vastness of time and space. Perhaps the most important political concept introduced by Daoists was the idea of *wuwei* (or "nonaction"), implying to those in power that the best form of governance was a minimalist approach that avoided interfering in the lives of their subjects.

Counter to the Daoist tradition and Confucianism ran the school of thought known as **Legalism**, the focal point of which was the accumulation of power. Legalists argued that governments drew power from a written legal code backed by an expansive system of rewards and punishments to ensure enforcement and order. A few of its exponents, like the thinker Han Feizi, studied Confucianism first, but came to see its proponents and teachings as too idealistic and naïve. Legalists downplayed the need for morality and asserted that the bedrock of a good government was a "rich country and a strong army."

While Confucianism, Daoism, and Legalism remained distinct, they borrowed liberally from each other and incorporated values, themes, and terminology to round out their own philosophies. All were open, eclectic systems reacting to historical circumstances and conditions. Moreover, each of these schools of thought and even the more minor traditions formed a common frame of reference within which Chinese rulers, philosophers, scribes, and even hermits expressed their own views. Confucianism and Legalism encouraged the study of texts over mystic rites, or society and its history over the supernatural and the afterlife, while other thinkers continued to ponder the yin and yang and work out principles applicable to astronomy, medicine, and the calendar. The world of spirits, ancestor worship, and folktales was no less prevalent than before. Still, it was the emergence of these new systems and their contributions that make this era an "axial age," a critical stage in the evolution of not just Chinese civilization but the world.

The Warring States Era and Qin Unification

Over the course of the long Eastern Zhou era (771–256 BCE), the means and methods of warfare changed, with dramatic consequences for ancient China. Initially war was regulated by chivalrous codes of conduct, complete with rituals of divination conducted before and after battle. Battles were fought according to a set of established rules by armies of a few thousand soldiers fighting for small Chinese states. The seasons and the rhythms of agricultural life limited the scope of campaigns. Victorious armies followed the precedent set by the early Zhou conquerors, sparing aristocratic leaders in order to maintain lines of kinship and preserve an heir who would perform rites of ancestor worship.

With the advent of the Warring States era (475–256 BCE), these rules were cast aside, and values such as honor and mercy went out of fashion. New military technologies provided the catalyst for these changes. The invention of the crossbow made the advantages once owned by cavalry and chariots nearly obsolete. The result was ballooning conscript armies of hundreds of thousands, making military service nearly universal for men. Protected by leather armor and iron helmets, soldiers skilled in the art of mounted archery trickled into Chinese states from the steppes. Discipline, drilling, logistics, organization, and strategy became paramount to success. Treatises on deceptive military maneuvers and the art of siege craft proliferated among the various states of the Zhou.

Not all the changes wrought by war in the late Zhou period were unwelcome. For example, common farmers gained the right to include their family names on registration rolls and pressure sovereigns for improvements to their lands such as new irrigation channels. Iron technology was developed for weapons, but was also used for new agricultural tools. Together, increasing agricultural productivity and advancements in iron technology were part of a late Zhou surge in economic growth. Mobilization for war stimulated a cross-regional trade in furs, copper, salt, and horses. And with that long-distance trade came increased coinage. The destruction of states through war also created social volatility, reducing the status of formerly great aristocratic families while giving rise to new forms of gentry and a more powerful merchant class. The only way back up the social ladder was through merit, and many lower-level aristocrats proved themselves as eager bureaucrats in the service of new sovereigns.

One of the many warring states in this period, the state of Qin, capitalized on these economic and social changes by adopting Legalist reforms to justify an agenda of power and expansionism. The arrival of Lord Shang, a migrant born in a rival territory in approximately 390 BCE, who soon took the position of prime minister, was the turning point, when Legalism came to dominate the thinking of Qin's elite. Before this, the Qin state had been a marginal area within the lands of the Zhou, a frontier state on the western border charged with defending the borderlands and raising horses. The Qin state leveraged this location by trading with peoples from central Asia. At the same time, their vulnerability on the periphery kept them in a state of constant alert and readiness for war, creating a more militaristic culture and an experienced army that proved invaluable when set against their Chinese neighbors in the east.

To offset their initial disadvantages, the Qin leaders wisely embraced immigrant talent such as Lord Shang and solicited help from advisors, militarists, and diplomats from rival domains. They adopted new techniques of governance, appointing officials and delegates to centralize rule rather than relying on hereditary nobles. Theirs became a society with new opportunities for social advancement based on talent and merit. Under Shang's advisement, the Qin scorned tradition and introduced new legal codes, unified weights and measures, and applied a system of incentives for able administrators that helped create an army and bureaucracy based more on merit than on birth. Over time, these changes produced an obedient populace, full coffers, and higher agricultural productivity.

The Qin state's rising strength soon overwhelmed its rivals, propelling to victory its king Ying Zheng, who anointed himself China's first emperor and was known as Qin Shi Huang, or Shihuangdi, literally "first emperor" (Figure 5.7). The Qin war machine defeated the states of Han, Wei, Zhao, Chu, Yan, and Qi in less than a decade. Under Shihuangdi's rule, the tenets of Legalism fostered unity as the emperor standardized the writing system, coins, and the law throughout northern China. Defeated aristocratic families were forced to uproot themselves and move to the new capital near Xi'an. To consolidate political control and reverse the fragmentation of the Zhou era, officials appointed by the emperor were dispatched to govern on his behalf, which cast aside the older feudal system of governance. Officials who performed poorly were removed and severely punished. Those who did well wrote regular detailed reports closely read by the emperor himself.

FIGURE 5.7 Qin Shi Huang. This image of China's first emperor was painted by an anonymous eighteenth-century Chinese artist for an album of emperors' portraits. Shihuangdi's reign was typified by expansionist campaigns and

enormous construction projects such as his tomb. (credit: "A portrait painting of Qin Shi Huangdi, first emperor of the Qin dynasty" by Richard R. Wertz/18th century album of portraits of 86 emperors of China, with Chinese historical notes, British Library/Wikimedia Commons, Public Domain)

Qin militarism also turned outward, enlarging the bounds of Chinese territory as far as the Ordos Desert in the northwest. In the south, Shihuangdi's armies ranged into modern-day Vietnam, laying a Chinese claim to the people and territory in this area for the first time in history. These expansions and the need for defense generated new infrastructure, such as fortified towns and thousands of miles of new roads to transport the Qin's armies to the borders. Northern nomadic and tribal civilizations known to Chinese as the Hu (or Donghu) and Yuezhi were seen as formidable threats. To guard against these "barbarians," hundreds of thousands of laborers, convicts, and farmers were sent to connect a series of defensive structures of rammed earth built earlier by states in northern China. Once completed, the Qin's Great Wall illustrated how fortifying the north and guarding against the steppes became the focal point of statecraft in ancient China. Successive empires in China followed a similar wall-building pattern. The walls commonly referred to as the Great Wall of China today are in fact Ming dynasty walls built between the fourteenth and seventeenth centuries CE.

Shihuangdi was also ruthless in defending himself from criticism at home. Informed by his chancellor in 213 BCE that literate Chinese were using commentary on classical texts and literary works to critique his rule, the emperor ordered the destruction of thousands of texts, hoping to leave in print only technical treatises on topics such as agriculture or medicine. An oft-cited story of Shihuangdi's brutality credits him with calling for the execution of hundreds of Confucian and Daoist intellectuals by burying them alive. Recent scholars have scrutinized these tales, questioning how much about his reign was distorted and exaggerated by the scholars of his successors, the Han dynasty, to strengthen their own legitimacy. In studying the ancient past, we must likewise always question the veracity of historical sources and not just reproduce a history "written by the winners."

Another monumental feat of Shihuangdi's reign was the creation of the **Terracotta Army**, thousands of life-sized clay soldiers fully armed with bronze weaponry and horses. From the time he was a young boy, the emperor had survived a series of assassination attempts, leaving him paranoid and yearning for immortality. Trusted servants were sent in search of paradise and magical elixirs, while hundreds of thousands of others were charged with the years-long process of constructing an enormous secret tomb to protect him in the afterlife. Almost immediately upon ascending the throne in 221 BCE, Shihuangdi began planning for this imperial tomb to be filled with clay replicas of his imperial palace, army, and servants. The massive underground pits, which cover an area of approximately thirty-eight square miles, were discovered with their innumerable contents near Xi'an in the 1970s (Figure 5.8). Labor for projects such as the Great Wall and the Terracotta Army came from commoners as a form of tax or as a requirement under the Qin's law codes. Penalties for violating the criminal code were severe—forced labor, banishment, slavery, or death.

(a)   (b)

FIGURE 5.8 The Terracotta Army. (a) Discovered in the 1970s, the buried treasures of China's first emperor, Qin Shi Huang, include thousands of life-size clay soldiers, known today as the Terracotta Army. (b) Small details of their dress and facial features distinguish the individual soldiers. (credit a: modification of work "Terracotta Soldier Panorama" by Walter-Wilhelm/Flickr, CC BY 2.0; credit b: modification of work "Terracotta warriors exhibit" by "scott1346"/Flickr, CC BY 2.0)

⊘ **LINK TO LEARNING**

Shihuangdi's mausoleum has been designated a UNESCO World Heritage site. Use the tabs at the UNESCO website to view pictures and to access the videos of the Terracotta Army (https://openstax.org/l/77Terracotta) to learn more.

The Qin Empire quickly collapsed in the wake of the emperor's death in 210 BCE. Conspiracy within the royal court by one of the emperor's sons led to the deaths of his rightful heir, a loyal general, and a talented chancellor. Beyond the court, the Legalist philosophy and practices that had helped the Qin accrue strength now made them brittle. Imperial power exercised in the form of direct rule and harsh laws inspired revolts by generals and great families calling for a restoration of the aristocratic feudal society of the Zhou.

The armies of the Qin's second emperor failed against Liu Bang, a commoner who rose to become Emperor Gaozu of the newly formed Han dynasty. The Han's early emperors distanced themselves from Shihuangdi's legacy by reducing taxes and burdens on the common people. But the Qin's imperial blueprint—uniform laws, consistent weights and measurements, a centralized bureaucracy, and early focus on expansionism to ward off "barbarians" in the north—provided the scaffolding for the Han's greatness.

5.2 The Steppes

LEARNING OBJECTIVES

By the end of this section, you will be able to:
- Discuss the role climate played in the ancient history of the steppes
- Describe the daily life of people who lived in the region of the steppes
- Analyze the relationship between the people of the steppes and nearby civilizations

The Eurasian Steppe is a vast stretch of grassland running from Eastern Europe over the top of central Asia and China into Mongolia. For much of human history, the area was home to traveling bands of nomadic pastoralists who grazed herds and collided with settled agricultural societies in Persia, Russia, and China. Geographers divide the Eurasian Steppe into two zones: One is in the west near Ukraine, Russia, and Kazakhstan, and the other is in the east, close to China and Mongolia (Figure 5.9). In both areas, the vastness of the land supported large herds of goat, cattle, and sheep. The prevalence of horses enabled powerful warriors of many cultures to rule from the saddle but also gave their people the freedom to roam, migrate, and resist absorption into a large unified state. While much of their history is still debated, these various tribes of the steppes provided the origins for a great number of Turkic, Iranian, Mongolic, Uralic, Tibeto-Burman, and multiethnic peoples today.

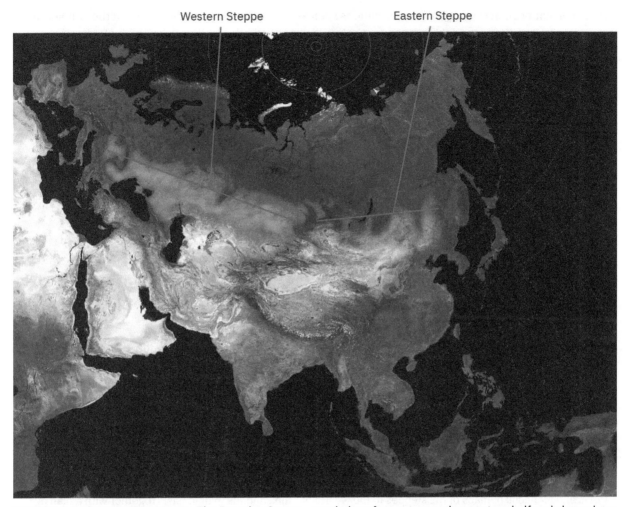

Western Steppe   Eastern Steppe

FIGURE 5.9 The Eurasian Steppe. The Eurasian Steppe, consisting of a western and an eastern half and shown here in light blue, reaches from the Caspian Sea in Europe to the Pacific Ocean. Its distinctive climate and vegetation are well-suited to pasturing livestock but less welcoming to settled agriculture. (credit: modification of work "Approximate extent of the Eurasian Steppe grasslands ecoregion, and Eurasia cultural region" by "Mdf"/Wikimedia Commons, Public Domain)

The Nomadic Culture of the Steppes

The eastern half of the Eurasian Steppe, sometimes referred to as the **Inner Asian Steppe**, now contains vast grasslands, mountains, and deserts not suitable to agriculture and only sparsely populated. Its history has been shaped to a great extent by climate change. Rainfall across the grasslands in Mongolia once supported pasturing herds of sheep, camels, goats, and horses, but in periods of a cooling climate, the grasslands could shrink, forcing nomads to roam in search of new pastures. Or droughts could drive them to desperate measures: If nearby societies were unwilling to trade, the nomads were often left with no choice but to make raids on farms and cities as a means to survive. Scholars now theorize that shifts to a colder, drier climate around 1500 BCE forced many peoples living here to abandon agriculture for livestock herding. However, grazing animals required mobile human communities that could readily find new pastures and protect their herds from predators. Thus the need to care for livestock forced cultural adaptation as people mastered the art of horseback riding.

As livestock herders, many people of the Inner Asian Steppe consumed a great deal of meat and dairy and made products from animal flesh and furs that could be traded in agricultural villages. They spoke languages unrelated to Chinese, such as Turkic or Mongolic, but a few such as the Jie may have even spoken Indo-European tongues. Due to the constraints set on pastoralism by a changing climate, the peoples of the steppes were in constant contact with agrarian civilizations such as the Chinese, who often looked on the nomads and their herds as a pestilence and threat to their own livelihoods. Yet while Chinese and Koreans for centuries tried to erect physical and cultural barriers between their civilizations and the "foreign" groups on the steppes, the ethnic and ancestral lines between Asia's nomads and their neighbors were porous.

Prizes taken by peoples of the steppes during raids, such as silk, lacquerware, grain, and war captives, were distributed by chieftains to their loyal supporters, who in turn conferred upon their leaders new titles such as *chanyu*, or **khan**, signifying a supreme leader with claims to spiritual and military supremacy. The khans' command over thousands of horses in an age of cavalry warfare further enhanced their power. Tribal confederations of the steppes wielded control over the **Silk Roads**, a series of trade routes circulating luxury goods to and from China and parts of central Asia, India, and the Middle East. To a mobile society, manufactured and luxury goods had material, social, and political value of enormous worth. Silk, for example, was treasured by nomads because its lightness was ideal for clothing in hot summers and its softness was desirable for lining beds. Powerful generals and khans who amassed huge quantities of the fabric used it as an indicator of their power. The same was largely true of other luxury goods such as wine.

THE PAST MEETS THE PRESENT

China's New Silk Road

For hundreds of years, the Silk Roads connected China to central Asia, India, and the Middle East and made prized Chinese goods such as silk available to the people of the steppes. The Silk Roads also created great wealth for China. Although trade over these routes ended in the fifteenth century, in 2013, China laid plans for creating a "New Silk Road," better known as the Belt and Road Initiative (BRI).

The BRI is a development project that includes the building of highways, railroads, and energy pipelines across central Asia, Pakistan, India, and Southeast Asia as part of a Silk Roads economic belt. When completed, it is meant to integrate the nations of central Asia—Kazakhstan, Turkmenistan, Uzbekistan, Tajikistan, and Kirghizstan—into the global economy, just as the Silk Roads established during the Han dynasty connected the Turkic and Mongolic nomads of the steppes to the wealth of China and the Middle East. Together with a plan by China to develop ports on the Indian Ocean (a project known as the Twenty-First Century Maritime Silk Road), the BRI is intended to increase exports for Chinese companies, provide China with a secure connection to the oil of the Middle East, and assist in the economic development of the country's western regions, which are poorer than other parts of the country.

Critics in the West as well as in India and Japan claim that the New Silk Road will also allow China to expand its political influence around the world. And not all the nations that China hopes will participate in the project have greeted it with open arms. Some have claimed it is too expensive. Chinese development assistance often comes in the form of loans, and some countries fear ending up in debt. This is especially likely if they are required to do business with Chinese companies that charge inflated prices for their goods and services. There is also concern about China's record on human rights. In 2019, crowds in Kazakhstan protested Chinese plans to build factories in their country partly because of China's much-criticized treatment of Uyghurs, an ethnic minority group in Xinjiang province.

- Why might leaders in China want to encourage an association between the modern economic initiatives and the older Silk Roads?
- Is it fair to suggest, as some have, that the Belt and Road Initiative and the Twenty-First Century Maritime Silk Road are imperialist in nature? Why or why not?

Most nomadic groups in Asia lived in small units of families or in a **clan**, a small group of several families that shared an encampment and herded or hunted together. Clans were united by loyalty to a chieftain selected for prowess as a mounted warrior. Compared with many other cultures in the ancient world, however, the societies of the steppes were more egalitarian. Role and status differences between men and women were more muted than in cities or farming settlements. Recent archaeological discoveries of female skeletons from the Xiongnu, Xianbei, and Turkic peoples of the steppes show evidence that women engaged in horseback riding and combat skills such as archery. They likely formed the historical basis for folktales about legendary female warriors such as Mulan that began circulating in Chinese society in the sixth century. Mobile lifestyles put a limit on the acquisition of wealth and its display in the form of architecture and clothing, which might explain why the development of written scripts was less common as well. Conversely, it was also true that most cultures of the Inner Asian Steppe readily absorbed technologies, goods, and ideas from neighboring civilizations.

Where the peoples of the steppes pioneered was in domesticating the horse, giving them a significant military advantage over their neighbors. Horseback riding and hunting provided the education in martial arts needed for war, and people began both activities at an early age. Hunting was a fixture of nomadic culture and the core of rituals that marked progress from child to adult, or from lowly member of society to one of the higher ranks. Touching both Europe and Asia, the steppes formed a bridge from which developments such as the chariot and cavalry warfare slowly spread to the rest of Asia. Chariots and mounted warriors in turn sparked the development of confederations that constituted a formidable military threat. Campaigns led by conquerors from the steppes—such as Modun, who came to power in 209 BCE—thus marked a turning point in the relationship between the Inner Asian Steppe, the rest of China, and the developing Silk Roads as arteries of exchange across the ancient world.

⊘ LINK TO LEARNING

This site provides an extensive history of the various nomadic tribes (https://openstax.org/l/77NomadicTribes) of the Eurasian Steppe. Consult the section about the Silk Roads to understand how these routes influenced the formation of tribal confederations and larger empires led by nomadic groups.

Tribes, Confederations, and Settled Neighbors

The earliest written records about many non-Chinese people living along the steppes come from Chinese sources, which referred to these people collectively as the Hu (or Donghu) and divided them into five large groups. These were the Xiongnu, the Di, the Qiang, the Xianbei, and the Jie. Later inhabitants of the steppes in the ancient world included the Khitan and many smaller groups.

Among the more powerful confederations noted by Chinese scribes were the Xiongnu, who controlled the lands near Mongolia from the third to the first century BCE. The Xiongnu became the dominant military confederation after forcing their rivals the Yuezhi to migrate west. In many periods, the relationship between the Xiongnu and Chinese dynasties such as the Han was complicated. Sometimes the Xiongnu and the Chinese were natural trading partners, exchanging horses for grain and silk. Access to Chinese civilization normally demanded that the Xiongnu submit tribute, accepting inferior status in return for trade rights and other rewards such as Chinese brides to establish stronger ties between the two cultures. At other times, the Xiongnu preferred to assert military and cultural dominance by raiding China and inciting war as well as constructing defenses such as the many northern fortification walls built by successive dynasties. At several points in their history, the Xiongnu were strong enough militarily to force the Chinese to adopt a policy of appeasement, exacting huge sums of silk, rice, and cash for peace. As a result, the tribute flowing between Xiongnu and Han Chinese often became a bribe meant to appease the nomadic tribes.

Simultaneously, tribal chieftains could often be employed as vassals of the Chinese, acting as a buffer to protect their border with the steppes or to sow division and conflict between various other bands of the Xiongnu. Chinese officials and soldiers also often found it convenient to defect to the Xiongnu, marrying into powerful families who sought their skills and expertise as administrators. For all these reasons, the border between the steppes and China was fluid and constantly changing, even as Han historians began to refer to groups such as the Xiongnu as "barbarians" and the antithesis of what it meant to be Chinese. Conversely, the nomads and tribes of the steppes often looked on Chinese farmers as lowly, weak, and servile peoples, in contrast to their own identity and values.

Critical to the struggle between the two were the Silk Roads. The balance of power, which initially favored the Xiongnu, shifted as two Han military expeditions went in search of allies in central Asia. These campaigns succeeded in subjugating the Xiongnu and gaining control over the eastern terminus of the Silk Roads. The Xiongnu were later weakened by years of civil war over their system of succession during the middle of the first century BCE. Less powerful groups in these wars tended to move toward the frontier of the Chinese empire and try to secure Chinese support against their rivals.

Thus the Southern Xiongnu, with their homeland threatened by natural disasters and resource scarcity, became vassals of the Han fighting against the Northern Xiongnu. Acceptance of tributary status required sending an aristocratic prince as hostage to live in the Han capital and be given a classical Chinese education, part of the continued cultural exchange between the Inner Asian Steppe and China. Channels between the two cultures widened as the later Han moved settlers west and tried to create military colonies along the frontiers for defense, staffed by non-Chinese auxiliary forces. Hundreds of thousands of Xiongnu lived inside the borders of China's empire, often becoming more settled and assimilated in their lifestyles and cultural practices.

Following the collapse of the Han dynasty, various branches of the Xiongnu tribes founded dynastic states across northern China during a period known as the Six Dynasties (220–589 CE). With innovations such as the stirrup and new forms of armor covering the whole of the mounted warrior and his horse, heavy cavalry units made these nomadic groups the supreme fighting force in Asia for the next two centuries. During this time, much of northern China and the Inner Asian Steppe was dominated by large, multiethnic conquest states ruled by chiefs claiming mixed ancestry from both Chinese and nomadic groups. Dynasties such as the Later Zhao and the Han Zhao were founded by powerful Xiongnu chiefs such as Shi Le and Liu Yuan, respectively. However, these dynasties often invoked claims to legitimacy staked in their ancestral and cultural ties to the Han dynasty. The ethnic markers and identity of the Xiongnu as distinct from Chinese and other groups on the steppes slowly melted away in these centuries. At the same time, an economy rooted in ranching and herding spread from the Inner Asian Steppe to northern China in a period that saw long-distance trade and grain agriculture decline.

Meanwhile, another ethnic nomadic group known as the Xianbei also emerged as a powerful force in the world of East Asia in this period. Originally hailing from southern Manchuria, the Xianbei were once subordinate to larger nomadic groups on the steppes such as the Xiongnu. After the fall of the Han, the Xianbei grabbed territory inside China proper by conducting raids for horses, war captives, and herds of cattle and sheep. Their military might forced a massive reshuffling of populations in northern China, while many Chinese sought employment with the Xianbei as advisers and administrators.

Drawing on the wealth of Chinese farmers, a branch of the Xianbei known as the Tuoba clan founded the Northern Wei dynasty (386–534 CE). Adopting the imperial title of emperor, Xianbei rulers such as Xiaowen in the late fifth century tried to remake their society into a true Chinese dynasty along the blueprint of the Han (Figure 5.10). During Xiaowen's reign, for example, elite Xianbei families arranged marriages between their daughters and wealthy, well-educated Chinese from the Southern dynasties. Such reforms proved dangerous. The opulence and culture of the courtly center of the Northern Wei alienated Xianbei soldiers of the garrisons along its frontier, who rebelled in 524 CE. The result was years of civil war and the sack of the capital in Luoyang. Still, the Xianbei proved a considerable force in the affairs of East Asia well into the later Sui and Tang dynasties.

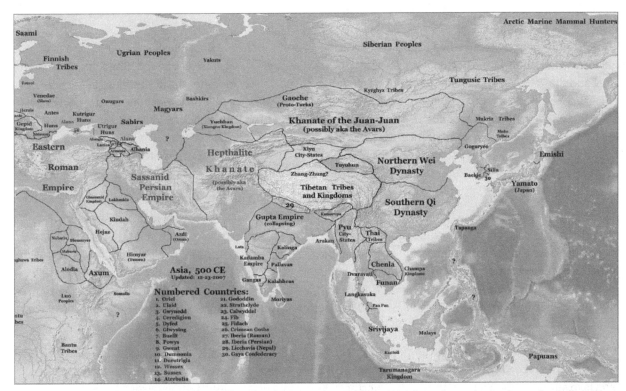

FIGURE 5.10 Northern Wei Dynasty. Xiaowen's reign over the Northern Wei dynasty marked a dynamic period of cultural exchange and assimilation between Xianbei and Han Chinese royals and nobility, but it also led to rebellion and violence by nomadic warriors charged with guarding the kingdom. (credit: modification of work "Map of the Eastern Hemisphere 500 CE" by Thomas Lessman/Wikimedia Commons, CC BY 3.0)

While the Xianbei and Xiongnu faded, after the fourth century another group known as the Khitan began a slow steady ascent toward power on the steppes and beyond. Organized for centuries as small clans of hunters, fishers, herders, and warriors in an area stretching from Mongolia to Siberia, the Khitan later founded the Liao dynasty (907–1125). Even more impressive were later empires that conquered the entirety of the Inner Asian Steppe and all of China, founded by the Mongols and Jurchen.

5.3 Korea, Japan, and Southeast Asia

LEARNING OBJECTIVES

By the end of this section, you will be able to:
- Discuss how geography and climate change influenced the early history of Korea, Japan, and Southeast Asia
- Describe the cultural exchanges between ancient Korea and Japan
- Compare daily life in ancient Korea, Japan, and Southeast Asia

Korea, Japan, and Southeast Asia were notable in the ancient world as homes to cultures uniquely engaged with the wider world. Via trade, religion, and diplomacy, Korea and Japan borrowed and adapted from Chinese civilization, but even more importantly from each other. Ties between Southeast Asia and India likewise proved formative in the eras in which many cultures evolved from small cities and agrarian villages into trade-post empires with monumental architecture. Conversely, geography, climate, and the early cultural forms produced by the first migrants meant that each area also produced its own indigenous systems. For example, Buddhist missionaries traveled from the Indian subcontinent across the Silk Roads and pilgrims trekked to temples to study and eventually bring home tools to convert their native cultures, but in each destination the faith was transformed into hundreds of new sects and interpretations of the path to enlightenment.

Ancient Korea

The earliest humans to reach the Korean peninsula did so around thirty thousand years ago. The land is very hilly, and mountains in the north form a barrier with Manchuria. Important rivers include the Daedong, the Han, and the Yalu. Winters are cold and snowy in the north, while summer months in the south feature blistering heat and torrential rains. Archaeologists have found evidence of bronze weapons dating back to 1300 BCE, but no clear proof that Korea at that time produced a Bronze Age civilization. The earliest written records of the first Koreans come from China, where the *Book of Documents* recounts the creation of a fief known as Joseon, located in northern Korea and awarded to a Chinese noble referred to as Gija. Later records in Chinese documents from 200 BCE to 313 CE provide descriptions of various small states in areas of Korea and Manchuria.

Seen from the vantage point of Chinese authors, our picture of ancient Korea begins to take shape during China's Han dynasty, when the peninsula was home to a number of small tribes, cultures, and communities living near the borders of the Chinese empire. From these Chinese records it is also clear that the earliest Koreans were in constant contact and exchange with not just the Chinese but also Inner Asian Steppe peoples like the Xiongnu as well as settlers in Japan. Thus, ethnicity in ancient Korea was quite fluid and prone to change. Groups borrowed liberally from each other's cultures, traded, and were absorbed and transformed by conquest.

The transformation of Korea into a unified culture and civilization is a story with many stops and starts. Historians often begin with the narrative of the Han dynasty historian Sima Qian, which tells of the dynasty's efforts to suppress the Xiongnu by invading northern Korea and establishing four garrisons there, from the Liao River to near today's Seoul. The presence of Chinese generals, troops, and settlers spurred exchange with societies on the Korean peninsula, which borrowed from Chinese culture the ideas of coins, seals, artwork, and building techniques to make roads and mounded tombs. Adopted by tribal chieftains and aristocratic warrior families, Chinese culture provided a wealth of material needed to engineer the first Korean states by controlling large areas of the northern half of the peninsula.

When unable to trade, Korean tribal societies mimicked the Xiongnu and raided the Chinese settlements, drawing strength and forging their own war bands. Among the early Korean polities noted in Chinese records in the north were Joseon, Goguryeo, and Buyeo, a frequent ally of the Han. With the collapse of the Han, each of these Korean societies lost a valuable partner and source of weapons, technology, and wealth. In the fourth and fifth centuries CE, all three struggled to defend themselves against rising powers in the north, such as the Xianbei.

In roughly the same time frame, in the central and southern parts of the Korean Peninsula, and therefore beyond the reach of Chinese administration, three groups known collectively as the **Three Han** established their territories. Chinese sources from the time refer to people in the southwest as the Mahan, those in the southeast as Jinhan, and between them a group known as the Byeonhan. These societies were ruled by aristocratic families that chose a chief and controlled the lives of lower-ranking commoners, servants, and enslaved people.

The Three Han were far less formidable military powers than their counterparts to the north, in part because they lacked horses and fought primarily on foot. On the other hand, they showed considerable cultural fluidity and knowledge of their neighbors. In Jinhan, many tattooed their bodies in decorative patterns like those found on the bodies of the Wa living in Japan, not surprising given that groups moved relatively freely between Japan and Korea in this age. Residents of Korea traveled to Japan, sometimes as traders and fishers and other times as migrants and permanent settlers. In Mahan, clothing and hairstyles mimicked a style used by the Xianbei on the Inner Asian Steppe, even as their lifestyles revolved around farming rather than a nomadic culture lived on horseback. Indeed, it appears that early Korean societies were quite selective in their borrowing.

Practices such as the *levirate*, in which a young male marries his elder brother's widow, were used widely by Inner Asian Steppe peoples and adopted by a number of early Korean ruling families. But the decision whether to emulate the Chinese, Japanese, or other neighbors presented a range of options and cultural choices for chieftains and elite families to build on in this age.

The decline of Chinese power in the fourth century unleashed a wave of refugees that proved pivotal in speeding up the process of state-building in Korea, opening an age known as the Three Kingdoms (313–668 CE). The three kingdoms in questions were Goguryeo, Baekje, and Silla (Figure 5.11). Chinese immigrants resettling within the bounds of Korea provided a source of knowledge about political practices that strengthened the rule of elites, transforming them into kings. These kings commanded large armies, drawing legitimacy from their military prowess and creating mounded tombs that required vast resources and labor. From the struggles against groups such as the Khitan and Xianbei in the north emerged the kingdom of Goguryeo. In the late fourth century, under the leadership of King Gwanggaeto, this kingdom drove southward in a series of expansionist wars against its main rival, the Korean kingdom of Baekje and its allies from Japan, the Wa. In doing so, Goguryeo managed to make the third of the Three Kingdoms, Silla, a vassal by the early fifth century.

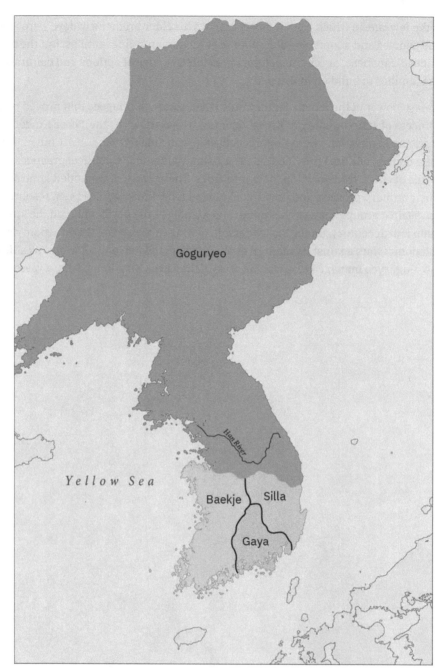

FIGURE 5.11 Ancient Korea. Three pivotal kingdoms—Goguryeo, Baekje, and Silla—dominated trade and cultural exchange with China and Japan and vied to unify all of Korea under their rule. A fourth kingdom, Gaya, remained relatively weak in this period and in 532 CE was absorbed by Silla. (credit: modification of work "Map of Goguryeo (476)" by "solicitatia"/Wikimedia Commons, CC0 1.0)

Beyond Goguryeo's militarism, its expansion was marked by two other critical developments. The first was its skillful use of diplomacy and regional politics to manage alliances and threats, playing off groups within and around the Korean peninsula to secure its power. The second was the adoption of a written script from China, evidenced by 414 CE in a stone slab inscribed to note the accomplishments of King Gwanggaeto upon his death. Goguryeo's elites also learned from the Chinese the art of adorning their large, mounded tombs with colorful murals depicting the lives of royals surrounded by dancers, servants, and enslaved people. Images of large battles, wrestling matches, and mythical creatures such as the phoenix in other mural scenes suggest the emergence of a rich courtly life.

During the Three Kingdoms era, the Chinese writing system spread throughout Korea, allowing those excluded from the ranks of aristocratic families a chance to seek appointment as scribes. The literacy necessary to study Confucian texts or Buddhist sutras, teachings of the Buddha, was a rare and very valuable skill. Knowledge of Chinese culture was another means to a life within the Korean courts, especially when writing poetry became a favorite pastime of Korean royalty and composing an eloquent verse was a critical sign of nobility and refinement. Many kingdoms sent royals, aristocrats, traders, scholars, and monks to China as apprentices to acquire skills and expertise they could bring home. These groups had an indelible impact on early Korean culture and society, particularly as Buddhism developed and grew into distinct sects and traditions. A few Korean Buddhist monks even traveled as far as India and central Asia, while others worked as teachers in the Three Kingdoms, inspiring new forms of painting, sculpture, and jewelry, and later the famed Buddhist monument, the first-century Seokguram Grotto (Figure 5.12).

FIGURE 5.12 The Seokguram Grotto. Created in the eighth century CE, this Buddhist monument lies in an enormous temple complex on the slopes of Mount Toshan, an architectural marvel and exemplar of Buddhist motifs that modern Koreans consider a national treasure. (credit: "Front view of Seokguram from front chamber" by Cultural Heritage Administration/Wikimedia Commons, Korea Open Government License Type I: Attribution)

These changes to the Korean political, social, and spiritual landscape also powered Gogoryeo's rival state Baekje. The kingdom of Baekje emerged from its home near the Liao River in Manchuria to conquer and absorb the Mahan territory in 369. To consolidate their control over the southwestern area of the peninsula, Baekje's rulers created a Chinese-style bureaucracy with a chief minister and carried on a successful maritime trade with China and Japan. Demand for Chinese culture, weapons, and Buddhism gave Baekje influence and prestige in Japan. However, a military defeat by Goguryeo and Silla in 475 kept Baekje hemmed in below the Han River. Afterward, Baekje turned its energy to upsetting the balance of power on the Korean peninsula by entreating Silla to rise against Goguryeo, its protector and overlord.

Ultimately, however, it was Silla that emerged from these plots to unify a larger share of today's Korea than any kingdom that preceded it. The smallest kingdom at the beginning of the era, located in the southeastern corner of the peninsula, Silla was ruled by powerful families that, like their neighbors, eventually copied models from China to wield power. Silla's rulers created Chinese-style ministries and codes of law and supported the practice of Buddhism to enhance their prestige and legitimacy. Maritime trade later proved a channel for Silla to form an alliance with a reunified China under the Sui and then the Tang dynasties. Conflict between Goguryeo and the Sui began in the 590s and lasted for decades. Later, the Tang supplanted the Sui and renewed Chinese ambitions to dominate the Korean peninsula.

By the 640s, the skillful diplomacy of Queen Seondeok of Silla (Figure 5.13) had leveraged the hostility between Goguryeo and the Chinese into the means for a Silla alliance with the Tang. Her kingdom's ships proved invaluable in ferrying Chinese armies onto the peninsula to lay conquest. Together, Silla and the Tang first subjugated Baekje and then eliminated Goguryeo in the north. Then, while the Tang set up bureaucracies to administer Korea, Seondeok's successors in Silla conspired with the defeated forces of their rivals to evict the invaders. Together, the remnants of the Baekje and Goguryeo's armies under the sway of Silla expelled Chinese forces in 676, ushering in a new era of unified rule over much of the peninsula that lasted from 668 to 892 CE. For a time, Silla severed its relations with the Tang, forgoing a critical resource that had powered its survival for centuries. But by the eighth century, new threats to both the Tang and Silla had emerged in the north. As a result, Silla once again sent tribute to the Chinese in return for protection and trade.

FIGURE 5.13 The Gold Crown of Silla. The kingdom of Silla left behind examples of its impressive and famous gold working skill. This gold crown, likely owned by a queen in the fifth century BCE, was found in a tomb in the early twentieth century in Gyeongju, the capital of Silla. While we can't know for sure, Queen Seondeok likely wore a similar crown. (credit: "Gold Crown of Silla Kingsom" by Gary Todd/Flickr, Public Domain)

Part of Queen Seondeok's legacy was a period of unprecedented female rule, during which new art forms emerged that in later centuries became distinctive Korean traditions. In ancient Korea, women wielded power as royal princesses, and affluent women often served as advisors and regents. But Queen Seondeok's reign paved the way for future queens of Silla, Jindeok, and Jinseong, to inherit the throne. Over time, Korean artisans learned from China how to make celadon ceramic, known for its lustrous green glaze, creating exquisite vases, jugs, bowls, and even pillows with Buddhist motifs such as cranes and clouds. In later centuries these works helped support a robust trade network running from China through Korea to Japan.

BEYOND THE BOOK

The Tombs of Goguryeo

Chinese rulers were not the only ones to build tombs that provide us with clues about what they valued in life. The rulers of the Korean kingdom of Goguryeo also constructed tombs decorated with murals depicting everyday scenes, presumably representing the lives they had lived and the lives they hoped to have after death. Shown here (Figure 5.14) are murals from the tomb of a Goguryeo man who was buried in the fourth century CE, not long after the end of China's Qin dynasty. As you study the images, consider what they tell us about life among the Goguryeo elite at this time.

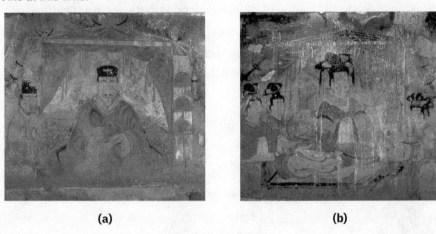

(a)   (b)

(c)

FIGURE 5.14 A Tomb of Goguryeo. (a) The tomb's owner is depicted. (b) A woman, most likely his wife, is shown, which was painted on the wall close to the image of the man so that she faces him. Image (c) shows a procession, complete with carts and mounted soldiers, from the tomb's corridor. (credit a: modification of work

"A drawing in one of the chambers of the Goguryeo tombs. Painting in Anak Tomb No. 3" by Unknown/Wikimedia Commons, Public Domain; credit b: modification of work "Mural Art in Anak Tomb No. 3. Painting in Anak Tomb No. 3" by Unknown/Wikimedia Commons, Public Domain; credit c: modification of work "Preserved wall mural of Anak tomb 3 (procession scene)" by Unknown/Wikimedia Commons, Public Domain)

- What do these murals tell you about the lives of Goguryeo's elite? What did they value and what were their concerns?
- Do you see any Chinese influences in these depictions? If so, where are they?

Ancient Japan

As in Korea, geography shaped much of Japan's early development and history. Four main islands make up Japan. The northernmost is Hokkaido. Then comes Honshu, which is home to Tokyo and the largest present-day population. Continuing south, the next island is Shikoku, and finally Kyushu, which is closest to the Asian mainland. Japan today also includes the islands of Okinawa and thousands of others strewn across the Pacific. But much of the story of ancient Japan concerns only the main isles, the inland Sea of Japan, the country's countless mountains, and a few fertile plains fed by monsoon rains that sustain agriculture.

Critical to the formation of the main islands and their geographical features is the belt known as the **Ring of Fire** (Figure 5.15), mapped by a horseshoe-shaped line drawn around the rim of the Pacific Ocean to mark a zone of frequent earthquake and volcanic activity that has generated countless tsunamis in Japan's distant past and modern day.

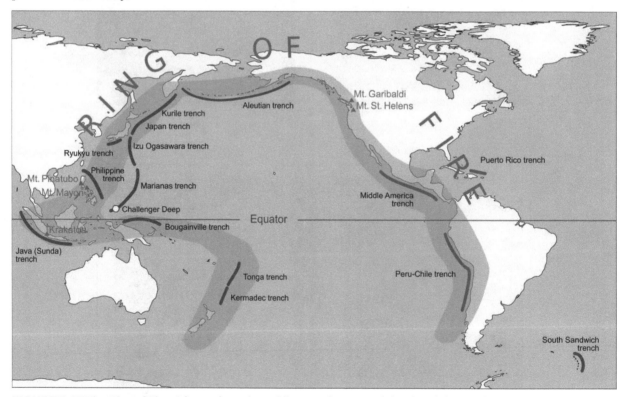

FIGURE 5.15 The Ring of Fire. A horseshoe-shaped line running around the rim of the Pacific Ocean marks the Ring of Fire, an area where frequent shifts of tectonic plates cause earthquakes, volcanic activity, and tsunamis that have plagued Japan for centuries. (credit: "Pacific Ring of Fire" by "Gringer"/Wikimedia Commons, Public Domain)

The story of prehistoric Japan is typically divided into two halves: the era of Jōmon hunters, ranging from 14,500 to 300 BCE, and that of the Yayoi agriculturalists who emerged after them to dominate the centuries from 300 BCE to 300 CE. These groups had no concept of themselves as "Japanese" in a sense recognizable to us today. But they left their imprint on the main isles via migration, settlement, and the development of practices for making the fertile plains, mountainous forests, and innumerable ocean bays and rivers their homes. Without written records, our knowledge of the Jōmon and Yaoyi is almost wholly based on the archaeological evidence and contemporary theories about the pathways humanity followed out of Africa and across the world. Early hominids likely made their way to the Japanese archipelago when it was still connected to the Asian continent, perhaps over 100,000 years ago. Hunting giant mammals such as elephants, wolves, and enormous deer, many of these early hunters moved to an area near today's Sea of Japan. Much later, changing climates led ocean levels to slowly rise and cover the stretches of land that connected Japan to the Asian mainland.

Linguists theorize that ultimately three early waves of foragers and hunters made their way overland or across the Tsushima Strait that separates the four main isles from the Asian mainland. These groups were descended from Ural-Altaic, Chinese, and Austro-Asiatic peoples. The climate shift that severed Japan from the Asian continent around twelve thousand years ago transformed the newly formed isles and the game these people once hunted. Grasslands for bison disappeared, for example, and wolves became smaller.

But the early inhabitants adapted, inventing new technologies to enhance their chances for survival. In the caves of Kyushu, archaeologists have found evidence of one of the world's earliest technological breakthroughs, the development of pottery. Known for its elaborate handles and distinctive cord patterns around rims, this pottery allowed Japan's inhabitants to become more sedentary and less dependent on finding wild game and foraging for edible plants. First used to store vegetables and boil water from the sea to make salt, the pottery called Jōmon was likely later used for rituals to promote unity and cooperation (Figure 5.16). The increasingly sophisticated culture of the people, also called Jōmon, was characterized by settlements with shared spaces for burials, food storage, and elaborate ceremonies. Among the important cultural symbols were earthenware figurines known as *dogu*.

(a)   (b)

FIGURE 5.16 Jōmon Artifacts. (a) This Jōmon pottery food container (c. 3500–2500 BCE) is among the earliest examples of the craft of pottery found in the world. (b) The *dogu* figurine (c. 1000–300 BCE) likely represents a female god, hinting at the spiritual life of the early inhabitants of Japan's main isles. Such figures are thought to have served as forms of sympathetic magic that healed illness and helped with childbirth. (credit a: modification of work "Deep Vessel" by The Harry G. C. Packard Collection of Asian Art, Gift of Harry G. C. Packard, and Purchase, Fletcher, Rogers, Harris Brisbane Dick, and Louis V. Bell Funds, Joseph Pulitzer Bequest, and The Annenberg Fund Inc. Gift, 1975/Metropolitan Museum of Art, Public Domain; credit b: modification of work "Dogū (Clay Figurine)" by The Harry G. C. Packard Collection of Asian Art, Gift of Harry G. C. Packard, and Purchase, Fletcher, Rogers, Harris

Brisbane Dick, and Louis V. Bell Funds, Joseph Pulitzer Bequest, and The Annenberg Fund Inc. Gift, 1975/
Metropolitan Museum of Art, Public Domain)

Skeletal remains of the Jōmon people suggest that despite their diverse diet of fruits, nuts, and seafood such as clams and fish, they lived with the constant threat of starvation and malnutrition. Another shift in the region's climate produced a deadly drop in temperatures that led to a decline in the populations of game such as deer and boar. To survive, many Jōmon moved to the coastal areas to supplement their food supply by fishing. Others likely began experimenting with early forms of agriculture; evidence suggests the cultivation of yams and lily-bulbs in the years from 3000 to 2400 BCE. Further evidence of early agriculture comes from traces of rice found in jars dated to the later years of the Jōmon era.

Agriculture and the Yayoi

The next phase of Japan's prehistory is marked by the leap into agriculture and is known by the name of a separate people and culture, the Yayoi. Beginning in 300 BCE, a new wave of migrants descended from groups in northern Asia began arriving on the southern island of Kyushu. They brought with them knowledge about cultivating barley, buckwheat, and later rice, and gradually they overwhelmed and replaced the Jōmon. Later, the Yayoi built impressive storehouses for grain and domesticated horses and dogs. Other archaeological sites show that, as Yayoi culture spread, the people developed the capacity to engineer the landscape for farming by creating irrigation canals, wells, and pits. Agriculture brought stability and growth, and the Yayoi population is estimated to have ballooned to more than half a million people by the first centuries of the common era.

The Yayoi period marked a turning point in Japan's prehistory. From this point forward, Korea, China, and Japan were in more consistent contact than in the centuries before. This was especially the case because in the Bronze Age, with copper in short supply on the islands of Japan, the Yayoi were forced to import much of the material. The Yayoi period also marked the beginning of a written record of Japan.

Han conquests and the construction of garrisons on the Korean peninsula began a period of trade in bronze mirrors, iron weapons, and agricultural practices transmitted via Korea to Japan. The Han dynasty (206 BCE–220 CE) and later the kingdom of Cao Wei (220–265 CE) also sent occasional envoys to Japan (which the Han called the Wa kingdom). These envoys left behind the first written records of the lives and cultures of the Yayoi. Their observations show a slow but gradual transformation of society and politics. Despite increasing food surpluses and material abundance, the Yayoi people at first remained largely communal, sharing wooden tools and public spaces. Over time, the appeal of certain areas and sites for agriculture led to competition and increasing warfare and, by extension, the emergence of states to provide for defense.

Chinese records also note the distinctive style of dual governance—in which power was shared between male and female rulers—that developed in early Japanese states at the end of the Yayoi era. Among the notable rulers was Queen Himiko, who ruled in the early third century and, in return for paying tribute to the Chinese emperor, was recognized as an ally and given a golden seal. Ruling alongside Himiko was her younger brother, who handled the administration of her realm. The Cao Wei's records show that Himiko was at war with a neighboring king and staked the legitimacy of her rule on her spiritual powers, expressed in elaborate burials, the practice of divination, and other sacred rituals. Through such specialization, ancient Japanese women exercised political power and influence, possibly built upon the legacy of the Jōmon, whose *dogu* figurines depicted women as deities ensuring fertility and safety.

Chinese envoys noted that Japan was also home to an increasingly stratified society that included aristocratic families, merchants, skilled divers and fishers, farmers, and other commoners. With warfare constant, palaces looked more like garrisons, but granaries and markets were full and lively. And while these early Japanese lacked a written script, the Yayoi did develop a rich art form literally written on their bodies, as the practice of tattooing patterns to denote rank, status, and family was widespread in this era.

The Dawn of the Yamato Age

Records of Queen Himiko's era also suggest a growing concentration of political power and control over territories held by a loose confederation of states and powerful families. This period, known as the Yamato era, was marked by the construction of tombs for deceased royals like Himiko, who were buried with an impressive array of treasures and human sacrifices to accompany them in the afterlife.

It may be that the onset of the Yamato era was produced by a changing climate and constant turmoil in Japan, as a result of which many of the island's inhabitants despaired and abandoned deities who seemed negligent in their duty to protect them. Instead, new gods associated with an imported technology—mirrors from China and Korea—arose to take their place. Powerful rulers and a new military class forged from warfare associated themselves with these new gods, or more importantly, with the female god of the Sun, Amaterasu, who soon became the ancestral figurehead of the imperial household. Yamato kings further accrued power by brokering alliances, managing trade, giving symbolic gifts, and presiding over ceremonies designed to forge a common culture across Japan.

As co-rulers of a kingdom or heads of households, women continued to wield political clout by using expertise in sorcery via items such as mirrors and often expressing their triumphs in gold jewelry and earrings. Many spiritual practices were imported from earlier Chinese dynasties such as the Shang dynasty. For example, during the burial of Queen Himiko, Chinese envoys recorded that Japanese employed the art of divining the future with heated bones by reading their cracks to foretell the outcome of harvests and wars. Other burial practices such as water purification were more indigenous to Japan and left an imprint on later religions such as Shintoism. Later, new foreign religions such as Buddhism were used by women such as Empress Suiko, who ruled in the early seventh century CE and sought to preserve women's role in politics through practices such as piety, rigorous study of sutras, and the construction of shrines and temples.

Regardless, it was the construction of large keyhole-style tombs and control over the burial rituals that brought the Yamato rulers power over the area stretching from western Honshu to northern Kyushu. Employing laborers and skilled artisans such as blacksmiths, the Yamato tomb makers showed their wealth and organizational capacity, skills they used later to create capital cities with large markets and highways to the countryside and the coastal ports. To centralize power, kings soon began issuing law codes, such as Prince Shotoku's Seventeen Article Constitution in 604. The emphasis on law as the basis for rule, the creation of a bureaucracy to help rulers govern, and Confucian values embedded in the document show the Yamato's reliance on Chinese culture as a source of ideas and inspiration. Borrowing from the Chinese model for imperial statecraft, the Yamato strengthened their rule with mythology and bejeweled regalia, elevating kings to godlike status and eventually transforming them into emperors. Later legal codes such as the Kiyomihara Codes in 689 organized monasteries, created a judiciary, and managed relations between the king's advisors and vassals. These set the stage for the evolution of Japan's culture and political system in the later Heian and Nara periods.

⊘ LINK TO LEARNING

Prince Shotoku's "Seventeen Article Constitution" was an effort to reform the Japanese state along the lines of the Chinese imperial model. Read the translated law codes (https://openstax.org/l/77LawCodes) at Columbia University's Asia for Educators site.

To the north, beyond the lands of the Yamato, was another group descended from the early Jōmon foragers who had lived on and resisted the sweep of Yayoi settled agriculture. Later, they continued to forage and hunt and practice their own spiritual beliefs, rejecting the Yamato cultural sphere and its borrowings from China, such as Buddhism, Confucianism, and the idea of large states governed by kings and emperors. While the later Japanese imperial courts in Nara and Heian deepened ties with China's Tang dynasty, these northern people existed in another orbit defined by contact with smaller northern Asian cultures, such as the Satsumon people of Hokkaido. Relations with the descendants of the Yamato to the south soured over these centuries, as Nara and Heian came to call the northerners *Emishi*, or "barbarians." The Emishi survived from the seventh to the eleventh century despite repeated attempts by emperors and militarists from the south to subjugate them. They resisted via war, moved to remote areas, and used other forms of evasion, but the culture of Japan's south moved inexorably north, and the smaller remnants of the Emishi were subdued by the end of the ninth century.

Southeast Asia

The term "Southeast Asia" describes a large area in subtropical Asia that can also include thousands of islands in the Pacific. Today it often refers to Brunei, Burma, Thailand, Laos, Cambodia, Vietnam, Malaysia, Singapore, and Indonesia. For much of human history, travel across this area was far easier by boat along the shore and between islands than overland. Lands were more sparsely populated than in India, China, Japan, and Korea, and most communities were isolated from their closest neighbors by forests and mountains. Early on, however, they became able to engage with other peoples through the sea lanes.

In general, communities in Southeast Asia settled first along coastlines near rivers, lakes, and the oceans and seas. But archaeological sites in Thailand, Burma, and Laos prove that many chose to make upland regions their homes as well. As in India, early agriculture was driven by the rhythms of monsoon season. Farmers developed rainwater tanks to manage their supply of water and learned how to grow rice in paddies. A reliance on slash-and-burn agriculture meant that many Southeast Asians had to migrate after the soil had been exhausted, making the population fluid as people moved from one area to the next. The social structure, too, was less stratified than in India and China. Only with the later arrival of new religions such as Buddhism and Hinduism did priestly and kingly classes start to form and play a central role in religion and politics.

Despite its great territorial expanse and varying climates and topography, the region does have broad commonalities that make it useful to see Southeast Asia as one geographic and cultural zone (Figure 5.17). For example, its location between India and China led to the growth of royal courts that borrowed from foreign traditions to develop rituals and diplomatic relations, assert control over ordinary farmers and fishers, and create trading-post empires. The region's geography and climate also made sailing a universally efficient craft. For centuries, merchants and adventurers traveling from the Indian landmass along the coastlines of Asia have exploited monsoon winds from June to November that easily push boats all the way to the Malaysian peninsula. Return voyages were made possible by a second set of monsoon winds blowing in the opposite direction from December to May. The holdover period between the two monsoon seasons proved ample time for merchants and missionaries to transplant customs, religion, and art from India to new environs in Southeast Asia. At the same time, the arrival of boats and merchants traveling from Vietnam and Malaysia to China and back as early as 300 BCE meant residents of Southeast Asia enjoyed a rich marketplace of ideas, goods, and cultures at a very early stage in world history.

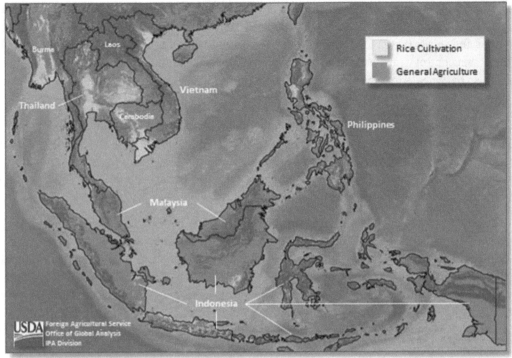

Source: Agricultural land cover, Geocover LC 2000

FIGURE 5.17 Southeast Asia. The expanse of Southeast Asia includes varied topographies and climates but also some common historical and cultural features, such as the practice of wet-rice agriculture and religions such as Buddhism. (credit: "SE Asia: Distribution of Agricultural Lands" by Agricultural land cover, Geocover LC 2000"/USDA: Foreign Agricultural Service, Public Domain)

While the influx of foreign ideas was critical to the development of societies across Southeast Asia, each local community made selective adaptations and preserved its indigenous customs. For example, the importance of the individual family was a point of commonality for many societies in Southeast Asia, in contrast to the weight given extended families and clans in India and China. Most peasant communities in Southeast Asia also afforded women higher status than their counterparts in China were allowed under the stricter Confucian values system.

Archaeological remains of the region's prehistory show that inhabitants of northeast Thailand used bronze and mastered agriculture as early as 3000 BCE. Evidence found at Non Nok Tha shows that they grew rice and cast bronze in factories using molds, later producing iron objects. The spread of rice cultivation produced densely populated centers along the region's smaller fertile plains. Expanding populations were often forced into hilly regions, which they made suitable for farming by creating terraces. Migration chains and artifacts such as simple tools suggest that by the time the inhabitants of India began making contact with Southeast Asia, the islands and coastline settlements there were dominated by peoples related to Malays, who had made their way from southern China. Expert sailors working with finished stone tools and navigating by the stars, these peoples developed long, narrow boats that navigated Southeast Asia's water with speed and grace. Moreover, they left behind cultures with maritime traditions that echo today with Malaysians, Indonesians, and the people of Singapore.

The archaeological record of Southeast Asia's prehistory is less clear than that of many other areas of the world, however, and its study has been hampered by many circumstances, including the political volatility of countries such as Vietnam and Cambodia after 1945. As a result, historians often look to the region's villages and families for insights into its remote past. For example, cultivating rice in terraced rice paddies requires skill and cooperation among many families, likely making this task the basis for village leadership and unity. Elders with experience in selecting breeds, transplanting young plants, and negotiating water resources likely used their authority to foster consensus around values and politics oriented toward giving deference to seniority. It is also possible that growing rice is particularly suited to cultures with animist religions, which venerate deities and spirits thought to inhabit nature. Rites and festivals to honor grains and timber and to appease forces that control wind and rain are still important to local cultures in Southeast Asia today, even as many people also participate in universal religions such as Buddhism.

Occupations offer another important point of continuity. Fishing, farming, and craftwork in fabrics are depicted in carvings found in caves, temples, and mountainsides and remain the primary labor activities of rural peoples today. For example, in Brunei many people still live much of their life on the water—at work as fishers and divers as well as at play when racing boats and swimming. Houses and many other buildings are still situated in the hills or on stilts to protect them from flooding, and many people share a diet of fish, simple grains, and coconut, just as their ancestors did.

In early Southeast Asia, trade and the arrival of outside religion were critical to the development of larger states and powerful kingdoms. Even in the interior, Buddhist artwork and texts flowed in steadily from 300 to 600 CE. The mouths of great rivers linked the interiors and the coasts, and capitals and small principalities that developed there taxed the trade on goods traveling to and from the wider world. During these centuries, Southeast Asians also traveled to India to trade and learn Sanskrit. When Indian elites and literate Buddhists arrived, they came to be known as *purohita*, advisers to Southeast Asia's powerful chiefs and nobility. Other immigrants became teachers and founded temples across the region's landscape, critical hubs that promoted travel, learning, and commerce.

As they did in India, Buddhism and Hinduism coexisted with local religions in much of Southeast Asia. In areas such as the kingdom of Srivijaya, which ruled over the island of Sumatra and southern Malaya Peninsula from the seventh to the twelfth centuries CE, Indian merchants and missionaries were welcomed, while the people retained their own religious traditions rooted in the worship of spirits that inhabited trees, rocks, water, and various physical features of the land. Proclaiming themselves "Lord of the Mountains," Srivijaya's rulers patronized Buddhism to foster trade relations across the Malaccan Straits and Indian Ocean.

Other communities, such as nearby Borobudur, which controlled central Java in Indonesia, were more firmly devoted to Buddhism. There, Buddhism inspired countless converts and the later Shailendra Kings (775–860 CE) to erect the world's largest Buddhist monument, a structure more than one hundred feet above the ground and adorned with magnificent artwork (Figure 5.18). Buddhists from all over Southeast Asia made pilgrimages to Borobudur, leaving behind thousands of clay tablets and pots as offerings. Wreckage from a nearby ship dated to the ninth century shows that the people of Borobudur were engaged in commerce that connected them to Islamic and Arabic cultures in the Middle East. Like many heads of Southeast Asian states, Borobudur rulers staked their political legitimacy on setting a pious example for their subjects and thrived economically by opening their ports to the wider world. Thus India's centrality to much of Southeast Asia in the ancient world was founded on trade, religion, and art. India was a repository of desired goods and a source of inspiration for religion and state-building, but also a bridge to the wider Eurasian world.

FIGURE 5.18 Borobudur. This 1913 photograph of the temple of Borobudur shows one side of the massive Buddhist structure with the local mountains in the background. In the upper left, one can see several of the seventy-two perforated stupas surrounding the central dome. Behind and to the left of the man posing for the photograph are just some of the over 2,600 decorated relief panels that adorn the site. (credit: modification of work "A terrace on the temple of Borobudur, Java, Indonesia, 1913" by State Library of New South Wales, PXD 162/150/Wikimedia Commons, Public Domain)

While much of Southeast Asia faced west toward India as the center of trade, culture, and religion, the area near today's Vietnam fell within the orbit of China's cultural sphere emanating from the east. The natural geography of Vietnam creates three distinct zones that shaped the evolution of the country from ancient times to the present: one area in the north surrounding the Red River delta; below that, in the south, another densely populated center on the Mekong River delta; and lastly, a long narrow land bridge along the coast squeezing between mountains to join the other two areas together. Humans practicing wet-field rice agriculture developed settlements in the northern zone sometime around 2500 BCE, and a millennium after, there is evidence of bronze-making by the region's inhabitants. But the most notable contribution to world history from this area in northern Vietnam came from the Dong Son culture (c. 600 BCE–200 CE), defined by its remarkable bronze drums decorated with cords and images of animals such as frogs. Dong Son drums have been found at sites all over Southeast Asia.

Whether the Dong Son culture and its drums originated in Vietnam or inside China near Yunnan province is the subject of debate. Evidence suggests that southeast China below the Yangtze River was once home to peoples who were more strongly linked, culturally and linguistically, to Southeast Asia than to the dynasties in the north such as the Shang and Zhou. During the Zhou dynasty, many non-Chinese societies and kingdoms inhabiting provinces such as Fujian and Yunnan were known as the Yue, the Mandarin version of "Viet." These areas and groups remained independent of Chinese control for centuries. Chinese records of the Yue demonstrate their sophistication and diversity. They were known for practicing wet-field rice cultivation, adorning their bodies with tattoos, and traveling widely by boat along the seas and the Red River that linked China to Vietnam.

These Chinese records further indicate that many early Vietnamese groups spoke a multitude of languages and were divided into as many as one hundred small polities, kingdoms, tribal clans, and autonomous villages. Unlike in northern China, there appears to have been no successful drive to centralize power under a unified dynasty in Vietnam's prehistory. In later centuries, many Vietnamese accepted the mythological lore of a mighty king known as Van-Lang, who in the seventh century BCE united the various tribes of the Yue and established a dynastic line of Hung kings. This origin tale eventually evolved to include a divine origin for the Vietnamese people, telling of a union between a dragon lord and a female mountain deity that produced the Hung royalty.

At best, Vietnam's prehistoric record can only validate the idea that chiefdoms grew increasingly large around 258 BCE. By then, the rulers of a new kingdom known as Au Lac had constructed an impressive capital arranged in the shape of a widening spiral near today's Hanoi. Later, around 179 BCE, Au Lac was conquered by another kingdom, Nam Viet, an offshoot of China's Qin dynasty. The area was later retaken by the Han dynasty, which attempted to establish permanent control by dividing its territory spanning southern China and northern Vietnam into nine administrative units. In 40 CE, Han control of the Red River delta ran afoul of two rebellious daughters of a Vietnamese general known as Trung Trac and Trung Nhi. The uprising launched by these women rallied native resistance from southern China to central Vietnam (Figure 5.19). Briefly victorious, the Trung sisters' rebellion was eventually squashed. Their legacy was indelible, however, and stories of their exploits riding elephants into battle became a source of Vietnamese nationalist pride and rejection of encroachment by outsiders such as the Chinese and, much later, the French.

FIGURE 5.19 Trung Trac and Trung Nhi. The sisters Trung Trac and Trung Nhi launched a short-lived rebellion against Chinese domination that has lived on popular memory as a potent symbol of Vietnamese national identity. Images such as this folk painting of them riding elephants into battle have long been a source of inspiration for resistance to foreign empires and, more recently, helped promote a role for women in politics and the military. (credit: "Hai ba trung Dong Ho painting" by "LuckyBirdie"/Wikimedia Commons, Public Domain)

The end of the Trung sisters' uprising began a period of more direct Chinese governance, with the aim of assimilating the region and its inhabitants. Over time, however, the families of the Han generals and officials who were sent as administrators took on many local habits and customs, blurring the boundaries between Chinese and Vietnamese culture in the ancient world. By that time, the area around the Red River delta had become critical to the Han's maritime trade in Southeast Asia. Thus, even after the dynasty collapsed, China's political dominance of northern Vietnam lasted into the next few centuries. Sporadic uprisings continued, occasionally resulting in independence for rulers in northern Vietnam. But the Sui and Tang relaunched campaigns to reabsorb the Red River delta. Thus, northern Vietnam remained on the border of the Chinese imperial frontier for centuries.

Farther south, an area known in the ancient world as Champa was settled by a wave of people arriving from the sea around 500 BCE. Distinct from the Dong Son culture, these people engaged in trade across the waterways of Asia, from India to the Philippines. Chinese records of a civilization in this central region of Vietnam describe a unique people who reserved a higher status for women than for men, and who used an Indian script written on leaves from trees. Indeed, all the remaining inscriptions on artifacts found within this region until the ninth century are written in Sanskrit.

Another import from India to central Vietnam was the idea of a society led by a priestly Brahman class and deities such as Shiva, identified with the Champa kings. Still, indigenous spirits and ancestors were worshipped as well, coexisting alongside the Indian imports whose foreignness faded slowly over the centuries. Lacking a large agricultural region to supply a powerful state, Champa may have been a region with many centers, loosely knit by trading networks exchanging rice, salt, horns, and sandalwood.

Even farther to the south, people known as the Khmers had made the Mekong River delta their home by the early centuries of the common era. Chinese texts referring to this region named it Funan, and its history shows many similarities to that of Champa, its neighbor to the north. Funan too was engaged in wide trade. Archaeological remains show items that made their way to Vietnam from India, the Middle East, and Rome. Funan's inhabitants and rulers imported features of Indian culture such as Sanskrit to help create royal courts, but little writing survived until the development of the powerful Khmer empire in the ninth century.

5.4 Vedic India to the Fall of the Maurya Empire

LEARNING OBJECTIVES

By the end of this section, you will be able to:
- Explain the caste system and the way it functioned in Indian society
- Identify the main elements of Buddhism
- Describe India's faith traditions: Brahmanism, Buddhism, and Hinduism

Few areas of the world are as important to our understanding of the emergence of human civilizations as India. Occupying an enormous subcontinent in South Asia, India has three distinct geographic zones: a northern area defined by the Himalayas that forms a natural barrier to the rest of the Asian mainland, the densely populated river valleys of the Indus and Ganges Rivers that lie to the south and northwest of that area, and lastly the tropical south, cut off from those valleys by many mountains and thick forests (Figure 5.20).

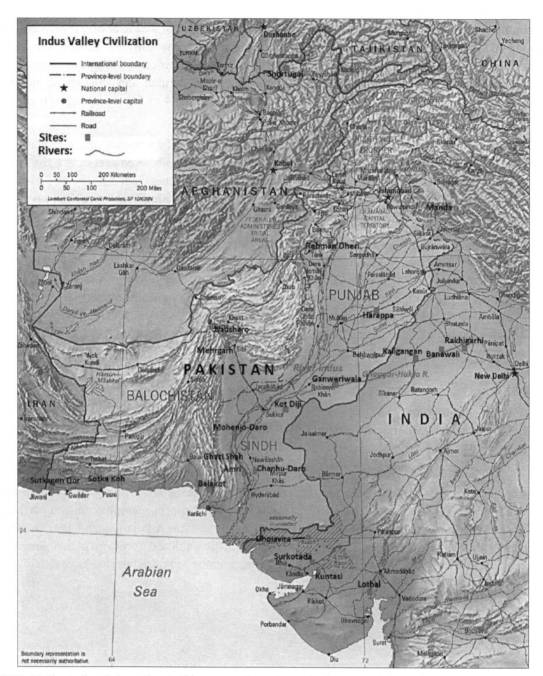

FIGURE 5.20 The Indian Subcontinent. This map outlines the major features of the Indian subcontinent, where the Himalayas stand as a northern border with the rest of Asia. (credit: "The major sites of the Indus Valley Civilization (https://en.wikipedia.org/wiki/Indus_Valley_Civilization) fl (https://en.wikipedia.org/wiki/fl.) 2600–1900 BCE (https://en.wikipedia.org/wiki/BCE) in Pakistan (https://en.wikipedia.org/wiki/Pakistan), India (https://en.wikipedia.org/wiki/India) and Afghanistan (https://en.wikipedia.org/wiki/Afghanistan)" by US Federal Central Intelligence Agency (CIA)/Wikimedia Commons, Public Domain)

Early humans traveled into Asia in waves around sixty thousand to eighty thousand years ago, moving from Africa to the Arabian Peninsula into India and beyond, on routes that hugged the coast. Some of the earliest evidence of this migration was found at Jwalapuram, India. Here, hundreds of stone tools dating to 74,000 BCE were discovered that resemble those of roughly the same age found in Africa, Laos, and Australia. But the roots of India's ancient civilizations lie in the north, amid the archaeological remains of two ancient cities, Harappa and Mohenjo-Daro.

Harappa and Mohenjo-Daro

Unlike ancient cultures in Mesopotamia (3500–3000 BCE), Egypt (3500–3000 BCE), and China (2200–2000 BCE), the Indus valley civilization shows little evidence of political power concentrated in the hands of hereditary monarchs. Yet its culture and technology spread, in an area running from parts of present-day Afghanistan into Pakistan and western India. There, early human communities capable of agriculture flourished near the fertile plains around the Indus River and other waters fed annually by the region's monsoons.

Farmers harvested domesticated crops of peas, dates, and cotton, harnessing the power of draft animals such as the water buffalo. The archaeological record shows few traces of any kind of elaborate monumental architecture, burial mounds, or domination by warriors and kings. Instead, a common culture grew that was defined by urban planning, complete with advanced drainage systems, orderly streets, and distinctive bricks made in ovens. Equipped with those tools, the Indus River valley produced two of the ancient world's most technologically advanced cities, Harappa and Mohenjo-Daro. Within them, residents developed a highly urban society and rich spiritual life, with altars featuring fire and incense, practices such as ceremonial bathing, and a symbolic vocabulary using elephants and bulls as revered animals. Dedicated artisans made jewelry and fabrics. All these aspects of the Indus valley culture left an imprint on later Indian civilizations.

How did a civilization with a high degree of labor specialization and the coordination necessary for irrigated agriculture and large urban centers manage such complexity without a powerful centralized state? There is no consensus answer, though the Indus valley civilization may have developed as a series of small republic-like states, dominated by religious specialists such as priests presiding over an intensely hierarchical class system. It does seem likely, however, that the environmental toll the civilization inflicted upon the surrounding areas led to its decline. Over time, irrigation replaced fertile soil with soil having greater quantities of salt, lowering crop yields. The use of wood as a fuel source, such as for making the oven-fired bricks, led to rapid deforestation and even greater soil erosion. It appears that most communities in and around Harappa and Mohenjo-Daro abandoned the sites around 1700 BCE, when they became unable to feed and supply themselves. Before their decline, however, the two cities housed perhaps as many as forty thousand residents each, most of whom lived in comparatively luxurious homes of more than one story that featured indoor plumbing and were laid out in an orderly pattern along grid-like streets. Public buildings such as bathhouses were quite large, as were the protective city walls and citadels.

The development of a written script, found on clay seals and pottery at the sites, likely made such feats possible. The written language of the Indus valley civilization featured more than four hundred symbols that functioned as pictures of ideas, words, and numbers. While many of the symbols have yet to be deciphered, one of the primary functions of writing appears to have been commerce because many finished goods were stamped with written seals. Writing used as a means of communication and recordkeeping probably also helped the Indus valley civilization profit from long-distance trade with Mesopotamia and Egypt.

Merchants from Sumer traveled to the Indus River valley to establish trade in luxury items such as lapis lazuli. In return, it appears that traders and merchants from cities such as Harappa took up residence in cities in Mesopotamia to facilitate exchange. In this way, Mesopotamia exerted a recognizable influence on India's art and culture. Scholars have identified aspects of Greek naturalist art in sculptures found in Harappa, combined with local preferences for representing human bodies in motion rather than adopting the Greek emphasis on anatomical correctness. Art from these early cities helped usher in artistic styles and motifs that created a continuous tradition ingrained within Indian culture. Stone seals with fantastic beasts and anthropomorphic deities were later associated with Indian traditions such as yoga and Hindu deities.

Significant archaeological evidence suggests that urban women in the Indus valley were influential figures who functioned as specialists in rituals. More figurines were found depicting female than male deities, and women were typically buried with female relatives—their mothers and grandmothers—and not with their husbands. This is not to suggest that all women were equals. The prevalence of contrasting hairstyles and clothing on many surviving figurines indicates that women were differentiated by a great number of class and ethnic markers.

Among the more intriguing clues to the way women fared in the Indus valley is a tiny artifact from Mohenjo-Daro called *Dancing Girl*, a bronze and copper figurine about 4.5 inches tall and dating from around 2500 BCE (Figure 5.21). Created by a method of casting bronze known as the "lost wax" method, the nude figure appears in a confident and relaxed pose, with her hair gathered in a bun. She may have represented a royal woman, a sacred priestess of a temple, or perhaps a lower-born tribal girl. That scholars can draw such a wide array of plausible conclusions speaks to the fact that the Indus valley likely had a very fluid class structure and a highly complex society.

FIGURE 5.21 Dancing Girl. A bronze and copper figurine from India, the tiny *Dancing Girl* found at Mohenjo-Daro stands as one of the most enigmatic artifacts from ancient Asia. (credit: modification of work "Bronze 'Dancing Girl,' Mohenjo-daro, c. 2500 BC" by Gary Todd/Flickr, Public Domain)

The Aryans and Brahmanism

The Aryans entered the Indian subcontinent as conquerors beginning in 1800 BCE. With them came a new religion, Vedic, named for their hymns called Vedas. Vedas were sung in rituals to celebrate a pantheon of gods representing various aspects of nature and human life and were a useful way of teaching, given that the Aryans were illiterate. Gods such as Varuna ruled the sky, while Indra was the god of war. The Aryans offered ritualistic sacrifices to their gods and built enormous altars of fire, imposing a hierarchy on the people they conquered that emphasized strict observance of the law. The Vedas, along with poems and prayers, were first transmitted orally from one generation to the next; later they were recorded in the written language of Sanskrit. Over time, the Indian peoples added new dimensions to the Vedic religion, changing the nature of Aryan society as well. New gods such as Soma, associated with magical elixirs, storehouses for grain, and the moon, grew in importance as the practice of ritual became ever more meaningful.

A later series of treatises known as the *Upanishads*, written by a priestly class called Brahmans, developed new expressions of the Vedic religion, gradually transforming it into what many scholars refer to as Brahmanism. These new expressions include **samsara** and **karma**. Samsara was a view of humanity and the universe in which the soul left the body after death to be reborn. Karma represented the idea that all human actions, moral and immoral, were counted and weighed, ultimately governing whether a person was reborn higher on the spiritual ladder in the next life, perhaps as a king or priest, or—if ruined by immoral acts—as a lower life form, perhaps a detested reptile, to try again. The ultimate goal of a person's earthly life was to achieve union with Brahman, the ultimate and universal reality. Even gods needed to perform good acts such as penance or meditation to transcend to a higher plane of existence. Belief in reincarnation supported the idea that a person's status in the present life came about not by chance, but rather as a consequence of past lives. Thus the authority of elites such as the Brahmans was sanctified as reflecting the divine will of the cosmos.

In this way, the Vedic religion of the Aryans religion produced the *varna*, a strictly hierarchical society based on inherited status. At the highest level were the Brahmans, who exerted authority by virtue of their knowledge of the sacrificial rituals and their role as guardians of the poems, hymns, and later texts that carried on the Vedic traditions. Below them were aristocratic warriors, Kshatriya, members of noble families who fought in small but effective armies to protect their kingdoms and carry conquest into new areas. Members of the third class living in the upper half of society were merchants and Aryan commoners, Vaishya, who along with the other two enjoyed privileges based on the idea that in their late childhood they underwent a rebirth.

The fourth major group were the Shudras, non-Aryan servants and peasants who were denied the opportunity to read or listen to Vedic hymns and accounted for more than half the population. At the bottom of society were the Dalits, a class of "untouchables," who were likely the descendants of the populations that lived in parts of south India before the arrival of the Aryans. They were effectively outside and hierarchically below the four-tiered caste system. Prohibitions against marrying Indians from another caste were just one element of a constellation of provisions designed to keep everyone locked in their inherited class from birth to death. Taxes on the lower classes ensured that wealth remained at the top. In truth, the Indian subcaste system was quite complex. Distinctions between groups within each caste mattered a great deal as well, creating sub-castes that came with separate privileges, obligations, and social circles that fixed where people lived and who they could marry.

The caste system reflected Hindu religious beliefs by ensuring that people performed their proper role in this life based on their actions in the past. The laws preventing upward mobility and protecting the privilege of elites were seen as guaranteeing order. They kept the low-born from escaping the divine plan and the cosmic justice that allowed for a slow, steady advancement up the spiritual scale over a series of lives. The ultimate goal was release from the wheel of life, the never-ending transmission of the soul to ultimate peace. Thus the arrival of Aryans and the gradual emergence of Brahmanism created a new social blueprint for India.

Buddhism

Indian culture, religion, and art were forever transformed with the life of Buddha Sakyamuni around 563 BCE. The son of a royal family living near India's eastern border with Nepal and sometimes known as Siddartha or Gautama, Sakyamuni abandoned a life of luxury in his family's palace after experiencing an awakening, upon which he embarked on a spiritual journey that lasted the rest of his life. He came to be called the Buddha, meaning "enlightened," because his teachings offered an alternative to the then-dominant Brahmanist values.

Buddhism explores the depths of human suffering, desire, envy, decadence, and death, offering adherents a way out of an eternal cycle of misery if they adopt the Four Noble Truths leading to the Eightfold Path. The Four Noble Truths acknowledge that pain and disappointment are an unavoidable part of life and that by focusing on spiritual matters via the Eightfold Path, pain and suffering can be overcome. By adopting Buddha's teachings about how to think, speak, and act with respect for all life, and many other practices, followers eventually arrive at an enlightened salvation called *nirvana*. Nirvana is a state of ultimate peace found in the extinction of all desire and transcendence of the person's very being. Without nirvana, upon death the soul is reincarnated into a new life that will again run the gamut of suffering, misery, and the search for enlightenment.

The teachings of Buddha and his followers issued a direct challenge to the status quo in ancient India. In his time, Buddha relished criticizing the Brahmans, questioning their authority and their dependence on ritualism. Continued generations of teachers, missionaries, and lay Buddhists used his teachings to assail the Brahmanist-based caste system. Female Buddhists were attracted by ideas promoting the opportunity for women to achieve enlightenment on an equal basis with men.

Before Buddhism, Brahmanist teachings had supported a system of gender that in the first centuries of the common era pronounced women's genitalia foul, leading women to be excluded from public rituals and worship. Buddhism protected women from being seen as spiritually unclean, promising them an elevated status and greater participation in the community's spiritual life. The same was true for members of the lower castes despite their inherited class. Both women and lower castes were drawn to Buddhism by the greater independence and freedom they found in it. But women adopting Buddhism often found the religion just as patriarchal: Buddhist monasteries were segregated into spheres for male monks and female nuns, and women were given lower positions and fewer privileges.

Buddhism never supplanted Brahmanism as the dominant religion in India. In later centuries, Buddhist thought and institutions were influenced by Brahmanism, incorporating deities such as Shiva and concepts such as karma. Boundaries between the two religions became blurred, a development that helped followers of Brahmanism and Buddhists find a means for coexistence and even cooperation. Buddhism arose in a historical context dominated by a Brahmanist society, and many Buddhist teachings and practices such as meditation reflect the influence of Brahmanism. Likewise, Brahmanism was greatly influenced by Buddhism and its popularity with certain classes in India. As a result, over several centuries between around 400 BCE and 200 CE, Brahmanism evolved into more of a devotional religion, allowing individual practitioners to communicate directly with the gods, not just through the Brahman priests. Worship became more personalized and private, centered on prayer and songs within the home. In this way, Brahmanism emerged as Hinduism, which retained the caste system and belief in the Vedas while also offering a prescription for common followers seeking to live a moral and fulfilling life. What emerged as the central text of Hinduism was called the *Bhagavad Gita*. Finished around 300 CE, it taught that commoners, not just Brahmans, could lead exemplary moral lives by abandoning bodily desires and seeking inner peace.

Both Buddhism and Hinduism were and remained diverse, branching into hundreds of schools of thought and sects that were each quite adaptable to local contexts. As it became institutionalized, however, Buddhism lost some of its early character as a means for liberation of the lowly of India. Instead it attracted the patronage of elites, who elevated it into Asia's most influential source of inspiration for monumental architecture and high art. Buddhism made inroads across all of Asia, coming to be adopted by millions in China, Korea, Thailand, Japan, and many other communities in Southeast Asia.

DUELING VOICES

Hinduism and Buddhism in Ancient India

The first excerpt, concerning the Hindu tradition, is from the *Bhagavad Gita*, titled "Perform Action, Free from Attachment." The second, "Basic Teachings of the Buddha," includes a version of Buddhism's teachings on the Four Noble Truths and the Eightfold Path. Notice how each spiritual system conceived of immorality, the proper way to demonstrate right conduct and living, and the purpose of life.

> 8. Perform thou action that is (religiously) required;
> For action is better than inaction.
> And even the maintenance of the body for thee
> Can not succeed without action.
> 9. Except action for the purpose of worship,
> This world is bound by actions;

Action for that purpose, son of Kunti,
Perform thou, free from attachment (to its fruits)
10. Therefore unattached ever
Perform action that must be done;
For performing action without attachment
Man attains the highest. . . .
21. Whatsoever the noblest does,
Just that in every case other folk (do);
What he makes his standard,
That the world follows.
35. Better one's own duty, (tho) imperfect,
Than another's duty well performed;
Better death in (doing) one's own duty;
Another's duty brings danger.

—*Bhagavad Gita*, translated by Franklin Edgerton

What, now, is the Noble Truth of Suffering? Birth is suffering; Decay is suffering; Death is suffering; Sorrow, Lamentation, Pain, Grief, and Despair, are suffering; not to get what one desires, is suffering. . . .

What, now, is the Noble Truth of the Origin of Suffering? It is that craving which gives rise to fresh rebirth, and, bound up with pleasure and lust, now here, now there, finds ever fresh delight.

What, now, is the Noble Truth of the Extinction of Suffering? It is the complete fading away and extinction of this desire, its forsaking and giving up, the liberation and detachment from it. . . .

It is the Noble Eightfold Path, the way that leads to the extinction of suffering, namely: 1. Right Understanding, 2. Right Mindedness, which together are Wisdom. 3. Right Speech, 4. Right Action, 5. Right Living, which together are Morality. 6. Right Effort, 7. Right Attentiveness, 8. Right Concentration, which together are Concentration. This is the Middle Path which the Perfect One has found out, which makes one both to see and to know, which leads to peace, to discernment, to enlightenment, to Nirvana.

. . .

—*Buddha, the Word*, edited by Nyanatiloka

- Based on these excerpts, what does it mean for one to lead a moral life in each of these distinct traditions?
- How is the Eightfold Path in the Buddhist excerpt similar to or different from the call for action in the Hindu excerpt?

The Mauryan Empire

The initial spur to Buddhism's migration across Asia occurred with the rise of the Mauryan Empire (326–184 BCE). This entity grew out of the smaller Indian kingdom of Magahda once its ruler, Chandragupta Maurya, managed to unify much of north India from a capital near the city of Patna and pass it on to his descendants, founding the Maurya dynasty. A Greek historian named Megasthenes visited the seat of Chandragupta's power around the end of the fourth century BCE, marveling at its palaces replete with grottoes, bathing pools, and gardens filled with jasmine, hibiscus, and lotus.

Ruling over a population nearing fifty million, Chandragupta's successors conquered all but the southern tip of the subcontinent in a series of military campaigns. The Mauryan Empire's political structure employed a large and well-run army, administered by a war office with branches for a navy and for raising horses and elephants for cavalry warfare. A civilian bureaucracy ran the ministries overseeing industries such as weaving, mining, and shipbuilding as well as organizing irrigation, road construction, and tax collection. The Mauryan rulers lived in constant fear of assassination and intrigue against their rule, however, which forced them to rely on an elaborate network of spies to monitor officials throughout the empire.

The high point of Mauryan greatness came with the ascension of Emperor Ashoka in approximately 268 BCE, opening a period of monumental architecture that left its mark on the ancient world. Ashoka's personal grandeur came from the story of his transformation from a ruthless warrior general to a devout man of peace with a universal mission (Figure 5.22). As the head of the Mauryan army laying siege to the kingdom of Kalinga, he won a great battle that caused an estimated 100,000 deaths. The carnage brought an awakening that led Ashoka to Buddhism and to reforms intended to promote harmony and compassionate rule throughout India. To that end, he supported missionary efforts to spread Buddhism to Burma and Sri Lanka. His new law code gave protections to the vulnerable—the ill and diseased, the poor and powerless, and travelers making their way across the empire. His ministers put their sovereign's will into action by building hospitals, digging wells, setting up rest-houses along India's roads, and sending out traveling magistrates to resolve disputes and bring justice to remote areas.

FIGURE 5.22 Ashoka in Splendor. This stone representation of the Mauryan ruler Ashoka visiting a Buddhist pilgrimage site with his entourage is from a large commemorative monument begun in his lifetime to house relics of Buddha. It illustrates the many strategies he adopted to magnify his rule. (credit: modification of work "King Asoka visits Ramagrama" by Anandajoti Bhikkhu/Flickr, CC BY 2.0)

Ashoka also had a lasting influence on the world of art. He decreed that his sayings and teachings on morality be inscribed on stone pillars erected throughout India (Figure 5.23). The Pillars of Ashoka demonstrate the Indian empire's character as a spiritual and political system. Through Buddhism, patronage of the arts, and monumental architecture, the Mauryans wished to demonstrate morality and benevolence to their subjects and exercise less direct rule. Leaders such as Ashoka hoped the people's loyalty and duty in turn would be motivated by admiration of their achievements, if not by the money and other gifts given to reward the virtuous and charm supporters. The Pillars of Ashoka also demonstrate the flexibility of the Mauryan system of rule. Those closest to the capital were inscribed with detailed summaries of the Mauryan codes for behavior and an orderly society. Farther away, in newly won territories, the pillars promoted very simple teachings, a mark of the ruler's intent to allow room for local autonomy and customs to prevail as long as his subjects met certain universal norms and tax obligations.

FIGURE 5.23 The Pillars of Ashoka. The incised stoned pillars with Ashoka's decrees about morality were erected throughout the Mauryan Empire and demonstrate how his message and role as sovereign were conditioned by local customs. (credit: "Asoka's Pillar, Monolith in Fort, Allahabad" by Thomas A. Rust/Wikimedia Commons, Public Domain)

At the end of Ashoka's reign, the Mauryans left a legacy for future generations of Indian rulers to try to emulate so as to rule a diverse society. When the Mauryan Empire finally collapsed in 185 BCE, India entered another period of fragmentation and rule by small competing states and autonomous cities and villages. By the early centuries of the common era, it was a multitude of smaller regional kingdoms that shared with each other a common culture linked by Hinduism, Buddhism, a canon of Sanskrit texts, and the caste system.

The Gupta Dynasty

From the fourth to the seventh centuries, an empire founded by the Gupta dynasty (320–600 CE) ruled over northern India. As revealed by the name he took, Chandragupta, the founder, emulated the Mauryans and its famous founder, Chandragupta Maurya. He hired scribes working in Sanskrit to promote learning and the arts, and during this age, Sanskrit became the basis for a classical literature that influenced generations of Indians and the world. Texts such as the *Mahabharata* and *Ramayana* glorified ideas about duty, valor, and performing a proper role in society (Figure 5.24). The first was a collection of thrilling poems featuring feuding rulers and powerful families, the other an epic tale of a warrior prince's journey to recover his honor.

FIGURE 5.24 The Humiliation of Draupadi. The *Mahabharata* is possibly the longest poem even written, with over 200,000 verse lines describing the lives and conflicts of several noble families. One of the main women featured in the stories is Draupadi, known for her beauty and morality. This eighteenth-century watercolor painting depicts a story in the epic when Draupadi's enemies attempt to humiliate her by stripping her naked. However, she's saved by the Hindu god Krishna who miraculously clothes her anew each time her dress is removed. (credit: "The disrobing of Draupadi" by Howard Hodgkin Collection, Purchase, Gift of Florence and Herbert Irving, by exchange, 2022/Yousef Jameel Centre for Islamic and Asian Art/Wikimedia Commons, Public Domain)

In *Ramayana*, Rama, an avatar for the Hindu deity Vishnu, triumphs over the demon Ravana on the island of Sri Lanka and rescues his wife Sita before going on to found a perfect Indian society from his capital of Ayudha. His noble virtues and ideal society became models for Hindus to aspire to as rulers and aristocrats, while his exploits were retold for centuries in countless paintings, sculptures, carnivals, plays, and shadow theatres.

The Sanskrit classics *Mahabharata* and *Ramayana* soon spread far and wide in Southeast Asia, where they became part of the cultural fabric for a multitude of non-Indians as well. Other intellectuals of the Gupta era proved themselves in the field of mathematics by using decimals and a mark to denote the concept of zero for precise measurements and recordkeeping. Among the more notable was the astronomer Brahmagupta, who in the seventh century CE pioneered the use of multiplication and division and the idea of negative numbers.

⊘ LINK TO LEARNING

You can read a brief synopsis of the *Ramayana* and a description of the epic's major characters (https://openstax.org/l/77RamayanaSyn) at the British Library website.

An animated English-language version of the epic (https://openstax.org/l/77RamayanaVid) is also available.

In politics the Guptas were innovators as well. In return for their loyalty, rulers granted tracts of land as gifts to powerful families, Brahmans, and temple complexes, guaranteeing these followers a share of the harvest and consolidating their own control. In return, the Brahmans elevated the Gupta rulers to new heights in rituals honoring Vishnu and Shiva. Yet as these deities became more important, worship among the commoners turned more personal and private; singing as a form of prayer and ritualism inside the home became essential to daily lives. Many Indians began to believe in the sanctity of *bhakti*, a direct personal relationship between a follower and the deity. This idea bypassed the role of Brahmans as intermediaries, displeasing the Brahmans but gaining popularity in southern India, where poems written in the Tamil language became foundational to the new practice of personalized worship among Hindus.

The Gupta's dynasty marked a flourishing of art and religion and the heyday of Buddhism in India. Painted caves with beautiful sculptures found in the Ajanta caves illustrate the sophistication of the artists patronized by the dynasty. While Hinduism remained the official religion of the state and the Guptas, Buddhist universities such as Nalanda were among the first of their kind in the ancient world and attracted throngs of students and pilgrims from China. India's educated classes ranked among the most learned and knowledgeable of the ancient world, and at times they turned their attention from math and morality to explore the depths of passion, love, and eroticism. During this period, the *Kama Sutra*, a treatise on courtship and sexuality, became a seminal piece of Indian literature, inspiring and titillating generations worldwide ever since.

The opulence and stability provided by the Guptas dissipated under the threat of invaders from the north known as the Huns. While northern India fractured into smaller states after this point, southern India's ties and trade with South Asia deepened and matured. By the eleventh century, the region's profitable exports of goods such as ivory, pepper, spices, Roman coins, and even animals like the peacock had led to the formation of notable southern kingdoms, such as the Tamil Chola dynasty. But the most influential exports from India to the rest of South Asia—Hinduism, Buddhism, and the art and learning each inspired—long outlived these states.

Key Terms

"Mandate of Heaven" the favor of the gods that conferred a right to rule but could be lost by those less worthy

clan a small group of several families that shared an encampment and herded or hunted together and formed the basic social unit of the seminomadic peoples of Eurasia

Confucianism a Chinese school of philosophical thought shaping morality, governance, education, and family life

Daoism a Chinese religion that emphasized veneration of nature, the cosmos, and mysticism

Inner Asian Steppe the eastern half of the Eurasian Steppe that stretches into Mongolia and runs along the northern border of China

karma a Hindu concept emphasizing the influence of good deeds and moral behavior on a person's status in life and rebirth after death

khan a title claimed by warrior-kings to unite various tribes into powerful confederations and empires

Legalism a school of philosophical thought that helped dynasties such as the Qin use uniform laws and codes to reform and strengthen rulers

Peking Man a subspecies of *Homo erectus* identified by fossil remains found in northern China

Ring of Fire the boundary line of a zone of intense seismic activity in the Pacific Ocean

samsara a Hindu concept explaining the continuance of the soul after death and its transformation

Silk Roads a series of trade routes circulating luxury goods to and from China and parts of central Asia, India, and the Middle East

Terracotta Army a collection of life-size clay statues of soldiers, officials, servants, and horses of the Qin emperor and buried in his tomb near Xi'an

Three Han the three groups (the Mahan, Jinhan, and Byeonhan) in southern Korea that were among the earliest with tribal chieftains

Section Summary

5.1 Ancient China

Parts of today's People's Republic of China were home to many migrant groups from disparate cultures who arrived in waves over hundreds of years. But many of these cultures left behind the tools necessary for others to centralize political control and create forms of common culture, such as a written script and schools of thought and religion such as Confucianism, Daoism, and Legalism. Together, China's first dynasties—the Shang, Zhou, and Qin—produced an imperial blueprint for harnessing the power of an agrarian civilization that succeeding generations of Chinese adopted and modified to found their own dynasties.

5.2 The Steppes

Around 1500 BCE, climate change forced many ethnic groups living in the eastern portion of the Eurasian Steppe to abandon farming and turn to a nomadic lifestyle, herding livestock and hunting from horseback. They alternately traded with and raided the settled agricultural societies of China and Korea. Several formed military confederations. The Xiongnu, for instance, fought with the Chinese for control of the Silk Roads. The Han dynasty first sought to appease the Xiongnu but later sent military expeditions to defeat them.

Following internal dissension within the Xiongnu confederation in the middle of the first century BCE, the Southern Xiongnu became vassals of the Han dynasty and assisted them in their fight against the Northern Xiongnu. After the collapse of the Han dynasty, Xiongnu tribes established their own states in northern China, as did the Xianbei. In 439 CE, the Touba clan of the Xianbei established the Northern Wei dynasty. As the Northern Wei adopted Chinese culture and intermarried with wealthy Chinese families, however, they alienated other members of the Xianbei, who rose against them in 524 CE. Following the collapse of the Xiongnu and Xianbei, the Khitan rose to prominence, establishing their own Liao dynasty in 907.

5.3 Korea, Japan, and Southeast Asia

By the end of the ancient era, Korea, Japan, and Southeast Asia were home to a number of impressive states that channeled written languages, trade, and cultural exchange from their larger neighbors to power distinctive cultures and royal courts. As seafaring cultures, all three areas were also well positioned to engage a wider world than just India and China. Moreover, the achievements of Koreans and Southeast Asians in monumental architecture, such as the Seokgoram Grotto and Borobudur, are some of the richest and most artistically dynamic of the ancient world. At the same time, the geographic constraints these areas faced hindered cultural unity and social stability, as natural disasters, porous borders, and vibrant trade networks brought an array of problems difficult to solve without the machinery of a modern government.

5.4 Vedic India to the Fall of the Maurya Empire

A sophisticated civilization developed in the Indus River valley, centered on cities such as Harappa and Mohenjo-Daro. These cities were abandoned around 1700 BCE, however, possibly because of deforestation and a decline in soil productivity. India was then invaded by a people called the Aryans, whose social structure was based on hereditary social castes and the Vedic religion. This religion, incorporating a belief in reincarnation and karma, developed into Hinduism.

In the sixth century BCE, an Indian prince named Siddhartha Gautama founded the religion of Buddhism as an alternative to Hinduism and taught people how they might escape the suffering of the world. Buddhism spread beyond India following the conversion in the third century BCE of Ashoka, a king of the Mauryan dynasty, which had unified northern India in the preceding century. After the collapse of the Mauryan Empire, a new empire was established by Chandragupta of the Gupta dynasty, and Indian art and culture flourished. Despite their accomplishments, however, the Guptas lost control of northern India when the Huns invaded, and the area was broken into smaller independent kingdoms.

Assessments

Review Questions

1. What purpose did jade *not* serve in the early Neolithic cultures of China?
   a. artwork
   b. currency
   c. funeral rites and religious rituals
   d. jewelry

2. What key piece of evidence convinced scholars that the Shang dynasty was not a mythical dynasty, as was once believed?
   a. oracle bones
   b. chariots
   c. bronze weapons
   d. agriculture

3. What was one of the major tenets of early Confucian thought?
   a. the need for clearly defined law codes
   b. the search for natural beauty and immortality
   c. the right of sovereigns to rule based on the favor of heaven
   d. the need for rulers to exhibit moral leadership and virtuous conduct

4. In what way did the mobilization for war during the Warring States Period contribute to economic growth in China?
   a. Mercenary work became a primary occupation for commoners.

b. Conquered rulers were forced to pay heavy taxes.

c. War encouraged more cross-regional trade in things like copper and horses.

d. To avoid fighting, aristocrats transformed themselves into merchants.

5. What Chinese tradition from the Hundred Schools of Thought encouraged "nonaction" as an important political concept?

a. Confucianism

b. Legalism

c. Mohism

d. Daoism

6. Which was *not* one of the nomadic cultures that lived on the Inner Asian Steppe in the ancient world?

a. Di

b. Xiongnu

c. Xianbei

d. Yangshao

7. What Inner Asian Steppe peoples founded the Northern Wei dynasty?

a. Xiongnu

b. Xianbei

c. Di

d. Jie

8. Why do scholars think that the people of the Inner Asian Steppe began to abandon agriculture for livestock herding around 1500 BCE?

a. climate change

b. war between clans

c. introduction of the horse

d. pressure from the Shang dynasty

9. What early culture was known for its bronze drums that spread widely across Southeast Asia?

a. Yayoi

b. Dong Son

c. Emishi

d. Baekje

10. What climatic condition supported the transfer of culture between India and Southeast Asia?

a. warm summers

b. torrential rails

c. monsoon winds

d. dust storms

11. What group in Japan invented new technologies like pottery in an effort to adapt to the climate changes occurring around twelve thousand years ago?

a. the Jōmon

b. the Yayoi

c. the Yamato

d. the Silla

12. Which of the Three Kingdoms of Korea, though originally the smallest and least powerful, came to

dominate the others with the help of China?

   a. Goguryeo

   b. Baekje

   c. Silla

   d. Mahan

13. What imported technology from China and Korea seems to have been connected to the religious transformations occurring in Japan during the beginning of the Yamato era?

   a. mirrors

   b. rice cultivation

   c. bronze

   d. gold jewelry

14. What cultural practice of the people in Jinhan (Korea) suggests they were in contact with Japan?

   a. They tattooed their bodies.

   b. They practiced Buddhism.

   c. They used Chinese script.

   d. They built stone temples.

15. What is the name of the hymns the Aryans brought to India?

   a. Bhakti

   b. Ashoka

   c. Vedas

   d. Brahmans

16. What Indian ruler promoted the spread of Buddhism after his own conversion?

   a. Chandragupta

   b. Megasthenes

   c. Rama

   d. Ashoka

17. What do Buddhists call the state of ultimate peace found in the extinction of all desire?

   a. brahman

   b. karma

   c. nirvana

   d. samsara

18. What group occupied the highest tier in the Indian caste system?

   a. Kshatriya

   b. Vaishya

   c. Shudra

   d. Brahman

Check Your Understanding Questions

1. What were some of the legacies or characteristics of each of the three dynasties of ancient China?

2. What effect did the Warring States period have on the development of Confucianism and Legalism?

3. How did Daoist concepts help the Chinese people deal with the chaos of the Warring States period?

4. Describe a few of the ways in which nomadic cultures and societies differed from their agrarian neighbors.

5. How would you describe the relationship between the Xiongnu and the Han dynasty of China?

6. What role did changing climatic conditions play in the lifestyle of the people of the Inner Asian Steppe?

7. Compare and contrast the roles of women in politics in ancient Korea and Japan, including Queen Himiko (Japan) and Queen Seondeok (Korea).

8. How might climate change have affected the development of early Japanese culture?

9. How did Chinese and Korean culture influence the development of Japanese culture during the Yayoi and Yamato periods?

10. To what extent was Buddhism liberating for women in India?

11. Following the development of Buddhism, how did changes in Brahmanism reduce the influence and prestige of the Brahman class as it evolved into Hinduism?

Application and Reflection Questions

1. Most scholars today still hold that the Xia dynasty was a mythical dynasty developed during the Zhou dynasty period. Given what you've learned about the Mandate of Heaven, how might the Zhou rulers have benefited from encouraging belief in the Xia?

2. Some scholars mark the end of the Warring States period in 256 BCE with the collapse of the Zhou dynasty, while others use the date for the establishment of the first Chinese empire, 221 BCE. Given what you've learned about the features of the Warring States period, which date seems more appropriate?

3. How would you characterize the relationship between the peoples of the steppes and their neighbors—was it primarily about conflict, war, and competition? Or were its purposes economic exchange and cultural adaptation? Explain your answer.

4. Given what you've learned about the environment of the steppe and the lifestyle practiced there, why was the horse and the use of the horse in battle such an important part of their daily life?

5. What were some of the geographical barriers to the development of agrarian societies in Japan, Korea, and Southeast Asia? What technologies and social practices allowed each culture to make the transition from hunting, gathering, and fishing to farming?

6. The religion of Buddhism from India ultimately made a huge impact on the people of China, Korea, Japan, and across Southeast Asia. Why do you think Buddhism was so attractive to the people in these different places?

7. Compare Buddhism and Hinduism to Chinese religions such as Daoism and philosophical schools such as Confucianism and Legalism. Are there any ideas or values that made the Chinese traditions more advantageous to political stability and empire? Alternatively, what Buddhist and Hindu teachings promoted local autonomy and regionalism in India?

FIGURE 6.1 Alexander the Great. This first-century CE portrayal of the Macedonian king Alexander the Great is part of a large mosaic depicting the Battle of Issus (333 BCE) that was discovered in a home excavated in Pompeii, Italy. (credit: modification of work "Alexander and Bucephalus - Battle of Issus mosaic" by Museo Archeologico Nazionale – Naples/Wikimedia Commons, Public Domain)

CHAPTER OUTLINE

6.1 Early Mediterranean Peoples
6.2 Ancient Greece
6.3 The Hellenistic Era
6.4 The Roman Republic
6.5 The Age of Augustus

INTRODUCTION In the first century CE, a wealthy Roman in the southern Italian town of Pompeii decorated his home with an elaborate mosaic portraying the decisive victory of the Macedonians, led by Alexander the Great, over the Persian Empire at the Battle of Issus (in modern Turkey) in 333 BCE (Figure 6.1). Why would a Roman invest in such expensive decoration to commemorate the three hundred–year-old victory of a foreign king in a distant land?

Beginning approximately 3,500 years before our time, the lands that border the Mediterranean Sea became increasingly linked by commerce and cultural interaction. These links culminated in the emergence of the Roman Empire, which had united all these regions by the first century CE. Greek colonists had settled the region of Pompeii some seven hundred years before this mosaic was produced, and Alexander, the hero of the battle, was a champion in Greek culture. With his iconic victory over the Persian "barbarians," he represented the shared cultural legacy of Greeks and Romans. The history of the ancient Mediterranean world shows how this common culture developed over time.

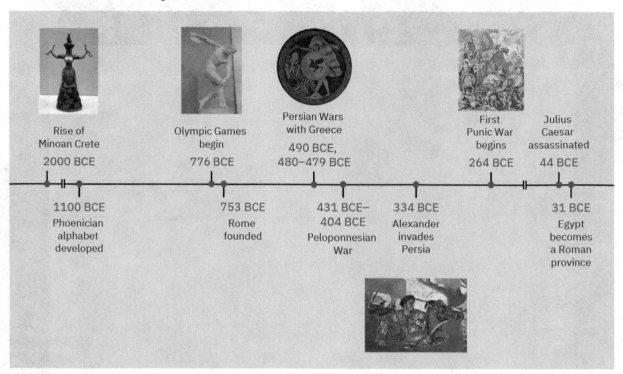

FIGURE 6.2 Timeline: Mediterranean Peoples. (credit "2000 BCE": modification of work "Figurine of the Snake Goddess. Archaeological Museum of Herakleion" by O.Mustafin/Wikimedia Commons, CC0 1.0; credit "776 BCE: modification of work "Discobolus side 2" by Ricky Bennison/Wikimedia Commons, CC0 1.0; credit "490 BCE, 480–479 BCE": modification of work "Persian Warrior (Left) and Greek Warrior (Right) in a Duel" by National Museums Scotland/Wikimedia Commons, Public Domain; credit "334 BCE": modification of work "Alexander and Bucephalus - Battle of Issus mosaic" by Museo Archeologico Nazionale – Naples/Wikimedia Commons, Public Domain; credit "264 BCE": modification of work "Heinrich Leutemann - Hannibals Übergang über die Alpen (cropped)" by Musée Dauphinois Grenoble/Wikimeida Commons, Public Domain)

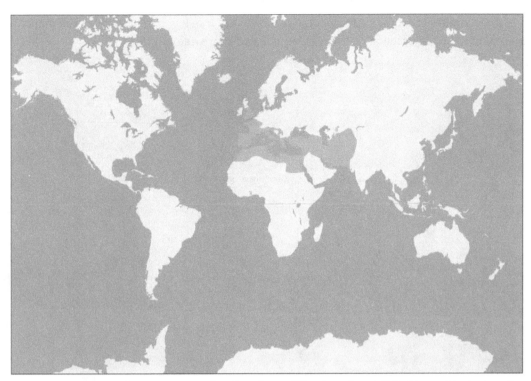

FIGURE 6.3 **Locator Map: Mediterranean Peoples.** (credit: modification of work "World map blank shorelines" by Maciej Jaros/Wikimedia Commons, Public Domain)

6.1 Early Mediterranean Peoples

LEARNING OBJECTIVES

By the end of this section, you will be able to:
- Identify the regional peoples of the Mediterranean before 500 BCE
- Discuss the technological achievements of the early Mediterranean peoples
- Describe the interconnectedness of the early Mediterranean peoples

During the Bronze Age (c. 3300–1200 BCE), trade connected the peoples and cultures of Greece and the Aegean islands such as Crete. By the third millennium BCE, the inhabitants of these lands were already producing wine and olive oil, products in high demand in ancient Egypt and the Near East. The Aegean Minoan and Mycenaean civilizations of the Late Bronze Age (c. 1600–1100 BCE) thus shared in the economic prosperity and cultural interaction that linked the eastern Mediterranean with the ancient cultures of western Asia.

The eventual collapse of the Late Bronze Age world coincided with the development of new technology that allowed people to devise iron tools and weapons. During the new Iron Age, the Phoenicians not only preserved Bronze Age cultural traditions but they also developed a revolutionary new communication tool, the alphabet, that vastly expanded literacy. They established trading posts across the Mediterranean as far as Spain, often in search of new sources of iron ore and other metals such as tin. The arrival of the Phoenicians and Greek traders in the western Mediterranean brought them into contact with the Etruscans in the Italian peninsula. Thus, the period from the Bronze Age through the Iron Age witnessed the development of numerous cultures across the Mediterranean.

The Late Bronze Age World

Egypt was the dominant economic and military power of the Late Bronze Age, for the most part a time of economic prosperity and political stability. Other powerful kingdoms included Minoan Crete, Mycenaean Greece, the Hittites of Asia Minor (modern Turkey), the Mitanni and Assyrians in northern Mesopotamia, and the Kassites and Elamites in southern Mesopotamia and western Iran (Figure 6.4). While each maintained its own unique culture, their interactions created a shared Late Bronze Age culture.

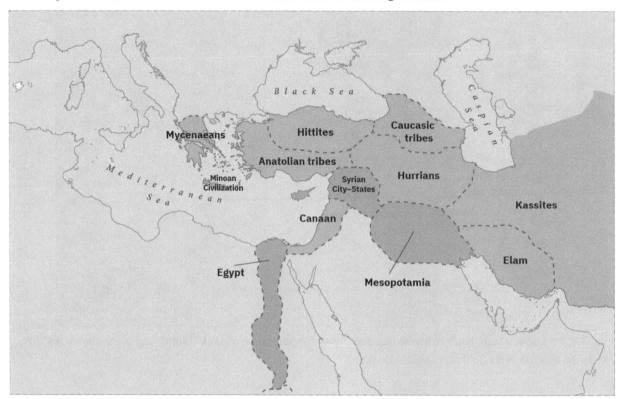

FIGURE 6.4 The Bronze Age World. While Egypt was the dominant power in the relatively peaceful Late Bronze Age, many other cultures thrived during this time. (credit: modification of work "Near East and Mediterranean in 2000 BCE" by "Briangotts"/Wikimedia Commons, CC BY 2.5)

For instance, they all used a redistributive economic system in which agricultural goods were collected from local farmers as taxes, stored in the palace or temple, and redistributed to urban artisans, merchants, and officials who could not grow food. They all possessed military forces of elite warriors trained to fight from horse-drawn chariots. They interacted using a common set of diplomatic practices: Official correspondence was often written in Akkadian cuneiform, military alliances were sealed by arranged marriages between the royal families of allied states, and vassal states paid tribute to dominant states to avoid military assault.

These civilizations also exchanged prized goods, such as wine and oil from Greece, cedar logs from the **Levant** (modern Israel, Jordan, Lebanon, Palestine, and Syria), and copper from the island of Cyprus. Great cultural achievements resulted from their interaction. For example, in the small maritime kingdom of Ugarit (now Syria), scribes modified Egyptian hieroglyphics to suit their local Semitic Canaanite language, creating an ancestor of our alphabet. They used this script to record traditional epic poetry featuring myths of their main deity, the storm god Baal.

Minoan Crete and Mycenaean Greece

By 2000 BCE, a unique culture had developed on the Aegean island of Crete, reaching the height of its power at the beginning of the Late Bronze Age around 1600 BCE. The later Classical Greeks told the myth of King Minos of Crete, who built a giant maze known as the Labyrinth and imprisoned there a half-man, half-bull called the Minotaur (the "Bull of Minos"). To avenge his own son's death, Minos forced young men and women from Athens in Greece to enter the Labyrinth and be eaten by the monster. Historians see in the myth a distant memory of the earlier civilization on Crete and use the term Minoan, derived from Minos, to describe it.

The Minoans built spacious palaces on Crete, the largest at Knossos. Since these were usually unfortified, historians believe Crete was generally peaceful and united under a single government with Knossos as the capital. The Minoans also established settlements and trading posts on other Aegean islands such as Thera and along the Anatolian coast. Their palaces were huge complexes that served as economic and administrative centers. To keep records for these centers the Minoans developed their own script, written on clay tablets and known to scholars as **Linear A**. It has not yet been deciphered.

A common weapon and symbol in these palaces was the *labrys*, or double ax, from which the word "labyrinth" arose. In the courtyards, young men and women participated in bullfights that may be the basis for the myth of the Minotaur. Frescoes on the palace walls depict these fights as well as sea creatures and scenes from nature (Figure 6.5). The Minoan religion revered bulls and a goddess associated with snakes, nature, and fertility. The abundance of figurines of this snake-wielding female deity and other artistic depictions of women may mean that at least some women enjoyed high social status in Minoan society. Religious rituals were practiced in small shrines as well as on mountain tops and in caves and sacred forests.

FIGURE 6.5 A Leaping Bull. This small Minoan fresco (c. 1600–1450 BCE) shows a leaping bull with one acrobat on its back and two others alongside. It is one of five discovered in the Knossos palace on Crete. (credit: "Toreador Fresco (Bull-Leaping Fresco)" by "Jebulon"/Wikimedia Commons, CC0 1.0)

🔗 LINK TO LEARNING

For a thorough examination of the art and archaeology of the Aegean Bronze Age, visit Dartmouth University's Aegean Prehistoric Archaeology (https://openstax.org/l/77AegeanPre) website.

Sometime around 1500 BCE, the palaces on Crete were destroyed. Knossos was rebuilt, and scribes there began employing a new script scholars call **Linear B**, apparently derived from Linear A and found to be an early form of Greek. Linear B clay tablets discovered on the Greek mainland led historians to conclude that Greeks from the mainland conquered Crete and rebuilt Knossos.

The Bronze Age culture that produced Linear B is called Mycenaean since the largest Bronze Age city in Greece was at Mycenae. Bronze Age Greeks appear to have migrated from the Balkans into mainland Greece around 2000 BCE and adopted Minoan civilization around the beginning of the Late Bronze Age, in 1600 BCE. Unlike the Minoans, the Mycenaean Greeks were divided into a number of separate kingdoms. Immense palace complexes like those at Knossos have been found at Mycenae, Tiryns, Thebes, Pylos, and Sparta, sometimes surrounded by monumental fortifications. These locations correspond to the powerful kingdoms described in the later Greek epic poem the *Iliad*, attributed to the poet Homer. This poem tells the story of the Trojan War, in which the Greek kingdoms, led by King Agamemnon of Mycenae, waged war against the city of Troy. Archaeologists have also uncovered the Bronze Age city of Troy in western Turkey, which suggests the *Iliad* was loosely based on oral traditions that preserved the memory of these ancient Bronze Age kingdoms. The Linear B tablets indicate that the ruler of these palaces was known as the *Wanax* or "lord," the same word used to describe the heroic kings of the *Iliad*.

The Collapse of the Bronze Age World

The last century of the Late Bronze Age, after 1200 BCE, was a period of wars and invasions that witnessed the collapse of many powerful states. The palaces of Mycenaean Greece were destroyed, perhaps following revolts by the lower class and natural disasters like climate change and earthquakes. In the centuries that followed, the population declined drastically, writing and literacy disappeared, and Greece entered a "Dark Age."

Later ancient Greek historians reported that Greek-speaking tribes known as the Dorians migrated from northwest Greece to the south after the Trojan War. The instability in Greece and the Aegean resulted in much migration by people in search of new homes. For instance, ancient Egyptian inscriptions tell us that the "Sea Peoples" destroyed the Hittite Empire and numerous kingdoms in the Levant to the north of Egypt. One particular group known as the Philistines (Peleset), who attacked Egypt, eventually settled just north of Egypt along the coast of the southern Levant. But there were many others, including the Akawasha, Lukka, Shardana, Tursha, and more who washed across the eastern Mediterranean during the Late Bronze Age Collapse (Figure 6.6).

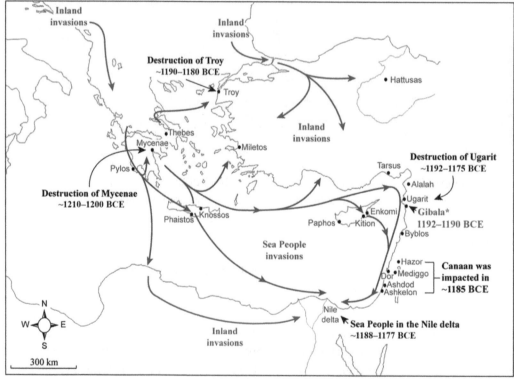

FIGURE 6.6 The Path of the Sea Peoples. The "Sea Peoples," as they were called in Egyptian records, came largely from the Aegean region. By studying the remains of pottery and other archaeological traces, scholars have concluded that these groups moved through Greece and Crete and into North Africa, Cyprus, and the Levant (as shown by the blue arrows) at the close of the Late Bronze Age. (credit: modification of work "Map of the Sea People invasions in the Aegean Sea and Eastern Mediterranean at the end of the Late Bronze Age" by David Kaniewski, Elise Van Campo, Karel Van Lerberghe, Tom Boiy, Klaas Vansteenhuyse, Greta Jans, Karin Nys, Harvey Weiss/"The Sea Peoples, from Cuneiform Tablets to Carbon Dating"/Wikimedia Commons, CC BY 2.5)

Other groups were also on the move. Libyans, who inhabited the North African coastal region west of Egypt, invaded the northern Nile River valley and settled there. The attacks of the Sea Peoples and Libyans contributed to the later collapse of Egypt's central governments after 1100 BCE, ending the New Kingdom period. Phrygians, who inhabited the Balkans in southeast Europe, migrated into Asia Minor (Turkey). The Aramaeans, nomadic tribes who spoke a Semitic language and inhabited the Arabian Desert, migrated into Syria and Mesopotamia.

These wars and invasions coincided with an important technological innovation, the birth of sophisticated iron-making technology. For thousands of years, bronze had been the metal of choice in the ancient world. But the disruptions caused by the Late Bronze Age Collapse made it difficult for metal workers to access tin, a crucial ingredient in bronze. Without a sufficient supply of tin, artisans experimented for centuries with iron ore. In the process, they developed the techniques of steeling (adding carbon to the iron to make it stronger), quenching (rapidly cooling hot iron with water), and tempering (heat treating) to produce a metal far superior in strength to bronze. By around 900 BCE, the Iron Age had begun in the eastern Mediterranean.

Phoenicians, Greeks, and Etruscans

The Phoenicians were descended from the Bronze Age Canaanites and lived in cities like Sidon and Tyre (in today's Lebanon), each ruled by a king. They were great sailors, explorers, and traders who established trading posts in Cyprus, North Africa, Sicily, Sardinia, and Spain. They sailed along the west coast of Africa and to the British Isles in search of new markets and goods such as tin (See Figure 6.7).

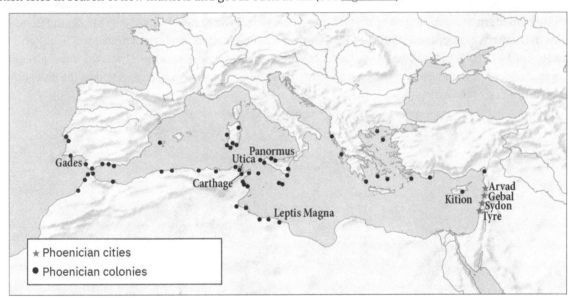

FIGURE 6.7 Phoenician Cities and Colonies. The Phoenicians were great mariners and explorers. This map shows the many cities and colonies they founded across the Mediterranean Sea. (credit: modification of work "Mediterranean at 218 BC" by "Megistias"/Wikimedia Commons, Public Domain)

Around 1100 BCE, the Phoenicians also invented the world's first known alphabet, using symbols that represented consonant sounds. Strung together, these consonants created words in which vowel sounds were interpreted by the order of the consonants. Because the Phoenician alphabet simplified the earlier script of the Canaanites, more people could now become literate, not just a small, specialized group of scribes. The Phoenicians' commercial success was undoubtedly partly a result of their better, more efficient record-keeping system that a larger population could learn and employ. Other cultures like the Aramaean peoples and the Israelites quickly adapted the new script to their own languages. By the eighth century BCE, the Greeks had also adopted and later adapted the Phoenician alphabet to write their language.

Beginning with the Assyrian Empire's expansion in the eighth century BCE, the Phoenician kingdoms became subjects of the successive Iron Age empires of western Asia: the Assyrians, the Chaldeans (Neo-Babylonian), and the Persians. The Phoenicians continued to flourish, however. The Assyrians valued Phoenician artists, and finely crafted Phoenician wares such as jewelry and furniture became popular among the ruling elites. The Persians relied largely on Phoenician sailors and ships to serve as the naval forces, especially in their campaigns to conquer Greece in the early fifth century BCE. When Phoenician city-states such as Sidon and Tyre became subject to foreign rule, many Phoenicians immigrated to the city of Carthage (in modern-day Tunisia), founded by Phoenician merchants around 700 BCE as a stopping place on the long but profitable voyage to Spain. Given this influx of immigrants, Carthage grew large and wealthy, and by the fifth century BCE the southern Italian peninsula was the dominant power in the western Mediterranean.

The Phoenicians were not the only people establishing colonial outposts around the wider Mediterranean world. Beginning in the eighth century, Greeks began founding colonies in North Africa, in coastal Spain and France, on the shores of the Black Sea, and on the Italian peninsula. Many of these colonies were built in resource-rich areas and commonly produced grain, tin, or timber for export back to Greece. Others served more mercantile interests, trading with major and minor powers across the Mediterranean. It was through these colonial ventures that Greeks and Phoenicians came into contact with the Etruscans of the northern Italian peninsula.

The Etruscans were organized into independent city-states such as Veii and Vulci, much like the Greeks were, and each city was ruled by its own king and council of elders. In their art and architecture, the Etruscans followed Greek models (Figure 6.8). They modified the alphabet the Greeks had acquired from the Phoenicians to write their language, which scholars have not yet fully deciphered. By 600 BCE, they had expanded beyond their base in modern Tuscany and colonized Rome, which became an Etruscan city. They also founded new colonies in northern and southern Italy. The Etruscan states remained the dominant power in the Italian peninsula until 474 BCE. In that year, at the Battle of Cumae off the coast of southern Italy, the naval forces of the Greek city-state of Syracuse won a decisive victory over the Etruscan fleet and emerged as the chief power in the region, along with Carthage.

FIGURE 6.8 Greek Influence in Etruria. This Etruscan antefix (roof tile) was created in the fourth century BCE and found in the Italian city of Cerveteri, northwest of Rome. The almost twenty-inch-tall piece of terracotta art depicts a maenad, a Greek mythological figure associated with the Greek god Dionysus. In its style and symbolism, it reflects the cultural exchange between the Etruscans and the Greeks. (credit: "Terracotta antefix (roof tile) with head of a maenad" by Purchase by subscription, 1896/Metropolitan Museum of Art, Public Domain)

Since ancient Rome began as an Etruscan city-state, the Etruscans strongly influenced the development of Roman culture. For example, Roman priests divined the will of the gods by examining a sacrificed animal's entrails, a custom adopted from the Etruscans. The Etruscans honored their dead with elaborate tombs, and the Romans did the same, maintaining that the spirits of their ancestors watched over them. Gladiatorial contests in Rome had origins among the Etruscans, who at funerals forced prisoners of war to fight to the death as human sacrifices to their dead. The *fasces*, a bundle of rods and an ax that symbolized the authority of Roman magistrates, originally denoted the authority of Etruscan kings. Finally, the Roman alphabet, still used in western and central Europe today, was based on Etruscan modifications to the Greek alphabet.

6.2 Ancient Greece

LEARNING OBJECTIVES

By the end of this section, you will be able to:
- Identify the historical factors that shaped the development of the Greek city-state
- Describe the evolution of the political, economic, and social systems of Athens and Sparta
- Discuss the alliances and hostilities among the Greek city-states during the Classical period
- Identify the major accomplishments of Ancient Greek philosophy, literature, and art

In the centuries following the collapse of the Bronze Age Mycenaean kingdoms around 1100 BCE, a dynamic new culture evolved in Iron Age Greece and the Aegean region. During this period, the Greek city-states developed innovative consensual governments. Free adult males participated in their own governance and voted to create laws and impose taxes. This system of government contrasted with the earlier monarchies of the ancient Near East, in which rulers claimed to govern their subjects through the will of the gods.

The degree of political participation in the Greek city-states varied from monarchy and oligarchy, or government by a small group of wealthy elites, to democracy, literally "rule by the people," a broader-based participation that eventually included both rich and poor adult males. These systems influenced Ancient Roman and European political thought through the centuries. The Greek Classical period (500–323 BCE) witnessed constant warfare among rival city-states, yet it was marked by the creation of enduring works of literature and art that inspired centuries of European artists and writers. Greek philosophers also subjected the human condition and the natural world to rational analysis, rejecting traditional beliefs and sacred myths.

Archaic Greece

The Greek Dark Ages (1100–800 BCE) persisted after the collapse of the Mycenaean civilization but began to recede around 800 BCE. From this point and for the next few centuries, Greece experienced a revival in which a unique and vibrant culture emerged and evolved into what we recognize today as Classical Greek civilization. This era, from 800 to 500 BCE, is called Archaic Greece after *arche*, Greek for "beginning."

The Greek renaissance was marked by rapid population growth and the organization of valleys and islands into independent city-states, each known as a **polis** (Greek for city-state). Towns arose around a hill fortress or *acropolis* to which inhabitants could flee in times of danger. Each polis had its own government and religious cults, and each built monumental temples for the gods, such as the temple of Hera, wife of Zeus and protector of marriage and the home, at the city-state of Argos. Though politically disunited, the Greeks, who began to refer to themselves as Hellenes after the mythical king Hellen, did share a common language and religion. The most famous of their sacred sites were Delphi, near Mount Parnassus in central Greece and seat of the oracle of Apollo, the god of prophecy, and Olympia in southern Greece, sacred to Zeus, who ruled the pantheon of gods at Mount Olympus (Figure 6.9). Beginning in 776 BCE, according to Aristotle, Greeks traveled to Olympia every four years to compete in athletic contests in Zeus's honor, the origin of the Olympic Games.

FIGURE 6.9 Zeus. This larger-than-life marble bust of the Greek god Zeus is believed to be a Roman copy of a fourth-century BCE Greek original. It was found in Otricoli, Italy, in 1775. (credit: "So-called "Zeus of Otricoli". Marble, Roman copy after a Greek original from the 4th century" by "Jastrow"/Wikimedia Commons, Public Domain)

THE PAST MEETS THE PRESENT

The Olympic Games

Postponed a year because of the COVID-19 pandemic, the 2021 Games of the XXXII Olympiad in Japan included more than three hundred events in thirty-three sports, including new entries like skateboarding, rock climbing, and surfing. Modern games have been held since 1896, when the new International Olympic Committee started the tradition, but as the name suggests, the inspiration came from Ancient Greece.

Athletic events in Ancient Greece were important displays of strength and endurance. There were contests at the sanctuaries at Delphi and Nemea (near Argos), but none was as renowned as the Olympic Games, held at the sanctuary in Olympia that was dedicated to Zeus. Contestants came from all over the Greek world, including Sicily and southern Italy.

Unlike the skateboarding and surfing of modern games, the ancient games focused on skills necessary for war: running, jumping, throwing, and wrestling. Over time, sports that included horses, like chariot racing, were also incorporated. Such events were referenced in Homer's *Iliad*, when the hero Achilles held athletic contests to honor his fallen comrade Patroclus and awarded prizes or *athla* (from which the word "athlete" is derived). The centerpiece of the ancient games was the two-hundred-yard sprint, or *stadion*, from which comes the modern word "stadium" (Figure 6.10).

FIGURE 6.10 The Original Olympic Track. These are the ruins of the original Olympic *stadion* at Olympia. The track was made of hard-packed clay for a race to be won by the fastest athlete in the Greek world. (credit: "Olympic Race Track in modern Olympia, Greece" by "Dwaipayanc"/Wikimedia Commons, Public Domain)

Unlike the modern games, where attendees pay great sums to watch athletes compete, admission to the ancient games was free—for men. Women were forbidden from watching and, if they dared to attend, could pay with their lives. Competitors were likely locals with proven abilities, though over time professional athletes came to dominate the sport. They could earn a good living from prizes and other rewards gained through their talent and celebrity, and their statues adorned the sanctuary at Olympia. The poet Pindar in the early fifth century BCE was renowned for composing songs to honor them when they returned home as victors. The Olympic Games continued to be celebrated until 393 CE, when they were halted during the reign of the Christian Roman emperor Theodosius.

- Why might the organizers of the modern Olympic Games have named their contest after the ancient Greek version?
- How are the ancient games similar to the modern Olympic Games? How are they different?

The start of the Archaic period also witnessed the reemergence of specialization in Greek society. Greek artists became more sophisticated and skilled in their work. They often copied artistic styles from Egypt and Phoenicia, where Greek merchants were engaging in long-distance trade. At the site of Al-Mina, along the Mediterranean coast in Syria where historians believe the Phoenician alphabet was first transmitted to the Greeks, Greek and Phoenician merchants exchanged goods. Far to the west, on the island of Ischia off the west coast of Italy, Greeks were competing with Phoenician merchants for trade with local peoples, whose iron ore was in strong demand. Thanks to their contact and trade with the Phoenicians, Greeks adapted the Phoenician alphabet to their own language, making an important innovation by adding vowels (a, e, i, o, u). The eighth century BCE thus witnessed the return of literacy and the end of the Aegean world's relative isolation after the interlude of the Greek Dark Ages.

The eighth century BCE was also the period in which the epic poems the *Iliad* and the *Odyssey* were composed, traditionally attributed to the blind poet Homer. While historians debate whether Homer was a historical or a legendary figure, they agree the epics originated in the songs of oral poets in the Greek Dark Ages. In the eighth century BCE, using the Greek alphabet, scribes wrote these stories down for the first time.

As the population expanded during the Archaic period, a shortage of farmland brought dramatic changes. Many Greeks in search of land to farm left their homes and founded colonies along the shores of the Black Sea and the northern Aegean, in North Africa at Cyrene in Libya, and in southern Gaul (modern France) at Massalia (Marseille). The largest number were on the island of Sicily and in southern Italy, the region the Greeks referred to as Magna Graecia or "Greater Greece." When Greeks established a colony, it became an independent polis with its own laws. The free adult males of the community divided the colony's land into equal lots. Thus, a new idea developed in the colonies that citizenship in a community was associated with equality and participation in the governing of the state.

In the society of Archaic Greece, the elite landowners, or *aristoi*, traditionally controlled the government and the priesthoods in the city-states. But thanks to the new ideas from the colonies, the common people, or *kakoi*, began demanding land and a voice in the governing of the polis. They were able to gain leverage in these negotiations because city-states needed troops in their wars for control of farmland. The nobility relied on the wealthier commoners, who could afford to equip themselves with iron weapons and armor. In some city-states, the *aristoi* and the *kakoi* were not able to resolve their differences peaceably. In such cases, a man who had strong popular support in the city would seize power and rule over the city. The Greeks referred to such populist leaders as tyrants.

In the sixth century BCE, the difficulties caused by the land shortage were relieved by the invention of coinage. A century before, adopting a practice of the kings of Lydia in western Asia Minor (Turkey), Athens stamped silver pieces with the image of an owl, a symbol of wisdom often associated with the goddess Athena (See Figure 6.11). Instead of weighing precious metals to use as currency or arguing over the value of bartered goods to trade, merchants could use coins as a simple medium of exchange. The *agora*, or place of assembly in each city-state, thus became a marketplace to buy and sell goods. In the sixth century BCE, this rise of a market economy stimulated economic growth as farmers, artisans, and merchants discovered stronger incentives to produce and procure more goods for profit. For example, farmers learned how to produce more food with the land they already possessed rather than always seeking more land. The economic growth of this period is reflected in the many new temples the Greek city-states constructed then.

FIGURE 6.11 Athenian Money. This Athenian silver coin from the fifth century BCE depicts Athena on one side and an owl, Athena's symbol, on the other. (credit: "Athens owl coin" by "yuichi"/Wikimedia Commons, CC0 1.0)

Sparta and Athens

In the Archaic period, Athens and Sparta emerged as two of the most important of the many Greek city-states. Not only did their governments and cultures dominate the Greek world in the subsequent Classical period; they also fired the imaginations of Western cultures for centuries to come. Athens was the birthplace of democracy, whereas Sparta was an oligarchy headed by two kings.

The Rise and Organization of Sparta

Sparta in the eighth century BCE was a collection of five villages in Laconia, a mountain valley in the Peloponnese in southern Greece. Due to the shortage of farmland, the citizens (adult males) of these villages, the *Spartiates*, all served in the military and waged war on neighboring towns, forcing them to pay tribute. The Spartiates also appropriated farmland for themselves and enslaved the inhabitants of these lands, most famously the Messenians, who became known as the *helots*. Just as Greek colonists at this time divided land among themselves into equal lots, the Spartiates likewise divided the conquered land equally and assigned to each landowner a certain number of helot families to work it. Helots, unlike enslaved people in other parts of Greece, could not be bought or sold but remained on the land as forced laborers from generation to generation. In the seventh century BCE, Sparta conquered the land of Messene to its west and divided its farmland equally among the Spartiates.

By the late sixth century BCE, the wealth from the rich agricultural land that Sparta then controlled had made it the most powerful state in the Peloponnese. Sparta also organized the city-states of this region and parts beyond into a system of alliances that historians refer to as the Peloponnesian League. Its members still had self-government and paid no tribute to Sparta, but all were expected to have the same friends and enemies as Sparta, which maintained its dominance in the league. Sparta also used its army to overthrow tyrants in the Peloponnesian city-states and restore political power to the *aristoi*.

The Spartans were proud of their unique system of government, or constitution, which was a set of laws and traditional political practices rather than a single document. It was said to have been created by a great lawgiver named Lycurgus around 800 BCE, but modern historians view its development as an evolutionary process during the Archaic period rather than the work of a single person.

Sparta had two hereditary kings drawn from rival royal families. Their powers were very limited, though both sat as permanent members of the Council of Elders and were priests in the state religion. On occasion, the Spartan kings also led armies into battle. The Assembly of Spartiates passed all laws and approved all treaties with the advice of the Council of Elders. This Assembly also elected five judges every year who administered the affairs of state, as well as the members of the Council of Elders.

The unique element of Spartan culture was the *agoge*, its educational system. At the age of seven, boys were separated from their families and raised by the state. To teach them to live by their wits and courage, they were fed very little so they had to learn how to steal food to survive. At the age of twelve they began an even more severe regimen. They were not allowed clothes except a cloak in the wintertime, and they bathed just once a year (Figure 6.12). They also underwent ritual beatings intended to make them physically strong and hardened warriors. At the age of eighteen, young men began two years of intense military training. At the age of twenty, a young Spartan man's education was complete.

FIGURE 6.12 **Spartan Youth.** The design of this nineteenth-century painting by French impressionist Edgar Degas was based on a passage from Plutarch's *Life of Lycurgus* and depicts Spartan girls encouraging and challenging Spartan boys. Here the boys prepare to compete in running and wrestling exercises. (credit: "Young Spartans exercising" by National Gallery, 1924: purchased from Courtauld Fund/Wikimedia Commons, Public Domain)

Women of the Spartiate class, before marrying in their mid-teens, also practiced a strict physical regimen, since they were expected to be as strong as their male relatives and husbands and even participate in defending the homeland. Spartan women enjoyed a reputation for independence, since they managed the farms while men were constantly training for or at war and often ran their family estates alone due to the early deaths of their soldier husbands. The state organized unmarried women into teams known as *chorai* (from which the term *chorus* is derived) that danced and sang at religious festivals.

When a Spartiate man reached the age of thirty, he could marry, vote in the Assembly, and serve as a judge. Each Spartiate remained in the army reserve until the age of sixty, when he could finally retire from military service and became eligible for election to the Council of Elders. Spartan citizens were proud to devote their time to the service of the state in the military and government; they did not have to work the land or learn a trade since this work was done for them by commoners and helot subjects.

The Rise and Organization of Athens

Athens, like Sparta, developed its own system of government in the Archaic period. Uniquely large among Greek city-states, Athens had long enclosed all the land of Attica, which included several mountain valleys. It was able to eventually develop into a militarily powerful democratic state in which all adult male citizens could participate in government, though "citizenship" was a restricted concept, and because only males could participate, it was by nature a limited democracy.

The roots of Athenian democracy are long and deep, however, and its democratic institutions evolved over centuries before reaching their fullest expression in the fifth century BCE. It was likely the growing prosperity of Athenians in the eighth century that had set Athens on this path. As more families became prosperous, they demanded greater say in the functioning of the city-state. By the seventh century BCE, Athens had an assembly allowing citizens (free adult males) to gather and discuss the affairs of the state. However, as the rising prosperity of Athenians stalled and economic hardship loomed by the end of the century, the durability of the fledgling democracy seemed in doubt. Attempts to solve the economic problems by adjusting the legal code, most notably by the legislator Draco (from whose name we get the modern term "draconian"), had little effect, though codifying the law in written form brought more clarity to the legal system.

With the once-thriving middle class slipping into bankruptcy and sometimes slavery, civil war seemed inevitable. Disaster was avoided only with the appointment of Solon in 594 BCE to restore order. Solon came from a wealthy elite family, but he made it known that he would draft laws to benefit all Athenians, rich and poor. A poet, he used his songs to convey his ideas for these new laws (Figure 6.13).

FIGURE 6.13 Solon. This idealized portrait in oils represents Solon, poet and legislator of Athens. It was made in the early nineteenth century by Merry-Joseph Blondel, a French painter of the Neoclassical school. (credit: "Portrait of Solon Legislator and Poet of Athenes" by Musee de Picardie/Wikimedia Commons, Public Domain)

One of Solon's first measures was to declare that all debts Athenians owed one another were forgiven. Solon also made it law that no Athenian could be sold into slavery for failure to repay a loan. These decrees did much to provide relief to farmers struggling with debt who could now return to work the land. Under Solon's new laws, each of Athens's four traditional tribes chose one hundred of its members by lot, including commoners, to sit in the new Council of Four Hundred and run the government. There were still magistrates, but now Solon created the jury courts. All Athenians could appeal the ruling of a magistrate in court and have their cases heard by a jury of fellow citizens. Solon also set up a hierarchal system in which citizens were eligible for positions in government based on wealth instead of hereditary privilege. Wealth was measured by the amount of grain and olive oil a citizen's land could produce. Only the wealthiest could serve as a magistrate, sit on the Council, and attend the Assembly and jury courts. Citizens with less wealth could participate in all these activities but could not serve as magistrates. The poorest could only attend the Assembly and the jury courts.

Solon's reforms were not enough to end civil unrest, however. By 545 BCE, a relative of his named Pisistratus had seized power by force with his own private army and ruled as a tyrant with broad popular support. Pisistratus was reportedly a benevolent despot and very popular. He kept Solon's reforms largely in place, and Athenians became accustomed to serving in Solon's Council and in jury courts. They were actively engaged in self-government, thus setting the stage for the establishment of democracy. Pisistratus also encouraged the celebration of religious festivals and cults that united the people of Attica through a common religion. To further help the farmers Solon brought back, Pisistratus redistributed land so they could once again make a living.

After Pisistratus's death, his sons tried to carry on as tyrants, but they lacked their father's popularity. Around 509 BCE, an Athenian aristocrat named Cleisthenes persuaded the Spartans to intervene in Athens and overthrow these tyrants. The Spartans, however, set up a government of elites in Athens that did not include Cleisthenes. Consequently, he appealed to the common people living in the villages, or *demes*, to reject this pro-Spartan regime and establish a "*demo*cracy." His appeal was successful, and Cleisthenes implemented reforms to Solon's system of government. He replaced the Council of Four Hundred with one of five hundred and reorganized the Athenians into ten new tribes, including in each one villages from different parts of Attica. Every year, each tribe chose fifty members by lot to sit in the new Council. This reform served to unite the Athenians, since each tribe consisted of people from different parts of Attica who now had to work together politically. Each tribe's delegation of fifty also served as presidents for part of the year and ran the day-to-day operation of the government.

By the end of the Archaic period, Athens had developed a functioning direct democracy, which differs from modern republics in which citizens vote for representatives who sit in the legislature. All citizens could sit in the Athenian Assembly, which then was required to meet at least ten times a year. All laws had to be approved by the Assembly. Only the Assembly could declare war and approve treaties. Athens had a citizen body of thirty to forty thousand adult males in the Classical period, but only six thousand needed to convene for meetings of the Assembly. Citizens could also be chosen by lot to sit in the Council. Since they were permitted to serve for just two one-year terms over a lifetime, many Athenians had the opportunity to participate in the executive branch of government. All citizens also served on juries, which not only determined the guilt or innocence of the accused but also interpreted the way the law was applied. Women, enslaved people, and foreign residents could not participate. However, women of the citizen class were prominent in the public religious life of the city, serving as priestesses and in ceremonial roles in religious festivals.

Classical Greece

The Greek Classical period (500–323 BCE) was an era of great cultural achievement in which enduring art, literature, and schools of philosophy were created. It began with the Greek city-states uniting temporarily to face an invasion by the mighty Persian Empire, but it ended with them locked in recurring conflicts and ultimately losing their independence, first to Persia and later to Macedon.

The Persian Wars

The Persian Wars (492–449 BCE) were a struggle between the Greek city-states and the expanding Persian Empire. In the mid-sixth century BCE, during the reign of Cyrus the Great, Persian armies subdued the Greek city-states of Ionia, located across the Aegean from Greece in western Asia Minor (Turkey) (Figure 6.14). To govern the cities, the Persians installed tyrants recruited from the local Greek population. The resident Greeks were unhappy with the tyrants' rule, and in 499 BCE they rose in the Ionian Rebellion, joined by Athens and the Greek cities on the island of Cyprus. But by 494 BCE Persian forces had crushed the rebellions in both Ionia and Cyprus. For intervening in Persian affairs, the Persian king Darius decided that Athens must be punished.

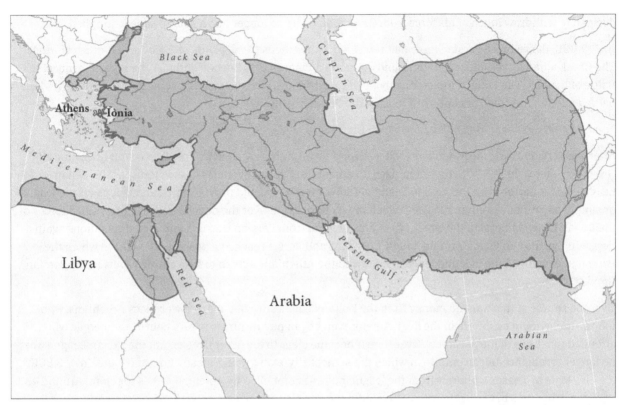

FIGURE 6.14 Persia and the Greeks in 499 BCE. The Greek world was on the edge of the massive Persian Empire at Persia's height around 500 BCE. Persian rulers likely thought little of the Greeks, but that changed in 499 BCE when Athens intervened in the rebellion in Ionia, a region located just across the Aegean Sea from Athens. (credit: modification of work "Persian Empire, 490 BC, showing route of Cyrus the Younger, Xenophon and the 10.000" by The Department of History - United States Military Academy/Wikimedia Commons, Public Domain)

In 490 BCE, Darius assembled a large fleet and army to cross the Aegean from Asia Minor, planning to subdue Athens and install one of Pisistratus's sons as tyrant there. These Persian forces landed at Marathon on the west coast of Attica. They vastly outnumbered the Athenians but were drafted subjects with little motivation to fight and die. The Athenian soldiers, in contrast, were highly motivated to defend their democracy. The Persians could not withstand the Athenians' spirited charge in the Battle of Marathon and were forced back onto their ships. Leaving the battle, the Persians then sailed around Attica to Athens. The soldiers at Marathon raced by land across the peninsula to guard the city. Seeing the city defended, the Persians returned to Asia Minor in defeat.

In 480 BCE, Xerxes, the son and successor of Darius, launched his own invasion of Greece intended to avenge this defeat and subdue all the Greek city-states. He assembled an even larger fleet as well as an army that would invade by land from the north. At this time of crisis, most of the Greek city-states decided to unite as allies and formed what is commonly called the Hellenic League. Sparta commanded the armies and Athens the fleet. A small band of the larger land forces, mostly Spartans, decided to make a stand at Thermopylae, a narrow pass between the mountains and the sea in northeastern Greece. Their goal was not to defeat the invading Persian army, which vastly outnumbered them, but to delay them so the rest of the forces could organize a defense. For days the small Spartan force, led by their king Leonidas, successfully drove back a vastly superior Persian army, until a Greek traitor informed the Persians of another mountain pass that enabled them to circle around and surround the Spartans. The Spartan force fought to the death, inspiring the Greeks to continue the fight and hold the Hellenic League together.

After the Battle of Thermopylae, the Persian forces advanced against Athens. The Athenians abandoned their city and withdrew to the nearby island of Salamis, where they put their faith in their fleet to protect them. At the naval Battle of Salamis, the allied Greek fleet led by Athens destroyed the Persian ships. Xerxes then decided to withdraw much of his force from Greece, since he no longer had a fleet to keep it supplied.

In 479 BCE, the reduced Persian force had retreated from Athens to the plains of Boeotia, just north of Attica. The Greek allied forces under the command of Sparta advanced into Boeotia and met the Persian army at the Battle of Plataea. The Persian forces, mostly unwilling draftees, were no match for the Spartan troops, and the battle ended in the death or capture of most of the Persian army.

The Athenian Empire and the Peloponnesian War

After the Persian Wars, the Athenians took the lead in continuing the fight against Persia and liberating all Greek city-states. In 477 BCE, they organized an alliance of Greek city-states known today as the Delian League, headquartered on the Aegean island of Delos. Members could provide ships and troops for the league or simply pay Athens to equip the fleet, which most chose to do. Over the next several decades, allied forces of the Delian League liberated the Greek city-states of Ionia from Persian rule and supported rebellions against Persia in Cyprus and Egypt. Around 449 BCE, Athens and Persia reached a peace settlement in which the Persians recognized the independence of Ionia and the Athenians agreed to stop aiding rebels in the Persian Empire.

Over the course of this war, the money from the Delian League enriched many lower-class Athenians, who found employment as rowers in the fleet. Athens even began paying jurors in jury courts and people who attended meetings of the Assembly. Over time it became clear to the other Greeks that the Delian League was no longer an alliance but an empire in which the subject city-states paid a steady flow of tribute. In 465 BCE, the city-state of Thasos withdrew from the league but was compelled by Athenian forces to rejoin. Around 437 BCE, the Athenians began using tribute to rebuild the temples on the Acropolis that the Persians had destroyed. Including the Parthenon, dedicated to Athena Parthenos, these were some of the most beautiful temples ever built and the pride of Athens, but to the subject city-states they came to symbolize Athenians' despotism and arrogance (See Figure 6.15).

FIGURE 6.15 The Parthenon. The large and sumptuous Parthenon, seen here as it is today, was built on the Athenian Acropolis in the fifth century BCE in honor of Athena. Following the temple's destruction in the Persian War, Athens set out to rebuild it using tribute money, which angered some of the other Greek city-states. (credit: "The Parthenon Athens" by Steve Swayne/Flickr, Public Domain)

The wealth and power of Athens greatly concerned the Spartans, who saw themselves as the greatest and noblest of the Greeks. The rivalry between the two city-states eventually led them into open conflict. In 433 BCE, the Athenians assisted the city-state of Corcyra in its war against Corinth. Corinth was a member of the

Peloponnesian League and requested that Sparta, the leader of this league, take action against Athenian aggression. Thus, in 431 BCE, the Peloponnesian War began with the invasion of Attica by Sparta and its allies (See Figure 6.16).

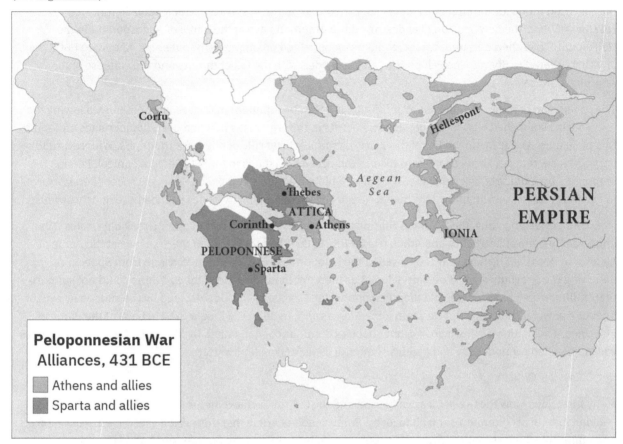

FIGURE 6.16 The Peloponnesian War. Athens and its allies controlled the coasts and islands of the Aegean, making it a powerful naval force to contend with. Sparta and its allies were largely land based, though they eventually were able to outmaneuver the Athenians at sea in some important battles. (credit: modification of work "The Alliances of the Peloponnesian War" by U.S. Army Cartographer/Wikimedia Commons, Public Domain)

The political leader Pericles persuaded his fellow Athenians to withdraw from the countryside of Attica and move within the walls of Athens, reasoning that the navy would provide them food and supplies and the wall would keep them safe until Sparta tired of war and sought peace. Pericles's assessment proved correct. In 421 BCE, after ten years of war, the Spartans and Athenians agreed to the Peace of Nicias, which kept the Athenian empire intact. The cost of the war for Athens was high, however. Due to the crowding of people within its walls, a plague had erupted in the city in 426 BCE and killed many, including Pericles.

LINK TO LEARNING

We know of the 426 BCE plague in Athens from the writings of Thucydides, the ancient chronicler and historian of the Peloponnesian War. But what was the mysterious illness? And how did it affect Athenian society and politics? Take a look at this article about the plague in Athens from The National Geographic (https://openstax.org/l/77AthensPlague) for some modern answers.

Several years later, arguing that the empire could thrive only by expanding, an ambitious young Athenian politician named Alcibiades (a kinsman of Pericles) inspired a massive invasion of Sicily targeting Syracuse, the island's largest city-state. Just as the campaign began in 415 BCE, Alcibiades's political enemies in Athens accused him of impiety and treason, and he fled to Sparta to avoid a trial. Without his leadership, the expedition against Syracuse floundered, and in 413 BCE the entire Athenian force was destroyed. In exile, Alcibiades convinced the Spartans to invade Attica again, now that Athens had been weakened by the disaster in Syracuse. In the years that followed, the Spartans realized they needed a large fleet to defeat Athens, and they secured funds for it from Persia on the condition that Sparta restore the Greek cities in Ionia to Persian rule. In 405 BCE, the new Spartan fleet destroyed the Athenian navy at the Battle of Aegospotami in the Hellespont. The Athenians, under siege, could not secure food or supplies without ships, and in 404 BCE the city surrendered to Sparta. The Peloponnesian War ended with the fall of the city and the collapse of the Athenian empire.

The conclusion of the Peloponnesian War initially left Sparta dominant in Greece. Immediately following the war, Sparta established oligarchies of local aristocrats in the city-states that had been democracies under the Delian League. And it set up the Era of the Thirty Tyrants, a brief rule of oligarchs in Athens. With regard to Persia, Sparta reneged on its promise to restore the Greek city-states in Ionia to Persian control. Persia responded by funding Greek resistance to Sparta, which eventually compelled Sparta to accept Persia's terms in exchange for Persian support. This meant turning over the Ionian city-states as it had previously promised.

Now with Persian backing, the Spartans continued to interfere in the affairs of other Greek city-states. This angered city-states like Thebes and Athens. In 371 BCE, the Thebans defeated the Spartans at the Battle of Leuctra in Boeotia. The next year they invaded the Peloponnese and liberated Messene from Spartan rule, depriving the Spartans of most of their helot labor there. Without the helots, the Spartans could not support their military system as before, and their Peloponnesian League collapsed. Alarmed by the sudden growth of Thebes's power, Athens and Sparta again joined forces and, in 362 BCE, fought the Thebans at the Battle of Mantinea. The battle was inconclusive, but Thebes's dominance soon faded. By 350 BCE, the Greek city-states were exhausted economically and politically after decades of constant warfare.

The Classical "Golden Age"

Many historians view the Greek Classical period and the cultural achievements in Athens in particular as a "Golden Age" of art, literature, and philosophy. Some scholars argue that this period saw the birth of science and philosophy because for the first time people critically examined the natural world and subjected religious beliefs to reason. (Other modern historians argue that this position discounts the accomplishments in medicine and mathematics of ancient Egypt and Mesopotamia.) For example, around 480 BCE, Empedocles speculated that the universe was not created by gods but instead was the result of the four material "elements"—air, water, fire, earth—being subjected to the forces of attraction and repulsion. Another philosopher and scientist of the era, Democritus, maintained that the universe consisted of tiny particles he called "atoms" that came together randomly in a vortex to form the universe.

Philosophers questioned not only the traditional views of the gods but also traditional values. Some of this questioning came from the sophists ("wise ones") of Athens, those with a reputation for learning, wisdom, and skillful deployment of rhetoric. Sophists emerged as an important presence in the democratic world of Athens beginning in the mid-fourth century BCE. They claimed to be able to teach anyone rhetoric, or the art of persuasion, for a fee, as a means to achieve success as a lawyer or a politician. While many ambitious men sought the services of sophists, others worried that speakers thus trained could lead the people to act against their own self-interest.

Many thought Socrates was one of the sophists. A stonecutter by trade, Socrates publicly questioned sophists and politicians about good and evil, right and wrong. He wanted to base values on reason instead of on unchallenged traditional beliefs. His questioning often embarrassed powerful people in Athens and made enemies, while his disciples included the politician Alcibiades and even some who had opposed Athenian democracy. In 399 BCE, an Athenian jury court found Socrates guilty of impiety and corrupting the youth, and he was sentenced to death (Figure 6.17).

FIGURE 6.17 The Death of Socrates. Socrates (center with upraised arm) was forced to drink hemlock, a poison. His last moments were imagined to great dramatic effect in this large oil painting of 1787 by the French artist Jacques-Louis David. (credit: "The Death of Socrates" by Metropolitan Museum of Art, Catharine Lorillard Wolfe Collection, Wolfe Fund, 1931/Wikimedia Commons, CC0 1.0)

Socrates left behind no writings of his own, but some of his disciples wrote about him. One of these was Plato, who wrote dialogues from 399 BCE to his death in 347 BCE that featured Socrates in conversation with others. Through these dialogues, Plato constructed a philosophical system that included the study of nature (physics), of the human mind (psychology and epistemology, the theory of knowledge), and ethics. He maintained that the material world we perceive is an illusion, a mere shadow of the real world of ideas and forms that underlie the universe. According to Plato, the true philosopher uses reason to comprehend these ideas and forms.

Plato established a school at the Academy, which was a gymnasium or public park near Athens where people went to relax and exercise. One of his most famous pupils was Aristotle, who came to disagree with his teacher and believed that ideas and forms could not exist independently of the material universe. In 334 BCE, Aristotle founded his own school at a different gymnasium in Athens, the Lyceum, where his students focused on the reasoned study of the natural world. Modern historians view Plato and Aristotle as the founders of Western (European) philosophy because of the powerful influence of their ideas through the centuries.

Athens in the Golden Age was also the birthplace of theater. Playwrights of the fifth century BCE such as Sophocles and Euripides composed tragedies that featured music and dance, like operas and musicals today (Figure 6.18). The plots were based on traditional myths about gods and heroes, but through their characters the playwrights pondered philosophical questions of the day that have remained influential over time. In Sophocles's *Antigone*, for example, Antigone, the daughter of Oedipus, must decide whether to obey the laws or follow her religious beliefs.

FIGURE 6.18 Dionysus. This terracotta representation of a theatrical mask a Greek actor might have worn dates from the first or second century BCE and portrays Dionysus, Zeus's son and the god of wine. (credit: "Terracotta figurine of a theatrical mask representing Dionysos" by Marie-Lan Nguyen/Wikimedia Commons, Public Domain)

🔗 LINK TO LEARNING

For an example of Greek theatre, watch this modern performance of *Lysistrata* (https://openstax.org/l/ 77Lysistrata) by the comic poet Aristophanes. In this comedy, first performed in 411 BCE, the women of Greece plot to end the Peloponnesian War. In the Greek original, the actors would have worn masks and sung their parts, as in a modern opera.

The study of history also evolved during the Golden Age. Herodotus and Thucydides are considered the first true historians because they examined the past to rationally explain the causes and effects of human actions. Herodotus wrote a sweeping history of wide geographic scope, called *Histories* ("inquiries"), to explore the deep origins of the tension between the Persian and Greek worlds. In *History of the Peloponnesian War*, Thucydides employed objectivity to explain the politics, events, and brutality of the conflict in a way that is similar in some respects to the approach of modern historians.

Finally, this period saw masterpieces of sculpture, vase painting, and architecture. Classical Age Greek artists broke free of the heavily stylized and two-dimensional art of Egypt and the Levant, which had inspired Greek geometric forms, and produced their own uniquely realistic styles that aimed to capture in art the ideal human form. Centuries later, and especially during the European Renaissance, artists modeled their own works on these classical models.

BEYOND THE BOOK

Ancient Greek Sculpture and Painting

In the Archaic period, the Greeks had more contact with the cultures of Phoenicia and Egypt, and artists modeled their work on examples from these regions. For instance, ancient Egyptian artists followed strict conventions in their heavily stylized works, such as arms held close to the sides of the body and a parallel stance for the feet. Greek artists adopted these conventions in their statues of naked youths, or *kouroi*, which were often dedicated in religious sanctuaries (Figure 6.19).

(a)   (b)

FIGURE 6.19 The Early Influence of Egyptian Sculpture. This basalt statue (a) is one of only seven statues of Cleopatra to survive from the ancient world. Its conventions like arms close to the body and parallel feet are mirrored in a Greek marble statue of a youth from about 580 BCE (b). (credit a: modification of work "Cleopatra statue at Rosicrucian Egyptian Museum" by E. Michael Smith Chiefio/Wikimedia Commons, Public Domain; credit b: modification of work "Marble statue of a kouros (youth)" by Metropolitan Museum of Art, Fletcher Fund, 1932/ Wikimedia Commons, CC0 1.0)

During the Classical period, Greek sculptors still produced statues of naked youths for religious sanctuaries, but in more lifelike poses that resembled the way the human body appears naturally (Figure 6.20).

(a)   (b)

FIGURE 6.20 Realism in Ancient Greek Art. In the mid-fifth century BCE, the Greek sculptor Myron produced a lifelike bronze statue of an athlete throwing a discus. Here (a) is a Roman marble copy of his statue. Approximately one century later, the Greek sculptor Praxiteles produced a similarly realistic statue (b), possibly depicting the Greek god Hermes holding Dionysus as a baby. (credit a: modification of work "Discobolus side 2" by Ricky Bennison/Wikimedia Commons, CC0 1.0; credit b: modification of work "Hermes of Praxiteles" by Dottie Day/Flickr, CC BY 2.0)

Greek painting is most often preserved on vases. In the Archaic period, artists frequently decorated vases with motifs such as patterning, borrowed from Phoenician and Egyptian art (Figure 6.21).

(a)   (b)

FIGURE 6.21 The Influence of Phoenician Decorative Art. This Phoenician silver bowl from the seventh century BCE (a) features lotus flowers and palm trees, which were Egyptian motifs, and repetitive patterning. A Greek jug from the same period (b) also uses repetitive patterns for decoration. (credit a: modification of work" Dish with Tambourine Players" by Cleveland Museum of Art, Purchase from the J. H. Wade Fund/Wikimedia Commons, CC0 1.0; credit b: modification of work "Corinthian jug 620 BC Staatliche Antikensammlungen" by Bibi Saint-Pol/ Wikimedia Commons, Public Domain)

By the Classical era, especially in Athens, vase painters were relying less on patterning and instead depicting realistic scenes from myths and daily life (Figure 6.22).

FIGURE 6.22 **Greek Realism in Art.** A Greek terracotta cup from the sixth or fifth century BCE (a) depicts charioteers. A wine jug from the fifth century BCE (b) depicts a scene from Greek mythology. (credit a: modification of work "Red-figured Kylix Greek 6th-5th century BCE terracotta (2)" by Mary Harrsch/Flickr, CC BY 2.0; credit b: modification of work "5th century BC Psykter" by Giovanni Dall'Orto/Wikimedia Commons, CC BY)

In the Classical period, Greek artists thus came into their own and no longer borrowed heavily from the art of Egypt and Phoenicia.

- What do the many artistic influences on Greece suggest about its connections with other parts of the ancient world?
- Why might Greek art have relied heavily on mythical symbols and depictions? What does this indicate about Greek culture?

6.3 The Hellenistic Era

LEARNING OBJECTIVES

By the end of this section, you will be able to:
- Explain the events that led to the rise of Alexander the Great
- Analyze Alexander the Great's successes as a military and political leader
- Discuss the role that Alexander the Great's conquests played in spreading Greek culture

The Classical period in Greece ended when Greece lost its freedom to the Kingdom of Macedon and Macedon's king Alexander the Great conquered the Persian Empire. The period that followed Alexander's death is known as the Hellenistic period (323–31 BCE). Alexander's empire was divided among his top generals, including Seleucus, Ptolemy, and Antigonus. During this time, Greeks, also called Hellenes, ruled over and interacted with the populations of the former Persian Empire. The resulting mixture of cultures was neither Greek nor non-Greek but "Greek-like," or **Hellenistic**, a term that refers to the flourishing and expansion of Greek language and culture throughout the Mediterranean and Near East during this period.

The Kingdom of Macedon

The ancient Kingdom of Macedon straddled today's Greece and northern Macedonia. The Macedonians did not speak Greek but had adopted Greek culture in the Archaic period, and their royal family claimed to be descended from the mythical Greek hero Heracles.

King Philip II of Macedon, who reigned from 359 to 336 BCE, transformed the kingdom into a great power. He recruited common farmers and developed them into a formidable infantry, with trained aristocrats as cavalry. His tactical skills and diplomacy allowed Philip to secure control of new territory in Thrace (modern-day northern Greece and Bulgaria), which provided access to precious metals and thus the economic resources to expand his military power.

In 338 BCE, Athens and Thebes finally put decades of conflict aside to ally against the rising power of Macedon. At the Battle of Chaeronea (338 BCE), the Macedonians crushed this allied army. Philip sought to unite the Greek city-states under his leadership after this victory, and he organized them toward the goal of waging war against the Persian Empire. However, in 336 BCE, Philip was killed by an assassin with a personal grudge.

Philip II was succeeded by his twenty-year-old son Alexander III, later known as Alexander the Great, who immediately faced an invasion by Thracian tribes from the north and a rebellion in Greece led by Thebes and Athens. Within a year, the young king had crushed these opponents and announced he was carrying out his father's plan to wage war against Persia. Darius III, the Persian king, amassed armies to face him, but they were mainly draftees from the subject peoples of the Persian Empire. At the battles of Issus (333 BCE) and Gaugamela (330 BCE), these forces collapsed against the Macedonians, commanded by Alexander himself.

At first, Alexander envisioned his campaign as a war of vengeance against Persia. Although he was Macedonian, he saw himself as a Hellene and often compared himself to the hero Achilles of the *Iliad*, from whom he claimed to be descended through his mother. In 330 BCE, Alexander's forces sacked and later burned Persepolis, the jewel of the Persian Empire. After the assassination of Darius III by disgruntled Persian nobles that same year, however, Alexander claimed the Persian throne and introduced Persian customs to his court, such as having his subjects prostrate themselves before him. To consolidate his control of the Persian Empire, in 330–326 BCE he advanced his army deep into central Asia and to the Indus River valley (modern Pakistan) (Figure 6.23). In 326 BCE, his exhausted troops mutinied and refused to advance to the Ganges River in central India as Alexander desired. He led his army back to Babylon in Mesopotamia, where he died in 323 BCE at the age of thirty-three, probably due to the cumulative impact of injuries experienced during the campaign.

FIGURE 6.23 The Conquests of Alexander the Great. Alexander advanced his army as far as central Asia and the Indus River, but he was unable to reach the Ganges River as he desired. (credit: "Map of the Empire of Alexander the Great (1893)" by Unknown/Wikimedia Commons, Public Domain)

DUELING VOICES

Why Did Alexander Burn Persepolis?

When Alexander reached Persepolis after the Battle of Gaugamela, he saw what was possibly the most beautiful city in the entire Persian Empire. Over the centuries Darius, Xerxes, and others had adorned it with colorful palaces, public buildings, and artwork. Within a few months of his arrival, however, Alexander had reduced the once-stunning imperial city to ashes and ruins. Why?

Historians have pondered this question for thousands of years. Though there are several accounts, the earliest was penned centuries after the actual events. The most common explanation cites a long night of drunken revels and a Greek woman named Thaïs (Figure 6.24). This account is by the first-century BCE Greek historian Diodorus Siculus:

> Alexander held games to celebrate his victories; he offered magnificent sacrifices to the gods and entertained his friends lavishly. One day when the Companions [fellow cavalry soldiers] were feasting, and intoxication was growing as the drinking went on, a violent madness took hold of these drunken men. One of the women present [Thaïs] declared that it would be Alexander's greatest achievement in Asia to join in their procession and set fire to the royal palace, allowing women's hands to destroy in an instant what had been the pride of the Persians.

—Diodorus of Sicily, *Library of World History*

FIGURE 6.24 Thaïs Burns Persepolis. This 1890 painting by the French artist Georges Rochegrosse imagines Thaïs, held aloft while brandishing a torch, leading the maddened crowd as they burn the city in a drunken spectacle. (credit: "The burning of Persepolis, 1890, by Georges-Antoine Rochegrosse" by Unknown/Wikimedia Commons, Public Domain)

Later Roman historians such as Quintus Curtius Rufus and Plutarch provide similar accounts, saying the fire was the result of an out-of-control party and lit at Thaïs's insistence. But at least one ancient writer disagrees. Relying on sources from Ptolemy and other contemporaries of Alexander, the historian Arrian of Nicomedia makes no mention of Thaïs or a night of heavy drinking. In *Anabasis*, he says the destruction of the city was intentional, the product of calculated revenge "for their invasion of Greece...for the destruction of Athens, the burning of the temples, and all the other crimes they had committed against the Greeks."

What really happened at Persepolis? Was Thaïs the instigator or merely the scapegoat? Thousands of years later we may be able only to speculate about the cause of this catastrophic event.

- Given what you've read, who do you think was responsible for the burning of Persepolis? Why?
- If Thaïs wasn't responsible, why do you think some ancient historians were convinced of her culpability?

Though his Bactrian wife Roxane was pregnant when he died, Alexander had made no arrangements for a successor. Members of his court and his military commanders thus fought among themselves for control of the empire in what historians refer to as the Wars of the Successors. One of the more colorful contestants was Pyrrhus, who was not Macedonian but was the king of Epirus and Alexander's cousin. Pyrrhus temporarily seized the throne of Macedon and attempted to carve out an empire for himself in Sicily and southern Italy. He never lost a battle, but he lost so many troops in a campaign defending Magna Graecia in southern Italy from Rome that he was never able to capitalize on his success. (Today the term *pyrrhic victory* refers to a win so costly that it is in effect a loss.) In 272 BCE, Pyrrhus died after being struck by a roof tile thrown at him by an elderly woman during a street battle in the city of Argos. His death marked the end of the wars among Alexander's generals.

By the middle of the third century BCE, certain generals and their descendants were ruling as kings over different portions of Alexander's empire (Figure 6.25). Antigonus and his descendants, the Antigonids, ruled Macedon and much of Greece. Some city-states in Greece organized federal leagues to maintain their independence from Macedon. The Achaean League was in the Peloponnese and the Aetolian League in central Greece. Another Macedonian general, Ptolemy, was king of Egypt. To win the support of the Egyptian people, Ptolemy and his successors assumed the title of pharaoh and built temples to Egyptian gods. Yet another Macedonian general, Seleucus and his descendants, the Seleucids, ruled as kings over much of the former Persian Empire, from Asia Minor in the west to central Asia in the east. They adopted many practices of the Persian Empire, including honoring local gods, as revealed by cuneiform records of the offerings they made.

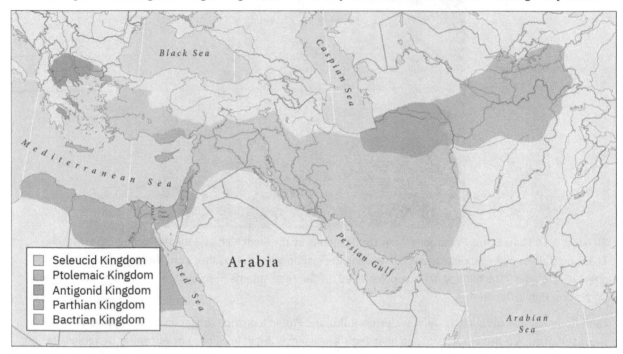

FIGURE 6.25 **The Hellenistic World.** The conquests of Alexander and conflicts over the spoils that raged for decades after his death resulted in the reordering of what had once been the Persian Empire. While the borders regularly shifted over the years, this map provides a snapshot of the Hellenistic kingdoms in about 263 BCE. (credit: modification of work "The Hellenistic World in late 281 BC" by "Cattette"/Wikimedia Commons, CC BY 4.0)

The Seleucid Kingdom was an enormous and complicated region, stretching from the Aegean Sea to today's Afghanistan, with a population of some thirty million people of various ethnic and linguistic groups. Keeping control over the vast kingdom proved difficult, and some of the far eastern portions like Bactria and Parthia began to break away around 250 BCE. Both became separate Hellenistic kingdoms, ruled initially by former Greek governors of the areas. Around 200 BCE, the Bactrian kingdom invaded and conquered the Indus River valley. The most famous of the Bactrian kings of India was Menander I, whose kingdom stretched from the Indus River valley to the upper Ganges in central India. Menander converted to Buddhism and became a holy man, known in India as Milinda. The Greek colonists who settled in Bactria and India introduced their art into the region, which influenced Indian sculpture, painting, and architecture. By the end of the second century BCE, however, the Bactrian kingdom had collapsed due to constant civil wars between rival claimants to the throne. We know of their existence only through the coins they issued as kings (Figure 6.26).

FIGURE 6.26 A Greco-Bactrian Coin. Even after the Bactrian kingdom split away from the Seleucid Empire in the third century BCE, Greek influence there remained. This Greco-Bactrian coin, likely from the second century BCE, shows a Greek goddess and Greek letters on one side and a humped bull, an Indian symbol, and Kharosthi script (Indo-Persian) on the other. (credit: "Bactrian coin, 1st or 2nd century BC" by Jean-Michel Moullec/Flickr, CC BY 2.0)

In these Hellenistic kingdoms, where peace treaties and alliances could be secured through arranged marriages, elite women might achieve political power unimaginable in Classical Greece. In Egypt, for example, Ptolemy II married his sister Arsinoe, as was the custom for pharaohs, and installed her as co-ruler. Dynastic queens also often ruled when the designated heir was just a child. In 253 BCE, the Seleucid king Antiochus II ended his war for control of Syria with a treaty by which he married Berenice, the daughter of his opponent Ptolemy II. However, Antiochus's former wife Laodice murdered Berenice and her children upon Antiochus's death in 246 BCE to secure the succession for her own young son Seleucus II. Ptolemy III subsequently declared war to avenge the death of his sister and her children.

In 194 BCE, Antiochus III ended yet another war for control of Syria by giving his daughter Cleopatra I in marriage to Ptolemy V. Upon Ptolemy's death in 180 BCE, Cleopatra ruled because their sons and daughter were still children. The most famous of the powerful Hellenistic queens was this Cleopatra's descendant, Cleopatra VII, who reigned from 51 to 31 BCE. The last of the Ptolemies, Cleopatra VII reigned as co-ruler with her brothers Ptolemy XIII and Ptolemy XIV, as well as with Ptolemy XV, also called Caesarion, who was her son with the Roman general Julius Caesar.

Hellenistic Culture

A characteristic cultural feature of the Hellenistic period was the blending of Greek and other cultures of the former Persian Empire. The Seleucid and Ptolemaic dynasties both employed Greeks and Macedonians as soldiers and bureaucrats in their empires. Alexander the Great and subsequent Hellenistic kings founded Greek cities in the former Persian Empire for Greek and Macedonian colonists, often naming them in honor of themselves or their queens. These cities included the institutions of the Greek cities of their homeland—temples to Greek gods, theaters, *agora* (marketplaces), and gymnasia—so the colonists could feel at home in their new environment. At the site of Ai Khanum in modern Afghanistan, archaeologists have uncovered the impressive remains of one such Hellenistic city with a gymnasium.

Alexandria in Egypt, founded by Alexander himself in 331 BCE, was the capital of the Ptolemaic kingdom and the largest Hellenistic city, with a population that reached one million. There the Ptolemies founded the *Museon*, or "home of the Muses," from which the term "museum" derives. They modeled this on Aristotle's Lyceum, as a center for scientific research and literary studies. These same kings also patronized the Alexandrian Library, where they assembled the largest collection of books in the ancient world. Antioch, in today's southeastern Turkey, was the largest city of the Seleucid kingdom, with a population of half a million. In cities such as Alexandria and Antioch, the Greek-speaking population became integrated with the indigenous population.

Most Greek cities in this period were no longer independent since they were usually under the control of one of the Hellenistic kingdoms. The city-states of the Achaean and Aetolian Leagues in Greece were the exception, fiercely maintaining their independence against the Antigonid rulers of Macedon. Having lost the right of self-government, many Greeks in cities under the rule of kings no longer focused on politics and diplomacy but turned to the search for personal happiness. New religions emerged that promised earthly contentment and eternal life and combined Greek and non-Greek elements. For example, the worship of the Egyptian goddess Isis became common in many Hellenistic cities.

Mithras was a Persian sun god worshiped by the Medes, but in the second century BCE, Greeks in Hellenistic cities came to believe Mithras would lead them, too, to eternal life. His followers built special chapels decorated with symbols whose meaning is still disputed. The emphasis on secret religious rituals, or *mysteries*, about which followers were sworn to silence, lends the worship of Isis and Mithras in this period the name **mystery religions** (Figure 6.27).

FIGURE 6.27 Mithras. This stone relief from the second century CE depicts the Persian sun god Mithras, who became the center of a mystery religion. (credit: modification of work "Cult Relief of Mithras Slaying the Bull (Tauroctony)" by Yale University Gallery/Wikimedia Commons, CC0 1.0)

Another religion practiced in Hellenistic cities was Judaism, whose followers included migrant Jewish people and new converts. By the second century BCE, the Hebrew Bible had been translated into Greek under the Ptolemies, since ancient Judea was within their control for much of the Hellenistic period and many Jewish people had immigrated to Alexandria.

Some Greeks preferred new philosophies to religion as a means to achieve happiness. Hellenistic philosophy emphasized the search for internal peace and contentment. Stoicism, for example, maintained that the universe was governed by divine reason (*Logos*), which determined the fate of all people. Happiness therefore resulted from learning how to cope with life and accepting fate while avoiding extreme negative emotions such as fear and anger. Epicureans, however, maintained that the key to happiness was to avoid physical and mental pain by pursuing pleasure. The founders of these two philosophical schools, Zeno and Epicurus respectively, both lived in the early third century BCE and taught in Athens, which continued to be a center of learning in this period. The Stoics were so named because Zeno instructed his students in the *stoa poikile*, or "painted porch" in the Athenian *agora*. The mystery religions and philosophies of the Hellenistic era continued to flourish as these cities became incorporated into the expanding Roman Empire.

6.4 The Roman Republic

LEARNING OBJECTIVES

By the end of this section, you will be able to:
- Identify the key institutions of the Roman Republic
- Discuss class differences and conflict in the Roman Republic
- Analyze the challenges that strained democratic institutions in the Roman Republic, including the Punic Wars

Many elements of early Roman culture and society resulted from Greek influence on the Italian peninsula. Later, when the Roman state expanded and built an empire, its people transmitted their culture—heavily indebted to Ancient Greece—to the Celtic and Germanic tribes of central and western Europe. They also transmitted their language, which is why French, Portuguese, Italian, and Spanish are known as "Romance" languages: They are descended from the Latin language spoken by the Romans. The classical civilizations of Ancient Greece and Rome were therefore the foundation for what became known as Western civilization.

The Foundation and Function of the Roman Republic

During the Archaic period, Greeks established colonies on Sicily and in southern Italy that went on to influence the culture of Italy. By around 500 BCE, the inhabitants of central Italy, who spoke Latin, had adopted much of Greek culture as their own, including the idea that citizens should have a voice in the governance of the state. For example, the people of the small city-state of Rome referred to their state as *res publica,* meaning "public thing" (to distinguish it from the *res privata*, or "private thing," that had characterized oligarchical and monarchical rule under the Etruscans). *Res publica*—from which the word "republic" derives—signified that government happens in the open, for everyone to see. Early Romans also adopted Greek gods and myths as well as other elements of Greek culture.

The Romans passed down many traditions about the early history of their republic, recorded by historians such as Livy in the first century BCE. These stories often reflected the values that the Romans revered. According to Roman tradition, the city was founded in 753 BCE by the twin brothers Romulus and Remus, sons of Mars, the god of war (Figure 6.28). It was said that Romulus killed his brother when Remus mocked his construction of a wall around the new city and jumped over it. This story brought into focus for Romans their respect for boundaries and private property.

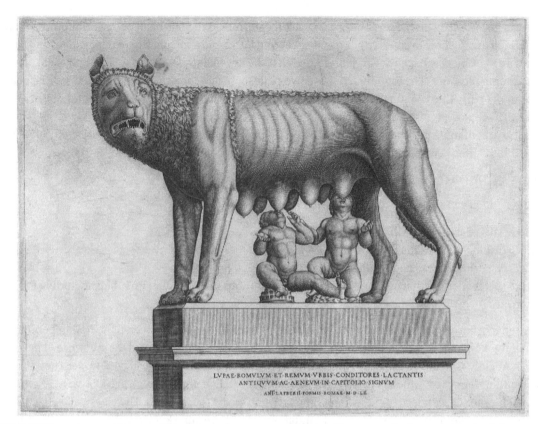

FIGURE 6.28 Romulus and Remus. This sixteenth-century engraving illustrates the legend that the infants Romulus and Remus, later the founders of Rome, were suckled by a she-wolf after a jealous king ordered them abandoned to die. (credit: modification of work "Speculum Romanae Magnificentiae: Romulus and Remus" by Metropolitan Museum of Art, Rogers Fund, Transferred from the Library, 1941/Wikimedia Commons, CC0 1.0)

Romulus assembled a group of criminals and debtors to inhabit his city, and, to secure wives for them, he invited the neighboring Sabines to attend a festival with their unmarried daughters and sisters. The Romans seized the women, and when the Sabines returned with an army to recover them, the women, now Roman wives, said they had been treated with respect and wished to remain. The Sabines and the Romans then joined together in a single city-state. This story showed that a person did not have to be born a Roman to receive the rights of citizenship. It also reflected women's social status in Rome, which was higher than their status in other ancient cultures. They couldn't vote or hold public office, but they could own property and freely participate in public events such as banquets.

These stories also include details of Roman ideas about government. For example, they note that in its early centuries, Rome was a monarchy, with the first king being Romulus. After the passing of the fourth king, the throne was assumed by Lucius Tarquinius Priscus, an Etruscan. The next two kings were also Etruscan. The last of these, Tarquin the Proud, was the final king of Rome, whose son raped a young Roman woman named Lucretia. This act triggered a rebellion against the monarchy, which ultimately ousted the Etruscan king. In 509 BCE, the victorious Romans declared their government to be a republic and vowed never to be subject to tyranny again. This story emphasized the Roman respect for the rule of law. No one, no matter how powerful, was above it.

IN THEIR OWN WORDS

Lucretia's Sacrifice for Rome

Like many stories about Rome's early history, the story of the rape of Lucretia emphasizes Roman values, in this case, virtue. Revered as a model Roman woman, Lucretia embodied sexual purity and loyalty to her husband at the expense of her safety, her autonomy, and even her life. According to the story, Sextus Tarquinius, the son of the king, is staying at Collatinus and Lucretia's home. During the night, Tarquinius enters Lucretia's chambers with his sword in hand, He threatens her with successive acts of violence and disgrace before raping her. While recounting the events, Lucretia asks her family to pledge that they will avenge her, and then she dies by suicide. Scholars debate the reason for her suicide, with some indicating it was related to shame, others viewing it as Lucretia asserting control, while still others see it as an allegory for the death of the Roman monarchy.

The historian Livy's account of Lucretia's suicide, written in the first century BCE, shows the story's enduring value in Roman culture. It begins as Lucretia's husband and father run to her aid after hearing she has been raped by Sextus Tarquinius, son of the king. Lucretia they found sitting sadly in her chamber.

> The entrance of her friends brought the tears to her eyes, and to her husband's question, "Is all well?" She replied, "Far from it; for what can be well with a woman when she has lost her honor? The print of a strange man, Collatinus [her husband], is in your bed. Yet my body only has been violated; my heart is guiltless, as death shall be my witness. But pledge your right hands and your words that the adulterer shall not go unpunished. Sextus Tarquinius is he that last night returned hostility for hospitality, and armed with force brought ruin on me, and on himself no less—if you are men—when he worked his pleasure with me." They give their pledges, every man in turn. They seek to comfort her, sick at heart as she is, by diverting the blame from her who was forced to the doer of the wrong. They tell her it is the mind that sins, not the body; and that where purpose has been wanting there is no guilt. "It is for you to determine," she answers, "what is due to him; for my own part, though I acquit myself of the sin, I do not absolve myself from punishment; not in time to come shall ever unchaste woman live through the example of Lucretia." Taking a knife that she had concealed beneath her dress, she plunged it into her heart, and sinking forward upon the wound, died as she fell. The wail for the dead was raised by her husband and her father.

—Livy, *Ab Urbe Condita* (*The History of Rome*)

- Why does Lucretia choose death?
- What does her choice say about Roman values concerning the conduct of women, chastity, and reputation?

Archaeological evidence seems to indicate at least some historical basis for these accounts of Rome's founding. In 1988, a wall was discovered around the Palatine Hill where Romulus reportedly built his fortification. Archaeologists also found Greek pottery from this period at the same location, suggesting trade took place. The city of Rome is located along the Tiber River where it was no longer navigable to sea-going vessels. Greek merchants would have sailed up the Tiber from the Mediterranean Sea and traded with the native peoples there. Greek merchants and colonists arriving in Italy at this time influenced the Iron Age culture in northern and central Italy, which then evolved though Greek influence into the Latin and Etruscan cultures. Around 600 BCE, the Etruscans colonized Rome, which became an Etruscan city-state. The story of the Tarquin dynasty reflects this Etruscan period of Roman history. Modern historians maintain that the story of the expulsion of the Tarquins is loosely based on historical events, which saw the Roman city-state free itself from Etruscan domination and establish an independent republic around 500 BCE.

In the early republic, Rome was ruled by elected magistrates instead of kings, and by a Council of Elders or Senate. Roman society was divided into two classes or orders, patricians and plebeians. The patricians were the aristocratic elite, who alone could hold public office and sit in the Senate. From the beginning of the republic through the third century BCE, the plebeians, or common people, worked to achieve equality before the law in Roman society. The political conflict between these two classes is known as the **Struggle of the Orders**.

Rome was located on a coastal plain known as Latium. East of it were the foothills of the Apennine Mountains, inhabited by warlike tribes that made periodic raids. When Rome was under threat, the plebeians could gain leverage with the patricians by refusing to fight until their demands were met. In 450 BCE, the plebeians went on strike for the first time. They feared that patrician judges were interpreting Rome's unwritten laws to take advantage of ignorant plebeians, so they demanded the laws be written down. The patricians agreed. In the **Twelve Tables**, published in the Forum, Rome's laws were written for the first time and were then accessible to all citizens.

⊘ LINK TO LEARNING

Read excerpts from Rome's Twelve Tables of law (https://openstax.org/l/77TwelveTables) from Fordham University's Ancient History Sourcebook. What do these laws tell us about Roman society in 450 BCE, when they were first written down?

After 450 BCE, the plebeians met in a Plebian Assembly that annually elected ten officials known as tribunes. These tribunes attended meetings of Rome's assemblies, the Senate, and the law courts. If they saw any public body or official taking action that would bring harm to plebeians, they could say "*Veto*" or "I forbid" and stop that action. This power to veto gave plebeians a way to protect themselves and put a check on the power of patrician officials.

In the fourth and third centuries BCE, plebeians won more concessions by again seceding from the patrician state. After 367 BCE, one of the two consuls, the highest officials in the republic, had to be a plebian. After 287 BCE, the Plebian Assembly could pass laws for the republic that were introduced to it by the tribunes, and their laws applied to all Roman citizens. By the third century BCE, the Struggle of the Orders had effectively concluded, since it was now possible for plebeians to pass laws, serve as elected officials, and sit in the Senate, equals of the patricians under Roman law. The Struggle of the Orders did not bring equality to everyone in Rome, however. Rather, it gave well-off plebeians access to positions of power.

Romans were a very conservative people who greatly venerated the *mos maiorum* or "way of the ancestors." Their political system was a combination of written laws and political traditions and customs that had evolved since the birth of the Republic. By the third century BCE, this system was being administrated by a combination of public assemblies, elected officials, and the Senate.

The Roman Republic had three main public assemblies—the Plebian Assembly, the Tribal Assembly, and the Centuriate Assembly—that elected various officials every year. Only plebeians could attend the Plebian Assembly, organized into thirty-five regional tribes with a single vote each. It was this assembly that annually elected the ten tribunes, who possessed veto power and could present laws to the assembly for approval. The Tribal Assembly was likewise divided into thirty-five tribes based on place of residence, with each tribe casting one vote, but both plebeians and patricians could attend. Every year, the Tribal Assembly elected the Quaestors, treasurers in charge of public money.

Only the Centuriate Assembly could declare war, though the Senate remained in control of foreign policy. Both plebeians and patricians could attend this assembly, which was organized into blocs. The number of votes assigned to each bloc was based on the number of centuries—meaning a group of one hundred men in a military unit—that bloc could afford to equip with weapons and armor. Wealthier citizens had more votes because they could pay more to support the military. This assembly also elected military commanders, judges, and the censor, whose main task was to conduct the census to assess the wealth of Rome's citizens.

All elected officials joined the Roman Senate as members for life after their term in office. By far the most powerful institution in the Roman state, the Senate decided how public money was to be spent and advised elected officials on their course of action. Elected officials rarely ignored the Senate's advice since many of them would be senators themselves after leaving office.

The patron-client system was another important element in the Roman political system. A patron was usually a wealthy citizen who provided legal and financial assistance to his clients, who were normally less affluent citizens. In return, clients in the Roman assemblies voted as directed by their patrons. Patrons could inherit clients, and those with many wielded great influence in Rome.

The Expansion of the Roman Republic

The early Romans did not plan on building an immense empire. They were surrounded by hostile city-states and tribes, and in the process of defeating them they made new enemies even as they expanded their network of allies. Thus they were constantly sending armies farther afield to crush these threats until Rome emerged in the second century BCE as the most powerful state in all the lands bordering the Mediterranean Sea.

The Roman Senate developed certain policies in conducting wars that proved quite successful (Figure 6.29). One was to divide and conquer. The Romans always tried to defeat one enemy at a time and avoid waging war against a coalition. Thus they often attempted to turn their enemies against each other. Another tactic was to negotiate from strength. Even after suffering enormous defeats in battle, Rome would continue a war until it won a major engagement and reach a position from which to negotiate for peace with momentum on its side. Yet another successful strategy was to establish colonies in recently conquered lands to serve as the first line of defense if a region revolted against Rome. Well-constructed roads were also built to link Rome to these colonies, so armies could arrive quickly in a region that rebelled. Thanks to these networks across Italy, the language and culture of Rome eventually spread throughout its empire as well. Romans also transformed former enemies into loyal allies who could enjoy self-government as long as they honored Rome's other alliances and provided troops in times of war. Some even received Roman citizenship.

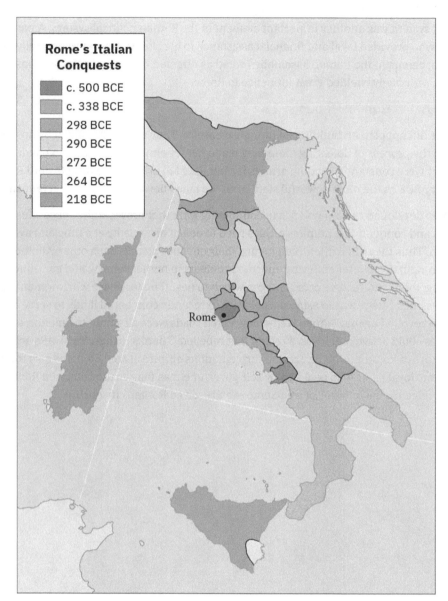

FIGURE 6.29 Rome's Conquests in Italy. This map shows the expansion of Rome across Italy over time and its addition of new allies. (credit: modification of work "Map of the Roman conquest of Italy" by "Javierfv1212"/Wikimedia Commons, Public Domain)

The Roman Conquest of the Mediterranean

After conquering most of the Italian peninsula, Rome came to challenge the other major power in the region, Carthage. A series of wars ensued, called the Punic Wars, in which Rome and Carthage vied for dominance. During the First Punic War (264–241 BCE), Rome and Carthage battled for control of the island of Sicily. Although Carthage had the largest fleet at the time, the Romans won by dropping a hooked plank on the deck of an opposing ship and using it as a causeway to cross over, transforming a sea battle in which they were at a disadvantage into a land battle where they could dominate. After the destruction of its fleet, Carthage sued for peace, and the war ended with Rome annexing Sicily.

Carthage desired revenge. In the Second Punic War (218–201 BCE), the Carthaginian general Hannibal marched his army, along with dozens of war elephants, from Hispania (modern-day Portugal and Spain), across southern Gaul, and then over the Alps into Italy. Hannibal hoped Rome's allies would abandon it and leave the city at his mercy. Most of Rome's Italian allies remained loyal, however, even after Hannibal repeatedly defeated Roman armies, and after his decisive victory at the Battle of Cannae. As Hannibal's army was rampaging through Italy, Rome sent an army across the Mediterranean to Africa to attack Carthage, which summoned Hannibal back to defend his homeland (Figure 6.30).

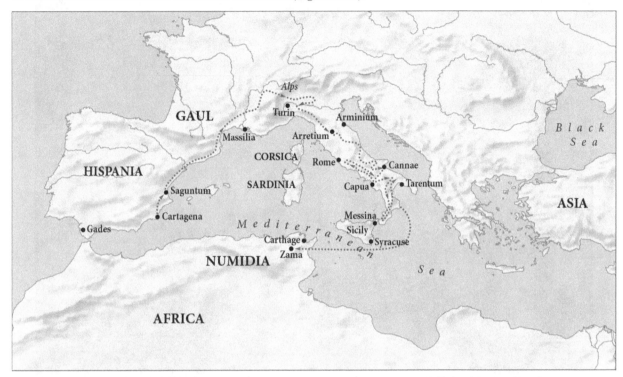

FIGURE 6.30 Hannibal's Invasion of Rome. This map shows the route Hannibal followed from Hispania over the Alps to attack Italy before finally returning to defend Carthage in the Second Punic War. (attribution: Copyright Rice University, OpenStax, under CC BY 4.0 license)

At the Battle of Zama in 202 BCE, the Roman army defeated Hannibal, and the Roman commander Scipio earned the nickname "Africanus" (Figure 6.31). Carthage sued for peace and was stripped of all its overseas territory. Rome thus acquired Carthage's lands in Hispania.

FIGURE 6.31 Hannibal and Scipio. This classical battle scene, painted by the Italian artist Bernardino Cesari in the early 1600s, is believed to represent Hannibal's defeat by the Roman commander Scipio in 202 BCE. (credit: "Hannibal and Scipio Africanus" by Bernardino Cesari/Wikimedia Commons, Public Domain)

During the war, King Philip V of Macedon, concerned by the growth of Rome just across the Adriatic Sea from his own kingdom, made an alliance with Carthage. After Rome's victory against Carthage, Rome declared war against this new enemy. Philip's Macedonian troops won numerous victories over Roman armies, but in 196 BCE at the Battle of Cynoscephalae in northern Greece, Philip suffered a defeat and lacked the resources to continue. Consequently, he agreed to become an ally of Rome. Rome also liberated all regions in Greece formerly under Macedonian control.

Philip's defeat emboldened the king of the Seleucid Empire, Antiochus III, to advance his army into Greece, hoping to obtain the territory Philip had vacated. Rome feared that Antiochus's occupation of Greece posed a threat to Italy, just as Philip had. In 190 BCE, Roman armies smashed the forces of Antiochus III at the Battle of Magnesia in western Asia Minor. Antiochus then agreed to withdraw from Asia Minor.

Rome discovered in the second century BCE that there was no end to the threats from hostile powers. Perseus, the son of Philip V, renounced the alliance with Rome. When he made alliances with Balkan tribes that threatened to invade Italy, Roman armies invaded Macedon and defeated his army at the Battle of Pydna in 168 BCE. Rome then dissolved the monarchy in Macedon, which soon afterward became a Roman province, and Perseus died of starvation as a prisoner in Rome. When the Achaean League in the Peloponnese in Greece challenged Roman control of Greece and Macedon, Rome declared war and sacked Corinth, the League's largest city, in 146 BCE. In that same year, Roman armies also destroyed the city of Carthage in the Third Punic War, fearing the city's revival as an economic and military power. After 146 BCE, no power remained in the Mediterranean that could challenge Rome (Figure 6.32).

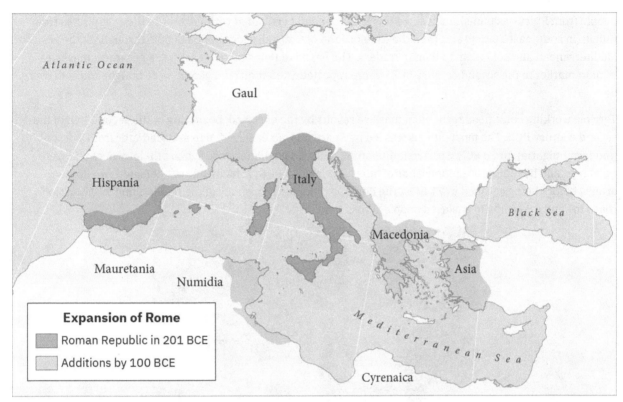

FIGURE 6.32 The Expansion of Rome. This map shows Rome's expansion in the second century BCE as it responded to perceived threats to its power from neighboring kingdoms. (credit: modification of work "Expansion of Rome, 2nd century BC" by The Department of History, United States Military Academy/Wikimedia Commons, Public Domain)

A Republic of Troubles

Rome's constant wars and conquests in the third and second centuries BCE created a host of social, economic, and political problems for the republic. The Roman people grew dissatisfied with the leadership of the Senate and the aristocratic elite, and they increasingly looked to strong military leaders to address the problems.

A number of factors contributed to these problems and transformations. From the foundation of the republic, most Roman citizens had owned and operated small family farms. Indeed, to serve as Roman soldiers, men had to own property. However, the Punic Wars had strained this traditional system. Roman soldiers were often away from home for long periods of time, leaving the women and children to maintain their holdings. When they ultimately did return, many found their property in another's hands. Others decided to sell their neglected farms and move their families to the expanding city of Rome, where they joined the growing ranks of the landless working class known as the **proletariat**. By the first century BCE, the population of the city of Rome may have exceeded one million.

The growth of the proletariat disrupted the Roman political system and invited large-scale corruption. The traditional patron-client system collapsed, since landless Romans didn't need the assistance of patrons to settle property disputes. Politicians therefore had to win the support of the urban masses with free food and entertainment, such as gladiatorial combats, and promises to create jobs through public works projects. Some even organized the poor into violent gangs to frighten their political rivals. These conditions resulted in widespread dissatisfaction with the government of the republic.

To meet the growing demand for grain, wine, and olive oil to feed the urban population, large landowners bought land from poor Roman farmers and leased public land from the Roman state to create large plantations. These were very profitable because landowners could cheaply purchase enslaved people, who were plentiful. For example, after the defeat of Perseus of Macedon in 168 BCE, the Romans enslaved 150,000 people from Epirus as punishment since this kingdom had been allied with Perseus in the war. Pirates from Cilicia (in southeast Turkey) and from the Greek island of Crete also kidnapped people throughout the eastern Mediterranean and sold them to Roman traders. The island of Delos in the Aegean Sea became a massive human market in the second century BCE, where reportedly ten thousand people were bought and sold every day.

Terrible working conditions resulted in massive revolts by the enslaved, beginning in the second half of the second century BCE. The most famous was led by Spartacus, an enslaved man and gladiator from Thrace (modern Bulgaria). In 76 BCE, Spartacus and other enslaved gladiators rose against their owners and were quickly joined by hundreds of thousands of others (Figure 6.33). Spartacus's forces defeated two Roman armies before being crushed in 71 BCE. The Romans crucified thousands of the rebels along Italy's major roads to send a warning to enslaved people across Italy.

FIGURE 6.33 Spartacus. This is a detail of a larger-than-life marble statue by the nineteenth-century French sculptor Denis Foyatier, showing Spartacus breaking his chains. Now in the Louvre, the statue originally stood in Paris's famous Jardin des Tuileries on the Avenue of Great Men. (credit: "Spartacus, Denis Foyatier, 1830" by Gautier Poupeau/Flickr, CC BY 2.0)

In addition to the proletariat and enslaved people, new classes of wealthy Romans were also unhappy with the leadership of the traditional elite. The most profitable enterprise for these new Roman entrepreneurs was acting as bankers and public contractors, or publicans. The republic relied on publicans to construct public works such as aqueducts and theaters, as well as to operate government-owned mines and collect taxes. Roman governors often looked the other way when publicans squeezed additional tax revenues from the populations of the provinces.

This tumultuous and complicated environment led to the rise of two of the Late Republic's most intriguing political figures, Tiberius and Gaius Gracchus. The Gracchi, as they are collectively known, were plebian brothers whose families had been members of the elite for generations (Scipio Africanus was their grandfather). Tiberius, the elder brother, was concerned to see the large plantations being worked by enslaved foreigners rather than Roman farmers. He feared Rome's military was in danger since Rome relied on its land-owning farmers to equip themselves and serve in the army. In 133 BCE, as a tribune, he proposed a law to distribute public land to landless Romans. This measure struck a blow at the senatorial class, many of whom had accumulated huge swaths of land formerly owned by independent farmers who had gone to war. The assembly voted to approve the proposal, but many senators were horrified not only because they stood to lose land but also because, to win the vote, Tiberius had violated the traditions of the Republic. The Republic was ruled by the upper classes, and in courting popular opinion, the brothers had challenged elite control over high political institutions. Convinced he was assuming too much popular support and violating the traditions of Rome, the Senate declared a state of emergency and a group of senators beat Tiberius to death.

Ten years later Tiberius's brother Gaius, an astute politician as well, was also elected tribune. He won over poor Roman farmers with his proposal to establish new colonies to give them land. He also provided free grain for the poor and called for new public works projects to create jobs for the working class and lucrative contracts for wealthy publicans. His measures passed the Plebian Assembly. Gaius was also elected tribune for two years straight, in violation of Roman political tradition. The final straw for the Senate was Gaius's proposal to establish a new court system that could try senators for corruption. In 121 BCE, the senators took action to subdue Gaius. He attempted to use force himself to resist the Senate, but in the end his supporters were massacred and he died, either by his own hand or at the hands of senators who had opposed his rise to power.

The Rise of Client Armies

After the assassination of Gaius Gracchus, Rome's political class was divided into two warring factions. The **populares** were politicians who, like Gaius, sought the political support of discontented groups in Roman society, whereas the **optimates** were the champions of the old order and the traditional leadership of the elite in the Roman Senate. In 112 BCE, Rome went to war against Jugurtha, the king of Numidia (modern Algeria/Tunisia) in North Africa, after he slaughtered Romans there who had supported his brother as king. Roman armies suffered defeat after defeat, and due to the decline in numbers of Roman farmers, Rome was having difficulty filling the ranks.

Gaius Marius was a plebian and commoner who rose up the ranks of the Roman army and emerged as the leader of the *populares*. In 107 BCE, he ran for consul by denouncing the traditional Roman elites as weak and ineffective generals and promising to quickly end the war with Jugurtha. Such rhetoric was wildly popular with the common people who supported him. Once in power, Marius reformed the entrance requirements for the army to open it to proletariats, extending them the opportunity for war gains and even land for their service. These reforms led to the emergence of professional client armies, or armies composed of men more loyal to their commander than to the state.

By 105 BCE, Jugurtha was captured and then paraded through the Roman streets in chains. That same year, Rome faced new threats from the north in the form of Germanic tribes crossing the Rhine River and seeking to invade Italy. The Romans elected Marius consul for five consecutive terms (105–101 BCE) to lead his professional army against these enemies. After his victories, however, his enemies in the Senate wanted to embarrass him politically, so they prevented his proposal to give veterans land from becoming law. Marius was intimidated by these events and retired from politics.

In 90 BCE, Rome was again in turmoil when its Italian allies revolted after years of providing troops without having any voice in governing. During this "Social" War (90–88 BCE), the Romans under the leadership of Sulla, an *optimate*, defeated the rebels. Shortly thereafter, in 88 BCE, Rome's provinces in Greece and Asia Minor also revolted, after years of heavy taxes and corrupt governors. The rebels massacred thousands of Roman citizens and rallied around Mithridates, the Hellenistic king of Pontus in north Asia Minor. *Optimates* in the Senate appointed Sulla to lead an army against Mithridates. Like Marius, Sulla had promised his recruits land in return for their service. *Populares* in the Plebian Assembly, however, assigned command of the army to Marius, who had come out of retirement.

Sulla, then outside Rome with his client army, convinced his soldiers to choose personal loyalty to their general and his promise of land over their allegiance to Rome, and they marched on the city. Sulla's army hunted down and murdered many *populares*, and after establishing his own faction in charge of Rome, Sulla marched against Mithridates (Figure 6.34).

FIGURE 6.34 Rome and King Mithridates. As Rome expanded far beyond Italy, keeping its citizens in distant provinces safe could be a challenge. That was the case when parts of Greece and Asia Minor rebelled and rallied around King Mithridates of Pontus. This 1911 map of the eastern Mediterranean in 88 BCE shows Rome and its allies (red) and King Mithridates's kingdom and his allies (gray). (credit: modification of work" Asia Minor at the time of the First Mithridatical War" by The Historical Atlas by William River Shepherd, University of Texas Libraries/ Wikimedia Commons, Public Domain)

In 87 BCE, Marius, who had been in hiding, rallied his old veterans and marched on Rome, marking the second time in two years that Roman soldiers had chosen personal loyalty to their general over obedience to Rome's laws. Marius's men now hunted down and murdered *optimates*. After winning his seventh term as consul in 87 BCE, Marius died in office from natural causes. Having forced Mithridates out of Greece and restored Roman rule there, Sulla led his army back to Rome in 83 BCE to overthrow the *populares* who were still in charge. While in Rome, he compelled the Senate to appoint him **dictator**. The office of dictator was an ancient republican office used only during emergencies because it granted absolute authority for a limited time to handle the emergency. When Sulla assumed the office, it hadn't been used since the Second Punic War.

During Sulla's time as dictator, he ordered the execution of his political enemies and reformed the laws. In 79 BCE, he relinquished the office and retired from public life, convinced he had saved the republic and preserved the power of the traditional elite in the Senate. Instead, however, within half a century the Roman Republic was dead.

6.5 The Age of Augustus

LEARNING OBJECTIVES

By the end of this section, you will be able to:
- Identify the key events of the First and Second Triumvirate
- Analyze the personal charisma and leadership styles of Julius Caesar and Augustus
- Explain the fall of the Roman Republic and the rise of the first emperor

The social troubles that rocked Rome following the Punic Wars led to populists like the Gracchi and military leaders like Sulla, who marched on Rome in his attempt to restore order. Such events made it clear to many that Rome's republican institutions were no longer able to adapt to the transformed landscape produced by decades of territorial expansion. These problems also presaged the political transformations Rome was to suffer through in the following decades. Between 60 BCE and 31 BCE, a string of powerful military leaders took the stage and bent the Republic to their will. In their struggle for power, Rome descended further into civil war and disorder. By 27 BCE, only one leader remained. Under his powerful hand, the Republic became a mere façade for the emergent Roman Empire.

The First Triumvirate

Sulla was unable to crush the *populares* completely since some discontented groups still opposed the Senate leadership. After his retirement, new military and political leaders sought power with the support of these groups. Three men in particular eventually assumed enormous dominance. One was Pompey Magnus, who became a popular general, and thousands of landless Romans joined his client army on the promise of land. In 67 BCE, Roman armies under Pompey's command suppressed pirates in the eastern Mediterranean who had threatened Rome's imported grain supplies. Pompey next conclusively defeated Mithridates of Pontus, who had again gone on the attack against Rome. By 63 BCE, Pompey had subdued Asia Minor, annexed Syria, destroyed the Seleucid kingdom, and occupied Jerusalem.

Another politician and military commander of this era was Crassus. He had served under Sulla, achieved popularity in Rome by fighting against Spartacus, and used the support of disaffected wealthy Romans such as publicans to amass a huge fortune. The third influential figure was Julius Caesar, whose original source of popularity was the fact that Marius was his uncle. When Sulla took control, Caesar lost much of his influence, but by 69 BCE he was making a political comeback and winning the support of *populares* in Rome.

The *optimates* in the Senate distrusted all these men and cooperated to block their influence in Roman politics. In response, in 60 BCE the three decided to join forces to advance their interests though a political alliance known to history as the First Triumvirate ("rule by three men"). Together its members had the wealth and influence to run the Roman Republic, but they were all very ambitious and each greatly distrusted the others. After serving as consul in 60 BCE, Julius Caesar took command of the Roman army in Gaul (modern France). Over the next ten years, his armies conquered all Gaul and launched attacks against German tribes across the Rhine, and on the island of Britain across the English Channel. The Roman people were awed by Caesar's military success, and Pompey and Crassus grew jealous of his popularity. In 54 BCE, Crassus invaded the Parthian Kingdom in central Asia, hoping for similar military and political triumphs. The invasion was a disaster, however, and Crassus was captured by the Parthians and executed.

The Roman Empire had now grown large, thanks to Pompey's and Caesar's conquests (Figure 6.35). After Crassus's death, Pompey decided to break with Caesar and support his old enemies the *optimates*. In 49 BCE, the *optimates* and Pompey controlled the Senate and demanded that Caesar disband his army in Gaul and return to Rome to stand trial on various charges. Instead, Caesar convinced his client army to march on Rome. In January of that year he famously led his troops across the Rubicon River, the traditional boundary between Italy and Gaul. Since Caesar knew this move would trigger war, as it was illegal to bring a private army into Rome proper, the phrase "crossing the Rubicon" continues to mean "passing the point of no return." In 48 BCE, Caesar defeated Pompey at the Battle of Pharsalus in northern Greece. Shortly after this, Pompey fled to Egypt, where he was murdered by the Egyptian pharaoh Ptolemy XIII, who hoped to win Caesar's favor.

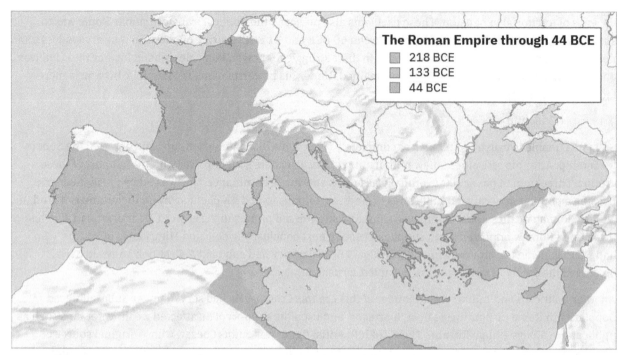

FIGURE 6.35 The Roman Empire through 44 BCE. Some of the areas marked in purple, like Gaul and Syria, were added to the Roman Empire by the victories of Julius Caesar and Pompey, respectively. (attribution: Copyright Rice University, OpenStax, under CC BY 4.0 license)

To prosecute the war against Pompey, Caesar had himself appointed dictator in 48 BCE. Despite the tradition that dictatorship was to be temporary, Caesar's position was indefinite. In 46 BCE, he was appointed dictator for a term of ten years, and in 44 BCE his dictatorship was made permanent, or for life. These appointments and other efforts to accumulate power unnerved many Romans, who had a deep and abiding distrust of autocratic rulers that stretched all the way back to the period of Etruscan rule. Caesar had hoped to win over his former enemies by inviting them to serve again in the Senate and appointing them to positions in his government. However, these former *optimates* viewed him as a tyrant, and in 44 BCE two of them, Brutus and Cassius, led a conspiracy that resulted in his assassination.

🔗 LINK TO LEARNING

In Shakespeare's play *Julius Caesar*, written in about 1599, Marc Antony gives one of the most famous speeches in English literature, based in part on the work of ancient Roman historians like Plutarch. In this short clip of that speech from the 1970 film adaptation (https://openstax.org/l/77AntonySpeech) of the play, Charlton Heston plays the part of Marc Antony.

From Republic to Principate

Octavian was only eighteen when Caesar was killed, but as Caesar's adopted son and heir he enjoyed the loyalty and political support of Caesar's military veterans. In 43 BCE, Octavian joined forces with two seasoned generals and politicians, Marc Antony and Lepidus, who both had been loyal supporters of Caesar. Marc Antony had been particularly close to him, as evidenced by the fact that Caesar left his legions under Antony's command in his will. Together these three shared the power of dictator in Rome in a political arrangement known as the Second Triumvirate. Unlike the First Triumvirate, which was effectively a conspiracy, the Second Triumvirate was formally recognized by the Senate. In 42 BCE, the army of the Second Triumvirate, under the command of Antony, defeated the forces of Julius Caesar's assassins Brutus and Cassius at the Battle of Philippi in northern Greece. The Second Triumvirate also ordered the execution of thousands of their political opponents.

After crushing the remnants of the *optimates*, the three men divided the Roman Empire between them: Octavian took Italy, Hispania, and Gaul; Lepidus Africa; and Antony Macedon, Greece, and Asia Minor. Soon they quarreled, however, and civil war erupted once again. Having greater support from Caesar's troops than his two opponents, in 36 BCE Octavian forced Lepidus into retirement. Antony countered by forming an alliance with Cleopatra VII, the Macedonian queen of Egypt, whom he married. Cleopatra was at that time co-ruler with Ptolemy XV, her son by Julius Caesar. With her financial support, Antony raised an army and fleet. In 31 BCE, in the naval Battle of Actium off the coast of northern Greece, Octavian defeated the forces of Antony and Cleopatra. When he afterwards invaded Egypt, the pair died by suicide (Figure 6.36), and Octavian installed himself as the new Egyptian pharaoh after executing Ptolemy XV. Octavian used the wealth of his kingdom in Egypt to finance his restructuring of the Roman state.

FIGURE 6.36 Cleopatra and the Asp. This mid-seventeenth-century painting by the Italian artist Cuido Cagnacci was modeled on one of many ancient accounts about how Cleopatra died. In this version, she allows a poisonous Egyptian snake, an asp, to bite her. If the story is true, she may have been incorporating Egyptian symbolism in her final act, the asp being associated with the Egyptian god Re. (credit: "The Death of Cleopatra" by Purchase, Diane Burke Gift, Gift of J. Pierpont Morgan, by exchange, Friends of European Paintings Gifts, Gwynne Andrews Fund, Lila Acheson Wallace, Charles and Jessie Price, and Álvaro Saieh Bendeck Gifts, Gift and Bequest of George Blumenthal and Fletcher Fund, by exchange, and Michel David-Weill Gift, 2016/Metropolitan Museum of Art, Public Domain)

One of Octavian's primary tasks after 31 BCE was to consolidate his position in order to preserve the peace and stability he had created. To avoid the fate of his adopted father, he successfully maintained a façade that the Roman Republic was alive and well, assuming titles and powers traditionally associated with it. After stacking the Senate with his supporters, in 27 BCE Octavian officially stepped down as dictator and "restored" the Republic.

The Senate immediately appointed him proconsul or governor of all Roman frontier provinces, which made him effectively the commander of the entire Roman army. The Senate also recognized him as the *Princeps Senatus*, or "leader of the Senate," meaning the senator who enjoyed the most prestige and authority due to his service to the Republic. (The name of this political order, the **principate**, derives from this title.) Finally, the Senate voted to honor Octavian with the title of *Augustus* or "revered one," used to describe gods and great heroes of the past. As these honors and titles suggest, Octavian, traditionally referred to as Augustus after 27 BCE, had assumed enormous power. Despite his claim that he had restored the Republic, he had in fact inaugurated the Empire, with himself as emperor possessing almost godlike authority (Figure 6.37).

FIGURE 6.37 **A Temple in the Roman Empire**. The power of Augustus laid the foundation for the emergence of the imperial cult, in which Roman emperors were worshiped during their reigns (largely in the east) and assumed demigod status after their deaths. At temples like this one in Vienne, France, built during Augustus's lifetime, people demonstrated their loyalty to the Roman Empire through the rituals of this cult. (credit: "Temple of Augustus and Livia in Vienne" by O.Mustafin/Wikimedia Commons, CC0 1.0)

After 27 BCE, Augustus held elected office as one of the two consuls, so he could sit in the Senate, oversee the law courts, and introduce legislation to the Centuriate Assembly, but the senators disliked this arrangement because it closed the opportunity for one of them to hold this prestigious office instead. In 23 BCE, therefore, the Senate gave Augustus several powers of a tribune. He could now veto any action taken by government officials, the Senate, and the assemblies, and he could introduce laws to the Plebian Assembly. He could wield political and military power based on the traditional constitution of the Republic.

As emperor, Augustus successfully tackled problems that had plagued Rome for at least a century. He reduced the standing army from 600,000 to 200,000 and provided land for thousands of discharged veterans in recently conquered areas such as in Gaul and Hispania. He also created new taxes specifically to fund land and cash bonuses for future veterans. To encourage native peoples in the provinces to adopt Roman culture, he granted them citizenship after twenty-five years of service in the army. Indigenous cities built in the Roman style and adopting its political system were designated *municipia*, which gave all elected officials Roman citizenship. Through these "Romanization" policies, Augustus advanced Roman culture across the empire.

Augustus also finally brought order and prosperity to the city of Rome. He began a vast building program that provided jobs for poor Romans in the city and reportedly boasted that he had transformed Rome from a city of brick to a city of marble. To win over the masses, he also provided free grain (courtesy of his control of fertile Egypt) and free entertainment (gladiator combats and chariot races), making Rome famous for its bounty of "bread and circuses." He also established a permanent police force in the city, the Praetorian Guard, which he recruited from the Roman army. He even created a fire department.

Augustus provided wealthy Romans outside the ranks of the Senate with new opportunities for advancement via key positions he reserved for them, such as prefect (commander/governor) of the Praetorian Guard and prefect of Egypt. These officials could join the Senate and become members of the senatorial elite. Augustus thus created an effective new bureaucracy to govern the Roman Empire. Emperors who followed him continued these practices.

Augustus was keenly aware that the peace and prosperity he had created was largely built upon his image and power, and he feared what might happen when he died. As a result, the last few decades of his life were spent arranging for a political successor. This was a complicated matter since there was neither an official position of emperor nor a republican tradition of hereditary rule. Augustus had no son of his own, and his attempts to groom others to take control were repeatedly frustrated when his proposed successors died before him. Before his own death in 14 CE, Augustus arranged for his stepson Tiberius to receive from the Senate the power of a proconsul and a tribune. While not his first choice, Tiberius was an accomplished military leader with senatorial support.

Despite the smooth transition to Tiberius in 14 CE, problems with imperial inheritance remained. There were always risks that a hereditary ruler might prove incompetent. Tiberius himself became dangerously paranoid late in his reign. And he was succeeded by his grandnephew and adopted son Gaius, known as Caligula, who after a severe illness became insane. The prefect of the Praetorian Guard assassinated Caligula in 40 CE, and the guard replaced him with his uncle Claudius (40–54 CE). The Roman Senate agreed to this step only out of fear of the army. Claudius was an effective emperor, however, and under his reign the province of Britain (modern England and Wales) was added to the empire.

The government of Claudius's successor, his grandnephew Nero (54–68 CE), was excellent as long as Nero's mother Agrippina was the power behind the throne. After ordering her murder, however, Nero proved a vicious despot who used the Praetorian Guard to intimidate and execute his critics in the Senate. By the end of his reign, Roman armies in Gaul and Hispania were mutinying. The Senate declared him an enemy of state, and he died by suicide. During the year after his death, 68–69 CE, four different generals assumed power, thus earning it the name "Year of the Four Emperors."

Of the four, Vespasian (69–79 CE) survived the civil war and adopted the name Caesar and the title Augustus, even though he was not related to the family of Augustus or their descendants (the Julio-Claudian dynasty). On Nero's death, he had been in command of Roman armies suppressing the revolt of Judea (Roman armies eventually crushed this revolt and sacked Jerusalem in 70 CE). In his administration, Vespasian followed the precedents established by Augustus. For example, he ordered the construction of the Colosseum as a venue for the gladiator shows he provided as entertainment for the Roman masses, and he arranged for his two sons, Titus (79–81 CE) and Domitian (81–96 CE), to succeed him as emperor. Domitian, like Nero, was an insecure ruler and highly suspicious of the Senate; he employed the Praetorian Guard to arrest and execute his critics in that body. In 96 CE, his wife Domitia worked with members of the Senate to arrange for his assassination. Thus the flaws of the principate continued to haunt the Roman state long after its founder was gone.

Key Terms

dictator a Roman Republican office with absolute authority over the state for a limited time during emergencies

Hellenistic a description of Greek history, language, and culture in the period 323–31 BCE

Levant a historical geographical term referring to an area in the eastern Mediterranean consisting roughly of modern Israel, Jordan, Lebanon, Palestine, and Syria

Linear A a script developed by the Minoans but not yet deciphered by modern scholars

Linear B a Mycenaean script developed from Linear A that was used to write an early form of the Greek language

mystery religions religious cults that featured secret rituals (the so-called mysteries) and became popular in Hellenistic cities

optimates politicians who supported the old order and the traditional leadership of elites

polis a city-state in Ancient Greece

populares politicians who sought the political support of discontented groups in Roman society

principate the political system established by Augustus Caesar after 27 BCE, which relied on Rome's traditional institutions and practices to legitimize a military dictatorship

proletariat the landless working class

Struggle of the Orders a political contest during the first centuries of the Republic in which Rome's commoners sought equal rights with elites

Twelve Tables the first set of written laws in Rome, from about 450 BCE

Section Summary

6.1 Early Mediterranean Peoples

The Late Bronze Age witnessed the development of a common culture that linked the diverse states of the eastern Mediterranean from Asia to the Aegean region. The Minoan and Mycenaean civilizations emerged on the Aegean island of Crete and on mainland Greece. Minoan culture strongly influenced the art and culture of the Mycenaean civilization that followed it. Around 1200 BCE, these Late Bronze Age states collapsed in a wave of wars and migrations.

The Iron Age began with the development of technology to produce iron tools and weapons. During this transition, the Phoenicians built their civilization and invented the alphabet around 1100 BCE, establishing trade networks that linked the entire Mediterranean basin. The arrival of Phoenicians and especially Greeks in central Italy after 700 BCE contributed to the evolution of a new culture in Italy, the Etruscans. Their civilization made a deep impact on the later development of ancient Rome.

6.2 Ancient Greece

During the Archaic period that began the Greek renaissance, the city-state, or polis, developed its defining characteristic—self-government. Sparta was an oligarchy whose elite class of soldier-citizens alone participated in government, while Athens developed a democracy in which all adult male citizens participated. During this period, well-known features of Greek culture emerged such as the Greek script, the epic poems of Homer, and the Olympic Games.

The Classical period of Greece was marked by increased creativity and innovation, especially in Athens. The philosophical schools of Plato and Aristotle, the histories of Herodotus and Thucydides, the plays of Athenian dramatists, and the art of Greek sculptors, architects, and painters have inspired European thinkers and artists for centuries. These developments were partially a result of the success the Greek city-states achieved in their efforts to withstand two invasions by the Persian Empire. Following these wars, however, the Greek city-states turned on themselves. Sparta and its allies first fought the Athenian empire in the Peloponnesian War. Following this long and destructive conflict, Sparta and Thebes struggled for dominance in Greece, often with meddling from the Persian Empire. By 350 BCE, the many decades of fighting had left the Greek city-states exhausted and vulnerable.

6.3 The Hellenistic Era

By 338 BCE, King Philip II's empire of Macedon had become the ruling power in Greece. Philip's son Alexander the Great adopted his father's plan to unite the Greek city-states in a war of revenge against the Persian Empire. He defeated the Persians at the battles of Issus (333 BCE) and Gaugamela (330 BCE), and after the assassination of the Persian king Darius III, he claimed the Persian throne for himself and advanced deep into central Asia and India. After his own soldiers mutinied, however, Alexander withdrew to Babylon, where he died in 323 BCE.

Alexander's generals and their children competed for control of his empire between 323 BCE and 272 BCE. The descendants of Alexander's generals, Antigonus, Seleucus, and Ptolemy, ruled over separate kingdoms in Macedon and Greece, western and central Asia, and Egypt, building new Greek cities for their Greek colonists. Alexandria in Egypt, the largest Hellenistic city, was a center of Greek science and literature, with its massive library and museum. Having lost sovereignty and self-government, many Greeks sought personal happiness through new philosophies such as Epicureanism and Stoicism.

6.4 The Roman Republic

The Romans overthrew the Etruscan dynasty at the close of the sixth century BCE and became a republic. The Struggle of the Orders ended with the plebeians winning equality with the patricians under the law, and by the third century BCE Roman citizens were electing officials and passing legislation through various assemblies under the watchful eye of the Senate. By the third century BCE, Rome had united the Italian peninsula by pledging to defend all new allies from their enemies. With these allies, Rome possessed the military resources to crush the other Mediterranean powers, Carthage and the Hellenistic monarchies of the eastern Mediterranean.

By the mid-second century BCE, Rome was the dominant power in the Mediterranean. But the wars had created a number of social problems tearing the Republic apart. These conflicts led to the rise of the Gracchi and later the partisan battle between the *populares* who opposed the governing elite and the *optimates* who supported it. By the end of the second century BCE, powerful military commanders and their client armies had assumed great authority in the republic. One of these commanders, General Sulla, twice marched on Rome to secure power for his political faction, the *optimates*. In 79 BCE, he retired, but his marches on Rome and his resurrection of the office of dictator laid the groundwork for the permanent overthrow of the Republic later.

6.5 The Age of Augustus

United by their opposition to the *optimates*, in 60 BCE, Pompey, Crassus, and Julius Caesar formed a political alliance, the First Triumvirate. After Crassus was killed in a failed conquest of the Parthians, Pompey joined his former enemies to oppose Caesar, whose success against the Gallic and Germanic tribes had made him popular. In 49 BCE, Caesar marched on Rome and initiated a civil war that ended in Pompey's defeat. Considering Caesar a tyrant, Pompey's former supporters assassinated him in 44 BCE.

Caesar's heir Octavian formed the Second Triumvirate in 43 BCE with Lepidus and Marc Antony. The three defeated Caesar's assassins but afterwards quarreled. With the support of Caesar's veterans, Octavian emerged the sole inheritor of Roman power. In 27 BCE, he announced the restoration of the Republic but in form only, receiving the honorary title of Augustus. He set up a system of government, the principate, in which the traditions of republican government legitimized his position as de facto emperor. In power, Augustus provided land for veterans; secured jobs, free grain, and internal order for the urban proletariat; and offered wealthy Romans political and social advancement. However, he was not able to create an orderly system of succession, and the hereditary monarchs who succeeded him were often weak and ineffective.

Assessments

Review Questions

1. On what Aegean island did Minoan civilization develop?
   a. Crete
   b. Sardinia
   c. Cyprus
   d. Rhodes

2. The Etruscan culture arose in the central area of what modern country?
   a. Greece
   b. Anatolia
   c. Spain
   d. Italy

3. Who developed the first alphabet?
   a. Egyptians
   b. Akkadians
   c. Greeks
   d. Phoenicians

4. What is an example of the Greeks borrowing and adapting Phoenician cultural traits?
   a. Greeks adopted the Phoenician *fasces* to symbolize power.
   b. Greeks adopted the Phoenician alphabet.
   c. Greeks adopted Phoenician deities to worship as gods.
   d. Greeks adopted Phoenician warfare tactics in their athletic competitions.

5. What likely set Athens on the path toward democracy as early as the eighth century BCE?
   a. the decline in literacy
   b. the decline in population
   c. its growing prosperity
   d. a rising conflict with Phoenicia

6. What Athenian leader played an instrumental role in the founding of a democracy in Athens in the late sixth century BCE?
   a. Socrates
   b. Cleisthenes
   c. Pericles
   d. Alcibiades

7. Though unsuccessful, the Spartans inspired the Greeks with their defense against the Persian army of what mountain pass in 480 BCE?
   a. Salamis
   b. Mantinea
   c. Thermopylae
   d. Leuctra

8. What two Greek city-states led their respective alliances on either side in the Peloponnesian War?
   a. Corinth and Thermopylae
   b. Athens and Corcyra

    c. Thebes and Syracuse

    d. Sparta and Athens

9. What Greek philosopher founded his own school at the Lyceum in Athens?

    a. Aristotle

    b. Plato

    c. Socrates

    d. Democritus

10. At what battle did the forces of Philip of Macedon defeat the allied armies of Athens and Thebes in 338 BCE?

    a. Thermopylae

    b. Chaeronea

    c. Leuctra

    d. Salamis

11. What land did Alexander the Great and the Macedonians conquer?

    a. Egypt

    b. Italy

    c. Sicily

    d. Carthage

12. What Greek city was the largest in the Hellenistic period?

    a. Alexandria

    b. Carthage

    c. Athens

    d. Sparta

13. Around what Persian sun god did a mystery religion form?

    a. Zeus

    b. Isis

    c. Baal

    d. Mithras

14. In what branch of government was Rome's Council of Elders?

    a. Senate

    b. praetors

    c. censors

    d. tribunes

15. What Roman officials could veto the actions of Roman law courts, the popular assemblies, and the Senate?

    a. consuls

    b. praetors

    c. censors

    d. tribunes

16. The common people of the Roman Republic were known as:

    a. patricians

    b. *optimates*

    c. plebeians

d. senators

17. With what group did Rome fight a war for control of the Mediterranean?
    a. Latins
    b. Carthaginians
    c. Samnites
    d. Etruscans

18. What were private contractors called who constructed public works and collected taxes in Rome?
    a. publicans
    b. equestrians
    c. *populares*
    d. proletariat

19. Who were the members of the First Triumvirate?
    a. Lepidus, Caesar, Octavian
    b. Caesar, Pompey, Crassus
    c. Marc Antony, Octavian, Lepidus
    d. Pompey, Lepidus, Marc Antony

20. What event led to the establishment of the Second Triumvirate?
    a. the assassination of Caesar
    b. the succession of Tiberius
    c. the retirement of Lepidus
    d. the suicide of Cleopatra

21. Julius Caesar won popularity among the Roman people for his successful military campaigns in _____.
    a. Pontus
    b. Parthia
    c. Carthage
    d. Gaul

22. Octavian's success in the civil war was due largely to support from _____.
    a. Pompey's veteran soldiers
    b. *optimates*
    c. Julius Caesar's veteran soldiers
    d. Julius Caesar's assassins

23. Octavian's naval forces defeated those of Antony and Cleopatra at the Battle of _____.
    a. Pharsalus
    b. Actium
    c. Philippi
    d. Zama

Check Your Understanding Questions

1. What were the three major Phoenician cities and where were they located?

2. What explains why iron replaced bronze as the metal of choice between 1200 and 900 BCE in the Near East and eastern Mediterranean?

3. What evidence suggests that Minoan civilization was conquered by the Mycenaeans?

4. What was the primary reason that Greeks established colonies overseas in the Archaic period?

5. What were Athens's and Sparta's expectations of their respective allies before and during the Peloponnesian War?

6. Under Athens's democracy in the Classical period, how were Athenian citizens (free adult males) able to participate in the government?

7. In what ways did the efforts of Philip II ultimately lead to the success of Alexander the Great?

8. What were the boundaries of Alexander the Great's empire by the time of his death in 323 BCE?

9. Why was there a period of wars following Alexander's death in 323 BCE?

10. Who were the tribunes and what were their main powers as elected officials?

11. How did the plebeians win concessions from the ruling patricians during the Struggle of the Orders?

12. During the Punic Wars and the wars fought by Rome thereafter, why did Rome's farmers come under stress?

13. What did Augustus actually accomplish with his efforts to "restore" the Republic?

14. Why did some Roman senators assassinate Julius Caesar?

15. During the wars between the members of the Second Triumvirate, what advantage did Octavian enjoy over his rivals?

Application and Reflection Questions

1. Given that iron, when properly manufactured, was far superior in strength to bronze, why did it take a civilizational collapse for metalworkers to experiment with it? Does the absence of tin seem sufficient to explain the shift to iron? Why or why not?

2. Historians and archaeologists have long recognized connections between different Mediterranean cultures like the Greeks, Etruscans, and Phoenicians. Why do you think these different cultures borrowed from each other? What might encourage one culture to adopt elements from another?

3. People often associate advancements in technology with human progress. Why did the development of iron technology and the alphabet occur at a time of societal collapse at the end of the Late Bronze Age?

4. How does the development of the Athenian political system over the course of the Archaic period compare to that of Sparta? In which of these cities would you have preferred to live? Why?

5. Alliances led the Greeks to victory during the Persian Wars but also contributed to the Peloponnesian War between the Greek city-states. What does this suggest about the role of alliances in the Greek world? Would Greece have been better off without them? Why or why not?

6. Many influential philosophies and celebrated works of art emerged from the Greek world in the fifth century BCE, when the Greeks were busy fighting Persia and each other. What does this suggest about the connection between conflict and the arts?

7. Alexander's march into India has been celebrated as a great achievement because of its boldness and as a terrible mistake because it led his troops to mutiny, and he died not long after. What do you think of this move? How might things have played out differently if Alexander hadn't tried to extend his empire in this way?

8. In the aftermath of Alexander's conquest and death, much of the former Persian Empire remained in the hands of Greek and Macedonian rulers. Why do you think this happened? Why didn't local rulers and dynasties reestablish their rule over these lands?

9. The Romans believed they had overthrown Etruscan kings in the sixth century BCE to establish their republic. What does this feature of their own history suggest about their reaction to the stresses on the Republic in the second century BCE and to the rise of military leaders like Sulla?

10. Given the problems experienced by small farmers and the lower classes in Rome as a result of the wars of expansion, why did Rome continue the wars? Why didn't populist leaders like the Gracchi suggest an end to them?

11. How did Sulla's march on Rome in 88 BCE set the stage for the civil wars of the First and Second Triumvirates?

12. To what extent were Octavian's political and military successes due to the achievements of his adoptive father Julius Caesar? Explain your answer.

13. What was the primary cause of the fall of the Roman Republic? Could modern republics such as the United States collapse for the same reason? Why or why not?

FIGURE 7.1 The Colosseum in Rome. The largest standing amphitheater in the world, the Colosseum is a perpetual reminder of the power and culture of the Roman Empire at its height. (credit: modification of work "Colosseum - Rome - Italy" by Sam Valadi/Flickr, CC BY 2.0)

CHAPTER OUTLINE

INTRODUCTION The ancient city of Rome gave its name to an empire that stretched from Britain to the Arabian Peninsula. While political life was centered in the city of Rome—the seat of the Senate and of the emperor—"Rome" came to represent a much broader geographic expanse. From the second century BCE to the third century CE, Rome's magnitude was reflected in the diversity of experiences of all those who lived within the empire's borders, not just those who lived in the shadow of the great Colosseum (Figure 7.1).

Rome was a patriarchal society that achieved success through military dominance, patriotism, and respect for authority. Romans prided themselves on the status and reputation they achieved through military or political service, as well as through their claims of noble ancestors. This arrangement largely benefited upper-class Roman men, while others struggled to navigate the system and were subject to domination by the elite. Roman women and enslaved people were held to restrictive cultural standards for their behavior, though many were able to overcome these and hold real influence in Roman society. The complexity of daily life in Rome is key to understanding the way the empire functioned and flourished at its height.

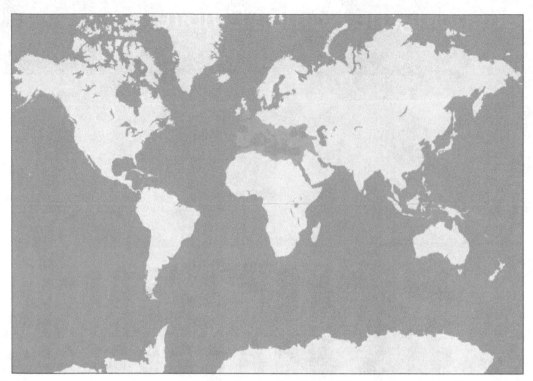

FIGURE 7.2 Locator Map: Experiencing the Roman Empire. (credit: modification of work "World map blank shorelines" by Maciej Jaros/Wikimedia Commons, Public Domain)

7.1 The Daily Life of a Roman Family

LEARNING OBJECTIVES

By the end of this section, you will be able to:
- Describe a typical Roman home
- Discuss gender roles in Roman families
- Analyze the influence of social class on daily life in Rome

The family was an important element of life during the Roman Empire. The male patriarch was the head of the household, which consisted of the immediate and extended family, as well as adjacent groups, including dependents and enslaved people. While men held ultimate authority in the family, women were also expected to maintain family order, with responsibilities in and often outside the household. Pride in a family's prosperity was a crucial Roman value, which motivated both the honoring of ancestors and the securing of a future for descendants. Romans looked to their ancestors for examples of correct moral behavior and worked diligently for the family's continuing stability.

The Structure of Roman Families

Family life was oriented around the **paterfamilias**, the male head of the household. According to tradition, this patriarch had the power of life and death over all his dependents, an authority referred to as *patria potestas* ("paternal power"). Members of the extended family subject to this authority included the patriarch's wife, their children, anyone descended through the family's male line, and all enslaved people belonging to the household. With his authority, the patriarch was both the judge and rule maker of the family, with the power to sell his dependents into bondage or destroy their property (Figure 7.3).

FIGURE 7.3 A Roman *Paterfamilias*. This painting by the seventeenth-century Dutch artist Ferdinand Bol depicts the Roman general Manlius, who had his own son executed for disobedience. Though produced in a much later period, Bol's work illuminates some traditional Roman values: The patriarch's power is indicated in Manlius's outward indifference as he looks away from his son's death, and his loyalty to Rome is demonstrated by his looking toward his troops instead. (credit: "Consul Titus Manlius Torquatus Orders the Beheading of his Son" by Rijksmuseum/Wikimedia Commons, CC0 1.0)

Ultimately, however, the goal of the *paterfamilias* was to promote his family's welfare. His power worked through consensus and deliberation with the other family members. As the primary provider, he expected respect from his family but could also reward good behavior. In this way, an entire family might benefit by working together to further their social or financial prosperity.

The securing of a Roman family's reputation began with the education and training of children. In early Rome, children were educated in the home; later, grammar schools enrolled boys and girls from wealthy families until around the age of twelve. Education usually centered on reading and writing Latin and Greek as well as arithmetic. Around age fifteen, boys donned the *toga virilis* ("toga of manhood"), a plain white toga representing their enrollment as citizens and entrance into manhood. Roman citizenship was highly coveted and was bestowed either at birth to children of citizens or by special decree. Sons of prominent families could then go on to a civil or military career. After a son inherited his father's property (as well as his debts), it became his responsibility to maintain the family's reputation and prosperity.

By contrast, girls commonly married at a young age, usually between fourteen and eighteen years old, and often to a much older man. Younger girls were viewed as more sexually pure and therefore easier to control. In the most common form of marriage, a wife brought a dowry that became her husband's property. Thus, a woman from a wealthy background with a large dowry had some sway in making marriage arrangements. She also had the protection a powerful family could offer should her husband prove to be less than ideal. Lower-class women were more reliant on their husband's status to enhance their own. In any case, marriage represented a woman's coming under the legal control of her husband's household.

The vast legal and age imbalance between husband and wife was reflected in the cultural restrictions on Roman women. Yet, though a Roman man's work was an important contributor to the family's success, women devoted much of their efforts to the same goal. Women were responsible for the management of the household, which included ensuring provisions for the family, overseeing any enslaved people and other dependents, and looking after the children. Spinning wool was viewed as the activity of an ideal Roman woman, and many wives were expected to occupy themselves with this work. Despite these expectations, there is evidence that many women, particularly non-elite women, held professions outside the home, including in medicine, trade, and agriculture.

A Day in the Life of a Roman Family

Romans lived and worked in a variety of contexts across the empire. Most of our evidence of the practical elements of their daily lives comes from archaeological evidence uncovered at Pompeii. The remains of this once-bustling city (which was destroyed by a volcanic eruption in 79 CE) show us the occupations, architecture, and lifestyles of different social classes. In addition, though most of what we know is about wealthy estates, life in the countryside outside the city constituted another important part of imperial Roman society.

Daily life was dominated by aristocratic men who enjoyed careers in politics, law, and the military. Wealthy Romans were part of two property-based classes: the senatorial and the equestrian ranks. Only those above a certain property threshold were allowed to be members of these upper classes, and they occupied privileged social positions with access to prestigious careers denied to the lower classes. An elite Roman man's day began at home in the ***domus***, a traditional single-family house that served both practical and symbolic roles (the term *domus* refers not only to the physical residence but also to the family). It was a place of display in which a family could take pride and where the father would conduct official business. Every morning, in the role of **patron**, he would receive a number of **clients** in his home who sought his aid in exchange for loyalty. The late morning was usually consumed by responsibilities outside the home, including business and political meetings. During the afternoon, wealthy Roman men spent their time socializing and pursuing leisure activities, such as attending public entertainment performances or visiting the bathhouse.

BEYOND THE BOOK

The Plan of a Typical Roman Household

The most common type of Roman house was the *atrium* house, which could include two or more stories. Based mostly on evidence from Pompeii, we know that each house contained several key features. The *fauces* or *vestibulum* was the entryway. The *atrium* was the open-air reception hall where the patron of the house met with his clients; this area was often decorated with a colorful mosaic on the floor. The *tablinum* was a small room separated from the atrium by a wooden screen or curtain and contained family records and portraits.

The partial roof over the atrium, or the *compluvium*, was slanted to drain rainwater into the shallow *impluvium* pool. This water was collected in an underground cistern for use by the family, or, if left in the pool, it helped to ventilate other rooms in the house. The *triclinium* ("three couches") was the dining room, where members of the household ate in the Roman fashion, reclining around a small table. *Alae* were the smaller recesses in a house that stored masks or busts of a family's ancestors.

Fountains, peristyle (columned) courtyards, gardens, and other lavish features were located across the atrium from the doorway, to make sure guests could see them upon arrival. This floor plan emphasized the power relationship between a patron and his clients, as well as the authority and prestige of the *paterfamilias* (Figure 7.4).

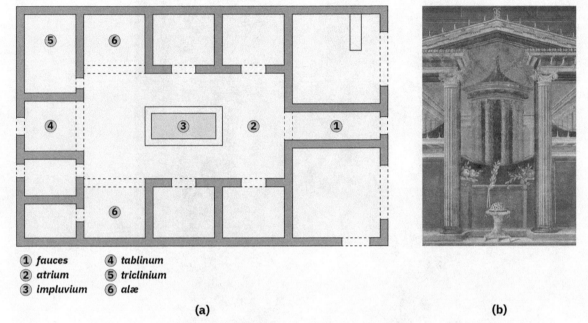

① *fauces*   ④ *tablinum*
② *atrium*   ⑤ *triclinium*
③ *impluvium*   ⑥ *alæ*

(a)   (b)

FIGURE 7.4 A Typical Roman Home. A typical Roman home was oriented around an atrium, or open-air reception hall (a). There were four styles of wall paintings or frescoes in Roman homes. The "architectural" style (b) was meant to serve as a window onto an imaginary public scene, framed by columns. This fresco is from the villa in Naples that is believed to have belonged to Publio Fannio Sinistore and was buried by the eruption of Mount Vesuvius in 79 CE. (credit a: attribution: Copyright Rice University, OpenStax, under CC BY 4.0 license; credit b: modification of work "Fresco from the villa of Publio Fannio Sinistore in Boscoreale" by Metropolitan Museum of Art, Rogers Fund, 1903/Wikimedia Commons, Public Domain)

- What are the key features of an atrium house and what do they tell us about daily life in Rome?
- How does the architecture of a typical Roman home reflect important aspects of Roman culture and society?

🔗 LINK TO LEARNING

Explore the ruins of the city of Pompeii (https://openstax.org/l/77Pompeii) to learn more. Remarkably preserved after the eruption of Mount Vesuvius in 79 CE, the city is our finest source of information about daily life in a Roman city.

The wealthiest Romans had both houses in the city and villas in the countryside. Suburban villas were located just outside a city's walls, and villas located in the countryside typically originated as agricultural estates. Large estates, known as **latifundia**, were agricultural operations in which enslaved people worked the land for the owner's profit. In the imperial period, these estates came to contain villa residences that functioned more as places of recreation and a means to display wealth. Many elements of luxury displayed in townhouses also appear in villas, such as gardens, fountains, and mosaics. Hadrian's villa outside Rome is an opulent example of luxury at the very top of the Roman social order, incorporating elements of this emperor's travels in the second century CE (Figure 7.5).

FIGURE 7.5 How Wealthy Romans Lived. The architecture of Hadrian's second-century villa outside Rome recalls elements of the emperor's travels, including a Greek Temple of Venus, a small lake resembling an Egyptian canal, and numerous statues. (credit: "Hadrian villa ruins" by "Entoaggie09"/Wikimedia Commons, CC BY 2.5)

Life for the lower classes was not as luxurious or as stable. Clients formed a largely educated class in Rome who supported themselves through gifts from their patrons and meager employment. Though Romans typically had a six-hour workday, the urban poor relied more on occasional work or odd jobs. In large cities, many lived in *insulae*, apartment complexes of three to four levels that occupied a rectangular city block. *Insulae* had a reputation for being overcrowded and having limited facilities, however.

What Family Meant in Rome

The power of the *paterfamilias* was mirrored in the power of Roman politicians and magistrates. Romans' personal respect for authority, dispensing of justice, and honoring of the family influenced the way they conducted themselves publicly. The desire to further the family's prosperity also extended into other facets of daily life. The family as a unit worked to achieve status and prosperity, and everyone had a role to play.

Politics was certainly an extension of Roman family principles. Holding a coveted and powerful political position, Roman senators were referred to as "conscript fathers" (*patres conscripti*), and their authority, dispensed through legislation and legal judgments, was much like that of a father over his household. Laws about marriage and childbirth made once-private matters a concern of the Roman state. For example, the emperor Augustus made adultery a public crime, setting out to promote childbirth in Rome and protect legal marriages. Yet, like the expectations for women in Roman society, this legislation disproportionately punished women, who could be exiled for adultery as a result.

Augustus's Laws Governing the Family

During his reign, which lasted from 27 BCE to 14 CE, the emperor Augustus enacted numerous moral laws to encourage proper Roman marriage and behavior, including those concerning adultery, discussed in the following accounts by the Roman historian Tacitus and by Suetonius, the biographer of the early Roman emperors. The question was, if Augustus could not ensure good behavior in his own family as *paterfamilias*, how could he expect Roman citizens to follow his strict moral guidelines? As you read, note the tone of each and what each author says about public perceptions of Augustus's treatment of the women in his family.

Fortune, staunch to the deified Augustus in his public life, was less propitious to him at home, owing to the incontinence of his daughter and granddaughter, whom he expelled from the capital while penalizing their adulterers by death or banishment. For designating as he did the besetting sin of both the sexes by the harsh appellations of sacrilege and treason, he overstepped both the mild penalties of an earlier day and those of his own laws [the laws concerning adultery passed in 18/17 BCE].

—Tacitus, *Annals*

But at the height of his happiness and his confidence in his family and its training, Fortune proved fickle. He found the two Julias, his daughter and granddaughter, guilty of every form of vice, and banished them. . . . After [his daughter] was banished, he denied her the use of wine and every form of luxury, and would not allow any man, bond or free, to come near her without his permission, and then not without being informed of his stature, complexion, and even of any marks or scars upon his body. It was not until five years later that he moved her from the island to the mainland and treated her with somewhat less rigor. But he could not by any means be prevailed on to recall her altogether, and when the Roman people several times interceded for her and urgently pressed their suit, he in open assembly called upon the gods to curse them with like daughters and like wives.

—Suetonius, *Life of Augustus*

- Why do you think Augustus went beyond the penalties of his own laws to punish adultery within his own family?
- What do his actions say about the cultural values of Roman men?

Emperors were especially interested in maintaining their family's stability, for the practical purpose of ensuring dynastic continuity but also to garner positive public opinion. Rulers took special interest in finding an heir and exercising tight control over family matters. Augustus worked diligently to name an heir to rule after him, appointing several before being succeeded by his stepson Tiberius. Having an unstable household could mean a quick end to an emperor's reign if the situation became too tumultuous. In the later Roman Empire, when there was significant turnover of rulers, emperors named an heir soon after coming to power.

Similarly, public figures who embodied Roman family values were looked on favorably. Cornelia, a noblewoman in the second century BCE, is remembered for devoting herself to motherhood above all else. She gave birth to twelve children, and after her husband died she refused to remarry and focused instead on raising her surviving children. Her sons Tiberius and Gaius Gracchus led influential political careers before they were both assassinated. Cornelia is reported to have said of her sons, in conversation with another woman displaying her jewelry, "*These* are my jewels." Cornelia was noted for embodying feminine virtues in her motherly devotion and for her indirect impact on Roman politics.

By contrast, public figures who disregarded Roman family values were infamous. For example, Agrippina the Younger, great-granddaughter of the emperor Augustus, was viewed as a power-hungry woman in her time.

She married her uncle, the emperor Claudius, who was twenty-five years older than she. She then convinced him to adopt her son Nero from a previous marriage, an act that eventually implicated Agrippina in Claudius's murder in 54 CE and led to Nero's reign as emperor. Instead of holding more power as empress after Nero's ascension, Agrippina saw her relationship with her son flounder. Nero plotted to have her killed, first in a sinking boat, from which she escaped, and then by an assassin. The violence and treachery of the imperial family especially tarred Agrippina as a disreputable woman.

Finally, respect for ancestral custom and precedents known as *mos maiorum* ("the way of the ancestors") and for deceased members of the family were epitomized in funeral parades. In these public rituals, the deceased was carried from home to the city center, or *forum*, where the body was laid out. A eulogy was delivered by the heir, surrounded by others wearing ancestor masks that represented deceased family members. The procession linked the living family to the past, and the route through the city gave the ritual public and communal significance (Figure 7.6).

FIGURE 7.6 A Roman Funeral. This relief from the first century BCE depicts a Roman funerary procession. The deceased's high status is clear from the presence of soldiers, musicians, and politicians heading toward the sanctuary on the right, where an animal sacrifice is prepared. (credit: modification of work "Etruscan-Roman cinerary urn from Volaterrae circa 100 BC" by "TimeTravelRome"/Flickr, CC BY 2.0)

7.2 Slavery in the Roman Empire

LEARNING OBJECTIVES

By the end of this section, you will be able to:
- Describe the legal and social structures that supported slavery in the Roman Empire
- Discuss the different experiences of enslaved men, women, and children
- Explain the importance of gladiators in Roman culture

Slavery was a fundamental part of Roman daily life. Enslaved people came from many parts of the large empire and had been enslaved in many different ways. They worked in a variety of contexts and were subject to their master's whims and punishment. Many were trained as **gladiators**, professional fighters paid to battle before an audience, sometimes to the death, but others worked in the cities and countryside in a variety of roles. The freeing of enslaved people was a common practice, and freed people were important to the continued functioning of the Roman economy and political order.

The Structures of Roman Slavery

Enslavement was the result of a variety of circumstances in the Roman world; there was no single mechanism that sustained the system. During the Roman Republic, it appears that most enslaved people were former soldiers captured in war. Slave dealers purchased these captives from defeated armies and brought them to various slave markets throughout the empire for sale to buyers in need of slave labor. Following the civil wars during the reign of Augustus, however, prisoners of war were fewer, and the system relied more heavily on other sources.

Some historians believe natural reproduction accounted for a large number of new enslaved people; the children of enslaved women were considered the property of the household in which the mother lived. Enslavement could also be the result of kidnapping and piracy. Some enslaved people were sold into bondage through *patria potestas*. Others had been abandoned as infants by families that did not want to or could not care for a child; these children often ended up in the hands of slave traders. Finally, while involuntary debt bondage had been outlawed since the time of the early Roman Republic, people could sell themselves into slavery to pay off debts. Slave markets, often kept supplied by piracy, were an important element of the system, and the one at Delos (which was most active in the second and early first century BCE) was the largest; upwards of ten thousand enslaved people might be sold in a single day.

The freeing of enslaved people through **manumission** was an expected practice in Rome, though the rate at which it occurred is difficult to assess. It usually happened when a person was around eighteen years old, but not simply in return for good behavior. Some of the enslaved were allowed to keep part of their earnings in order to purchase their freedom. And enslaved women could also be freed after producing a certain number of children. Manumission was made official before a Roman magistrate or in a slaveholder's will. It was often accompanied by a sum of money so that the newly freed could more assuredly begin their lives as freed persons. The debt of obligation was clear, however, since a freed person became the client of their former master.

Freed people formed a substantial class in Rome, but with a fair number of restrictions on their conduct. They were often beholden to their former master's influence and prevented from holding most important political or religious positions. Many did go on to become independently wealthy professionals in trade, agriculture, and education, and some were even slaveholders themselves. A few occupied prominent positions in powerful households. They were denied the full rights of Roman citizenship, however, though their children were considered full citizens.

Enslaved people were subject to brutal treatment, and a series of revolts illustrates their efforts to seek freedom. In the late second century BCE, rebellions in Sicily inspired uprisings elsewhere in the Mediterranean, notably in the Greek mines. A few decades later, Spartacus instigated the most famous slave revolt. Originally from Thrace or Greece, Spartacus was enslaved after being captured in battle and was trained as a gladiator in Capua in central Italy. In 73 BCE, he planned to escape, along with a substantial number of other enslaved people. Though their original plan may have been only to get away, they took up weapons and fought for their freedom. Spartacus eventually raised an army of more than seventy thousand and defeated a number of armies sent by the Roman Senate. Finally, the Roman general Crassus defeated Spartacus in battle, putting an end to the revolt in 71 BCE (Figure 7.7). However, Spartacus's rebellion was the tipping point. Following these violent conflicts, there seems to have been some effort by Rome to avoid future revolts, as seen in the laws of Augustus that controlled the practice of manumission.

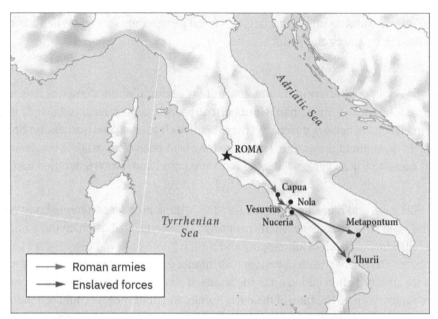

FIGURE 7.7 Spartacus's Revolt. Spartacus's revolt began in 73 BCE, in Capua in central Italy. As more enslaved people were recruited to the cause, Rome sent armies to subdue them. The rebels were besieged on the slopes of Mount Vesuvius but were able to outwit their opponents, defeat the initial Roman forces sent against them, and eventually expand their raiding territory farther south. (attribution: Copyright Rice University, OpenStax, under CC BY 4.0 license)

Life under Slavery

Enslaved people led lives that varied across the empire, depending on their age and gender and whether they lived in rural or urban areas. They worked as unskilled laborers, artisans, and assistants to merchants and shopkeepers. Many were trained as teachers, doctors, musicians, and actors. Others helped build public works such as bridges and roads and even served as imperial administrators. In the city, and in the household especially, they had more advantages and avoided the brutal physical labor demanded in mines, quarries, and *latifundia* across the empire. There, more than one hundred enslaved persons might labor, their harsh life evidenced by their poor clothing, cruel treatment, and inability to raise funds to buy their freedom.

Still, enslaved people in any context were a moment away from punishment by slaveholders, who were perpetually concerned with avoiding conspiracy and rebellion. A culture of uncertainty, coercion, and submission was the result of the constant threat of potential violence. Enslaved people could be whipped, beaten, or tortured and were often sexually abused. In Petronius's *Satyricon*, a novel written in the first century CE, the freed Trimalchio discusses the services he offered while enslaved: "Still, I was my master's favorite for fourteen years. No disgrace in obeying your master's orders. Well, I used to amuse my mistress too. You know what I mean; I say no more, I am not a conceited man." Enslaved people who ran away and were caught could be branded or forced to wear a collar with their owner's name on it.

Though the enslaved were denied the official rights of marriage, they could form families and have children, which often occurred in urban settings. The slaveholder could always manipulate the relationships between enslaved people for personal ends. Enslaved children were put to work, perhaps with simple duties in the house, and over time enslaved people might be promoted to different roles within a household.

IN THEIR OWN WORDS

Slavery in the Ancient Novel
Roman novels, which would have been read primarily by the upper classes, give us a glimpse of the lives of

enslaved people during the empire. *The Golden Ass* by Apuleius, written in the mid-second century CE, follows the adventures of a wanderer named Lucius after he is magically transformed into a donkey; the first passage here is Lucius's observation of enslaved people. In the second passage, an excerpt from Petronius's *Satyricon*, the formerly enslaved Trimalchio mistreats his own enslaved people during a lavish dinner party.

> The pale welts from chains crossed every patch of their skin like brush-strokes. Their flogged-up backs under sparse patchwork were no better covered than stretches of ground that shade falls on. Some of them had thrown on an exiguous vestiture, which extended only to the loins, yet all were calm so that their scraps of tatters kept no secrets. Their foreheads were inscribed with brands, their hair half-shaved, their ankles braceleted with fetters, their pallor hideous, their eyelids gnawed by gloomy smoke of the murky fumes, which left them less able to access light at all. Like boxers who fight bathed in fine dust, these men were filthy white with floury ash.

> —Apuleius, *The Golden Ass*

> As he was speaking, a boy dropped a cup. Trimalchio looked at him and said, "Quick, off with your own head, since you are so stupid." The boy's lip fell and he began to petition. "Why do you ask me?" said Trimalchio, "as if I should be hard on you! I advise you to prevail upon yourself not to be stupid." In the end we induced him to let the boy off. As soon as he was forgiven the boy ran round the table.

> —Petronius, *Satyricon*

- What do you learn from these fictional accounts about the treatment of enslaved people and Roman attitudes toward them?
- What do these passages reveal about the conduct of slaveholders?

Gladiators

Gladiatorial combat was an important element of Roman culture and a prominent part of public entertainments. Matches originated in central Italy in the third century BCE and were originally part of funeral games, spectacles that honored the deceased. The first games in the city of Rome occurred in 264 BCE, with three pairs of gladiators fighting. In the centuries that followed, the number of games increased until, under the emperors, they included hundreds of gladiators.

Gladiators came from a variety of backgrounds, and though some were volunteers, enslaved people forced into the role formed a substantial number. A team of gladiators was called a *familia* and was trained in a gladiatorial school by a **lanista**, the manager of the group. The *lanista* and other trainers assessed new recruits and picked the weapons they would use in combat. Daily training was strenuous, but gladiators were expected to fight only a handful of times over a year.

Matches usually consisted of differently armed gladiators fighting one another. In one common type of match, gladiators armed with swords fought a *retiarius*, who was armed with a net and a trident (Figure 7.8). Gladiators did not usually fight to the death, but the crowd played a major role in the fights, often encouraging gladiators to kill their wounded opponents. The emperor, if in attendance, could also influence the outcome by giving a "thumb up" or "thumb down," meaning allow the opponent to live or die, respectively. The most talented and successful gladiators could acquire a devoted following of fans as well as earn money for fighting.

FIGURE 7.8 Gladiators in the Arena. This third-century CE mosaic tells the story of a gladiatorial match in ancient Rome. The fight begins in the bottom panel with the *retiarius* Kaliendio throwing his net over Astyanax and thrusting his trident at him, but in the upper panel Kaliendio has been wounded, his trident has missed, and he is surrendering by raising his knife. The caption "Astyanax vicit" at the top indicates that Astyanax has won, while "Kaliendio Ø" tells us that Kaliendio was killed. The two toga-clad figures are *lanistae* (plural of *lanista*). (credit: "Astyanax vs Kalendio mosaic" by James Grout/Encyclopaedia Romana/Wikimedia Commons, Public Domain)

🔗 LINK TO LEARNING

Explore a newly discovered gladiatorial training camp (https://openstax.org/l/77Gladiator) in Austria.

There is also evidence that both senators and women participated in gladiatorial combat, possibly to ceremonially reenact scenes from myth. A law enacted by the emperor Tiberius in 19 CE declared that no senator or person of equestrian rank could take part in the fighting, suggesting that their participation had been an ongoing issue. That women took part is clear in a stone relief from the first or second century CE, showing two female gladiators fighting (Figure 7.9).

FIGURE 7.9 Female Gladiators. The two women gladiators facing off in this stone relief from the first or second century CE are identified below as "Amazon" on the left and "Achillea" (a version of the name Achilles) on the right. Stage names like these were often adopted for the reenactment of mythological scenes in the arena. (credit: "Two female gladiators, named as Amazonia and Achillea" by "Xastic"/Wikimedia Commons, Public Domain)

The **Colosseum** was a massive structure in the middle of the city of Rome that was the site of many public entertainments, including gladiatorial matches. Built between 69 and 79 CE, it was named the Flavian Amphitheater, after the ruling dynasty at that time. It was also known as the Colosseum because a colossal statue of the emperor Nero stood nearby. (Well over one hundred feet tall, the statue was later rededicated to the Roman sun god Sol.) The amphitheater was officially dedicated in 80 CE by the emperor Titus in a ceremony that included one hundred days of games. Its design featured a rising arrangement of columns in different styles and a complicated network of barrel vaults. Up to fifty thousand spectators could be seated within the structure, and spectacles included gladiator matches, mock naval battles, and animal hunts. The impressive displays of showmanship were intended to be entertainment, but they also served an important political function. As part of a policy mockingly called "bread and circuses," these epic games (and the distribution of free wheat) were meant to distract the people from potential weaknesses in Roman governance. The idea was that those whose immediate needs were being met with food and entertainment were less likely to notice social inequality, become discontented, or foment rebellion. The games were also a way to bolster popular enthusiasm for the sitting emperor, who usually attended regularly.

LINK TO LEARNING

Explore a virtual reality reconstruction of the Colosseum (https://openstax.org/l/77Colosseum), the site of public spectacles in Rome, including gladiatorial matches. This video gives a sense of the Colosseum's scale and what Romans may have seen when they entered the structure as gladiators or as spectators.

7.3 The Roman Economy: Trade, Taxes, and Conquest

LEARNING OBJECTIVES

By the end of this section, you will be able to:
- Identify key trade routes in the Roman Empire
- Explain how the Roman Empire used taxes to raise revenue and influence behavior
- Analyze the importance of conquest in the Roman economy

The Roman economy was a massive and intricate system. Goods produced in and exported from the region found their way around the Mediterranean, while luxury goods brought from distant locales were cherished in the empire. The sea and land routes that connected urban hubs were crucial to this exchange. The collection of taxes funded public works and government programs for the people, keeping the economic system functioning. The Roman army was an extension of the economic system; financing the military was an expensive endeavor, but the Romans saw it as a critical tool in dominating the Mediterranean.

Trade

Sea routes facilitated the movement of goods around the empire. Though the Romans built up a strong network of roads, shipping by sea was considerably less expensive. Thus, access to a seaport was crucial to trade. In Italy, there were several fine seaports, with the city of Rome's port at Ostia being a notable example. Italy itself was the producer of goods that made their way around the Mediterranean. Most manufacturing occurred on a small scale, with shops and workshops often located next to homes. Higher-value goods did find their way to distant regions, and Italy dominated the western trade routes (Figure 7.10).

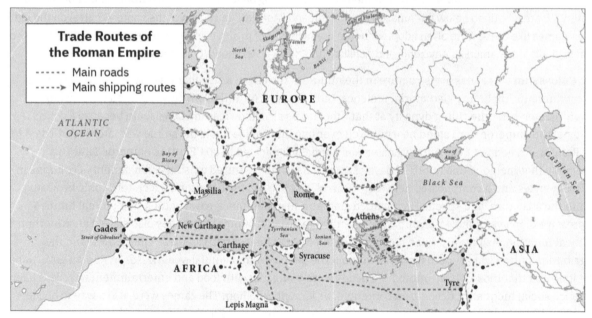

FIGURE 7.10 Trade Routes of the Roman Empire. As this map demonstrates, the Romans were able to harness an extensive system of roads and waterways to import and export both practical and luxury goods. (attribution: Copyright Rice University, OpenStax, under CC BY 4.0 license)

Italy was known for its ceramic, marble, and metal industries. Bronze goods such as cooking equipment and ceramic tableware known as red pottery were especially popular items. Red Samian pottery made its way to places around the Mediterranean and beyond, including Britain and India. Iron goods produced in Italy were exported to Germany and to the Danube region, while bronze goods, most notably from Capua, circulated in the northern reaches of the empire before workshops also developed there. These industries likewise relied on imports, including copper from mines in Spain and tin from Britain for making bronze.

Other Roman industries balanced their production with imported goods from foreign markets. Textiles such as wool and cloth were produced in Italy, while luxury items like linen came from Egypt. Several trading routes existed in addition to the famous Silk Roads. The monsoon-driven Indian Ocean network linked Asia and the Mediterranean and provided the Romans with silk from China and India and furs from the Baltic region. The eastern empire was known for its luxury goods, including purple dye, papyrus, and glass from Egypt and Syria. For a time, central Italy did manufacture and export glass products northward, until manufacturing in Gaul (present-day France) and Germany took over the majority of its production in the second century CE. Building supplies such as tiles, marble, and bricks were produced in Italy.

Agricultural goods were an important aspect of the Roman economy and trade networks. Grain-producing Egypt functioned as the empire's breadbasket, and Italian farmers were therefore able to focus on other, higher-priced agricultural products including wine and olive oil. Wine was exported to markets all over the Mediterranean, including Greece and Gaul. Both wine and olive oil, as well as other goods, were usually shipped in amphorae. These large storage vases had two handles and a pointed end, which made them ideal for storing during shipment. They may have been tied together or placed on a rack when shipped by sea (Figure 7.11).

FIGURE 7.11 A Roman Amphora. Amphorae (the plural of *amphora*) were large vessels essential for shipping liquid goods in the Mediterranean world. Their slender shape and pointed base made for easy storage whether they were placed upright in a ship's hold or set in the soft ground. (credit: "Roman Amphora" by Mrs. Elvi Adamcak/ Smithsonian, National Museum of Natural History, CC0)

The government's official distribution of grain to the populace was called the **annona** and was especially important to Romans. It had begun in the second century BCE but took on new importance by the reign of Augustus. The emperor appointed the *praefectus annonae*, the prefect who oversaw the distribution process, governed the ports to which grain was shipped, and addressed any fraud in the market. The prefect and his staff also secured the grain supply from Egypt and other regions by signing contracts with various suppliers.

The Roman government was also generally concerned with controlling overseas trade. An elite class of shipowners known as the *navicularii* were compelled by the government to join groups known as *collegia* (corporations) so they could be easily supervised. For signing contracts to supply grain, these shipowners received benefits including exemption from other public service. By the third and fourth centuries CE, control of the *navicularii* had intensified, and signing contracts to supply the *annona* was compulsory.

The *annona* kept the populace fed but was also a political tool; the emperor hoped his generosity would endear him to the people. The distribution of grain was thus heavily tied to the personality of the emperor. For instance, like many emperors, Hadrian, who ruled from 138 to 161 CE, associated himself with the *annona* to create a positive image before the public (Figure 7.12).

FIGURE 7.12 The *Annona* as Political Tool. On this coin issued by Hadrian, the emperor's likeness is on one side (left); the other side portrays Annona, the representation of the grain supply, holding a cornucopia in one hand and grain ears in the other. In the background is the prow of a ship, likely a reference to the grain supply entering the city of Rome. (credit: "Vespasian Dupondius" by Guy de la Bedoyere/Wikimedia Commons, Public Domain)

Taxes

Collecting taxes was a chief concern of the Roman government because tax revenues were a necessity for conducting business and funding public programs. Taxes fell into several categories, including those calculated with census lists in the provinces, import and customs taxes, and taxes levied on particular groups and communities.

Upper-class investment in the provinces drove the economy and facilitated the collection of taxes. An important role in this system was played by the **publicani**, who operated as tax collectors in the provinces. These contractors first bid for the right to collect taxes by making a direct payment to the Roman government, which functioned as a *de facto* loan. To recover their investment, the *publicani* then collected taxes from provincial residents, keeping any money in excess of their original bid in addition to a percentage paid by the Roman government.

The *publicani* ran an effective system of tax collection, but it was imprecise and they were often accused of fraud. During the reign of Augustus, the *publicani* system was essentially abolished. In the revised system, provincials had to pay roughly 1 percent tax on their wealth, which included their assets in the form of land, as well as a flat poll tax. This new tax structure was assessed through census lists and administered by procurators, imperial officials who made collections and oversaw the payment of public officials in the province.

Other taxes included those on inheritances and legacies. To raise funds for paying veteran soldiers, in 6 CE, Augustus codified a new 5 percent tax on money inherited through a will. The rule excluded inheritances from close relatives, however, and was directly aimed at traditional patron-client relationships. With this tax, Augustus disrupted elite patron-client networks that had relied on the formation of social bonds outside the immediate family. As a result, the elite were compelled to coalesce around the figure of the emperor as the ultimate patron.

Despite these attempts at collecting taxes, by the third century CE the empire had entered a period of financial crisis. Constant wars meant a never-ending need to sustain large armies. As less new land was acquired, troop payments came more often from the central treasury than from newly conquered territory. The financial pressure proved critical. The emperor Diocletian implemented a series of measures to address the problems. For example, in 301, to combat inflation, Diocletian issued the Edict on Maximum Prices, which set a price ceiling for certain goods and services. Diocletian's reforms also increased the money collected by the government with two new taxes, on agricultural land and on individuals. The inclusion of property in Italy in the land tax for the first time, as well as Diocletian's standardization of a five-year census, dramatically increased revenue for the empire. Replacing some of Rome's revenue shortfall through these taxes helped stabilize the economy in the short term.

Conquest

Periods of conquest contributed to the Roman economy in a number of ways. The Romans sought to control natural resources and attain wealth from the regions they conquered. By harnessing the revenues of conquest, they could support their goals of keeping the populace fed and the troops paid.

In early Rome, the army was a volunteer force mustered during times of conflict. By the time of the empire, however, it had become a standing professionalized force. The Roman **legion** was the cornerstone of the army. Though its organization changed over time, this military unit consisted of about five thousand soldiers and was commanded by a legate. A legion also included craftspeople and those assisting in building projects. Following the reforms of Augustus, twenty-eight legions were stationed throughout the provinces of the empire and on the frontier. They were numbered but also had nicknames based on their place of origin or service. Since legions could move around the empire, the First German legion might be found in Spain, for example. Soldiers served a sixteen-year term, though this was later raised to twenty, and they were paid a set amount at the end of their service. Soldiers and military staff received a large portion of the wealth secured during wartime, and some were also occasionally promised land taken in the various conflicts that Rome engaged in.

Many military engagements were clearly intended to secure resources and capital. For instance, the empire's grain supply was vastly expanded by its conquest of Egypt in the first century BCE, as well as of Sicily and Sardinia early in Rome's history. In addition, people captured in conquest were often sold in the Roman slave markets. Since the work of enslaved and freed people was the backbone of Roman industry, enslaved people too contributed to the functioning of the economy.

But there were trade-offs in this arrangement. The increasing size of the Roman military and the empire's expanding frontier made conflict more costly. While earlier in its history, Rome's soldiers might expect to campaign only part of the year, by the imperial period, conflict had become a regular situation on the frontier. Campaigns could last for months on end, and in some situations wars may have seemed endless. The distance from the city of Rome also contributed to the cost of running the military; far-flung military campaigns were expensive. The machinery of running and paying the army necessitated further conquest, a situation that ultimately strained the Roman military.

In addition, there were clearly societal disadvantages to continuous conflict. Though Romans took pride in their military superiority, the loss of life and property must have been a burden for many. Conflict abroad disrupted regional markets that Italy depended on. For example, an interruption in the grain supply in 190 CE resulted in famine and riots in the city of Rome. Elites were largely able to benefit from the economic arrangement of conquest, but those in the lower classes no doubt shouldered the burden of its negative consequences.

7.4 Religion in the Roman Empire

LEARNING OBJECTIVES

By the end of this section, you will be able to:
- Identify the major cults and religions found in the Roman Empire
- Discuss how Romans accepted and adapted religions from other areas of the Empire
- Explain the rise of Christianity in Rome

Religious belief and practice were enmeshed in Roman daily life. The presence of the divine suffused the physical world, and Romans sacrificed to their many gods as a way to gain their favor. Roman religion was multifaceted and based initially on the Greek pantheon, adapted for Rome's culture and language. While Romans took pride in the traditional elements of their religious system, they were also able to incorporate new features in it to accommodate cultural or political change. Some new gods were added, and it was common for certain sectors of Roman society such as soldiers to have favorite gods or patron deities. The flexibility of Roman religion set the stage for new religious groups to emerge, including Christians in the first century CE.

The Emperor and the Virgins

Roman *religio* (from which the English word "religion" derives) signified an obligation to the gods. According to this principle, Romans were expected to pay attention to divine and religious matters, including the most important aspect of religious practice, sacrifice. By offering animals to the gods, Romans hoped to receive good fortune or gain insight into a question or problem. While their religion certainly had private elements, its public rituals often intertwined faith with politics. That connection was also, and especially, visible in the worship of the emperor.

The **imperial cult** was a group of rites and practices that praised a deceased emperor's divine status. Emperors were often deified (made gods) after they died, by order of their successors and with approval by the Senate. This formal process of deification was known as *apotheosis* and was extended to emperors who were remembered favorably (Figure 7.13). The process of deification had become so routine among later emperors that when the emperor Vespasian was dying, he is reported to have said, "Alas! I think I am becoming a god!"

FIGURE 7.13 The Apotheosis of Emperor Antoninus Pius and Empress Faustina. This detail of a carved marble column from the second century CE shows the *apotheosis*, or elevation to divine status, of the emperor Antoninus Pius and his wife Faustina. A winged *genius* (an attendant spirit) in the lower right carries the two to heaven. (credit: "Column Base of Antoninus Pius (II)" by Institute for the Study of the Ancient World/Flickr, CC BY 2.0)

In this period, priesthoods were created specifically for the worship of a defied emperor. A number of priesthoods already existed that were attached to specific gods and that organized the religious affairs of the city, such as the festival calendar. Priesthoods for the imperial cult were added to this group of religious offices that men could join to further their public careers.

The worship of living emperors was much more muddled because Romans were wary of changing the custom of deifying only deceased individuals. Julius Caesar seems to have intended to be worshiped as a god in his lifetime, and later emperors may have been aware of this plan because many routinely pushed for deification during their own reigns. In the city of Rome, emperors were often closely associated with the gods, but only stereotypically "corrupt" emperors such as Caligula declared themselves gods during their lifetimes. Still, many compromises were made so living emperors were not directly worshiped. These included associating the emperor with the goddess Roma, the divine representation of the city, or making sacrifices for the emperor's well-being rather than directly to him. In the provinces, however, divine honors were sometimes given to living emperors; locals might equate a living emperor or a member of the imperial family with a deity in order to gain the emperor's favor, particularly in the Greek east.

A few women could serve in a priestly office as **vestal virgins**. The six members of this female priesthood were chosen at an early age to serve in the Temple of Vesta, the goddess of the hearth, for ten to thirty years. Their chief duty was to protect the sacred eternal fire that symbolized eternal Rome. Letting the flame go out was a punishable offense because the fire's absence meant Vesta had abandoned the city. Vestals swore a vow of chastity, and the punishment for breaking it was severe, illustrating the symbolic importance of their virginity, which was linked to the preservation of Rome. A vestal who lost her virginity could be punished by being buried alive or having hot metal poured down her throat. As a result, political crises could result from the murder of a vestal, while miracles were attributed to their magical virginity.

The story of the vestal virgin Claudia Quinta represents one such instance. To win favor during Hannibal's invasion of Italy in 204 BCE, the Romans brought the goddess Magna Mater ("Great Mother") by ship from her shrine in Asia Minor, in the form of a black stone. During its reception at Ostia, the ship was grounded on a shoal, but Claudia Quinta was able to miraculously pull it to safety. She had been suspected of breaking her vow of chastity, but her actions proved her virginity. According to the Roman historian Herodian of Antioch, "she took off her sash and threw it onto the prow of the ship with a prayer that, if she were still an innocent virgin the ship would respond to her. The ship readily followed, attached to the sash. The Romans were astounded, both by the manifestation of the goddess and by the sanctity of the virgin" (Figure 7.14).

FIGURE 7.14 *The Vestal Virgin Claudia Quinta.* This large sixteenth-century painting by the Belgian artist Lambert

Lombard imagines Claudia Quinta's rescue of the ship carrying Magna Mater to Rome. Lombard had visited Rome, and this work demonstrates that the story of the vestal virgin remained an inspiration there long after the empire had fallen. (credit: "Claudia Quinta" by Lambert Lombard, Eglise St-Armand à Stokrooie/Wikimedia Commons, Public Domain)

Religions of the Empire

In addition to performing public service and ritual, Romans participated in the private practice of religion. In the home they maintained a *lararium*, a shrine in which the spirits of ancestors were honored. Tiny statues, or *lares*, within the shrine represented these ancestors, and Romans made daily offerings to them. In addition, the *penates*, figurines of household gods, were put on the dining table during meals and worshipped as protectors of the home. Finally, the *genius* signified the household itself, represented as a snake in religious imagery.

More esoteric religious practices included the use of curse tablets and spells. With these, individuals hoped to mobilize supernatural powers to influence the living by writing an invocation. Many curse tablets, aimed at ensuring the writer's way in love, justice, and competitions, have survived. The tablets were placed in graves, in water sources such as rivers and springs, and in the homes of targeted individuals. An example found in Egypt with a pierced female figurine ordered a spirit to "not allow [Ptolemais] to accept the advances of any man other than me alone [Sarapmmon]. Drag her by the hair, the guts, until she does not reject me."

Mystery cults allowed individuals to become initiated in the worship of a specific deity. These groups were devoted to a single god or goddess who was often worshipped to the neglect of traditional Roman gods. Their adherents carried out secret initiation rites and practices, and there were often hierarchical levels of initiation. The cult devoted to the god Mithras originated in ancient Persia (now Iran) and found its way to Rome by the second century CE. Its beliefs centered on the idea that life originated from a sacred bull sacrificed by the god Mithras, often associated with the Sun (Figure 7.15). The practices of the cult are obscure and difficult to reconstruct, but it seems that initiations took place in a cave. The cult was especially popular among Roman soldiers.

FIGURE 7.15 Mithras. In this second-century CE relief from a Mithraic sanctuary in Nersae, Italy, the intricate iconography typical of the cult of Mithras shows the god sacrificing the sacred bull, alongside other imagery important to Mithraic belief. (credit: "Tauroctony: Mithras killing the sacred bull" by Marie-Lan Nguyen/Wikimedia Commons, Public Domain)

Originating in Egypt, the cult devoted to the goddess Isis spread to the western Roman Empire in the first century BCE. The veneration of Isis included hymns of praise and initiation rituals, and priests of the cult usually shaved their heads. The exclusive worship of Isis was reflected in her perceived omnipotence and identification with other gods. She appears in the second-century Roman novel *The Golden Ass*, rescuing the protagonist Lucius. Her speech begins, "Behold, Lucius, here I am, moved by your prayer, I, mother of all Nature and mistress of the elements, first-born of the ages and greatest of powers divine, queen of the dead, and queen of the immortals, all gods and goddesses in a single form." The popularity of mystery cults may have been a precursor to monotheism in Rome, as seen in the rise of Christianity.

BEYOND THE BOOK

The Temple of Isis in Pompeii

The Temple of Isis was one of many temples in Pompeii and was located just behind the city's theater. Originally erected during the reign of Augustus, it was rebuilt following an earthquake in Pompeii in 62 CE (Mount Vesuvius erupted seventeen years later). Its proximity to other public buildings illustrates the temple's incorporation into the city, but its structure and relatively small size emphasize the esoteric rituals of Isis worship.

Though employing a Roman architectural style, the temple also fused Egyptian and Greek elements in its design (Figure 7.16). It stands in a small courtyard, with an altar and a small building known as a *purgatorium* in front of it. Here, a basin containing water said to be from the Nile River was used in rituals of purification.

FIGURE 7.16 Temple of Isis, Exterior. This is the front of the excavated Temple of Isis, in its small courtyard, as it looks today in Pompeii. (credit: modification of work "Pompeii. Temple of Isis" by Istvánka/Wikimedia Commons, Public Domain)

At the top of the steps, the entrance to the temple consisted of a portico, or a porch supported by columns, and was flanked by Egyptian statues. Inside, the inner area contained statues of Isis and her spouse Osiris, as well as wall paintings depicting the myths of Isis. There was a large gathering area in the rear of temple for initiates (*ekklesiasterion*), as well as living quarters for the priests of Isis, more altars and recesses, and a subterranean room used for initiating members (Figure 7.17).

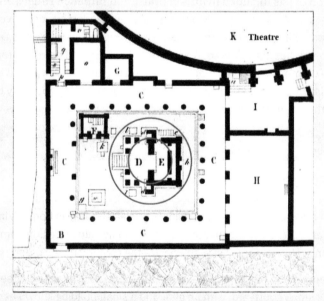

FIGURE 7.17 Temple of Isis, Interior. This layout plan of the Temple of Isis shows its proximity to the theatre (labeled K in this image), suggesting the popularity of the cult of Isis in Pompeii. (credit: modification of work "Temple of Isis, Regio VIII, Insula 7, Pompeii, plan" by Unknown/Wikimedia Commons, Public Domain)

- What elements of the Temple of Isis and its location in the city suggest the public role it and structures like it played in Roman society?
- Can you connect anything in these images to identified characteristics of Roman religion? Which ones?

Christianity

Religious experiences in Rome were varied and diverse. In the first century CE, Christians joined this landscape, but their relationship with traditional Roman religion was often strained. Christians themselves did not form a cohesive group at first, but their general unwillingness to adhere to some aspects of traditional rituals often set them apart from mainstream religion.

Christians generally disapproved of animal sacrifice and worship of the emperor. Instead, their customs focused on prayer and meetings in house churches (proper churches and basilicas appeared in Rome only in the late third and fourth centuries). The emphasis on gathering for worship was important to the formation of a communal identity. Christians also participated in communal feasting, addressed each other as "brother" and "sister," and adopted the practice of baptism. This initiation practice varied across the empire, but it focused on cleansing of the spirit and was performed by those in the church's hierarchy, namely bishops or deacons.

Less concerned with the possible threat Christian beliefs might pose to traditional religion, Roman officials often viewed the new faith's practices as a challenge to their worldly authority instead. For example, they characterized Christians as "atheists" because of their refusal to perform animal sacrifice, and a period of persecution singled this group out for punishment. The earliest record of such violence was made during the reign of Nero, when the emperor chose to punish Christians for a fire in the city of Rome in 64 CE. Over the next two centuries, local authorities grappled with what to do with Christian groups. For example, the letters of Pliny the Younger, a provincial governor in Asia Minor in the early second century, ask the emperor Trajan for advice about local Christians. Pliny writes that he has arrested and questioned those he suspects of being Christian; Trajan responds by telling him not to seek out the Christians actively but to punish those who have been caught and who do not renounce their faith.

Later, the persecution of Christians was formalized. The Edict of Caracalla in 212 extended citizenship across the empire but seems to have made everyone responsible for making sacrifices on behalf of the Roman state. The emperor Decius called for universal sacrifice in 250. As a result, it became a crime for Christians across the empire not to sacrifice to the emperor, with torture and death as likely punishments. Finally, persecution under the emperor Diocletian in 303–311 focused on destroying churches in favor of restoring traditional Roman cults.

The reign of the emperor Constantine ended this period of persecution. Following a civil war, Constantine attributed his victory in 312 to the Christian God, claiming to have had a vision of a cross (a symbol of Christianity) in the sky. The Edict of Milan he issued in 313 outlined a policy of religious toleration in which Christianity was no longer illegal and most traditional Roman religious practices could continue. Constantine also christened Constantinople as a new capital of the empire, decorating the city with images of himself and religious iconography.

IN THEIR OWN WORDS

The Martyrdom of Perpetua

The Passion of Saints Perpetua and Felicity is a third-century diary begun by Perpetua, a Christian noblewoman, and completed after her death. Perpetua and her fellow Christians are sentenced to die during the games in Carthage, in celebration of the emperor Septimius Severus's son Geta in 203. After surviving the arena, Perpetua wills her own death at the hands of the executioner as an act of martyrdom.

Perpetua was first thrown, and fell upon her loins. And when she had sat upright, her robe being rent at the side, she drew it over to cover her thigh, mindful rather of modesty than of pain. Next, looking for a pin, she likewise pinned up her disheveled hair; for it was not meet that a martyr should suffer with hair disheveled, lest she should seem to grieve in her glory. So she stood up; and when she saw Felicity smitten down, she went up and gave her hand and raised her up. And both of them stood up together and the (hardness of the people being now subdued) were called back to the Gate of Life. There Perpetua being received by one named Rusticus, then a catechumen [a recent convert to Christianity], who stood close at her side, and as now awakening from sleep (so much was she in the Spirit and in ecstasy) began first to look about her; and then (which amazed all there), When, forsooth, she asked, are we to be thrown to the cow? And when she heard that this had been done already, she would not believe till she perceived some marks of mauling on her body and on her dress. Thereupon she called her brother to her, and that catechumen, and spoke to them, saying: Stand fast in the faith, and love you all one another; and be not offended because of our passion. . . .

And when the people besought that they should be brought forward, that when the sword pierced through their bodies their eyes might be joined thereto as witnesses to the slaughter, they rose of themselves and moved, whither the people willed them, first kissing one another, that they might accomplish their martyrdom with the rites of peace. . . . Perpetua, that she might have some taste of pain, was pierced between the bones and shrieked out; and when the swordsman's hand wandered still (for he was a novice), herself set it upon her own neck. Perchance so great a woman could not else have been slain (being feared of the unclean spirit) had she not herself so willed it.

—Perpetua, *The Passion of Saints Perpetua and Felicity*

- How would you characterize the martyrdom of Perpetua? Why?
- What aspects of early Christian identity can you identify in the actions and words of the Christian martyrs?

7.5 The Regions of Rome

LEARNING OBJECTIVES

By the end of this section, you will be able to:
- Identify the regions of the Roman Empire and the way they related to the center of power
- Describe the various peoples who made up the Roman Empire

The expansion of Rome's borders created a process in which local communities both emulated and resisted Roman culture, and in which some cultural elements were imposed by the Romans themselves. In the western empire, the army spread Roman culture, and local life coexisted with the presence of Roman people and goods. In the eastern empire, including Egypt and the Levant, complex local life likewise persisted even as elites hoped to gain prominence in the imperial system. The exclusion or incorporation of foreigners was a perennial problem for the empire as it interacted with a wide swath of different cultures. Citizenship was a prized Roman cultural value, and its changing definition reflected the way Rome managed its empire.

The Culture of the Roman Empire

The Roman Empire was divided into administrative units called provinces, the number of which seems to have always been in flux as new territories were lost or gained. A province was governed by a magistrate chosen by the Senate or personally by the emperor. The term for governing a senatorial province was one year, while that for administering an imperial province was indefinite. Provincial governors had *imperium*, or jurisdiction over a territory or military legion. They were also relatively autonomous in managing their territory, having a staff of lieutenants and other officials to conduct administrative business.

By the first century CE, the western empire had undergone several periods of conquest by the Romans. The regions of Britain and Gaul (the latter is now France and some areas east of it) witnessed many cultural changes after the invasions of Julius Caesar in the 50s BCE. The process of Romanization in Gaul shaped the unique culture that developed there. Local Gallic elites and Romans, generally members of the military for a time, contributed to a fusion of cultures. Characteristic Roman features such as roads and **centuriation**, a process of mapping the land onto a grid for development, demonstrated the integration of Gaul into the wider Roman economy. The production of local goods increased in order to supply the Roman army. Gauls constructed villas with Roman features such as tiled roofing, stone masonry, and peristyle or columned courtyards. Urban spaces also became characteristically Roman in their architecture. This shifting culture in Gaul shows the adoption of a Roman way of life following the period of conquest.

Following Julius Caesar's invasion of Britain in 55 BCE, the region came into increasing contact with Roman culture, though the Roman army did not have a permanent presence there. So, in 43 CE, the emperor Claudius invaded Britain and incorporated the southern region of the island into the empire. Unlike the case in Gaul, centuriation and the construction of roads in Britain were an attempt at direct control of the local population. The militarization of the province reflected the imposition of Roman culture. In addition to roads, the Roman army also constructed forts and camps, including the immense fortification called Hadrian's Wall, built to establish a frontier in the early second century (Figure 7.18). Still, a local community was able to flourish in small towns, which increased their agricultural production and adopted a limited version of Roman culture. For example, the town of Silchester included a forum, possibly an early Christian church, and an amphitheater that may have hosted gladiatorial matches.

FIGURE 7.18 Hadrian's Wall. The massive Roman fortification built in Britain by the emperor Hadrian in the second century CE is roughly seventy-four miles long, with small forts known as milecastles placed at every mile along its entire length, as in the foreground of this photo. (credit: "Milecastle 39 on Hadrian's Wall" by Adam Cuerden/ Wikimedia Commons, Public Domain)

In the eastern empire, the relationship between locals and Rome was similarly complex. Even before its conquest in the second century BCE, Greece and its classical past had fascinated Romans. **Hellenism**—a high regard for the Greek cultural institutions of philosophy, religion, and system of education—influenced Roman views of this region. Greek culture inspired Romans with both reverence for and anxieties about literature, language, and even fashion. For instance, to some, Latin was in a power struggle with Greek after the latter language became popular among the Roman elite and educated. And even the Roman toga was contrasted with the Greek *pallium* cloak, in an effort to articulate Roman identity. Emperors such as Augustus and Hadrian praised classical Greece, attempting to preserve its past greatness; they imposed a Roman view of Greekness by contributing to monument building in the region, and local Greek elites sought imperial favor and grants in their cities.

North Africa also had a long history of interaction with Rome. Through a series of conflicts with the Carthaginians, the Romans had taken control of the coastal regions by the second century BCE. Following the conquest, local settlements in the west underwent a period of intense urban building as the Romans attempted to set up the frontier. In the east, Egypt, like Greece, had a profound influence on the Romans. In addition to Egyptian religious cults that became popular, Egyptian art and architecture gained a foothold, with motifs such as crocodiles and hippos appearing in the art of wealthy Roman homes. The Egyptian practice of embalming the dead may also have gained some prominence among Romans in the first century CE. Furthermore, the encaustic portraits that adorned coffins reflect the multiethnic identity of people in Roman Egypt. This artistic style, in which pigments mixed with wax were painted on wood, originated in ancient Egypt. But the subjects of the portraits wear Roman dress and bear Greek and Egyptian names (Figure 7.19).

FIGURE 7.19 A Funerary Portrait. This life-size Egyptian funerary portrait from about 170–180 CE was painted in encaustic on wood and shows the deceased as they wished to be remembered. Its naturalistic style demonstrates the influence of Roman culture in Egypt at the time. (credit: modification of work "Mummy Portrait of a Bearded Man" by Walters Art Museum, Acquired by Henry Walters, 1912/Wikimedia Commons, Public Domain)

Cleopatra in Popular Culture

As the Roman Empire expanded, its population became increasingly diverse. There are several examples of racially and ethnically diverse peoples playing significant roles in Roman history. For example, Cleopatra VII was a ruler of Egypt from 51 to 30 BCE and the final member of the Ptolemaic dynasty, named for descendants of Ptolemy, general under Alexander the Great. An ambitious woman of exceptional intelligence, she courted Julius Caesar and married Marc Antony—breaking up his existing marriage in the process. She sought power in her own right and flaunted the wealth of her kingdom.

Her identity, however, has remained a contentious issue in academia and in popular culture. She is particularly controversial because she was all the following: female, foreign, and famous. Cleopatra challenged nearly every aspect of stable Roman society, from the family home to the halls of the emperors. Thus she is an interesting case study of the cross-sections of gender, race, and power. The retelling of her story is not yet done; a new film about her starring Gal Gadot is underway and will likely not be the last.

In 1987, Martin Bernal published the first volume of his controversial three-volume work *Black Athena: The Afroasiatic Roots of Classical Civilization*. This book's main claim, which has little evidence, was that the Egyptians colonized Greece sometime in the second millennium BCE, and that this event and Egypt's subsequent influence on Greece has been erased by scholars. Following the book's publication, Afrocentric models of the ancient world gained ground and addressed the way Africa and Blackness had been written out of classical studies. Specific topics were the origin of Greek philosophy, the possibly "stolen legacy" of Egyptian philosophy, and Cleopatra's Blackness (Figure 7.20). Debates about these issues also moved into the public sphere.

(a)   (b)

FIGURE 7.20 Who was Cleopatra? These two images of Cleopatra show drastically different interpretations of the Egyptian ruler. (a) The limestone figurine from the first century BCE shows Cleopatra dressed as pharaoh. (b) The U.S. silent film star Theda Bara portrayed Cleopatra in the film *Cleopatra* in 1917. The queen's racial identity remains a mystery to this day. (credit a: modification of work "Busto de soberano" by Ángel M. Felicísimo/Flickr, CC BY 2.0; credit b: modification of work "Theda-Bara-Cleopatra6" by Gordon Edwards (director)/Wikimedia

Commons, Public Domain)

- Identify some of the questions around Cleopatra's ancestry, ethnicity, and appearance. Why are these still an issue today?
- Why do you think these questions are important? Would they have been as important in ancient Rome? Consider the Roman view of family, obedience, and citizenship.

LINK TO LEARNING

Read comments from the Oxford University Press blog post on "Cleopatra's true racial background" (https://openstax.org/l/77CleoRace) and check out ancient views on Cleopatra's beauty (https://openstax.org/l/77CleoBeauty) to learn more.

The People of the Empire

The diversity of those living in the Roman Empire meant that Romans felt compelled to define the status of different groups. Not everyone was considered a proper Roman. As the definitions of foreigner and citizen shifted during Rome's long history, the empire accommodated new peoples in different ways.

Citizens and Foreigners

The Roman Empire policed both its cultural and physical borders. In addition to maintaining their frontier with an army, Romans carried on a perpetual debate about citizenship, or *civitas*, and whether to extend its benefits to different groups. To gain *civitas* at birth, a person needed to be the child of two citizens. Citizenship conferred voting rights, the right to perform military service, the right to run for public office, and certain marriage and property rights, among others. The extent to which non-Romans were barred from enjoying these rights was not always clear. Foreigners themselves were categorized into different groups, including free provincials, or *peregrini*, who were not Roman citizens; army recruits; and those living beyond the Roman border. Foreignness was not a stable category, however; a person could move from one group to another, and the definitions were always changing.

People could gain citizenship through other means than being born to Roman citizens. Enslaved people who had been manumitted and allied fighters in times of conflict were likely to be granted citizenship. "Latin Rights," a limited form of citizenship, were often extended to existing communities when they were brought under Roman control. Finally, in 212 CE, the emperor Caracalla issued an edict that extended citizenship to all free people of the Roman Empire. Its effects are not clear; the emperor was accused of having an ulterior motive, and the surviving text of the edict appears to exclude a group of stigmatized foreigners or freed people. In any case, differences in status and ethnicity persisted among Romans despite the edict.

A person could also lose the privileges of citizenship. Exile and expulsion were a common punishment for criminals. In a series of works, Ovid, a poet during the reign of Augustus, lamented his own exile to a city on the Black Sea. The reasons for his banishment are unclear, but he seems to have angered the emperor, alluding to "a poem and an error" (*carmen et error*) as the cause of his exile. People could also exile themselves voluntarily to avoid further punishment from Rome, especially the death penalty. There were eventually degrees of exile in which a person might lose their property or in fact be able to return to Rome. Finally, whole groups of people could be expelled from the city of Rome, including Jewish people and followers of Isis in 19 CE, as well as astrologers, philosophers, and actors during the reigns of the emperors Nero and Domitian.

A Special Case: The Jewish People in the Roman Empire

The Jewish people had a deep history in the Mediterranean by the time of the Roman Empire. For a considerable length of time, they had occupied the region of the Levant, which was founded as the Roman province of Judaea in 6 CE. Roman writers expressed varied attitudes toward Jewish people; some were sympathetic, while others were overtly hostile. There was often respect for the long tradition of Judaism, but it was offset by slander and violence.

After the creation of the province of Judaea and the incorporation of the local ruling dynasty into the empire, various Jewish uprisings occurred. Inspired by the region's reorganization, riots occasionally broke out in the cities of the eastern empire. For instance, when images of the emperor were placed in synagogues in Alexandria, riots occurred in 38 CE. There must have been dissatisfaction with the general treatment of Jewish people by the Roman state, but the worship of the emperor was clearly an issue. Further riots occurred in 40; only the death of the emperor Caligula in the next year prevented real war from breaking out.

Several wars did occur between Rome and the Jewish people in the first two centuries CE. Revolts against taxation and the Roman looting of the Second Temple in Jerusalem led to war in 66 CE. Roman forces besieged Jerusalem, and in 70 the Temple was destroyed during the conflict. Following the war, the Arch of Titus was erected in Rome in 81 to honor the emperor Vespasian and his son Titus for leading the Roman forces (Figure 7.21). The Arch of Titus and the Colosseum (the latter was built in 79) were paid for with wealth looted from Jerusalem and the Temple. The destruction of the Temple led to a profound change in Judaism; the Temple had functioned as a symbolic center for the Jewish people, and its destruction led to their splintering into different communities based in synagogues around the Mediterranean.

FIGURE 7.21 The Arch of Titus. This recreation of a relief panel from the Arch of Titus, constructed in Rome in 81 CE, shows the Roman looting of the Jewish temple. (credit: "Arch of Titus Menorah" by "Steerpike"/Wikimedia Commons, CC BY 3.0)

Roman views of the Jewish people were complex and contradictory. The historian Tacitus, for example, narrates the events of Titus's capture of Jerusalem and the suppression of the Jewish revolt in his *Histories*. He begins by giving an overview of Jewish custom and history: "To establish his position over the race for the future, Moses introduced novel rites, quite different from those of the rest of the human race. In them everything we hold sacred is profane, and conversely they permit what for us is taboo." Tacitus goes on to discuss Jewish fasting, observance of the Sabbath, and abstention from pork, all in hostile terms his Roman readers would identify with. He also reports that the Jewish people were from either Mt. Ida on Crete or Egypt, a common view among Romans.

Official Roman attitudes to the Jewish people were not consistently hostile, and the Jewish view of Roman treatment also varied depending on the political and cultural climate. Philo, an Alexandrian Jewish ambassador sent to Rome following the riots of 38 CE, recounts in his *Embassy to Gaius* that he explained to the emperor Caligula how past emperors and officials granted his people particular privileges: "[Augustus] knew that the large district of Rome across the river Tiber was owned and inhabited by Jews. Most of them were Roman ex-slaves; brought to Italy as war captives, they had been set free by their owners, without being forced to alter any of their ancestral customs."

Philo contrasts Caligula's hostility toward Jewish people with Augustus's apparent approval of Judaism. But we also learn about the Jewish population in the city of Rome. Philo explains that there was a particular district of the city in which Jewish people lived, and that there were synagogues within the city. He also suggests that many Jewish people in Rome were formerly enslaved people who had been captured in conflict. It seems therefore that a substantial portion of the Jewish population was made up of freed people. Confirming some of these claims, archaeological evidence of the existence of synagogues and Jewish catacombs in Rome suggests that there was a substantial Jewish population during the imperial period.

Key Terms

annona the Roman government's distribution of grain to the population, which was also a political tool for the emperor

centuriation the Roman practice of dividing land into a grid in preparation for development and agriculture

clients less well-off Romans who relied on a patron's gifts for subsistence

Colosseum a large structure in Rome that was the site of gladiatorial matches and other entertainments

domus the name for a typical Roman house, as well as the family unit

gladiator an enslaved professional fighter paid to battle before an audience, sometimes to the death

Hellenism a high regard for the cultural institutions of Greece including its religion, philosophy, and system of education

imperial cult the religious cult that venerated the Roman emperors as gods

lanista the trainer and manager of a group of gladiators

latifundia large agricultural estates in the countryside, worked by enslaved people to produce profit for the owner

legion the basic unit of the Roman army, made up of around five thousand soldiers

manumission the process of releasing a person from slavery, usually in front of a magistrate or via a slaveholder's will, or through a person's purchasing their own freedom

paterfamilias the patriarch of an extended Roman family, with authority over his wife, children, and any other dependents

patron a wealthy Roman aristocrat sought by clients in need of assistance

publicani provincial contractors who bid for the right to collect taxes and profited from the excess money they gathered

vestal virgins the priesthood of six women who took a vow of chastity and maintained the sacred fire in Rome

Section Summary

7.1 The Daily Life of a Roman Family

The family unit was the cornerstone of Roman life. Since the father held the ultimate authority to dispense justice within a family, its members sought to further the family's prosperity through various means. While elite Roman men served in politics or in the military, women oversaw the household. Children were trained for this arrangement from a young age; boys were educated with these careers in mind, while the marriage of a family's girls was of prime concern. Yet women could and did hold occupations outside the home, and lower-class Romans had to rely on less stable employment. The *domus*, or family home, was where wealthy Romans conducted much of their business; a Roman patron would invite his clients to his home, and luxurious estates were places of wealth display. Roman values about the family were mirrored in politics and culture, where those who embodied Rome's cultural ideals were looked upon favorably. This especially applied to emperors, their families, and others in the public eye.

7.2 Slavery in the Roman Empire

Rome relied on the labor of enslaved individuals who were mostly war captives but who might also have been born into slavery, kidnapped, or abandoned in infancy. Manumission was common, and freed people formed a substantial class in a number of skilled professions. Enslaved life was often brutal, however, and the wars of the first century BCE show the frequency with which the enslaved chose violence as a way to escape. Gladiators were often enslaved men made to fight in violent spectacles that remained hugely popular throughout the imperial period.

7.3 The Roman Economy: Trade, Taxes, and Conquest

The Roman Empire produced, imported, and exported a variety of goods. The government attempted to control this trade through several means, including enticing shipowners to sign contracts with the state and supplying grain to the populace. The collection of taxes was carried out by *publicani* at the local level, but the system was imprecise, and reforms by Augustus and Diocletian show that taxation was an ongoing issue.

In many ways, the military was an extension of Rome's attempts at economic domination. Areas conquered by the army could contribute resources to the economy, especially Egypt as Rome's primary supplier of grain. Rome was in perpetual conflict by the time of the later empire, and despite the incentives for service in the army, these military engagements must have taken a toll on the Roman people.

7.4 Religion in the Roman Empire

Traditional Roman religion had both public and private elements. In the public sphere, the imperial cult that worshipped deified emperors was a representation of the power of the imperial throne. The vestal virgins were a way for a few women to hold a priesthood, though the occasional punishments inflicted on them shows their precarious status. Romans also practiced religion in private, especially with rituals in the home.

Mystery cults were a means to participate in esoteric religious rituals. The cults of Mithras and Isis were especially popular, with secret initiation rituals and a hierarchical membership. Unlike members of mystery cults, early Christians suffered periods of persecution, especially in the third century, because of their refusal to participate in traditional Roman religious practices such as animal sacrifice.

7.5 The Regions of Rome

As the borders of the Roman empire grew, Britain and Gaul became sites of conquest and militarization. But their local communities were able to thrive as they interacted with the military, trading with them and embracing aspects of Roman culture. In the east, Romans maintained a measured reverence for Greek culture, embracing some elements of Hellenism. And elite Romans adopted facets of Egyptian art, architecture, and religion.

Citizenship was a complex issue in Rome, and Romans were perennially concerned with how to incorporate foreigners, eventually extending citizenship to all residents of the empire in 212. The Jewish people were a special case. Romans occasionally expressed respect for the deep history of the Jewish people, but this was offset by negative attitudes that culminated in wars during the first century and the destruction of Second Temple by the Romans.

Assessments

Review Questions

1. How did the noblewoman Cornelia represent traditional Roman values of femininity?
   a. She remarried immediately after becoming a widow.
   b. She was punished under Augustus's law against adultery.
   c. She entered politics and had much influence on legislation concerning marriage.
   d. She devoted herself to raising her children above all else.

2. What was the toga *virilis*?
   a. a garment worn by senators who had recently come into office
   b. a veil worn by girls during their wedding ceremony
   c. a garment worn by boys to mark the transition into manhood and citizenship
   d. a shawl worn at funeral processions to honor the dead

3. What characterized Romans' relationship to their ancestors?
   a. Ancestors were viewed with skepticism and apprehension.
   b. Ancestors served as examples of correct moral behavior.
   c. Ancestors were quickly forgotten after their funeral parades.
   d. Ancestors of emperors were the only ones viewed favorably.

4. In what sort of occupations did freed people typically serve?
   a. government and magistrate positions
   b. professions in trade, agriculture, or education
   c. military commanders and officers
   d. trainers at gladiatorial schools

5. How did rural life under slavery compare to experiences in the city?
   a. Enslaved people in rural areas worked only on large villas.
   b. Life under slavery in rural areas was harsh and offered fewer advantages.
   c. Enslaved people in rural areas were granted full Roman citizenship.
   d. There were no enslaved people in rural settings.

6. What was the most common source of enslaved people?
   a. abandoned infants
   b. family members who were sold into bondage
   c. members of gladiatorial schools
   d. people who were enslaved during wartime conquest

7. What is a likely modern analogy for the Roman gladiator?
   a. football players
   b. political leaders
   c. workers
   d. artisans

8. How did Diocletian reform the Roman tax system?
   a. He taxed provincials on the amount of olive oil they exported.
   b. He introduced an agricultural land tax.
   c. He forbade land from being taxed in any way.
   d. He taxed shipowners by the weight of grain their ships carried.

9. What was the nature of Augustus's inheritance tax?
   a. It taxed the inheritance of veteran soldiers after a period of service.
   b. It taxed money inherited by *publicani* in certain provinces.
   c. It taxed patrons who had a certain number of clients.
   d. It taxed inheritances received from persons outside the immediate family.

10. Why was proximity to a seaport important to Roman trade?
    a. Shipping by sea was less expensive than by land.
    b. No road network existed outside Italy.
    c. Shipowners had a monopoly on the entire trade network.
    d. Romans were interested only in luxury goods from overseas.

11. What was an important feature of Roman mystery cults?
    a. strict devotion to the leader of the group
    b. adherence to worship of multiple deities
    c. hierarchical structure of initiation
    d. use of curse tablets to appease a deity

12. How did the imperial cult venerate a living emperor?
    a. by sacrificing on behalf of the emperor's well-being

    b. by converting to Christianity

    c. by worshipping the emperor only when he was outside the city

    d. by sacrificing to the emperor in secret

13. What did the Edict of Milan accomplish?

    a. It established Milan as the capital of Constantine's empire.

    b. It made Christianity the official state religion.

    c. It outlawed animal sacrifice in Rome.

    d. It legalized Christianity.

14. How could a person obtain Roman citizenship?

    a. It was given to provincial governors after a period of service.

    b. It was given to those who returned from exile.

    c. It was given to a person whose parents were both citizens.

    d. It was given to gladiators who had won a certain number of matches.

15. How did the Romans fortify the frontier in Britain?

    a. They built only luxurious villas there.

    b. They refused to buy goods produced by non-Roman locals.

    c. They forced locals to join the Roman army.

    d. They built forts, camps, and walls.

16. What does the Arch of Titus in Rome commemorate?

    a. the end of the riots in Alexandria

    b. the extension of citizenship to all free residents of the empire

    c. the Roman victory over the Jewish rebellion in Judaea

    d. the victory of Titus in a gladiatorial match in the Colosseum

Check Your Understanding Questions

1. What privileges did the wealthy upper class have in Rome, and how did their lives compare to the lives of the lower classes?

2. How did politicians and emperors show respect for Roman family values by their actions and discourse?

3. How did Romans acquire enslaved people?

4. What types of work did enslaved people do?

5. Could enslaved people be freed, and if so, how?

6. Which goods came to Rome, and from where?

7. What was the structure of trade in the Roman Empire?

8. How did Rome accommodate the coexistence of many religions and cults?

9. What made Christianity different from other Roman religions?

10. How was citizenship used as a tool to incorporate or exclude people from participation in the life of the Roman Empire?

11. What were the most prevalent Roman attitudes toward the Jewish people?

Application and Reflection Questions

1. Would you have rather been a man or a woman in Roman society? Why? How could women exercise power in Rome's patriarchal society?

2. What parallels can you identify between the ideal Roman family and the ideal Roman government, which were intended to mirror one another? What characteristics would have strengthened both, and what problems could cause both to break apart?

3. Write a diary entry describing one day in the life of an enslaved or freed person in ancient Rome.

4. Is there a modern event with the social and political importance of the Roman public games? Do you think political leaders still try to pacify the public with "bread and circuses?" If so, how?

5. How did the emperors use the economic system to inspire loyalty among the Roman people?

6. How did conquest contribute to the Roman economy?

7. Compare and contrast religious cults and beliefs in Rome. What shared and different features made traditional Roman religion and the mystery cults appealing?

8. What key elements of Roman religion can you connect to the chapter's earlier discussion of the Roman family?

9. What were the major differences and similarities between the peoples of the eastern and western Roman Empire?

10. How did Romans interact with different local populations throughout the empire, and how did Roman culture influence these peoples?

FIGURE 8.1 Machu Picchu. Nestled between two peaks high in the Andes Mountains, the Inca fortress of Machu Picchu was built in the fifteenth century CE and once looked out over an expansive empire. (credit: modification of work "Machu Picchu" by Roger Canals/Wikimedia Commons, CC0 1.0)

CHAPTER OUTLINE

8.1 Populating and Settling the Americas
8.2 Early Cultures and Civilizations in the Americas
8.3 The Age of Empires in the Americas

INTRODUCTION The stunning ruins of Machu Picchu, situated in the Andes Mountains between two sharp peaks almost eight thousand feet above sea level, continue to attract visitors from around the world (Figure 8.1). Once a palace and royal retreat for the conquering Inca ruler Pachacuti Yupanqui, the complex was begun in the mid-fifteenth century CE and remained occupied until shortly after the Spanish arrived in the following century. Under Pachacuti Yupanqui, from their Andean home city of Cuzco, the Inca extended their control and built a large empire in Peru. Later rulers continued this expansion, bringing much of western South America under their rule. While the Inca Empire was impressive and politically, religiously, and technologically sophisticated, it was merely the last of many Andean civilizations and cultures stretching back thousands of years. Indeed, these South American civilizations were part of an even larger number of cultures, empires, and architectural traditions that spanned the entire Western Hemisphere and were built by the descendants of migrants who reached the Americas several thousand years ago.

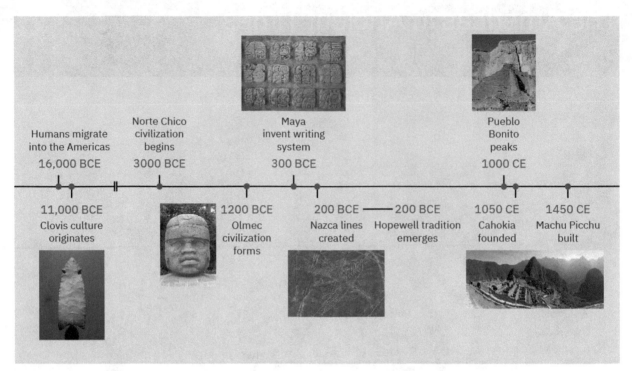

FIGURE 8.2 Timeline: The Americas in Ancient Times. (credit "11,000 BCE": modification of work "Clovis point" by "Daderot"/Wikimedia Commons, CC0 1.0; credit "1200 BCE": modification of work "An Olmec colossal head at the Xalapa Museum of Anthropology, in Veracruz, Mexico" by "Maunus"/Wikimedia Commons, Public Domain; credit "300 BCE": modification of work "Maya stucco glyphs displayed in the museum at Palenque, Mexico" by "Kwamikagami"/Wikimedia Commons, Public Domain; credit "200 BCE": modification of work "The Condor" by Roger Canals/Wikimedia Commons, CC0 1.0; credit "1000 CE": modification of work "Chaco Canyon - Taaqa 'man' at Pueblo Bonita" by "Kyleson1"/Wikimedia Commons, CC BY 4.0; credit "1450 CE": modification of work "Machu Picchu" by Roger Canals/Wikimedia Commons, CC0 1.0)

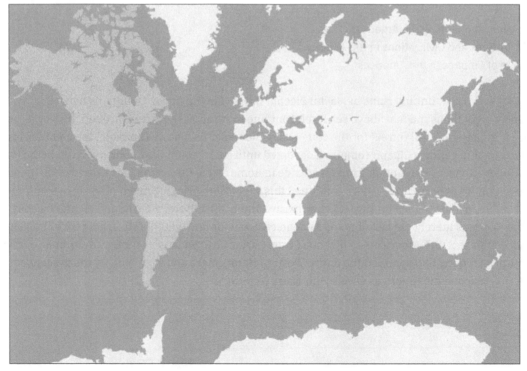

FIGURE 8.3 Locator Map: The Americas in Ancient Times. (credit: modification of work "World map blank

shorelines" by Maciej Jaros/Wikimedia Commons, Public Domain)

8.1 Populating and Settling the Americas

LEARNING OBJECTIVES

By the end of this section, you will be able to:

- Identify patterns of early migration to the Americas
- Describe the lifestyles of people living in Archaic America
- Explain how and when the Neolithic Revolution occurred in different regions of the Americas

Ancestral humans like *Homo erectus* migrated out of Africa almost two million years ago and made their way around Asia, the Near East, and Europe. But so far, no solid evidence has placed them in the Americas. It was only with the rise of *Homo sapiens* that the populating of the Americas began. Exactly when this occurred is not clear, but it likely started around eighteen thousand years ago at the earliest. Within a few thousand years, modern humans had expanded in small numbers around North America, Central America, and South America. There they developed their own agricultural traditions, independent of those that emerged in the Near East, China, and Africa. They also established a range of unique cultural traditions and later a number of sophisticated civilizations characterized by refined religious practices, monumental architecture, large urban populations, and in some cases, writing systems.

Populating the Americas

About eighteen thousand years ago, the last glaciation period was entering its peak stage, and sea levels globally were far lower than they are today. It was likely during this period that the first *Homo sapiens* reached the Americas, crossing the then-existing land bridge between modern Alaska and Russia known as **Beringia**. Beringia has since been consumed by rising waters and now lies under the Bering Strait. But then it was a low-lying land of sand dunes and spotty vegetation. It is possible that *Homo sapiens* had lived there for thousands of years before venturing into North America, but solid evidence for that theory has not yet been found.

Regardless of how long humans lived in Beringia or when they crossed, they began spreading farther south into the Americas as the glacial ice retreated. They made their way through a corridor between two melting ice sheets and spread out in waves into what is now the continental United States. Some made their way to the western coast. Others migrated into the northeast and southeast regions. Still others made their way through the center of the continent into modern Mexico, Central America, and South America. By around fifteen thousand years ago at the earliest, human populations had reached as far as the tip of South America and were living throughout the Western Hemisphere (Figure 8.4).

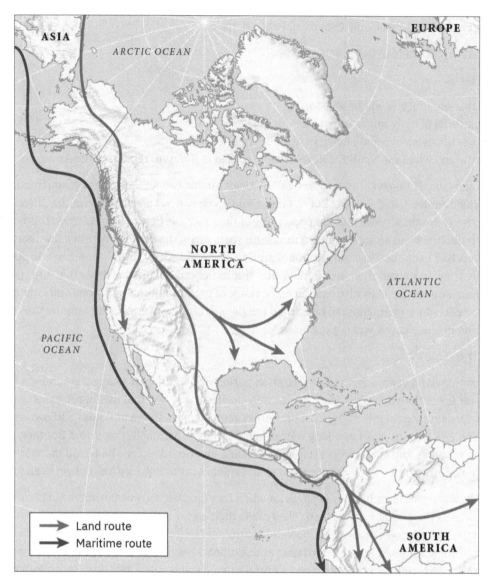

FIGURE 8.4 The Populating of the Americas. While the precise method of migration is unclear and still debated, it seems certain that by around fifteen thousand years ago, human populations had expanded throughout both North and South America. This map shows land and coastal routes they might have taken. (attribution: Copyright Rice University, OpenStax, under CC BY 4.0 license)

Who Was Kennewick Man?

When two young men discovered a human skull along the Columbia River near Kennewick, Washington, in 1996, they assumed it was old. After an archaeologist retrieved the rest of the skeleton and analyzed it, however, people were shocked to realize just how old. Carbon dating revealed that the person now called Kennewick Man had lived nine thousand years ago.

The discovery of one of the oldest humans ever found in the Americas was just the beginning of the long and contentious history of Kennewick Man. Analysis of the remains revealed he was likely related to Asian groups that currently live in Japan and Polynesia. This startling finding caused a reevaluation of migration theories about the earliest Americans. It also stirred controversy and legal debate.

On one side were Native Americans who claimed Kennewick Man was one of their ancestors and should therefore be buried according to tribal custom. The Umatilla tribes of the Pacific Northwest insisted, "Our elders have taught us that once a body goes into the ground, it is meant to stay there until the end of time. If this individual is over nine thousand years old, it only substantiates our belief that he is Native American."

On the other side were scientists. Although they understood the argument made by Native Americans, they maintained the find was so important to efforts to understand the past that they should be able to continue studying it. Anthropologist Elizabeth Weiss wrote in 2001, "Consider having dedicated a large part of one's life to unearthing the materials that are now being examined. Even casts and other important works—such as videotapes, photos, and excavation records—are in increasing danger of confiscation. Some scientists have expressed fear that their federal grants would be in jeopardy if they objected too openly to current policies. Under such circumstances, most scientists do not even begin 'high-risk' projects."

Despite scientists' claims, Native Americans stood firm and began a protracted legal battle over the remains. In 2016, the U.S. Army Corps of Engineers resolved the issue in their favor with a DNA analysis that confirmed the remains demonstrated a sufficient genetic relationship with them. In 2017, the bones were buried according to tribal custom at an undisclosed location in Washington State.

- What do you think further analysis of Kennewick Man might have revealed about his origins?
- Do you support the decision to allow the Native American groups to rebury the remains? Why or why not?

There are aspects of the migration we may never fully understand but can be fairly certain happened. It is very likely, for example, that some populations moved down the west coast via a combination of land travel and coastal skirting by raft or canoe. Solid evidence has not yet been discovered, however, because at that time the coast extended a number of miles west of its current location. As sea levels rose following peak glaciation, the water covered these routes in the same way it covered Beringia. Yet we do have evidence for later coastal travel along similar routes. And these 10,000-year-old sites, discovered on high ground in coastal Alaska and Canada, have convinced many that similar and older evidence may now be beneath the sea.

The Clovis People

As long as thirteen thousand years ago, groups of hunter-gatherers had spread across North America south of the remaining ice sheets. Named after the site in Clovis, New Mexico, where the first evidence of their existence was discovered, the **Clovis culture** consisted of mobile bands of hunter-gatherers who camped at resource-rich locations in modest-sized populations. Since the earliest discovery in the 1920s, archaeologists have found many other sites traceable to Clovis culture in Texas, Virginia, South Carolina, Oregon, and Pennsylvania. Recent DNA analysis conducted on remains discovered in Central and South America suggest that the Clovis culture also extended far to the south.

The most striking artifacts the Clovis people left behind are the many finely worked, fluted stone points they made. They created these so-called Clovis points by chipping and shaping various types of high-quality stone into sharp-sided projectiles, which they attached to shafts that were probably made of wood (Figure 8.5). Once assembled, the tools could serve as spears or other types of thrown hunting tools like darts. These weapons were part of a larger Clovis toolkit that included hand axes and implements made of bone. Items that were small and portable were a necessity for a people regularly on the move.

FIGURE 8.5 A Clovis Point. Clovis points discovered in North America have a distinctive appearance and were highly effective tools for hunting big game. This point found in modern Utah is between 11,000 and 13,000 years old. (credit: "Clovis point" by "Daderot"/Wikimedia Commons, CC0 1.0)

As they migrated, the Clovis people hunted mammoths, mastodons, giant bison, and many small animals. They likely also fished in coastal waters and in lakes and rivers. The places where they did settle for long periods typically had reliable access to fresh drinking water, animals for hunting and fishing, and rocks for making their signature points. Archaeologists have even discovered burial sites that appear to have been carefully designed and decorated with red ocher, a native earth containing iron oxide, suggesting a spiritual belief that required occasional ritual burial.

The world in which the Clovis people lived held a great variety of large animals like giant sloths, bears, tortoises, lions, wolves, beavers, armadillos, and various types of large bison. Then, about the same time people began migrating and hunting across North America, these giant species all went extinct. Some have argued that overhunting by the Clovis likely caused the extinction. An alternate hypothesis, however, suggests that rapid temperature rise at the end of the last ice age was the primary culprit. Both theories have weaknesses, and the debate continues. However, it seems at least plausible that both human intervention and climate change were factors.

The Clovis culture that spread across North America around thirteen thousand years ago vanished after only a few centuries. Its people settled in a number of different areas and produced new cultures as they responded to the environmental conditions in which they found themselves. These groups were then joined by other waves of migrants spreading across the Americas and settling in different areas. Between 9000 and 2000 BCE, during what is called the Archaic period, a great many different cultural traditions existed across North America and Mexico, Central America, and South America. They adapted to their many geographical settings: the Pacific Northwest, the Great Plains, the Eastern Woodlands, the Southwest, the jungles of southern Mexico and Central America, and the Andes region of South America.

Peopling the Pacific Northwest

The groups that settled along the resource-rich Pacific Northwest developed into complex hunter-gatherer societies keenly adapted to the abundant marine life in the region. They likely migrated into the area by following caribou, which they hunted. Once they settled in the densely forested region, they learned to survive on beaver, elk, seals, birds, sea lions, and salmon and a great many other fish species.

Salmon were an important resource. When they migrated upstream in the fall to spawn, they were so numerous they could be easily captured with traps, crude dams, or spears. They were then eaten immediately or dried to preserve the food for later. Halibut was another important fish species the peoples of the Pacific Northwest made into a staple of their diets.

The landscape also provided a great many resources for tools. From bone, the hunter-gatherer peoples designed harpoons useful for hunting large marine mammals like whales. They polished the rocks from the region into woodworking tools and used them to carve dugout canoes from the available trees. They also perfected a sophisticated woodcarving technique for producing art, created special bone and wood fishhooks, and used certain types of tree bark to create cloth and baskets.

Because of the great abundance of resources along the Pacific Northwest coast, the groups that settled there could accumulate wealth far more easily than many other hunter-gatherer societies. We know they developed complex societies in which wealth and social status were connected. Evidence from the few discovered burial sites dating to around 2000 BCE supports the suggestion that wealth contributed to social differentiation even then. In the burial sites of the very wealthy, for example, archaeologists have found carved tools made of antler and other objects made from shells. As time went on, the graves of the wealthy came to include even more objects indicating their higher social status. There is also evidence of high population density in some areas, made possible by the large supply of food resources and the ability to accumulate and store them.

Peopling the Great Plains

Within the expansive Great Plains region in the center of the North American continent, settlers hunted large bison herds that grazed on the short grasses growing there. Unlike the animals hunted by the Clovis people, the bison were able to adapt to the warming climate conditions and flourished in the plains. The groups that followed and lived off them practiced a seminomadic lifestyle requiring relatively few belongings; thus, their culture had far less social stratification than existed in the Pacific Northwest. Hunting bison was dangerous and required keeping a distance in order to not startle the animals or allow them to grow reflexively fearful of human presence. We know from archaeological sites in central Canada, Texas, Montana, Wyoming, and Colorado that as long ago as 8000 BCE, hunters used a strategy of driving herds of bison over cliffs to their death. Once the animals had been killed or immobilized in this way, sometimes by the hundreds, the hunters could carefully process the carcasses for their meat, bones, and hides. Other strategies included cornering the bison herds in a way that allowed the hunters to approach them with spears.

In addition to bison, the plains peoples also hunted antelope, deer, and small animals like rabbits and birds. Hunting birds sometimes required the use of bird decoys designed with feathers to allow hunters to approach and make the kill. The hides of some animals, especially soft ones like rabbit, could be used for clothing when stitched together with plant materials. Edible plants included various types of seeds, berries, nuts, acorns, and tubers like yampa and biscuit-root, which could be unearthed with digging sticks. People carried and stored these foods in coiled baskets made of plants or bags made of leather.

Peopling the Eastern Woodlands

To the east of the Great Plains lie the wetter and lusher Eastern Woodlands, extending from the Mississippi River basin to the Atlantic coast. The groups that lived there found a great variety of plants and animals to feed on and exploit. The many rivers and lakes of the region provided fresh water that encouraged settlement along their shores. The same was the case with the oxbow lakes, U-shaped pools created as river courses stabilized in the warmer conditions. These locations also served as excellent hunting and fishing grounds for catfish, deer, birds, rabbits, and many others. Edible plants included nuts from oak, chestnut, and beech trees. Near coastal areas, there was access to saltwater marine life.

Not only was there less need for mobility here, so that settlements could be sustained, but populations also began to rise around 6500 BCE, and people constructed large earthworks in Arkansas, Louisiana, Mississippi, and Florida. The oldest discovered, Watson Brake in northern Louisiana, dates from around 3900 BCE and includes several human-made earth mounds as high as twenty-five feet and set in a circular formation. Archaeologists believe the site was likely used by hunter-gatherers on a seasonal basis. While no burial remains have been found there, large cemeteries from the period have been discovered in many other woodland locations including Illinois and Tennessee. Some sites include the remains of more than a hundred individuals, some with personal items like weapons and art. They are evidence of not only rising populations but also an increasingly sedentary lifestyle.

Peopling Mesoamerica

To the south and west of the Eastern Woodlands, the climate is much more arid and less green. This desert scrubland extends down the center of Mexico to the tip of the Central Mexican Plateau. South of there, in the region often described as Mesoamerica, the environment is warmer, greener, and wetter. The formerly large-game-hunting peoples settled there after around 8000 BCE as the game disappeared and the bison followed the retreating grassland north. Evidence of Archaic peoples in this area has been found in several coastal sites along the Gulf of Mexico and the Pacific Ocean, as well as in the Tehuacán Valley south of modern Mexico City. They lived largely in small groups and hunted and gathered over large areas. During the dry season, they relied mostly on wild game like lizards, snakes, and insects, and edible plants like the agave. During the rainy season, they ate avocados, nuts, various types of fruit, and small game, like rabbits.

Beginning around 8000 BCE, some groups of hunter-gatherers began periodically occupying a site known as El Riego Cave in the Tehuacán Valley. Excavations there have uncovered numerous stone tools, woven baskets and blankets, and even elaborate burial sites. These burials suggest the existence of a complex spiritual practice. Other evidence in the Tehuacán Valley indicates that by around 5000 BCE, the settlers' earlier reliance on wild game had given way to a more plant-based diet that included beans, squash, maize (corn), and bottle gourds. By 2600 BCE, the gathering of wild plants had waned considerably as groups adopted agricultural practices, cultivating maize, beans, and squash.

Peopling the Andes Mountains Region

The Andes Mountains run along the western side of South America, rising to more than twenty-two thousand feet in some areas and punctuated by arid deserts and dozens of rivers. It is unclear when the first humans reached South America. At the Monte Verde site in Chile, archaeologists excavating a peat bog recovered remnants of shelters, butchered animal remains, and even scraps of clothing made from hides. Testing dates these to about 12,000 BCE, well *before* the arrival of Clovis culture in the north. It is unclear exactly what this information means, and it leaves the story of how the Americas were populated incomplete. But whenever they came, the first hunter-gatherers who arrived appear to have spread quickly down the continent, likely because its unique geography encouraged north–south rather than east–west migration (Figure 8.6).

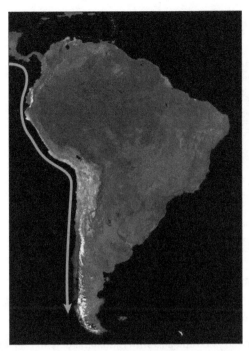

FIGURE 8.6 A Natural Migration Path. The Andes Mountains hug the west coast of South America, creating a narrow coastal passage that runs north–south. Scholars have hypothesized that this narrow passage enabled early American migrants to spread quickly down the length of the continent on its western side. (credit: modification of work "South America - Blue Marble orthographic" by Blue Marble by Reto Stockli, NASA/GSFC/Dave Pape/ Wikimedia Commons, Public Domain)

The earliest hunter-gatherer groups reached as far as southern Chile and often camped near streams to hunt llamas, guanacos (similar to llamas), and deer. By 8000 BCE, some had begun regularly occupying certain sites. One such site is Guitarrero Cave, located at an altitude of 8,500 feet near the small town of Mancos in central Peru. There, archaeologists have recovered projectile points, modified bone and antler, and textiles. Those who lived in and around Guitarrero Cave likely survived by hunting animals and gathering beans, peppers, and a variety of tubers. In the narrow, low-lying areas along the Pacific coast, people relied on marine resources like fish and mollusks. The site called Quebrada Jaguay in coastal southern Peru may have been used by fishers as early as 10,000 BCE. There, archaeologists have discovered what are believed to be cord and fishing nets as well as the remains of fish and other exploited marine life. Obsidian found at the site, originating about one hundred miles away, is even more surprising; it suggests that long-distance trade may have been occurring in the region many thousands of years ago.

BEYOND THE BOOK

The Chinchorro Mummies

The Chinchorro settled in coastal Chile and southern Peru around 5800 BCE. They were largely fishers who left evidence in the form of fishing hooks and harpoons. However, their most striking cultural feature was their practice of mummifying the dead. Indeed, the oldest mummies known so far were those created by the Chinchorro, predating Egyptian mummies by at least two thousand years (Figure 8.7).

FIGURE 8.7 A Chinchorro Mummy. The earliest Chinchorro mummies, from about 5000 BCE, were painted black, though later mummies were painted red or left unpainted. (credit: modification of work "Cultura chinchorro año 3000 AC" by Pablo Trincado/Flickr, CC BY 2.0)

The organs of the dead were removed and replaced with reeds and clay to help dry the bodies and complete the mummification process. Once dry, the bodies were painted and adorned for burial. A clay mask was placed over the faces. The oldest Chinchorro mummy discovered dates from about 5000 BCE and was painted black before burial. Around 2500 BCE, the Chinchorro began painting their mummies red and using different methods for removing organs. They also appear to have aided drying by heating the bodies with hot coals. By around 2000 BCE, the process changed again, and the mummies were left unpainted.

The Chinchorro have not left records to explain why they created mummies, so scholars study more recent Andean mummification practices to try to understand. For example, we know from Spanish records that on certain festival days, the Inca, who ruled Peru thousands of years after the Chinchorro, decorated the mummified bodies of their old rulers and displayed them publicly, feeding them cups of corn beer. Scholars believe these ceremonies were intended to help the deceased transition to the afterlife. Might the Chinchorro mummies have served a similar purpose?

Some Chinchorro mummies had clay face masks with open mouths. It is possible these aided in feeding ceremonies, not unlike the later Inca rituals. Evidence also suggests the Chinchorro mummies were occasionally repainted and repaired, leading some to conclude they were a type of religious art form and possibly used to communicate with the afterworld or to celebrate certain gods or ancestors.

We may never fully understand the mummies' significance for the Chinchorro. But it seems clear the process was somehow related to spiritual practices, possibly an indication of ancestor worship or even belief in an afterlife.

- How does the Chinchorro mummification practice reflect a connection between culture and environment?
- Why do you think the process for painting and preparing the bodies of the dead changed over time?

The Neolithic Revolution in the Americas

As noted earlier, Beringia was submerged under the Bering Strait about eleven thousand years ago, effectively cutting off the Western Hemisphere from the rest of the world. For this reason, technological and cultural developments in Asia, Africa, and Europe were not disseminated to the Americas for many thousands of years. Nor did similar developments in the Americas reach the Eastern Hemisphere. This meant the shift to agriculture in North and South America occurred entirely independently, in three distinct regions that developed agricultural traditions of their own. These were the Andean region, Mesoamerica, and the upper reaches of the Mississippi River valley in the Eastern Woodlands.

The earliest evidence for the shift to agriculture, or the Neolithic Revolution, in the Americas has been found in the Andean region (Table 8.1). There, the domestication of plants and animals developed piecemeal and gradually, and its precise origins are not entirely clear. In some parts of the region, the domestication of camelids such as llamas, guanacos, and alpacas for meat and later wool may have begun as early as 7400 BCE. Similarly, the domestication of the guinea pig for food may have begun as early as 6200 BCE, or as recently as 4400 BCE depending on the evidence used. As for edible plants, some discoveries place the earliest cultivation of squash and bottle gourds at around 8000 BCE. The dates scientists have discovered for domesticated plants like the potato are also remarkably early. Genetic testing of the potato indicates that this rugged tuber may have been domesticated from a wild variant between 8000 and 6000 BCE. Another Andean cultivated plant, quinoa, may have been grown as animal feed about 5000 BCE and later eaten by humans.

8000 BCE	Domestication of squash and bottle gourds
8000–6000 BCE	Domestication of the potato
7400 BCE	Domestication of camelids (llamas, guanacos, alpacas)
6200–4400 BCE	Domestication of the guinea pig
5000 BCE	Domestication of quinoa

TABLE 8.1 The Neolithic Revolution in the Andean Region. The earliest evidence for the domestication of plants and animals in the Americas comes from the Andean region.

Regardless of when or how the process began, by 3000 BCE, at least partially settled agricultural communities were becoming more common in the Andes region. The similarities among sites in central coastal Peru have led archaeologists to describe them as belonging to one larger culture, sometimes called the **Norte Chico** or the Caral civilization. A few sites were quite large, such as Aspero, El Paraiso, and Caral (Figure 8.8). Each included multiple mounds and was topped by architectural complexes arranged in a U-shaped pattern. Of the three, Caral is the largest, with a great number of mounds spread across a large area. The largest mound, or the main temple, measures ninety-two feet high and is almost five hundred feet long at its base. Building such a mound would have required a dedicated workforce, suggesting a highly organized society.

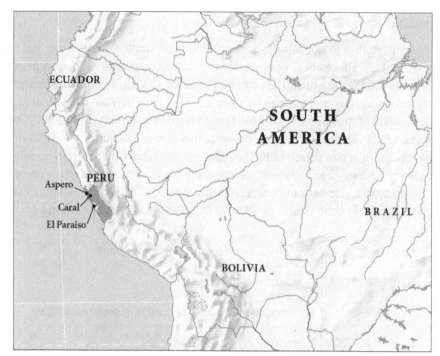

FIGURE 8.8 Norte Chico Sites. The ancient settlements at Aspero and Caral were near each other in coastal Peru, while El Paraiso was to their south. (attribution: Copyright Rice University, OpenStax, under CC BY 4.0 license)

Archaeological evidence indicates that the people who lived at Caral relied primarily on fish and both wild and domesticated crops, such as squash, beans, avocados, and potatoes. As for the social organization of the Norte Chico, we can only speculate, but based on an examination of the burial sites and the likely ritual significance of many of the ruins, there appear to have been social divisions and organized spiritual or religious practice (Figure 8.9). Given the large-scale architecture and the need for laborers, it is also almost certain there was some type of powerful hereditary leadership. And, apart from the structural similarities across the different sites, evidence suggests there were connections between them. For example, the smaller sites along the coast appear to have supplied the larger inland Caral site with necessary marine resources. There may then also have been some type of ruling system over all the various sites, rather than just a similar culture that united them. However, there is no solid evidence to date to support that conclusion.

FIGURE 8.9 **The Caral Culture**. The ruins of the ancient Caral temples in Peru still stand at the site of one of the earliest urban centers in the Americas, with a history going back five thousand years. (credit: modification of work "Piramide de la Huaca, Caral" by Jose C./Wikimedia Commons, Public Domain)

Given the great distance and climate differences between the Andean region and Mesoamerica, the agricultural traditions developed in South America were not easily disseminated north into Mesoamerica in Neolithic times. However, it does appear that at least one important Mesoamerican domesticated crop did reach the Andes. This crop was maize, colloquially called corn in the United States. Maize was domesticated from a type of wild edible grass known as *teosinte* between 5000 and 3000 BCE. While debate continues about how exactly that process occurred, it is generally accepted that human intervention transformed the thick wild grass into the large, sturdy, cob-producing plants we know today. Once domesticated, maize became an important staple carbohydrate in Mesoamerica and led to the rise of large populations. The earliest domesticated maize emerged in either the Tehuacán Valley or the highlands of Oaxaca, from which it was disseminated around Mesoamerica and eventually far beyond. Evidence for Mesoamerican maize in the Andean region dates to about 1600 BCE. There it was commonly used to make a fermented alcoholic drink and popcorn, but it never became an important part of the diet in the way it did in Mesoamerica.

By around 2500 BCE, a shift toward cooler and wetter conditions in Mesoamerica, combined with the availability of domesticated maize, gave birth to a number of agricultural villages in the region. The residents of these villages typically continued hunting and gathering, but they soon recognized the great advantage of growing maize. Over time, the labor demands of doing so and the caloric value of maize led to a steady decline of gathering activities, resulting in exclusively sedentary agricultural communities. Populations grew, necessitating more farmland to raise even more maize. In this way, maize cultivation expanded across the core regions of Mesoamerica, including southern Mexico and parts of Guatemala. By 2000 BCE, sedentary agricultural settlements had become common across these areas. As occurred in regions around the world during the shift from hunting and gathering to sedentary agriculture, new social hierarchies developed as work became more specialized. These hierarchies were related to not only wealth accumulation but also the rise of leadership power.

At some point in the late third millennium BCE, maize was eventually disseminated to what is now the southwestern United States. There, groups began using a form of the plant that had been adapted to the drier environment. At this time, it was merely a supplement to other gathered plants, so peoples in this area remained mostly migratory for some time. Over many centuries, they experimented with varieties of maize. They found ways to grow it in high-elevation areas, and they discovered which areas produced the best results, such as floodplains where irrigation occurred naturally.

In the Eastern Woodlands, people had been experimenting for thousands of years with naturally occurring edible plants like goosefoot, sunflower, bottle gourds, and squash (Figure 8.10). The use of bottle gourds as containers was an ancient practice in the Eastern Woodlands, and the cultivation of bottle gourds may have been encouraged as long ago as 5000 BCE. Similarly, the domestication of sunflowers, useful for their oily and nutritious seeds, appears to have begun by about 2300 BCE. However, by about 2000 BCE, groups in this region began making concerted efforts to increase their food supply by altering the physical environment, clearing small plots of land to more carefully cultivate these wild plants. Through migration, some transported seeds for certain plants to other areas. Successful techniques for encouraging the growth of these plants were passed from generation to generation. In this way, agricultural cultivation emerged in the Eastern Woodlands independently.

FIGURE 8.10 Goosefoot. Goosefoot grew wild in North America and was one of the many edible plants gathered by people in the Eastern Woodlands. When consumed, these plants were an important source of vitamins A and C, iron, magnesium, and other minerals. (credit: "Strawberry Goosefoot (*Blitum virgatum*)" by Peter de Lange/Wikimedia Commons, CC0 1.0)

By the time Eastern Woodlands peoples began cultivating their own native plants around 2000 BCE, they had also begun living in more clearly defined territories. Yet there was communication and trade between different areas. Certain types of stone, copper materials, and shells from the coastlines could pass from one small group to another and in the process move many hundreds of miles. Groups from around a localized region may also have participated in certain ceremonies together. Over time, the increasing availability of food and exposure to wealth in the form of traded materials led to social transformations like a reduction in the egalitarianism common among hunter-gatherers. Burial sites and the increasing number of earthen mounds built from the period demonstrate this.

Groups in the Eastern Woodlands remained small, likely no more than one hundred or so members in most places. There were a few exceptions, such as at the large Poverty Point site in northern Louisiana (Figure 8.11). There, beginning around 1000 BCE, several U-shaped concentric mounds were constructed to form an impressive and unusual ceremonial site. The exact purpose of the site and the social organization of the people who built it are not known, but it likely had some ritual significance, and those who lived in and around it employed both hunter-gatherer and agricultural strategies. It was an active site for about three hundred years before being abandoned for reasons unknown.

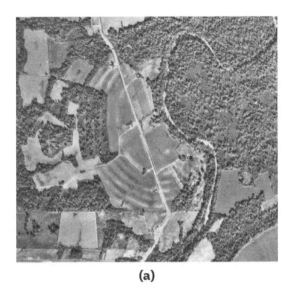
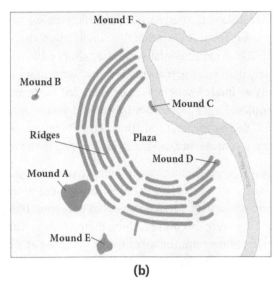

(a)   (b)

FIGURE 8.11 **Poverty Point.** (a) The aerial photograph shows what the Poverty Point site in Louisiana looks like today. (b) The schematic shows what it may have looked like at its height. (credit a: modification of work "Povery Point Site, Louisiana, Aerial Photograph" by USDA Agricultural Stabilization and Conservation Service/Wikimedia Commons, Public Domain; attribution b: Copyright Rice University, OpenStax, under CC BY 4.0 license)

8.2 Early Cultures and Civilizations in the Americas

LEARNING OBJECTIVES

By the end of this section, you will be able to:
- Describe how civilizations in the Americas adapted to their environments
- Discuss the contributions of the Olmec civilization to culture and religion in Mesoamerica
- Identify the key components of early cultures in North and South America

At the start of the third century BCE, after thousands of years of hunter-gatherer existence, the peoples living in the Americas began to form complex agricultural-based societies. Over the next few thousand years, the early settled communities gave way to large and architecturally impressive settlements from the Andean region to the Eastern Woodlands of North America. These led to local similarities in art, architecture, religion, and pottery design.

Complex Civilizations in Mesoamerica

By the year 1200 BCE, farming had become well established across southern Mexico, especially in the gulf lowland areas where there was sufficient water for irrigation. The many societies there were not exclusively agricultural; they continued to rely on hunting and gathering to supplement their diets. One of them, the Olmec culture, emerged around this time as Mesoamerica's first complex civilization with its own monumental architecture.

Olmec Culture

The start of the Olmec civilization, at a site known as San Lorenzo in the modern Mexican state of Veracruz, stretches back to about 1350 BCE and the construction of a large earthen platform rising some 164 feet above the flat landscape. Upon this platform, the Olmec built ceremonial and other structures, water reservoirs, a system of drains, numerous stone works of art, and a number of massive sculpted stone heads. One of the structures has become known as "the red palace" because of the red ocher pigment on the floor and walls. It was likely a residence for the elite and included large stone columns and aqueducts. The massive stone heads and other sculptures, some weighing as much as fifty tons, were carved from volcanic basalt that came from as far as ninety miles away and was likely brought by raft for part of the way and on rollers over land.

Because little of the San Lorenzo site remains, we can only speculate about the organization of the Olmec civilization, but it is clear that their civilization shaped those that followed. For example, the great earthen platform and monumental sculptures shaped liked step pyramids attest to a highly sophisticated culture, with a clearly defined elite that could control large labor forces. Relying on pottery fragments and population density estimates, scholars have concluded that most workers were probably free laborers working to accomplish larger goals. They likely lived well beyond the elevated center reserved for the elite, in villages surrounded by gardens and other agricultural zones where the Olmec grew maize, avocados, palm nuts, squash, tomatoes, beans, tropical fruits, and cacao for chocolate.

The stone heads themselves are remarkable (Figure 8.12). Seventeen have been found across all the Olmec sites; some stand eleven feet tall. All are generally similar in form and style, depicting men's faces with large lips and noses with flared nostrils, but they were likely intended to be realistic portraits of rulers of the sites where they were discovered. Upon their heads are helmets of various styles, some with coverings for the ears. Given the effort required to transport the stone and carve the heads, these works were likely intended to emphasize the power of the rulers, both to the Olmec people and to outsiders.

FIGURE 8.12 An Olmec Head. Some of the enormous Olmec carvings of heads discovered in Mexico are as tall as eleven feet and weigh as much as fifty tons. (credit: "An Olmec colossal head at the Xalapa Museum of Anthropology, in Veracruz, Mexico" by "Maunus"/Wikimedia Commons, Public Domain)

Evidence of possible vandalism on some of the heads has led some scholars to suspect an invasion occurred in the tenth century BCE, with desecration of the images as a result. Others, however, believe this is evidence of reworking that was never completed. We may never know for sure, but we do know that during the tenth century BCE, San Lorenzo declined in importance. At the same time, another Olmec site rose in significance, some fifty miles to the northeast at La Venta.

La Venta was built around 1200 BCE on a high ridge above the Palma River less than ten miles from the Gulf of Mexico. By 900 BCE, it had become the dominant Olmec city in the region. At its height, La Venta covered almost five hundred acres and may have supported as many as eighteen thousand people. Its central monuments included several large earthen mounds, plazas, a possible sports arena, several tombs, and numerous stone heads and other sculptures. The complexity of this urban complex reflects a major development in Mesoamerican civilizational and architectural design. It was likely built as a sacred site, with its temples and other complexes organized on a north–south axis believed to enhance the rulers' authority by connecting them to supernatural environments. This style of urban design was later adopted by other Mesoamerican civilizations like the Maya.

Olmec art depicts numerous deities, such as a dragon god, a bird god, a fish god, and many fertility deities like a maize god and water gods. The Olmec also clearly recognized many types of supernatural mixed beings, like a feathered serpent and the were-jaguar, a cross between a jaguar and a human. These artistic images imply that the Olmec had a sophisticated pantheon of gods who controlled the universe and expected certain rituals be performed, perhaps by Olmec leaders themselves, who may have functioned as shamans empowered to communicate with the spirit world. The rituals were performed in the temples and plazas of the sacred cities like La Venta and San Lorenzo, as well as in sacred natural sites like caves and mountaintops.

Other rituals were connected to a type of ball game played in a special court with balls made from the abundant natural rubber of the region. Sports contests often existed to bring communities together, to allow men to show prowess and strength in times of peace, and to entertain. It is also likely that in times of heightened spiritual need, such contests could take on greater meaning and might have been choreographed to play out supernatural narratives and perhaps connect people to the gods. Like some later civilizations, the Olmec also saw bloodletting as a link to the spirit world. Blood sports may have been used to create pathways to understanding the will of their gods.

⊘ LINK TO LEARNING

The ritual ball game of the Olmec became a cultural feature of Mesoamerica over the centuries, and various forms of it were played by the Maya, the Aztec, and many others. Read more about the history of the Mesoamerican ball game (https://openstax.org/l/77MesoamBall) and see pictures of related artifacts from different Mesoamerican cultures at the Metropolitan Museum of Art website.

The Olmec were clearly in contact with other groups around southern Mexico and Central America. There is evidence of a robust trade in pottery and valued materials like obsidian, magnetite, and shells, likely carried out by merchants traveling across the larger region. Over time, this trade exposed other Mesoamerican cultures to Olmec ideas about religion, art, architecture, and governance. Some scholars thus conclude that Olmec civilization was a "mother culture" for later large and sophisticated Mesoamerican states. Cultural similarities exist among these, such as ritual ball games, deities, and calendar systems. Olmec-style artifacts have also been found at sites as far away as what are now western Mexico and El Salvador. Like much related to the Olmec, however, the extent of their influence is a question we may never answer with certainty. By the time this civilization disappeared around 400 BCE, a number of other Mesoamerican cultures were emerging.

The Zapotec civilization appeared in the valleys of Oaxaca in western Mexico beginning around 500 BCE, with the construction of the regional capital known today as Monte Albán (Figure 8.13). Set on a flattened mountaintop overlooking the larger region, Monte Albán likely had a population of about five thousand by around 400 BCE and as many as twenty-five thousand by around 700 CE. As it grew over the centuries, so too did its stone temples and other complexes. The city exerted influence on the hundreds of much smaller communities scattered across the Oaxaca Valley. The region was highly suitable to maize cultivation, thus allowing for larger populations and monumental architecture. From the defensive walls created around their settlements, it seems the Zapotec lived in a world where warfare was especially common. Monte Albán itself was likely selected for defensive reasons.

FIGURE 8.13 Monte Albán. Perched on a flattened mountaintop and serving as the Zapotec capital between 500 BCE and 800 CE, Monte Albán in today's Oaxaca, Mexico, was an easily defensible city. (credit: "Roman architecture ruins" by Andrew McMillan/Wikimedia Commons, Public Domain)

The structures built at Monte Albán after 300 CE reflect the influence of another major Mesoamerican civilization about thirty miles northeast of Mexico City. The massive city of Teotihuacán dominated trade in obsidian, salt, cotton, cacao, and marine shells across southern Mexico and greatly influenced cultures like that of the Zapotec. The origins of the Teotihuacán settlement date to about 400 BCE, but major building at the site did not begin until centuries later. By 300, the growing city had a population of about 100,000, making it one of the largest cities in the world at the time (Figure 8.14). It exercised enormous cultural and military influence across large portions of Mesoamerica until it declined in the sixth and seventh centuries CE.

FIGURE 8.14 Teotihuacán. The enormous size of the ruins of Teotihuacán, northeast of Mexico City, is enduring evidence of the power of this city in ancient times. This photograph was taken from the top of the Pyramid of the Moon (c. 250 CE) looking down the Avenue of the Dead and toward the Pyramid of the Sun (c. 100 CE) on the far left side. (credit: "View of the Avenue of the Dead and the Pyramid of the Sun, from Pyramid of the Moon (Pyramide de la Luna)" by"Jackhynes"/Wikimedia Commons, Public Domain)

The Teotihuacanos built numerous stone temples and other structures organized around a north–south passageway known as the Avenue of the Dead. The largest temples are known as the Pyramid of the Sun and the Pyramid of the Moon. Both are multitiered stone structures, 197 and 141 feet tall, respectively. The site also includes a large royal residence known as the Citadel, which includes the elaborate Temple of Quetzalcoatl, the feathered serpent. Elite military leaders and others lived in large apartment compounds decorated with colorful artwork depicting priests, gods, or warriors. The remaining population was spread across the roughly ten thousand square miles that surrounded the city and produced trade goods as well as agricultural products.

The size of Teotihuacán denotes its wealth and regional influence at its height. This wealth came from trading in crafts, agricultural products, obsidian tools, cloth, ceramics, and artwork. The many preserved frescos and murals show the city's rulers dressed in elaborate clothing, including iridescent quetzal bird feathers from as far away as Guatemala, testifying to Teotihuacán's long reach. To influence areas so far away, the city wielded power through its control of trade and use of military force and diplomacy. Sculptures at Monte Albán show Teotihuacano diplomats meeting with the Zapotec elite, reflecting mostly peaceful contact between the two civilizations. Evidence from Maya sites also demonstrates that the Teotihuacanos commonly intervened in Maya affairs deep in Central America, sometimes militarily. They may even have orchestrated a coup in the powerful Maya city of Tikal in 378.

Maya Culture

While Maya civilization was clearly influenced by the Teotihuacanos beginning in the fourth century CE, evidence of urban development and rapid population growth in the Maya heartland of Central America dates to before 600 BCE. Village life may go back much further, but in any case, by 600 BCE, the lowlands of Central

America were full of small villages, each showing evidence of sophisticated pottery, architecture, irrigation techniques, and religious traditions. By 250 BCE, a handful of powerful Maya city-states had emerged. The major cities of this Early Classic period (250–600 CE) include Tikal, Calakmul, El Mirador, and a few others.

El Mirador was a dominant city before 150 CE, with a population of about 100,000 at its height. But Tikal and Calakmul were equally impressive. All had numerous large pyramid-like structures creating an impressive skyline across the spaces cleared of jungle. Most of the major cities were built next to large, shallow lakes, since access to water for drinking and irrigation was important in the lowlands, where rainfall was often insufficient. The tropical soil in the area is also insufficiently fertile, and the Maya developed a style of slash-and-burn agriculture to raise maize, squash, beans, and cacao for the growing urban populations in these cities.

LINK TO LEARNING

Tour the ruins of Tikal (https://openstax.org/l/77TikalRuins) by exploring this immersive video.

The Maya were certainly influenced by Olmec civilization, though likely not directly. For example, some examples of Maya art include Olmec-derived features like the were-jaguar. The Maya also played a ritual ball game based on the earlier Olmec variety. Another possible Olmec influence was the Maya calendar. This consisted of two different parts—the 260-day Sacred Round calendar and the 365-day Vague Year calendar—that functioned together to create a 52-year cycle for measuring time and tying the dates for ceremonies to important mythological events performed by the gods.

THE PAST MEETS THE PRESENT

Did the Maya Predict the End of the World?

The premise of a 2009 science fiction movie was that the Maya calendar predicted the end of the world would occur in the year 2012. While the film (called *2012*) was a commercial success, the idea that the Maya predicted when the world would end has been largely discredited.

The Maya had a sophisticated calendar system evolved from earlier Mesoamerican versions, possibly the Olmec. Because it used two different calendar rounds working together, it revealed important ritual days and cycles over long periods of time (Figure 8.15). For example, one full cycle covered a space of fifty-two solar years, often called a bundle. But to explore longer chunks of time, the Maya relied on what scholars call the Long Count Calendar. This had cycles that included the *winal* (20 days), the *tun* (360 days), the *k'atun* (7,200 days), and the *bak'tun* (144,000 days). The Great Cycle occurred every thirteen *bak'tun*, or about every 5,125 years. And this is where the idea of the significance of 2012 comes from.

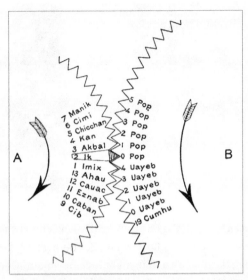

FIGURE 8.15 The Maya Calendar. The two Maya calendar rounds were intended to function together in order to reveal important dates years in advance. (credit: modification of work "Diagram showing engagement of tonalamatl wheel of 260 days and haab wheel of 365 positions by An Introduction to the Study of the Maya Hieroglyphs" by Sylvanus Griswold Morley/Wikimedia Commons, Public Domain)

According to scholars' calculations, the Maya Great Cycle would have begun in 2012 CE. But did that really mean the Maya thought this was the end of the world? Most historians and archaeologists say the answer is a resounding "no." Rather, that year would simply have started a new cycle, though the Maya would have seen great importance in the event and celebrated it with major festivities. It appears that only Hollywood and some imaginative modern writers have read an Earth-ending catastrophe into this date.

- What does the cyclical nature of the Maya calendar system suggest about their rituals and cosmology?
- Why do you think the concept of an apocalypse occurring in 2012 was so attractive to modern people?

The era of Maya greatness begins with the Classic period, starting around 250 CE and lasting until about 900. During this time, urbanization in the Maya world expanded greatly, with approximately forty different city-states emerging in different areas. Some of the most powerful were older sites like Tikal and Calakmul, along with newer locations like Palenque, Copan, Yaxchilan, and Piedras Negras (Figure 8.16). Each had its own rulers, referred to as "divine lords." These powerful chieftains exercised their authority over the city-state through their control over religious rituals and ceremonies, the construction of temples, and especially wars they waged with other Maya city-states. Such wars were common for weakening rivals and keeping neighbors in line, and they may even have served important ritual purposes. They also allowed for the exacting of tribute from subdued enemies in the form of animal products, salt, textiles, artwork, and agricultural goods like cacao and maize. Tribute could be paid through labor as well, when defeated enemies supplied workers for the victorious city-state. Only rarely did rulers seek to control conquered city-states, however. These generally remained independent, though they all shared many cultural attributes.

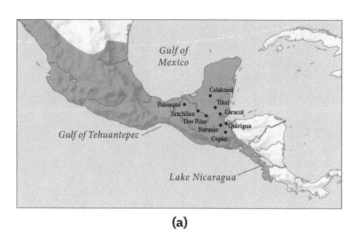

(a)   **(b)**

FIGURE 8.16 The Maya World. (a) At its height, the Maya civilization included as many as forty city-states. (b) Today the ruins of Palenque and other Maya sites appear ghost-white. But during their heyday in the seventh century, their temples were painted in bright colors. (attribution a: Copyright Rice University, OpenStax, under CC BY 4.0 license; credit b: modification of work "Palenque Palace" by "Candiderm"/Wikimedia Commons, Public Domain)

At the heart of Maya religious practices was the veneration of family ancestors, who were considered bridges between heaven and earth. Homes had shrines for performing ritual bloodletting and prayers directed to the ancestors, and deceased family members were typically interred beneath the floor. Indeed, the large stone temples themselves were in some ways grander versions of these family shrines, usually with large tombs within them, and deceased kings were effectively ancestors for the entire city-state. Ritual practices were tied to the complicated Maya calendar, and gods could act in certain ways depending on the time of year and the location of certain heavenly bodies. Shamans and priests guided rituals like bloodletting, which allowed for communication with the ancestors by releasing a sacred essence in the blood called *chu'ulel*. The same principle applied to the human sacrifice of war captives and especially captured rival leaders.

While we can only speculate about how the Olmec played their ritual ball game, we know more about the Maya and later versions (Figure 8.17). The intention was to reenact aspects of Maya mythology, and the game held a significant place in religious practice. Two teams of four wore ritual protective padding and passed the ball to each other without using hands or feet on long I-shaped courts flanked by sloping walls. The object appeared to be to move the ball through a stone ring without letting it hit the ground. As the use of padding indicates, the game could be quite dangerous; the ball was solid rubber and could weigh more than seven pounds. But the true danger came at the end, when losing team leaders or sometimes the entire losing team could expect to be sacrificed to fulfill the game's ritual purpose.

FIGURE 8.17 A Maya Ball Court. Maya ball court designs varied from city to city, but like this one in front of a pyramid in Peten, Guatemala, all had the same I-shaped layout. (credit: "Tikal Ballcourt" by Gary Todd/Flickr, Public Domain)

One of the reasons we know so much about the Maya is that, unlike some other Mesoamerican civilizations, they created a writing system that scholars have been able to decode and read (Figure 8.18). This system was phonetically based, with complex characters, and was far more developed than any other writing system discovered in Mesoamerica. It allowed the Maya to record their own history in stone monuments, including invaluable political histories, descriptions of rituals, propagandistic records of battles, and genealogies.

FIGURE 8.18 The Maya Writing System. The phonetically based Maya script baffled researchers for years and was decoded only after decades of careful work. These stucco characters are from Palenque and were likely created between the fifth and eighth centuries BCE. (credit: "Maya stucco glyphs displayed in the museum at Palenque, Mexico" by "Kwamikagami"/Wikimedia Commons, Public Domain)

Classical Maya civilization entered a period of decline in the ninth century CE and then deteriorated rapidly. Over a period of about a century, alliances broke down, conflicts became more common, the production of luxury goods slowed to a stop, and cities went from thriving urban centers to depopulated shells. The reason for this collapse has been a topic of debate among historians and archaeologists for many years, and much remains uncertain. Among the proposed causes are epidemic diseases, invasions, natural disasters, internal revolutions, and environmental degradation. Several of these may have been influential; it is unlikely there was a single cause.

For example, studies over the last few decades have pointed to the environmental problems created by demographic growth. This growth led to large-scale deforestation, which in turn produced soil erosion. Large populations that required high agricultural yields made Mayan civilization more vulnerable to variations in climate or a string of bad harvests caused by crop disease. Such problems would have put enormous pressure on elites and commoners alike and contributed to disorder, war, and perhaps internal revolts. However it happened, by 900 CE the Classic period of Maya civilization had come to an end. But this was not the end of the Maya. In the Yucatán Peninsula, well north of the old centers of power, Maya civilization would experience a rebirth that extended into the sixteenth century and the arrival of the Spanish.

Early Cultures and Civilizations in South America

South of Mesoamerica and north of the Andes lies a dense tropical jungle that long prevented any regular communication or cultural transmission between the two areas. As a result, the early cultures and civilizations in South America developed in different ways and responded to different environmental factors. Neolithic settlements like Norte Chico in today's Peru had already emerged by 3000 BCE. However, in the centuries following this, others proliferated in the Northern Highlands as well. These include sites known today as

Huaricoto, Galgada, and Kotosh, which were likely religious centers for offering sacrifices. There was also Sechin Alto, built along the desert coast after 2000 BCE. Then, around 1400 BCE, groups in the Southern Highlands area around Lake Titicaca (on the border between Peru and Bolivia) began growing in size after adopting agricultural practices. The construction of a large sunken court in this area around 1000 BCE indicates they had their own sophisticated ceremonial rituals.

Around 900 BCE, the Andes region experienced a transformation when a single society, often called the Chavín culture, expanded across the entire area, opening what archaeologists call the Early Horizon, or Formative, period. The Chavín culture is known for its distinctive pottery style, which spread throughout the entire region and depicted numerous people, deities, and animals in a flowing and balanced manner (Figure 8.19).

FIGURE 8.19 Chavín Pottery. The Chavín culture produced a distinctive pottery style. This ceramic piece (c. 1000–800 BCE) shows a stylized caiman, an alligator-like reptile species that inhabits parts of Mexico and South America. (credit: "Bottle with caiman" by The Michael C. Rockefeller Memorial Collection, Purchase, Nelson A. Rockefeller Gift, 1967/The Metropolitan Museum of Art, Public Domain)

🔗 LINK TO LEARNING

Read or listen to a short expert description of the Chavín bottle with caiman (https://openstax.org/l/77Chavin) presented by the Metropolitan Museum of Art, which holds this item in its collection.

In addition, you can explore a number of other artifacts (https://openstax.org/l/77Artifacts) from the period at the Met website.

The name Chavín comes from Chavín de Huántar, possibly the culture's most important religious center. This site is more than ten thousand feet high in the Andes Mountains, to the east of the older Norte Chico settlements. Its dominant architectural feature was its large temple complex, which faced the rising sun and included a maze of tunnels snaking through. Deep within the tunnels was a large sculpture of possibly this culture's chief deity, called *El Lanzón* ("great lance") because of its long lance-like shape. The image of *El Lanzón* mixes both human and animal features, with flared wide nostrils, bared teeth, long fangs on either side of the mouth, and claws protruding from fingertips and toes. The temple was also decorated with many other sculptures of animals, human heads, and deities bearing the features of both, all probably intended to awe residents and visitors alike.

The inhabitants of Chavín de Huántar numbered about twenty-five hundred by 200 BCE as it slipped into decline. The site's importance lay in its role as a religious or ceremonial site, not as a population center. But by around 400 BCE, the Chavín religion and culture had spread far and wide across the Andes region. Whether these influences were transmitted by trade or warfare is unclear. Eventually, however, they replaced other architectural and artistic styles and burial practices. Innovations in textile production and metalworking in gold, silver, and copper also proliferated around the region. Craftspeople in towns and villages produced textiles and metal objects, and traders moved them from place to place along improved routes and with the aid of llamas as pack animals (Figure 8.20).

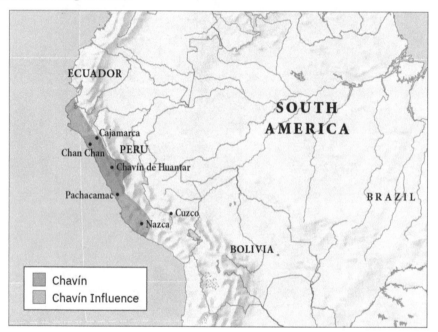

FIGURE 8.20 Chavín Culture and Its Influence. Between about 900 and 200 BCE, the Chavín culture exerted a strong influence over much of what is today coastal and Andean Peru. (attribution: Copyright Rice University, OpenStax, under CC BY 4.0 license)

Beginning around 200 BCE, the influence of Chavín cultural styles and religious symbols began to wane. This came at a time of increased regional warfare among many groups, evidenced by the increasing use of defensive features like walls around settlements. The broader Chavín-influenced region then fragmented into a number of regional cultures that grew to full-fledged civilizations like the Moche, Nazca, and Tiwanaku (Figure 8.21).

FIGURE 8.21 Moche, Nazca, and Tiwanaku Cultures. The Moche and Nazca civilizations both emerged around 200 BCE in different parts of what had formerly been Chavín areas of influence. The Tiwanaku civilization also traces its roots back to about 200 BCE, but its major building period started around 100 CE. (attribution: Copyright Rice University, OpenStax, under CC BY 4.0 license)

The Moche civilization emerged in northern Peru and made major settlements with large pyramid-style architecture at Sipán, Moche, and Cerro Blanco. Its people were agriculturalists with a keen knowledge of irrigation technology, which they used to grow squash, beans, maize, and peppers. They were also a highly militaristic society; their art depicts warriors in hand-to-hand combat, scenes of torture, and other forms of physical violence (Figure 8.22). The Moche formed a politically organized state with a sophisticated administration system. Their cities and burial practices reflect a hierarchical organization, with powerful divine kings and families of nobles ruling from atop large pyramids. Below these two tiers was a class of many bureaucrats who helped manage the state. Near the bottom of the social order were the large numbers of workers, agricultural and otherwise, who lived in the many agricultural villages controlled by the elite.

FIGURE 8.22 The Moche at War. The Moche commanded a highly militaristic state that used war as well as ceremonial violence to subjugate surrounding populations. This colorful reproduction of a scene originally painted on a piece of Moche pottery (300–700 CE) shows a ceremony in which a Moche lord hands a cup to a high priest (top) as bound prisoners endure bloodletting at the hands of their captors (bottom). (credit: "Mural de la cultura Moche" by SCALA/Wikimedia Commons, CC0 1.0)

Far to the south of the Moche, along the dry coast of southern Peru, were the Nazca, whose culture also emerged around 200 BCE. While the terrain there is parched, with rainfall virtually unknown in some areas, the rivers that carry water from the mountains provided the Nazca with sufficient water for irrigation. Unlike the Moche in their large cities, the Nazca people lived mostly in small villages. However, they maintained important ceremonial sites like Cahuachi, where villagers made pilgrimages and witnessed elaborate fertility and other rituals.

Politically, the Nazca may have adopted a type of confederation made up of a number of important families. Apart from many human-altered hills, called *huacas*, they also left behind hundreds of geoglyphs, large artistic representations imprinted in the dry desert ground. These are sometimes referred to as the **Nazca Lines**, and they can be either geometric patterns or images of animals like birds, fish, lizards, and cats (Figure 8.23). Some are as large as twelve hundred feet long and were created by clearing stones away from the desert floor to reveal the different-colored ground beneath.

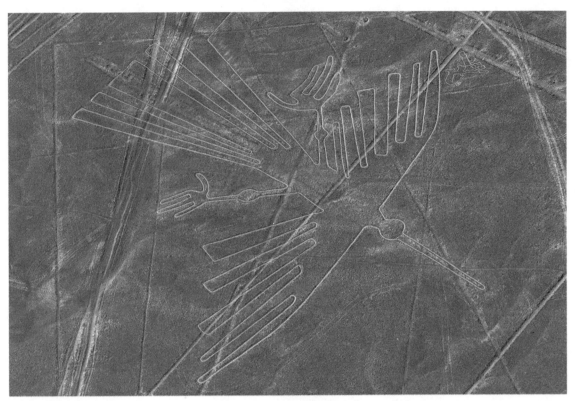

FIGURE 8.23 Nazca Lines. Between 200 BCE and 600 CE, the Nazca in modern southern Peru created massive images of animals and other shapes like this bird by moving rocks to reveal the different-colored desert floor beneath. (credit: "The Condor" by Roger Canals/Wikimedia Commons, CC0 1.0)

🔗 LINK TO LEARNING

The Nazca Lines in Peru have baffled scholars for many years. Watch this video about the Nazca Lines (https://openstax.org/l/77NazcaLines) to learn more about how some are trying to understand these giant geoglyphs today.

Whereas the Nazca lived in the arid coastal desert, the Tiwanaku civilization thrived high in the mountains near Lake Titicaca. Like the Moche and Nazca societies, this culture emerged in the wake of the collapse of Chavín culture around 200 BCE. Beginning around 100 CE, it entered a period of sustained building at its key city of Tiwanaku. There, residents built two large stone structures topped by additional buildings and carved stone artwork. A signature feature of the structures at Tiwanaku is the many "trophy heads" that poke out from among the stone blocks (Figure 8.24). Noting the different facial features on each head, some scholars have concluded that they represent important ancestors of the Tiwanaku elite or possibly the gods of various conquered groups.

FIGURE 8.24 Tiwanaku "Trophy Heads." So-called trophy heads decorate the face of this wall built between the third and sixth centuries CE at Tiwanaku, near Lake Titicaca between Bolivia and Peru. (credit: modification of work "Tiwanaku23" by Alexson Scheppa Peisino (AlexSP)/Wikimedia Commons, Public Domain)

At its height, the city supported perhaps as many as forty thousand people and oversaw at least four smaller cities in the surrounding area. It may even have been the center of a type of imperial system, with colonies on both the Pacific coast and the eastern side of the Andes. To support Tiwanaku and the other related cities, the people irrigated massive fields with a network of canals to grow potatoes. They also raised domesticated llamas and used them as pack animals for long-distance trade.

Tiwanaku survived until about 1000 CE and may have declined as the water level in Lake Titicaca rose to flood its farmland. The other civilizations of this period—the Moche and the Nazca—had disappeared long before, between 500 and 600 CE, for reasons that likely included environmental transformations. Other Andean civilizations emerged in their wake, including the Wari of the highlands of southeastern Peru and the Chimor of coastal Peru. These later groups built upon the earlier cultures' innovations in agriculture, art, manufacturing, and trade. While Wari declined around 800 CE, Chimor survived into the fifteenth century. It was only in the 1400s that Chimor was conquered by a new and expanding imperial system, the Inca.

North America in the Formative Period

The earliest complex societies in North America began to emerge in the Ohio River valley around 1000 BCE, at the start of the Formative period, when mound-building cultures with large populations in the Eastern Woodlands became more common.

Mound-Building Cultures in the Eastern Woodlands

The mound-building culture of the Ohio River valley area is often referred to as the Adena, after a mound excavated in 1901 in Ross County, Ohio. This and the hundreds of others discovered in the area were burial sites. They started small, with the burial of one or two important people, but grew over time as more were buried and more earth was used to cover them. Some of the mounds had a large circular ditch surrounding them and logs lining the interior. Evidence of postholes indicates that structures once stood there as well, suggesting the locations may have been meeting or ceremonial spots. The bodies of the dead themselves were often decorated with red ocher and other pigments. Grave objects included jewelry, weapons, stone tools, marine shells, and pipes for smoking kinnikinnick (a mixture of leaves and bark) and perhaps tobacco (Figure 8.25).

FIGURE 8.25 Owl Pipe of the Adena Culture. Carefully carved pipes like this one dating from 900–1300 CE could be buried with their owners in the mounds built by the ancient Adena culture in the Ohio River valley. (credit: "Owl effigy pipe" by "Wmpearl"/Wikimedia Commons, CC0 1.0)

Communities of mound builders in the valley remained small at first, sometimes erecting no more than a couple of structures. The mounds themselves were also relatively small when compared with those of later cultures like the **Hopewell tradition**, a civilization that emerged around 200 BCE and eventually spread across the Eastern Woodlands through a common network of trade routes. Named for a large earthwork complex occupying 130 acres in today's Ohio, the Hopewell tradition emerged around 200 BCE and is one of the most impressive of many of this period in the Woodlands. The site encloses thirty-eight different mounds within a large earthen D-shaped rectangle. The largest are three conjoined mounds; before centuries of erosion occurred, together they measured about five hundred feet wide and thirty feet high. Large platforms once supported wooden structures and were likely used for ritual purposes.

Another Hopewell site located near Newark, Ohio, is equally impressive, with earthen enclosures, mounds, and an observation circle all organized to align with the movement of the moon and likely used to predict lunar eclipses and other seasonal events. Building such mounds with the available technology would have been a labor-intensive task and indicates the culture responsible was highly organized.

The mound complexes were used for ceremonial purposes and do not appear to have been the site of urban settlements. Instead, most people of the Hopewell culture lived in small dispersed communities consisting of only a few extended families. They employed both hunter-gatherer strategies and the cultivation of domesticated plants like sunflowers and bottle gourds. Neighboring groups likely came together to participate in hunting, gathering, and religious events at their ceremonial sites. Religious traditions included the veneration of ancestors, such as those buried in the mounds.

Different communities from the wider area buried their dead leaders in the same mounds, likely as a way to establish symbolic connections across kin groups. Evidence from sites like the one at Newark suggests that ceremonies for burial and veneration were probably connected to seasonal changes and important astronomical observations. The items deposited in the mounds included a number of artistic depictions of animals like beavers, bears, dogs, cats, and even supernatural mixtures of these. These likely had symbolic importance for the individual kin groups and were connected to both their religious practices and specific ancestral ceremonies.

Politically, the settlements of the Hopewell tradition were decentralized and mostly egalitarian. The leadership structure of individual kin groups may have revolved around shamans or shamanistic practices, but there were no powerful rulers. There were, however, some divisions of labor based on specialization, including healers, clan leaders, and those who possessed certain spiritual qualities necessary for interpreting astronomical signs, preparing burials, and preserving important religious traditions. Ceremonial objects made of copper, bone, stone, and wood and shaped into bird claws and totem animals aided shamanistic figures in their duties and were often buried with them. Items within the mounds also provide evidence of extensive long-distance trading. Those discovered in the Ohio River valley include copper from Lake Superior, quartz from Arkansas, mica from the Appalachian region, marine shells from the Gulf coast, and obsidian from as far away as the Rocky Mountains. Trade in these objects was carried out by individuals moving along rivers or the networks of village paths.

BEYOND THE BOOK

Turtle Island

The earthen mounds of the Eastern Woodlands region had a number of symbolic meanings and purposes. They served as burial sites, provided connections to ancestors, and were settings for religious rituals. But what do ancient stories suggest about these mounds? Because the Native Americans who built them did not leave behind written records, their legends are one tool modern scholars can use to understand their symbolic importance.

Consider one of the ancient origin stories common to many Indigenous groups of the Eastern Woodlands. Preserved orally in numerous versions, it tells of the construction of the world by the accumulation of earth upon the shell of a large turtle, which grew over time and supported life. Some versions of the story begin with a great flood, after which animals work diligently to bring up earth from below the water to place on the turtle's back. Other versions refer to a woman with supernatural powers who falls or travels from the heavens and creates the world on a turtle's back (Figure 8.26). Across all the versions, the symbolic importance of the turtle, representing life, is paramount.

FIGURE 8.26 *Sky Woman*. In some versions of the Turtle Island story, a woman descends from the heavens to create the world on the back of a turtle. This 1936 oil painting called *Sky Woman* by the twentieth-century Seneca artist Ernest Smith illustrates such a moment. (credit: "'Sky Woman', by Ernest Smith. 1936" by Unknown/Wikimedia Commons, Public Domain)

While we cannot know for sure, the Woodlands mounds may have been connected to this ancient origin story. They certainly would have provided safety from river flooding in low-lying areas. During such times, the connection between the mound and the turtle floating in the water would have been difficult to miss.

- What purpose do you think origin stories like these served for the ancient people of the Eastern Woodlands?
- Do you think using preserved origin stories is a good way to understand ancient peoples and customs? Why or why not?

The Hopewell tradition settlements began to decline in the fourth century CE, evidenced by a waning of mound building and trade. The precise reason is not clear, but larger kin group alliances may have broken down as a result of underlying religious issues. Beginning around 600, groups in the Midwest built a number of so-called effigy mounds. These are earthen mounds formed in the image of animals like wolves, bears, snakes, and birds. Like many earlier mounds, the effigy mounds were also burial sites, but they usually contained only a few individuals. In comparison to the earlier Hopewell mounds, they were generally constructed with less labor and in a shorter amount of time, possibly by just a few dozen people working for a few days.

Early Cultures of the American Southwest

Far to the west of the mound-building cultures, a very different cultural tradition formed in the arid landscape of the Southwest. Here, people began experimenting with maize varieties as early as the third millennium BCE. By that time, some groups in the region had begun planting maize in small plots along riverbanks and using it to supplement their hunter-gatherer existence. Exactly how maize reached the American Southwest from southern Mexico is not clear, but there must have been some sporadic contact between cultivators in the south and hunter-gatherer adopters farther north. However, for many centuries after maize was introduced into the Southwest, its cultivation remained limited to one small part of a lifestyle firmly rooted in hunting and gathering. It is possible that the arid conditions of the region necessitated greater mobility and thus made the advantages of maize cultivation less obvious.

Some of the earliest evidence of maize cultivation in the area dates from about 2250 BCE and comes from what is now northwestern New Mexico. By around 1200 BCE, groups in the Las Capas area, by the Santa Cruz River near modern Tucson, Arizona, had developed a sophisticated irrigation system for cultivating maize. The people at Las Capas built a network of canals that directed water from the river into their fields. Around this agricultural base, they constructed oval-shaped homes and pits for roasting the maize they grew. Over time, the homes became more elaborate and were organized in rings around courtyards. But even here the cultivation of maize remained only a small part of a largely hunter-gatherer lifestyle, which included gathering goosefoot and piñons as well as hunting rabbits, bison, and deer.

By around 500 BCE, the cultivation of beans was adding to the growing diversity of foods consumed in the Southwest. This change helped to encourage more dependence on maize since, nutritionally speaking, these two foods are complementary—beans are a source of lysine, a necessary amino acid that maize lacks. Growing beans with maize also increases the nitrogen in the soil and preserves its fertility for longer periods. However, even after the introduction of beans, settled and solidly agricultural communities in the Southwest did not begin to emerge until around 200 CE. Once they did, the region entered a transformational period that resulted in the development of the Anasazi or Ancestral Pueblo societies.

8.3 The Age of Empires in the Americas

LEARNING OBJECTIVES

By the end of this section, you will be able to:
- Describe the expansion of pre-Columbian civilizations like the Aztec and Inca
- Identify key features of the Aztec and Inca civilizations
- Identify key features of the Anasazi and Mississippian traditions in North America

The arrival of the Spanish at the end of the fifteenth century inaugurated a new age in the Americas, but in Mexico and Peru, the Spanish entered areas already under the control of large and sophisticated empires. The Inca in the Andes and the Aztecs in Mesoamerica were the cultural inheritors of thousands of years of civilizational development that included the heritage of the Moche, Nazca, and Tiwanaku in the Andes and the Olmec, Maya, and Teotihuacanos in Mesoamerica. Likewise, the Mississippian tradition chiefdoms of the Eastern Woodlands, where the early Spanish explorers also trod, were the product of ancient cultural and civilization developments going back to the mound-building traditions of Adena, Hopewell, and even earlier cultures.

The Aztec Empire

The early origins of the Aztecs are cloudy, partly because this culture did not have a fully developed writing system for chronicling its history. Instead, the Aztecs relied on artistic records and oral traditions passed from generation to generation. They also used codices, book-like records drawn on bark paper that combined both images and pictograms. Based on information from these sources, historians have been able to place Aztec origins within the context of the collapse of the Toltec civilization.

Ⓖ LINK TO LEARNING

Aztec codices are similar to modern books, but instead of words they use images and icons to relay oral traditions. An example is the Codex Mendoza (https://openstax.org/l/77CodexMendoza) that was created around the year 1541. By scrolling through its pages, you will see both Aztec pictograms and Spanish translations.

The Toltec were an earlier Mesoamerican culture that filled the power vacuum created by the decline of Teotihuacán. From their capital at Tula, the Toltec dominated central Mexico between the tenth and twelfth centuries CE. When their civilization collapsed internally or was possibly conquered, a number of nomadic and warlike groups descended into the area, one of which appears to have been the Aztecs. A new period of cultural transformation and violent wars followed. The Aztecs clearly excelled in these military conflicts, likely acting as mercenaries. Ultimately, they were permitted to settle on a collection of islands within a large but shallow ancient lake called Lake Texcoco, one of five contiguous lakes that once spread across the Valley of Mexico.

BEYOND THE BOOK

The Aztec Origin Story

Much of our information about the Aztecs was recorded by the Spanish after they arrived in the sixteenth century. This is problematic for historians because Spanish religious leaders and conquistadores destroyed Indigenous records, particularly those that seemed to have religious significance. Since the Europeans viewed the Indigenous people through their own worldview and transformed Mesoamerica politically and culturally, their written accounts are often an imperfect means for understanding this people. Only by carefully studying the records we have, including Spanish accounts and Aztec codices, have scholars been able to piece together the story the Aztecs told themselves and their subject peoples about their origins.

The word *Aztec* is derived from their mythical original home, Aztlan. According to the Aztecs' own origin story, they migrated from Aztlan centuries before their rise to greatness in the Valley of Mexico. This long period of wandering in search of a new home included a number of important events, such as battles, encounters with sorcerers, significant tribal divisions, and the birth of important gods like Huitzilopochtli, the Aztec war god. The story culminates in a dramatic clash on the shore of Lake Texcoco. There the Aztec migrants faced an alliance of rebels who sought their destruction. They survived only because Huitzilopochtli intervened by sending his priests to kill the leader of the enemy alliance and rip out his heart. Huitzilopochtli then instructed the Aztec priests to throw the heart far into the lake. It landed on the island of Tenochtitlán and sprouted a cactus, on which an eagle holding a snake landed. This was where Huitzilopochtli said the Aztecs should settle and build their great city (Figure 8.27).

FIGURE 8.27 The Aztec Origin Story. This colorful page of the sixteenth-century Aztec Codex Mendoza, written using traditional Aztec pictograms, shows the mythical battle with rebels on the shore of Lake Texcoco in the lower panel, and the eagle perched on the cactus above. (credit: "Codex Mendoza depicting the coat of arms of Mexico" by Bodleian Libraries/Wikimedia Commons, Public Domain)

While archaeological evidence contradicts some of this legend, origin stories do have special cultural and political significance. Not only did the Aztecs' migration story reinforce the important idea that they had emerged from obscurity to dominate the world, but different leaders also curated the history regularly to demonstrate that their reign was the culmination of earlier events. In this way, the story could change over time to support different rulers, general Aztec dominance, and specific cultural practices.

- Why might the Aztecs have wanted to emphasize that they came from a distant land?
- What other practical purposes might such an origin story serve?

The Aztecs began constructing their home city of Tenochtitlán among the islands within Lake Texcoco around 1325. During the following century, they survived by trading goods they could produce as well as continuing to serve as mercenaries for the surrounding powers. In this way, they accumulated wealth and supplied themselves with stone, which they used to transform their small island settlement into a large and architecturally sophisticated city. After acquiring some influence in the region, they formed an alliance with two neighboring city-states, Texcoco and Tlacopan. Then, in 1428, this **Triple Alliance** launched a surprise attack on the powerful city-state of Atzcapotzalco and made itself the dominant regional power. Over the next several decades, the Triple Alliance, with the Aztecs at its head, expanded its control of central Mexico to include Oaxaca in the west, parts of modern Guatemala in the south, and the areas bordering the Gulf of Mexico. By 1502, the newly crowned emperor of the Aztecs, Moctezuma II, was ruling an expansive empire from his capital city of Tenochtitlán (Figure 8.28).

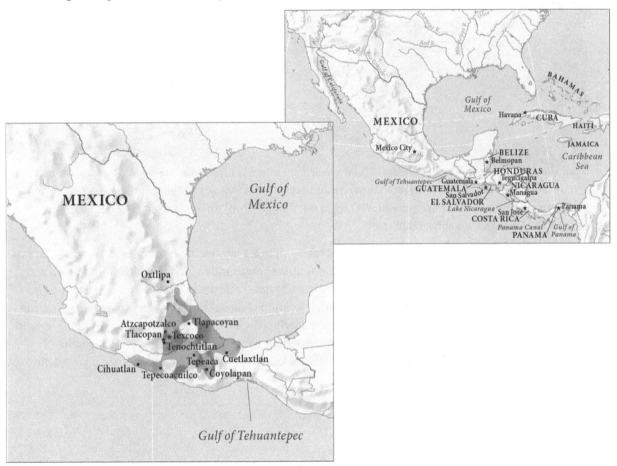

FIGURE 8.28 The Triple Alliance. By 1502, the Aztec-led Triple Alliance held sway over a large portion of central Mexico (shown in green). (attribution: Copyright Rice University, OpenStax, under CC BY 4.0 license)

At its height in the early 1500s, Tenochtitlán had a population of at least 200,000 people. It was a massive island city with large causeways that connected it to the shores of the lake. Some of the city's land had been made by human intervention, which included creating artificial agricultural islands called *chinampas* around the city that were crisscrossed by canals for irrigation and transportation. These chinampas produced food for the city's occupants. Toward the center of the island where the land was more firm were the homes of the city's occupants, made mostly of adobe with flat roofs and built around small courtyards. At the center of the island were large temples, a ball court, administration buildings, homes for the elite, and the palaces of the rulers. The most impressive of the temples was the Templo Mayor, which was expanded numerous times during its long history. By the early 1500s, it was a dual stepped pyramid standing about ninety feet tall (Figure 8.29). One side was dedicated to the city's patron Tlaloc, the god of rain. The other side was dedicated to

Huitzilopochtli, the god of war. Priests climbed a long staircase to the temple to perform important state rituals.

FIGURE 8.29 Tenochtitlán. At their height in the sixteenth century, the temples at Tenochtitlán were beautifully painted, as this modern model shows. (credit: "Model of the Templo Mayor (main temple) of Tenochtitlan" by "schizoform"/Wikimedia Commons, CC BY 2.0)

One of the most important ceremonies performed at the Templo Mayor and other temples in Tenochtitlán was the ritual of human sacrifice. Like many Aztec traditions, this rite was widely practiced in Mesoamerica and had roots going back to the Olmec culture and likely earlier. Human sacrifices occurred on important days identified on the Aztec calendar and during the commemoration of new temples or the expansion of existing ones. Contemporary descriptions note that long lines of sacrificial victims were led up the steps to the temple platform. There they were laid on a sacrificial stone, where their chests were opened with a sharp flint or obsidian knife and their hearts removed by the executioner (Figure 8.30). The bodies were then tossed down the steps of the temple.

FIGURE 8.30 An Aztec Ritual. Like many pre-Columbian civilizations, the Aztecs considered human sacrifice an important part of their religious traditions. This image is from a sixteenth-century codex. (credit: "Aztec Human Sacrifice 10" by latinamericanstudies.org modification of "Image 242 of General History of the Things of New Spain by Fray Bernardino de Sahagún: The Florentine Codex. Book II: The Ceremonies" by Library of Congress/Wikimedia Commons, Public Domain)

These rituals were closely tied to Aztec cosmology and the people's understanding of their role in the universe. The gods were believed to participate in the practice of sacrifice and to have used it to create the world and perpetuate its existence (Table 8.2). They often needed the assistance of human beings, who were created to serve and feed them through human sacrifice and other means. The sacrifices were thought to ensure that the sun stayed in the sky, the harvests continued to be bountiful, illnesses were kept at bay, and the military power of the Aztecs remained supreme.

Centeotl	The Aztec god of maize
Huitzilopochtli	The Aztec god of war
Quetzalcoatl	The "feathered serpent" and Aztec god of wind, dawn, merchants, and knowledge
Tlaloc	The Aztec god of rain
Coatlicue	The Aztec goddess of fertility and rebirth
Xiuhtecuhtli	The Aztec god of fire and creator of life

TABLE 8.2 The Aztec Gods

Human sacrifice was also an important means of preserving and expanding the empire and keeping conquered territories in line, since sacrificial victims were often those captured in battle. Thus, the goal in warfare was often to seize the enemy alive. Aztec war had important ritual purposes too. In some instances, it could be highly theatrical and consisted of paired individuals fighting each other, rather than large armies. Young boys began training to serve in the Aztec military from an early age. They drilled regularly with javelins for throwing, leather-covered shields, and clubs fitted with obsidian blades. Until they were old enough and experienced enough to become warriors themselves, they worked in the service of veteran warriors (Figure 8.31).

FIGURE 8.31 An Aztec Warrior. Aztec warriors, like this one shown in a detail from the Codex Mendoza (c. 1542), trained from childhood to fight in wars for the empire. (credit: "Tlacochcalcatl" by Unknown/Wikimedia Commons, Public Domain)

The Aztec Empire also exacted tribute payments from its conquered territories. At its height, the empire consisted of thirty-eight provinces, each expected to submit specific tribute to the imperial capitals. Occasionally, regions that resisted incorporation into the empire were given harsh terms. More often, the type of tribute demanded was related to the location of the tribute state and the goods it typically produced. For example, the Gulf coast area was known for natural rubber production and was assessed a tribute payment of sixteen thousand rubber balls for use in the Aztec ball game. Locations much closer to the capitals commonly provided goods like food that were expensive to transport over long distances. Those much farther away might be expected to provide luxury goods the Aztec elite gave as gifts to important warriors. Typical tribute items included cloth, tools like knives and other weapons, craft goods of all types, and of course, food. Tribute items could also include laborers to work on larger imperial projects. The Aztec tribute system functioned much like a crude system of economic exchange. Goods of all types flowed into the centers of power and the hands of elites. But they also made their way to commoners, who benefited from the diversity of the items the system made available.

As a highly militarized society, Aztec culture prized perceived male virtues like bravery, strength, and fighting ability. Warriors were expected to sacrifice themselves to perpetuate the glory of the state. When they were successful in battle, they were adorned with rich cloth and celebrated by the masses. Aztec women operated within a more circumscribed world. They could not serve in the military or attain high positions within the state, yet they did not necessarily occupy a lower status than men. Rather, Aztec state culture emphasized the complementarity of women and men, with men expected to fill roles outside the home like farming and fighting and women responsible for domestic chores like cooking and weaving.

Aztec women thus often spent long hours grinding corn into meal and weaving clothing for the family. Their work could sometimes take them outside the home, such as to the markets where some gained considerable wealth as traders and served in leadership roles. As midwives and healers, women ensured that healthy children were born and that the sick were treated with medicines backed by centuries of knowledge about the medicinal properties of certain plants.

Aztec society was made up of a number of social tiers. At the bottom was a large number of enslaved people and commoners with no land. Above these were the commoners with land. Before the imperial expansion, landed commoners had some limited political power. However, within the imperial system they were relegated to providing food and service for the military. Above them were the many specialized craftspeople, merchants, and scribes. And above all commoners were the nobles, who used conspicuous displays of wealth to elevate themselves. They served in the most important military positions, on the courts, and in the priesthood.

The members of the Council of Four also came from the noble class. The council's primary task was to select the Aztec emperor, or *Huey Tlatoani*, from the ranks of the nobility. The emperor occupied a position far above everyone else in Aztec society. His coronation included elaborate rituals, processions, speeches, and performances, all meant to imbue him with enormous power. Even high-ranking nobles were obliged to lie face down in his presence.

The Aztec rulers had not always been so powerful or elevated so far above the masses. Their great authority and the ceremony of their office increased with the expansion of the empire. By the coronation of Moctezuma II in 1502, the office of emperor had reached its height, as had the empire. The expansion of the preceding decades had slowed, and demands for tribute and captives for ritual sacrifice were taking their toll and stirring resentment in many corners of the empire. It was into this context that the first Spanish explorers came. They were able to exploit the weaknesses in the empire and eventually bring about a new Spanish-centered order built on top of the old Aztec state.

The Inca Empire

At around the same time the Aztec Empire was expanding across Mesoamerica, an equally impressive new civilization was on the rise in the Andes region of South America. Known today as the Inca, its cultural and technological roots extend back to the earlier Andean cultures of the Moche, Nazca, and Tiwanaku. The heart of what became the Inca Empire was the city of Cuzco, located more than eleven thousand feet above sea level in the central Andes and northwest of the shores of Lake Titicaca. But centuries before it became an imperial city, it was a relatively modest agricultural community where the predecessors of the Inca farmed potatoes and maize and raised llamas and guanacos.

According to one Andean tradition, the origin story of the Inca began with a great flood that displaced four brothers and their wives and sent them on a mission to find fertile land where they could settle. During the journey, one of the brothers acquired incredible and supernatural strength. Consumed with jealousy, the other brothers sealed him in a cave and left him to die. They continued on, somewhat remorseful, but on the outskirts of Cuzco, two were mysteriously turned to stone. This left only one brother, Ayar Manco, who reached Cuzco, dipped his golden cane into the ground, and founded the city (Figure 8.32).

FIGURE 8.32 Ayar Manco. This eighteenth-century depiction of Ayar Manco, by Inca tradition the founder of the city of Cuzco, names him its first king and shows him with his golden staff. (credit: "Manco Capac, First Inca, 1 of 14 Portraits of Inca Kings" by Dick S. Ramsay Fund, Mary Smith Dorward Fund, Marie Bernice Bitzer Fund, Frank L. Babbott Fund, The Roebling Society, The American Art Council, Anonymous, Maureen and Marshall Cogan, Karen B. Cohen, Georgia and Michael deHavenon, Harry Kahn, Alastair B. Martin, Ted and Connie Roosevelt, Frieda and Milton F. Rosenthal, Sol Schreiber in memory of Ann Schreiber, Joanne Witty and Eugene Keilin, Thomas L. Pulling, Roy J. Zuckerberg, Kitty and Herbert Glantz, Ellen and Leonard L. Milberg, Paul and Thérèse Bernbach, Emma and J. A. Lewis, Florence R. Kingdon/Brooklyn Museum/Wikimedia Commons, Public Domain)

The fantastical story of the Ayar brothers, with its descriptions of magic and supernatural events, is clearly partly fictional, and it is not the only origin myth about the Inca. However, it may preserve a kernel of truth about the early group that founded Cuzco, perhaps after some type of migration prompted by changes in climate. We may never fully know, but based on historical and archaeological evidence, we do know the people of Cuzco emerged as agricultural villagers by around 1000. Through both peaceful and violent means, they assumed a dominant position in the larger surrounding region. Over time, their numbers grew, and they became one of a number of small military powers in the Andean region, centered on the growing city of Cuzco. As master stonemasons, the Inca were capable of carefully carving stones so they fit tightly together (Figure 8.33). At its height in the early sixteenth century, Cuzco was an impressive stone city built high in the Andes.

FIGURE 8.33 Inca Stonework at Sacsayhuamán. While many of the Inca-built parts of Cuzco were destroyed in later centuries, the sixteenth-century site of Sacsayhuamán nearby preserves its ancient walls of stones, so skillfully hewn as to fit together tightly without mortar. (credit: "Peru - Cusco Sacred Valley & Incan Ruins 005 – Sacsaywamán" by McKay Savage/Flickr, CC BY 2.0)

The leap to imperial expansion is explained by another Inca legend, this time telling of a military challenge from a rival group known as the Chanka and involving real historical figures. When the Chanka arrived at Cuzco, King Wiraqocha fled the city with his heir, leaving only a small group of nobles aligned with another son, Yupanki, to stand their ground. The defenders' act of courage inspired the creator god of the Inca to intervene by transforming the surrounding stones into warriors who helped Yupanki defeat the Chanka. In the aftermath of the victory, the story goes on, Yupanki assumed the additional title of Pachacuti, meaning "cataclysm." But the victory also led to an internal dispute between Pachacuti Yupanki and the reigning king, his father. This was ultimately resolved in Pachacuti Yupanki's favor, and he assumed control of Cuzco and the Inca, whereupon he began a series of wars of expansion that gave birth to the Inca Empire.

While this story was partly contrived, there is no doubt that Inca expansion did occur, and Pachacuti appears to have been a real leader. The empire's growth began in earnest around 1430 during his reign, and as king he oversaw the conquest of much of modern Peru. His successors, Thumpa and Wayna Qhapaq, further expanded the empire by adding territory far to the south in today's Chile and Argentina, to the east in the edges of the Amazon basin, and to the north in Ecuador and Colombia. These wars were costly in lives and material, but they were also important for sharpening the skills of the Inca military.

Inca warriors wore helmets and cloth armor, carried shields, and were equipped with weapons like clubs, spears, slings, and axes (Figure 8.34). Typically, they could use their great numbers to overwhelm and awe the enemy into capitulation. If that failed, they rushed into the fray, often with little discipline but with great courageous resolve. Apart from the sheer power of numbers, the Inca military excelled in its ability to move swiftly along the empire's complicated highland road systems to surprise the enemy and put down any emerging rebellions.

FIGURE 8.34 Inca Soldiers. The Inca armies could use their vast numbers to intimidate rivals into capitulation. In this seventeenth-century image by Huamán Poma de Ayala, a Peruvian chronicler of the Spanish conquest, the Inca soldiers in their feathered helmets are on the right, and their enemy faces them on the left. (credit: "Huamán Poma de Ayala's picture of the confrontation between the Mapuches (left) and the Incas (right)" by Unknown/Wikimedia Commons, Public Domain)

The empire created through conquest was divided into four administrative regions controlled by close relatives of the emperor (Figure 8.35). Each region was then broken down into a number of provinces, organized generally along ethnic lines and ruled by an imperial governor selected from the Inca nobility. A great variety of crops were produced across the empire including potatoes, coca, cotton, and maize. Surpluses were held in large storehouses to feed the armies and provide sustenance in times of famine. The subjects of the empire were also expected to provide labor for the construction of roads, bridges, palaces, and religious structures and to serve as messengers, transport food to storehouses, or serve in the military. Certain members of each household submitted their labor tax while others stayed home to manage the family's affairs.

FIGURE 8.35 The Inca Empire. At its height in the early sixteenth century, the Inca Empire controlled an enormous area that reached from modern Columbia down into modern Chile and Argentina. It was divided into four administrative regions: Chinchansuyu, Antisuyu, Cuntinsuyu, and Collasuyu. (attribution: Copyright Rice University, OpenStax, under CC BY 4.0 license)

IN THEIR OWN WORDS

Inca Quipus: Writing with String

Unlike the Maya, the Inca did not have a writing system that could be inked into a codex or carved in stone. But they did have an ingenious recordkeeping and communication system that relied on a portable device called a *quipu* ("kee-poo"), made of a great number of knotted strings (Figure 8.36).

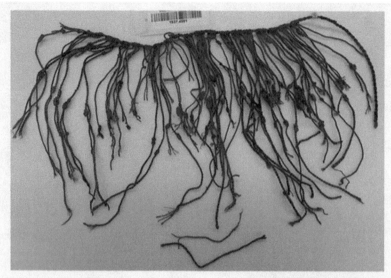

FIGURE 8.36 An Inca Quipu. The quipu of knotted string was a complex but portable Inca recording device. This fragment was made between 1400 and 1600. (credit: "Quipu fragment" by Yale University Art Gallery/Wikimedia Commons, Public Domain)

While many were destroyed by the Inca and later the Spanish, and much knowledge necessary to decipher them has been lost, surviving quipus have been carefully studied. They could record quantitative information like census and tax data, land allocations, the movements of armies, and astronomical observations. They also held qualitative information like ideas and possibly even poems. Different-colored strings and different types of knots that could be tied, untied, and retied made many thousands of combinations possible.

The Spanish were reluctant at first to believe that quipus accurately preserved information. The sixteenth-century explorer Pedro de Cieza de Léon reported:

> When I was at Marcavillca, in the province of Xauxa, I asked the lord Guacarapora to explain it in such a way as that my mind might be satisfied, and that I might be assured that it was true and accurate. He ordered his servants to bring the quipus, and as this lord was a native, and a man of good understanding, he proceeded to make the thing clear to me. He told me to observe that all that he, for his part, had delivered to the Spaniards from the time that the governor Don Francisco Pizarro arrived in the valley, was duly noted down without any fault or omission. Thus I saw the accounts for the gold, the silver, the clothes, the corn, sheep, and other things; so that in truth I was quite astonished.
>
> —Pedro de Cieza de Léon, *The Second Part of the Chronicle of Peru*, translated by Clements R. Markham

According to Garcilasco de la Vega, born in the sixteenth century to Spanish and Inca parents, quipus could even record poems:

> They were composed in accordance with a fable they had, as follows: they say that the Creator placed a maiden, the daughter of a king, in the sky with a pitcher full of water which she spills when the earth needs it, and that one of her brothers breaks it occasionally, and the blow causes thunder and lightning. . . . The fable and verses, Padre Blas Valera says he found in the knots and beads of some ancient annals in threads of different colors.
>
> —Garcilasco de la Vega, *Royal Commentaries of the Incas and General History of Peru*, translated by Harold V. Livermore

- Why might the Spanish have destroyed many quipus?
- How would you go about translating a quipu? What methods might you employ?

Apart from military violence and an organized imperial administration system, the Inca used religious symbolism to hold their empire together. A complex ritual calendar was overseen by religious experts whom the king and nobles regularly consulted before making political or military decisions. The Inca used human sacrifice in some rituals, but apparently not as readily as the Aztec of Mesoamerica. Among their most important deities was the sky god, who could manifest in a number of different forms such as the creator god Wiraqocha, the thunder god Illapa, and the sun god Inti. Inti was of particular importance because Inca rulers claimed direct descent from him. They constructed temples to Inti around the empire, encouraged his worship, and incorporated representations of conquered peoples into Inti's key temple in Cuzco. In this way, the Inca cemented stronger ties between their rulers and the large and diverse empire they had created.

🔗 LINK TO LEARNING

In the fifteenth century, the Inca built a large palace complex high in the mountains above Cuzco that is now called Machu Picchu. You can tour the impressive ruins of Machu Picchu (https://openstax.org/l/77MachuPicchu) at this link.

One of the empire's most important features, and one that held its expansive territory together, were the many roads and bridges that laced through its vast domains. Unlike the Aztec Empire, which expanded across a far more topographically consistent landscape, the Inca Empire included large mountain ranges, canyons, deserts, and narrow coastal valleys. Travel and communication were difficult in this extreme landscape and necessitated a technologically sophisticated road and bridge system. While elements of the network predated the Inca, it was under Inca rule that the larger network was expanded and greatly improved. At the height of the empire, the system may have included as many as twenty-five thousand miles of roads. These roads were as diverse as the landscape itself, including straight passages across flat land, winding paths and staircases around and up mountains, and numerous canyon-spanning bridges made of rope, stone, and wood (Figure 8.37). On them the Inca armies traveled, and goods produced in the provinces made their way to the imperial storehouses.

FIGURE 8.37 An Inca Road. The mountainous terrain of the Inca Empire necessitated roads like this one to connect the many important cities and regions.(credit: "Stone steps and mountains on the Inca Trail" by "Mx._Granger"/Wikimedia Commons, CC0 1.0)

Like the Aztec Empire, the Inca Empire had just reached its height on the eve of the Spanish arrival in the early

1530s. Diseases brought by Europeans had already weakened it by then, even leading to the untimely death of Emperor Wayna Qhapaq in 1528. Just a few years later, the Spanish conqueror Francisco Pizarro reached Ecuador with his small army. There he found new Inca subjects eager to ally themselves with a possible enemy of the empire, while the Inca themselves were in the midst of a minor civil war over who would ascend the newly vacated throne. By 1532, the Spanish had entered the conflict and emerged masters of the empire, upon which they constructed their own system.

Complex Societies in North America

After many centuries of cultivating maize to supplement their hunter-gatherer lifestyle, around 500 BCE, groups in the American Southwest began to establish permanent villages supported by farming. Over the next few centuries, settled villages with permanent homes supplied with large storage pits for maize proliferated across the region. The agricultural peoples of these villages are often subdivided into three major cultural groups: the Mogollon tradition in the south, the Hohokam tradition in the west, and the Anasazi or Ancestral Pueblo tradition in the north (Figure 8.38). They were in contact with each other and shared a number of similarities. Their early settlements consisted of a number of oval and circular pit houses, partly underground and built of wooden poles covered in dried mud. These could be ventilated by rooftop openings accessible by internal ladders. Such homes were especially well suited to the sun-drenched environment and provided a cool escape from the hot outside temperatures. They also efficiently preserved heat during winter, when conditions could get exceedingly cold.

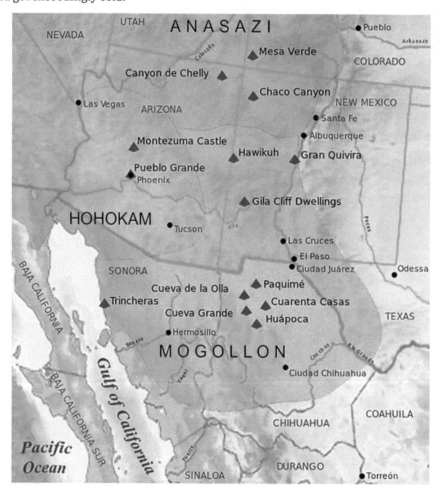

FIGURE 8.38 Traditions of the American Southwest. Three large and distinct cultural traditions emerged in the Southwest beginning around 500 CE: the Mogollon, the Hohokam, and the Anasazi. (credit: modification of work "Regions of ancient regional tribes in the southwestern United States and Northwestern Mexico" by "Ricraider"/Wikimedia Commons, CC BY 3.0)

Settlements varied in size from a handful of homes to as many as sixty. The design of the dwellings and the complexity of the settlements varied as well, with both generally increasing over time. By around 700, for example, large ceremonial meeting-house structures called *kivas* had become common in the central and northern areas. These were likely the local centers of religious ceremonies and civic life. In the centuries after 700, the settlements evolved into larger collections of multiroom structures built of dried adobe clay and stone. By 900, similar permanent settlements dotted the larger southwestern landscape, including in modern New Mexico, Arizona, Colorado, Utah, Texas, and the Mexican state of Chihuahua.

Some of the most impressive settlements that remain include Pueblo Bonito in New Mexico, Cliff Palace in Colorado, and Casas Grandes in Chihuahua. Pueblo Bonito in Chaco Canyon began to expand into the large masonry settlement visible in its ruins today around 800, when its residents abandoned their pit houses for the larger pueblo-style rooms. **Pueblo architecture** used stone or wooden frames covered in adobe clay. The houses and other buildings made in this way tended to have flat roofs that could be used as terraces.

At Pueblo Bonito, the houses were organized in a U-shape around the old pits from the pit houses, which were then used as kivas. This settlement reached its peak around 1000, which may have meant a modest population of about one hundred people, though its six hundred pueblo rooms could have housed as many as one thousand. In addition to being an important agricultural settlement, Pueblo Bonito was a major ceremonial center and likely attracted groups from the surrounding area for significant events. Some residents were clearly of particular importance, as indicated by the 130 burial sites and associated objects discovered there.

In addition to Pueblo Bonito, at least seventy other communities of varying sizes were scattered across the larger Chaco Canyon area. The total population of these settlements may have included as many as 5,500 people. Connections between them are suggested by shared pottery and architectural styles, and by the network of roads that pass through some settlements while radiating outward from the canyon like spokes on a wheel.

A long period of drought after 1130 led the residents of Chaco Canyon and Pueblo Bonito to abandon their settlements for other areas that promised sustenance. By about 1200, the old settlements were empty. Some eighty miles to the north in Mesa Verde, conditions were wetter and natural resources more plentiful, and groups there built a number of impressive cliffside dwellings. Construction of one of the largest settlements, today called Cliff Palace, began around 1190. Archaeologists believe this settlement was made as a defensive measure when competition for scarce resources was becoming more intense. Similar cliffside settlements were built in other places in the region for the same reason. Cliff Palace had twenty-three kivas and 220 rooms made of sandstone, mortar, and wood. They extend up the side of the cliff, some towering twenty-six feet tall (Figure 8.39). Like Pueblo Bonito, Cliff Palace also likely had a population of about one hundred people. And for just over a century, the settlement prospered, until expanding drought conditions forced the residents to abandon it and the many other Mesa Verde settlements around 1300.

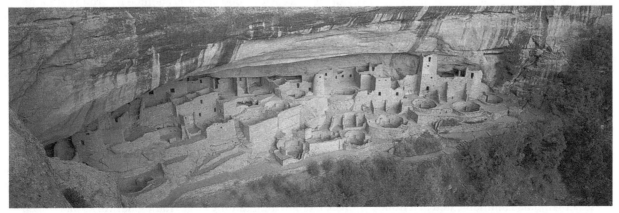

FIGURE 8.39 The Cliff Palace. Construction of the impressive cliffside dwellings at the Cliff Palace site in modern southwest Colorado began about 1190. Residents used wooden ladders to reach their elevated homes. (credit:

"Trail of the Ancients - Cliff Palace at Mesa Verde National Park" by U.S. National Archives and Records Administration/Wikimedia Commons, Public Domain)

Far to the south of Mesa Verde were the settlements of the Mogollon tradition. One of the more impressive is known today as Casas Grandes or Paquimé (Figure 8.40). Set in a flat arid portion of northern Chihuahua, Mexico, near the modern U.S. border, Casas Grandes emerged as an important agricultural settlement in the fourteenth century. Far more agriculturally productive than its northern Anasazi neighbors, Casas Grandes may have had a population of almost 2,300 people at its height. These people lived in adobe structures clustered close together and surrounded by a large enclosure wall.

FIGURE 8.40 Casas Grandes. The ruins of Casas Grandes stand as a testament to the productivity of this once-large city. Its population—more than two thousand at its height in the fourteenth century—was far larger than that at settlements like Pueblo Bonito or Cliff Palace. (credit: "Wide view of Paquime" by Luis Serrano/Wikimedia Commons, Public Domain)

Because of its adobe design, Casas Grandes bears a superficial resemblance to some Anasazi communities. But the site actually has more in common with the Mesoamerican civilizations far to its south. For example, there are no kivas at Casas Grandes, but there are ruins of a large I-shaped Mesoamerican-style ball court. Among the valuable trading goods produced at Casas Grandes were colorful macaw feathers commonly used in Anasazi rituals. These indicate that trading networks existed between Casas Grandes and the Anasazi to their north. By the start of the fifteenth century, however, Casas Grandes was entering a period of decline; by the end of the century, it had been abandoned.

Around the same time that settled agricultural communities were becoming common in the Southwest, the Eastern Woodlands region was going through its own cultural transformations. On the former site of the Adena and Hopewell traditions, a new mound-building culture called the **Mississippian tradition** began to emerge around 700. This large and sophisticated culture constructed some of the biggest and most impressive of all the ceremonial mounds in the region.

The Mississippian tradition was apparently sparked by the adoption of maize agriculture from much farther south. Maize may have arrived in the Eastern Woodlands as early as 800 and was adopted by groups already accustomed to farming edible plants like sunflowers and bottle gourds. By 1000, its cultivation had become common throughout the region, even among groups that had not used agricultural techniques before. Bean cultivation was also spreading around the Eastern Woodlands, and at about the same time, people in the area began to use the bow and arrow, especially for hunting small animals like birds.

Combined, these changes brought about a major cultural shift in the Eastern Woodlands marked by the appearance of large settled agricultural communities and the spread of common cultural, architectural, and technological practices. A number of settlements arose throughout the Mississippi River valley and as far away as Georgia and Florida. Most were small chiefdoms built around one or just a few earthen mounds. Occasionally, smaller settlements were grouped into larger chiefdoms, and in a few important places, the settlements were exceptionally large, with populations in the thousands. Archaeological discoveries reveal that these settlements communicated and traded with each other, maintaining large trading networks that linked their many urban centers. Artifacts have been found many hundreds of miles from the site of their manufacture, and common architectural and artistic details suggest that cultural ideas too were disseminated far and wide.

The Mississippian site at Cahokia near modern St. Louis is possibly the most elaborate and important researched thus far. Earlier settlements nearby were smaller and date to about 600. But around 1050, the large urban center of Cahokia began to emerge, reaching its peak about 1250 before experiencing a gradual decline. At its height, Cahokia and its surrounding settlements covered nearly four square miles, had a population as large as sixteen thousand people, and included well over one hundred different mounds. At the center was a network of large mounds organized around a 100-foot-tall temple mound, built in stages with a wooden structure at its summit and a large staircase leading up from the surrounding plaza (Figure 8.41). Wood and thatch houses of various sizes radiated out from the central plaza and into the surrounding maize fields. Around the central complex of mounds and the homes of the elite was a large defensive wall, with watchtowers spaced at intervals around it.

FIGURE 8.41 Monks Mound at Cahokia. The terraced remains of Monks Mound at Cahokia, completed around 1100, stand today as the largest human-made earthen mound in North America. It rises almost one hundred feet above the surrounding landscape. (credit: "Monk's mound panorama" by Tim Vickers/Wikimedia Commons, Public Domain)

Other mounds at Cahokia served as burial mounds and platforms for ritual performances. Some of the rituals included human sacrifice, not unlike those common in Mesoamerica. One of the excavated mounds at the site contained the remains of several dozen sacrificial victims. At the base of this mound, archaeologists found the remains of two men, one buried face down, one face up. The man facing up had been placed on a bed of more than twenty thousand shells arranged in the shape of a large bird, suggesting that he was a particularly important person. Among the items buried with this "birdman" were hundreds of arrowheads, copper pieces, and a number of stones, elements of a ritual ball game called *chunkey* that may have had the same significance for the Mississippians as the rubber ball game had for Mesoamerican civilizations (Figure 8.42).

FIGURE 8.42 The Game of Chunkey. In this painting by the widely traveled nineteenth-century artist George Catlin, Native Americans living in North Dakota are shown playing the game of chunkey. The roots of this game, played with sticks and a rolling disk, go back to the time of Cahokia and perhaps much earlier. (credit: "Tchung-kee, a Mandan Game Played with a Ring and Pole" by George Catlin/Smithsonian American Art Museum/Wikimedia Commons, Public Domain)

The "birdman's" identity is not clear, but whether a leader, a shaman, or even an important warrior, he was a member of Cahokia's elite. Cahokia and other large Mississippian settlements had a distinct nobility with access to luxury goods and a surplus of food produced by a large population of commoners who did agricultural work. Sites like Cahokia likely derived their power from their ability to exact tribute from surrounding groups, and from their control of long-distance trade routes that brought exotic items such as marine shells, rare stones, copper goods, and the feathers of colorful birds from distant lands.

⊘ LINK TO LEARNING

Learn more about the history and archaeological discoveries of Cahokia (https://openstax.org/l/77Cahokia) at the Cahokia Mounds Museum Society website. You can also explore an interactive map of Cahokia (https://openstax.org/l/77CahokiaMap) at this link.

Despite Cahokia's obvious power, the settlement was relatively short-lived. By 1250, it had entered a period of decline, and ultimately it was abandoned. This did not mark the end of the Mississippian tradition itself, however. Sites like Moundville in Alabama, Etowah in Georgia, and many others bloomed in the wake of Cahokia's demise. However, by about 1375, these large chiefdoms had begun to collapse as well. As the larger Mississippian tradition declined, so too did the long-distance trade routes. The people who had once lived at the large settlements became more dispersed across the Eastern Woodlands, leading to the emergence of a number of new groups. By the time the first Spanish explorers arrived in 1539, Cahokia was long gone. But from the records the Spanish kept, we know there were still a number of smaller chiefdoms scattered across the Eastern Woodlands. These were clearly different from the earlier Mississippian chiefdoms, but they still displayed many of the cultural traditions that had arisen centuries before.

Key Terms

Beringia a section of low-lying land between modern Alaska and Russia, now underwater, that once served as a land bridge between continents

Clovis culture a culture consisting of mobile bands of hunter-gatherers who camped at resource-rich locations in modest populations across North America

Hopewell tradition a widely dispersed mound-building tradition that emerged in the Eastern Woodlands around 200 BCE, linked by a network of trade routes

Mississippian tradition a widely dispersed mound-building tradition that created a number of urban settlements linked by trading networks in the southeastern United States around 700

Nazca Lines a group of geoglyphs made on the desert floor in southern Peru representing both geometric patterns and images of animals

Norte Chico the culture of partially settled agricultural communities in the Andes region; also known as the Caral civilization

Pueblo architecture a building style of the early American Southwest that relied on stone or wooden frames covered in adobe clay

Triple Alliance an alliance formed in 1428 between the Aztecs and two neighboring city-states, Texcoco and Tlacopan

Section Summary

8.1 Populating and Settling the Americas

During the last glacial period, modern humans crossed Beringia and entered the Americas for the first time, migrating across North, Central, and South America. They relied on hunting large game and may have contributed to the extinction of some animals. Later they became more settled in a number of regions, adapting their hunter-gatherer strategies to their environments and the available resources.

About nine thousand years ago, groups like those in the Andes region began experimenting with animal domestication. Later they began to cultivate edible plants like squash, bottle gourds, and later the potato. In Mesoamerica, the shift to maize-based agriculture began at some point between 5000 and 3000 BCE. By around 2500 BCE, the use of domesticated maize had become more common and enabled the settlement of agricultural villages that combined the strategies of hunting and gathering with maize cultivation. Over time, the advantages of maize agriculture became more obvious, and exclusively sedentary agricultural communities emerged. In the Eastern Woodlands, a different agricultural tradition emerged independently by 2000 BCE. In each area, plant domestication allowed Neolithic settlements to begin, from which larger cultures and civilizations later grew.

8.2 Early Cultures and Civilizations in the Americas

The Olmec civilization formed around 1200 BCE and developed sophisticated religious traditions, a calendar system, and a ritual ball game. The Olmec influenced Mesoamerican cultures that followed, including the Zapotecs of Oaxaca, the Teotihuacanos of the Valley of Mexico, and the Maya of southern Mexico and Guatemala. By 300 BCE, Teotihuacán was among the largest cities in the world and controlled a vast trading network. By that time, a handful of powerful Maya city-states like Tikal, Calakmul, and El Mirador had grown to large urban centers and were using their own sophisticated writing and calendar system.

In the Andes region of South America, Chavín culture began expanding around 900 BCE, spreading its distinctive artistic and religious traditions. In the wake of the Chavín collapse in 200 BCE, new states like the Moche, the Nazca, and the Tiwanaku emerged and thrived in the Andes.

In North America, the complex societies of the Adena tradition emerged in the Ohio River valley around 1000 BCE and built a number of earthen burial mounds. This tradition was followed by other mound-building cultures like the Hopewell tradition. Very different traditions developed in the Southwest, where maize agriculture was incorporated into a largely hunter-gatherer existence as early as the third millennium BCE. But in this dry environment, settled and entirely agricultural communities did not begin to emerge until around 200 CE.

8.3 The Age of Empires in the Americas

In Mesoamerica in the fifteenth century, the Aztec Empire expanded to control central Mexico from its island city of Tenochtitlán. In addition to building large temples, ball courts, and palaces, the Aztec practiced human sacrifice as an important religious ritual. In the Andean region, the Inca Empire expanded to control a large swath of western South America from its capital at Cuzco, eleven thousand feet above sea level. The empire was created by trained warriors, employed a tribute system, and was held together by a vast network of roads through its largely mountainous terrain.

Intensive agriculture of maize in the Southwest and Eastern Woodlands led to enormous changes in both regions. By around 900, a number of settlements had grown in the Southwest, such as Pueblo Bonito in Chaco Canyon, the cliffside dwellings at Cliff Palace in Mesa Verde, and the larger Casas Grandes settlement in northern Mexico. In the Eastern Woodlands, the adoption of maize agriculture around 800 led to the rise of the Mississippian tradition and large agricultural communities across the Mississippi River valley. Most were small chiefdoms, but a few like Cahokia were exceptionally large, with populations in the thousands.

Assessments

Review Questions

1. Why has evidence of earlier coastal migrations down the west coast of North America not been discovered?
   a. There is resistance to these theories.
   b. The likely sites are now covered by water.
   c. The migrants probably did not follow the coast.
   d. The legal fight over Kennewick Man prevented it.

2. What activity best characterizes the Clovis people?
   a. They were settled agriculturalists.
   b. They lived on the salmon abundant in the areas where they lived.
   c. They were mobile big-game hunters.
   d. They were prolific mound builders.

3. Where did maize agriculture initially begin?
   a. Mesoamerica
   b. Eastern Woodlands
   c. Pacific Northwest
   d. Andean region

4. What edible plant was domesticated in the Eastern Woodlands?
   a. sunflower
   b. maize
   c. potato
   d. quinoa

5. For what ancient method of hunting bison have archaeologists uncovered evidence in places like Texas and Montana?
   a. using large reed traps
   b. shooting bison with bows and arrows
   c. driving bison over cliffs

    d. chasing bison with horses

6. What species was an important source of protein for the people of the Pacific Northwest?
    a. llamas
    b. salmon
    c. guanacos
    d. guinea pigs

7. What does it mean to call Olmec civilization a "mother culture?"
    a. Its expansion led to the creation of other similar cultures.
    b. It expanded from San Lorenzo to La Venta.
    c. It encouraged the production of stone heads in northern Mexico.
    d. It founded important Maya city-states.

8. What was the political organization of the larger Maya world?
    a. It was a large empire.
    b. It was a confederation with one elite city.
    c. It was a collection of independent city-states.
    d. It was made up of two large multicity kingdoms.

9. What South American culture gave birth to the Early Horizon period?
    a. Chavín
    b. Tiwanaku
    c. Moche
    d. Nazca

10. How did the Hopewell tradition people transform the environment to suit their needs?
    a. They built large stone temples.
    b. They farmed maize in river deltas.
    c. They created animal depictions in the desert.
    d. They created earthen mounds.

11. What two Mesoamerican civilizations were contemporaries?
    a. Olmec and Zapotec
    b. Teotihuacano and Zapotec
    c. Olmec and Teotihuacano
    d. Maya and Olmec

12. What Mesoamerican civilization created a complex writing system for recording its history and genealogies?
    a. Olmec
    b. Teotihuacáno
    c. Maya
    d. Zapotec

13. What conclusions have scholars drawn from the art left behind by the Moche?
    a. They were a highly militaristic people.
    b. They were a nonagricultural people.
    c. They engaged in peaceful religious expansion.
    d. They maintained a strong relationship with the Maya.

14. Where did the Aztec establish their city?
    a. Lake Texcoco
    b. Oaxaca
    c. Gulf lowlands
    d. Aztlan

15. In what role did Aztec women serve?
    a. soldiers
    b. farmers
    c. healers
    d. diplomats

16. According to Inca legend, what event brought Yupanki to power in Cuzco?
    a. He placed his golden staff in the ground.
    b. He defeated the Chanka offensive.
    c. He turned his brothers to stone.
    d. He constructed a temple to Inti.

17. What was a major reason for the cultural shift in the Mississippian tradition?
    a. the adoption of maize agriculture
    b. the start of earthen mound building
    c. the construction of cliffside dwellings
    d. the use of human sacrifice

18. What serves as strong evidence that the builders of Casas Grandes were culturally influenced by Mesoamerican civilizations farther south?
    a. the presence of kivas
    b. the presence of an I-shaped ball court
    c. the presence of macaw feathers
    d. the presence of adobe structures

Check Your Understanding Questions

1. What were the societal consequences of abundant and available resources in the Pacific Northwest for the hunter-gatherers who lived there?

2. What recent discoveries have challenged earlier views about how migrations to the Americas occurred?

3. What evidence supports the conclusion that Teotihuacán wielded great influence in the larger Mesoamerican world during its height?

4. How did Maya civilization adapt to the environmental conditions of its surroundings?

5. What was the significance of human sacrifice for the Aztec?

6. What practical purpose did the construction of Inti temples have for the administration of the Inca Empire?

Application and Reflection Questions

1. Why do you think maize agriculture became very common in Mesoamerica but was of only minor importance in South America?

2. If evidence of 15,000-year-old rafts and canoes was found along the Pacific coast, how might this change our understanding of early migration in the Americas?

3. Do you think the Olmec culture was a "mother culture" for the later Mesoamerican civilizations? Why or why not?

4. If you were a visitor to an Olmec or Maya city, what would you experience from the start of your stay to the end?

5. What do you think life was like for the Anasazi living in the cliffside dwellings? What might a member of the community experience during a typical day?

6. How might you have responded to acts of human sacrifice if you lived in the Aztec Empire? Why?

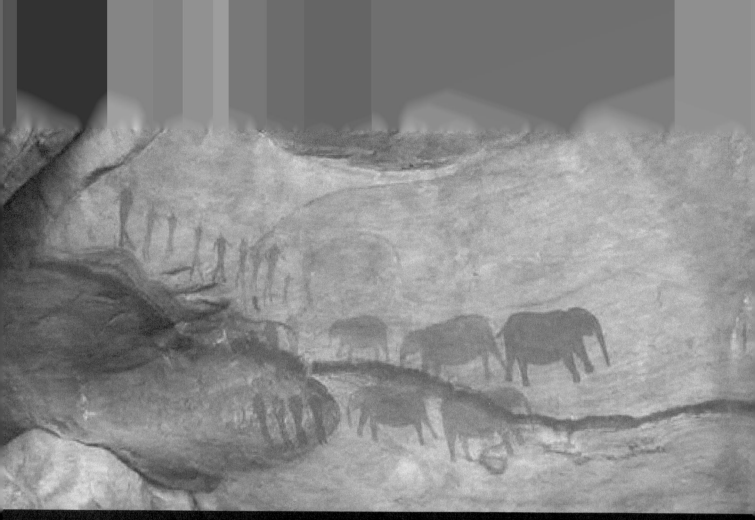

FIGURE 9.1 San Men among Elephants. This rock art in the Cederberg Caves, South Africa, depicts a group of twenty San men interacting with a group of six elephants. In the center of the image, a small elephant extends its trunk as if to sniff one of the men. Painted around 5500 BCE, the artwork likely depicts the special bond between the San people and the elephants, and it demonstrates that even thousands of years ago these African peoples had developed a keen understanding of elephant behavior and characteristics. (credit: modification of work "Cave painting created by the San people in the Cederberg Cave near Stadsaal" by "Valroe"/Wikimedia Commons, Public Domain)

CHAPTER OUTLINE

9.1 Africa's Geography and Climate
9.2 The Emergence of Farming and the Bantu Migrations
9.3 The Kingdom of Kush
9.4 North Africa's Mediterranean and Trans-Saharan Connections

INTRODUCTION More than eleven million square miles in size, Africa is Earth's second-largest continent and home to a huge diversity of geographies and climates. Its environments range from arid desertscapes with sand dunes hundreds of feet high to lush tropical rainforests blanketed by impenetrably dense foliage. Its peoples have adapted to these environments over millennia (Figure 9.1), and their achievements were great, but extreme climates wreak havoc on the historical record. Ancient Africa was nevertheless a marvelous mosaic of unique civilizations, and the more historians work at uncovering their pasts, the clearer our picture will be of their accomplishments and contributions to world history.

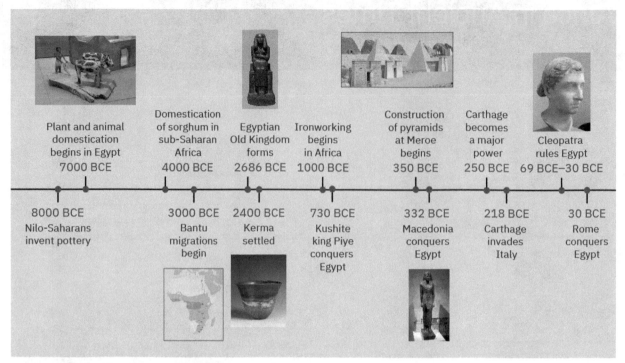

FIGURE 9.2 Timeline: Africa in Ancient Times. (credit "7000 BCE": modification of work "Ancient Egypt Wooden Farmer & Oxen Model, Middle Kingdom, c. 2000 BC" by Gary Todd/Flickr, CC0 1.0; credit "3000 BCE": modification of work "'Spread of the "Early Iron Age' in Eastern, Central and Southern Africa, a proxy for the Bantu migrations" by Kevin Shillington/Wikimedia Commons, Public Domain; credit "2686 BCE": modification of work "Statue of princess Redji" by Museo Egizio/Wikimedia Commons, CC0 1.0; credit "2400 BCE": modification of work "Classic Kerma Beaker" by Rogers Fund, 1920/The Metropolitan Museum of Art, Public Domain; credit "350 BCE": modification of work "Pyramids N26 and N27" by "Wufei07"/Wikimedia Commons, Public Domain; credit "332 BCE": modification of work "Ptolemy III Euergetes" by Szilas/Wikimedia Commons, Public Domain; credit "69 BCE–30 BCE": modification of work "Marble bust of Cleopatra VII of Egypt" by Altes Museum Berlin/Louis le Grand/Wikimedia Commons, Public Domain)

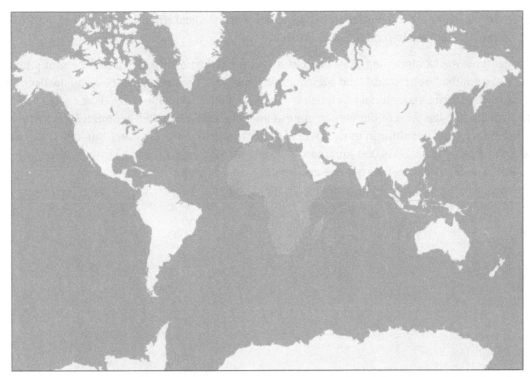

FIGURE 9.3 **Locator Map: Africa in Ancient Times**. (credit: modification of work "World map blank shorelines" by Maciej Jaros/Wikimedia Commons, Public Domain)

9.1 Africa's Geography and Climate

LEARNING OBJECTIVES

By the end of this section, you will be able to:
- Describe the way geography and climate shaped Africa's ancient societies
- Discuss the various Neolithic and hunter-gatherer societies in early Africa

Geography played a vital part in shaping early human societies. Landscape, climate, wildlife, vegetation, and the availability of natural resources all helped influence what early societies looked like, whether they were nomadic units that kept animals and survived by hunting and foraging or settled communities that grew crops, tended herds or flocks, and built shelters. Such characteristics depended on factors like weather patterns and soil fertility, as well as the proximity of drinking water and toolmaking resources.

Well-watered regions in Africa, such as the grassy plains of the savannas and the northern and southern fringes of the continent, have historically produced environments that foster settled human communities. Here abundant rain, adequate forestation, and a host of wildlife provided conditions that could support ever-growing populations over long periods of time. More arid regions, such as the narrow transitional belts separating the savannas from Africa's deserts, experience less rain and have less fertile soil, producing land that cannot be successfully farmed. These areas lent themselves to nomadism and the herding of grazing animals to provide many of the necessities of life, from milk and meat for food to leather and fur for clothing and bones for toolmaking. Throughout most of human history, geography has been an important factor in human development. As a result, exploring Africa's diverse geography opens a window into the development of the earliest human civilization on the continent.

Geographic Diversity on the African Continent

Owing to its position across the equatorial and subtropical latitudes of both the northern and southern hemispheres, Africa is home to a range of climates, including searing deserts, frozen glaciers, sweltering rainforests, and lush grasslands. These divergent environments exist because most of the continent lies between the Tropic of Cancer and the Tropic of Capricorn, in the tropical climate zone. Only its northernmost and southernmost fringes are beyond the tropical area.

Across the center of Africa, stretching like a band from Guinea in the northwest to parts of Mozambique in the southeast, lies a swath of wet, tropical land subject to extremely heavy rainfall. Here we find the deep canopy and undergrowth of Africa's equatorial rainforest (Figure 9.4). Centered on the Congo River Basin, the rainforest is densest in the present-day central state of the Democratic Republic of Congo. Here there is very little space between trees, resulting in thick layers of leaf covering that prevent much sunlight from reaching the forest floor. Approximately 386,000 square miles in extent, the Congo rainforest is the second largest in the world. Overall, it receives between sixty-three and seventy-eight inches of rain every year.

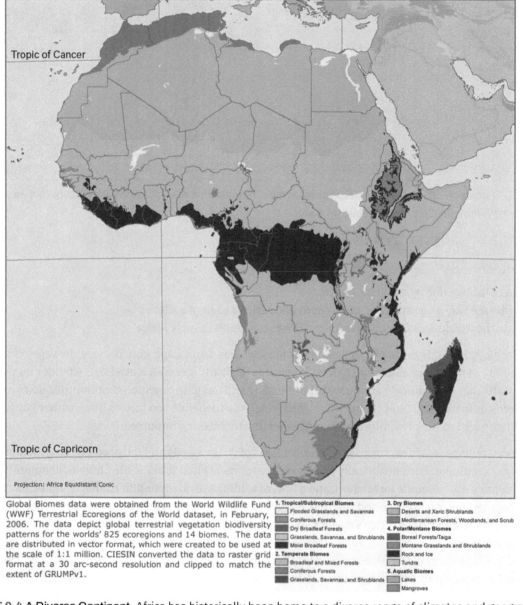

Global Biomes data were obtained from the World Wildlife Fund (WWF) Terrestrial Ecoregions of the World dataset, in February, 2006. The data depict global terrestrial vegetation biodiversity patterns for the worlds' 825 ecoregions and 14 biomes. The data are distributed in vector format, which were created to be used at the scale of 1:1 million. CIESIN converted the data to raster grid format at a 30 arc-second resolution and clipped to match the extent of GRUMPv1.

1. Tropical/Subtropical Biomes
Flooded Grasslands and Savannas
Coniferous Forests
Dry Broadleaf Forests
Grasslands, Savannas, and Shrublands
Moist Broadleaf Forests
2. Temperate Biomes
Broadleaf and Mixed Forests
Coniferous Forests
Grasslands, Savannas, and Shrublands

3. Dry Biomes
Deserts and Xeric Shrublands
Mediterranean Forests, Woodlands, and Scrub
4. Polar/Montane Biomes
Boreal Forests/Taiga
Montane Grasslands and Shrublands
Rock and Ice
Tundra
5. Aquatic Biomes
Lakes
Mangroves

FIGURE 9.4 A Diverse Continent. Africa has historically been home to a diverse range of climates and geographies, ranging from savannas and deserts to tropical rainforests and temperate zones. Notice that the bands of climate patterns above the equator are a near-mirror image of those below it. (credit: modification of work "Africa: Biomes" by SEDACMaps/Flickr, CC BY 2.0)

The Congo River, which forms the heart of the rainforest region, is the second-longest river in Africa; only the Nile is longer. The geographic differences between the environments of these rivers produced vastly different societies. The Nile River and its predictable flood patterns allowed Egyptian civilization to flourish for centuries. Large cities and grand architecture were features of the region due to readily available and plentiful food supplies, and hieroglyphs remained that left a clear and permanent record of key moments of its history. The Congo, however, flows through a tropical region, where dense forests created a very different kind of society, and the moist environment did not allow for recorded history but rather oral stories passed down through generations. Thus, while both regions had a human past, we know far more about one than we do about the other.

Africa's tropical band is further divided into the monsoon area and the tropical savanna. Wetter than temperate savannas, tropical savannas are characterized by tall grasses, sparse trees, and greater rainfall and are found bordering the equator. The monsoon area is subject to seasonal wind changes that produce wetter and drier periods in isolated locations of the West African coast and the Central African interior. In the tropical savanna, on the other hand, rainfall diminishes considerably, and the dense stands of thickly layered trees that characterize the rainforest give way to forested pockets and lush grasslands.

The **savanna** is a grassy plain that constitutes another of Africa's immense biomes. A **biome** is a community of vegetation and wildlife adapted to a particular climate. At around five million square miles in size, the savanna covers almost half the surface of the continent and has been home to more people and history than any other part of Africa. Stretching from the warm and humid reaches of the rainforest to the torrid zone of the Sahara, it is wetter than the desert but drier than the rainforest and presents a striking geographic contrast to the landscapes of the desert and rainforest. Unlike those areas, the savanna landscape encompasses snow-capped mountains, vast expanses of grassy plains dotted with trees, and marshy tropical areas.

Geographers consider the savanna a region of transitions, with three successive belts running east–west: the Sahel, the tropical grassland savanna, and the woodland savanna. The **Sahel**, the northernmost band, is a semiarid belt between the Sahara and the grassland savannas to the south (Figure 9.5). It is the driest part of the savanna and experiences rain only periodically during six months of the year.

FIGURE 9.5 The African Sahel. This photograph shows acacia trees that grow on the road to Timbuktu in the African Sahel, between the Sahara and the grasslands. (credit: modification of work "The road to Timbuktu in the Sahel, Mali" by Annabel Symington/Wikimedia Commons, CC BY 2.0)

The people of the Sahel have historically been seminomadic—that is, they have adopted a mixed-farming system of crop production and the breeding and raising of livestock. Although the soil of the Sahel lacks sufficient nutrients to grow forests of trees, it is rich in the kind of nutrients that support the growth of plants in gardens as well as those that allow for small-scale farming and foster the growth of abundant grasses for the grazing of larger animals, particularly cattle and sheep. These herding animals also provide a key ingredient to help African farmers grow crops: manure. With the use of manure and the process of composting, the people of the region successfully navigate the challenges posed by their environment. Its conditions have tended to produce limited agriculture and smaller homesteads that are spaced farther apart to accommodate livestock. Many people of the region continue to live a seminomadic lifestyle rooted in animal husbandry. They do not cling to the past, a recurring myth about Africa; rather, their lifestyle is still the best way to harness what their climate provides.

The Sahel gradually gives way in the south to a grassland savanna carpeted by short grasses and studded by scattered trees. At the extreme, this area can see as much as forty-eight inches of rain per year (the rainy season lasts from May to October). The most famous of all Africa's tropical savannas is the Serengeti. Located in northern Tanzania, the Serengeti is a tremendously diverse ecosystem that witnesses some of the world's largest mass migrations of animals. In January each year, for example, nearly 1.75 million wildebeests begin migrating out of the Ngorongoro Conservation Area at the southern extreme of the Serengeti, following the rainfall in search of food (Figure 9.6).

FIGURE 9.6 Migrating Wildebeests. Every year between January and November, nearly two million wildebeests migrate in a great circular sweep across the Serengeti, arcing from northern Tanzania through southern Kenya and returning to the Ngorongoro Conservation Area nearly eleven months later. (credit: "Wildebeest Migration in Serengeti National Park, Tanzania" by Daniel Rosengren/Wikimedia Commons, CC BY 4.0)

Moving clockwise in a northerly direction toward the Masai Mara Reserve in Kenya, along the way these wildebeests encounter hundreds of thousands of other animals, including zebras and gazelles, that preceded them on their migration. They confront many obstacles and dangers on their trek, including rivers that hide dangerous hippopotamuses and crocodiles, not to mention numerous predators they face on land. When they finally arrive in Kenya, the female wildebeests birth around half a million calves. Their migration comes to an end in early November, after months spent grazing in the savanna grasslands of the Masai Mara Reserve. The herds then migrate south on their return trip to northern Tanzania from Kenya.

LINK TO LEARNING

The Serengeti migration is one of the most impressive movements of animals anywhere on earth. Watch a short video of the annual wildebeest migration (https://openstax.org/l/77WildebeestMig) of over a million of these animals across the Serengeti.

The woodland savanna is the last of the belts separating the great northern desert from the equatorial rainforest. It is characterized by tall grasses occasionally interrupted by scattered trees, and corridors of gallery forests along streams and rivers. The area receives plentiful rainfall, usually nine months of the year, and farmers in the region cultivate palm oil trees and root crops such as yams.

As distance from Africa's tropical zone increases, so too does the unpredictability of the rainfall. Progressively, to the north and south of this region, the bands of tropical and temperate climate give way to increasingly drier environments. Limits on resource availability in the more arid parts of Africa, as elsewhere in the world, have necessarily restricted the growth and expansion of civilizations. Regions that lack accessible supplies of water in the form of underground aquifers or wells, rivers, or lakes or that receive little rainfall are ill-suited to farming. Because only farming can support larger human population centers, the lack of accessible water is a barrier to human settlement. This helps explain why no large civilizations emerged in the more obviously arid parts of Africa, such as the Sahara and the Kalahari Desert and also why certain of the drier transitional zones between savanna and desert remain so thinly populated.

The Sahel transitions to desert in the extreme north of the savanna belt. Deserts are the sunniest and driest parts of the continent. Africa's largest desert—in fact, the world's—is the Sahara. At 3.6 million square miles, about the size of the United States, the Sahara covers much of North Africa (excluding the fertile coastal zones along the Mediterranean and the Nile delta) and stretches from the Red Sea in the east to the Atlantic Ocean in the west. The Sahara has not always been a vast desert, however. In the period following the last Ice Age, this was a lush region that experienced monsoon-like weather conditions and was home to pastoralists and large herds of cattle. In fact, the earliest evidence we have of the domestication of cattle was discovered on Saharan rock art. But between 6000 and 2500 BCE, the region witnessed a great drying, which resulted in the retreat of the rainforest and the expansion of desert zones. These changes prompted crises for the human inhabitants of the formerly tropical zones, who found their old hunting and gathering techniques no longer suitable in the changed environment.

This desertification is what produced the modern Sahara, which receives less than an inch of precipitation per year with variations of some regions experiencing up to four inches per year, while other places go decades with no rain(Figure 9.7). The average daytime high is 99°F, and average nighttime lows are as cool as 68°F, but highs can reach up to 120°F during the warmer months from April to June, and lows can dip below 37°F in the cooler period between December and January. The only plants that can survive in this hostile environment rely on the water that collects in dry riverbeds during the exceptional periods of rain, but they are few.

FIGURE 9.7 The Sahara Desert. Aside from its rare oases, the Sahara is one of the most inhospitable places on earth, with sparse rainfall and extreme temperature swings from day to evening. (credit: modification of work "Sahara" by "Not So Dusty"/Flickr, CC BY 2.0)

Among the Sahara's thousand-foot-tall sand dunes, hard stony surfaces, and vast mountain ranges with peaks as high as eleven thousand feet are oases, green dots of civilization formed around underground water sources that reach the surface via wells or springs. Although together these oases take up only eight hundred square miles—about 0.02 percent of the desert's total landmass—they are home to some three-quarters of the people living in the desert. The remainder of the population are nomads, including the Tuareg and Teda. These peoples engage in a range of economic activities, such as farming and herding, but on a severely restricted basis. Pasturage, for example, exists only in marginal areas such as mountain borders and the somewhat moister areas to the west, limitations that govern the herders' nomadic lifestyle.

As famous as it is, the Sahara is not Africa's only desert; there is also a desert region in the African Horn (the area corresponding to Somalia, Ethiopia, and northern Kenya), as well as the Namib and the Kalahari Desert, Africa's great southwestern desert (Figure 9.8). The Kalahari Desert presents perhaps the most interesting contrast to the extremes of the Sahara.

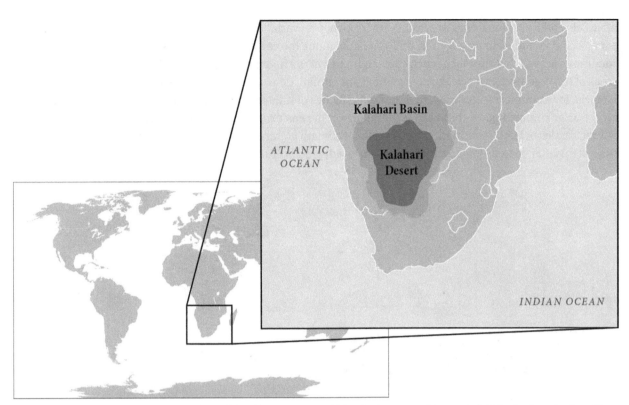

FIGURE 9.8 The Kalahari Desert. The Kalahari in southwest Africa is the second largest of Africa's deserts. (credit: modification of work "Kalahari Desert and Kalahari Basin map" by "Quadell"/Wikimedia Commons, Public Domain)

The Kalahari is a semiarid sandy savanna some 350,000 square miles across. Occasionally referred to as the southern African equivalent of the Sahel, it stretches south from modern-day Namibia into South Africa's Northern Cape province, extends deep into the interior of the South African veld or grassland, and covers almost the whole of Botswana. While Saharan sand dunes are typically large, in the Kalahari they are much smaller, ranging between twenty and two hundred feet high and measuring at least one mile in length and several hundred feet in width. The landscape is also distinguished by numerous "dry lakes" or pans, evidence of a wetter period earlier in the region's history. Even today, some of the northeastern parts of the Kalahari receive more than ten inches of water per year and thus climatically do not qualify as "desert." However, they do lack surface water. When they experience rain, it drains instantly through the deep sands, leaving the soil completely devoid of moisture.

Precipitation in the Kalahari depends largely on weather patterns influenced by the Indian Ocean and is highly variable. While the northeastern part receives comparatively abundant rainfall, the southern fringe of the desert sees less than five inches of rain per year. This rainfall accompanies severe thunderstorms, which often appear suddenly and produce violent downpours that deluge the landscape. Still, for six to eight months of the year, the region receives no rainfall. As a result, there is very little ecologically to distinguish the southwestern landscape beyond flat sand plains—aside from a few drought-resistant shrubs and bushes. On the other hand, the central Kalahari, which enjoys more rain, is dotted with scattered trees, shrubs, and grasses. At the extreme end, the northern reaches of the Kalahari appear to be an entirely different biome with woodlands, palm trees, and forests.

The final major climate in Africa is the Mediterranean climate, found only on the northernmost and southernmost fringes of the continent in the coastal regions of Morocco, Algeria, and Tunisia in the north, and in South Africa. The combination of dry summers with lower humidity (relative to the tropical band) and mild rainy winters makes them ideal environments for the growing of olive trees, cereal grains, and grapes—the so-called Mediterranean triad of crops that dot the landscapes of both regions. The temperatures there are pleasant, with average daily highs of 77°F and average nightly lows hovering around 60°F.

Africa also offers regional climates, each with its own local variations. East Africa, for example, straddles the equator and includes Kenya, Uganda, and Tanzania. Along the coast and around Lake Victoria, hot and humid conditions prevail, but there are much cooler climates in the highlands and mountains (Figure 9.9). Many areas of the region experience extreme amounts of rainfall. Coastal islands and the tropical area around Lake Victoria, for example, receive upward of fifty-nine inches of rain per year. To the north, the Ethiopian highlands form a drier climate region, thanks to the influence of the eastern desert. Locally, Africa's diverse microclimates belie the continent's broad regional climate patterns and suggest the impressive variety of ecosystems that span it—and to which people have adapted over the millennia.

FIGURE 9.9 Lake Victoria. Hot and humid Lake Victoria, home to one of Africa's regional climates, is centrally located in East Africa and bordered by Uganda, Kenya, and Tanzania. (credit: modification of work "Lake Victoria 1968" by U.S. Army/Wikimedia Commons, Public Domain)

A staggering variety of wildlife has also adapted to these climates. Because of the abundance there of grasses as sources of food, Africa's savannas are home to a range of large grazing mammals including gazelles, wildebeests, elephants, ostriches, and zebras. Large herds of these animals are commonly seen in the savanna, none more spectacular than the wildebeests on their annual migration in East Africa. Although giraffes, elephants, hippopotamuses, and rhinoceroses can be found in many places on the continent, including modern-day Botswana, Zimbabwe, and Zambia in the interior of south-central Africa and East Africa, one of the greatest concentrations of these animals on the continent is found in the sub-Saharan savanna.

Types of Ancient African Societies

The variety of African climates directly influenced the evolution of human societies there. People adapted to these climates in many ways, developing techniques and technologies that both helped them survive and altered their surroundings. Understanding the connection between climate, geography, and humans opens the way to understanding Africa's early history.

Before the domestication of plants and animals, life in prehistoric Africa was characterized by the hunter-gatherer stage of human civilization. Hunter-gatherers survive by hunting prey and foraging for fruits and vegetables, or by exchanging game for crops grown by others. In some regions, such as Tanzania and Kenya in East Africa and Botswana in southern Africa, hunter-gatherers followed the seasonal migrations of large game animals, such as wildebeests and elephants. Hunter-gatherers do not plant crops or build permanent shelters but rather live nomadic lifestyles guided by the seasons, limited resource availability, conflict with other groups, or a combination of these factors. They must be highly mobile so their communities tend to be small, consisting of only several dozen interrelated people. Their mobility means that they often play an important role in connecting different regions and cultures and in transmitting goods and ideas across great distances.

Hunting and gathering peoples of Africa have historically included the rainforest-dwelling Baka of Central Africa and the San people of the Kalahari Desert. The Baka, found today in Cameroon, Gabon, and northern Congo, eat wild roots, nuts, fruits, vegetables, a variety of insect species, fish, and wild game they hunt using bows, poison-tipped arrows, and traps (Figure 9.10). Baka villages are made up of small single-family huts of branches and leaves, built predominantly by women and usually dismantled after about a week so the Baka can follow the available food supply. Baka society has a well-defined structure. In addition to building the family hut, women also dam small streams to catch fish and carry material gathered while foraging with their husbands. Men hold a higher social status derived from the fact that they engage in the more hazardous task of hunting and trapping animals.

FIGURE 9.10 The Baka People of Central Africa. Peoples such as the Baka have historically dwelled in the rainforest regions of Gabon, Cameroon, and northern Congo. This photo of Baka people was taken in 1904. (credit: modification of work "Group of Pygmies from the Department of Anthropology at the 1904 World's Fair) by Missouri History Museum/Wikimedia Commons, Public Domain)

Like that of many other African peoples, the Baka religion was and remains centered on a belief in animism—that is, it teaches that certain objects, places, and creatures have spirits. Those who can interpret what those spirits desire have positions of leadership. Animism is also polytheistic, meaning it has numerous gods, each of whom typically personifies a natural force such as rain, wind, or lightning. Given the impact of weather on survival, it is not surprising that trying to control the natural environment was a key factor in religious observance. Among the gods of the Baka are Kamba, the creator of all things, and Jengi, the spirit of the forest. The Baka live in and rely on the forest for their survival, so they view Jengi as a parental figure and, perhaps most importantly, the protector of the forest.

Although ancient African religions were remarkably complex, and their rituals, practices, and beliefs varied greatly among the continent's diverse populations, some commonalities can be identified in the pre-Judaic, pre-Christian, and pre-Islamic periods, including polytheism. Another typical feature of the pantheon of traditional African deities is a supreme being, like the Ngai of the Kikuyu, held to be the creator god from whom the universe originated. The supreme being was a distant deity who played no role in the ordinary affairs of Africans. Instead, management of the day-to-day fell to specialized secondary deities, such as Obatala, the Yoruba god of earth, and Makasa, the Baganda god of harvest and fertility. Other shared features of many ancient African religions include the worship of ancestors as protectors and guides and ceremonial practices to mark important life events, such as the Bantu Okuyi, a rite of passage celebrating the transition between youth and adolescence.

The San people of southwest Africa were and remain seminomadic hunter-gatherers and are polytheistic (Figure 9.11). Their diet is dictated by the arid conditions in which they live. Lack of water in the Kalahari Desert means there are fewer vegetables and fruits to forage, although seasonal nuts, plant buds, and certain roots are food staples. The San also hunt a variety of big game animals, including giraffe and antelope species such as kudu and hartebeest, using poison-tipped arrows and traps. They do not build permanent homes. Rather, their shelter types vary by season: they erect nightly rain shelters in the spring, when they move constantly in search of budding greens, and in the dry season, when water is scarce and most plants are dead or dormant, they congregate around the only permanent water holes in the area.

FIGURE 9.11 The San. A San family in present-day South Africa. (credit: "Bushman family" by Aino Tuominen/ Wikimedia Commons, CC0 1.0)

The hunt is a key part of San society, and all the San gods have jobs related to it. The supreme deity Cagn ensures a successful hunt, often by protecting the San hunters from animals or people who could endanger the hunt. Hei-tusi the hero god assists Cagn in leading and protecting the hunt. To these are added a host of lesser spirits, including predators and tricksters.

The most important of the San religious rituals depends on the hunt. The curing or great trance dance is initiated by a San shaman through the hunting of a "power animal" such as an antelope, whose fat is believed to have supernatural potency and is used in different ritualistic settings, including rites of passage. The shaman enters a trance-like state after a night-long dance around a fire surrounded by clapping women. The

San believe the trance dancers can be affected physiologically and mystically by the ritual, giving them powers to heal or provoking in them an out-of-body experience. The dance, often depicted on ancient San rock art, is the key source of all spiritual knowledge for the San and is often prompted at times of great social stress such as during times of settler incursion, outbreaks of disease or illness, and poverty.

9.2 The Emergence of Farming and the Bantu Migrations

LEARNING OBJECTIVES

By the end of this section, you will be able to:
- Discuss the introduction and emergence of farming in Africa
- Analyze the origin and impact of ironworking technology in Africa
- Describe the geographic extent and impact of the Bantu migrations

For tens of thousands of years, people across Africa lived in relatively small groups and relied on hunting and gathering. This lifestyle began to change dramatically beginning around 7000 BCE when plant and animal domestication methods from the Fertile Crescent were first adopted in Africa. Often called the Neolithic Revolution, the adoption of domestication led some groups to build permanent settlements and support large populations. Over thousands of years, these methods spread up the Nile River and across North Africa. Below the Sahara, plant domestication was developed independently in both the east and the west as the people in those areas learned to cultivate their own unique plant varieties. By approximately 1000 BCE, large populations in both north and sub-Saharan Africa supported themselves by working the land. This wave of transformation effectively transformed the continent and over time led to the emergence of a number of large and sophisticated civilizations.

The Emergence of Farming

Although scholars still debate the origins of agriculture in Africa, there is a general consensus that agriculture emerged in three distinct regions: along the Nile River in Egypt, in the eastern Sahara of Sudan, and in the great bend of the Niger River of West Africa. The oldest evidence for agriculture in Africa can be found in Egypt along the Nile River valley. There, sometime after 7000 BCE, agricultural technology and knowledge about the domestication of wheat, barley, sheep, goats, and cattle were introduced into the region, likely from southwest Asia. The introduction of these methods transformed the region and put Egypt on the path to greatness. Over the next few thousand years, these practices were disseminated west across North Africa to Libya, Tunisia, Algeria, and Morocco.

In the grasslands south of the Sahara, agriculture emerged independently. The origins of that process can be traced to as early as 9000 BCE, when the Nilo-Saharan people of the region began to adopt the grain-collecting and grinding techniques of their northern neighbors and applied them to sorghum and pearl millet, the tropical grasses of the Nile region. These changes were made possible by a millennia-long wet phase beginning around 11,000 BCE. During this period, monsoon-like weather conditions prevailed, drenching the region of the Sahara and creating lakes and a lush landscape covered in grasses and acacia forests that was home to countless varieties of wildlife. By around 8000 BCE, the Nilo-Saharans had domesticated wild cattle of the Red Sea hills and had begun to produce pottery they used to store and cook these grains. By as early as 6000 BCE, the gathering of these wild grains had begun to evolve into deliberate domestication. Over the next few thousand years, the Nilo-Saharans domesticated a host of other plants, including watermelons, cotton, and gourds.

Agriculture also emerged independently, far to the west of the Nilo-Saharans in the bend of the Niger River of West Africa. There, the domestication of yams by the Niger-Congo peoples developed gradually and likely in a piecemeal fashion beginning possibly around the same time the Nilo-Saharans of the eastern Sahara were adopting agriculture. Certainly, by 3000 BCE, the Niger-Congo peoples of West Africa were actively clearing land with stone tools to plant crops such as yams, the oil palm, peas, and groundnuts. Over the next couple thousand years, the Niger-Congo peoples also domesticated a uniquely African variety of rice, which they grew in the wetlands of the Niger River region.

 LINK TO LEARNING

In this article, the ancient climate and geography of the Congo River Basin (https://openstax.org/l/77CongoBasin) are examined.

The impact of farming was enhanced by advances in metallurgy. Bronze was introduced into Egypt from the Near East and Eastern Mediterranean a little before 3000 BCE. From there, bronze technology was gradually disseminated west across North Africa as well as south up the Nile into sub-Saharan Africa. Being far harder than the farming materials these populations were previously using, the introduction of bronze greatly increased agricultural production. Unlike wooden plows, which allow only scratch farming, bronze-bladed plows pulled by oxen could dig deep into the ground and turnover large amounts of earth.

Iron tools in Egypt during the Bronze Age were not unknown. Indeed, an iron dagger was placed in Pharaoh Tutankhamun's tomb in 1323 BCE, and archaeologists have found several hundred iron objects in sites around the Near East and Eastern Mediterranean which date to centuries before the start of the Iron Age. Most of these iron objects, however, were ornamental and include things like iron jewelry. It was only after about 1000 BCE that the number of iron tools began to overtake the number of bronze tools across the Near East. The reason for this is that iron is far more difficult to produce than bronze. The types of iron objects that could be produced earlier were inferior to bronze in strength, which is why the early objects tended to be ornamental. Only during the Late Bronze Age Collapse (1200–1100 BCE), when tin was difficult to acquire, did people begin experimenting with iron more seriously. By about 900 BCE, numerous blacksmiths around the Near East had mastered the art of creating iron tools that were far superior in strength to bronze. Evidence of sophisticated ironworking technology in Egypt dates to the seventh century BCE, introduced to the area from other parts of the Near East.

For many years, modern historians assumed that ironworking technologies spread to other parts of Africa from Egypt. The prevailing consensus now, however, is that ironworking technology was likely developed independently in sub-Saharan Africa. Most modern scholars agree that iron smelting in sub-Saharan Africa likely preexisted its introduction into Egypt by a few centuries. The earliest evidence dates to about 1000 BCE and comes from Central Africa—modern Chad, the Central African Republic, and South Sudan. From there the technology appears to have spread west to the Niger River area and, by 500 BCE, was being used by the Nok culture of West Africa.

Settling around the confluence of the Benue and Niger Rivers in present-day Nigeria, the Nok initially used iron to fashion jewelry. Eventually they began using it to make farming tools and weapons as well. The obvious utility of iron for fashioning tougher and more durable tools used to clear forests, aerate land, and dig trench-based irrigation systems led others to adopt the new material. As a result, over the next several centuries, ironworking technology spread around West Africa and later far beyond. In the hands of migrating Bantus, iron technology was indispensable. They used iron tools to clear the surrounding trees and extended prehistoric irrigation systems by digging deeper furrows, shored up with embankments, to create Iron Age farms. In the process, they spread ironworking technology throughout equatorial and subequatorial Africa.

BEYOND THE BOOK

The Iron Age in Africa
It had been thought that ironworking originated in modern-day Turkey around 1500 BCE. However, new evidence suggests that the discovery of iron metallurgy happened in Central Africa—modern Chad, the Central African Republic, and South Sudan—around the same time, likely as a by-product of firing ceramics. Today, most modern scholars agree that iron smelting in sub-Saharan Africa likely preexisted its introduction into Egypt by a few

centuries with the earliest evidence dating to about 1000 BCE.

Ironworking revolutionized human civilization in Africa. It helped make large-scale agriculture possible because it produced stronger tools for farming, including shovels and furrow-diggers. Iron axes and knives enabled Africans to clear paths through the densest parts of the Central African rainforest. In so doing, they exposed new areas for settlement and opened corridors between historically isolated regions, connecting them for the first time.

These corridors allowed for migration as well as the diffusion of cultures, a process that introduced to other prehistoric peoples not only new technologies but also new languages and the innovations of the Neolithic Revolution: the domestication of plants and animals. The advent of iron metalworking was a vital component in the laying of common cultural foundation throughout much of southern Africa and utterly transformed the societies found there.

Watch this short video about the origins of ironworking in Africa (https://openstax.org/l/77Ironwork) to learn more. Pay close attention to the circumstances that led to the discovery of iron smelting in Africa and why iron metallurgy proved so revolutionary to the societies that adopted it.

View multimedia content (https://openstax.org/books/world-history-volume-1/pages/9-2-the-emergence-of-farming-and-the-bantu-migrations)

- How was iron discovered in Africa? What were some of the first uses of iron?
- In what ways did iron transform African societies?
- Can you name other discoveries/innovations that had a similar impact on human civilization? What were they, and what was their impact?

The Bantu Migrations

The word "Bantu" is a modern term invented by linguists who have studied the languages of Africa. The word is made up of the common stem "ntu" and the plural prefix "ba" which put together literally means "people." It describes a large and geographically widespread subfamily of African languages that make up part of the larger Niger-Congo language family. There are well over four hundred known Bantu languages spoken today across a large portion of the southern half of Africa (Figure 9.12). Linguists believe that these similar languages derived from an ancient parent language often described as "proto-Bantu."

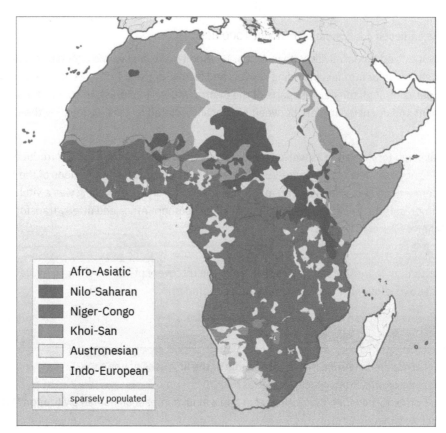

FIGURE 9.12 Africa's Wealth of Languages. This map shows the distribution of language groups in Africa that resulted from ancient migrations. The Bantu subfamily is part of the Niger-Congo family and extends from western Africa to the far south. (credit: modification of work "Languages of Africa map" by "Seb az86556"/Wikimedia Commons, CC BY 3.0)

Theories about the spread of the Bantu speakers have changed over the last several decades. For example, it was once believed that the spread occurred relatively recently, meaning over the last several centuries. It was also assumed that the process took the form of conquering bands of Bantu speakers who subjugated or even annihilated those they came into contact with. We know now that the process began several thousand years ago and proceeded in a piecemeal fashion as small groups of Bantu speakers spread across the larger area, integrating and intermarrying into the largely hunter-gatherer communities they met.

It is generally accepted today that the original proto-Bantu speakers emerged and lived in the area between modern-day Nigeria and Cameroon in West and Central Africa. A Neolithic people, the proto-Bantu were farmers who subsisted by cultivating pearl millet and yams and extracting oil from the abundant palm and bush candle trees of the region's luxuriant rainforests. Gradual changes in weather patterns caused the rainforests to recede and, together with increasingly seasonal (rather than constant) rainfall, opened tracts of savanna between forested areas. Over time, these open patches merged to form the Sangha River Interval, a 200-mile-wide grassland running north–south between modern-day southeastern Cameroon, southern Central African Republic, and northern Republic of Congo. This grassland corridor allowed the previously forest-dwelling Bantu to move southward, through what had once been impenetrable tropical rainforest.

The expansion of the Bantu speakers beyond that region and across other parts of sub-Saharan African likely began between 3000 and 2000 BCE and is referred to as the **Bantu migrations** (Figure 9.13). Although scholars debate the precise timing, motivation, and directions of these migrations, linguistic evidence and archaeological traces of pottery and ironmaking technology suggest there were multiple waves. The earliest seems to have consisted of two phases: an initial eastern stream or "early split," and a somewhat later western "rivers and coasts" stream. In both phases, pioneering groups moved gradually and sporadically, first proceeding eastward across the northern reaches of the Congo Forest and arriving in the Great Lakes region of East Africa around 1500 BCE.

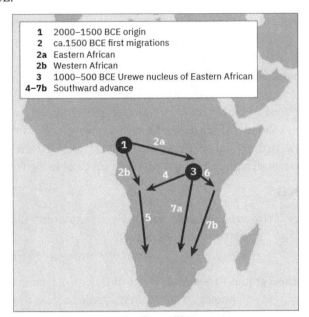

FIGURE 9.13 The Bantu Migrations. Two streams of ancient Bantu migration originated in the Bantu homeland, located in West and Central Africa: (1) an eastward "early split" (2a) and a southward "western" expansion (2b). In later waves of migration, Bantu groups moved on from the Great Lakes region (3) in a generally southward advance (4–7). (credit: modification of work "Map showing the Bantu expansion" by Derek Nurse und Gérard Philippson/"Botev"/Wikimedia Commons, Public Domain)

Dominated by the Urewe culture, the Great Lakes region was one of the oldest centers of iron smelting in Africa. It was likely from the Urewe that the Bantu learned the iron-forging techniques that enabled them to later produce carbon steel. The Urewe also produced the earliest East African Iron Age pottery, called Urewe ware. Confidently dated to between the second and fifth centuries CE, Urewe ware is found in the Great Lakes region and is recognizable by the distinctive indentation on the bases of its bowls and pots, which gives it the name "dimple-based" pottery. Kwale ware, a related style, has been discovered in the region to the east of the Rift Valley, in southern Kenya and northern Tanzania. Kwale ware appears to be an offshoot of the earlier Urewe ware and dates to the Early Iron Age, around the third century. Archaeologists and historians have traced the southward thrust of the eastern stream of Bantu in the third and fourth centuries by uncovering Iron Age slag sites and related styles of pottery in Malawi and Mozambique.

As small clusters of Bantu advanced into modern Kenya and Tanzania, some turned toward Congo, while other groups pushed southward in the direction of southern East Africa. By the seventh century, Bantu communities stretched from the extreme southern reaches of Somalia in the north to Natal and Eastern Cape in present-day South Africa. Along the way, they created key cultural elements that were the bases for later civilizations, including the Swahili speakers of the East African coast.

The western stream of Bantu migration progressed considerably more slowly than the eastward stream, advancing south along the West African coast into modern Gabon and the Democratic Republic of Congo, with small groups branching off to follow the Congo River system inland as early as 1500 BCE. Early Iron Age farm settlements dating from around the second century CE have been uncovered in southwestern Congo, near Kinshasa, but some of the most impressive and revealing evidence of Iron Age Bantu settlements comes from the savanna woodlands around Lake Kale in southeastern Congo. Here, archaeologists have uncovered evidence of extensive copper and iron smelting, with copper used for trade and to fashion jewelry, while iron was forged into tools and weapons. The westward stream penetrated deeper into the south-central African interior, where Kalundu and Dambwa pottery, Early Iron Age styles specific to this flow of Bantu, have been identified in the Zambezi valley. This evidence dates to the same period of southward expansion that has been linked to the eastward early split Bantu.

It was not until the early centuries of the Common Era that the western stream penetrated Angola in the far southern extreme of West Africa. Around this time, East Africa witnessed a third phase of Bantu expansion, with groups moving through and settling in parts of modern Mozambique, Botswana, and eastern South Africa. It appears that all three streams of Bantu migration—the western stream, the early split, and its later southward-bound branch—converged on the Zambezi valley (Figure 9.13). By 500 CE, all parts of the vast tropical rainforest had been settled by Bantu farming communities. Populations of Bantu-speaking peoples could now be found throughout southern Africa, from the savanna woodland south of the Congo forest and that of northern Namibia in the west, to the Great Lakes region of East Africa, western Tanzania, and eastern Botswana in the east, to the Transvaal high veld, Natal, and Eastern Cape in the south.

⊚ LINK TO LEARNING

As the Bantu migrated, did they arrive as conquerors, colonizers, or explorers? Listen to the BBC's "The Story of Africa" (https://openstax.org/l/77StoryAfrica) and learn more.

The Bantu were among the earliest groups to benefit from the diffusion of farming, herding and animal keeping, and advanced metalworking technologies, and they dispersed across the continent changing its linguistic and cultural landscape along the way. Pioneers originating in West and Central Africa advanced sporadically as small groups of people moving from one point to another. During the earliest centuries of expansion, groups of Bantu arrived in regions that were only thinly populated by groups of nomadic hunter-gatherers. The land was unsettled, enabling the Bantu to select the best sites for their farms, and because there was no need to clear thick forest or adopt new techniques to suit a difficult environment, their expansion across the subcontinent proceeded relatively rapidly. New generations could simply move to new areas. Initially, then, Bantu farm settlements were typically confined to fertile river valleys and regions with favorable rainfall—which helps explain why they moved toward the southeast, a path that avoided the much drier southwest.

The situation changed, however, as the birth of each new generation put pressure on a given area's limited resources. Growing needs necessitated further expansion, and as the Bantu advanced into the rainforest—their path helpfully cleared with new iron tools—they began to adjust their cultivation techniques to a variety of conditions. Although it may seem so, the tropical rainforest is not—and has never been—a uniform ecosystem: its topography and climate vary greatly from river valleys and swampy regions to dense forest canopies and plateaus, and across highlands and lowlands. Each of these environments requires different cultivation techniques, knowledge the Bantu acquired only after their gradual occupation of all parts of the rainforest and centuries of experimentation and adaptation. Their efforts were so effective that by the sixth century CE, Bantu farming communities had settled in virtually all parts of the tropical rainforest.

But the Bantu did not stop at the rainforest. Rather, they continued to drift southward and eventually emerged into the southern savanna, where they found an environment not unlike the grasslands they had encountered north of the rainforest. Like the rainforest, southern Africa was also lightly populated by foragers and hunter-gatherers, leaving vast swaths of land open for the Bantu farmers to inhabit. They expanded into this region seeking new land, a migratory process repeated by generations of their successors. Initially, the diffusion of the Bantu speakers south of the rainforest followed an easterly direction and hugged the southern and eastern edges of the rainforest. When they began to settle around Lake Victoria, the Bantu acquired cattle. From there, a general dispersal into eastern and southern Africa began.

Although the areas into which the Bantu migrated were only sparsely populated, interactions with the peoples who already lived there were unavoidable. It is not entirely clear what these meetings were like, but evidence suggests that interactions were complex and included elements of cultural absorption and assimilation as well as displacement, often at the same time. Early on, the Bantu moved in relatively small numbers, so there were no large-scale displacements of hunter-gatherer societies. It was some time before the Iron Age farmers came to dominate their Neolithic contemporaries.

At first, there was enough room for both societies to coexist in relative harmony. Oral tradition and linguistic evidence indicate that the Bantu intermingled with some of these populations, including rainforest-dwelling peoples such as the Twa and the Khoekhoe herders of South Africa. Had it not been for the rainforest dwellers, the Bantu may have had a far more difficult time adjusting to the environment. Indeed, Bantu oral tradition holds that it was rainforest dwellers like the Twa who taught them to adapt. It is also likely that the Bantu acquired their cattle—or at least their cattle-herding techniques—from the Khoisan, a cattle- and goat-herding people who preceded them in southern Africa. In fact, many of the words in the southern Bantu language that relate to cattle and cattle-herding practices are derived from Khoisan. This linguistic heritage is reinforced by the presence today of Khoisan "click" sounds in certain Bantu languages, particularly those of the south.

Yet displacements did occur. The peoples who dwelled in the rainforest had all descended from a common population, but the arrival of the more technologically advanced Bantu farmers caused them to scatter into separate groups. On entering San territory, for example, the Bantu farmers displaced the previously dominant San and Khoekhoe peoples, the first inhabitants of South Africa. Forced from their home territories by the Iron Age farmers, the San and Khoekhoe embarked on their own widespread migrations. The Bantu were not dominant everywhere in southern Africa, however. In the drier, sandier areas of the western Kalahari Desert and Namibia, Khoisan speakers remained the dominant group until more recent times.

Overall, the Bantu migrations had a significant impact on Africa's economic and cultural practices. As they migrated, the Bantu encountered different groups whose adaptations to their environments had produced innovations in plant and animal husbandry and metalworking. The Bantu borrowed and adapted these over a generations-long expansion across and throughout sub-Saharan Africa, forging a package of common cultural advances that they gradually diffused among the peoples in the areas they settled. In the long term, the Bantu laid a common cultural framework throughout much of sub-Saharan Africa. This enabled them to forge complex settled societies that later became the bases of large African states, such as medieval Great Zimbabwe, that could dominate whole regions.

9.3 The Kingdom of Kush

LEARNING OBJECTIVES

By the end of this section, you will be able to:
- Explore the origins and rise of the Kingdom of Kush
- Describe the relationship between the Kingdom of Kush and Egyptian culture
- Analyze the transformations in Nubia following the founding of Meroe

The traditional southern boundary of Ancient Egypt was the first cataract of the Nile. A **cataract** is a place in a river where the otherwise placid flow is upset by a waterfall, a shallow portion, or the presence of boulders that make the river impassable by boats. Downriver of the first cataract, the river is largely unobstructed and serves as a fertile highway skirting through an otherwise desert and connecting the Egyptian settlements and facilitating the dissemination of a uniform Egyptian culture. Since the cataract served as a physical barrier, it largely limited Egyptian influence south of it and thus allowed distinct cultures and kingdoms to emerge along the upper reaches of the Nile.

Nubia was the name Egyptians gave to the expansive area south of the first cataract and extending into sub-Saharan Africa. The kingdom that first emerged in Nubia was called Kush. Because of its location along the Nile, throughout its long history the Kingdom of Kush was culturally influenced by Egypt. However, because it was sufficiently distant from Egypt, it also had the liberty to develop its own traditions, culture, language, and impressive history.

The Origin and Rise of the Kingdom of Kush

The history of the Nubian Kingdom of Kush is bound up in the history of Egypt, its northern neighbor. It was heavily influenced by Egypt throughout much of its long history. And at one point during the eighth century BCE, a line of Kushite kings even sat on the throne of Egypt. At that time, the kingdom stretched from the Nile delta south to the confluence of the Blue and White Niles outside Khartoum, the capital of present-day northern Sudan (Figure 9.14). But the origins of the Kingdom of Kush date back almost two thousand years before that impressive period.

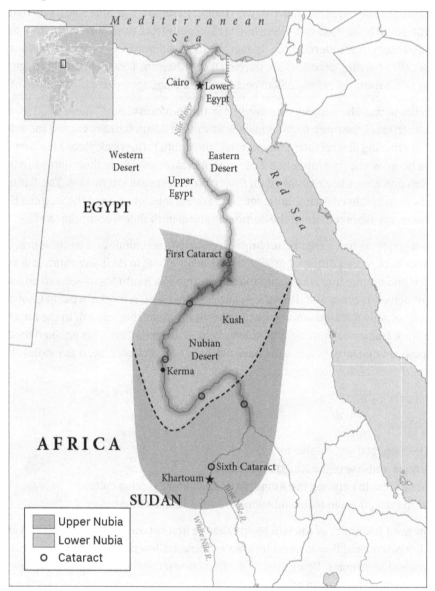

FIGURE 9.14 The Kingdom of Kush. Africa's ancient Kingdom of Kush originated to the south of Upper Egypt in the northern (lower) part of Nubia. This is the area that today straddles the border between Egypt and Sudan. In later centuries, the Kingdom of Kush moved its center farther south into southern (upper) Nubia. (credit: modification of work "Political Middle East" by CIA/The World Factbook, Public Domain)

Although the earliest period of Nubian history is shrouded in mystery, we do know that kingdoms from Nubia engaged in trade with the Egyptian Old Kingdom (c. 2686–2181 BCE). Goods of particular interest to the Old Kingdom Egyptians seem to have been ostrich feathers, ivory, ebony, incense, and especially gold, a commodity that played a vital role in pharaonic ritual and ceremony. For example, craftspeople used Nubian gold to fashion the sarcophagus mask of Tutankhamun, arguably Egypt's most famous pharaoh.

The earliest Nubian state arose sometime around 2400 BCE and was organized around the city of Kerma (in present-day northern Sudan) located just south of the Nile's third cataract in a lush floodplain ideal for agriculture and the pasturage of animals. The city's wealth and prosperity were symbolized by its great walls, behind which lay a palace, religious buildings, dwellings, and roads, as well as a funerary complex that included a temple and chapel. At the heart of the urban center lay a large temple known today as the Western Deffufa. A **deffufa** is a form of mud-brick architecture specific to Nubia. There are three known deffufas in the area today. Of these, the two best known are the large Western Deffufa and less well-preserved Eastern Deffufa some two kilometers away. The Western Deffufa is an impressively large three-story temple reaching nearly sixty feet in height. Religious ceremonies (possibly involving ancestor worship, although we do not know their actual nature) were held in this massive structure (Figure 9.15). At its height, around the eighteenth century BCE, Kerma may have supported a population of about ten thousand people.

FIGURE 9.15 The Western Deffufa. Kerma's Western Deffufa is one of three such massive temples known to exist. It is fifty-nine feet tall, and its complex extends over fifteen thousand square feet. (credit: "Western Deffufa – Kerma" by Walter Callens/Wikimedia Commons, CC BY 2.0)

It seems to have been the Egyptians who first referred to the Nubian city-state of Kerma as "Kush." Beginning during the rise of Egypt's Middle Kingdom (2040–1782 BCE), the Egyptian state initiated a centuries-long but intermittent expansion southward, a process that entailed the establishment of fortresses to consolidate its control over regional trade. Over time, its trade with Kush grew, and the area became increasingly wealthy. Although the Egyptians' southward advance was periodically stymied, usually by internal political problems occasioned by the death of a pharaoh and the chaos that ensued, their progress seemed inexorable.

When the Middle Kingdom collapsed and the Second Intermediate Period (1782–1570 BCE) began, trade and Egyptian contact with Kush declined. This left the Egyptian fortresses to fend for themselves. For a short time, the fortress communities attempted to become independent entities. But by at least 1650 BCE, the expanding power of the emerging Kingdom of Kush absorbed them. As this happened, the Kingdom of Kush also adopted elements of Egyptian culture, integrating Egyptian artistic styles and technology into their practices. Additionally, the leaders of Kush during this time cooperated with Hyksos-controlled Lower Egypt to keep the native Egyptian center of power located at Thebes weak.

Leaders in Kush had good reason to believe that a strong Egypt threatened their survival. And when the native Egyptian rulers began to grow their power and inaugurated the New Kingdom (1570–1069 BCE), they soon expanded into Kush. By the time Pharaoh Thutmose I came to the throne in about 1506 BCE, the Egyptians had extended their control of the Nile valley as far as the Nile's second cataract. Thutmose was determined to conquer Kerma. His forces sacked and burned the city, desecrating its great temple with the unsettling inscription, "There is not one of them left. The Nubian bowmen have fallen to slaughter, and are laid low throughout their land." Decades later, Thutmose III built a temple to the god Amun at Napata, just below the fourth cataract of the Nile. For the next five hundred years, Egypt controlled Nubia, and the region was further Egyptianized—that is, it was made Egyptian in character. The Kingdom of Kush was crushed as New Kingdom pharaohs asserted their control over Nubia, constructed Egyptian-style architecture, and promoted the use of Egyptian hieroglyphs on temples and Demotic (ancient Egyptian) script by the region's Egyptian administrators.

IN THEIR OWN WORDS

The Nubian Travels of Harkhuf, Egyptian Governor of Aswan

Nubia was rich in resources, and Egyptian pharaohs often sent provincial governors there to trade for gold, ivory, and feathers and recruit soldiers. Following is an excerpt from the travel writings of Harkhuf, an Egyptian noble from Aswan in southern Egypt. Harkhuf held many titles, including governor of the south and ritual priest. A caravan trader by profession, he made multiple journeys into Nubia for the Old Kingdom monarchs, the details of which were inscribed on his tomb.

> The majesty of Mernere, (my) lord, sent me together with (my) father, the "sole companion" and lector-priest Iri, to(wards) Yam (Upper Nubia) in order to explore the way to this country. I accomplished it within seven months, and I brought all kinds of products therefrom, beautiful and exotic. I was much praised about it.

> When his majesty sent me a second time, I was alone: I went forth on the "Ivory Road" and I descended from Irthet, Mekher, Tereres, Irtheth in a period of eight months. And I went down, and I brought (back) of the product from this country very much, the like of which had never been brought to this land (i.e. Egypt) before.

> And when his majesty sent me a third time to Yam, I departed from the Thinite districts on the Oasis Road. I discovered that the chief of Yam had gone by himself to the land of Temeh in order to beat Temeh to the western corner of heaven. When I had gone out in his support to the land of Temeh, I appeased him, so that he was praising all gods for the sovereign . . .

> I descended with three hundred asses loaded with myrrh, ebony, heknu, grain, leopard skin, ivory tusks . . . (and) all beautiful products. And when the chief of Irthet, Sethu, and Wawat saw that the troops of the Yamians, who had descended with me for the Residence, and the soldiers, who had been sent with me, were strong and numerous, then this chief supported me and gave me cattle and goats and showed me the ways of the ridges of Irthet, as the vigilance which I carried out was more excellent than that of any associate-overseer of mercenaries sent to Yam before.

> —Harkfuf's tomb inscription

- Why were the Egyptian kings interested in Nubia?
- What does the excerpt suggest about the strength of the Nubian army?

With the decline of the New Kingdom and the beginning of Egypt's Third Intermediate Period (1069–525 BCE), local leaders in Nubia were able to reassert their independence. As Egypt withdrew, Nubians built up a new independent Kushite kingdom around the city of Napata, just above the fourth cataract and beyond the Nile floodplain but within the zone of tropical summer rainfall and a region of fertile soil. Despite efforts to assert a specifically Nubian culture, the rulers at Napata were still largely Egyptianized—they built temples to Egyptian gods in Egyptian styles, increased trade with Egypt, and governed their state along Egyptian lines.

By the year 736 BCE, the Kushite kingdom centered on Napata was growing in power and influence, as evidenced by the fact that a Kushite king named Piye managed to install his own sister as high priestess of Amun in Thebes. Such a move was tantamount to an assertion of Kushite authority over Upper Egypt itself and appears to have precipitated a war. During the war, King Piye of Kush marched his army down the river to the Nile delta, effectively conquering all of Egypt. This move inaugurated a period of Nubian rule in Egypt that lasted for several decades. Egyptologists refer to this unique period as the Twenty-Fifth Dynasty or the Ethiopian dynasty.

The Nubian leaders who ruled Egypt during this period were thoroughly Egyptianized in culture and religious traditions. As a result, they ruled as Egyptian leaders, carefully preserving Egyptian cultural practices and traditions as a way to strengthen legitimacy. Like other pharaohs, the Kushite pharaohs wore the traditional double crown, promoted the worship of Egyptian deities, and constructed architectural testaments to their rule in the Egyptian style (Figure 9.16).

FIGURE 9.16 Pharaoh Chabaka. Like pharaohs before and after, the Kushite pharaohs of the Twenty-Fifth Dynasty inscribed their names on temples using traditional Egyptian hieroglyphics. This stone remnant displays the name of the Kushite pharaoh Chabaka. (credit: modification of work "Cartouche au nom du pharaon Chabaka (Ägyptisches Museum Berlin AM 31235)" by "Tangopaso"/Wikimedia Commons, Public Domain)

The Meroitic Period in Nubia

The rise of the Neo-Assyrian Empire and completion of its conquest of Egypt in 656 BCE brought an end to Nubian rule in Egypt. The Kushite leadership fled Thebes and reconstituted their kingdom at a new capital, Meroe, located well south of the fifth cataract. This effort inaugurated the Meroitic period of the Kingdom of Kush. Sometimes called the Island of Meroe because of the way the Nile and Atbara rivers flowed around it, the new capital had several distinct advantages. One advantage was its distance from Egypt, which helped to protect it from raiding and conquests coming from the north. Another advantage was the plentiful iron ore in the surrounding land. As discussed previously, iron smelting technology had only recently reached Egypt in the early 600s BCE. But after facing the well-trained iron-wielding army of Assyria, the Kushite leadership came to appreciate the utility of this metal both as a part of their economy and as a defensive measure against possible invasion. Over time, the iron workers in Meroe earned a reputation for producing high-quality tools well regarded by kingdoms and empires far beyond its boundaries.

Archaeological work done at Meroe suggests that the site was occupied at least a couple hundred years before the Assyrians arrived in Egypt. There is evidence of possibly royal or at least elite tombs at the site which have been dated to the early ninth century BCE. While the earliest inhabitants may not have recognized the benefits of the rich iron ore deposits, they surely would have appreciated the environmental conditions. Unlike lower reaches of the Nile, which were known for wide floodplains and insufficient rainfall, Meroe is far enough south to receive natural watering from the sub-Saharan tropical rains. This meant that the agriculturalists of Meroe were not entirely reliant on the waters of the Nile. Instead, they could expand their farms of sorghum and millet out across the landscape and depend on the plentiful rainfall.

Given its proximity to the Red Sea, Meroe became an important trading center. Evidence from Persia, Egypt, and Rome indicates that iron, wood, elephants, and ivory flowed from Meroe to the wider world. Meroe was also known for its distinctive jewelry produced by highly skilled artisans and made with a great variety of materials. As the goods flowed out, wealth flowed back in. According to some accounts, the wealth of Meroe was so well known that Persia in the sixth century BCE once attempted to conquer the kingdom and add it to its enormous empire. Whether this story is based in fact is up for debate, though it is undeniable that the Persians were quite familiar with the wealth of Meroe. Records indicate that ivory from Meroe was used to decorate the palace of Darius I at Susa. Additionally, stone reliefs at Persepolis appear to show a Nubian delegation bringing gifts of ivory and exotic animals to the Persian king.

Having had many centuries of cultural contact with Egypt, it is no surprise that Egyptian influences in writing, architecture, and religion persisted despite the great geographic distance. The use of Egyptian hieroglyphs, for example, continued for centuries until it was ultimately replaced by Meroitic, an alpha-syllabic script derived from the Egyptian Demotic script. Similarly, the Meroitic rulers constructed pyramids for their rulers just as they had seen and clearly admired in Egypt. Unlike the much older pyramids in Egypt, however, the Meroitic variants were smaller, with steep sides and blunt tops (Figure 9.17). Finally, traces of Egyptian religious practices endured throughout Meroe's long history, albeit gradually and predictably deviating from the original practices as time went on. For example, the Kushite religious traditions eventually included the worship of the lion-headed god Apademak. This was a war god worshipped exclusively by the people of Kush, though it was often depicted in an artistic style clearly influenced by Egyptian culture.

FIGURE 9.17 Pyramids at Meroe. The royal necropolis at Meroe contains distinctive burial pyramids for dozens of royal officials including kings, queens, and crown princes. The tallest is ninety-six feet high. Two other cemeteries contain more than a hundred additional pyramids. (credit: "Pyramids N26 and N27" by "Wufei07"/Wikimedia Commons, Public Domain)

🔗 LINK TO LEARNING

Through trade and conflict, Egypt left a deep mark on Nubian culture, manifesting in architecture, art, architecture, religion, and even language. Yet Nubian culture was not entirely subsumed by Egyptian influences, and the two often coexisted in the same work of art.

Use these links to explore the Nubian art collection (https://openstax.org/l/77NubianArt) and Egyptian collection (https://openstax.org/l/77EgyptArt) at the Museum of Fine Arts, Boston.

The majority of people worked in the fields and the grazing pastures. They lived in mud homes within small rural villages overseen by minor chiefs of family clans. The elite, ruling families, and artisans, on the other hand, lived in larger towns. The entire kingdom was ruled by monarchs from the reigning family. However, unlike in Egypt where succession to the throne tended to flow from father to son, in the Meroitic kingdom, the monarch was carefully selected by a group made up of local chiefs, military officials, and other high officials. While theoretically the ultimate authority in the land, the power of the kings was limited by customs, taboos, and the consent of the nobility and the priestly class. Unpopular monarchs could be and were removed if they fell out of favor with either of these groups. There was also the position of the **kentake**, or queen mother. The *kentake* exercised a degree of official power somewhere above the highest officials and below that of the king. On several occasions, the *kentakes* themselves, given the right circumstances, could assume complete power and even lead armies into battle.

DUELING VOICES

Witnessing Kush: Kushite and Greek Perspectives

Eyewitness accounts of ancient civilizations provide invaluable primary source evidence for historians. Such sources are far scarcer than modern ones, and written accounts of ancient sub-Saharan Africa are even rarer. Often, what source material we have comes not from Africans but from outsiders—travelers, invaders, or occupiers (perhaps all three).

The first excerpt that follows is an inscription attributed to Aspalta, king of Kush (c. 600 BCE), and the other is an account by the Greek historian Herodotus (c. 430 BCE). Consider the approaches they adopted to documenting Kush and what the differences suggest about the values of their respective societies.

Now then, the trusted commanders from the midst of the army of His Majesty were six men, while the trusted commanders and overseers of fortresses were six men. [. . .] Then they said to the entire army, "Come, let us cause our lord to appear, for we are like a herd which has no herdsman!" Thereupon this army was very greatly concerned, saying, "Our lord is here with us, but we do not know him! Would that we might know him, that we might enter in under him and work for him, ..." Then the army of His Majesty all said with one voice, "Still there is this god Amon-Re, Lord of the Thrones of It-Tjwy, Resident in Napata. He is also a god of Kush. Come, let us go to him. . . . .

So the commanders of His Majesty and the officials of the palace went to the Temple of Amon. . . . They said to [the priests], "Pray, may this god, Amon-Re, Resident in Napata, come, to permit that he give us our lord, to revive us, to build the temples of all the gods and goddesses of Kemet, and to present their divine offerings! We cannot do a thing without this god. It is he who guides us. . . . Then the commanders of His Majesty and the officials of the palace entered into the temple and put themselves upon their bellies before this god. They said, "We have come to you, O Amon-Re, Lord of the Thrones of It-Tjwy, Resident in Napata, that you might give to us a lord, to revive us, to build the temples of the gods of Kemet and Rekhyt, and to present divine offerings. That beneficent office is in your hands—may you give it to your son whom you love!"

—attributed to Aspalta, king of Kush (c. 600 BCE)

I went as far as Elephantine [Aswan] to see what I could with my own eyes, but for the country still further south I had to be content with what I was told in answer to my questions. . . .

The Ethiopians . . . are said to be the tallest and handsomest men in the whole world. In their customs they differ greatly from the rest of mankind, and particularly in the way they choose their kings; for they find out the man who is the tallest of all the citizens, and of strength equal to his height, and appoint him to rule over them. [. . .] The spies were told that most of them lived to be a hundred and twenty years old, while some even went beyond that age—they ate boiled flesh, and had for their drink nothing but milk. Among these Ethiopians copper is of all metals the most scarce and valuable. Also, last of all, they were allowed to behold the coffins of the Ethiopians, which are made (according to report) of crystal, after the following fashion: When the dead body has been dried, either in the Egyptian, or in some other manner, they cover the whole with gypsum, and adorn it with painting until it is as like the living man as possible. Then they place the body in a crystal pillar which has been hollowed out to receive it. . . . The next of kin keep the crystal pillar in their houses for a full year from the time of the death, and give it the first fruits continually, and honor it with sacrifice. After the year is out they bear the pillar forth, and set it up near the town. [. . .]

Where the south declines towards the setting sun lies the country called Ethiopia, the last inhabited land in that direction. There gold is obtained in great plenty, huge elephants abound, with wild trees of all sorts, and ebony; . . . . The Ethiopians were clothed in the skins of leopards and lions, and had long bows made of the stem of the palm-leaf, not less than four cubits in length. On these they laid short arrows made of reed, and armed at the tip, not with iron, but with a piece of stone, sharpened to a point, of the kind used in engraving seals. They carried likewise spears, the head of which was the sharpened horn of an antelope; and in addition they had knotted clubs. When they went into battle they painted their bodies, half with chalk, and half with vermilion.

—Herodotus, *The Histories*, Book III

• What do these accounts tell us about how Nubian civilization had changed from Aspalta's time to that of

Herodotus?

- Consider how the authors' viewpoints may have influenced their accounts and why. Is one voice more dependable than the other? Why or why not?

During the second and first centuries BCE, Roman power spread across the Mediterranean and, in the year 30 BCE, assumed control of Egypt. Around this same time, the Kushite kings of Meroe were also expanding their power northward. These two expanding powers inevitably clashed as Rome sought to secure its southern border and prevent further Meroitic expansion. In one reported encounter, the Romans came face-to-face with a possibly battle-scarred *kentake* leading an army. In another encounter at Syene (modern Aswan in southern Egypt), the Kushite forces of Meroe appear to have gotten the better of the Romans. Kushite soldiers pillaged the city and took with them a number of statues and other valuables, including a bronze head of the Roman emperor Augustus.

Not a group to leave such an affront unanswered, the Romans counterattacked and nearly destroyed Napata. When they finally left, they took with them several thousand Kush subjects whom they sold into slavery. Historians debate the nature of the subsequent relationship between Rome and the Meroitic Kingdom of Kush. Evidence suggests that at some point during the Augustan period, Kush was a client state of the Roman Empire. In exchange for its internal autonomy, Kush helped Rome secure its East African frontier by providing soldiers and support for garrisoned legions stationed in the kingdom.

The Kingdom of Kush reached a new high-water mark in its power and artistic achievement a few decades later under King Natakamani, in the early first century CE. During his reign, Kush also attained its maximum geographic extent, stretching from the Ethiopian foothills in the south to the Nile's first cataract in the north. Testifying to its wealth and influence during this period are the pyramids built under Natakamani as well as the temples that were constructed and restored, including one for the lion-headed god Apademak and the Egyptian god Amun (Figure 9.18).

FIGURE 9.18 Apademak, God of War. This small fragment of a votive plaque was carved from red siltstone in about

100 BCE and honors the Kushite war god Apedemak, who has a lion's head and carries a scepter with a small seated lion on top. (credit: "Votive Plaque of King Tanyidamani" by Walters Art Museum/Wikimedia Commons, Public Domain)

Despite earlier tensions, Meroe and Roman Egypt enjoyed mostly friendly relations for the next two centuries. During this time, however, Meroe's power began to wane, and the kingdom came to an end sometime in the fourth century CE. Scholars are uncertain what caused its decline, although environmental degradation due to the overuse of timber for charcoal manufacture may have been a factor. Trees were being cut down faster than they could replace themselves, which would likely have led to erosion and reduced fertility of the soil, so the land could no longer support a large urban population.

In addition, the weakening of the Roman Empire and its economic contraction in the third century led to a steep decline in demand for the types of luxury goods traded through Kush, especially the ivory, enslaved peoples, perfume, exotic animals, and hardwoods on which its economy depended. Having no partners of similar size and wealth with whom to trade African goods on a large scale, the kings of Kush found that Rome's economic crisis triggered a fiscal crisis for them. Perhaps the final blow was the rise of the kingdom of Aksum. Better placed to take advantage of the Red Sea trade, Aksum starved Kush of regional commerce. Sometime around 350, the Aksumite king Ezana invaded Meroe but found the island capital of the Kingdom of Kush had been abandoned.

9.4 North Africa's Mediterranean and Trans-Saharan Connections

LEARNING OBJECTIVES

By the end of this section, you will be able to:
- Describe the interactions between North Africa, the Levant, and Europe
- Analyze the trade routes from North Africa to the Mediterranean, the Sahara, and the Levant

The Mediterranean coast of North Africa has been a crossroads of civilizations for millennia. Beginning in the first millennium BCE, it was occupied successively by a string of invaders, including the Phoenicians, Greeks, Romans, Vandals, and Arabs, and it has been the site of countless internal migrations, as in the case of the Mauri and Massylii peoples. One result of these interactions was a long-term process of cultural commingling, reabsorption, and acculturation that has left a rich tapestry of human societies in its wake.

North Africa and Egypt

The Phoenicians were responsible for the earliest known trade network that unified the Mediterranean world. A Semitic-speaking and seafaring people originally from the Levant, or eastern Mediterranean coast, the Phoenicians emerged initially from the areas around Tyre in what is present-day Lebanon (or Canaan in the Bible, which refers to the Phoenicians as the Canaanites). Around the end of the tenth century BCE, the Phoenicians began to found a series of trading posts and colonies along the Mediterranean coast, a loop of interconnected settlements that eventually stretched from Byblos in the east to Nimes and Gadir (Cadiz) in the west and Libdah (Leptis Magna) in the south (Figure 9.19). In 814 BCE, they established what would become their greatest settlement, Carthage. Located on the North African coast in modern-day Tunisia, Carthage was in an ideal position to dominate the trade activities of the western Mediterranean.

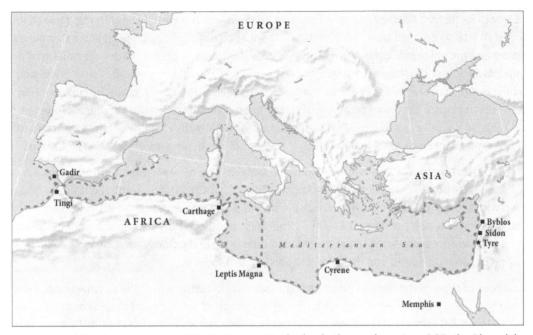

FIGURE 9.19 Phoenician Settlements and Trade Routes. Beginning in the tenth century BCE, the Phoenicians established colonies and trading outposts along the Mediterranean coasts of North Africa and southern Europe. Areas that experienced either Phoenician contact or settlement are those identified with the green dotted line. Carthage, the most impressive Phoenician settlement, juts out into the western Mediterranean from the North African coast, making it an ideal place to manage and control trade in the sea. (attribution: Copyright Rice University, OpenStax, under CC BY 4.0 license)

The government of Carthage was originally a monarchy, but by the turn of the fourth century BCE, it had given way to a republic. The Carthaginian republic was singled out for praise by the Greek philosopher Aristotle, who considered it the perfect balance between monarchy, aristocracy, and democracy. By this time, Carthage had been the dominant military power of the western Mediterranean for almost a century. By 300 BCE, the city controlled dozens of the trading towns that dotted the North African coast. Thus, by the start of the third century BCE, Carthaginian power and influence could be felt along a thousand-mile stretch of the Mediterranean.

At the time of Carthage's founding, the population of the **Maghreb**—the western half of North Africa, including most of present-day Morocco, Algeria, Tunisia, and Libya—spoke indigenous languages and had adapted their lives to the landscape. Those who lived on the coastal plains were mostly settled farmers, while those who lived in the Atlas Mountain range were seminomadic pastoralists, and nomadic peoples lived in the Sahara. To the Carthaginians, Greeks, and Romans, these North African natives were collectively known as **Berbers**[1], a pejorative term equating to "barbarian." This simplification belies the political, social, and cultural complexities of what was actually a wide range of different African ethnic groups and societies, including the Mauri, Massylii, Musulamii, Masaesylii, Garamantes, and Gaetuli. These groups had built impressive societies of their own. For example, the Garamantes developed a major urban society in the Libyan Fezzan, and the Masaesyli established the kingdom of Numidia. Over centuries of interaction, cooperation, and tension, a rich tapestry of customs, values, and traditions developed among these groups—who typically refer to themselves as Amazigh, or Imazighen, rather than Berber—to produce societies and cultural practices well suited to the Maghreb region of North Africa.

A city like Carthage, with its republican form of government and leaders who exercised political authority, levied taxes, enforced laws, and employed armed forces for defense, was foreign to the indigenous systems of

---

1   There is a growing awareness about the use of the term *Berber* to describe indigenous North Africans, many of whom self-identify as Amazigh, or Imazighen (plural). With this understanding, although we have introduced the term *Berber* as the most commonly used name in English, we have generally preferred to use the term *Amazigh* in this text.

the area. Early in its history, Carthage adopted a pragmatic relationship with its neighbors; it paid tribute to them to forestall attacks and facilitate good relations. But that changed after 480 BCE, when Carthage stopped paying tribute and moved to subjugate the region's peoples. In time, not only were the coastal towns dominated by Punic-speaking elite of Carthaginian origin, but the peoples of the inland towns began to adapt and adopt Carthaginian culture. Not only did they speak Punic, the language of the Phoenicians, but on occasion they also spoke Greek, particularly if they held positions of power or engaged in trade with Carthage. Moreover, the urban elite in these towns began to emulate Carthage, and eventually they founded their own states inland, such as Mauretania, which was established by the Mauri and Massylii peoples of the Atlas Mountains.

Carthaginian control over North Africa did not go unchallenged. The most significant threat to its dominance emerged with the rise of the Roman Republic in the third century BCE. To that point, the Romans had been preoccupied with consolidating their control over the Italian peninsula south of the River Rubicon, a process finally brought to an end with the defeat of Magna Graecia (as southern Italy was then called) in the Pyrrhic War in 275 BCE. Rome's encounter with Carthage led to three long and exhaustive conflicts known as the Punic Wars. The first began in 264 BCE, and the third wrapped up in 146 BCE.

The most famous of these is the Second Punic or Hannibalic War, during which the Carthaginian general Hannibal Barca (Figure 9.20) invaded Italy with tens of thousands of soldiers and dozens of war elephants. For over a decade, Hannibal terrorized the Romans, destroying their armies at Trebia (218 BCE), Lake Trasimene (217 BCE), and, in one of the most lethal battle days in history, the village of Cannae in 216 BCE. The Carthaginians were unable to inflict a decisive defeat on the Romans, however, and the deadlock remained unbroken until the Roman general Publius Cornelius Scipio took the war to Carthage, forcing Hannibal to return from Italy to North Africa to defend it.

FIGURE 9.20 Hannibal. This marble bust, believed to be of the Carthaginian general Hannibal Barca, was found in Capua, Italy, and may have been made in Hannibal's lifetime. (credit: "Image from page 299 of 'Republican Rome; her conquests, manners and institutions from the earliest times to the death of Caesar' (1914)" by Havell/Internet Archive Book Images/Flickr, Public Domain)

Carthage was finally defeated at the Battle of Zama in 202 BCE, a victory that earned Scipio the honorary name *Africanus* (Figure 9.21). Five decades later, urged on by the conservative senator Marcus Portius Cato (known to history as Cato the Censor), Rome returned to finish the job. The Third Punic War (149–146 BCE) ended with the destruction of Carthage. Tunis, some twenty miles inland, became the capital of Rome's new African province.

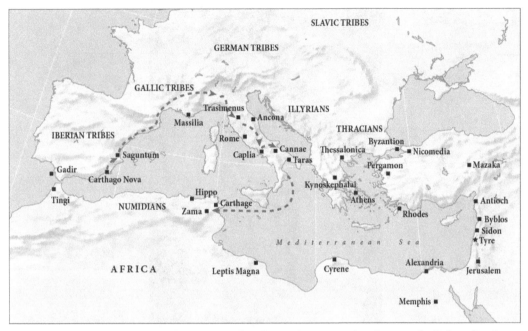

FIGURE 9.21 Hannibal's War (218–203 BCE). This map shows the route taken by Hannibal's invading forces in the Second Punic War. (attribution: Copyright Rice University, OpenStax, under CC BY 4.0 license)

The absorption of North Africa into the Roman Empire greatly affected the Indigenous African peoples of the region. Carthage had needed very little from the peoples who lived beyond its hinterland. What food the population required was supplied by Carthaginian estates located on the outskirts of the city. Rome, on the other hand, needed a great deal from the Maghrebi interior, including grain and olive oil to feed the capital's growing urban population. Decades of Roman development of the inland territory resulted in farms that, by the first decades of the Common Era, were generating hundreds of thousands of gallons of olive oil and millions of tons of wheat per year—all destined to feed the residents of Rome. This bounty earned North Africa the nickname "the breadbasket of Rome."

The intensification of agricultural production in the Maghreb led to the institution of individual land ownership and huge seasonal migrations of nomads and their animals to the coastal plains for work. To help control the flow of people during these periods and to protect crops from migrating cattle, the Romans established *limes* (lee-meis), or lines of fortified frontier posts that marked out the territorial limits of Roman occupation. Agricultural production also led to new growth for the old Phoenician coastal cities, which became commercial centers for shipping produce and livestock to Rome.

Eastern North Africa was also the site of great change in antiquity. In 332 BCE, Alexander the Great, king of Macedon in Greece, conquered Egypt, and before leaving to continue his advance into western Asia, he founded the great city of Alexandria on the Nile River. Following Alexander's death in 323 BCE, his generals warred with each other over control of the empire and eventually divided the vast territory among themselves. One officer, Ptolemy, took Egypt and founded a dynasty that ruled it for the next three centuries. Of necessity, the Ptolemies styled themselves as pharaohs to demonstrate continuity from pharaonic times through Alexander to themselves (Figure 9.22). They adapted the Egyptian style partially because they were awed by the history and grandeur of Egypt and also because the Ptolemies wanted the people to see them as legitimate rulers of Egypt, not foreigners. Like all the Hellenistic (or Greek-like) monarchs of the three-hundred-year period following the death of Alexander, they encouraged Greeks from around the Mediterranean to settle in one of the three Greek city-states established by the Macedonian conquerors, including Alexandria. The

Ptolemies also enticed Jewish people from Palestine to settle in northern Egypt, making Alexandria one of the most cosmopolitan cities in all antiquity.

FIGURE 9.22 Ptolemy III. As the Macedonian Greek rulers of Egypt, the Ptolemies styled themselves as pharaohs. This basalt statue from about 220 BCE is believed to be of Ptolemy III and shows him wearing Egyptian clothes and a pharaonic headdress. (credit: "Ptolemy III Euergetes" by "Szilas" in the Neues Museum, Berlin/Wikimedia Commons, Public Domain)

The focal point of Greek culture in Egypt was the *Museon* or Museum of Alexandria. This "Home of the Muses" was much more than a place to see artifacts from the past; it was also the world's largest library, housing some 700,000 scrolls representing all the knowledge of the known world. It had laboratories for the study of human anatomy and astronomy and was the home of dozens of intellectuals, who studied everything from geography and physics to literature and geometry. In many ways, it displaced the Academy at Athens as the ancient world's center of learning. It was at the *Museon*, for example, that the canonical versions of Homer's *Iliad* were identified, and that Eratosthenes developed his geographic understanding of the earth and estimated its circumference as between 24,500 and 29,000 miles (today we know it is 24,900 miles).

Day-to-day governance of Ptolemaic Egypt was in the hands of Egyptian officials and of Greek officials who brought Egyptian translators. To convincingly style themselves as pharaohs, the Ptolemies turned to religion. One of Ptolemy's first acts as ruler of Egypt was to seize the body of Alexander the Great as it was being transported from Babylon home to Macedonia. Ptolemy had an elaborate tomb built for Alexander and made it a focal point of the capital at Alexandria. He then declared Alexander a god, a move fully in keeping with the status bestowed upon him in life by Egypt's priests of Amun at Siwah in 332 BCE. In addition, Ptolemy had a temple dedicated to the new god Serapis built in the capital city. Serapis was an extraordinary deity demonstrating how astute Egypt's Greek rulers were. A fusion of the Egyptian deities Osiris and Apis and the Greek deities Zeus and Helios, Serapis allowed the very different subjects of Ptolemaic Egypt to find common ground in worship. To further cement their position as Egypt's legitimate rulers, the Ptolemies carried out the religious duties of the pharaoh, including dedicating new temples to Egyptian gods, visiting shrines throughout the country, and declaring themselves the inheritors of Alexander's godlike mantle.

The last of the Ptolemies was Cleopatra VII (Figure 9.23). A brilliant politician with a strong character, Cleopatra spoke upward of a dozen languages and was the only Greek ruler of Egypt fluent in Egyptian. Politically ambitious, she was determined to preserve what autonomy she could in the face of Rome's growing dominance of the Mediterranean. To this end, she had an affair with the Roman general and dictator Julius Caesar and bore him a child named Caesarion. When Caesar fell afoul of the Roman Senate (whose members suspected him of wanting to be king) and was assassinated in 44 BCE, Cleopatra shifted her affection to the inheritor of Caesar's armies, Marc Antony. This strategy was ill-fated, however, because Marc Antony was increasingly embroiled in a conflict with Octavian, Caesar's adopted son, which soon erupted in an all-out civil war between the two.

FIGURE 9.23 Cleopatra. This marble bust of Cleopatra (69–30 BCE), the last of the Ptolemaic rulers of Egypt, was made during her lifetime. (credit: "Marble bust of Cleopatra VII of Egypt" by Altes Museum Berlin/Louis le Grand/ Wikimedia Commons, Public Domain)

The climax of the war came at the Battle of Actium in 31 BCE, during which the naval forces of Octavian and Marcus Agrippa met to defeat those of Marc Antony and Cleopatra. Octavian pursued the vanquished pair, and soon after he invaded Egypt in 30 BCE, Marc Antony and Cleopatra died by suicide. Cleopatra's death ushered in the start of Roman rule in Egypt as it marked the end of the Ptolemaic dynasty.

THE PAST MEETS THE PRESENT

Ancient Perspectives on Cleopatra

Can we ever know history with certainty? Only the smallest fraction of anything ever written in antiquity survives today, and much of that was set down long after the events and people it describes, possibly by writers hostile to their subject matter. Figures such as Cleopatra have been the source of endless ancient propaganda and character assassinations. Read the following excerpts by ancient writers describing Cleopatra, and consider the information they provide.

> Why Cleopatra, who heaped insults on our army, a woman worn out by her own attendants, who demanded the walls of Rome and the Senate bound to her rule, as a reward from her obscene husband? . . . Truly that whore, queen of incestuous Canopus, a fiery brand burned by the blood of Philip, dared to oppose our Jupiter with yapping Anubis, and forced Tiber to suffer the threats of Nile, banished the

Roman trumpet with the rattle of the sistrum, chased the Liburnian prow with a poled barge, spread her foul mosquito nets over the Tarpeian Rock, and gave judgements among Marius' weapons and statues.

—Propertius, *Poems III*

It would have been wrong, before today, to broach the Caecuban wines from out the ancient bins, while a maddened queen was still plotting the Capitol's and the empire's ruin, with her crowd of deeply-corrupted creatures sick with turpitude, she, violent with hope of all kinds, and intoxicated by Fortune's favor. But it calmed her frenzy that scarcely a single ship escaped the flames, and Caesar reduced the distracted thoughts, bred by Mareotic wine, to true fear, pursuing her close as she fled from Rome, out to capture that deadly monster, bind her, as the sparrow-hawk follows the gentle dove or the swift hunter chases the hare, over the snowy plains of Thessaly.

—Horace, *Cleopatra*

For she was a woman of surpassing beauty, and at that time, when she was in the prime of her youth, she was most striking; she also possessed a most charming voice and a knowledge of how to make herself agreeable to every one. Being brilliant to look upon and to listen to, with the power to subjugate every one, even a love-sated man already past his prime, she thought that it would be in keeping with her rôle to meet Caesar, and she reposed in her beauty all her claims to the throne. She asked therefore for admission to his presence, and on obtaining permission adorned and beautified herself so as to appear before him in the most majestic and at the same time pity-inspiring guise. When she had perfected her schemes she entered the city (for she had been living outside of it), and by night without Ptolemy's knowledge went into the palace.

—Cassius Dio, *Roman History* XLII

For her beauty, as we are told, was in itself not altogether incomparable, nor such as to strike those who saw her; but converse with her had an irresistible charm, and her presence, combined with the persuasiveness of her discourse and the character which was somehow diffused about her behaviour towards others, had something stimulating about it. There was sweetness also in the tones of her voice; and her tongue, like an instrument of many strings, she could readily turn to whatever language she pleased.

—Plutarch, *Life of Antony* XXVII

- Who was Cleopatra? What was her character like? What might have motivated these widely varying descriptions of her?
- How might have these ancient accounts gotten Cleopatra wrong? How much do you think we are likely to "know" about ancient people?

⊘ LINK TO LEARNING

The tradition of interpreting and depicting Cleopatra (https://openstax.org/l/77Cleopatra) is presented in this article.

Rome's conquest of Egypt added yet another layer of complexity to Egyptian society. While Latin-speaking governors and administrators continued to run the affairs of state from Alexandria, they did so in Greek, which remained the language of government. Rome invested heavily in the development of Egypt's largest cities and creating inviting cosmopolitan spaces eventually inhabited by Greeks, Jewish people, Romans, and assimilated Egyptians. Still, under the Romans, the majority of Egyptian subjects lived in rural areas. In more than two thousand villages scattered throughout the Nile delta and along the Nile valley, people labored to produce the tons of grain that supplied the imperial capital with bread. These people were also hardest hit by Roman taxation, a circumstance that inspired periodic revolts against the empire.

Roman imperial administration over North Africa remained constant until the fourth and fifth centuries CE, when the weakened Western Roman Empire confronted a new series of challenges, including widespread barbarian invasions. One invading group was the Vandals. A Germanic people originating in present-day Poland, the Vandals migrated westward in the second century CE and settled in the region of Silesia. By the third century, they had been contained in the Roman province of Pannonia (a sizable territory that included parts of modern-day Hungary, Austria, Croatia, Serbia, Bosnia and Herzegovina, and Slovenia), but they pushed west in the face of the advance of the Huns, nomadic steppe people from central Asia.

By the fifth century, Vandals had migrated to Gaul and the Iberian Peninsula. Around 430, under their leader Genseric, they were invited by Bonifacius, Rome's governor in North Africa, to help him establish himself as a ruler independent of Rome. For the next several years, the Vandals fought Rome's imperial forces on behalf of Bonifacius, who died at the Battle of Remini in Italy in 432. Rome finally agreed to a peace treaty that granted the Vandals control of Mauretania and the western half of Numidia. Unsatisfied, Genseric then pursued a plan to extend his control over Roman North Africa by breaking the treaty and invading Carthage, which he seized in 439.

The Vandals remained in control of the Maghreb region of Roman North Africa until the early sixth century, when Byzantine forces under the general Belisarius reconquered the territory and forced the Vandal king Gelimer to surrender in 534. Less than a century later, a new power from the east threatened the Byzantine position in North Africa. Beginning in the 640s, the armies of Islam advanced, conquering Byzantine Egypt in 642. Using Egypt as a forward position, they then launched successive invasions across the region until the final Byzantine strongholds of North Africa including Carthage fell. By 709, the whole of North Africa had been conquered.

North African and Trans-Saharan Trade

Trans-Saharan trade—the movement of goods between oases and larger settlements in North and West Africa—has existed in one form or another since at least the ninth century BCE. Over time, this system grew from the relatively localized trade in agricultural products and iron goods centered on the Phoenician city of Carthage. It became a continent-wide system of exchange that moved commodities such as copper, salt, ivory, enslaved people, textiles, and gold between what is now Senegal in West Africa and Egypt in the east, reaching as far south as Niger and as far east as Somalia in the Horn of Africa (Figure 9.24). At its height, the trans-Saharan exchange of goods influenced commerce and finance across the whole of North Africa, as well as the economies of Europe and the Near East. This system of trade was made possible by the nomadic peoples of North and West Africa.

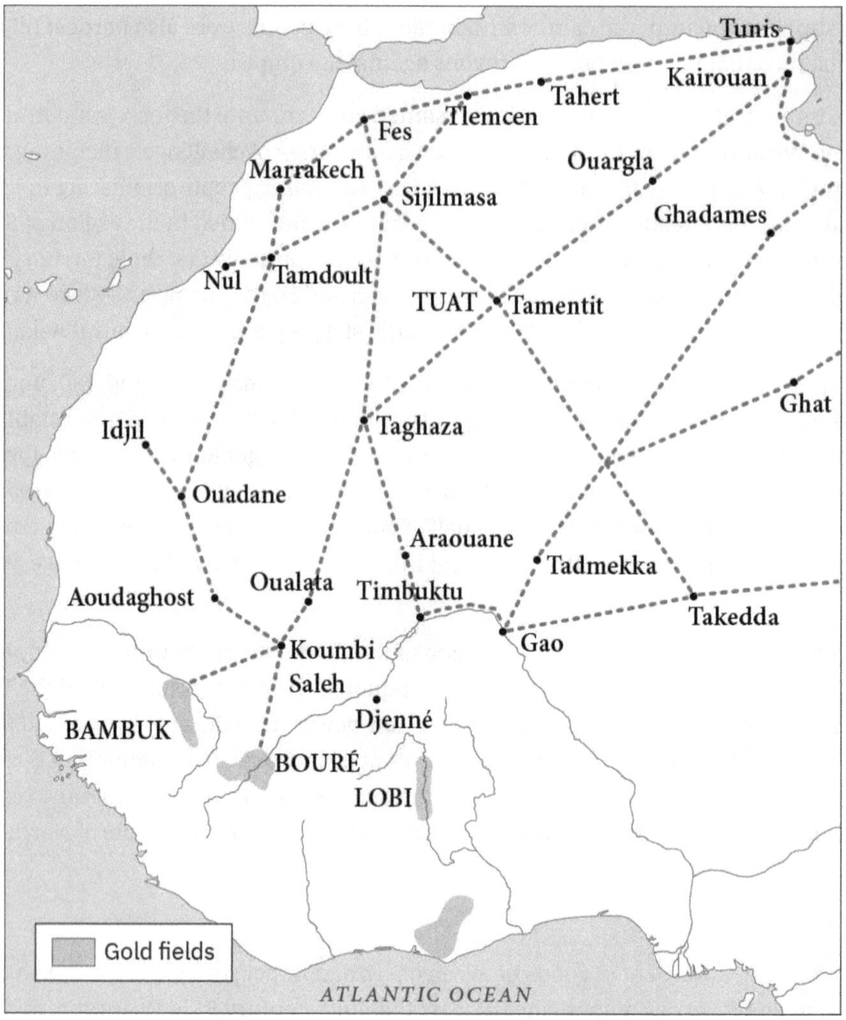

FIGURE 9.24 Trans-Saharan Trade. This map shows the historical trans-Saharan trade routes that crisscrossed ancient North Africa, linking cities on both sides of the Sahara in a network that grew and expanded over several hundred years. (credit: modification of work "Trade routes of the Western Sahara c. 1000-1500" by "Aa77zz"/Wikimedia Commons, CC0 1.0)

In the ninth century BCE, African farmers supplied the Phoenician towns of North Africa with food. In exchange, the Phoenicians introduced these peoples to innovative technologies such as ironworking. Over centuries of interaction, the two groups intermarried and became an integral part of North African society. From around the seventh century BCE, Phoenician merchants relied on the herders of the Atlas Mountains (in present-day Morocco) and the stretch of the northern Sahara to the south.

Indigenous peoples of North Africa had long maintained contact across the Sahara, but it could be tenuous due to the inherent risks of desert travel, including attacks on trading caravans and slave raids by the Garamantes desert people of Libya. Helping facilitate contact in the desert extremes were small settlements of seminomadic peoples at a fragile line of oases forging a point-to-point trading system. Thus, early trade in the Sahara was a matter not of transporting goods across the vast desert expanse but rather of passing them from oasis to oasis. A principal commodity exchanged during this early stage of trade was salt, which was carried to the south and acted as a sort of currency. Salt was highly prized in the agricultural communities south of the Sahara where the mineral is scarce. This is because humans require salt to maintain healthy bodily functions and must regularly consume salt to replace its loss through sweat and urination. The Saharan traders knew where the salt was located, accessed it for themselves, and traded in the substance for goods they could otherwise obtain. Only gradually were highly valuable trading goods introduced, such as gold and copper, which were then brought across the desert from tropical West Africa to the far reaches of the North African coast.

During the period of Carthaginian dominance in Tunisia, goods were carried by pack animals such as mules, horses, and donkeys between the Phoenician imperial capital and the independent African kingdoms in the mountainous and coastal regions to its west. These kingdoms, known to the Romans as Mauretania and Numidia, had extended their control of much of North Africa by the second century BCE as Carthage declined and Rome ascended. For a time, the Romans and the North African kingdoms enjoyed a relatively peaceful and prosperous alliance, but gradual Roman interference in the domestic political affairs of the Numidian state caused their relations to sour, and eventually Rome conquered both Numidia and Mauretania.

In typical fashion, the Romans established large estates as well as towns in the newly conquered territories. Their administration outside these enclaves reached only so far, however. Beyond them, the region remained under the dominance of the people native to the area, in both language and culture. But it was in the strategic interests of Rome to secure the southernmost frontiers of these new provinces. Doing so effectively required not only establishing a border but also patrolling it. This was impossible with horses, so the Romans used the dromedary camel (one-hump camel) (Figure 9.25). Biologically equipped to survive desert extremes, the camel was the ideal means to help secure Rome's new southernmost frontier.

FIGURE 9.25 The Dromedary Camel. The widespread use of dromedary camels by the Romans in North Africa helped to popularize the animal's use in trans-Saharan trade. (credit: "Animals of Iran - Kavir National Park - Qom Province - Deir-e Gachin Caravansarai 20" by Mostafameraji/Wikimedia Commons, CC0 1.0)

The introduction of the dromedary camel originally from Arabia into North Africa revolutionized the trans-Saharan trade, but its adoption across the region was slow. The first camels in North Africa may have reached Egypt by as early as the ninth century BCE, but it was not until the third and fourth centuries CE that its use spread to the African nomad groups of the northern Sahara, likely helped along by Roman use of the animal. By the fifth century, it had become a major form of transportation in the region. The camel had many advantages over other pack animals. It could maintain a steady pace over much longer distances than oxen, and it could carry upward of three hundred pounds of goods an average of fifteen to eighteen miles a day. Further, the camel's capacity to store fat and water enabled it to travel up to ten days without stopping for fresh water, more than twice the time and distance of almost every other pack animal. Added to this was the camel's unique splayed foot, which allowed it to walk easily in the soft, sandy conditions of the Saharan environment.

The camel enabled desert nomads to reach more distant oases than ever before and so open entirely new routes across the desert. Although desert travel remained precarious and filled with risk, it certainly became more reliable. For the first time, it was possible for desert travelers to consider dispatching large-scale and regular long-distance trading caravans across the Sahara. Despite this, desert transport remained largely in the hands of the nomadic peoples of the region, principally the Sanhaja in the west and the Tuareg of the central and southern Sahara. Although trans-Saharan trade was growing at this time, it was not yet full-time work, so these groups remained largely nomadic pastoralists, harvesting date palms and grazing their flocks and herds at oases.

In many cases, they tended goats and sheep, but they often also had camel and cattle and occasionally horses. These animals all had to graze, and when they were unable to do so at oases because of either distance or weather, the nomads were forced to find other grazing land. This was particularly the case during the hottest and driest seasons, when the nomads migrated their flocks and herds to the better grazing areas of the Maghreb in the north or the Sahel in the south. Inevitably, this brought them into contact with the more settled agricultural peoples of these areas, and often into conflict as they competed for precious resources in a hostile environment. Beyond these settlements, the nomadic pastoralists dominated the Sahara. Yet there were other peoples in the desert, including small groups such as the Haratin who also called the oases home. They harvested dates and dug salt to exchange for food but were often kept in a subordinate position by the nomads, who controlled the oases.

As the camel transformed desert transport, the products of sub-Saharan Africa became more readily available to the Mediterranean world. Trade in West African gold expanded, demand increased for such goods as ivory and ostrich feathers, and large animals were hunted to extinction in North Africa. As cross-desert traffic grew, several new settlements developed to aid the movement of goods north and south of the Sahara, including Sijilmasa, Ghat, Gao, Awdaghust, and Kano. At sites such as these, goods were exchanged, and camel caravans were unloaded and replenished to continue their journey across the desert. While the desert traffic in goods remained in the hands of nomads, the actual demand for and exchange of goods was largely the work of peoples of settled societies to the north and south of the Sahara.

Key Terms

Bantu migrations the millennia-long expansion of Bantu-speaking peoples southward from West and Central Africa, spreading a common cultural foundation that included language, farming, and ironworking

Berbers the name used by Carthaginians, Greeks, and Romans to describe the native peoples of the Maghreb; today, this population generally self-identifies as Amazigh, or Imazighen

biome a community of vegetation and wildlife adapted to a particular climate

cataract a place in a river where the otherwise placid flow is upset by a waterfall, a shallow portion, or the presence of boulders

deffufa a type of monumental mud-brick structure unique to Nubian civilization and believed to have served a religious function

kentake a Kushite title that roughly translates to "queen mother" and was a powerful position in Meroitic Kush

Maghreb the western half of North Africa, including most of present-day Morocco, Algeria, Tunisia, and Libya

Nubia the name Egyptians gave to the expansive area south of the first cataract and extending into sub-Saharan Africa; it included the Kingdom of Kush

Sahel an east–west belt of semiarid grassland that forms a transitional zone between the Sahara to the north and the equatorial rainforest to the south

savanna a grassy plain with scattered trees found to the north and south of the tropical African rainforest

Section Summary

9.1 Africa's Geography and Climate

Geography played a critical role in the development of early human civilization in Africa. Climate conditions such as temperatures and rainfall dictated agricultural growing seasons, and soil fertility governed what crops—if any—could be grown in a particular area, as well as the availability of fodder for grazing animals. In particular, the availability of water dictated the likelihood of fixed settlement. A wide range of peoples populated Africa's diverse geography, from the desert-dwelling San to the Baka people of the rainforest. All developed lifestyles and cultures that were not only suited to their geography but were also greatly influenced by it.

9.2 The Emergence of Farming and the Bantu Migrations

The earliest evidence of plant domestication in Africa has been uncovered in three different areas: Egypt, the eastern Sahara, and West Africa. In Egypt, agricultural technologies were introduced from southwest Asia, where the Neolithic Revolution first occurred. From there, wheat and barley agriculture spread across North Africa over thousands of years. In the other two locations, plant domestication appears to have emerged independently. In these locations, early Neolithic societies grew crops of sorghum, yams, watermelons, and African rice. In Central and West Africa, the farming of these crops was aided greatly by iron technology.

Once believe to have been introduced to Africa through Egypt, scholars now generally agree that iron smelting was developed independently in Central Africa. Iron tools allowed sub-Saharan African farmers to more efficiently clear forested areas to establish farms. By at least 500 BCE, Bantu-speaking peoples migrating across Africa were using iron tools to aid them in their gradual expansion.

The Bantu speakers likely originated in West and Central Africa and began spreading east and south as early as 3000 BCE. Their migrations were gradual, protracted, and took a few different routes. As they spread, they established farms, introduced others to agricultural practices, and dramatically transformed the linguistic makeup of much of subequatorial Africa.

9.3 The Kingdom of Kush

Long the center of prehistoric African civilization, the region of Nubia, between Aswan in southern Egypt and the confluence of the Blue and White Nile Rivers in northern Sudan, flourished thanks to its links with Nile-based trade and its well-watered hinterland. Beginning with the city-state of Kerma in the early second millennium BCE, the Nubian people of Kush steadily absorbed Egyptian culture, including its language, religious practices, and architecture. During periods of Egyptian weakness, such as during the Second Intermediate Period, the Kingdom of Kush was able to achieve political independence. Similarly, during periods of great Egyptian regional strength, Kush was again subjugated by Egypt. Incredibly, in the eighth century BCE, the Kushite king Piye turned the tables on Egypt and placed himself on the Egyptian throne.

Once Egypt was conquered by Assyria in seventh century BCE, the Kingdom of Kush retreated to Meroe far to the south of Egypt. There they built up a kingdom known for its iron production and trade goods. For many centuries, the kingdom blended its many Egyptian cultural practices with Nubian traditions to develop its own distinctive styles and even writing system. After confronting Rome in Egypt in the first century BCE, it settled into a centuries-long trading relationship with the imperial Roman province of Egypt until it finally declined and died out sometime in the fourth century CE.

9.4 North Africa's Mediterranean and Trans-Saharan Connections

From the earliest Phoenician forays across the sea in the first millennium BCE, North Africa played an increasingly prominent role in the trade-based economies of the Mediterranean and the polities that surrounded it. It was the source of rare and valuable commodities such as salt, gold, and ivory, transported from the African interior across the Sahara by Indigenous nomadic peoples and long sought after by Egyptians, Carthaginians, Greeks, Romans, Vandals, and Arabs, each in their turn. Many parts of the Mediterranean coastline of North Africa were also renowned for their fertility, particularly the Maghrebi region immediately surrounding Carthage and the Egyptian Nile delta, whose bountiful lands constituted the "breadbasket" of Rome.

Egypt's stability was thus critically important. When Cleopatra of Egypt began influencing Roman officials, including Julius Caesar and Marc Antony, to the benefit of her kingdom, Rome responded with force, and Egypt came under Roman rule. Three hundred years later, the Romans' introduction of the camel to North Africa enlarged the practical scope of truly trans-Saharan trade from the far south of the great desert to the Mediterranean coast.

Assessments

Review Questions

1. What is the Serengeti?
    a. a desert in southern Africa
    b. a climate pattern in the Horn of Africa
    c. a grassy plain in Africa that witnesses some of the world's largest annual animal migrations
    d. a semiarid transition zone between the Sahel and the Mediterranean coast

2. What is a key characteristic of Africa's Mediterranean climate?
    a. It is very similar to the climate of the Sahel.
    b. It is arid and known for its sandy soils.
    c. It is tropical.
    d. It is sunny and well suited for farming.

3. What characteristic best describes the traditional religious beliefs of the Baka people?
    a. animistic
    b. monotheistic
    c. pre-Islamic
    d. ritualistic

4. For the San people of southern Africa, religion _____.

    a. included elements of animism

    b. was polytheistic and intimately bound up in the hunt for prey

    c. was based on early Christian models

    d. centered on ritualized foraging for plant buds and seasonal nuts

5. What African region independently developed agriculture based on yams?

    a. West Africa

    b. the eastern Sahara

    c. North Africa

    d. South Africa

6. In what part of Africa did sophisticated ironworking technology develop independently?

    a. South Africa

    b. the eastern Sahara

    c. Central Africa

    d. North Africa

7. How was ironworking technology likely disseminated throughout sub-Saharan Africa?

    a. It was introduced by Egyptian traders.

    b. It was introduced by Nilo-Saharan farmers.

    c. It was introduced by Near Eastern conquerors.

    d. It was introduced by migrating Bantus.

8. What was the likely original location of the proto-Bantu speakers?

    a. the area west of Egypt

    b. the area between Nigeria and Cameroon

    c. the Ethiopian highlands

    d. the central Sahara region

9. What areas remained largely untouched by Bantu migrants until recent times?

    a. the western Kalahari Desert

    b. the Lake Victoria region

    c. Western Tanzania

    d. Eastern Botswana

10. What city was the site of the earliest iteration of the Kingdom of Kush?

    a. Thebes

    b. Meroe

    c. Kerma

    d. Napata

11. During what period did the Kingdom of Kush cooperate with the Hyksos rulers of the Nile delta to keep the Egyptian rulers at Thebes weak?

    a. the Old Kingdom

    b. the First Intermediate Period

    c. the New Kingdom

    d. the Second Intermediate Period

12. What two items of trade helped the Kingdom of Kush become wealthy and powerful in its early centuries?

    a. iron and gold

b. diamonds and copper

c. fish and dates

d. wheat and rice

13. What is the Kushite king Piye most famous for?

    a. defeating the Romans

    b. giving tribute to Persia

    c. conquering Egypt

    d. trading with Greece

14. The Kingdom of Kush was most heavily influenced by its long connection with which culture?

    a. Persian

    b. Egyptian

    c. Greek

    d. Nok

15. During the Meroitic period, what high-quality item did the Kingdom of Kush gain a reputation for producing?

    a. bronze

    b. iron

    c. pottery

    d. cloth

16. Where was the Phoenician city of Carthage located?

    a. the Sahel

    b. Egypt

    c. the plains of the Atlas Mountains

    d. the coast of present-day Tunisia

17. How did the Ptolemaic rulers of Egypt seek to legitimate their rule?

    a. by enslaving all Egyptians

    b. by adopting Egyptian religious practice and styling themselves as pharaohs

    c. by employing Egyptians in high-level administrative positions

    d. by learning to speak Egyptian

18. What animal transformed trade across the Sahara?

    a. horse

    b. cattle

    c. camel

    d. sheep

19. Why did early trans-Saharan traders move salt across the desert into sub-Saharan Africa?

    a. Salt was used to mine gold.

    b. Salt was heavily taxed by the Romans.

    c. Salt was necessary and scarce in the region.

    d. Salt was prized for its religious properties.

Check Your Understanding Questions

1. What do you think was the most important climatic feature in the evolution of African societies?

2. What are the traditional gender roles followed by Baka society?

3. What distinguished hunter-gatherer societies in Africa from settled societies?

4. How did the Neolithic Revolution affect African societies?

5. Why did earlier scholars believe that ironworking technologies were disseminated to sub-Saharan Africa, and what evidence leads most scholars today to accept that these societies independently developed ironworking?

6. In what ways did the Bantu migrations affect African civilization?

7. How did the decline of Egypt after the Middle Kingdom affect the Kingdom of Kush?

8. What role did trade play in the relationship between Egypt and the Kingdom of Kush?

9. What were some of the advantages for Kush of relocating to Meroe?

10. What effect did the rising power of Rome in North Africa have on Maghreb?

11. Why did the Ptolemies, who were Macedonian Greeks, style themselves as Egyptian pharaohs?

12. What made early trans-Saharan trade possible?

Application and Reflection Questions

1. The geography and climate of Africa have greatly influenced the different societies that have emerged across the continent. This is because the climate and geography generally determine the available resources of an area. But is this always true? Can you think of an example in which an African society defied those geographic and climactic limitations?

2. Given what you now know about the variety of climates and geographies of Africa, has your perception of the continent changed? If so, how?

3. What were some of the ways environmental conditions in different parts of Africa influenced the emergence of agriculture? How does this account for the differences in crops and ways agricultural practices were disseminated or developed independently?

4. Why do you think scholars were reluctant for many years to accept that sub-Saharan societies independently developed ironworking technology? What does this suggest about how people have traditionally evaluated African historical developments?

5. In what ways did geography and climate affect the Bantu migration?

6. How do you think scholars use linguistic evidence to trace the movement of Bantu speakers over thousands of years?

7. Why did the Nubian pharaohs of Egypt during the Twenty-Fifth Dynasty embrace Egyptian culture, rather than attempt to impose Nubian culture on Egypt?

8. Why do you suppose that the *kentake* (or queen mother) position was such an important role in Meroitic Kush?

9. In what ways might North Africa have influenced the cultures of Europe and the Near and Middle East?

10. Given the great risks involved in crossing the Sahara, why do you think some groups would have engaged in such endeavors?

FIGURE 10.1 Sasanians in Victory. This rock relief carving from Naqsh-e Rostam (in modern Iran) depicts the Sasanian victory over the Romans at the Battle of Edessa in 260 CE. On the right, King Shapur I looks down from his horse at the kneeling Valerian, the first Roman emperor ever taken captive in battle. (credit: modification of work "Naqsh i Rustam. Shapour" by Unknown/Wikimedia Commons, CC BY 2.5)

CHAPTER OUTLINE

10.1 The Eastward Shift
10.2 The Byzantine Empire and Persia
10.3 The Kingdoms of Aksum and Himyar
10.4 The Margins of Empire

INTRODUCTION The later Roman Empire was a time of profound cultural, political, and religious transformations. Various crises in the Roman government, as well as the rise of Christianity, propelled these changes. In the third century CE, the emperor Valerian's capture by the Sasanians was an indication of how easily the Roman Empire's prominence could fluctuate and fissure (Figure 10.1). Stretching from the island of Britannia (Britain) in the Roman West to Syria in the Roman East, the empire continually struggled in its relationships with foreign groups on its eastern and western frontiers. The threatening presence of the Sasanians and other marginal states in the Mediterranean, including various Germanic kingdoms in the west and Palmyra in the east, reflected a new state of affairs.

The empire shifted its focus eastward, a trend signaled most prominently by its reorientation around its new capital in Constantinople (today's Istanbul). The Romans then saw their power and sphere of influence shift as well. With a growing Christian population and shrinking borders, the entity that now became the Byzantine Empire persisted in the eastern Mediterranean. Yet it had to grapple with the migration of different groups through its territory as well as the disintegration of the western empire into small independent states. In addition, smaller states such as Aksum in sub-Saharan Africa and the Kushan Empire in central Asia came onto the scene during this period, establishing their own thriving societies away from the Mediterranean while being interconnected as neighbors and trade partners. The interrelationships among this multitude of states reflect the complicated circumstances of the Late Antique world.

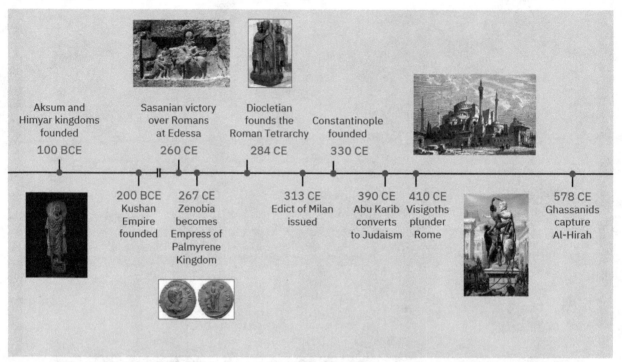

FIGURE 10.2 Timeline: Empires of Faith. (credit "200 BCE": modification of work "Buddha" by Purchase, Denise and Andrew Saul Gift, in honor of Maxwell K. Hearn, 2014/The Metropolitan Museum of Art, Public Domain; credit "260 CE": modification of work "Naqsh i Rustam. Shapour" by Unknown/Wikimedia Commons, CC BY 2.5; credit "267 CE": modification of work "Zenobia" by Classical Numismatic Group Wikimedia Commons, Public Domain; credit "284 CE": modification of work "Portrait of the Four Tetrarchs" by Jean-Pol Grandmont/Wikimedia Commons, CC BY 4.0; credit "330 CE": modification of work "Lithography of the Hagia Sophia, Istanbul, 1857" by Dmitry Makeev/Wikimedia Commons, Public Domain; credit "410 CE": modification of work "The Sack of Rome in 410 by the Barbarians" by *Das Königreich der Vandalen*/Wikimedia Commons, Public Domain)

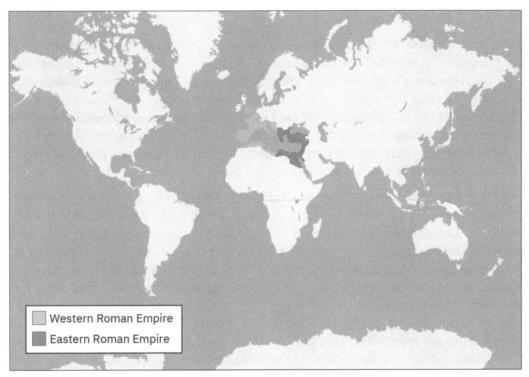

FIGURE 10.3 Locator Map: Empires of Faith. (credit: modification of work "World map blank shorelines" by Maciej Jaros/Wikimedia Commons, Public Domain)

10.1 The Eastward Shift

LEARNING OBJECTIVES

By the end of this section, you will be able to:
- Explain how and why the political focus of the Roman Empire shifted eastward during Late Antiquity
- Discuss how the adoption of Christianity as the official religion of the Roman Empire altered Mediterranean society
- Explain the collapse of Roman authority in the West, including the role of Germanic migrations and invasions

From the third through the seventh centuries CE, the culture of the Roman Empire transformed itself profoundly and in fundamental ways. The rise of Christianity marked a seminal moment, and from the time of the emperor Constantine in the fourth century, the government advocated monotheism, the worship of one God to the exclusion of others. With a Christian government and a new capital at Constantinople in the eastern Mediterranean, the Byzantine Empire grew from the old Roman state. At the same time, the fracturing of the Roman Empire's government led to various new regional alliances and rivalries. Germanic kingdoms flourished in the West, while the Byzantines attempted to maintain order among the burgeoning Christian population within their borders.

The Roman Empire's eastward shift epitomized the major cultural changes occurring during this period. Because of these shifts, **Late Antiquity** has been characterized as a transitional period between the ancient and medieval worlds that occurred from roughly 150 to 750 CE. On the one hand, Late Antique culture remained influenced by the classical past, with the maintenance of certain ancient institutional values. While still calling themselves "Romans," the Byzantines simultaneously attempted to maintain Christian orthodoxy. On the other hand, the appearance of new religious identities and the breakdown of the Roman state led to conflicts among different regional and cultural groups. The empire's borders were in constant flux, and its territory slowly diminished as numerous powers vied for regional dominance.

Constantinople and the Roman East

The third century was a period of upheaval and change for the Roman government, often referred to as the Crisis of the Third Century. From 235 to 284, a span of only forty-nine years, the empire was ruled by upward of twenty-six different claimants to the imperial throne. New emperors were often declared and supported by Roman soldiers. As a result, civil wars—as well as wars on the eastern frontier—were nearly constant. Economic problems became more apparent after the devaluation of currency, in which coins issued by the government became increasingly less valuable, led to a rapid rise in the price of goods. The high turnover of leadership led to periods of reform and attempts to bring stability to the government and economy, but progress toward securing the empire was limited.

In 284, however, Diocletian, a military official from Illyria in the Balkans, was declared emperor by his troops. His reforms, unlike those of his predecessors, had a lasting impact on the empire and its eventual eastward shift. Diocletian divided his rule with a co-emperor, who like him bore the title *augustus*, and with two junior emperors given the title *caesar*. This shared rule between the four emperors was called a **tetrarchy**. While there was no formal geographic division of leadership, each emperor or tetrarch had his own sphere of influence. Each also had a regional capital city located near the empire's borders from which he governed and organized military defense. There were familial and legal ties among the tetrarchs, who utilized imagery to send a message of strength (Figure 10.4). Diocletian also aimed to fix the empire's economy, issuing several edicts to curb inflation and promote trade within the empire. For example, in 301, he issued the Edict on Maximum Prices, which had two goals. First, to curb inflation, the edict placed an upper limit on the price at which certain goods could be sold. Second, to combat currency devaluation, it set specific values for coinage issued by the government.

FIGURE 10.4 The Four Tetrarchs. This sculptural portrait of the Roman tetrarchs from St. Mark's Basilica in Venice

shows the cooperation the four co-rulers hoped to achieve. The figures, carved in about 300 CE, are for the most part indistinguishable, and their rigid features contrast with the idealism of the classical style that had been prevalent in early Roman society. (credit: "Portrait of the Four Tetrarchs" by Jean-Pol Grandmont/Wikimedia Commons, CC BY 4.0)

It is unclear if when Diocletian established his tetrarchy, he expected to eventually abdicate as a means of making the succession of future emperors more uniform. In any case, after he and his co-emperor Maximian formally left office in 305, the remaining two tetrarchs took their place alongside two new junior emperors. Civil wars soon engulfed the empire as infighting among the emperors resulted in the advancement of Constantine, son of the emperor Constantius Chlorus. Upon his father's death, Constantine claimed the imperial throne in 306. Making his way from the city of York in Britannia, he first gained control of the western provinces before arriving in Italy in 312. In the city of Rome, he defeated Maxentius, his final rival to the throne, at the Battle of Milvian Bridge.

During his reign, Constantine attributed his victory over Maxentius to the Christian God. According to the emperor's official biographer Eusebius, Constantine had seen an image of the labarum, the Greek symbols of "Chi" and "Rho" that make up the first letters of "Christ," in the sky that commanded him, "By this sign, conquer." Whether this was a message specifically designed to appeal to the empire's Christian populace is disputed, but Constantine showed clear Christian sympathies. From early in his reign, however, he sent out a carefully balanced message aimed to please Christians and traditional polytheists alike. For example, the design and inscription of the Arch of Constantine in Rome express a new synthesis of Roman tradition with Christianity that balanced the emperor's competing interests. The arch contains images from existing Roman monuments, while the inscription regarding a divine being is deliberately ambiguous (Figure 10.5).

FIGURE 10.5 The Arch of Constantine. The Arch of Constantine in Rome was dedicated in 315 CE. Its incorporation of material from earlier monuments shows Constantine's desire to place himself at the pinnacle of Roman history, while the deliberately ambiguous inscription caters to a religiously diverse audience by attributing the emperor's victory to "divine inspiration" and not to a specific deity. (credit: modification of work ""DSC_0787; Arco di Constantino Rome Italy February 2013" by Bengt Nyman/Flickr, CC BY 2.0)

To further celebrate his rule, Constantine refounded the city of Byzantium (modern-day Istanbul) as Constantinople in 330 CE, and it eventually became the new imperial capital. The city's location on the empire's eastern frontier was advantageous for its proximity to trade routes and to the sites of many Roman military campaigns (Figure 10.6).

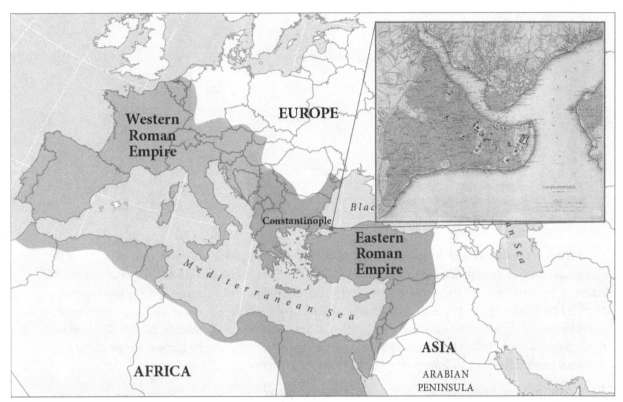

FIGURE 10.6 The Roman Empire Moves East. Constantinople's location shifted the empire's geographic focus eastward. The city was near the sites of frequent Roman military campaigns in the lower Danube and significantly closer than Rome to the frontiers along the Euphrates (in modern Iraq). It was also a hub of trade and travel because it was connected to western Europe, the Near East, and the Balkans. (credit: modification of work "Political Europe" by CIA/The World Factbook, Public Domain; credit inset: modification of work "Constantinople. Stambool" by *Maps of the Society for the Diffusion of Useful Knowledge*/Wikimedia Commons, Public Domain)

BEYOND THE BOOK

Constantinople: The "New Rome"?

Though not initially intended to replace Rome, Constantinople ("city of Constantine") was formally dedicated as a city in 330 CE, and the emperor Constantine was celebrated with various monuments. On the day of the dedication, Constantine erected a porphyry column with a statue of himself as Apollo on top. He collected other pieces of art from across the empire to decorate the newly christened city, including the Serpent Column from Delphi, an Augustan victory monument from Nicopolis, and an Egyptian obelisk. These represented Constantine's attempt to mark the city as both the continuation and culmination of Roman history to that point, giving legitimacy to Constantinople and to his reign.

The Colossus of Constantine was a massive statue that once occupied the west apse of the Basilica of Maxentius in Rome. Constantine may have wanted it to portray him as having an otherworldly or divine quality, apparent in its sheer size—the head alone is more than eight feet high—but also in its enlarged eyes that look toward heaven. The rigid facial features show the changing style of portraiture at the time (Figure 10.7a).

(a)   **(b)**

FIGURE 10.7 The Colossus of Constantine and The Column of Constantine. (a) The remaining pieces of the enormous statue of Constantine are on view in the Capitoline Museum in Rome. (b) Although the enormous statue of Constantine that once topped this column was destroyed in a fall centuries ago, the two together probably surpassed 160 feet in height. (credit a: modification of work "Fragments of the fourth-century colossal acrolithic statue of the Emperor Constantine" by Michael Squire/Wikimedia Commons, CC BY 4.0; credit b: modification of work "Image from page 276" by *A History of All Nations from the Earliest Times; Being a Universal Historical Library* by John Henry Wright/Flickr, Public Domain)

The Column of Constantine originally served as the base for a large statue of the emperor in Constantinople. Erected after he became sole emperor in 324, the statue, now lost, may have shown him dressed as his favored god Sol Invictus (the "Unconquered Sun"). Constantine seemed to hold that his devotion to this god was compatible with his preference for Christianity (Figure 10.7b).

The Serpent Column was dedicated to Apollo in the fifth century BCE by the Greeks in Delphi, then considered the center of the world. Its removal to Constantinople may have been intended to reclaim that status for the emperor's city and to show again his affinity for the sun god (often equated with Apollo). The column's original purpose as a monument to the Greeks' victory over the Persians allowed Constantine to hint at his own victories in the recent civil wars (Figure 10.8).

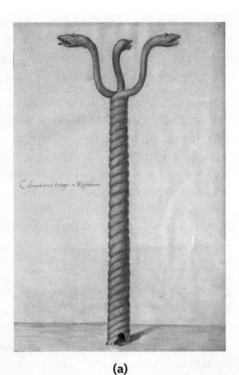

(a)   (b)

FIGURE 10.8 **The Serpent Column.** A drawing from the sixteenth century (a) shows the Serpent Column as it looked in antiquity. The photo (b) shows the column as it stands today in Istanbul. (credit a: modification of work "Freshfield Album, Serpent Column (fol 6)" by Trinity College Library/Wikimedia Commons, Public Domain; credit b: modification of work "Snake column Hippodrome Constantinople 2007 by "Gryffindor"/Wikimedia Commons, Public Domain)

- What message did each monument send about Constantine's reign?
- How was Christianity incorporated into Constantine's monuments in Constantinople?

Constantine ruled until his death in 337, and his legacy was cemented during the reigns of his sons who succeeded him. They waged military campaigns to maintain the frontiers of the empire, promoted Christianity, and enacted laws against pagan practice. Only Julian, a nephew of Constantine, attempted a brief resurgence of paganism in the Roman government during his rule, from 361 to 363. He enacted a series of reforms, wrote a number of philosophical works, and carried out a military campaign against the Sasanians. But after reaching the Persian capital of Ctesiphon, Julian's army was effectively in retreat when the emperor suffered a mortal wound from a spear. Any vision for a renewed polytheist empire ended with his death. Thus, Constantine had effectively ushered in a new era of Christian governance. Rulers for the rest of the empire's history were explicitly Christian, acting as de facto heads of the church and controlling church policy.

The Rule of Roman Christianity

The Christian Church attracted a large influx of new members during the reign of Constantine. The Edict of Milan, issued in 313, allowed citizens to worship any deity they wished, but it was mainly intended to embrace Christians living in the empire who were now given back their confiscated property and legal rights. Christianity was not made the official religion, but the edict effectively ended any state-sanctioned persecution of its adherents within the empire's borders. The religion's new privileged status brought about profound changes for its institutions and their relationship to the imperial government.

Emperors generally did not interfere in the self-regulation of the church, except for religious belief. They exercised this control chiefly by organizing **ecumenical councils**, meetings of bishops to discuss religious doctrine. (The word "ecumenical" comes from the Greek *oikoumene*, meaning the entire inhabited world.) Ecumenical councils brought together bishops from the Roman East and West and issued decisions designed to be adopted universally. They were venues for hammering out matters of Christian orthodoxy, addressing questions of Jesus's divinity, and eliminating emerging heretical movements within the church.

In 325, for example, Constantine convened the first ecumenical council, the Council of Nicaea, to settle the question of Jesus's divine nature and his relationship to God. The bishops were most concerned with addressing the Arians, followers of the priest Arius, who held that Jesus was created out of nothing but had a beginning. The bishops at the council worried that this thinking detracted from Jesus's divinity and after much debate decided against the Arians. They adopted the Nicene Creed, a statement of dogma that declared Jesus was "begotten, not made" and was "consubstantial" with God, expressly embracing his divinity. These types of religious debates remained at the center of the numerous ecumenical councils thereafter, and emperors sometimes used them to exercise control over church-related matters. But while the emperors self-styled themselves as priestly rulers, the bishops sometimes contested this role, and emperors then had to compete with them for religious authority.

The steady bureaucratization of the empire made its governance more complicated because it meant that power could only be usurped at various levels of government. One way in which emperors attempted to balance local, regional, and imperial power was by formally codifying laws. For example, in 429, the emperor Theodosius II established a commission to compile what became known as the **Theodosian Code**, a single publication containing all laws issued after 312 CE from across the empire. This code was the first attempt to create a unified system of government for the empire since the days of the Republic. It further solidified Christianity in Roman society because it featured laws that adhered to Christian beliefs and practice. It also brought about a transformation of social morals and placed power in the hands of the church to police morality, a practice that had not been seen in antiquity.

The Theodosian Code represented a trend of emperors attempting to address religious issues through laws and edicts. Constantine, for instance, seems to have banned animal sacrifice, a major feature of traditional Roman religion, though it was already in decline by this time. In several imperial edicts, notably the Edict of Thessalonica in 380 that made Nicene Christianity the state religion of the Roman Empire, Theodosius I attempted to suppress religious controversy outside the church, treating pagans and heretics (those holding unorthodox beliefs) as threats to the imperial state. The First Council of Constantinople, convened in 381, reestablished the Nicene Creed and addressed the topic of the Holy Spirit, suggesting that the problem of Arius's sympathizers had not completely disappeared. Jewish people were also viewed skeptically during this time but were not a major concern to imperial authorities. Finally, responding to an appeal from the Christian population of Athens, the emperor Justinian closed that city's philosophical schools in 529. The dismantling of pagan temples, removal of statues of pagan divinities, and discontinuation of traditional practice and priesthoods throughout the empire were a common pattern of authority during this time (Figure 10.9).

FIGURE 10.9 A Winged Victory. Made by the Italian sculptor Antonio Canova in the early nineteenth century, this bronze figure of a winged Victory atop a globe may resemble a statue that once stood outside the Roman Senate house. As a representation of pagan worship, that statue was removed twice by Christian emperors, in 357 and 382 CE, a decision that was controversial among many pagan senators at the time. (credit: modification of work "Winged Victory by Antonio Canova" by "Daderot"/Wikimedia Commons, CC0 1.0)

The relationships between pagans and Christians were unquestionably strained. Elite pagans could still pursue a career and hold public office, as did the noted intellectuals Libanius and Symmachus. These public figures viewed their Christian counterparts, such as the theologian Gregory of Nazianzus, as holding the same general philosophical assumptions as themselves, so they could debate religion together. Yet episodes of violence also occurred in the cities of the empire where bishops wielded both religious and political power. The murder of the influential pagan scholar and teacher Hypatia in Alexandria in 415 demonstrates how a bishop could wield extralegal authority. Bishop Cyril viewed Hypatia, who had a large friendship network of Christians and pagans, as a political threat, and he was able to convince the Christian populace to attack and kill her. This secured his own position as a substantial political and religious authority in the city.

LINK TO LEARNING

Learn more about the pagan teacher and scholar Hypatia of Alexandria (https://openstax.org/l/77Hypatia) in this video. Hypatia's teaching of mathematics and philosophy was viewed as a threat to the Christian order in the city, which ultimately led to her demise.

The Fall of the Roman West

Theodosius I was the last emperor who reigned over a united empire. After his death in 395, power passed to his two sons; Arcadius ruled the eastern half of the empire from Constantinople, while Honorius controlled the western half from Ravenna in northern Italy. The geography of each region dictated its fate. With a shorter stretch of the Danube River to guard against foreign invaders, the East was able to thrive by paying off these groups with its wealth and discouraging them from entering their territory. The West suffered various setbacks along its more extensive and chaotic frontier that brought both political and social disruption. There were simply more foreign groups to contend with, and the traditional barrier of the Rhine and Danube Rivers was long and continuously crossed by Germanic groups during this period. The West was also less urbanized than the East, resulting in less social cohesion in parts of this region. This allowed different, outsider cultures to infiltrate and transform it (Figure 10.10).

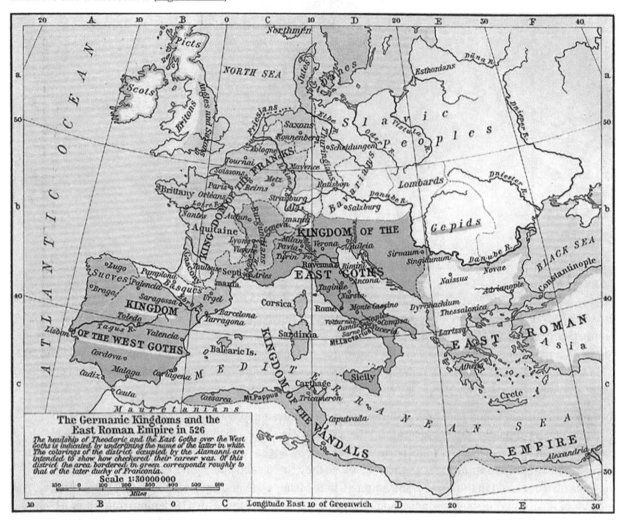

FIGURE 10.10 Germanic Kingdoms. The increasing influx of Germanic peoples into the western empire brought about a fracturing of Roman power as a series of independent kingdoms took control of the Italian peninsula, Gaul (modern-day France and Belgium), the Iberian Peninsula, and North Africa. This map from cartographer William R. Shepherd's *Historical Atlas* (1923) shows the Germanic kingdoms as they were in 526 CE. (credit: "Germanic kingdoms 526CE " by Historical Atlas by William R. Shepherd/Wikimedia Commons, Public Domain)

As the western empire came into increasing contact with these outsider groups, the state dealt with them in various ways. It deemed many Germanic groups ***foederati***, meaning they were bound by a treaty that allowed them semiautonomy in exchange for their military service on behalf of the Roman Empire. Mercenaries thus came from the various tribes and foreign states allied with the empire, serving alongside Romans in an increasingly diverse military. After completing their military service, foreign soldiers were given the opportunity to participate in Roman civic life, to live in Roman territory, and to integrate into Roman society. Some Germans were also able to settle in Roman territory, leading to periods of peaceful coexistence and cooperation, while others were not so fortunate because they were captured in conflict and forced into Roman households as enslaved people. As Germans were brought into the Roman cultural fold through various means, rivalries among ambitious and newly integrated outsiders often disrupted Roman society.

In the early 400s, Germanic groups made their way into Gaul and Italy, negotiating and fighting with the Romans. Originating in central Europe around modern-day Poland, the Vandals crossed the Rhine in 406, settling in Gaul before being pushed into Spain and finally forming a kingdom in North Africa. A notable Roman military commander of Vandal origin was Stilicho, who was appointed guardian of the young emperor Honorius. Stilicho had aims to control the western empire himself, having married into the imperial family and attained some popularity due to his military victories.

Stilicho fell out of favor, however, because of his mismanagement of another outsider group, the Visigoths, one of several Gothic groups from eastern Europe. The Visigoths had come into increasing contact with the Romans after crossing the Danube River in the fourth century, ultimately defeating Rome at the Battle of Adrianople in 378. By the early 400s, the Visigoth leader Alaric had negotiated various agreements with the Roman government to settle his people in Roman territory. Stilicho urged the Roman Senate to honor the agreements and pay Alaric to pacify him, which the Senate did despite preferring a military solution against the Visigoths. As the situation disintegrated, Stilicho was blamed for the unfavorable outcome, and his increasingly strained relationship with the Senate eventually resulted in his execution. Alaric then invaded Italy, attacking Rome over the course of three days in 410. Remembered as a seminal moment in the empire's decline, this "sacking" of the city of Rome itself produced little physical damage but plundered a good deal of the city's wealth and further damaged the prestige of the grand old city. After Alaric's death soon thereafter, the Visigoths ultimately settled in Gaul as *foederati* of the Roman Empire.

Many of the migrations of Germanic peoples during this period were a result of the influx of the Huns. A nomadic group originating in the Eurasian Steppe, the Huns made their way west from central Asia toward Europe around 450. As they reached the edge of Europe, they conquered and occupied the frontiers of the Roman Empire, placing pressure on groups already there to move into the continent's interior. These migrations eventually pushed Germanic groups and others into Roman territory. The Huns were led by their ruler Atilla, who gained a reputation among the Romans for being ruthless as he plundered much of Europe. Atilla oversaw a vast empire, conquering and integrating various peoples as the Huns moved westward. Reaching as far as Gaul, the Hun Empire ultimately collapsed due to Atilla's death in 454.

Other migratory groups during this period settled in Gaul, including the Franks. A one-time ally of the Roman Empire, the Frankish kingdom eventually expelled the Romans and ruled the region in some form until the ninth century. Roman troops were likewise pushed out of Britain for the final time by the invasion of Germanic peoples who included the Angles and the Saxons. Coming from modern-day southern Denmark and northern Germany, they occupied southern Britain in the late fifth century. Originally two distinct groups, they are more commonly known as Anglo-Saxons, a name applied to them in the eighth century to distinguish them from similarly named Germanic groups on the European continent.

DUELING VOICES

The End of Rome

Since the publication of Edward Gibbon's *The History of the Decline and Fall of the Roman Empire* in 1776, historians of Rome have debated what the fall of Rome actually means. An English historian during the Enlightenment, Gibbon presented it as a period of moral decline marked by barbarian invasions and an intolerant Christianity. Newer scholarship takes into account the primary sources from this period. More recent scholars ask what exactly "fell." For example, many third- and fourth-century crises and reforms began much earlier, and the survival of paganism shows that Christianity's rise was not inevitable.

> The decline of Rome was the natural and inevitable effect of immoderate greatness. Prosperity ripened the principle of decay; the causes of destruction multiplied with the extent of conquest; and, as soon as time or accident had removed the artificial supports, the stupendous fabric yielded to the pressure of its own weight. The story of its ruin is simple and obvious; and, instead of inquiring why the Roman empire was destroyed, we should rather be surprised that it had subsisted so long.

—Edward Gibbon, *The History of the Decline and Fall of the Roman Empire*, 1776

To study such a period one must be constantly aware of the tension between change and continuity in the exceptionally ancient and well-rooted world round the Mediterranean. On the one hand, this is notoriously the time when certain ancient institutions, whose absence would have seemed quite unimaginable to a man of about [250 CE], irrevocably disappeared. . . . On the other hand, we are increasingly aware of the astounding new beginnings associated with this period: we go to it to discover why Europe became Christian and why the Near East became Muslim. . . . Looking at the Late Antique world, we are caught between the regretful contemplation of ancient ruins and the excited acclamation of new growth. What we often lack is a sense of what it was like to live in that world.

—Peter Brow, *The World of Late Antiquity*, 1971

At the very same time as some sought new modes for understanding the classical elements of late antique culture, another revolution was taking place, . . . whose method was to seize as objects of study elements that were 'new' in Late Antiquity. . . . much of what has been identified as 'new' falls within the domain of religion, and within that sphere attention has focused on those Christian beliefs and practices that had some claim to novelty in this era: asceticism, monasticism, pilgrimage, and episcopacy foremost among them. But few things are new under the sun, and I worry that scholars, whether from ignorance or naïveté, or in pursuit of some contemporary agenda, too often have credited the ideologically motivated claims to novelty put forward by Christian polemicists at the time.

—Clifford Ando, "Decline, Fall, and Transformation," *Journal of Late Antiquity*, 2008

- How do the scholars quoted here differ in their approaches to the study of Late Antiquity?
- Would they agree on what makes this period unique or the best way to study it? Why or why not?

10.2 The Byzantine Empire and Persia

LEARNING OBJECTIVES

By the end of this section, you will be able to:
- Explain the evolution of the Byzantine Empire in Late Antiquity
- Describe Sasanian culture and society in Late Antiquity
- Analyze the relationship between the Roman Empire and Sasanian Persia in Late Antiquity

The period of Late Antiquity witnessed the height of two great competing empires. The Roman Empire morphed into the Byzantine Empire, possessing a culture that looked to both its Roman past and its Christian present. This duality was exemplified in the reign of the emperor Justinian, who sought to reconquer the old empire. Meanwhile, in the East, the Sasanian Empire emerged with its own vibrant culture and vied with the Byzantines for supremacy. This situation set the stage for the emergence in the following period of smaller but still disruptive states.

Late Antique Rome

Historians have carved out roughly 150 to 750 CE as the period of Late Antiquity and view it as a time of vibrant transformation in the Mediterranean, rather than simply Rome's decline and fall. The cultural focus on the eastern Mediterranean, the rise of Christianity, and new forms of Roman governance indicate some ways in which people from this period thought of themselves as being different from what was seen in the ancient world.

Yet the Roman state continued to function, at least in the East, and many still saw themselves as a part of the classical Mediterranean order. The later Roman Empire was in many ways an extension of the earlier period, replicating and repeating similar trends in governance, culture, and even religion. This interplay between continuity with the ancient world and stark differences from it makes Late Antiquity a unique historical period.

In the late 400s and early 500s, the culture of the empire was changing profoundly as Christianity grew in influence. The centralization of imperial power was coupled with intense growth of the empire's bureaucratic system, in which the wealthy classes were able to control government at the expense of the poor. The Roman senatorial class in particular had changed. While in earlier centuries the Senate had played an important administrative role for the entire state, it now acted largely as a type of aristocratic "city council" for the city of Rome itself, making few meaningful decisions beyond city management and with many members choosing not even to attend. Urban growth continued in some places, despite various setbacks due to war on the eastern frontier, while public spaces in some cities fell into disrepair. In contrast, the Christian Church thrived as a social and economic force in the cities of the eastern Mediterranean, and the construction of monasteries and churches overseen by bishops continued.

Art and architecture produced during this period underwent a similar transformation. Much of the new construction across the empire consisted of the building of churches, many erected with material salvaged from dismantled pagan temples. Churches generally followed the plan of a Roman basilica, with a central nave (aisle) and an apse (small chapel) at one end of the building. Art was also produced in the Christian mode, with icons that depicted holy people or places. Paintings, mosaics, and in later periods stained-glass windows functioned as aids to worship and also as a means of teaching the mostly illiterate people about the Bible stories central to their faith. Mosaics, a hallmark of Roman art, became more elaborate during this period, and artists were able to play with light and color in their designs (Figure 10.11). In much the same way, the classical past influenced Late Antique literature as writers continued to produce histories and works in genres that had enjoyed prominence in earlier times. But literature from this period also represented the Christian present because it was dominated by conversations about theology.

FIGURE 10.11 Empress Theodora. This mid-sixth-century mosaic from the Basilica of San Vitale in Ravenna, Italy, depicts the empress Theodora, wife of the emperor Justinian, presenting a chalice as a symbol of her charity. Theodora's image and the nearby panels depicting her husband emphasized their high status and Christian devotion. (credit: "Mosaic of Empress Theodora, Basilica of San Vitale, Ravenna" by Sharon Mollerus/Flickr, CC BY 2.0)

These cultural and societal trends were prominent in the reign of Justinian I, who was the Eastern Roman emperor from 527 to 565. A devout Christian, Justinian expressed his piety by drafting laws that specifically addressed religious matters. He showed a special interest in religious debates and theology, publishing a series of theological discourses during his reign. In addition, he funded the construction of numerous churches in Constantinople. The most impressive was certainly the Hagia Sophia, or the Church of Holy Wisdom. This church was located next to the imperial residence and hippodrome (a stadium for horse and chariot racing) and was a central point in the city where the emperor could carry out his duties (Figure 10.12).

FIGURE 10.12 Hagia Sophia. Built on the layout of a cross, the Hagia Sophia or Church of Holy Wisdom in Constantinople is massive in size; its main dome is 105 feet in diameter. This lithograph of the exterior was made in 1857; mosaics decorated the rich interior. (credit: modification of work "Lithography of the Hagia Sophia, Istanbul, 1857" by Dmitry Makeev/Wikimedia Commons, Public Domain)

Justinian also focused on maintaining the empire's connection to its past. Among the legal reforms he instituted to preserve its laws, the **Code of Justinian** aimed to compile the laws issued since the early second century. Unlike the Theodosian Code, however, the Code of Justinian regulated imperial edicts by addressing any inconsistencies among them. Though laws were increasingly being issued in Greek by this time, the Code of Justinian also preserved past laws in their original Latin. Thus, while Greek was the dominant language spoken in the empire, Latin continued as the language of legislation and formed part of upper-class education. It also functioned as a means to link the empire to its past. Though the language slowly fell out of use, fluency in Latin was still a status symbol among the wealthy, educated class. In addition to his compilation of edicts, Justinian carried out other legal projects that brought together the written opinions of jurists, legal professionals in the Roman Empire.

Justinian's ambitions also extended to reconquering the West. Though by this time the Byzantine Empire was focused on the eastern Mediterranean, regaining Italy, the earlier seat of the empire, held strong appeal. Following the successful capture of Carthage in Vandal-controlled North Africa, the emperor planned to invade Italy, by that time controlled by the Ostrogoths. He sent his trusted general Belisarius to Italy, and despite having a relatively small force, Belisarius occupied Rome in 536. He made headway in recapturing the cities of Italy, including Milan and Ravenna, and he continued his campaign until 540 when he was recalled to the east to command the troops against the Persians. Justinian completed the conquest of Italy in the 550s, also making inroads against the Visigoths in southern Spain (Figure 10.13).

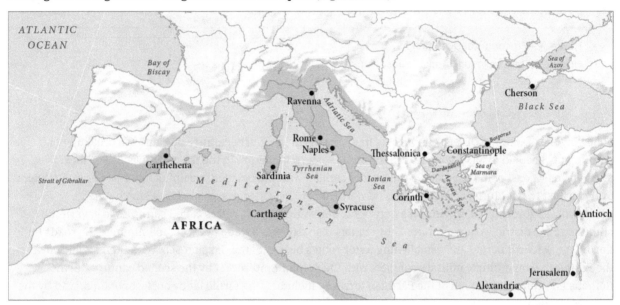

FIGURE 10.13 The Reconquests of Justinian. Justinian's plan to reconquer the western empire (the areas in green) proved effective with a relatively small force, but it ultimately strained his realm, which had to deal with growing problems with the Persians in the East. (attribution: Copyright Rice University, OpenStax, under CC BY 4.0 license)

IN THEIR OWN WORDS

Procopius and the Portrayal of Theodora

Procopius was a prominent scholar in the sixth-century Byzantine Empire whose writings are our key source for many events of the time. He published works such as *The Wars* and *The Buildings* that praised Justinian, but his scandalous work the *Anecdota* ("Secret History") claims to expose Justinian and Theodora as conniving, deceitful rulers. Likely unpublished during the author's lifetime because of its shocking content, *Anecdota* describes the pair as victims of demonic possession, and Theodora as a woman of humble but disgraceful background who used dishonest (and inappropriate) means to become empress. The content is clearly embellished, but its critical viewpoint allows readers to understand how the author may have become disillusioned with Justinian's reign.

> But as soon as she [Theodore] came of age and was at last mature, she joined the women of the stage and straightway became a courtesan, of the sort whom men of ancient times used to call 'infantry.' For she was neither a flute-player nor a harpist, nay, she had not even acquired skill in the dance, but she sold her youthful beauty to those who chanced to come along, plying her trade with practically her whole body . . . . And as she wantoned with her lovers, she always kept bantering them, and by toying with new devices in intercourse, she always succeeded in winning the hearts of the licentious to her; for she did not even expect that the approach should be made by the man she was with, but on the contrary she herself, with wanton jests and with clownish posturing with her hips, would tempt all who came along, especially if they were beardless youths. . . .

> Then at length Justinian set about arranging a betrothal with Theodora. But since it was impossible for a man who had attained to senatorial rank to contract marriage with a courtesan, a thing forbidden from the beginning by the most ancient laws, he compelled the Emperor [Justinian's uncle the emperor

Justin I] to amend the laws by a new law, and from then on he lived with Theodora as his married wife, and he thereby opened the way to betrothal with courtesans for all other men; and as a tyrant he straightway assumed the imperial office, concealing by a fictitious pretext the violence of the act.

—Procopius, *Anecdota*, translated by H.B. Dewing

- How does Procopius depict Theodora's past as scandalous?
- How does this depiction implicate Justinian as an unfit ruler?

From Parthian to Sasanian Persia

Following Alexander the Great's conquest of the Persians in the fourth century BCE and the breakup of his empire, the Seleucid dynasty governed much of his eastern kingdom. In the third century BCE, a local tribe along the east coast of the Caspian Sea came into conflict with the Seleucids, gaining more power in the region over the next two centuries. The Parthians, as they came to be called, were ruled by a king but had a decentralized government, relying on a network of semiautonomous rulers called *satrapies* to govern the administrative districts of the empire. They managed an extensive trade network, maintaining the roads built during the Seleucid period and establishing water routes by way of the Caspian Sea. With their skilled cavalry, the Parthians won multiple military conflicts with the Roman Empire. Yet by the second century CE, the Romans had conquered much of the Parthian territory including the fertile lands of Mesopotamia, won by the emperor Trajan.

This turmoil spurred the Parthians to found a new empire in 224. Ardashir was the first king of the Sasanians, a name derived from the ruler's family name, Sasan. Throughout their history, the Sasanians were in perpetual conflict with the Romans as well as other groups as they attempted to maintain the borders of their empire. Notable events included Shapur I's capture of the Roman emperor Valerian in 260 and, in the fourth century, Shapur II's fortification of the western and eastern borders against encroachment, especially by nomadic groups like the Huns. By the fifth century, priests had largely taken over the administration of the empire after a series of weak kings.

Dubbed the "King of Kings," the Sasanian ruler maintained a centralized state in which local officials reported directly to him. The Sasanians ruled the area of the former classical Persian Empire, including the modern-day country of Iran. The empire extended beyond this region, however, stretching from the modern-day country of Georgia in the west to the Indus River in the east (Figure 10.14). It contained both heavily urbanized centers and various nomadic tribes, especially on the Iranian plateau. The Sasanians were able to leverage their location between the Roman Empire and China to facilitate trade. Their empire's trade network extended far beyond its borders, and it was the Silk Roads that gave the Sasanians the greatest advantage because these land routes linked the empire with numerous regional trading partners.

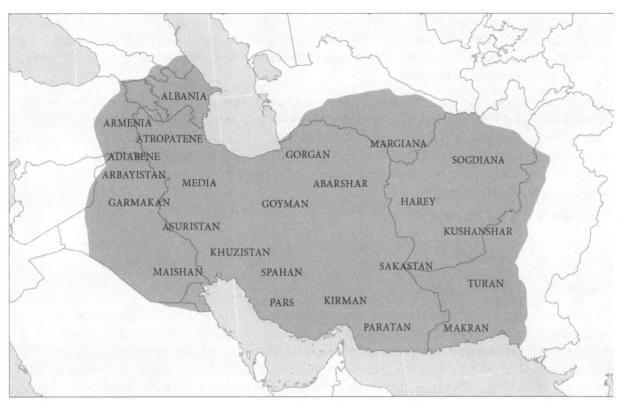

FIGURE 10.14 Sasanian Persia. The Sasanian Empire stretched from modern-day Armenia and Georgia in the west to the Indus River in the east. At its greatest extent in the seventh century, it encroached into once-Byzantine territory through a series of conflicts. (credit: modification of work "Map of the Sassanid Empire just before the Arab conquest of Iran" by "DieBuche"/Wikimedia Commons, Public Domain)

Because of its massive size, the empire was linguistically and culturally diverse. While the west was characterized by interactions with the Byzantines, in the east evidence from inscriptions suggests a diversity of languages and cultures. For example, the use of Greek continued as a remnant of Alexander the Great's empire, and Bactrian was an Iranian language from what is now Afghanistan. In cities throughout the empire, a hierarchical class structure prevailed, with the educated priestly class on top, followed by those who served in the military, agriculturalists, artisans, and finally enslaved people.

As in the Roman and Byzantine worlds, women's legal status was very low, and many laws controlled their behavior. However, women could inherit property from their family and conduct low-level business. Punishments were a way to control Sasanian society and were often tied to sins as defined by the state religion. Incestuous relationships and even marriages were known, particularly among the religious elite, although descriptions of incest as commonplace may be an attempt by successors to belittle the Sasanians in later centuries. There were no opportunities for women to become involved in Sasanian politics, with the single exception of Queen Boran's brief rise just before the collapse of the Sasanian state in the seventh century. The daughter of the previous ruler Khosrow II, she was hailed as ruler despite being a woman because of her connection to Khosrow rather than because of her capability or her status as a woman. While she attempted to build a positive relationship with the Byzantines and to stabilize the Sasanian state, she was ultimately unsuccessful in her efforts before being murdered by her own people, a demonstration of the instability that followed the Sasanian loss in the war.

Ardashir, the first king, instituted Zoroastrianism, the religion of the ancient Persians, as the state religion, encouraging loyalty to the government and to the royal family through religious practice. Zoroastrianism is a universal faith with both monotheistic and dualistic elements, and with rituals and beliefs based on the teachings of the prophet Zoroaster, who lived sometime in the first millennium BCE. Adherents to the faith focus their daily lives on carrying out good deeds, holding good thoughts, and practicing rituals of purification in preparation for their judgment and resurrection after death. Zoroastrian iconography is based on images of fire and water in devotion to the creator god Ahura Mazda. The faith also supposes a perpetual struggle between the dual elements of good and evil. According to Zoroastrian teachings, this struggle will ultimately end in the assured triumph of the good.

The Sasanian kings were intimately involved in the religious affairs of the empire, instituting religious policy and maintaining fire temples across the empire. Yet the population also included Jews and Christians, who could be maligned for their lack of devotion to the state religion. The Sasanian government viewed residents of the western empire as difficult to manage in terms of religion; they may have been seen as particularly susceptible to Byzantine influence because Byzantine rulers claimed dominion over all Christians, including those outside their empire's borders.

LINK TO LEARNING

Learn more about Sasanian art and culture (https://openstax.org/l/77Sasanian) in this presentation.

The Last Great Empires of Antiquity

In the sixth and seventh centuries, the Byzantines and Sasanians lived through their longest period of sustained conflict. Though there were intervals of peace, and even of alliance, military conflict largely characterized the relationship between the two powers. Khosrow I was a particularly adept military leader, thwarting several incursions of nomadic peoples into the Sasanian Empire. He also negotiated peace with the Byzantines in 532. This peace did not last, however, and Khosrow moved westward into Byzantine territory while Justinian was preoccupied with reconquering Italy. During this long war from 541 to 557, the Sasanians won various portions of Byzantine-controlled lands, including Armenia and Syria. The truce signed in 557 ended in 565 with the death of Justinian and the renewal of hostilities.

Khosrow II was the last Sasanian king to conduct a lengthy war with the Byzantines. He originally had a friendly relationship with them, having recovered his throne from a rival with the aid of the Byzantine emperor Maurice. When Maurice was murdered, however, Khosrow used this event as a pretext to invade Byzantine territory in 602. The Sasanians once again occupied Armenia and Syria but now extended their sway further, into Palestine and Egypt, and even reached Libya by 619. The Byzantines retaliated successfully, recovering all their lost territory, and as a result Khosrow II was deposed in 628.

Despite these hostilities, the Sasanians and the Byzantines shared some court rituals and participated in cultural exchange. Each was present in the other's court, and they communicated nearly constantly via embassies, even in times of conflict. The rituals around the court included exchanging gifts and observing processions and games. Both cultures also adopted similar methods of symbolic communication: They used their capital cities (Constantinople and Ctesiphon) as centers of power, relied on a link to their empire's past glory, and created art to communicate legitimacy. They each recognized the other's legitimacy as a rival state, even as they vied for universal power.

In this period of seemingly perpetual war between the two empires, both also used smaller states as proxies in conflicts. The Armenians, despite religious rivalries as Christians, often requested the assistance of the Sasanians, and the Byzantines were able to play different nomadic groups against one another. Gradually, however, the two great empires saw their geographic might dwindle. The states on their peripheries had an important role to play.

10.3 The Kingdoms of Aksum and Himyar

LEARNING OBJECTIVES

By the end of this section, you will be able to:
- Discuss how Aksum and Himyar participated in cultural and economic exchange with other societies
- Explain how issues of religion influenced Aksumite and Himyarite culture
- Describe the religious changes that occurred around the Afro-Eurasian world during Late Antiquity

Beyond the borders of the Byzantine and Sasanian Empires, several smaller states flourished. They established cultural contacts with the large empires, but they were also able to participate in long-distance trade with Asia. Two kingdoms, Aksum in northeastern Africa and Himyar in southern Arabia, had distinct religious identities that informed their governments and cultures. During much of Late Antiquity, faith played a crucial role in shaping people's identities, and the religions of these two kingdoms—Christianity in Aksum and Judaism in Himyar—were no exception.

The Kingdom of Aksum

Aksum flourished in sub-Saharan Africa as a counterpoint to the Byzantine and Sasanian Empires. Located in modern-day Ethiopia and Eritrea, Aksum was able to take advantage of its location adjacent to the Red Sea, expanding across it into southern Arabia for a time. Similarities in architecture and polytheistic practices suggest that the Aksumites may have originally descended from the Sabaean people of southern Arabia. In any case, Aksumites were present in East Africa from at least the first century BCE. At its height, from the third to the sixth century CE, Aksum was a powerful economic force, trading luxury goods with Egypt, Arabia, and the eastern Mediterranean (Figure 10.15).

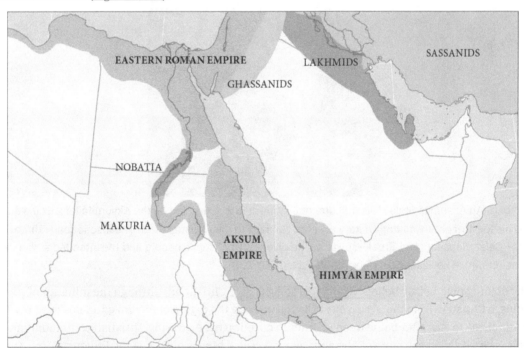

FIGURE 10.15 The Aksum and Himyar Empires. Aksum occupied the region of modern Ethiopia, while Himyar was located on the other side of the Red Sea in modern-day Yemen. The locations of the two empires allowed them to dominate trade in the region. (credit: modification of work "Map of the Sassanid Empire just before the Arab conquest of Iran" by "DieBuche"/Wikimedia Commons, Public Domain)

Aksumite society was hierarchical, with the king and nobility at the top. The lower classes at the bottom worked as artisans and farmers, though little evidence of Aksumite family life has survived to confirm class distinctions. There is some evidence that owners of large wealthy estates existed. To work the land, Aksumite society relied on enslaved people, who were likely criminals or foreigners captured in war. The empire was organized around several urbanized centers with monumental architecture including grand royal palaces, as well as lower-class homes made from stone or mud with thatched roofs. A written Semitic language known as Ge'ez survives in inscriptions from this period. Prior to the arrival of Christianity, the Aksumites held polytheistic beliefs, and numerous religious sanctuaries and temples exist from this early period. A priestly class oversaw the state religion, and the king may have held a prominent role in the religious hierarchy.

King Ezana came to power in the mid-fourth century, and what we know about the Christianization of Aksum comes largely from his reign. Ezana conducted successful military engagements against the Beja and Nubian people, subduing the Kingdom of Kush that had ruled southern Egypt for at least the previous millennium. A great builder, Ezana is also likely responsible for the construction of several obelisks. Inscriptions on *stelae* (commemorative slabs or pillars) and obelisks erected in Aksumite cities describe his exploits and profess his faith, while coinage shows the Christian cross gradually replacing other symbols (Figure 10.16).

FIGURE 10.16 An Aksumite Stela. This monumental stone slab was erected by the Aksumite king Ezana and attributes his fourth-century military victory over the Nubians to the Christian God. The inscription in three languages—Ge'ez, Sabaean, and Greek—suggests the diversity of Aksum's people and the intended audience for this monument. (credit: "The Ezana Stone" by Alan/Flickr, CC BY 2.0)

Originally holding polytheistic beliefs, Ezana was converted to Christianity through the initiative of Frumentius, a Christian from the Syrian city of Tyre. Entering the region of Aksum as an enslaved man, Frumentius chose to stay after being freed in order to encourage the growing Christian community, and Athanasius, the Christian patriarch of Alexandria, consecrated him as bishop of the Ethiopian Church. This custom of patriarchs ordaining bishops for foreign cities often strained their relations with local rulers. But it showed that the Christian powers outside Aksum were interested in controlling religious policy there, and Ezana's conversion may have been a means for Aksum to become more closely allied with the Roman Empire.

Interference from the Christian community abroad culminated in the arrival of proselytizing missionaries from the Roman world in the fourth and fifth centuries, who were working to spread the message of their faith with new peoples. While Christianity had largely been adopted in urban centers thanks to the activity of

Frumentius, these later missionaries were able to spread the faith into the Aksumite countryside. They established hermitages and monasteries in traditionally pagan sites and occasionally suffered persecution by the local inhabitants. Yet Christianity continued to spread, and inscriptions of the time show biblical passages being translated into Ge'ez. Because of infrequent oversight by the patriarchs in Alexandria, however, Ethiopian Christianity developed unique characteristics, blending local beliefs in its own church ceremonies and holidays.

The Judaic group living in Aksum was known as Beta Israel. Probably founded by artisan traders visiting Aksum in the first century, Beta Israel was isolated from other Jewish communities outside the empire. Therefore, like those of Aksumite Christianity, its religious practices were sometimes distinct from the way the faith was practiced in other contexts. In several traditions, Aksum was the kingdom of the biblical figure the Queen of Sheba and the location of the lost Ark of the Covenant, an important artifact supposedly brought from Jerusalem by Ethiopia's first emperor, Menelik. Still, the Ethiopian Jewish community experienced periods of both tolerance and persecution within Aksum.

Christianity continued to flourish in Aksum into the sixth-century reign of King Kaleb. By this time, churches were a common feature in Aksumite cities, and many of the most prominent examples were built in the sixth century with inscriptions claiming that Kaleb had contributed to their construction. The floor plans of Aksumite churches generally followed that of Byzantine churches or basilica, meaning they were oblong in shape with a rounded apse at one end. Still, some were unique in their design, with a circular plan that might have been based on local house types.

The apex of Aksumite society, in the sixth century, coincided with the extension of its cultural and political influence into southern Arabia. Kaleb had already established more connections overseas, initiating a silk trade with China. In Arabia, he sought to aid the local Christian communities with a military campaign against the Himyarite king Dhu Nuwas. Owing to their claimed lineage from the biblical figures King Solomon and the Queen of Sheba, the Aksumites may have felt some pull to conquer the biblical kingdom of Sheba in southern Arabia. These overtly Christian motivations allowed for an alliance with the Byzantines in the campaign against the non-Christian Himyarites. With the Byzantine emperor Justin (uncle of the future emperor Justinian), Kaleb subdued Dhu Nuwas, and Aksum controlled southern Arabia until the Sasanian conquest in 572.

After the reign of Kaleb, the Aksumite Kingdom fell into decline, having failed to garner enough resources from working the land to sustain its population. Although it is unclear why this decline occurred so quickly, the climate may have been a factor because the region appears to have become especially arid after the middle of the eighth century. Economic difficulties in the kingdom may have also contributed. Kaleb's campaign in Arabia could have overextended its finances and military strength, and the Sasanian occupation of the regions around the Red Sea might have disrupted Aksum's trade network. There appears to have been growing dissatisfaction among the ruling class, and evidence from inscriptions suggests that revolts occurred in some Aksumite cities. As a result of these contributing factors, Aksum fell from political and cultural prominence in the mid-600s.

⊘ LINK TO LEARNING

Explore Ethiopia's Aksumite rock churches (https://openstax.org/l/77RockChurch) and the continuing practice of Christianity in Ethiopia today.

The Kingdom of Himyar

The Kingdom of Himyar flourished in southern Arabia from the first century BCE to the sixth century CE, on the coast of modern-day Yemen (Figure 10.15). The Himyarites originated from the kingdom of the Sabaeans, a Semitic people who had occupied southern Arabia from at least 1000 BCE. The Himyarites, however, were able to form their own kingdom because of the discovery of a prosperous trade route on the Red Sea coast. From the first century BCE to the second century CE, the Himyarites absorbed the Sabean and Qataban kingdoms, as well as several local tribes, and created their own capital in Zafar. This centralization of power unified the entire region of southern Arabia under a single government for the first time.

Once Himyar had become unified, it sought to maintain good relations with its neighbors by focusing on the exchange of goods from abroad. Unlike the Sabaeans, who had earlier dominated trade in the region through overland routes, the Himyarites shifted their focus to maritime trade. They had access to a port on their southern coast that lay along an important sea route from Egypt to Asia, and they traded luxury goods such as ivory and spices, acting as a waypoint between the Roman Empire, East Africa, and India.

The Himyarites had traditionally practiced a polytheistic religion, but in Late Antiquity the kingdom experienced a religious transformation when King Abu Karib As'ad chose to convert to Judaism in the early years of his reign, around 390 CE. The conversion of the people followed, and Judaism spread among the elite Himyarites first, perhaps as a means of appeasing the king and gaining political goodwill. However, some scholars have speculated that Himyar's focus on Judaism was politically motivated, because it appears that a substantial Jewish population already existed in Arabia. The king may have felt compelled to create a Jewish state when one was no longer possible in Palestine because the Christian Byzantines controlled it. Much like the Byzantine emperors, who were religious reformers, the kings of Himyar publicly displayed their religious devotion. Several inscriptions from this period are dedicated to "the one God of Heaven and Earth." Kings also constructed synagogues for the burgeoning Jewish community.

Himyar came into increasing contact with Christian missionaries inside its borders, and several churches were built in Himyarite cities in the fourth and fifth centuries. The earliest known Christian missionary was the diplomat Theophilus, sent as an ambassador by the Roman emperor Constantius II around 354. Because of Himyar's access to lucrative trade routes, the Byzantines sought to influence the local population by converting them to Christianity, much as they had done in Aksum. The Himyarites responded to this outside interference in their kingdom by dealing with the Christians violently. Christian missionaries, Byzantine merchants, and other perceived outsiders were seized and put on trial. Overseen by the king and other religious officials, the trials resulted in the execution of numerous Christians in the late fifth century. Political rather than religious motivations spurred much of this violence, but in the following period that rationale changed, and the violence against Christians escalated.

In 522, King Dhu Nuwas began to conduct a military campaign against any Ethiopians or Christian sympathizers in the kingdom. Priests were killed and churches burned or dismantled and converted into synagogues. At Najran, home to a large Christian population, Dhu Nuwas set up a blockade in an effort to turn the population against the city's Christians. He ultimately executed hundreds of Christians there and in Zafar. Hoping to form a larger Jewish state, Dhu Nuwas also sought alliances with the Sasanians and Jewish residents in Palestine. As previously discussed, this violence and political maneuvering in Himyar piqued the interest of Aksum, which was the kingdom's chief rival because of its nearby location across the Red Sea.

The conquest by the Aksumites in the 520s was followed by the rule of Abraha, the Ethiopian who had commanded the Aksumite forces. A staunch Christian, Abraha sought to eradicate Judaism and other faiths in Himyar, attempting to wipe out idolatry and any lingering elements of paganism in the region. His major building projects included a grand church and the reconstruction of the Marib Dam. Abraha's rule was brief, however, and Sasanian loyalists controlled Himyar until the arrival of Islam in the seventh century.

THE PAST MEETS THE PRESENT

South Arabian Geography and Agriculture

The Arabian Peninsula is largely a desert landscape, experiencing hot temperatures and little rain year-round. In the southwest, however, in what is today Yemen, the highlands allow for somewhat cooler temperatures and consistent rainfall. This makes for a fertile and hospitable region. There is much evidence that crops were grown in ancient Arabia, mainly date-palms, olives, grapes, and other fruits. But farmers also cultivated wheat, cotton, and henna. What made this farming possible were feats of engineering that allowed the local population to harness water.

For example, in the city of Marib in central Yemen, a great dam was constructed to provide water for local agriculture. Marib was the capital of the Sabaean kingdom, which used the dam to great purpose for farming in the city by means of an intricate irrigation system. However, the construction of the dam may predate the Sabaeans, perhaps having begun in the eighteenth-century BCE. In the 520s CE, the conquering Himyarites took control of the structure and raised the height of its walls, though it later collapsed in 570.

The ability to harness water was important to sustaining prolonged settlements in Arabia in Late Antiquity. In addition to constructing dams and irrigation systems, the people of this region collected water from flash floods and used terracing in hilly regions.

Of all Yemen's most famous agricultural products, however, few have had as large an impact on world history as coffee. From the medieval period onward, central Yemen in particular became known for the growing and trade of *Coffea Arabica*, or Arabica coffee beans. While it is believed that these beans originated in the Horn of Africa before crossing the Red Sea, it was in Ottoman-controlled Yemen during the fifteenth century that the hot beverage known as coffee was first consumed. Even today, more than half of all coffee beans grown and consumed throughout the world are these Arabica beans.

- What agricultural products come to mind when you think of the Arabian Peninsula?
- What does the spread of Arabica coffee and its popularity around the world say about the interconnectedness of people throughout history?

🔗 LINK TO LEARNING

Learn more about the Marib Dam and agriculture (https://openstax.org/l/77MaribDam) in South Arabia.

Religious Influence at the End of Antiquity

The arrival of new traditions of faith was a defining feature of Late Antiquity, and state-sponsored religion was a critical element in the conduct of empires' relations with one another and with their own subjects. An increasing number of individuals in Late Antiquity came to identify themselves not as citizens of a particular location or even an empire, but as members of the community associated with their religion.

Unlike paganism, Christianity was a proselytizing religion; that is, Christian leaders hoped to convert others to their faith. Elite Christian thinkers disseminated religious knowledge to a wide audience and strove to construct a single agreed-upon narrative of what Christian identity meant. Theological writings, ecumenical councils, and the interpretation of Christian rituals were all part of this meticulous effort, and ongoing participation in the defining of belief and practice were instrumental in Christianity's spread during this period.

The running of the state also became intimately tied to religion and religious policy, as the policies of Justinian and other Christian emperors and the institution of Zoroastrianism in the Sasanian Empire show. The Aksumites and Himyarites too, although they embraced different faiths, used religious imagery in their inscriptions and monumental buildings. Each empire's elite endorsed this kind of religious messaging, converting to the new faith in great numbers, while the general populace in Late Antique communities often remained religiously diverse.

Judaism became a religion without a firm geographic center after the Romans destroyed the Second Temple in

Jerusalem in the first century CE. The **Jewish diaspora** refers to the subsequent dispersion of believers out of the traditional Jewish homeland of Israel/Palestine, which led Jewish groups around the Mediterranean to feel a sense of displacement and the need to form a community. Though some of their individual practices may have differed, those in locations as varied as Spain and southern Arabia could largely agree on the tenets of their faith. In Late Antiquity, Christian theologians' attitudes toward Jewish people hardened, and restrictive laws were instituted by the Byzantine emperors. Yet despite these hostilities, Jewish culture flourished, especially in Palestine, resulting in the construction of many new synagogues and art (Figure 10.17).

FIGURE 10.17 The Finding of Moses. This wall painting from a third-century synagogue in the city of Dura-Europos, in modern-day Syria, is one of many with biblical themes. It depicts the discovery by the pharaoh's daughter of the infant Moses in the Nile River. (credit: "Dura Europos fresco Moses from river" by Unknown/Wikimedia Commons, Public Domain)

Christians marked their devotion in numerous ways during this period. One was **asceticism**, a form of self-denial that includes foregoing bodily pleasures and adopting a life of chastity, virginity, and renunciation of normal society. Monasteries that housed groups devoted to the ascetic life spread across the empire, usually in remote locations and often in the desert. Despite their isolation, however, many accepted visitors, so that the reputation of various holy people might spread to Christians everywhere. Many ascetics played a leading role in their communities, sometimes extending beyond the realm of civil behavior. For example, Late Antiquity witnessed a surge in violence carried out by ascetic monks against nonbelievers in cities of the empire, in an effort to preserve a sort of "pure" Christianity.

Despite continuing efforts to define proper Christian orthodoxy, regional differences among religious sects persisted during this time. For example, a crucial divide developed between urban and rural devotion. Saint Anthony was perhaps the most famous of the so-called Desert Fathers who in the third century chose to give up his possessions and practice asceticism in the Egyptian desert. These ascetics attracted followers, and as a result monasteries and hermitages flourished in less hospitable areas. Monasteries such as Kellia in the Egyptian desert housed a community of monks who lived together but had some contact with the surrounding region, while hermitages were places of more extreme seclusion for the religiously devout. By contrast, churches and synagogues were located in often crowded cities, where attendance at services was a daily life for laypeople. But these religious centers had to compete with other concerns for people's attention. Evidence suggests that elements of religious devotion that originated from the polytheistic environment of earlier centuries also persisted, such as home shrines, magical spells, and other private practices.

On a larger scale, geographic divisions produced different types of devotion. Aksum in Ethiopia embraced a unique version of Christianity because of its relative isolation from the rest of the Christian world. In the Mediterranean as well, people of the same faith could differ in their experience of the same religion. For example, Nestorian Christianity emerged in the fifth century in the debates about Christ's divinity, claiming that Jesus existed as two individuals—human and divine. Though officially rejected by the church in the ecumenical Council of Chalcedon in 451, Nestorius's teachings flourished in Persia and spread eastward due to the efforts of missionaries.

10.4 The Margins of Empire

LEARNING OBJECTIVES

By the end of this section, you will be able to:
- Discuss the economic and cultural exchange between the Kushan Empire and other societies
- Explain Palmyra's relationship with the Roman Empire and how it was able to become an independent state
- Analyze the way Arab tribes interacted with the Roman Empire and Sasanian Persia

On the Silk Roads linking Europe and Asia in Late Antiquity, several small kingdoms functioned as important intermediaries for goods and people entering the Mediterranean world, as well as being trade partners, military adversaries, and allies of the great Byzantine and Sasanian Empires. The Kushan Empire served as an important cog in the trade route linking the Mediterranean and East Asia, but the ethnic and religious diversity of its population is also important in understanding this empire's role in Late Antiquity. Palmyra was a major trading partner in the Mediterranean world, but the rule of Queen Zenobia shows how quickly a city-state could take advantage of its geographic position and a tumultuous political situation to expand its borders. Finally, the diversity of groups in the Arabian Peninsula provided the context for the rise of Islam in the following period. The peoples discussed in this section demonstrate the complexity of the wider world of Late Antiquity. They made connections far beyond their borders, and their multiregional societies often had culturally diverse populations.

The Kushan Empire

The Kushan Empire was located in northwest India and flourished from the second century BCE to the third century CE. The empire initially arose from the Yuezhi people's uniting of several nomadic tribes into a single state. Eventually renamed Kushan after its ruling dynasty, this state gradually took territory from the Parthians' eastern empire. Sometime in the first century BCE, the Kushans moved south, establishing the dual capital cities of Kapisa and Pushklavati near the modern-day cities of Kabul and Peshawar. Under the control of the emperor Kanishka, who ruled the empire during the mid-second century CE (the exact dates are uncertain), the Kushan Empire reached its greatest extent and cultural influence. Kanishka conducted military campaigns, extending Kushan into central China and northern India, and the empire eventually included parts of Pakistan, Afghanistan, and Uzbekistan, as well as northern India (Figure 10.18).

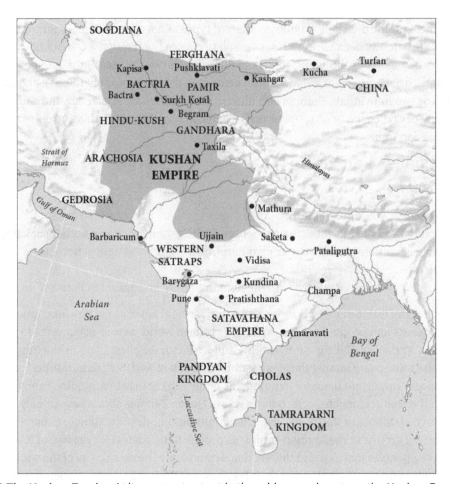

FIGURE 10.18 The Kushan Empire. At its greatest extent in the mid-second century, the Kushan Empire stretched from modern-day Uzbekistan to northern India, with two capital cities: Kapisa and Pushklavati. (attribution: Copyright Rice University, OpenStax, under CC BY 4.0 license)

At the confluence of several rivers in a valley plain, the Gandhara region of Kushan was home to a particularly vibrant culture whose influence extended across the Indus River into the rest of Kushan. The people of Gandhara produced a unique artistic style, incorporating Greco-Roman elements but focused on Buddhist subjects. This blending of cultures extended to the region's population; as a result of multiple conquests made before the Kushan Empire, the people of Gandhara claimed lineage from the Macedonian Greeks at the time of Alexander, from the Parthians, and from Indian peoples.

IN THEIR OWN WORDS

The Diverse Culture of Kushan: An Outsider's Perspective

There was a literary tradition in central Asia during the period of the Kushan Empire, but anything that could have provided primary information about Kushan has been lost. The region was fascinating for outsiders, however, who wrote extensively about its different peoples, its diverse culture, and its extensive trade network. *The Periplus of the Erythraean Sea*, written in Greek by an anonymous Egyptian merchant around 70 CE, is a firsthand account of trade routes beginning in Egypt and covering east Africa and Arabia before finally focusing on the east coast of India. The author discusses the nature of each route, the goods imported and exported, and the nature of local people in each region.

> The country inland from Barygaza is inhabited by numerous tribes, such as the Arattii, the Arachosii, the Gandaraei and the people of Poclais, in which is Bucephalus Alexandria. Above these is the very war-like

nation of the Bactrians [Kushan], who are under their own king. And Alexander, setting out from these parts, penetrated to the Ganges, leaving aside Damirica [Limyrike] and the southern part of India; and to the present day ancient drachma [Greek coins] are current in Barygaza, coming from this country, bearing inscriptions in Greek letters, and the devices of those who reigned after Alexander, Apollodotus and Menander." (47)

"After this region under the very north, the sea outside ending in a land called This, there is a very great inland city called Thinae [China], from which raw silk and silk yarn and silk cloth are brought on foot through Bactria to Barygaza, and are also exported to Damirica [Limyrike] by way of the river Ganges. But the land of This is not easy of access; few men come from there, and seldom. The country lies under the Lesser Bear [Ursa Minor] and is said to border on the farthest parts of Pontus and the Caspian Sea, next to which lies Lake Maeotis; all of which empty into the ocean.

—Author unknown, *The Periplus of the Erythraean Sea*, translated by Schoff

- What sense do you get about the extent and diversity of the Kushan trade network based on this author's account?
- What features of this account demonstrate that it was written by an outsider, rather than an indigenous member of Kushan society?
- What challenges do historians face if these are the only types of accounts available to teach Kushan history?

Kushan played a crucial role along the Silk Roads, acting as the link between the trading partners China and the Roman Empire. Its connections to Rome are clear from the Roman coins found in the Kushan region, as well as from written evidence that several Kushan embassies were sent to Roman emperors. Romans in turn received various luxury goods from Asia via Kushan, including jewelry, furs, and silk. In addition, Kushan protected a mountain pass that linked its empire to central China, allowing people and goods to easily enter this region. Its trade and cultural ties in China extended as far as Mongolia. Through its proximity to the sea to the south via the Indus River valley, Kushan also connected maritime and overland trade routes, and Kushan materials have been found in locations from Scandinavia to Ethiopia.

The religious identities of the region were likewise diverse, with a mix of people practicing Buddhism and Zoroastrianism among other faiths. Religious accommodation was a hallmark of Kushan, and its rulers might have felt compelled to embrace various faiths to win over people newly integrated into the empire. For example, some coinage of Kushan rulers shows a fire altar that bears a striking resemblance to Zoroastrian iconography. Yet Buddhism appears to have been important to the rulers of Kushan, who gave this religion special preference. For example, Emperor Kanishka undertook several initiatives to promote Buddhism. He made Buddhist texts more widely available and had many translated into other native languages such as Sanskrit. Around 100 CE, he convened the Fourth Buddhist Council in Kashmir. This council decided to recognize two sects of Buddhism, Mahayan and Hinayan, and compiled the Sarvastivadin Abhidharma texts, a systematic presentation of Buddhist doctrines. Kanishka also contributed to the production of art in Kushan. In what may have been a further attempt at accommodating different beliefs, Kushan art includes the first images of the Buddha in human form (Figure 10.19).

FIGURE 10.19 The Buddha. This skillfully made third-century sculpture, about three feet high, depicts the Buddha in human form. The flowing drapery of his dress may have been influenced by the Greek toga, suggesting the multiethnic makeup of the region of Gandhara where it was made. (credit: "Buddha" by Purchase, Denise and Andrew Saul Gift, in honor of Maxwell K. Hearn, 2014/The Metropolitan Museum of Art, Public Domain)

The pass connecting Kushan and China also allowed Buddhist monks to bring their religion to China in the second century. The most prominent example of this religious transmission was the activity of the Kushan monk Lokaksema, who traveled to China sometime in the 180s. Originally from Gandhara, Lokaksema was a Buddhist scholar who spent his time in China at the court of the Han dynasty, translating Mahayana Buddhist texts with his students. Once they were available in Chinese, these *sutras,* representing a genre of Buddhist scripture, could reach a wider audience. Thus Kushan's links allowed Buddhism to grow both intentionally and organically, given that the presence of Buddhists on the area's extensive trade routes surely led to its spread.

After the death of the emperor Vasudeva I in the early third century, the Kushan Empire split into eastern and western halves that were ruled separately. Centered in modern-day Afghanistan, the western half of the empire fell under the control of the Sasanians in 248, who replaced the ruling dynasty with loyal chiefs referred to today as Indo-Sasanians. The Indo-Sasanian kingdoms were given partial autonomy, so they were self-governing for a time while also paying tribute to the Sasanians. The activities of Buddhist monasteries and the production of art appear to have persisted despite the political changes of this period.

The Gupta Empire campaigned against Kushan's eastern half, centered in the Punjab region of modern-day northern India, leading to its eventual absorption into this empire around 375. The final remnants of the Kushan Empire were eventually taken over by the Hephthalites (the White Huns) in the fifth century.

Palmyra as Rival to the Roman Empire

Located in south-central Syria, the city of Palmyra rose in influence in the third century BCE because of its proximity to a newly built east–west road. As a result, the city was linked to a wider trade network between the Roman state and the east via both the Silk Roads and the Persian Gulf. By funneling goods to the Roman state, the city came to the special attention of the Romans in the first century BCE. Though there is evidence that Roman officials and military were in the city at this time, Palmyra's government remained semiautonomous throughout the period.

Palmyra was made part of the Roman province of Syria in the first century CE, and it eventually achieved the status of a Roman colony. This designation meant that its inhabitants were Roman citizens, and at least on the surface, public life was culturally Roman. The city continued to receive imperial favor, being visited by several Roman emperors. Palmyra became the site of architectural adornment with the construction of several remarkable monuments and structures. These included the Great Colonnade, the city's main street, and a famous temple dedicated to the god Baal. Several different Mesopotamian civilizations worshipped Baal, who was considered the chief deity of weather and fertility.

The emperor Trajan added the Nabataean Kingdom, inhabited by a Semitic people of northern Arabia, to the Roman Empire in 106 CE. As a result of this annexation, the Nabataeans' trade network seems to have disintegrated, an event that greatly benefited the Palmyrenes who no longer had to compete against them. However, the growing power of the Parthian Empire at this time led some trade routes to the east to become cut off. To address these sorts of threats to Palmyra's trade network, the city allied itself more closely with the Roman Empire. In 267, the leader of Palmyra, Septimius Odaenathus, was assassinated while fighting the Parthians as an ally of the Roman Empire. His widow Zenobia took over as regent of the Palmyrene Kingdom, declaring herself empress.

In 269, Zenobia broke off ties with the Roman state and expanded the borders of her kingdom, first taking Anatolia and then Egypt. Because of the disarray of the Crisis of the Third Century, during which their empire split into three separate states for a time, the Romans had left these regions relatively unguarded. Palmyra benefited greatly, now having links to extensive trade networks via the Red Sea. Her kingdom's independence was short-lived, however, since the Roman emperor Aurelian conquered Palmyra in 272 and took Zenobia captive. Sources differ on her ultimate fate, but one famous anecdote tells of her being led through Rome in gold chains, a sign of the wealth she had accumulated as the leader of this prosperous kingdom (Figure 10.20).

FIGURE 10.20 Queen Zenobia. Issued in 272 CE, this rare silver coin names its subject Zenobia and shows her as queen of Palmyra wearing a royal diadem (left). The reverse of the coin (right) says "Regina" (queen in Latin) and shows the Roman goddess Juno, wife of Jupiter, holding a dish for pouring offerings and a scepter. (credit: "Zenobia" by Classical Numismatic Group/Wikimedia Commons, Public Domain)

🔗 LINK TO LEARNING

Though the emperor Aurelian returned and sacked the city of Palmyra in 273, a vast archaeological site there remained well preserved until relatively recently. Explore the consequences of ISIS's occupation of Palmyra (https://openstax.org/l/77Palmyra) and destruction of this ancient city between 2015 and 2017, and the recent efforts to restore it.

Following the capture of Zenobia, Palmyra's influence in the region dwindled. The city remained under Roman control, since Aurelian had left behind a military garrison whose soldiers formed a major part of the city's population. In the late third century, the eastern frontier of the empire was reorganized, and the changed arrangement of forts and roads put Palmyra at a disadvantage for participating in trade. Certain emperors took some interest in the city; Diocletian had a public baths complex constructed, and Justinian is said to have had the city's walls rebuilt. Palmyra's Christian population also appears to have grown during this period. The first church there dates from the fourth century, and Christians took over the temple of Baal in the fifth century. Despite continued habitation, however, Palmyra now had less regional influence, and the nearby city of Nisibis became the region's main trade hub.

The Arab Tribes

Nomadic tribes have a deep history in the region of Arabia. From at least the early first millennium BCE, they survived in this somewhat harsh environment through pastoral farming, raising livestock such as sheep and goats to produce milk, wool, and other goods. They are known as **Bedouin,** from the Arabic word *badawī* meaning "desert dwellers," and their nomadic lifestyle was a key part of their Arab identity. Bedouin tribes consisted of familial clan groups that were patriarchal (ruled by men) and patrilineal (inheritance was through the father). Because of their familial relationships, tribes were tight-knit groups that had skeptical views of outsiders, occasionally coming into violent conflict with other tribes ([Figure 10.21](#)).

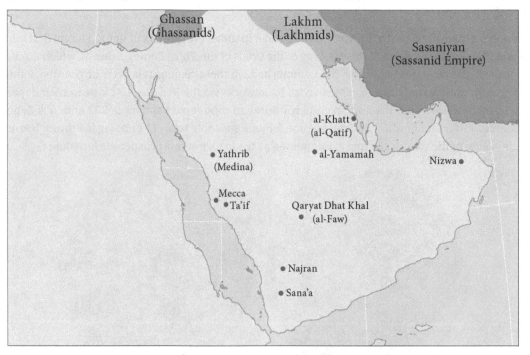

FIGURE 10.21 Territories of Arab Tribes. The map shows approximate locations of some of the numerous Arab tribes that competed for regional control around 600 CE. These tribes were semi-independent kingdoms susceptible to Byzantine and Sasanian influence, especially in northern Arabia. (credit: modification of work "Map of Arabia 600 AD" by "Murraytheb"/Wikimedia Commons, Public Domain)

After military conflict brought them to the eastern empire in the first century BCE, the Romans allowed Arab tribal chiefs of both sedentary town-dwellers and nomadic Bedouin groups to govern themselves. By the second century CE, however, the Roman Empire had begun to absorb the northern regions of Arabia, reflected in its subduing of the Nabataeans and the emperor Trajan's creation of the Arabian province. But the Romans never made true headway in this region, occupying only the northwestern fringes of Arabia, and for a relatively short period. Instead, Arab tribes continued to be a problem for the Roman Empire on its frontier as they migrated to the outskirts of Syria by the third century.

The Arabs served as clients, a type of ally, of the Sasanians, especially in the fifth and sixth centuries, as well as *foederati* of the Byzantine Empire in its long conflict against the Sasanians. For example, the Lakhmid kingdom in northern Arabia was at its height during this period. As an ally of the Sasanian Empire, Lakhmid used its military might to control the northern Arabian tribes. In addition, the Sasanian Persian king Khosrow I cooperated with the Lakhmids in the conquest of Yemen in the sixth century. In a similar role, the Ghassan kingdom was allied with the Byzantines and functioned as a buffer between the eastern empire and the Sasanians. The Ghassanids often clashed with the Lakhmids, whom they defeated in 554, eventually capturing their capital city (Al-Hirah) in 578.

Since there were several Arabian groups in the region, its pre-Islamic culture was diverse and multifaceted. As the most prominent group by the end of the sixth century, the Ghassanids are thought to have contributed to the creation of a somewhat cohesive Arab identity, which included kinship organization, the growth of cultural traditions such as poetry, and the use of languages that later became Arabic. Possibly settled by this time, the Ghassanids constructed monumental buildings in their urban centers and governed a diverse Arab culture.

The religious life of Arabia was diverse. The peninsula was home to those practicing Christianity, Judaism, Zoroastrian, and polytheism. Traditional polytheistic views included animism, or the recognition of a spiritual essence in natural objects such as plants, animals, and rivers. Arabian polytheists worshipped idols and totems, physical representations of divine spirits. Containing a variety of religious idols, the Kaaba sanctuary in the city of Mecca was the site of religious pilgrimage during this period, perhaps setting the stage for Islamic pilgrimage in the following centuries. Members of the Jewish diaspora had begun to migrate into Arabia in the first century CE. New converts to Judaism in this region as well as the influence of Himyar led to the development of a substantial Jewish population here. By Late Antiquity, Christianity had also gained a foothold, especially in the north, as the influence of the Byzantine and proselytizing missionaries contributed to the growth of the Christian population.

The composition of poetry was a major feature of pre-Islamic culture and formed part of an oral tradition that passed poems from generation to generation. Performers memorized often lengthy poems for recitation before public and private audiences. These works express tribal identity because their content often concerns the nature of nomadic life and descriptions of the natural world. In addition to this oral tradition, pre-Islamic literature began to be written down more often by Late Antiquity, and Arabic script was increasingly in use by the sixth century. Papyrus documents surviving from cities like Petra show Arabic script alongside Greek and Latin, pointing to the region's diversity and transitional state.

Key Terms

asceticism the practice of self-denial and rejection of pleasures as a way to express religious devotion

Bedouin the name given to nomadic tribes of Arabia

Code of Justinian a legal project carried out by Emperor Justinian to compile and edit Roman edicts issued from the second to the sixth century CE

ecumenical councils meetings organized by emperors that gathered Christian bishops from around the empire to settle matters of doctrine within the Church

foederati foreign states and tribes that were given semiautonomy as Roman allies in exchange for pledging military service to the Roman Empire

Jewish diaspora the dispersion of the Jewish people beyond their ancestral homeland of Israel/Palestine following the Romans' destruction of the Second Temple

Late Antiquity a transitional period between the ancient and medieval worlds that occurred from roughly 150 to 750 CE

tetrarchy the rule of four emperors, two senior and two junior, established by the emperor Diocletian to quell the Crisis of the Third Century

Theodosian Code a document initiated by the emperor Theodosius II compiling laws from around the empire that had been issued since the early fourth century

Section Summary

10.1 The Eastward Shift

After the political tumult of the third century, the emperor Constantine reinvigorated the Roman Empire by establishing a new capital in Constantinople and embracing Christianity. Both Constantine and the Christian emperors who succeeded him attempted to manage the church and Christian orthodoxy through ecumenical councils, new laws, and increased bureaucratization in the Roman government. This new religious culture resulted in the neglect of traditional Roman polytheism, and the empire's eastward shift came at the expense of the western empire. In the Roman West, Germanic peoples became both allies and enemies of the Roman state. The imperial government was able to manage these groups for a time, but by the fifth century, the Roman West had fragmented into various Germanic kingdoms.

10.2 The Byzantine Empire and Persia

The two great superpowers of Late Antiquity, the Byzantine Empire and the Sasanian Empire, vied for supremacy in the fifth and sixth centuries. Though the Byzantine Empire had to contend with the Sasanians as a particularly formidable challenge, the reign of Justinian witnessed the zenith of Byzantine culture. Justinian carried out monumental building projects, codified Roman law, and oversaw the reconquest of parts of the Roman West. The Sasanians meanwhile consolidated control over a vast region of central Asia, overseeing a large trade network and instituting Zoroastrianism as the state religion. Military conflict characterized the relationship between these two empires, but there were also periods of peace and cultural exchange.

10.3 The Kingdoms of Aksum and Himyar

Two kingdoms flourished on the periphery of the Byzantine and Sasanian Empires in Late Antiquity. In East Africa, Aksum oversaw a trade network with a wide geographic scope. King Ezana's conversion to Christianity in the fourth century was a seminal moment for the empire because it was then able to use religious motivation to conduct a military campaign in southern Arabia. Here, the Himyarite Empire subsumed local groups to become a unified state that converted to Judaism sometime in the fifth century CE.

These two kingdoms demonstrate the diversity of Late Antique societies because each had to manage its disparate populations and interact with different regional powers. Their history also shows the political motivations of their governments' religious policies. While the use of religion to justify administrative and military campaigns was a hallmark of Late Antique life, ordinary people expressed their individual faiths in a variety of ways.

10.4 The Margins of Empire

The Kushan Empire in central Asia is an example of the diversity found beyond the Mediterranean during Late Antiquity. The Kushan Empire dominated trade along the Silk Roads, was home to a religiously diverse population, and promoted the burgeoning religion of Buddhism within and outside its borders. The city of Palmyra was able to rival the Roman Empire for a short time in the third-century eastern Mediterranean. By taking advantage of a tumultuous political situation, Queen Zenobia expanded her empire, and Palmyra flourished as a nexus of trade in the region. The peoples of pre-Islamic Arabia likewise interacted with the major superpowers of Late Antiquity. The Arabian Peninsula was a culturally diverse region and home to a mix of different religions and distinct tribal groups.

Assessments

Review Questions

1. What made the Western Roman Empire more prone to societal disruption than the Eastern Roman Empire?
   a. The West had a larger population of Christians.
   b. The West had a longer frontier and was less urbanized.
   c. Western cities were ruled exclusively by bishops.
   d. German kings rejected Christianity.

2. How did the Huns affect the migration of Germanic peoples?
   a. They bribed the Visigoths to invade Italy and sack Rome.
   b. They put pressure on the frontier, pushing people into Roman territory.
   c. They forced the Vandals to attack the Saxons.
   d. They spread Christianity past the frontier of the empire.

3. What role did bishops play in Roman governance?
   a. They served in the Roman military.
   b. They instituted monetary reforms in periods of crisis.
   c. They participated in ecumenical councils and dominated local politics.
   d. They collaborated with pagans in public education.

4. Through what means did the Sasanian kings rule their empire?
   a. direct centralized control
   b. semiautonomous rulers in the eastern empire
   c. proxy governments, such as that of Armenia
   d. Zoroastrian priests controlling city governments

5. What regions did the Sasanians take from Byzantine control in the seventh century?
   a. Italy and Spain
   b. Bactria and Armenia
   c. Syria and Palestine
   d. Yemen and Mesopotamia

6. How did the Sasanians and Byzantines practice cultural exchange?
   a. They both participated in Christian ecumenical councils.
   b. They both refused to conduct trade with China.
   c. They attempted to invade Italy as a joint military force.

    d. They sent embassies to each other's courts.

7. In what century did the Parthian Empire collapse?
    a. the first century
    b. the second century
    c. the third century
    d. the fourth century

8. What body of water allowed Himyar and Aksum to conduct long-distance sea trade?
    a. Black Sea
    b. Danube River
    c. Caspian Sea
    d. Red Sea

9. How did Christianity initially reach the kingdom of Aksum?
    a. It was brought by the Syrian teacher Frumentius.
    b. It was introduced by violent ascetic monks.
    c. It was practiced by an embassy from the Byzantine court.
    d. It was spread by Jewish people from Himyar.

10. How did Aksumite and Himyarite leaders publicly express their religious devotion?
    a. by creating inscriptions and building monuments to their faith
    b. by trading only with empires that shared their faith
    c. by forbidding nonbelievers to enter their territory
    d. by making Zoroastrianism the state religion

11. To what biblical figure was Aksum possibly connected?
    a. King David
    b. Esther
    c. Queen of Sheba
    d. Moses

12. To what area was the Kushan Empire able to introduce Buddhism?
    a. Georgia
    b. Caspian Sea
    c. Uzbekistan
    d. China

13. On what trade routes was Palmyra able to capitalize because of its location?
    a. Caspian Sea and Danube
    b. Silk Roads and Persian Gulf
    c. Black Sea and Bosporus
    d. Aegean Sea and Cyprus

14. Of what event was Palmyra able to take advantage, to the detriment of the Kushan Empire?
    a. third-century crisis
    b. fourth-century arrival of Christianity
    c. fifth-century monastic violence
    d. sixth-century Byzantine reconquest

Check Your Understanding Questions

1. What relationship did Germanic peoples have with the Roman state?

2. Why was Constantinople an ideal location for a new Roman capital city?

3. Did Rome really "fall" in the fifth century CE? Why or why not?

4. What made the period of Late Antiquity different from that of the ancient world?

5. What similarities did Aksum and Himyar share in Late Antiquity?

6. What characteristics made Aksum and Himyar powerful states in East Africa and Arabia, respectively?

7. What were the clearest influences on the development and decline of the Kushan Empire?

Application and Reflection Questions

1. Of all the factors that brought about the administrative disintegration of the Roman West, which do you think was the most important? Why?

2. How did the spread of Christianity and its acceptance by emperors alter Roman society from what it was in earlier antiquity?

3. Should we continue to refer to the Byzantine Empire in this period as the Roman Empire? Why or why not?

4. What marked Zoroastrianism as unique among religious traditions in Late Antiquity?

5. How did religious beliefs serve as both unifying and divisive factors in Late Antiquity?

6. How did religious issues in Aksumite and Himyarite culture affect the development of these societies?

7. How were Aksum and Himyar affected by their relationships with the Byzantines and Sasanians, and what influence did each have on other states?

8. Do you think people were focused more on religion or on politics in Late Antiquity? Why?

9. Why did both the Sasanians and the Byzantines create alliances with Arab tribes in the fifth and sixth centuries CE?

10. In what way did outsiders to the former Roman Empire affect its successors?

11. What role did long-distance trade play in the development of the Palmyra, Kush, and Arab societies?

FIGURE 11.1 The Prophet Abraham. This illustration from al-Biruni's fourteenth-century history called *al-Athar al-Baqiyah* depicts the prophet Abraham destroying idols that were being worshipped instead of the one God. Abraham holds an important place as a common ancestor in Jewish, Christian, and Muslim traditions. (credit: Centre for Research Collections, University of Edinburgh, shelfmark Or.Ms.161, folio number f.88v., used with permission)

CHAPTER OUTLINE

11.1 The Rise and Message of Islam
11.2 The Arab-Islamic Conquests and the First Islamic States
11.3 Islamization and Religious Rule under Islam

INTRODUCTION The modern monotheistic religions of Judaism, Christianity, and Islam have a great deal in common with one another, including a number of traditions and beliefs. At the center of these shared traditions is the worship of one god, but the leadership of the prophets—individuals who were chosen to receive messages to humankind from God—is shared, too. Perhaps no prophetic figure is quite as central in all three faiths as the prophet Abraham (Figure 11.1). Abraham was a patriarch of the Israelites in Jewish and Christian tradition, a common ancestor known for his intense commitment to the worship of the one God in the scripture, the book of Genesis. In one of the best-known stories from the scripture featuring him, he was willing to sacrifice his own son if necessary in order to obey his God. Islamic tradition holds that he is also the ancestor of all the Arabs, and the house of worship he constructed in Mecca, in western Arabia, has become a revered site of pilgrimage for Muslims around the world.

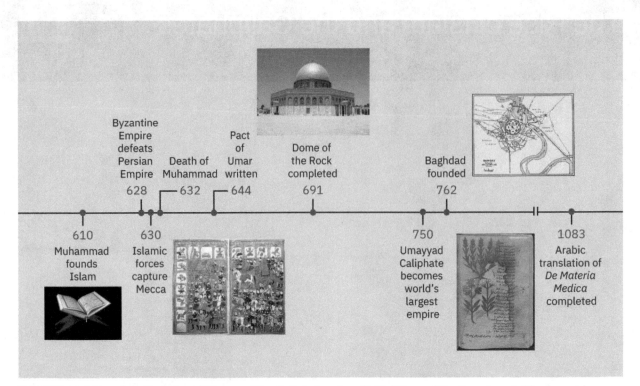

FIGURE 11.2 Timeline: The Rise of Islam and the Caliphates. (credit "610": modification of work "Qur'an and Rehal" by "sayyed shahab-o- din vajedi"/Wikimedia Commons, CC BY 4.0; credit "630": modification of work "Muhammad destroying idols" by Histoire Geographie 5ieme Nathan/Wikimedia Commons, Public Domain; credit "691": modification of work "Exterior of Dome of the Rock or Masjid Al Sakhrah, in Jerusalem" by Thekra A. Sabri/ Wikimedia Commons, CC BY 2.0; credit "762": modification of work "Baghdad 150 to 300 AH" by www.muhammadanism.org/Wikimedia Commons, Public Domain; credit "1083": modification of work "Kitāb al-Ḥašāʾiš fī hāyūlā al-ʿilāg al-ṭibbī Or. 289" by Universitaire Bibliotheken Leiden/Leiden University Libraries, CC BY)

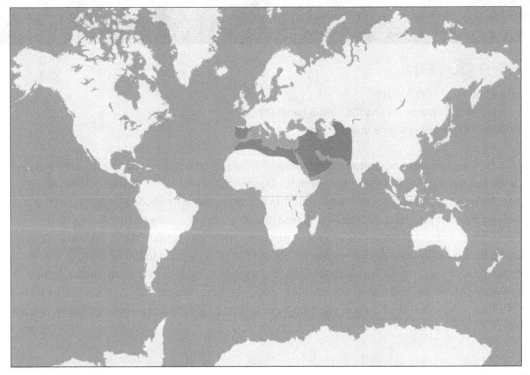

FIGURE 11.3 Locator Map: The Rise of Islam and the Caliphates. (credit: modification of work "World map blank shorelines" by Maciej Jaros/Wikimedia Commons, Public Domain)

11.1 The Rise and Message of Islam

LEARNING OBJECTIVES

By the end of this section, you will be able to:
- Describe the political, geographic, and economic circumstances within the Middle East during the rise of Islam
- Discuss the origins of Islam and the career of the prophet Muhammad
- Explain the uniqueness of the community Muhammad built

The story of Abraham, called Ibrahim, within Islam is an important one. Not only was he a monotheist at a time when his people had embraced polytheism and begun to worship various idols, but according to Islamic tradition, he was the first person to settle in what later became the city of Mecca. Abraham arrived there with his servant and concubine Hagar and their son Ishmael. There he constructed the Kaaba, considered by Muslims to be the house of God and the most sacred site in Islam.

Muslims believe that as generations passed, however, the descendants of Ishmael, the Arabs, forgot their monotheism and began to worship idols, entering a period of ignorance known as the *jahiliyyah*. There they remained until God sent a new prophet, Muhammad, to correct their religious practices and deliver them from ignorance and disbelief. This lapse and deliverance, according to the faithful, is the story of Islam.

Arabia on the Eve of Islam

Seen from the outside, the Arabian Peninsula of the fifth and sixth centuries CE was a seemingly marginal space, on the southern fringes of the last great realms of antiquity, the Byzantine (Roman) and Sasanian (Persian) Empires. The geography of much of Arabia was harsh; the peninsula was filled with many dry and inhospitable places where rainfall, access to water, and cultivatable land were in short supply. Even today, a large portion of the center of modern Saudi Arabia is taken up by the "Empty Quarter," the Rub' al-Khali, a 250,000-square-mile sand desert that barely sustains the few local Arab tribes that continue to live in the region. To many, the Arabian Peninsula might not seem like an obvious setting for the rise of a ruling empire and one of the world's largest religious traditions (Figure 11.4).

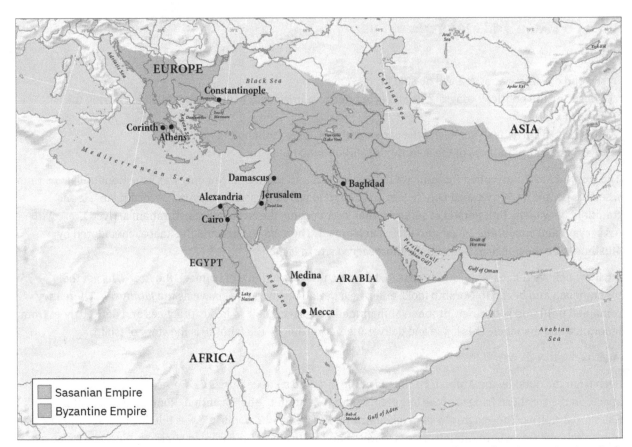

FIGURE 11.4 The Byzantine and Sasanian Empires. This map shows the Byzantine (Roman) and Sasanian (Persian) Empires at the beginning of the seventh century CE. Note the long border the two empires shared, and the southern borders with Arabia that remained out of their direct control. (attribution: Copyright Rice University, OpenStax, under CC BY 4.0 license)

The reality, however, is that the Arabian Peninsula is—and was—more diverse than it might immediately seem. In the fifth, sixth, and early seventh centuries, it was the home of disparate tribes often united by the bonds of kinship typical of nomadic and seminomadic peoples around the world, and divided for the same reason. As they do with the Celts, Iroquois, Mongols, and Persians (to name but a few), historians often group peoples together because of their use of a common language, their habitation of a specific geographic area, and aspects of culture they share such as food, dress, and religious practices. But beyond these shared features, little unified the peoples of the Arabian Peninsula prior to the seventh century. Many communities in the region were divided along tribal lines while vying with one another for power, prestige, influence, and available resources.

The great Byzantine and Persian Empires to the immediate north had a history of expansion and conflict. Despite their strength, however, neither desired to dominate Arabia. To those classical states, much of Arabia appeared as a backwater occupied by migratory and aggressive Arab tribes and offered no reason for them to turn their imperial ambitions southward. Few resources were produced in the region that suggested conquest would be worthwhile, even if western Arabia did play a role in the caravans of trade goods that traveled between east and west.

However, the region was a tapestry of unique cultures and history. The Bedouin were migratory Arab tribes that largely subsisted on animal herding and, in some instances, on the raiding of trade caravans and settled communities. Many Bedouin and other seminomadic Arabs practiced polytheism, the worship of many gods and goddesses who were often considered patrons of certain tribes or residents of certain locales. Polytheistic religions were not all that was found in the Arabian Peninsula: the monotheistic faiths of Judaism and Christianity were both present in the region before the arrival of Islam, and they influenced its formation.

Given the harshness of the environment, in fact, during the ancient and late antique periods, important monasteries were founded for Christian worship, allowing the monks there to fully dedicate themselves to an ascetic life detached from the earthly world (Figure 11.5).

FIGURE 11.5 St. Catherine's Monastery. Perhaps the most famous Christian monastery of the Arabian Peninsula is St. Catherine's, constructed in the sixth century CE and adjacent to Mount Sinai (in the background of the photo), where the prophet Moses is said to have received from God the religious laws known as the "Ten Commandments." (credit: "Saint Catherine's Monastery on the Sinai Peninsula in Egypt" by Joonas Plaan/Wikimedia Commons, CC BY 2.0)

In the very south of the Arabian Peninsula, in what is Yemen today, was a kingdom known as Himyar. Its rulers controlled some of the most fertile lands in the region. They built their state on agricultural produce, on luxury goods such as frankincense and myrrh, and on their role as intermediaries in both East African and Indian Ocean trade. The Himyarites and their predecessors the Sabaeans played significant roles in long-distance trade, using camel caravans along the western coast of Arabia to bring goods from Africa and Asia to the markets in places such as Alexandria, Damascus, Jerusalem, and beyond (Figure 11.6). Their cultural influence was important, too, with a number of the southern Arab tribes connecting their history and lineage directly with these prestigious states. The decision by the Himyarite rulers to convert to Judaism in the late fourth century CE made monotheism more prominent in the region.

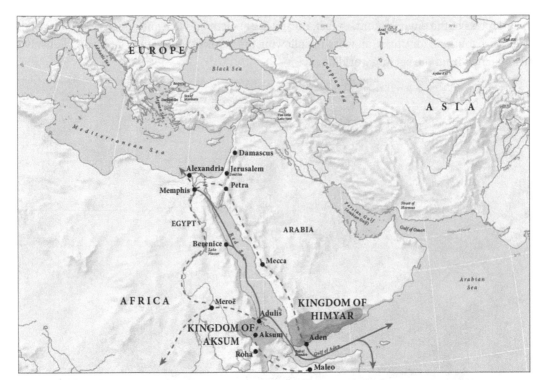

FIGURE 11.6 Himyar and Aksum. The Arabian Kingdom of Himyar (shaded green) and the African Kingdom of Aksum (orange) both played important roles in the overland and oversea Silk Roads trade, bringing goods northward to markets in Egypt, Palestine, and beyond. (attribution: Copyright Rice University, OpenStax, under CC BY 4.0 license)

In the very north of Arabia, along the southern borders of the Byzantine and Sasanian Empires, were the Arabs who had the most sustained interactions with those two imperial powers. While tribes in the region had long acted as trade intermediaries between the Mediterranean world and the Indian Ocean states, those of northern Arabia were most regularly engaged in harassing the trade caravans that brought goods to and from the urban imperial centers. To combat this aggression on their southern borders, both the Byzantines and the Persians opted to employ certain Arab confederations to create a buffer between the settled peoples and the raiders from the south. Best known were the Ghassanids and the Lakhmids, who were brought into the service of the Byzantines and Persians, respectively, by the sixth century CE and became increasingly acculturated to them.

The Ghassanids adopted many elements of Byzantine culture, including Christianity. In fact, it was among Christian Arabs specifically that historians have found some of the earliest surviving uses of the Arabic script, from the seventh century. The Byzantine emperors also formally recognized and rewarded the Ghassanids, at least for a time. The Ghassanid ruler was documented as a *phylarch* (local ruler or chieftain) and given titles of honor by the Byzantine emperor Justinian during the sixth century.

The Lakhmids established themselves in the central Iraqi city of Al-Hirah and were recognized as allies of the Sasanian Persians from the late fourth century onward (Figure 11.7). Some of the Lakhmids embraced a form of Christianity known as Nestorianism and, like the Ghassanids, were able to thrive on the patronage of the great empire while protecting its southern borders from other Arabs. Both tribes were more than just servants of their larger patrons, however. They were allies with a certain degree of autonomy that allowed their societies to flourish. The money and support they received allowed them to become powerful confederations in comparison to other Arab tribes, and their conversion to Christianity allowed the further spread of monotheism in the region.

FIGURE 11.7 The Lakhmid Fort at Kharnaq. This late fifteenth-century manuscript page by the renowned Persian miniaturist Kamal al-din Bihzad shows the construction of the fort at Kharnaq, a castle near the Lakhmid capital of Al-Hirah. (credit: "The construction of the palace of Khavarnaq" by British Museum/Wikimedia Commons, Public Domain)

The relationship between the Byzantines and the Sasanian Persians was very often tense, however. Both empires had ambitions to expand their influence, and they regularly skirmished with one another and attempted to meddle in each other's politics, including by supporting rival claimants to the throne. Their combative relationship was not unique in late antiquity. When Rome was still a united empire and Persia was ruled by the Parthian dynasty, conflict between those two sides occurred regularly. By the sixth century, however, such conflicts between the two great powers of the region were increasingly costly and risky. Both states had a good deal to lose from open warfare, and much of their conflict played out through proxies, often the Arab Ghassanids and the Lakhmids. This arrangement was beneficial for the Arab tribes so long as payment and recognition of their role was forthcoming. By the beginning of the seventh century, however, much had changed.

The borderlands between the Byzantine Empire and Sasanian Persia were often where conflicts broke out, and this happened several times during the sixth century, especially in places like Iraq and Armenia (now called the Caucasus). In the year 602, however, the conflict exploded. The Byzantine emperor Maurice, who had helped the Sasanian ruler Khosrow II regain the throne of Persia and brought peace between the two sides, was murdered by his own troops. They installed a new emperor, Phocas, and Khosrow vowed revenge, using the coup as a reason to begin what historians call "the last great war of antiquity" (Figure 11.8).

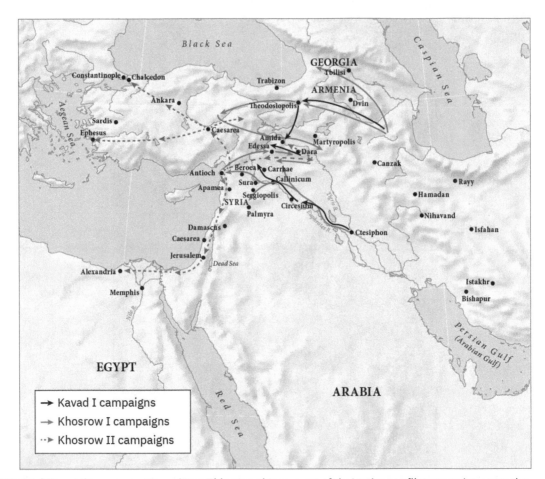

FIGURE 11.8 Byzantines versus Sasanians. This map shows most of the major conflict zones between the Byzantines and Sasanians during their wars of the sixth and seventh centuries. Think about how much time was spent in regular conflict and what life must have been like for noncombatants in places like Theodosiopolis, Dara, and Sergiopolis. (attribution: Copyright Rice University, OpenStax, under CC BY 4.0 license)

Between 602 and 628, the Byzantines and Persians waged a devastating conflict that had long-lasting repercussions for the entire region. In the first phase, Khosrow and the Persians overwhelmed the Byzantines and claimed much of their eastern Mediterranean territory, including Iraq, Syria, Jordan, Palestine, and crucially, the vital agricultural province of Egypt. Phocas, facing upheaval within his empire aside from the war with the Persians, was deposed and then executed in 610 by the newly declared emperor Heraclius. Desperate to claim back lost territory, return stability to the state, and rebuild the army to face the Persians, Heraclius was able to lead the Byzantines to victory and end the conflict in 628 (Figure 11.9).

FIGURE 11.9 The Victorious Emperor Heraclius. This inlaid copper plaque is a twelfth-century depiction of the Byzantine emperor Heraclius (right) overcoming the Persian Sasanian Shahenshah Khosrow II (left) during the war between the two sides. Note the symbolism of the heroic warrior-ruler Heraclius knocking the crown from the head of his rival. Despite the short-lived victory of the Byzantines in the war, depictions of their success remained popular images throughout the Middle Ages. (credit: "Sassanid King Khosrau II submitting to the Byzantine Emperor Heraclius" by "Jastrow"/Louvre Museum/Wikimedia Commons, Public Domain)

Heraclius and the Byzantines did not go on to destroy the Sasanian dynasty, however. While Khosrow II was overthrown in a civil war at the end of the conflict, neither side was truly capable of continuing a long and costly fight against the other. The Byzantines were ultimately victorious, but the war was devastating for both sides politically, militarily, and economically. Despite his accomplishments, Heraclius had placed all his focus and state expenditures on the war itself rather than on truly governing the empire. Both sides had lost an enormous number of soldiers over more than fifteen years of conflict, and those who survived were war-weary and ready for retirement. Neither side had the money to rebuild the army or their defenses when they had put so much of the state's resources toward victory—and survival.

With so much upheaval occurring despite the Byzantine victory, the war affected many aspects of society, including the state and nobility's ability to patronize scholarship, historical writing, and the arts, leading this period to be known as the "Byzantine Dark Age" because of the severe lack of historical writing that survived in the seventh and eight centuries. Finally, the borders were constantly changing, and many civilians just attempting to live their lives were likely tossed between sides as the tides of war changed. More war would have taken an exhausting toll even on the people living in seemingly safe places like Jerusalem, Antioch, and Damascus.

As it was, the impacts of the conflict were far-reaching. The later Byzantine chronicler Theophanes wrote in the early ninth century about how the conflict had changed the relationship between the Byzantines and the Arabs in the year 630–631, including, almost certainly, tribes like the Ghassanids that had enjoyed special privileges and payments from the state. Theophanes wrote, "There were some nearby Arabs who received modest allowances from the emperors for guarding the desert pathways. A eunuch came to distribute to the soldiers' allowances; but this time, when the Arabs came to receive theirs, as was their custom, the eunuch drove them away. 'The ruler can hardly afford to pay his troops,' he said, 'much less give money to such dogs as these.' The Arabs were outraged, went to their comrades, and showed them the route to the district of Gaza, the pathways toward Sinai, which were extremely rich."

The timeline and circumstances of this long final conflict between the Byzantines and Sasanians, and the exhausted state in which both sides were left, were also significant for future events. While these great powers were distracted by the devastating war between them, their southern border was likely far from their rulers' minds. Yet at the same time, the Arabs of western Arabia were being united for the first time in history, through the leadership of a man named Muhammad and the religion of Islam, with direct repercussions for the survival of the two ancient empires.

The Religious Tradition of Islam

While the conflict between the Byzantines and the Sasanians raged at the beginning of the seventh century, western Arabia began to take center stage in the creation of a new world religion deeply influenced by the environment, people, and cultures of the late antique Middle East. That religion was Islam, a word meaning "submission [to the one God]." Islam is a monotheistic faith that shares many features with both Judaism and Christianity, while at the same time having many features that were uniquely Arabian and that eventually brought the culture and traditions of the Arabian Peninsula to greater prominence.

Understanding Islam's origins and early decades can be challenging. Much of what we know about the earliest community of Muslims comes from sources within the community itself that often assume the reader is already a believer, so they omit important details. And because many people were illiterate at this time and not writing their history as it happened, we have less evidence outside religious scripture to help us reconstruct it. While the Arabs placed great emphasis on remembering the events and people of the area's past, they transmitted this information primarily through a process of memorization and oral recitation, and memory aids, such as poetry, were vital methods as material was passed down through generations. Written histories of the past for future generations were seen as less important than the living "performance" of information through the oral tradition.

While other contemporary societies had become increasingly focused on writing for centuries before the seventh century, the Arab commitment to oral transmission in this period was not unprecedented. The history of early Judaism was similarly transmitted before being committed to writing much later, and historians also face challenges trying to reconstruct the origins of Christianity when little contemporaneous writing survives. Memorializing, memorizing, and transmitting events of the past through epic poetry also has precedent in the Mediterranean world, as seen in the preservation of works such as *The Iliad* and *The Odyssey*, attributed to the Greek poet Homer, and the ancient Indian world, as in the case of the *Mahabharata*.

At the center of the founding of Islam are the city of Mecca, the worship of one God—Allah—and the leadership of the prophets. Even to Muslims today, Allah is not considered to be a god separate from the God of Judaism and Christianity; *Allah* is simply the Arabic word meaning "the one God." In fact, Christians who live in the Middle East and speak Arabic today refer to the God of the Christian Bible by using the word "Allah" in their own worship. Belief in the one God and the message of the Islamic prophet Muhammad is the first and most important of the "Five Pillars of Islam," known as the *shahada*, the profession of faith. To embrace Islam as their religion, adherents must recognize the creed that "There is no god but Allah, and Muhammad is the messenger of God." Muhammad, as recognized by Muslims, was the final prophet in a long list with whom the one God had communicated throughout history, including figures such as Adam, Noah, Abraham, Moses, and Jesus. Muhammad was a divinely chosen man who is not, nor ever has been, worshipped as a God or as a relative of God himself.

Many of the other pillars of Islam also have features in common with other world religions such as ritual fasting, charity, and daily prayer. For Muslims, these acts are specified as daily prayer while facing the direction of the holy mosque in the city of Mecca; almsgiving, the donation of money and goods to the community and people in need; fasting (if able) during Ramadan, the holy month during which the Muslim scripture of the Quran was first revealed to Muhammad; and participating at least once (if able) in the pilgrimage to Mecca—the **hajj**—to relive important moments in the life of Abraham and his family's arrival in Arabia and to circle the house of God, the Kaaba, in prayer.

THE PAST MEETS THE PRESENT

Hajj: The Islamic Pilgrimage to Mecca

One of the core tenets or "Five Pillars" of Islam is participation in the pilgrimage to the holy city of Mecca. This event, when undertaken during the month of Dhu al-Hijja, is known as the hajj. Each year millions of Muslims travel to the holy city to take part in a process that has been going on for almost fourteen hundred years.

While Mecca was the home of the prophet Muhammad, for Muslims the pilgrimage is about much more. The rituals and events in which they participate are intended to reenact important events in the life of a different prophet, Abraham. The sacred mosque that is the focus of much of the pilgrimage is the holiest site of Islam, built to surround the Kaaba, the black-shrouded cube structure at the center that is believed to be the original home of monotheism (Figure 11.10). Some Muslims believe the Kaaba was constructed by Adam, the first man, and then reconstructed by Abraham.

FIGURE 11.10 **The Sacred Mosque in Mecca.** This photo shows the sacred mosque in Mecca, Islam's holiest site, with a large crowd of pilgrims surrounding the Kaaba, the black-shrouded building in the center. (credit: modification of work "Mekke Suudi Arabistan" by "Konevi"/Pxhere, CC0 1.0)

The five- to six-day hajj recognizes the long history of monotheism in Arabia, acknowledging that Muhammad's career and message were the correction and perfection of monotheistic worship begun centuries earlier. In addition to Adam, Abraham, and Muhammad, other great figures of history have been adopted and associated with worship at the Kaaba, including Iskandar, more recognizably known as Alexander the Great.

Islamic law recognizes that the hajj is not a trip every Muslim will be able to take. Some may not be healthy enough, and Islamic charitable organizations around the world collect donations to support those who cannot otherwise afford it. Pilgrims may also travel to the holy mosque during other times of the year, which is not considered as having made the hajj but is instead called the *umra*, the "lesser pilgrimage."

- What are the historical implications of the pilgrimage to Mecca being one of the core tenets of Islam?
- How might the obstacles to making such a pilgrimage today be greater or smaller than in the past?

Muslims have believed throughout their history that Islam and its holy writings are not a new faith created in the seventh century. Instead, the faith that Muhammad brought to the Arabs in the early 600s was merely a corrective to the monotheistic religions that had come before. From the perspective of most Muslims, Islam is the same faith as Judaism and Christianity, with adherents of all three traditions worshipping the same God and recognizing divine intercession in humanity through the leadership of the prophets. Muslims also recognize the holy scriptures of Judaism and Christianity as having been given to humans by God but then corrupted over time. Islam thus sees itself as a purer form of these faiths and directly connected to both. The shared history and lineage of the three run through the prophet Abraham, whom all list as an ancestor. Many modern scholars of religion thus refer to Judaism, Christianity, and Islam as the **Abrahamic faiths**.

For all the influence that other monotheistic worship in the region may have had on the formation of Islam in the seventh century, however, the faith has many features we might consider uniquely Arab or Arabian. First, of course, is the setting itself. While the land that is modern Israel and Palestine played a central role in the narratives of Judaism and Christianity, much of the story of the formation of Islam as a distinct religion is found in western Arabia, a region of the peninsula known as the Hijaz. Its holiest sites lie in this region, and the life of its founder was spent almost entirely there.

The faith is firmly connected to Arabic, the indigenous language of the region, especially in its holiest scriptures and also in cultural features like the survival of Arabic poetry as a means of recording the past. The tribal structure of pre-Islamic Arabian society also defined the first several decades of the religion and the states it inspired, which included a social hierarchy that made it nearly impossible to convert to Islam for the better part of the first century of the faith unless an individual was first embraced as a member of an Arab tribe. In this way, conversion was connected to the old ways of the Arabs, which did not require a convert to be of a particular ethnicity or bloodline but did require the adoption of the cultural traditions and markers of the Arabian tribal society. For these earliest adherents of the faith, it seems likely that they felt the one God had chosen the western Arabian peoples and their traditions for special recognition, and embracing these features was a prerequisite for being among the "chosen" people. But more influential than anything, perhaps, was the Muslims' belief in the leadership and message of the man whom God chose as his final prophet, an Arab of the early seventh century from the Hijaz of western Arabia.

The Islamic Prophet Muhammad

Muslim tradition tells us that Muhammad was a merchant from a prominent Arab tribe called Quraysh in the Hijaz region. Born in the city of Mecca, he spent his early life engaged in the trade that passed along the north–south trade routes through his city, a hub that had become a waystation and a good place to conduct business (Figure 11.11). The tribe of Quraysh dominated leadership and trade in the region in large part because its members were the protectors of the sacred Kaaba, which in this period, we are told, had become a house of idol worship, a center of polytheism among the Arabs. Long-distance trade of luxury goods could be risky because of raiding that occurred along trade routes, and the Kaaba had become a sanctuary where fighting was illicit, making it a safe place to conduct business. The Quraysh were enriched as the stewards of this important sanctuary and had a keen interest in protecting its role in society.

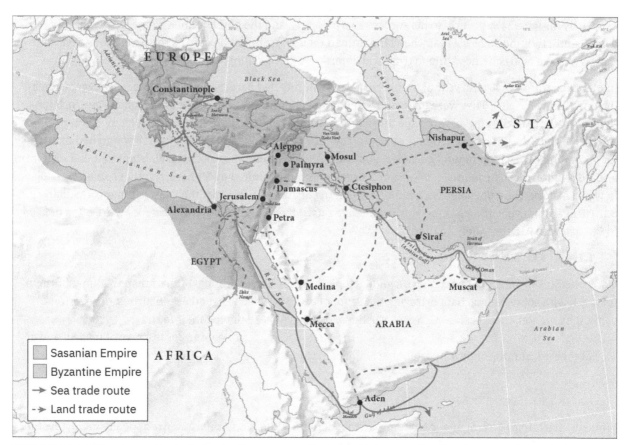

FIGURE 11.11 Mecca as a Trade Hub. Muslim sources tell us that Muhammad's tribe, the Quraysh, made the city of Mecca an important waystation for those trading luxury goods by land and sea. (attribution: Copyright Rice University, OpenStax, under CC BY 4.0 license)

According to Muslim belief, in the year 610 the middle-aged Muhammad, who had traveled to a cave just outside Mecca for contemplation, received contact from God through the intermediary of the angel Gabriel (Jabrīl in Arabic). Muhammad was told to recite the first revelations of a scripture that became the Muslim holy book, the **Quran**. He returned home amazed and surprised by what he had experienced. As a well-traveled and successful trader in the region, he had much to lose from undertaking a religious mission with a novel message. For one thing, a new religion would threaten the balance of power within his Arab tribe by plainly rejecting the polytheism that many in the community practiced and the financial benefits that came with the Kaaba. However, Muhammad essentially abandoned a financially stable and comfortable life as a merchant to embrace what he believed was required by God: becoming a preacher and working to save the souls of his family and kin from a coming day of judgment.

There has been much disagreement throughout history over who was the first man to convert to Islam after hearing Muhammad's message, but there is no debate among Muslim sources about who was the first *person* to do so: his first wife Khadija. As a successful merchant in her own right—who had lifted Muhammad's standing in their community by marrying him and bringing him into her caravan business—Khadija too would have had much to lose in supporting the new religion. The earliest biographer of Muhammad, Ibn Ishaq, described the critical support she provided Muhammad by saying, "Khadija believed in him and accepted as true what he brought from God, helping him in his work . . . through her, God lightened the burden of his prophet."

While many of Muhammad's confidants and family members embraced Islam shortly after the revelations began and continued, his career as a prophet, especially the first twelve years, was fraught with challenge. His preaching of monotheism upset the political status quo and was often resisted. The support of his family, especially his wives, was critical to his success as a preacher, and the guidance of Khadija was especially significant. Tradition suggests that when Muhammad thought he might be mad as the revelations first came to him, it was she who convinced him to trust and embrace his new calling.

In 622, Muhammad's twelfth year of prophecy, his community fled persecution and increasing aggression by the polytheist Meccans. They were invited to join another community of Arabs in a city called Yathrib, later known as Medina, "the city" or more specifically "the prophet's city." There they were welcomed among other Arab tribes, including some practicing Judaism. This **hijra**, meaning "emigration," was a watershed moment for Muhammad's early community. At a low ebb and without any certainty of survival, Islam now changed from a small religion mostly confined to Mecca to a larger community united by Muhammad that solidified its place in world history. The *hijra* holds such importance in the history of Islam that the Islamic lunar calendar counts 622 CE as its first year. (Dates in the Muslim calendar, used by many around the world today, are often labeled in English with AH, for "After the Hijra.")

LINK TO LEARNING

Many Muslims throughout history have avoided depicting the Islamic prophet Muhammad in human form in their art, with some feeling that portraying the Prophet could be misconstrued as idolatrous, or revering something (or someone) besides God. But Muslim artists have also depicted their founder Muhammad in words and calligraphic art (https://openstax.org/l/77MuhammadArt) for centuries, as a sign of respect and as part of their recounting of the important narrative of his life.

Muhammad's Community

While the narrative of Islam under Muhammad's leadership centers on Arabs and Arab society in the seventh century, many factors influenced his message, his leadership, and the growth of the community of Muslims, called the **ummah**. The Muslim emigration to Medina was one step in a wider process as Muhammad sought shelter for his community, an opportunity to spread the message of Islam outside his region, and ultimately the unification of Arab tribes into a confederacy the region had never seen.

Even before fleeing Mecca, some from Muhammad's community sought refuge and support wherever they could find it as they attempted to expose more of the region to the monotheistic message of Islam. One support was found across the Red Sea, in East Africa in the Christian Kingdom of Aksum. There, the Negus—the leader of Aksum in what is modern-day Ethiopia—provided shelter for Muslims fleeing Meccan persecution and allowed them to practice their faith under his protection. Many remained there until they were able to return to Muhammad and emigrate to Medina, too. This support from the Aksumites was important to the survival of Islam, and in fact the decision by some early Muslims to seek refuge in Ethiopia is sometimes referred to as "the first *hijra*."

In Medina, the previously polytheist Arabs, Jewish Arabs, and Muhammad's *ummah* formed an alliance for their common defense. Muhammad served first as an arbiter of disputes between the tribes and, soon after, as the city's de facto leader. Under his guidance, the community devised the Constitution of Medina as a means to solidify the agreement between the tribes and their mutual responsibility to protect their city and its people from outside attack. Later Muslim rulers saw the constitution as a blueprint for the creation of a religious society that tolerated those of other faiths while supporting the worship of the one God, mutual defense for the community, and Muhammad's leadership.

The constitution stated that "the believers and Muslims of [the tribe of] Quraysh and Medina and those who join them . . . form one *ummah* to the exclusion of others." It goes on to explain that the Jewish Arabs of the tribe of Banu Awf "are secure from the believers [the Muslims]. The Jews have their religion and the Muslims have theirs." The phrases most commonly used in the constitution to describe Muhammad's followers are "Muslims" ("those who have submitted to God") and "believers" (*al-Mu'minun*). For this reason, some historians have described the earliest *ummah* as a "community of believers" that was open to most monotheists. In these earliest decades of Islam, Muhammad's new community had much in common with the monotheistic Jewish people and Christians, and we find little evidence of the distinctive Muslim identity that formed over the next several centuries.

IN THEIR OWN WORDS

Jewish and Christian Narratives in the Quran

The holy scripture of Islam, the Quran, is deeply intertextual, meaning it has a relationship with and is often in dialogue with other texts, namely the Jewish Tanakh and the Christian Bible. Here in translation are excerpts from Surah (Chapter) 5 that, in part, address Muhammad's community about where their faith fits with the other monotheistic traditions, Judaism and Christianity.

> The Jews and Christians say, "We are the children of God, the ones He loves." Say: "Then why does He punish you for your sins? No. You are mortals, of those He has created. He forgives those whom He wishes and He punishes those whom He wishes. God has sovereignty over the heavens and the earth and what is between them. To Him is the journeying."

> O people of the Scripture, Our messenger has come to you, making things clear to you after an interval between messengers, so that you cannot say, "No bearer of good tidings or warner has come to us." A bearer of good tidings and a warner has come to you. God has power over everything.

> And [recall] when Moses said to his people, "O my people, remember the blessings of God to you when He placed prophets amongst you and made you kings and gave you what He had not given to anyone [else] among created beings. O my people, Enter the holy land which God has prescribed for you. Do not turn your backs, lest you return as losers."

> And recite to them in truth, the tale of the two sons of Adam [Cain and Abel], when they offered sacrifices, and it was accepted from one of them and not from the other. [The latter, Cain] said, "I shall kill you." [Abel] replied, "God accepts only from those who are god-fearing.

> If you stretch out your hand to me to kill me, I shall not stretch out my hand to kill you. I fear God, Lord of created beings.

> I wish you to take on both your sin and my sin and become one of the companions of the Fire. That is the recompense of evil-doers."

> Then his soul prompted him to kill his brother; so he killed him, and became one of the losers.

> Then God sent a crow, which scratched into the earth to show him how he might hide the corpse of his brother. He said, "Woe on me. Am I unable to be like this crow, and hide the corpse of my brother?" And he became one of the repentant.

> Because of that, We have prescribed for the Children of Israel that whoever kills a soul, other than in retaliation for [another] soul or for corruption in the land, will be as if he had killed all the people; and whoever saves one will be as if he had saved the life of all people.

> Our messengers have come to them in the past with the clear proofs; but even after that many of them commit excesses in the land.

> —Sura 5 of the Quran, verses 18–21 and 27–32, translated by Alan Jones

- Who is the "messenger" referenced here, and what is their goal on earth?
- What lessons do you think are being communicated to believers in this reading?
- What might the references to Moses and Cain and Abel tell us about Quran's early audience?

The even-handed approach to members of this new *ummah* was critical to the ultimate success of Muhammad and his community. Much of the last ten years of Muhammad's life was spent with this new Muslim community in Medina, engaged in conflict with their former brethren in Mecca. Fighting between the two sides was fierce, and there were also tensions within Medina and the early *ummah* as Muhammad's followers grew in number and prominence at the expense of other Arabs in the city, in particular, the Jewish contingent. Many on both sides were related by blood even if their religious beliefs had altered. Muhammad's community continued to grow and win more supporters until, on the eve of battle outside Mecca in 630, his former tribe of Quraysh surrendered, and the population of the city converted to Islam. Muhammad and his followers were then able to return to Mecca, where he entered the holy sanctuary of the Kaaba, now filled with the polytheist idols worshipped by the Arabs, and smashed them all, echoing a famous story about the biblical prophet Abraham (Figure 11.12). From the perspective of Muslims, the original house of Abraham, which had always been dedicated to the worship of the one God, was now cleansed.

FIGURE 11.12 Cleansing the Sanctuary of Mecca. In this early nineteenth-century depiction from Kashmir, India, the Muslim army triumphantly enters the sanctuary of Mecca to destroy the idols kept there, which are shown on the top and left edges of the scene. Muhammad is not himself depicted in the image, though the National Library of France, which holds this work, indicates he is depicted as a flame. (credit: "Muhammad destroying idols" by Histoire Geographie 5ieme Nathan/Wikimedia Commons, Public Domain)

Muhammad had succeeded in uniting the majority of Arab tribes of western Arabia under his leadership. He spent the next two years continuing to expand his community and spreading the message of Islam, until his death from natural causes in the year 632.

11.2 The Arab-Islamic Conquests and the First Islamic States

LEARNING OBJECTIVES

By the end of this section, you will be able to:
- Explain the motivations for Islamic expansion during the seventh and eighth centuries
- Identify where and how Islam expanded during the seventh and eighth centuries
- Discuss the establishment of the first Islamic dynasty in the Middle East
- Describe the nature of Islamic society during the seventh and eighth centuries

When Muhammad died in 632 CE, members of the early Muslim *ummah* needed to immediately answer several important questions. Who was capable of now leading the community, of following in the footsteps of a leader who claimed prophecy—the ability to communicate with God—when none of those who remained could do so? Another critical question was about the survival of the community: what, exactly, had Muhammad accomplished by uniting the Arab tribes, and where would they go from here? The first few years following Muhammad's death tested the community's resolve while its members sought to articulate what made this moment in their history unique.

The Arab-Islamic Conquest Movement

Arab tribes had come together for a common cause in the pre-Islamic period, such as a war against another tribe or recognition of the strength of a chieftain. But once that cause had been accomplished or that chieftain had died, the confederacy typically disbanded, its purpose fulfilled. In the wake of Muhammad's death, at least some Arab tribes likewise believed the community's purpose had been completed. His accomplishment in bringing people together under the banner of Islam was not one the surviving leaders of the community intended to be temporary, however.

There were urgent questions about the leadership of the community, and immediate disagreements about it as well. In many tribal- and clan-based societies like that of the Arabs, leadership was not hereditary, meaning it did not immediately pass to the heir upon the death of the leader. Thus, as Muhammad was dying, two primary claimants for leadership emerged: his son-in-law Ali ibn Abi Talib, and a friend and confidant of Muhammad's named Abu Bakr. Ali, related to the Prophet by blood and marriage, was comparatively young in a society that saw leadership in its elders, although he claimed to have been chosen by Muhammad as his heir and successor. Abu Bakr, in contrast, was one of the elders of the community, well respected and popularly chosen. Both had been among the first to convert to Islam.

Members of the community had concerns about their own standing. Some were the earliest converts who had joined Muhammad when he was still in Mecca, some had welcomed his community in Medina when they needed shelter, and still others had not converted until shortly before Muhammad's death. In the end, Abu Bakr was chosen to be the first successor to Muhammad, the **caliph** or religious and political leader of the Muslim community. This was accomplished through popular acclamation by tribal leaders, who ultimately won out over those who favored the lineage of Ali. Islam had weathered this first hurdle, although the question of leadership had longer-term implications for the unity of the *ummah*. Ali, believed by some to have been chosen by Muhammad as his heir, was likely aggrieved at the decision, although he accepted it. Other stakeholders may also have felt slighted, including a number of Muhammad's wives, several of whom were shunned despite their close relationship as members of the family of the Prophet. And while this new role of caliph would provide leadership to the young community at a critical juncture, there seems to have been near immediate recognition that things without Muhammad would be different, not least of which because the caliph was not assuming the mantle of another prophet capable of communicating directly with God as Muhammad had.

Tensions arose after Muhammad's death not just over leadership and inheritance, but also over whether the alliance was ever intended to last beyond its founder. Some Arab tribes left to return to their homes, while others may have believed they could discard their commitment to the worship of the one God and membership in this confederation. From the perspective of the Muslims, however, this was apostasy, and a conflict known as the Ridda Wars then began in an attempt to force these Arab tribes to continue to honor their agreements with the Muslims. The Ridda Wars also appear to have been expansionist, bringing into the fold, whether by treaty or force, Arab tribes that had never been aligned with Muhammad's community during his lifetime. This effort was the first step of a wider movement called the Arab-Islamic or Arab-Muslim conquests, and by 633 the entirety of Arabia had been brought under the control of this first Islamic state.

Abu Bakr did not live long after Muhammad, and the conquest movement did not stop with his leadership, nor with uniting just the Arab tribes under the banner of Islam. The new state's expansionist desire seems to have existed from the outset, and the Arab-Muslim armies turned their attention northward to the old empires of Sasanian Persia and Byzantium. They were likely inspired by the richness of these lands, where they knew resources were more plentiful and luxury trade goods regularly traveled. But there were other factors, too. The Arab-Muslims may have felt emboldened by their successes in Arabia, seeing them as recognition of God's favor and of their destiny to rule the world.

Religious belief and zeal are difficult for historians to quantify, but we have seen throughout history that nomadic and seminomadic societies must forcefully seek the resources they need to survive while defending themselves against threats that sedentary societies face less often. The hardiness and capability of the Arab-Muslims as a fighting force during this period was also a factor. The weakness of the empires to the north would have been seen as a clear opportunity for the raiders who had long supported themselves by harrying the frontiers. And there was the timing: Muhammad and his successors were creating and expanding the new Muslim community in the 620s and 630s, as the war between the Byzantines and the Sasanian Persians was entering its last stages and leaving both empires weakened at a critical juncture.

Conquering Persia and the Byzantine Empire

It was not always clear that the Arab-Muslims would be successful against the Byzantines and the Persians, the last empires of antiquity. Nonetheless, starting in 634 and continuing into the early eighth century, they found enormous success conquering much of the territory around the Mediterranean basin and central Asia, going as far west as Spain and Portugal and all the way to the Indus River valley in the east. The new Islamic state, or **caliphate** (an area under the control of a caliph), was larger than the realm of Alexander the Great, the Romans, or the Han Chinese; it was the largest empire the world had yet seen (Figure 11.13).

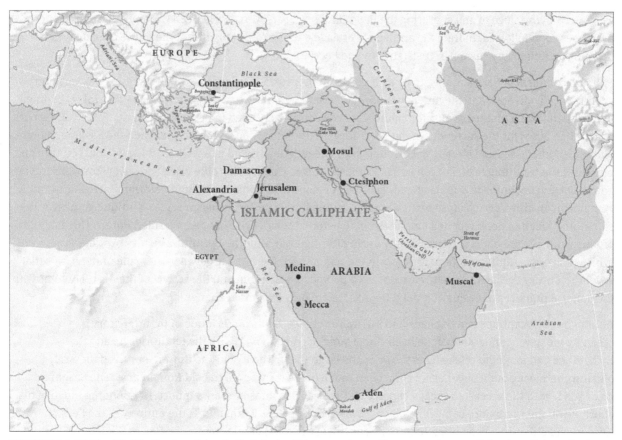

FIGURE 11.13 The Eighth-Century Islamic Caliphate. This map shows the extent the new Islamic caliphate had achieved by the end of its first dynasty, the Umayyads. During the eighth century CE, the Umayyads ruled the world's largest empire. (attribution: Copyright Rice University, OpenStax, under CC BY 4.0 license)

The crucial early years of Islamic expansion were overseen by the first four caliphs, a group of rulers who came to be called the "rightly guided" or **Rashidun**. These four figures—Abu Bakr, Umar, Uthman, and the originally overlooked son-in-law of Muhammad, Ali—ruled between 632 and 661, a period when much Byzantine and Persian territory was conquered, and the message of Islam spread throughout a predominantly Christian Middle East. While the Byzantines and the Persians had employed the Arabian Ghassanids and Lakhmids to guard their borders and serve in their wars, the arrival of the Arab-Muslim armies was unlike anything either empire had seen before.

The Byzantine emperor Heraclius, heralded for bringing victory over the Persians, was not able to enjoy his triumph for very long. Meanwhile, defeated Sasanian Persia was coping with the effects of a destabilizing civil war. The ruler who ultimately emerged in 632, Yazdegerd III, was little more than a puppet king, a child figurehead, and the once-unified Sasanian state devolved into a fractured entity ruled by the noble families.

⊚ LINK TO LEARNING

This brief audio essay from BBC Sounds discusses the development of the Arab-Islamic conquests (https://openstax.org/l/77ArabIslamic) and their long-term successes.

The Arab-Muslim armies began their invasion with the provinces of Iraq and Syria before moving eastward into the Iranian plateau and westward into Egypt. On all fronts, the first decades of the conflict proved extraordinarily successful for the conquerors. Shortly after winning several skirmishes and capturing the Syrian city of Damascus, the Arab-Muslims bested the Byzantine army at the Battle of Yarmuk in 636. Unable to defend the remaining cities of the region, the Byzantines then abandoned Greater Syria, consisting of what are today Israel, Jordan, Lebanon, Palestine, and Syria. The Arab-Muslim armies continued northward and westward, laying siege to and capturing the Egyptian port city of Alexandria in 641. Many other Byzantine provinces soon followed. In Iraq, the armies of Persia lost to the Arab-Muslims at the Battle of Qadisiyya, bringing an end to any sustained resistance by the Persians.

Still, the conquest of Persia proved to be a longer-term process. Sasanian-controlled territory was vast and geographically diverse, and the independence the Sasanian nobility had wrested from the central government following the war with the Byzantines meant the Arab-Muslims needed to negotiate with many local governors and landed elites for the surrender of their territory. At the same time, dynamics between the Sasanian nobility and the lower classes had already begun changing. The nobility existed in a well-established court culture and practiced the traditional Persian religion of Zoroastrianism. Outside this elite circle, however, Zoroastrianism had long been declining in popularity, while other religious traditions, including Nestorian Christianity and Manichaeism, grew. The collapse of the Sasanian ruling family in Persia also provides a unique glimpse into something that had not happened among the elite before: the brief rise of a female ruler, Boran. The daughter of Khosrow II, Boran came to power briefly during the civil war after the Byzantine victory over her father. While such opportunities for female power in the region were few and far between, her rule underscores that seventh-century Persia was already a state and a people in transition, and the arrival of the Arab-Muslims with the cultural practices of Arabia and the religion of Islam only expedited change.

Although the Byzantines and Persians had put up resistance, by the 650s much of their territory had been taken by the new Islamic state of the Rashidun. Heraclius died in 641, with the territories he and the Byzantines had fought to retake from the Persians largely lost. The Byzantine Empire survived the Arab-Muslim conquests, but it never again controlled much of the territory of the old Roman east. The Sasanian ruler Yazdegerd III fled east to escape capture by the Arab-Muslims or their supporters, spending much of his short life on the run before being killed by his own people in 651. By that time, the entirety of the Persian Empire had effectively been brought into the control of the new Islamic state.

The Conquerors and the Conquered

From the perspective of the Arab-Muslims, the conquest movement had been enormously successful, a demonstration of the power of God and his favoring of their *ummah*. From the perspective of Christians who were not aligned with the Muslims during this period, the arrival of the Arab-Muslims was also seen as an act of God, a God who was angry at the sinfulness of the Christians and who had sent the Arab-Muslims as a punishment they needed to bear.

Calling these events the "Arab-Muslim conquests" is somewhat misleading, however. While the first years of expansion did see several major battles, including Yarmuk and Qadisiyya, most of the territory came under Islamic control through peace agreements. Cities and regions agreed to terms of surrender that protected their residents, many of their belongings, and their right to practice their religion. Peaceful agreements made sense for non-Muslim populations. Especially during the seventh century, the Muslims maintained a policy of noninterference toward the religious practices of subject populations. As long as they paid taxes to their new Muslim government, the conquered could live in the Islamic state and still practice their religion somewhat freely.

The Muslims developed a legal classification for the Jewish people, Christians, and Zoroastrians who lived under their rule. They referred to them as *ahl al-kitab*, or People of the Book, which recognized them as monotheists who had received a revealed scripture from God in the past, and who were worthy of protection by the Islamic state so long as they paid taxes and submitted to Muslim rule. For many, this situation was an improvement on their earlier lives. Under Byzantine rule, for instance, those who did not follow the official Christian religion of the empire were often discriminated against. They could be barred from holding certain jobs, charged extra taxes, and otherwise be badly treated as heretics. For Jewish populations, the situation had often been even harsher. Many had been unable to openly practice their faith or gather outside the synagogue. While they were not officially monotheists and were not seen as having a revealed scripture, Zoroastrians under the Muslims were still treated as People of the Book, likely for pragmatic reasons owing to their noble status in Persian society.

Reaction to the Arab-Islamic Conquests

With the arrival of the Arab-Muslims in Persia, Christian leaders vied with one another for prestige, followers, and perhaps preferential status with the new ruling Muslim elite. Sophronius, the author of the first excerpt presented next, was Patriarch of Jerusalem (one of the most senior roles within the Eastern Orthodox Church) from 634 until his death in 638. The second writer, Ishoyahb III, was Patriarch of the Church of the East, or the Nestorian Church, from 649 to 659, leading the most popular Christian denomination of the former Persian Empire.

> Why do barbarian raids abound? Why are the troops of the [Arab-Muslims] attacking us? Why has there been so much destruction and plunder? . . . That is why the vengeful and God-hating [Arab-Muslims], the abominations of desolation clearly foretold to us by the prophets, overrun the places which are not allowed to them, plunder cities, devastate fields, burn down villages, set on fire the holy churches, overturn the sacred monasteries, oppose the Byzantine armies arrayed against them, and in fighting raise up the trophies [of war] and add victory to victory. . . . Yet these vile ones would not have accomplished this nor seized such a degree of power as to do and utter lawlessly all these things, unless we had first insulted the gift [of baptism] and first defiled the purification, and in this way grieved Christ, the giver of gifts, and prompted him to be angry with us, good though he is and though he takes no pleasure in evil, being the fount of kindness and not wishing to behold the ruin and destruction of men. We are ourselves, in truth, responsible for all these things and no word will be found for our defense.

> —Sophronius, Patriarch of Jerusalem, translated by Robert G. Hoyland

> As for the Arabs, to whom God has at this time given rule over the world, you know well how they act towards us. Not only do they not oppose Christianity, but they praise our faith, honor the priests and saints of our Lord, and give aid to the churches and monasteries. Why then do your [inhabitants of Merv, a city in the former Persian Empire] reject their faith on a pretext of theirs? And this when the [inhabitants of Merv] themselves admit that the Arabs have not compelled them to abandon their faith, but only asked them to give up half of their possessions in order to keep their faith. Yet they forsook their faith, which is forever, and retained the half of their wealth, which is for a short time.

> —Ishoyahb III of Adiabene, translated by Robert G. Hoyland

- What was the experience of Christians under the rule of the new Muslim conquerors?
- Who were the audiences for these two letters? Why does the audience matter to their messages?
- Why might the writers have such different perspectives on their treatment by the Arab-Muslims?

The term "Arab-Muslim conquest" has another drawback in that some participants were non-Arabs, including people from East Africa, North Africa, and Persians who chose to join the Muslim armies. Among them were some Amazigh (Berber) tribes from North Africa and the elite Persian cavalry, the *asawira*. Other fighters *were* Arabs but had not necessarily formally converted to Islam. These included Arab members of devout Christian tribes such as the Banu Taghlib. There are likely many reasons for non-Arabs and non-Muslims to have contributed to the Muslim effort. Joining in the conquests would at least have entitled the participant to a portion of the spoils of war and standing in the new society, both of which were immensely beneficial.

In the end, the most important differentiator of status in this earliest society was not Arab versus non-Arab or Muslim versus non-Muslim, but rather conqueror versus conquered. Thus, in the first centuries of Islamic history, society was organized into those who paid tax for the protection and benefit of the state, and those who received that payment and provided that protection and those benefits. Those who were ethnically Arab had opportunities to enjoy special preferences within government and society in the earliest decades, but by the end of the eighth century, this distinction eroded as more non-Arabs became involved in the affairs of state.

Islam's First Dynasty

The Rashidun caliphs are remembered not just for overseeing the process of conquest in the region but also for helping to articulate what Muhammad's *ummah* should look like, and what made Islam different from other monotheistic religions such as Judaism and Christianity. The first four caliphs committed to writing a canonized Quran and helped interpret and articulate the religious law. For matters of faith the Quran did not directly address, they played a crucial role in transmitting the **hadith**, the sayings and actions of Muhammad and his closest confidants, to help answer those questions. Together, the Quran and the hadith make up the bulk of religious law for Muslims to the present day, and the Rashidun caliphs have long been regarded as interpreters of this material for later Muslims who were not able to interact with Muhammad themselves. Critical for the transmission of the hadith were those who had spent the most time in Muhammad's presence, not only the Rashidun but also his wives. Among the most important for the hadith was Muhammad's youngest wife Aisha, whose achievements as a transmitter and interpreter of Islamic law in the decades following her husband's death cannot be understated.

The rule of the "rightly guided," despite their name, did not escape challenge and controversy. The reign of the fourth caliph, Ali ibn Abi Talib, resulted in the first Islamic civil war, which proved devastating for the long-term unity of the new religion. The war was fought over the murder of the third caliph, Uthman, in 656, and his successor's inability to bring the killers and their collaborators to justice. Uthman's family—the tribe of Umayya—rose to resist Ali's claim to the caliphate. It was a conflict that deeply wounded the unity of the Islamic world and saw many early family members and supporters of Muhammad take up arms against one another. For example, Aisha played a leading role in opposing Ali at the Battle of the Camel at the outset of the civil war. The eventual murder of Ali in 661 deepened the divide between his supporters and other Muslims.

With Ali's death, the Umayyads, led by Mu'awiya ibn Abi Sufyan, established Islam's first hereditary dynasty. Moving the capital of their state from the Prophet's city of Medina to the Syrian city of Damascus, they became a major imperial power in the region while beginning to articulate what made Islam different from other religious traditions in the region. As the founder of the dynasty, Mu'awiya proved to be a particularly shrewd politician, but his preference for nepotism meant his family's long-term legacy was mixed. Despite a second civil war in the 680s and 690s, his successors continued to favor their own, while at the same time the conquest of further territory slowed and then stopped.

After the Muslims met defeat at the walls of the Byzantine capital of Constantinople, the later Umayyad period, which ended in 750, was defined by the dynasty's struggle for legitimacy. At first the Umayyads followed the tactics of the Rashidun, creating everything from art to buildings with forms and symbols that were familiar to the Byzantine and Persian worlds. In doing so, they attempted to provide continuity with the old empires they replaced, while at the same time earning authority among the largely non-Muslim population they now ruled. Within the running of the state, too, many government officials in these early decades—in positions from tax collector to scribe at the court of the ruler—were non-Muslim holdovers from the Byzantines and Persians. They helped the early Muslim rulers establish and administer a government the size of which they had never experienced.

As time passed, however, the Umayyads achieved a more successful demonstration of what made Islam distinct. They did this by changing the symbols and style of their art, embracing written Arabic—the language of the Quran—as unique to Muslims, centering the Islamic prophet Muhammad as the "seal" on a long line of Rabbinic (Jewish) and biblical (Christian) prophets, and asserting an anti-Trinitarian message. This last decision, about the nature of Jesus in the Christian tradition, proved the source of growing tension between Muslims and Christians as time passed.

Early Islamic Art and Architecture

Little written material of the seventh-century Arab-Muslim conquerors survives. As the century waned, however, Arabic script began to appear on coins and buildings, offering important sources for historians.

The earliest Islamic caliphs had mimicked the styles and motifs of their Byzantine and Persian rivals to justify their rule and demonstrate a continuity of government. What would have happened, for instance, if they had immediately minted coins utterly different from those their citizens were using (Figure 11.14)? Would anyone accept them?

(a)   **(b)**

FIGURE 11.14 Byzantine Gold Solidus. A gold coin called a *solidus* from about 608 CE shows the (a) Byzantine emperor Heraclius the Elder and his son on the front and (b) a Christian cross on the reverse. The coin, minted by Byzantine rulers in today's Turkey or Cyprus, includes inscriptions in Greek celebrating victory over a usurper. (credit: "Revolt of the Heraclii solidus, 608 AD" by Classical Numismatic Group, LLC/Wikimedia Commons, CC BY 2.5)

The culture started to change after the second Islamic civil war in the early 690s. The victors, a branch of the Umayyad family, began to make the empire look increasingly Arab. Their governmental reforms included the gradual removal of signs and symbols associated with the old Byzantine and Persian rulers, such as Christian crosses on coins).

Another reform was the introduction of Arabic as the official language of the Islamic empire. Here again, gold coins demonstrate how widely this change was made, and how inscriptions specific to Islam began to appear (Figure 11.15).

(a)   **(b)**

FIGURE 11.15 Umayyad Gold Dinar. (a) (b) On this gold dinar minted by the Umayyad caliph around 700, images common on Byzantine and Sasanian coins have disappeared and Greek replaced by the Umayyads' official language, Arabic. The inscriptions are invocations of the Muslim faith, including "There is no God but God, He is Alone, He has No Associate." (credit: "Gold dinar of Abd al-Malik 697-98" by American Numismatic Society/ Wikimedia Commons, Public Domain)

It took time for the Muslims to dramatically change the style and forms of their art. In the intermediate period—as illustrated by two of the earliest mosques constructed by the Muslims, the Dome of the Rock in Jerusalem and the Umayyad Mosque in Damascus—rulers married the old empires' traditions with new design elements (Figure 11.16, Figure 11.17). These examples reveal an early Islamic state beginning to articulate its own identity.

FIGURE 11.16 Dome of the Rock, Exterior. The Dome of the Rock mosque in the Old City in Jerusalem is one of Islam's holiest sites. Its hexagonal shape is very unusual, but it had a precedent in nearby Byzantine Christian churches. (credit: "Exterior of Dome of the Rock or Masjid Al Sakhrah, in Jerusalem" by Thekra A. Sabri/ Wikimedia Commons, CC BY 2.0)

FIGURE 11.17 Dome of the Rock, Interior. Mosaics inside the Dome of the Rock include depictions of the mythological Senmurv bird, popular in Sasanian Persia, while the medium of mosaic tile itself was Byzantine. Arabic inscriptions from the Quran are found throughout the interior—a distinctly Islamic feature. (credit: "Mosque Of Omar 1914" by National Geographic/Wikimedia Commons, Public Domain)

- Why did the Arab-Muslims finally change their gold coins more dramatically at the end of the seventh century from the imitative versions they first minted?
- How can art and architecture help historians understand this early period of Islamic history? What do coins and the Dome of the Rock reveal?

The Umayyads also struggled within the *ummah*, however, when it came to their treatment of Arab ethnicity. As they worked to establish a new empire that was quickly growing beyond their ability to administer on their own, the Arab-Muslims relied on the continued employment of former Byzantine and Persian bureaucrats to help with the running of the state. These non-Muslim and primarily non-Arab government officials were critical to the early governance of the Rashidun and the Umayyad dynasty, but by the eighth century they were rapidly being shunned in favor of Arabs. In some cases, non-Muslims were passed over for the best positions, while in other situations, new converts to Islam grew increasingly frustrated at not being considered full members of the conquering elite.

As more people encountered the message of Islam, interest grew among non-Arabs wanting to convert to the new faith. The Umayyads largely pushed back against this trend, and not just because for the upkeep of the state they relied on revenue from taxes Muslims did not have to pay. They also perceived their faith as a religion by Arabs for Arabs. As they saw it, God had sent the Arabs his last prophet—Muhammad, an Arab—to spread his message in their language, Arabic. Becoming a Muslim was not just a religious conversion but a cultural one as well. Non-Arab converts needed, in essence, to convert to an ethnically Arab culture, to be adopted by an Arab tribe as a protected member called a ***mawali***, before any religious conversion could occur. This was an onerous process that discouraged conversion. But as more Arab-Muslims settled in the conquered regions and intermarried with the Indigenous population, more children were born of mixed parentage, bringing the increasing focus on "Arabness" and pure Arab dominance of the Umayyads under even greater scrutiny. It was the treatment of *mawali* as second-class citizens that proved the Umayyads' undoing, and that ushered in a more universalist view of Islam that further solidified the religion's hold in the region.

11.3 Islamization and Religious Rule under Islam

LEARNING OBJECTIVES

By the end of this section, you will be able to:
- Explain how the Abbasids established themselves as the dominant state in the Middle East
- Discuss the formation of sects within the Islamic community
- Analyze how Islam influenced the religious and cultural experience of people living under Abbasid rule

The Rashidun and Umayyads played an important role in articulating the new religion of Islam while establishing the Islamic state in the Middle East. But the dynasty that followed them in 750 CE was the one that solidified Islam's place in the region and in world history. While the Abbasid caliphate did not greatly extend the borders of the Islamic state, its achievements included overseeing and building on the transmission of ancient knowledge that had gone unseen in much of world history until then. The Abbasids presided over what was arguably the end of antiquity in the Middle East and its transition to the Middle Ages, becoming one of the most important powers of their time. They also faced the fracturing of their authority over the outlying provinces, and the growth within Islam of distinct sects with different theological beliefs and goals.

The Abbasid Caliphate

The last decades of Umayyad rule were defined by factionalism and infighting. Arab tribes vied for power and influence, while non-Arab converts to Islam became increasingly frustrated over being marginalized, especially in the far east of the empire. There, in the province of Khurasan, Arab-Muslims had settled after the conquests, often intermarrying with the Indigenous Persians (Figure 11.18). By the mid-eighth century, several generations of these mixed-ethnicity Muslims had come to feel disenfranchised in the region, and Khurasan became a hotbed of revolutionary activity. Many who were frustrated with Umayyad rule and ready for a change met to imagine a more open Islamic community, one in which all ethnicities could enjoy the full benefits of Islamic society, and marginalized groups like the supporters of the fourth caliph Ali and his family would have more opportunity.

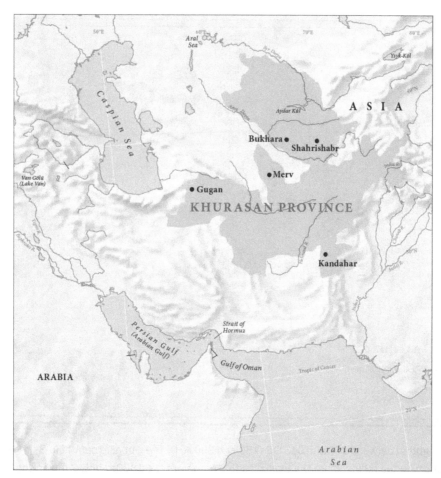

FIGURE 11.18 Khurasan Province. The province of Khurasan (shaded orange) made up the northeastern extent first of the Sasanian Empire and then of the realm of the early Islamic caliphates. Discontent among the mixed-ethnicity Muslims living there grew during the eighth century. (attribution: Copyright Rice University, OpenStax, under CC BY 4.0 license)

This revolutionary group championed the right of the family of Muhammad to hold the position of caliph. Its members supported the claims of the descendants of Ibn Abbas, a first cousin of Muhammad, and thus came to be known as the Abbasids. In 749, after several years of growing dissatisfaction, they rose in rebellion against the Umayyads, overthrowing Islam's first dynasty within a year and establishing themselves as the new rulers of the Middle East. Abbasids claimed the title of caliph from the year 750 through to the early sixteenth century, although the power they sought waxed and waned over time.

Shortly after coming to power, the Abbasids of the eighth century reoriented the focus of the Islamic world, pulling it away from Arabia and closer to the East by founding their new capital, Baghdad, in central Iraq (Figure 11.19). Especially with the prominence of Khurasan and the Islamic East in the rise of the Abbasids, shifting the capital city closer to the East also made a great deal of sense. Baghdad was a planned city intended to take advantage of the immense wealth and talent the Islamic state had accumulated over almost a century and a half of conquest and consolidation under the Umayyads. It was built on the banks of the Tigris River in Mesopotamia, a land that had supported some of the earliest human civilizations because of its remarkable fertility. As the Abbasid state grew wealthier and more powerful, Baghdad became a prominent center of trade and culture, and the city sprawled outward along the banks of the river and into the fertile farmland that surrounded it.

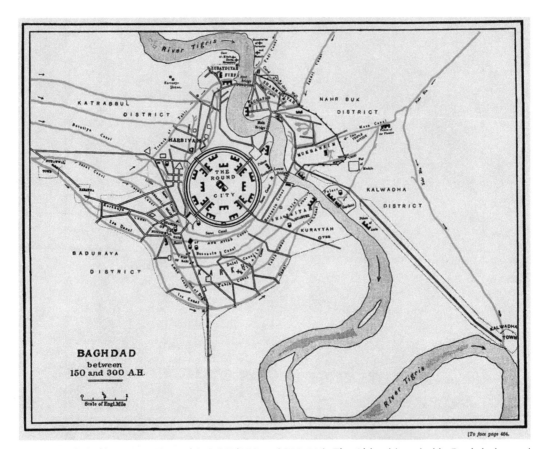

FIGURE 11.19 Baghdad between 767 and 913 CE (150 and 300 AH). The Abbasid capital in Baghdad was designed to be the greatest city in the region, if not the world. As this map from the 1880s shows, it was constructed with a circular layout, and those who lived inside the walls of the main city, closest to the caliph's palace, enjoyed special prestige. (credit: "Baghdad 150 to 300 AH" by www.muhammadanism.org/Wikimedia Commons, Public Domain)

The decision to move the focus of Islamic rule further east also signaled a significant shift in the region's politics and economics. The inhabitants of the former Persian Empire had played an integral role in helping the Abbasids to rise, and they became a major power base for the dynasty as it advanced. Persian language, culture, and traditions came to exert a greater influence on early Islamic society, especially at the court in Baghdad. And as Baghdad overtook traditional Mediterranean cities such as Alexandria, Antioch, Constantinople, Damascus, and Jerusalem in prominence, the center of trade moved further east along the Silk Roads that connected with the Indian Ocean world and a continually growing China.

⊛ LINK TO LEARNING

What would it have been like to live in medieval Baghdad? In some ways, it was a bit like living in New York City. This brief video describes the culture and status of medieval Baghdad (https://openstax.org/l/77Baghdad) in the Abbasid period.

The Abbasid Translation Movement

The society the early Abbasids created was one of the great marvels of the Middle Ages, and the growth of Baghdad and its courtly culture played a major part in that achievement. But as central as Baghdad was to the advancement and success of the Abbasids, so too were the people who made up their cosmopolitan empire. The early Abbasids strongly supported learning, especially in their capital, and fostered what is now called the Abbasid Translation Movement, or the Greco-Arabic Translation Movement. Few people were literate at this time, but it was an especially important moment in world history thanks to new technology and opportunities that improved access to education and literacy more generally. Especially important was the introduction of

Chinese papermaking techniques into the Middle East. These methods allowed for the creation of significantly less expensive books, and the Abbasids' patronage of scholarly work proved the catalyst for an explosion of medieval learning.

The Abbasids sought to preserve the knowledge of past societies by translating the works of the ancient world into Arabic, especially from Greek and Persian, as the Islamic world transitioned from an oral to a writerly society during the ninth century. Writing and scholarly research were not always well funded in the premodern world, so wealthy patrons, including the caliph himself, provided financial support to scholars capable of completing this work. As a result, the Abbasid elite were able to attract the best and brightest to participate, and a culture of learning grew among the upper echelons of society and especially in Baghdad. Scholars were often native speakers of Greek and Syriac who were generally non-Muslim. The Abbasids' support of this multicultural and multiethnic community ultimately increased the number of works produced in Arabic during the first centuries of their rule, while at the same time providing exceptional educational opportunities as Islamic schools called *madrasas* were founded and grew.

The achievements of the translation movement were considerable, preserving many incredibly important astrological, geographic, mathematical, medical, and other scientific and philosophical texts in Arabic at a time when non-Arabic copies had become increasingly rare. These texts included seminal works by the Greek thinkers Aristotle, Dioscorides, Galen, Hippocrates, and Ptolemy that were given advanced study in the Muslim world when their popularity and even availability were extremely limited in the rest of the Mediterranean (Figure 11.20).

FIGURE 11.20 The Abbasid Translation Movement. This is a page from an Arabic translation of the first-century Greek physician Dioscorides's treatise, *De materia medica* (*On Medical Material*). It dates from the eleventh century, but many manuscripts like it were first rendered from the original Greek into Arabic during the Abbasid Translation Movement. (credit: "Kitāb al-Ḥašā'iš fī hāyūlā al-'ilāg al-ṭibbī Or. 289" by Universitaire Bibliotheken Leiden/Leiden

From the Persian world, the Abbasids focused on the translation of materials related to statecraft, etiquette, the history of kings, and economics. All these were topics considered essential for a professional education, especially for a class of state bureaucrats known as "secretaries" whose job was to administer the empire and its people on behalf of the ruler. Yet the Abbasids were not simply having the great texts of ancient peoples brought into their language and their madrasas during this period. The manuscripts, especially works of science, were in some cases many centuries old. So, a major goal of the translation movement was not just to preserve but also to correct and expand them. Baghdad, then, became the "house of wisdom" through this emphasis on learning and continued scholarly endeavor. Although the scholars who improved these traditional works often go uncredited in the new volumes they produced, their work allowed the Abbasids to apply contemporary knowledge and understanding to the ruminations of previous generations. Early Abbasid society was a time and place of learning and openness to considering old, new, and foreign ideas; to making them a part of the "Islamic sciences"; and to bringing material from the Mediterranean, Central Asian, and Indian Ocean worlds into the empire.

Sect Formation in the Middle East

The early Abbasid period brought stability to the Islamic world, but it was not permanent. Although there had been contention within the Islamic *ummah* from the very beginning, it was during the Abbasid rule that more distinct sects formed, based on doctrinal differences and questions about the leadership of the community that traced back to the first century of Islamic history.

The catalyst for the formation of denominations within Islam was a growing divide between the groups now known as the **Sunni** and the **Shia** (sometimes written as *Shi'ite*), the two primary "umbrella sects" within Islam. The Sunni take their name from the *sunna* or customs of the Islamic prophet Muhammad. Adherents follow a canonized, common form of the hadith and interpretation of the Quran, although different schools of law exist that provide variable interpretation and guidance to the religious faithful. Today the largest group of Muslims around the world, the Sunni also came to be identified as those who accepted the decision, following Muhammad's death, that the first leader of the community would be his father-in-law Abu Bakr rather than his son-in-law Ali. The Shia derive their name from the Arabic phrase *Shiat Ali* or "the followers of Ali," who eventually became the fourth caliph. They began as those who believed in the claim by Ali and the Prophet's family that Ali had been designated the new leader of the Muslim community following Muhammad's death.

Tensions between the two groups continued to escalate through the first Islamic civil war, fought between the caliph Ali and the Umayyad ruler Mu'awiya, and escalated with the massacre of a large portion of Muhammad's family, including his grandson Husayn ibn Ali, at Karbala as the second Islamic civil war was beginning. The commemoration of these events in the early Islamic period remains a major feature of the denominations of Shia Islam. The Shia came to revere the family of the Prophet, seeing in them a role beyond providing a new caliph. They believe members of Muhammad's family transmit divine knowledge, charisma, and authority, and they afford certain of them the title of **imam**, signifying the religious leader of the community of Muslims. At the center of this focus on the Prophet's family in the faith's earliest century was the lineage of Muhammad through his daughter Fatima, the wife of Ali, and her children, who included Husayn. As time passed, however, and as Islam became increasingly more patriarchal in the Abbasid period, the emphasis shifted to the male members of Muhammad's family and their lineage through Ali specifically.

In the medieval period, the divide between the Sunni and Shia was not complete. The issue of succession following Muhammad's death was not irreconcilable, and the Sunni respected the family of the Islamic prophet Muhammad even if they did not see an automatic or exclusive right to rule through Ali's bloodline. The early Shia supported the Abbasids' claim to leadership because the Abbasids required the caliph to be a member of the Prophet's family, but Ali's kin were eventually overlooked in the line of succession. As rivalry grew between these early Shia and the Abbasids, it seems likely that the Shia then articulated that the authority of the imam specifically passed through the family of the Prophet through Ali, and not through anyone less closely related to him—likely to support their own claims to rule.

The role of the caliph as a leader in the Islamic world also began to change dramatically in the Middle Ages. This shift was due not just to the Shia conception of the imam. Rather, as the Abbasids came to power, a religious clerical class also arose within Islam. Known as the **ulama** (literally "the scholars"), they came to hold an increasingly important role as the interpreters of Islamic law within non-Shia, Sunni Islam during the Abbasid period (Figure 11.21).

FIGURE 11.21 A Member of the *Ulama* as Teacher. This thirteenth-century image of a group of students learning from a teacher (far right) in a library depicts religious education in the Abbasid period. (credit: "Les Makamat de Hariri" by Bibliothèque nationale de France/Wikimedia Commons, Public Domain)

Before the Abbasid period, the early caliphs had successfully made a case for being vested with both secular and religious authority, including the ability to interpret the scripture and issue religious proclamations. As the *ulama* acquired a more prominent role in Abbasid society, however, they claimed more of this power and authority for themselves, diminishing the religious entitlements that earlier caliphs had claimed. As the centuries passed, the religious role of the caliph weakened further, and the decision to compile and write down the hadith, which had been transmitted only orally for the bulk of the first two centuries, gave further authority to the keepers and teachers of this material at the expense of the caliph within early Sunni Islam.

Islamization before the Crusades

What was it like for Indigenous peoples of captured territories to live under Islamic rule during the Umayyad and Abbasid periods? Perhaps unsurprisingly, the experience was variable, especially considering the size of the empire the Abbasids came to rule. What *is* surprising is that the majority of these inhabitants were not Muslims themselves.

The largest group belonged to eastern Christian denominations, including Melkites, Jacobites, Copts, and

Nestorians, but significant minority populations of Jewish people and Zoroastrians also lived throughout the empire. We have seen that non-Muslims were allowed to keep their religion and continue to live under Islamic rule by paying a special tax. Early on, the Muslims instituted a series of rules to limit the interactions between themselves and non-Muslims, and a later series of regulations regarding religious intermarriage and child-rearing slowly converted more of the population to Islam over time.

For example, a Muslim generally could not marry a non-Muslim under Islamic law, but if such a marriage occurred, a Muslim woman's future husband had to convert to Islam to marry her, and the children of a Muslim husband had to be raised as Muslim. Thus, it seems likely that the process of conversion to Islam at this time was quite slow and that the Muslims remained a numeric minority for centuries even though they wielded the majority of power in the empire.

IN THEIR OWN WORDS

The Pact of Umar

The "Pact of Umar" is a legal document detailing the rights and responsibilities of Christians living under early Islamic rule. Often attributed to Umar, the second Rashidun caliph who ruled from 634 to 644, it may date anywhere from the seventh to the early ninth century.

In the name of God, the Merciful and Compassionate. This is a letter to the servant of God Umar, Commander of the Faithful, from the Christians of such-and-such a city. When you came against us, we asked you for safe-conduct for ourselves, our descendants, our property, and the people of our community, and we undertook the following obligations toward you:

We shall not build, in our cities or in their neighborhood, new monasteries, Churches, convents, or monks' cells, nor shall we repair, by day or by night, such of them as fall in ruins or are situated in the quarters of the Muslims.

We shall keep our gates wide open for passersby and travelers. We shall give board and lodging to all Muslims who pass our way for three days.

We shall not give shelter in our churches or in our dwellings to any spy, nor bide him from the Muslims.

We shall not teach the Quran to our children.

We shall not manifest our religion publicly nor convert anyone to it. We shall not prevent any of our kin from entering Islam if they wish it.

We shall show respect toward the Muslims, and we shall rise from our seats when they wish to sit.

We shall not seek to resemble the Muslims by imitating any of their garments, the qalansuwa [a type of headwear], the turban, footwear, or the parting of the hair. We shall not speak as they do, nor shall we adopt their kunyas [a part of an Arab name].

We shall not mount on saddles, nor shall we gird swords nor bear any kind of arms nor carry them on our- persons.

We shall not engrave Arabic inscriptions on our seals.

We shall not sell fermented [alcoholic] drinks.

We shall clip the fronts of our heads.

We shall always dress in the same way wherever we may be, and we shall bind the zunar [a type of belt] round our waists

We shall not display our crosses or our books in the roads or markets of the Muslims. We shall use only clappers in our churches very softly. We shall not raise our voices when following our dead. We shall not show lights on any of the roads of the Muslims or in their markets. We shall not bury our dead near the Muslims.

We shall not take slaves who have been allotted to Muslims.

We shall not build houses overtopping the houses of the Muslims. . . .

We accept these conditions for ourselves and for the people of our community, and in return we receive safe-conduct.

If we in any way violate these undertakings for which we ourselves stand surety, we forfeit our covenant, and we become liable to the penalties for contumacy and sedition.

—"The Status of Non-Muslims Under Muslim Rule"

- Who is said to be writing this agreement, and why does that matter? Why was it written?
- You may see the pact as onerous and limiting for Christians. Can it be read differently? How?

Even during the Abbasid period, Islam was still a new religion. The Muslims benefited from allowing non-Muslim communities a certain amount of autonomy and segregation, so long as this did not limit or infringe on the rights and privileges of the ruling Muslim elite. They even allowed non-Muslim religious courts to adjudicate many cases among Jewish people and Christians. They may also have feared a temptation among adherents to stray from the new faith to older traditions like Christianity and Judaism, which had a great deal in common with Islam at that time.

Along with religious conversion to Islam, cultural conversion, which took place much more rapidly, formed part of the process of **Islamization** in the Middle East and North Africa. As the early Islamic state grew wealthier and more powerful through continued expansion, and as the Arab-Muslim conquerors became a clearer and stronger elite in the new society, members of the nobility of Indigenous populations were keen to maintain their own wealth and status in whatever ways they could. Thus, they began to bring aspects of Arab and Islamic culture into their daily lives while retaining their commitment to their own religious communities.

It became common, then, for Christians in places like Jordan and Egypt to adopt the Arabic language while outside their homes or churches, and a native language such as Syriac or Coptic within their own communities and for their worship. Non-Muslim men and women also adopted styles of dress and grooming similar to those of the Muslim elite (even if there was anxiety among religious leaders about this type of acculturation, as seen in the Pact of Umar), along with naming practices, especially in places like Islamic Spain. They also began to embrace aspects of Islamic art and architectural design. In the same way as the Rashidun and the first Umayyad caliphs had relied upon imitative design and symbols to legitimize themselves in the earliest period of Muslim rule, so did non-Muslims now adopt features of Islamic culture to gain, maintain, or regain status within the Abbasid world.

Key Terms

Abrahamic faiths the religions of Judaism, Christianity, and Islam, which all trace their origins through a common ancestor, the prophet Abraham

caliph an Islamic title designating a spiritual and secular leader

caliphate an area under the control of a Muslim ruler called a caliph

hadith the words and actions of the Islamic prophet Muhammad and his immediate successors that, along with the Quran, form the fundamental basis for Islamic law

hajj the Islamic pilgrimage to Mecca

hijra an Arabic term meaning "emigration" that describes a defining moment for early Muslims as they fled Mecca for Medina in 622 CE

imam the religious leader of Shia Muslims

Islamization the religious and cultural conversion of those living under Islamic rule

mawali non-Arab converts to Islam in the early Islamic period who had to be adopted by an Arab tribe as part of the conversion process

Quran the holy scripture of Islam, which Muslims believe was given to humanity by God through Muhammad

Rashidun a term meaning "rightly guided" that describes the first four caliphs after Muhammad's death: Abu Bakr, Umar, Uthman, and Ali

Shia one of the two umbrella sects of Islam, whose members believe leadership of the Muslim community should reside in the family of Muhammad only through his son-in-law Ali

Sunni the larger of the two umbrella sects of Islam, whose adherents did not require leadership of the community to come specifically from the descendants of Muhammad through Ali

ulama a class of religious clerics and scholars who act as the primary interpreters of Islamic law

ummah the community of Muslims

Section Summary

11.1 The Rise and Message of Islam

While the Arabs of northern Arabia were uniting as a capable fighting force looking for opportunities to expand, the Byzantines and Sasanian Empires were at a low ebb. In the early seventh century, the Byzantine Empire had won a long and costly war against the Sasanians, sometimes fought on both sides by proxies from northern Arabia, but now the combatants were exhausted and financially drained. Meanwhile, Muhammad's historic unification of the majority of Arab tribes under the single leader of a monotheistic faith was only the beginning of the story of Islam. After Muhammad and his followers were forced to flee Mecca for Medina in 622, fighting between the two communities continued for several years before those in Mecca converted to Islam, and Muhammad made a triumphant return to the city. The stage was now set for a significant shift in the balance of power in the region.

11.2 The Arab-Islamic Conquests and the First Islamic States

The issue of leadership following Muhammad's death caused immediate tensions within the Islamic *ummah* even as the first four caliphs, the Rashidun, oversaw significant territorial expansion. Tensions between the family of Muhammad—especially his son-in-law Ali, the fourth caliph—and the Umayyads resulted in a civil war that brought Islam's first dynasty to power.

Within a century of Muhammad's death, an Islamic state ruled over the world's largest empire at that time, first unifying the Arabian Peninsula through the Ridda Wars and then taking territory previously ruled by the flagging Byzantine and Sasanian Empires. Mimicking the leadership and culture of their Byzantine and Persian predecessors as a means to legitimize their own role, the Umayyads began the process of articulating what made Islamic culture unique among the other cultures of the region. By the later period of their rule, they began to privilege the position of the ethnically Arab members of the empire and to increasingly "Arabize" the government and its functions, despite the fact that the Arab-Muslim conquerors remained a minority population and did not promote or support the conversion of non-Muslims to the new faith.

11.3 Islamization and Religious Rule under Islam

Through a process of conquest, conversion, and coexistence, the early Abbasids created a cosmopolitan medieval empire centered at their new capital of Baghdad. By assimilating the late antique traditions of the Byzantines and Persians before supplanting them, integrating Arab culture northward throughout the region, and overseeing the preservation and dissemination of knowledge from the ancient world, the Muslims of the Middle East created a thriving cultural hub with considerable impact on world history in this period and beyond. While religious conversion to Islam remained slow, a process of cultural conversion and an increased openness to non-Arab converts to the faith saw the escalation of Islamization throughout the Abbasid empire from Spain and Portugal in the west to India in the east.

Assessments

Review Questions

1. What two empires were at war during much of Muhammad's prophetic career?
   a. the Mughal and the Sasanians
   b. the Byzantines and the Sasanians
   c. the Byzantines and the Aksumites
   d. the Himyarites and the Holy Roman Empire

2. According to Muslim belief, which of the following statements is true?
   a. Muhammad was the first in a long line of monotheistic prophets.
   b. Moses, Jesus, and Muhammad were the same person.
   c. Muslims worship the same God as Jewish people and Christians.
   d. Islam is a polytheistic faith.

3. What is the holy scripture of Islam?
   a. Quran
   b. Torah
   c. Bible
   d. Kaaba

4. What united the members of Muhammad's *ummah*?
   a. the use of the Arabic language and service to the Byzantine Empire
   b. the belief in one God, Muhammad's leadership, and mutual defense
   c. previous membership in the Jewish faith
   d. residence in the city of Mecca

5. What state was defeated and assimilated into the early Islamic state?
   a. Han China
   b. Aksumite Ethiopia
   c. Byzantine Empire
   d. Sasanian Persia

6. In the earliest decades of Muslim rule, what was the most important differentiator of status?
   a. Muslim versus non-Muslim
   b. Arab versus Persian
   c. conqueror versus conquered
   d. Byzantine versus Roman

7. Who were the *mawali* in early Islamic society?
   a. non-Arab converts to Islam
   b. religious leaders of the young Muslim community
   c. caravan traders traveling along the Silk Roads
   d. the first dynasty of Islam

8. What were the Ridda Wars?
   a. a conflict between Muslims and other Arab tribes that began the conquest of Arabia
   b. the Arab-Muslim invasion of Sasanian Persia
   c. the first Islamic civil war
   d. an uprising of enslaved people against the Umayyad dynasty

9. Why did the Muslims create Baghdad as a new capital city?
   a. No other cities were hospitable to the Arabs, so they needed to build their own.
   b. The Abbasids wanted to return the capital of their empire to Arabia.
   c. The Byzantines recaptured the old capital city of Damascus.
   d. The center of the Islamic world was shifting eastward after the Abbasid Revolution.

10. Where was the province of Khurasan located?
    a. Western Arabia
    b. Northeastern Persia
    c. Southeastern Persia
    d. North Africa

11. What did the process of Islamization look like during the early Abbasid period?
    a. Christians adopted the Arabic language and Islamic forms of dress while not necessarily converting to Islam.
    b. The entire Indigenous population of the Middle East and North Africa converted to Islam.
    c. People feared Muslims and the Muslim faith more generally.
    d. Arab-Muslims refused to allow any non-Arabs to convert to Islam.

12. What was a defining feature of the earliest supporters of Ali, who became the Shia?
    a. the refusal to recognize Muhammad as an Islamic prophet
    b. the elevation of the family of Muhammad through his son in-law Ali
    c. a belief in multiple gods that are subservient to the one God of Islam
    d. the refusal to support the Abbasid family over the Umayyads in the Abbasid Revolution

Check Your Understanding Questions

1. What role did the cities of Mecca and Medina play in the formation of Islam?

2. Look at the following map (attribution: Copyright Rice University, OpenStax, under CC BY 4.0 license) and identify the Kingdom of Aksum, the Byzantine Empire, the Kingdom of Himyar, and the Sasanian Empire. For what reasons was Mecca not aggressively sought as a target of conquest by these neighboring states?

3. How did monotheistic faiths spread through the Arabian Peninsula before the rise of Islam?

4. Discuss the factors that led to the success of the Arab-Islamic conquests of the seventh and eighth centuries.

5. What issues did the Muslim community have to consider in choosing Muhammad's first successor?

6. Why did the earliest Arab-Islamic conquests first focus on the Arabian Peninsula?

7. What differences separated the two umbrella sects of Islam, the Sunni and the Shia, in the Abbasid period?

8. What features of Abbasid society helped make the Abbasid Translation Movement such a successful intellectual endeavor?

Application and Reflection Questions

1. What were the most important historical influences on the formation of Muhammad's community, and what was their impact on Islam?

2. What made Islam different from Judaism and Christianity as a monotheistic religion in the region?

3. Why were some religious communities of the Middle East accepting of Muslim rule despite not converting to Islam themselves?

4. What benefits were provided by the early Umayyads' decision to run their empire like that of the Byzantines and Sasanian Persians? Why did they change?

5. Who were the minority communities of the early medieval Middle East? What did it mean to be a minority?

6. What did the process of cultural conversion by non-Muslims during the first centuries of Islamic history look like?

FIGURE 12.1 A Caravansary. Along the Silk Roads, caravansaries were vital outposts where merchants traveling between Turkey and China could stay and meet other traders to exchange goods, commodities, and ideas. The Shah Abbasi caravansary shown here is now a national heritage site in Nishapur, in modern Iran. (credit: modification of work "Abbasi caravanserai of Nishapur" by Sonia Sevilla/Wikimedia Commons, CC0 1.0)

CHAPTER OUTLINE

12.1 The Indian Ocean World in the Early Middle Ages
12.2 East-West Interactions in the Early Middle Ages
12.3 Border States: Sogdiana, Korea, and Japan

INTRODUCTION The early Middle Ages was a time of increased connections across continents. This period was marked by the continued development of the maritime networks centered on the Indian Ocean, and of the Silk Roads—a series of trade routes linking China and parts of central Asia, India, and the Middle East. A globally connected medieval world was emerging, one united by long-distance trade networks and enhanced by the exchange of ideas. An important element of this system was the **caravansary**, an inn funded by the state or wealthy individuals where travelers could spend the night and store their goods securely (Figure 12.1). In addition to providing shelter, caravansaries were a place for merchants to meet other traders to exchange goods as well as share and spread Islamic ideas and traditions.

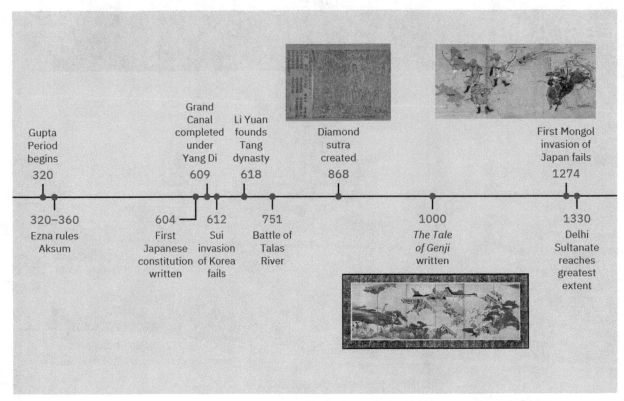

FIGURE 12.2 Timeline: India, the Indian Ocean Basin, and East Asia. (credit "868": modification of work "Jingangjing" by British Library/Wikimedia Commons, Public Domain; credit "1000": modification of work "Scenes from the three chapters of The tale of Genji [Genji monogatari]" by Art Gallery of South Australia/Wikimedia Commons, Public Domain; credit "1274": modification of work "Mōko Shūrai Ekotoba 2" by Unknown/Wikimedia Commons, Public Domain)

12.1 The Indian Ocean World in the Early Middle Ages

LEARNING OBJECTIVES

By the end of this section, you will be able to:
- Identify important political developments in South Asia
- Discuss religious and social practices in South and East Asia
- Describe the rise and fall of the Sui and Tang dynasties in China

Beginning in the eighth century, the Khyber Pass, renowned as the means by which Alexander the Great and his army traveled from Afghanistan to India, made it possible for a new religious tradition to enter northern India. This tradition was Islam, which soon came to dominate the areas of modern-day Pakistan and Bangladesh as well as portions of India. In time, Muslims created the powerful Delhi Sultanate, which stretched from the Punjab in the northwest to Bengal in the northeast.

Islam arrived in China during the early Tang period (618–690 CE) by way of the Silk Roads trade as well as through diplomatic missions sent to the Tang court at Chang'an by the Umayyad caliph at Damascus. Before Islam's appearance in China, the Tang dynasty, like its predecessor the Sui, had been influenced by the Indian tradition of Buddhism; the Sui emperor and his Tang cousins adhered to many Buddhist precepts. Monumental constructions such as the Grand Canal and the Huaisheng Mosque, which was built in the seventh century CE and stands today in Guangzhou, demonstrate the grandeur of these two dynasties. Yet, in the end, their expenses outran their income, leading to their ultimate collapse.

South Asia in the Early Middle Ages

India, usually referred to as South Asia, shares the Asian subcontinent, culture, and history with several countries in the modern period, including Pakistan and Bangladesh. Before the Middle Ages, two powerful religious and philosophical traditions emerged there, Hinduism and Buddhism, the latter spreading by traveling merchants via the Silk Roads, both overland and overseas.

In the fourth century BCE, Alexander the Great, his army, and his people came to what is today Afghanistan and the region of the Hindu Kush. Although they did not remain there, for the next three centuries this Hellenistic Seleucid kingdom continued to trade with India and spread Greek ideas. The arrival of Alexander's army in the region was a crucial step in the process of bringing the Afro-Eurasian world closer together. Long-distance travel in this period was still arduous and undertaken primarily by merchants, but important cultural shifts were beginning. Although Alexander's death shortly after his Indian campaigns meant that neither he nor his successors came to rule over this part of the world, disparate and previously separate cultures and peoples began sharing material goods, technologies, and ideas in ways that only continued as the centuries passed. This change was accelerated by the rise of the Mauryan Empire, the first major kingdom to dominate the Asian subcontinent. The Mauryan Empire was founded by Chandragupta Maurya in 322 BCE and lasted until around 185 BCE. During that time, the region saw great intellectual developments, such as the implementation of place value in numbers and the addition of zero to the numbering system, while long-distance trade continued to expand and widen the spread of these new ideas and concepts.

While India experienced a time of unity and great success during the Mauryan age, the subcontinent again broke into separate kingdoms following invasions by the White Huns, which fatally weakened the empire. One of the more stable regimes to emerge in this period was the northern kingdom of Thanesar, under its Buddhist ruler Harsha Vardhana, whose reign lasted from 606 to 647 CE. We know a great deal about Harsha thanks to contemporary accounts by the Indian poet Bana and the Chinese Buddhist monk Xuan Zang. According to both, Buddhism had penetrated the region surrounding Thanesar to a considerable degree, despite the Guptas' earlier favoring of Hinduism. It was also clear, though, that Buddhism had declined as a result of Gupta neglect because its monasteries throughout India were in a state of disrepair. Still, Xuan Zang found Harsha's kingdom well run, wealthy, and justly administered. As far as the monk was concerned, Thanesar was a model state. It did not outlive its king by many years, however. Soon after Harsha's death, the Arab advance that began in the early part of his reign had become a wave that, in the early eighth century, swept across northern India.

In the early seventh century, the new religion of Islam had begun to expand, encompassing Arabia and soon spreading even farther. By 659, Muslim forces were advancing eastward and clashed with the rulers of Sindh in modern-day Pakistan; by the early eighth century, armies of the Umayyad Islamic state had conquered the region. Under increasing pressure from foreign invaders, India splintered into rival principalities ruled by independent rajas, or princes. These kingdoms, which extended from the Indus River valley in northwestern India to the Ganges River in the northeast, flourished for a time. However, long centuries of fending off invasions by Islamized Turkic warlords from central Asia had taken their toll.

The career of Mahmud of Ghazna is a good example of these developments. The son of a Turkic mamluk, or military slave, who ruled from 998 to 1030, Mahmud was intent on developing his region as an important Islamic state and launched dozens of campaigns against the princes of northern India from his base in Afghanistan. The onslaught was quite successful, for by the twelfth century, the Muslim Ghaznavid dynasty ruled an area that stretched from the Aral Sea in the north to Lahore in the east and encompassed the vital Silk Roads conduit of Khurasan in the southwest (Figure 12.3). The Muslim advance did not end with the establishment of the Ghaznavid state, however. Wars raged across northern India, and by the end of the twelfth century, the remaining independent Indian princes had become fatally weakened. Vulnerable to conquest, the kingdoms of the rajas collapsed.

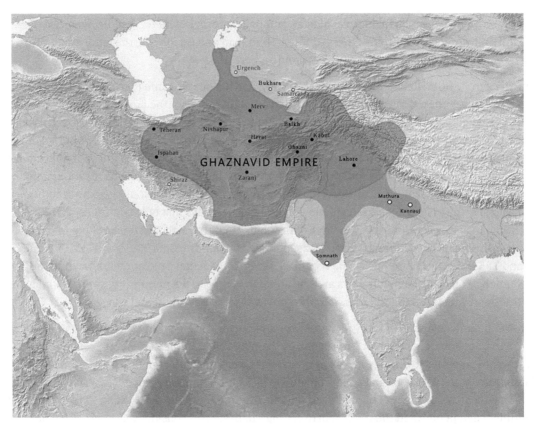

FIGURE 12.3 The Ghaznavid Dynasty. At its height, the Ghaznavid Empire encompassed a vast swath of central Asia and included parts of modern Iran, Afghanistan, and the historical region of Turkestan. With several vital trade centers such as Samarkand and Merv, the state for a time played a key role in maintaining Silk Roads connections between the East and West. (credit: "Map of the Ghaznavid Empire" by Unknown, created in DEMIS World Map Server/Wikimedia Commons, CC BY 4.0)

In the twelfth century, a new line of Turkic invaders arose in present-day Afghanistan, led by Muhammad of Ghur (Ghur was an especially important town in the region). A Persian ruler subject to the Ghaznavids, Muhammad declared his independence from Ghazna and conquered most of the lands of his former lords. In 1192, his forces defeated an army of some 100,000 Rajputs, considered Hindu India's most ferocious warriors, in one of the most violent engagements of his increasingly bloody career. The crowning achievement of Muhammad's campaigns was establishing a Muslim state at Delhi, deep in the heart of northern India. It endured as the Delhi Sultanate for more than three centuries (1206–1526), during which time it was the center of Islamic India (Figure 12.4).

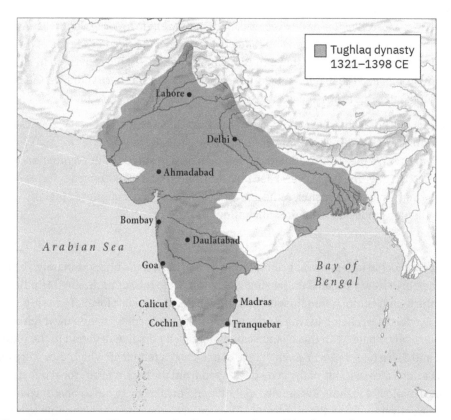

FIGURE 12.4 The Delhi Sultanate. The orange shading shows the Delhi Sultanate in 1330, at its greatest extent. Its size allowed it to control much of the Indian Ocean trade on the western side of the subcontinent. However, the absence of larger cities in the center and south-center of the subcontinent meant that Indigenous peoples there were less likely to come into contact with Islam and its practitioners, so this region was not under the control of an Islamic state. (attribution: Copyright Rice University, OpenStax, under CC BY 4.0 license)

Thus, through a series of invasions over the course of some five hundred years, Arab and then Turkic invaders made their way into northern India, bringing Islam and stimulating political integration in the process. Because the minority Muslim rulers did not enforce cultural homogeneity, the invasions also strengthened the cultural diversity that was already a hallmark of Indian social order. For example, the Islamic rulers of the sultanate gave Hindu subjects the status of *dhimmis*, which protected their rights as non-Muslims, although they still had to pay the special tax, the *jizya*, placed on non-believers. The sultans of Delhi often employed Hindu laborers on construction projects such as the building of mosques, which led Muslims to integrate certain forms of Hindu symbolism and motifs such as trees and plant life into the structures. In the fourteenth century, Sultan Muhammad bin Tughluq expanded and even encouraged Hindu religious freedom, himself participating in Holi, the annual celebration of spring, while he allowed Hindu pilgrimages to the Ganges River, Hinduism's holiest site.

Before the arrival of Islam in South Asia, Hinduism was the dominant religion in the subcontinent. The result of a synthesis of beliefs that occurred after the Vedic period of Ancient India (c. 1500–500 BCE) and a response to Buddhism's commercial and urban influence, Hinduism developed a philosophy and belief system more widely accessible to the rural and agrarian peoples of India. An elaborate universe of Hindu deities was also established that included divinities from other religions, widening Hinduism's accessibility and appeal. Perhaps most importantly, Hinduism stressed personal devotion to a particular deity to obtain a truly individualized religious experience.

The Muslim Turks who arrived in India in the twelfth century recognized the Hindus as a protected people, allowing them to practice their own religious traditions and govern individual territories so long as they paid taxes and tribute. Buddhists, however, were not given the same measures of religious freedom, although it is not clear why. They were forced to flee or be executed, and many went to areas of Southeast Asia, Nepal, or Tibet, where Buddhism remains a major religion today. Over time, in the northern areas of the Indian subcontinent, which include modern Pakistan and Bangladesh, many Hindus converted to Islam, which then became the majority religion of the region. In the Vijanagar Empire in southern India, on the other hand, far fewer conversions took place, perhaps due to its distance from the centers of Islam.

In 1221, the province of Khurasan, which had invaded the Punjab in the tenth century, was itself invaded by the Mongols from China, led by Chinggis Khan (often referred to as "Genghis Khan" in the West). The Mongols then turned their attention to the Delhi Sultanate, which managed to successfully weather an attempted Mongol invasion in 1222. Over the next several decades, northern India experienced a series of invasions accompanying renewed Mongol expansion. Although most were repelled, countless Muslims were displaced and resettled on sultanate lands deeper in the subcontinent's interior.

A Multicultural South Asia

Throughout the decline of the independent principalities of northern India and, ultimately, the conquest of the Delhi Sultanate, the north slowly became increasingly Muslim, while the south retained Hindu cultural beliefs and ideas. By the thirteenth century, Buddhism had diminished as a popular form of worship in India and Hinduism had evolved from a religion in which only priests offered sacrifices to one in which a wider array of people could actively participate. With this change came increased personal devotion to the individual gods, including Vishnu and Shiva (Figure 12.5). Each village usually had a temple in which they were enshrined and worshipped, and various incarnations of the gods developed from these numerous local beliefs. For example, Krishna was an incarnation of Vishnu. Eventually, Vishnu and Shiva came to have consort wives, and their powers could not be activated except through union. Thus, many female deities also came to be worshipped. In contrast, Christianity, Islam, Buddhism, and Confucianism all feature male-centered systems.

FIGURE 12.5 The Hindu God Vishnu. This eighteenth-century painting on paper shows the poet Jayadeva (left) bowing to Vishnu, the beneficent preserver. Vishnu is one of three major Hindu gods; the others are Brahma (creator of the universe) and Shiva (giver and destroyer of life). (credit: "Jaydev worshipping lord Vishnu" by The Government Museum and Art Gallery, Chandigarh/Wikimedia Commons, Public Domain)

The Hindu religion evolved to become the dominant religion likely because it was a belief system with broader appeal than Buddhism. Originating in the period following the Vedic Age (c. 1500–500 BCE) and evolving over centuries, Hinduism developed from much older traditions, especially those of the Aryan peoples who arrived in India beginning in the third millennium BCE. One particularly distinctive facet of Hindu tradition that originated among these peoples was the Indian caste system. At its origin, the caste system was limited, and all of society was organized into four categories known as *varnas*. The four major *varnas* were Brahman (priests), Kshatriya (warriors), Vaishya (merchants and farmers), and Shudra (servile people). In these early days of the system, a person's *varna* was determined by their profession but also their **dharma**—their adherence to proper behaviors for their caste as stipulated by cosmic law, including avoiding contact with lower castes—and the karma they accrued by virtue of their dharma (Figure 12.6).

FIGURE 12.6 **Bodhisattvas.** In Buddhism, bodhisattvas are people who are seen as spiritually advanced and on the path toward Buddhahood. This detail of a twelfth-century manuscript painting depicts Maitreya, a bodhisattva who, according to Indian tradition, is the teacher of dharma. (credit: "Astasahasrika Prajnaparamita Maitreya Detail" by Unknown/Wikimedia Commons, Public Domain)

Karma worked both ways: A believer's failure to follow their dharma resulted in negative residue, whereas faithful obedience resulted in positive residue. At the personal level, the incentive behind amassing karma was samsara, the continuance of the soul after death and the soul's transformation. The more positive karma someone built up, the greater the chances of being reincarnated in a higher *varna* in the next life—with the ultimate goal being the attainment of **moksha**, or release from the karmic cycle and the achievement of a complete understanding of the world. If too much bad karma accumulated, on the other hand, the opposite occurred: reincarnation at a lower *varna*.

Yet the ramifications of the caste system went far beyond the personal. Nothing less than the continued existence of the universe was at stake. Adherence to dharma helped ensure the universe remained in balance, while failure to do so risked chaos and destruction. A rigidly hierarchical system of social segregation maintained this belief system. However, the *varna* communities created by the caste system also provided social support to their members and a vital stabilizing element in an Indian society otherwise rocked by political upheaval, foreign invasion, and war (Figure 12.7).

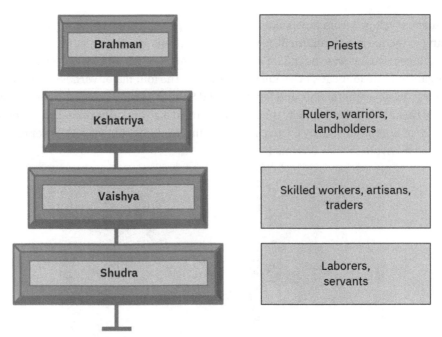

FIGURE 12.7 The Indian Caste System. The Indian caste system was a hierarchical one, with ranked *varnas* that, in the system's earliest days, related to a person's profession. Someone could move up or down within this hierarchy depending on their dharma and their accrual of karma during their lifetime. Still, such mobility came primarily through reincarnation at the end of a person's life. (attribution: Copyright Rice University, OpenStax, under CC BY 4.0 license)

The basic social unit of Indian society and the focus of life was the extended family, which included parents, grandparents, aunts, uncles, cousins, and in-laws. Most peasant families lived in villages and worked as farmers. Farming was more important than cattle raising for several reasons, not least the prohibition against eating cows. Hindus believe these animals to be sacred but also used them as draft animals on farms. Their manure helped fertilize crops, and their milk was a sustaining element of the Hindu diet. Key crops were rice, millet, wheat, barley, lentils, and peas. The extended family's large web of relationships encouraged everyone to work together for the betterment of the community. Villages were usually walled, with gates that were shut at night after the farmers returned from the fields.

Like Confucianism in China, Hinduism fostered a patriarchal family structure in which women were subservient. Men were viewed as stronger than women and less governed by their emotions, while older men, due to age and presumed experience, were thought to be wiser than younger men and thus superior to all others. Male domination of Hindu family life was reinforced by the fact that the oldest male was head of the household and might have several wives, who generally came to live with their husband's parents.

Although children often assisted the family in daily work such as farming, in wealthier homes the basics such as reading, writing, and arithmetic might be taught. Daughters were often married at a young age, and finding the ideal husband—who could provide for the family financially—was a key concern. A wife had no life apart from her husband, and if widowed, she might shave her head, sleep on the floor, eat only a single meal a day, and avoid attending family festivals. A wealthier widow, particularly from the Kshatriya or warrior caste, might throw herself on her husband's funeral pyre in an act of ritual suicide known as *sati*.

IN THEIR OWN WORDS

Crime and Punishment in Tenth-Century India

Abu Zayd al-Sirafi was a sailor from Sirafi, a center of the spice trade, who traveled throughout the Indian Ocean during the tenth century. The following is his account of how Indians used ordeal by fire to allow the gods to decide whether an accused person was guilty. As you read, note whether Abu Zayd felt this was an effective system and consider what biases may exist in his account.

> Moving now to India, if a man accuses another of an offense for which the mandatory penalty is death, the accuser is asked, "Will you subject the person you have accused to ordeal by fire?" If he agrees to this, a piece of iron is first heated to such a high temperature that it becomes red-hot. The accused man is told to hold out his hand, palm up, and on it are placed seven leaves from a particular tree of theirs; the red-hot iron is then placed on his hand, on top of the leaves. Next, the accused has to walk up and down holding the iron, until he can bear it no longer and has to drop it. At this point, a leather bag is brought out: the man has to put his hand inside this, then the bag is sealed with the ruler's seal. When three days have passed, some unhusked rice is brought, and the accused man is told to husk it by rubbing it between his palms. If after this no mark is found on his hand, he is deemed to have got the better of his accuser, and he escapes execution. Moreover, his accuser is fined a maund [about 82 pounds] of gold, which the ruler appropriates for himself. On some occasions, they heat water in an iron or copper cauldron until it boils so furiously that no one can go near it. An iron finger-ring is then dropped into the water, and the accused man is told to put his hand in and retrieve the ring. I have seen a man put his hand in and bring it out unharmed. In such a case, too, his accuser is fined a maund of gold.

—Abu Zayd al-Sirafi, *Accounts of China and India*

- What biases do you see in this account?
- Does Abu Zayd feel ordeal by fire is an effective system? Why or why not?
- Why do you think ordeal by fire was once a common method of identifying guilt around the globe?

Toward the end of the Gupta period, in the sixth century, rulers began giving land grants to officials and Brahman priests to help stimulate local economies. Often entire villages were included in the gifts, and their inhabitants came under the control of the grantees. Eventually, land grants were also awarded to temples and monasteries, in the hope that this could encourage wider economic growth and lessen dependence on the central state.

Although this was a politically chaotic period, new ideas and belief systems spread and many cultural and technological advances occurred. Improvements in shipbuilding and textile manufacturing stimulated coastal trade, for example, especially in Southeast Asia. Paradoxically, many such developments were the result of the same forces that destabilized India's politics, for the continual invasions and migrations of foreigners in the north cross-fertilized the region's cultural base, producing new ideas and practical innovations. The diffusion of ideas was enhanced by India's annual monsoon winds, which lengthened maritime traders' exposure to Indian society and culture by preventing those who arrived in summer from returning home until the winter monsoon season.

One of the most influential and enduring effects of trade was the spread of Buddhism, which began to take hold elsewhere as it competed with, and in some ways reshaped, Hinduism. Many Southeast Asian regions adopted it, from what is now Thailand up to the Mekong Delta in Vietnam and down to Java. By the first century BCE, there were two branches of Buddhism: Theravada ("the path of the elders," the oldest extant form of Buddhism) and Mahayana ("the greater vehicle"). Mahayana, the larger branch, spread along the great trade routes of Asia into the borderlands of the Parthian Empire, eventually reaching China, Korea, and Japan, where it was gradually infused with local ideas. Theravada Buddhism established itself in Sri Lanka, southern India, and parts of Southeast Asia. Unlike Hinduism, Buddhism did not emphasize the caste system and in many instances opposed it, thus strengthening its influence abroad. It therefore appealed to lower-caste individuals as well. Nonetheless, Hinduism influenced many monarchies, particularly through the concept of dharma. Sanskrit, the written language of India, also spread to many southeast Asian courts, cementing the broad influence of Indian culture.

Sui and Tang China

Following the collapse of the Han Empire in 220 CE, three states ruled over China: the Wei in the north, the Wu in the south, and the Shu in the west. A temporary reunification occurred under the Western Jin dynasty from 265 to 316, but from 316 to 589 China was again divided, this time into north and south. Along the Silk Roads, merchants established monasteries, convents, and shrines, bringing Buddhist traditions into China. Many Chinese traders therefore adopted Buddhism, particularly under the Sui dynasty (Figure 12.8).

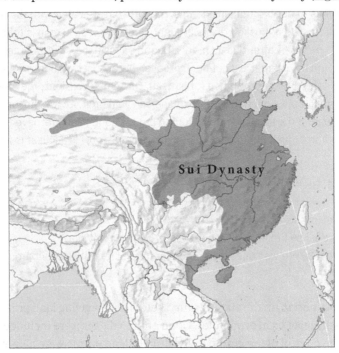

FIGURE 12.8 The Sui Dynasty. This map shows the extent of the Sui dynasty in 609. Like the Qin before them, the Sui pursued empire-building and vast public works projects such as the Grand Canal, which was vital to the movement of Sui armies during campaigns in the south. (attribution: Copyright Rice University, OpenStax, under CC BY 4.0 license)

🔗 LINK TO LEARNING

Read the Metropolitan Museum of Art's brief overview "Buddhism along the Silk Road" (https://openstax.org/l/77BuddhismSilk) to follow the trade routes of the Silk Roads in East Asia and to explore the images, iconography, and ideas of Buddhism as it traveled those routes.

A Mongol general from northern China, Yang Jian, was an affirmed Buddhist. His military abilities allowed him to gain such fame that he was able to create a marriage alliance between one of his daughters and a northern prince. With growing power, at the death of the ruler, he claimed the role of regent to his grandson before later deposing him. Yang then made himself the first emperor of the new Sui dynasty in 581 and adopted the name Wen. Emperor Wen gained his soldiers' allegiance by granting them lands acquired through conquest, a years-long process that reunified most of the old Han lands. To consolidate his control over the empire, Emperor Wen created a powerful centralized government, with loyal bureaucrats appointed to rule its many territories. To eliminate the risk that these powerful regional administrators could amass followers into a rebellious army, Wen periodically moved them to different territories, forcing them to build new networks from scratch.

Emperor Wen was succeeded by his son Yang Guang. Like his father before him, Emperor Yang Di, as Yang was known, was ambitious and grandiose. During his reign, he continued his father's practice of building large public works through forced labor, completing the Grand Canal in 609 to connect Luoyang in central China with Hangzhou in the south. The canal made the movement of foodstuffs and supplies between north and south possible on an unimaginable scale. From the south, with its warmer and wetter climate, came rice; from the drier and cooler north came crops such as wheat and millet (Figure 12.9). A crucial step in the economic integration of overland trade was taken when the canal was connected to the Sui capital and eastern terminus of the Silk Roads in Chang'an, finally extending all the way north to Beijing. Construction of this arm of the canal took seven years and required as many as five million workers, sometimes including entire populations conscripted to labor on the project. An early form of a police force supervised, enforcing corporal punishment on anyone refusing to work.

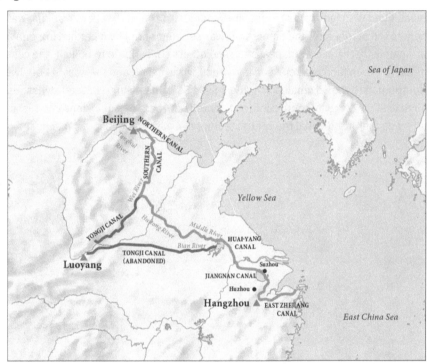

FIGURE 12.9 China's Grand Canal. This map of China's Grand Canal shows how it connects the country's north and south, just as rivers connect the east and west. The canal became critical to centralizing control of the Sui Empire. Its primary route is shown in orange, while the purple indicates shorter-lived expansions constructed to connect the southern Chinese provinces with this important economic thoroughfare. (attribution: Copyright Rice University, OpenStax, under CC BY 4.0 license)

The Grand Canal was essential to the economic and administrative integration of the newly reunified Chinese empire under the Sui. The canal made it easier for goods to be transported and provided increased revenue by allowing the government to tax the products being shipped. It also greatly improved communication and the effectiveness of the government, as officials were able to travel quickly between north and south and to send communication more easily across the Chinese interior. The canal was also a vital tool of Sui foreign policy, allowing Chinese armies from the north to travel to the borders of Korea, from which Yang Di launched his futile campaigns of conquest.

THE PAST MEETS THE PRESENT

The Grand Canal
The modern city of Hangzhou, situated at the head of a large bay extending out into the East China Sea, has a

population of almost twelve million and is known around the country and world for its robust economy. One of the keys to Hangzhou's success is the busy canal that extends northward from the city and is plied around the clock by numerous barges carrying bulk materials to distant locations in the interior. The origins of the canal date back over two thousand years to pre-imperial China, and its use today is a reminder of the enduring legacy of ancient Chinese engineering and determination.

Commonly referred to as the Grand Canal, this man-made waterway has portions that were built in the fifth century BCE. But it was during the Sui dynasty when these older canals were connected, refurbished, and extended to create a continuous water route stretching 1,100 miles from Hangzhou to Beijing. Built with conscripted workers, it was intended to supply southern-produced grain to the large cities in the north, facilitate the movement of troops, and to generally better integrate the northern and southern portions of the vast empire.

Completing the canal, fitted with lock gates to regulate water levels over different elevations, was an engineering feat and a testament to the boldness of the emperor. It was supplemented by a parallel imperial road dotted with post offices. Unfortunately for the enslaved, peasants, and others conscripted to build it, the costs were enormous. An estimated two million workers died constructing the canal; and the cost in both lives and taxes almost certainly contributed to the downfall of the short-lived Sui dynasty in 618. Later dynasties, however, found the canal quite useful. By the fifteenth century, hundreds of years of expansions and technological improvements had made the Grand Canal the central feature of a vast and indispensable inland transportation network (Figure 12.10).

FIGURE 12.10 Touring the Grand Canal. This image from a larger scroll shows the canal as it looked in the late eighteenth century. Created by court painter Xu Yang in 1770, the scroll commemorates the emperor's 1751 tour of south China. Here you can see the emperor's large touring boat moving through the city of Suzhou on a now defunct portion of the canal. (credit: "The Qianlong Emperor's Southern Inspection Tour, Scroll Six: Entering Suzhou along the Grand Canal" by Purchase, The Dillon Fund Gift, 1988/Metropolitan Museum of Art, Public Domain)

During the nineteenth century, the canal entered a period of decline as a result of a change in the course of the Yellow River and the rise of competing transportation routes made possible by railroads and steam-powered ships. Today, ships can no longer travel the full length of the canal. North of Jining, the canal is too shallow. Nonetheless, the canal remains an important transportation route, facilitating the flow of many millions of tons of raw materials through the interior. And improvement efforts have been underway for decades.

- What does the construction of the Grand Canal suggest about the ambitions of the Sui rulers, especially given the enormous costs involved in building the canal?
- In a modern world where so much freight is moved by air, rail, and highway, why do you think the Grand Canal continues to be a vital transportation route?

In the end, and despite the great benefits of the Grand Canal, its construction overextended the Sui. Enormously costly in labor and materiel, the waterway became a great source of grievance among the Chinese people, millions of whom were forced to work on it and neglect their families and farms. The situation was worsened by the combined effects of a natural disaster—the Yellow River flooded the North China plain and triggered famine throughout the countryside—and military defeat—the Sui invasion of Korea was repelled in 612. Undaunted, Yang Di pushed ahead with a second invasion campaign, stopping only when the exhausted military revolted. The emperor was assassinated in a period of turmoil in the region before Li Yuan, a provincial governor, acceded to the throne and announced the founding of the Tang dynasty in 618.

The Tang Empire, which lasted until 907, emerged just as Islam exploded out of Arabia and swept across North Africa and the Iberian Peninsula and into central Asia. Like the great Islamic empires that thrived during this period, the Tang promoted a cosmopolitan culture, a character greatly enhanced by wider international developments. In 674, for example, the advancing tide of Arab armies from the west forced members of the Sasanian royal family to flee to the safety of the Tang court at Chang'an, at the eastern terminus of the Silk Roads. This event inspired whole communities of merchants to move from Sasanian Persia to the Chinese capital, bringing all manner of exotic products and luxury goods, from silver artwork to Arab, Persian, and central Asian musical forms and dance.

It did not take long for the Tang elite to develop a taste for these items, creating an impressive industry of Persian-Arab-inspired goods and services to meet the growing demand. As a taste for Persian-Arab culture spread, trade relations between the Tang and India blossomed, bringing everything from mathematics to new sciences and medicines to China. These different cultural streams met in Tang China's major cities, which soon generated a diverse international culture greatly enhanced by the presence of merchant communities of Jewish people, Christians, Zoroastrians, peoples of the major Indian traditions, and a sizable minority of Muslims.

For much of its duration, Tang China was the most powerful empire in existence, and among its priorities was completing the consolidation and expansion begun under the Sui. To this end, the Tang embarked on a series of military campaigns into central Asia. Their large professional army was organized around a core of aristocratic cavalry of some seven million troops who routinely clashed with the mounted nomads of the Inner Asian Steppe, and an immense peasant infantry several million strong and garrisoned in the interior. By the 750s, Tang frontier units increasingly relied on pastoral nomadic peoples from the steppes, such as the Uyghurs, Turkish-speaking peoples who constituted the empire's most potent military force. Over time, Tang forces pushed into Manchuria (the area immediately north of the Korean Peninsula), Vietnam, and Tibet. At its height in the late ninth century, the Tang army controlled more than four million square miles of territory, an area roughly the size of the entire Islamic world during the same period.

The Tang achieved several early foreign policy successes, including reestablishing Chinese rule over Korea in 668, resulting in a tributary relationship with the peninsula's Silla dynasty. The Tang also opened diplomatic relations with Japan, which proved so effective that in 645 Japan embarked on its "Great Reform"—an all-encompassing adoption of Tang culture, including its imperial institutions (which the Silla also adopted), Confucian bureaucracy, and Buddhism.

The spread of Tang culture was greatly enhanced by several major innovations in China, including the world's first block-printing process, which proved opportune for printing Buddhist scriptures (Figure 12.11). Like the Sui, the Tang embraced and promoted Buddhism, the scriptures of which were usually hand-copied by scribes and disseminated among students. The scarcity of these works meant that most commoners and even many elites had no access to them. China's artisans, however, devised a way to carve the mirror-image of a text into a block of wood, add ink, and then press the block onto paper. Scriptures and other forms of writing now became more accessible, spreading ideas from the elites to the masses. Block-printing remained the major method of transferring images onto paper until the end of the nineteenth century.

FIGURE 12.11 The First Block-Printed Book. This is a page from the *Diamond Sutra*, the world's first block-printed book, made in China in 868. Note the image of the Buddha in the center, and consider how the production of multiple copies of documents such as this could lead to wider knowledge of Buddhism. (credit: modification of work "Jingangjing" by British Library/Wikimedia Commons, Public Domain)

Buddhism was important not only under the Sui. The Tang period witnessed the rapid growth of two forms of Mahayana Buddhism in particular: Pure Land, which had originated much earlier in India and had found adherents in China since the fifth century, and Chan, which developed during the fifth and sixth centuries but became popular under the Tang. **Pure Land Buddhism** was a school of popular devotion to Amida (or Amitabha), the Buddha of the "pure land" or the uncorrupt plane of existence believers anticipated reaching on their rebirth. Like the Hindu *bhakti* sects in India, Pure Land Buddhists held that to achieve salvation it was necessary not to study sacred texts but rather to engage in practices accessible to everyone, especially by invoking Amida's name.

Chan Buddhism, like Pure Land, deemphasized scriptural study but rejected the notion of personal devotion to a savior. Instead, Chan Buddhism, known more popularly by its Japanese name Zen, stressed the disciplined practice of meditation and following the example of a Chan master, who underwent great hardships performing humble tasks and wrestling with paradoxical questions, to achieve enlightenment. Chan Buddhism was austere and monastic in character, whereas Pure Land was the more popular form observed by lay people.

Buddhism's popularity became a flashpoint for violence in Tang China, however. In the mid-ninth century, the Tang Empire cracked down on what it perceived as the threat that hundreds of thousands of Buddhist monks and nuns posed to its Confucian and Daoist leaders, who argued that Buddhism represented an alien influence on the state. Although this prompted the active suppression of Buddhist monasteries and the confiscation of their wealth, it was not enough. Blatant persecution unfolded under Emperor Wuzong, resulting in the destruction of some forty thousand temples and shrines, the closure of more than four thousand monasteries, and the forced secularization of hundreds of thousands of Buddhist monks and nuns. Culturally, the state moved to expunge the impact of Buddhism by reviving classical prose styles and the teachings of Confucius and his followers (Figure 12.12).

FIGURE 12.12 Emperor Wuzong. Emperor Wuzong, represented in an ink drawing from a Chinese encyclopedia of the early seventeenth century, engaged in widespread persecution of Buddhist monks and nuns in ninth-century (attribution: Copyright Rice University, OpenStax, under CC BY 4.0 license) China. (credit: modification of work "Emperor Wuzong of the Tang dynasty" by Baidu/Wikimedia Commons, Public Domain)

The Tang period also produced a great deal of poetry, much of it influenced by the prevalent religious and philosophical traditions. For example, in the eighth century the poets Wang Wei, Li Bai (Li Bo), and Du Fu were influenced by Buddhism, Daoism, and Confucianism, respectively, and many people could recite their poems from memory. Along the Silk Roads during this period, poetry spread along with China's religious and philosophical traditions, first to Korea and from there to Japan. Neither area had a written script of its own yet, so admirers learned the poets' works in Chinese.

Entrance into the Tang bureaucracy was based on passage of a merit-based exam administered every three years. This civil service exam, the first fully written such exam in history, had been developed from the Sui dynasty and tested sophisticated literary skills and knowledge of Confucian and Daoist classics. In theory it was open to all; in practice, however, until the late Tang period, women, the sons of merchants, and those who could not afford a classical education were excluded. Most laborers were also excluded because of their circumstances, as they could not take time away from their fields to study. In the end, people became government officials thanks to their literary achievements or the influence of their prestigious families.

Tang China also witnessed contradictory trends in personal behavior and relations between the sexes. In 665, Emperor Gaozong, infirm and sickly, handed power to his second wife, Wu Zetian. Following Gaozong's death in 683, Wu ruled as empress dowager and regent for her son, though she held all the real power of the state. A devout Buddhist, she declared Buddhism the state religion, ordered scholars to write biographies of famous women, and in 690 took the extraordinary step of founding her own dynasty, the Wu Zhou (not to be confused with the much earlier Zhou dynasty). Three years later, Wu assumed the Buddhist title "Divine Empress Who Rules the Universe." Although she was an intelligent and competent ruler, the founding of her own dynasty and the adoption of imperial titles felt to many like usurpation. Resistance soon followed, prompting her abdication and the restoration of the Tang dynasty.

Wu's reign was remarkable in China's male-dominated society. Still, the Tang Empire has been described as a "golden age" for women in China, perhaps because lingering contact with the nomadic peoples of the north and their relatively egalitarian society encouraged a somewhat similar view among the Chinese. As evidence of the increased prominence of women, historians also point to a flourishing culture of poetry written by courtesans, the careers of Empress Wu and her daughter-in-law Empress Wei, and the practice of using diplomatic marriages of Tang daughters to prominent foreign officials to forge political alliances. However, sumptuary laws dictated what women could and could not wear, elite men kept concubines, and the Tang legal system considered women property.

The Tang Empire reached its zenith in the early eighth century (Figure 12.13). By mid-century, however, internal and external challenges had set in motion the empire's terminal decline. Externally, the Tang were defeated at the Battle of Talas River in 751. There, Tang forces were beaten by the combined Turkic and Arab armies of the Abbasid Caliphate, which was expanding the frontiers of the Islamic empire deep into central Asia after overthrowing the Umayyads. Internally, China faced revolts in Korea, Yunnan (in extreme southern China), and Manchuria, which distracted and weakened the state.

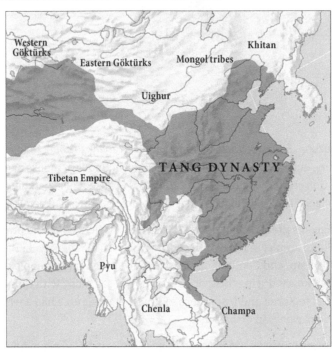

FIGURE 12.13 The Tang Dynasty. This map shows the extent of China's Tang dynasty at its height in the eighth century. (attribution: Copyright Rice University, OpenStax, under CC BY 4.0 license)

Then, in 755, the Tang Empire was rocked by the massive An Lushan rebellion. Some 150,000 frontier troops led by the Tang commander An Lushan revolted against Emperor Xuanzong and the decadent court at Chang'an. It took eight years for the Tang to crush the rebellion, by the end of which China was both militarily and economically exhausted. The empire carried on in an enfeebled state, but over the ensuing decades, Chang'an ceded much military and civil authority to provincial warlords. In 906, following additional civil wars, the Tang dynasty collapsed, leading to a period of disunity until the Song rose to dominance in 960.

12.2 East-West Interactions in the Early Middle Ages

LEARNING OBJECTIVES

By the end of this section, you will be able to:
- Discuss the trade in goods, technology, and ideas that occurred along the Silk Roads
- Describe how Islam spread in South and Southeast Asia
- Discuss the role of East Africa in Indian Ocean trade

The Silk Roads made up one of the greatest trade routes in world history, linking east and west in a vast interlocking network that reached its heyday between the fifth and eighth centuries. It had begun to form a few hundred years before, when the Chinese Han dynasty sought to placate and control the great Xiongnu nomadic peoples to the north by trading with them, and with other nomadic peoples such as the Yuezhi in Bactria (modern-day Afghanistan). The Silk Roads eventually connected China, central Asia, South Asia, the Middle East, and even the Mediterranean basin, facilitating the exchange of goods such as silk and spices, technologies such as papermaking, and cultural traditions and religions such as Buddhism and Islam.

These road networks were critical to the spread of Islam, as seen in the wake of Muslim raiders entering the Sindh area of northwest India in the early eighth century. Maritime networks centered on the Indian Ocean also played a large role in this expansion. From India and through both the Persian Gulf and the Red Sea, Muslim sailors began to dominate much of the Malabar Coast of western India and the Swahili coast of eastern Africa, becoming fixtures in the lucrative Indian Ocean trade all the way to China and beyond. The influence of Muslim traders throughout the region went far beyond commercial exchange, however. One of the most significant results of this trade-based diffusion of Islamic culture in South and East Asia was the emergence of powerful states such as Indonesia, which has the world's largest Muslim population today.

Travel and Exchange along the Silk Roads

By the first century BCE, China had become firmly established as the eastern end of the Silk Roads, with Rome as the western end. The Romans also traveled by sea to secure the goods that came through the ports of western India, the Red Sea, and the Persian Gulf, as well as trading through key centers in Syria such as the great caravan cities of Petra and Palmyra, the Nabatean city famed as the main entry point for Chinese silk and eastern incense. In exchange for such goods, the Roman provinces of North Africa traded Roman glassware, wool, gold, and silver through intermediaries in the Middle East and central Asia and even into India (Figure 12.14).

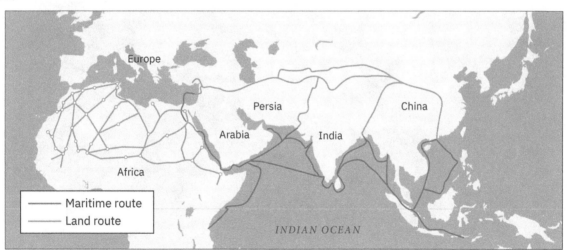

FIGURE 12.14 The Silk Roads in the First Century CE. The Silk Roads network was not a single route but many, including caravan routes that linked to the main trading regions, oasis towns, and overseas routes—the so-called Maritime Silk Roads—throughout the Indian Ocean. (credit: modification of work "World map blank shorelines" by Maciej Jaros/Wikimedia Commons, Public Domain)

Before they reached the Romans, trade goods from the east were largely in the hands of the Kushan Empire. The Yuezhi confederacy in Bactria had unified to form this empire, trading with both China and the Indian subcontinent and providing a conduit between the two, particularly from the city of Taxila. The Kushan Empire managed to stabilize the trading routes connecting the Parthian western leg of the road with that of the central Asian steppes, spreading its control halfway down the Indian subcontinent in the process and ideally positioning itself to handle trade between India, China, and the Mediterranean.

By the third century CE, many empires using the Silk Roads had begun to decline, including the Romans, the Kushans, the Parthians, and the Han. The Kushans and Parthians were replaced by the Sasanids in Persia, who also annexed the northern portion of the Kushan Empire. The Gupta soon controlled the southern portion of India. The Mediterranean world was changing too; the Silk Roads' new trade destination was the surviving Eastern Roman Empire, known as the Byzantine Empire from the late fifth century onward, following the fall of Roman dominance in western Europe. These new players continued and extended the trade network.

Long-distance trade during the early and later Middle Ages was fraught. The Silk Roads were not a four-thousand-mile-long superhighway outfitted to bridge eastern and western markets from Rome to China but rather a series of interconnected roads, many ill maintained, that were built up over time and eventually linked dozens of oasis towns and market cities such as Palmyra in the west and Bactria in the east. It is most useful to imagine it as a network of "legs" on a journey, along which merchants and traders traveled via caravan with their wares, pausing to rest at caravansaries along the way. Goods changed hands many times over these long distances, being exchanged between merchants who each traveled only part of the "road," and their price increased the farther they went from their origin.

Buddhism arrived in China sometime during the period known as the Six Dynasties (220–589 CE). Monks traveling the Silk Roads between northern India and Afghanistan brought its universalizing message of a lifestyle open to all and offering salvation to any willing to listen, and they found a receptive audience among countless merchants traveling between China and central Asia. Over time, Buddhist monks established themselves in small communities and set up monasteries at a string of oases the length of the Taklamakan Desert—a chain that ran all the way to the Great Wall in northern China. At one of these, Yungang, weary travelers were greeted by five huge Buddhas carved from the cliffs and surrounded by tens of thousands of statues representing Buddhist deities and patrons (Figure 12.15). This great religious complex offered not only an opportunity to rest and recover but also an entry point to the Chinese market.

FIGURE 12.15 Buddha Statues at Yungang. These huge statues of Buddha were carved along the Silk Roads by the Northern Wei dynasty in China around the fourth century. They clearly demonstrate the importance of trade routes in the spread of culture and ideas. (credit: "Yungang Grottoes 2008" by Mirinda K./Wikimedia Commons, Public Domain)

Many legs of the Silk Roads were perilous in the extreme. For example, upon departing Chang'an, the Tang capital and eastern terminus of the network, travelers almost immediately confronted the Gobi, the largest desert in Asia. Its terrain is compacted and rocky and thus ideal for long-distance travel by camel, but the lack of water necessitated the establishment of caravansaries, usually about a day apart along the road connecting China to the central Asian interior. To geographic and environmental hazards, travelers could add warring tribes and roving bandits and thieves. A menace since the beginning of the Silk Roads, robbers targeted the convoys of precious cargoes as they headed across open and unprotected terrain. While small armies and groups of archers accompanied some larger and better-funded caravans, and caravans sometimes merged into "super-caravans" for safety, these were the exceptions, not the rule. Most travelers undertook a caravan journey at great risk to themselves and the goods they carried.

Despite its dangers, however, the overland route was more appealing for many than the alternative, a hazardous and costly voyage across the sea. Pirates lurking in coastal waters harassed ships on the Maritime Silk Roads, and shifting weather and poorly charted waters posed enormous challenges to even the sturdiest vessels and hardiest merchants. The loss of a ship to a sudden storm or shallow reef (as happened repeatedly at the Gelasa Strait in Indonesia) could mean not only the deaths of crew and passengers but also the ruin of the merchants whose goods were sunk. To most merchants and traders, the risks posed by seaborne trade, not to mention the cost of hiring a ship and its crew, made it the less appealing of the two Silk Road routes open to them. As land empires such as the Sasanian Persians' realm in central Asia grew more stable, the overland route became even more attractive.

⊘ LINK TO LEARNING

Read the short article "Unearthing the Islamic Relics of China's Medieval Port City" (https://openstax.org/l/77ChinaPort) for more information about the importance of trade to the spread of religious ideas.

The Sasanian Persians were able to provide a great deal of security, allowing for more peaceful and effective trading. Much of their power in fact relied on and was derived from this trade. The Sasanian Empire was soon displaced by the Islamic Umayyad Caliphate, however, which came to control trade and produce textiles and other goods of its own to sell along the route, although demand for Chinese silks continued. In 750, the Umayyads in turn were overthrown by the Abbasids (749–1258), a new Islamic dynasty that sought to expand eastward from the Middle East even as the Tang dynasty drove westward from China. The Abbasids moved their capital to Baghdad, along the Tigris River in what is modern-day Iraq. This change streamlined their dominance of the Silk Roads, letting them use the Persian Gulf to effectively bypass the Red Sea, which was the seaborne trade route closest to the former Umayyad capital in Syria.

Despite their ambitions, the Abbasids' eastward expansion was halted in 751 when a combined Arab-Tibetan army met Tang forces in the Battle of Talas River near the town of Atlakh (Figure 12.16). Initially a stalemate, the battle turned in favor of the Abbasids when Turkic forces that were allied with the Tang switched allegiances and joined the Abbasids. Although the Abbasids were victorious, the engagement marked the end of expansion for both empires.

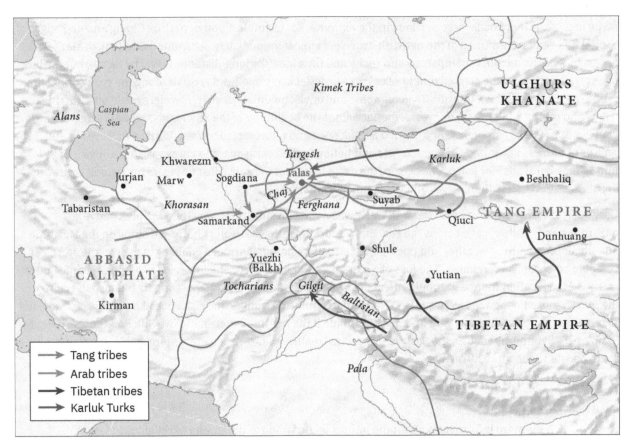

FIGURE 12.16 The Battle of Talas River. Note the centrally located site of the 751 Battle of Talas River, between the Abbasids in the west and the Tang in the east. (attribution: Copyright Rice University, OpenStax, under CC BY 4.0 license)

Throughout the rise and fall of these empires and others, control of trade routes, particularly the Silk Roads, was paramount. For example, people from the central Asian steppes exchanged hides, wool, and livestock for Chinese manufactured goods such as lacquerware, silk, floss, paper, porcelain, and iron tools. These goods and commodities were then traded for similar items along the way, eventually reaching buyers as far away as the Sanhaja tribes of West Africa and the Egyptians and Ethiopians in East Africa. The Silk Roads were never as vital to the Chinese economy, however, as they were to the others. The domestic Chinese economy was large enough to meet all the needs of the state and its people without imports, frustrating European powers intent on breaking into the Chinese economy well into the modern period. At the same time, there was great desire for Chinese goods by western peoples, meaning that the balance of power in trade was almost always skewed in favor of East Asia.

The silk that gave the Silk Roads their name may have originally come from China, but it was not long before many other states began raising silkworms and processing the silk thread from their cocoons into luxurious cloth. The Byzantines, legend has it, acquired silkworms clandestinely in the sixth century when Christian monks visiting China spirited some cocoons away in hollowed-out walking sticks. Much of the labor of producing silk fell to women, who grew the mulberry trees needed to feed the silkworms, unraveled the cocoons, and wove the threads into textiles. They were vital to the trade that led to Chinese dominance of the luxury goods market that the Silk Roads were so famous for. The men were responsible for the upkeep of the tree farms and the sale and exchange of the finished products. Many rural and even urban areas survived by producing silk cloth in this way, like the cottage industries that thrived later in Europe.

The Art of Papermaking

Before the invention of paper, the key writing material in China was bamboo strips, which were very bulky and took up a great deal of room (Figure 12.17). For centuries, however, the Chinese had been perfecting the art of papermaking. During the second century CE, craftspeople took the bark from the mulberry tree (whose leaves were fed to silkworms) and pounded the fibers into a pulp. By spreading the mixture as sheets to dry, they created paper. Later they discovered they could add hemp rags or fishing nets or any number of similar items to the pulp to strengthen the paper, which was then sometimes called parchment. Unlike bamboo, paper and parchment could be rolled up and were much easier to carry.

FIGURE 12.17 Bamboo Strips as Writing Material. This set of bamboo strips dating from the Warring States Period (fifth to third centuries BCE) illustrates how writing was achieved in China before the invention of paper. (credit: "Strip no. 22 of Kǒngzǐ Shīlùn" by Shanghai Museum/Wikimedia Commons, Public Domain)

Before the Battle of Talas River in 751, some of this paper had already made its way to Mecca in Arabia. Some Chinese prisoners of war from the battle were said to be papermakers who were taken to Samarkand and Khurasan, where they began to build paper mills. Evidence suggests this may be merely a legend, however, and that papermills were probably already in existence in Samarkand by this time. Nonetheless, the first paper mill in the Abbasid Caliphate was built in 794–795, and Spain began producing paper as early as the tenth century.

- What does the story of Chinese papermaking suggest about the ways in which ideas and technologies can be diffused to other cultures?
- How was this diffusion of ideas and technologies connected to, but not a product of, trade via the Silk Roads?

🔗 LINK TO LEARNING

Watch this video to view a specialized technique of papermaking (https://openstax.org/l/77Papermaking) that differs from the one discussed in the preceding "Beyond the Book" feature.

Religion and Trade in South and Southeast Asia

The growth of Islam gave Muslims a considerable role in world trade, particularly along the Silk Roads and in the Indian Ocean. By the middle of the eighth century, Islam had moved into northern India, and when the Abbasids overthrew the Umayyad dynasty and then moved their capital from Damascus to Baghdad, they established what became one the most important cities along the Silk Roads and a location that allowed them to dominate the growing Indian Ocean trade.

This new capital was situated along the Tigris River, a vital trade conduit to the Persian Gulf and to the Indian Ocean beyond. In the ninth century, the city of Siraf on the Persian Gulf coast was regularly sending ships to China and back and became one of the most important trading ports of this period. However, Siraf's hold on trade weakened when an earthquake struck and damaged it in 997. Other regions stepped in, including Hormuz, Omar, and particularly Qeys, an island city in the Persian Gulf. Arab expansion into the Indian Ocean trade initially filtered through these ports, but it eventually expanded along the African coast as well (Figure 12.18).

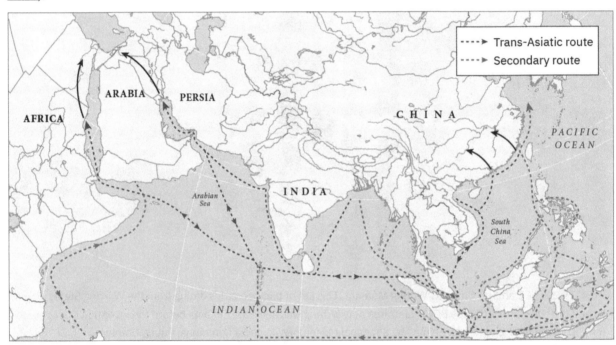

FIGURE 12.18 Indian Ocean Trade Routes. In the tenth century, Indian Ocean trade spread from the Red Sea and Persian Gulf down to Africa and around India to China. (attribution: Copyright Rice University, OpenStax, under CC BY 4.0 license)

The Muslim presence in northwest India was also an important link in the chain of Indian Ocean trade. Muslim raiders invaded India in the eighth century and came through Khurasan and Ghazni in the late tenth and eleventh centuries and many of the local inhabitants converted to Islam. In Gujarat, just south of the Sindh region, the Hindu Chalukya dynasty still controlled much of the Indian Ocean trade through their key city of Khambhat. However, by the end of the twelfth century, their power was waning. When the Turkic peoples from present-day Afghanistan began to rule the area of Delhi independently as the Delhi Sultanate in 1206, this region slowly came under their influence.

Generations of incursions from Persian dynasties into South Asia meant that Persian influence deeply affected the region. That Persian influence can still be seen today in the language of Urdu in modern-day Pakistan, which combines Hindu and Farsi elements. One portion of the Delhi Sultanate was Gujarat, which the sultan Ala al-Din annexed in 1304 after years of ransacking Gujarati cities. When the central Asian warlord Timur (also called Tamerlane in the West) sacked and captured Delhi at the end of the century, Gujarat split off from the weakened state to become an independent Muslim sultanate under the Tughluq dynasty. The Tughluqs set about subduing the region's Hindu Rajput chieftains and building a navy at Diu, strategically located along important trade routes between the Arabian Sea and Indian Ocean. Thus, much of the Indian Ocean trade in northwest India fell into the hands of this Islamic state.

From the decline of the Guptas to the rise of powerful northern Muslim sultanates such as Gujarat, peninsular India was home to the Hindu Chola kingdom, a maritime trade empire. With its vassal states including parts of the modern-day Maldives and Sri Lanka in the south, Chola dominated trade in the nearby portion of the Indian Ocean from about 970 to 1300. Crucially important to its dominance was control of the Palk Strait between Sri Lanka and southern India. The strait acted as a choke point where vessels had to stop to pay taxes, usually a portion of their cargo. Many of these vessels were known as *dhows* and carried twelve to twenty-four sailors (Figure 12.19).

FIGURE 12.19 An Arab *Dhow*. This is an image of a ship called a *dhow*, with lashed and stitched hull construction and a lateen (triangular) rigged sail, such as Arab merchants used en route to India. (credit: "Arab Dhow" by The New Gresham Encyclopedia, Vol IV, Part 1/Project Gutenberg, Public Domain)

Secondary trading also occurred, in which authorized middle merchants conducted exchanges between these larger ships and smaller port cities, a system known as **cabotage**. In the eleventh century, the Chola were trying to extend and consolidate their control over regional trade. To this end, Rajendra I, the "Victor of the Ganges" (1019–1021), sailed up east India's Coromandel coast and seized ports with the goal of deepening commercial ties with China, where trade in items such as ivory and glassware were common.

The Chola enjoyed an artistic, architectural, and literary flowering during the tenth and eleventh centuries. This "Imperial Golden Age" saw an explosion in the construction of monumental temples, like the one at Thanjavur on the southeastern coast, in the so-called Chola style—identifiable by such elements as high surrounding walls and stepped, pyramidal towers (Figure 12.20). Many of these sites housed intricately ornamented bronze statues of deities commissioned by the rulers, signifying their prominence, wealth, and devoutness. The golden age of the Chola is also known as the greatest epoch in South Indian literary tradition. One notable work of this tradition is the *Ramavataram*, a twelfth century Tamil epic written by the poet Kambar that was based on the *Ramayana*, the Sanskrit epic that told of the exploits of Prince Rama. All of this is a clear reminder that throughout world history, art and architecture tend to flourish when there is economic and political stability to support and sustain those efforts.

FIGURE 12.20 Chola Architecture of the Golden Age. This Hindu temple dating from the Chola dynasty's golden age represents the distinctive stepped-pyramidal shape that was a common feature of Chola architecture. (credit: "A Surya temple from Eastern Chalukyas of Vengi era" by G.N. Subrahmanyam/Wikimedia Commons, CC0 1.0)

Their golden age would not have been possible had the Chola not controlled trade through the Palk Strait, which generated enormous revenues. The monopolization of choke points was essential to anyone wishing to profit from maritime trade, as the founders of the Srivijaya Empire discovered with their command of the Malacca Strait. Traders sailing from the eastern Indian Ocean to Southeast Asia had to travel through this strait, between today's Sumatra in the Indonesian archipelago and Malaysia (Figure 12.21). From around 650, Srivijaya profited by managing and taxing the lucrative trade that passed through the strait.

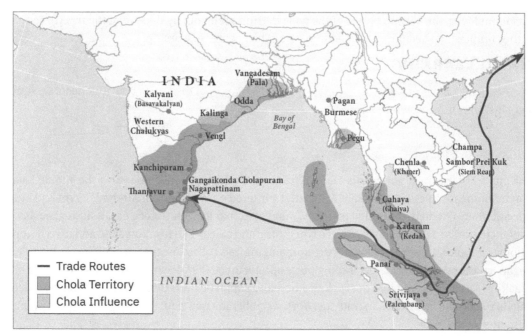

FIGURE 12.21 Srivijaya Trade Routes. This map shows the maritime trade route of the Srivijaya Empire, which went through the Strait of Malacca, the narrow stretch of water between the Malay Peninsula and the island of Sumatra. For a time, Srivijaya, with its capital at Palembang, controlled most of Southeast Asia's waterborne trade. (attribution: Copyright Rice University, OpenStax, under CC BY 4.0 license)

During its early history, Srivijaya was highly influenced by both Buddhist and Hindu traders coming from India. For example, in the Srivijaya capital of Palembang in southern Sumatra stands a magnificent Buddha statue dating from the seventh or eighth century. Sculpted in the highly ornate and detailed Amaravati style still popular in contemporary India and named after the southeastern region where it originally developed, this work attests to the role of trade in spreading art, culture, and ideology. Hindu shrines and temples that still stand also show the depth to which Hinduism penetrated Srivijayan culture and society during this formative period.

By the tenth century, Srivijaya controlled all trade between the Indian Ocean and China. Alarmed by the exorbitant taxes on trade and the threat of piracy the Srivijaya posed, however, the Cholas sent a maritime expedition against them in 1025, crushing their major ports including Palembang and reducing Srivijaya's power and influence for a time. Although Srivijaya managed to recover somewhat, its grip on maritime trade soon weakened permanently. By the thirteenth century, it had largely been displaced by the port of Malacca, which came to dominate a region that included modern-day Singapore.

The thirteenth century marks a time of considerable Islamic expansion into Southeast Asia; the Acehnese peoples on the northern tip of Sumatra were the first to embrace the religion. Many merchants in particular converted to Islam, which ensured the safe movement of their goods and protections against loss, especially in the states on the northeast coast of Sumatra such as Perlak and Aru, followed by Pasai in the north, and Malacca, the new maritime center. A further stream of Islamization came with Sufi missionaries. Sufism, a branch of Sunni Islam, blended Islam with local religious traditions, encouraging non-merchants to convert. Over time, Islam came to dominate much of the Malay Peninsula as well as Sumatra and, particularly in the fifteenth century, northern Java.

Hinduism, like Islam, grew in Southeast Asia during the later Middle Ages. In the twelfth century, for example, construction began on the great temple complex of Angkor Wat in Cambodia. Dedicated to Vishnu, Angkor Wat was meant to serve as the state temple, funerary complex, and capital city of the reigning monarch Suryavarman II. Hindu motifs decorated the exterior of the structure in bas relief form, featuring images of the gods and scenes from the epic Indian poem *Mahabharata*, while the temple's five towers were meant to represent Mount Meru, the dwelling place of the gods in Hindu religion. By the end of the twelfth century, however, the complex had been transformed into a Buddhist center of worship.

🔗 LINK TO LEARNING

This illustrated magazine article (https://openstax.org/l/77Indonesia) discusses how Indonesia became one of the largest Muslim countries in the world.

East Africa and the Indian Ocean Trade

East Africa played a large role in the Indian Ocean trade network that connected it with the Middle East, China, and East and Southeast Asia. Trade in East Africa first centered on the Red Sea. After all, Egypt had been a Hellenistic and then a Roman-controlled territory, making exchange with Greece and Rome especially important and lucrative. Luxury goods such as ivory, furs, and spices like frankincense and myrrh were traded with the Roman Empire. However, following the Roman Empire's collapse, other groups from areas such as Arabia began to take over this trade. As trading ports sprang up farther down the east coast of Africa and as Bantu-speaking Africans moved into the region, a new and sophisticated culture arose on the Swahili coast, expanding its role in the Indian Ocean trade network, establishing powerful city-states, and connecting with the African interior via trade.

Aksum and Ethiopia in the Middle Ages

During the period of the Roman Empire, trade between Rome and China crossed central Asia on the Silk Roads. However, there was also a demand for goods from the Indian Ocean, Arabia, and Africa. The route for this trade centered on the Red Sea for a time and was controlled by the Kingdom of Aksum (Figure 12.22).

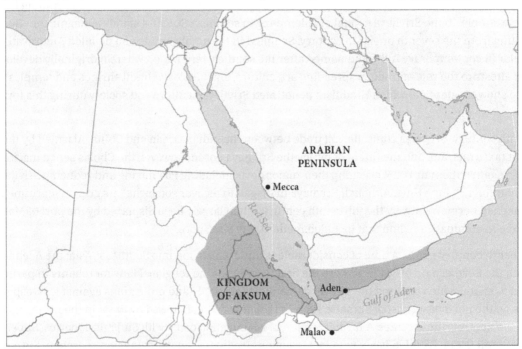

FIGURE 12.22 The Kingdom of Aksum. This map shows the Kingdom of Aksum at its greatest extent in the early sixth century CE. Though it appears to separate Africa and Arabia, the Red Sea was in fact a conduit of regular cultural exchange and movement of goods and people throughout the premodern period. For most of Aksum's existence, however, the kingdom did not control the fertile lands of southern Arabia, which today form part of Yemen. (credit: modification of work "Map of the Sassanid Empire just before the Arab conquest of Iran" by "DieBuche"/Wikimedia Commons, Public Domain)

The Red Sea connects the Gulf of Suez and the Sinai Peninsula with the Indian Ocean. In the third century CE, traders from Saba, the Yemeni area of the Arabian Peninsula, crossed the Red Sea to the coast of Eritrea. They began focusing much of their trade in the city of Adulis, which became the most important port of the Kingdom of Aksum. The city of Aksum, the capital of the kingdom, was eight days' journey south from Adulis, over a mountain range to the Ethiopian plateau.

The Kingdom of Aksum owed its power to this Red Sea trade, particularly in the fourth century CE. Traded goods included gold, silver, iron tools, cotton cloth, tortoise shells, and, above all, ivory and spices such as frankincense and myrrh. The fourth-century king Ezna expanded the kingdom to its farthest extent through conquering peoples south of Egypt and north of Ethiopia. In 350, toward the end of his reign, Ezna was converted to Christianity by the Syrian missionary Frumentius. Frumentius was later appointed bishop of Aksum by the patriarch in Alexandria, which meant the kingdom followed an Egyptian Coptic form of Christianity that held that Jesus had only a divine and not a mortal body.

During the reign of Ezna, caravans traveled from the interior to take part in the trade at Adulis, creating a constant stream into and out of the port city. The Kingdom of Aksum became increasingly wealthy and powerful. However, in the sixth and seventh centuries, all began to change. In 528, the Aksumites expanded their control as far as Yemen and were said to have reached the gates of Mecca in 571. However, they had evidently overextended themselves. With the help of the Sasanids from Persia, the king in the region of Yemen, Sayf ibn Dhi Yazan, rose up and pushed the Aksumites out of the peninsula.

In the seventh century, the Sasanids were in turn conquered by the Arab Muslim population, particularly the Umayyads. Arabs quickly expanded their control over the peninsula and into North Africa, especially Egypt, and thus access to the Red Sea naturally came into their hands. Particularly as Islam expanded to the Sindh region of northern India, the Persian Gulf became increasingly important for oceangoing vessels, which began bypassing the Aksumite port of Adulis.

Simultaneously, internal problems, some of them environmental, racked the Aksumite Kingdom. For centuries, if not longer, trees had been chopped down and agricultural fields planted, and the land was becoming increasingly barren due to soil erosion. Given this threat to the food supply and the decline in Red Sea trade, which is evidenced in the archaeological record by the reduced number of Aksumite coins used in this period, groups in the interior such as the Beja peoples began to rebel. The Aksumite Kingdom quickly collapsed into a smaller entity centered on the capital city of Aksum. Slowly the Kingdom of Ethiopia incorporated this area, and Aksum became an agricultural community ruled by a landed aristocracy.

Culturally, Ethiopia combined traditional pre-Islamic Jewish traditions with polytheistic ones and, as of the fourth century CE, with Christianity. Owing to its important location and support of long-distance trade, East Africa would prove to be a thriving cultural hub with proud heritage and history that linked them to the many peoples who traveled to and through the region. The legendary Christian kingdom led by Prester John was said to be hidden there, for example. And, until the 1970s, tradition held that Ethiopia's rulers were descendants of both the Queen of Sheba and King Solomon of Jerusalem and had even brought the treasured Ark of the Covenant to Aksum. Thus, while the economic power of the region may have declined, its cultural significance continued well into the modern era.

The Swahili Coast and Indian Ocean Trade

Following the decline of the Kingdom of Aksum, the Indian Ocean trade shifted in part to the East African states. Factors that helped elevate the role of maritime trade in this region included improved shipbuilding, the rise of the Umayyad and Abbasid caliphates, the decline of the Tang dynasty—which disrupted overland trade—and even environmental changes such as desertification that made some areas of Africa uninhabitable.

While the Kingdom of Aksum was in decline, the internal migration of Bantu peoples was making its way from Africa's northwest to its east and southeast. The Bantu brought their language, their cultural traditions, and especially the technology of ironmongering. Many began settling in coastal communities in East Africa, where they displaced or mixed with the Khoisan and other indigenous African peoples, particularly on the coasts of modern Tanzania and Kenya. They also traveled south, establishing many fishing and trading villages. These exported ivory, hides, quartz, and gems in return for cotton, glass, jewelry, and other items the Bantu people were unable to make themselves. Port towns such as Shang and Manda began growing into major port centers. Soon Arab merchants began living among the Bantu peoples to participate in the newly developing trade (Figure 12.23).

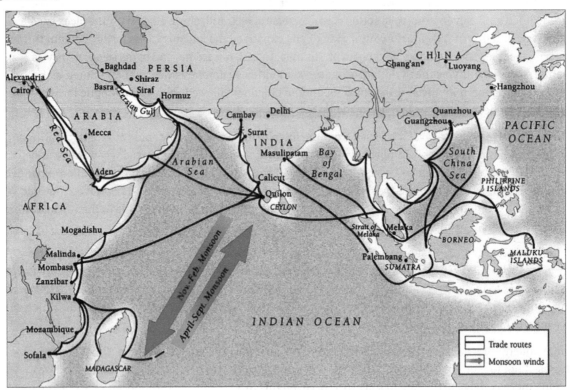

FIGURE 12.23 The Swahili Coast. Key cities along the Swahili coast included Mombasa, Zanzibar, and Kilwa. They were in the path of the monsoon winds and therefore ideally placed to participate in the Indian Ocean trade. (credit: modification of work "Muslim countries Trade" by Muslim countries/Wikimedia Commons, Public Domain)

Yemeni traders began arriving along the coast in East Africa in the eighth century and settled in such important areas as Mogadishu (in modern-day Somalia) and the island of Zanzibar. Some of the earliest of these traders were the Kharijites, dissidents from Arabia who held very different opinions from the mainstream on the role of the caliph and the centralization of Muslim society. Many settled in Oman; there and in eastern Africa they developed complex networks of exchange with merchant families and villages and towns along the coast. Over time, the Muslim traders married into these families, mixing cultures and languages, particularly those of Arabs, Persians, and the Bantu-speakers of East Africa, and produced the Swahili (from the Arabic for "of the coast") civilization.

Thanks to expanding trade with the Muslim world, coastal African traders and port cities from Mogadishu in the north to Sofala in the south adapted to long-distance trade and to Islamic civilization. This adaptation shaped what is known as the Swahili coast, a region of the East African coast dotted by dozens of city-states such as Zanzibar that date from the Middle Ages and served as centers of exchange, particularly of luxury goods.

After 1050, a new wave of Muslim immigrants arrived from the Iranian capital city of Shiraz and pushed many of the previous settlers farther south along the coast. They retained their Islamic cultural heritage and adopted much of the Bantu language, adding Arabic words and creating the language of Kiswahili, which is today a main language of modern Tanzania. The newcomers were eager to trace their Persian heritage as a means of legitimating themselves in the eyes of the peoples of the area, to which end some even claimed descent from the prophet Muhammad himself. In time, these Shirazi Muslims came to dominate trade along the coast, such as at Mombasa, Malinda, Lamu, and Sofala. Many chose to move onto the islands of the coast, particularly Pemba, Mafia, and Zanzibar. Those who dominated trade and claimed descent from the Middle East were known as patricians.

About forty new Muslim towns formed, many of them city-states independently ruled by their own sultans. A council of other patricians often served as advisors or sometimes simply ran the town without a sultan. In either case they formed an elite, hereditary merchant class, speaking Arabic or Kiswahili and trading with Africans in the interior for such items as ivory, furs, and gold. Gold came from Sofala, the southernmost settled point at that time, and was shipped to the northern part of the Swahili coast, where it was traded to the city-states and from there to the Indian Ocean trade network. The merchants of the city-state of Kilwa sought to bypass intermediaries and purchase gold directly. They therefore established the trading colony of Sofala in the region of the same name. Mostly due to its domination of the gold trade, Kilwa became the most important of the Swahili towns, although Zanzibar proved nearly as powerful. For periods in the fourteenth century, in fact, Kilwa ruled over many other towns.

The development of the Swahili city-states also had the effect of connecting the interior of central southern Africa with the wider trade of the Indian Ocean basin. Merchants from city-states such as Sofala, for example, traveled up the Zambezi and Limpopo Rivers to the great fairs that took place on the Zimbabwean plateau, a region dominated by the Bantu peoples of Great Zimbabwe (Figure 12.24). There they exchanged shells, ceramics, and coins from the East African coast for such high-value luxury goods as gold and ivory. Archaeologists have found everything from ancient Indian coins to fourteenth-century Longquan Chinese ceramics in the region of the Zimbabwean plateau, testifying to the reach of Swahili-borne oceanic trade in the African interior.

FIGURE 12.24 Great Zimbabwe. Great Zimbabwe was an advanced trade-based civilization established by Bantu speakers between the Limpopo and Zambezi Rivers in the south-central African interior. Shown here are the remains of the one of the walls of Great Zimbabwe. (credit: "Inside of the Great Enclosure which is part of the Great Zimbabwe ruins" by Jan Derk/Wikimedia commons, Public Domain)

The Bantu societies of eastern and south-central Africa tended to be more matrilineal than Arabic or Persian societies were. Many Middle Eastern immigrants cemented their power by marrying the daughters of local ruling elites. But eventually a culture began to form in which women in the city-states veiled themselves and lived in separate quarters. Even the smallest city-state had a mosque, and many of these can still be seen today.

Many of the more powerful city-states, such as Kilwa, began to mint their own money in the form of copper and silver coins. Generally not used internationally, these coins were nonetheless useful among the coastal people themselves.

If the merchant ruling class were the elite and upper class, the second class comprised the townspeople, the artisans, clerks, and other non-elite workers. They were generally non-elite because they could not trace their genealogy in a line of descent from Shirazi Muslims. Many non-Muslims also resided in the towns and were even lower in social status, such as servants or other manual laborers.

The lowest class of all were the enslaved, people purchased from the mainland who performed much, if not all, the necessary agricultural labor. Slavery played as much of a role in East Africa at this time as it did in the Atlantic world later, following European colonization of the Americas. Enslaved people also became a key trade item in the Indian Ocean trade route and remained long after the arrival of Portuguese sailors and other Europeans in the sixteenth century. Merchants purchased enslaved Bantu peoples from the interior through African intermediaries; they then shipped them to southern Iraq. During the ninth century, these enslaved people, whom the Muslims called *Zanj*, labored to drain the swamps near the mouths of the Tigris and Euphrates rivers and to grow sugarcane and rice. But one of the greatest uprisings of enslaved people in history began in 868 when the Zanj rebelled against their enslavers. Although it was eventually crushed in 883, this unrest effectively ended much of the large-scale slave trade between the Swahili coast and the Persian Gulf in this period. The trade in enslaved people continued throughout the Indian Ocean networks, but this form of slavery never again took hold in the Persian Gulf.

By the twelfth century, East Africa had become a key center of Indian Ocean trade. The combination of monsoon winds that allowed ships to sail toward India in the summer and toward Africa in the winter facilitated the spread of Islam and the unifying culture it created among the merchant classes. Trade-based societies developed along the great arc of land that encircled the Indian Ocean basin. The ivory, animals, skins, rhinoceros' horns, and gold that played such a large role in this trade came from East Africa to be exchanged for luxuries such as silks, glassware, and tools.

12.3 Border States: Sogdiana, Korea, and Japan

LEARNING OBJECTIVES

By the end of this section, you will be able to:
- Discuss the rise of the kingdoms of Sogdiana, Korea, and Japan
- Explain how long-distance trade along the Silk Roads influenced the growth of border states like Sogdiana
- Describe the cultural influence of China on the states of Korea and Japan

Sogdiana, in modern Uzbekistan and Tajikistan, traded both with the Chinese and, increasingly in its long history, with other nomadic peoples such as the Turks. The Chinese, in turn, influenced both Korea and Japan. Both already participated in oceanic trade, but the additional benefits of the Silk Roads' interchange of ideas came to Korea and Japan through the Chinese as Koreans studied writing, Confucianism, and Buddhism in China and brought back the ideas and methods that suited them best. These innovations and ideas then spread to Japan, especially Buddhism.

Sogdiana and Silk Road Trade

East of the Sasanian Empire and west of Tang China, in what is now Uzbekistan and Tajikistan, lay the region of Sogdiana, a territory whose documented history stretches back to the fifth century BCE. Inhabited primarily by nomadic groups, Sogdiana was subject to the rule of a succession of empires and kingdoms throughout antiquity, from the Achaemenid Persians, Alexander the Great, and the Hellenistic successor kingdoms to the Kushan Empire. As a result, the region became a cultural melting pot. Indeed, under first the Seleucids and then the breakaway kingdoms of the Bactrian and Sogdian rulers, Greek learning flourished in Sogdiana, prompting later Islamic rulers to recruit scholars from the area. The Kushan Empire in central Asia was key to stabilizing the heartland that connected the eastern and western ends of the Silk Roads. After Kushan's fall in 375 CE, the Sogdians came to control an array of vital oasis towns, including Bukhara and Samarkand (both in modern-day Uzbekistan), from which they dominated regional trade for hundreds of years.

Although Sogdiana was never unified into a single polity and was almost always ruled by larger states, its long exposure to so many different cultures produced a multilingual population of merchants and skilled craftspeople. The Sogdians were able to use these traits to dominate their portion of the Silk Roads from their city-states such as Panjikent (in Tajikistan). So effective was their control that Sogdiana became the richest country in central Asia. Archaeological excavations of the palace complex at Panjikent have revealed large and elaborate buildings with interiors bearing frescoes of armored cavalry engaged in combat, clearly showing the influence on Sogdian culture of the warrior aristocracy of the Sasanids (Figure 12.25).

FIGURE 12.25 A Sogdian Fresco. This Sogdian fresco (wall painting) of the sixth or seventh century CE depicts a warrior on horseback. It was discovered on a wall of the palace complex at Panjikent in what is today Tajikistan. (credit: "Panjikent mural (6th-7th century CE)" by "Pendjikent"/Wikimedia Commons, Public Domain)

🔗 LINK TO LEARNING

Visit this Smithsonian site (https://openstax.org/l/77Sogdiana) to learn more about Sogdiana and the Sogdian people, including their religious and cultural diversity, the skills of their craftspeople, and their place in the history of the Silk Roads.

Sogdiana reached the peak of its wealth and influence between the fourth and eighth centuries CE. Concentrated in a patchwork of oasis towns and city-states among larger kingdoms, the Sogdians traded frequently with Romans to the west and with nomadic peoples of the steppes and the Chinese to the east. Sogdian communities that exchanged leather and animal products for Chinese silk and manufactured goods were also found in thriving Chinese river ports like Dunhuang and Chang'an.

The Sogdians were also keen agents of cultural transmission throughout this period. As early as the fourth century, for example, Sogdian merchants and traders helped spread Buddhism beyond the borders of South Asia. By the sixth century, Sogdians had followed the Silk Roads into Europe, bringing Nestorianism, the branch of Christianity from Asia Minor and Syria that believed Jesus had two separate natures. Sogdians also brought Manichaeism, a dualistic philosophy of good versus evil that emerged in the Sasanid Empire and blended Persian Zoroastrianism, Buddhism, and Christianity. Manichaeism was the chief competitor of Catholic Christianity in Late Antiquity until the arrival of Islam.

Sogdian traders also established alliances with some of the peoples they encountered in the west, including groups of nomadic Turks who adopted not only Manicheanism but also Sogdian, which was the language of the Silk Roads until the seventh century when it was replaced by Persian. By the eighth century, however, parts of Sogdiana including Samarkand were ruled by the expanding Islamic caliphate, which saw the potential in monopolizing the central Asian corridor of the Silk Roads. The diffusion of Muslim culture into Sogdiana prompted many Sogdian merchants and traders to convert, seeing benefits that included reliable contracts among believers to safeguard goods moving along the Silk Roads. By the middle of the century, the revolutionary Abbasid caliphs who overthrew their Umayyad predecessors had extended their Muslim empire all the way to Tang China, against whose forces they engaged in the Battle of Talas River in 751. For all its significance in ending Abbasid expansion eastward, the battle is also noteworthy in the story of Sogdiana for one unexpected reason: the response of the rebellious Tang general An Lushan.

Although An's biological parentage is shrouded in mystery, the record suggests he was adopted by a Turkic-speaking mother and a Sogdian father and swiftly rose to prominence in the Tang army as an interpreter in the military markets along the Silk Roads. His aggressive nature endeared him to no one, but by the 730s, An had come to the attention of Emperor Xuanzong and ingratiated himself into court politics. He and the emperor became fast friends, but An's fears about his future should the emperor die led him to rebel against the Tang state following its defeat at Talas River. An Lushan's rebellion decided the fate of the Tang presence in central Asia, for it prompted the Tang to withdraw from the region. The story of An reminds us yet again of the interconnected nature of the premodern world.

By the end of the eighth century, much of Sogdiana was ruled by the Abbasid Caliphate, and Sogdian communities abroad gradually assimilated, as in China, for example. Still, Arab, Byzantine, Chinese, and Armenian sources refer to Sogdians as the "great traders of Inner Asia," while caravanners' graffiti in India and the presence of Sogdian loanwords in the Turkish vocabulary testify to the intensity and durability of their commercial interactions long after their absorption into the Islamic world.

The dual Muslim/Chinese control of the Silk Roads that began in the eighth century was shaken by the coming of the Mongols in the thirteenth century. Chinggis Khan's second son Chagatai and his descendants controlled central Asia as the Chagatai Khanate from the mid-thirteenth century onward, until the Turkic warlord Timur (Tamerlane) took over in 1363 and made his capital at Samarkand, the old Sogdian center of the Silk Roads.

Early Korea

The Korean peninsula is a mere six hundred miles long, from the Yalu River in the north to the Korean Strait in the south. Manchuria is located north of it and has historically been home to many nomadic peoples; at times it was part of the kingdoms that made up the lands of Korea. Situated so close to China and at the crossroads of much oceangoing traffic in East Asia, Korea and Manchuria have been influenced a great deal by Chinese culture, from landscape painting techniques to city planning, as well as by ideas such as Confucianism and Buddhism.

Before the common era, an early Korean state was established in the northwest portion of the peninsula and part of Manchuria. This was the state of Gojoseon, and its people founded their capital at the site of Pyongyang, the current capital of North Korea. During the period of the Han in China (220 BCE–220 CE), three separate kingdoms formed in the peninsula: Goguryeo in the north (37 BCE–668 CE), and in the south Baekje (18

BCE–660 CE) and Silla (57 BCE–935 CE). The northern kingdom of Goguryeo had been overrun by the Han, but in 313 CE it was able to throw off the Chinese and reestablish independence. A fourth state, the confederacy of Gaya (42–532 CE), was also established in this period, but it remained relatively weak and in 532 CE was absorbed by the kingdom of Silla (Figure 12.26).

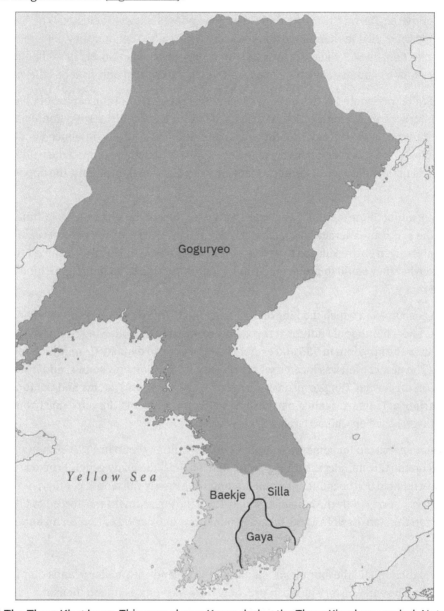

FIGURE 12.26 The Three Kingdoms. This map shows Korea during the Three Kingdoms period. Note the locations of the three—Baekje, Silla, and Goguryeo—which all vied to unify Korea under their own rule. Eventually the Kingdom of Silla absorbed the confederacy of Gaya in 532 and allied with the Tang to defeat Baekje in 660, and then Goguryeo in 668. (credit: modification of work "Map of Goguryeo (476)" by "solicitatia"/Wikimedia Commons, CC0 1.0)

It was during this Three Kingdoms period that cultural influences such as Buddhism were being spread along the Silk Roads. One of the Chinese dynasties to succeed the Han, the Jin, sent Buddhist missionaries into Goguryeo in 372. Many elites soon converted, and the kingdoms of Baekje and Silla followed suit. Other cultural innovations that influenced the three kingdoms were Confucian teachings and Chinese writing; Chinese became the official governmental language. The three kingdoms soon fell to quarreling among themselves, however. The southern two allied against Goguryeo in 550, though their victory was delayed for quite some time.

When the Sui reunified China in 589, they also sought to regain control of Korea, finding themselves in conflict with Goguryeo but repeatedly defeated. In 612, for example, when the Sui attacked with 300,000 soldiers, only 2,700 were reported to have survived. This and other failed attempts to conquer Korea weakened the Sui and were among the key reasons for the dynasty's collapse and replacement by the Tang in 618.

The second Tang emperor, Taizong, also attacked Goguryeo and was likewise defeated. The Tang therefore allied with the Kingdom of Silla in their bid to dominate the peninsula. Together they defeated Baekje in 660, and then Goguryeo in 668. By 668, Silla was the sole remaining kingdom in Korea. In exchange for victory, however, Korea was now a tributary state of the Tang, although it extended only as far as the city of Pyongyang.

The new capital of Silla was located at Geumseong. Basing their city on the Tang capital of Chang'an, the Silla built many Confucian schools, and many Koreans traveled to China to acquire a solid Confucian education and learn more about Buddhism. The ideas of Confucianism and Buddhism slowly influenced and altered Korean culture. For example, Korea had been relatively matrilocal, with the husband joining the wife's family after marriage. But thanks to the influence of Confucianism and its patriarchal traditions, the opposite now began to occur.

The Koreans did not adopt Chinese values wholesale. Although they accepted aspects of China's examination system for filling the state bureaucracy based on merit, for instance, aristocratic control remained strong. High aristocrats were often given entire villages to govern and directly chose the local governing officers, and many of these nobles did what they could to protect their indigenous identities. And although China had few enslaved people, Korea had many.

In 780, an uprising occurred in which the king of Silla was killed. This event marked the beginning of the kingdom's decline, and a number of additional revolts occurred over the following century. A general named Wang Geon overthrew the kingdom in 935 and established the Goryeo dynasty (from which modern Korea derives its name). The new capital was located where the city of Kaesong now stands, and its administration was based largely on the former Tang governmental system; examination systems and Confucian education increased in importance. To guard against northern nomadic invaders, the Goryeo dynasty built a wall just south of the Yalu River, based on China's Great Wall.

The new Korean state persisted for some two centuries until a military coup in 1170. Although the Goryeo dynasty remained on the throne, successor kings were figureheads; the army generals held real power and maintained a powerful hold on the military establishment. In the early thirteenth century, however, the Korean capital in Kaesong was besieged by the Mongols, and in 1231 the government was forced to flee southward. The Mongols overran the state itself in 1258, bringing this formative period of Korean history to an end.

Early Japan

East of Korea and Manchuria lie the four major islands and thousands of smaller islands that make up modern Japan (Figure 12.27). The early history of Japan probably began as long as fifteen thousand years ago, when the islands are thought to have physically separated from Korea at the end of the last ice age. But archaeological research in Japan has uncovered artifacts such as arrowheads and spearpoints made from bone and antlers that date from even earlier, closer to 16,500 years ago. This early time is known as the Jōmon period, which lasted until the fourth century BCE.

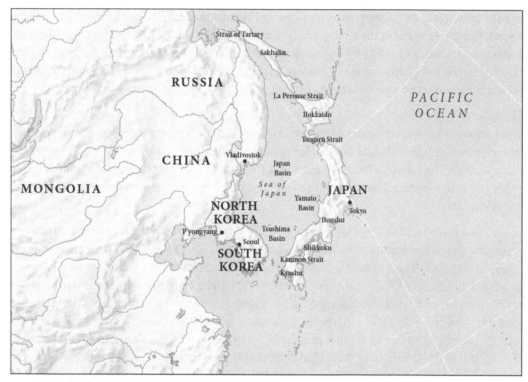

FIGURE 12.27 Japan, Korea, and China in Context. This modern map of Japan and Korea shows their proximity to each other and to China. Their closeness explains how Buddhism and other cultural elements such as writing were able to spread from China to Korea and then to Japan in the premodern period. (attribution: Copyright Rice University, OpenStax, under CC BY 4.0 license)

The centuries from about 300 BCE to roughly 300 CE marked a new agricultural era in Japan known as the Yayoi period. Crops such as millet and rice began to be cultivated, both probably from Korea and China. After around 300 CE, we have evidence of a complex urban culture, such as burial mounds of a large new ruling class. These *kofun*, meaning "old mounds," give this era of Japanese history its name, the Kofun period. Lasting until the sixth century CE, this time saw an intensification of cultural exchange and foreign relations between Japan and Korea. In either 538 or 552, for example, King Seong of Baekje in western Korea sent emissaries to Japan along with Buddhist scriptures and a statue of the Buddha, marking the introduction of Buddhism into the country. About a century later, intense warfare on the Korean Peninsula prompted the migration of countless Koreans to Japan, most of whom were welcomed there. In fact, Emperor Tenji employed many skilled Korean technicians and craftspeople to build fortresses along his coastline.

During the Kofun period of the late third to sixth centuries, the arrival of Buddhism in Japan coincided with the rule of the Yamato clan, a group said to have descended from the goddess Amaterasu. The Yamato began to dominate the island of Honshu, one of the four large islands of Japan where another aristocratic clan, the Nakatomi, supervised the court's religious ceremonies at the imperial palace. The indigenous religion of Japan, Shintoism, held that many gods and spirits must be revered and honored, such as the spirits of trees, rocks, mountains, streams, and former rulers and chieftains. Amaterasu, for example, was the Shinto goddess of the sun. The Nakatomi clan, along with the Mononobe clan, opposed any religion, particularly foreign, that might threaten the dominance of tradition. However, the Soga clan chose to support Buddhism, in opposition to the other two clans.

In the seventh century, the ruler of Japan was Empress Suiko, the daughter of a Soga mother who came to power in 593 after the assassination of her brother King Sushun. For the next three decades, she ruled with her nephew and adviser, Prince Shotoku. In 594, early in her rule, Buddhism became a state religion. This was not the end of Shintoism, but it began a parallel system that continued to the present. In short, by the end of the sixth century, both Shintoism and Buddhism were influencing the cultural makeup of Japan.

In keeping with the ancient East Asian tradition of embracing and borrowing from Chinese culture, the Soga rulers of Japan, like the Koreans in the sixth century, sent envoys to China. These envoys brought back Confucianism, which soon became a way to govern based on principles of appropriate and ethical behavior, as happened in China and Korea. An unusual feature of government in Japan at this time, however, was the adoption of a cap-rank system, which marked an official's rank by the color of cap worn; purple was the most prestigious.

In 604, Prince Shotoku wrote a statement of seventeen articles of government, sometimes referred to as Japan's first constitution. The state was then under great stress, divided among semiautonomous clan-based units. Not surprisingly, the constitution emphasized the Chinese Confucian precepts of a unified state ruled by one sovereign, the meritocratic rather than hereditary system of civil service, and the rights and obligations of the rulers and the ruled.

The Soga clan came to a violent end in 645, marking the rise of the Nakatomi family and the Fujiwara clan. Agitation and civil war persisted until 672, when King Temmu and Jito, his wife and later successor, came to the throne and initiated the Taika Reforms. Seeking to adopt the centralization instituted by the Tang, who came to power in China in 618 CE, Temmu and Jito started to build a capital at Fujiwara-kyo in 694. When it burned down a few years later, they built another at Nara to resemble the Tang capital of Chang'an, inaugurating the Nara period in Japanese history, which lasted until 794. Other reforms included a system of taxation, conscription, and labor service that came to be known as the Taihoo Code (701). An administrative and penal code system based on that of Tang China was established in 718.

After the death of Emperor Shomu in the mid-750s, conflict characterized the remainder of the century. In 794, Emperor Kammu moved his capital about twenty miles north to Heian-kyo, the site of today's Kyoto, ending the Nara period. Heian-kyo remained the capital of Japan until 1868. This larger city symbolized Japan's increasing power over all the major islands, with the exception of the northern island of Hokkaido. Emperor Kammu took his Fujiwara patron with him to the new capital. Throughout the ninth century, Fujiwara advisers became increasingly powerful at the expense of the emperors, many serving as regents and even as emperors themselves.

Gender roles became more rigidly defined during this period, and many non-elites were officially categorized as peasant, artisan, or merchant. Even the system of writing changed. Chinese script had been the traditional writing style, particularly among scholars. However, many words in Japanese were pronounced differently than Chinese writing allowed. Thus a new script called kana began to develop, to more accurately depict the way the words were pronounced in Japanese.

The most famous work written in kana is *The Tale of Genji*, the story of the romantic escapades of Hikaru Genji, a fictional emperor's son. Genji is removed from the line of succession for political reasons, and now a commoner, he decides to pursue a career as an imperial officer. Along the way, he has various romantic entanglements, secret love affairs that produce offspring believed to be the emperor's, and something like a midlife crisis, a reflection of the Buddhist belief in the transience of life. Widely considered the world's first novel, *Genji* was composed in the eleventh century by Murasaki Shikibu, a noblewoman and lady-in-waiting in the Heian Court. It skillfully portrays the forms of entertainment, manner of dress, daily routines, and moral code of the Heian nobility at the height of the Fujiwara clan's power. While the facts surrounding much of Murasaki's life and the composition of her magnum opus are not known, what is not disputed is *Genji's* critically important place in the literary canon of world literature, with the work often considered one of the world's oldest complete novels and a master class of Japanese literature. What is also not in dispute is that the work was composed by a woman from a powerful family at a time when the role of women around the world was still secondary to their male counterparts. It leaves us to wonder how much powerful and influential literature could have been composed by other women should they have been given the opportunity and resources that Murasaki was able to leverage during her career.

The Tale of Genji and Japanese High Society during the Heian Period

Composed in the eleventh century and attributed to female writer Murasaki Shikibu, *The Tale of Genji* opens a unique window into the culture of Japan during the late Heian Period from the eighth to twelfth centuries. The story reveals many aspects of aristocratic life at court, from the styles of clothes worn to the musical instruments played and the mores and values that guided interpersonal and public relationships.

The scenes and events described in *The Tale of Genji* have been depicted in paintings and drawings over the centuries, weaving the story more deeply into Japanese identity by bringing to vivid life the setting for this ancient tale. One of the central themes in the story is of love and unrequited love. Genji finds his ideal woman in the form of Lady Fujitsubo, who is his stepmother, and therefore his love for her is forbidden. At one point in the story, he kidnaps a young girl (Murasaki), who he discovers is actually Lady Fujitsubo's niece. To satisfy his desire for Lady Fujitsubo, he educates the young Murasaki to be like his womanly ideal before finally marrying her (Figure 12.28).

FIGURE 12.28 Scene from *The Tale of Genji*. This scene from a seventeenth-century paper album rendered on paper and consisting of twenty-four album leaves shows the young female servants playing in the snow as Genji and Murasaki watch from their veranda. This scene of childish play was likely intended by the artist to emphasize the youthfulness of Murasaki. (credit: "The Tale of Genji (Genji Monogatari)" by Gift of Mary L. Cassilly, 1894/ Metropolitan Museum of Art, Public Domain)

Many of the illustrations that accompanied the novel's texts provide exquisite detail on the novel's content and reveal both a close reading of the text as well an intimate knowledge of imperial customs. Consider this mid-seventeenth-century handscroll fragment showing the funeral of Lady Aoi, Genji's first wife (Figure 12.29).

FIGURE 12.29 **The Funeral of Lady Aoi.** This funeral scene from chapter nine of *The Tale of Genji* dates to the mid-seventeenth century CE and was rendered on a paper handscroll in ink and gold. Here we see a high-ranking Tendai monk wearing orange and performing rituals in front of an ornamented altar as many priests from various temples gather around. The attending monks are arranged hierarchically and are recognizable by their elaborate clothing. (credit: "'Leaves of Wild Ginger' (Aoi), from the Phantom Genji Scrolls (Maboroshi no Genji monogatari emaki)" by Metropolitan Museum of Art, Rogers Fund, 1912/Wikimedia Commons, Public Domain)

The story of Genji was enormously popular in Japan and illustrations of him and about the story continue to be made. In the nineteenth century, artists using woodblock printing often elaborated on the themes in the story by putting Genji in more modern scenes (Figure 12.30).

FIGURE 12.30 **Modern Illustrations from** *The Tale of Genji*. In this colorful three-panel woodblock print, Genji (left) is shown entering the Gankiro Teahouse, one of the most famous brothels in nineteenth-century Yokohama. Here the artist, Utagawa Kunisada, is likely blending the sensual imagery in the story of Genji with the sensual atmosphere of the teahouse. (credit: "Prince Genji Visits the Gankirō Tea House" by Bequest of William S.

- What do the images suggest to you about gender and social relations during the Heian period?
- The details in many of the images, like the preceding funeral scene, are sometimes more elaborate than the story itself. What does this suggest about the way the story had become an important part of Japanese culture over time?

Throughout the Heian period, the court supported obscure forms of Buddhism such as Tendai (Tiantai in China) and Shingon. Shintoism retained its status as a key religious tradition (Figure 12.31), but so did these forms of Buddhism. Emperor Shomu had encouraged the spread of Buddhism by ordering a temple to be built in every province and block printings of Buddhist scriptures to be disseminated to the general populace.

FIGURE 12.31 The Itsukushima Shrine. Originally built in the twelfth century, the Itsukushima Shrine pictured here is an important Shinto symbol of the indigenous religion of Japan and a UNESCO World Heritage Site. The prominence of shrines such as this shows that the religion is still a vibrant aspect of cultural life in Japan today. (credit: "The torii gate at the Itsukushima Shrine in Miyajima" by Balon Greyjoy/Wikimedia Commons, CC0 1.0)

🔗 LINK TO LEARNING

One of the key religious traditions of Japan is Shintoism. Read this article, particularly the first section, "What is Shinto?" (https://openstax.org/l/77Shinto) and consider why early people like the Japanese might have developed such a keen connection to nature and the environment. What other religious traditions beyond those of Japan uphold the importance of nature?

During the late eleventh century, a unique facet of Japanese government developed called *insei*, or cloistered rule, in which the emperor retired from public life to live in a monastery but continued to rule behind the scenes. Initially, at least, this practice was meant to establish a regency of sorts; that is, the cloistered emperor could direct the affairs of state until his son came of age to rule in his own right. In time, however, cloistered rule became unwieldy and prompted chaos in the Japanese state. Often there were several retired emperors at the same time, each with their own troops, who exerted (or attempted to exert) control through cloistered rule. At this time, Heian-kyo began to be called Kyoto, meaning "the capital city."

An upsurge of violence began in the late 1150s when two families, the Taira and the Minamoto, vied for power. In 1160, the Taira were ascendant, but a generation later, in the uprising known as the Genpei War, the

Minamoto triumphed, winning the naval Battle of Dannoura in 1185. The Kamakura period of Japan's history then began and lasted until 1333. In this period, the imperial capital remained at Heian-kyo, but the warrior families, first the Minamoto and then the Hojo, were headquartered in Kamakura.

From 1180 to 1185, with the help of the **samurai**, the warrior aristocracy of Japan, Yoritomo, the heir of the Minamoto clan, successfully wiped out all rivals, even eradicating the northern branch of the Fujiwara in 1189. In 1192, he gave himself the title of **shogun**, or commander in chief. From then on, the military shogun exercised the power of state, while the emperor was little more than a figurehead. Regional lords also had samurai retainers. Samurai adhered to a strict code of behavior called *bushi*, or "way of the warrior." One of the expected behaviors was disdain for capture, leading to ritual suicide known as *seppuku*.

DUELING VOICES

Origins and Evolution of the Samurai Class: A Historical Debate

Historians seeking to understand the changing nature of armed force and military organization in early Japan and the origin of the samurai look at the ways in which Japanese society, culture, and economy were influenced by military matters before the eighth century and how this influence prompted the emergence of a new class of warrior-administrators.

The prevailing view today is that the samurai emerged in the mid- to late-Heian period as the result of a weakened imperial system. The imperial court had modeled its administration on institutions imported from Tang China, which included a governing ideology based on Confucianism and a military establishment that depended on a peasant-conscript army. This system proved ineffective in Japan, however, resulting in an inept central government that failed amid warfare and regional rebellion beginning in the early tenth century. The subsequent breakdown in public order prompted people in the countryside to take matters into their own hands. Provincial families armed themselves to defend and advance their private interests, allowing them to reclaim land and gain influence at the Heian Court by acting as regional warlords who could impose stability and security over rebellion. By 1100, therefore, samurai organized in regional bands were emerging as a major force in Japan's military and political arenas.

Other historians argue that the Heian Court was not inept or inactive and that the growth of private regional armies was well underway by the Heian period rather than being a product of it. This development too, they believe, was a return to familial authority patterns already deeply rooted in Japanese culture. Finally, these scholars contend that the rise of provincial warrior families and emergence of the samurai class was nothing more than the outcome of their being coopted by the central imperial authority, which sought to use them to perform essential military service.

The debate surrounding the origins and evolution of the samurai class may never be resolved. With that in mind, watch the following video of *The Evolution of Samurai through Japanese History* (https://openstax.org/l/ 77Samurai) and then answer the questions that follow.

View multimedia content (https://openstax.org/books/world-history-volume-1/pages/12-3-border-states-sogdiana- korea-and-japan)

- According to the video, what were the origins of the samurai?
- How does this explanation fit into the discussion of the origins and development of the samurai in this feature box?
- The video talks about some of the cultural influences that led to the development of the samurai. What were they?
- What were the symbols of the samurai class? What was the preferred philosophy of the samurai?

In 1268, envoys arrived in Kamakura on behalf of some new rulers in Asia, the Mongols. Though they declared friendly intentions, these emissaries were ignored by the court. In response the Mongols sailed to Japan and invaded in 1274, only to be repelled when a storm arose following bitter fighting (Figure 12.32). Knowing they would return, the ruling Hojo clan built several land- and sea-based fortifications to halt any future invasion. When the Mongols did reappear in 1281, there was no clear victor, but a typhoon arose and scattered the Mongol ships, convincing many that divine winds, or *kamikaze*, were being sent by the gods to protect Japan.

FIGURE 12.32 **The First Mongol Invasion of Japan.** This scene from an illustrated scroll called *Mōko Shūrai Ekotoba* from the late thirteenth or early fourteenth century shows the first Mongol invasion of Japan in 1274. It depicts the combatants using arrows as well as bombs. (credit: "Mōko Shūrai Ekotoba 2" by Unknown/Wikimedia Commons, Public Domain)

Key Terms

cabotage a system wherein groups or individuals are granted the right to trade in another's territory

caravansary an inn funded by the state or wealthy individuals where travelers could spend the night and store their goods securely

Chan Buddhism a form of Mahayana Buddhism that emphasizes meditation; it is widely practiced in Japan where it is known as Zen Buddhism

dharma the Hindu concept of the right way of living as defined by cosmic law

moksha the release from samsara and the karmic cycle together with the attainment of a complete understanding of the world

Pure Land Buddhism a branch of Mahayana Buddhism holding that all believers can be reborn into a place of salvation, the Pure Land

samurai a member of the elite warrior class of Japan, governed by a strict code of behavior

shogun a Japanese military commander-in-chief

Section Summary

12.1 The Indian Ocean World in the Early Middle Ages

The new religion of Islam came into India with waves of invaders, from Turkic speakers of central Asia to Arabs from the distant west. In the process, northeastern India became increasingly Muslim and influenced by Islamic culture owing to the arrival of these Turkic peoples. An Islamic state was established at Delhi—the Delhi Sultanate—which lasted more than three hundred years and became the center of Islamic India. However, because the minority Muslim rulers did not enforce cultural homogeneity, the invasions strengthened the cultural diversity that was already a hallmark of Indian social order. Despite Muslims beginning to engage in the Indian Ocean trade soon after their arrival in northern India, carrying goods and ideas with them throughout the subcontinent, the south remained Hindu in its cultural beliefs and ideas.

East Asia, particularly China, was affected by all this trade. Buddhism also began to take hold along the overland routes of the Silk Roads, particularly those linking India with China. The Sui dynasty not only adopted Buddhism but also expanded and strengthened trade across central Asia. Overextending themselves, however, the Sui were replaced by the Tang, who strengthened trade routes and ties with Buddhism even further. The An Lushan rebellion weakened the Tang, however, and eventually the Tang fell.

12.2 East-West Interactions in the Early Middle Ages

The Silk Roads originated in the Han dynasty's trade with nomadic peoples from the Inner Asian Steppe and grew into a vast network that crisscrossed much of central Asia, linking China with the West. Beyond the obvious economic benefits, trade along the Silk Roads also facilitated cultural exchange, such as Buddhism's spread from India to China and onward. Beginning in the seventh century, Arab expansion led to the conquest of Sasanid-controlled portions of the route, and much of southwest Asia was unified by an Islamic caliphate, putting large portions of the network in the hands of a single empire. In the east, the powerful Tang dynasty ensured protection of trade on the Silk Roads. But in 751, the Tang and Abbasid empires clashed at the Talas River, marking the end of expansion in central Asia for both. However, both Hinduism and Islam grew in Southeast Asia during the later Middle Ages, playing a large role in the Indian Ocean trade.

East Africa connected the Indian Ocean trade network of the Middle East to China, India, and Southeast Asia. From the seventh century onward, Islamized Arab traders were vital in bringing the regional trade that characterized the East African Aksumite economy into the wider maritime trade of the Indian Ocean basin, a feat accomplished through linkages between the Red Sea and the Gulf of Aden and beyond. In the seventh century, the Swahili culture blossomed along the East African coast. Arab traders from North Africa and Iran intermingled with local Bantu populations and built a thriving trade-based civilization along the coastline between Mogadishu in modern Somalia and Sofala in Mozambique. The city-states there deepened trade connections with the Middle East and East and Southeast Asia, bringing cultures and goods from as far away as

China to the African interior and sending gold, ivory, and rare animals from southern Africa to China.

12.3 Border States: Sogdiana, Korea, and Japan

Sogdiana was vital to the operation of the Silk Roads beginning in the fourth century CE. Over the course of some four hundred years, Sogdian city-states like Samarkand and Panjikent grew into key markets, and Sogdian trading communities were established in China. At its height, Sogdiana was the wealthiest region in central Asia.

Like many other states in East Asia, Korea was greatly influenced by Chinese civilization. Korean students were educated in Confucian schools, and Korean culture took on the patriarchal character and traditions favored by Confucianism. China's meritocratic civil service system was incorporated into Korea's bureaucratic state system, and the Korean capital built by the Silla dynasty at Geumseong was modeled on the Tang capital at Chang'an.

China likewise influesnced ancient Japan, though less directly. In the sixth and seventh centuries, countless Korean artisans and craftspeople emigrated to Japan, where their knowledge was put to use. Foreign relations with Korea introduced Buddhism to Japan in the sixth century, and Japanese contact with China brought Confucianism to the island chain, as well as Chinese-influenced written language. Still, unique cultural traditions emerged in Japan, from Shintoism and the development of obscure forms of Buddhism to the institutions of *insei*, the samurai, and the shogun.

Assessments

Review Questions

1. What group of people originated the Hindu caste system?
   a. Aryans
   b. Kshatriya
   c. monks
   d. Vedic Brahmans

2. The ultimate goal of the Hindu caste system was to attain what?
   a. dharma
   b. karma
   c. moksha
   d. samsara

3. The rulers of the Delhi Sultanate in India were followers of what religious tradition?
   a. Christianity
   b. Buddhism
   c. Hinduism
   d. Islam

4. Yang Jian, founder of the Sui dynasty, was an adherent of what religious tradition?
   a. Christianity
   b. Buddhism
   c. Hinduism
   d. Islam

5. What was the likely reason the aristocracy opposed the rule of Empress Wu Zetian?
   a. She was female.
   b. She was a peasant.

    c. She was Hindu.

    d. She opposed Confucian teachings.

6. Why did Tang emperor Wuzong persecute Buddhist monks and nuns?

    a. Buddhism was illegal under the Tang.

    b. Wuzong believed Buddhism threatened the Confucian state and the imperial order.

    c. Buddhist monks and nuns routinely protested the religious intolerance of the Tang.

    d. Many civil servants in the bureaucracy were Buddhist, which threatened Tang control.

7. Sumptuary laws enacted under the Tang emperor Gaozong were meant to achieve what purpose?

    a. restrict the foods women could eat at the Tang Court

    b. enshrine legal proscriptions on women scholars

    c. tighten laws governing the types of clothes women could wear

    d. censor the language used by female courtesans in the poetry they wrote

8. Who were the successors to the Umayyads?

    a. the Abbasids

    b. the Sasanids

    c. the Parthians

    d. the Tang

9. What was a key result of the Battle of Talas River?

    a. the conquest of the Tang by the Abbasids

    b. the end of Abbasid expansion into China

    c. the spread of Hinduism

    d. the conquest of the Abbasids by the Tang

10. During the reign of what king did Aksum's trade with the African interior expand considerably, making the kingdom wealthy and powerful?

    a. Prester John

    b. Solomon

    c. Ezna

    d. Frumentius

11. What was a key export from East Africa?

    a. ivory

    b. cotton

    c. glassware

    d. silk

12. During the Middle Ages, what was a patrician in East Africa?

    a. an African living in Arabia

    b. a Muslim who could trace their Middle Eastern descent

    c. a pagan who could trace their Middle Eastern descent

    d. a settler on the east coast of Africa

13. What kingdom succeeded because of its ability to monopolize trade through the Palk Strait?

    a. Srivijaya

    b. Chola

    c. Swahili

    d. Delhi Sultanate

14. What group replaced the Sasanid Empire?
   a. Tang
   b. Umayyads
   c. Abbasids
   d. Byzantines

15. What two religious traditions were practiced in Japan during the Yamato period?
   a. Buddhism and Catholicism
   b. Catholicism and Hinduism
   c. Hinduism and Shintoism
   d. Buddhism and Shintoism

16. What Asian country did *not* adopt Chinese writing?
   a. China
   b. Japan
   c. Korea
   d. Sogdiana

17. What was the language of the Silk Roads until the seventh century CE?
   a. Chinese
   b. Japanese
   c. Sogdian
   d. Korean

Check Your Understanding Questions

1. In what ways did the Muslim rulers of the Delhi Sultanate embrace other cultures?

2. How did the Grand Canal lead to greater centralization in China?

3. In what ways did women thrive in Tang China?

4. How did the Silk Roads help in the diffusion of culture?

5. What were some of the risks faced by travelers along the Silk Roads? Why do you think these travelers would be willing to face these risks?

6. How did the Kingdom of Aksum enhance trade in Africa during the early Middle Ages?

7. How did trade along the Swahili coast connect the cultures of the African interior with those of East Asia?

8. What cultural influences did China have on both Korea and Japan?

9. How did the Silk Roads encourage the growth of Sogdiana?

10. Why did Chinese culture spread to Japan by way of Korea?

Application and Reflection Questions

1. Why did the Indian subcontinent remain largely segmented and decentralized from the eighth through the tenth centuries, while many neighboring states (such as China) became increasingly centralized?

2. Consider the role the internet now plays in international commerce. What are some of the similarities and differences between the internet and historic trade networks?

3. How do the luxury goods of the late Middle Ages compare with our luxury goods today? If the Silk Roads still existed, what might be the most important goods traded along this route?

4. Did the interactions between the Tang and Abbasid states positively affect one, both, or neither? Why?

5. How did the arrival of Islam in South and Southeast Asia affect the indigenous populations there?

6. In what ways did the cultural blending on the Swahili coast make it an ideal region of exchange between the east and the peoples of Africa?

7. How did their relative openness to foreign innovation and culture affect the development of border states like Sogdiana, Japan, and Korea?

8. How did states like Japan and Korea benefit from having common cultural traits in this era?

FIGURE 13.1 *Harun al-Rashid Receiving a Delegation of Charlemagne.* The nineteenth-century German artist Julius Köckert painted this imaginary scene in which representatives of the Frankish Christian ruler Charlemagne (on horseback) meet with the Islamic ruler Harun al-Rashid (seated at left). Both leaders helped shape the history of western Afro-Eurasia in the post-Roman world. (credit: modification of work "Harun al-Rashid receiving a delegation of Charlemagne in Baghdad" by Maximilianeum Foundation/Wikimedia Commons, Public Domain)

CHAPTER OUTLINE

INTRODUCTION Western Afro-Eurasia faced a number of challenges in the early Middle Ages, the period from about 500 to 1000 CE. With the collapse of Roman authority came a time of political instability and insecurity. Cities declined, and institutions of learning weakened. Western Europe became increasingly rural. Because there was no longer a strong centralized state to develop and police the roads, travel became more difficult and more dangerous, harming commerce. However, this is not the whole story. Trade and urban life flourished in the early Islamic kingdoms, which eventually extended from Spain to India. The Byzantine Greeks maintained some classical traditions, and their capital in Constantinople was a center of global trade for centuries. Germanic kings sought to form new alliances with Christian leaders and participate in world trade and diplomacy.

Perhaps no figure better exemplifies the merging of cultures in western Europe than Charlemagne, a Germanic ruler who reigned from 768 to 814. Charlemagne dreamed of reviving the Roman world in terms of territory, education, and art. Despite his belief in spreading Christianity through conquest, he sent embassies to Muslim leaders and even received the sumptuous gift of an elephant from the Abbasid ruler Harun al-Rashid in 802 (Figure 13.1). It might be tempting to see this period as one of just conflict, but as Charlemagne's reign demonstrates, it was also a dynamic time of merging cultures and social transformation.

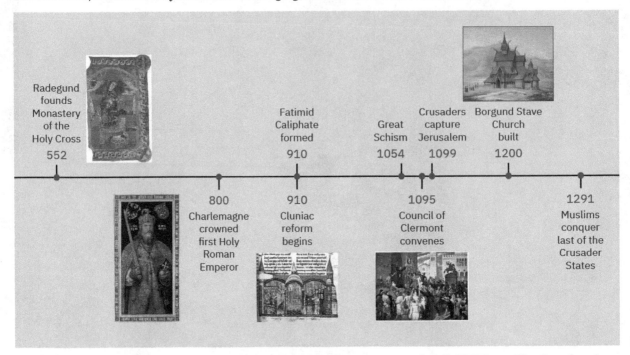

FIGURE 13.2 Timeline: The Post-Roman West and the Crusading Movement. (credit "552": modification of work "Saint Radegonde" by Poitiers Municipal Library/Wikimedia Commons, Public Domain; credit "800": modification of work "Emperor Charlemagne and Emperor Sigismund" by Germanisches Nationalmuseum/Wikimedia Commons, Public Domain; credit "910": modification of work Consécration de Cluny III par Urbain II" by Bibliothèque Nationale de France/Wikimedia Commons, Public Domain; credit "1095": modification of work "Peter the Hermit Preaching the First Crusade" by Cassell's History of England, Vol. 1 (of 8)/Wikimedia Commons, Public Domain; credit "1200": modification of work "Franz Wilhelm Schiertz Borgunds Kirke i Lærdal i Sogn" by Norge fremstillet i Tegninger fra Digitalarkivet/Wikimedia Commons, Public Domain)

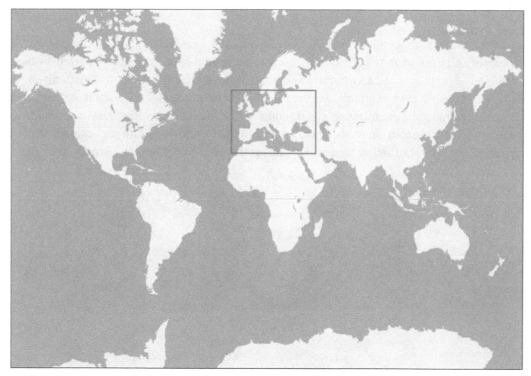

FIGURE 13.3 Locator Map: The Post-Roman West and the Crusading Movement. (credit: modification of work "World map blank shorelines" by Maciej Jaros/Wikimedia Commons, Public Domain)

13.1 The Post-Roman West in the Early Middle Ages

LEARNING OBJECTIVES

By the end of this section, you will be able to:
- Analyze the foundations of medieval society that emerged in the post-Roman world
- Define feudalism in western Europe
- Describe the role of religion in medieval European culture and society
- Discuss the establishment of Muslim rule in western Europe and the religiously diverse society in Spain

Of all the regions in the post-Roman world, western Europe experienced arguably the most dramatic change. Its political order fragmented under Germanic warlords empowered mainly by their ability to provide loot for their followers. In this world of soldiers, the Roman church, directed by the pope, worked to secure military assistance from kings and convert various groups to Christianity. The church's goal was to ensure that its vision of Christian beliefs and practices eclipsed those of other sects such as the Arians, Christians who questioned the Roman church's basic tenet that Jesus was divine. The merging of these two antithetical cultures—the religious and the military—helped prepare the ground for a new civilization we call the medieval culture, which emerged between the end of Rome and the rise of the modern world.

Europe after the Roman Empire

There was no exact date when the Roman Empire fell, and the eastern half of the empire did not collapse until the fifteenth century. In fact, the Germanic peoples who settled in the former Roman Empire were not hostile to its culture, so in some places, Roman culture lasted longer than Roman political authority. Latin remained the language of the educated, for example, and Germanic peoples gradually adopted the Latin alphabet for their own languages, including English. Traditionally, though, the end of the empire is fixed at 476, when a German general named Odoacer deposed the emperor Romulus Augustulus and established himself not as a Roman emperor but as King of Italy. Even that date may be arbitrary, but by the late fifth century, traditional Roman authority had ceased to be the basis of political power in much of western Europe.

German Successor States

What replaced Roman political authority was the authority of the successor kingdoms (Figure 13.4). The Germanic peoples and the Roman population they conquered were able to create a new society by blending cultural traditions—a process called *acculturation*—in three ways. First, conversion to Christianity helped reduce differences between the two groups. Second, the Christian Church and the Roman aristocracy offered a useful example of bureaucratic organization and diplomacy that the successor kingdoms adopted. Finally, the erosion of Roman society enabled a new society to emerge in the Middle Ages. Although other Germanic kingdoms existed, those established by the Franks, Ostrogoths, and Visigoths demonstrate these three forms of acculturation most vividly.

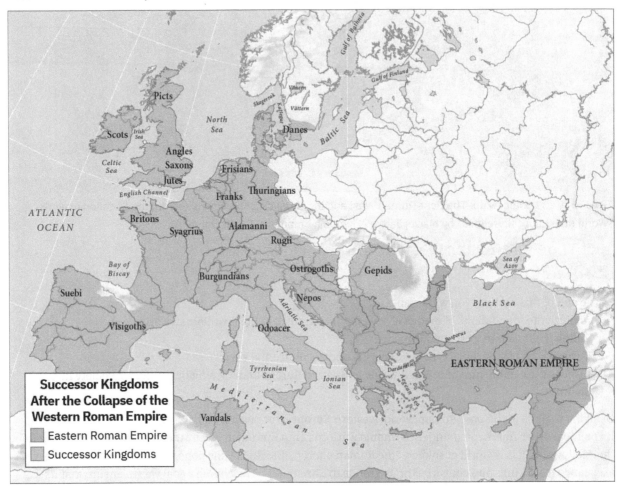

FIGURE 13.4 Post-Roman Western Eurasia. This map shows the Eastern Roman Empire as dominant in the eastern Mediterranean around 500 CE, and the division of western Europe among various successor kingdoms at this time. (attribution: Copyright Rice University, OpenStax, under CC BY 4.0 license)

"German" was the term Romans used for all the peoples beyond their northern borders, and for them, it was interchangeable with "barbarian," meaning not Romanized, although there was a great deal of cultural exchange between the two groups. The relationship between the term "German" and the peoples to whom it has been applied is complex. Some of those who invaded the Roman Empire did not speak a Germanic language at all, such as the Huns and Avars. There were few rigid ethnic boundaries between the groups, and the armies of any leader often included warriors from other tribes.

The Germanic peoples generally did not read or write and instead transmitted information and traditions orally. Famous tales that eventually found their way into written form, such as the *Song of Hildebrand* and the *Song of the Nibelungs,* had their beginnings as spoken epics. Oral culture celebrating warriors facing their fate on the battlefield and scornful queens plotting revenge reflected real possibilities in this society.

⊘ LINK TO LEARNING

The Anglo-Saxon peoples who settled in the British Isles, a mix of many cultures including Germanic, are famous for their literary output, both in Latin and in their own language, now called Old English. In particular, they loved riddles. The following links present an Anglo-Saxon riddle 1 (https://openstax.org/l/77riddle1) and riddle 2 (https://openstax.org/l/77riddle2) related to food. Can you guess the answers?

Across all Germanic societies, warfare was an important tool for building social prestige. There were no formal hierarchies, so advancement was possible for any willing to serve a powerful chieftain or king. In return, leaders promised loot and the chance to do great deeds. A king who could not ensure material or social resources would lose followers and could not expect to be obeyed. While gold and glory motivated fighters and kings alike, Germanic law and custom tried to limit the destructive cycles of violence by instituting a "blood price" or *wergild*, under which the injured were compensated according to their social status. These laws tell us much about Germanic society. Chieftains and men of fighting age carried a higher blood price than older men, for example, and women of childbearing age were valued more than older women.

Women were often responsible for running the household and doing the bulk of the farming work, especially when men were called to fight or travel. Men might hunt, but their contributions were often the spoils of war, including enslaved people captured in battle who then worked in the household. Germanic society was fully patriarchal, and tribes like the Alemanni beat women whose clothes were deemed immodest (showing the leg above the knee). Germans were also often polygynous; men might have multiple wives at once and be able to divorce at will, while women's options were severely limited.

The Germans were polytheistic, worshipping various deities such as Wodan, a god of war, wisdom, and death, and his consort Frigg, a goddess of motherhood, marriage, and magic. By the third century, individual Germans were already converting to Christianity. Many, like the Goths and Vandals, adopted Arian Christianity, adhering to the teaching that Jesus and the Father were not identical entities. Once within the Roman Empire, they encountered competing forms of the faith that could become a source of further conflict with Christians and non-Christians alike.

As an example of acculturation, Theodoric the Great, king of the Ostrogoths, was one of the most dynamic leaders of the post-Roman world. When he became King of Italy in 493, he relied on Roman aristocrats to administer his kingdom, such as the scholar and writer Cassiodorus and the historian and philosopher Boethius. Theodoric also rebuilt Roman infrastructure, including repairing aqueducts and city walls in his kingdom. He used diplomacy to secure alliances with other German kings, often through marriages. To form an alliance with the Franks, for instance, he himself wed Audofleda, the sister of Clovis I, king of the Franks, and he gave his daughters in marriage to other Germanic kings. Envisioning himself as the heir to Roman rule in the west, he maintained ties with the eastern Roman emperors and strove to revive trade with the eastern Mediterranean world. Despite the struggle to maintain order, most rulers attempted to connect with distant civilizations and learned from the peoples around them.

To create common bonds between Romans and Germans, Theodoric settled the Ostrogoths among the Roman population, although religious differences kept them from fully integrating. Toleration was possible and even desired in the early Middle Ages, but distrust between religious groups could spark outright violence and persecution. While he was an Arian Christian, Theodoric tolerated the Catholic population of Italy and attempted to mitigate conflict between the two groups until late in his reign, when his distrust of Catholics led him to persecute them. After his death in 526, the Ostrogoths struggled in Italy, and invasion by both the Byzantines and new invaders called the Lombards left the land devastated and divided.

The most successful Germanic kingdom was that of the Franks. Clovis I, a member of the Merovingian dynasty, founded the kingdom in the early sixth century and offers a striking contrast to Theodoric. Ruthless and violent, Clovis was nevertheless a cunning leader who saw the advantages of diplomacy and the support of the Catholic Church and who was tolerant of religious differences until his conversion to Catholicism. He also worked with Gallo-Roman aristocrats and clergy to strengthen the administration of his kingdom and ensure that Roman institutions continued where they could. Shortly before his death, he convened the first council of Catholic bishops at Orleans, whose proclamations were binding on both the Gallo-Roman population and the Franks. In this case, religion helped unite the two groups.

Over time, the Merovingian rulers fell to violent infighting, leaving their sons or nephews as young and often ineffective successors. A chief source of conflict was the practice of partible inheritance, whereby each son received an equal share of his father's estate. Estates thus became smaller with each successive generation unless new lands were conquered, often by being taken from siblings, in-laws, or cousins. Kings without land and resources to offer as reward lost the ability to attract fighters. Real power lay with the aristocrats, and eventually a new dynasty called the Carolingians took control of the Frankish kingdom. With the support of the pope, Pépin le Bref (Pippin the Short) became the first Carolingian king of the Franks, deposing his Merovingian rival. In return, he confirmed a grant of lands in Italy to the pope. This grant, known as the Donation of Pepin, provided the legal basis for the establishment of the Papal States and helped ensure that the **papacy**, the set of administrative structures associated with the government of the Catholic Church, was not just a religious institution but also a territorial power (Figure 13.5).

FIGURE 13.5 The Donation of Pepin. An artist's rendering of the Donation of Pepin in 754, in which the pope granted legitimacy to Pépin le Bref as the first Carolingian king of the Franks in exchange for a grant of lands in Italy that would ensure the territorial power of the Papal States in the centuries to come. (credit: "The donation of Pepin the Short to Pope Stephen II (or Treaty of Quierzy)" by États pontificaux/Wikimedia Commons, Public Domain)

Their alliance with the popes allowed the Carolingian rulers to work independently of the Byzantine Empire, which became an important factor in their desire to conquer new territory and revive the idea of empire. It also indicates that even in the chaotic period after the collapse of Roman authority, diplomacy, religious movements, conflict, and opportunity still connected the Mediterranean world and western Europe.

Pépin's son Charles, known as Charlemagne ("Charles the Great"), was the most influential ruler in the early European Middle Ages and one of its best-known figures. Charlemagne was fortunate, as his father had been, in that he did not need to fight his siblings for control of the kingdom. He was tall and energetic and had a profound belief in his role as a Christian ruler, with a will to conquer others and convert them to Catholic Christianity. He campaigned nearly every year of his reign, conquering land and subjugating peoples across central Europe. He reorganized his government and attempted to revive learning, reform the church, and extend his influence beyond his own realm. His vast empire eventually extended from modern France to Germany, northern Italy, and parts of northern Spain and central Europe, uniting western Europe for the first time since the collapse of Roman authority. On Christmas Day in the year 800, Charlemagne was crowned Emperor of the Romans by Pope Leo III. This coronation angered Byzantine rulers and set the stage for conflict between east and west in their quest for prestige and territory. It also enabled both cooperation and conflict between popes and emperors, because each saw an advantage in working together to fight mutual enemies.

IN THEIR OWN WORDS

Charlemagne Receives an Elephant

This excerpt from *Vita Karoli Magni*, or *The Life of Charles the Great*, describes how the Abbasid ruler Harun al-Rashid sent Charlemagne an elephant as a gift. The writer is the scholar Einhard, who knew Charlemagne personally, served in his administration, and considered Charlemagne a great king, often excusing his faults and praising his accomplishments.

It added to the glory of his reign by gaining the good will of several kings and nations; so close, indeed, was the alliance that he contracted with Alfonso [II 791–842] King of Galicia and Asturias, that the latter, when sending letters or ambassadors to Charles, invariably styled himself his man. His munificence won the kings of the Scots also to pay such deference to his wishes that they never gave him any other title than lord or themselves than subjects and slaves: there are letters from them extant in which these feelings in his regard are expressed. His relations with Aaron [Harun al-Rashid, 786–809], King of the Persians, who ruled over almost the whole of the East, India excepted, were so friendly that this prince preferred his favor to that of all the kings and potentates of the earth, and considered that to him alone marks of honor and munificence were due. Accordingly, when the ambassadors sent by Charles to visit the most holy sepulcher and place of resurrection of our Lord and Savior presented themselves before him with gifts, and made known their master's wishes, he not only granted what was asked, but gave possession of that holy and blessed spot. When they returned, he dispatched his ambassadors with them, and sent magnificent gifts, besides stuffs, perfumes, and other rich products of the Eastern lands. A few years before this, Charles had asked him for an elephant, and he sent the only one that he had. The Emperors of Constantinople, Nicephorus [I 802–811], Michael [I, 811–813], and Leo [V, 813–820], made advances to Charles, and sought friendship and alliance with him by several embassies; and even when the Greeks suspected him of designing to wrest the empire from them, because of his assumption of the title Emperor, they made a close alliance with him, that he might have no cause of offense. In fact, the power of the Franks was always viewed by the Greeks and Romans with a jealous eye, whence the Greek proverb 'Have the Frank for your friend, but not for your neighbor.'

—"Einhard: The Life of Charlemagne," translated by Samuel Epes Turner

- How distant are the territories Einhard mentions? What does this suggest about medieval communication?
- Why might Einhard emphasize that Harun al-Rashid favored Charlemagne above all others? What does the gift of the elephant signify?
- Why were the Greek rulers anxious about Charlemagne?

Like Theodoric, Charlemagne was more than a conqueror. He hoped to revive Roman institutions, reform the church, and convert people to Christianity. The period of intellectual activity and reorganization of educational and religious institutions that began in his reign is often called the Carolingian Renaissance, meaning a "rebirth" of culture and learning (and "Carolingian" being a reference to Charlemagne). The Carolingian aristocracy supported the building of new palaces and monasteries and promoted artists to decorate these buildings as well as to illustrate (or "illuminate") books, and the increased emphasis on learning was a way to ensure that the court of the Carolingians was filled with highly educated advisers and associates (Figure 13.6).

FIGURE 13.6 *In Praise of the Holy Cross*. This page from the ninth-century poetry collection *In Praise of the Holy Cross* shows its author, the Frankish monk and teacher Rabanus Maurus (left), presenting the book to Otgar, archbishop of Mainz (seated at right). The connection between books, clergy, and art is a hallmark of cultural works from the Carolingian era. (credit: "Raban Maur (left), supported by Alcuin (middle), dedicates his work to Archbishop Otgar of Mainz (Right)" by De laudibus sanctae crucis/Österreichischen Nationalbibliothek/Wikimedia Commons, Public Domain)

Intellectuals and monks flocked to Charlemagne's court, where they put their talents to use copying the classical works of ancient Greek and Roman authors and serving in the emperor's administration. One of the most important of these scholars was Alcuin of York, an Anglo-Saxon who perfected the Carolingian minuscule script. This standard form of handwriting was clearer and easier to read than earlier Roman and Merovingian forms. Carolingian scholars also popularized punctuation marks, like the sentence-ending period. These innovations made it easier for people to learn Latin and contributed to the revival of classical education.

Charlemagne was also a globally minded ruler. He corresponded with the Byzantine rulers, received gifts from the Abbasid caliph, and facilitated the trade of enslaved people taken on his eastern frontier with Al-Andalus (modern Spain).

The Collapse of the Carolingian Empire and the Rise of Feudal Society

Charlemagne's empire did not last. The emperor was succeeded by his son Louis the Pious, who continued the revival of learning and was deeply involved in church reform. Members of the church's hierarchy, like the monk Benedict of Aniane, believed that both spiritual and administrative matters had declined, so Louis gave Benedict authority to reform all monasteries in the Frankish empire by promoting the strict observance of rules about what monks could eat and when and how they should work and pray. Carolingian reformers took inspiration from the monks of Ireland, who brought with them both their ascetic style of religious practice and their handsomely copied books of classical literature. The reform of the monasteries thus helped to preserve Carolingian cultural developments and classical learning.

Louis's religious and intellectual projects were influential, but the weaknesses of the Carolingian state worked against him. He was not viewed as the imposing warrior his father had been, so soldiers looked elsewhere for glory and loot. And his sons, impatient to rule, rebelled against him in his lifetime. They eventually forced him to abdicate, and under the principle of partible inheritance, in 843 they divided the empire among them in an agreement called the Treaty of Verdun.

The Frankish empire became three territories: the Kingdom of the West Franks (west of the Rhine River), the Kingdom of the East Franks (east of the Rhine), and a middle region called Lotharingia that included Italy. None of Louis's sons found the settlement acceptable, and their need for more land to reward their supporters ensured further conflict. When they died, their own sons faced diminished holdings, and an ever-increasing need to wage war ensured that the stability of the kingdoms weakened. Thus, Charlemagne and Louis's efforts to resurrect the Roman Empire as a Christian state guided by Germanic leaders crumbled.

These internal problems were worsened by external ones, especially new invaders emboldened by the collapse of Carolingian strength. From the east came nomadic raiders, the Magyars, a non-Germanic people who migrated from the steppes of central Asia. At the end of the ninth century, they settled in what is today Hungary, and from there they launched devastating raids for plunder into Germany. Only in 955 did the German king Otto the Great manage to break the power of the Magyars at the Battle of Lechfeld. From the south, the fragmentation of Islamic political unity led petty rulers to raid the now-weakened coasts of Christian Europe. North African dynasties like the Aghlabids pushed into Sicily in the ninth century, and by 846, Islamic raiders had sacked churches on the outskirts of Rome.

Perhaps more famous today than the Magyars and Islamic raiders were the Norse who raided northern Europe from Scandinavia, called the Vikings. The peoples of Scandinavia, who spoke Germanic languages, had a culture similar to that of the Germanic peoples who settled in the Roman Empire. For example, Scandinavians were polytheistic, worshipping gods like Odin and Freyja who were similar to earlier Germanic deities like Wodan and Frigg. The aristocracy practiced polygyny (having many wives), and local chieftains rewarded their followers with lands and gifts. The growth of the population in the eighth century and the relative lack of arable land in Scandinavia compelled groups of Danes, Norwegians, and Swedes to travel in search of plunder. Some went eastward, using their shallow-drought ships (ships that could navigate rivers), and made trading connections along the Dnieper River, establishing settlements at Kiev that eventually became one of the first Russian states. They reached Constantinople, and some served as the personal bodyguard to the Byzantine ruler. These Vikings were known as Varangians, and they settled in eastern Europe. Although violent, they were also traders, interested in paving the way for new settlements and connections beyond western Europe.

In the west, the arrival of the Norse raiders was less benign. They attacked in small groups that could travel far upriver and surprise settlements, destroy them, and be gone before resistance could be organized. They specifically targeted churches and monasteries, not only for their loot but also because they lacked defenses. Vikings destroyed the monastery of Lindisfarne in the Anglo-Saxon kingdom of Northumbria, which had been a celebrated center of learning. Their reputation for ferocity may have been exaggerated by clerical authors, but the sudden nature of the violent raids, and the inability of Frankish or Anglo-Saxon armies to defeat them, instilled fear in the population of western Europe.

Eventually, the Norse raiders began to settle in regions rather than just raid them. In 865, a substantial army of Vikings invaded Britain and destroyed most of the Anglo-Saxon kingdoms except for Wessex. In 911, they settled in northern France, establishing the duchy of Normandy. By the end of the tenth century, Vikings had also established settlements throughout the British Isles, including Ireland and Scotland, farther west in Iceland and Greenland, and even (though briefly) in North America. Not just raiders, they promoted trade throughout northern Europe and beyond, extending their trading routes to the Byzantine Empire and the Abbasid Caliphate. Like the earlier Germanic peoples, they eventually converted to Roman Christianity, and their kings began to build more centralized kingdoms that enabled them to curb the violence of the raiders. Their conversion did not mean a wholesale abandonment of their existing culture and tradition. Early Scandinavian churches were decorated with images of heroes and villains from Norse mythology. This overlap of tradition and innovation reflects the persistence of cultural exchange between Germanic peoples and Greek and Roman cultures that created the foundation for medieval society.

BEYOND THE BOOK

Norse Art and Christian Architecture

Stave churches were Christian churches built in Scandinavia early in the period of conversion to Christianity. Their interior and exterior decoration often depicted themes and images from the pre-Christian era, such as heroes from the sagas of the Vikings. The Borgund Stave Church, built around 1200 in Norway, is adorned with four dragon heads on the top ridges of the roof (Figure 13.7).

FIGURE 13.7 Borgund Stave Church. This nineteenth-century rendering of Borgund Stave Church was made by the Norwegian author Christian Tønsberg. (credit: "Franz Wilhelm Schiertz Borgunds Kirke i Lærdal i Sogn" by Norge fremstillet i Tegninger fra Digitalarkivet/Wikimedia Commons, Public Domain)

- Why would people converting to Christianity want to keep art and imagery from their earlier history?
- Why would Christian clergy accept pre-Christian images to decorate their churches?
- What appeal and use would such imagery have for both the religious authorities and the patrons who designed medieval churches? What about for the newly converted?

In the ashes of the Carolingian world, medieval Europe embraced a social system called **feudalism** that emerged from the basic need for security and was defined by unequal relationships. Looking to protect their territories and their peasants, lords began to grant lands to fighters as their *fiefs*, whose produce the warriors could enjoy so long as they served the lord. For their part, fighters became *vassals* of the lord, sworn to perform service in exchange for the land. This service was chiefly military in nature, but it could also include other obligations like advising the lord and attending his court when called. Bishoprics and monasteries behaved the same way; abbots and abbesses could be lords who were owed service and also owed service to greater lords.

While feudalism was not a political system, warriors owed service to lords who owed service to the king, who in theory was the largest landowner in the kingdom and the guarantor of rights and privileges. For example, the late Carolingian king Charles the Simple granted the Duchy of Normandy to the Viking leader Rollo, so long as Rollo protected northern France from other Vikings. However, the need to placate their feudal lords ensured that kings gave away lands and privileges, often weakening them and driving them to look for ways to maximize their resources. They might consider advantageous marriages, for example, in which women were expected to bring a dowery of property or money. In other cases, crushing rebellious vassals was a way of taking back needed land.

On their fiefs, the warriors oversaw the work of agricultural laborers. Some laborers might own their own land and be self-directed, but most in western Europe were unfree, servile laborers called **serfs** who were tied to the land. They were not enslaved and could not be bought or sold, but they occupied the lowest rung of the social ladder, could be physically abused by the lord, were forced to provide labor and goods for the lord, and rarely had any rights a lord was obligated to acknowledge. All these limitations existed despite the serfs' being the largest class of people in European society at the time (Figure 13.8).

FIGURE 13.8 Medieval European Society. This illuminated initial letter from a thirteenth-century French manuscript shows the key members of the medieval European social order: a member of the clergy, a warrior, and a laborer (left to right). (credit: "Cleric-Knight-Workman/MS Sloane 2435, folio 85" by British Library/Wikimedia Commons, Public Domain)

The lord was required to protect the serfs, resolve their disputes, and administer their work. Serfs owed their lord a set number of days of service a year (these were many) and could not leave the land, marry, or undertake other work without the lord's permission. Under **manorialism** or the manor system, named for the manor house occupied by the lord, serfs (or other varieties of servile, unfree workers) were brought together into villages where their labor could be cooperative. They tended both their own and their lord's land, sharing draft animals and farm implements to undertake the planting and harvesting of crops. Women tended smaller livestock and vegetable gardens near their homes. Although cities on the coast often maintained commercial or networking ties with each other, society in western Europe was overwhelmingly rural, and production was largely at the subsistence level. People produced what they were going to consume, and surplus went to the lord or the church as a mandatory tax, usually 10 percent, called the *tithe*.

This system of social obligations and ties between the serfs and their lords, and the lords and the kings, framed the economic and political world of the Middle Ages. By the tenth century, the old Roman Empire was largely forgotten by the general population, while medieval kings and nobles had reimaged and transformed the idea of the Roman Empire to serve and legitimize their own purposes. A new society began to emerge based on a combination of Roman, Christian, and Germanic traditions.

Religion and Society in Medieval Europe

While Christianity had developed in an atmosphere of antagonism to the Roman state, by the fifth century, the church had become the preserver of classical Greek and Roman law, literature, and philosophical ideas. Language and cultural differences existed between the eastern and western churches, and in the eighth century, their political and theological ties became strained. One dispute was over the use of images in Christian worship, which the popes supported but some emperors rejected. The popes had also been building up an argument for their supremacy over the church, based partly in scripture and partly in tradition. Early medieval popes like Leo I laid the groundwork for the power of the Bishops of Rome, a power the eastern churches largely rejected or ignored. Once they had made an alliance with the Frankish kings, however, the popes looked to western Europe for the church's future.

The papacy was not the only church institution in Europe; local traditions and needs shaped a variety of Christian beliefs and practices in the early Middle Ages. There were three ways in which the church helped transform the old Roman world into the new. First, the institutional church, often under the guidance of the popes, worked to convert the Germanic peoples to Christianity. Second, it helped to preserve the classical tradition. Finally, it worked with the new rulers to help legitimize their rule and Christianize their populations.

Missionary work was undertaken by men and women devoted to Christian beliefs and intent on incorporating new peoples into the society of Christian nations. Pope Gregory (also known as Gregory the Great) commissioned monks from Italy, led by Augustine of Canterbury, to convert the Anglo-Saxons. (Monks are men who do not marry, often live in community with each other, and devote their lives to serving God. Their female counterparts are called nuns.) The laity (nonclergy) often engaged in missionary work, and the wives of kings were especially influential in promoting widespread conversion to Christianity. Contemporaries noted the success of Clothilde's persuasion in the conversion of her husband King Clovis, and Bertha, the wife of King Ethelbert of Kent, likewise encouraged her husband to convert. Both supported the efforts of the missionary (and later bishop) Augustine of Canterbury. Missionaries often worked closely with Christian rulers, whose conversion could be critical in expanding the frontiers of Catholic Christianity.

Monasticism (the way monks live and their communal institutions) had developed in the Mediterranean world and flourished in western Europe among religious men and women. The most influential monastic leader was Benedict of Nursia, who composed a guidebook or "rule" for monastic life that stressed moderation, a balance between prayer and useful work, the self-sufficiency of communities, and enough education for monks to copy out books in Latin. Many communities were "double monasteries," containing a community of men and a community of women and often operating under the regulation of an abbess. Monasticism gave women a role in society that was not based on their relationship to a father or husband, and some women enjoyed considerable influence as abbesses. Radegund was a Frankish queen who fled the court when her husband murdered her brother. She became famous as the founder and abbess of the Monastery of the Holy Cross in Poitiers and was widely venerated as a saint after her death. Women like Radegund found religious life preferable to the intrigue of the court and the whims of a violent husband (Figure 13.9).

FIGURE 13.9 Queen Radegund. This eleventh-century image shows Radegund, queen of the Franks and later founder of a monastery, seated with a book, demonstrating her learning and piety. Religious women like Radegund were influential in the Middle Ages. (credit: "Saint Radegonde" by Poitiers Municipal Library/Wikimedia Commons, Public Domain)

Monastic communities were often critical to the preservation of learning in the post-Roman world. There, monks copied out books by hand to foster the work of missionaries and preserve knowledge they thought was useful from the ancient world. Monasteries also served as refuges in times of crisis and could become valued centers of administration and nodes in communications networks. They were often the only place for the training of priests to serve newly converted peoples. While bishops were the undisputed authorities, especially the bishop of Rome (the pope), monasticism was equally crucial for both missionary work and the development of a Christian population.

Finally, Christianity helped legitimize new rulers. Germanic kings could better integrate themselves with their Roman population once they converted to the Catholic Christianity their subjects practiced. Bishops could serve as administrators, and monasteries were places of education for the new elite. One issue raised by the career of Charlemagne, though, was the relationship between rulers and the papacy. Leo III had crowned Charlemagne, and clergy often performed an anointing ceremony when a king was invested with the symbols of office.

Aside from the rivalry between the eastern and western churches, an important non-Christian religion was present in the form of Judaism, which was given latitude by the Romans on account of its antiquity. With the collapse of Rome and the growing dominion of Catholic Christianity, however, Jewish communities faced new challenges as clergy and kings instituted restrictions on their behavior and practices. Christians often viewed Jewish people as outsiders no matter how long they may have lived in a given area. The mistaken belief that Jewish people were to blame for the death of Jesus led to rumors that they wanted to harm Christians. In some cases, as in Visigothic Spain, Jewish residents faced the threat of either converting to Christianity or being expelled from the kingdom. Hostility was never uniform, however, and kings like Louis the Pious granted Jewish people considerable freedoms. Rulers might also feel compelled to protect Jewish communities because of their connections, especially trade connections, to other communities across the Mediterranean. Still, the position of Jewish communities in the Middle Ages was often precarious.

The Iberian Peninsula and the World of Al-Andalus

Like the Ostrogoths, Visigoth rulers attempted to emulate Roman institutions in Spain by creating written law codes, but their relationship with their Hispano-Roman subjects was largely uneasy, and unlike Theodoric and Clovis, they tended to remain apart from them. The Visigoths were Arian Christians who tolerated their non-Arian subjects, but the need to better integrate themselves with the population eventually compelled King Recared to convert to Catholicism and gain the support of the church. In 711, however, the armies of the Umayyad Caliphate crossed the Strait of Gibraltar and overran the kingdom.

The Umayyad armies that invaded Spain never succeeded in controlling the entire peninsula, just as the Visigoths had not. Christian kingdoms persisted in the north, though they were weak and often fought with each other. Another reason was that non-Arabic soldiers, like the North African Amazigh (Berbers), always felt shortchanged when Arab leaders divided the spoils of conquest. This ethnic and regional conflict played an important role in the collapse of the Umayyad dynasty, but it also led an offshoot of it to take root in Spain.

The Muslims called the region Al-Andalus, and it was governed by members of the Umayyad dynasty who had fled the collapse of their power when the Abbasid dynasty overthrew them. Abd al-Rahman I, fleeing the destruction of his family in Syria, capitalized on the discontent felt by non-Arab soldiers following the conquest of Spain. With their help, he was able to build alliances and defeat his enemies to become the ruler of Al-Andalus. He established his capital at the city of Cordoba and began to form a new society, based on Islamic law and dedicated to expanding into Christian territory. Abd al-Rahman and his successors created a remarkable community that was multireligious and multiethnic and that sustained diplomatic and commercial ties throughout the Mediterranean world and beyond, a testament to the global context of the early Middle Ages. Soon Cordoba rivaled Constantinople and Baghdad as a center of trade, learning, and the arts. Connections to North Africa and the Middle East ensured the revival of trade and, consequently, the revival of urban life (Figure 13.10).

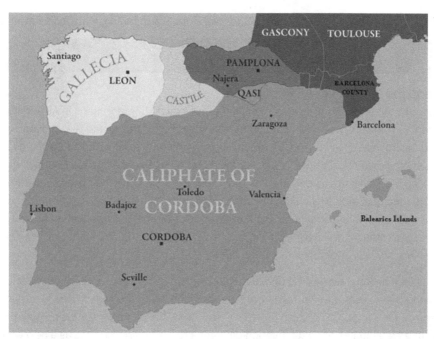

FIGURE 13.10 Medieval Cordoba. This map shows (in green) the extent of the Caliphate of Cordoba in Iberia at its height in the tenth century, but with Christian kingdoms still controlling the north. (credit: "Al Andalus & Christian Kingdoms" by Alexandre Vigo/Wikimedia Commons, CC0 1.0)

Many Christians there, whether they converted or not, adopted Islamic culture by speaking Arabic, dressing as their Amazigh and Arab rulers did, and adopting their practices. For this reason, they are called "Mozarabs." In some ways, this period, in which Christians, Muslims, and Jewish people lived and worked in proximity, is a good example of medieval toleration, but violence by the dominant group, as we have seen in the conflict between Arians and Catholics, was always possible.

Al-Andalus reached its peak in the tenth century. It was a dynamic society whose population prospered and created its own hybrid culture from the ways of the ethnic and religious peoples who lived in the Iberian Peninsula. Under Abd al-Rahman III, trade expanded into sub-Saharan Africa and across the Mediterranean. This link to the broader Mediterranean world enabled contacts that were often absent from the Germanic kingdoms and brought new agricultural goods like citrus fruit, sugar, and cotton to the peninsula from as far away as India. Cordoba became famed for its orange, lime, and lemon groves.

The growth of trade and commerce also encouraged the revival of cities, another difference from the Germanic kingdoms. By the year 1000, for example, Cordoba had nearly 100,000 inhabitants, making it one of the most populous cities in Europe. Its close connections to the Mediterranean world brought scholars, craftspeople, merchants, and emigrants in greater numbers than to the Germanic north. Even so, Germanic merchants and traders also made connections with Spanish states, those ruled by Christians and by Muslims.

The caliphs established schools of Islamic jurisprudence and hired scholars and linguists to help administer the kingdom. These scholars scoured Spain for older Greek and Latin manuscripts to translate. Jewish and Christian scholars also found the caliphate a place of learning, and a flowering of Jewish religious thought and poetry developed. Under Islamic law, Christians and Jewish people were considered "protected." This meant that because they also believed in one God, they could not be compelled to convert so long as they did not challenge the beliefs of Muslims. Some historians have viewed this period of toleration, now called *convivencia* ("living together"), as a particular example of coexistence and nonviolent interaction among people of different faiths. The antagonism of the Christian kingdoms in the north, however, and the growth of zealous Islamic leaders in North Africa show that once again, while toleration was always possible, it depended on the presence of willing leaders for whom peace was desirable. When conflict between Christians and Muslins was exacerbated, religious tensions could make toleration less desirable. Islamic dynasties and Christian rulers who found religious identity a source of inspiration for warriors, for instance, whittled away at *convivencia*.

DUELING VOICES

Convivencia and the Memory of Al-Andalus

Convivencia describes the time during the early Middle Ages in which different faiths in Al-Andalus experienced a peaceful coexistence. The name was developed in the early twentieth century and is associated with the Spanish historian Américo Castro, who believed the toleration he saw in the medieval world could serve as a contrast to the political and ethnic problems in his own time. For example, rulers like the famous Rodrigo "El Cid" de Vivar found it wise to keep both Muslim and Christian allies in order to consolidate their control over territory. Muslim rulers also found it difficult to simply wipe out Christian kingdoms in the north, so compromises were made between religious goals and political realities that permitted toleration to exist between Christians, Muslims, and Jewish people. Seen in this light, medieval Spain offered an example of people of different ethnicities and religions living in harmony.

When the last Muslim kingdom fell in 1492, Christian rulers reversed course and instituted policies of intolerance to ensure that Catholicism became a central part of Spanish identity. For this reason, the history of Spain could be written in terms of the triumph of Spanish Christians over non-Christian communities. Some historians instead point to Al-Andalus as a period of general toleration between groups, of *convivencia*, as a new way of framing Spain's history. Still others believe this is a romanticized view of a period when religious hostility contributed to armed conflict and violence. The legacy of Al-Andalus and *convivencia* is still being shaped by modern conversations about religion, toleration, community identity, and the past.

- What conditions favored religious toleration in the early medieval examples you have encountered so far? What conditions tended to push rulers to demand greater religious conformity?
- Why would religion be so important to identity in the medieval world?

Despite the ongoing toleration that rulers of one faith could show to subjects of another, conflicts between rulers of different faiths persisted. The Islamic rulers of Al-Andalus succeeded in disrupting the Christian kingdoms in the north of the peninsula until the eleventh century. For example, in the 990s, the powerful general al-Mansur sacked Barcelona on the eastern coast and Leon in the northwest, both important centers of Christian political power. Despite its successes in the north, however, the Caliphate of Cordoba collapsed due to infighting after the death of al-Mansur, and regional aristocrats broke up the unity of Al-Andalus, creating smaller successor states that often fought as much against each other (and in alliance with Christian fighters) as against Christianity. The conflicts in the eleventh century were still largely about knights, fast-moving heavily armored soldiers on horseback, winning plunder and fame, but the stage was set for wars of cultural conquest and the struggle for religious supremacy. The destruction of the Christian states in Spain had gained the attention of the popes, and this helped shape the church's promotion of a religiously sanctioned fight against Islam.

LINK TO LEARNING

Use this link to hear a journalist interview people about the legacy of toleration (https://openstax.org/l/77alandalus) during the period of Muslim rule in Spain, when it was called Al-Andalus. Note how the issues of toleration and acceptance shape the way people view the past.

13.2 The Seljuk Migration and the Call from the East

LEARNING OBJECTIVES

By the end of this section, you will be able to:
- Explain why the Islamic world began to fragment along political and religious lines
- Contrast the Fatimids and Seljuks with other Islamic states
- Discuss the challenges the Byzantine Empire faced prior to the First Crusade

The Abbasid Caliphate was a remarkable state that increased both the wealth of Islam and Muslims communities' contacts with peoples across Afro-Eurasia, from China to sub-Saharan Africa. Wealthy, cosmopolitan, and deeply influenced by Persian culture, the Abbasid caliphs invested heavily in reviving science and literature. However, the complications of ruling a large empire ensured that challengers from within the empire and beyond would eventually wear them down. The Abbasids, their Islamic competitors, and a powerful new Turkic empire set the stage for conflict with the Byzantine Empire and the Christian kingdoms of Europe.

The Breakdown of Abbasid Authority and the Turkic Migration

Having overthrown the Umayyad caliphs, the Abbasid rulers moved east, establishing a capital at Baghdad. There the ruling elite were able to foster a time of immense creativity and intellectual achievement that allowed cultures, languages, and ethnicities to blend in the course of building an empire.

The Abbasid Caliphate kept intact the Persian and Byzantine administrative apparatus, which ensured wealth for the elite and promoted the revival of cities and trade. While Arabic continued as the language of administration and religion, Persian language and literary forms also began to influence Arabic and helped to create a rich tradition of both secular and religious works, housed at the Great Library of Baghdad. The caliphate became cosmopolitan. Syriac Christians translated Greek works into Arabic, Persians served as administrators, and Jewish people and Christians alike were bankers and physicians. Wealth flowed in from the trading routes that connected the Mediterranean with India and China, and Baghdad became the center of the empire, a cosmopolitan city with a reputation as a place of learning, commerce, and trade. (Figure 13.11)

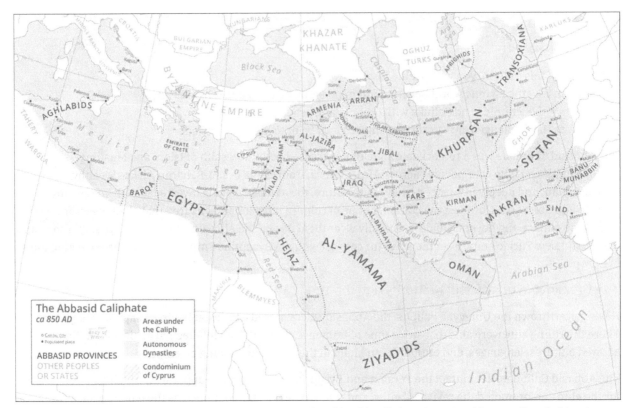

FIGURE 13.11 The Abbasid Caliphate. This map shows the Abbasid Caliphate in 850, with areas listed either by their regional name in Arabic or by the ruling dynasty. The caliphate stretched from the territory in North Africa held by the Aghlabids in the west to the region of Transoxiana in the east. The heartland was in Iraq in the center. (credit: modification of work "Abbasid Caliphate 850AD" by "Cattette"/Wikimedia Commons, CC BY 4.0)

The early Abbasid caliphs were successful in establishing a centralized administration and easing some of the ethnic tension that had undone the Umayyad dynasty. Other problems went unresolved, however, and new ones arose that the Abbasid rulers struggled to manage. To create an army that was loyal solely to the Abbasid ruler, early ninth-century caliphs began to use enslaved men of Turkic origins. These soldiers, called **mamluks**, were often young boys taken from their homes, converted to Islam, and trained as soldiers. Their education was provided and their social status assured; in return, they were expected to be loyal to the caliph alone.

The mamluks were initially useful for quelling rebellions, attacking Byzantine rivals, and enabling caliphs such as al-Mutasim to gain some security against hostile aristocrats. Al-Mutasim's predecessors had tried to strike a balance between Persian and Arab elites, but his own power rested on the militaristic force of the mamluks. The wealth and favor shown the military, however, and especially to these Turkic soldiers, only served to erode the caliph's position with the traditional elite. To solve this problem, al-Mutasim moved his capital from Baghdad to Samarra in northern Mesopotamia in order to segregate the Turkic soldiers from the rest of the population. After his death, the mamluks supported different successors in a vicious civil war that lasted nearly ten years. Their power and influence had become a permanent fixture in the Abbasid heartland.

The Abbasid rulers also faced religious divisions and criticism, even as the cosmopolitan nature of the caliphate sparked the growth of speculative philosophy and rationalizing thought. For example, philosophers like al-Farabi and Ibn Sina delved deeply into the philosophy of the ancient Greeks, including their systems of logic and medicine. They promoted new ways of approaching philosophy and made contributions to science, law, and theology that later influenced the thought of Christian philosophers in Europe. These Islamic scholars translated ancient philosophical texts into Arabic that Christian scholars later translated into Latin. However, the fact that these two leading figures were not Arabs, and that they applied human reason to the truths of

Islam, antagonized religious conservatives and fostered discontent with the worldly caliphs. The Abbasid cultural renaissance was a remarkable achievement, but the Abbasid leadership was not celebrated by all.

One of the most important and enduring religious developments in the Abbasid period was the growth of a mystical form of Islam known as **Sufism**. Sufism was organized into "brotherhoods," each of which followed the teachings and practices of its founders in the pursuit of heartfelt and personal worship of God. Sufis behaved like monks in other religions, renouncing the artificial performance of religious duties, as well as luxury and worldliness, to embrace a life dedicated to mystical union with God. Some Sufis also rejected the rationalization of religion and criticized the incorporation of Greek philosophy into Islamic theology. Though Sufism was not a political movement, its search for spiritual purity and rejection of classical philosophy weakened the position of the Abbasids.

IN THEIR OWN WORDS

Poetry from the Abbasid Period

Omar Khayyam was a mathematician, philosopher, and poet who lived during the transition from Abbasid rule to the rise of the Seljuk Turks. He is famous for writing poetry that was often controversial in its day, so much so that he was accused of being irreligious at the Seljuk court. For example, drinking wine was forbidden by the Quran, but Khayyam often refers to drinking wine in terms that seem both literal and metaphorical. Other contemporaries viewed his poetry as reflecting the Sufi value of moving beyond external religious conformity to a more personal spirituality.

Following are excerpts from his most famous work, *The Rubaiyat*. Khayyam uses imagery related to drinking to express both the joy of life and its fleeting nature. He also considers life experience more precious than formal education, showing a disdain for the teachings of sages and scholars. (Note: The word *sans* is French for "without," and a *muezzin* is the person who makes the call to prayer five times a day at a mosque.)

> XXI
> Lo! some we loved, the loveliest and best
> That Time and Fate or all their Vintage pressed,
> Have drunk their Cup a Round or two before,
> And one by one crept silently to rest.
> XXII
> And we, that now make merry in the Room
> They left, and Summer dresses in new bloom,
> Ourselves must we beneath the Couch of Earth
> Descend- ourselves to make a Couch- for whom?
> XXIII
> Ah, make the most of what we yet may spend,
> Before we too into Dust descend;
> Dust into Dust, and under Dust to lie,
> Sans Wine, sans Song, sans Singer, and- sans End!
> XXIV
> Alike for those who TO-DAY prepare
> And those that after some TO-MORROW stare,
> A Muzzein from the Tower of Darkness cries,
> "Fools, your Reward is neither Here nor There"
> XXV
> Why, all the Saints and Sages who discuss'd
> Of the Two Worlds so wisely- they are thrust

> Like foolish Prophets forth, their Words to Scorn
> Are scatter'd, and their Mouths are stopt with Dust.
>
> —Omar Khayyam, *The Rubaiyat of Omar Khayyam*, translated by Edmund Fitzgerald

- What does Khayyam mean when he speaks of the "Couch of Earth" in XXII?
- In the lines of XXV, why does he chide "Saints and Sages?" What might be his issue with these wise or holy men?

As the Abbasid rulers struggled to maintain control over the heartland in Mesopotamia and Persia, the political and cultural unity of the Islamic world began to decline. Dynasties that viewed the Abbasids as too corrupt or too distant began to splinter off. In Spain and North Africa, the Amazigh Idrisid dynasty in Morocco and the Aghlabids in Algeria drifted away from Abbasid control. On the eastern fringes, Persian and Turkic dynasties openly contested the authority of the Abbasid Caliphate without formally dissolving it. This process of growing disunity is called political devolution, in which powers once assumed by a centralized state are taken over by local authorities.

The worldliness of the Abbasid culture offended religious conservatives. For example, the scholar al-Ghazali criticized the incorporation of Greek speculative thought when speaking of Islamic beliefs. The caliphs' support for Persian culture and literature, as well as the power given to Persian families and scholars, alienated the Arab elites. An entrenched and powerful bureaucracy, as well as the use of the mamluks, made the Abbasid government look corrupt and weak. The most significant blow to Abbasid power was the ability of rivals to establish their own states and claim the title of caliph, as well as the arrival of powerful Turkic tribes like the Seljuks in the Abbasid heartland.

The Fatimid Caliphate and the Seljuk Sultanate

The Abbasids had overthrown the Umayyads with support from non-Arabs who felt cheated of the spoils of conquest, and from Shia Muslims who were opposed to the Umayyads for religious and political reasons. The Abbasids then worked to address the grievances held by different sections of Islamic society. Despite their best efforts, however, the size and complexity of the empire and the various political, ethnic, and religious tensions within it blunted the caliphs' effectiveness. Power often rested in the hands of local governors, who exploited regional tensions or weaknesses to establish their own dynasties and even their own rival caliphates, as in Al-Andalus. In Persia and on the eastern frontiers, dynasties close to Baghdad threatened the Abbasids themselves.

This process of political devolution became critical in the rise of rivals who seized Abbasid territory. Muslim factions also sought to wrest power from the caliphs or replace them altogether. Two of the most important rivals for control were the Fatimids and the Seljuk Turks.

The Fatimid Caliphate

Observing the challenges the Abbasids faced on the eastern frontier, and the success of the Umayyad Caliphate in Spain, the early tenth-century Shia leader Abu Muhammad Abdullah declared himself the proper leader of the Shia and successor to Muhammad's son-in-law Ali. Not all Shia agreed; Abdullah's claims to be descended from Ali were questionable. His leadership and charisma, however, along with the support of dedicated Amazigh soldiers, helped him establish the first and only Shia caliphate in North Africa in 910, which challenged the political power of the Abbasids and their religious influence.

The state Abu Muhammad Abdullah established is called the Fatimid Caliphate because his dynasty claimed descent through Ali's wife and the Islamic prophet Muhammad's daughter Fatima. The Fatimid caliphs also claimed to be imams, Shia with spiritual authority over Muslims, based on either their biological descent from Ali or their manifestation of God's will on earth. In 969, the Fatimids conquered Egypt, which became the center of a powerful state that controlled most of North Africa. Then they began to threaten the Abbasid heartland by taking Syria and parts of the Arabian Peninsula, including the holy city of Mecca (Figure 13.12).

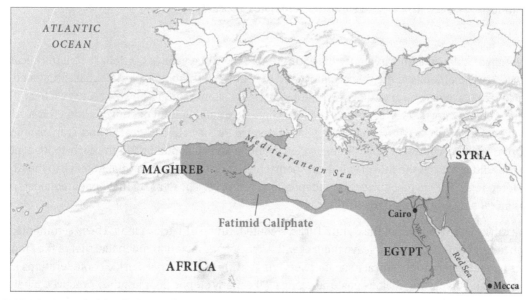

FIGURE 13.12 The Fatimid Caliphate. The tenth-century Fatimid Caliphate (in pink) was based in North Africa with its capital of Cairo in Egypt, but it managed to take control of the holy city of Mecca on the Arabian Peninsula. (attribution: Copyright Rice University, OpenStax, under CC BY 4.0 license)

The Shia believed their caliphs held not just secular authority but also spiritual power and insight as imams. This concept was different from the Abbasid view in which the caliph was meant to lead the faithful but was not a spiritual guide. Thus, in the Fatimid Caliphate, the ruler's religious view could lead to arbitrary (or eccentric) leadership. For example, Abu Muhammad Abdallah encouraged the Fatimid concept of caliph by taking the title of al-Mahdi, denoting an apocalyptic figure who would vanquish evil and usher in the end of time. Caliph al-Hakim bi-Amr Allah intensified preaching against the Sunnis and instituted restrictive measures on Christians and Jewish people. Rumors persisted that he considered himself divine, and his sudden disappearance at age thirty-five added to his religious mystique. Despite their religious view of the caliph, the Shi'ites were tolerant of other faiths, and Christians and Jewish people occupied important administrative posts (Figure 13.13).

FIGURE 13.13 A Fatimid Gold Coin. This tenth-century gold coin from the rule of Abu Muhammad Abdullah was issued under his royal name of al-Mahdi. Coins were an important way of ensuring his subjects understood his claims to spiritual authority. (credit: "Calif al Mahdi Kairouan 912 CE" by "PHGCOM"/Wikimedia Commons, CC0 1.0)

As a powerful state and religious rival, the Fatimid Caliphate posed an existential threat to the Abbasids. Seeing how powerless the Abbasids were to prevent the loss of North Africa, the Umayyad emir of Al-Andalus declared himself to be caliph of a third state, the Caliphate of Cordoba.

The Seljuk Empire

The devolution of Abbasid authority under the Fatimids and the Umayyads at Cordoba is striking because both dynasties had rival claimants to the title of caliph, and the Fatimids established a state that threatened Sunni Islam. This breakdown of central authority was not limited to distant regions, however. By the late ninth century, the Abbasids permitted, or were forced to accept, the establishment of emirs within their territory. A dynasty called the Samanids controlled the regions of eastern Persia called Khorasan and Transoxiana, and the Buyid dynasty took control of Abbasid territories in Persia and Mesopotamia in the early tenth century. Although they did not claim the title of caliph for themselves, they paid only minimal homage to the Abbasid state and forced its rulers to recognize their independent authority. The dynasty that benefited most from this chaos was an outside group called the Seljuks.

The Seljuk Turks were a branch of the Oghuz Turks, a confederation of Turkic clans. These seminomadic clans could form larger confederations or leave them at will, a type of organization much like that of the Mongols. The Oghuz had migrated from central Asia after surviving conflicts with other Turkic confederations in the eighth century and displacing various pastoral groups. Like many steppe peoples, they practiced a polytheistic religion, with a hierarchy of gods and spirits headed by Tengri the sky god. Specialists called shamans were believed to possess powers to negotiate for favor and fortune with these deities.

The initial contact between the Oghuz and the world of Islam was not peaceful. Raids between the two became the source of enslaved men who served the Abbasids as mamluks. The Seljuk dynasty is named for the clan leader Saljuq, who moved south from the Oghuz state in the tenth century and came into contact, often violent, with other Turkic peoples and Abbasid emirs. The leaders of the Seljuks converted to Islam, a development that may have been a source of conflict with the Oghuz but drew them into the orbit of the Abbasids. Under leaders like Tughril, they began to establish their own state within and beyond the Abbasid domains in the eleventh century. They drove off other Turkic peoples in Afghanistan, pushing them toward India. They fought successfully against the Byzantine Empire and some of its client states, especially the Kingdom of Georgia. Under Alp Arslan, they seized Anatolia from the Byzantines and posed an existential threat to Constantinople. By the middle of the eleventh century, the Seljuks had created an empire through conquest that extended from India to the Mediterranean (Figure 13.14).

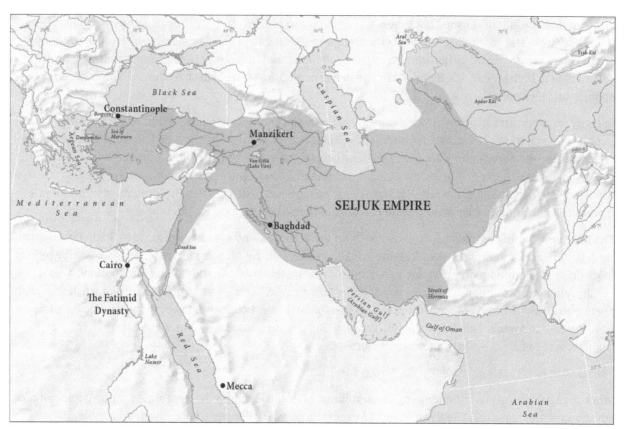

FIGURE 13.14 The Seljuk Empire. The Seljuk Empire (in green) extended from India to Anatolia, taking territory away from the Byzantine Empire and ruling over Persia, Mesopotamia, Syria, and much of Anatolia." (attribution: Copyright Rice University, OpenStax, under CC BY 4.0 license)

The Seljuk leaders did not take the title of caliph from the Abbasids but instead adopted the name **sultan**, meaning "the authority." Because they were new converts to Islam who were not Arabs and had no connection to the family of Muhammad, the title of caliph seemed out of their reach. They acknowledged the position of the caliph, but real authority was in their own hands. Eager to show their zeal by fighting against Christians and Fatimids, the Seljuks now controlled the heart of the Islamic civilization, and considerable Byzantine territory.

The Seljuks built their legitimacy by defending Sunni Islam and investing in cultural and artistic projects. They built mosques and supported the work of religious scholars and missionaries. The famous philosopher al-Ghazali served in the courts of Seljuk sultans. Despite his opposition to the way Ibn Sina (known in the West as Avicenna) had applied Greek logic to matters of faith, he nevertheless worked in natural sciences and mathematics. Like the Abbasids before them, the Seljuks patronized the arts and built mosques, madrasas, and palaces. They supported the work of scholars like the mathematician and poet Omar Khayyam. Like the earlier Arab conquerors, they also adopted Persian as a literary language and embraced urban living.

They participated in the exchange of culture, and the promotion of Islamic cultural institutions revolved around the courts of the aristocracy, mosques, and madrasas. The Seljuks also stand out as promoters of the caravansaries, inns along the trade routes that had long offered a safe place to stay for those traveling long distances.

LINK TO LEARNING

Caravansaries were an important element of travel and trade in the medieval world, serving merchants, diplomats, and pilgrims as hubs for news and rest. In this video, more information about caravansaries (https://openstax.org/l/77caravansary) is presented, including their architecture and the services they offered.

Strict Sunnis, the sultans pushed back the Shia Fatimids and took control of Jerusalem and eventually Mecca. While they were still generally tolerant of other religions like Judaism and Christianity, they ensured that Sunni Islam was dominant by insisting on regular payments from non-Muslim communities and by refusing to permit Shia in high offices. The Seljuks' success in fighting against Christian states fueled claims of religious oppression in western Europe.

In many ways, the arrival of the Turkic peoples and their conversion to Islam helped to revive the fortunes of Sunni Islam and the fight against Christian states. Despite the victories of leaders like Alp Arslan, however, by the end of the eleventh century, conflicts over the succession were taking their toll. Members of the dynasty began to fight each other and break the empire into smaller states. One of the most important successor states was established in Anatolia, near the Byzantine Empire, and was called the Seljuk Sultanate of Rum, a name that reflects the region's past as part of the Roman and then the Byzantine Empires.

The infighting among the Seljuks, their conflict with the Fatimids, and the rival caliphate in Spain fragmented the Islamic world. Attempts by the Abbasids to take effective control of their empire led to more complications for Seljuk rule. Fatimid power was threatened by internal instability when the caliphs incorporated Turkic cavalry, alienating traditional Amazigh cavalry. The Islamic world continued to produce brilliant scholars and poets who engaged with Persian, ancient Greek, and Indian ideas. Politically, however, the Islamic kingdoms were divided and weak. This fragmentation enabled Christians from western Europe to establish their own colonies in the Islamic world by means of the Crusades.

The Battle of Manzikert and the Call from the East

While the Islamic world was undergoing the devolution of Abbasid power, the Byzantine Empire could not take advantage of its weakness. The Byzantines had experienced an earlier period of cultural and military dominance under the powerful Macedonian dynasty (867–1025), whose warrior-emperors had been able to push back against Muslims to the east and Slavic peoples to the west. The resulting stability had brought a period of cultural production and innovation sometimes called the Macedonian Renaissance. Its artwork later influenced Italian art and anticipated developments in the Italian Renaissance (Figure 13.15).

FIGURE 13.15 The Macedonian Renaissance. This image is from a tenth-century illuminated manuscript made in Constantinople and called the Paris Psalter (for its current location). It depicts the biblical King David (seated with harp) composing psalms or sacred songs. The realism of the setting and the individualized faces and postures were innovations of the art of the Macedonian era. (credit: "Paris Psalter" by Bibliothèque nationale de France/Wikimedia Commons, Public Domain)

At the end of the Macedonian period, the Byzantine emperor's ability to navigate the economic and military situation deteriorated. Ineffective rulers and conflict over successors to the Macedonian dynasty rendered the empire less militarily capable. The Byzantines also lost control of their overseas territories, especially southern Italy and Sicily, which had been sources of trade and revenue. Islamic and Italian navies began to dominate trade in the Mediterranean. As direct trade between the Christian West and the Islamic world increased, the economic position of the Byzantine Empire as an intermediary began to decline. Byzantine rulers attempted to establish marriage alliances with Slavic rulers and even Norman adventurers who were active in Sicily and southern Italy. Although such allies were eager to associate themselves with the prestige of the Byzantine Empire, they were just as likely to gain it by attacking the empire and carving out a state for themselves. All around them, the Byzantine emperors saw inconstant allies and ferocious enemies.

The challenges the Byzantine Empire faced were not limited to external rivals. Its rulers faced the same problem as the Abbasid caliphs: powerful actors within their own empire who sought to exploit the weaknesses of the rule to enrich their families. Macedonian emperors such as Basil II had issued legislation to curb the power of these elites, called the **dynatoi**, by ensuring they were taxed heavily, and their massive estates were broken up and distributed to the peasants who served in the armies. Basil was succeeded by less competent or less secure emperors who were compelled to rely on the *dynatoi* for support and reversed his policies. This harmed the peasant backbone of the army and emboldened the elite, who rewarded the patronage of the emperors with schemes to control or replace them. Like the Abbasids, the rulers then had to balance external threats and challenges with internal ones in a complex search for stability.

One of the *dynatoi* became Emperor Romanos IV in 1068. Romanos was a capable general who wanted to reverse the empire's losses to the Seljuks. The neglect of the army by previous emperors meant that he had to rely on foreign mercenaries, who did not get along with each other and who plundered Byzantine territory if they were not paid on time. Romanos had some earlier successes against the Seljuks, whose raids under Alp Arslan had become bloody and bitter affairs. He hoped to take back strategic areas in eastern Anatolia while Alp Arslan was fighting the Fatimids.

Alp Arslan was not as far away as Romanos had hoped, however, and the armies met near the town of Manzikert. Some of Romanos's mercenaries abandoned him before the battle, and at a decisive moment, he was betrayed by his own aristocratic rivals who failed to protect the army during a retreat. Romanos was then captured by the Seljuks, and instead of executing him—the typical fate for one considered a dangerous foe—to humiliate him, Alp Arslan spared the emperor's life and set him free, after he agreed to concede territory and pay a hefty ransom.

The military defeat might not have been disastrous, but problems within the empire exacerbated the loss. Romanos was deposed and killed by his own aristocracy, and for the next twenty years, the Byzantine rulers struggled to restore order to their empire. One of Romanos's successors, Alexios I, called on the popes for assistance against the Seljuks. He was expecting a mercenary force, but instead Pope Urban II framed the conflict between Byzantine and Seljuk as a fight between religions, culminating in the crusading movement.

13.3 Patriarch and Papacy: The Church and the Call to Crusade

LEARNING OBJECTIVES

By the end of this section, you will be able to:
- Describe the East-West schism within the Christian Church
- Explain why Pope Urban II called for the First Crusade
- Discuss the concept of religiously motivated warfare in Christianity and Islam
- Identify the reasons western Christians traveled to the Middle East as crusaders

The image of holy war has often colored the history of the Middle Ages. We can view it either positively in terms of warriors engaged in an altruistic struggle, or in a more negative light as a conflict rooted in bigotry and ignorance. The factors that justified holy war existed in Christianity well before the Crusades, but the Crusades helped shape specific ideals that sanctioned armed conflict based on religious beliefs. These ideals were both internal to Christian Europe and reactions to developments in the Islamic world.

The East-West Schism

The chaotic aftermath of the collapse of the Carolingian Empire led to a complicated situation between secular rulers and the Christian Church. According to German law, lords had the right to control everything on their land, including churches and monasteries. This control even extended to the appointment of officeholders to church positions such as abbot or bishop. To ensure they had the loyalty of church officials, lords staffed these offices with their family members or even sold them to the highest bidder. The consequence was that those without religious vocations, or even familiarity with Christian doctrine, could be installed into church leadership. Even the position of the pope, the bishop of Rome, could come up for sale.

Revulsion at this treatment of religious office led to a reform movement intended to remove the influence of secular lords from the management of the church. The movement is often associated with the monastery of Cluny in France, which managed to get independence from the local aristocrat. Other monasteries around France flocked to be included in the rights and privileges that Cluny had earned, creating a movement called the **Cluniac reform**. The Cluniac movement eventually drew in other clergy who wanted the church to control the election of bishops, independent of secular influence. This desire for independence finally reached the top of the Catholic Church and the office of the bishop of Rome (Figure 13.16).

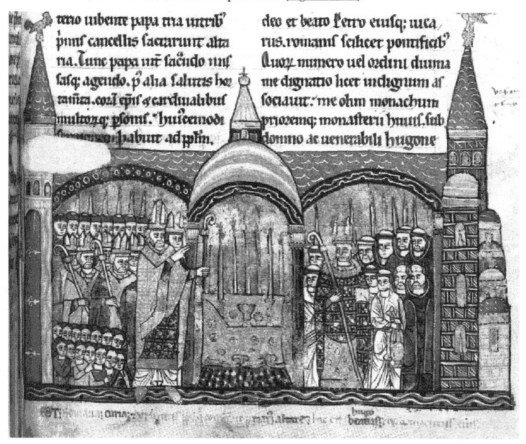

FIGURE 13.16 **The Abbey of Cluny.** This twelfth-century image shows the consecration by Pope Urban II (in gold robes on the left) of the third Abbey of Cluny. Popes developed their reforming platform from Cluny's program. (credit: "Consécration de Cluny III par Urbain II" by Bibliothèque Nationale de France/Wikimedia Commons, Public Domain)

The bishops of Rome were eventually influenced by the Cluniac movement to reform the church. They condemned the sale of offices as a sin called simony and insisted that bishops should be elected by clergy, independent of a lord. Any clergy member who had bought an office or had it bought for them could be removed. To end the practice of treating church positions like a fief to be passed on to the officeholder's children, priests were told to practice celibacy and were forbidden to marry. While celibacy was not a new concept in the Catholic Church, reforming monks and popes began to enforce it with energy. These changes caused bitter conflict with the rulers of Europe, so the church declared that a king who tried to appoint a bishop or asked for a bribe could be excommunicated (placed outside the church, its communion, and the sacraments, in hopes of reforming the offender). Excommunication could threaten the king's position and lead to rebellions.

The reformers were also interested in creating a thoroughly Christianized society by distinguishing between legitimate and illegitimate warfare. The church argued that Christian soldiers, especially knights, should obey a code of conduct that reflected the church's values. For example, they should not loot monasteries or hold clergy for ransom. They should protect the church as well as women and the defenseless. They should observe periods of publicly declared truces and not fight on religiously significant days like Easter. These principles contributed to the ideals of **chivalry**, a code of conduct that was meant to Christianize knightly violence and behavior. Although it was never successful at curbing violence, the idea of Christianized warfare was only one strand of a broader, secular interest in a newly defined chivalric culture of knighthood, and images of Christian knights helped popes justify their directing the military classes of Europe to act against peoples deemed to be enemies of the church, and therefore also of God.

The reform movement gained the church some moral prestige, but the growing power of the pope also worsened the relationship between the eastern and western halves of the faith. By the time of the Middle Ages, five ancient seats of Christianity were recognized as the most prestigious: Jerusalem, Antioch, Alexandria, Rome, and Constantinople. Each was led by a bishop with the honorary title of "patriarch." In the tenth century, only Rome and Constantinople were in territory not controlled by Muslims.

While the pope in Rome and the patriarch of Constantinople believed many of the same things, linguistic and cultural differences helped drive a wedge between them. For example, the church in the west operated in Latin, insisted on a celibate clergy, and elevated the pope as the final authority for all matters regarding the church everywhere. The church in the east used Greek, permitted priests to marry (although tradition held that bishops should be unmarried), and believed other patriarchs were just as authoritative as the pope. The reform movement unintentionally made divisions sharper.

In 1054, the pope sent representatives to the patriarch of Constantinople to discuss the differences between the two halves of the church. The pope's chief representative felt the patriarch was not cooperating with or even recognizing the embassy, so he issued a letter excommunicating the patriarch and his followers. Soon after, the patriarch issued his own letter excommunicating the pope's representatives. Following this **Great Schism of 1054**, the eastern church became known as the Eastern Orthodox Church, and the western half the Catholic Church.

The Great Schism was not the only cause of their division, given that tensions and disagreements had been growing over time. But it did help to highlight the way Christianity was being shaped by different forces in different parts of Europe. From this time on, the popes hoped to reunite the two halves under their authority and impose their vision of a reformed church on the Orthodox Church. While Orthodox bishops might accept the pope as "first among equals," the papacy insisted on being the supreme authority in the church.

Pope Urban II and the Council of Claremont

In 1095, facing invasion on all sides, the Byzantine ruler Alexios I sent ambassadors to plead for help from the pope and an opportunity for a reconciliation between the two churches. Pope Urban II was a supporter of church reform, and that put him at odds with German emperors like Henry IV, who insisted on his own right to appoint bishops, even the bishop of Rome. To avoid being in Italy when Henry was, Urban traveled throughout western Europe, preaching repentance from sins and obedience to the church. He answered the Byzantine emperor's call for aid, but in a way Alexios was probably not expecting.

Urban II presented his idea of religious war in response to the Byzantine request for aid at a council in Clermont, France, in 1095. While the council was ostensibly about reform, Urban also issued a call for Christians from all walks of life to undertake an "armed pilgrimage" to liberate the Christian Holy Land (the lands of the eastern Mediterranean associated with the life of Jesus and the biblical prophets, including Jerusalem) from "Turkic" control. Urban's goal at this point was to free the Holy Land from non-Christian rulers in defense of the Christians living there; it was not a blanket endorsement of violence against Muslims. These limitations were later eased, however, as the popes discovered the power of calling repeated crusades to promote the reforming goals of the church and to compete with political rivals in Europe, like the German emperors.

While the Byzantine emperor wanted aid for his realm, Urban instead sent the crusaders to Jerusalem. Urban's directive to "liberate Jerusalem" and support the Christians in the Middle East was clever. Few Europeans knew or cared about the problems of Constantinople, but the church's reforming and educational efforts had made the life of Jesus in Jerusalem and the early Christian community there a focal point in people's imaginations. Catholics prized relics of saints as a means of fostering their devotion and bringing them closer to the divine, and Jerusalem was in effect an enormous relic, a gateway to heaven itself. Preachers like Peter the Hermit whipped up crowds of men and women with the idea of a glorious pilgrimage to the most sacred of cities (Figure 13.17). The call to crusade stirred western Christians into action, soldiers and knights as well as poor peasants and zealots.

FIGURE 13.17 *Peter the Hermit Preaching the First Crusade.* This painted illustration from a world history published in the early twentieth century imagines Peter the Hermit giving a rousing speech to attract men and women to go on crusade. In many ways, it is representative of a modern perception of the popularity (and virtue) of the crusading movement from the perspective of western Christian society of the period. The reality, however, was much more nuanced. (credit: "Peter the Hermit Preaching the First Crusade" by Cassell's History of England, Vol. 1 (of 8)/Wikimedia Commons, Public Domain)

Urban also hoped to restore unity to the church by offering help to the Byzantine Empire. What we know of his speeches shows how he tied this effort together with his reform program. Freeing Jerusalem from "the wicked" would mirror the rallying cries to free the church from aristocratic control. After all, the reason Urban called for the crusade while in France was that he had to contend with a rival pope, supported by the German emperor, who had occupied Rome since before Urban became pope. Urban was also likely concerned about guarding the frontiers of Christianity, which compelled him to insist that Spanish Christians should not go on this pilgrimage because they were needed at home in the persistent struggle against Islam in the Iberian Peninsula.

Finally, Urban's ability to inspire the people of Europe signaled the influence he wielded over Christians at large. The popes had no armies, and they often had to depend on the unreliable aristocracy for protection when disagreements over church policy resulted in armed conflict with the princes of Europe. If they were to maintain their control over the church in contests with kings and emperors, it would be useful to see what happened when a pope rallied common Christians to a religious cause as a test of faith. Thousands were willing to stitch a cross onto their clothes, a sign that they were on this special pilgrimage and the source of the word "crusade."

The Rhetoric of Holy War

The use of religion to justify war was not new in Christianity, or in human history. For Christian theologians, however, acts of violence put believers in the difficult position of committing a grave sin and endangering their soul. Most Christian thinkers, like Augustine of Hippo (354–430), had argued that some forms of violence had to be tolerated for the good of the community, such as punishing criminals and defending against invasion. Above all, a recognized public authority like a king was needed to publicly call for war. From this point of view, Christians had tried to identify what would be an acceptable or "just war," but the idea of a "holy war" did not exist until the crusading period. A crusade, then, was a "just war" called by the pope, who offered spiritual rewards.

This technical definition of crusade does not mean that Christian rulers had always sought the pope's blessing before attacking their non-Christian enemies. Very little prevented earlier rulers from claiming God supported their military efforts, especially against non-Christians, or from believing God condoned specific acts of violence. Charlemagne claimed as much in his wars against non-Christian peoples, forcing Saxons to convert to Christianity when he was victorious. But the idea of fighting a war against other religions was outside the boundaries of classical Christian thinking. The Christian view of violence was that it should be as limited as possible and justified as defensive. The Crusades made that technical definition problematic, and the earlier notion of crusade expanded to include Muslim kingdoms in Spain or elsewhere, non-Christian settlements in Europe, and even the domains of the pope's political enemies in Europe. The result of the Crusades was a belief that warfare on behalf of God, even if it was neither defensive nor approved by the people, was a "just war."

The images conjured by Urban, Peter the Hermit, and others implied that the Muslim occupation of the Holy Land was unjust and oppressed the Christian community. This idea of Christian suffering was linked to the earliest days of the church when, as members of an underground religion, Christians were persecuted by Rome.

DUELING VOICES

The Rhetoric of Holy War

There were no newspapers, radio, television, billboards, or social media to promote the Crusades. Preachers needed to speak over and over to multiple crowds and stir the individuals in them to join. To do so, they relied on several tactics to inspire anger, fear, or fervor.

We do not have an exact copy of Urban's speech in Clermont that launched the First Crusade, but others grafted their own ideas onto what they had heard, what others said they had heard, or what some people thought Urban should have said. We do not know how accurate any of these texts are. One version, the earliest, has Urban emphasizing that the crusade will be good for the souls of those who go to Jerusalem. In another, written by Robert the Monk, Urban tries to stir his audience with tales of persecution, saying Christians are being forced to accept circumcision and "blood of the circumcision they [the Seljuk Turks] either spread upon the altars or pour into the vases of the baptismal font." He tries to inspire them with tales of Charlemagne and other kings, who in their time "have destroyed the kingdoms of the pagans and have extended in these lands the territory of the holy church." Finally, he deplores the violent tendencies of the aristocracy by pointing out "that you murder one another, that you wage war, and that frequently you perish by mutual wounds." Pity for the victims, hunger to revive glorious deeds, and a call for unity are all employed to inspire warriors to go on crusade.

- Although we cannot definitively know the content of Urban's speech, what rationales did commentators offer for going on crusade in the years following the call in 1095?
- In what ways do modern public speakers rely on these same methods of persuasion to change people's minds?

🔗 LINK TO LEARNING

You can read the exact texts of the speeches attributed to Urban II (https://openstax.org/l/77UrbanII) by various authors to see the way they attempt to persuade the audience to answer the call to crusade. You can also read the arguments made by a Muslim scholar (https://openstax.org/l/77Sulami) Ali ibn Tahir Al-Sulami, and compare his approach to persuading rulers and warriors to fight against the Christians.

Although some historians have speculated that it was only the younger sons of aristocrats, those who could not hope to inherit anything from their fathers, who fervently joined the crusade, the reality was more complicated. Commoners (even poor ones), women, the sick, and the elderly all joined alongside knights, and powerful nobles also answered the call. Many sacrificed their own land and property to gain the resources needed to join the crusading movement. The trek to Constantinople alone was arduous, with few amenities or roads to guide the way. Some may have hoped to gain land if they remained in the Holy Land, and others were motivated simply to see the earthly Jerusalem as a way of experiencing the heavenly Jerusalem that awaited them when they died, and then returned home.

Others had less altruistic motives. The rhetoric preached about non-Christians made Jewish communities, like those in the Rhineland, vulnerable to attack by crusaders seeking plunder, who extorted bribes from Jewish communities to leave them in peace. Even those whose motivations were clearly religious, like Peter the Hermit, compelled German Jewish people to render supplies for their crusading bands. Although the church condemned violence, the Crusades mark the beginning of precarious times for Jewish communities in Christian Europe, when they were subject to abuse, expulsion, and sudden violence.

Unlike classical Christianity, Islam from its earliest days had a concept of holy war called **jihad**. Jihad, meaning "struggle" in Arabic, can have different meanings or uses. For the Sufi mystics, the struggle against internal doubt and weakness could be a form of jihad. In other circumstances, the struggle was against evil, in which Christians, Muslims, and Jewish people could participate as allies. Defining jihad is similar to the problem of defining crusade and distinguishing it from other conflicts. In the Quran, Muslims were enjoined to avoid conflict with Christians and Jewish people unless they provoked Muslims in some way. Like the notion of "crusade," jihad had to be called by a proper authority, such as the caliph or a high-ranking Muslim cleric. In some ways, then, jihad is similar to the idea of a "just war" for Christianity. In practice, however, Muslim rulers, like Christian rulers, could certainly wage war against their nonbelieving neighbors without a formal declaration of jihad, while still claiming their actions were for the benefit of Islam and supported by Allah.

According to Islam, Jewish people and Christians should be tolerated because they are monotheistic. In most instances, though, the idea of endeavoring to realize the will of God meant that armed conflict and conquest were also options. A ruler who was not concerned with striving against non-Muslims was viewed as failing in his duties. Similar ideas began to color Christian views of their own conflicts with Islam, especially in places like Spain. One such thought was that territories that had once been Christian should always belong to Christians, and this was considered particularly true of the Holy Land, even though the area was significant to Muslims and Jewish people as well. It was difficult to find nuance when attempting to carry out the will of God.

13.4 The Crusading Movement

LEARNING OBJECTIVES

By the end of this section, you will be able to:
- Describe the centrality of the city of Jerusalem to Judaism, Christianity, and Islam
- Explain how the Crusader States in the Middle East complicated the relationships between the Christian churches of the east and west
- Discuss the Muslim and indigenous Middle Eastern reaction to the crusading movement
- Explain how the crusading movement developed after the First Crusade

The call to crusade had profound consequences for Islamic and Christian societies. The military fortunes of the crusaders were watched carefully by Muslims and Christians alike, and while the success of the First Crusade was shocking to everyone, to Christians it was also a clear sign of God's favor. The flaws in the crusading movement grew or became better known over time, however. Fewer Christians joined later crusades, even though the legend and romance of the venture became more popular in the European imagination.

Jerusalem and the Holy Land

Judaism, Christianity, and Islam all have a concept of pilgrimage. Sacred journeys can be undertaken to enhance a person's connection with God, as an act of penance, or in gratitude. In many ways, they are meant to be transformative.

Jerusalem drew pilgrims from the three monotheistic religions. Pilgrimage had been obligatory for Jewish people until the destruction of the Second Temple in 70 CE, but even after that time, the city continued to play a special role in Jewish life. In the earliest decades of the first century, it had also become the location for some of the most dramatic and important scenes in the life of Jesus and the early Christian community. In the time of Constantine, a church had been built over the site of what was believed to be Jesus's tomb, called the Holy Sepulchre. As the place where it is believed Jesus was crucified and resurrected, Jerusalem was bound up with the most essential Christian beliefs. Even in the ancient world, Christians undertook pilgrimages to this holiest of cities (Figure 13.18).

FIGURE 13.18 Shrine of the Holy Sepulchre, Jerusalem. This nineteenth-century lithograph of the interior of the Church of the Holy Sepulchre depicts the Shrine of the Holy Sepulchre. Christians believe the shrine contains both the tomb in which Jesus was buried and the rock thought to have sealed it. (credit: "Shrine of the Holy Sepulchre April 10th 1839 / David Roberts (https://commons.wikimedia.org/w/index.php?curid=78866711)" by Library of Congress Prints and Photographs Division/Wikimedia Commons)

Mecca, in the Arabian Peninsula, is the holiest city in Islam and the site of the annual pilgrimage called the *hajj*. The Al-Aqsa Mosque, built on the old Temple Mount in Jerusalem, is the third holiest site in the faith, and it is believed to be mentioned several times in the Quran as "the furthest shrine." Muhammad is said to have made a special journey to be able to pray in Jerusalem and to be allowed to glimpse God before he continued his mission to convert others to Islam. Another shrine, called the Dome of the Rock, was also built near the Al-Aqsa Mosque, which is associated with Muhammad's journey and with the biblical Abraham, an important figure to Muslims, Christians, and Jews alike. Jerusalem, then, was a city unlike others in its spiritual appeal to people of different faiths.

In Christian Europe, the reforms of the church emphasized the earthly life of Jesus, and the idea of being able to see and touch the physical land where he walked filled the imagination of both the clergy and the laity. The image of heaven as a "heavenly Jerusalem" in the writing of monks and nuns heightened the common desire to see the earthly Jerusalem. The report that the Fatimid caliph al-Hakim had destroyed the Church of the Holy Sepulchre outraged Christians, even though his son permitted its rebuilding. It is no coincidence, then, that the term medieval people most often associated with the crusading movement (before the term "crusade" was coined) was pilgrimage, or more specifically, armed pilgrimage.

The First, Second, and Third Crusades

Historians have categorized the different crusades and given them numbers for convenience and to distinguish between various developments within the crusading movement (Figure 13.19). The Crusades were rarely well organized, however, and one of the challenges they all faced was trying to move people from one end of Europe to the other. For example, during the First Crusade, the followers of Peter the Hermit arrived in Constantinople first. They did not wait for other groups to arrive and were ferried over to Anatolia (the Asian part of today's Turkey) by Alexios, the Byzantine ruler. The Turks destroyed this army, and very few survived to return to Constantinople. Later crusaders understood that gathering intelligence in Constantinople was crucial to avoiding Peter's fate.

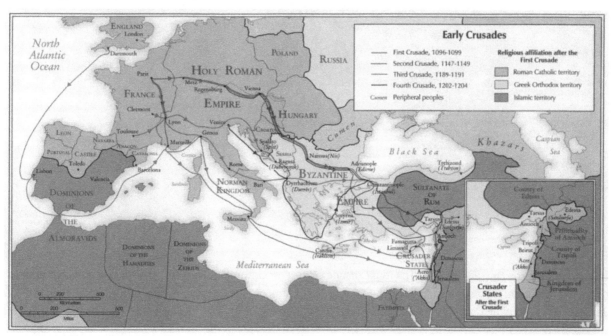

FIGURE 13.19 Routes of the Early Crusades. The First through Fourth Crusades all faced logistic and other challenges and met with varying degrees of success. (credit: "Early Crusades (https://collections.leventhalmap.org/search/commonwealth:q524n6167)" by United States. Central Intelligence Agency/Norman B. Leventhal Map Center Collection at the Boston Public Library)

The bulk of the First Crusade was directed by powerful aristocrats whose armies were better organized and prepared to fight than Peter's, even if most of its participants were not the most senior nobles of Western society. Alexios promised them aid in exchange for the return of Byzantine territory held by Muslims, which most initially agreed to. The crusaders crossed Anatolia and, after laying a bloody siege with little help from the Byzantines, took control of the port of Antioch, an ancient seat of Christianity in the Holy Land. After their victory, they felt Alexios was undeserving of either the city or their fidelity. The city was thus given to a Norman crusader who had no intention of delivering it to Alexios, straining the relationships between the crusaders and the Byzantine Empire.

The First Crusade finally reached Jerusalem in the summer of 1099. Before attacking the city, the crusaders fasted and walked around its walls as penitents, an act that shows the blending of pilgrimage with armed conflict. The crusaders then took the city, and in an act that shocked Muslims and Christians alike, they massacred the Muslim and Jewish inhabitants. The crusading armies then took other important cities in the area, and to secure their control they established the four Crusader States: the County of Edessa, the Principality of Antioch, the County of Tripoli, and the Kingdom of Jerusalem. These Crusader States were also called **Outremer** (literally "overseas") by the French, and they claimed Jerusalem as their capital (Figure 13.20). Of all the Crusades, this was the only one that accomplished its objective.

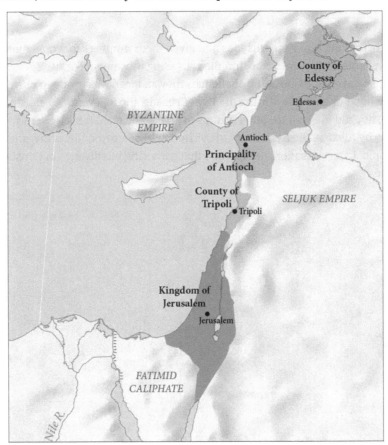

FIGURE 13.20 The Crusader States. The four Crusader States, or Outremer, were the territories seized by members of the First Crusade: the County of Edessa, the Principality of Antioch, the County of Tripoli, and the Kingdom of Jerusalem. (attribution: Copyright Rice University, OpenStax, under CC BY 4.0 license)

Despite the surprising success of the First Crusade, Outremer suffered some critical problems from the beginning. The crusaders had alienated the Byzantine Empire by not returning to it important cities like Antioch or lands in the Middle East as they had promised. The European aristocrats and knights were eager to acquire lands for themselves, which meant they often fought with each other even when faced with a common enemy. And while there was always at least a trickle of warriors who made it to Outremer, the elite remained in desperate need of soldiers to defend their new territories.

🔗 LINK TO LEARNING

Recent media representations have tried to portray a realistic view of the Crusades that includes their internal factionalism and intolerance, but realism often gives way to a filmmaker's need for a more compelling character, a more stylish scene, or the inclusion of inappropriately modern sentiments. Follow the link to read a historian's review of the 2005 Ridley Scott crusader film (https://openstax.org/l/77scottfilm) *Kingdom of Heaven.*

The Muslims' confusion about the nature and goals of the crusaders, as well as internal conflicts among them, initially dampened their political and military response. The Muslims adapted quickly, however, especially the Seljuks who prevented many of the newly arriving knights from ever reaching Outremer. A Turkic aristocrat named Imad al-Din Zengi began to cultivate the image of a holy warrior opposing the crusaders. While he spent most of his career ruthlessly scheming against other Muslim rulers, he managed to take the city of Edessa, in the northernmost of the Crusader States. He was praised as a defender of Islam, but he was assassinated before he could continue his campaign against the crusaders. The loss of Edessa posed a serious threat to the remaining Crusader States, however, and prompted the pope to call the Second Crusade.

The Second Crusade, from 1147 to 1149, was heralded by a new generation of preachers like Bernard of Clairvaux who inspired believers to "take up the cross." Bernard also wrote the rules for the Knights Templar, one of the new crusading orders, religious orders of monks devoted to protecting Christian pilgrims and fighting to support Outremer. This crusade was led by powerful rulers, including King Louis VII of France and King Conrad III of Germany (Figure 13.21). The armies of the Second Crusade were defeated in Anatolia in separate battles, and few soldiers reached the Holy Land. The kings accomplished very little, and many blamed the Byzantine emperor, who had learned to be distrustful of European armies. Bernard of Clairvaux was humiliated and apologized to the pope, claiming the sins of the crusaders had caused the defeat. It was a disaster that seemed as complete as the First Crusade had looked miraculous.

FIGURE 13.21 King Louis VII on Crusade. This illustration from a fifteenth-century chronicle of the Crusades shows King Louis VII, in blue and wearing a gold crown, being welcomed to Antioch during the Second Crusade. (credit: "Raymond Of Poitiers Welcoming Louis VII in Antioch" by Passages d'Outremer/Wikimedia Commons, Public Domain)

After this loss, the situation for Outremer only became more dire. Imad al-Din Zengi's successors were well liked, even by crusaders, and they strove to unite the Muslim princes in jihad. The most famous of these successors was Salah al-Din, or Saladin in the Christian world. He was known for being humane, fair-minded, and, in Christians terms, chivalrous. He expanded his territory from Syria into Egypt and founded a new dynasty called the Ayyubids from the ashes of the Shia Fatimid Caliphate. He also took up his religious calling to wage jihad against the crusaders. In 1187, after years of gathering allies and eroding the military power of Outremer, he destroyed the crusaders at the Battle of the Horns of Hattin (in today's Israel). Within months, Jerusalem fell to Saladin.

The Christians' response was the Third Crusade (1189–1192). This crusade was prompted both by the fear that Outremer was about to be wiped off the map and by the desire to retake Jerusalem. Kings from England, the Holy Roman Empire, and France as well as other powerful princes answered the call. When they arrived in the last remaining Christian outposts in the Middle East, they quickly fell to squabbling with each other and the aristocracy of Outremer. As a result, the Christians were able to conquer the island of Cyprus and the coastline of the Holy Land but were unable to move farther inland. Eventually, Richard I of England, known in popular stories as Richard the Lionhearted, negotiated a treaty with Saladin that left Jerusalem under Muslim control but allowed Christian pilgrims to freely visit the city. Both Saladin and Richard were praised as examples of chivalric virtue in Europe and heroes of their respective religions. But this was one of the last successes the crusaders were to have in the Holy Land.

Experiencing the Crusades

Despite the relatively brief existence of the Crusader States, they offered an example of Christians, Muslims, and Jewish people living and working together in a Christian kingdom surrounded by hostile states. Initially, however, the ignorance and religious bigotry of the crusaders led them to expel populations of Muslims or Jewish people from holy sites or places of strategic importance. In several cases, they perpetrated violent expulsions, killing civilians.

European Catholics also found in the conquered areas native Christian populations with a variety of different creeds. In most cases, these Christians were permitted to stay, but eventually, conflict over religious authority developed as Catholic bishops were named (by the pope or by the Latin Patriarch of Jerusalem) as heads of communities with few Catholics. The Christians of the Middle East had also been acculturated by centuries of living under Muslim rule, which meant the Christianity of the east looked very different from that practiced in Europe. In some communities, Christians spoke Arabic, dressed like their Muslim neighbors, and worshipped in ways different from those of Catholics in Europe. The Greek Orthodox Byzantines were unhappy with the establishment of a well-organized religious rival in the Holy Land. Many native communities distrusted the crusaders not because they were of a different religion but because they arrived with brutality and did not share the cultural practices of the area.

Despite the initial violence by crusaders that scarred and scattered some Jewish and Muslim communities, policies of toleration and protection emerged. These had less to do with the crusaders' growing familiarity with the religious and ethnic groups in Outremer and more to do with the lack of settlers from Europe. Lords needed workers, and if they could not be had, then native communities had to be preserved, not brutalized. Even when Europeans began to adopt local cultural habits and grew familiar with Islamic practices, distrust of the unfamiliar remained common on all sides. The Islamic poet and warrior Usama ibn Munqidh, for example, could count Christians among his friends, but he admonished his readers never to trust the "Franks," or the newly arrived crusaders, whose ignorance he highlighted in his writing.

IN THEIR OWN WORDS

A Muslim View of the Crusades

Usama ibn Munqidh was a Muslim poet and warrior who fought during the Crusades. Like many Muslims, he believed the crusaders were barbarians and invaders, but he came to know some of them very well. He understood that they were different from the Christians of the Middle East, who shared common cultural traits with Muslims. In the following passage, Usama records his experiences in Jerusalem when he tried to pray facing Mecca and was accosted by a Christian who tried to make him face east, as a Christian would.

Everyone who is a fresh emigrant from the Frankish lands is ruder than those who have become acclimated and have held long association with the Moslems. Whenever I visited Jerusalem I always entered the Aqsa Mosque, beside which stood a small mosque which the Franks had converted into a church. When I used to enter the Aqsa Mosque, which was occupied by the Templars, who were my friends, the Templars would evacuate the little adjoining mosque so that I might pray. One day I entered this mosque . . . and stood up in the act of praying, upon which one of the Franks rushed upon me, got hold of me and turned my face eastward saying 'This is the way thou shouldst pray.' A group of Templars hasted to him, seized him and repelled him from me. I resumed my prayer. The same man, while the others were otherwise busy, rushed once more on me and turned my face eastward, saying, 'This is the way thou shouldst pray!' The Templars again came in . . . and expelled him. They apologized to me, saying 'This is a stranger who has only recently arrived from the land of the Franks and he has never before seen anyone praying except eastward.' Thereupon I said to myself 'I have had enough prayer.' So I went out and have ever been surprised at the conduct of this devil of a man, at the change in the color of his face, his trembling . . . at the sight of one praying towards [Mecca].

—Usama ibn Munqidh, *Memoirs of an Arab-Syrian Gentleman at the Time of the Crusades*, translated by P.K. Hitti

- Why do you think the Templars, Christians devoted to defending Outremer, would be so friendly with ibn Munqidh, a Muslim?
- What parts of this passage show the acclimation of western Europeans to life in the Middle East?

The crusaders organized their government in feudal terms, but the native populations never became serfs owing service to their lords. Instead, they paid their taxes in cash or in goods. This form of payment was based on existing practices, and in many ways, the crusaders left rural agricultural production unchanged. Christian landlords used forms of taxation and village administration similar to those their Muslim predecessors had, and they relied on Muslim scribes and interpreters given the diversity of the people and languages in the region. Islamic and Jewish communities maintained their own schools and legal institutions. Despite the earlier violence and ongoing religious and ethnic tensions, the desire for trade and prosperity helped ease some of the tensions between the crusaders and native communities.

The lack of settlers from Europe ensured that the number of soldiers in Outremer was small. This was why the church promoted the crusading orders, and why the crusaders built imposing fortresses and castles, like the famous Krak des Chevaliers in Syria, that could be defended by a relatively small number of soldiers (Figure 13.22). Some European families, especially aristocrats with a family connection, went on sending crusaders, such as the dukes of Burgundy who continued to support the crusading movement. Many crusaders wrote letters to loved ones describing the military engagements in which they had taken part, often using provocative language to cast Muslims in a negative light. Often their expectation was that they would return home, and many pilgrims and crusaders did so rather than settling in the Holy Land.

FIGURE 13.22 Krak des Chevaliers. This is a nineteenth-century artist's drawing of the compact fortress of Krak des Chevaliers in Syria, built to be defensible by a small number of fighters. (credit: "The Krak des Chevaliers as it was in the Middle-Ages" by Guillaume Rey : Étude sur les monuments de l'architecture militaire des croisés en Syrie et dans l'île de Chypre (1871)/Wikimedia Commons, Public Domain)

While European settlers in Outremer remained few, other types of Europeans kept the cities and ports busy, both during the period of the Crusader States and after their fall. In addition to pilgrims, administrators, and scholars, merchants from the Italian city-states like Venice and Genoa benefited from the crusading movement. They profited by shipping pilgrims and fighters to Outremer and wrested lucrative concessions to establish their mercantile outposts in cities like Constantinople, Antioch, and Acre. Their contact with the trading emporiums of the Middle East connected Europe to the trade routes that extended across Afro-Eurasia and increased Europeans' consumption of spices, silk, lacquerware, and ceramics from China.

These trading connections were not the only result valued by the Italian merchants. They were also eager for better knowledge of the peoples and geography of the lands, with an eye to establishing direct trading contacts with the distant civilizations that produced luxury goods Europeans began to demand. The best example is the fourteenth-century merchant and explorer Marco Polo, who followed the land routes to China. The Italian merchants kept up their trade and contact with different Islamic kingdoms, and the wealth of their mercantile cities inspired the kings of Europe to patronize their own merchants and explorers to help them capitalize on the riches of the world that flowed into the Mediterranean. This age of exploration and trade was accelerated by European experiences in the Crusades.

Later Crusading

The crusading movement continued after the Third Crusade, but enthusiasm waned. Pope Innocent III, one of the most powerful medieval popes, called for a new crusade in 1202. The crusaders wanted to avoid the overland routes through Anatolia that had been a problem from the start. They hoped to avoid the Byzantine Empire too, because tensions between crusader leaders and the Byzantine emperors had been worsened by religious conflict and accusations of betrayal. These crusaders ordered ships from Italian cities to carry them directly to the Holy Land. In return, the Venetian leader asked the crusaders to attack a port city named Zara on the Dalmatian coast, which was Christian but Venice's rival. When the crusaders agreed, the pope was furious and excommunicated them.

The crusaders continued to Constantinople, where they became involved in the internal politics of the Byzantine Empire and attacked the city, sacking it after a complicated attempt to put a pro-crusader emperor on the throne. A city that had stood against countless enemies for nearly a thousand years had been crushed. The event marked a deep betrayal of the Greek Christians and of crusading ideals. While the Catholics established the short-lived Latin Empire of Constantinople, considerable damage had been done to the crusading movement and to relations between the Greek Orthodox and Catholic churches.

Later calls for crusades were met with some enthusiasm, but the object of the fight became Egypt, recognized as an important base for controlling the Holy Land. Nevertheless, later crusades became increasingly French and less successful at accomplishing their goals, at least as far as establishing Christian control of the Holy Land went. The French crusader-king Louis IX led the Seventh and Eighth Crusades against Muslim rulers in North Africa and died of illness there. (He was later canonized as St. Louis.) When the port city of Acre in present-day Israel fell in 1291, the last of the Crusader States fell with it.

The crusading ideal was also transformed by practice and experience. The popes now called holy wars not just to liberate Jerusalem but to fight against the enemies of the church. Crusades were called against non-Christians in the Baltic regions, against heretics in France, and even against the pope's personal enemies in Italy (Figure 13.23). Crusaders came to expect standard privileges like the indulgence, a means to reduce the penance owed for sinning by giving money directly to the church or paying for masses or other clerical services. They could also rely on the protection of their property and relief from feudal dues or taxes. Crusading become commonplace by the thirteenth century, and generations of families made going on crusade a family tradition. The popes frequently called on Christian knights and aristocrats to fight against Muslims in a conflict that now seemed to be waged everywhere, not just in the Middle East, and against non-Christians of all types. Conflict was never the sole characteristic of relationships between Christians, Muslims, and Jewish people in the medieval period, but the image of Muslims and Jewish people as perennial enemies of Christian culture that developed in the crusading era had a lasting negative impact in Europe and elsewhere, even to the present day.

FIGURE 13.23 Crusade in the Baltics. This relief carving from the early fourteenth century shows Germanic knights, members of a crusading order, fighting against Lithuanians in the Baltic Crusades. (credit: "Lithuanians fighting Teutonic Knights" by Unknown/Wikimedia Commons, Public Domain)

Toward the end of the Middle Ages, the crusading ideal declined in popularity. This was due in part to the decline of the power of the papacy and in part to the revival of royal power in the fourteenth century. The Crusades had been launched by popular popes viewed as reformers and men of virtue. Over time, they came to seem more concerned about their own power and prestige and less like the hard-working clerics who had battled kings for the freedom of the church. In the early fourteenth century, the king of France accused the Knights Templar, one of the more popular crusading orders, of committing crimes such as blasphemy and apostasy (the rejection of Christianity). The order's leaders were executed as heretics, and the popes disbanded the order, largely to please the French king.

THE PAST MEETS THE PRESENT

The Modern Crusade?

As part of the secularization of society that occurred with industrialization and the rise of the nation-state, most modern Western cultures reject the idea of warfare for religious regions. Romanticized images of the Crusades persist in movies like *Kingdom of Heaven* (2005) and in video games like Ubisoft's *Assassin's Creed*.

The rhetoric of holy war, and the memory of it in Islamic and Christian communities, also persist in modern political discourse in many Western countries, but in different contexts. As the medieval scholar Matthew Gabriele has argued, after 9/11, the concept was revived in the United States to describe its conflict with terrorism. "The consensus of American opinion now holds that, in the minds of Al Qaeda and other 'radical Islamists,' the attacks were part of a religious war, a cosmic, Manichean struggle that would only end with complete and utter victory of one side over another."[1]

Gabriele argues that use of the term "holy war" is complicated because of all the assumptions that go with it, especially the way it "omits the messiness of everyday life in the spaces in which Muslims and Christians lived side-by-side in the medieval world—tensions, violence, and coexistence captured by Ibn Jubayr, Usama ibn Munqidh, and the Templar of Tyre among many others."[2] A study of the Crusades, then, must take into account the lived history of religious toleration in the Middle Ages as well as the points of conflict.

- Why would video games and action films revisit the Crusades in the modern period?
- In what ways can a simplistic view of the Crusades be misleading to modern audiences?

---

1   Mathew Gabriele. "Debating the 'Crusade' in Contemporary America." *The Medieval Journal* vol. 6 no. 1. 2016.
2   Mathew Gabriele. "Debating the 'Crusade' in Contemporary America." *The Medieval Journal* vol. 6 no. 1. 2016.

While Christian kingdoms expanded in the Baltic regions and in the Iberian Peninsula, the rise of powerful Islamic kingdoms in the Middle East, like the Mamluks in Egypt and later the Ottoman Turks in Anatolia, ensured that crusades to control Jerusalem became impractical. Kings and aristocrats turned their attention to building up nation-states and warring against their dynastic rivals at home. The rhetoric of crusade still colored fights between Christians and non-Christians, but these conflicts often served the political goals of kings and monarchs willing to deal with the papacy in return for its blessing.

Key Terms

chivalry a code of ideal conduct meant to validate the practices of noble warriors by Christianizing knightly violence and behavior

Cluniac reform a movement that aimed to limit the influence of aristocrats in church matters

dynatoi members of the Byzantine elite who often compromised imperial authority

feudalism a collection of practices that bound lesser lords to greater lords through land and privileges given in return for personal and military support

Great Schism of 1054 the conflict that solidified the separation of the eastern and western Christian churches

jihad a religiously infused conflict waged on behalf of Islam, or any struggle a Muslim undertakes in the name of Allah

mamluks educated, formerly enslaved men who served as soldiers and administrators in Islamic societies beginning in the ninth century

manorialism a medieval economic system of agricultural production directed by a lord and carried out by serfs or other varieties of unfree laborers

Outremer the French name for the four Crusader States created after the First Crusade, the County of Edessa, the Principality of Antioch, the County of Tripoli, and the Kingdom of Jerusalem

papacy the set of administrative structures associated with the government of the Catholic Church primarily—but not exclusively—linked with the city of Rome

serfs unfree peasants who owed labor to a feudal lord and lived under the lord's authority

Sufism the mystical expression of Islamic faith

sultan a ruler who claims authority over the Islamic community but not necessarily the title of caliph

Section Summary

13.1 The Post-Roman West in the Early Middle Ages

The early Middle Ages helped set the stage for a new society to emerge from Roman, Christian, and Germanic traditions, and for a revival of the classical world to influence the rise of Islamic culture. Kings, clergy, and scholars helped to preserve the classical past and maintain diplomatic and economic ties across western Afro-Eurasia. The growth of cultural and religious cohesion through western Europe and the crude but effective institutions of the feudal world laid the groundwork for a period of stability and growth to come in the High Middle Ages.

13.2 The Seljuk Migration and the Call from the East

The Abbasid rulers had established their control over the Middle East and created a multiethnic, multireligious society that promoted trade, scholarship, and urbanization. By the tenth century, however, the caliphs' sphere had been reduced to Syria and Iraq. Religious and political rivals like the Fatimids, who established the only Shia caliphate, weakened the Abbasids. The arrival of the Seljuk Turks helped to push back the Fatimids and dealt a devastating blow to the Byzantine Empire. The Seljuks enjoyed their status as protectors of the Abbasid realms, and like other conquerors before them, they eagerly embraced Persian culture, art, and literature. The Byzantine emperors, suffering a loss of prestige and territory, looked west in the hope that renewed alliances with the Germanic kingdoms could help restore their power in Anatolia.

13.3 Patriarch and Papacy: The Church and the Call to Crusade

The period of recovery from the collapse of the Carolingian Empire brought about the ordering of society from the lowliest serf to the kings of western Afro-Eurasia. Popes wanted to reform the church and used their authority to challenge the secular rulers of European kingdoms. Those same rulers worked to create stability by integrating their warrior culture with Christian beliefs, both to justify and to restrain violence. The Byzantine emperor's call to the pope for aid leaned on all these complex developments and helped to launch the Crusades, a new chapter in the history of conflict fueled by religion.

13.4 The Crusading Movement

The Crusades were a movement that signaled the growth of the papacy's influence in western Europe and helped to stimulate trade, the growth of the Italian city-states, and contact with peoples across Afro-Eurasia. They were also complicated by the ways in which they failed their own ideals: the massacre of innocents, the betrayal of other Christians, and the too-frequent use of warfare to meet political or economic goals. The Crusades persisted in the European imagination for the rest of the Middle Ages, and in many ways, their legacy shapes the modern world today.

Assessments

Review Questions

1. What was the relationship between the Germanic kings and the non-German aristocracy they ruled?
   a. They could not find common ground and were often at war.
   b. They could work together when religious differences were not a point of contention.
   c. They viewed each other as so similar that there were no differences between them.
   d. They were able to preserve the Roman Empire until the end of the Middle Ages.

2. How did the Visigoths' conversion to Christianity change their relationship with the Jewish people?
   a. The Visigoths became more tolerant of Jewish people.
   b. The Visigoths did not change their policies toward Jewish people.
   c. Jewish people joined the Visigoths in converting to Christianity.
   d. The Visigoths began to insist that Jewish people convert or suffer consequences.

3. Which is not a key feature of feudalism?
   a. the *wergild*
   b. serfs
   c. fiefs
   d. manorialism

4. Feudalism developed after the collapse of what empire?
   a. the Byzantine Empire
   b. the Roman Empire
   c. the Carolingian Empire
   d. the Caliphate of Cordoba

5. What state was founded in North Africa and was eventually centered in Egypt?
   a. the Abbasid Caliphate
   b. the Byzantine Empire
   c. the Caliphate of Cordoba
   d. the Fatimid Caliphate

6. What religious movement rejected the worldliness of the Abbasid Caliphate and instead pursued spiritual union with God?
   a. Sufism
   b. Shi'ite Islam
   c. Mamluk
   d. Shaman

7. Legitimate caliphs in Shia Islam had to be descended from what early figure in Islamic history?
   a. Abu Bakr

    b. Ali

    c. Moses

    d. Constantine

8. What dynasty established the only Shia caliphate?

    a. Fatimids

    b. Buyids

    c. Seljuks

    d. Macedonians

9. What challenge did both the Abbasid Caliphate and the Byzantine Empire face?

    a. They both had to find military alternatives to their own elite.

    b. They both had to prove they were descended from a religious authority.

    c. They both had to take control of Italy to ensure their wealth.

    d. They both had to develop systems of writing to record their scriptures.

10. What event marked the separation of the eastern and western churches?

    a. the First Crusade

    b. the Great Schism

    c. the fall of Rome

    d. the Islamic conquest of Spain

11. Why did Pope Urban call for the First Crusade while in France and not in Rome?

    a. France had more Christians than Italy.

    b. Rome was occupied by a rival pope supported by the German emperor.

    c. France had better systems of communication than Rome.

    d. Rome had a significant Muslim population, and the pope did not want them harmed.

12. What does the term jihad mean?

    a. just war

    b. conversion

    c. struggle

    d. pilgrimage

13. What religious communities did the crusaders attack before they had even left Europe?

    a. Christian communities

    b. Monasteries

    c. Islamic communities

    d. Jewish communities

14. What site in Jerusalem is considered of particular importance to Christians?

    a. the Holy Sepulchre

    b. the Al-Aqsa Mosque

    c. the Temple Mount

    d. the Pope's Palace

15. Why was the Byzantine emperor unhappy with the development of Outremer?

    a. The emperor had controlled Jerusalem, and the crusaders took it from him.

    b. The emperor was Muslim and believed Jerusalem should stay under Muslim control.

    c. The emperor expected the crusaders to return to him the territory they conquered.

    d. The emperor did not approve of mixing religion and warfare.

16. What two groups were targets of massacres and expulsions after the establishment of Outremer?
    a. Jewish people and Christians who were not Catholic
    b. Jewish people and Muslims
    c. Muslims and the Greek Orthodox
    d. Catholics and Muslims

17. What was a reason for the decline in crusading in the later Middle Ages?
    a. the decline of the power and influence of the popes
    b. the control of Jerusalem by a Christian state
    c. the disinterest in religion felt by many Europeans
    d. the good relationship between Muslims and Christians

Check Your Understanding Questions

1. What were the chief weaknesses of the Carolingian Empire?

2. Under what circumstances did peoples of different ethnic or cultural background encounter each other in the early Middle Ages?

3. In what ways was the Caliphate of Cordoba different from Germanic kingdoms?

4. What were the causes of the devolution of Abbasid power?

5. Why did the Seljuks assume the title of sultan rather than caliph?

6. What caused the Byzantine Empire to seek aid from the Christian West?

7. What differences between the eastern and western Christian churches in the eleventh century led to the Great Schism?

8. What motivations did western Christians have for leaving their homes and participating in the Crusades?

9. Why was Jerusalem so important to Jewish people, Christians, and Muslims in the medieval period?

10. Why did many eastern Christians and Jewish people not welcome the arrival of the crusaders into the Holy Land?

Application and Reflection Questions

1. What challenges did people face in the period of time after the collapse of Roman authority in western Europe?

2. How did religion influence political life in the early Middle Ages?

3. What roles did women play in early medieval societies?

4. How did the Germanic tribes transform the western Roman Empire?

5. What external and internal forces challenged the stability of states, Christian or Islamic, in this period?

6. In what circumstances were peoples of different faiths tolerated in this period? Under what conditions were people more divided over religion? Why?

7. In what ways were the Germans, the Byzantine Empire, and the Muslim states all inheritors of Roman and Greek culture?

8. How did religious reform shape relationships between different Christian communities?

9. What do the Christian ideas of crusade have in common with the Islamic ideas of jihad? What complicates

these ideas as notions of "just war"?

10. What stated goals did the crusading movement achieve, and what unintended consequences arose from them?

11. In what way did the Crusades bring peoples from across Afro-Eurasia into contact with each other?

12. In what ways did the Crusades change the relationship between Christian, Muslim, and Jewish communities in the Middle East? What impact have the Crusades had on subsequent ideas of religious toleration?

13. How did geography affect the crusaders, the Byzantine Empire, or the Muslim states?

FIGURE 14.1 Kublai Khan. This image is from a silk scroll painting made in 1280 CE by Liu Guandao, known as Zhongxian, an artist of Kublai Khan's court. It depicts Kublai (center in a white fur coat) with his wife and others on a traditional hunt, demonstrating the value the Mongols continued to place on their origins even after their empire spread far from their ancestral steppe lands. (credit: modification of work "Kublai Khan on a hunting expedition, painted on a silk handscroll (fragment)" by Cambridge Illustrated History of China (1999) by Patricia B. Ebrey/ National Palace Museum/Wikimedia Commons, Public Domain)

CHAPTER OUTLINE

14.1 Song China and the Steppe Peoples
14.2 Chinggis Khan and the Early Mongol Empire
14.3 The Mongol Empire Fragments
14.4 Christianity and Islam outside Central Asia

INTRODUCTION The years between 1000 and 1350 CE were a time of extreme highs and lows for the people living in the Eurasian land mass. China came close to industrializing and creating a Confucian meritocracy. An increasing percentage of Eurasia's population converted to Islam, even as Christian military forces pushed Islamic civilization to the southern tip of Iberia and tried to wrest the eastern Mediterranean—the territory viewed by Jews, Christians, and Muslims as "the Holy Land"—from Muslim rule. Europeans grappled with creating governments strong enough to protect the population but with robust enough checks on centralized authority to keep at least the elites from being abused. Enslaved people revolted and began to rule in the Nile delta and Indian subcontinent.

Nowhere, however, was change more dramatic and consequential than among the scattered seminomadic people of the Inner Asian Steppe. One of their number, written off and enslaved as a child, emerged to unite and lead a large faction of them into such a potent force that his descendants, who included Kublai Khan (Figure 14.1), marched as conquerors through the palaces of the Chinese Son of Heaven, the Caliph of God's messenger, and countless cities. This leader was known to the world as Chinggis (Genghis) Khan. Uniting a million or so of the world's 400 million people into the Mongol Empire, he not only altered the trajectory of their lives, he also unleashed forces that swept many old ways aside and laid the foundations for the modern world to emerge.

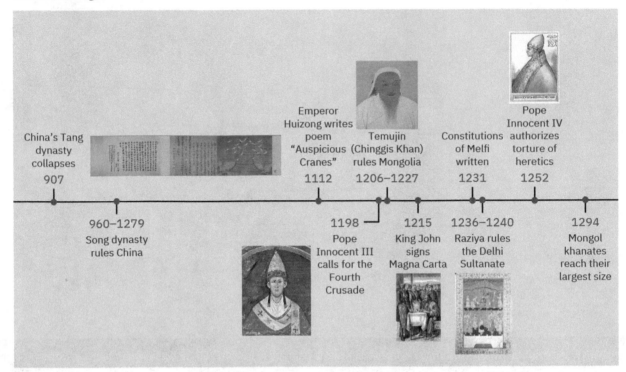

FIGURE 14.2 Timeline: Pax Mongolica: The Steppe Empire of the Mongols. (credit "1112": modification of work "Auspicious Cranes" by Liaoning Provincial Museum/Wikimedia Commons, Public Domain; credit "1198": modification of work "Pope Innocent III wearing a Y-shaped pallium" by Fresco at the cloister Sacro Speco/ Wikimedia Commons, Public Domain; credit "1206–1227": modification of work "Emperor Taizu of Yuan, better known as Genghis Khan" by National Palace Museum/Wikimedia Commons, Public Domain; credit "1215": modification of work "King John of England signing Magna Carta" by The Granger Collection, New York/Wikimedia Commons, Public Domain; credit "1236–1240": modification of work "Sultana Razia Begum" by Salar Jung Museum, Hyderabad/Museums of India, Public Domain; credit "1252": modification of work "Pope Innocent IV" by The Lives and Times of the Popes by Chevalier Artaud de Montor, New York: The Catholic Publication Society of America, 1911/Wikimedia Commons, Public Domain)

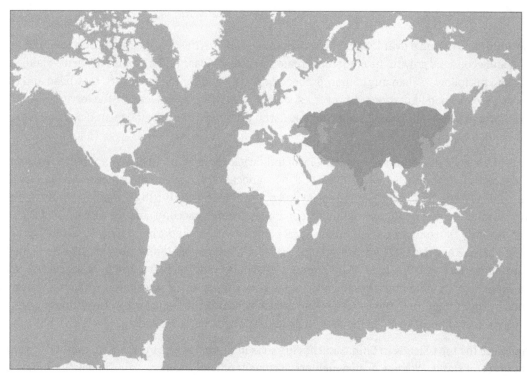

FIGURE 14.3 Locator Map: Pax Mongolica: The Steppe Empire of the Mongols. (credit: modification of work "World map blank shorelines" by Maciej Jaros/Wikimedia Commons, Public Domain)

14.1 Song China and the Steppe Peoples

LEARNING OBJECTIVES

By the end of this section, you will be able to:
- Describe the political and economic structures of Song China
- Describe the way of life of Song China's northern neighbors
- Discuss Chinggis Khan's role as unifier and empire builder

The disintegration of China's Tang dynasty in 907 CE left a chaotic power vacuum in the territory it had ruled. Generals turned the jurisdictions they could control into small independent sovereign states. More traditional seminomadic peoples from the sparsely settled semiarid grasslands and mountains to the north of China's borders, such as the Khitan Liao and the Xia, seized control of many former Tang domains. As they occupied these areas, some groups switched from migrating periodically for animal grazing and hunting, with the occasional raid on neighbors, to living a more agrarian life with urban centers and formal government, which would become hallmarks of Chinese civilization. The absence of central authority and legitimate succession led to frequent conflicts within and between these groups. Other seminomadic people located farther from China such as the Tatars and Mongols in the west and north, however, continued to live in loosely organized groups that were fluid in composition and unsettled in duration. They built no permanent structures and had only sporadic interaction with those to the south, occasionally exchanging or plundering goods.

Meanwhile, in the central and southern parts of what had been Tang China, the Zhao family convinced the fractured political units that they held the Mandate of Heaven—the favor of the natural order that sustained them but could be lost by those less worthy—thus beginning the Song dynasty in the 960s. The Khitan Liao and Xia, who ruled much of northern China, refused to recognize the Zhao patriarch as the Son of Heaven, the rightful Chinese ruler. Attempts to force such recognition failed, leaving the Song with a much smaller realm than the Han or Tang. Despite this, Song China was largely stable, with a steadily rising population and standard of living. In the 1120s, military reversals led to the loss of substantial territory and set back economic growth, but the Song were able to recover, only to be faced with the Mongol invasion in the 1230s.

Song China to the Thirteenth Century

While the Song dynasty ruled over less territory than other major dynasties, it experienced tremendous population and economic growth. Its emperors created a system closer to the ideals and virtues laid out by Confucius and his followers than any of their predecessors had, and for the most part, they lived and ruled by them. Those precepts had limitations, however, especially when it came to securing the territory against the increased power of the seminomadic steppe peoples, who were now adopting the technology and lifestyle of their more settled neighbors.

Securing the dynasty's rule required replacing local military leaders with imperially appointed **mandarins**, civilian government officials who could advise and, when necessary, restrain the generals on matters of foreign policy. Mandarins were the key class in the social and political hierarchy during times of stability in the more than two thousand years of Confucian dominance in China, from the second century BCE to 1911 CE. Starting as allies of the early Han emperor who oversaw local landed gentry, mandarins were selected by a process that by the height of the Tang dynasty had evolved into a system of exams on Confucian texts. The Song made great progress bringing the Confucian ideal of government by scholar-officials to fruition by enacting reforms that made the exam process more merit based and less subject to nepotism or favoritism. While the system was interrupted by the Mongol Yuan dynasty, the Song reforms became the basis for the way Chinese government officials were selected until the fall of the monarchy in the early twentieth century.

Mandarins were the top officials in China, and having sons in this class was the primary method of gaining or maintaining social status. Women, even daughters of current officials, were not able to benefit. Although existing mandarin families had significant advantages in preparing their sons to succeed on the exams, it was not unheard of for a village to recognize talent in a peasant or artisan family's child and support that child's study. Not only would this step elevate that family into a higher social class, it would also give the village better access to government officials.

The Song dynasty's founding brothers, Emperors Taizu and Taizong, had both served in the military, yet they structured a government in which the mandarins applied their Confucian pacifism to protect the state by bribing potentially hostile neighbors either not to attack them or to attack hostile neighbors for the Song. This policy stemmed from the belief that the Tang dynasty had fallen because it expanded into areas populated by non-Chinese peoples who refused to adopt orderly Confucian values. Pacifying those areas took unsustainable amounts of resources. The Song attitude toward the military was summed up in a saying from the era: "Do not waste good iron making nails; do not waste good men making soldiers."

At the same time, Song engineers were the first to develop effective military uses for gunpowder, creating flamethrowers, handheld projectile-launching early guns, and shrapnel-laden bombs, hurled first by catapults and later by rockets. The Song had powerful military technology, but their predisposition toward Confucian pacifism and fear of a strong military that could endanger civilian rule prevented them from effectively using it much of the time.

While Tang dynasty China had emphasized increasing wealth through territorial expansion, the Song relied instead on internal economic development. Agriculture focused not on mere subsistence farming but on creating a food surplus that then supported a considerable expansion in population and, in turn, an increase in urbanization. At the same time, rural, farming households had increased purchasing power. Much of this was due to improvements in agricultural technology, which increased both the amount of available cultivatable land as well as crop yields. For example, irrigation made possible by the invention of chain-driven pumps turned unused hillsides into arable land (Figure 14.4). Peasants began planting new strains of rice that ripened quickly enough to yield two harvests per year. The Song government aided this economic development by stabilizing agricultural markets and food prices and taking advantage of new technologies that greatly increased the productivity of irrigation. It also maintained transportation and irrigation systems and spread the seeds of more efficient crops. In short, more land was open to farm, and the result was an increase in harvests and the availability of produce.

FIGURE 14.4 Terraced Rice Paddies. These terraced rice paddies in Longsheng, China, demonstrate how, with irrigation, hilly land can be cultivated. (credit: "Paddy fields of Longsheng, China" by "Drolexandre"/Wikimedia Commons, CC BY 3.0)

🔗 LINK TO LEARNING

Machinery to move water uphill was a key part of the irrigation technology that fueled the agricultural revolution in Song China. Read this brief text about the history of the chain pump and its connections to China (https://openstax.org/l/77chainpump) to learn more.

The resulting increase in China's food supply fueled a huge population boom, freeing labor to work in economic sectors outside agriculture. The first complete Song census showed around fifty-five million people in the early eleventh century. One hundred years later, there were around 120 million. At its height, Song China had at least three cities with populations of more than one million and dozens of cities with more than 100,000 people; in the same period in Europe, no city other than the Byzantine capital of Constantinople even approached these sizes after the fall of the western Roman Empire.

Some scholars contend that by the twelfth century, Song China was experiencing an industrial revolution similar to that of eighteenth-century Britain. Surplus labor from the population boom provided significant opportunities for the expansion of the production of industrial goods, and the dynasty saw iron production rise from around 65 million pounds around the year 1000 to more than 250 million pounds by 1100. This was almost double what would be produced in Britain even seven hundred years later. Large-scale factory production and water-powered textile and paper-making machinery were in use in some larger cities. These developments, along with the construction of better roads and canals, allowed the Song to become a more mobile and interconnected society. The increase in productivity meant that goods could be traded over greater distances, and there was more need (and opportunity) for merchants and other support workers to interact and move these goods, thus distributing the economic benefits that came with the use of machines.

Urban Society in the Song Period

One of the most famous depictions of urban daily life in Song China is a hand-painted scroll from the first decades of the twelfth century, attributed to Chinese painter Zhang Zeduan. The title of this scroll is generally translated as *Along the River During the Qingming Festival*, although some suggest that Qingming refers not to a specific festival but to a more generic time of peace and order.

The Qingming scroll illustrates the prosperity and economic development of the Song period by showing a variety of everyday social and economic activities undertaken by people of all classes in an unspecified Chinese city. Traditional interpretations suggest it is a realistic portrayal of daily life in Bianjing (modern Kaifeng), the Song capital from 960 to 1127. More modern critical analysis suggests instead that the scroll dates from a generation or more later and represents a yearning for a more idealized time in the past. For example, specific features of the capital have been omitted, and the images lack the signs of crime, poverty, and homelessness that are generally typical of large cities in any civilization.

It is not difficult to understand why well-known landmarks and characteristics of the capital are absent. While the scroll was likely intended to present a realistic visual depiction of the capital, those seeking to portray places of which they are proud often show them in their best light. Thus, the exclusion of the seedier sides of life makes sense; it is a truthful representation of aspects of Song society during this period, but one that does remain dishonest by omission, and a reminder to us as modern historians to carefully analyze and think about the sources from the past on which we rely for information.

Whether the scroll was intended to reflect what the artist chose to see in the city in which he lived or was an homage to an earlier and better time, it does show several aspects of daily urban life and Song dynasty technology. Watch the animated video (https://openstax.org/l/77SongDynasty) to learn more.

View multimedia content (https://openstax.org/books/world-history-volume-1/pages/14-1-song-china-and-the-steppe-peoples)

- Contrast the types of businesses and modes of transportation depicted in the scroll with those in contemporary U.S. towns and cities.
- Does the omission of some aspects of Song society mean we should consider the scroll untrustworthy as a historical document for reconstructing the past? Why or why not?

The Inner Asian Steppe and Chinese Dynastic Struggles

Steppe peoples organized themselves under widely varying degrees of centralized authority. At one end were small self-governing nomadic clans with fluctuating membership and modest herds in remote parts of the steppe. At the other extreme were settled societies with fixed capital cities, centralized administrations funded by routine taxation, and a writing system for their language. In between were larger groups of seminomadic tribes that were mostly preliterate, with more loosely fixed memberships and territorial ranges than the settled societies. In the wake of the Tang dynasty collapse at the beginning of the tenth century, some seminomadic tribes seeking the prosperity and technology of China transitioned to more settled and centralized civilizations.

Taking advantage of the power vacuum caused by the collapse of the Tang dynasty, two steppe peoples extended their rule from the Inner Asian Steppe into northern China: the Khitan Liao, linguistically a Mongolian people who formed the Liao kingdom, and the Xia, sometimes called the Tangut, linguistically a Tibetan people who formed the Xi Xia kingdom. These kingdoms became a bridge between the long-established, highly centralized, and sedentary civilization of China and the nomadic tribes of the steppe (Figure 14.5).

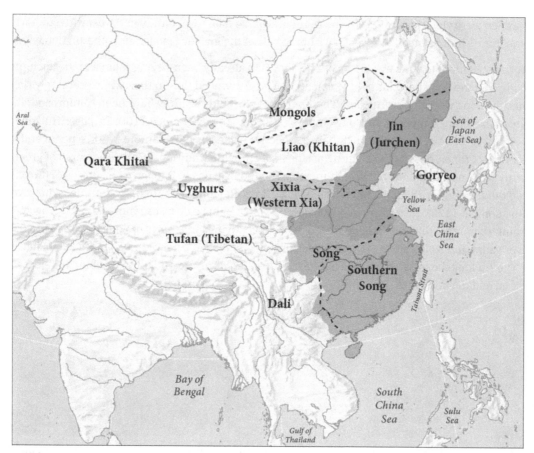

FIGURE 14.5 The Collapse of the Tang Dynasty. Multiple sovereign political units emerged from the chaos of the Tang dynasty's collapse in the early tenth century. Note the loss of Song territory—which previously occupied much of the blue area in the northeast—as a new dynasty, the Jurchen Jin, expanded southward, displacing the Khitan Liao and taking many Song lands. (attribution: Copyright Rice University, OpenStax, under CC BY 4.0 license)

The eight tribes of the Khitan Liao spent the chaotic years between the Tang and the Song making a transition to life as a settled people with administrative institutions. Establishing a permanent capital city in the north in 918, their leader abandoned the traditional elections in favor of a hereditary monarchy. A dual system of administration was adopted, using traditional tribal practices of governance in areas populated predominantly by steppe people, while a system of exams similar to that used by the mandarins selected officials in the majority-Chinese parts of the kingdom. The processes of centralized administration required a written script, which was finalized in 920. The Liao dynasty also promoted economic development by moving Chinese workers skilled in technologies that steppe people did not practice, like metallurgy, to teach their crafts to those living in the steppe.

In 1004, the Song and the Liao agreed to the Treaty of Shanyuan. This pact highlighted the changing relationship between the steppe people and the Chinese between the Tang and the Song dynasties. In it, both the Song and the Liao emperors were referred to as Sons of Heaven. The two states were recognized as equals, each having the rights and obligations of border control and extradition, and neither allowed to alter the waterways that flowed between them. Tellingly, however, on the issue of tribute, the Song were obligated to give the Liao an annual payment of 200,000 bolts of silk and 130,000 ounces of silver (worth about USD$2.7 million in 2020 prices). No reciprocal obligation of the Liao to give tribute to the Song was specified.

The Song resented this relationship with the Liao, and in 1120 they bankrolled the revolt of one of Khitan Liao's tributary states, the Jurchen, a steppe people who were themselves transitioning to more centralized, sedentary structures apart from their traditional tribal organization. Once the Liao and the Jurchen were locked in combat, the Song attacked from the south. Exploiting divisions within the Liao kingdom, the Song and the Jurchen were victorious by 1125. The remnants of the Liao royal family fled west with supporters and founded the Kara-Khitan state. The Jurchen assumed rule of the former Liao lands as the Jin dynasty.

The Jin were not content to supplant the Liao. The Song had already been paying them a modest tribute of luxury goods, and the Song need for help to defeat the Liao convinced the Jin that, while seemingly rich and prosperous, the Song were militarily weak. Their perception would certainly have been reinforced if they had been aware of the temperament of the Song emperor Huizong. In power since 1100, Emperor Huizong was more renowned as a Daoist poet and artist than an effective ruler. His most famous work, a poem and painting titled *Auspicious Cranes*, depicts the sighting of a flock of cranes, a traditional Chinese symbol of greatness and longevity and one of the links between humanity and the heavens in Daoism (Figure 14.6). Huizong interpreted the sighting as a sign his reign would be glorious and long. The Jin had other ideas, however, and attacked the Song in 1126. Huizong quickly abdicated in favor of his eldest son, Qinzong, who proved no more adept in military matters than his father. With Jin forces occupying large parts of Song territory north of the Yellow River valley and laying siege to the capital, Qinzong dispatched a peace mission, led by his half-brother Gaozong. The Jin took the mission hostage and extracted a hefty ransom and annual tribute to release its members and end the hostilities.

FIGURE 14.6 *Auspicious Cranes*. Emperor Huizong's poem and painting from 1112 uses ink and paint on silk to commemorate a good omen , the reported sighting of a flock of cranes on one of the palace buildings. (credit: modification of work "Auspicious Cranes" by Liaoning Provincial Museum/Wikimedia Commons, Public Domain)

The peace proved short-lived as Qinzong tried to entice the former Liao mandarins, who were now working in service to the Jin, to revolt. They reported Qinzong's clumsy intrigues to the Jin emperor, who launched a more protracted attack. Bent on conquest and revenge this time, the Jin refused to be bought, and in 1127 they took the Song capital and seized the entire imperial household, goods, and people, including Huizong and Qinzong. In what became known as the Jingkang incident, the Jin went on a three-week rampage of raping and looting throughout the city.

Gaozong, who proved much more politically adept than his father or his brother, had been sent south to lead reinforcements back to the capital. Upon learning of the capital's fall, Gaozong united the military and mandarins behind him, proclaimed himself emperor, and rallied Song forces to halt the Jin advance. This event is considered the beginning of the Southern Song dynasty. War continued to rage until the 1140s, when the two sides agreed to the Treaty of Shaoxing, in which Gaozong ceded all Song territory north of the Huai River to the Jin, acknowledged the Song's tributary status to the Jin, and agreed to pay an annual tribute of 250,000 bolts of silk and 325,000 ounces of silver (more than USD$6.7 million today). Huizong died in captivity before the treaty was signed. Perhaps as a statement of contempt for his incompetence, Gaozong did not negotiate for his elder half-brother's release, condemning him to live out his remaining twenty years as a Jin captive.

Within a dozen years of conquering the Liao Empire, the Jin began embracing the institutions and structures of the Song Confucian state. Landed aristocrats, generally descended from tribal chieftains, were replaced by mandarins selected by Confucian exams. The capital was relocated from the traditional Jurchen homeland in northeast Asia to Zhongdu, around contemporary Beijing. Confucian texts and Chinese literature were translated into Jurchen to speed the spread of Chinese culture and values, and the mandarin exams began to be given in Jurchen as well as proto-Chinese. Jurchen families were bribed (or forced) to relocate into former Liao and Song areas to mix with the Han population.

Meanwhile, despite the huge setbacks and defeats of the second quarter of the twelfth century, Gaozong and his immediate successors were able to unite and stabilize the Song dynasty. The long period of warfare allowed many ethnic Chinese to move south as refugees, where government assistance enabled them to find land or employment. By 1200, the Southern Song population was roughly the same size as it had been under the last census of the Song, despite encompassing much less land, and the economy seemed to have recovered to prewar levels.

The Rise of Chinggis Khan and Mongol Unification

While an increasing number of steppe people gathered in settled communities, many still lived as nomads. The clan, a small group of several families that shared an encampment and herded or hunted together, was the basic unit of steppe society. Each clan had a ruling lineage from which leaders were selected and that intermarried with other lineages to avoid in-breeding. Thus, the ruling lineages formed an aristocracy of sorts. Clans could split apart, creating a ruling lineage for a new clan, so it was possible to move from commoner to aristocrat, although founding and leading a clan was no small feat.

Given the high mortality among the steppe peoples, the adoption of children and widows was commonplace. Polygamy was practiced by men who could support multiple wives and the children they would produce, and most households included some enslaved people. Children, wives, enslaved people, and livestock were often obtained by raiding weaker, underprepared clans.

Clans joined together to form tribes under a single leader to better protect their herds and households, cooperate on resource management and migration, and engage in united actions like raids on other clans. Eurasian tribes were loosely organized, often multiethnic and multilingual, not exclusive to a kinship network, and open to any who were willing to obey the leader. Clans drifted in and out of tribes depending on their needs and wishes. Multiple tribes periodically united around a single skillful or charismatic leader, creating a larger confederation. This unity was very short-lived, rarely lasting beyond a generation or two.

Many clans and dozens of tribes occupied the Mongolian grasslands in the late twelfth century (Figure 14.7). Settled peoples like the Jin and Song had long incited these nomadic groups against one another, adding to the turmoil of incessant clan raids. In 1161, concerned that a confederation led by Mongolian speakers was growing too powerful, the Jin encouraged and supported a confederation led by Tatars to attack the Mongol-led confederation. Tatar was a Turkish language spoken by many inhabitants of the grasslands north of China. (The fluidity of membership in clans, tribes, and confederations makes it problematic to consider a group led by a speaker of one language as truly having a common ethnic heritage or long-standing communal bond such as a modern nation has. Nevertheless, perhaps for the sake of simplicity, scholars tend to refer to confederations of seminomads by the primary language of their leader.)

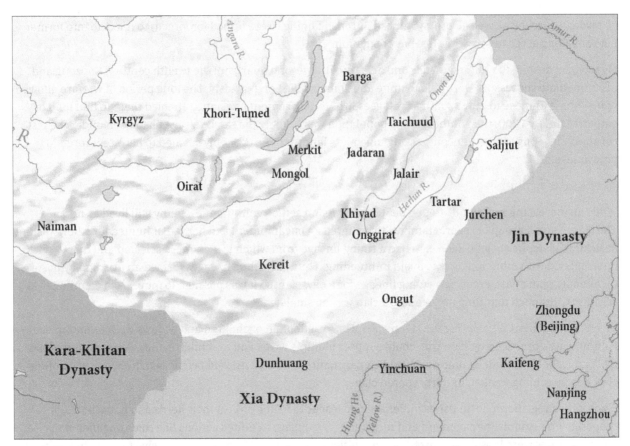

FIGURE 14.7 Mongol Tribes and the Three Steppe Kingdoms. This map shows (in yellow) the areas that various Mongol tribes considered their lands in the late twelfth century and where they were in relation to the three settled kingdoms of the Kara-Khitan, Xia, and Jin between the steppe and the Southern Song dynasty. (attribution: Copyright Rice University, OpenStax, under CC BY 4.0 license)

The Tatar attack on the Mongol confederation scattered its clans, forcing them to form new tribes and seek to join other confederations. It was in this context that a son was born to Hoelun, primary wife of one of the clan leaders of the recently defeated Mongol confederation in their camp between the Onon and Herlen Rivers. The child, born as Temujin, is better known today by the title he acquired later in life and that history most remembers him by: Chinggis Khan, meaning "universal ruler." He completely altered the relationships between the nomadic groups on the Eurasian Steppe and radically changed the trajectory of world history.

There are no historical records of Temujin before he became known as Chinggis Khan, the powerful ruler of the world's largest empire in his time. A work called *The Secret History of the Mongols*, likely written after his death, is the most potentially reliable source, though it is suspect because it is based solely on oral history interpreted by non-Mongols.

Whereas *The Secret History of the Mongols* recounts many heroic exploits in Temujin's family's struggle to survive, it paints a bleak picture of their existence on the steppe. Temujin was briefly enslaved by the rival clan until a sympathetic family helped him escape. Not long after Temujin married, raiders from the Merkit Mongol tribe attacked and kidnapped his wife, Borte. Temujin sought help from Ong Khan, leader of the Kereit Mongol confederation, to retrieve her, and she gave birth to a son not long after. The timing made it unclear who the father was; nevertheless, Temujin accepted the child as his. At some point in the early 1180s, Temujin broke with his friend and clan leader Jamukha and formed a new clan with himself as head.

IN THEIR OWN WORDS

Jamukha and Temujin Pledge Eternal Friendship and Loyalty

The Secret History of the Mongols is silent on how Temujin and his close friend Jamukha became blood brothers when Temujin and his family were roaming clanless on the Inner Asian Steppe. In the aftermath of the battle in which they fought together to free Temujin's wife, Temujin joined Jamukha's clan. The selection that follows is an account from *The Secret History of the Mongols* describing their pledges of unity and loyalty. As you read, think about how the two depict their relationship and what obligations they pledge to each other. Consider also how they symbolically confirm their new relationship, and how they celebrate it.

This is how they declared themselves friends by oath for the second time.

They said to each other, "Listening to the pronouncement of the old men of former ages which says: "Sworn friends—the two of them Share but a single life; They do not abandon one another: They are each a life's safeguard for the other." We learn that such is the rule by which sworn friends love each other. Now, renewing once more our oath of friendship, we shall love each other."

Temujin girdled his sworn friend Jamukha with the golden belt taken as loot from Toqto'a of the Merkit. He also gave sworn friend Jamuqa for a mount Toqto'a's yellowish white mare with a black tail and mane, a mare that had not foaled for several years. Jamuqa girdled his sworn friend Temujin with the golden belt taken as loot from Dayir Usun of the U'as Merkit, and he gave Temujin for a mount the kid-white horse with a horn, also of Dayir Usun. At the Leafy Tree on the southern side of the Quldaqar Cliff in the Qorqonaq Valley they declared themselves sworn friends and loved each other; they enjoyed themselves revelling and feasting, and at night they slept together, the two of them alone under their blanket.

—Igor de Rachewiltz, *The Secret History of the Mongols: A Mongolian Epic Chronicle of the Thirteenth Century*

- What personal values and behaviors in the oath Temujin and Jamukha swear to each other are important to the Mongolian-speaking peoples?
- What do the gifts they exchange suggest Mongolian speakers greatly value?

By 1187, Temujin had such an impressive force and reputation that Ong Khan turned to him when the Jin induced Ong Khan to attack the Tatar Confederation. Ong Khan and Temujin defeated the Tatars and acquired goods more luxurious than Temujin's people had ever seen. This drew even more people to his clan. As the clans allied with Temujin grew, Jamukha expanded his clan to keep up with him. Soon those in the Mongol-speaking part of the steppe were left with the choice of joining Temujin, joining Jamukha, or risking attack by one or the other.

Temujin made drastic changes to traditional Mongol practices, in part as a reaction to the hardships he suffered growing up, which laid the groundwork for his creation of a huge multiethnic empire. As he engaged in warfare with a wider array of rivals, he considered class differences. He punished those who led any resistance and executed the leaders of rival clans, but he often spared the common people and integrated the men into his army. He ordered his fighters to refrain from looting and raping and instead to pursue any fleeing warriors to capture or kill them, minimizing future retaliatory raids by those who escaped. Rather than enslaving the captured adult males, he put the members of aristocratic lineages on trial for committing whatever affront he had used to justify the attack. Once found guilty, which was the general outcome, they were executed. Temujin then divided the spoils of the raid equally between the participants and the households of his men killed in the raid. By assuring his soldiers that their widows and orphans would not be at the mercy of whoever took them in, he reduced the incentive to desert.

Temujin also divided his warriors into units of ten, each bound to the others by oaths of loyalty, and then units of one hundred and one thousand that chose their own leaders and swore similar oaths. Only at the highest level, ten units of one thousand warriors, did he appoint commanders, and he did so on the basis of merit and loyalty to him, not kinship or clan identity. The groups drilled precision moves and learned simple musical chants that identified the formations their commanders desired in the heat of battle. This innovative organization not only forged a deadly, efficient fighting force; it also provided all males with a shared and classless role in society and unified an increasingly ethnically and linguistically diverse portion of the steppe people, whom Temujin began to call the **People of the Felt Walls** in a reference to their fabric-covered homes.

Temujin's reforms introduced a new division in steppe civilization that today might be called class warfare. People from aristocratic lineages began to fear Temujin and joined with Jamukha, but commoners sought the protection and rewards of joining the People of the Felt Walls. The aging Ong Khan disapproved of Temujin's attack on tradition and aristocratic privilege and began favoring Jamukha. After Ong Khan tried to lure him into a trap, Temujin fled to a rendezvous with his top leaders, who swore renewed loyalty to each other in the Baljuna Covenant. The covenant became a rallying point and symbol of Mongol nationalism for future generations.

The men who swore to the covenant came from nine different clans and represented at least four religions: Buddhism, Christianity, Islam, and the traditional Mongol worship of Tengri, the Eternal Blue Sky. The glue that held the People of the Felt Walls together was not kinship, ethnicity, or religion but devotion to the civil society Temujin had created. Word went out from Baljuna to the scattering People of the Felt Walls to regroup and to find Temujin and the others in a remote part of the steppe.

Ong Khan believed Temujin was hiding out a weeks' ride away in the east. Temujin and his followers were much closer, however. They surrounded Ong Khan's forces, using the element of surprise to launch an attack that lasted three days. Demoralized, many of Ong Khan and Jamukha's followers began to join Temujin. Ong Khan was killed while crossing alone into territory controlled by the Naiman, the last confederation that could oppose Temujin.

With Temujin expanding and the Naiman harboring Jamukha and other refugees from Ong Khan, war between the two groups was inevitable. Temujin's discipline and tactical training of his troops paid off, and in 1204 the Naiman collapsed, its leadership dead or in flight. The survivors joined the People of the Felt Walls. Jamukha was eventually turned in by his followers and executed, along with those who had betrayed him, since Temujin felt their treachery to their lord deserved punishment.

14.2 Chinggis Khan and the Early Mongol Empire

LEARNING OBJECTIVES

By the end of this section, you will be able to:
- Describe the new civilization Chinggis Khan created for the Mongols
- Analyze the trajectory and motivations of the conquests made under Chinggis, Ogedei, and Mongke Khan
- Explain the actions Ogedei Khan took to bring about Chinggis Khan's vision for a Eurasian trading empire
- Identify the obstacles the Mongols faced in their efforts to unify and expand their empire

With no remaining rivals to Temujin's rule over the People of the Felt Walls, nothing stood in the way of his vision of a better world for his followers; Chinggis Khan, or "World Leader," had truly been born. His vision was twofold. On one hand, Chinggis wanted to end the constant strife and warfare that characterized life on the steppe. Despite being a practitioner of violence and warfare, he also wanted to promote the peaceful acquisition of goods. He spent the rest of his life forcefully promoting those objectives, regardless of whether others desired them, with a bloody ruthlessness that seems at odds with those very same goals.

The *Yassa* and Mongol Life

To allow bitter feelings to subside after years of struggle, Chinggis waited until 1206 to call a *kurultai* to consolidate and confirm his rule over all Mongols. A **kurultai** was a meeting of those loyal to the leader of a seminomadic confederation, convened to confirm acceptance of a major change the leader wanted to make in relations within the group or between the group and others. Attendance signaled acceptance, and not attending meant not just disagreement but possibly withdrawal of loyalty to the leader. Temujin's *kurultai* was unprecedented in its scale. *The Secret History of the Mongols* records that nearly all the million or so People of the Felt Walls attended, setting up encampments that spread for miles. Unlike almost all previous coronations in recorded history, Temujin's was a highly inclusive event, not just for the elites and population of the capital. A shaman proclaimed him Chinggis Khan and confirmed that Tengri, a god revered by many central Asian peoples, granted him authority and would bless his people with prosperity and good fortune as long as he governed wisely and fairly, an idea similar to the Confucian Mandate of Heaven.

To prevent conflict over succession and maintain the democratic spirit of the *kurultai* where members had a say in selection, Chinggis Khan decreed that any future great khan, that is, any leader over the entirety of what he began to refer to as the "great Mongol nation" and the superior of all lesser khans, could be chosen only by a *kurultai* and not familial succession alone. Chinggis Khan now filled the role of clan and tribe leader. He put forth rules known as the **yassa** to govern relations between households; later, as the empire grew, he ordered the development of a written script for the Mongol language—based on that used by Uyghur tribes from areas north of China and Mongolia—so the *yassa* and records pertaining to it could be recorded (Figure 14.8).

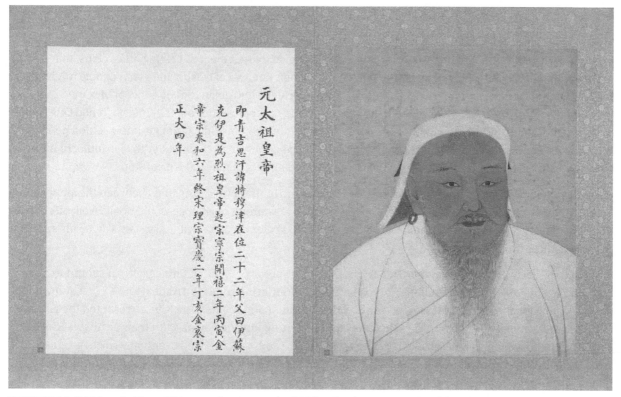

FIGURE 14.8 Chinggis Khan. This oversized portrait of Chinggis Khan was made with paint and ink on silk and comes from a fourteenth-century album of royal portraits that is today held in the National Museum in Taipei, Taiwan. The description on the left page provides brief details about Chinggis, primarily about when he reigned. (credit: "Emperor Taizu of Yuan, better known as Genghis Khan" by National Palace Museum/Wikimedia Commons, Public Domain)

The *yassa* made theft and robbery—the objectives of incessant raiding between clans—capital offenses. Enslaving Mongols was outlawed, as were adultery and kidnapping women and selling them for marriage. No one could kill more animals than their household could use, hunting was banned during animals' mating seasons, and specified butchering methods ensured that maximum use was made of the animal. The *yassa* favored no religion and prohibited discrimination and favoritism on the basis of religion, perhaps the first law code to do so. Chinggis Khan, who continued to worship Tengri, granted tax and labor service exemptions to all religious leaders and holders of church lands, privileges later extended to those in secular occupations requiring literacy, such as medicine and law.

The family was the center of life for a Mongol woman, yet she had little if any say about how her family was formed. Marriages were arranged, and polygamy was common, although a man was not supposed to have more wives than he could support. Adult males in the household could sleep with any of the women in the household if this did not violate incest taboos, and it is unclear the degree to which a woman's consent was necessary. Because the *yassa* defined adultery as occurring only between married people of different households, it codified the potential for sexual assault within households.

Mongol women did have some power, however. They were often left to oversee the household when the men went to herd, hunt, and raid. A widow beyond childbearing years was often considered a household head and took her husband's place in the clan's collective decision-making institutions. When Chinggis Khan was away on extended campaigns, his wife Borte was the de facto leader of the civilians of the Mongol Empire, and the wives and mothers of later Mongol rulers could hold significant power over a khanate following this model. Such instances of female leadership were far, far rarer—or entirely unheard of—in most other Afro-Eurasian societies of the same period.

The Conquest Movement of Chinggis Khan

The *yassa* and the social-military organization put in place by Chinggis Khan removed many sources of strife from the Mongol Empire. But they also prohibited traditional activities, such as raiding other clans, that had led to social mobility. Chinggis Khan believed that without new sources of wealth and glory, people might grow restless and reject the peace he tried to create. His life experience had given him no concept of settled economic development or ways to redirect his people's energy to that goal. From the time he joined Ong Khan's attack on the Tatars and saw the luxuries acquired from the Jin and the Song, Chinggis knew settled peoples were a source of wealth ripe for the Mongol Empire to take, and for him as their leader to distribute. In his eyes, conquering these peoples or intimidating them into giving tribute was the next logical step.

As word spread of Chinggis Khan's coronation, some warriors in the settled kingdoms between the steppe and Song China left to join the Mongol Empire. The Kara-Khitan, assuming resistance would not go well, offered tribute to Chinggis Khan. After a coup in 1210, the new Xi Xia ruler accepted tributary status on terms similar to those of the Kara-Khitan.

The Jin, however, were another matter. In 1210, a new Jin emperor demanded Chinggis Khan submit to him and send tribute, so Chinggis marched his smaller but superior army south to invade (Figure 14.9). A master at exploiting his opponents' weaknesses, he realized that his linguistic cousins, the Khitan, resented the rule of the Jurchen Jin dynasty, so he portrayed his army as a liberating force for them. With their army swelling with Jin defectors, the Mongols were able to lay siege to Zhongdu, the Jin capital, and eventually seize the starving city. Chinggis Khan ordered the city thoroughly looted, tens of thousands enslaved, and untold numbers of others massacred.

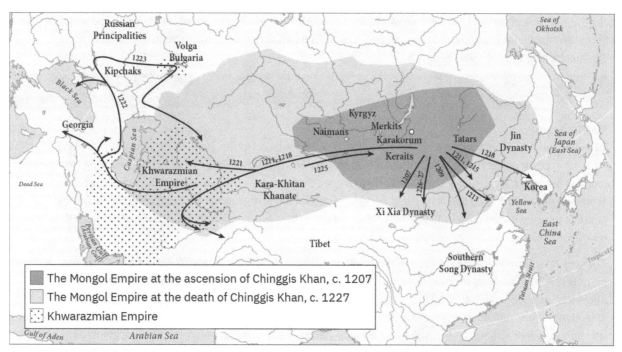

FIGURE 14.9 The Mongol Empire. This map shows the areas conquered by the Mongol Empire under Chinggis Khan's leadership from 1207 to 1227. The black arrows depict the paths his army took, including exploratory campaigns outside the empire's boundaries to the west. In areas of northern China, Chinggis Khan had to invade areas he had already conquered that rebelled. (attribution: Copyright Rice University, OpenStax, under CC BY 4.0 license)

Once the spoils from Zhongdu had been gathered, Chinggis Khan and his army headed back to the steppe, leaving the campaign against the Jin mostly in the hands of his Khitan allies. Forces loyal to Chinggis Khan continued to subdue the Yellow River basin and expanded north into the Jurchen homeland, even venturing to the Korean Peninsula. By 1223, these areas were pacified and providing tribute to the Mongol Empire and its allies who occupied them. Ironically, this vast amount of looted goods forced Chinggis Khan to build the first permanent structures on the steppe, a warehouse complex to hold war booty so it could be preserved and distributed or traded over time.

The Kara-Khitan kingdom caught Chinggis Khan's attention in 1213 when the son of the Naiman leader he had defeated a decade earlier took control. The Kara-Khitan were already not meeting tribute expectations, and now a once-defeated rival led them. The Mongols quickly triumphed over the Kara-Khitan and absorbed them into the empire. Their conquests were wide, however, and not limited to China and the East. Mongol armies moved westward and likely seemed an unstoppable force to many.

The vast amount of wealth seized from the Jin fundamentally changed the mindset of the Mongol leadership, which demanded ever more goods, food, grazing lands, and raw materials. These new needs prompted Chinggis Khan to seek trading and raiding opportunities farther west. The absorption of the Kara-Khitan into the Mongol Empire had provided a direct border with the Islamic world through Khwarazmia, a realm stretching from Persia through central Asia. Around 1218, Chinggis Khan sent a caravan of a few hundred of his Muslim subjects to the leader of Khwarazmia, Allah al-Din Muhammad, with a letter requesting the establishment of trade relations and a great many valuable goods to show what he could offer.

Before the caravan reached the Khwarazmian ruler, however, his governor of Otrar confiscated the goods and killed the traders. In a grave miscalculation, Allah al-Din Muhammad then killed most of the emissaries Chinggis Khan sent to demand compensation, returning only a couple of them, disfigured. This did not just mean war to Chinggis Khan; it meant a war of revenge of the utmost brutality. This included the decimation of the cities of Herat, Merv, and Nishapur, which for centuries had been three of the most important and prominent cities of the eastern Islamic world. By 1223, Allah al-Din Muhammad had been killed while fleeing Mongol troops on an island in the Caspian Sea. Chinggis Khan divided the Khwarazmian state up to be administered by his sons and generals.

THE PAST MEETS THE PRESENT

World Trade

In the present day, the World Trade Organization (WTO) has seen countries from around the world join together with the support of the United Nations to develop and expand trade over long distances. Recognizing that the world is becoming increasingly globalized and that goods are moving across borders and between people more than ever before, the WTO has played a major role in streamlining, regulating, and supporting international commerce since its founding in 1995. But can we view the WTO as a contemporary version of Chinggis Khan's vision for world trade?

Chinggis Khan's messages to the ruler of Khwarazmia indicate that he genuinely sought trade, not tribute. In one he notes, "I have no need to covet other dominions. We have an equal interest in fostering trade between our subjects." In a second letter, after the sultan had responded by sending a trade caravan, Chinggis Khan notes, "Merchants from your country have come among us . . . we have likewise dispatched to your country in their company a group of merchants in order that they may acquire the wondrous wares of those regions; and that henceforth the abscess of evil thoughts may be lanced by the improvement of relations and agreement between us, and the pus of sedition and rebellion removed."

Both Chinggis Khan's messages convey that trade promotes peace among countries and people. While the sultan did not see it that way, this idea is now the basis for many actions in international relations, where the concept of liberalism—which contends that the way to a peaceful world is to promote economic growth by barrier-free economic exchange between countries—holds great sway. While the WTO works through collaboration rather than by edict, the logic and intent are the same: allow goods to be exchanged throughout the world with a single set of rules, and people will live in harmony with one another.

- What benefits might Chinggis Khan have seen in supporting a free flow of trade between his empire and the Khwarazmians, even when they fought one another?
- Should we consider the formation of an organization like the WTO an innovation of the twentieth century or an outcome directly connected to the trade networks of the past? Why?

Reconnaissance for launching surprise attacks against Khwarazmia brought the Mongols into unfamiliar territory. To the south, they discovered India's Delhi Sultanate in one of its rare periods of unity and growth. These Muslims were not part of the Khwarazmian realm, however, so attacking them would have been an unnecessary distraction. Seeking a route to surprise the Khwarazmians from the north, two of Chinggis's most trusted generals, Jebe and Subutai, had crossed through the Georgian Kingdom, then the lands of the Rus, Slavic ancestors of modern Russians who had ruled the agricultural lands east of Hungary and Poland. They quickly annihilated the Khwarazmian and Rus forces, forcing both groups to become tributaries to Chinggis Khan.

Ogedei Khan's Great Mongol Nation

Chinggis Khan spent his remaining years reasserting control over his Chinese conquests. The Jin, for example, regained tenuous sovereignty over the areas between Zhongdu and the coast. The Xi Xia refused to send troops to aid the war against the Khwarazmians, an act Chinggis saw as a betrayal. After defeating the Khwarazmians, he invaded the Xi Xia lands to punish them for this disloyalty. He was unable to enjoy the vengeance finally brought upon these uncooperative subjects, however, dying several months before the completion of his conquest, possibly as a result of being thrown from a horse.

As was Mongol custom, Chinggis Khan's estate was to be divided between his four sons by his primary wife Borte. His estate was a huge chunk of the Eurasian continent with millions of people to rule and a great deal of annual tribute. To preserve this wealth and the harmony the *yassa* had created for at least the population of the Mongol Empire, Chinggis had insisted that one of his sons be the next great khan. This son was to not only run one-fourth of the empire directly but also command the military, serve as the final court of appeal, and control a central government consisting largely of postal stations for communication and warehouses for spoils and tribute.

🔗 LINK TO LEARNING

This web page has a simplified chart of Chinggis Khan's male line of descent (https://openstax.org/l/77KhanDescent) through his grandchildren, many of whom are referenced in this chapter. The site uses a different method of transliteration, so some names appear differently (for instance, Qubilai = Kublai and Cayatai = Chagatai). The German text reads "Mongol Grand Khans. The wife of Ogedei, Torgene, led the state from 1241 to 1246; Oyul Gaimis, the wife of Guyuk, was regent from 1248 to 1251."

At a *kurultai* of his family and closest advisers years before Chinggis' death, Ogedei was chosen to be this great khan. That decision was respected, demonstrating just how successful Chinggis had been in uniting the steppe peoples. The division of the empire between Chinggis Khan and Borte's sons also occurred. Ogedei received the conquered lands of the Xi Xia and Jin. The heirs of the oldest of Chinggis Khan's sons, Jochi, who had died a few months before his father, were given portions of the Mongol lands in central Asia, the territory of the Rus in modern Russia, and adjacent areas in northwest Eurasia. Led by Chinggis's oldest grandson, Batu, they became known as the **Golden Horde**, *horde* being one of the most common terms used for the tribal organization of the Mongols. The youngest son, Tolui, was granted the Mongol homeland, and the rest went to the second son, Chagatai.

Ogedei's coronation as khan reflected his reputation as a partier, with weeks of celebrations and feasting that involved virtually the entire nation and carefree depletion of the treasury by distributions of generous gifts to attendees. Tribute collections had fallen off, however, especially once word of Chinggis's death spread. After Ogedei's reckless spending, the Mongols were suddenly in financial trouble and unable to satisfy either the population's growing expectations of living standards or their new leader's ostentatious ambitions. Ogedei needed a way to quickly find more money.

To intimidate the tributary states, Ogedei attacked and defeated the Jin by 1234. The Jin civilization's wealth flowed into the Mongol treasury, but it was not enough. More than pursuing a life of conquest, Ogedei wanted to siphon off wealth as tribute through control of Eurasia's trade routes. To do that, he needed a capital, which he stored near Chinggis Khan's warehouses in the Mongol heartlands; this was the origin of Karakorum as a city. Funding its construction required yet more tribute, however. In 1235, Ogedei called a *kurultai* to decide which lands should be conquered to provide it. After much debate, it was decided to attack both Europe and Song China.

The war against the Song was inconclusive. Both sides suffered heavy losses, and peace negotiations began in 1241. The Mongols fared better in the west. They reestablished control over areas they had subdued earlier, conquered Kyiv (Kiev) in 1240, and essentially wiped out most Christian armies east of the Holy Roman Empire, looting major cities such as Krakow and Buda in modern-day Poland and Hungary. As they entered Bohemia in early 1242, word came that Ogedei had died the previous December. To participate in the expected *kurultai* to replace him, the Mongols abruptly retreated before bringing full destruction to eastern Europe, though leaving devastation in their wake.

While Ogedei's reign had mixed success, his extravagance and hedonism reflected the lifestyle the Mongol Empire adopted in the decades of unity brought by Chinggis Khan's *yassa*. Ogedei instituted practices that allowed fairly effective extraction of resources and imposed stability and order in the lands he and his father had conquered. The details are generally credited to a Khitan mandarin named Yelu Chucai, whom Chinggis Khan first took notice of in 1215 and whom Ogedei tapped to expand the burgeoning system of taxation and recordkeeping for the whole empire. Yelu is credited with convincing Ogedei that "an empire can be conquered from horseback, but it cannot be ruled from horseback," setting the stage for the bureaucratization of Mongol rule.

Ogedei embraced Yelu's plans of systematic recurring taxation to replace tribute. He saw his empire as the center of world trade and expanded the infrastructure to support that. Primarily for military communication, Chinggis Khan had established a system of horse relay stations called **yam** on the long-distance roads throughout his realm. These *yam* were located at one-day intervals from one another and included rest areas and supply depots. Ogedei expanded the system, extending its use to merchants and diplomats and lavishly rewarding traders who brought items he had never encountered before. This hospitality and his spendthrift ways attracted many merchants.

In addition, Ogedei created the Pax Mongolica, or Mongol Peace, which united a large part of the world through the exchange of goods and the long-distance travel of people and ideas. This was accomplished through a twofold approach: it was facilitated by the peace and justice imposed by Mongols on those who accepted or embraced their rule and was funded by the taxation of all producing people. At the same time, it was assured by clear instances of unabashed brutality against any who would dare resist their spread into new lands. Many recognized that resistance was not worth the risk.

Ogedei had given no thought to succession, however, and almost a decade of infighting occurred after his death, calling forth a great effort to maintain what had already been conquered. A battle between Chinggis Khan's grandsons Guyuk and Batu seemed imminent when the forty-two-year-old Guyuk mysteriously died.

THE PAST MEETS THE PRESENT

Chinggis Khan, Mongol National Identity, and the Hu

Although several clans and tribes of the Inner Asian Steppe spoke a common language, it was not until the reign of Chinggis Khan that they became a unified nation. From that point on, except for roughly three generations of Soviet rule in the twentieth century, during which symbols and figures with a strong local nationalist focus were often banned, Chinggis Khan has been inexorably linked to Mongol national identity.

A recent pop culture example is the breakout Mongolian heavy-metal band The Hu. Their 2019 debut album was called *Gereg*, after the medallions that granted merchants the use of the Mongols' system of rest and supply areas on the roads. The Hu were the first Mongolian band to have a song lead the Billboard Top 100 list. In the fall of 2019, they finished a twenty-three-city European tour, and for their contributions in spreading Mongol culture globally, the Mongolian government gave them the country's highest award, the Order of Chinggis Khan. Almost every song on their album harkens back to the days of the Mongol Empire of the thirteenth century.

The second verse of "The Great Chinggis Khaan" (simply an alternative spelling of "khan") sums up both Chinggis Khan's vision of the world and the way the Mongolian people view him. Here is the official music video of The Hu song (https://openstax.org/l/77HuSong) "The Great Chinggis Khaan." You may want to turn on the closed captioning to read the lyrics in English.

View multimedia content (https://openstax.org/books/world-history-volume-1/pages/14-2-chinggis-khan-and-the-early-mongol-empire)

- Why might The Hu have chosen Chinggis Khan as a focus for their first album?
- What aspects of the status of Chinggis Khan in both contemporary Mongolian society and world history more generally do you think explain why this song proved so popular?

The Last Gasp of Mongol Expansion

It took until 1251 for majority support to coalesce around Chinggis Khan's grandson Mongke. While Mongke successfully expanded Mongol domains, his reign would mark the end of continued conquest while also signaling the end of a united Mongol Empire.

Blending the best elements of Chinggis Khan and Ogedei, Mongke was poised to re-create the greatness of unified Mongol rule. He stabilized the empire, ordering a census to assess not just taxes but also the natural and human resources of his domains. To increase the empire's wealth and dissipate potential restless energy that might be turned on him, he undertook multidirectional expansion. His brother Hulagu Khan was asked to subdue the Islamic world, while another brother, Kublai Khan, was sent to Song China.

Hulagu was enormously successful; like his grandfather in northern China, he exploited existing conflicts, which included resentment by the minority Shia Muslims against the Sunni caliph. Combining this strategy with the Mongols' usual offer to spare from destruction those who would acknowledge Mongol rule and submit tribute without struggle, Hulagu was able to gain control of much of the caliph's lands, especially Shia areas. By late 1257, his forces had surrounded Baghdad, and the city fell in early 1258, its physical defenses undermined. Tens, possibly hundreds, of thousands were massacred, and the caliph himself was killed.

Meanwhile, Kublai was also successful, conquering areas of Tibet and southwestern China. During the campaign, he began to favor Tibetan Buddhism, although not to the point of dismissing or persecuting other faiths. Mongke then moved him to administer the former Jin areas that were conquered by his grandfather, while Mongke himself, seeing the Song's vulnerability, launched a broader attack against them in 1256. In 1259, as reports reached Mongke that Kublai was establishing a power base in northern China, he ordered Kublai to join him in the war against the Song, probably also wanting to keep close watch over him.

Before Kublai could reach him, however, Mongke died, likely from dysentery. His cousin Ariq Boke, another of Chinggis Khan's grandsons and the one who had been left to administer the Mongol homeland, declared himself the new khan of the Mongol Empire ahead of a *kurultai*. Upon hearing this, Kublai, who was returning for the *kurultai*, also declared himself the new khan. While Kublai would prove a powerful and capable ruler, much had begun to change since the days of Chinggis, and the stage was set for the end of a unified Mongol Empire and a single khan who dominated the entirety of the territories they had conquered. Continued success in conquest had been a major factor in keeping rivals from unnecessarily challenging the rule of the chosen great khan or devolving his power. With this period of expansion over, these rivals were presented with new opportunities to claim more power for themselves, especially with the size and diversity of the empire the Mongols now ruled.

The last *kurultai* of the Mongol Empire failed and led to the permanent splitting of the realm. Hulagu stood with his brother Kublai. The Golden Horde, now led by Batu's younger brother Berke, supported Ariq Boke. This left Orghina, sister-in-law to Hulagu and granddaughter of Chinggis Khan, in a position to choose which of her cousins would rule the Mongol Empire. Orghina, acting as regent for her son who was too young to assume a leadership role, chose neutrality, endorsing neither claimant. The fact that she was making this decision, not advising a man who would make the choice, shows the strides women had made under the *yassa*. Kublai ultimately prevailed, since his bonds with the army conquering China and his resource-rich power base in the northeast left him well situated to repulse Ariq Boke's attacks. In 1264, Ariq Boke rode to Kublai's capital and surrendered. He died under house arrest a couple of years later, probably having been poisoned.

Hulagu recognized Kublai as the great khan, calling himself *il-khan* (lesser khan) and his realm the Il-Khanate. He and his successors pursued their own policies independently, however, and Kublai's hold on the Chagatai Khanate remained only as strong as the armies he devoted to enforcing it. The Golden Horde was well out of his reach. From this point on, the parts of the once-united Mongol Empire were administered separately and evolved differently (Figure 14.10). Historians refer to them as khanates—the Khanate of the Golden Horde, Il-Khanate, Chagatai Khanate, and the Khanate of the Great Khan—to distinguish them from the prior period of unity.

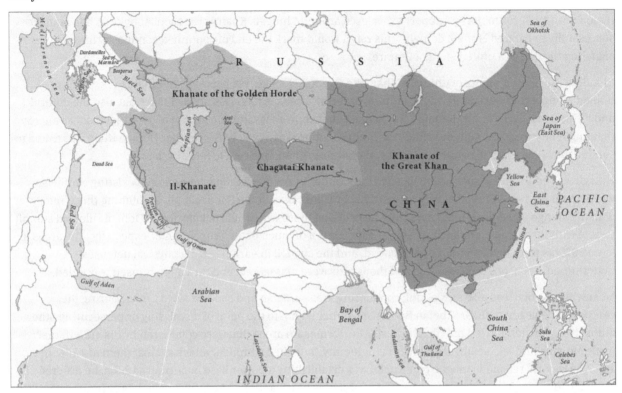

FIGURE 14.10 The Four Khanates of the Mongol Empire. This map shows the areas ruled by the four Mongol khanates after the death of Kublai Khan in 1294. For all intents and purposes, these were separate sovereign states. Hulagu's Il-Khanate was the only one to recognize Kublai as great khan. (attribution: Copyright Rice University, OpenStax, under CC BY 4.0 license)

The struggle for power between Kublai and Ariq Boke also reflected a divide between Mongols willing to live as settled people and those who sought to preserve traditional nomadic ways. Kublai and Hulagu represented Mongols willing to adopt some aspects of settled life. Their successors, especially Kublai's, embraced the settled lifestyle even more. Ariq Boke embodied the spirit of their traditional nomadic culture, the weaknesses of which had been under attack since Temujin had become Chinggis Khan and had sought to promote harmony and justice in ways traditional Mongol customs and practices did not. While Mongol armies were a formidable force in open battles on broad plains, it was only with the help of settled people and their technologies that they could take down the world's richest cities and bring their riches to the Mongolian plain and, more importantly, create bureaucratic systems to keep it flowing and distribute it.

14.3 The Mongol Empire Fragments

LEARNING OBJECTIVES

By the end of this section, you will be able to:
- Analyze the extent to which Chinggis Khan's vision for the future of Eurasia was realized by his grandsons
- Explain why Islam was successful in gaining converts in the Mongol Empire
- Analyze the degree to which Yuan China was a continuation of traditional Chinese civilization

While the ascension of Mongke Khan in 1251 gave hope for the realization of a Mongol Empire overseeing Eurasian trade, it proved only a temporary rebirth, since a lust for power consumed Chinggis Khan's grandsons. The rulers of three of the four khanates—the Chagatai Khanate, the Khanate of the Golden Horde, and the Il-Khanate—eventually converted to Islam along with many of their people, but having a common religion did not keep them from fighting one another. By the mid-fourteenth century, two khanates had completely fragmented. Sporadic efforts were made to expand against the Delhi Sultanate but failed. Kublai conquered China and established the Yuan dynasty, also known as the Great Khanate of Yuan China, in the 1270s. However, in the fourteenth century, China too was dealing with serious internal divisions.

Islam and the Mongols

While the lands of the Eurasian Steppe were always a place of great religious heterogeneity, Islam was the faith of most of the people living there. Except in the Slavic areas of the Golden Horde, the lands west of the Volga River, the endorsement of the ruling Mongol elite added to the attractions of Islam, leading the majority of the population to convert. The other faiths were relegated to small, scattered communities (Figure 14.11).

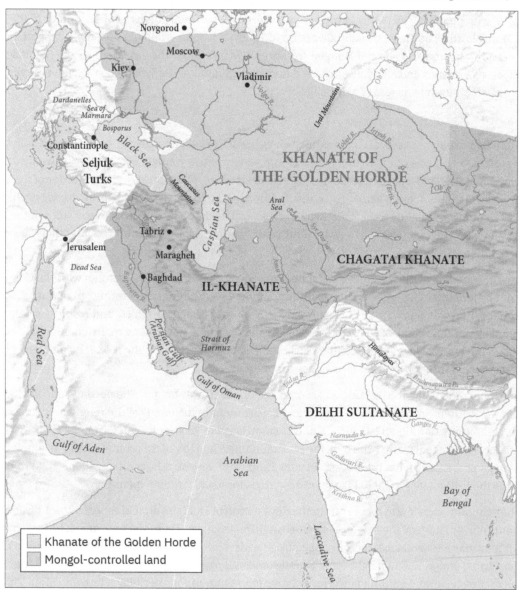

FIGURE 14.11 The Western Mongol Empire. This map shows the western Mongol Empire after its final fragmentation into four parts, which included the Great Khanate of the Yuan in China (not depicted here). The areas west of the Volga River, populated largely by Orthodox Christians, were the only ones that did not see the majority convert to Islam, and they remain so to this day. (attribution: Copyright Rice University, OpenStax, under CC BY 4.0 license)

By spreading throughout much of western and southern Asia over the centuries since its founding, Islam had often influenced—and been influenced by—local cultures. This exchange could lead to the formation of unique sects of the faith. One such set of beliefs was Sufism, a strain of Islam that emphasized asceticism and meditation as the path to a level of divine understanding that brought a rapturous feeling of love for God. Sufism played an important role in the Islamification of the Mongols and other peoples of the Inner Asian Steppe. While Sufis often sought to live lives of spiritual and moral perfection, their ultimate belief was that God was best worshipped through deep thought and reflection. Living a life strictly adhering to Quranic law was not an end in itself but a means to remove distractions so that the intense contemplation necessary to know God at the level they sought could occur.

Sufis were instructed in the movement's practices by spiritual guides and often formed communities. The disruptions of the Mongol conquests caused many of these communities to scatter into the steppe, where they intermingled with people of the Mongol Empire, and where Sufi spiritual guides seemed similar to the shamans Mongols knew as the guardians of worship of Tengri. The Sufi emphasis on a mystical path of meditation and reflection also allowed Mongols to continue to live under the y*assa* and accept Sufi teachings and practices. As Muslims and Mongols interacted and formed families, Sufism made the conversion to Islam seem more of an evolution and less of a dramatic change.

The Fate of Hulagu's Il-Khanate

Hulagu Khan had to balance several conflicts once civil war broke out after the death of Mongke Khan in 1259. The most serious threat was war with the Golden Horde, led by Batu's younger brother Berke. A convert to Islam, Berke had become deeply disturbed by Hulagu's destruction of Baghdad and the murder of the caliph. There were also disputes about whether Hulagu or the Horde should receive tribute from areas on which Hulagu had reimposed stability. Not surprisingly, Hulagu and Berke ended up on different sides of the civil war to succeed Mongke. Their conflict lasted nearly four years, until both men died in 1265, and their successors moved on to other pursuits.

For decades, the leaders of the Il-Khanate remained in frequent but intermittent conflict with the Golden Horde and the Mamluks of Egypt, who were sometimes joined by the Seljuks operating out of Anatolia and the Chagatai khans. Repulsing these attacks consumed most of the Il-Khanate's efforts and resources, a situation compounded by periodic bouts of civil war over succession and making further expansion out of the question. The Il-Khans constantly struggled to hold the Tigris-Euphrates basin, leaving the Nile delta and lands holy to the Abrahamic religions in the Levant forever beyond their grasp.

Most of the population of the Il-Khanate had become Muslim centuries before. The need to concentrate on defense led the Il-Khans to leave most of the work of government in the hands of the religious scholars called the *ulama*, reinforcing traditional Islamic law and custom. Ghazan Khan, who ruled from 1295 to 1304, firmly favored Islam. His brother Oljaitu (who took the Muslim name Khodabandeh) promoted Shia Islam, further entrenching its presence in what is today eastern Iraq and Iran. Despite this, conflict with its Muslim neighbors continued as the Il-Khanate sought to take more resources for itself at their expense.

Overall, the economy was slow to recover from the devastation of Hulagu's attack, especially with frequent warfare continuing to destroy the irrigation and urban infrastructure. There were chronic labor shortages in the first generations after Hulagu's conquest because of wide-scale murder, enslavement, and relocation, as well as substantial emigration to neighboring Islamic lands. Ghazan's reign laid the groundwork for a generation of prosperity and cultural flowering relative to the tumultuous periods before and after. This prosperity was centered east of Baghdad and the Tigris-Euphrates basin, around Maragha and Tabriz in modern Iran. The Il-Khanate rulers tried to live up to Chinggis and Ogedei Khan's dream of a world united in trade by negotiating trade deals, most famously with Venice and Genoa on the Italian Peninsula. They were also able to maintain secure trade with Mongolian China. This prosperity, however, was not enough to overcome the peril of succession struggles. After the son of Ghazan died without an heir in 1335, the Il-Khanate fell into a civil war from which it never emerged. While several men claimed to be *il-khan* in subsequent years, none exercised control over more than a fraction of the lands Hulagu had conquered.

European Portraits of Chinggis Khan

Following are depictions of Chinggis Khan by two famous European writers. The first, from Geoffrey Chaucer's *Canterbury Tales*, was written around 1400 as entertainment and likely reflected popular beliefs about the long-dead Mongol ruler. The second, from Montesquieu's *Spirit of the Laws*, was written in 1748 as a work of social science aimed at Enlightenment intellectuals. Montesquieu's disdain for absolute authority undoubtedly influenced his view of the great khan.

> This noble king was known as Cambinskan, [Chinggis Khan]
> Who in his time was of so great renown
> That there was nowhere in the wide world known
> So excellent a lord in everything;
> He lacked in naught belonging to a king.
> As for the faith to which he had been born,
> He kept its law to which he had been sworn;
> And therewith he was hardy, rich, and wise,
> And merciful and just in all men's eyes,
> True to his word, benign and honourable,
> And in his heart like any center stable;
> Young, fresh, and strong, in warfare ambitious
> As any bachelor knight of all his house.
> Of handsome person, he was fortunate,
> And kept always so well his royal state
> That there was nowhere such another man.

—Geoffrey Chaucer, *The Canterbury Tales*

The Tartars appear to be mild and humane among themselves; and yet they are most cruel conquerors: when they take cities they put the inhabitants to the sword, and imagine that they act humanely if they only sell the people, or distribute them among their soldiers. They have destroyed Asia, from India even to the Mediterranean; and all the country which forms the east of Persia they have rendered a desert . . . . These people having no towns, all their wars are carried on with eagerness and impetuosity. They fight whenever they hope to conquer; and when they have no such hope, they join the stronger army. With such customs, it is contrary to the law of nations that a city incapable of repelling their attack should stop their progress. They regard not cities as an association of inhabitants, but as places made to bid defiance to their power.

—Montesquieu, *The Spirit of the Laws*

Thus the Tartars under Jenghiz Khan [Chinggis Khan], among whom it was a sin and even a capital crime to put a knife in the fire, to lean against a whip, to strike a horse with his bridle, to break one bone with another, did not believe it to be any sin to break their word, to seize upon another man's goods, to do an injury to a person, or to commit murder.

—Montesquieu, *The Spirit of the Laws*

- How are these two depictions different and similar? What might account for their differences?
- What do these excerpts suggest about how western Europeans saw the East—and the khanates in particular?

The Golden Horde

The areas the Golden Horde ruled, northwest Asia and the lands of the Rus, were less economically developed. People had a greater diversity of lifestyles and less centralized authority than imposed by the Il-Khans, and they were able to avoid splintering into civil war until outside factors intervened more than a generation after the Il-Khanate fell.

Batu and Berke, the foundational leaders of the Horde, established a capital for the storage of tribute as their grandfather had done, but they mainly roamed with their armies, raiding neighbors or defending against attacks. The people conquered by the Golden Horde varied from Turkish peoples like the Kipchaks, seminomads similar to the Mongols, to settled Slavic peasants in small urban centers. The Mongols ruled over the Turks indirectly, allowing local leaders to enforce the *yassa*, collect taxes, and conscript labor and soldiers. Mongol officials in the capital received and distributed tribute and heard appeals of local decisions. The Rus and other Slavic peoples were ruled more directly, with Mongol overseers assigned to each local ruler to make sure taxes flowed in and rebellion was kept down.

While Berke was the first Mongol ruler and khan of the Golden Horde to embrace Islam, not all his successors were Muslim. Islam continued to gain adherents among the Horde's Mongols, however. In 1313, Uzbeg made Islam the official religion of the Golden Horde, but he did not remove the *yassa's* tax exemption for other religions. Uzbeg's promotion of Islam undoubtedly strengthened the Islamic community throughout the Golden Horde's lands.

At the same time, the Horde's rule strengthened the Orthodox Christian church in its Slavic regions. The church came to represent Rus national identity as people turned to Christianity to distinguish themselves from, and perhaps subversively resist, the Mongols. The tax and service exemptions the *yassa* gave religious institutions and those running them surpassed those the church received from Rus nobles. Church-owned land expanded under the Horde, whether because of donations to help the church provide increasing amounts of spiritual solace and identity, or because of fraud that enabled elites to live free of Mongol taxation and obligation by donating their land and then becoming the church officials in charge of the donation. By the collapse of Mongol rule in the late fifteenth century, the Russian Orthodox church's holdings had grown to about one-third of the arable land in the areas formerly ruled by Rus nobles.

The Golden Horde both benefited from and contributed to the prosperity brought about by the Pax Mongolica. Direct European trade was under their control. Whether an import to the Mongol world in the east was produced by the Rus or brought from the continent by Italian merchants, it almost certainly entered through the Golden Horde, which had the first opportunity to buy it. The *yam* that facilitated the movement of goods throughout the empire was maintained for hundreds of years after Mongol rule had dissipated.

The troubled Chagatai Khanate lay in the middle of Mongol lands. Conflict with the other Mongol Khanates and Kublai's Yuan dynasty was inevitable. At various times, separately or in combination with each other, the other Mongol states supported usurpers against the Chagatai Khans. While most had no long-term success, they kept the khanate in turmoil until it splintered into small states in the mid-fourteenth century. In addition to fighting other Mongols, some Chagatai Khans raided and on a couple of occasions tried to conquer the Delhi Sultanate. These efforts proved futile and weakened the regime, inviting more challenges and instability.

The most important long-term impact of the Chagatai Khanate was its solidification of Islam's hold over western central Asia. Central Asia had always been a place of religious diversity, given that merchants of different faiths traversed its trade routes. It was a major factor in spreading Buddhism from India and Islam beyond the borders of the caliphate. Asian versions of Christianity, different from the Catholic and Orthodox traditions in Europe, thrived there as well. The last ruler to have governed the unified Chagatai Khanate, Tarmashirin, instituted policies that favored the displacement of other faiths by Islam and replaced the *yassa* with the more restrictive **sharia**, or Islamic religious law. While this change provoked resentment among the non-Muslim populations, Islamic law continued to be in force in lands given to the Chagatai after that khanate collapsed into small states that were in constant conflict.

Yuan China

In Yuan China, even as Kublai Khan was lining up forces against Ariq Boke, he demanded the Song emperor recognize him as the Son of Heaven in exchange for autonomy over the Han Chinese people. Not unexpectedly, the Song Son of Heaven declined to submit to vassalage under a man he considered a barbarian, and war broke out. Eventually, Kublai's forces were victorious, prompting him to declare that the Mandate of Heaven had shifted to him, and the Yuan dynasty was proclaimed. As might be expected for the champion of Mongols adapting to a settled lifestyle, Kublai set up a capital city close to the old Jin capital of Zhongdu, both part of modern Beijing. China proved very difficult to govern, however; by the 1330s, the Yuan dynasty was in decline.

The Conquest of Song China

Although Kublai attempted to subdue the Song while fighting Ariq Boke, he did not begin serious efforts to conquer them until 1265. It took over a dozen years, but by 1279, the Song military was broken and its royal family dead or in hiding.

The Mongols, with allied peoples from north China and other parts of the steppe, dominated the Song on land. The Song military never developed good cavalry, perhaps hoping their fiery and explosive weapons would intimidate enemy horses and render their opponent's cavalry useless. Retreating to the cities was not an option, because the Mongols were extremely adept at siege warfare. One area in which the Mongols were almost completely inexperienced, however, was naval warfare. The long and expansive river systems in southern China posed serious obstacles to the Mongols' ability to completely conquer the Song.

Through the 1270s, the Song still tried to function as a working, mobile government, moving up and down river systems until finally pushed out to sea, whereupon they moved from port to port with a huge fleet of ships. A combination of the geography of the region, previous developments in hydraulic and irrigation technology, and Song seafaring skills allowed them to resist the arrival of the Mongols for many years. Tens of thousands of civilians loyal to the Song traveled with them. In a great irony of history, the increasingly settled Yuan Mongols had turned the Song into aquatic seminomads. The Mongols adapted to naval warfare by relying on loyal non-Mongol experts. They controlled the labor of skilled craftspeople who built warships and had sailors who could maneuver them.

In the year 1279, many Song loyalists, approximately 250,000 people in over a thousand ocean-capable boats, anchored off a remote bay near modern Yamen, China. There they began building a capital and prepared for a last stand, hoping that if they won, their victory would rally the Chinese to revolt against the Mongols. Mongol forces secured the land behind the Song ships, leaving them dependent on only the supplies they had on board. Within a few days, the Songs' supply of fresh water ran out. Weakened by dehydration, they were no match for the Mongols. As a few ships fell to Mongol boarding parties, morale among the Song collapsed, and most of them committed suicide by jumping into the sea. China was united again for the first time in more than three hundred years, not by a Han Chinese Son of Heaven, but by the Mongol Kublai Khan.

Politics, Economy, and Society in Yuan China

Although retaining some Song policies such as the rotation of officeholders, the Yuan dynasty operated very differently from the way earlier Chinese dynasties had done. Kublai Khan's most drastic change was to replace the Confucian system of class distinctions based on economic function with one based on ethnicity. At the top of the Yuan class structure were Mongols, followed by non-Chinese people, who were Europeans or previous steppe inhabitants like the Jurchen, Tangut, and Khitan. The bottom two classes were Chinese people: those of Han ethnicity who had been ruled by the Jin in the north, and the remaining Song Chinese who lived in the south. Mongols could not marry people from these bottom two classes. Everyone's place in this new class system was noted in census records for each family, along with each head of household's occupation, which was sometimes assigned if a shortage of certain types of labor occurred.

Adopting the Khitan idea of ruling different types of people differently, the Yuan dynasty had separate types of administration for its varied peoples. Even though an increasing number of Mongols were literate, including Kublai who was the first Mongol great khan to read, the mandarin written exam system fell into disuse. Mongols were subject to the *yassa*, as were the next two classes, who were ruled over by administrators appointed by the chief local Mongol administrator or the emperor himself. The Song Chinese, who were at the bottom of the four-class system, were governed by two administrators, one a Chinese person and one a Mongol or non-Chinese person. Both were imperial appointees. The Chinese administrator was under the supervision of and responsible to his counterpart. People in all these positions were rotated periodically, so they could not build up a power base.

Some non-Chinese administrators over the Song had not intended to work in the Yuan government. They came seeking some favor, often the right to trade, in exchange for which the emperors required them to perform administrative tasks. Literate Europeans came to know of the riches of Yuan China through one of these bureaucrats, Marco Polo, a young merchant, and member of a Venetian trade caravan who, along with several of his family members, ended up spending almost twenty-five years in Mongol lands and who wrote a popular account of the merchants' experiences. While the Polos were the most famous of these hostage bureaucrats, serving for about twenty years, most were Muslim traders from other parts of the Mongol Empire. Regardless of how well they did their jobs, such bureaucrats were not likely to bond with the population and create a power base from which to challenge imperial authority.

Following Kublai's death in 1294, his system's flaws became apparent. In 1315, his great-grandson Buyantu reinstated the mandarin exam system, which now reflected the dual nature of the administration. Non-Chinese people took different (and shorter) exams than the Chinese people, and between 25 and 50 percent of those who passed had to be non-Chinese people. The effect of this quota was magnified because Song Chinese people made up more than 90 percent of the population, according to Yuan censuses. Between the differences in the exams and the quota system, it was much easier for Mongols and non-Chinese to pass than for Chinese.

Although travelers like Marco Polo, and to a lesser degree the North African Muslim traveler Ibn Battuta, wrote of the impressive wealth of Yuan China, economic growth had at best stagnated, thanks to a decline in consumer purchasing power caused by inflation and heavy taxation. The use of paper currency was a major contributor to inflation. While paper money was theoretically convertible to metal or silk, the Yuan government issued much more of it than it had metal or silk to redeem it with. Kublai decreed that currency must be used in transactions with the government, thus ensuring that paper money featured in at least some economic activity. This meant the population could not escape increasing inflation, however, as successive Yuan governments issued more paper currency to pay their bills and forced the population to obtain such money to pay their taxes. As more paper money entered the system without objects of value to back it up, ever more of it was required to purchase the same amount of goods and labor.

⊘ LINK TO LEARNING

Beyond official histories, we have descriptions of the Mongol Empire (https://openstax.org/l/77MongolEmp) recorded by travelers through its domains, most famously Marco Polo and Ibn Battuta. This video contains a comparison of the men's accounts of China and their impacts on their respective civilizations. Note the differences in the purposes of their travel, the content of their accounts, and their impacts.

The increasing taxes that partly resulted from inflation were pumped back into the economy through narrow and unproductive sectors, draining wealth from the rest of the economy. The Yuan spent lavishly on grandiose but failed military ventures that bankrupted the government. These were mainly Kublai's projects. Kublai twice tried to conquer what is now Vietnam, and in even more costly ventures, he attempted complex sea invasions, two of Japan and one of Java. There were also periods of chaos and instability because of succession struggles. After Kublai's appointed successor and grandson died in 1307, seven emperors reigned over the next twenty-six years. Resentment, especially among the Song population, seethed beneath the surface as government extraction of resources increased and inflation eroded the standard of living. As if all that was not challenge enough for the Yuan, in 1331 people outside the capital in the Hebei area began to sicken and die in large numbers. Within three years, 90 percent of that area's population was dead from a strange new illness, later known as the Black Death. The Mongol Yuan government, like many of its people, did not survive long.

14.4 Christianity and Islam outside Central Asia

LEARNING OBJECTIVES

By the end of this section, you will be able to:
- Explain the evolving relationship between the Western Christian church and the rulers and people of Europe
- Identify the factors that led to the strengthening of Muslim control over the Middle East
- Discuss the limits of Mongol expansion and the states in North Africa and South Asia that remained independent

Largely oblivious to events in the Inner Asian Steppe, the thirteenth-century followers of the teachings of Jesus and Muhammed continued their struggle for control of the once-mighty Roman Empire in Europe and the Middle East. Islamic rule was slowly ending in the Iberian Peninsula (present-day Spain and Portugal), as new Christian kingdoms in the region rose and pushed the remaining Islamic states southward to a small strip around Granada. In the East, Christian forces continued their retreat before the successors of Salah al-Din (known in the west as "Saladin"), while Catholics of western Europe dealt near-fatal blows to those who considered themselves to be Rome's true heirs in Byzantium.

The Christian Pope and the Papal States

Politically, thirteenth-century Europe was a series of confederations of warriors who had sworn oaths of *vassalage*, or loyalty, to one of the titular European kings. There were no real centralized governments, courts, or bureaucracies. The real power of kings rested on the resources they could draw from their own personal lands, and on the willingness of their vassals to provide them with the support they had pledged, which in turn depended on the willingness of lesser nobles who had sworn vassalage to *them*. The church was more unified, having a multinational bureaucracy ostensibly to meet the spiritual needs of the population, but also to extract society's wealth for church leaders. This gave the church a direct and recurring relationship with the people that few lords had with the vassals on whom they relied for defense and order. Most people saw their parish priest much more often than their feudal lord.

In the 1230s, Pope Gregory IX created an Office of Papal Inquisition to centralize the persecution of heresy throughout Western Christendom. Thus began the **Inquisition**, a centuries-long effort to impose religious homogeneity on western Europe, through torture and execution, if necessary. In 1252, Pope Innocent IV authorized the use of torture on suspected heretics, who had to prove their innocence, confess, or face execution, sometimes by being burned at the stake. The fact that inquisitors could seize the lands and property of the condemned provided an unfortunate incentive to keep the persecution going.

Church-State Relations

Citing the precedent of Pope Leo III's coronation of Charlemagne, the church argued that kings held their position because the pope granted it to them. The kings and their vassals did not see it that way. Some insisted they had the right to appoint and control church officials in their lands. While the church did not gain total control of the appointment and supervision of its officials, it obtained substantial protection against arbitrary monarchial rule and some leverage over kings in most countries.

The Hohenstaufen family ruled both the Holy Roman Empire and the Kingdom of the Two Sicilies, which encompassed much of the southern half of the Italian peninsula and the island of Sicily. Thus, the papal lands in Rome were surrounded by the Hohenstaufens, causing recurring conflict between the two. In 1241, the Hohenstaufens gained the upper hand when two popes died in quick succession while Hohenstaufen armies were laying siege to Rome. As a result, the papacy remained vacant for two years. A new pope incited revolt throughout the Holy Roman Empire, however, and the last Hohenstaufens succumbed to malaria in 1254. Their fall ushered in a long period known as the Great Interregnum, in which no Holy Roman emperor existed and Germanic nobles swore oaths of vassalage to rival kings. With such divisions in place, the papacy on occasion intervened—sometimes successfully, sometimes not—in political matters as well.

The church-state conflict played out differently in the Two Sicilies, where the monarchy established secular political control through the 1231 **Constitutions of Melfi**, considered the oldest surviving written constitution in the world. The Constitutions of Melfi increased the power of the monarch by replacing vassals and church officials with royal bureaucrats as local administrators and judges. The bureaucracy was funded by revenue from royal monopolies on essential products like salt, iron, and copper, along with tariffs and tolls. This revenue also allowed the king to build infrastructure, including fortifications in strategic parts of the kingdom staffed with soldiers paid from the royal coffers. The state created by the Constitutions of Melfi resisted church encroachment on its authority better than the Holy Roman Empire had.

Tension between the Rulers and the Ruled

A stronger central government also emerged in France over the thirteenth century. As in the Two Sicilies, this resulted from a restructuring of local government so that royal bureaucrats replaced vassals and church officials, and the monarchy had sufficient income to pay for their loyalty. Beginning with King Phillip II in the late twelfth century, French monarchs exploited opportunities to add to their royal holdings by taking land from their nobles. These new lands were managed by salaried royal appointees, not vassals who could pass their holdings to heirs. By the early fourteenth century, much of France was under direct royal control, greatly enhancing the resources French kings could call upon in conflicts with their vassals and the church.

By the reign of Phillip IV, which began in 1285, the French crown's relationship with the church had drastically deteriorated. The crisis escalated until 1303, when Phillip sent soldiers to Rome to remove Pope Boniface. This act so intimidated church officials that when it came time to select Boniface's successor in 1305, the cardinals picked a Frenchman allied with Phillip who then moved the papacy from Rome to Avignon, France, where it remained under the watchful eyes of French kings until 1376.

England developed differently than other European states. The monarch's power over its vassals and the church was limited from the thirteenth century onward, and the basic rights of commoners, generally interpreted to mean adult males not bound as servants or apprentices, were protected. After King John was forced to become the pope's vassal and pay him tribute, John's vassals, emboldened by his capitulation, compelled him in 1215 to reaffirm those rights and expand them in **Magna Carta**, a document that reiterated existing rights and relationships of vassals. The document confirmed the papal position that the church was above the state and "shall have its rights undiminished, and its liberties unimpaired . . . by our heirs in perpetuity." Among the rights spelled out in Magna Carta, perhaps the most important was that "no free man shall be seized or imprisoned, or stripped of his rights or possessions, or outlawed or exiled, or deprived of his standing in any way, nor will we proceed with force against him, or send others to do so, except by the lawful judgment of his equals." This requirement created a precedent for trial by jury, which remains a staple of the judicial system in the West to the present day.

The other key development leading toward centralized government with limited and specified powers was the creation of a deliberative body of nobles, clergy, and commoners that replaced the Great Council of the king's vassals and high clergy. This new body evolved into Parliament, designed to represent the interests of the people. Membership was expanded to representatives elected by the vassals of the king's vassals, and starting in 1265, selected towns could send representatives to speak for the interests of merchants.

Parliament had two primary powers. One was to approve all tax increases. To establish uniform rule by the monarch, as opposed to a decentralized set of laws from the nobility and a potentially conflicting set from the church, Edward I asked Parliament to also approve laws. Parliamentary approval made the laws England's laws, not just the king's laws. Even if the king had drafted them, the nobles, clergy, and wealthy commoners had to agree to them. Edward I called his first Parliament in 1275, and the body met forty-six times during his thirty-five-year reign.

In the thirteenth century, the Iberian Peninsula was split between Christian kingdoms and parts of the Islamic Almohad Caliphate. The Christian kingdoms of Portugal, Leon, Navarre, Castile, and Aragon held about three-fifths of the land. Not only did these kingdoms fight each other and their Islamic rivals, but the same conflicts occurred between vassals and king and between monarch and church that existed in other Christian kingdoms. The church and vassals joined together to provide the king with revenue they deemed sufficient to keep the kingdom safe and orderly. Further resources had to be agreed upon by a council of vassals, clergy, and merchant representatives called the Cortes. As in England, the church and vassals were able to avoid being bypassed by kings and to assert checks on royal finances and power.

The Almohad Caliphate

Since the 1170s, Islamic Iberia had been ruled by the Almohad Caliphate, but they struggled to unify Muslims throughout the region and at times struggled to assert their authority. The Almohads were Imazighen (Berbers) from what is now southern Morocco. Leadership positions and economic advantage disproportionately went to members of the tribe from which the Almohad movement originated, often causing resentment. Support for the Almohads among other Muslims in North Africa and Iberia was broad but not especially strong.

Pope Innocent III arranged a truce among the Iberian Christian kingdoms in the early thirteenth century, convincing them to crusade to restore Christian rule to Iberia. In 1212, the Christian kingdoms devastated the Almohads at the Battle of Las Navas de Tolosa. Within a year, the Almohad caliph died without an heir, plunging the Muslim states in Iberia into a civil war from which they never recovered.

⊘ LINK TO LEARNING

This four-minute animation depicts the back-and-forth between Christian and Muslim control of Iberia, from the first Muslim invasion in the early eighth century to the final Christian conquest of Granada in 1492. This final success of the Christians in the peninsula is often called the Reconquista (https://openstax.org/l/77Reconquista) (reconquest), but historians have been moving away from that term because it privileges a Western Christian worldview on the period.

Squabbling among Iberia's Christian kings caused their alliance to collapse. Nevertheless, over the next forty years or so, each kingdom expanded independently into what had been Almohad territory. By the late 1260s, only the area around Granada, about 5 percent of the peninsula, remained under Muslim control. Even there, however, the rulers swore vassalage to the secular kings of Castile.

Iberian Muslims now under Christian rule were generally not driven out and could work and practice Islam. The less fundamentalist Islamic law of pre-Almohad days was brought back for them, though church law called for discriminatory segregation in dealing with non-Christians. To ensure that minimal interaction occurred, for instance, Muslims were required to wear distinctive dress. They also had to pay taxes to the Christian church and observe Sabbath restrictions on Sundays, although they were not compelled to work on their own holy day of Friday. Muslims could work in Christian businesses but not in Christian households. Marriage between Christians and Muslims and Jews was forbidden, as was trying to convert Christians.

The Later Crusades and the Limits of Mongol Rule

Although Muslims lost ground to Christians in Iberia in the early thirteenth century, they were much more successful against them in their heartland. Despite incessant conflicts over which individuals should rule the Levant for Islam, Muslims rebuffed Christian attempts to reassert control of the Holy Land (modern Israel). Meanwhile, Catholic and Orthodox Christians killed each other in the struggle that mortally wounded Byzantium, known as the Fourth Crusade. By midcentury, several more crusades had been defeated, and

Muslims seemed well positioned to expel Christians from the Levant and make gains against the dying Byzantine Empire.

After the Third Crusade, crusaders held only Tyre, Acre, and scattered fortifications in the interior of the Holy Land. Pope Innocent III, hoping to regain the Holy Land for western Christendom, and by virtue of that victory to convince the eastern churches to accept papal sovereignty, called for a Fourth Crusade soon after assuming the papacy in 1198. The plan was to attack the Muslims through Egypt to seize Jerusalem, as the last two (failed) crusades had attempted.

The Fourth Crusade never made it to Egypt, however, much less the holy lands of the eastern Mediterranean. The expense of transportation and supplies left the crusaders in debt to Venetian merchants, who insisted they settle the obligation by reconquering the city of Zadar (in modern Croatia, called "Zara" by the Venetians) for Venice. Pope Innocent was opposed to the idea. Not only was it a distraction from retaking the Holy Land, but Zadar was a Catholic city. Nevertheless, the crusaders agreed, taking the city in 1202.

While wintering in Zadar, the crusaders were offered the opportunity to make more money and recruit Byzantine soldiers for the crusade if they installed the son of a recently deposed Byzantine emperor on the throne in Constantinople. Perhaps to forestall Innocent's objections, the Byzantines' offer also included subordination of the Orthodox churches to Catholicism, a long-term goal of the western crusaders. Pope Innocent ordered the crusaders to go on to the Holy Land, but they accepted the Byzantines' offer and made their way to Constantinople instead (Figure 14.12).

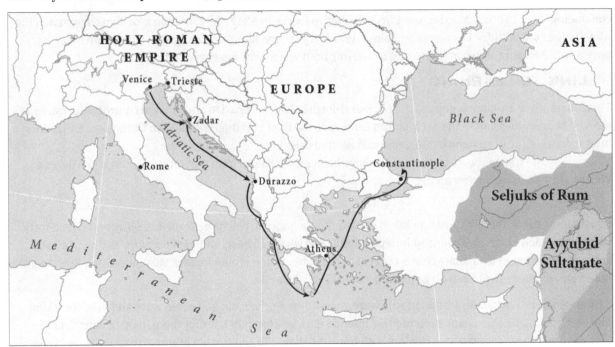

FIGURE 14.12 The Fourth Crusade. This map shows the route of the Fourth Crusade in the early thirteenth century. Distracted by other goals in Zadar and Constantinople, the crusaders never reached the Holy Land. (attribution: Copyright Rice University, OpenStax, under CC BY 4.0 license)

After a great deal of bungling and confusion on both sides, the crusaders were able to put their young patron on the throne of Byzantium as Alexius IV in the summer of 1203. It turned out, however, that Alexius could come up with only half the promised money, and his attempts to raise the remainder provoked a coup that ended in his death. As they awaited payment from the Byzantines, the crusaders found their expenses increasing, and getting to Egypt looked increasingly daunting. Defeating the heirs of Salah al-Din would be no easy task. The Byzantine army had already fled before them, and many crusaders had not seen their homes for almost three years. Clergy among them pointed out, however, that bringing a usurper (Salah al-Din) to justice was a holy cause that could fulfill their vows of fighting for causes aligned with Christian principles and God's will, and one that would guarantee their entrance into heaven. However, restoring a legitimate ruler to the Byzantine Empire became the mission of the Fourth Crusade, accomplished in short order in the spring of 1204.

This new mission of the Fourth Crusade was radically different from that of the previous crusades, which had focused on expelling Muslim rulers from formerly Christian lands. The First Crusade, near the end of the eleventh century, had been the most successful, reestablishing Christian control over areas of Palestine and Syria and creating four Christian-ruled sovereign states in the Levant. After Muslims reclaimed much of the area, two more crusades occurred in the late twelfth century. Neither was able to reassert Christian dominance over Jerusalem or other key Christian sites. The Fourth Crusade had sought to complete the mission, but now it shifted to righting the supposed moral wrongs of Byzantium's latest internal intrigues.

Once they had stripped Constantinople bare, the crusaders appointed a new Byzantine emperor and one of their own priests as Patriarch of Orthodox Christianity, thus putting the leadership of the Byzantine church in the hands of someone loyal to the papacy. Within a year, most of them had drifted back to their original homes, taking a share of Byzantium's wealth with them. As they expected, Pope Innocent accepted the reimposition of Catholicism on Eastern Christianity as sufficient for fulfilling a crusader's vows, even if not a single drop of Muslim blood had been shed or an inch of Islamic territory added to Christendom.

The Ayyubids and the Crusaders

The land the crusaders had intended to invade was ruled by the heirs of Salah al-Din and called the Ayyubid dynasty. Although Salah al-Din had directed that his empire be split among his brothers and sons upon his death in 1193, his brother al-Adil I had centralized it under his own control by around 1200. The actual power of any Ayyubid ruler rested on his ability to maintain the loyalty of mamluk armies; mamluks were soldiers, generally enslaved men taken from the peoples of the Eurasian Steppe as boys or adolescents. They had limited property and marriage rights and could move into high administrative and leadership posts if talented. They had no loyalties to the populations they policed and defended, and they were much less likely to rebel than members of communities that might become unhappy with the caliph's rule. Their position and future completely depended on the continuation of their owner's rule. Many caliphs thus preferred mamluk armies to civilian ones.

With Jerusalem still in Muslim hands after the Fourth Crusade, Pope Innocent called for a Fifth Crusade, dedicating church funds to avoid the financial issues that had lured the Fourth Crusade off course. Reusing the intended strategy of the Fourth Crusade, the Fifth Crusade departed for Egypt in 1217. Taking advantage of the turmoil caused by al-Adil I's death in late 1218 and the ensuing rebellion against his son al-Kamil, the crusaders captured Damietta in 1219. With his lands in disarray, al-Kamil tried to bribe the crusaders to leave Egypt. He offered them all of what had been the former crusader state centered around Jerusalem and a thirty-year truce between Muslims and Christians in the Holy Land.

Confident they could defeat him, the crusaders rejected al-Kamil's offer, a choice that proved unwise. By 1221, al-Kamil and his brothers had reasserted control over their father's empire and joined together to trap the crusader army in the Nile delta. Faced with the threat of death by arms or by drowning, the crusaders agreed to withdraw from their conquests and return to Europe, ending the Fifth Crusade in yet another failure.

To placate the papacy, Hohenstaufen ruler Frederick II agreed to lead a new crusade, but personal misfortune and lack of enthusiasm among Europe's vassals hindered his ability to get underway. The delays were so severe that the exasperated Pope Gregory IX excommunicated him, cutting him off from the church and its sacred rites. Even after Frederick set sail in 1228, Gregory condemned his venture as an unjust war, not a holy crusade.

Breaking with the strategy of the four previous crusades, Frederick landed in Acre, the main port still in Christian hands. His slow pace allowed word of his excommunication to precede him, causing him to be greeted with suspicion by his fellow Christians. Recognizing the power balance between Christians and the Ayyubids, Frederick fell back on his highly effective diplomatic skills to obtain the crusade's objectives, concluding the Treaty of Jaffa with Sultan al-Kamil in 1219 (Figure 14.13).

FIGURE 14.13 Al-Kamil and Frederick II. This image from a fourteenth-century Italian manuscript depicts the Holy Roman emperor, Frederick II (second from left), and the Ayyubid sultan al-Kamil (center) signing the Treaty of Jaffa decades earlier in 1229. Although the figures are similar in appearance, note the turban and curved swords that identify the two on the right as Muslims. (credit: "Friedrich II. mit Sultan al-Kamil" by I Villani illustrato/Wikimedia Commons, Public Domain)

The agreement allowed Frederick to be the titular king of Jerusalem, though with limited power. Muslims were under the rule of local Islamic scholars, not Christian officials; they could not be expelled or have their wealth confiscated, they could practice Islam, and the Islamic holy sites of the Al-Aqsa Mosque and Dome of the Rock remained under Muslim control. The treaty prohibited Jerusalem's city walls, destroyed in the course of the crusades, from being rebuilt, leaving the city defenseless if Muslims attacked. A ten-year truce between Muslims and Christians was put in place.

The agreement was widely seen as a capitulation by both Muslims and Christians. Frederick's decision to favor negotiation over battle sapped morale among the crusaders and furthered mistrust of him among the Holy Land's Christians. Nevertheless, a Christian was king of Jerusalem, more Christians were under Christian rule than had been the case for at least two generations, and all had been accomplished without spilling a single drop of human blood.

By the time the truce expired, al-Kamil's sons were fighting each other and ambitious generals for control. New crusaders arrived sporadically, augmenting Christian forces in the area. They tried to expand Christian territory by playing rival Ayyubid factions against each other, but it was all for naught. Al-Kamil's son al-Salih stabilized his rule over the Ayyubid Empire, retook Jerusalem, and pushed the Christians back to a strip of coastal ports by 1244. He owed much of his success to bands of wandering Turks who had been displaced by Mongol expansion into central Asia and whom he incorporated into the Ayyubid mamluk army. While helpful for the moment, however, these additional soldiers entered the status of mamluk as independent adult refugees, not as adolescents with no life experience to compare mamluk service to.

While al-Salih consolidated his power, the French king Louis IX called for another crusade to liberate Jerusalem from Islamic rule, hoping to repeat the initial successes of the Fifth Crusade by taking Damietta in Egypt. He succeeded, but while Salih's death in 1249 gave the crusaders hope, they met the same fate as their predecessors almost thirty years earlier. The Ayyubid mamluk army, led by al-Salih's son Turan Shah, trapped the crusaders in the unfamiliar terrain of the Nile delta, capturing Louis and much of his army in 1250. Those deemed sick or unworthy of ransom were killed. Louis and the vassals with him were held hostage until Damietta was abandoned by the crusaders and a ransom of 6.4 million ounces of silver (more than USD$134 million at 2020 prices) was paid in advance, with the crusaders pledging to pay an equal amount later. This and the later crusades were often failures for a variety of reasons, which included unfamiliarity with the land and its peoples and more than a century of distrust that had continued to build between the crusaders and the indigenous eastern Christians.

The Rise of Egypt's Mamluk Dynasty

Turan Shah did not live long enough to enjoy the fruits of his success. The wandering Turks turned mamluks who were the backbone of his army were convinced that the ransom money from the crusaders would be used to replace them with more traditional mamluks from Africa. To secure their position and gain control of the ransom money for themselves, they overthrew Turan Shah. His stepmother, al-Salih's surviving widow Shajar al-Durr, briefly assumed the throne, but the mamluks were not willing to follow a female sultan, so they forced her to marry their leader Izz al-Din Aybak and abdicate in his favor. Historians consider the ascension of Aybak to be the end of the Ayyubid dynasty and the beginning of the Egyptian Mamluk dynasty. The Ayyubids left important marks on the history of the Islamic Levant. They restored the primacy of Sunni Islam after over two hundred years of Shia Fatimid rule. They built new madrasas—Muslim schools of learning, often with an emphasis on studying the Quran—in Aleppo, Cairo, and Damascus.

While Christians and Muslims were fighting each other, Hulagu Khan and his troops were ready to return to expanding Mongol domains. Satisfied with their looting of Baghdad and the security of their supply routes, they moved north to lands more hospitable to the enormous herds the army required. Hulagu decided the Mamluk areas of Syria and Egypt would be his next targets and demanded the Mamluk sultan become his vassal and pay tribute. The sultan declined. In 1259, after securing cooperation (or at least noninterference) from Islamic forces in Anatolia and crusader forces in the area, Hulagu attacked the Mamluks. Initially he had great success, taking Aleppo, which was annihilated as Baghdad had been, and Damascus, which surrendered unconditionally and was largely spared. Hulagu's participation was short-lived, however. In early 1260, he received word that his presence was needed at a *kurultai* in Karakorum.

Hulagu appears to have underestimated Mamluk military prowess. Despite withdrawing possibly 90 percent of his forces as he returned to Karakorum, he still ordered Kitbuqa, one of his top generals and a Nestorian Christian, to take twenty thousand troops to conquer Egypt. Augmenting Kitbuqa's forces were Christian Armenians and some of the remaining crusaders. In the fall of 1260, the Mamluks attacked the invading Mongols at Ain Jalut and soundly defeated them, killing Kitbuqa and most of his force. While the loss was relatively small compared with Hulagu's overall force, it was enough to save parts of the unconquered Islamic world from further Mongol attack. Hulagu soon had his hands full defending his territory from his fellow Mongols, especially those of the Golden Horde. Meanwhile, the Mamluks were able to liberate Syria and Palestine from both the Mongols and the remaining crusaders and give some support to the Golden Horde in its conflicts with the Il-Khanate.

The Delhi Sultanate

There are many parallels between Mamluk Egypt and the Delhi Sultanate (in present-day India). The Delhi Sultanate had been created by the inhabitants of what is modern Afghanistan and was led by Muhammed of Ghur, who conquered the sultanate established by Mahmud of Ghazna in the late twelfth century. When the

Mongols encountered it, the sultanate was ruled by a dynasty of former mamluks whose founder, Quṭb al-Din Aybak, had seized power after Muhammed's death in 1206. Perhaps his efforts served as inspiration for the mamluk general Izz al-Din Aybak, who led the overthrow of Egypt's Ayyubid dynasty almost fifty years later.

A feature the Delhi Sultanate shared with both its Mongol neighbors and the later Egyptian Mamluk dynasty was frequent bouts of civil war over succession. Aybak died from an injury after falling from a horse in 1210, leaving the task of stabilizing the sultanate to his son-in-law Iltutmish. Iltutmish did a remarkable job, asserting authority over other commanders of mamluk armies. After his death in 1236, however, decentralization and turmoil reigned for sixty years. During that time, there were ten sultans, only one of whom died from natural causes. The population suffered the disruption of economic activity and the destruction of crops, goods, and production centers during these multiyear struggles for leadership.

The conflict after the death of Iltutmish foreshadowed the turmoil of the Mamluk seizure of power from the Ayyubids and the role played in each case by a talented and forceful Muslim woman. Among the Mamluks this was al-Salih's surviving widow, Shajar al-Durr. In the Delhi Sultanate, it was Raziya, Iltutmish's daughter, whom he considered the most capable of his children to rule. A half-brother seized power with help from factions unwilling to accept a female sultan. Raziya, who had administered Delhi when her father was away on campaign, outmaneuvered her half-brother by directly appealing to the people of Delhi. When the army saw the public behind her, they deposed her decadent and incompetent brother.

Raziya ruled as sultana for four years and is remembered as a capable administrator, even leading successful military campaigns (Figure 14.14). Politically shrewd, she came to power despite the objections of nobles primarily because of popular support from her people. Breaking with Islamic convention, she dressed as a man, wore pants and no veil, and kept her hair short. This was too much for some Muslims in the sultanate. Another half-brother capitalized on their discontent and organized a rebellion of several military units, which drove Raziya into hiding. She was, however, cunning; she was eventually captured by one of the generals and married him; whether the marriage was a romantic alliance or a case of political opportunism is unknown. Ultimately, the couple was defeated and killed.

FIGURE 14.14 Sultana Raziya. This nineteenth-century painted miniature depicts Sultana Raziya in the center of the top row. Notice that she is the only female in the throne room, including her attendants, who appear to her right. (credit: modification of work "Sultana Razia Begum" by Salar Jung Museum, Hyderabad/Museums of India, Public Domain)

To keep down rebellion and internal power struggles, the later Delhi sultans developed a series of authoritarian policies. For example, a secret police network was established to watch civilian administrators and military officials. Rules were so strict that these elites were banned from having celebratory gatherings with their peers, because sultans feared coups were planned at such events. Although already prohibited by the Quran, alcohol was officially outlawed, at least in the administrative area of Delhi. Peasants were largely spared in an effort to prevent rebellions, but other classes lost their financial independence and were placed under state control. Land that had been given to soldiers and war widows was confiscated, and bureaucrats' salaries were kept low. Price controls limited merchants' profit potential, and high taxes prevented the accumulation of large amounts of private capital. All these policies deprived subjects of wealth to fund rebellions and gave the sultan the ability to control people by cutting off their income.

Despite frequent internal turmoil, the Delhi Sultanate performed well against external foes and expanded greatly during the hundred years after Iltutmish's rule. When he died in 1236, the sultanate controlled the area from the Himalayas through the Ganges River valley to the Narmada River at the northern edge of the Deccan Plateau. By the end of Muhammad Bin Tughlaq's conquests in 1336, it held almost all the subcontinent's land as well (Figure 14.15). This expansion not only enlarged the territory Muslims ruled from Delhi; it also facilitated the conversion to Islam of more of the Indian population. A per-person tax was imposed on Hindus, but it was graduated based on income. Those at the extremes of wealth and poverty, the Brahmans and the Pariah, respectively, were largely exempt. Furthermore, no sultan imposed sharia, which would likely have caused resentment. Those like the Pariah and Sudra, who felt caste discrimination, could easily find a home and increase their social standing by converting to Islam, and a good number chose to do so.

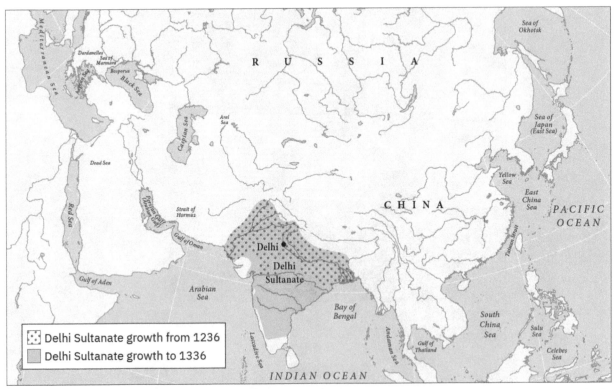

FIGURE 14.15 The Growth of the Delhi Sultanate. This map shows the growth of the Delhi Sultanate in the hundred years from 1236 to 1336. (attribution: Copyright Rice University, OpenStax, under CC BY 4.0 license)

The Delhi Sultanate was also effective at repulsing Mongol attacks. While Chinggis Khan had bypassed it in his war against the Khwarazmians, both the Il-Khanate and the Chagatai Khanate, despite their own domestic turmoil and conflict with neighboring Mongol khanates, launched periodic raids against it for plunder. It was not until the 1290s that the Chagatai Khan Duwa made the first of several attempts not just to pillage but to conquer at least parts of the Delhi Sultanate. Duwa never led these efforts himself because he was engaged against the Yuan dynasty for most of this period. At least six attempts failed between 1296 and 1306, however, in no small part because Duwa had chosen to attack when the sultanate had one of its most capable rulers, Alauddin Khilji.

Tarmashirin made one last attack on the Delhi Sultanate for the Chagatai Khanate in 1327. Taking advantage of Sultan Tughlaq's moving his capital and the bulk of his forces south to the center of his expanded empire, Tarmashirin, while struggling to assume the Chagatai Khanate throne, laid siege to Delhi. After extorting a great deal of tribute from Sultan Tughlaq, useful in raising an army to complete his own ascension to power back home, Tarmashirin withdrew his forces. Some scholars suggest his subsequent conversion to Islam was an attempt to minimize the possibility of a major retaliatory strike by the sultanate. Regardless, the fracturing of the Chagatai Khanate after Tarmashirin's death ended any serious efforts by Mongols to conquer the Delhi Sultanate.

Key Terms

Constitutions of Melfi the oldest surviving written constitution in the world, which increased the power of the monarch of the Kingdom of the Two Sicilies by replacing vassals and church officials with royal bureaucrats

Golden Horde the Mongol group that ruled over portions of central Asia, the former lands of the Rus, and northwest Asia

Inquisition a centuries-long effort by the church to impose religious homogeneity on Western Europe through torture and execution, if necessary

kurultai a proto-democratic gathering of a Mongol leader's followers, called to reach agreement on major political decisions

Magna Carta an English document that reiterated existing rights of vassals, confirmed the papal position that the church is above the state, and spelled out some basic rights of commoners

mandarins top officials in the Imperial Chinese bureaucracy, selected by a series of exams on Confucian texts

People of the Felt Walls Temujin's name for his ethnically and linguistically diverse followers

sharia Islamic religious law

yam horse relay stations established by Chinggis Khan for long-distance communication on military campaigns; they were later expanded into rest areas and supply depots

yassa Chinggis Khan's law code, designed to eliminate the sources of conflict in steppe society and bring harmony to his people

Section Summary

14.1 Song China and the Steppe Peoples

The Song dynasty revived and strengthened Confucian civilization in the areas it ruled. Technology improved agricultural yields and laid the groundwork for a type of industrial revolution to occur long before the one that took place in the Western world. The emphasis on Confucius's pacifist vision led to a neglect of the military, however, at a time when China's neighbors were becoming more organized and powerful. The Khitan, Xia, and Jurchen all adopted elements of Chinese civilization but did not lose their appetite for raiding and war. Once the Jurchen Jin dynasty displaced the Liao, it realized the weaknesses of the Song and reduced it to an even smaller slice of China's traditional territory.

Meanwhile, in Mongolia, Temujin used military innovations to gain control of increasing numbers of commoners at the eastern end of the Eurasian Steppe, building a force loyal and powerful enough to bring about his vision of a better life for his people. By 1204, Temujin was the unchallenged ruler of the People of the Felt Walls.

14.2 Chinggis Khan and the Early Mongol Empire

Chinggis Khan ruled the Mongol Empire for twenty-one years. In that time, he established a law code, the *yassa*, that he hoped would allow his seminomadic people to live in harmony. He saw the people living in settled areas, such as the Xi Xia, Jin, and Khwarazmians, as a source of wealth and tribute. The empire changed enormously during Chinggis Khan's reign, becoming more inwardly peaceful but also much more materialistic in its tastes. The military changed as well, becoming a sophisticated war machine capable of surprise attacks and deadly sieges.

Chinggis Khan's son Ogedei steered the empire toward his father's vision of a united people, overseeing a peaceful Eurasia-wide exchange of goods and collection of taxes, and he expanded the empire to make it happen. Equally important, Ogedei undertook the development of the bureaucracy and infrastructure necessary to support trade on a large scale. Due to Ogedei's lack of foresight in planning for succession, however, the reign of Chinggis Khan's grandson Mongke marked the end of a united Mongol Empire. When Mongke's brother Kublai succeeded him as great khan, the empire was beginning to divide into those who preferred the old nomadic ways and those who had adopted a settled lifestyle of wealth and trade.

14.3 The Mongol Empire Fragments

While Kublai's Yuan dynasty reunited China and gave it the same ruler as the Mongol homeland and much of central Asia, it revived neither the prosperity of China nor the robustness of the steppe people. Trade continued to flow, and the effects of earlier economic growth were still apparent, but less wealth was subsequently produced. This meant less went to the steppe, and those producing wealth saw increasingly fewer returns on their labor. The seemingly invincible armies of the Mongol Empire had proven unable to conquer Southeast Asia and were even less skilled at long-distance sea invasions. Perhaps most contrary to Chinggis Khan's desired legacy, his descendants succumbed to a lust for power and were quick to abandon the strength of a unified Mongol people under one leader for their own bid to be that leader for a few years.

14.4 Christianity and Islam outside Central Asia

The forces of centralization and conformity in Western Christendom scored important victories, crushing heretical movements and formalizing institutions such as the Inquisition to keep them down. On the other hand, crusaders and kings alike often ignored the papal will with virtual impunity. Monarchs in France and the Two Sicilies laid the groundwork for strong royal bureaucracies to keep the nobility in check. In other areas, nobles and merchants in places like England and Iberia created institutional arrangements to protect their rights and resources from royal abuse.

The Muslim-held portions of the Mediterranean saw frequent struggles over who would govern as institutions to ensure orderly succession failed to develop. Whoever had the military strength to impose law and order did so until they were displaced. Perhaps nothing demonstrated this pattern more than the rise of the Mamluk dynasty, founded by the mercenaries long used in struggles by different descendants of Salah al-Din. In North Africa, this failure of succession and changing military realities led to a collapse of centralized power and a yielding of land in Iberia to growing Christian states. In both areas, however, Sunni Islam emerged stronger than it had been at the beginning of the thirteenth century, although the strength of Muslim governance in the Iberian Peninsula was on a precipitous decline from which it would not recover.

Assessments

Review Questions

1. The saying "Do not waste good iron making nails; do not waste good men making soldiers" reflects the attitude of the _____ toward their military.
   a. Jin dynasty
   b. Liao dynasty
   c. Naiman Confederation
   d. Song dynasty

2. What caused the sizable population rise in Song China during the eleventh century?
   a. the use of strains of rice that ripened quickly enough to allow for two harvests in a single year
   b. Mongolian soldiers protecting trade routes that allowed more food to be imported
   c. the invention of horse-drawn plows that allowed more land to be cultivated
   d. the immigration of refugees from Chinggis Khan's conquests

3. What empire maintained a dual system of governance in which formerly seminomadic peoples were governed in their traditional manner, while Chinese populations were governed by mandarins?
   a. Jin
   b. Liao
   c. Song
   d. Tatar

4. How did Temujin change traditional seminomadic practices for dealing with men captured from the clans

or tribes he defeated?
   a. He ordered all captured enemies killed, sparing no one regardless of class.
   b. He ordered all captives enslaved.
   c. He ordered commoners killed but spared the leadership of his defeated rivals.
   d. He tried and executed the leaders but spared the commoners, even allowing them to join his army.

5. What was the intention of Chinggis Khan's *yassa*?
   a. to reinforce the objectification of women
   b. to force all Mongols to worship Tengri
   c. to remove sources of conflict and strife among Mongols
   d. to make the Mongolian economy self-sufficient

6. Who ultimately conquered the Jin dynasty?
   a. Chinggis Khan
   b. Mongke
   c. Hulagu
   d. Ogedei

7. What does the term *kurultai* mean?
   a. a medallion carried by Mongol government officials to identify them as under the great khan's protection
   b. Chinggis Khan's law code
   c. rest areas that provided lodging, supplies, and fresh horses for those on official business
   d. a proto-democratic gathering of a Mongol leader's followers to reach agreement on major political decisions

8. Why is Ariq Boke important?
   a. because he conquered the Abbassid Caliphate
   b. because his challenge to Kublai ended the unity of the Mongol Empire
   c. because he conquered Song China
   d. because he succeeded Chinggis Khan

9. What Mongol khanate was the first to fragment beyond recovery after a succession struggle?
   a. the Il-Khanate
   b. the Khanate of the Golden Horde
   c. the Chagatai Khanate
   d. the Khanate of the Great Khan

10. What was the only part of the Mongol world in which the rulers did not convert to Islam?
   a. the Il-Khanate
   b. the Khanate of the Golden Horde
   c. the Chagatai Khanate
   d. the Khanate of the Great Khan

11. Economic growth in Yuan China was _____.
   a. even greater than in Song China
   b. less than in Song China
   c. unchanged from Song China
   d. hard to evaluate because no records were kept

12. Jerusalem was temporarily restored to Christian control by _____.
    a. the Fourth Crusade
    b. the Treaty of Jaffa
    c. the Fifth Crusade
    d. the crusade led by Louis IX

13. What was the purpose of the Constitutions of Melfi?
    a. strengthen the king's control over his vassals and the clergy
    b. require the Cortes to meet every year
    c. ensure all free adults were tried by juries of their peers
    d. ensure that no free people were deprived of property without due process

14. Where did the Almohads rule?
    a. Mesopotamia and Persia
    b. Byzantium
    c. Iberia and North Africa
    d. Egypt and the Levant

15. Under what name did Salah al-Din's descendants rule Egypt and Syria?
    a. Almohads
    b. Hohenstaufens
    c. Ayyubids
    d. Mamluks

16. What Mongol khanate weakened itself in several failed attempts to conquer the Delhi Sultanate?
    a. the Il-Khanate
    b. the Khanate of the Golden Horde
    c. the Chagatai Khanate
    d. the Khanate of the Great Khan

Check Your Understanding Questions

1. To what degree were the emperors of the Song dynasty effective at running a thriving civilization? Why?

2. How did the way the Khitan Liao lived, once they established a more settled empire, compare with that of the Jurchen Jin once they did so as well?

3. Did succession to the position of great khan work out as Chinggis Khan had hoped in the decades after his death?

4. Using the map provided, identify each part of the Mongol Empire. (credit: modification of work "Map of the Mongol Empire c. 1300, after its four subdivisions" by "Gabagool"/Wikimedia Commons, CC BY 3.0)

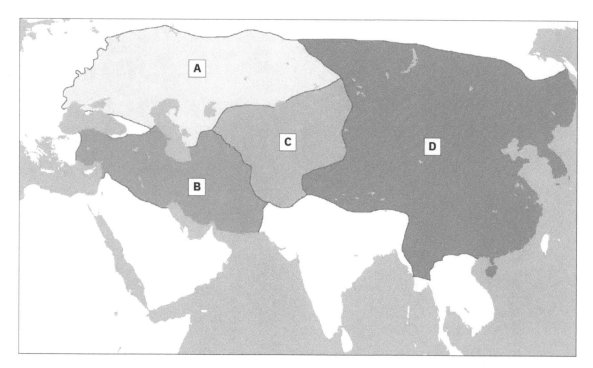

5. How did the rivers and hydraulic infrastructure of China allow the Song dynasty to prolong their rule and stave off defeat by the Mongols for many years?

6. Why did the Mongol Empire break apart?

7. What was a common source of instability among both Christian and Islamic monarchies in the thirteenth century?

8. Why were the Ayyubids and Mamluks able to repel the crusades of the first half of the thirteenth century?

9. Why might members of the Sudra and Pariah castes convert to Islam under the Delhi Sultanate?

Application and Reflection Questions

1. How did the Song dynasty differ from earlier periods of unified Chinese history such as the Tang and Han dynasties, and how did these differences change Chinese society for the better?

2. How was Chinggis Khan able to unify the peoples of the eastern end of the Eurasian Steppe?

3. What were some of the factors that prevented the Mongols from conquering more lands in South Asia, Africa, and the Middle East?

4. How did Chinggis Khan's *yassa* change the traditional practices of the Mongol people, and what motivated him to make these changes?

5. To what degree did Yuan dynasty government and policy differ from the administration of the Song dynasty?

6. What effect did the Mongol conquests have on the spread of Islam?

7. Did the crusading movement, both in Iberia and the Levant, do more to help or harm the relationship between the Christian church and the rulers of western Europe in this period? Why?

8. What were some of the reasons the Mongols failed to make meaningful inroads in South Asia? What may have helped make their attempts more successful?

FIGURE 15.1 Mansa Musa. This composite of images from the fourteenth-century *Catalan Atlas* depicts several pages of maps in the background, with a detail from the left-most page superimposed on top that shows the Malian king Mansa Musa enthroned, holding a golden scepter and orb and wearing a gold crown as symbols of his wealth and power. (credit background: modification of work "Catalan Atlas" by Bibliothèque Nationale de France/Wikimedia Commons, Public Domain; credit center: modification of work "Detail from the Catalan Atlas Sheet 6 showing Mansa Musa" by Gallica Digital Library/Wikimedia Commons, Public Domain)

CHAPTER OUTLINE

15.1 Culture and Society in Medieval Africa
15.2 Medieval Sub-Saharan Africa
15.3 The People of the Sahel

INTRODUCTION "This king is the greatest of the Muslim kings of the Sudan. He rules the most extensive territory, has the most numerous army, is the bravest, richest, the most fortunate, the most victorious over his enemies, and the best able to distribute benefits." So wrote al-Umari of the fourteenth-century Malian king Mansa Musa. An official of the Mamluk Sultanate and Mansa Musa's contemporary, al-Umari was in a unique position to describe the great Sudanic king of West Africa and his legendary wealth. At this time, Mansa Musa's kingdom was the latest state in the history of West Africa to exploit its strategic location astride the trans-Saharan trade routes (Figure 15.1).

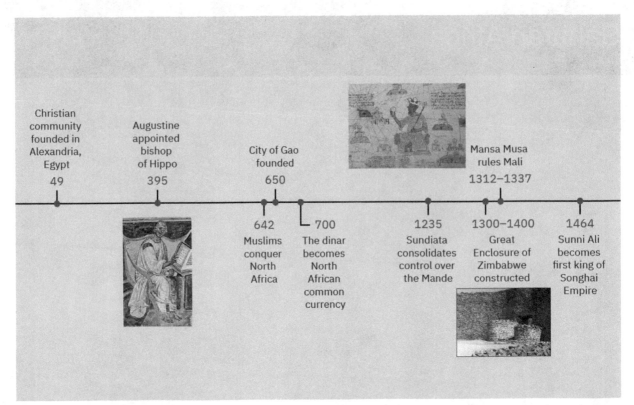

FIGURE 15.2 Timeline: States and Societies in Sub-Saharan Africa. (credit "395": modification of work "Augustine Lateran" by Unknown/Wikimedia Commons, Public Domain; credit "1312–1337": modification of work "Detail from the Catalan Atlas Sheet 6 showing Mansa Musa" by Gallica Digital Library/Wikimedia Commons, Public Domain; credit "1300–1400": modification of work "Great Zimbabwe, Main enclosure entrance" by "damien_farrell"/Flickr, CC BY 2.0)

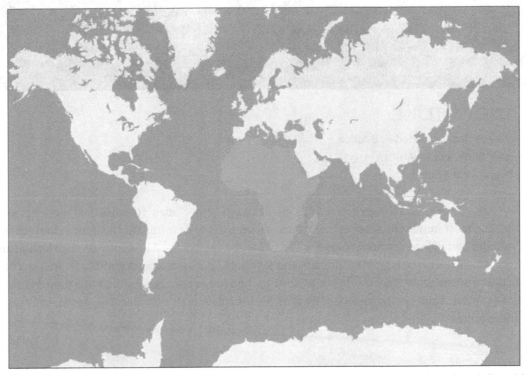

FIGURE 15.3 Locator Map: States and Societies in Sub-Saharan Africa. (credit: modification of work "World map blank shorelines" by Maciej Jaros/Wikimedia Commons, Public Domain)

15.1 Culture and Society in Medieval Africa

LEARNING OBJECTIVES

By the end of this section, you will be able to:
- Analyze the relationship between the physical geography of Africa and the migration of peoples like the Bantu
- Discuss how Christianity and Islam arrived and spread throughout western Africa

As the second-largest continent on the planet, Africa's vast landmass possesses a great variety of different terrains and climatic regions. In some cases, these regions have inhibited the movement of people, technologies, languages, cultures, and religions. For example, the Sahara stretches from the Atlantic coast of northwest Africa to the Red Sea in Egypt and forms a nearly impassable barrier between the Mediterranean world and sub-Saharan Africa. Only with considerable effort have some groups been able to penetrate this arid zone. For this reason, the people of North Africa have historically had stronger cultural, political, and religious connections to the Mediterranean world than the peoples south of the desert. Other regions like the Sahel (the environmental threshold that is the southern portion of the Sahara) and the tropical woodland savanna are spread across large portions of the continent and have in some ways encouraged the migration of groups. The migrating Bantus, for example, spread their languages and ironworking technology throughout this region.

African Geography, Migrations, and Settlement

North of the Sahara is a thin strip of forest and scrubland hugging the southern shores of the Mediterranean Sea. Like other parts of the Mediterranean world, it has a relatively mild climate with sufficient rainfall, wet winters, and dry summers. For this reason, the arable land there is suitable for growing grains like wheat and barley, originally domesticated in the Fertile Crescent and disseminated around the sea over thousands of years. Likewise, this northern African region has had a long history of cultural contact with other Mediterranean cultures like the Greeks, Phoenicians, and Romans. As a result, the cultural practices, religions, and languages of the larger Mediterranean world have had, and continue to have, a huge impact on this region.

South of the Sahara is the Sahel, a semiarid belt of land that separates the desert in the north from the savanna in the south. The Sahel is a transitional zone that stretches some 3,300 miles across the continent. The farther south, the longer is the rainy season (four months on average), the more temperate is the climate, and the greater is the abundance of pasturage and forage plants for livestock (especially cattle and sheep), including grasses, thorny shrubs, and baobab trees. The word *Sahel* is derived from the Arabic *sahil*, meaning "shore." This is a reference to the view held by many that the Sahara was a vast sea of sand that could be navigated only with great difficulty.

The Sahara's extremely dry conditions are hostile to both plants and animals, so only small-scale human settlements are possible. These are clustered around the desert's oases, which amount to a fraction of a percentage of its total landmass. During the Middle Ages, these oases were crucial hubs connecting trade routes across the desert, nowhere more so than in West Africa, where medieval kingdoms competed for control over markets and the movement of goods across the region.

During the medieval period, the Sahara provided powerful West African kingdoms with a vital commodity: salt. Almost completely unobtainable in the inland regions south of the Sahara, salt was mined from sites such as Taghaza and transported in enormous slabs on the backs of camels in caravans that crossed the desert to West African villages and beyond (Figure 15.4). Salt became the second most prized good traded across the Sahara—the first being gold. Indeed, salt was such a valuable commodity that the king of Ghana stored it in the royal treasury alongside gold nuggets.

FIGURE 15.4 A Precious Commodity: Salt. This early twentieth-century photograph shows a caravan of camels laden with sixty-pound slabs of salt crossing the Sahara near Timbuktu. In medieval Africa, salt was second only to gold in value and was transported in much the same way. (credit: modification of work "Tombouctou-Arrivée d'une caravane de sel (AOF)" by Collection particulière/Wikimedia Commons, Pubilc Domain)

The southern frontier of the Sahel is marked by the transition to grasslands and tropical woodlands of the savanna. While the Sahara is dry and arid, the savanna is more temperate and wetter, carpeted with grasses and studded by scattered trees. At its extreme end near the West African rainforests stretching from modern-day Sierra Leone to Ghana, the savanna can see as much as forty-eight inches of rain per year (the rainy season lasts from May to October), which is similar to the average annual rainfall of New York City in the United States. Alongside a greater abundance of vegetation, the savanna is also home to a wider range of wildlife, including cattle, antelope, and giraffes. Endowed with a hospitable environment, climate, and geography, the plains of the savanna have historically been the region with the greatest concentration of human settlement in Africa.

Winding through the savanna and Sahel regions of West Africa is the Niger River. Along its fertile banks, people have grown staple crops like sorghum, African rice, and millet for hundreds of years. Approximately 2,500 miles in length, the Niger is West Africa's longest river. It was critical to the development of medieval West African kingdoms, both for its ability to sustain intensive agriculture and as a crucial transport conduit for goods and commodities (Figure 15.5). It was in the areas drained by the Niger River where West Africa's great empires emerged, profiting from the flows of salt from the north and gold from the south. In this way, these empires grew fabulously wealthy.

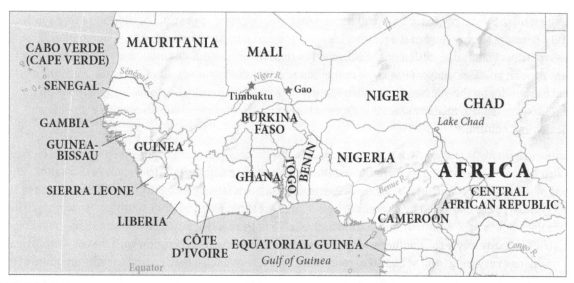

FIGURE 15.5 The Niger River. From its source in the Guinea Highlands, the Niger, the third-longest river in Africa (after the Nile and the Congo), travels through a great part of the interior of West Africa before emptying into the Atlantic Ocean in southern Nigeria. As the major source of water for both the western Sahara and Sahel, the Niger was crucial to the establishment and development of trading centers at Gao and Timbuktu. (attribution: Copyright Rice University, OpenStax, under CC BY 4.0 license)

To the south of the savanna lies the tropical rainforest, Africa's third major environment alongside the desert and the savanna. Relative to the Sahara, the African rainforest covers a far smaller geographic footprint: some two million square miles, or roughly 10 percent of the continent's total landmass. Nevertheless, the rainforest is rich in biodiversity, including pygmy hippopotamuses, giant forest hogs, canopy monkeys, and chimpanzees, as well as thousands of species of plants. In West Africa, dense stretches of rainforest can be found in Sierra Leone, Liberia, and Côte d'Ivoire. In this area, the Bantu initially encountered the Nok people, from whom they acquired the metallurgical knowledge that enabled them to move into and later emerge from the equatorial rainforest between 500 and 1000 CE. The gradual dispersal of the Bantu throughout much of southern Africa followed.

Bantu speakers had been migrating from this area possibly since as early as 3000 BCE. But with the adoption of ironworking technology from the Nok, these ironworking farmers were able to travel throughout much of the eastern, western, and southeastern regions of the subcontinent. Their Iron Age economy was dominated by farming, mostly of sorghum and millet, with some livestock including cattle, pigs, and chickens, although animal husbandry tended to be secondary to farming. Because the regions into which they moved were only thinly populated by roving bands of hunter-gatherers, the Bantu were able to choose the most suitable land for farming. Early Iron Age Bantu settlements tended to be small, typically consisting of a dozen or so round houses encircling a livestock pen of cattle or goats. Larger settlements (sometimes in the range of several hectares) could be found in regions such as Natal, favored by large Bantu kinship groups because of the combination of rich biodiversity and sparse population. Settlements were placed close to iron ore and wood for the smelting of carbon steel. The early Iron Age Bantu economy necessarily focused on self-sufficiency with little potential for trade, although some small-scale trade did take place, particularly of sought-after commodities like copper and salt in regions of the Congo and Tanzania.

Until about the eighth century CE, the Bantu developed and exploited the resources of the more favorable areas and adapted the local environments. Throughout, they remained a stateless society organized along kinship lines. Women tended crops, prepared food, and minded the smaller children, while men tended livestock, hunted for meat and for animal skins for clothing, and engaged in trade with other villages. Women leaders were the exception; archaeological evidence of male dominance is considerable. Authority was decentralized in any case, with no rigidly hierarchical power structure to exercise central authority.

From the tenth century, relatively powerful Bantu kingdoms began to appear in the savanna to the south of the Central African rainforest, and in the plateau between the Zambezi and Limpopo Rivers in the interior of southern Africa. Their large settlements displaced the region's earlier inhabitants. This revolution in the ancient African political landscape was the combined result of the introduction of Neolithic cultivation and animal husbandry on the one hand, and the adoption of Iron Age technologies, tools, and weapons on the other. The succession of medieval Bantu kingdoms that emerged dominated these regions economically, politically, and culturally.

Migrating originally from West Africa, the Bantu would have recognized much of the geography and climate of southern Africa: there is desert, such as the Kalahari and Namib in southwest Africa, and vast savanna. Entire regions of the modern countries of Angola, Democratic Republic of the Congo, Zimbabwe, Zambia, Tanzania, and Mozambique are blanketed by grassland, as is a large area that extends from southern Mozambique into northeastern South Africa. Both the vegetation and wildlife of the southern African savanna resemble that of West Africa in many ways. The southern African climate also has much in common with that of West Africa, encompassing everything from semiarid to temperate zones, with each experiencing varying amounts of rain. Broadly speaking, the eastern area of the region (including Mozambique and eastern South Africa) is wetter than the western area. The west is sapped of moisture, in part by the Atlantic Ocean's cold Benguela Current. The resulting dryness of western South Africa was a key factor in the development of the Kalahari and Namib Deserts (Figure 15.6).

FIGURE 15.6 The Kalahari Desert. Parts of the Kalahari Desert are especially dry, making life there quite a challenge. (credit: modification of work "Kalahari" by Quinn Norton/Flickr, CC BY 2.0)

Throughout the Middle Ages, the river systems of southern Africa were exploited by the large civilizations developing there. For example, the Limpopo River basin spreads across the southern reaches of today's Mozambique and Zimbabwe, the northern extreme of South Africa, and the eastern edge of Botswana. The basin's temperate climate and well-watered landscape encouraged the migration of San hunter-gatherers from southwestern Africa and the settlement of Bantu peoples. The Bantu, who arrived from the north, brought with them the knowledge of ironworking, farming, and livestock herding they had acquired over generations of migrations throughout sub-Saharan Africa. From the tenth century onward, they used this knowledge to cultivate farms across extensive field systems along the basin and to accumulate large herds of cattle.

As the settlements around the Limpopo River grew, so too did the need to manage the basin's resources and govern the affairs of the people there. As a result, centralized systems of governance emerged among the Bantu peoples in the region, particularly in the Iron Age culture of Leopard's Kopje in Zimbabwe. This cattle-keeping culture, whose name derived from the site where it was identified (*kopje* means "small hill"), dominated the area for nearly two centuries, but by the thirteenth century, it had given way to an even larger and more complex state, Great Zimbabwe.

The Expansion of Christianity in Africa

Throughout its history, North Africa's fate and fortunes have been connected to the Mediterranean Sea and the peoples who share its borders. Whether economic, political, or spiritual, changes and innovations occurring in this region have had lasting and important consequences for Africa. These changes often went hand in hand; as the Roman Empire grew and expanded, for instance, so did Christianity.

Christianity emerged as a distinct religion in the second half of the first century and soon spread into communities around the Roman-controlled Mediterranean world. Being part of the Roman Empire, North Africa became home to some of the world's earliest Christian communities. According to Christian tradition, Saint Mark traveled to the Egyptian city of Alexandria and founded the first Christian community in Africa there around the middle of the first century. Regardless of whether we accept this tradition as factual or not, it is indisputable that by the third century Alexandria was a major center of Christianity. By that time, the influential School of Alexandria was an important center for theological research, and the bishop of the Church of Alexandria was held by Christians to be as important as the pope (the bishop of Rome). It was from Alexandria that Christianity spread south along the Nile, penetrating the reaches of Upper Egypt.

The growth of the church in Africa mirrored its expansion across the Mediterranean and drew the attention of Roman officials. In general, the Roman Empire was not interested in persecuting the followers of the many religions practiced around the empire, even members of new religions like Christianity. However, some actions of early Christian communities were seen by Roman officials as disruptive to peace and stability in the empire. For example, Christians refused to participate in the state cults that honored the Roman gods and protected Roman society. Such refusal was interpreted as treason and occasionally punished accordingly, such as under Emperor Nero, who ruled from 54 to 68. But during the reign of Emperor Decius in 250, official empire-wide persecution noticeably increased, reaching its height under Emperor Diocletian in 303. During this time, Rome undertook a series of official persecutions meant to restore the primacy of ancient pagan religious worship and practice throughout the empire.

In Africa, these persecutions prompted many orthodox Christians to flee the relative security of the Nile and seek refuge in the western desert. There, some chose to dwell in solitude as hermits while others chose to build monasteries and live as part of communities of the faithful. One of the latter was Antony of the Desert, who, around the year 300, chose to end his life of isolation and welcomed the company of those who wished to live with him and follow his teachings. Soon, numerous religious settlements cropped up throughout the desert (Figure 15.7).

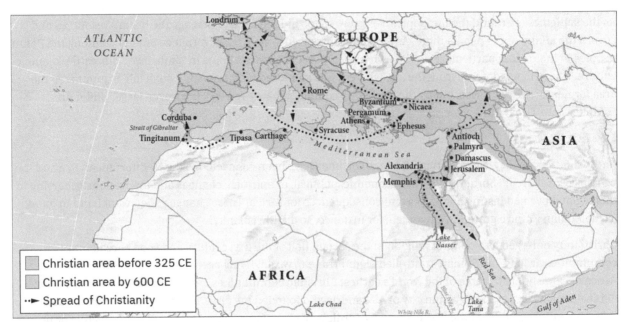

FIGURE 15.7 The Early Spread of Christianity. The Christian faith spread widely throughout the Mediterranean world, including in northern Africa, from the first through the sixth centuries. (attribution: Copyright Rice University, OpenStax, under CC BY 4.0 license)

Within a hundred years, three distinctive forms of monasticism had emerged in northeast Africa. Many isolated hermits continued to dwell in northern Egypt. In southern and northwestern Egypt, however, religiously devout men and women preferred to live a communal existence. Monks in southern Egypt gathered together as bands of "brothers" who lived together and shared their daily work. Another type of monasticism emerged in northwestern Egypt. West of the Nile delta monasteries were more hierarchical in structure. At the head of the monastery was a man known as the abbot ("father"). Around him he gathered other men willing to live according to his directions and his teachings. Religious women also chose to engage in the monastic lifestyle. Like men, some chose to live in communities of the faithful, where they sometimes assumed leadership roles. Others, like Amma (Mother) Sarah, preferred a more solitary existence. According to legend, for sixty years Amma Sarah lived a severely ascetic existence in a small dwelling beside a river, probably the Nile, at which she never looked because she was so focused on the state of her soul that little else held interest for her. The way of life pioneered by the devout men and women of North Africa would be imitated by Christians in Europe and elsewhere.

Christianity quickly spread beyond Egypt southward to Ethiopia. The eventual rise of the Christian Kingdom of Aksum was due in large part to the efforts of the missionary Frumentius. Shipwrecked on the Eritrean coast, Frumentius was brought to the royal court and in the role of tutor converted King Ezana, then a devout polytheist. Following his baptism, Ezana sent Frumentius to Alexandria to ask that the head of the Christian Church in Egypt name a bishop for Ethiopia. The bishop of Alexandria, Athanasius, duly appointed Frumentius, who assumed the name "Selama." It was likely Bishop Selama who founded Ethiopia's first Christian monastery.

It was also from Egypt that Christianity spread westward in the second and third centuries along the North African coast to the Maghreb, the region of northwest Africa lying between modern-day Morocco and Libya and encompassing a vast tract of the Sahara. One of the places in this region where Christianity appears to have flourished was Carthage. Like Christians in Egypt, the community in Carthage was also subject to Roman persecution during the third century. Most of the evidence we have of this community comes to us in the form of martyr stories. One such story, passed down through a diary, tells of the life of Perpetua, a young Christian mother imprisoned along with her infant and her pregnant servant Felicitas, who gave birth while in prison. Perpetua and Felicitas were executed with other Christians in the arena at Carthage.

To avoid a similar fate, many Christians in North Africa chose to renounce their faith openly while still practicing it in safety. Often the Roman authorities would be satisfied if church leaders simply handed over their scriptures. While this practice seemed preferable to execution for some Christians, others found the refusal to accept martyrdom for their faith an inexcusable offense. Once the persecutions ceased in 313 with the Edict of Milan, which granted religious toleration to Christianity throughout the Roman Empire, many in North Africa refused to recognize those who had renounced their faith as leaders. They further held that any sacramental acts performed by these leaders after they had renounced the faith were invalid, including baptisms, weddings, and even the consecration of clergy. This caused a huge rift in the North African Christian community that became known as the **Donatist controversy**, named after a Carthaginian bishop named Donatus who led the movement. The problem grew to such proportions that Emperor Constantine had to intervene. Yet even after Donatus was exiled to Gaul (modern France) in 347, the controversy in North Africa continued.

The man who ultimately brought an end to the Donatist rift was one of Christianity's most influential thinkers, Augustine of Hippo. Augustine was born to a Roman colonist father and indigenous African mother in Tagaste, Roman Numidia (present-day Souk Ahras, Algeria). At the age of seventeen, he took up his studies in Carthage and then went on to become a teacher of rhetoric at the imperial court in Milan. During his time in Italy, Augustine read an account of the life of Antony of the Desert, the famous Egyptian hermit, and was inspired to convert to Christianity (Figure 15.8).

FIGURE 15.8 St. Augustine. An influential Christian philosopher and theologian who was later made a saint, Augustine was born in Roman Numidia in the fourth century. This image from a sixth-century fresco, the earliest known of him, shows him as darker skinned, an acknowledgment of his origins as a Romanized African. (credit: "Augustine Lateran" by Unknown/Wikimedia Commons, Public Domain)

Augustine returned to North Africa and was appointed bishop of Hippo (present-day Annaba, Algeria) in 395. By this time, the Donatist controversy had been roiling North Africa for approximately a century. A fierce critic of the Donatist view, Augustine was determined to wipe it out. He was the chief opponent of the Donatists at the 411 Council of Carthage, assembled by the emperor to finally resolve the thorny issue. As a result of Augustine's efforts, the council ordered the Donatists expelled from the church. Despite this fatal blow, elements of the Donatist sect persisted in North Africa until the seventh century.

In addition to his success in combating the Donatists, Augustine left an indelible mark on the early church by writing hundreds of works about Christian doctrine. Perhaps the most influential of these was *The City of God*, which he wrote in response to the Visigoths' sack of Rome in 410. In this work, Augustine argued that any kingdom created by humans—including Rome—could fall, but the Kingdom of God, composed of the people who embraced the Christian faith, would persist forever. In effect, Augustine was reassuring the Christians who had witnessed the near-destruction of Rome that it was not the end of the world. The Christian society that had been created over the centuries—the Kingdom of God—would carry on.

LINK TO LEARNING

Learn more about Augustine's concept (https://openstax.org/l/77Augustine) of the two cities—the earthly and the heavenly—by reading excerpts from his early work of Christian philosophy, *The City of God*.

Augustine was a major force in helping Christianity assume a more uniform character across the empire. Also, as the Roman Empire became more Christian, religious persecution by Christians against pagans became more common throughout the empire. One of the most violent acts of Christian persecution occurred in Alexandria. In 415, a mob of Christians set upon Hypatia, a pagan philosopher, as she traveled the streets of the provincial capital in her chariot. Pulled from the cart, she was dragged to a nearby temple where she was tortured, flayed alive with shards of roof tiles, and then dismembered. Her body parts were carried to a nearby site and burned. Hypatia's murder in Roman North Africa was a signal event in the assertion of Christian dominance in the empire, which had witnessed a dramatically violent shift in the tide of persecution throughout the Mediterranean world. So recently pagan, the Christian Roman state now embarked on pogroms and persecutions of pagans and unbelievers meant to eradicate every semblance of the ancient Roman belief systems. An essential feature of this program was the fact that violence against pagans was both actively and passively tolerated by the central administration and provincial governors, leading to the abuse and murder of pagans and the destruction of their temples, altars, and sanctuaries by Christians across the Roman world.

The persecution of pagans in the empire coincided with efforts by the church leadership to reel in aspects of the faith that some considered unorthodox. This process culminated with the Council of Chalcedon in 451 and its decision concerning the nature of Christ. Since the early years of the church, the faithful had been of two minds about the precise nature of Jesus. Some believed he was both fully divine and fully human—the Dyophysite position—while others believed Jesus's humanity was inseparable from his divinity—the Monophysite position. The Monophysite position dominated in Egypt, but the council decreed it heretical, triggering a schism that brought the ejection of monks and church members throughout Egypt. From that point, the Christian Church in Egypt followed a more independent path and gradually became more isolated from the wider Christian world. It became known as the Coptic Church, reflecting the acceptance of Coptic as both the major literary language and the language of public worship in Egypt at the time.

By the eighth century, following the direction of the patriarch of Alexandria, the Coptic Church had uniformly adopted Monophysite Christianity and was flourishing in the upper reaches of the Nile valley. The Christian Kingdom of Aksum thrived until its final destruction by the Zagwe queen Gudit in the tenth century. Queen Gudit and her descendants established the Zagwe Kingdom with its capital at Roha. Later, under King Lalibela, who ruled from 1181 to 1221, Roha became a major pilgrimage center for Christians, styled "the new Jerusalem." Lalibela renamed the stream flowing through his capital the River Jordan and built new churches by having them carved out of solid rock. By the thirteenth century, Monophysite Christianity was well-established in northeastern Africa.

The Expansion of Islam in Africa

By the start of the seventh century, Christianity seemed firmly entrenched across Egypt and the Maghreb. But by the end of that century, the situation had changed dramatically as the religion of Islam swept across the region. Founded in the early seventh century, within a few decades, Islam had gathered armies that consolidated control of the Arabian Peninsula and the region of the Levant and established a bridgehead in Byzantine Egypt from which to launch the conquest of North Africa. As Muslim conquerors advanced across the region, they established settlements that eventually developed into the towns and cities that would house the officials of the Islamic Caliphate, the area ruled over by the leader of the Islamic state, the caliph (Figure 15.9).

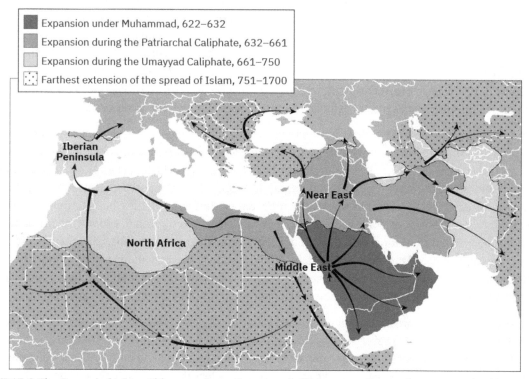

FIGURE 15.9 **The Spread of Islam.** This map shows the spread of Islam over time and across North Africa, the Iberian Peninsula, and the Near and Middle East. (credit: modification of work "Age of the Caliphs (version with more surrounding space)" by Brian Szymanski/Wikimedia Commons, Public Domain)

In 661, the Umayya family of Mecca assumed control of the caliphate and combined the previous conquests into a functioning state with a capital at Damascus in Syria. Under their rule, the position of caliph changed from being a family member or close associate of the prophet Muhammad into a dynastic, heritable position passed from father to son. The Umayyad dynasty extended the reach of the caliphate through military conquest until it encompassed all of North Africa's Mediterranean coast. With Egypt as its launching pad, the Muslim conquest of Byzantine-controlled territories in the Maghreb region of North Africa proceeded in three stages between 642 and 709.

The earliest Arab accounts of the conquest date from some two hundred years later and are not very detailed, although they serve as the basis of our understanding of these events. After Egypt was conquered, the Islamic advance across North Africa stalled because of the thousand-plus miles of desert between the Nile delta and the Byzantine province of Africa centered on Carthage. But by 647, tens of thousands of Muslim soldiers had begun their march to the Maghreb. That same year, they engaged with and defeated the forces of the Byzantine governor at Tripolitania (in modern-day Libya).

By 665, a second invasion of North Africa was underway. Once again, an army of tens of thousands of Arab soldiers marched from Egypt, this time determined to take Carthage. Reinforced later by forty thousand soldiers from Damascus, the Islamic advance established a beachhead at Kairouan in modern-day Tunisia. Kairouan, which became the capital of the Islamic province of Ifriqiya, was the center of Islamic operations that plunged Arab armies into the heart of North Africa, including Libya, Tunisia, and Algeria. After prolonged campaigns against indigenous tribes and the forces of the Byzantine provincial government, Carthage finally fell to a third Arab invasion in 698.

After taking Carthage, Arab armies continued their sweep across North Africa. Along the way, their numbers were swelled by African soldiers. Many were forced to join the Arabs while others volunteered, hoping to share in the spoils that would result from a planned invasion of Spain, which took place in 711. That year, armies of the Umayyad Caliphate sailed across the Strait of Gibraltar and invaded the Iberian Peninsula. A few years later, Islamic forces had occupied all the major towns in the peninsula and advanced as far north as Narbonne, France. In less than a century, Islam went from being a novel religious movement centered on the Arabian Peninsula to an empire that stretched from Iraq in the east to the Atlantic coast of North Africa in the west. Despite its spectacular success, however, the Umayyad dynasty was unable to hold onto power and fell to revolution in 750. That year, the Abbasid family from Mecca seized control of the Islamic Caliphate and relocated its capital from Damascus to Baghdad, where it would remain for five centuries.

The Islamic military conquest of North Africa might have ended in the eighth century, but the spread of Islam did not. Islam was diffused throughout West, East, and sub-Saharan Africa primarily by merchants, traders, scholars, and missionaries. Muslim Berbers (Amazigh) carried the ideas of Islam from North Africa along the many trans-Saharan trade routes they used. In this way, the ideas of the religion penetrated the arid desert and reached West African trading towns like Gao and Koumbi Saleh, the capital of the Ghana Empire. Over time and through increased exposure, some ruling sub-Saharan African elites began to adopt it, and in some cases, they blended it with their traditional beliefs. Although the Ghanaian kings themselves did not convert, they recognized the importance of the Muslim-led trans-Saharan trade to their economy and so tolerated Islam. In acknowledgment of this fact, they allocated a second town of their capital to Muslim merchants and traders. This district took on a distinct Islamic character, a fact borne out by the presence of mosques within it.

By the eleventh century, the broader Islamic world extended across North Africa and the western Sahara into Ghana in the western Sudan. However, even by this late date, Islam had made only a limited impact in West Africa, and many Amazigh groups tended to mingle both Islamic traditions and native African religious practices. Some more orthodox Muslims in the region found this less than satisfactory and sought to rectify the problem. What emerged were reformist Islamic kingdoms in West Africa. The earliest was the Almoravid state, which arose in the eleventh century. Centered in Morocco and led by a radical Islamic scholar, the Almoravid state grew rapidly through Islamic fervor and military conquests. By the 1070s, the Almoravids controlled a vast portion of West Africa from the Mediterranean coast of Morocco to the edges of the Ghana Empire. In the process, many groups in these areas were more thoroughly Islamized. In this period, Islam truly began to expand among the people of Ghana.

By the middle of the twelfth century, the religious enthusiasm of the early Almoravid conquests had largely died down. The descendants of the early founders preferred the peace and luxuries of settled life in Morocco to jihad (war on behalf of Islam). This situation was unsettling to some of the Amazigh, who then launched a successful war of religious reform against the Almoravids and established their own reformist West African kingdom, the Almohad Kingdom. The empire forged by the Almohad Caliphate was short-lived, however, and by the thirteenth century, it had been fatally weakened by internal rebellions.

As the geopolitical configuration of the West African kingdoms changed, the center of the regional economy shifted away from Ghana. By the thirteenth century, the kingdom of Mali had become the dominant political and economic force in the region. Unlike the rulers of Ghana, the Malian elite—including the *mansa* or king—converted to Islam. Mansa Musa, perhaps the most famous ruler of Mali, drew the attention of observers from Arabia to Spain when he went on pilgrimage to Mecca in 1324–1325. Renowned for the wealth of his kingdom, Mansa Musa distributed so much gold during a stopover in Cairo that the Egyptian economy suffered high inflation for more than a decade according to some reports. On his return to Mali, Mansa Musa brought with him Muslim scholars, architects, and books, all of which helped deepen the Islamic character of Mali. At Timbuktu, for example, the Djinguereber Mosque was built, and schools and universities specializing in the study of the Quran were established, cementing that city's growing international status as a place of Islamic scholarship and learning (Figure 15.10).

(a)

(b)

FIGURE 15.10 The Djinguereber Mosque. (a) (b) Fourteenth-century Timbuktu was a great center of learning specializing in Islamic law, philosophy, and science. These photos show two views of the famous Djinguereber Mosque, built there in 1327. (credit a: modification of work "Djinguereber Mosque, Timbuktu" by "upyernoz"/Flickr, CC BY 2.0; credit b: modification of work "Timbuktu Mud Mosque, Mali, W. Africa" by Emilio Labrador/Flickr, CC BY 2.0)

By the end of the fourteenth century, West African rulers from Mali to Hausaland (present-day Nigeria) had adopted Islam and completed the Islamic encirclement of sub-Saharan Africa. Islam also spread throughout East Africa, although its progress there was checked by entrenched Christianity among the kingdoms of Nubia and the Ethiopian Kingdom of Aksum. By the 1200s, however, such resistance had been severely weakened, and many Christian kingdoms had become Muslim. An important exception was the Kingdom of Abyssinia, the Christian successor state of Aksum and Zagwe. Farther east, in the African Horn, the Muslim sultanates of Ajuran and eventually Adal rose.

Islam faced less competition farther south. In the eighth century, Muslim traders from Arabia and Egypt began to settle in towns and trading centers along the Swahili coast, the part of eastern Africa that stretches along the Indian Ocean. By this time, it was home to countless settled Bantu communities, many of which prospered thanks to their role in connecting regional and burgeoning international trade. The Arab incomers intermingled and mixed with the Bantu peoples, creating a unique blended language and culture in an urban, trade-based society.

By the tenth century, the Swahili coast was acknowledged as an important commercial center. Writing in 915, the Arab traveler al-Masudi described the area's vigorous trade, which included exports of everything from ambergris and ivory to gold and leopard skins and such imports as stone bowls, Islamic pottery, and glass vessels. By the 1200s, a distinct Swahili civilization had emerged, speaking a distinct Arabic-Bantu dialect, oriented toward the sea rather than the African interior, dominated by independent city-states that specialized in trade, and Islamic in faith. This Swahili language and culture had a powerful influence in the towns of the east African coast. Yet despite Islam's success along the coast during the medieval period, it made virtually no impact on the peoples of the East African interior until many centuries later.

The spread of monotheistic belief systems like Christianity and Islam throughout Africa proceeded along many fronts, including military conquest, commercial exchange, and cultural diffusion. At no time was the process straightforward and uncomplicated, and conquerors and merchants alike confronted unique challenges. While people adopted these religions for different reasons, whether a firm belief in a better afterlife or the tangible commercial benefits that accompanied conversion, the medieval period of African history nevertheless witnessed a revolution in the nature of belief. This is not to say that ancient African belief systems were eradicated. Indeed, while Christian missionaries and Muslim teachers had little respect for traditional religious practice in Africa, the adoption of Christianity or Islam was often the product of adaptation to the traditional practices and rituals of African peoples.

The Africanization of these faiths was largely circumstantial, of course. For example, whereas Christianity emphasized monogamy, Islam allowed a man to take several wives. Thus, Islam would find a more receptive audience among African societies that already practiced polygamous marriages, which were otherwise forbidden in the Christian tradition. The cross-pollination of religious tradition helped to perpetuate ancient African belief systems in both rural and urban communities. Indeed, the Africanization of Islam among the peoples of the Swahili coast produced a distinctive form of the faith, one that included ancestor worship and the appeasing of spirits, as well as the development of unique grave-marking habits and the placement of traditional offerings in mosques.

15.2 Medieval Sub-Saharan Africa

LEARNING OBJECTIVES

By the end of this section, you will be able to:
- Discuss the uniqueness of West African civilization in the premodern world
- Explain the source of wealth and power held by Ghana and Mali
- Describe how Mapungubwe and Great Zimbabwe developed as a result of the Bantu migrations

For nearly seven hundred years, medieval empires and kingdoms dominated the economies and politics of West Africa and southern Africa. The wealth of these states and thus their power came from their control of trade in commodities such as gold, ivory, salt, silk, horses, and enslaved people. In West Africa, the empires of Ghana and Mali moved these goods along a sprawling network of trade that stretched across North Africa, eastward into Ethiopia, and southward as far as the grassland savanna, connecting West Africa to the Mediterranean world, Europe, the Near East, southwest Asia, and beyond. In southern Africa, Mapungubwe and then Great Zimbabwe consolidated their control over local and regional trade and connected their economies with the coastal civilization of the Swahili peoples through a network of waterways that included the Limpopo and Zambezi Rivers. In so doing, they linked the southern African interior with the distant and overlapping nodes of oceanic commerce that connected East Africa with Asia and Arabia.

The Ghana Empire

By the turn of the ninth century, Arab rulers in Morocco were minting gold coins called dinars on behalf of the Islamic Caliphate. The official currency of the Muslim world since the end of the seventh century, the dinar was an important link connecting the sprawling Arab empire then centered on Baghdad. The gold used to mint those coins in Morocco came from a kingdom south of the Sahara known as Ghana, a realm the Arab governor of Morocco attempted and failed to conquer (and not to be confused with the modern nation-state of Ghana).

The Ghana Empire dominated the region between western Mali and southeastern Mauritania from the sixth to the thirteenth centuries. Although ancient trade-based societies had existed in the region for some time by enriching themselves on the area's lucrative salt and gold, the introduction of the Arabian camel by the Romans between the third and fifth centuries CE, and the consequent regularization of trade between Morocco and the Niger River, allowed larger political entities to emerge. Until then, the development of farming and ironworking technology had supported West African clan-based societies in small, simple villages. Sometime around the fifth century, however, a group of chiefdoms in the Sahel grassland south of the Sahara formed a loosely knit empire—that is, the empire or kingdom of Ghana (Figure 15.11).

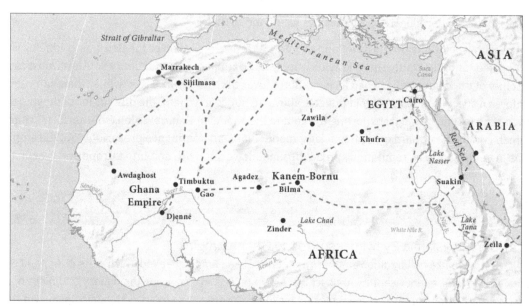

FIGURE 15.11 Ghana and the Trans-Saharan Trade. The growth and development of Ghana, the first of the great medieval West African empires, were tied to its trade in goods and commodities across North Africa. (attribution: Copyright Rice University, OpenStax, under CC BY 4.0 license)

Although the origins of the Ghana Empire are shrouded in mystery, one theory holds that it was founded by Soninke speakers from Senegal who referred to their kingdom as Wagadu (Ghana, the name by which it was known to outsiders, was one of the titles of its king). Soninke oral tradition tells us that the kingdom was founded by Diabe Cisse, a powerful figure whose father Dinga, a nomadic mystic, was said to have conquered a female water genie. Dinga subsequently wed the genie's daughters. Sons resulted from the union of these women and Dinga, and their descendants established important Soninke families. Cisse's arrival as a son of Dinga, an outsider, marked a turning point in the history of the region, then subject to the destabilizing effects of nomadic raids.

With the drying out of the Sahara, the Sanhaja people of southern Morocco pressed deeper into the Sahel in their search for water and seasonal grazing land. During drought years, their migrations took the form of violent raids on settled agricultural communities, including those of the Soninke. In response, Soninke cavalry commanders turned to Cisse; tradition holds that Cisse unified the Soninke in a loose federation to combat the raiders and to expand the kingdom.

The early growth of Ghana was a slow process of conquering independent chiefdoms and kingdoms and then absorbing them into the empire. At the empire's core were four central provinces established by Diabe Cisse when he first unified the Soninke. Conquered vassal chiefdoms and kingdoms occupied the periphery of the kingdom. Some of these vassal states operated fairly independently of the central administration and paid only a small amount of tribute; other states were controlled to some extent by the capital. As the kingdom expanded, so too did its military. When Ghana reached the apex of its power in the early eleventh century CE, its king had some 200,000 soldiers at his command.

The Soninke response to nomadic raiders was only one factor that may have stimulated unification during the early period of Ghanaian history. Historians believe Ghana's position with regard to trade was another. Ghana grew powerful, and its kings became wealthy on the strength of the trans-Saharan trade, which the Soninke were ideally placed to exploit. Situated in the western Sahel, they stood halfway between the desert—the principal source of salt—and the territory of Bambuk—where goldfields were located along the upper reaches of the Senegal River. Initially, the Soninke had exchanged their gold surplus for salt harvested by the Taghaza people of the Sahara, but soon cross-desert traffic by camel allowed North Africans access to West African gold. As the trans-Saharan demand for gold increased, the Soninke were able to act as intermediaries, passing

Saharan salt to the gold producers of the savanna woodland to their south.

Despite stories that celebrate Ghana as a "land of gold," its kings' control over the Bambuk goldfields was tenuous. Located far to the south, the goldfields were beyond Ghiyaru, the kingdom's southernmost trading post. The chief of the nearest village had local authority over the mining area, and while Ghanaian rulers were able to enforce a strict monopoly on gold nuggets above an ounce in weight, the difficulties of digging mine shafts up to sixty feet deep and transporting the gold to the capital at Koumbi Saleh (southern Mauritania today), which could take upward of eighteen days, made Ghanaian dominance precarious. Yet the empire's wealth was legendary, and its reputation spread throughout North Africa and into Europe and reached Muslim scholars as far away as Baghdad.

IN THEIR OWN WORDS

Eleventh-Century Islamic Eyewitnesses to the Ghana Empire

Arab writers and Soninke oral tradition emphasize that the Ghana Empire derived much of its power and wealth from gold. Al-Hamdani, a tenth-century Arab scholar, described Ghana as having the richest goldmines on earth. al-Bakri, his near-contemporary who spent most of his life in Cordova and Almeria in Islamic Spain, wrote about Ghana after gathering information from merchants and visitors. In the following excerpt from the *Book of Roads and Kingdoms* (1067–1068), al-Bakri describes Koumbi Saleh and the appearance and customs of the king and the court.

> Ghana consists of two cities situated on a plain. One of these, which is inhabited by Muslims, is large and possesses twelve mosques, in which they assemble for the Friday prayer. There are salaried imams [prayer leaders] and *muezzins* [prayer callers], as well as jurists and scholars. In the environs are wells with fresh water, from which they drink and with which they grow vegetables. The king's town is six miles distant from this one [. . .] In the king's town, and not far from his court of justice, is a mosque where the Muslims who arrive at his court pray. Around the king's town are domed buildings and groves and thickets where the sorcerers of these people, men in charge of the religious cult, live. In them too are their idols and the tombs of their kings. [. . .]
>
> The king's interpreters, the official in charge of his treasury, and the majority of his ministers are Muslims. Among the people who follow the king's religion, only he and his heir apparent (who is the son of his sister) may wear sewn clothes. All other people wear robes of cotton, silk, or brocade, according to their means. All of them shave their beards, and women shave their heads. The king adorns himself like a woman, wearing necklaces and bracelets, and he puts on a high cap decorated with gold and wrapped in a turban of fine cotton. [. . .] When the people who profess the same religion as the king approach him they fall on their knees and sprinkle dust on their head, for this is their way of greeting him. As for the Muslims, they greet him only by clapping their hands . . . .

—al-Bakri, *Book of Roads and Kingdoms*

- What does this reading suggest about the expansion of Islam into this area by this time?
- What aspects of this excerpt suggest that the king of Ghana was both wealthy and powerful?

Ghanaian wealth derived from other commodities as well, including copper (on which the king levied a hefty custom duty) and captives. Many captives were often prisoners of war. Others had been seized in enslavement raids. In the twelfth century, the Moroccan geographer al-Idrisi, recounted a Ghanaian slave raid on a region named Lamlam: "The people of . . . Ghana make excursion in Lamlam bringing natives into captivity, transporting them to their own country and selling them to merchants." Al-Idrisi's observations were confirmed by his contemporary, al-Zuhri. Scholars have estimated that during the height of the Ghana Empire, some five thousand captives were transported across the Sahara to slave markets in North Africa every year.

During the eleventh century, the Ghanaians' tolerance was sorely tested, however. The people welcomed Muslim traders, but radical reformist Islamic sects in Morocco threatened their peace and prosperity. Early in the century, the kingdom had expanded to take over the Islamic town of Awdaghost, an oasis north of the capital. At about the same time, a militant Islamic Almoravid movement emerged among the Sanhaja people of the southern Sahara, who soon established an empire centered on Morocco. In 1055, they captured Awdaghost, and in the ensuing religious strife and sectarian warfare, the Soninke Ghanaians converted to Islam. The wider destruction caused by violence had so weakened Ghana's trading links that by the end of the twelfth century, it had lost its dominant position over the region's trade. Having been thoroughly Islamized, Ghana began to produce Muslim scholars, lawyers, and Quran readers of some repute, many traveling to Islamic Spain to study or going on pilgrimage to Mecca.

The eleventh and twelfth centuries were a transitional time in the history of the kingdoms of West Africa. As Ghana expanded and was in turn conquered, new goldfields were opened at Bure in the woodland savanna south of Bambuk, well beyond Ghana's commercial reach. Itinerant Soninke traders transported the gold from Bure to the Middle Niger region on new trans-Saharan trade routes east of Awdaghost that bypassed the Ghanaian capital and shifted the caravans of North Africa to Oualata (Walata). These changes provided the southern Soninke and Malinke chiefdoms the chance to assert their independence. In the early 1200s, the southern Soninke chiefdom of Sosso took over most of former Ghana as well as the Malinke people. This set the stage for a struggle for Malinke independence against the Sosso, which ultimately led to the creation of the Sudanese kingdom of Mali.

The Mali Empire

The kingdom of Sosso benefited the most from the dissolution of the Ghana Empire, a process furthered by the collapse of the Islamic Almoravid state in present-day Morocco in the mid-twelfth century. Yet the Sosso Kingdom was short-lived; it was defeated by Sundiata Keita in 1235. Five years later, Prince Sundiata (also spelled Sunjata) captured Koumbi Saleh, laying the foundation for the great Mali Empire, the largest and richest that medieval Africa had yet seen (Figure 15.12).

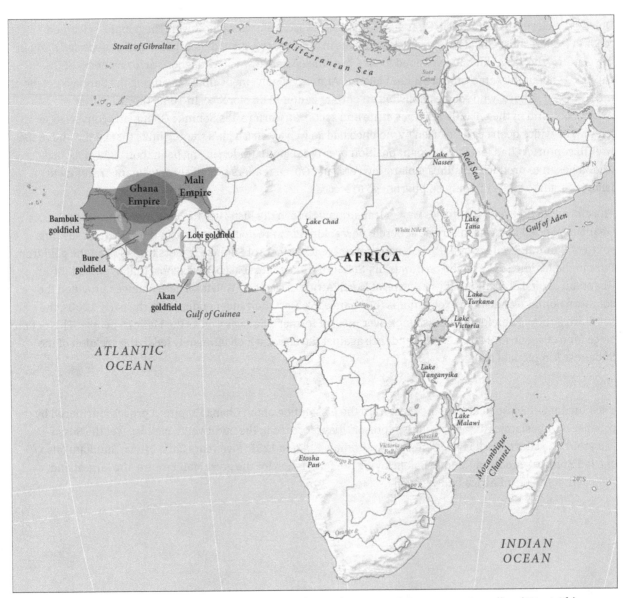

FIGURE 15.12 The Ghana and Mali Empires. This map shows the extent of the two great medieval West African empires: Ghana and Mali. At its height, Mali extended farther west and south than Ghana. (attribution: Copyright Rice University, OpenStax, under CC BY 4.0 license)

In the twelfth century, the main source of gold in West Africa had shifted from Bambuk to Bure, located to the southeast in the savanna country. This shift not only ended Ghanaian control over trans-Saharan trade, it also brought new groups into the great Sudanese trading network of West Africa, notably the southern Soninke and Malinke-speakers of the savanna. The Sosso, a branch of the southern Soninke, were the first to take full advantage of these changed circumstances. Sometime around 1200, they broke away from Ghana and established a successor state under Soumaoro, their sorcerer-king. During its brief existence, their Sosso Kingdom earned a grim reputation for violence by raiding and conquering neighboring kingdoms, killing their rulers, and seizing tribute. During the 1220s, the Sosso army made raids on the Malinke-speaking Mande people to the south and then attacked the northern Soninke of Ghana, sacking their capital in about 1224.

In response to the incursions against the Mande, Prince Sundiata of the Keita clan, a survivor of one of Soumaoro's raids, rallied several of the region's small Mande kingdoms and united them against the invaders. The exploits of Sundiata Keita, a near-mythical figure in the Mande oral tradition, have been passed down by generations of bards. Beginning around 1235, Sundiata set about consolidating his control over the heartland of the Mande people, a region centered on the upper reaches of the Senegal and Niger Rivers. He then moved to expand the kingdom of Mali by taking control of all the Soninke peoples recently conquered by the Sosso. Their territory comprised much of the former kingdom of Ghana and its nominally independent vassal states, including Mema and Wagadu. These newly conquered territories were often administered indirectly, leaving friendly puppet regimes in place to do the bidding of the Malian monarch (a political strategy that bred resentment among certain of the Malian vassal states, including Takrur and Songhai).

When forming alliances against the Sosso, Sundiata convinced the other Malinke kings to surrender their title, *mansa*, to him. He thus became the sole *mansa*, the religious and secular leader of all the Malinke people. In a few short years, he had built up a vast realm. Its imperial capital was advantageously situated at Niani, in the southern savanna country of the upper Niger valley near the goldfields of Bure. Within Sundiata's lifetime, the Mali Empire extended from the forested margins of the southwest through the grassland savanna country of the Malinke and southern Soninke to the Sahel of former Ghana.

Awdaghost, the one-time trade center at the western extreme of trans-Saharan trade, remained in the hands of nomads, and its role was taken by the more easterly commercial center of Oualata, now the main southern desert port for trade traversing the Sahara. The kings of Mali were less interested in conquering the various small kingdoms and chiefdoms of the grasslands than in taking the Sahelian trading towns that linked the regional economy to the vast trans-Saharan trade. These towns were key prizes and included Oualata, Gao, Timbuktu, and Djenné.

Control of the towns and the trade routes they connected was one of several components in Mali's diverse economy, which included access to the Bure goldfields and the agriculturally rich rural areas, particularly those around Niani in the south of the country. Unlike in Ghana, rainfall in Mali, located in the southern savanna, was more abundant, and the farmers of Mali had no difficulty growing enough food to sustain the population. Different areas of the empire specialized in different crops. For example, sorghum and millet grew on the savannah, and rice flourished in the Gambia valley and around the upper Niger floodplain. Meanwhile, the more northerly and drier Sahelian grasslands specialized in the grazing of camels, sheep, and goats.

Control over the gold-producing towns could present challenges for Mali's rulers. When a king conquered a region and attempted to spread Islam, the gold producers who refused to convert ceased mining operations, thereby threatening the Malian gold supply. This posed a serious risk to the imperial economy, so Malian rulers allowed gold areas to remain quasi-independent vassal states. Mali's gold trade was bolstered by events taking place elsewhere in the world. European kingdoms were again producing gold coins as the medieval economy improved. To meet the new demand, merchants from southern Europe sought to buy gold from their counterparts in North Africa. At the same time, new southerly trade routes were opened into the goldfields of the Akan forest (in present-day Ghana), from which sellers brought gold to the settlements of the Middle Niger. These developments to the north and south of Mali allowed the trans-Saharan gold trade to attain its greatest heights in the fourteenth century.

DUELING VOICES

Perspectives on Mali

What was life like for the people living and trading in West Africa in the fourteenth century? These two excerpts describe life in the Mali Empire. In the first, al-Umari, a Syrian scholar employed by the Mamluk sultan in Cairo, describes an aspect of Malian rule. In the second, Arab traveler Ibn Battuta describes the salt-mining center at Taghaza.

[The kingdom] is square, its length being four or more months' journey and its width likewise. It lies to the south of Marrakesh and the interior of Morocco and is not far from the Atlantic Ocean. . . . Under the authority of the sultan of this kingdom is the land of Mafazat al-Tibr. They bring gold dust [*tibr*] to him each year. They are uncouth infidels. If the sultan wished he could extend his authority over them, but the kings of this kingdom have learned by experience that as soon as one of them conquers one of the gold towns and Islam spreads and the muezzin calls to prayer, there the gold begins to decrease and then disappears, while it increases in the neighboring heathen countries. When they had learned the truth of this by experience, they left the gold countries under the control of the heathen people and were content with their vassalage and the tribute imposed on them.

—al-Umari, *Corpus of Early Arabic Sources for West African History*, translated by J. F. P. Hopkins

After twenty-five days, we arrive at Taghaza. . . . One of its marvels is that its houses and mosque are of rock and salt and its roofs of camel skins. It has no trees, but is nothing but sand with a salt mine. They dig in the earth for the salt, which is found in great slabs lying one upon the other. . . . A camel carries two slabs of it. No one lives at Taghaza except the slaves of the Massufa tribe, who dig for the salt [. . .] The people [of Mali] possess some admirable qualities. They are seldom unjust and have a greater abhorrence of injustice than any other people. Their sultan [the mansa] shows no mercy to any one guilty of the least act of it. . . . Neither traveler nor inhabitant in it has anything to fear from robbers or men of violence.

—Ibn Battuta, *Travels in Asia and Africa*

- What do these excerpts suggest about traveling in the Mali Empire?
- What do they suggest about the Malian king's access to commodities such as gold and salt?
- What happened to the goldfields when Malian kings conquered gold-producing areas?

The pilgrimage of Mansa Musa to Egypt and Mecca in 1324–1325 represents the golden age of the Mali Empire. Mansa Musa, the most famous of the Malian kings and reputed to be fabulously wealthy, arrived in Cairo at the head of a huge caravan that accounts tell us included sixty thousand soldiers, five hundred captives, and a hundred camel-loads of gold. Received with great respect by the sultan of Egypt as a fellow Muslim, Mansa Musa spent lavishly, giving away so many gifts that the value of gold in Cairo fell and did not recover for twelve years.

🔗 LINK TO LEARNING

At the ARCGIS website, trace the caravan route of Mansa Musa (https://openstax.org/l/77MansaMusa) and consider the legacy of his pilgrimage to Mecca.

Mansa Musa's journey captured the attention of people from Spain to Syria, including the Muslim geographer Ibn Battuta, who, after years traveling throughout Asia, visited Mali during the reign of Mansa Musa's brother Mansa Suleyman. Ibn Battuta's account has become a major source of our knowledge about fourteenth-century Mali.

As a marker of Mali's enduring fame in the fourteenth century, the Majorcan mapmaker Abraham Cresques featured it in *The Catalan Atlas* in 1375. One of the maps, which in part depicts the trade routes of North Africa, shows Mansa Musa enthroned (Figure 15.1). His royal status is proclaimed by his gold crown and scepter. In one hand he holds an immense piece of gold, proof of his kingdom's wealth. The caption reads, "The black lord is named Mussa Melly, lord of the Blacks of Guineas. This king is the richest and most noble lord of all this country by reason of the abundance of gold taken out of his land."

The strength and success of the Mali Empire depended on its ruler. During the late fourteenth century, a series of weak rulers, brief reigns, and dynastic civil wars opened the empire to conquest. With their power weakened, the *mansas* of Mali were unable to maintain unchallenged control of the trade routes on which they depended. Opposition from the Mossi people in the country south of the Niger, coupled with attacks from the Tuareg to the north of the Niger bend and regular uprisings by the Songhai people who controlled the city of

Gao (on the edge of the empire), led Mali to abandon both Gao and Timbuktu in 1438. At the same time, Mema, one of the kingdoms that had formed an alliance with Sundiata, broke away and became independent once more. Although weakened, Mali retained control of the Mande heartland and the nearby southern grasslands. However, the emerging Songhai Empire centered on Gao was beginning to take control of the lucrative trade across the Sahara.

The Zimbabwean Plateau

In the Later Iron Age (c. 900–1600), the Bantu who migrated to southern Africa developed several polities around the Zimbabwean plateau. These included the kingdoms of Mapungubwe and Great Zimbabwe. Although scholars debate which aspects of these societies are derived from the Bantu, the region's linguistic heritage and archaeological record (in the form of ironwork, enclosure walls, and burial customs) show clear links to the eastern Bantu subgroup.

The Kingdom of Mapungubwe

The precise relationship between them remains controversial, but Mapungubwe, which flourished between the eleventh and thirteenth centuries, is often considered the initial stage in the development of Great Zimbabwe. It has been called southern Africa's first state (Figure 15.13). The origins of Mapungubwe date to around the tenth century with a cattle-keeping culture known as Leopard's Kopje. In a region of relatively high rainfall near present-day Bulawayo in Zimbabwe, the people of Leopard's Kopje developed a complex mixed economy of livestock-keeping and herding and agriculture. Like other kingdoms in southern Africa, theirs produced ample food and a surplus they traded for other goods. A unique feature of their farming was a method of terracing the hillsides on the southern slopes of the large sandstone plateau to prevent soil erosion. One such site was Mapela Hill, where during the twelfth century extensive hillside terracing featured dry stone-walling (without mortar) for housing, defense, and cultivation.

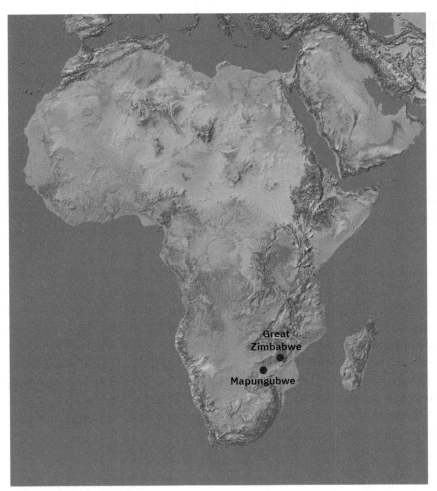

FIGURE 15.13 **Mapungubwe.** This map shows the location of Mapungubwe and Great Zimbabwe in the interior of southern Africa. (credit: modification of work "Topographic map of Africa" by NASA/JPL/NIMA/Wikimedia Commons, Public Domain)

Archaeological investigation of the region has revealed the presence of large cattle herds from around the ninth century. Because cattle were the traditional source of wealth and political power in southern Africa, the finding is suggestive of the influence the people of Leopard's Kopje could exercise. In the tenth century, the economy underwent several important changes, including significant growth in the number of cattle, the development of cotton cultivation and weaving (as indicated by the discovery of spindles), and the introduction of gold mining. The western plateau was rich in gold-bearing rock and was worked intensively by Later Iron Age miners. Narrow shafts were sunk deep into the ground, following the course of seams some ninety feet down. The rock was cracked by alternating use of fire and water and broken out with iron wedges.

Although little is known about the organization and control of this mining work, it is probable that it was largely forced labor. The mining of gold led to a flourishing production of goods for local consumption by elites as well as trade farther afield. A unique type of gold ornamentation found at Mapungubwe (and elsewhere only at Great Zimbabwe) is beaten gold sheets. Decorated with geometric patterns, the sheets seem to have been used to cover wooden pieces, although these have long since rotted away. Other gold objects found at the site include beads, bangle bracelets, and animal figurines.

Despite its setting in the southern African interior, Mapungubwe engaged in long-distance trade. Large finds of ivory splinters and animal hides indicate these were being stockpiled for trade (elephants were plentiful in the region). The most probable route for trade was up the Limpopo River to the coastal areas toward Sofala, one of the southernmost regions of the Swahili coast. Other finds, including glass beads from India and fragments of brightly colored India cloth and Chinese celadon (green-glazed) pottery, support this connection with the

Swahili coast and its seaborne trade with Arabia, China, and East Asia. While it is possible that Mapungubwe was a terminus for this type of international trade, it was certainly a hub for interregional trade in southern Africa.

Because the Mapungubwean people left no written record, scholars rely on the physical remains of the site to glean hints of its social structure. Mapungubwe is thought to be the first class-based social system in southern Africa, with sharp distinctions between wealthy rulers and their subjects. Commoners lived in mud and thatch dwellings in low-lying areas, district leaders occupied small hilltops on the outskirts of the capital, and the chief or king resided with his court in a stone enclosure at the capital atop Mapungubwe Hill, an imposing structure some 98 feet high and 328 feet in length. The royal wives lived in separate dwellings removed from the king, and the entire royal complex was surrounded by a wooden palisade (Figure 15.14).

FIGURE 15.14 Mapungubwe Hill. Mapungubwe Hill became the center of the Mapungubwe kingdom in the eleventh century, after the population outgrew the earlier center at Leopard's Kopje. (credit: modification of work "Mapungubwe, Limpopo, South Africa" by South African Tourism/Flickr, CC BY 2.0)

Mapungubwe fell into terminal decline around the end of the thirteenth century. The precise cause is a matter of speculation, though evidence suggests that the region was subject to a dramatic period of climate change at this time that led to a series of intense droughts. As weather patterns changed and rainfall became less predictable, it caused the land to dry and lose fertility. Pasturage used for livestock dwindled, and the surrounding agricultural farmland, which had once supported a large population, shrank. The failure of crops meant that the once-abundant farms could no longer support the same number of inhabitants, leading to overpopulation and resource scarcity. Around the turn of the fourteenth century, the center of medieval southern African civilization shifted northward where a new polity emerged: Great Zimbabwe. In Bantu, *Zimbabwe* (*dzimba dzamabwe*) means "stone buildings," a telltale marker of the debt the Zimbabweans owed to their southern Mapungubwean neighbors, who had a tradition of building in stone.

Great Zimbabwe

Great Zimbabwe was founded by the Shona, an Iron Age Bantu-speaking people who first migrated to southern Africa around the second century CE. As at Leopard's Kopje and Mapungubwe, the first settlers were livestock-herders drawn to the location by its abundant natural resources and location on the southwestern edge of the Zimbabwean plateau. Here, amid temperate grasslands ideal for seasonal grazing, the Shona found ample supplies of timber for firewood and for building, as well as well-watered fertile soil for cultivation. There is some evidence that they had domesticated goat, sheep, and cattle as early as the third century. The Shona were not the first inhabitants of the region; that distinction belongs to the small bands of hunter-gatherers who stalked game and foraged the plain in the centuries before the Bantu speakers' arrival. Despite having superior iron technology, the Shona were unable to completely dislodge these hunter-gatherers, resulting in tension and conflict that persist to the modern era.

The five hundred years between the fourth and ninth centuries witnessed the development of Bantu communities that farmed the valley and mined and worked iron. They lived in reed thatch or mud houses and represent the earliest Iron Age settlers in the area so far identified by archaeologists. During this period, the Shona manufactured simple pottery and produced leather for clothing, jewelry from copper and gold, and weapons and farming tools from iron. Many of these goods they traded with members of coastal settlements for commodities like salt, glass beads, and seashells. By the eleventh century, the society of the Zimbabwean plateau was thriving, and **drystone** buildings—that is, buildings constructed using interlocking stones rather than mortar—began to emerge. The people had established a prosperous mixed farming economy, engaging in animal husbandry and hunting the region's abundant game.

Above all, trade was the most important factor in Great Zimbabwe's wealth and power. Situated at the head of the Sabi River valley, the capital was ideally positioned for exploiting the long-distance commerce between the goldfields of the western plateau and Sofala, a Swahili center that connected Zimbabwean trade goods to the island of Kilwa. Zimbabwean gold made Kilwa the wealthiest of all the Swahili city-states. In exchange for gold, copper, and ivory, Swahili merchants bartered such exotic luxury goods as Chinese Ming porcelain and carved faience (ceramicware) from Persia at the markets and fairs established on the Zimbabwean plateau.

Construction of major stone buildings began sometime in the eleventh century and continued for about three hundred years. These stone structures are the most famous ancient ruins in southern Africa. The oldest is the Hill Complex. Located on a natural rise approximately 260 feet high, this citadel likely provided the Shona people with a space to perform rituals and find safety in uncertain times; however, the exact purpose of the site is still a matter of debate. Some scholars have suggested it functioned as a religious site for ancestor worship, while others have suggested it was a burial ground for chiefs or possibly even the site of a royal palace. Whatever its intended purpose, the site is an impressive one, and its prominence certainly ties it to some important aspect of Zimbabwean culture.

The ruins of Great Zimbabwe have impressed visitors for centuries. The Great Enclosure at the heart of the civilization dates from the thirteenth to fourteenth centuries and is still partially intact today, a massive elliptical building with drystone walls thirty-five feet high and as much as seventeen feet thick. Located in the area of the valley below the Hill Complex, it is the largest ancient monument in Africa south of the Sahara (Figure 15.15). Upon seeing the ruins, the sixteenth-century Portuguese explorer Vicente Pegado wrote, "Among the gold mines of the inland plains between the Limpopo and Zambezi rivers there is a fortress built of stones of marvelous size, and there appears to be no mortar joining them [. . .] This edifice is almost surrounded by hills, upon which are others resembling it in the fashioning of stone and the absence of mortar, and one of them is a tower more than twelve fathoms high. The native of the country call these edifices Symbaoe, which according to their language signifies court."

FIGURE 15.15 **The Great Enclosure.** The Great Enclosure at the heart of the Zimbabwean civilization, which dates from the thirteenth to fourteenth centuries and is still partially intact today, is the largest ancient monument in Africa south of the Sahara. (credit: "Photo of the Great Enclosure from the hilltop Great Zimbabwe" by Amanda/Flickr, CC BY 2.0)

Between the thirteenth and fourteenth centuries, the Great Enclosure underwent major renovation, most notably the addition of its elliptical drystone wall. The wall pitches slightly inward at the top and is punctured by a main entrance doorway that looks out across the valley toward the Hill Complex. The existence of multiple other doorways suggests the wall was not a fortification. Inside the Great Enclosure, a subsidiary wall forms a corridor and channels visitors to a conical stone tower some sixteen feet across and thirty-two feet high. The purpose of the Great Enclosure, which has a total circumference of 820 feet, is unknown, although its size suggests it was a royal residence and the tower was a granary (grain was a common form of tribute used by Shona rulers). Between these two sites—the Hill Complex and the Great Enclosure—archaeologists have found the most impressive and luxurious artifacts, including figurines made of soapstone, elaborately worked ivory, copper ingots, and bracelets.

Numerous other stone buildings lie in the valley between the Hill Complex and the Great Enclosure. These ruins are enclosed by high stone walls, along with the remains of imposing circular mud houses approximately thirty-two feet in diameter and nearly twenty feet high. The existence of these Valley Ruins suggests that the settlement along the valley floor grew significantly as Great Zimbabwe flourished. All told, the three sites cover some 1,700 acres, and the spatial organization of their structures suggests a hierarchical civilization of around eighteen thousand people ruled by an elite class or some type of central authority.

BEYOND THE BOOK

Architecture and Urban Design in Great Zimbabwe

The ruins of the massive stone structures of Great Zimbabwe are among the largest and oldest in sub-Saharan Africa (Figure 15.16). Much debate surrounds the identity of those who built the sprawling complex and why they did so. Some scholars have suggested that the site was used for religious purposes, while others believe it was a military fortification or even a palace. Whatever the reason, the drystone technology used to erect these magnificent structures is deceptively simple. The structures are enormous and have stood for hundreds of years.

The walls of the Great Enclosure, the structure at the heart of the settlement, measure dozens of feet in height and encircle an area some 820 feet in circumference. A second set of walls on the interior of the enclosure traces the outside wall, creating a channel that directs visitors toward a massive tower some thirty feet high. In addition to the Great Enclosure, the older Hill Complex includes ruins of mud houses with stone foundations and an enclosing wall; a further valley settlement, with remains of mud houses measuring as much as thirty-two feet in diameter, radiates away from the Great Enclosure and Hill Complex. All told, it is an impressive site.

(a)   (b)

FIGURE 15.16 Great Zimbabwe Walls. (a) The Zimbabwean plateau features many impressive ancient structures constructed of drystone, that is, walls that do not rely on mortar. (b) The interior of the Great Enclosure can be seen in this photo of the entrance to the main enclosure. (credit a: modification of work "Great Zimbabwe 8" by Mike/Wikimedia Commons, CC BY 2.0; credit b: modification of work "Great Zimbabwe, Main enclosure entrance" by "damien_farrell"/Flickr, CC BY 2.0)

- What do you believe the Great Enclosure's purpose was?
- What evidence leads you to this conclusion?
- What additional evidence might be useful in helping you interpret the site?

⊘ LINK TO LEARNING

Watch the video clip about Great Zimbabwe (https://openstax.org/l/77GreatZimb) titled "The City of Great Zimbabwe: Africa's Great Civilizations," and consider what the archaeological remains of Great Zimbabwe suggest about Zimbabwean culture and the organization of its society.

Great Zimbabwe flourished between the thirteenth and sixteenth centuries. Like many other aspects of the civilization, the exact makeup and nature of its government and society are unclear. Scholars have argued that it was male dominated, and that male heads of family competed for power and influence based on the size of their cattle herds. Herd size also correlated to the number of wives and thus the amount of labor at a man's disposal. Women in this society were expected to tend and harvest crops, prepare food, and get water. Single men hunted, herded animals, and made clothing. Males without property often became dependent on the wealthier men in the society.

Politically, Zimbabwean society was led by a chief or a king who was also likely the wealthiest member, although Shona tradition held that the position was hereditary, so being chief may not have indicated great wealth. That the chief had no army suggests that he had to govern by reaching consensus with the community's leading male figures and whatever subordinated chiefs may have existed. All this is speculative, but the existence of grandiose stone monuments is indicative of some sort of political authority—at least the kind that could organize and control resources and labor.

Medieval African society developed along similar lines in both West Africa and southern Africa. Beginning in the sixth century, regions with small groups of livestock-herders and keepers became home to growing and increasingly complex political entities. Agricultural and metallurgical innovations supported societies around the Niger River in West Africa and the Limpopo River in South Africa. The growth of these settlements was linked to the expansion and exploitation of trade, beginning with localized segments of trade routes connecting trading centers and culminating in control over vast territory. Although some of these kingdoms were short-lived (Mapungubwe, for example, lasted only about eighty years), they were vitally important to the development of medieval Africa, connecting it to peoples, places, and cultures thousands of miles away. In the end, these kingdoms linked local and regional African economies to a network of trade and commerce that touched Europe, Asia, and Arabia.

15.3 The People of the Sahel

LEARNING OBJECTIVES

By the end of this section, you will be able to:
- Discuss the development of the Gao and early Songhai states
- Explain why the people of the Sahel were able to take advantage of long-distance trade routes
- Explain why some nomadic African tribes settled at the edges of the Sahara

Among the peoples of the Maghreb and Sahel in West and North Africa, a group known as the Berbers (Amazigh) played an outsized role in the region's history. This assortment of nomads, settled agriculturalists, and merchants and traders who in ancient times inhabited modern-day Morocco, Algeria, Mauritania, Tunisia, Mali, and northern Niger, included many ethnic tribes—such as the Sanhaja, Masmuda, Zenata, Kutama, and Tuareg, among others—who called various pockets of the Maghreb, Sahel, and Sahara home. Each had a distinct culture, and often unique language and social structures. These Amazigh groups were crucial to the creation and longevity of the trans-Saharan trade, the control of which led to the rise and ultimately the fall of multiple medieval African kingdoms and empires. Eventually these peoples Islamized and became great empire builders themselves.

The Gao Dynasty and Early Songhai

In the seventh century CE, the region of the Middle Niger was home to a number of different peoples including the Gabibi, Gow, and Sorko, all of whom had migrated to the area to live off its abundant resources. Each group exploited the region for different reasons: the Gabibi were settled agriculturalists who farmed the fertile banks along the Niger; the Gow hunted the river's animals, including crocodile; the Sorko were warrior fishers and hunters of hippopotamus. The different purposes for which these peoples used the river and its resources ensured a relative balance between themselves and their environment.

Of these groups, the Sorko were best positioned to exercise control over the area. The canoes from which they hunted and fished gave them mastery of the river, which they used as a trading route to exchange food along this section of the Niger. They soon extended their territory upstream toward the Niger bend, establishing villages along the banks to help facilitate trade. From these trading post villages, the Sorko dominated the nearby communities of Gabibi farmers, raiding their granaries and pillaging their settlements. The dynamic in the region changed sometime in the ninth century, with the arrival of a nomadic horse-riding people who spoke Songhai, a dialect of the Nilo-Saharan language family. Gradually, the Sorko, Gabibi, and Gow peoples adopted the language of their conquerors, and collectively their cultures formed the basis of Songhai identity and the state of Songhai, with its capital at Kukiya. As the emerging Songhai state coalesced, its people were in steady contact with Muslim traders at Gao in the north.

At the eastern edge of the Niger bend, an area of historical significance to both the Ghana and Mali Empires, the trading city of Gao was founded in the seventh century by African and Egyptian merchants attracted by the Bambuk gold trade in Ghana. It soon became an important link in the trans-Saharan trade of gold, copper, enslaved captives, and salt in the eastern and central regions of the Sahara. The earliest mention of Gao dates from the ninth century; by the 870s, it had already grown into a regional power.

By the tenth century, Arab travelers had noted Gao's strategic location as a hub in the trans-Saharan trade route between Egypt and ancient Ghana. As Gao grew, so too did its needs. Songhai farmers and fishers provided the city's merchants with food in exchange for salt, cloth, and other products from North Africa. As a result of their contacts with Muslim traders, the rulers of Songhai were exposed to Islam and converted in the eleventh century, making theirs one of the first West African states to do so. This conversion marks the beginning of the Gao imperial period.

The earliest dynasty of kings of the Songhai state was the Za dynasty, which tradition and later historical record suggest ruled the kingdom during the eleventh and twelfth centuries. The Za are an obscure dynasty; what evidence exists comes to us in the form of myths and legends, the seventeenth-century *History of the Sudan*, the oral tradition of the Songhai written down by Abd al-Sadi, and some tombstone inscriptions dating to the fourteenth and fifteenth centuries. According to al-Sadi's history, the mythical founder of the dynasty was Za Alayaman, who settled in Kukiya sometime before the eleventh century. Za Alayaman and his immediate successors bore the title *malik* or "king." Evidence suggests that later rulers, possibly a second dynasty, bore the title *zuwa*, hence the name Zuwa dynasty.

Tradition holds that the first fourteen rulers of the Songhai state, which was initially centered on Kukiya, were *jahiliyyah* (literally "in ignorance [of Islam]"). Sometime in the 1000s, the dynasty Islamized, possibly under Za Kusay, whom the *History of the Sudan* remembers as the first Muslim ruler of Songhai. This timeline is contested, however. Modern scholars believe the Islamization of the Songhai rulers occurred toward the end of the eleventh century with the arrival of the Sanhaja Almoravids from Morocco. In any event, it was sometime during this period that the political focus of the kingdom shifted from Kukiya to Gao. Due in large part to its position as a terminus in the caravan route connecting the northern Sahara, Gao became the center of a significant Islamized kingdom (Figure 15.17).

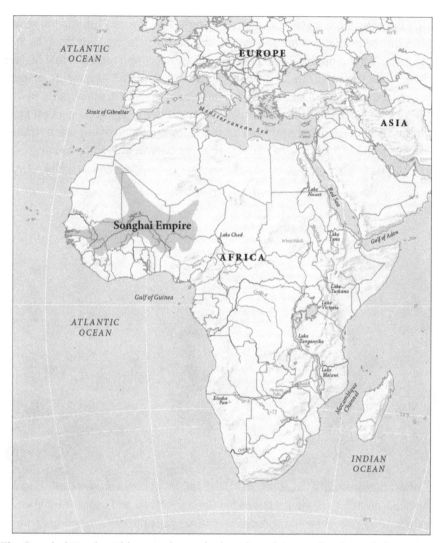

FIGURE 15.17 The Songhai Empire. This map shows the location of the medieval Songhai Empire in West Africa. (attribution: Copyright Rice University, OpenStax, under CC BY 4.0 license)

As goods such as kola nuts, dates, enslaved captives, ivory, salt, leather, and of course gold passed through the capital on their way to and from the kingdom of Ghana, traders and merchants, including the Songhai themselves, prospered. Gao's prosperity also drew the attention of the new and expansionist West African kingdom of Mali, which annexed Gao around 1325. This was the golden age of imperial Mali, and for the next century, its rulers profited from Gao's trade and collected taxes from its kings. When the explorer Ibn Battuta arrived at Gao from Timbuktu in 1353, he described it as a "great town on the Nile [Niger], one of the finest, biggest, and most fertile cities of the Sudan."

The annexation of Gao greatly expanded the Mali Empire, but only temporarily. Periodic rebellions by the peoples of Timbuktu, Takedda, and Gao, coupled with civil war, a struggling economy, and incursions by Almoravids from the north, caused Gao's Malian rulers to withdraw in the 1430s. The leader of the Songhai rebels, Sunni Ali, became the first king of the Songhai Empire. Under him, Songhai became one of the greatest empires of medieval Africa. From his capital at Gao in the heart of the kingdom, Sunni Ali engaged in a war of conquest against his Muslim neighbors. Marshaling his massive cavalry and fleet of war canoes, the king extended his empire deep into the desert in the north and as far as Djenné in the southwest. His near-constant harassment and pursuit of the Tuareg nomads resulted in his capture of Mali's great religious and scholarly center in Timbuktu, the trading town of Djenné, and almost the whole of the Middle Niger floodplain and the Bandiagara uplands.

Despite being Muslim himself, Sunni Ali campaigned against Muslim forces. This and his general lack of respect for Islam led to his being highly criticized by Arabic historians. In the *History of the Sudan*, al-Sadi characterized Sunni Ali as "a great oppressor and notorious evil-doer" and reported that he "tyrannized the scholars and holy men, killing them, insulting them, and humiliating them." As a result, many of the scholars in Timbuktu fled to Oualata, leading to a significant diminishment in Islamic scholarship in the city (Figure 15.18). Nevertheless, in Songhai oral tradition, Sunni Ali is remembered as a great general and conquering hero, as well as the founder of the Songhai Empire. Through his domination of important trade routes and urban areas, he enriched his kingdom and enabled it to become even wealthier than Mali.

FIGURE 15.18 Timbuktu. This artist's rendering shows the German scholar and explorer Heinrich Barth approaching Timbuktu in 1853, one of the first Europeans to do so. Note the city's baked-mud mosques and centers of learning in the background. The image was published in Barth's famous five-volume travel journal of Africa. (credit: "Timbuktu seen from a distance by Heinrich Barth's party, September 7, 1853" by Heinrich Barth, Reisen und Entdeckungen. Gotha 1858, vol. 4./Wikimedia Commons, Public Domain)

IN THEIR OWN WORDS

Timbuktu in the Sixteenth Century

Al-Hasan ibn Muhammad al-Wazzan al-Zayyati, known as Leo Africanus, was born in Spain in 1485, educated in Fez (a city in present-day Morocco), and traveled widely in North Africa, including Ghana. Returning from Mecca in 1518, he was captured and enslaved by Christian pirates before being presented to Pope Leo X because of his education and abilities. Leo X baptized him and commissioned him to write a detailed survey of Africa in Italian. This survey, published in 1526, was the basis of European knowledge of Africa for the next several centuries.

The houses of Timbuktu are huts made of clay-covered wattles with thatched roofs. In the center of the city is a temple built of stone and mortar, built by an architect named Granata, and in addition there is a large palace, constructed by the same architect, where the king lives. The shops of the artisans, the merchants, and especially weavers of cotton cloth are very numerous. Fabrics are also imported from Europe to Timbuktu, borne by Amazigh merchants.

The women of the city maintain the custom of veiling their faces, except for the slaves who sell all the foodstuffs. The inhabitants are very rich. [. . .] There are many wells containing [fresh] water in

Timbuktu; and in addition, when the Niger is in flood, canals deliver the water to the city. Grain and animals are abundant, so that the consumption of milk and butter is considerable. But salt is in very short supply because it is carried here from Tegaza, some five hundred miles from Timbuktu. [. . .]

The royal court is magnificent and very well organized. When the king goes from one city to another with the people of his court, he rides a camel and the horses are led by hand by servants. [. . .] When someone wishes to speak to the king, he must kneel before him and bow down; but this is only required of those who have never before spoken to the king, or of ambassadors. The king has about three thousand horsemen and infinity of foot-soldiers armed with bows made of wild fennel which they use to shoot poisoned arrows. This king makes war only upon neighboring enemies and upon those who do not want to pay him tribute. When he has gained a victory, he has all of them—even the children—sold in the market at Timbuktu. [. . .]

The people of Timbuktu are of a peaceful nature. They have a custom of almost continuously walking about the city in the evening (except for those that sell gold), between 10 pm and 1 am, playing musical instruments and dancing. The citizens have at their service many slaves, both men and women.

—Leo Africanus, *Description of Africa*

- What can you tell about Timbuktu from this description?
- What can you tell about the economic connections between Timbuktu and North Africa and Europe?

Cross-Cultural Interaction in the Sahel

From the late seventh century, the African communities of West and North Africa were under increasing pressure from the forces of Islam. Home to some Christian communities since the second century, as well as to groups of settled and nomadic pagans, North Africa lay in the path of the powerful and expansionistic new Muslim power centered on the Arabian Peninsula. Egypt, an early bastion of Coptic Christianity and a bulwark of Christian Roman power in North Africa, was conquered by the armies of Islam around the middle of the century. From there, Muslim Arab armies marched steadily across the northern quadrant of the continent. When Byzantine Carthage fell to Umayyad armies in 698, Islamic forces turned to al-Kahina, "the Queen of the Berbers" and likely a Christian convert, who forged a coalition of indigenous African forces against the Islamic onslaught. With her power based in Algeria, al-Kahina roundly defeated an Islamic army sent from Egypt in 698, but five years later, a more determined Islamic vanguard bested her at Tabarka in Tunisia. The way was now clear, and with the help of pockets of Islamized Africans, Arab control of North Africa was achieved in 709.

🔗 LINK TO LEARNING

A great deal of art originated during the Islamic period, but archaeologists have also discovered troves of pre-Islamic art in the Sahel, including beaded jewelry, pottery, and figures. Follow this link to explore the Sahel collection (https://openstax.org/l/77SahelArt) at New York's Metropolitan Museum of Art.

Conversion of the nomads did not mean their submission, however. Heavily taxed subjects in conquered provinces whose daughters were sometimes enslaved, the Islamized Africans were treated as second-class Muslims. Nevertheless, many Africans regarded themselves as better Muslims than their elite Arab rulers, whom they believed had been corrupted by wealth and luxury and were no longer devoted to Islam. They insisted that cruel rulers be removed from power and replaced by pious men. Widespread opposition took the form of revolts that erupted across North Africa in 739 and 740 and shattered the Islamic Caliphate. In the end, control over the region fell to a variety of Islamic sects and ruling families. It took nearly two hundred years for North Africa to unite under Muslim rulers again. These rulers were known as the Fatimids, Shia Muslims who did not recognize the authority of the Abbasids who had succeeded the Umayyads in 750.

The Fatimids

Fatimid missionaries had long been active in Iraq and Syria before converting the Kutama in Algeria. Beginning in the tenth century, the Fatimids started capturing Muslim strongholds throughout the Maghreb. By the end of the century, armies had captured Egypt and seized control of Palestine, Syria, and parts of the Arabian Peninsula including Mecca and Medina. The Fatimids established a Shi'ite caliphate in Cairo, but their ultimate goal was to conquer the Sunni Abbasid Caliphate in Baghdad and establish a caliphate that was the center of the Muslim world.

The founder of the Fatimid Caliphate, Abdullah al-Mahdi Billah, had relied on indigenous African soldiers in his conquest of the Maghreb. These soldiers, so crucial to victories in Africa, were no match for the Turkish soldiers of the Abbasid Caliphate, who were often enslaved captives. Taking a page from the Abbasids, the Fatimids diversified their army, enlisting free and enslaved Turks alongside indigenous African soldiers and transforming their tribal force into a multiethnic one. In the short term, this proved a decisive strategy, but in the long term, competition for positions within the military manifested along ethnic lines and resulted in a civil war in Egypt in the 1060s.

Having experienced persecution and status as outsiders, the Fatimids were religiously tolerant and did not attempt to forcibly convert Christians, Jewish people, or Sunni Muslims. Coptic Christians even continued to dominate the financial and administrative realms of the Fatimid Caliphate. The Fatimids sought the spread of Shia Islam through education (they built many madrasas) and an increase in Shia mosques, such as the Al-Azhar Mosque in Cairo, where students could study Islamic law and jurisprudence, astronomy, philosophy, and Arabic grammar. These were effective steps, for by the end of the tenth century, the majority of people in Egypt were Muslim.

Unable to directly rule over the region of the Maghreb, the Fatimid rulers at Cairo appointed emirs or governors from the Zirid family. Like the Fatimids, the Zirids followed Shia Islam. At first, they ruled in the name of the Fatimids, but in the middle of the eleventh century, they declared their independence and aligned themselves with the Sunni Abbasid Caliphate. The Fatimid caliph attempted to reassert Shia Muslim control by encouraging tens of thousands of Arabs to migrate westward, pressuring the frontiers of the breakaway Ziridi state and causing war. Although enormously destructive, the Fatimids failed to achieve their desired ends, and the Maghreb had gone beyond their control.

In addition to their western troubles, the Fatimids faced challenges from Europe in the form of Christian crusaders, who captured Jerusalem from them in 1099. Gradually, the caliphate of the Fatimids shrank to only Egypt. The Fatimids were further weakened in the 1160s when they were divided by a power struggle between two competing factions. One of the contenders appealed to Christian crusaders for assistance, and Egypt subsequently became a crusader protectorate for a short time as a result. His rival reached out to a Sunni Muslim army for aid. By 1169, the Muslim army, under the leadership of a Kurdish general named Saladin, had expelled the crusaders. When Saladin pledged allegiance to the Abbasids a few years later, this brought Egypt back into the Sunni-dominated Islamic Caliphate.

The Almoravids

As the Fatimid Caliphate tried to wrest control of the Maghreb back from the Zirid family, the center of power in the region shifted away from the coast and toward the Atlas Mountain range in Morocco. This part of West Africa was occupied by the Sanhaja, Islamized Africans subdivided into distinct ethnic tribes including the Djuddala and the Lamtuna. It was among these groups that the Islamic jurist Ibn Yasin settled in 1039 at the instigation of Yahya ibn Ibrahim, who sought to reform the tribes to the "true" Islamic religion (that is, Sunni Islam as he saw it). Ibn Yasin worked for over a decade to impose on the Djuddala the Malikite interpretation of Sunnism, which was based on a literal reading of the Quran and the *sunna* (the deeds and sayings of the prophet Muhammad). Anyone who fell short of Ibn Yasin's strict demands for discipline and the observation of religious duties was severely punished.

After more than a decade among the Djuddala, during which time he alienated several leading members of the tribe, Ibn Yasin himself was expelled. While in exile, he received a steady stream of followers from both the Lamtuna and Djuddala Sanhaja, forming a group he soon came to call the Almoravids. Under Ibn Yasin's direction the Almoravids became zealous reformers committed to imposing his version of Islam on the people of the Maghreb. In 1052, Ibn Yasin and the Almoravids embarked on a years-long campaign to defeat the other tribes of the region, assembling an impressive army in the process.

By 1054, the Almoravids had captured the trans-Saharan trading route between Sijilmasa and Awdaghost. After the death of Ibn Yasin in battle in 1059, his followers continued their northward advance all the way to Fez (in modern-day Morocco), which they captured in 1069. In 1070 they established their capital at Marrakesh. After tightening their grip on Morocco, the Almoravids launched an invasion of Umayyad Spain, conquering the Islamic states of Al-Andalus to create the Almoravid Empire. From 1085, the Almoravid Empire, ruled by the Sanhaja, encompassed all the territory from Awdaghost in the southern Sahara to Zaragoza on the Ebro River in Spain (Figure 15.19). Maliki legal doctrine dominated interpretations of Islam, and study of the Quran and the prophetic traditions contained in the *sunna* were largely abandoned. Unlike the Fatimids of Egypt, the Almoravids were intolerant of any other faith, including mystic Islamic Sufism and sects of Sunni Islam.

FIGURE 15.19 The Almoravid Empire. The Almoravid Empire was founded in the early eleventh century. At its height around the end of the century, it stretched from Zaragoza in the north to the oasis town of Awdaghost in Mauretania to the south. (attribution: Copyright Rice University, OpenStax, under CC BY 4.0 license)

The Almohads

The Almoravids did not remain in power for long. Ibn Tumart, a member of the Masmuda (an Amazigh tribe) from the Atlas Mountains, launched a countermovement that rejected the legalistic formality of the Almoravids. Through his studies at mosques and madrasas across the Muslim world, Ibn Tumart had developed a broader outlook than Ibn Yasin, and Ibn Tumart's cosmopolitan approach challenged Ibn Yasin's scriptural literalism. A reformer, he sought a return to what he believed was the original, uncorrupted Islamic faith and rejected all of the schools of Islamic law because he considered their pronouncements to be heretical interpretations of the teachings of the prophet Muhammad. Ibn Tumart's followers adopted the name Almohads, meaning "those of the oneness," a reference to their belief in the transcendental unity of God. Despite the more cosmopolitan outlook of his movement, Ibn Tumart was no less strict than Ibn Yasin in insisting upon what he considered to be the appropriate way to practice Islam. He once pulled his sister off the horse she was riding because she was not wearing a veil. He was also a frequent visitor to Marrakesh, where he routinely mocked Almoravid government officials and ridiculed their beliefs.

The reach of the Almoravids in the southern extreme of their empire was tentative. Their mounted armies encountered difficulties fighting and maneuvering in the heights of the Atlas Mountains, so the Masmuda nomads who lived there largely escaped Almoravid control. It was among these nomads that Ibn Tumart began to recruit the Masmuda tribes into a force to oppose the Almoravids. By 1130, his control extended across the region. Those groups initially reluctant to join the Almohad cause were persuaded into an alliance by Ibn Tumart's military. In 1147, the Almohads captured Marrakesh, destroyed what they believed were the symbols of a decadent and corrupt empire, including the Almoravid mosque, and moved on to the coastal region of the Maghreb, which they conquered as far as Tripoli by 1160. At the end of the century, the Almohad Empire extended across all of Muslim Spain (Figure 15.20).

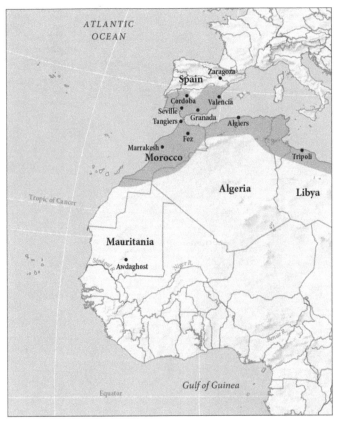

FIGURE 15.20 The Almohad Empire. At its height around the year 1200, the Almohad Empire stretched from the Atlas Mountain range in the south eastward across the Mediterranean coast to Tripoli in Libya, and north to Granada in Spain. (attribution: Copyright Rice University, OpenStax, under CC BY 4.0 license)

Like the Sanhaja before them, the Masmuda dominated both the administration and the military of Almohad Spain. The manuals of Malikite legal doctrine were banned and later burned, to be replaced by the teachings of Ibn Tumart, who died in 1130. Like their predecessors the Almoravids, the Almohads made no attempt to integrate the conquered and subject peoples of Spain into the administration. Almohad dominance turned out to be short-lived, however. No sooner did it reach its peak around 1200 than the empire of the Masmuda started to crumble, due in part to pressures from Christians to the north. By the middle of the thirteenth century, Christian forces had captured all of Spain north of Granada (which fell in 1492). Meanwhile, insurgencies in the Maghreb and the sacking of Marrakesh by rebels in 1275 brought the Almohad Empire to an end.

For two hundred years, the Almoravids and Almohads controlled the Maghreb. Despite being rivals, they had much in common: they shared militant reformist origins, they were independent of Arab rulers (Fatimid Egypt in the case of the Almoravids, Abbasid Baghdad in the case of the Almohads), and they both retained indigenous African cultural attributes (Sanhaja continued to be veiled, Masmuda maintained their Council of Fifty chiefs that adjudicated tribal matters). Yet they were also very different: the Malikite legalism of the Almoravids was in contrast to the cosmopolitanism of Ibn Tumart's ideology. In the end, although both empires were relatively short-lived, they left lasting legacies in North Africa and along the Mediterranean coast in the form of the spread of Islam and the Arabic language.

LINK TO LEARNING

The article, "These West African Artifacts Tell Stories of Great Forgotten Empires but Also the Battle to Own Africa's Art," looks at the ownership of African art (https://openstax.org/l/77AfricanArt) found in collections held in European museums.

Key Terms

Donatist controversy the Christian schism in North Africa springing from the belief that church leaders who had renounced their faith to avoid persecution held no authority to perform sacraments

drystone a construction method that uses interlocking stones rather than mortar

Section Summary

15.1 Culture and Society in Medieval Africa

Africa's ancient migrations diffused technological and cultural innovations that helped establish settlements later enriched by the spread of new belief systems. Beginning with both Judaism and Christianity in the early centuries of the Common Era and continuing with the long tradition of Islam, monotheism had taken root throughout much of North Africa by the end of the eighth century and gradually penetrated the sub-Saharan region. By the medieval period, the nature of religious belief throughout much of the continent had been utterly transformed. Islam in particular made great advances in the Sudanic region of West Africa and along the Swahili coast. Nevertheless, ancient African belief systems continued to be practiced in many rural communities. In other areas, monotheistic beliefs were blended with prehistoric religious practices to create truly unique cultural expressions, such as the Africanized Islam practiced by the Muslims of the Swahili coast.

15.2 Medieval Sub-Saharan Africa

Medieval African kingdoms and polities controlled vast territories, used emerging technologies, and governed populations that were heterogeneous and cosmopolitan. In every kingdom, trade was vital not only to longevity and prosperity, but also to their dynamic cultures. Ghanaian control over trans-Saharan trade in West Africa led to a thriving relationship between Muslim traders and the empire's rulers, who never converted. After Ghana's fall, the larger kingdom of Mali emerged, whose *mansas* converted to Islam.

As an Islamic kingdom, Mali was far better integrated in the wider world of Muslim-dominated trade in Africa and the Near and Middle East than Ghana had been. Through trade, Ghana and Mali's southern African contemporaries Mapungubwe and Great Zimbabwe likewise connected peoples, places, and cultures thousands of miles distant. As goods and people flowed to and from the central South African interior, the Shona civilization of the Zimbabwean plateau used the wealth it generated to expand its territory and to build medieval Africa's largest stone structures, many of which stand to this day.

15.3 The People of the Sahel

During the Mali Empire's period of decline, the Soninke-speaking people of the Niger established a new polity centered on the trade city of Gao, which soon became the capital of the Songhai kingdom. During the sixteenth century, Songhai grew into a larger and wealthier state than even the fabled Mali. Its prosperity depended on controlling the trans-Saharan trade routes of West Africa. This trade was made possible largely by nomadic and seminomadic peoples such as the Sanhaja and Tuareg who acted as caravan leaders, merchants, and traders. They had long maintained contact across the Sahara and were familiar with the oases and settlements along the way.

The conversion to Islam of North African peoples followed the Arab conquests of the seventh century, but over time, their loose interpretation of and adherence to Islamic law, custom, and practice made them a target for radical and militant religious movements, particularly in the Maghreb region of northwest Africa. These movements, the Almoravid and later the Almohad, sought to reform the prevailing Sunni Islam then propagated by the Umayyad Caliphate. The result was decades of conflict, amounting to civil war, centered on Morocco, during which the Almoravids wrested control of the region from the Umayyads. The Almoravid Empire was short-lived; its traditionalism alienated many, who rebelled and overthrew the Almoravids when they conquered their capital at Marrakesh. The Almohads had no greater luck than their predecessors, and their dynasty soon collapsed under the weight of internal conflict and rebellion.

Assessments

Review Questions

1. What made cultural contact between the Sahel and the Mediterranean peoples of North Africa difficult?
   a. Red Sea
   b. Kalahari Desert
   c. Sahara
   d. the Nile

2. In what African ecological system did the migrating Bantus likely adopt ironworking technology from the Nok?
   a. tropical rainforest
   b. desert
   c. semiarid grassland
   d. savanna

3. What is the name of the branch of Christianity that emerged in Egypt?
   a. Maghrebi
   b. Visigothic
   c. Sufi
   d. Coptic

4. What does the "Africanization" of Christianity and Islam in the medieval period refer to?
   a. the process of converting African communities to monotheism
   b. the development of holy books written in indigenous African languages
   c. the blending of traditional African beliefs with those of Christianity and Islam
   d. the diffusion of traditional African beliefs among the Abrahamic faiths of the Near and Middle East

5. The Ghana and Mali Empires were centered on what two capital cities, respectively?
   a. Ouagadougou and Accra
   b. Koumbi Saleh and Niani
   c. Koubmi Saleh and Bure
   d. Niani and Cairo

6. Who was Mansa Musa?
   a. a Christian ruler of the Swahili coast who traveled to China
   b. a Muslim ruler of the Ghana Empire who followed the trans-Saharan trade route to Egypt
   c. a pagan tribal chief who led a revolt against Islamized Africans in West Africa
   d. a Muslim ruler of the Mali Empire who made a pilgrimage to Mecca in the fourteenth century

7. What were the two principal goods the medieval empires of West Africa were renowned for trading in?
   a. furs and ceramics
   b. gold and salt
   c. metalware and textiles
   d. porcelain and ivory

8. What characterized the political systems of the West African empires?
   a. A formerly independent kingdom incorporated into a larger empire often retained its identity and internal political structure.
   b. When empires declined in power, they left anarchy behind.

    c. Empires were indivisible organizations with stable borders.

    d. Empires were synonymous with chiefdoms and engaged in nearly constant tribal warfare.

9. Bantu-speaking peoples brought innovations to southern Africa that led to the foundation of which medieval kingdoms?
    a. Songhai and Mali
    b. the Swahili coast and Natal
    c. Mapungubwe and Zimbabwe
    d. Mozambique and Lesotho

10. The Sanhaja and Masmuda founded what West African kingdoms, respectively?
    a. Mali and Ghana
    b. Ghana and Egypt
    c. Almoravid and Almohad
    d. Almohad and Al-Andalus

11. The Fatimid Caliphate followed _____ Islam.
    a. Shia
    b. Sunni
    c. Sufi
    d. Al-Wabbi

12. Gao was the capital and important trading center of what kingdom?
    a. Ghana
    b. Songhai
    c. Maghreb
    d. Almoravid

Check Your Understanding Questions

1. Why was the Sahara vital to the prosperity of medieval West African kingdoms despite its hostile environment?

2. What were some of the controversies that gripped Christianity in medieval Africa?

3. Which were the most important factors that helped spread Islam in Africa?

4. What explains the origins of Ghana, the earliest Sudanic West African kingdom?

5. How did the success of Mali differ from that of Ghana?

6. In what ways did medieval African societies in West and sub-Saharan Africa develop along similar lines?

7. Why were nomadic Africans essential to the operation of the trans-Saharan trade?

8. What circumstances led to the rise of the Fatimid Caliphate?

Application and Reflection Questions

1. How might the history of Africa have been different if the Sahara did not exist and the savanna region extended up to the Mediterranean coast?

2. Which African groups likely benefited most from the spread of new belief systems during the Middle Ages? Which probably benefited least? In both cases, why?

3. How did trade connect West Africa to a wider network that included Europe, North Africa, and the Middle

East? What did this mean for the development of the region?

4. What evidence do we have of the wealth and power of the medieval kingdoms in southern Africa? Why are these kingdoms important?

5. Compare the territory of Songhai to that of Ghana and Mali. Why are the three empires oriented differently and different in size?

6. How were the Almoravid and Almohad movements both reformist and reactionary?

7. In what ways were the Bantu kingdoms of Mapungubwe and Great Zimbabwe similar and dissimilar to the West African Sahelian kingdoms?

FIGURE 16.1 The Bubonic Plague. Thanks to modern scientific tools, the remains of fourteenth-century bubonic plague victims, such as those being buried in this image, have yielded much insight into the course and impact of historical pandemics, and their short- and long-term consequences on human society. This painting is a miniature from a manuscript of the mid-fourteenth century. (credit: modification of work "Gilles li Muisis, Antiquitates Flandriae (Tractatus quartus)" by Belgian Art Links and Tools/Wikimedia Commons, Public Domain)

CHAPTER OUTLINE

16.1 Asia, North Africa, and Europe in the Early Fourteenth Century
16.2 Famine, Climate Change, and Migration
16.3 The Black Death from East to West
16.4 The Long-Term Effects of Global Transformation

INTRODUCTION Climate change, global pandemics, and political upheaval may seem more characteristic of the modern era than of the premodern world, but the first decades of the 1300s did in fact witness a rapid succession of such crises, prompting historian Barbara Tuchman to dub the period "the calamitous fourteenth century" in her book *A Distant Mirror*. From the ravages of the so-called Little Ice Age to the bubonic plague (Figure 16.1) and the rapid decline of the once-mighty Mongol Empire, the 1300s were marked by an array of extraordinary challenges that not only radically altered the world's demographic and political landscape but also showcased the strength and vigor of human resilience.

Although any one of these catastrophes might have crushed the societies upon which they descended, in each case, people adapted, rebounded, and rebuilt. Due to their remarkable grit, the fourteenth century offers an unprecedented opportunity for historians to understand critical facets of the human experience, such as the impact of environmental change, infectious disease, and the ravages of military conflict.

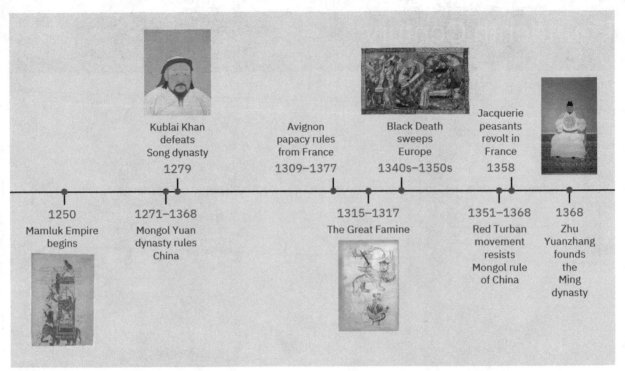

FIGURE 16.2 Timeline: Climate Change and Plague in the Fourteenth Century. (credit "1250": modification of work ""The Elephant Clock", Folio from a Book of the Knowledge of Ingenious Mechanical Devices by al-Jazari" by Bequest of Cora Timken Burnett, 1956/Metropolitan Museum of Art, Public Domain; credit "1279": modification of work "Yuan Emperor Album Khubilai Portrait" by National Palace Museum/Wikimedia Commons, Public Domain; credit "1315–1317": modification of work "Death ("Mors") sits astride a lion whose long tail ends in a ball of flame (Hell). Famine ("Fames") points to her hungry mouth" by "Mariule"/Wikimedia Commons, Public Domain; credit "1340s–1350s": modification of work "Gilles li Muisis, Antiquitates Flandriae (Tractatus quartus)" by Belgian Art Links and Tools/Wikimedia Commons, Public Domain; credit "1368": modification of work "Official court painting of the Hongwu Emperor" by Unknown/Wikimedia Commons, Public Domain)

16.1 Asia, North Africa, and Europe in the Early Fourteenth Century

LEARNING OBJECTIVES

By the end of this section, you will be able to:
- Analyze the impact of the Mongol conquest on China
- Describe changes that took place in Mongol rule of the Middle East in the fourteenth century
- Identify the causes of instability in Europe in the fourteenth century

The fourteenth century was a period of great instability in Asia, North Africa, and Europe. Although much of this precariousness was caused by climate change, famine, and epidemic disease, these natural phenomena might not have been so devastating if strong political and social institutions had existed to provide support for the people affected by these events. However, in China, the Middle East, North Africa, and Europe, war and conquest, conflicts among rulers, and the weakness of political and religious institutions affected the ability of kingdoms and empires to respond effectively to these challenges.

China in the Early Fourteenth Century

By the beginning of the fourteenth century, the Mongol realm had expanded its reach through a broad swath of Eurasia, effectively becoming the largest land-based empire in history. First uniting the Mongol tribes into a common fighting force with a goal of expanding their control beyond their homeland, the Mongols extended their conquest into China across the North China plain in 1212–1213, leaving many cities in ruin. It was not until Chinggis Khan's grandson Kublai Khan came to power, however, that the Mongol invasion of southern

China was complete (Figure 16.3).

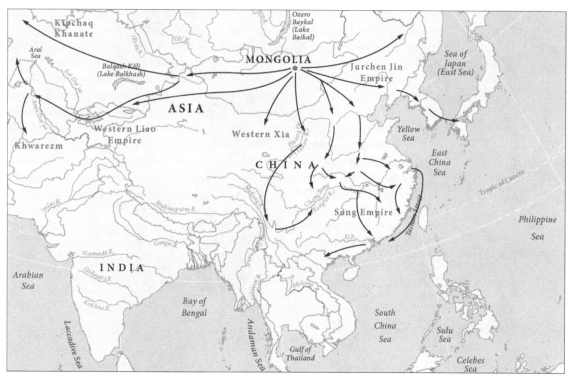

FIGURE 16.3 Mongol China and Beyond. This map depicts the Mongol conquest of Chinese regimes over the course of the thirteenth century, as well as the movement of Mongol armies westward toward the Middle East and beyond. Notice how the movement of the Mongol conquests varies, owing to both the geographic size of China and the resistance within each region. (attribution: Copyright Rice University, OpenStax, under CC BY 4.0 license)

Having transferred his capital from Karakorum in Mongolia to what is now Beijing in 1264, Kublai Khan began his conquest of China by adopting the Chinese name Yuan for his empire in 1271. Meaning "origin," the term *Yuan* cemented the Mongols' political legitimacy in China by reinforcing their connection to the Mandate of Heaven, an ancient political philosophy that emphasized the divine source of governmental authority. After fully conquering the Song dynasty in 1279, Kublai Khan became the first ruler over all of China who was not of Chinese origin. In addition to his role as Yuan emperor, he claimed the title of "great khan," asserting his claims to supremacy over the entire Mongol Empire, even though the Mongols had regional khans responsible for their own territories.

The Yuan dynasty not only incorporated China into the vast Mongol domain, but it also made it a nominal capital of the empire. China had long been a target of Mongol conquest. Its combination of strategic placement at the terminus of the interconnected Eurasian trade routes known as the Silk Roads, its abundant croplands, and a sophisticated bureaucracy provided a ready-made foundation for Mongol governance. The Mongols' traditional nomadic ways had given them little experience in managing sedentary agriculture, so they began by absorbing many Chinese practices of taxation and administration into their government, which they staffed mainly with foreigners rather than with their Chinese subjects. Although some Chinese officials maintained their positions at the local level, the most lucrative and prestigious jobs were primarily held by Mongols and non-Chinese outsiders. Mongol leaders favored those of Mongolian descent, but they also exhibited tolerance for those they considered outsiders and supported the ethnic and religious diversity of Yuan China, particularly in urban areas. By developing policies favorable to trade, adopting the practice of Buddhism, and expanding the circulation of paper money, Mongol leadership fostered economic expansion and a cosmopolitan spirit that attracted many foreign traders to China (Figure 16.4).

FIGURE 16.4 An Early Passport. This late-thirteenth-century iron and silver plaque, known as a *paiza*, served as one of the world's first passports. The writing appears in the script used to record the Mongol language in Yuan China and was derived from that used by the Uyghur tribes of central Asia. *Paizi* such as this were carried by Mongol diplomats or officials to permit them safe passage and access to supplies wherever they traveled in the Mongol realm. (credit: "Safe Conduct Pass (Paiza) with Inscription in Phakpa Script" by Purchase, Bequest of Dorothy Graham Bennett, 1993/Metropolitan Museum of Art, Public Domain)

🔗 LINK TO LEARNING

An initiative called "The Mongols in China" (https://openstax.org/l/77MongolsChina) is presented by the Weatherhead East Asian Institute at Columbia University. It includes links to an interactive timeline of the Mongol presence in China. It also contains an introduction to the Mongol influence on Chinese society and narratives and visual depictions of life in China under Mongol rule.

Although Yuan rulers incorporated some elements of Chinese political culture into their governmental organization, such as the Confucian emphasis on filial piety and the veneration of ancestors, they also sought to maintain cultural distance from their Chinese subjects by forbidding them to adopt Mongol dress or learn the Mongol language. They enforced rigid hierarchies based on ethnicity and capitulation to their rule. Their four-tiered social structure placed Mongols at the top, followed by non-Mongol foreigners known as *Semu ren*. Their ethnic Chinese subjects were relegated to the bottom two categories; those who had submitted to Mongol rule earlier, the Han Chinese in the north, were ranked higher than those in the south who held out longer.

Although the social policy of the Mongols generated a great deal of resentment from their ethnic Chinese subjects, in other respects, the Yuan rulers instituted more benevolent policies. By creating granaries that provided food in times of famine, forgiving the tax burden for villages hit by natural disasters, and reducing the number of crimes that had traditionally resulted in the death penalty, for example, Mongol rulers likely alleviated the hardships faced by many of their subjects. By reducing banditry and making trade safer, particularly along the Silk Roads, they also boosted commerce and improved the lives and fortunes of merchants.

Despite Kublai Khan's dominance in China, his attempts to hold a unified Mongol Empire together were largely in vain. The realm had already begun to unravel by the time he took the reins of power in China. Not only had a sharp divide occurred when some Mongols converted to Islam, but the empire itself had splintered into four separate sections known as khanates, each governed by a military ruler or governor known as a khan and who linked his ancestry to the sons of Chinggis. Yuan rulers also faced unrest from their Chinese subjects, particularly when a string of weak emperors after Kublai Khan's death in 1294 resulted in a succession crisis that left Yuan leadership vulnerable to revolt.

Mongol taxation practices and the expropriation of agrarian land had proved financially ruinous for many Chinese peasants and farmers, though taxation benefited merchants and artisans. Despite modest efforts to shore up roads, bolster the postal service, and rebuild the Grand Canal, which provided a means of trade and transportation between northern and southern regions of China, Mongol attempts to bolster infrastructure did not reduce the resentment of their Chinese subjects. Aside from the implementation of some favorable economic and social policies, the notion of foreign rule was an affront to Chinese subjects, who were also offended by Mongols' dietary and bathing practices. Many Chinese people likely felt affronted by their subjugation to a people they would have viewed as lesser for having such different cultural practices.

By the middle of the fourteenth century, aversion to Mongol rule had led to widespread local rebellions that ultimately hastened the collapse of the Yuan dynasty. Rapid inflation, the devastating impact of the bubonic plague, and intensifying Mongol factionalism all contributed as well. In 1368, the Yuan dynasty officially came to an end when rebel forces triumphed over the Mongol leaders and established the Ming dynasty in its stead.

The Middle East and North Africa in the Early Fourteenth Century

Although China served as the heart of the Mongol Empire, in the early fourteenth century, the Mongol presence also extended across the Middle East and central Asia. Political instability and shifting relationships with conquered peoples increasingly characterized the remaining khanates. For example, in the Il-Khanate, a division of the Mongol Empire that extended from the northern border of the Indian subcontinent to the eastern edge of Anatolia in modern Turkey, the nature of Mongol leadership had shifted from remote detachment to embedded assimilation by the early 1300s (Figure 16.5).

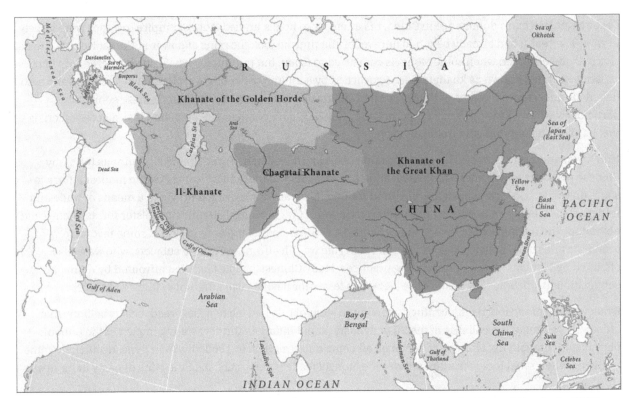

FIGURE 16.5 The Mongol Empire. This map depicts the four khanates that made up the Mongol Empire in 1335: the Khanate of the Golden Horde, the Il-Khanate, the Chagatai Khanate, and the Khanate of the Great Khan, or Yuan dynasty. Although each was nominally under the control of the Great Khan of the Yuan, their rulers had relative independence and autonomy; in some cases, they rivaled each other for influence. (attribution: Copyright Rice University, OpenStax, under CC BY 4.0 license)

When the Mongols occupied portions of the Middle East, their regional leader, Chinggis Khan's grandson Hulagu, used the title *il-khan* (lesser khan); his realm, therefore, became known as the Il-Khanate. Founded in 1256, the Il-Khanate was primarily centered in Persia, and its rulers resurrected the ancient title of "Iran" for this core of their domain, where they sought to maintain Mongol nomadic ways and generally neglected the khanate's economic welfare. Early on, Mongol leaders largely imposed their traditions and practices as the dominant culture, little appreciating the cultural traditions of their subjects. In addition to experiencing this cultural alienation, many peasants found the first decades of Il-Khanate rule financially disastrous as they lost their livestock and farmlands to Mongol nomads. However, after Mahmud Ghazan, the seventh ruler of the Il-Khanate, converted to Islam in 1295, the *il-khans* became increasingly embedded within the Muslim communities they governed.

Although Ghazan's conversion may have been based solely on religious conviction, it also enabled him to appeal to the growing numbers of Mongols and members of the Persian elite who had become Muslims. Mongols living in the Il-Khanate had already begun intermarrying with their Muslim subjects, but this practice greatly increased as they gradually became less culturally distinct from them. This transformation marked a significant shift in the cultural identity of Mongols, who now increasingly became part of the sedentary societies they conquered and eventually abandoned their roles as military conquerors.

Eventually the transition from foreign interlopers to fully integrated members of the community shifted Il-Khanate priorities. Although the northern regions of the khanate had been badly damaged in the early years of Mongol invasions, Ghazan and his successors focused on rebuilding the agricultural infrastructure in the southern portions of their territory, including the Iranian provinces of Fars and Khuzistan. They channeled resources into rehabilitating the empire's economy and cosmopolitan urban life through the construction of schools, mosques, and bazaars. These policies not only enabled Islamic culture and scholarship to flourish, but they also further cemented the cultural bond between Mongol rulers and their subjects in Persia.

Despite the success of early attempts to rehabilitate the empire's economy, by the middle of the fourteenth century, the Il-Khanate began to succumb to struggles for supremacy after the *il-khan* Abu Sa'id died in 1335. Clashes between Mongol, Arab, Persian, and Turkic factions ultimately split the former Il-Khanate into several successor states. Although fragments of the Mongol Empire, such as the Golden Horde, persisted in name until the sixteenth century, after the overthrow of the Yuan dynasty in 1368, the Mongol Empire ceased to exist as a unified political entity.

BEYOND THE BOOK

Depictions of Royalty across Borders and Cultures

Portraiture has long served to legitimize political leaders and convey an image of their character as rulers. Each image in this selection (Figure 16.6) is associated with a ruler from a different region of the Mongol Empire in the fourteenth century: from left to right, Mahmud Ghazan of the Il-Khanate; Ayurbarwada, the fourth emperor of the Yuan dynasty in China; and Jani Beg, khan of the Golden Horde.

Although all three rulers were tied genealogically and politically to the Mongol Empire, they each adapted to the unique cultural contexts of their jurisdictions by recognizing and embracing the dominant religious and intellectual views of their subjects. This included having themselves depicted in a way that their indigenous subjects would see as befitting the power and status of their royalty. The differing character of their reigns and the distinctive relationship each developed with the traditions of their respective regions are reflected in the three images presented. Whereas Ghazan, who was born a Buddhist, converted to Islam shortly after ascending to the Il-Khanate throne, Ayurbarwada embraced the Confucian practices of his Chinese subjects. Jani Beg, by contrast, remained a Muslim, but he also granted concessions to the Christian Church toward the end of his reign when, according to tradition, his mother Taidula's blindness was cured by a Christian bishop named Alexius. Look closely at the images, and consider the differing messages they might convey and the ways in which they reflect the unique circumstances of each region.

(a)

(b)

(c)

FIGURE 16.6 Imperial Rulers. This depiction (a) of Ghazan's conversion from Buddhism to Islam shortly after ascending to the throne of the Il-Khanate appears in Rashid al-Din's fourteenth-century masterpiece of world history, the *Jāmi' al-Tawārīkh*. (b) The silk painting of Ayurbarwada, the Yuan emperor Renzong, first appeared in a fourteenth-century album of Yuan imperial portraits. Renzong, who was strongly influenced by Confucian political culture, reinstated the civil service examination system in China after previous Mongol emperors had shunned the Confucian educational model. (c) The last image depicts Alexius, metropolitan bishop of Kyiv, curing the blindness of Taidula Khatan, the mother of Jani Beg, khan of the Golden Horde. (credit a: modification of work "Conversion of Ghazan to Islam" by Rachid Ad-Din, Claude Mutafian/Wikimedia Commons, Public Domain; credit b: modification of work "Renzong a.k.a. Ayurbarvada a.k.a. Buyantu Khan" by National Palace Museum in Taipei/ Wikimedia Commons, Public Domain; credit c: modification of work "Metropolitan Alexis healing Queen Taidula from blindness" by Tretyakov Gallery/Wikimedia Commons, Public Domain)

- How do these depictions of the rulers differ?
- Why might two of the images depict religious events? Drawing upon what you know about religion in China, explain why a Mongol ruler of that country might have chosen not to depict himself as affiliated with a particular religious tradition?

As the Il-Khanate regime began its steady decline in the fourteenth century, one of its chief rivals, the Mamluk Sultanate of Egypt, rose to a position of greater influence in the eastern Mediterranean. Founded by formerly enslaved soldiers of Turkish origin who first emerged as elite fighters in the Abbasid Caliphate, the Mamluk Sultanate eventually became the foremost center of Muslim scholarship and learning in the fourteenth century (Figure 16.7). The Mamluks' reputation for military prowess gained them the respect of Muslims throughout North Africa and the Middle East, especially after they repelled the Mongol army at the Battle of Ain Jalut in Syria in 1260, stopping Mongol southwestern expansion. The Mamluks, under their military commander Baybars, then gained control of Egypt and Syria. In the process, they not only managed to protect their empire from subsequent Mongol attacks, but they also made significant contributions to the Islamization of Africa.

FIGURE 16.7 Muslim Scholarship in the Mamluk Sultanate. This page from a 1315 treatise on mechanical devices

by Syrian author al-Jazari depicts the high sophistication of Islamic scientific scholarship and mechanical knowledge at the height of the Mamluk Empire. The image depicts a fantastical elephant clock that was to generate a chain reaction every half hour in which the bird at the top would whistle, the man would drop a ball into the dragon's mouth, and the driver would prod the elephant with a goad. (credit: ""The Elephant Clock", Folio from a Book of the Knowledge of Ingenious Mechanical Devices by al-Jazari" by Bequest of Cora Timken Burnett, 1956/ Metropolitan Museum of Art, Public Domain)

During the period between 1260 and 1341, Cairo, the capital of the Mamluk Sultanate, became a prominent center of Muslim intellectual culture and architecture, drawing many merchants and scholars fleeing Mongol attacks in their Persian and Iraqi homelands. The age of Mamluk prosperity and prominence eventually came to an end with the death of Sultan al-Nasir Muhammad in 1341, which initiated a period of instability worsened by the onslaught of the bubonic plague in the late 1340s. While the Mamluks remained in power until their defeat by the Ottomans in the sixteenth century, a period of marked decline had begun.

Europe in the Early Fourteenth Century

While its eastern and southern neighbors struggled to overcome the challenges of the early fourteenth century, Europe was also undergoing widespread crises of authority and shifting axes of power in the face of famine, war, and eventually pestilence. At the beginning of the century, a period of worsening weather resulted in crop failures and food shortages that left Europe vulnerable to the ravages of the bubonic plague, a deadly bacterial disease. These crises resulted in demographic changes and economic troubles that signaled profound transformations in the religious and political foundations of medieval society. Not all regions of Europe experienced the same level of upheaval and economic decline—some areas such as the Italian Peninsula and the French city of Bourges continued to prosper—but the fourteenth century was generally an era of chronic conflict and instability for most of the continent (Figure 16.8).

FIGURE 16.8 The Fourteenth Century Begins. This map depicts the patchwork of kingdoms and political entities in Europe and beyond at the beginning of the fourteenth century. The many divisions ensured that political fragmentation rather than centralization defined the region throughout the medieval period, and many states depicted here still lacked a strong, centralized rule entirely. (credit: "Europe in 1328" by Lynn H. Nelson/Wikimedia Commons, Public Domain)

In contrast to the stability that had defined much of the thirteenth century for the European Christian Church, it began experiencing significant destabilization in the beginning of the fourteenth century, when tensions between the pope and national monarchs led to a weakening of papal authority and division within the church. A notable conflict occurred between Pope Boniface VIII and King Philip IV of France, after Philip sought to impose taxes on the clergy in his country without papal approval. As a result, Boniface issued an edict reinforcing papal supremacy over secular rulers, to which Philip responded by attempting to kidnap the pope in 1303. Although the papacy retained its political autonomy and independent bureaucratic structures after a series of pontiffs came to settle in Avignon, France, the time they spent there tarnished the pope's spiritual prestige and led many to question the integrity of the church's administrative structures.

Although Pope Gregory XI brought the papal court back to Rome in 1377, continuing disagreements between church factions about papal legitimacy led to the simultaneous appointment of three popes and inaugurated a period known as the **Great Western Schism** (1378–1417). Although this crisis of authority was eventually resolved when the Council of Constance (1414–1418) persuaded two of the popes to resign, by then the reputation of the papacy had deteriorated significantly.

The decline in respect for the Roman Catholic clergy can be seen in an English satirical poem known as *The Land of Cockaigne*. The poem calls attention to the church's purported gluttony during a time marked by food insecurity by depicting a monastery made of mouthwatering pastries and breads. The image of a church made of food suggested the greed of the clergy: "There is a fair abbey for monks, white and grey, and its chambers and halls have walls made of pies filled with fish and rich meats, the most delicious man can eat. The shingles on the church, cloisters, bowers and hall are wheat cakes, and the pinnacles are fat puddings, rich enough for princes and kings. All may be rightfully eaten without blame, for it is shared in common by young and old, strong and stern, meek and bold."

In the midst of the church's crisis of authority and status, many areas of Europe were further racked by political and military conflict through much of the fourteenth century. The Hundred Years' War (1337–1453) erupted between England and France over claims to French lands held by the English monarch. The tension was heightened in 1328 when King Charles IV of France died without a son. The crown was given to his nephew Philip, the Count of Valois, the son of Charles's younger brother. However, King Edward III of England, the son of Charles's sister and the older of the two claimants, maintained that he had the greater right to the throne of France. The conflict caused widespread political factionalism and devastation, particularly in France where most of the fighting occurred.

Although the war lasted 116 years, its periods of conflict alternated with times of truce. The new military technologies of the late medieval period shaped much of the conflict and rendered combat especially savage. While the English longbow, prized for its ability to send arrows farther and faster than the French crossbow, dominated the first decades, later in the war the use of firearms and gunpowder became more widespread and more destructive, thanks to the ability of these weapons to dismantle the protective walls of castles and cities. Despite England's dominance early in the conflict, the war's conclusion in 1453 ultimately left France in control as the dominant kingdom of western Europe.

LINK TO LEARNING

The British Library learning timeline (https://openstax.org/l/77Timeline) provides an interactive chronology including brief descriptions, sources, and images of key events in fourteenth-century European history, such as the Hundred Years' War.

Another center of political instability during this period was the Holy Roman Empire. In the fourteenth century, the Holy Roman Empire, which had been founded by Charlemagne in 800, comprised four main entities—the Kingdom of Italy, the Kingdom of Germany (including lands that now are part of Belgium, the Netherlands, Germany, Austria, and Switzerland), the Kingdom of Burgundy (a region in southeastern France), and the Kingdom of Bohemia (what is now the Czech Republic and part of Poland) under the nominal control of an elected emperor. Each of these kingdoms, in turn, was composed of a loose coalition of independent territories with different hereditary rulers. The emperor was chosen by a handful of these rulers known as electors.

Competition between noble families vying for the role of emperor often created instability. In 1314, for example, one group of electors chose the ruler of Austria to be emperor, but another group gave the title to the ruler of Bavaria. Later in the century, the **Golden Bull**, proclaimed by the emperor Charles IV in 1356 (*bull* is the Latin word for "seal"), attempted to simplify and clarify the process by which the emperor was elected. The document asserted that emperors would be selected by seven specific prince-electors, the secular rulers of four principalities and the archbishops of three cities within the empire. This practice of electing emperors stood in stark contrast to the hereditary monarchies of other European kingdoms such as France and England.

Rather than adopting a common currency, legal system, or representative assembly, the Holy Roman Empire remained a patchwork of semiautonomous principalities. Although each of these became relatively stable, the empire itself was a weak and decentralized political entity. By the end of the fourteenth century, it included more than one hundred principalities, each with varying degrees of power and autonomy. The emperor was now beholden to both the rulers who elected him and the pope, who in theory bestowed the imperial crown.

16.2 Famine, Climate Change, and Migration

LEARNING OBJECTIVES

By the end of this section, you will be able to:
- Explain how climate change affected Afro-Eurasian societies in the fourteenth century
- Discuss the reasons medieval people migrated and how they did so

Rising sea levels, extreme hurricanes, and seismic disruptions may call to mind apocalyptic scenes from sci-fi movies, but global climate change, adverse weather, and natural disasters all played a real and significant role in shaping the course of human history in the fourteenth century. Environmental conditions have consistently had a profound impact on the availability of resources and the development of human settlements, trade, and migration across the globe.

Cross-disciplinary collaboration between historians and paleo-scientists has yielded vital information about environmental change in the premodern world. Even subtle shifts in climate and temperature have historically resulted in widespread demographic and ecological transformations that now shed light on the ways in which forces of nature and human activity intersected in the past. Understanding these connections enables us as modern historians to track the short- and long-term causes and consequences of historical plagues, famines, and environmental events, such as those that defined much of the fourteenth century. Learning about the ways in which past societies adapted to environmental challenges also provides vital context for modern debates about the effects of climate change and ways in which the environment affects the continued settlement and development of peoples around the world.

The Effects of Climate Change in the Fourteenth Century

Perhaps the greatest challenge in grasping the impact of climate change on the past is the limitations of traditional historical sources. Texts and other written source materials often provide scant information about environmental fluctuations of earlier centuries. To overcome these barriers, the field of **historical climatology** focuses on reconstructing and analyzing climates of the past and comparing them with modern conditions, allowing scholars to expand the traditional source base of historical research. Historians study references to crop yields and weather fluctuations in weather journals and tax records, along with scientific data drawn from tree rings and organic material trapped beneath ice sheets in different parts of the world, which offer information about past temperature fluctuations and rainfall patterns (Figure 16.9).

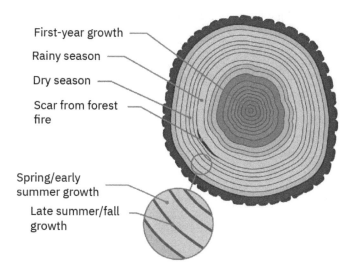

FIGURE 16.9 **Hidden Clues to History.** Because trees can live for hundreds or even thousands of years, during which they experience a variety of environmental fluctuations, clues about these changing conditions are often hidden within the rings in their stumps, which historical climatologists can analyze. (credit: modification of work "The color and width of tree rings can provide snapshots of past climate conditions" by /NASA Climate Kids, Public Domain)

The investigation of such historical clues hidden in the natural world has enabled scholars to identify the ways in which environmental conditions and patterns of human migration and settlement have together shaped the course of human history. In the case of the calamitous fourteenth century, a series of unusual climatic changes led to a chain reaction of competition for resources and desperate attempts to mitigate the damage and despair that defined the century's first decades.

At the beginning of the fourteenth century, subtle shifts in global mean temperature and rainfall had a profound impact on the climate of the Northern Hemisphere, unleashing devastating famines and plagues across Afro-Eurasia. These events caused significant human hardship, disrupted commerce, and contributed to the decline of once-great empires, even the seemingly impenetrable Mongol dynasty. Although premodern people did not understand these extraordinary environmental shifts, their lives were no less affected by them. In an era during which many people survived on subsistence agriculture, even the slightest change in seasonal weather patterns could devastate crops and result in widespread malnourishment and starvation. Poor nutrition weakens human immune systems, which—together with poor sanitation and the close quarters in which people lived in medieval towns—undoubtedly left many more vulnerable to the ravages of epidemic diseases. This was especially the case when the bubonic plague struck much of Afro-Eurasia by the middle of the century.

To place the dramatic meteorological changes of the fourteenth century in context, we must understand how they relate to larger climate patterns. Long-term weather fluctuations, during which periods of relative warmth and cold alternated over hundreds of years, have long been part of Earth's ecological landscape and the narrative of environmental history. Within these longer periods of gradual climatological change, however, less predictable short-term fluctuations have also resulted from rapid changes in wind patterns, ocean currents, and seismic activity. From time to time, such erratic climatological shifts resulted in devastating reversals of typical weather patterns.

In the fourteenth century in particular, the **Little Ice Age**, a period of unusually cold weather that affected most of the Northern Hemisphere (Figure 16.10), led to significant variations in normal rainfall and a general drop in the mean annual temperature. Preceded by a **Medieval Warm Period**, a span of more temperate climate across the globe from the tenth through the thirteenth century, the cool temperatures and, in some areas, droughts radically reduced available resources and food supplies. Aggravated by rising population levels and declining agricultural productivity, food shortages caused significant hardship and financial distress as famine became commonplace and competition for resources intensified.

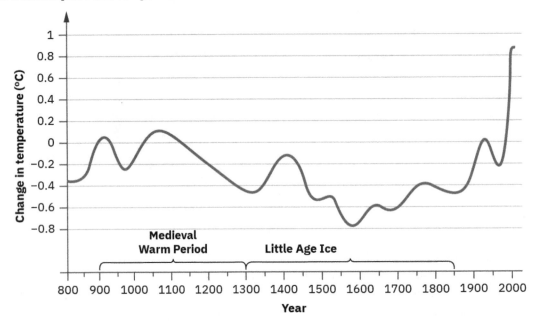

FIGURE 16.10 The Little Ice Age. This chart depicts the shift in the Northern Hemisphere's temperature over the last millennium, including the Medieval Warm Period that began in the tenth century and the Little Ice Age that ran from the fourteenth century to approximately 1850. (data source: Northern Hemisphere Temperature Reconstruction by Moberg et al., 2005) (attribution: Copyright Rice University, OpenStax, under CC BY 4.0 license)

⊘ LINK TO LEARNING

An overview of the field of historical climatology (https://openstax.org/l/77Climatology) is provided in "Little Ice Age Lessons: Towards a New Climate History." This overview includes a section about the ways in which the fourteenth-century Little Ice Age offers lessons about past, present, and future relationships between climate change and human affairs.

If you have a scientific background and would like to explore the subject in greater depth, a compilation of scientific information about the causes and impact of the Medieval Warm Period (https://openstax.org/l/77MedievalWarm) is provided by this ScienceDirect web resource. Charts and graphs are included that demonstrate the temperature and meteorological fluctuations of this period.

Although a consensus about the causes of the Little Ice Age remains elusive, possible triggers may have included changes in ocean circulation patterns, shifts in the earth's orbit, and several massive volcanic eruptions in the tropics that released clouds of sulfate particles into the atmosphere and reflected solar energy back into space at the end of the thirteenth century. Ultimately, these environmental changes resulted in an advance of mountain glaciers and an overall mean global temperature decrease of 0.6°C (with some areas experiencing as much as a two-degree drop in annual temperature). This decrease may seem insignificant, but in the absence of modern agricultural and irrigation techniques, it led to catastrophic crop failures and widespread famine in many parts of the Northern Hemisphere within the first few decades of the fourteenth century. The increase in glacier growth, moreover, affected many regions of the world, because the more water turned to ice, the less was available to evaporate and turn into rain. As a result, even areas far from glacial mountains suffered prolonged periods of drought.

Despite their global impact, the effects of the Little Ice Age were not the same everywhere. In the Mediterranean and West Africa, irregular rainfall and periods of drought dramatically reduced crop yields, whereas in China and northern Europe, cold weather and the freezing of lakes and rivers were especially pronounced. Elsewhere in Europe and Asia, in 1314, extraordinary rains began to fall that introduced a period of abnormally cold and wet winters. This deluge of precipitation resulted in poor harvests as people struggled to cultivate already overworked land. Outside Afro-Eurasia, evidence suggests that the North American interior also suffered when established agricultural systems faltered under hotter summers with less rain and colder winters, leading to severe population loss in the southwestern region.

Although the Little Ice Age was especially devastating in the 1300s, its effects persisted for many centuries. In addition to its immediate impact on crops, late medieval climate change led to longer-term deforestation because more wood was used for heating, in the Northern Hemisphere in particular. The climate shift not only altered building designs and clothing styles, which became adapted to colder temperatures, but in some places it also ultimately precipitated the eventual adoption of coal for heating and the beginning of human reliance on fossil fuels.

⊘ LINK TO LEARNING

"The Little Ice Age: Weird Weather, Witchcraft, Famine and Fashion" is a podcast discussing the historical climatology of the Little Ice Age (https://openstax.org/l/77LittleIceAge) and its connection with some of history's most critical events, such as the Black Death and the French Revolution.

The period known as the Great Famine of 1315–1317 was a direct result of the Little Ice Age in much of Europe north of the Alps, an area of roughly 400,000 square miles. This widespread and prolonged food shortage prompted one of the worst population collapses in Europe's recorded history. It is virtually impossible to know the actual death toll, but it is likely that up to 10 percent of northern Europe's population of more than thirty million perished. Even though crop yields began to rebound in 1317, it took several more years for them to return to prefamine levels. Beyond the devastating loss of lives and human suffering, prolonged food shortages also led to widespread political and economic instability. The prices of necessary food staples like grain skyrocketed, and competition for resources generated social tension, conflict, and an increase in crime. Ultimately, the Great Famine led many to question the ability of church officials and monarchs to respond effectively to crises and catastrophes, which had long-term effects on public trust in these institutions (Figure 16.11).

FIGURE 16.11 An Allegory of the Great Famine. This image from a fourteenth-century manuscript created in Erfurt, Germany, at the time of the Great Famine depicts Death sitting atop a legendary creature known as a manticore, with famine perched on the fires of hell at the end of the manticore's tail. (credit: "Death ("Mors") sits astride a lion whose long tail ends in a ball of flame (Hell). Famine ("Fames") points to her hungry mouth" by "Mariule"/Wikimedia Commons, Public Domain)

IN THEIR OWN WORDS

Johannes de Trokelowe

In 1315, Johannes de Trokelowe, an English monk and chronicler in the reign of King Edward II, wrote the following account of the impact of the Great Famine. Note how daily life was affected by rapidly rising prices and scarcity of food in the wake of devastating rains over northern Europe during the Little Ice Age.

In the year of our Lord 1315, apart from the other hardships with which England was afflicted, hunger grew in the land. . . . Meat and eggs began to run out, capons and fowl could hardly be found, animals died of pest, swine could not be fed because of the excessive price of fodder. A quarter of wheat or beans or peas sold for twenty shillings [in 1313 a quarter of wheat sold for five shillings], barley for a mark, oats for ten shillings. A quarter of salt was commonly sold for thirty-five shillings, which in former times was quite unheard of. The land was so oppressed with want that when the king came to St. Albans on the feast of St. Laurence [August 10] it was hardly possible to find bread on sale to supply his immediate household. . . .

The dearth began in the month of May and lasted until the feast of the nativity of the Virgin [September 8]. The summer rains were so heavy that grain could not ripen. It could hardly be gathered and used to bake bread down to the said feast day unless it was first put in vessels to dry. Around the end of autumn the dearth was mitigated in part, but toward Christmas it became as bad as before. Bread did not have its usual nourishing power and strength because the grain was not nourished by the warmth of summer sunshine. Hence those who ate it, even in large quantities, were hungry again after a little while. There can be no doubt that the poor wasted away when even the rich were constantly hungry. . . .

Four pennies worth of coarse bread was not enough to feed a common man for one day. The usual kinds of meat, suitable for eating, were too scarce; horse meat was precious; plump dogs were stolen. And, according to many reports, men and women in many places secretly ate their own children. . . .

—Johannes de Trokelowe, *Annales, 1315*

- How does Trokelowe describe the change in food prices, and to what does he attribute the poor harvests of 1315?
- Salt was an important staple for food preservation. How might a significant rise in the price of salt affect everyday life?
- How did people attempt to cope with food shortages? Why do you suppose Trokelowe came to believe that some even resorted to eating their own children?

With very few options to remedy the devastation wrought by years of poor weather and famine, most people had little practical recourse other than migrating in search of better conditions. The collective anxiety and social tension of the era sometimes led to scapegoating, including persecutions of supposed witches based on the premise that they had the ability to control the weather as a means of causing others harm. Historians have traced connections between peaks of the Little Ice Age and spikes in witch-hunting activities. Although this type of persecution was by no means universal, it demonstrates the desperation many people must have felt in the face of unrelenting strife.

Mobility and Human Society

Throughout history, economic opportunity and access to new and varied resources have inspired merchants and traders to travel. In the premodern world, this was especially the case along the trade routes of North Africa and the Silk Roads, an active network of trade and commerce that attracted merchants and traders from across Afro-Eurasia (Figure 16.12).

FIGURE 16.12 Traveling the Silk Roads. This detail from a page of the Mallorquin (meaning "from the island of Majorca off the coast of Spain") Atlas of 1375 shows the type of trade caravan that traveled through various legs of the Silk Roads journey. Given the length of the route, few merchants covered it in its entirety. (credit: "Caravan on the Silk Road" by Gallica Digital Library/Wikimedia Commons, Public Domain)

Travel was also a common requirement of religious devotion in the tradition of pilgrimage. Muslims desired and were even obligated, by one of the "pillars" of Islam, to complete the hajj, a visit to Mecca and Medina, the holy sites of their faith in modern Saudi Arabia. Many Christian faithful wanted to travel to sacred sites containing relics of the saints, believed to be imbued with special power, and also to the Holy City of Jerusalem, believed to be the site of Jesus's crucifixion and resurrection. The surrounding area was the birthplace of the Christian Church. Jerusalem was also the site of the holiest of holies of Judaism, the most sacred of spaces where the Temple of Solomon had stood until its destruction by the Romans.

Beyond the demands of trade and religion, however, travel was far less possible for all but a small elite who could afford the time and expense required. Travel narratives and journals written by the select few who could embark on voyages provide much of our knowledge of premodern travel. In particular, the chronicles of Ibn Battuta, a Moroccan scholar who traveled across much of the Muslim world of Asia and Africa in the fourteenth century, offer much insight into the conditions and challenges travelers faced.

🔗 LINK TO LEARNING

This interactive web resource from the University of California, Berkeley provides a virtual tour of Ibn Battuta's travels (https://openstax.org/l/77Battuta) in the fourteenth century. It also describes their historical context and offers suggested readings and links to related videos and primary sources.

At the same time, worsening environmental conditions necessitated travel by many who would rarely have ventured beyond their immediate surroundings but now migrated in search of the resources they needed to survive. Leaving behind all that was familiar in the hope of finding a more stable and hospitable environment, they faced a variety of perils, including regional disputes, adverse weather conditions, illness, and banditry. It was difficult to arrange travel between the many different political entities that existed in the fourteenth century, and crossing borders could be exceptionally risky without the security provided by the presence of established networks or patrons, especially when it came to bandits and lack of access to safe waystations to rest. Moreover, at a time when people were struggling to secure basic necessities, travel was very expensive. Horses, carts, camels, and seafaring vessels were beyond the means of most people, so walking became the most common means of transportation for those in search of new opportunities and resources. Walking eight to ten hours a day, on poor roads and at times in poor weather conditions, likely made the experience all the more grueling for migrants who were already malnourished, weak, and vulnerable to opportunistic infections.

Although some people traveled back and forth across borders, the difficulties and expense of fourteenth-century travel made round trips uncommon. Many were forced to abandon their homes knowing they would likely never return. In times of drought and food shortages, these climate refugees faced precarious situations and uncertain prospects. They could become "strangers in strange lands," foreigners whose unique customs and cultural practices—including religious traditions, dress, and language—marked them as "other" and worthy of scorn.

For those participating in commerce and bringing luxury goods over long distances for sale in faraway markets, however, the experience of travel could be very different. Though merchants and traders too were often seen as "other," the goods they carried and their need for logistic support along the way, like food and caravansaries (inns along the common trade routes), directly enriched local societies and gave these travelers a different status.

Whether they were pilgrims, refugees, merchants, or soldiers traveling great distances in the premodern world, people on the move brought with them both the goods and traditions of their homelands. In the fourteenth century, an increase in this long-distance travel by a greater swath of people across Afro-Eurasia helped bring new technologies and traditions over geographic and cultural divides, but the desperation of some travelers meant the process was not without tensions. Beyond this, however, a growing threat in the form of infectious disease traveled with them, too, and it soon had a disastrous impact on society even beyond the droughts and famine that had caused many to abandon their homes.

16.3 The Black Death from East to West

LEARNING OBJECTIVES

By the end of this section, you will be able to:
- Identify the origins and characteristics of the bubonic plague
- Describe the response to the Black Death in Asia and North Africa
- Describe the response to the Black Death in Europe

Imagine a world in which medicine was utterly defenseless against a disease that could kill within hours. Vaccines and antibiotics had not yet been discovered, nor was the existence of germs and their role in contagion understood. While treatments existed, their efficacy was limited, and medical knowledge was unequally understood across regions and within class structures. At times, the defenses against illness were prayers, divination, the protective aromas of flowers and spices, and for the select few who could afford to flee heavily populated areas, retreat to the countryside. Such was the world of the Mediterranean basin and Afro-Eurasia in the middle of the fourteenth century when the bubonic plague ravaged central Asia, the Middle East, North Africa, and Europe.

After the plague had run its course by the 1350s, it recurred in cyclical fashion several times during the second half of the fourteenth century. It was never fully eradicated, though subsequent waves were not as deadly as the initial outbreak, with the exception of the Great Plague of London in the 1660s and an especially virulent outbreak that began in China in 1894. Outbreaks have occurred more recently in parts of Asia, Africa, and Latin America, but surveillance, preventive measures, early diagnosis, and treatment with antibiotics remain the most effective approaches to preventing its spread.

The Origins and Spread of the Bubonic Plague

The bubonic plague, the most common variant of the disease caused by the bacterium *Yersinia pestis*, raises egg-shaped swellings known as buboes near an afflicted person's lymph nodes in the groin, underarm, and upper neck areas. Other symptoms include fever, nausea, vomiting, aching joints, and general malaise. For the vast majority in the Middle Ages, death generally occurred within three days. The bubonic plague pandemic, which had far-reaching economic, political, social, and cultural effects throughout Afro-Eurasia, came to be known as the **Black Death**. This name, inspired by the blackened tissue the disease caused on the body, also came to express the fear and awe brought by a disease with a mortality rate ranging from 30 to 80 percent. That is significantly higher than the deadliest smallpox, influenza, and polio pandemics of the modern era. Although in its bubonic form the plague could not be spread from human to human, the rat flea became a major plague vector, an organism that spreads plague from one organism to another.

The black rat was one of the most capable animal hosts for the plague-carrying fleas. It was highly susceptible to the disease itself and an especially inconspicuous stowaway on trade caravans and merchant ships. Cases of bubonic plague proliferated as rats spread through the international shipping and trades routes of the Silk Roads and the Mediterranean Sea, where they colonized crowded dwellings in towns and cities. The spread of the plague only increased owing to the increased movement of people. First it was the Mongol armies, traveling over enormous distances and unintentionally bringing small mammalian stowaways among their foodstuffs. Then, owing to the Mongols' protection of merchants and others traveling great distances during the Pax Mongolica, the disease spread further and in new directions. Finally, those forced to leave their homes for survival amid famine and environmental change created yet another pathway for the disease to spread.

Plague-bearing fleas generally preferred to feed on small rodents such as rats and marmots, but when their rodent hosts succumbed to the plague, they secured their next meal from the nearest human. Two even deadlier variants of the disease eventually emerged during the fourteenth century: pneumonic and septicemic. The pneumonic form directly infected the lungs and was spread from person to person by coughing, with a mortality rate of 95 to 100 percent. The septicemic variant, which resulted from plague bacteria circulating directly into the bloodstream, was invariably fatal and, according to contemporary observers, seemed to kill within hours of the first onset of symptoms. While historians had surmised for many decades that the plague had spread in primarily one form (bubonic) and in one direction (east to west), new evidence increasingly suggests there was a far greater diversity of spread.

Although in many regions where it struck the plague was eventually understood to be contagious, at first the means of transmission were not recognized. Some saw the epidemic as a divine punishment from God, and others speculated that it was caused by a rare conjunction of planets creating noxious atmospheric conditions on Earth. Others blamed foreign travelers, minority religious communities, or vagrants. The desperation incited by the plague's relentless assault often led to scapegoating of marginalized populations, particularly in Europe.

DUELING VOICES

The Origins of the Black Death

In the following excerpts are two different historical interpretations of the origins of the Black Death. In the first, medievalist Philip Ziegler discusses the central Asian origins of the fourteenth-century bubonic plague pandemic, arguing that abnormally high death rates near Lake Issyk-Kul point to the pandemic's beginnings. In the second selection, new research by medical historian Monica H. Green strongly suggests the disease first developed in the thirteenth century and was largely misunderstood amid the chaos of the Mongol conquests. Green argues that the plague outbreak of the mid-fourteenth century was actually one of four "explosive proliferations of *Yersinia pestis* into new environments" and that its origins go beyond a simplistic narrative of rats moving westward. As you read, consider what factors might have led each historian to take a particular point of view.

> Though it is impossible to be categorical about the origins of the medieval pandemic, investigations near Issyk-Kul, a lake in Central Asia, show that there was an abnormally high death rate in 1338 and 1339. Memorial stones attribute the deaths to plague. Since this area is in the heart of one of the zones in which bubonic plague lies endemic, it is likely that this was the cradle of the Black Death. From there it spread eastward into China, south to India, and west to the Crimea some eight years later.

—Philip Ziegler, *The Black Death*

> The combined approaches of evolutionary genetics—working from modern isolates of *Yersinia pestis* and the retrieved genetic fragments of the bacterium reclaimed from its premodern victims—have given new parameters to the history of plague. Currently, the biological archive, which has now yielded over three dozen complete *Yersinia pestis* genomes in evidence of Europe's late medieval and early modern experience of plague . . . supports the idea that one specific strain of *Yersinia pestis* . . . entered the Black Sea and the Mediterranean, and from there into Europe, in 1347–1348. . . . The climate crises and grain shortages of the early fourteenth century may well explain the intensity of that outbreak. . . . But the (west Eurasian) Black Death, as traditionally defined, was preceded by the terrors experienced at the sieges in Song China and western Asia [by the Mongols] in the thirteenth century. . . . The historian, working with documentary sources, will need to track the humans who are now implicated in plague's spread. In so doing, historians would do well to adopt epidemiologists' neutral stance toward the task of tracking infectious disease: this is not about assigning 'blame.' It is about documenting humans doing what humans do.

—Monica H. Green, "The Four Black Deaths"

- How do Ziegler and Green's arguments about the origins of the plague differ?
- Upon what sources is Green relying for her innovative conclusions?

Many historians have focused almost exclusively on the Black Death's impact on Europe, assuming that other regions were only minimally affected. The Americas and Australia were, indeed, entirely spared due to their geographic isolation. Other areas such as the Indian subcontinent experienced relatively mild outbreaks. However, we now know that the disease's spread affected much of Asia, the Middle East, Europe, North Africa, and possibly some regions of sub-Saharan Africa in what are now Ghana, Nigeria, Burkina Faso, and Ethiopia. And new scientific techniques such as genetic testing are strongly suggesting that the plague developed far earlier than modern historians had believed. In its most well-documented form, it ultimately spread along international sea and land trade routes in the 1340s and by 1409 had reached port cities of the Indian Ocean trade network in East Africa (Figure 16.13). Wherever it went, the Black Death left a trail of demographic destruction and long-term damage to social and economic networks, compounded by the combined effects of drastic climate changes, rebellions, and crop failures that preceded it in many parts of Afro-Eurasia in the early 1300s.

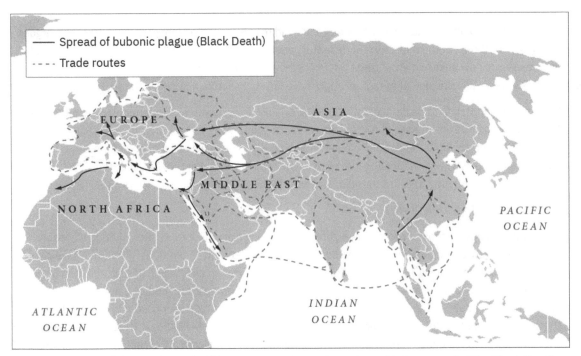

FIGURE 16.13 Route of the Black Death. This map compares trade routes with the spread of the Black Death across Asia, the Middle East, North Africa, and Europe. (credit: modification of work "TNM Download (v2.0)" by National Land Cover Database (NLCD)/United States Geological Survey (USGS)/U.S. Department of the Interior, Public Domain)

The Black Death in Asia and North Africa

Although the exact date of the Black Death's arrival in China remains unknown, Chinese historical records first refer to the appearance of a deadly epidemic in the years from 1331 to 1334. The accounts of the Chinese Imperial Maritime Customs Service, compiled in the late nineteenth century, suggest that roughly thirteen million people perished during this lethal outbreak. For those living in China, the devastation likely seemed to portend the withdrawal of the Mandate of Heaven from the rulers of the Yuan dynasty. Epidemics, droughts, and other catastrophes could be perceived as omens of divine displeasure and an indication that a ruler had lost divine support.

After ravaging China, the plague continued to spread west along trade routes by land and sea that eventually enabled it to engulf much of the Middle East. The Il-Khanate was heavily reliant on the trade networks of the Silk Roads and especially vulnerable to the plague's disruption of the trade communities therein. In the midst of a protracted conflict with the Golden Horde, a rival khanate to the north, the Il-Khanate was reeling from the shock of invasion, factional disputes, and the death of the ruler Abu Sa'id Bahadur Khan (possibly from plague) in 1335. The plague's devastating impact on trade and the population decline further compounded the deterioration of Il-Khanate Mongol rule after Abu Sa'id's death. Cities such as Tabriz in Iran that had long served as thriving centers of trade were largely abandoned by the 1340s, when foreign merchants abruptly fled the city and commerce plummeted. To put this into perspective, imagine what would occur if today's most renowned cosmopolitan centers of trade like New York, Tokyo, London, and Hong Kong fell suddenly into ruin as deserted ghost towns.

The decline of Tabriz was truly shocking to contemporary observers, but few cities were spared when infected fleas accompanying trade caravans were readily transported across central Asia and into the Middle East. Although the mortality rate across the Middle East was high, much of our knowledge of the plague's impact in the Muslim world comes from historical documentation of its impact on the Mamluk Empire (1250–1517), which suffered a population loss of roughly one-third.

Under the control of the Mamluk rulers, who were based in Cairo, the trade routes of the Nile delta were hit especially hard. As in Yuan China, the onset of plague in Egypt was intensified by localized famines that disrupted agriculture and sent many rural peasants to large cities like Cairo and Alexandria in search of employment as unskilled wage laborers. Being in these densely populated zones significantly increased their chances of contracting the plague. The nomads of the region had long known to avoid settled areas when strange diseases appeared, and they largely managed to outrun the disease by retreating into the desert. Although some of Cairo's Mamluk elite fled to rural areas north of the city in 1347, most decided to remain and protect their citadel from potential attacks from their rivals. In the process, however, they made themselves vulnerable to the plague and experienced high mortality rates.

Treatises written by Islamic scholars in the 1340s shed some light on the ways in which the Muslim world responded to the suffering. These texts, meant to serve as chronicles of the plague, also provided medical guidance and advice about proper conduct during epidemics. Doctors could neither define nor remedy the disease, so plague texts tended to frame the epidemic with religious explanations and recommendations derived from the Quran and religious law. Typically describing the plague as noncontagious, they instructed readers not to flee from it, declaring it a potential opportunity for martyrdom for faithful Muslims and a warning to infidels sent directly by God.

Other contemporary Arab writers described the plague as an apocalyptic catastrophe that resulted from a breach in the gate that separated humanity from Gog and Magog, the evil forces that, according to tradition, threatened to destroy the faithful. Even given the apocalyptic tone of this account, however, the Muslim response to the plague generally lacked the doomsday predictions and persecution of minorities that occurred in other regions such as Christian Europe. Although many undoubtedly fled the plague in spite of the treatises, Muslim writers tended to emphasize the importance of a collective and controlled response that promoted resignation and acceptance of God's will.

Many formerly thriving industries in Mamluk cities went into deep decline during the plague, but there was a sudden increase in the construction of madrasas, mosques, and tombs, which for those who survived were a means of expressing gratitude. As a result, urban artisans who worked on these tended to be compensated very well for their skill. The only other occupational group in the Mamluk Sultanate that prospered in the wake of the plague was the spice merchants, since Egypt continued to serve as an important depot in the international spice trade. As agriculture and trade in other industries plummeted, however, the golden age of the Mamluk rulers came to an abrupt end in 1341. Although the Mamluks continued to rule until 1517, fierce clashes and ethnic rivalries within their empire created significant political instability that ultimately led to its collapse.

The Black Death in Europe

As the plague began wreaking havoc in the Mamluk Sultanate, it was also making its way to the ports of Europe via Silk Roads trade caravans and merchant ships sailing the Black Sea in 1346–1347. After striking the Mongol-controlled cities of Astrakhan and Sarai (in present-day Russia), when bales of flea-infested marmot fur were unloaded, the plague then traveled down the River Don, where it reached the city of Caffa (present-day Feodosiya, Ukraine), a center of trade on the Crimean Peninsula.

The plague's entry point into Europe, Caffa was also the site of a Mongol siege targeting Genoese traders who had taken refuge in the city. Gabriele de Mussis, an Italian notary clerk who witnessed the siege, wrote a gruesome account of the Mongols' efforts to launch plague-ridden corpses into the city. Although its reliability is difficult to establish, the story nevertheless demonstrates that even though the role of microbes was not yet known, dead bodies were believed to be sources of contagion. But the plague was most likely spread to Caffa by flea-infested rats independent of the Mongol siege. Caffa had long served as an important administrative center of Genoese trade, and its port was a major hub of merchant activity.

From Caffa, the plague made its way to Italy in the summer of 1347, when plague-bearing rats boarded ships headed across the Black Sea, through the Dardanelles, and onward to the ports of Messina and Genoa. From there, the disease was carried to the port of Marseilles and spread into the European interior along rivers, paths, and roads, leaving perhaps as many as twenty-four million dead, roughly 30 percent of the continent's population at the time.

The plague's arrival in Europe occurred after a period of economic contraction following a series of famines and crop failures earlier in the fourteenth century. In the early 1300s, a rising population and a relative decline in agricultural productivity had created an economic crisis and falling standards of living for all but the most privileged elites. For the vast majority of people living at the lower end of the economic spectrum, falling wages led to limited resources, poorer diets, and widespread malnourishment. Well before the plague's arrival in the 1340s, the European population was reeling from years of economic decline and poor nutrition, which may have weakened immune systems and made some people more vulnerable to attacks of infectious disease.

In addition to the demographic and economic impacts of the Black Death era, modes of artistic and literary expression were significantly transformed in response to the plague's devastation. In the visual arts, the fears engendered by the omnipresence of death and decay initiated a new emphasis on realism that grappled with themes of salvation and mortality. Macabre representations of deathbed scenes and dancing skeletons became especially prominent reminders of the inevitability of death and fears of hell and damnation (Figure 16.14). Although the visual iconography of death reflected the collective cultural trauma associated with the plague, it also served as a potent reminder to celebrate life in the face of it.

FIGURE 16.14 Dance of Death. This fifteenth-century woodcut image from the *Nuremburg Chronicle* of Hartmann Schedel depicts Death dancing and celebrating. The personification of death as a dancing skeleton became a common theme in late medieval Europe that reflects the psychological toll of the Black Death. (credit: "The Dance of Death" by Michael Wolgemut, from the Nuremberg Chronicle of Hartmann Schedel/Wikimedia Commons, Public Domain)

Medieval writers also sought to make sense of the Black Death by documenting the experience of living through the pandemic and exploring themes of transience and mortality. For example, in Giovanni Boccaccio's famous collection of novellas, *The Decameron*, a fictional group of young men and women taking refuge from the plague in a villa outside Florence pass the time by trading stories that reflect upon love, loss, and the vagaries of fortune. *The Decameron* also calls attention to larger social responses engendered by the plague's demographic devastation, such as the growing prominence of merchants due to the continued growth of global trade and people's loss of confidence in the European Christian Church.

🔗 LINK TO LEARNING

Some of the stories that make up Giovanni Boccaccio's *The Decameron* (https://openstax.org/l/77Decameron) can be read at the Project Gutenberg website.

Although the Christian Church remained a bastion of spiritual solace for many during the Black Death, social responses to the plague in medieval Europe ranged from increased piety to hedonism to resigned acceptance of inevitable death. Those who could afford to do so fled the crowded urban centers, but most did not have this luxury. Medieval European cities remained hotbeds of infection despite the efforts of some Italian cities to impose quarantine and travel restrictions. Some cities even closed markets and prohibited gatherings for funerals; others required the removal of the infected to plague hospitals. Lacking a germ theory of contagion, however, medical practitioners were unable to fully explain or remedy the plague, although centuries of early scientific observations led many to attempt the techniques and approaches that had served in outbreaks of other diseases. Failing to fully grasp how and why the disease was spreading, however, many of the devout turned to the clergy, who were also dying in record numbers, mostly because of their efforts to care for the sick. But they too were unable to prevent the plague's relentless toll.

Although some blamed the plague on earthquakes, astrological forces, or poisonous fog, most people in Christian Europe agreed it was a sign of God's displeasure. In some towns, the belief that communities had to be purged of "morally contaminating people" such as prostitutes and beggars also led to the scapegoating of Jewish people, who were falsely accused of causing the plague by poisoning wells. Regardless of the fact that their communities also suffered from the plague, Jewish people faced widespread persecution, escalating in several cities to full-blown massacres (Figure 16.15). Driven by the fire-and-brimstone dogmatism of late medieval Christianity, those who led the persecution of marginalized populations sought to placate God by building churches, developing cults to plague saints like Saint Roche, and hunting heretics and outsiders they believed had provoked divine displeasure.

FIGURE 16.15 Scapegoating in a Pandemic. This image from a fourteenth-century Belgian manuscript shows Jewish people being burned alive on false accusations of spreading the plague. The anti-Semitism inflamed by the Black Death in many parts of medieval Europe sometimes had deadly consequences, and the scapegoating of Jewish and other marginalized communities led to full-blown massacres at times. (credit: modification of work "Burning of Jews during the Black Death epidemic, 1349" by Bibliothèque royale de Belgique from *A History of the Jewish People* by H.H. Ben-Sasson/Wikimedia Commons, Public Domain)

IN THEIR OWN WORDS

Strasbourg during the Black Death

This excerpt from *The Cremation of Strasbourg Jewry St. Valentine's Day, February 14, 1349* describe the destruction of the Jewish community in Strasbourg in the time of the Black Death and how city authorities who attempted to defend the city's Jewish population were overwhelmed by an angry mob.

In the year 1349 there occurred the greatest epidemic that ever happened. Death went from one end of the earth to the other, on that side and this side of the sea, And from what this epidemic came, all wise teachers and physicians could only say that it was God's will.

In the matter of this plague the Jews throughout the world were reviled and accused in all lands of having caused it through the poison which they are said to have put into the water and the wells—that is what they were accused of—and for this reason the Jews were burnt all the way from the Mediterranean into Germany, but not in Avignon, for the pope protected them there.

Nevertheless they tortured a number of Jews in Berne and Zofingen [Switzerland] who then admitted that they had put poison into many wells, and they also found the poison in the wells. Thereupon they burnt the Jews in many towns and wrote of this affair to Strasbourg, Freiburg, and Basel in order that they too should burn their Jews. But the leaders in these three cities in whose hands the government lay did not believe that anything ought to be done to the Jews. However in Basel the citizens marched to the city-hall and compelled the council to take an oath that they would burn the Jews, and that they would allow no Jew to enter the city for the next two hundred years. Thereupon the Jews were arrested in all these places and a conference was arranged to meet at Benfeld Alsace, February 8, 1349. The Bishop of Strasbourg [Berthold II], all the feudal lords of Alsace, and representatives of the three above mentioned cities came there. The deputies of the city of Strasbourg were asked what they were going to do with their Jews. They answered and said that they knew no evil of them. Then they asked the Strasbourgers why they had closed the wells and put away the buckets, and there was a great indignation and clamor against the deputies from Strasbourg. So finally the Bishop and the lords and the Imperial Cities agreed to do away with the Jews. The result was that they were burnt in many cities, and wherever they were expelled they were caught by the peasants and stabbed to death or drowned.

—*The Cremation of Strasbourg Jewry St. Valentine's Day, February 14, 1349*

- According to this source, why did the people of Strasbourg seek to destroy the city's Jewish population in response to the plague?
- Why might a minority community like Strasbourg's Jews become a scapegoat? What does this excerpt suggest about Jewish-Christian relations in this period?

The desperation and zealotry that inspired some responses to the plague in medieval Europe are perhaps best seen in the appearance of **flagellants**, people who believed that by publicly flogging themselves, they could atone for the sins of humanity and mitigate divine retribution. After this idea originated in Eastern Europe and took root in Germany, the flagellants traveled from town to town, reciting penitential verses and lashing themselves with leather whips until they drew blood. They were usually welcomed by townspeople who hoped they could bring an end to the plague epidemic. Occasionally, their rhetoric took an anti-Semitic turn, accusing the Jewish people of causing the plague to annihilate Christendom. The flagellants were active through much of Europe in the early years of the plague pandemic and may have even spread the disease through their contaminated blood. As a result of their increasingly radical orientation, however, by 1349 flagellants had been officially condemned by Pope Clement VI, and they ultimately faded into oblivion in the fifteenth century.

The plague left each region it affected with long-term economic and demographic consequences, including widespread depopulation and cyclic outbreaks of the disease in the fourteenth and fifteenth centuries. Old systems of belief came into question, and ancient social hierarchies shifted to accommodate the significant population losses that followed the plague. Peasants, laborers, and those at the lower end of the socioeconomic hierarchy tended to experience the greatest mortality, but for those who survived, pronounced labor shortages led to the demise of some industries and more favorable working conditions in others. The disadvantaged began to question whether social elites really did enjoy God's privilege, as the social hierarchy generally preached, since they too succumbed to the plague and failed to care for those to whom they bore responsibility.

16.4 The Long-Term Effects of Global Transformation

LEARNING OBJECTIVES

By the end of this section, you will be able to:
- Describe how the challenges of the fourteenth century affected the structure of European society
- Explain the reaction of religious communities throughout Afro-Eurasia to the challenges of the fourteenth century

As they recovered from plague, famine, and political conflict, people across many regions during the fourteenth century took the opportunity to rebuild and rebound. Although some empires fell and once-thriving trade routes were abandoned, other entities emerged to take their place and establish the foundations of a truly modern global society. As the crises of the fourteenth century came to an end, geopolitical boundaries shifted, religions expanded into many new areas, and social traditions transformed to meet the needs of an ever-expanding world. Many social and political structures of the fourteenth century, such as the Mongols' dominance and the economic and land-ownership conventions that made up the feudal system, ultimately ceased to exist. Although it may be tempting to assume the modern world has little in common with the fourteenth century, the growth of **globalization**—the interconnectedness of societies and economies throughout the world as a result of trade, technology, and the adoption and sharing of various aspects of culture—defined the later medieval period and the fourteenth century in particular as transregional exchange continued to expand.

Economic and Social Changes in Europe

Just as political entities and empires broke down or evolved over the course of the fourteenth century, so too did the social structures and hierarchies that defined much of the medieval period, especially in western Europe. In many medieval cities, the merchant class began to acquire increasing wealth and power, while in the countryside the political and social pyramid known as feudalism began to weaken. Feudalism had been defined by a small elite group of hereditary landowners governing the lives of the peasants known as serfs who worked their lands. In exchange for the privilege, serfs paid rent in the form of labor, which generally kept them tied to the land in servitude with little income to spare. This dependent relationship began to disintegrate, however, in the wake of the Great Famine, Black Death, and Hundred Years' War.

Given massive depopulation and the loss of resources they needed to survive, people increasingly chose to leave locations to which they had formerly been anchored. Peasants left the feudal estates on which their families had lived for generations, as landlords elsewhere offered more generous terms of labor to attract workers who could replace the dead. Many peasants also left the countryside to seek wage labor and employment in cities, which began experiencing significant labor shortages as a result of the plague's staggering death toll. Because the demand for labor was so high, peasants who remained in the countryside, especially males, were now able to press their employers for more money and rights.

However, power did not suddenly shift away from the noble landowners in favor of the peasantry and common people. European rulers sought to restore the status quo and ensure the nobility had sufficient access to peasant labor by passing laws that fixed wages at pre–Black Death levels. In 1349, an English law required laborers to accept wages at the level that would have been paid in 1346. Two years later, England's 1351 Statute of Labourers required all unemployed and able-bodied people under sixty years of age to accept whatever work was offered to them. Similar laws were enacted elsewhere in Europe.

In towns, where labor shortages were also a problem, rules requiring guild membership for artisans seeking to practice their crafts were often relaxed, making it easier for newcomers to engage in craft production. Guild masters often responded to the need for labor by shortening the time that apprentices had to serve, which may have helped to attract willing young men to their shops. The same masters, however, often changed the rules of their guild so that only the sons and sons-in-law of current masters could become masters themselves. The enterprising peasant might thus be able to find an apprenticeship in a trade, but he would not be able to advance to the highest level and become an independent master or the employer of others.

THE PAST MEETS THE PRESENT

The COVID-19 Pandemic

Although the devastation of the Black Death may seem difficult to fathom in an era with access to modern scientific knowledge and medical technologies, COVID-19 clearly overwhelmed contemporary public health systems across the globe in 2020–2021. Far more than a health crisis, the pandemic has also had disastrous social and economic effects. In addition to causing significant loss of life worldwide, it has disrupted global supply chains, food systems, and the world of work. The global recession of 2020 was the deepest since the culmination of World War II. Millions of people remain at risk of falling into extreme poverty, particularly in low-income countries. According to the World Bank, the COVID-19 pandemic pushed more than eighty-eight million people in South Asia and Sub-Saharan Africa into poverty in 2020 alone.

In addition to its impact on health and economic systems more generally, the pandemic laid bare the vulnerabilities of the global food system. Border closures, quarantine measures, and trade restrictions made it more difficult for workers to harvest crops and for farmers to reach their markets, leaving many people with reduced access to healthful and affordable food. And as millions of wage earners lost jobs or fell ill, rates of food insecurity and malnourishment continued to increase, while the logistic system through which goods traveled became strained, and many essentials became much harder to find.

The COVID-19 pandemic also radically altered the patterns of human interaction as social distancing requirements transformed everyday routines and forced many to avoid family members, friends, schools, workplaces, stores, and support networks and even to suspend their routine health care. The psychological effects of quarantine, financial loss, and infection fears led to a worsening of chronic health problems, increased substance use, and elevated risk of adverse mental health outcomes including depression.

- How would you compare the experience of living through the modern global pandemic of COVID-19 to the fourteenth century's experience of the plague?
- Considering the effects of both the plague and the COVID-19 pandemic, what can we say about the positives and negatives of an increasingly globalized world?

LINK TO LEARNING

The experience of infectious disease can be different depending on a variety of factors, especially access to wealth. While diseases do not discriminate between the poor and the rich, our ability to avoid exposure does. This article from TheConversation.com provides some fascinating contrasts (https://openstax.org/l/77PlagueCOVID) between the Black Death pandemic in the fourteenth century and the COVID-19 global pandemic in the modern world.

Emboldened by the shift in power and angered when the nobility attempted to limit their economic opportunities, peasants launched rebellions that further damaged the foundations of feudalism by calling into question the lords' traditional privileges. These popular revolts, such as the Jacquerie (a French word for a particular type of garment that came to be associated with peasants and peasant uprisings) of northern France in 1358 and the English Peasants' Revolt of 1381, included not only peasants but also merchants, craftspeople, and other common people. Although the landowning elites ultimately prevailed in most of these clashes, their role was changing rapidly. With fewer people to work their land and generate income for them, their collective wealth contracted significantly. The power of local nobles and landowners was also being eclipsed by more powerful monarchs and emerging urban economies that bolstered the growth of towns and cities.

In addition, the death of many members of the clergy during the Black Death made monarchs more dependent on the merchant class to perform services for which education was required. The rising prominence of the merchant class that resulted, coupled with the growing centralization of monarchical power, gradually eroded some of the traditional privileges and prerogatives of landed elites. Although some regions of the continent, particularly the German lands of the Holy Roman Empire, remained a largely decentralized and fragmented collection of principalities, by the end of the fourteenth century, England and France had begun to lay the foundations of the centralized modern nation-state to replace the power of the nobles.

Another impetus for the rise of centralized monarchies and the reduction of the nobility's authority was the

Hundred Years' War. This conflict not only reinforced budding notions of national identity, but it also changed the nature of warfare and minimized the nobles' traditional military role as expensively trained and outfitted cavalry officers. The use of new weapons and tactics rendered the cavalry-focused armies of the feudal era all but obsolete, because large professional standing armies paid for by monarchs could defeat mounted knights with the use of the longbow. Thus, the new type of warfare chipped away at the traditional feudal prerogatives and prestige of social elites. The growth of professional armies also offered peasants the potential for social mobility, because they were able to earn a regular wage for military service while also sharing in the spoils of war.

Ultimately, the combination of depopulation, shifting military practices, and centralization of monarchical power led to the demise of feudalism. Although profound social disparities persisted in the wake of its decline, increased opportunities for social mobility and the emergence of centralized monarchical bureaucracies began to erode the feudal divide between commoners, serfs, nobles, and the wealthiest landowners.

Religious Changes

Anxieties about spiritual redemption and conflicting doctrinal interpretations generated many transformations in religious life across Afro-Eurasia in the fourteenth century. While some religions splintered into subdivisions focused on reinforcing their own doctrinal purity and conformity of belief, others expanded in the face of adversity. In the wake of the plague and the demoralizing collapse of the Mongol Empire, for example, Islamic traditions in much of North Africa and central Asia did not deteriorate but increasingly solidified into institutional forms that helped develop a sense of common identity across a broad territory (Figure 16.16). To maintain this sense of community, Muslim scholars routinely corresponded with each other and traveled to Mecca to keep up with the latest theological teachings.

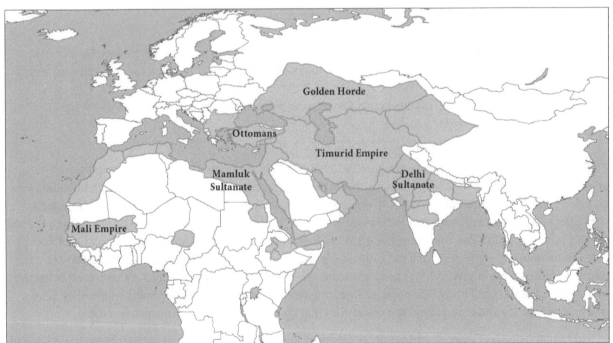

FIGURE 16.16 The Late Fourteenth-Century Islamic World. The shaded areas in this map depict the extent of the largest Islamic states at end of the fourteenth century. Despite the challenges of the Black Death and the Mongols' conquest and decline, Islam's scope and influence continued to expand into Africa and Asia in the fifteenth century. (credit: modification of work "TNM Download (v2.0)" by National Land Cover Database (NLCD)/United States Geological Survey (USGS)/U.S. Department of the Interior, Public Domain)

The Quran and the Hadith (the recorded actions and sayings of Muhammed) remained central components of all varieties of Islam, but different interpretations of ritual and the role of the mystical experience increasingly defined the contours of its myriad branches. In particular, Sufism, a mystical form of Islam that had first emerged in the eighth century, became increasingly integrated into everyday religious life. Although it could be expressed in a variety of ways, Sufism's emphasis on inner personal contemplation and the believer's connection with the divine became especially compelling during the period of instability and uncertainty following the collapse of the Il-Khanate.

By the end of the fourteenth century, the majority of the population from North Africa to eastern Persia was Muslim. This community of the faithful was increasingly defined by its diversity of languages and cultures. But allegiance to a shared historical tradition and set of core beliefs provided unity and coherence, as did believers' social networks, schools, and mosques. This cohesion and continued growth enabled Islam to expand into sub-Saharan Africa and Southeast Asia, setting the stage for Muslim ascendancy in the fifteenth century.

While Islam spread across central and southern Asia, China focused on recovering its religious and philosophical traditions after years of Mongol rule. Thus, the Ming era represented a period of introspection and isolation. Zhu Di took the imperial title of Yongle emperor and ruled from 1402 to 1424 as the third emperor of the Ming dynasty. He reinstated Confucian-based rituals and learning by sponsoring the compilation of a massive encyclopedia that incorporated writing from thousands of Confucian scholars. Although Confucianism coexisted with Buddhism and Daoism in Ming China, it effectively complemented these traditions rather than competing with them.

Meanwhile, western Europe was grappling with emerging cracks in the foundations of Christianity, its principal religious tradition. By the end of the fourteenth century, leadership crises associated with the Avignon papacy and the Great Western Schism had badly damaged the papacy's reputation and led many to question the church's piety and integrity. After the conclusion of the Great Schism, some attempts were made to resolve such doubts and misgivings by granting more authority to councils of clergy rather than popes through the conciliar movement. Although this movement offered some hope that the church could be reformed from within, it met with severe resistance from popes who insisted on absolute papal supremacy.

Beyond their larger misgivings about the integrity of church leadership, however, many Christians who survived the trauma of the Black Death were primarily concerned with their own salvation and the church's inability to appease God's anger or mitigate the plague's devastation. As a result, new forms of mystical and individualistic spiritual practices emerged that emphasized *asceticism*, a tradition of strict self-discipline and the denial of worldly goods, and that encouraged the rise of anticlerical groups such as the Spiritual Franciscans in Italy and the Lollards in England. Through their critiques of clerical wealth and corruption, these groups posed significant challenges to the authority of the church. Although the leaders of many anticlerical organizations were deemed heretics and suppressed by church leaders, they nevertheless laid the groundwork for the sixteenth-century religious revolution known as the Protestant Reformation. Born in central Europe, the Reformation came to emphatically divide the Christian Church.

Key Terms

Black Death a pandemic of the plague caused by the bacterium *Yersinia pestis* with far-reaching economic, political, social, and cultural effects that transformed Asia, Europe, and North Africa in the fourteenth century

flagellants penitents who ritually flogged themselves in response to the Black Death as a means of appeasing God and mitigating the spread of the disease

globalization the interconnectedness of societies and economies throughout the world as a result of trade, technology, and the adoption and sharing of various aspects of culture

Golden Bull a document issued by the Holy Roman emperor Charles IV in 1356 that recognized the role of seven princes in electing Holy Roman emperors

Great Western Schism the period from 1378 to 1417 during which three men simultaneously served as pope of the Roman Catholic Church in western Europe

historical climatology the study of historical temperature and climate changes and their effects on human society

Little Ice Age a period in the early fourteenth century during which global mean temperatures dropped an average of 0.6°C, resulting in droughts and decreased agricultural productivity

Medieval Warm Period a time of more temperate climate across the globe from the tenth through the thirteenth century

Section Summary

16.1 Asia, North Africa, and Europe in the Early Fourteenth Century

The fourteenth century was a time of profound political change across Afro-Eurasia. From the rise of the Yuan dynasty to the emergence of the Il-Khanate, the Mongol Empire began the fourteenth century in a period of growth and expansion. By the end of the century, however, plague, revolts, rebellion, and crises of authority had led to the decline of the once-massive empire. Elsewhere in Europe, conflict between England and France and the fragmented political structure of the Holy Roman Empire led to a deeply divided continent ready for change.

16.2 Famine, Climate Change, and Migration

The field of historical climatology has enabled historians to combine analyses of written sources with data about the ecological environment of the past. Thus, we know that at the beginning of the fourteenth century, a prolonged period of temperate climate was followed by a devastating period of lower temperatures and substantial changes in precipitation in the Northern Hemisphere that wiped out crops and led to widespread droughts and famines. Many were forced to migrate in search of the basic necessities of life.

16.3 The Black Death from East to West

From the 1340s to the 1350s, the Black Death unleashed a wave of death and devastation across Afro-Eurasia. This global pandemic of bubonic plague not only resulted in significant population loss, but it also led to profound social and economic transformation. The formerly thriving cities of the Mamluk Sultanate in Egypt quickly deteriorated, and in Europe, the psychological toll of the plague's trauma led many to question the traditional privileges of the clergy and nobility. Although afflicted regions of Afro-Eurasia eventually recovered from the plague's devastating impact, the Black Death radically altered the course of human history.

16.4 The Long-Term Effects of Global Transformation

The challenges and crises of the fourteenth century generated many social and cultural changes as the societies of Afro-Eurasia sought to recover and rebuild. The Ming dynasty represented an era of introspection during which traditional practices and beliefs such as Confucianism were reestablished to shed China of Mongol influence. Islam continued to expand across central Asia and North Africa, incorporating many new cultural traditions and regions into the community of believers. In Europe, growing anxiety about the church's leadership led to further stirrings of reformation that crystallized in the sixteenth century. While England and France squared off in the battles of the Hundred Years' War, peasants acquired some status and power as feudalism declined across western Europe. In each of the regions of Afro-Eurasia, the challenges of the fourteenth century created a climate of change that laid the foundations of the modern world.

Assessments

Review Questions

1. What was unique about the Yuan dynasty in Chinese history?
   a. The entire Chinese state was ruled by someone not of Chinese ancestry.
   b. Confucianism was fully embraced throughout the Mongol Empire.
   c. There were no rebellions or revolts.
   d. China closed its borders to foreign trade for the next several hundred years.

2. Following the conversion of the Il-Khanate ruler Ghazan to Islam in 1295, what occurred in the Il-Khanate?
   a. Intermarriage between Muslims and non-Muslims became illegal.
   b. Muslim subjects were required to adopt the nomadic lifestyle of the Mongols.
   c. Il-Khanate rulers embraced Islamic culture and civilization.
   d. Buddhism became the most widely practiced and embraced religion in the Il-Khanate.

3. How did Mongol leaders of the Il-Khanate become less distinct from their Muslim subjects in the fourteenth century?
   a. They intermarried with their subjects.
   b. They required their subjects to adopt traditional Mongol shamanistic beliefs.
   c. They chose to live in the same neighborhoods as the peasants.
   d. They replaced all languages and traditions in their realm with newly developed ones.

4. How did the Golden Bull clarify the process of selecting a new Holy Roman emperor?
   a. It declared that Holy Roman emperors would be selected by hereditary succession.
   b. It declared that only popes would be eligible to serve as Holy Roman emperors.
   c. It declared that the Holy Roman emperors would be required to reside in Rome.
   d. It declared that seven princes known as electors would select the Holy Roman emperor.

5. How did the period of the Avignon papacy affect the church in western Europe?
   a. It represented the growing power of secular monarchs and a weakening of papal authority.
   b. It enabled the pope to become the king of France.
   c. It marked a period during which the pope refused to travel to the city of Avignon.
   d. It encouraged many Europeans to abandon Christianity.

6. What did the Golden Bull attempt to clarify?
   a. The order of hereditary succession to the position of Holy Roman emperor.
   b. The nature of the Holy Roman emperor's duty to the pope.
   c. The method of electing the Holy Roman emperor.
   d. The assessment of taxes in the Holy Roman Empire.

7. The simultaneous appointment of three popes in 1378 began the period in the history of the Catholic Church known as what?
   a. the Conciliar Period
   b. the Avignon papacy
   c. the East–West Division

    d. the Great Western Schism

8. What may have caused the Little Ice Age, a period of global cooling during the fourteenth century?
    a. overpopulation and the growth of cities
    b. a lack of adequate livestock on farmlands
    c. volcanic eruptions and changes in the earth's orbit
    d. the encroachment of humans on land in the Arctic

9. What subject for analysis has the field of historical climatology incorporated into the investigation of historical climate change?
    a. fossilized firewood
    b. tree ring data
    c. weapons used by premodern armies
    d. remnants of medieval clothing

10. The Great Famine of 1315–1317 primarily affected what regions?
    a. northern Europe
    b. Central Africa
    c. Southeast Asia
    d. the Mediterranean

11. What caused many fourteenth-century people to migrate from their homes in search of more hospitable conditions?
    a. the low cost of travel in the medieval period
    b. the widespread availability of horses and carts
    c. an enormous growth in available wealth across the social hierarchy
    d. worsening environmental conditions

12. What was the primary factor that made travel in the fourteenth century far more difficult than today?
    a. a lack of interest in leaving the homeland
    b. the high cost and limited modes of transportation
    c. the difficulty of traveling with children
    d. the need to first obtain permission from the king or emperor

13. What did most medieval people believe was the cause of the Black Death?
    a. insect vectors
    b. religious, astrological, and supernatural factors
    c. lack of cleanliness
    d. a comprehensive germ theory

14. What was true of the plague's impact on the world of the fourteenth century?
    a. It began to have a significant impact only when it reached Europe.
    b. China was the only region in the world the plague did not reach.
    c. The plague had a devastating impact on Europe, Asia, the Middle East, and North Africa.
    d. The disease originated in Australia, where it decimated the population before reaching China.

15. What was the principal means of the plague's spread?
    a. the use of shared medicine
    b. contaminated water supplies
    c. small rodents traveling with foodstuffs and other transported goods

   d. rabid dog bites

16. What trade route played a pivotal role in enabling the plague to spread from central Asia to western Europe and North Africa?
    a. the Silk Roads
    b. the trade caravans of Sub-Saharan Africa
    c. commercial networks of the Rhine River
    d. merchant ships of the North Sea

17. The 1330s marked the beginning of the plague's appearance in which regions?
    a. the Mongol Empire and China
    b. Egypt and Libya
    c. Italy and France
    d. Ethiopia and Tanzania

18. Following the Black Death, the decline of feudalism in western Europe was hastened by what factor?
    a. Nobles became so wealthy that they no longer relied on peasant labor.
    b. The Christian Church abolished the practice of servitude.
    c. Monarchs began to appropriate feudal lands for the construction of plague hospitals.
    d. Many peasants left rural areas in search of employment in towns and cities.

19. How did Ming emperors such as Zhu Di seek to restore Chinese cultural traditions after the overthrow of the Mongol Yuan dynasty?
    a. by reinforcing the role of Confucianism
    b. by requiring their subjects to practice Daoism exclusively
    c. by creating a new religion known as Mingism
    d. by levying steep fines on all non-Chinese residents

20. What mystical Islamic tradition emphasized inner personal contemplation?
    a. Shamanism
    b. Buddhism
    c. Sufism
    d. Shi'ism

21. To address labor shortages caused by the Black Death, countries like England passed laws regulating workers'_____.
    a. hours
    b. wages
    c. working conditions
    d. religious preferences

22. How did the lack of laborers in towns and cities affect the European social structure?
    a. It made it easier for people to set up craft shops, undermining the guild system.
    b. It led to an increase in female artisans and business owners.
    c. It reduced the size of the merchant class.
    d. It led towns to pass laws forbidding apprentices to move elsewhere.

Check Your Understanding Questions

1. Why did the Yuan leaders select China as the center of their empire?

2. Why did England and France engage in the series of conflicts known as the Hundred Years' War?

3. What events weakened the power of the papacy in western Europe in the fourteenth century?

4. What types of methods have historical climatologists used to learn about the history of climate change?

5. What are some key differences between fourteenth-century and modern travel patterns?

6. How were different regions affected by the climate changes of the Little Ice Age?

7. What role did trade and commercial networks play in the spread of the bubonic plague?

8. How did responses to the plague differ in Christian Europe and the Muslim Middle East?

9. What conditions made populations more vulnerable to infectious disease?

10. How did the social structures and hierarchies that defined much of western medieval Europe shift in the aftermath of the Black Death?

11. How did the calamities of the fourteenth century affect religious life in Afro-Eurasia?

Application and Reflection Questions

1. How did the events of the fourteenth century contribute to the destabilization of the Europe?

2. What comparisons can you draw among the various political transformations and crises of authority that occurred across Afro-Eurasia in the fourteenth century? How were they similar, and how were they different?

3. Compare the Mongol establishment of rule in China to their establishment of the Il-Khanate in the Middle East. What actions did the Mongol conquerors of these regions take that likely angered or alienated the inhabitants of these regions? In which area were the Mongols more likely to have peaceful relationships with the inhabitants? Why?

4. How did climate change affect European culture and society in the fourteenth century? In what ways are these effects similar to (or different from) the ways in which climate change affects societies in the twenty-first century?

5. For what reasons did people travel or migrate from one region to another in the fourteenth century? Do people travel or migrate for the same reasons today? Why or why not?

6. Although germs do not select hosts based on their social status or relative wealth, how might such factors in the premodern world have influenced an individual's exposure and vulnerability to infectious diseases such as the plague? How do they affect the likelihood that people will contract infectious diseases today?

7. Many people have compared the COVID-19 pandemic to the bubonic plague pandemic of the fourteenth century. What similarities do you see between the two? What are some of the differences? In what ways is the modern world better able to cope with pandemics?

8. Were the political, social, and religious changes of the fourteenth century inevitable? Why or why not?

9. If you were a peasant in Afro-Eurasia during the fourteenth century, how do you think you would seek to explain the upheaval that had occurred in your lifetime?

FIGURE 17.1 Suleymaniye Mosque. The Suleymaniye Mosque in Istanbul, depicted here in an Ottoman miniature, structurally resembles the Greek Orthodox church Hagia Sophia in the same city. Its dome is intentionally higher however, in an effort to surpass the achievement of the Byzantine emperor Justinian who had it constructed and proclaimed that by erecting Hagia Sophia, he had outdone the Israelite king Solomon's construction of the temple to the one God in Jerusalem. (credit: modification of work "The carrying-in of a model of Süleymaniye Mosque (Detail from Surname-i Hümayun)" by Nakkaş Osman/Wikimedia Commons, Public Domain)

CHAPTER OUTLINE

17.1 The Ottomans and the Mongols
17.2 From the Mamluks to Ming China
17.3 Gunpowder and Nomads in a Transitional Age

INTRODUCTION The Ottomans rose to prominence at the end of what historians call the Middle Ages and the beginning of the early modern period, arriving on the scene in the thirteenth century. In defeating the Byzantine Empire, the last remnant of ancient Rome, the Ottoman Empire became a gatekeeper between East and West, occupying a central position politically, economically, and culturally in Eurasia. The meeting of the two worlds is represented in the architecture of Istanbul's Suleymaniye Mosque, which combines Islamic architectural elements such as minarets with a large central dome popularized in ancient Mediterranean temples and churches such as the Hagia Sophia in the same city (Figure 17.1). Hagia Sophia itself was transformed into a mosque by Mehmed the Conqueror when the city fell to Ottoman forces in 1453.

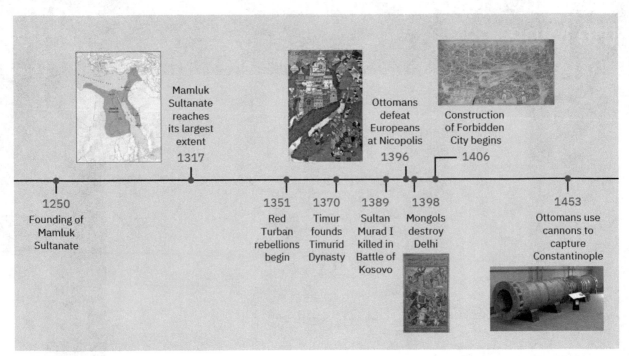

FIGURE 17.2 Timeline: The Ottomans, the Mamluks, and the Ming. (credit "1317": Copyright Rice University, OpenStax, under CC BY 4.0 license; credit: "1396": modification of work "Battle of Nicopolis, 1396" by Géza Fehér/ Wikimedia Commons, Public Domain; credit "1398": modification of work "Timur defeats the sultan of Delhi" by Zafarnama of Sharaf Al-Din 'Ali Yazdi/Wikimedia Commons, Public Domain; credit "1406": modification of work "Ming shi san ling tu" by Arthur W. Hummel/Library of Congress, Geography and Map Division, Public Domain; credit "1453": modification of work "Dardanelles Gun Turkish Bronze 15c" by "The Land"/Wikimedia Commons, Public Domain)

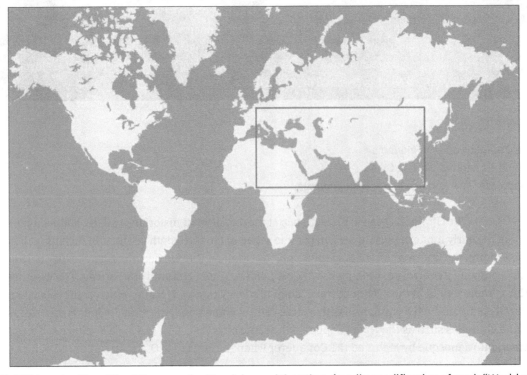

FIGURE 17.3 Locator Map: The Ottomans, the Mamluks, and the Ming. (credit: modification of work "World map blank shorelines" by Maciej Jaros/Wikimedia Commons, Public Domain)

17.1 The Ottomans and the Mongols

LEARNING OBJECTIVES

By the end of this section, you will be able to:
- Discuss the origins of the Ottoman Empire
- Describe how the conflict between the Ottomans and Timur influenced the development of the Ottoman state
- Describe the effect of the conquest of the Byzantine Empire on Europe and the Ottoman Empire
- Describe the intellectual, cultural, and artistic developments of the Renaissance

As the people of western Europe remade their societies following the collapse of the western half of the Roman Empire, the Byzantines in the east preserved Roman cultural practices for centuries, seeing themselves always as the continuation of a proud and strong Mediterranean empire. By the eleventh century, however, the Byzantines found their power challenged by the arrival of Turkic tribes such as the Seljuks, who settled in the eastern half of their domains and gradually wrested control of the area from them. As different Turkic tribes arrived and settled in the region, one group, the Ottomans, soon rose to prominence over others. Withstanding the last major Mongol onslaught, the Ottomans went on to dominate Asia Minor, invade Europe, and eventually deprive the Byzantines of their last remnants of power. The fall of the Byzantine Empire in 1453 sent many Greek scholars and theologians fleeing to the city-states of Italy, where they contributed to the intellectual and artistic transformation of western Europe in the period known as the Renaissance. By the end of the fifteenth century, the Ottomans had transformed the eastern Mediterranean.

Ottoman Growth

With an empire that bordered both the western and eastern worlds, the Ottoman Turks began to play an important role in Asian and European affairs in the thirteenth century. They were not the first Turkic-speaking people to do so, however. In the tenth and eleventh centuries, a group of Turkic speakers from central Asia arrived first through the Iranian plateau before continuing westward into the area that is now modern Turkey. This group, called the Seljuks after their ruler, converted to Islam in the tenth century. Accomplished archers and riders, they were originally employed by the armies of the Islamic Karakhanid and Ghaznavid dynasties of central Asia before carving out an empire of their own in Persia, Mesopotamia, and eastern Asia Minor. Seizing control of Baghdad, the capital of the Abbasid Empire and home to the Sunni caliph, in 1055, the Seljuks came to regard themselves as defenders of the Islamic faith and established the Seljuk Empire. Defeating the forces of the Byzantine Empire in 1071 at the Battle of Manzikert in eastern Anatolia (another name for Asia Minor), the Seljuks soon dominated that region as well (Figure 17.4).

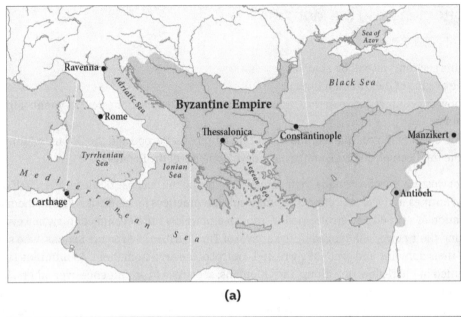

(a)

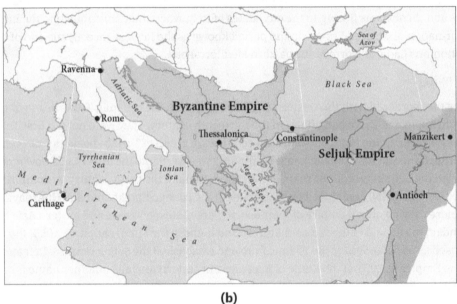

(b)

FIGURE 17.4 Incursions of the Seljuk Empire against the Byzantines. Before the arrival of the Seljuk Turks, the Byzantine Empire laid claim to most of Asia Minor (a). Over the course of the eleventh century, the empire's holdings in Asia Minor steadily shrank as the Byzantines were replaced by the Seljuk Turks (b). (attribution: Copyright Rice University, OpenStax, under CC BY 4.0 license)

In 1077, the Seljuks established a state in Anatolia they called the Sultanate of Rum ("Rome") because the territory had been taken from the Byzantine Empire, the Eastern Roman Empire. The sultanate steadily absorbed other Turkish tribes in Anatolia and brought them under its control, forming a confederation of tribes more than a unified state. The sultanate's ruler was primarily a military leader, and the provinces were governed by military commanders. Within the provinces, different regions were controlled by different groups of warriors who often fought with one another and sometimes sold their military services to Byzantine rulers.

Seljuk rulers built mosques and madrasas—schools where scholars taught subjects such as science, theology, and Islamic law—especially in Iconium (now Konya), one of the cities that served as the capital of the Sultanate of Rum. They also established caravansaries, inns where merchants traveling along the Silk Roads could safely rest and conduct business. Trade attracted merchants and artisans, and religious scholars took up residence in the Turkish cities. As the Byzantine Empire lost control of Anatolia, Orthodox Christian clergy and monks fled, loosening the peasants' ties to Christianity and making it easier for many to convert to Islam. Gradually, Anatolia became more Islamic in appearance and nature, and the Byzantine emperors' grip on the region grew ever weaker.

The Seljuk Empire, centered as it was in Baghdad in Mesopotamia, faced many struggles both from within and from outside forces. The arrival into the region of the western crusaders at the very end of the eleventh century and the establishment of the Crusader States caused major political and social shifts in the region, even though those states would eventually be defeated. The Seljuks were defeated by the Khwarezm-Shah, a central Asian dynasty, whose founder had been enslaved by the Seljuks.

As the Seljuk dynasty lost control of the region, the Seljuk Sultanate of Rum—a splinter state of the original group—was left as the sole center of Seljuk power in Anatolia. Even there, however, political and military change continued. Following the Mongols' invasion of eastern Anatolia and their decisive victory over the Seljuks at the Battle of Köse Dağ in 1243, the Sultanate of Rum splintered into numerous small, independent states called *beyliks*. In the fourteenth century, one of these *beyliks* began to rise to prominence as Seljuk fortunes declined in the wake of the Mongol invasions. This *beylik* was led by a man named Osman, and his followers came to be known as the "Osmanli" or "Ottomans."

The Ottomans were Turkic-speaking pastoralists who occupied lands in northwestern Anatolia. Like the Seljuks, they regarded themselves as *ghazis*, warriors who fought to expand and protect the borders and influence of Islam, and this recognition came to form an important part of Ottoman Turkish identity. The Ottomans had originally stepped into the power vacuum left in northwestern Anatolia by the attack on Constantinople in 1204, when European crusaders raided, ransacked, and demolished parts of the city. Civilians were brutally assaulted and killed. Priceless religious relics were looted and destroyed, erasing ties to the history of the Byzantine Empire. After this "sack" of Constantinople, Venice and its allies divided the empire, and political upheaval took place in the years that followed. Although the Byzantines attempted to rebuild their capital and state, they were no match for the Ottomans. The empire lasted another two hundred years, but it controlled relatively little territory in Anatolia. The Ottomans laid siege to the Byzantine cities of Anatolia, conquered them, and made one, Bursa, the capital of a growing Ottoman state with imperial ambitions. They built mosques and madrasas in the city, turning it into an important religious center.

Following Osman's death, his son Orhan I, who took the title of sultan, expanded Ottoman territory into Europe. In 1354, his troops established a base on the European peninsula of Gallipoli, on the northern side of the Dardanelles, one of the straits that separate Asia Minor from Europe. Control of Gallipoli gave the Ottomans control over oceanic traffic between the Mediterranean and the Black Sea. It also gave them the ability to interfere with ships bound for Constantinople, which sat on the European side of the straits of the Bosporus, should they so desire. The Ottomans steadily took control of the European portion of the Byzantine Empire, the area that is now northern Greece, southern Bulgaria, and Thrace, the western part of modern Turkey.

Orhan's son Murad I established a new capital at Edirne, on the European side of the Dardanelles, in 1362. Turks from Anatolia were invited to settle in Ottoman-controlled territory in Europe and take over the lands of fleeing European landowners. The European peasants who came under Ottoman control did not necessarily resent their new masters; the majority were Orthodox Christians, and they were allowed to practice their faith without interference so long as they paid the special tax, the *jizya*, and recognized their status as Ottoman subjects. The Ottomans also realized that non-Muslim clergy could help in the governing of their empire, because people were accustomed to turning to their religious leaders for direction on a variety of issues. To win the assistance of Christian clergy, therefore, the Ottomans refrained from efforts to stamp out their religion. Many peasants likely regarded the religiously tolerant Ottomans as better overlords than the European Roman Catholic soldiers, who had attacked the Greek Orthodox Byzantine Empire on more than one occasion. They also welcomed the lighter tax burden imposed by the Ottomans.

Murad sought to take advantage of the death of the Serbian king in 1355 and incorporate his land into the

Ottoman domains as well. At the Battle of Kosovo in 1389, the Ottomans defeated the Serbian army and made Serbia, the last major Orthodox Christian state, a vassal of the empire. Both Murad and the Serbian ruler Prince Lazar died in the battle, although Serbian myth claims that a Serbian soldier used trickery to secretly kill the Ottoman sultan in his tent (Figure 17.5).

FIGURE 17.5 Sultan Murad I. In this image created by an Ottoman artist two centuries after Murad's death, the sultan (left, followed by his guards) is described in the caption at the top as "the Kosovo martyr." (credit: modification of work "Sultan Murad I šahīd" by Unknown/Wikimedia Commons, Public Domain)

🔗 LINK TO LEARNING

The Battle of Kosovo in 1389 serves as a focus for Serbian national identity, and its anniversary is a national holiday. In this blog, you can learn more about how the Battle of Kosovo (https://openstax.org/l/77BattleKosov) has affected Serbian views about political independence.

Murad's son and successor Bayezid I (called "the Thunderbolt") attempted unsuccessfully to eliminate all remaining Byzantine governance in the region by capturing Constantinople. In 1396, the Ottomans blockaded the city, but the pleas of the Byzantine emperor led Pope Boniface IX to call for a crusade to rescue the Greek Orthodox Christians from the Muslim Turks. Roman Catholic knights from throughout Europe responded. Ottoman troops, fighting alongside Bayezid's Serbian vassals, crushed the crusader army at the Battle of Nicopolis on the Danube River (Figure 17.6). The blockade of Constantinople ultimately failed, however, for the Ottomans had no way to break through the city's walls, and Bayezid soon found himself facing a more formidable foe, the Mongol conqueror Timur.

FIGURE 17.6 The Battle of Nicopolis. This 1523 painted miniature by an Ottoman artist depicts the triumphant Ottoman army on the left, defeating the European knights who opposed them at the Battle of Nicopolis in 1396. A miniature painting such as this, which appeared in bound books and manuscripts, was a popular medium of artistic expression throughout Ottoman history. (credit: "Battle of Nicopolis, 1396" by Géza Fehér/Wikimedia Commons, Public Domain)

The Timurids and the Aftermath of the Battle of Ankara

Timur was a Mongol from the Barlas tribe, which had been exposed to and assimilated Turkic culture. He was born in central Asia, in a part of the Chagatai Khanate (now modern Uzbekistan), in the 1320s or 1330s. At some point early in his life, he suffered an injury that left him lame in one leg and without two fingers. According to some stories, he had been wounded while attempting to steal sheep, but he may well have sustained his injuries in battle.

Timur sought to rebuild the empire that Chinggis Khan had controlled at the time of his death. Because he could not establish descent from Chinggis, he could not claim the title of khan himself. In the 1360s, he gained control of part of the Chagatai Khanate and placed one of Chinggis's descendants, Soyurgatmish, on the throne, claiming to act in his name. He also married a female descendant of Chinggis and adopted the title "Royal Son-in-Law."

Timur soon looked beyond central Asia for lands to control. In the 1380s and 1390s, he conquered Persia, portions of Iraq and Afghanistan, and Syria. He taxed the inhabitants of vanquished cities heavily and sent skilled artisans to work in his capital in Samarkand, but he spared people's lives. Cities that did not submit were treated brutally, however. For example, when the city of Isfahan, in Persia, surrendered peacefully, he treated the residents leniently. However, when the people later rose in revolt, Timur responded unequivocally: he killed an enormous portion of the city's population, with some reports claiming that 100,000 to 200,000 people were killed. Eyewitness accounts report his soldiers amassing piles of severed heads. Timur's troops then turned north to the Russian territory controlled by a former follower named Tokhtamish, the khan of the Golden Horde, who sought the same lands in central Asia that Timur claimed. After destroying the Russian cities of Astrakhan and Ryazan, Timur defeated Tokhtamish's army in 1391.

In the late 1390s, Timur turned eastward toward India. In 1398, he attacked the city of Delhi, the capital of the Muslim-ruled Delhi Sultanate. The sultan's army rode into battle on war elephants clad in chain mail, frightening Timur's troops, who had not seen elephants before (Figure 17.7). Timur piled hay on the backs of his camels, set the hay on fire, and sent the burning, panicked animals into the enemy's lines, scattering the elephants. Victorious, Timur then destroyed Delhi.

FIGURE 17.7 Timur Defeats the Sultan of Delhi. In this image produced in India around 1600, Timur's Mongol forces, wearing golden helmets, defeat the troops of the sultan of Delhi, who are shown sprawled across the backs of their war elephants. (credit: "Timur defeats the sultan of Delhi" by Zafarnama of Sharaf Al-Din 'Ali Yazdi/ Wikimedia Commons, Public Domain)

Timur also coveted lands in Syria that were controlled by the Mamluk Sultanate and territory in Anatolia that was claimed by the Ottomans. Bayezid I had been steadily conquering weaker rulers in Anatolia and forcing them to become his vassals. In 1397, he defeated the ruler of the *beylik* of Karaman and went on to subdue smaller Anatolian states. Unwilling to submit to his domination, however, Turkish tribes and Ottoman vassals who Bayezid I believed owed allegiance to him turned to Timur, considering him their means of achieving independence from Ottoman rule. In turn, enemies of Timur such as Kara Yusuf, the leader of the Black Sheep Turks, and Sultan Ahmed, the ruler of the Persian Mongol Jalayir dynasty whose lands Timur had conquered, turned to Bayezid for assistance. Timur wrote to Bayezid, demanding that the Ottoman ruler cease aiding his enemies. Bayezid responded with insults and sent his forces to attack an ally of Timur's in Armenia.

In 1400, Timur struck back, destroying the city of Sivas in Anatolia, part of Bayezid's domain. He then went on to wage war against the Mamluk sultans in Egypt in Syria, preventing Bayezid from turning to them for help. He also entered into an allegiance with the Byzantines against the Ottomans, amassed forces from throughout his empire, and headed for Anatolia. Bayezid broke off his siege of Constantinople, which had begun in 1396, and rushed to meet him. In July 1402, Timur's troops clashed with the Ottoman army at the Battle of Ankara in Anatolia.

On the field at Ankara, one of the great weaknesses of Bayezid's Ottoman state was revealed. The Ottomans had built their empire in Anatolia by conquering other Turkish states and absorbing their rulers and the rulers' descendants into their administration. These men, Bayezid's unwilling vassals, had no wish to risk their lives for their Ottoman overlords. In addition, Bayezid had chosen to live primarily at Edirne, in Thrace. He had adopted elements of Greek culture and, as part of a strategy to build alliances with other rulers, had taken as wives or concubines a number of non-Turkish women, including the daughter of Prince Lazar. This decision further alienated him from the Turkish nobility of Anatolia. When Timur's forces attacked at Ankara, therefore, many of Bayezid's Turkish vassals abandoned the field and left Bayezid to his fate, happy to be free of Ottoman control. The Ottomans were defeated, and Bayezid and his sons Musa and Mustafa were captured by Timur. Bayezid remained Timur's prisoner until he died a few months later.

Following his rout of the Ottomans and having conquered most of the domains of Chinggis Khan and his sons and grandsons, Timur turned eastward to claim his last prize—China. In 1368, the Mongol Yuan dynasty in China had come to an end. Its successor, the Chinese Ming dynasty, sought to make a tributary vassal of Timur, but the Ming emissaries and the soldiers who accompanied them had instead been imprisoned in Samarkand, the capital of Timur's empire, in the Mongol heartland near the place of his birth. In December 1404, Timur set out to cross central Asia on his way to China. Within a few months, however, he fell ill, and in February 1405 he died. The invasion of China ended before it had begun, and the Chinese emissaries were released.

At the time of his death, Timur had conquered much of the land claimed in the original Mongol conquests of Chinggis Khan and his descendants. Unlike them, however, Timur made no real effort to rule the places he seized outside Persia. His armies conquered, plundered the riches of the defeated cities, seized artisans and whoever else might be of use to Timur, and sent the wealth and captives on to Samarkand. Thus, it was relatively easy for most places that Timur had conquered to regain their independence. Anatolia is a good example. Following his defeat of Bayezid I, Timur departed, leaving Bayezid's sons to battle among themselves for control of their father's lands. Although Bayezid's son Mehmed declared himself a vassal of Timur, Timur did not assist him in his civil war against his brothers. Following Timur's death, his own sons and grandsons fought over the lands he had conquered (Figure 17.8). In 1409, his son Shah Rukh emerged as his successor and the next head of the Timurids, the name given to the dynasty founded by Timur.

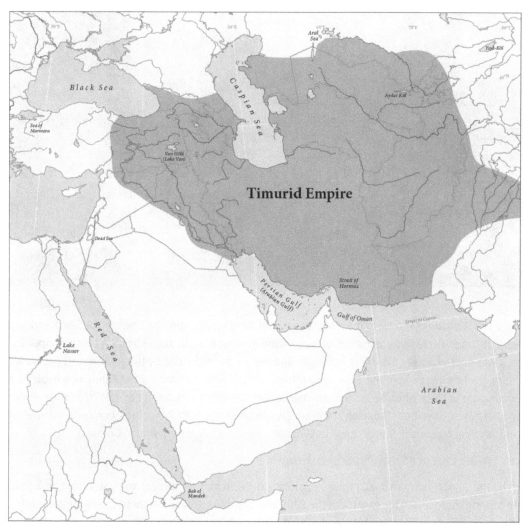

FIGURE 17.8 The Timurid Empire. By the time of Timur's death in 1405, his empire stretched from the border of Anatolia in the west to northern India in the east, and from modern Uzbekistan in the north to the Gulf of Hormuz in the south. (attribution: Copyright Rice University, OpenStax, under CC BY 4.0 license)

While many in Asia regarded Timur as a villain, he was a hero of the Turks and Mongols of central Asia. Ibn Khaldun, the North African Muslim historian, credited him with unifying the world's Muslims into a single empire. Timur's greatest legacy may be an artistic one. Although conquered people might have been met with brutality, artists, architects, and artisans were spared and sent to Samarkand. During Timur's lifetime, the city was in a constant state of construction, and buildings like the Bibi Khanum Mosque were erected or remodeled to please him. The Muslim traveler Ibn Battuta praised the city's beauty, and its gardens made visitors forget the arid lands that surrounded it (Figure 17.9). Timur's grandson Ulugbek built a madrasa (an Islamic school) and an observatory in Samarkand and invited Muslim mathematicians and astronomers to the city, making it an important site of learning in the fifteenth century. Many Europeans of the time also regarded Timur, whom they called Tamerlane ("Timur, the Lame"), as a hero.

(a)   (b)

FIGURE 17.9 The Registan. (a) A word meaning "country of sand" in Persian, the Registan of Samarkand was the public square of Timur's splendid capital city of Samarkand in what is today Uzbekistan. A center for public gatherings, it was also a center of learning in the city and region, as evidenced by the three madrasas flanking the central square. (b) This image from the *Zafarnama* ("Book of Victories"), an account of Timur's campaigns, depicts the construction of the Great Mosque for Timur's new capital in Samarkand. (credit a: modification of work "Samarkand, Registan, Sher-Dor Madrasah" by Arian Zwegers/Flickr, CC BY 2.0 ; credit b: modification of work "Building of the Great Mosque in Samarkand" by Bihzad/Wikimedia Commons, Public Domain)

The Ottoman Conquest of the Byzantine Empire

Following the Battle of Ankara in 1402, the sons of Bayezid who had remained free—Mehmed, Suleyman, and Isa—fought among themselves for control of the Ottoman domains. Suleyman held the Ottoman lands in Europe, Isa controlled Anatolia, and Mehmed I ruled Amasya, a region on the Black Sea coast. When Musa was released from Mongol custody, he also joined the fight, and Mustafa later contended for the throne as well.

In 1413, Mehmed emerged victorious in the civil war with his brothers. He and his son and heir Murad II reorganized and expanded the domains of the Ottomans. Members of the cavalry and other highly placed members of the Ottoman administrative and military elite were each granted a **timar**, the right to collect taxes from merchants, farmers, and artisans in a particular geographical area (Figure 17.10). Timars were awarded regardless of religion or ethnicity, and occasionally elite women were given them as well. At times, conquered local elites were allowed to retain control of their former lands as *timariots* (holders of a timar). The taxes they collected supported them, so the state did not need to pay them a salary or hire tax collectors.

FIGURE 17.10 A Member of the Ottoman Cavalry. Administrators and other elites, like this member of the light Ottoman cavalry, were granted timars to reward them for their service and enable them to support themselves. The image is from a mid-seventeenth-century book of miniature drawings of costumes, possibly made in Constantinople. (credit: "Ralamb Sipahi" by Unknown/Wikimedia Commons, Public Domain)

The practice of awarding timars to members of the military ensured their loyalty. The land ultimately belonged to the sultan, who would revoke a timar if the holder did not continue in his service. A timar might also be lost if the population of the land declined; this encouraged timariots to treat the people on their holdings well. Timariots also tried to make the lands they controlled more agriculturally productive. The more crops produced, the more taxes they could collect. They were responsible for maintaining order on their lands, but they could not impose punishments without the permission of a judge appointed by the sultan. The timar was nonhereditary; upon the timariot's death, the sultan awarded the vacant timar to someone else. This prevented the development of an independent hereditary class of timariots.

The main goal of Mehmed I and Murad II was to conquer Constantinople. Muslim rulers since the seventh century had attempted to capture the Byzantine capital and had always failed. Both Mehmed and Murad realized that in order to rebuild the Ottoman state, they had to drive out the Byzantine rulers. The Byzantine emperor Manuel II had assisted Mehmed's rivals for the Ottoman throne, attempting to keep the Ottomans weak by prolonging the civil war. The Byzantines were also close allies of the Venetians and Genoese, who controlled trade in the Aegean and the Black Seas and whose ships could interfere with Ottoman efforts to control both sides of the Dardanelles.

Murad II laid siege to Constantinople in 1422, but the effort failed because the Ottomans lacked artillery to destroy the city walls. Murad was also distracted from the siege by his need to combat yet another claimant to the Ottoman throne. As they had done before, the Byzantines called upon European Christians for assistance against the Ottomans. The pope called for a new crusade, and the Roman Catholic knights of Europe responded. Murad defeated them in 1444 at the Battle of Varna, in eastern Bulgaria (Figure 17.11). Nevertheless, Constantinople stood firm. The city was only a shadow of what it had once been. At its height, somewhere between 500,000 and one million people had lived within its walls, but the bubonic plague and Ottoman sieges had reduced the number to perhaps fifty thousand. Nevertheless, so long as Constantinople stood on the western shore of the Bosporus controlling access to the Black Sea, the Ottomans could not rest easy in their domains.

FIGURE 17.11 The Death of Władysław III. According to legend, at the Battle of Varna in which he led Ottoman forces against European Christians, Murad II prayed for victory. When the Polish king Władysław III charged Murad's troops, the sultan's guards beheaded him, an event depicted in this Ottoman miniature. (credit: "Murad II and the imaginary beheading of Władysław III of Poland" by Géza Fehér/Wikimedia Commons, Public Domain)

It fell to Murad II's son Mehmed II (also called Mehmed the Conqueror and Mehmed the Great) to destroy the Byzantine threat. He was better prepared than his father had been. In 1453, he summoned his Muslim and Christian vassals from Anatolia, Thrace, and the Balkans. With the vassals and a core of six thousand elite professional soldiers, he marched to the Bosporus. Ottoman forces included more than one hundred newly constructed ships to prevent Constantinople from receiving reinforcements and supplies via the sea. He also summoned European gunsmiths, the most important of whom was the Hungarian named Urban, to craft bombards, an early form of cannon. One gun was so large that it could fire a twelve-hundred-pound granite ball more than a mile. Constantinople's defensive walls, which had guarded the city since the fifth century, could not withstand the Ottoman artillery (Figure 17.12).

FIGURE 17.12 The Walls of Constantinople. The walls that protected Constantinople were massive. On the right is the inner wall, the city's last defense. In places it was up to six meters thick. On the left is the outer wall. Below this was yet a third wall, and beyond that a moat. (credit: modification of work "Theodosian Walls in Constantinople" by "CrniBombarder!!!"/Wikimedia Commons, Public Domain)

On the morning of May 29, 1453, after a siege of fifty-seven days, the Ottoman guns breached the walls, and Mehmed's soldiers rushed into the city. Perhaps twenty thousand people were left to defend it, including the last Byzantine emperor, Constantine XI Palaeologus, who died fighting for his city. After their Genoese commander was wounded, many defenders abandoned their posts along the walls, leaving them deserted during battle. Constantinople's residents carried religious icons to the walls and prayed for deliverance. However, they put up little resistance, and the city fell to the Ottomans.

DUELING VOICES

The Fall of Constantinople

Following are two accounts by European Christians of the fall of Constantinople in 1453 and the behavior of Mehmed II, the conquering sultan. The first excerpt is from a letter from the Convent of the Order of Saint John on Rhodes to the military commander of Brandenburg (present-day Germany), a principality of the Holy Roman Empire. The second is an eyewitness account of the event.

After the great Turk had besieged Constantinople by land and sea, on the twenty-ninth of the May just passed he seized the city by force of arms, killed the emperor of Constantinople, cut off the heads of many nobles, gave the entire city over to plunder, and cruelly tortured many. He then obtained the city of Pera, which the Genoese held, without force of arms, made it a tributary, and tore down its walls. This also happened to the walls of Constantinople. . . .

It is believed that he is preparing a new fleet from scratch, since he intends to make all the islands of the Aegean archipelago subject to him or to destroy them if he can. For his heart swells with pride and he boasts that he has equaled or surpassed the deeds of Alexander of Macedon. He also threatens that he will attempt to do what Alexander never did—push into Italy and the regions of the West with his arms and might and see whether fortune shall favor him there as it has throughout the East.

—a letter from the Convent of the Order of Saint John on Rhodes to the Margrave of Brandenburg, June 30, 1453, translated by W.L. North

The enraged Turkish soldiers . . . gave no quarter. When they had massacred and there was no longer any resistance, they were intent on pillage and roamed through the town stealing, disrobing, pillaging, killing, raping, taking captive men, women, children, old men, young men, monks, priests, people of all sorts and conditions. . . . This medley of all nations, these frantic brutes stormed into their houses. . . .

Temples were desecrated, ransacked and pillaged . . . sacred objects were scornfully flung aside, the holy icons and the holy vessels were desecrated. Ornaments were burned, broken in pieces or simply thrown into the streets. . . .

When Mehmed (II) saw the ravages, the destruction and the deserted houses and all that had perished and become ruins, then a great sadness took possession of him and he repented the pillage and all the destruction. Tears came to his eyes and sobbing he expressed his sadness. "What a town this was! And we have allowed it to be destroyed!" His soul was full of sorrow. And in truth it was natural, so much did the horror of the situation exceed all limits.

—"The Sack of Constantinople, 1453," *EyeWitness to History,* 2011

- In what ways are these accounts similar? How do their depictions of Mehmed II differ?
- How did the Ottomans create a multiethnic military force? Why would that be useful?

Many Muslim scholars believed the conquest of Constantinople had been predicted in a hadith, an account of the sayings and actions of the prophet Muhammad. After his capture of the city, Mehmed turned eastward, incorporating the Turkish state of Karaman, the home of the important Islamic religious center of Konya, and other lands ruled by Turkish tribes in eastern Anatolia. In 1461, he sent the Ottoman fleet to conquer Trebizond, an offshoot of the Byzantine Empire and an important trading center on the Black Sea. In Europe, he gained control of most of the southern part of Greece, defeating the Byzantine princes who ruled the area, as well as Bosnia and Albania. He also wrested the Black Sea port of Kaffa from the control of Genoese merchants. At his death, the Ottoman Empire controlled all of Anatolia and nearly all of the Balkans.

Mehmed II, despite being referred to regularly as "the Conqueror" by historians, was a builder more than a destroyer, however. Upon conquering Constantinople, he declared it the new capital of the Ottoman Empire, replacing the city of Edirne. He dispatched soldiers to clear away the ruins left from the siege and the Ottoman assault, and he immediately set about appointing a mayor and other important city officials to establish and maintain order. Rather than drive out the city's European merchants, he allowed them to stay, to retain their property, and to continue to worship in their churches. He demanded only that the Genoese merchants remove the walls that surrounded Galata, the Genoese trading quarter of Constantinople, and surrender their armaments. To protect his new Christian subjects, he forbade his Turkish troops to enslave the Europeans.

Mehmed regarded himself not as a usurper but as the rightful successor to the Byzantines. He declared himself Caesar, the heir to the old Roman imperial throne. He appointed a new leader of the Eastern Orthodox Church, Gennadius II, who in turn recognized Mehmed's claim as the legitimate heir of the last Byzantine emperor. The last emperor's actual heirs, his nephews, were taken into Mehmed's service and occupied important administrative positions in the empire. One served as Grand Vizier, or chief minister, under Mehmed's successor Bayezid II.

Mehmed embarked on an ambitious campaign to rebuild Constantinople, now called Istanbul. He built the new

Topkapi Palace, where he ruled the empire. The palace also contained his private household, or **harem**. He ordered that the Byzantine cathedral of Hagia Sophia be left intact and converted into a mosque. He rebuilt the city walls, constructed a weapons foundry, and established a hospital. He also ordered a new mosque, the Fatih Mosque ("Conqueror's Mosque"), to be built in the city (Figure 17.13). Near the mosque, he erected numerous madrasas in which Muslim scholars taught science, Islamic law, and theology.

FIGURE 17.13 Fatih Mosque. In Melchior Lorck's painting of Istanbul from 1559, the Fatih Mosque rises above the rooftops of the city. The building was destroyed by an earthquake in 1766, and a mosque built according to a different plan was subsequently constructed on the site. (credit: "Fatih Complex" by Melchior Lorichs/Wikimedia Commons, Public Domain)

🔗 LINK TO LEARNING

Visit this UNESCO site to learn more about Istanbul (https://openstax.org/l/77UNESCOIstan) and to view pictures of its famous historic sites.

Mehmed had a great thirst for knowledge. He spoke many languages and amassed a library filled with works in Turkish, Greek, Latin, Persian, and Arabic. He invited Muslim scientists to Istanbul and attended debates of religious scholars. He collected Greek antiquities and brought Greek scholars and Italian artists to Istanbul. Some of these artists, such as the Italians Gentile Bellini and Paolo Veronese, painted portraits of him (Figure 17.14).

FIGURE 17.14 **Mehmed II**. The meeting of East and West is evident in this portrait of Sultan Mehmed II. Painted in 1480 by the Italian artist Gentile Bellini, it depicts an Eastern ruler in a Western artistic style. (credit: "The Sultan Mehmet II" by Gentile Bellini/Wikimedia Commons, Public Domain)

As Mehmed conquered other parts of the Balkans and of Anatolia, including *beyliks* that had broken free of Ottoman control following Bayezid I's defeat at the Battle of Ankara, he brought artisans and prisoners of war to Istanbul to rebuild the city. As earlier Ottoman rulers had done, Mehmed allowed Christians and Jews in his lands to worship as they pleased. This arrangement was an early appearance of the Ottoman *millet* system, in which religious communities were allowed a substantial degree of autonomy and were governed by their own leaders and their own law codes. In addition to naming a head of the Eastern Orthodox Church, Mehmed established the position of *hakham bashi* ("chief rabbi") to lead the Ottoman Empire's Jewish community. He also invited the head of the Armenian Apostolic Church to establish a house of worship in Istanbul; because the Eastern Orthodox Church, the religion of the Byzantine rulers, regarded the Armenian church as heretical, it had been banned from the Byzantine capital. And although the Roman Catholic Church refused to recognize his right to rule Istanbul, Mehmed allowed Catholic clergy to travel throughout Ottoman lands and worship freely.

Mehmed also moved to exert authority over Islamic clergy in his domains. He made teachers at madrasas employees of the Ottoman state. He issued *kanun*, laws made by the sultan, as opposed to sharia (religious law) interpreted by Islamic judges, and compiled them in the *Kanun-name* ("Book of the Law"). *Kanun* dealt with issues that sharia often did not address, such as taxation or punishment for certain crimes. Mehmed also made use of *kanun* to centralize his authority and gain unchallenged control over the Ottoman state.

With the fall of the Byzantine Empire and the collapse of Timurid authority, the Ottoman state could now assert its authority in both the East and the West, effectively making itself a gatekeeper between the two worlds. Following their defeat of the Byzantine Empire and their capture of Constantinople, the Ottomans gained control of part of the Silk Roads that brought silk, spices, and other luxury goods from East Asia. Besides controlling the overland route, the Ottomans commanded Red Sea ports in Egypt after defeating the Mamluk Sultanate in 1517, which gave them additional control over the spice trade. By the late fifteenth century, Ottoman ships were trading with India, and goods such as Chinese silks and porcelains furnished the homes of the wealthy in Istanbul. The Ottomans also dominated trade on the Black Sea, which until then had been the province of the Venetians and Genoese. The exclusion of Italian merchants from their traditional trade routes, the heavy taxes imposed on goods that traveled overland, many Europeans' dislike for transacting business with Muslims, and the expense of overland trade led western Europeans to seek all-water oceanic routes to South and East Asia.

The Renaissance

The fall of Constantinople was lamented in Europe as signaling that no significant force remained to counter the Muslim advance westward. For many historians, it also marks the end of the European Middle Ages. As the Byzantine Empire collapsed, many Greeks sought refuge in other lands, often wealthy merchants and state officials who brought their riches with them. Many settled in Italy, especially in Venice and Rome. Those who came to Venice were assisted by Anna Notaras, a wealthy Byzantine noblewoman who had taken up residence in the city before Constantinople fell.

Byzantine scholars, theologians, artists, writers, and astronomers also fled westward to Europe, bringing with them the knowledge of ancient Greece and Rome that had been preserved in the eastern half of the Roman Empire after the western half fell. Among the texts they brought were the complete works of Plato and copies of Aristotle's works in the original Greek. Access to these and other writings, many of which had been either unknown in western Europe or known only in the form of Arabic translations that arrived at the time of the Crusades, greatly influenced the course of the Italian Renaissance.

The **Renaissance**, which means "rebirth" in French, was a period of intellectual and artistic renewal inspired by the cultural achievements of ancient Greece and Rome and marking the dawn of the early modern world. It began in the city-states of northern Italy that had grown wealthy through trade, especially trade with the Ottomans. Beginning in the 1300s, scholars there turned to the works of Western antiquity—the writings of the ancient Greeks and Romans—for wisdom and a model of how to live (Figure 17.15). Among these scholars was Petrarch, who encouraged writers to adopt the "pure" Classical Latin in which the poets and lawmakers of the Roman Empire had written instead of the form of Latin used by medieval clergy. He advocated imitating the style of the Roman orator Cicero and the foremost of the Roman poets, Virgil.

FIGURE 17.15 The Birth of Venus. Sandro Botticelli's 1485 painting *The Birth of Venus* shows the Roman goddess of love and beauty perched on a seashell after having emerged from the water. During the Renaissance, the depiction of scenes from Greek and Roman mythology became common in European art. (credit: modification of work "The Birth of Venus" by Sandro Botticelli/Wikimedia Commons, Public Domain)

Petrarch has been called the father of **humanism**. Humanism was a movement born in Italy in the fourteenth century that focused on the study of human beings, human nature, and human achievements, as opposed to the study of God. Humanists stressed the beauty and dignity of humanity instead of focusing on its sinful, "fallen" nature. They believed the classical worlds of ancient Greece and Rome could provide contemporary people with untold wisdom and a model for life.

BEYOND THE BOOK

The *Arnolfini Portrait*

Humanism influenced the manner in which people were depicted in works of art as well as the types of people who were portrayed. Many of the subjects of Renaissance paintings were wealthy members of the merchant class. Merchants might appear as worshippers in paintings with religious subject matter, but many paintings of the period also depicted such people in secular settings as well, often in a manner meant to display their wealth. This 1434 painting, by Jan van Eyck, an artist from the Netherlands, is believed to depict the Italian merchant Giovanni Arnolfini and his wife (Figure 17.16). The image may have been painted to commemorate the Arnolfinis' marriage. Mrs. Arnolfini (her exact name is unknown) is not pregnant. The fashions of the time featured gowns with cloth gathered at the front to give the illusion of a large belly, very different from what is considered stylish today.

FIGURE 17.16 The *Arnolfini Portrait*. This oil painting, believed to represent the merchant Giovanni di Nicolao di Arnolfini and his wife at their home in Bruges, was painted in 1434 by Jan van Eyck. (credit: modification of work "The Arnolfini Portrait" by Jan van Eyck/Wikimedia Commons, Public Domain)

- What details in the painting may indicate that the Arnolfinis are wealthy people?
- In what ways do the values of humanism seem to have influenced this painting?
- Why may artists of the time have included members of the merchant class in their paintings?

Before the arrival of Byzantine scholars and their copies of Plato and Aristotle, Italian humanists had focused primarily on the study of rhetoric and ethics. They displayed little interest in metaphysics, the philosophical study of the nature of existence. Access to Plato's complete works changed that, and many scholars were influenced by Byzantine Neoplatonism, an intellectual movement that sought to synthesize the ideas of Plato, Aristotle, the Stoic philosophers, and Arabic philosophy. One of the most important of the Italian Neoplatonists was Marsilio Ficino, who translated all of Plato's works from ancient Greek to Latin and synthesized Platonic thought with the teachings of Christianity.

In the Neoplatonic conception, the universe was an ordered hierarchy with God, "the One," at the top, and everything else existing as "emanations" of God at descending levels with the earth at the bottom. If God was perfect, the physical world in which humans lived was least perfect. However, Ficino argued, the human soul existed at the center of the universe, because it combined aspects of both the godly world and the physical world in which humans lived. Because humans possessed a soul, they were thus the center of creation. Ficino's ideas fit well with the humanist perception of human beings as special creatures and worthy of study.

Another Neoplatonist, Nicholas of Cusa (Nicholas Cusanus), also had a profound effect on the Italian Renaissance and one of its most important legacies, the Scientific Revolution of the sixteenth and seventeenth centuries. The Greek philosopher Aristotle had stressed the study of the world through direct observation, a method known as *empiricism*. For Plato, however, the world of ideas, of abstract concepts, was superior to the components of the physical world. Thus, mathematical thought was superior to sensory observation as a way of arriving at ultimate knowledge of the "truth" of the world. Nicholas also stressed that mathematical knowledge of the world was superior to knowledge derived from mere observation. He went so far as to state that through mathematics, humans could know the very mind of God.

The idea that the physical world could best be understood through mathematical formulas was espoused by Johannes Kepler, the German astronomer who believed the model of the universe that made the most sense mathematically was the true model. It was through mathematics that Kepler discovered three of the laws of planetary motion and was able to explain how the planets moved in the heliocentric, or sun-centered, model of the universe earlier proposed by Nicolaus Copernicus (Figure 17.17). This was the same view of the universe held by the Italian astronomer Galileo Galilei: the true nature of the universe could be discovered only through mathematics.

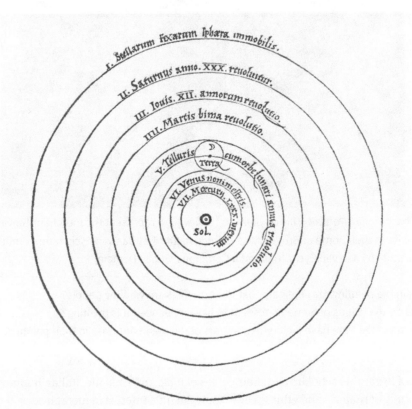

FIGURE 17.17 **The Heliocentric Universe.** In 1543, Nicolaus Copernicus proposed a model of the universe with the sun at the center, which differed from the medieval Ptolemaic model with the earth in the center. Copernicus's model does not show any planets beyond Saturn. In his model, beyond Saturn there are only fixed stars. (credit: modification of work "Image of heliocentric model from "De revolutionibus orbium coelestium"" by Nicolaus Copernicus/Wikimedia Commons, Public Domain)

Although the Neoplatonists did not value Aristotle's empiricism, they did not completely cast his ideas aside. First, his concept of "virtue" influenced the humanists' idea of human excellence. And his emphasis on acquiring knowledge through observation influenced scientists in fields other than astronomy. Observation of nature became of importance not only to scientists but also to the visual artists of the Renaissance. The fifteenth-century Florentine painter Masaccio was the first to incorporate the principles of linear perspective into painting (Figure 17.18). The use of linear perspective had been a "secret" known to the ancient Greeks and Romans but lost and then "rediscovered" by the Florentine architect Filippo Brunelleschi, whose drawings inspired Masaccio. This technique created a sense of realism in visual imagery that had been lacking in medieval art. Later artists such as Leonardo da Vinci conducted studies of animal and human anatomy to make their works more realistic. Michelangelo went beyond attempting to make human beings look realistic and instead idealized the body, in keeping with the new position into which the thinkers of the Renaissance had elevated humans.

FIGURE 17.18 Linear Perspective. The fresco *Trinity with the Virgin, Saint John the Evangelist, and Donors*, painted around 1427 in the church of Santa Maria Novella in Florence, shows Masaccio's use of linear perspective to create a realistic image of the interior of a building. (credit: modification of work "Holy Trinity" by Masaccio/Wikimedia Commons, Public Domain)

⊘ LINK TO LEARNING

These short videos from Khan Academy discuss Filippo Brunelleschi's experiment (https://openstax.org/l/77Khan1) with linear perspective (https://openstax.org/l/77Khan2) and demonstrate how linear perspective works. There is also an interactive feature (https://openstax.org/l/77Khan3) that enables you to experiment with linear perspective.

17.2 From the Mamluks to Ming China

LEARNING OBJECTIVES

By the end of this section, you will be able to:
- Describe the system of slavery that existed within the Islamic world
- Explain the unique political and social organization of the Mamluk Sultanate
- Describe Ming dynasty China in the fifteenth century and its responses to foreign influences

In the thirteenth century, a new state came into existence in Egypt and the Levant. Although it grew out of the existing Ayyubid Sultanate, the **Mamluk Sultanate** was unique among world societies in that it was administered and defended by educated, elite, formerly enslaved men. The Mamluk state grew so powerful that it was able to fend off the advances of the Mongols. At the opposite end of Asia, the Mongols also found themselves displaced by the Han Chinese of the Ming dynasty.

The Slave Soldier System

Many of the Islamic states formed in western Asia over the centuries relied upon a unique means of staffing their armies and administrations—the creation of a highly trained, foreign-born enslaved (or formerly enslaved) elite. Beginning in the ninth century in the Abbasid Caliphate, rulers purchased Turks from beyond the Oxus River in central Asia to serve as soldiers for the state. Enslaved adult men raised outside the state were loyal to their purchaser and not to the state itself, however, and thus they were more willing to revolt if they were not well treated. Briefly losing control of the state in the ninth century because of such uprisings was a lesson for Muslim rulers. Thereafter, they sought to enslave young boys who could be educated and trained within and by the state, ensuring they were more invested in the society they served as adults. Non-Muslim children were chosen because Islam forbade the enslaving of fellow Muslims.

Known as mamluks (from an Arabic word meaning "someone owned"), the boys were taken primarily from Turkic tribes in central Asia, as well as from the Caucasus and eastern Europe, and then converted to Islam and educated. Because they were freed upon completing their training, the rule against enslaving other Muslims was not violated. The largest part of their instruction consisted of training in riding, archery, and military tactics (Figure 17.19). Some were given a formal education in the bureaucracy, in a bid to develop smart and capable administrators for the state.

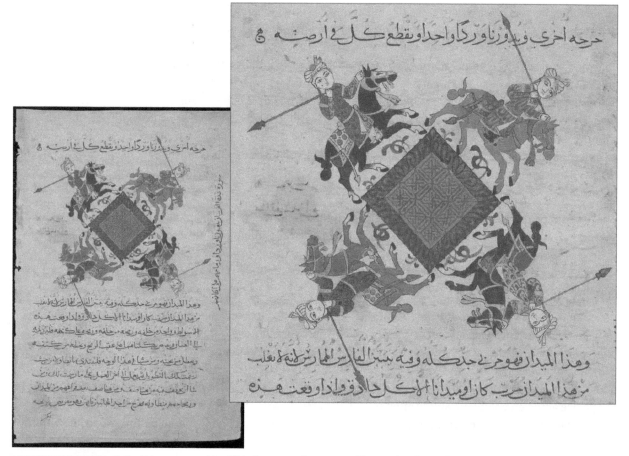

FIGURE 17.19 **The Art of Horsemanship.** This fourteenth-century illustration from the *Manual of the Arts of Horsemanship* by al-Aqsara'i depicts mounted competitors carrying spears in a game that required great physical skill. As part of their training, young mamluks were taught to ride at a gallop while aiming projectiles at a swinging target. (credit: modification of work "Manual on the Arts of Horsemanship by al-Aqsara'i" by Unknown/Wikimedia Commons, Public Domain)

When the young men's education was completed, they were set free in a special ceremony. They were then allowed to grow beards, marry, and establish their own households, into which they could introduce purchased mamluks of their own. They might, however, remain in the household of their former owner, the ruler to whom they were expected to remain loyal. In this way, the mamluks somewhat resembled the freed people of ancient Rome, who often retained ties to their former masters.

The relationship between mamluks and their masters was often conceived of as familial in nature, and mamluks often referred to one another as "brother" and to their master as "father." When their training had ended, their "father" would find a place for them in the ruler's service. Most mamluks found positions in the army, and from there they often went on to hold administrative positions. In the Ayyubid Sultanate, the mamluks eventually gained control over the government after deposing the sultan and proceeded to rule the state as the Mamluk Sultanate.

In Mamluk Egypt, having been an enslaved soldier was often the path to the greatest success and standing in society. Important positions were given to mamluks, such as provincial governor and commander of the yearly pilgrimage to Mecca. The sultan himself was a mamluk. Appointed mamluks were regarded as more entitled to positions of power and authority than were a man's biological sons, and while Egyptian mamluks married and produced children, it was considered inappropriate if these offspring were awarded important roles in government when true mamluks were available. The mamluks were displeased when this happened, and it was they who usually determined who became the sultan.

While it might seem like a risk to entrust important governmental and military positions to men who had once been enslaved, the Ayyubids, who had broken away from the Abbasid state to found their own dynasty in the eleventh century, adopted the system because of its advantages. The mamluks were highly trained and well educated, and thus well prepared to occupy the offices given to them. A ruler could pick and choose the most able of them, whereas biology might leave a sultan with children entirely unsuited to occupy positions of authority. The fact that the mamluks were of non-Arab origin and had been taken from their homes in foreign lands as children also meant they were likely to remain loyal to the "father" who had been responsible for their training, and to whom they owed their position in society. While the offspring of the Arab nobility might act to advance the fortunes of their families in ways that did not suit the interests of the sultan, the sultan usually did not need to fear that his mamluks would favor the interests of far-distant, long-absent biological relatives over his own.

Enslaved men occupied a similar position in the Ottoman Empire. Beginning in the fourteenth century, the Ottomans purchased enslaved people or used prisoners of war to fill the ranks of their armies. With their invasion of the Balkans, however, the Ottoman sultans soon turned to gathering Christian children from the European lands they occupied, in order to counter the power of the Turkish nobles who controlled the army and the state's administration.

In a system known as the **devshirme** ("gathering"), Ottoman agents recruited Christian boys as part of the tax imposed on their European subjects (Figure 17.20). Approximately every three to five years, agents of the sultan took boys, ideally aged between eight and ten, to serve the Ottoman state. They were taught to speak Turkish and brought to Istanbul where they were educated and made to convert to Islam. When they became adolescents, they were trained to become scribes, palace administrators, or soldiers. Those selected to serve in the palace at the end of their training often rose to occupy important positions, including Grand Vizier. In addition, many were awarded timars in exchange for their service and had the opportunity to become wealthy.

FIGURE 17.20 The *Devshirme*. In this Ottoman miniature painting from 1558, Christian parents look on as their sons are led away to be enslaved by the sultan. The children carry a few personal possessions in sacks over their shoulders as the seated Ottoman official registers them. (credit: "Janissary Recruitment in the Balkans" by Ali Amir Beg/Wikimedia Commons, Public Domain)

The majority of boys were trained as soldiers, some of whom became members of the elite infantry corps called the **Janissaries** (from the Turkish words *yeni cheri*, or "new soldier"). They accompanied the sultan into battle and served as his household guard. Like the mamluks, the Janissaries were expected to be loyal to their master, the Ottoman sultan. In fact, the sultans believed the Janissaries would prove more dependable than the noble vassals, because they were entirely dependent upon the sultans for their status and privileges, and because they had been cut off from the biological families to whom they might otherwise have owed their first loyalty. The risk of trusting in the Turkish nobility had become clear at the Battle of Ankara when Bayezid I's Turkish vassals fled, abandoning him to the Mongols.

IN THEIR OWN WORDS

Memoirs of a Janissary

The account that follows is by a Serbian named Konstantin Mihailović. Born in 1430, he was taken as a child to be trained as a Janissary and recorded his experiences in a book, *Memoirs of a Janissary*, written between 1490 and 1501.

And from there the Emperor [the Ottoman Sultan] marched and surrounded a city which they call Novo Brdo, "Mountain of Silver and Gold," and having attacked it, conquered it, but by means of an agreement: he promised to let them keep their possessions and also not to enslave their young women and boys . . . . Having arrived in the city the Turks ordered all the householders with their families, both males and females, to go out of the city through the small gate to a ditch, leaving their possessions in the houses. And so it happened that they went one after another, and the Emperor himself standing before the small gate sorted out the boys on one side and the females on the other, and the men along the ditch on one side and the women on the other side. All those among the men who were the most important and distinguished he ordered decapitated. The remainder he ordered released to the city. As for their possessions, nothing of theirs was harmed. The boys were 320 in number and the females 74. The females he distributed among the heathens, but he took the boys for himself into the Janissaries, and sent them beyond the sea to Anatolia, where their preserve is.

I was also taken in that city with my two brothers, and wherever the Turks to whom we were entrusted drove us in a band, and wherever we came to forests or mountains, there we always thought about killing the Turks and running away by ourselves among the mountains, but our youth did not permit us to do that; for I myself with nineteen others ran away from them in the night from a village called Samokovo. Then the whole region pursued us, and having caught and bound us, they beat us and tortured us and dragged us behind horses. It is a wonder that our soul remained in us. Then others vouched for us, and my two brothers, that we would not permit this anymore, and so they peacefully led us across the sea.

—Konstantin Mihailović, *Memoirs of a Janissary*

- How does Mihailović feel about the Ottomans? Why does he feel this way?
- How loyal a Janissary was he likely to have been? Why?
- While the Janissaries were elite members of Ottoman society, they remained enslaved people. What sense does this excerpt and the rest of the chapter give you of the Janissary experience?

The Janissaries held high status in Ottoman society. Although many parents protested the taking of their children and sometimes rebelled against the system, others who hoped to provide their sons with a means of advancing in society reportedly bribed Ottoman officials to select them. Some Muslim parents, whose sons were not subject to the *devshirme*, supposedly even lied about their religion to secure a spot for them in the sultan's service.

The sultans also kept other kinds of enslaved people. Christian women from foreign lands were purchased in slave markets, and others were given to the sultan as gifts or taken as prisoners of war. They were placed in the sultan's harem, where they lived among his children and female relatives and served the ladies of the court as attendants. Women in the harem were ranked according to a strict hierarchy in which they could advance based on talent and length of service. The minority chosen to become sexual partners of the sultan were also elevated, especially if they bore him children. Some became the mothers of future sultans and were given the title "lady." They might hold great power. While some of these women held great power, most remained servants, and after a few years of service, they were usually released from their duties and married to palace officials. Guarding the Ottoman harem were enslaved eunuchs, castrated men who were usually purchased in slave markets in Africa and whose perceived differences in sexuality led them to be assigned made them well suited to important roles such as managing the household of the ruler and other nobles. Despite their enslaved status, the control these men exerted over the harem gave them great power.

Although the mamluks and enslaved men and women who served the Ottoman sultan were considered among the elite of their societies and occupied relatively privileged positions, people other than sultans owned enslaved people who performed hard physical labor on farms or as domestic servants. They might be poorly fed and clothed and were neither paid nor educated. They also could not expect to gain their freedom. As property, they could be pawned or sold at their owner's whim, and regardless of age, they might be sexually abused. The experiences of these people were far more typical and representative of the enslaved, including Africans enslaved in the Americas beginning in the sixteenth century, than were those of the mamluks, the Janissaries, or the women of the Ottoman harem.

The Mamluk Sultanate

The mamluks of Egypt reached the pinnacle of their unusually high status in 1250. In that year, they deposed the last Ayyubid sultan, then only a child, and took control of the state.

The Ayyubids, who ruled the Levant and Egypt beginning in the eleventh century, had established their dynasty by breaking away from the Abbasid Caliphate. In the early 1200s, as the members of the Ayyubid ruling family competed with one another for supremacy, they amassed large numbers of mamluk guards and soldiers, consisting mostly of Kipchak Turks from the steppes north of the Black Sea, to assist them. When rulers defeated brothers and uncles in their quest for power, they also took control of their mamluk forces. Soon the mamluk troops vastly outnumbered the members of the Ayyubid Arab ruling class.

In 1249, Sultan as-Salih Ayyub died. His son replaced him but was assassinated by mamluks in 1250. As-Salih's widow, Shajur al-Durr, also ruled briefly, but she was soon deposed. The Ayyubid commander of the city of Aleppo in Syria initially challenged mamluk rule and took an army to Egypt to reclaim control of the state, prompting the mamluk commander Aybak, whom Shajur al-Durr had married to bolster her own claim to power, to place an Ayyubid royal child on the throne as a puppet ruler and his nominal "master." Following his defeat of the Ayyubid forces, Aybak deposed the child sultan and took power in his own right, permanently ending Ayyubid rule in Egypt and formally establishing the Mamluk Sultanate. When Aybak was assassinated in 1257, his teenage son took the throne, but true power in Egypt was wielded by another mamluk commander, Saif ad-Din Qutuz.

The new Mamluk Sultanate soon found its power tested by the arrival of invading Mongol forces. In 1258, Hulagu Khan attacked and destroyed Baghdad, the seat of the Abbasid Caliphate. His troops then took the city of Damascus, which lay within the territory claimed by the Mamluk Sultanate. Hulagu demanded that Qutuz surrender Egypt, but the sultan refused. In 1260, the Mongol and Mamluk armies clashed at the Battle of Ain Jalut, in what is today modern-day Israel, and the Mamluks were triumphant. This halted the Mongol advance in western Asia and prevented them from invading North Africa.

Qutuz did not live to relish the Mamluk victory over the Mongols, however. Shortly after his triumph at Ain Jalut, he was assassinated, and a rival mamluk commander, Baybars, claimed the throne as sultan. Baybars established the Bahri dynasty, named for the location in Cairo of the mamluk barracks from which he had come. The rulers of the Bahri dynasty were mamluks of primarily Turkish origin. Unlike members of most dynasties, they were not generally descendants of the founder. Two of Baybars' sons succeeded to the throne following his death, but they were quickly deposed by rival mamluk army factions. This was the case for most Mamluk sultans, who each ruled for an average of only seven years, and often much less.

Stability was a constant problem for the Mamluk Sultanate. Although it remained in control of Egypt and the Levant until it was defeated by the Ottomans in 1517, the sultans' rule was never secure. Sultans were routinely deposed—and often murdered—by rival claimants to the throne. Provincial administrators often rebelled against the authority of Cairo as well. The problem lay in the origin of the mamluks themselves. Having undergone rigorous training and the experience of enslavement, and having risen through the ranks based solely on their abilities, the mamluks were scornful of those who had not had a similarly harsh upbringing and won their position based on merit. Thus, when sultans attempted to establish their biological sons as their heirs, the army often regarded them as unworthy and refused to follow them. Furthermore, while mamluk soldiers were loyal to their masters, they did not feel similar loyalty to other commanders. When a sultan died or was deposed, his mamluks were not inclined to obey the person who took his place. The succession to the throne of the Mamluk Sultanate thus always remained uncertain as the army continued to assert its right to choose (and depose) the ruler. Mamluk history was marked by repeated attempts by individual commanders to seize power, and by the army's removal of "unworthy" rulers in favor of others.

Despite the fact that the line of succession always remained unclear, the Mamluk Sultanate was a force to be reckoned with, and its troops were successful at defeating their enemies. Beginning during the rule of Baybars, for example, the Mamluks gradually retook control of the Christian Crusader States in the Levant, either razing their fortresses or converting them to Mamluk garrisons. The final Christian stronghold, Acre, fell in 1291. The Mamluks also defeated the Christian Armenian Kingdom of Cilicia and stopped an attempted Mongol invasion of Syria in 1313 before establishing a peace treaty with the Ilkhanate Mongols in Persia in 1322 (Figure 17.21).

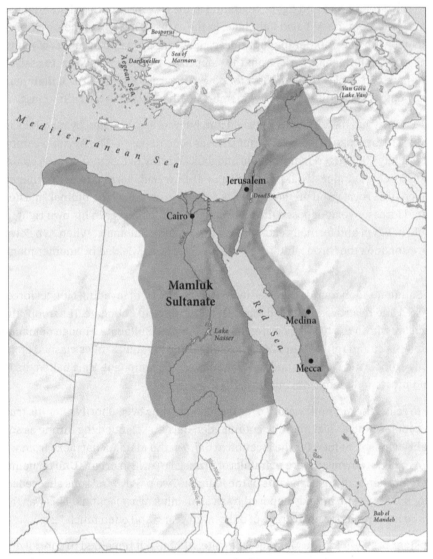

FIGURE 17.21 The Mamluk Sultanate. This map shows the territory claimed by the Mamluk Sultanate at its greatest extent in 1317. The empire controlled access to the eastern Mediterranean, the Red Sea, and the Nile as well as the holy cities of Mecca, Medina, and Jerusalem. (attribution: Copyright Rice University, OpenStax, under CC BY 4.0 license)

During the first century of Mamluk rule, the time of the Bahri dynasty, the empire flourished. Following the capture of Baghdad by the Mongols in 1258 and the execution of Caliph al-Musta'sim, members of the Abbasid family sought refuge in Egypt. In 1261, Baybars proclaimed al-Mustansir, the nephew of al-Musta'sim, the new caliph. In return, al-Mustansir recognized Baybars's authority to rule over the lands once held by the Abbasids.

Thus, while the Mamluk sultans never claimed the caliphate for themselves, they sought legitimacy for their rule through their role as protectors of the caliph.

Mamluk rulers were pious Muslims who protected pilgrims bound for the holy cities of Mecca, Medina, and Jerusalem. They built mosques and madrasas, and Cairo grew into an important center of religious scholarship. Unwilling to risk the displeasure of Muslim judges, the mamluks supported all four major schools of Islamic law. They also built hospitals, primary schools, and public fountains to provide the poor with clean drinking water. Their championing of Islam and their building of charitable institutions provided them with an important connection to their non-Turkish subjects, who might otherwise have resented their rule.

⊘ LINK TO LEARNING

Although the Mamluk Sultanate is known primarily for the military prowess of its armies, Mamluk society also produced unique architecture and prized works of art. You can learn more about Mamluk art and architecture (https://openstax.org/l/77MamlukArchi) at the Metropolitan Museum of Art website.

In the late fourteenth century, a new Mamluk dynasty came to power—the Burji, also named for the location of its mamluk barracks. The Burji sultans were mamluks of primarily Circassian and Georgian origin, unlike the Turks of the Bahri dynasty. The first Burji sultan, al-Zahir Barquq, assumed the throne in 1382. Almost immediately, plots emerged to remove him, one headed by the caliph who hoped to rule in his own right and another by Turkish tribes in Syria. Both attempts were defeated, but the peace did not last long. In 1399, 1434, and 1437, soldiers rioted in the streets of Cairo. Sometimes the riots began as conflicts between rival mamluk factions that spread to the streets and involved civilians. At other times, soldiers rioted when they had not been paid. In 1441, riots were sparked by food shortages and the perception that the grain trade, from which government officials profited, was inefficient and the prices unfair. Merchants' stores were plundered by angry mobs. In the second half of the fifteenth century, mamluk-initiated chaos erupted nearly every year as soldiers fought in the streets and attacked the homes of the wealthy and government officials. Even religious scholars were not safe.

Unable to maintain order in their own capital, Mamluk rulers also had to confront rebellions in more far-flung parts of their domain. The Mamluks had difficulty establishing control over Syrian Arabs and the nomadic and seminomadic Bedouin tribes of Upper Egypt. Bedouin rebels were punished severely; men were impaled or burned alive, while women and children were enslaved. The heads of rebels were placed on the gates of Cairo as a warning against future revolts. Syrian Arabs were punished less harshly because their assistance was needed to repel attacks by Mongols and the Ottomans.

Although they remained an elite class in Egypt until 1811, the Mamluks found their sovereignty over the region threatened when they lost control of Syria to the Ottomans in 1516. The Ottoman sultan Selim I then conquered Cairo in 1517. Rather than depose the Mamluks, however, the Ottomans allowed them to rule their old domains on their conquerors' behalf, though true power lay with the Ottomans in Istanbul.

Ming China and Its Neighbors

The ascendance of the Turks and the decline of Mongol rule in western Asia in the thirteenth century were soon followed by the decline of Mongol dominance in East Asia as well. By the second half of the thirteenth century, China found itself beset by problems. The Yuan dynasty emperor Kublai Khan waged a series of expensive campaigns against the kingdoms of Burma (now Myanmar), Annam, and Champa in Southeast Asia, and Java in the Indian Ocean. Two attempts to invade Japan failed, and revolts against Mongol rule erupted.

One of these revolts was the Ispah Rebellion, which began in Quanzhou. A major port city in southeastern China's Fujian Province, Quanzhou was on the Maritime Silk Road, an ocean trading route that connected China to other trading ports in Southeast Asia, the Indian Ocean, India, the Arabian Peninsula, East Africa, and Egypt. Along this route, highly sought-after Chinese goods like porcelain and silk flowed westward to Europe,

Africa, India, and western Asia.

Quanzhou had a population of more than two million, making it the largest port in China and likely in the world in the thirteenth century. Most of the population were foreign-born merchants from Arabia, Persia, India, Armenia, and other lands. The Muslims who lived in Quanzhou were among the many Arabs, Persians, and Turks from western and central Asia who had come to China to trade or to serve the Yuan government. Though they encouraged Muslims from elsewhere in Asia to settle in China, Yuan officials often discriminated against them, forbidding the butchering of animals according to Islamic law and interfering with Muslim marriage laws and efforts by the Muslim community to govern themselves. In 1357, Muslims in Quanzhou rose against the Mongols. The rebellion was not crushed until 1367.

Attempts to suppress such revolts, which continued after the death of Kublai, drained the treasury, as had Kublai's unsuccessful military campaigns. His successors often mismanaged the treasury and sometimes held the throne for only brief periods of time. By the first half of the fourteenth century, natural disasters were compounding the difficulties China already faced. Droughts and floods led to food shortages and famines. Inflation and scarcity combined to raise the price of food beyond the reach of many peasants. Unusually cold weather worsened people's suffering, and from the 1330s through the 1350s, epidemics swept through various parts of the country, killing millions. Bandits roamed the countryside, and the army made little effort to hunt down the numerous outlaws who preyed on the populace.

A number of religious sects arose foretelling the end of days. One of these was the White Lotus, a sect of Buddhism that announced the coming of a new Buddha and thus a new age (Figure 17.22). Seizing on the White Lotus prophecy, a secret peasant society named the **Red Turbans** called for the overthrow of Mongol rule and the return of the Song dynasty. Armed rebellion broke out in 1351. In 1352, a young wandering Buddhist monk named Zhu Yuanzhang joined the Red Turbans and married the daughter of one of its leaders. In 1356, his forces captured the southern Chinese city of Nanjing. After eliminating his rivals within the Red Turbans, in 1368 Zhu defeated the last Yuan emperor, who then abandoned China. Zhu destroyed the Yuan palace in the capital of Dadu (Beijing), proclaimed himself emperor with the name of Hongwu, meaning vast and martial, and dubbed his new dynasty the Ming ("bright").

FIGURE 17.22 The White Lotus Society. The White Lotus Society, a meeting of which is depicted in ink on this fifteenth-century paper handscroll, was originally established in China to spread the teachings of a novel sect of Buddhism that foresaw the coming of a new age. (credit: "White Lotus Society" by Unknown/John Stewart Kennedy Fund, 1913/The Metropolitan Museum of Art, Public Domain)

Hongwu began by enforcing his power and bolstering China's security as the Ming dynasty's first emperor (Figure 17.23). Although he tried to resolve social disparities by abolishing slavery and increasing taxes on the wealthy, the cost of his army put a significant strain on the Chinese economy. He was never able to fully bridge the gap between rich and poor, and his attempts to protect China from invasion and rebellion led to repressive domestic policies. Nevertheless, with the restoration of agricultural productivity and political stability, the early Ming era was a time of significant wealth and power for China.

FIGURE 17.23 Zhu Yuanzhang. This hanging scroll silk painting of the fourteenth century is an official court portrait of the first emperor of the Ming dynasty. It is about 8 feet high by about 5 feet wide. (credit: "Official court painting of the Hongwu Emperor" by Unknown/Wikimedia Commons, Public Domain)

Hongwu's reign was marked by efforts to consolidate his own power, to protect himself from attack, and to reassert and expand Chinese influence. He eliminated the office of chief minister so that he might govern without interference, established a force of secret police, and ordered the execution of thousands of people who he believed disagreed with his polices. He also acted swiftly to stamp out rebellions. A revolt by the Miao ethnic group in Hunan Province in the southwest was crushed. The Kingdom of Dali, where Mongol forces had taken refuge in what is now Yunnan Province in the southeast, was defeated and the region incorporated into China. In 1387, Ming forces invaded Manchuria in the northeast, where Mongols loyal to the Yuan dynasty had also established a foothold. To protect the borders in underpopulated areas, Hongwu made military service in these regions hereditary. He forced the mass relocation of peasants from the south to augment the population in parts of central and northern China that had been hard hit by crop failures and epidemics.

Hongwu's efforts to expand Chinese power continued under his successor, his son Zhu Di, known as the Yongle emperor. From 1406 to 1427, Chinese forces tried unsuccessfully to invade and subdue the kingdom of Vietnam, and to counter the continuing Mongol threat, the Great Wall of China was repaired and lengthened. In other ways, though, Zhu Di reversed his father's policies. Hongwu had wanted to isolate China from dangerous foreign influences and so had forbidden nearly all maritime trade. The Yongle emperor strove instead to establish relations with foreign lands in order to make their rulers aware of China's wealth and power. To this end, he dispatched Admiral Zheng He on seven naval expeditions between 1405 and 1433. Chinese fleets consisting of thousands of ships sailed to Southeast Asia, India, Arabia, and East Africa. Zheng He presented foreign rulers with gifts of porcelain, silk, and gold to impress upon them the splendor of the Ming dynasty, and he returned with tribute for the emperor in the form of ivory and exotic animals such as zebras and ostriches.

Zhu Di also established diplomatic relations with Shah Rukh, the son and heir of Timur, as well as with rulers in the Philippines and the Indian Ocean. China had no direct contact with the Ottoman state, however. When he ascended the throne, Hongwu sent an announcement to the Byzantine emperor, who he believed was still in power in Constantinople. After this, however, there was no correspondence or direct contact between the two states for at least a century.

The Yongle emperor moved the capital of China from Nanjing to Beijing, in the center of which he began construction of the new **Forbidden City**, a walled compound consisting of palaces, temples, and gardens for use by the emperor and the members of his household. In 1420, he also ordered the building of an elaborate tomb north of Beijing, where other members of the dynasty also built final resting places for themselves (Figure 17.24). All these structures conveyed an image of China's power, wealth, and magnificence.

FIGURE 17.24 Ming Tombs. Ming dynasty emperors built thirteen tombs at the foot of the Jundu Mountains near Beijing, shown here in a nineteenth-century ink and watercolor image. The three red arches in the lower left mark the beginning of the Spirit Way, a four-mile road that runs through the valley. (credit: "Ming shi san ling tu" by Arthur W. Hummel/Library of Congress, Geography and Map Division, Public Domain)

BEYOND THE BOOK

The Forbidden City

The construction of the Forbidden City (Figure 17.25) in the center of Beijing began in the reign of the Yongle emperor. Within its walls were gardens, palaces, and temples. Guards at its gates carefully limited access to only the important people who lived and worked inside it. The main entrance was the Meridian Gate, which had five separate gateways. The central one was reserved for exclusive use by the emperor with only two exceptions: the empress could use the central gate on her wedding day, as could men who had successfully passed the imperial examinations for entering into state service as an administrator.

The Ming emperors held court in the Hall of Supreme Harmony. During the Ming dynasty, the emperor lived in the Palace of Heavenly Purity, while the empress lived nearby in the smaller Palace of Earthly Tranquility. To either side of these palaces were the six western palaces and the six eastern palaces where the emperor's consorts lived.

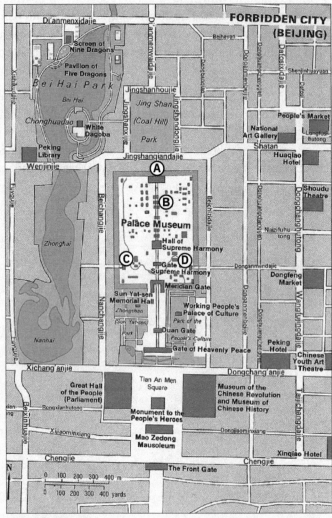

(A) Gate of Divine Might

(B) Palace of Heavenly Purity and the Palace of Earthly Tranquility

(C) Hall of Military Eminence

(D) Hall of Literary Glory

FIGURE 17.25 The Forbidden City. This map of central Beijing shows the location of the palace complex known as the Forbidden City, now a national museum. Note how the layout and names of important buildings and other structures within the compound compare to those of the surrounding area. (credit: modification of work "Map of Forbidden City, 1987" by Nathan Hughes Hamilton/Flickr, CC BY 2.0)

- Examine the layout of the Forbidden City and the names of its palaces, gates, and other structures. What does this compound tell you about the values of the Ming dynasty?
- Can you think of any complexes that are similar to the Forbidden City? If so, what and where are they?

Despite their wealth and power, the Ming emperors could still find themselves helpless in the face of Mongol aggression. The Yongle emperor tried unsuccessfully to subdue the Oirats, the westernmost of the Mongol tribes, who lived in what is now western Mongolia and the Altai region of Siberia. In 1449, the Oirat leader Esen took the twenty-one-year-old Ming emperor Yingzong hostage after the Mongol army defeated a much larger Chinese military force at the Battle of Tumu Fortress. The Ming responded by demoting Yingzong to the rank of "retired emperor" and placed his younger half-brother on the throne instead.

Esen's efforts to return Yingzong to Beijing—after conveniently marrying the captive emperor to his daughter—failed, and Mongol efforts to take Beijing by force were repulsed. Yingzong remained a prisoner of the Oirat until a member of his court ransomed him and returned him to Beijing, where he was placed under house arrest in a palace in the Forbidden City by his half-brother, who had no intention of giving up the throne. It was another seven years before Yingzong managed to unseat (and kill) his half-brother and reclaim his throne.

Yingzong was forced to confront Mongol forces again in 1461 when the Chinese general Cao Qin attempted a coup with the assistance of Mongol soldiers. The emperor was saved only when a timely downpour foiled efforts to burn the gates that blocked the rebels' entry to the Forbidden City.

17.3 Gunpowder and Nomads in a Transitional Age

LEARNING OBJECTIVES

By the end of this section, you will be able to:
- Describe gunpowder weaponry and its effect on early modern society
- Explain the reasons for the decline in nomadic societies in this period and beyond

The development of gunpowder and firearms technology in the late Middle Ages and early modern era had a tremendous impact on many societies. Firearms changed the nature of siege warfare and reduced the effectiveness of mounted warriors in battle, which in turn influenced the decisions of governments and the social organization of many states. Firearms also had an effect on nomadic societies that, before the early modern era, had often managed to dominate settled societies.

Social Change and the Adoption of Gunpowder

Societies like those of the Turks and the Mongols had originally gained power as a result of their prowess as mounted warriors. Turkish fighters, whether Janissaries or mamluks, were renowned for their archery and equestrian abilities. The Mongols also awed their opponents with their skills as archers and riders. In the tenth century, however, the invention of gunpowder transformed the manner in which these societies and others made war.

The first recorded use of gunpowder in battle occurred in China in 919. Scholars believe gunpowder was invented as a by-product of experiments conducted by Chinese alchemists, a group of people who pursued ways to turn ordinary metals into gold. A painting from Dunhuang in western China depicts a figure holding a tube from which flames are issuing forth (Figure 17.26). In 1126, a Chinese army was described as using similar tubes made of bamboo to fire projectiles at their opponents. Only six years later, another Chinese army made use of a bamboo cannon on wheels to destroy the walls of a city to which they had laid siege. By the thirteenth century, the Chinese were forging cannons from bronze.

FIGURE 17.26 An Early Image of Gunpowder? This mid-tenth-century silk painting from Dunhuang, China, believed to show Buddha tempted by the demon Mara, depicts a figure in the upper right holding a tube from which fire emerges. Below him, another figure holds what appears to be a flaming bomb or grenade. (credit: "First illustration of Fire Lance and a Grenade, 10th Century, Dunhuang" by Unknown/Wikimedia Commons, Public Domain)

Gunpowder and guns, along with the knowledge of how to manufacture them, spread westward from China with invading Mongol armies. This was not entirely new technology, however. The Arabs of this region already knew how to create flammable substances using petroleum, and the Byzantines employed a substance made from naphtha, called "Greek fire," to set enemy ships alight (Figure 17.27). Arab texts of the thirteenth century contain numerous recipes for gunpowder and descriptions of rockets and other weapons that made use of it. The Mongols employed gunpowder and incendiary devices when laying siege to cities but did not adopt guns for fighting on horseback. The Arabs and Turks did, however. At the Battle of Ain Jalut in 1260, the mamluk forces that successfully fought off a Mongol army and prevented it from conquering Egypt were armed with an early type of cannon.

FIGURE 17.27 Greek Fire. A twelfth-century codex illustration shows the Byzantines using Greek fire to burn an enemy ship during a rebellion of the ninth century. The use of Greek fire in a variety of forms was a critical weapon for the Byzantines for centuries and made them a formidable force on the seas. (credit: "Greek Fire, from Codex Skylitzes Matritensis" by Unknown/Wikimedia Commons, Public Domain)

Europeans probably first encountered early versions of firearms in Russia, where the Mongols had introduced Chinese technology. Western Europeans discovered recipes for gunpowder in Arabic texts brought back from the Crusades or, in the case of Spain, introduced by the Muslims who established kingdoms there from the eighth through the fifteenth centuries. By the fifteenth century, numerous European countries had begun to use gunpowder and guns in battle. Some of the earliest weapons employed exploding gunpowder to fire arrows. By the thirteenth century, European and Ottoman armies were using early cannons called bombards to destroy the walls of cities and fortresses.

The use of early firearms, cannons, and gunpowder transformed the ways in which wars were fought and also changed the societies that adopted this technology. On the battlefield, explosions could not only kill soldiers but also panic horses ridden by mounted warriors and thwart cavalry charges. Before the adoption of bombards and cannon, sieges of cities could drag on interminably; some lasted for years. So long as the people within the city walls had food and water, they would not surrender. Bombards and cannon allowed armies to breach stone walls, however; even a modest opening gave enemy attackers the opportunity to enter the city and do battle with the forces within. It was the use of cannon that finally allowed the Ottomans to destroy the walls of Constantinople and bring an end to the Byzantine Empire in 1453 (Figure 17.28). Earlier attempts to defeat the city had failed because armies could not break through the walls and were unable to carry on a prolonged siege that could reduce the Byzantines to starvation. The ability to destroy fortifications helped rulers assert power both in battle and at home. Nobles found it difficult to challenge the power of rulers whose cannon could destroy their castles.

FIGURE 17.28 **The Dardanelles Gun.** Cannons like this Dardanelles gun allowed the Ottoman Empire to conquer Constantinople in 1453. The Dardanelles gun was still in use nearly four hundred years later. (credit: "Dardanelles Gun Turkish Bronze 15c" by "The Land"/Wikimedia Commons, Public Domain)

The use of cannon also changed the nature of military defenses. To give added strength to city or fortress walls, earthen banks were built up inside them. Fortresses and city defenses were designed in the shape of stars so guns could be aimed in all directions, preventing an enemy from bringing artillery within reach of the walls (Figure 17.29). Engineers who knew how to build or destroy the new styles of fortress were in high demand. Paying for their expertise and for cannon, gunpowder, and cannon balls was expensive; rulers in societies that adopted guns taxed peasants heavily to pay for this new style of warfare.

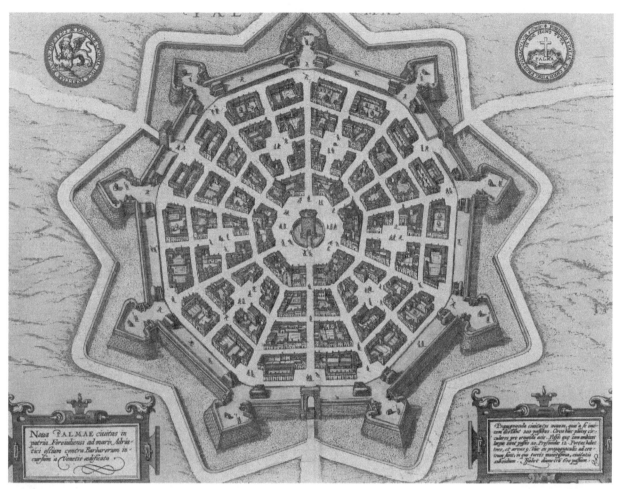

FIGURE 17.29 A Star Fort. This anonymous artist's seventeenth-century illustration of the Italian city of Palmanova shows its walls designed in the shape of a star for improved defense. (credit: "Palmanova1600" by Unknown/ Wikimedia Commons, Public Domain)

The nature of armies changed as well. Before the invention of gunpowder, cavalry were the most effective troops a commander could place in the field. Mounted warriors could attack and escape much faster than soldiers on foot, and they could reach down from horseback to deliver fatal blows to infantry or trample them underfoot. Guns deprived the cavalry of these advantages because they could kill riders and their mounts before they came within striking distance of opponents on the ground.

The development of handheld guns for individual soldiers lagged behind improvements in large artillery pieces like cannon. Early firearms were heavy and difficult to carry and maneuver. An **arquebus**, one of the earliest guns, had to be propped up on pieces of wood to be fired because it was too heavy to hold easily (Figure 17.30). Early firearms were also unreliable, inaccurate, and slow to load. A skilled archer like a mamluk soldier could fire several arrows in the time it took to reload a gun. Indeed, even after firearms were introduced, many armies still relied on infantry armed with bows and arrows. The Ottomans, for example, used peasant soldiers called *azebs* who carried bows and arrows, sabers, and sometimes halberds (weapons that combined a spear and an axe). *Azebs* bore the brunt of the enemy's frontal attack before moving to the side and allowing cannon and Janissaries with guns, who had been stationed behind them, to fire at the oncoming foe.

FIGURE 17.30 The Arquebus. The arquebus, an early gun, was so large and difficult to maneuver that it had to be propped on forked rods before it could be fired. (credit: "Dictionnaire raisonné du mobilier français de l'époque carlovingienne à la Renaissance - illustration Tome 6" by Viollet-le-Duc/Wikimedia Commons, Public Domain)

The adoption of firearms like the arquebus required the development of new military tactics to enable them to be used effectively in battle. For example, military commanders adapted the technique of volley fire, which had been used by archers and crossbow fighters, to the use of firearms. Because early guns like the arquebus were so inaccurate and took so long to reload, a row of soldiers was trained to fire and then immediately move to the rear behind other rows of troops who, in turn, stepped to the front, fired, and then moved back. The soldiers in the rear had time to reload their guns as others fired their volleys. To help soldiers remember the complex series of steps to be followed in loading their guns, the Ming general Qi Jiguang composed a song listing them in turn.

In most societies, male members of the nobility, often the only ones who could afford to purchase and pay for the upkeep of horses, had formed the core of the fighting forces. Their role as society's defenders helped to justify the exalted position their class occupied. When handheld guns became common, armed peasant infantrymen supplanted the mounted elite. The loss of their warrior role often marked the beginning of the decline in the power of the aristocracy, and the loss of privileges that other social classes had not shared.

As societies adopted the use of guns, some states developed a decisive advantage over others. Rulers who had access to metal to forge guns and the chemicals to make gunpowder were better able to impose their will on societies that did not. As the cost of handheld guns decreased, rulers such as Matthias I of Hungary created corps of armed infantry. Matthias armed approximately one-quarter of his foot soldiers with arquebuses in the fifteenth century. Countries with centralized governments and well-developed bureaucracies that were able to effectively tax their populations had the money to pay for these developments and found it easier to locate and recruit soldiers into the army. States with these advantages grew even more powerful.

Gunpowder thus helped to develop centralized states in Europe. These changes did not happen everywhere, though. States like the Ottoman Empire and Ming China already possessed centralized governments before they adopted gunpowder technology, and the use of firearms did not have a significant impact on the position of their nobility. In the Ottoman Empire, the non-noble Janissaries had formed the core of the Ottoman military before the widespread adoption of gunpowder and remained an elite force afterward. For the military portion of the Janissary corps, the adoption of gunpowder weapons combined with their intense training from a young age made them a formidable fighting force indeed, especially when using weapons that were not simple to use effectively. In Japan, the daimyo elite and their samurai vassals retained their privileged position in society until the nineteenth century, hundreds of years after the Japanese adopted guns. The arrival of guns brought change to a society, but not all societies responded in the same way.

The Age of the Nomad

The adoption of guns by societies in Europe, Asia, and Africa was the beginning of the end for some nomadic cultures. For centuries before this, nomadic societies had often played an important role in world history and were often important agents in bringing about historical change. For instance, life on the Indian subcontinent was transformed by the arrival of mounted Indo-Europeans around 1500 BCE. The sacred texts of the Indo-Europeans, the Vedas, were the basis on which the religion of Hinduism was built, and their social organization formed the basis for the Hindu caste system. Their language, Sanskrit, became the sacred tongue of both Hinduism and Buddhism.

The nomadic tribes of central Asia set in motion changes that contributed to the downfall of the Roman Empire. In the fourth and fifth centuries CE, the Huns, who occupied central Asia, the Caucasus, and eastern Europe, began to sweep westward, attacking and conquering Germanic tribes that lived on the borders of the Roman Empire. These tribes, the Goths, the Visigoths, and others, fled before their onslaught into Roman territory, destabilizing the empire. In East Asia, mounted nomads had a similar effect on Chinese society. Over the centuries, a variety of tribes—the Xiongnu, the Jurchen, and others—alternately traded with and attacked Han Chinese settlements. During the Qin dynasty (c. 221 BCE), construction of a wall began to protect the more settled areas of China from the roaming riders. When this failed, because the wall was built along only portions of the border between the lands settled by the Chinese and those occupied by nomadic tribes, Chinese emperors gave tribute in the form of gifts and Chinese princesses to mollify more aggressive tribes, which also demonstrated that the status of women was seen as being completely secondary to the agency and needs of men, even those from high social standing.

Beginning in the early modern era, nomadic societies increasingly began to settle down. The adoption of firearms by settled societies undoubtedly jeopardized the continued existence of nomadic societies. When firearms technology was perfected, meaning guns and artillery became more accurate and could fire farther and faster, mounted archers could not compete. This does not completely explain the disappearance of the nomadic way of life, however. Although early firearms were unwieldy and could not easily be fired from horseback, once they became more lightweight, they could have been adopted by nomads, and some nomadic societies, such as the Plains Indians of North America, did adopt them.

Not all nomads were mounted warriors. Mongols and Arab Bedouins were both, as were the Huns and the Xiongnu who plagued the Han dynasty. However, many nomadic groups neither rode horses nor formed armies. The Sami reindeer herders of Scandinavia and Russia and the Gaddi shepherds of the Himalaya were not traditionally warriors. Furthermore, settled societies, like those of Europe, also fielded mounted warriors. The European knights of the Middle Ages disappeared as a result of the widespread adoption of gunpowder and firearms. It also took several centuries after the development of firearms before mounted warriors no longer formed part of the world's armies. European and U.S. combatants in World War I made use of cavalry. It is thus perhaps more correct to say that gunpowder made cavalry (other than modern "cavalry" in the form of tanks) obsolete, than to say that gunpowder made nomads disappear. Finally, while mounted warriors are today a thing of the past, nomadic societies still exist across geographic boundaries around the world, although their numbers are much smaller. Many modern Mongols and Arab Bedouin, for example, still lead a nomadic lifestyle.

THE PAST MEETS THE PRESENT

Nomadic Lifestyles in the Twenty-First Century

In the twenty-first century, many people still lead nomadic lifestyles. Roughly one-quarter of Africa's population consists of nomadic pastoralists who graze herds of cattle and goats. In China, millions of Mongolians also live as herders on the Asian steppes, though the group has been gradually relocating to cities. Climate change, political conflicts, and economic factors are forcing nomadic groups to adopt new practices and are threatening their way of life. Desertification is expanding the size of Africa's Sahel desert region, making it more difficult for pastoralists in West Africa to find grazing lands for their flocks. As they search out grasslands, they have found themselves competing with both small farmers and commercialized agricultural enterprises for access to land and water. This has at times led to violence, just as clashes between nomadic herders and settled farmers did in past centuries. In Cote d'Ivoire in March 2016, such violence resulted in twenty-seven deaths. In the first eight months of 2018, conflicts between farmers and pastoralists cost more than 1,300 Nigerians their lives. Hundreds of thousands more have been displaced by such conflicts.

Just as gunpowder and firearms adversely affected some nomadic groups in the early modern era, so too did the development of land mines affect the Kuchi of Afghanistan and change their way of life. Their herds were destroyed, and armed conflict often made traveling dangerous. For the Kuchi, who are Sunni Muslims, being allied with the Taliban has worsened their situation. When the Taliban ruled Afghanistan before the U.S. invasion in 2001, the Kuchi were given rights to graze their animals on land claimed by the Shi'a Hazara ethnic group. When the Taliban were routed from power, the Hazara sought revenge by expelling the Kuchi from the pastureland they had been using. Now it is unclear what will happen to the Kuchi.

- In what ways are the problems that nomadic pastoralists face today similar to those of the past? In what ways are they different?
- What are possible solutions to some of the difficulties nomadic people encounter in the twenty-first century?

The rise of firearms played a role in forcing many nomads to adapt to changing military, political, and social realities, which in turn would lead many to move toward sedentarization. However, they were only the *means* by which some modern states enforced their will on nomads; guns were not the *reason* nomadic groups declined. The reasons modern states made war on nomads were various. Often, settled people feared nomads, especially those who waged war on them or who competed with settled people for natural resources. In the case of the North American Plains Indians, for example, settled people not only feared the mounted warriors, but they also coveted the lands they occupied. So long as the Plains tribes claimed extensive hunting grounds, the colonizing farmers, ranchers, and miners could not utilize the natural resources of the American West as they wished.

Modern nation-states with permanent borders also objected to nomads crossing at will from one nation into another. They regarded nomads as a threat to national security and sovereignty and forced them to settle. Modern nation-states also found it easier to tax people who were not always on the move. As nations industrialized, nomads' access to the grasslands and water sources that their herds needed was jeopardized. Private lands were fenced. Water sources were polluted. Grasslands were grazed by animals owned by commercialized livestock interests that produced meat to feed city dwellers. As industrialization made settled life more comfortable, many nomads willingly abandoned their traditional way of life.

Increasingly, in the twentieth and twenty-first centuries, climate change has also made nomadic life more difficult. Droughts and more severe weather are jeopardizing grasslands and water sources for animals. Lack of grass is disastrous for nomadic pastoralists. The soldiers of the Mamluk Sultanate made use of early cannons at the Battle of Ain Jalut. That was not what made them victorious, however. The Mongol force they faced was much smaller than such armies usually were. The arid climate of the Levant could not supply enough grass for the thousands of horses (five or six per person) that Mongol warriors traveled with, which forced the Mongols to field a smaller army. Now, more nomad homelands are experiencing desertification and harsh winter temperatures, and this may be the final blow for the world's few remaining nomadic societies.

⊘ LINK TO LEARNING

Read about the experiences of nomads in Mongolia (https://openstax.org/l/77MongoliaNom) who are making the decision to settle in cities.

Key Terms

arquebus an early gun that was large and difficult to maneuver

devshirme the system of acquiring Christian boys from the Balkans to be enslaved, converted to Islam, and trained to serve the Ottoman sultan

Forbidden City a walled complex of palaces, temples, and gardens built by the Ming dynasty emperors in the center of Beijing

harem the private household of the Ottoman sultan

humanism a movement born in fourteenth-century Italy that focused on the study of human beings, human nature, and human achievements rather than the study of God

Janissaries the elite enslaved infantry corps of the Ottoman army

Mamluk Sultanate a state in Egypt and the Levant administered and defended by educated, formerly enslaved men called mamluks

Red Turbans a secret peasant society that rose up against Mongol rule during the Yuan dynasty

Renaissance a period of intellectual and artistic rebirth inspired by the cultural achievements of ancient Greece and Rome

timar a right granted to subjects of the Ottoman sultan to collect taxes in a given area

Section Summary

17.1 The Ottomans and the Mongols

Following the sack of Constantinople by crusaders and the Mongols' defeat of the Seljuk Turks, the Ottomans emerged as a power in northwestern Anatolia. Under Osman's successors, they crossed the Dardanelles into Europe, defeating the Serbs at the Battle of Kosovo. When the Mongol conqueror Timur invaded the region, he defeated Bayezid, and the subsequent conflict among Bayezid's sons splintered the Ottoman state. Timur's empire came to include Persia, central Asia, and northern India, but Timur died before he could fulfill his plan to invade China.

Bayezid's son Mehmed I and his grandson Murad II rebuilt Ottoman possessions in Anatolia and Europe. In 1453, among other victories, Mehmed II conquered Constantinople. He rebuilt the city, thereafter known as Istanbul, and invited scholars and artists from Asia and Europe. He was tolerant of his non-Muslim and European subjects and allowed them to remain in Istanbul, though historians see the flight of many scholars to western Europe with the preserved knowledge of ancient Greece and Rome as one factor that helped to spark the Italian Renaissance and the transition to the early modern era. Meanwhile, western European traders began to seek all-water, oceanic routes to South and East Asia.

17.2 From the Mamluks to Ming China

The Abbasids, Ayyubids, and Ottomans all depended on enslaved or formerly enslaved people to staff their armies and run their administrations. Christian boys were taken from their parents, forced to convert to Islam, and trained as soldiers and administrators. In the Abbasid and Ayyubid states, they were called mamluks. In the Ottoman state they were Janissaries. Enslaved women might also become members of the sultan's harem and bear him children. Enslaved people were often placed in positions of trust because, having been taken from their families as children, they were entirely dependent on the ruler for their position and thus loyal to him.

In Egypt, the mamluk soldiers overthrew the Ayyubid sultan in 1250 and established the Mamluk Sultanate. Because succession to the throne was controlled and not hereditary, the Mamluk Sultanate could maintain sway over Egypt and the Levant and fight off challenges from the Mongols until it was defeated by the Ottomans in 1517.

The Ming dynasty came to power in China after revolts drove out the Mongol rulers of the Yuan dynasty. The Hongwu emperor eliminated all challenges to his rule by creating a secret police force, eliminating the position of chief minister, and putting down rebellions in distant provinces. He forbade most foreign trade in order to protect China from foreign influences. The Yongle emperor resumed foreign trade and collected tribute, and Chinese silks and porcelains were traded in Europe, Africa, India, and western Asia. Despite China's great power, the Ming had difficulty controlling the Mongols.

17.3 Gunpowder and Nomads in a Transitional Age

Early forms of guns were difficult to use and often inaccurate, but as they improved, rulers began to replace cavalry with infantry armed with guns. Where mounted warriors had been members of the aristocracy, this change often cost them their privileged position in society. Gunpowder also made it easier for armies to destroy fortifications, ending siege warfare. Centralized governments that adopted firearms technology and could levy taxes to pay for it grew more powerful and were able to dominate other states.

The adoption of firearms made the fighting style of nomadic societies less effective. These societies declined in size and number when governments forced them to settle. Sometimes settled people's fear of nomads forced governments to take action against them. The competition for natural resources also encouraged many nomadic pastoralists to abandon their way of life.

Assessments

Review Questions

1. What allowed for the development of an Ottoman state independent of the Seljuk Turks' Sultanate of Rum?
   a. the Mongol invasion of Anatolia
   b. the depopulation of Serbia by the bubonic plague
   c. the death of the Byzantine emperor Manuel II
   d. the Ottoman victory at the Battle of Kosovo

2. How did invasion by Timur influence the development of the Ottoman state?
   a. The death of all Bayezid I's sons at the Battle of Ankara left the Ottoman state without a ruler.
   b. Timur's invasion encouraged the Ottomans' vassals to rally to their aid, strengthening the Ottoman state.
   c. Timur's invasion and the defeat of Bayezid I encouraged Turkish vassals to break away from Ottoman rule.
   d. The need to rebuild the Ottoman military resulted in higher taxes for Ottoman subjects and subsequent revolts.

3. How did Europeans respond to the Ottomans' taking control of trade in the eastern Mediterranean and along the Silk Roads?
   a. The nations of western Europe launched a Crusade to retake control of the trade routes from the Ottomans.
   b. Venetian and Genoese traders welcomed Ottoman control because the Ottoman army protected the trade routes and made them safer.
   c. Europeans began to seek an all-water, oceanic route to South and East Asia.
   d. European merchants objected to paying taxes to the Ottomans and created overland routes to India and East Asia that bypassed Ottoman-controlled lands.

4. What area did the Ottoman state not control after the collapse of the Byzantine Empire?
   a. most of southern Greece
   b. Genoese trading posts on the Black Sea
   c. Bosnia and Albania in the Balkans
   d. southern Italy

5. How did Masaccio transform European art during the Renaissance?
   a. He was the first artist to paint in oils.
   b. He was the first artist to depict nonreligious subjects.
   c. He was the first artist to incorporate linear perspective into painting.
   d. He was the first artist to paint landscapes.

6. What was *not* a potential occupation for a child taken in the *devshirme*?
   a. scribe
   b. soldier
   c. palace administrator
   d. priest

7. What effect did the Battle of Ankara have on the Janissary system?
   a. It revealed the potential disloyalty of Janissary forces, leading to the demise of the system.
   b. It led the sultans to turn to Egypt as a source of new Janissary recruits.
   c. It demonstrated the danger of relying on the Turkish nobility for defense, thus encouraging the development of the Janissary system.
   d. It forced the Ottomans to rebuild their Janissary corps because so many were killed.

8. Why was political succession in the Mamluk Sultanate always unstable?
   a. Succession did not typically descend from a sultan to his sons, and the army usually chose the new sultan.
   b. The Ottomans routinely interfered in the choice of the new sultan.
   c. Mamluk sultans had numerous children who fought among themselves for the throne.
   d. Mamluk sultans rarely had children, so distant relatives competed who had no clear claim to the throne.

9. Why did the Mamluk sultans usually treat rebellious Syrian Arabs more leniently than they did rebellious Arab Bedouins in Egypt?
   a. The Syrian Arabs were protected by the caliph.
   b. The Mamluks needed the assistance of Syrian Arabs in fighting the Ottomans and the Mongols.
   c. The Bedouins were a greater threat to the lives and property of Egyptians.
   d. The leaders of the Syrian Arabs had once been mamluks themselves.

10. What was the main reason for the voyages of Zheng He in the fifteenth century?
    a. to impress other states with the power of China
    b. to encourage trade between China and Europe
    c. to explore the lands of the Arabian Peninsula
    d. to discover a new trade route to India

11. Why did members of the Mamluk army oppose rule by non-mamluks?
    a. They believed that only their biological relatives were fit to rule.
    b. They did not believe that non-mamluks were pious enough.
    c. They believed only those who had experienced rigorous training and enslavement were worthy.
    d. They resented rule by foreigners.

12. Which was *not* an example of foreign contact that took place during the Ming dynasty?
    a. the voyages of Zheng He
    b. conflict with the Mongols
    c. the invasion of Vietnam

    d. the invasion of Japan

13. Zhu Yuanzhang, the first emperor of the Ming dynasty, had sympathy for the poor because in his early life he had been what?
    a. a poor peasant
    b. a nomadic warrior
    c. a Daoist monk
    d. an aristocratic scholar

14. How did firearms technology affect the social structure of western European societies?
    a. It made it easier for small, decentralized states to challenge larger centralized ones.
    b. It completely eliminated nomadic herding as a way of life in Europe.
    c. It eventually made aristocratic mounted warriors obsolete.
    d. It led to the development of an elite class of aristocratic infantry.

15. What has *not* been a contributing factor in the demise of nomadic societies?
    a. climate change
    b. industrialization
    c. the desire of modern nations to control borders
    d. epidemic disease

16. How did firearms technology affect nomadic groups?
    a. Firearms eventually made the forms of warfare favored by nomadic groups less effective.
    b. The adoption of firearms by nomadic groups threatened the existence of settled societies.
    c. The adoption of firearms technology eliminated nomadism as a way of life.
    d. The need to pay taxes to support the armed forces of centralized states caused nomads to settle as farmers.

Check Your Understanding Questions

1. What motivation did Orthodox Christians have for accepting Ottoman rule?

2. Why did the Ottoman state grant timars?

3. In what ways did the empire founded by Timur geographically resemble that founded by Chinggis Khan?

4. Why do some historians regard the fall of Constantinople as the end of the Middle Ages and the beginning of the early modern era?

5. How did the intellectual movement of humanism affect Europeans' view of human beings?

6. Why did the Abbasid, Ayyubid, and Ottoman states prefer to train enslaved male children to become soldiers and administrators?

7. In what ways was the Janissary system of the Ottomans similar to the mamluk system in Egypt?

8. What was the main difference between the two Mamluk dynasties?

9. Other than religious piety, what motives did the Mamluk sultans have for establishing mosques and charitable institutions?

10. What effect did the Mongols have on the Ming dynasty?

11. How successful was Zhu Yuanzhang at improving life for China's poor?

12. What impact did the adoption of gunpowder have on the European aristocracy?

13. What impact did the adoption of gunpowder have on the Ottoman Empire?

14. Why did nomadic societies begin to decline beginning in the early modern era?

Application and Reflection Questions

1. What role did religion play in the development of the Ottoman Empire?

2. In what ways were the actions of Timur and Mehmed II toward conquered cities similar? How were they different?

3. What were some of the long-term effects of the Ottoman conquest of the Byzantine Empire?

4. How did the rediscovery of the works of ancient Greece and Rome influence European philosophy, art, and scientific inquiry during the Renaissance?

5. What was life like for enslaved people under the Ottomans and Mamluks?

6. What benefits did the Mamluk Sultanate derive from making use of formerly enslaved men as soldiers and administrators? What were the drawbacks of this system?

7. With which foreign powers did the Ming dynasty maintain relationships? What were these relationships like?

8. Think about other major technological changes that have taken place in the past hundred fifty, fifty, and five years. Have any of them had effects on human society similar to that of gunpowder? If yes, describe those effects. If not, why not?

9. How has the adoption of firearms technology affected nomadic societies? To what extent did it lead to their decline? What other factors have led to the gradual disappearance or reduction in size of nomadic societies?

APPENDIX A

Glossary

A

Abrahamic faiths the religions of Judaism, Christianity, and Islam, which all trace their origins through a common ancestor, the prophet Abraham

Acheulean tools stone tools made by carefully chipping away flakes of the stone core to make them into teardrop-shaped implements that replaced the cruder Oldowan hand-axes

animism the belief that a degree of spirituality exists not only in people but also in plants, inanimate objects, and natural phenomena

annona the Roman government's distribution of grain to the population, which was also a political tool for the emperor

arquebus an early gun that was large and difficult to maneuver

asceticism the practice of self-denial and rejection of pleasures as a way to express religious devotion

Australopithecus a very distant ancestor of modern humans who lived in eastern and southern Africa between 2.5 and 4 million years ago

B

Babylonian exile the deportation of Judeans to Babylon after the fall of Jerusalem

Bantu migrations the millennia-long expansion of Bantu-speaking peoples southward from West and Central Africa, spreading a common cultural foundation that included language, farming, and ironworking

Bedouin the name given to nomadic tribes of Arabia

Berbers the name used by Carthaginians, Greeks, and Romans to describe the native peoples of the Maghreb; today, this population generally self-identifies as Amazigh, or Imazighen

Beringia a section of low-lying land between modern Alaska and Russia, now underwater, that once served as a land bridge between continents

biome a community of vegetation and wildlife adapted to a particular climate

Black Death a pandemic of the plague caused by the bacterium Yersinia pestis with far-reaching economic, political, social, and cultural effects that transformed Asia, Europe, and North Africa in the fourteenth century

Bronze Age the period from 3500 to 1110 BCE when bronze, an alloy of copper and tin, was the preferred material for manufacturing tools and weapons

C

cabotage a system wherein groups or individuals are granted the right to trade in another's territory

caliph an Islamic title designating a spiritual and secular leader

caliphate an area under the control of a Muslim ruler called a caliph

caravansary an inn funded by the state or wealthy individuals where travelers could spend the night and store their goods securely

cataract a place in a river where the otherwise placid flow is upset by a waterfall, a shallow portion, or the presence of boulders

centuriation the Roman practice of dividing land into a grid in preparation for development and agriculture

Chan Buddhism a form of Mahayana Buddhism that emphasizes meditation; it is widely practiced in Japan where it is known as Zen Buddhism

chattel slavery a form of slavery in which one person is owned by another as a piece of property

chivalry a code of ideal conduct meant to validate the practices of noble warriors by Christianizing knightly violence and behavior

chronological approach an approach to history that follows a timeline from ancient to modern

city-state an independent political entity consisting of a city and surrounding territory that it controls

clan a small group of several families that shared an encampment and herded or hunted together and formed the basic social unit of the seminomadic peoples of Eurasia

clients less well-off Romans who relied on a patron's gifts for subsistence

Clovis culture a culture consisting of mobile bands of hunter-gatherers who camped at resource-rich locations in modest populations across North America

Cluniac reform a movement that aimed to limit the influence of aristocrats in church matters

Code of Hammurabi a list of judicial decisions that the Babylonian king Hammurabi had inscribed on stone pillars throughout his kingdom

Code of Justinian a legal project carried out by Emperor Justinian to compile and edit Roman edicts issued from the second to the sixth century CE

Colosseum a large structure in Rome that was the site of gladiatorial matches and other entertainments

Confucianism a Chinese school of philosophical thought shaping morality, governance, education, and family life

Constitutions of Melfi the oldest surviving written constitution in the world, which increased the power of the monarch of the Kingdom of the Two Sicilies by replacing vassals and church officials with royal bureaucrats

culture all the ways in which members of a human society interact with one another and with their environment and pass these ways from generation to generation

cuneiform a phonetic writing system based on the sounds of words and invented by the Sumerians in about 3000 BCE

D

Daoism a Chinese religion that emphasized veneration of nature, the cosmos, and mysticism

deffufa a type of monumental mud-brick structure unique to Nubian civilization and believed to have served a religious function

devshirme the system of acquiring Christian boys from the Balkans to be enslaved, converted to Islam, and trained to serve the Ottoman sultan

dharma the Hindu concept of the right way of living as defined by cosmic law

dictator a Roman Republican office with absolute authority over the state for a limited time during emergencies

domus the name for a typical Roman house, as well as the family unit

Donatist controversy the Christian schism in North Africa springing from the belief that church leaders who had renounced their faith to avoid persecution held no authority to perform sacraments

drystone a construction method that uses interlocking stones rather than mortar

dynatoi members of the Byzantine elite who often compromised imperial authority

E

ecumenical councils meetings organized by emperors that gathered Christian bishops from around the empire to settle matters of doctrine within the Church

Exodus the mass migration of Hebrews out of Egypt under the leadership of Moses

F

Fertile Crescent a crescent-shaped geographical area in the Middle East where agriculture first flourished

feudalism a collection of practices that bound lesser lords to greater lords through land and privileges given in return for personal and military support

flagellants penitents who ritually flogged themselves in response to the Black Death as a means of appeasing God and mitigating the spread of the disease

foederati foreign states and tribes that were given semiautonomy as Roman allies in exchange for pledging military service to the Roman Empire

Forbidden City a walled complex of palaces, temples, and gardens built by the Ming dynasty emperors in the center of Beijing

G

genus a taxonomic rank that includes several similar and related species

gladiator an enslaved professional fighter paid to battle before an audience, sometimes to the death

global citizen a person who sees themselves as responsible to a world community rather than only a national one

globalization the interconnectedness of societies and economies throughout the world as a result of trade, technology, and the adoption and sharing of various aspects of culture

Golden Bull a document issued by the Holy Roman emperor Charles IV in 1356 that recognized the role of seven princes in electing Holy Roman emperors

Golden Horde the Mongol group that ruled over portions of central Asia, the former lands of the Rus, and northwest Asia

great man theory the view that it is enough to study the deeds and impact of important leaders to paint an accurate picture of the past

Great Schism of 1054 the conflict that solidified the separation of the eastern and western Christian churches

Great Western Schism the period from 1378 to 1417 during which three men simultaneously served as pope of the Roman Catholic Church in western Europe

H

hadith the words and actions of the Islamic prophet Muhammad and his immediate successors that, along with the Quran, form the fundamental basis for Islamic law

hajj the Islamic pilgrimage to Mecca

Harappan a term describing the ancient Indus valley civilization, named for one of its largest cities and the first to be discovered by archaeologists

harem the private household of the Ottoman sultan

Hebrew Bible the holy book that, according to Jewish tradition, tells the history of the Hebrew people

Hellenism a high regard for the cultural institutions of Greece including its religion, philosophy, and system of education

Hellenistic a description of Greek history, language, and culture in the period 323–31 BCE

hieratic a simplified form of hieroglyphics employed by Egyptian scribes for recording everyday documents such as receipts and contracts

hieroglyphics a complex writing system developed around 3000 BCE in which written symbols represented both sounds and ideas

hijra an Arabic term meaning "emigration" that describes a defining moment for early Muslims as they fled Mecca for Medina in 622 CE

historical climatology the study of historical temperature and climate changes and their effects on human society

historical empathy the ability to see the past on its own terms, without judgment or the imposition of our own modern-day attitudes

historiography the study of how historians have already interpreted the past

Homo erectus a member of the genus Homo who emerged in East Africa around two million years ago, living entirely on the ground and walking exclusively in an upright position

Homo habilis the earliest member of the genus Homo, appearing in the archaeological record about two to three million years ago

Homo sapiens modern humans, members of the genus Homo who emerged in Africa first and later migrated to other areas

Hopewell tradition a widely dispersed mound-building tradition that emerged in the Eastern Woodlands around 200 BCE, linked by a network of trade routes

humanism a movement born in fourteenth-century Italy that focused on the study of human beings, human nature, and human achievements rather than the study of God

hunter-gatherers people who survive by employing the strategies of hunting animals and gathering wild plants rather than by planting crops and raising livestock

I

iconography the use of images and symbols in art

imam the religious leader of Shia Muslims

imperial cult the religious cult that venerated the Roman emperors as gods

Inner Asian Steppe the eastern half of the Eurasian Steppe that stretches into Mongolia and runs along the northern border of China

Inquisition a centuries-long effort by the church to impose religious homogeneity on Western Europe through torture and execution, if necessary

intellectual history the history of ideas, which looks at the philosophies that drive people to make certain choices

Iron Age the period beginning around 1200 BCE when iron became the preferred material for manufacturing tools and weapons

Islamization the religious and cultural conversion of those living under Islamic rule

J

Janissaries the elite enslaved infantry corps of the Ottoman army

Jewish diaspora the dispersion of the Jewish people beyond their ancestral homeland of Israel/Palestine following the Romans' destruction of the Second Temple

jihad a religiously infused conflict waged on behalf of Islam, or any struggle a Muslim undertakes in the name of Allah

K

karma a Hindu concept emphasizing the influence of good deeds and moral behavior on a person's status in life and rebirth after death

kentake a Kushite title that roughly translates to "queen mother" and was a powerful position in Meroitic Kush

khan a title claimed by warrior-kings to unite various tribes into powerful confederations and empires

kurultai a proto-democratic gathering of a Mongol leader's followers, called to reach agreement on major political decisions

L

lanista the trainer and manager of a group of gladiators

Late Antiquity a transitional period between the ancient and medieval worlds that occurred from roughly 150 to 750 CE

latifundia large agricultural estates in the countryside, worked by enslaved people to produce profit for the owner

Legalism a school of philosophical thought that helped dynasties such as the Qin use uniform laws and codes to reform and strengthen rulers

legion the basic unit of the Roman army, made up of around five thousand soldiers

Levant a historical geographical term referring to an area in the eastern Mediterranean consisting roughly of modern Israel, Jordan, Lebanon, Palestine, and Syria

Linear A a script developed by the Minoans but not yet deciphered by modern scholars

Linear B a Mycenaean script developed from Linear A that was used to write an early form of the Greek language

Little Ice Age a period in the early fourteenth century during which global mean temperatures dropped an average of 0.6°C, resulting in droughts and decreased agricultural productivity

lugal the Sumerians' term for their ruler

M

Maghreb the western half of North Africa, including most of present-day Morocco, Algeria, Tunisia, and Libya

Magna Carta an English document that reiterated existing rights of vassals, confirmed the papal position that the church is above the state, and spelled out some basic rights of commoners

Mamluk Sultanate a state in Egypt and the Levant administered and defended by educated, formerly enslaved men called mamluks

mamluks educated, formerly enslaved men who served as soldiers and administrators in Islamic societies beginning in the ninth century

mandarins top officials in the Imperial Chinese bureaucracy, selected by a series of exams on Confucian texts

"Mandate of Heaven" the favor of the gods that conferred a right to rule but could be lost by those less worthy

manorialism a medieval economic system of agricultural production directed by a lord and carried out by serfs or other varieties of unfree laborers

manumission the process of releasing a person from slavery, usually in front of a magistrate or via a slaveholder's will, or through a person's purchasing their own freedom

mawali non-Arab converts to Islam in the early Islamic period who had to be adopted by an Arab tribe as part of the conversion process

Medieval Warm Period a time of more temperate climate across the globe from the tenth through the thirteenth century

Mississippian tradition a widely dispersed mound-building tradition that created a number of urban settlements linked by trading networks in the southeastern United States around 700

moksha the release from samsara and the karmic cycle together with the attainment of a complete understanding of the world

monsoon the seasonal pattern of wind and rainfall across South Asia

Mousterian tools stone tools and hand-axes made beginning around 250,000 years ago and consisting of flakes rather than cores

mystery religions religious cults that featured secret rituals (the so-called mysteries) and became popular in Hellenistic cities

N

Nazca Lines a group of geoglyphs made on the desert floor in southern Peru representing both geometric patterns and images of animals

Neanderthals members of the genus Homo who evolved from Homo erectus and lived in Europe and western Asia between 30,000 and 200,000 years ago

Neolithic Age the final phase of the Paleolithic Age, beginning around twelve thousand years ago when human populations began growing crops and domesticating animals

Neolithic Revolution the shift from hunting and gathering to a life based primarily on agriculture

nomarchs regional governors in ancient Egypt

Norte Chico the culture of partially settled agricultural communities in the Andes region; also known as the Caral civilization

Nubia the name Egyptians gave to the expansive area south of the first cataract and extending into sub-Saharan Africa; it included the Kingdom of Kush

O

Oldowan tools sharpened stones used until about 1.7 million years ago for a variety of cutting, scraping, and chopping purposes

optimates politicians who supported the old order and the traditional leadership of elites

Outremer the French name for the four Crusader States created after the First Crusade, the County of Edessa, the Principality of Antioch, the County of Tripoli, and the Kingdom of Jerusalem

P

Paleolithic Age the period of time beginning as early as 3.3 million years ago until nearly twelve thousand years ago, when our distant pre-human ancestors began using stone tools for a variety of purposes

papacy the set of administrative structures associated with the government of the Catholic Church primarily—but not exclusively—linked with the city of Rome

papyrus a type of paper Egyptians made from a common reed plant growing along the Nile

pastoralists nomadic people who rely on herds of domesticated animals for subsistence

paterfamilias the patriarch of an extended Roman family, with authority over his wife, children, and any other dependents

patron a wealthy Roman aristocrat sought by clients in need of assistance

Peking Man a subspecies of *Homo erectus* identified by fossil remains found in northern China

People of the Felt Walls Temujin's name for his ethnically and linguistically diverse followers

pharaoh the title of the Egyptian ruler, translated as "big house"

polis a city-state in Ancient Greece

polytheists people who worship multiple gods, usually associated with different aspects of the natural world

populares politicians who sought the political support of discontented groups in Roman society

primary cause the most immediate reason an event occurred

primary source a document, object, or other source material from the time period under study

principate the political system established by Augustus Caesar after 27 BCE, which relied on Rome's traditional institutions and practices to legitimize a military dictatorship

progressive history a school of thought that views history as a straight line to a specific and more democratic destination

proletariat the landless working class

publicani provincial contractors who bid for the right to collect taxes and profited from the excess money they gathered

Pueblo architecture a building style of the early American Southwest that relied on stone or wooden frames covered in adobe clay

Pure Land Buddhism a branch of Mahayana Buddhism holding that all believers can be reborn into a place of salvation, the Pure Land

Q

Quran the holy scripture of Islam, which Muslims believe was given to humanity by God through Muhammad

R

Ramesside kings the line of kings that ruled New Kingdom Egypt following the reign of Ramses I

Rashidun a term meaning "rightly guided" that describes the first four caliphs after Muhammad's death: Abu Bakr, Umar, Uthman, and Ali

Red Turbans a secret peasant society that rose up against Mongol rule during the Yuan dynasty

Renaissance a period of intellectual and artistic rebirth inspired by the cultural achievements of ancient Greece and Rome

revisionism the process of altering our interpretation of historical events by adding new elements and perspectives

rhetoric the way words are used and put together in speaking or writing

Ring of Fire the boundary line of a zone of intense seismic activity in the Pacific Ocean

S

Sahel an east–west belt of semiarid grassland that forms a transitional zone between the Sahara to the north and the equatorial rainforest to the south

samsara a Hindu concept explaining the continuance of the soul after death and its transformation

samurai a member of the elite warrior class of Japan, governed by a strict code of behavior

satrapy one of twenty governing districts in Persia administered by royal governors called satraps, who answered directly to the king

savanna a grassy plain with scattered trees found to the north and south of the tropical African rainforest

secondary source a document, object, or other source material written or created after the time period under study

serfs unfree peasants who owed labor to a feudal lord and lived under the lord's authority

sharia Islamic religious law

Shia one of the two umbrella sects of Islam, whose members believe leadership of the Muslim community should reside in the family of Muhammad only through his son-in-law Ali

shogun a Japanese military commander-in-chief

Silk Roads a series of trade routes circulating luxury goods to and from China and parts of central Asia, India, and the Middle East

social constructs ideas such as class and gender created and accepted by the people in a society that influence the way they think and behave

social history a field of history that looks at all classes and categories of people, not just elites

social stratification the hierarchical order of society in which people sharing the same level of wealth and status make up a distinct class or strata

specialization a societal characteristic in which people perform specific tasks, such as farming (farmer) or producing tools and clothing (artisan), that contribute to the well-being of the community

Struggle of the Orders a political contest during the first centuries of the Republic in which Rome's commoners sought equal rights with elites

Sufism the mystical expression of Islamic faith

sultan a ruler who claims authority over the Islamic community but not necessarily the title of caliph

Sunni the larger of the two umbrella sects of Islam, whose adherents did not require leadership of the community to come specifically from the descendants of Muhammad through Ali

T

Terracotta Army a collection of life-size clay statues of soldiers, officials, servants, and horses of the Qin emperor and buried in his tomb near Xi'an

tetrarchy the rule of four emperors, two senior and two junior, established by the emperor Diocletian to quell the Crisis of the Third Century

Theodosian Code a document initiated by the emperor Theodosius II compiling laws from around the empire that had been issued since the early fourth century

Three Han the three groups (the Mahan, Jinhan, and Byeonhan) in southern Korea that were among the earliest with tribal chieftains

timar a right granted to subjects of the Ottoman sultan to collect taxes in a given area

Triple Alliance an alliance formed in 1428 between the Aztecs and two neighboring city-states, Texcoco and Tlacopan

Twelve Tables the first set of written laws in Rome, from about 450 BCE

U

ulama a class of religious clerics and scholars who act as the primary interpreters of Islamic law

ummah the community of Muslims

V

vassal state a state or kingdom that is nominally independent in the running of its internal affairs but must submit to the demands of a dominating empire and usually provide tribute to it

vestal virgins the priesthood of six women who took a vow of chastity and maintained the sacred fire in Rome

Y

yam horse relay stations established by Chinggis Khan for long-distance communication on military campaigns; they were later expanded into rest areas and supply depots

yassa Chinggis Khan's law code, designed to eliminate the sources of conflict in steppe society and bring harmony to his people

Z

ziggurat an immense stepped tower with a flat top built of mud-brick that served as a temple in Sumerian cities

Zoroastrianism the religion of the ancient Persians, named for its founder Zarathustra, pronounced *Zoroaster* in Greek

APPENDIX B

World History, Volume 1, to 1500: Maps and Timelines

Chapter 1: Understanding the Past

- The Whole World Figure 1.1

Chapter 2: Early Humans

- Migration of the Earliest Humans Figure 2.6
- The Most Recent Glaciation Period Figure 2.14
- Sites of Natufian Settlements Figure 2.23

Chapter 3: Early Civilizations and Urban Societies

- Locator Map: Early Civilizations and Urban Societies Figure 3.3
- Early Sumer Figure 3.8
- The Fertile Crescent Figure 3.4
- The World's First Empire Figure 3.13
- The Upper and Lower Kingdoms of Egypt Figure 3.17
- The Indus Valley Culture Figure 3.24
- Indus Valley Trade with Mesopotamia Figure 3.26

Chapter 4: The Near East

- Locator Map: The Near East Figure 4.3
- Hammurabi's Realm Figure 4.5
- The Hittite Empire Figure 4.6
- The Neo-Assyrian Empire Figure 4.8
- The Neo-Babylonian Empire Figure 4.9
- Three Kingdoms in Egypt Figure 4.18
- Trade Routes in the Eastern Mediterranean Figure 4.26
- The Persian Empire Figure 4.30
- The Divided Monarchy Figure 4.40

Chapter 5: Asia in Ancient Times

- Locator Map: Asia in Ancient Times Figure 5.3
- Topography of Ancient China Figure 5.4
- The Eurasian Steppe Figure 5.9
- Northern Wei Dynasty Figure 5.10
- Ancient Korea Figure 5.11
- The Ring of Fire Figure 5.15
- Southeast Asia Figure 5.17
- The Indian Subcontinent Figure 5.20

Chapter 6: Mediterranean Peoples

- Locator Map: Mediterranean Peoples Figure 6.3
- The Bronze Age World Figure 6.4
- The Path of the Sea Peoples Figure 6.6
- Phoenician Cities and Colonies Figure 6.7

Chapter 11: The Rise of Islam and the Caliphates

Chapter 12: India, the Indian Ocean Basin, and East Asia

Chapter 13: The Post-Roman West and the Crusading Movement

Chapter 14: Pax Mongolica: The Steppe Empire of the Mongols

Chapter 15: States and Societies in Sub-Saharan Africa

Chapter 16: Climate Change and Plague in the Fourteenth Century

Chapter 17: The Ottomans, the Mamluks, and the Ming

Timelines in Volume 1, to 1500

APPENDIX C

World Maps

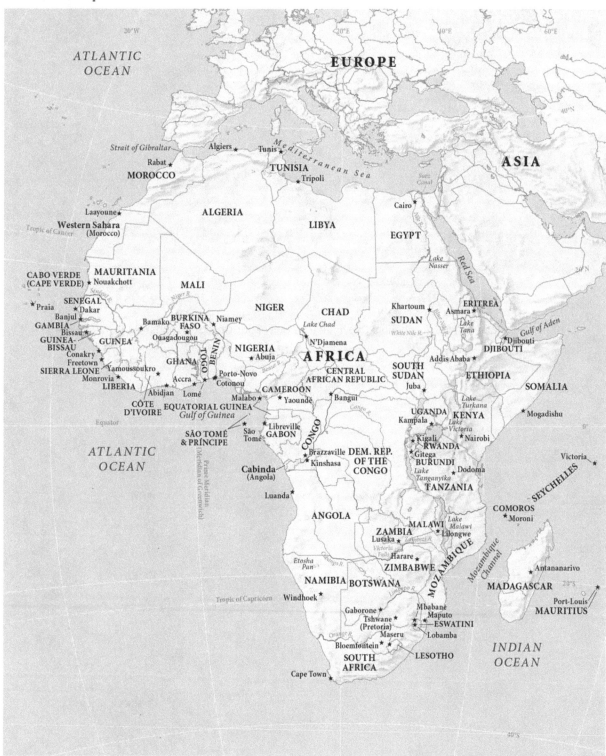

FIGURE C1 Map of Africa. (attribution: Copyright Rice University, OpenStax, under CC BY 4.0 license)

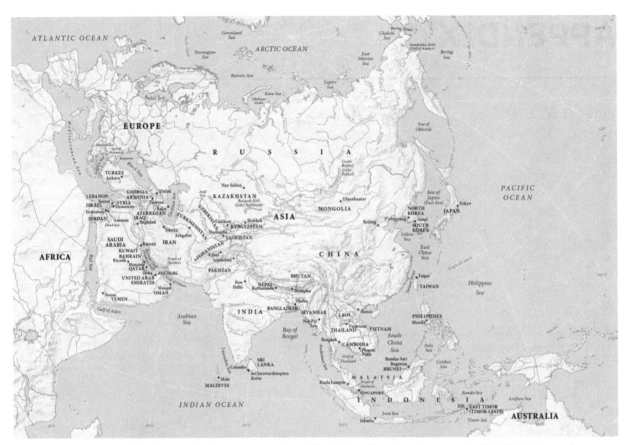

FIGURE C2 Map of Asia. (attribution: Copyright Rice University, OpenStax, under CC BY 4.0 license)

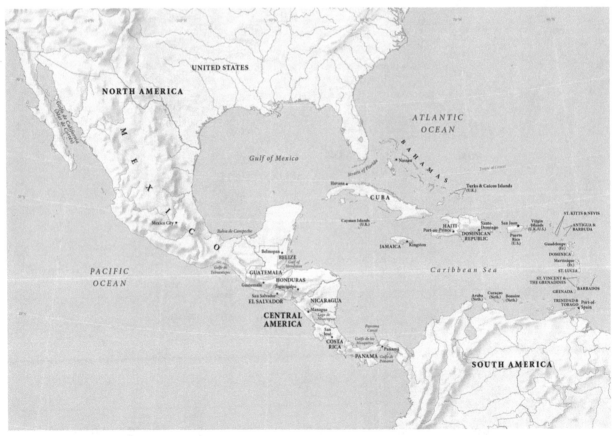

FIGURE C3 Map of Central America. (attribution: Copyright Rice University, OpenStax, under CC BY 4.0 license)

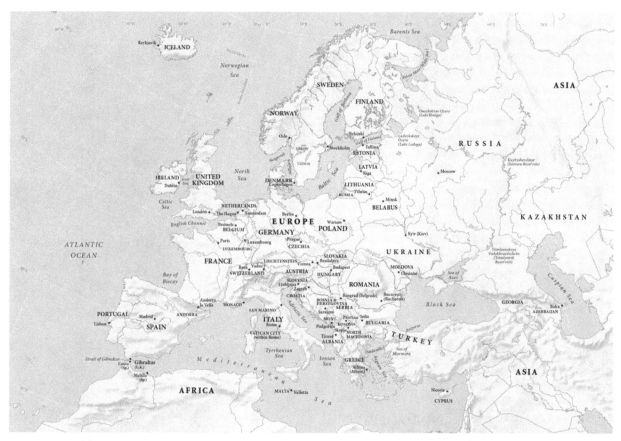

FIGURE C4 **Map of Europe.** (attribution: Copyright Rice University, OpenStax, under CC BY 4.0 license)

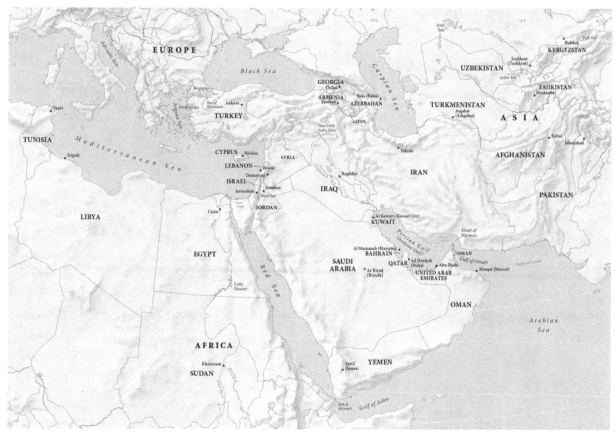

FIGURE C5 **Map of the Middle East.** (attribution: Copyright Rice University, OpenStax, under CC BY 4.0 license)

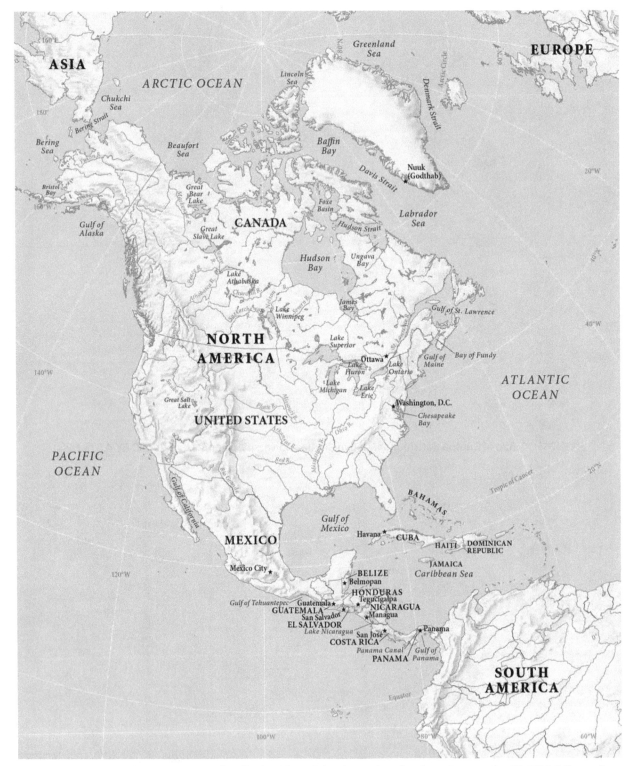

FIGURE C6 Map of North America. (attribution: Copyright Rice University, OpenStax, under CC BY 4.0 license)

FIGURE C7 Map of South America. (attribution: Copyright Rice University, OpenStax, under CC BY 4.0 license)

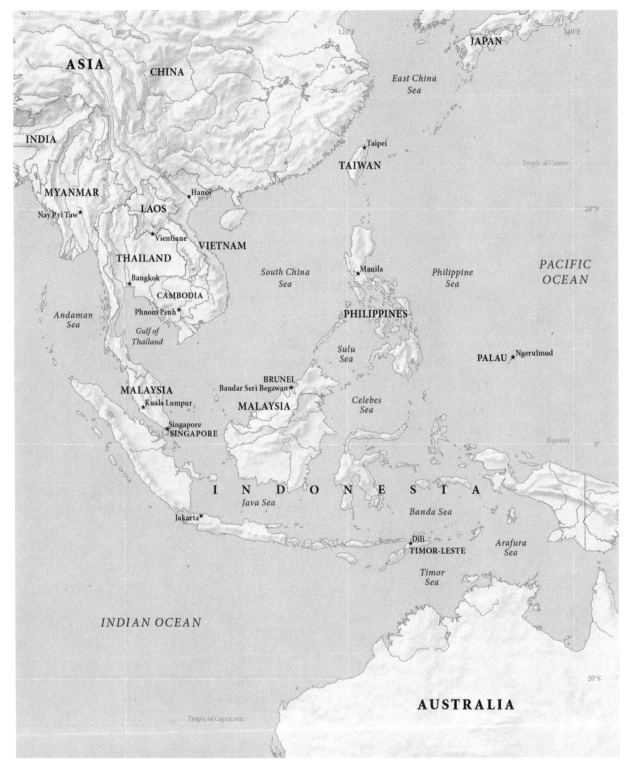

FIGURE C8 Map of Southeast Asia. (attribution: Copyright Rice University, OpenStax, under CC BY 4.0 license)

APPENDIX D

Recommended Resources for the Study of World History

How to Study World History

World History Sources (http://chnm.gmu.edu/worldhistorysources/index.html) includes various strategies for analyzing historical documents.

Resources for Primary Sources

World History Encyclopedia (https://www.worldhistory.org/) includes timelines and primary sources.

Digital Public Library of America: Primary Source Sets (https://dp.la/primary-source-sets) includes collections of primary sources.

DocsTeach (https://www.docsteach.org/) includes many primary sources.

Internet History Sourcebooks Project (https://sourcebooks.fordham.edu/) includes historical texts.

Library of Congress: World Digital Library Collection (https://www.loc.gov/collections/world-digital-library/about-this-collection/) presents various historical documents.

MIT Visualizing Cultures (https://visualizingcultures.mit.edu/home/index.html) aims to reconstruct the past.

Smithsonian Collections (https://www.si.edu/collections) showcases the Smithsonian's vast collection of objects from the natural and cultural world.

Resources for Maps

Geology.com Maps (https://geology.com/world/) includes many different maps.

CIA World Factbook (https://www.cia.gov/the-world-factbook/maps/) presents a variety of world, regional, and country maps.

National Geographic MapMaker (https://mapmaker.nationalgeographic.org/) connects to an interactive mapmaking tool.

Resources for Videos

CrashCourse World History (https://www.youtube.com/playlist?list=PLBDA2E52FB1EF80C9) includes brief educational videos on a variety of world history topics.

Website Collections

World History Matters (https://worldhistorymatters.org/) is a collection of various historical websites.

Roy Rosenzweig Center for history and New Media (https://rrchnm.org/our-work/) includes access to online resources for teachers, online collections, exhibits and collecting sites, and open-source software.

Resources for Art History

Heilbrunn Timeline of Art History (https://www.metmuseum.org/toah/) includes collections from various periods of world history.

SmartHistory (https://smarthistory.org/introductory-guides-overview) presents an art history overview and collections organized by religion and time period.

Magazine Articles

BBC's History Extra (https://www.historyextra.com/)

Podcasts

The Almost Forgotten (https://www.listennotes.com/podcasts/the-almost-forgotten-the-almost-forgotten-_5EyY-TBo6V/)

BBC's History Extra (https://www.historyextra.com/podcast)

The Fall of Civilizations (https://podcasts.apple.com/us/podcast/fall-of-civilizations-podcast/id1449884495)

Fifteen Minute History (https://15minutehistory.org/)

The History Chicks (https://podcasts.apple.com/us/podcast/the-history-chicks/id415983183)

The Ancients (https://podcasts.apple.com/us/podcast/the-ancients/id1520403988)

The History of Rome (https://podcasts.apple.com/us/podcast/the-history-of-rome/id261654474)

Not Just the Tudors (https://podcasts.apple.com/us/podcast/not-just-the-tudors/id1564113869)

Revolutions (https://podcasts.apple.com/us/podcast/revolutions/id703889772)

The History of the Twentieth Century (https://historyofthetwentiethcentury.com/)

The Cold War Vault (https://www.coldwarvault.com/)

The History of China (https://thehistoryofchina.wordpress.com/)

The China History Podcast (https://podcasts.apple.com/us/podcast/the-china-history-podcast/id489369498)

The History of Japan (https://podcasts.apple.com/us/podcast/history-of-japan/id635736811)

New Books Network (https://www.stitcher.com/search/%22new%20books%20in%22)

3D Tours

Virtual Rome: What Did Ancient Rome Look Like? (https://www.youtube.com/watch?v=NZ2NWXp-1Y4)

Virtual Tour in Ancient Athens (5th century BC) – 3D Reconstruction (https://www.youtube.com/watch?v=ulAxMLJ7O7M)

Virtual Museum Content

Natural History Museum (https://artsandculture.withgoogle.com/naturalhistorymuseum/)

The British Museum (https://britishmuseum.withgoogle.com/)

INDEX